THE LETTERS OF
CHARLES DICKENS

Charles Dickens in 1842
From the bust by Henry Dexter

THE PILGRIM EDITION

The Letters of Charles Dickens

Volume Three
1842–1843

EDITED BY
Madeline House   Graham Storey
Kathleen Tillotson

ASSOCIATE EDITOR
Noel C. Peyrouton

CLARENDON PRESS · OXFORD
1974

Oxford University Press, Ely House, London W.1

GLASGOW NEW YORK TORONTO MELBOURNE WELLINGTON
CAPE TOWN IBADAN NAIROBI DAR ES SALAAM LUSAKA ADDIS ABABA
DELHI BOMBAY CALCUTTA MADRAS KARACHI LAHORE DACCA
KUALA LUMPUR SINGAPORE HONG KONG TOKYO

ISBN 0 19 812474 0

PRINTED IN GREAT BRITAIN
BY BUTLER & TANNER LTD, FROME AND LONDON

CONTENTS

ILLUSTRATIONS

PREFACE

Since the publication of our second volume in 1969, the total of letters known to us has risen by over 300, from 12,758 to 13,074. This volume contains 772 letters (including extracts and mentions). Of these, 264 are published for the first time and many others have appeared in no previous collection. The texts of 509 have been transcribed from originals or photographs of originals.

Dickens's visit to America and its aftermath are inevitably the central subject of the volume. Of the newly published letters, about sixty belong to the four months of this visit; many of them add materially to what is known of his social life—first among the literati of Boston, two of whom, C. C. Felton and Long-fellow, remained his lifelong friends. Later letters hitherto unpublished or un-collected, such as those to Macready, Henry Austin, and Fonblanque, reveal his outspoken antipathy to much that he found in the States. But disillusionment makes its first appearance, a few weeks after his arrival, in the published letter to an American, Jonathan Chapman, Mayor of Boston, in whom Dickens had found a kindred spirit. The whole sequence as now presented makes it possible to trace much more precisely than before the different phases of his tour and the changes in his response from delighted gratification at his welcome to disenchantment and even repulsion. The mass of available illustrative material, in newspaper accounts and the private comments of those who met him, allows us also to see the varying impressions which in his turn Dickens made on Americans; and as the American visit has never been thoroughly examined, some amplitude of annotation has seemed to us justified.

His letters to John Forster still remain the fullest record—intended, as they were, to be used as the basis for *American Notes*. During much of his visit, he wrote long sections whenever he found time for writing, and these (often ended and posted to catch some particular mail-packet) summarized the events of the last week or more, and sometimes repeated facts or descriptions already written to other correspondents. When Forster came to write the *Life*, he quoted from them extensively, but saying he had made it his rule not to repeat passages that had already appeared in *American Notes*. As Dickens had omitted all mention of International Copyright, and descriptions of his reception and of individuals, Forster had here a clear field. But, outside these passages, he was astonished by the richness of what he could still print. "The *personal narrative* of this famous visit to America is in the letters alone", he wrote; and he regretted (and in fact frequently broke)[1] his "rule" not to include what had already been printed. The diary-letters, written at leisure on canal or steamboats, were those Forster prized most highly: he regarded them as "literature", and quoted them "exactly as they were written" with their "freshness of first impressions". He felt strongly

[1] As in Dickens's conversation with the Keeper of the Tombs, the description of the small boy on the roof of the Harrisburg Mail, and of the "little woman" and her baby on board the boat to St Louis.

that certain passages—particularly Dickens's description of Niagara—had not been strengthened by "rhetorical additions in the printed work".[1] That Forster "edited" the letters he quoted seems most unlikely; no discrepancies have been found between them and the other letters Dickens wrote from America, and only one misdating, the passage we have dated ?4 February.[2]

While still in England, Dickens, no doubt already aware of the strained relations existing between England and America over the Maine–Canadian Boundary dispute, had read in the English press in October 1841 alarming reports of the latest incident—a belated repercussion from the attack on the American ship *Caroline* in 1837—and had at first seen his approaching visit as only feasible if no "wars or rumours of wars" prevented it.[3] Ill-feeling continued. The *Westminster Review* of February 1843, in an article praising Lord Ashburton for the part he played in settling the Boundary dispute, described Anglo-American relations "a year ago" as "nothing but a state of unarmed hostility"; "Never since the conclusion of the late war had such a variety of causes combined to raise so general an animosity to Great Britain, as at the commencement of his mission" (in April 1842).[4] But after the Webster-Ashburton Treaty, signed on 9 August, relations improved.

Before setting sail Dickens had partly prepared himself for the visit, as his letters show, by reading with some care Harriet Martineau's three-volume works, *Society in America* (1837) and *Retrospect of Western Travel* (1838), and Marryat's *A Diary in America* (published in two series 1839); also James Silk Buckingham's three-volume *America: . . . the Northern and Free States* (1841). To Mrs Trollope's *Domestic Manners of the Americans* he referred admiringly, though only after his return to England. English travellers naturally read each others' books. Mrs Trollope read and commented on Captain Basil Hall's; Fanny Kemble on Mrs Trollope's; Marryat clearly knew Harriet Martineau's well, and agreement or disagreement with her runs through his volumes.[5] Dickens must have deplored Marryat's political views,[6] but he read his descriptions of travelling, particularly on steamboats, with attention. With Harriet Martineau's

---

[1] F, III, v, 244–5.

[2] It was probably after using them for the *Life* that Forster had the letters bound, with a lock fitted to the binding. The volume, with title "Letters from America" in gilt lettering, is in the Forster Collection at the Victoria & Albert Museum, but the letters are missing—presumably cut out and destroyed by Forster's executors: see K. J. Fielding in *Boston University Studies in English*, II (1956), 140–9.

[3] See Vol. II, pp. 405 and *n*, 415.

[4] *Westminster Review*, XXXIX, 165, 203. Some instances of this animosity appear in Dickens's letters: during his week in Washington, Mar 1842, he heard of the violent speech H. A. Wise had made against England in the House of Representatives (see p. 118); in Richmond, Virginia, he was forcibly struck by the hostility the Southern States felt towards England over the *Creole* affair, which involved slaves (see p. 142); in Cleveland he was incensed on reading a newspaper urging war against England "to the death" (see p. 209).

[5] See *Diary in America*, Second Series, I, 109, 130–1, 134, 204–9, 287.

[6] Those shown, for instance, in his declaration, when replying to the *Edinburgh Review*'s criticism of his first volumes, that his great object had been "to do serious injury to the cause of democracy" (*op. cit.*, Second Series, III, 293).

enthusiasm for the republican experiment he was predisposed to agree,[1] and in conversation with Ann Warren Weston in Boston described her work as "the best . . . that had been written on America".[2] Because of his knowledge of their books we draw on both Harriet Martineau and Marryat in our footnotes. We also occasionally quote comments by Lord Morpeth and Charles Lyell because both were in America at the same time as Dickens.

Doubtless it was to a large extent owing to his knowledge of earlier travellers' books that Dickens's four-and-a-half month stay in America and Canada was so largely spent in visiting places to which they, on their more leisurely visits of a year or more, had been before him—the Lowell Mills, the Perkins Institution, the Eastern Penitentiary, a Shaker colony; and like them he went on the Mississippi, to a prairie and inevitably to Niagara Falls. With the exception, perhaps, of certain prisons, he saw nothing new; nor, with the same exception, did he think very profoundly about what he saw; yet all his descriptions bore "Boz's peculiar colours", characteristic of his novels. In Macready's words, Dickens had "a clutching eye—gets his impressions at once—is given to activity, and would not care to linger for contemplation":[3] compare Forster's comment on his "unrivalled quickness of observation, the rare faculty of seizing out of a multitude of things the thing that is essential".[4] But his visit had the limitations inherent in its brevity. Unlike Harriet Martineau, he barely penetrated the slave states in his visit to Richmond, Virginia; and, unlike Marryat, when in Buffalo he made no attempt to visit the neighbouring Indian reservation.

Equipped, no doubt, with some of the "Various American Guide Books" mentioned in the 1844 inventory of his library,[5] Dickens set sail in the S.S. *Britannia* on 4 January 1842, and landed at Boston on 22 January, where a great welcome awaited him. He was the talk of the town—entertained by almost all the most eminent people in Boston, called on by many others, stared at and followed in the street, given a great public dinner; guest of honour, with Catherine Dickens, at a crowded Ball; described by every newspaper and in numerous private letters shuttling between one Bostonian and another.[6] It was not long before a note of criticism of such lionizing showed itself in both press reports and private comment. Several of Charles Lyell's American friends, he recorded in his diary on 1 February 1842, doubted whether "Walter Scott, had he visited the U.S., would have been so much lionised". Lyell added, "There may be no precedent in Great Britain for a whole people thus unreservedly indulging their feelings of admiration for a favourite author; but if so, the Americans deserve the more credit for obeying their warm impulses". Some might be actuated by vulgar curiosity, but the majority wished to applaud a man whose works were "here, as in his own country, an inexhaustible source of interest and amusement".[7] Inviting him to a public dinner, the Young Men of Boston wrote: "We

[1] For his later expression of preference for a liberal monarchy, see *To* Macready, 22 Mar and *fn.*

[2] Quoted in an unpublished article, "Boz and Boz-town", by the late Mr N. C. Peyrouton.

[3] Quoted in Lady Pollock, *Macready as I Knew Him*, 1884, p. 59.

[4] F, III, v, 245.   [5] MS Major Philip Dickens.

[6] There was general agreement that what was most striking about him were his wonderful, expressive eyes.

[7] *Travels in North America*, 1845, I, 199–200.

do not address you as a son of our fatherland, for 'genius has no country'; we claim your literary reputation as the property of the human race".[1]

In New York a more elaborate and ostentatious welcome was being prepared for him by the "fashionables"—the Boz Ball of 14 February, at which some sections of the press openly mocked. Meanwhile other sections were engaged in indignant attacks on him for his references in speeches at Boston and Hartford to American piracy of English works and his appeal for an International Copyright.[2] Dickens himself, apparently quite unruffled by either the mockery (if he read it) or the attacks,[3] was still in a state of euphoria at his reception (comparable with Lafayette's, many people said); and it carried him through the Ball and even induced him to consent to a repeat performance two nights later. But then he fell ill.

The change in his feelings for America clearly began while he was confined to his hotel, from 15 to 17 February, and able to read and reflect on reports and editorials in the newspapers. There he read, for instance, the mortifying statement that he was being used as a "raree-show"—made by papers ostensibly defending him, though perhaps more concerned to score a political point against the anglophile Whig "aristocracy" who had appropriated him; among these was the notorious *New York Herald*. But the greatest shock was the extent of the newspaper attacks on him for daring to hold forth in his public speeches on a subject as delicate as International Copyright; mercenary motives were imputed to him, and the "monstrous" suggestion made that this was the express purpose of his visit to America—a charge which had many repercussions. To Jonathan Chapman he wrote on 22 February of the "agony" (greater than any he had experienced since his birth) that such unfair and unexpected attacks had caused him: their "one good effect" would be to make him "iron" on the subject. Though two days later, when writing to Forster, he launched into a counterattack on the lack in America of its supposed "freedom of opinion",[4] clearly the whole incident had been a severe blow to his pride. From this time his attitude to the country was changed.[5]

In fact, despite his earlier excitement and elation, the papers that had castigated Dickens's hosts for overdoing their welcome (as well as the general public for "intruding themselves at seasonable and unseasonable hours")[6] did so—whatever their motives—with some justice. What Dickens seems most to have enjoyed were his quieter activities. The happiest part of his stay at Boston, he is reported to have said,[7] had been the day he spent with T. C. Grattan, the

---

[1] Quoted in W. C. Wilkins, *CD in America*, 1911, pp. 19–20.

[2] See *To* Forster, 14 Feb (p. 59).

[3] Though on 14 Feb, and more explicitly on 24 Feb, he asked Forster to enlist English support for his copyright campaign—from which emerged the Memorial he sent to American newspapers on 27 Apr.

[4] *To* Forster, 24 Feb (p. 81).

[5] It was probably during this period that (if the story is true) he suffered the indignity of having his nose pulled in a New York shop—an incident for which our only evidence is a report, quoted without date in the *Liverpool Mail*, 26 Mar, from the *Halifax Morning Herald* under the heading "Assault upon Dickens—Pusillanimous Conduct of Boz": he "offered no resistance" and would not prosecute.

[6] *New York Herald*, 6 Feb.

[7] See *To* Forster, ?4 Feb, *fn* (p. 50).

British Consul, at the Lowell Mills. In New York, he probably most enjoyed his informal meetings with Macready's friends, the David Coldens, with Washington Irving, Fitz-Greene Halleck and W. C. Bryant, and his jaunts with C. C. Felton. Certainly in Washington he said that his "pleasantest" evening was when he dined with Robert Greenhow, a mere translator in the State Department.[1] It was at the New York Dinner of 18 February that he announced (to cheers) that in future he would accept no public invitations. During their last five days in the city (while Catherine, now, was ill) he lay low, allowing it to be thought that he had already gone on to Philadelphia.

Although Dickens now sought privacy, he could not escape holding a "levee" at many of the places in which he stayed—the most notorious of them at Philadelphia.[2] Even when he set out for the "Far West"[3]—parts of the country where prominent visitors were comparatively rare—levees lay ahead, with hours of hand-shaking at Cincinnati and St Louis.[4] Nor could he escape such disagreeable incidentals of American life of the period as spitting, lack of hygiene, suffocating stoves, and the bolting of food (on all of which most English travellers commented).

After their days at St Louis, Dickens, Catherine, and her maid Anne, succeeded in travelling privately—as the reviewer of *American Notes* in *Blackwood's*[5] maintained they should have done throughout their whole visit if they wanted to see the people and country as they really were. But *Graham's Magazine* in a rhymed review (February 1843) took a different, facetious, line:

. . . we can't, for our lives, 'spite of warm admiration,
Discover the reason for one exclamation—
(It occurs at page fortieth, line twenty-one—)
"Delighted to find ourselves once more alone!"
Now to scrape an acquaintance with dear Mrs. D.,
Scarcely needed the risk of the treacherous sea;

In fact, Dickens did make the acquaintance of "dear Mrs. D." in a new kind of way while they were abroad together, and she for once not pregnant, nor involved in house-keeping, nor pushed into the background by her husband's work or social activities. All the Americans she met thought well of her. "An excellent woman", wrote the far from uncritical R. H. Dana; "She is natural in her manners, seems not at all elated by her new position, but rests upon a foundation of good sense and good feeling".[6] American comment shows that during the hectic weeks in Boston and New York she had risen to every social occasion with considerable poise; but only when he was at greater leisure did

[1] See *To* J. Q. Adams, 10 or 11 Mar, *fn* (p. 113).
[2] See *To* Gebler and others, 20 Feb, *fn* (p. 75).
[3] In 1842, Illinois and Ohio would have been considered Western. Beyond was Indian country (some under U.S. Territorial Government, some under Mexican rule, and some in the recently established [1836] Republic of Texas).
[4] Cf. J. K. Paulding's acccount of his tour with ex-President van Buren in May 42: they "shook hands with about 5000 people" (*Literary Life of James Kirke Paulding* by his son W. I. Paulding, New York, 1867, p. 286).
[5] See *To* Felton, 31 Dec, *fn* (pp. 412–13).
[6] *Journals*, ed. R. F. Lucid, Cambridge, Mass., 1968, I, 61.

Dickens himself write of the part she had been playing as his consort. "Imagine", he wrote to Maclise on 22 March, "Kate and I—a kind of Queen and Albert— holding a Levee every day"; to Mitton, on the same day, he confessed that, if he had not had a lady with him, he thought he would have had to throw up the sponge and return to England: after two hours of shaking hands and answering questions, they were "literally exhausted" and could "hardly stand". After mentioning to Frederick Dickens on 4 April his successful magnetizing of Catherine, he commented: "She will rather astonish you, when we come home, I can tell you"; to Forster on 26 May, describing the Montreal theatricals, he wrote "only think of Kate playing! and playing devilish well, I assure you!" Throughout some very rough travelling, Dickens found her invariably game— "an out and outer to travel".[1] His joking references to her frequent falls are plainly affectionate. He saw her restraint in not opening their eagerly awaited *Caledonia* mail until he returned from a dinner and could enjoy the letters with her as "heroic".[2]

After the exhaustion of his hurried tour in America, the fortnight spent at Niagara ("on the *English* side") and the month elsewhere in Canada came as a welcome respite. In *American Notes* he made it clear that he would not compare "the social features" of America with those of Canada; but in his letters he had not been so restrained. "English kindness is very different from American", he wrote to Forster on 12 May. "People send their horses and carriages for your use, but they don't exact as payment the right of being always under your nose." The Canadian press congratulated itself on not hunting him as a lion; and, apart from full and appreciative reports of the private theatricals he organized in Montreal, made very little of his visit.[3]

Once back in England, Dickens, within a week, returned to his agitation for an International Copyright law, following up the Memorial sent to certain American newspapers on 27 April, with a strong circular letter to British Authors and Journals, published in the *Morning Chronicle* on 7 July, which had little effect in England, but was angrily received in America. He then set to work on the book he had promised Chapman & Hall,[4] but had mentioned to none of his American friends—though in newspapers the question was frequently asked, "Will he write a book about us?". On 1 February, in the early glow after Dickens's arrival, the *New York Herald* could write of him: "His mind is American—his soul is republican—his heart is democratic"; but the Americans were now, in the words of Henry Petingale, an English emigrant, writhing "under the antici- pated malediction of Boz".[5] After all the wearisome flattery and "bore-ation" Dickens had endured, *Brother Jonathan* doubted whether a book favourable to the country could possibly be looked for.

Dickens's Introductory Chapter (discarded on Forster's advice)[6] shows his

---

[1] *To* Mitton, 26 Apr (p. 212)

[2] *To* Forster, 15 Mar (p. 132).

[3] Although the *Toronto Herald*, in November, protested strongly at his account in *American Notes* of violence in the Toronto elections of 1841.

[4] On 14 Sep 41 (Vol. II, p. 383).

[5] Letter to his sister from Rochester, N.Y., 22 Aug 42, quoted in Charlotte Erickson, *Invisible Immigrants*, 1973, p. 443.

[6] But quoted in F, III, viii, 284–6.

awareness of the hostility with which his book, like those by earlier English travellers, might be met, particularly from those sections of the press that he most detested. How well-founded this detestation was became clear two months after he left the country. On 11 August the *New York Evening Tattler* published a gross forgery,[1] purporting to be a letter written by Dickens to the *Morning Chronicle* on 15 July, and designed to show total ingratitude for the hospitality he had received in America and contempt for his hosts. This, confused with the genuine *Morning Chronicle* letter to British Authors of 7 July, in which Dickens had not minced words in a paragraph attacking the editors of the piratical "mammoth" papers (such as the *New World* and *Brother Jonathan*), brought him once more into the American limelight, as a villain, except to those wise enough to suspect forgery.[2] Next—ahead of the arrival of *American Notes*—came the October *Foreign Quarterly Review*, containing Forster's (unsigned) swingeing attack on the American press. This also was, at first, attributed to Dickens,[3] and increased resentment.

When *American Notes* at length arrived on 6 November, all—those who planned to pirate it, those who expected to hate it, and those who had been devoted readers of the novels—were on tenterhooks to see it.[4] Thousands of copies were sold.[5] The description of the city of Washington aroused the indignation of George Watterston,[6] who was "not sparing in his condemnation of the whole work",[7] the chapter on slavery and passages about spitting (and pigs) were deplored by many who in other respects found the work amusing; but the superficiality of a book written about a vast country, still in the early stages of the republican experiment, after so short a visit, was commented on on both sides of the Atlantic.[8] Harriet Martineau, after reading long excerpts in periodicals, wrote to Crabb Robinson (29 October) that she rejoiced to find "how far more moderate his tone is therein than in his speeches & conversations, & letters

---

[1] See *To* Forster, ?30 or 31 Aug, *fn* (pp. 311–12), and Appx, pp. 625–7.

[2] Not a new activity in the American press: in 1832, for instance, the *New York Evening Post* published "A Leaf from Mrs Trollope's Memorandum Book" (on New York) supposed to have been found among papers left at her lodgings (M. Parent-Fazee, *Mrs. Trollope and America*, Caen, 1969, p. 12). See also Forster's second article on the American press in the *Foreign Quarterly Review* (Apr 43, XXXIII, 278*n*) for O'Connell's "indignant disclaimer . . . of a forged letter with his signature that had 'gone the round' of the American press", and, as quoted in the *New York Herald*, included the remark "Thank God Dickens is not an Irishman". See also *Chuzzlewit*, Ch. 16.

[3] It undoubtedly drew on newspaper material he had collected for *American Notes* but not used, and Dickens's footnote to his final chapter, referring to it as "an able, and perfectly truthful article . . . to which my attention has been attracted, since these sheets have been passing through the press", was intentionally misleading in suggesting that it supplied independent confirmation of his own views.

[4] "How very funny it would appear at home", wrote J. R. Godley (*Letters from America*, II, 1844, 170), "to see people looking out in this way for the critique of a foreigner upon England".

[5] See *To* Jonathan Chapman, 15 Oct, *fn* (p. 346).

[6] See p. 122 and *fn*.

[7] According to the *National Intelligencer*, 18 Nov, which itself thought there was "good as well as evil" in the book.

[8] For the book's mixed reviews, see *To* Prescott, 15 Oct, *fn* (p. 348), and *To* Felton, 31 Dec, *fn* (pp. 411–2).

... I *have* an impression that it is humane, good tempered, faithful as far as it goes,—but superficial, rather affected in parts, likely to occupy the whole world for a month or two and then be absolutely forgotten in the superior merits of his fictions. Is this a good guess ?"[1] Emerson saw the book as "a lively rattle, readable enough, & very quotable in the philanthropic newspapers".[2]

The chapter devoted to slavery did in fact win the approval of the abolitionist press. Although, according to William Lloyd Garrison's *The Liberator* (18 Nov 42), Dickens "avoided" the abolitionists during his visit, the paper praised the "serious indignation" of "his testimony"; and the *Anti-Slavery Reporter* saw the chapter as "one of the most powerful, effective anti-slavery tracts yet issued from the press".[3] Both papers must have been aware but, for the sake of the cause, turned a blind eye to the fact that the chapter was largely composed of extracts from W. W. Weld's *American Slavery as It Is: Testimony of a Thousand Witnesses* (New York, 1839) and newspaper cuttings (collected by Edward Chapman).[4] This was evidently recognized by the New York *Ladies Companion*, which remarked (December 1842) that "when any thing approaching to solidity of judgment rises up, it is found to be based only upon public documents or newspaper report".[5] This was not wholly fair: in the Richmond section there is first-hand reporting of visits to a slave plantation and slave factory; and Dickens's letters show that, although warned to be silent on the subject of slavery while in the South, at Richmond[6] he found that "they won't let you be silent". He was relieved when he could turn his back on "this accursed and detested system".[7]

A sad aftermath of Dickens's visit to America was his loss of several friends. The absence of further correspondence suggests that Jonathan Chapman's strongly expressed affection, and Sumner's liking, did not survive the publication of *American Notes*. Washington Irving was wholly antagonized, either at the same time or after reading the American chapters of *Chuzzlewit*. In his own mind Dickens must have seen the American experience as something of a failure; for he enjoyed personal popularity yet knew from the falling off of friends and what he learned of newspaper attacks that, despite the brilliant beginnings of his visit, he had largely lost it. To attribute this to the wickedness of American newspapers was easy, but could not have entirely satisfied him.

His English friends welcomed him home in the way he would have most enjoyed—with a great dinner on 9 July at Greenwich; and he was quickly drawn back into his old pursuits, and with more than his old energy launched out into new ones. The brief interval between the completion and publication of *American Notes* was happily occupied with Longfellow's stay at Devonshire Terrace.[8] There followed the private celebration of Dickens's return—the

[1] MS Dr Williams's Library.

[2] *Letters*, ed. R. L. Rusk, Columbia, 1939, III, 100.

[3] Quoted by Forster in his *Examiner* review (8 Apr 43) of Longfellow's *Poems of Slavery*.

[4] See *To* Chapman, 16 Sep and *fns*.

[5] For Dickens's extensive use of the Perkins Institution's Annual Report in *American Notes*, Ch. 3, see *To* Felton, 1 Sep, *fn* (p. 317).

[6] As later at St Louis (*To* Forster, 15 Apr, p. 196).

[7] *To* Forster, 21 Mar (p. 141).

[8] "What a charming visit that was to me! a memory of delight for ever", Longfellow wrote to Forster, 17 Oct 48 (MS V & A).

jaunt to Cornwall with Forster, Maclise, and Stanfield, planned "by way of challenge to what he had seen while abroad".[1] Lasting only eight days, though expanded to twice the length in Forster's genial recollection, it was filled with adventure and merriment ("I never laughed in my life as I did on this journey")[2] and was clearly seen as a last fling before Dickens settled down in earnest to the promised new novel, due to start publication in January. At one stage, Cornwall was thought of as its initial setting; but in the event the only impress left by the tour was in the descriptions of autumn winds and weather, inn-parlours, and travel by coach and gig. Nothing in the first four numbers of *Martin Chuzzlewit* suggested to readers that the tale would be concerned with any but "English life and manners". But though America had been no part of the original plan, there had been premonitory hints of the possibility. Some of his American friends had supposed that he would use his experiences in future novels (fondly imagining that this would be preferable to a travel-book);[3] and the germ of his intention was surely present when, writing to Forster from the solitude of Niagara, he saw "a perplexingly divided and sub-divided duty, in the matter of the book of travels. Oh! the sublimated essence of comicality that I *could* distil, from the materials I have!"[4]

His letters from America show that there was indeed a rich hoard of comic material unused or only slightly touched upon in *American Notes*,[5] and in the winter after his return, increasing provocation to use it. (Particularly exasperating was the revival of the "copyright mission" rumour in the January *Edinburgh Review*.)[6] Forster was probably right in suggesting that Dickens was influenced less by the disappointing sales of the early numbers of *Chuzzlewit* than by "the challenge to make good his *Notes* which every mail had been bringing him from unsparing assailants beyond the Atlantic."[7] His decision, somewhat less abrupt than Forster makes out, was almost certainly taken by mid-March[8]—which gave him ample time, in his solitary Finchley retreat, to ponder the details of its operation and its relation to the main story. (Writing the "American episode", he said in June, took him "at least twice as long . . . as the ordinary current").[9] Martin's "desperate resolution" to go to America was dramatically placed at the

---

[1] F, III, viii, 278.

[2] *To* Felton, 31 Dec (p. 415).

[3] E.g. Fanny Appleton (see *To* Felton, 31 July 42, *fn*, p. 293) and Jonathan Chapman (see 15 Oct 42, *fn*, p. 345).

[4] *To* Forster, 26 Apr (p. 211)

[5] For example, the levees, with such details as the audience lining up "exactly like the Chorus to God Save the Queen" (p. 205); the "very queer customers" at their reception in the West, including the one who "stood in a corner, motionless like an eight-day clock" (p. 178); the "letters all about nothing, and all requiring an immediate answer" (p. 87); various "intensified bores", and above all, the "Literary Ladies".

[6] *To* the Editor of *The Times*, 15 Jan 43 and *fns* (p. 423).

[7] F, IV, ii, 302.

[8] For reasons he was "not at liberty to explain", he postponed, on 10 Mar, the writing of a pamphlet; by 14 Mar he had seen Chapman & Hall's accounts, and gave up the idea of buying a house out of town; instead, he explored Finchley, where by 21 Mar he had found rooms in a farmhouse, in which to "bury" himself; and on 22 Mar asked Mitton not to tell his publishers what he was "about in the writing way", so that it should come "(if it come at all) a surprise" (see pp. 461-6).

[9] *To* Mitton, 7 June (p. 501).

very end of the May number; and with nicely calculated suspense, expectation was prolonged through the June number, which ends with the voyage.

The July number "exploded upon them", in Forster's phrase, with the arrival of Martin and Mark Tapley in New York: the travellers' first impression of the land of liberty is the legion of newsboys swarming on to the steamboat, crying their wares (the violence and licentious slanders of "the New York Peeper", "the New York Spy", "the New York Sewer"), and their first encounter is with Colonel Diver of the *Rowdy Journal*. Little doubt could remain of Dickens's determination to concentrate on the seamy side of his experiences; into the visitors' first twenty-four hours is concentrated everything that he hated, and nothing that he liked except the sherry-cobbler. The single sympathetically drawn American, the enlightened observer from Massachusetts, is himself a plain-spoken critic of his own country; but Dickens half admits that this might not serve to placate his American friends, by making Mr Bevan say, "the best of us are something like the man in Goldsmith's comedy, who wouldn't suffer anybody but himself to abuse his master".

Chuzzlewit must have been a severe test of Dickens's firmest American friendships. Even Felton commented (in a letter not to him but to Forster)[2] in such terms as to convince Dickens that on this question they could never "agree on paper"—Dickens predicting, however, that one day Felton would admit "My dear Dickens you were right, though rough",[3] thus, for once, acknowledging some roughness. Two months later, he told Prescott that "the heartiest of Greek Professors has become strangely mute". Meanwhile Felton would have read the September chapters (which include the Watertoast Gazette, the levees in the West, and the arrival in Eden) and might well have noted Willis's tart comment on the July number: "The North American Review will be obliged to unfrock him of its high approbation and give us a new review of his 'American Notes' "[4] (i.e. in place of Felton's). But Felton must have written to Dickens with all his customary warmth in December, judging from Dickens's immediate reply, with only a joking reference to the subject, and the conclusion, "The Proscribed One. Oh, breathe not his name!"[5]

Dickens had nearly finished writing the September number when news reached him (from a correspondent unnamed in Forster's extract)[6] of the outburst in the American press.[7] Its only effect was to make him anxious on behalf of Macready, shortly leaving for America, for fear their known friendship might endanger the success of his season there.[8] But the charge of ingratitude to his former hosts and entertainers (made also by several English papers) evidently rankled, and was the one point on which he considered making a defence.[9] He

---

[1] 28 June.   [2] With whom he had established a correspondence.

[3] *To* Felton, 1 Sep (p. 547).

[4] *National Intelligencer*, 21 July.

[5] See 2 Jan 44 (N, I, 553).

[6] *To* Forster, 15 Aug 43 (p. 541).

[7] For *Brother Jonathan*'s review, see p. 541, *fn.* Others were on equally predictable lines, varying only between outraged abuse and contempt: "gross libel", "lies and blackguardism", "sad trash", "precious twaddle".

[8] See pp. 548–56 below; especially *To* Macready, 1 Sep.

[9] *To* Forster, 15 Aug (p. 541); as before, Forster dissuaded him.

must also have resented the continued imputation of mercenary motives: the accusation of having visited America on a "money making speculation"—not only to write "a catch-guinea book", but to increase his own profits by obtaining an international copyright law—was inevitably revived; he was thought to have been provoked by the failure of both ventures, and, moreover, to have found the popularity of his novels fading:

> From the returns of the sales of the earlier numbers of *Martin Chuzzlewit*, he must have received a fearful warning of the mutability of human affairs . . . Abuse of America would rally his market; and the more bitter and biting, the better for this effect.[1]

The one uncomfortable grain of truth, the disappointing sales of *Chuzzlewit*, should not have been common knowledge; but there had been earlier rumours in America of his financial difficulties, as well as wildly exaggerated statements about his profits, which some put as high as £30,000. The ingenious Willis supplied the answer: unexpected wealth had "lifted him irresistibly to an expensive level of life" which "not only absorbs his entire present income, but crowds hard upon the future . . . the bills of Messrs. Chapman & Hall for a thousand pounds have been discounted and used while the equivalent is still uncoined in his brain."[2] Something about the terms of the agreement of 7 September 1841 had evidently leaked out; and American visitors in the summer of 1843 may have sent back misleading reports of Dickens's style of living.[3] So, a year after his return, the intrusion of American journalists upon his private affairs still continued.

The actual financial anxiety which developed in the late autumn had additional causes, notably the "many, never-satisfied, constantly recurring claims" from the incorrigible John Dickens and other "blood-petitioners".[4] A few hitherto unpublished letters (and Dickens's accounts-book) supply more evidence of their extent—and, more strikingly, how they affected him. "Nothing makes me so wretched, or so unfit for what I have to do, as these things. They are so entirely beyond my own controul, so far out of my reach, such a drag-chain on my life, that for the time they utterly dispirit me, and weigh me down."[5]

The many letters unconnected with or only indirectly related to his American journey demonstrate the truth of Forster's recollection that "he returned from America with wider views . . . and with more maturity of mind".[6] America's political and social system was not the answer; but an answer had to be found— "in these times, when so wide a gulf has opened between the rich and poor, which, instead of narrowing, as all good men would have it, grows broader daily".[7] Questions of public health, and factory legislation, and above all, popular education, all engaged Dickens's attention and practical concern. In the

---

[1] *United States Magazine*, Oct 1843, in a review of *Change for American Notes*, pp. 347–9.

[2] *New Mirror*, 8 July; reprinted in the *National Intelligencer*, 12 July.

[3] See, for instance, *To* S. G. Howe, 19 May, *fn* (p. 493).

[4] *To* Forster, ?17 Nov and *fn* (p. 600), and *To* Mitton, 4 Dec (p. 604).

[5] *To* Mitton, 28 Sep (p. 576).   [6] F, IV, ii, 307.

[7] *To* the *Morning Chronicle*, 25 July 42 (p. 285).

last, he must have felt the challenge of the Americans' achievements.[1] He should also have approved of their relative freedom, in the education of the poor, from controversies over "creeds and formulas". His admiration for Channing, as well as his growing disgust with the established Church, clearly influenced his decision to join the Unitarians, "who *would* do something for human improvement, if they could; and who practise Charity and Toleration."[2] In the current schemes for "improvement" Dickens was increasingly active, and fertile in expedients and projects—joining committees, making speeches, writing and planning anonymous articles, even making overtures for the editing of a Liberal newspaper. His hard-hitting letter (now first attributed to him) attacking Lord Londonderry's opposition to the Mines and Collieries bill was his most direct incursion into political controversy; but equally important, and more far-reaching in their effect on his fiction, were his impassioned response to the Second Report of the Children's Employment Commission ("I am so perfectly stricken down by the blue book you have sent me"),[3] and his activities on behalf of Starey's Ragged School in Field Lane.[4] His letters enlisting the support of Miss Coutts, a churchwoman, convincing her that "creeds and forms" were inappropriate to the "desolate" condition of such children, and his public warning of the dangers of ignorance in his speech at the Manchester Athenaeum Soirée, mark further stages in a crusade which he would continue for several years. Its most telling stroke in 1843 was Scrooge's vision of the two children, Ignorance and Want, "meagre, ragged, scowling, wolfish . . . monsters horrible and dread"; and the writing of *A Christmas Carol* (its triumphant success as yet unalloyed) is a fitting climax to the year.

By December, America, to him as to Martin Chuzzlewit, was "a cloud upon the sea behind".[5] The more remote consequences of the visit, in Dickens's renewed determination to "enlarge [his] stock of experience and observation"[6] by further travel (and in countries where he would not be drawn into controversy) belong to the following year.

Problems concerning the dating of letters have been comparatively light in this volume. Dickens still occasionally, as indeed throughout his life, dated letters with only the day of the week; but usually external events or other letters have made the dating of these simple. Most interesting are his own misdatings during his first fortnight in the States: the excitement of his reception, and his crowded social life, threw out his time-sense to such an extent that he even forgot the date of his birthday, giving it more than once as 8 February.[7] Of 1843 all

---

[1] Cf. *Chuzzlewit*, Ch. 17: see *To* Macready, 22 Mar 42 and *fn* (p. 156).
[2] *To* Felton, 2 Mar and *fn* (pp. 455–6).
[3] *To* Southwood Smith, 6 Mar 43 (p. 459).
[4] *To* Miss Coutts, 16 Sep 43 (p. 562); cf. *To* Forster, 24 Sep (p. 572).
[5] *Chuzzlewit*, Ch. 34.   [6] *To* Forster, 1 Nov 43 (p. 587).
[7] For his most crucial misdating during his first week in Boston, see *To* Alexander, ?27 Jan, *hn* and *fns* (pp. 26–7).

that need be said is that in the Nonesuch edition and elsewhere several 1843 letters were placed in 1847 through the misreading of Dickens's loosely-written "3".

Our practice with Dickens's punctuation and spelling follows that of previous volumes; as with his own mis-spellings, those in letters written by G. P. Putnam, his secretary, are preserved and indicated in footnotes. But we have not footnoted Dickens's variations in the spelling of "via" on letter-covers.

MADELINE HOUSE
GRAHAM STOREY
KATHLEEN TILLOTSON

ACKNOWLEDGMENTS

We are again deeply grateful to the Pilgrim Trustees for their generous grant to make this edition possible; and to Mr Christopher Dickens, owner of the copyright in Dickens's letters, for giving us permission to use unpublished material.

It is with great sorrow at his recent death that we record our gratitude to Mr W. J. Carlton, whose unique knowledge of Dickens's family background and early career made him an indispensable prop of this edition from its beginning; our notes, particularly in Volume I, on the obscurer friends and acquaintances, owed most of their substance to his indefatigable researches; and he was still gallantly exploring unknown corners in Dickens biography and helping us, either directly or through the pages of the *Dickensian*, at an age when most scholars have to call a halt. We shall miss him greatly; but all future volumes will continue to draw on both his published articles and the wealth of detailed information he had sent us.

In this volume, we owe special thanks to those who have given us much-needed help in annotating Dickens's visit to America. First, we want to acknowledge our great debt to our Associate Editor, the late Mr Noel Peyrouton: besides combing through innumerable American sales catalogues, he gave us his time and skill in untiring research, and many of our American notes would have been impossible without him. His death in February 1968 was a great loss to us. We are extremely grateful to Mr Edwin C. Sanford, who generously continued Mr Peyrouton's help, in responding to a great many appeals for information. Professor Peter Morgan has put us greatly in his debt by allowing us to consult the proof sheets of his *Letters of Thomas Hood*; and Professor James J. Barnes has most kindly given us information in advance of his forthcoming book on copyright in America. We are indebted to Professor John Wallace, Dr Errol Durbach, Professor Paul B. Davis and Professor Peter S. Bracher, for their help with American and Canadian newspapers; and particularly to Mr Hugh Tulloch for helping us to find the "forged letter".

Our original helpers have continued to give us their support in a great many ways. We are particularly grateful to Sir Rupert Hart-Davis for his warm interest and for reading our proofs. The death in 1968 of our original indexer and valued adviser, Mr J. C. Thornton, was a severe loss to the edition: but we are fortunate in now having as his successor Mr Philip Wright, to whom we already owe much. We must especially thank Mr Alan Bell for his discovery of new letters and his valuable help in the National Library of Scotland.

For their generous permission to use their important Dickens collections and their continuing help when it is asked for, we are again greatly indebted to libraries in the United States mentioned in our earlier volumes and especially to the following: the Henry E. Huntington Library, California, and Miss Jean F. Preston; the Pierpont Morgan Library, New York, and Mr Herbert Cahoon; the Berg Collection in the New York Public Library and Mrs Lola L. Szladits; the

Miriam Lutcher Stark Library, University of Texas, and Mr F. W. Roberts; and the Free Library of Philadelphia (with its Benoliel Collection) in which we owe special thanks to Mr Howell J. Heaney for the kindness with which all new letters acquired are speedily photographed for our use. We particularly wish to acknowledge our debt to Yale University Library, and to thank its librarian Miss Marjorie G. Wynne for so swiftly providing us with photographs of those letters formerly in the possession of Colonel Gimbel which we had nevertheless not seen, and to Miss Suzanne Rutter and Mr John Podeschi for all their help in sorting and listing the collection when it came to Yale, and answering our queries.

Among English libraries and collections, our greatest immediate debt is to the Victoria & Albert Museum for allowing us access to all the invaluable manuscripts and newspaper cuttings in the Forster Collection; and to Dickens House where, as a gift from the Comtesse de Suzannet, a large part of the famous Suzannet Collection has joined the splendid collection of letters already there. We also thank its Curator, Miss M. E. Pillers, for her ready cooperation.

To the authorities of the following institutions we express our gratitude for permission to publish the letters they have recently made available to us:

Öffentliche Bibliothek der Universität Basel; Bodleian Library, Oxford; Brown University Library, Rhode Island; Cheltenham Ladies' College and Miss Sheila Knowles; Chicago Public Library; Clark University, Worcester, Mass.; the County Borough of Derby; Dunedin Public Library, New Zealand; University of Michigan Library; the Warden and Fellows of New College, Oxford; New Hampshire Historical Society; City of Norwich Museums; University of Rochester Library, New York; University of Reading; Rhode Island Historical Society; Alexander Turnbull Library, New Zealand; the Unitarian College, Manchester.

We are also most grateful to the following owners who have kindly allowed us to see letters in their possession or have sent us photographs of them:

Mr Nathan L. Bengis; Mr Nicolas Bentley; Commander J. Bickford-Smith, RN; Mr William Bridges; Mr Thomas Brown; Mr John Butts; Mrs Sheila Caton; Mr Edward Caulfield; Mrs Margaret Cleminson; Cockburn & Co. (Leith) Ltd; Mr C. F. Cork; Dr Noël J. Cortés, MD; Mr John J. Curran; Miss E. S. de Kock; Mrs Pauline Dower; Mr Alfred Essex; Mrs T. Evans; Mr Douglas C. Ewing; Mr J. F. Fields; Mr Paul Getty, Jnr; Mr Peter Goodricke; Mrs D. Harmer; Mr Charles F. Heindl; Mr Robert L. Henderson; Mr Richard Hobbs; Mr D. C. L. Holland; Miss H. R. Jackson; the Viscount Knutsford; Miss Susan Sidi Leon; Mrs M. Long-Fox; Mr I. H. Macdonald; McDowell Kent Books Ltd.; Messrs MacFarlan Smith & Co.; Mr W. Marriott; Trustees of the Hon. Mrs John Mildmay-White; Mr Conny Nelson; Dr Robert Newsom; Mrs Isabel Painter; Monsieur Jean Paladilhe; Mr A. H. Reed; Mr Robert B. Riss; Mr Alec Robertson; Miss Julia Rosenthal; Chas J. Sawyer Ltd; Mrs H. B. Sinclair; Brigadier Lord Stratheden and Campbell; Mrs Helena Taylor; Mr Thomas L. Twidell; Mr W. D. Varnals; Mrs Geoffrey Williams; Mr H. W. Woodward.

For help too varied to be specified we wish to record our grateful thanks to the following:

Mr Anthony Burton; Mrs John Butt; Dr Margaret Cardwell; Professor David

R. Cheney; Mr Randolph W. Church; Cincinnati Historical Society; Professor P. A. W. Collins; the Library of Congress; Dr John Cule; Mr George de Gex; the late Major Philip Dickens; Professor K. J. Fielding; Colin & Charlotte Franklin; Mr Eric Gaskell; Miss Freda Gaye; Professor Gordon S. Haight; Mrs Christian Hardie; Professor Barbara Hardy; the Rev. H. G. Herrington; Mrs John House; Mr T. L. Ingram; Dr Louis James; Mr Brian Jenkins; Mrs Elizabeth Kemp; Professor J. Kinsley; Mr G. Norman Knight; Miss Margaret Lane; Mrs L. Lee; Mr R. A. Leigh; the Archives and Local History Group of Lewisham Borough Library; Mr Raymond Lister; Miss Katherine Longley; Maggs Bros Ltd and Miss Hinda Rose; Mr Brian Maidment; Mr Dudley Massey; Professor Sylvère Monod; Dr A. N. L. Munby; Sir John Murray; the National Register of Archives, Scotland; Professor Ada B. Nisbet; the National Library, Ottawa; Pennsylvania Historical and Museum Commission; Mr A. J. Phelps; Mr Michael Pidgley; Pittsburgh Public Library; Mr Ernest Raymond; Mr Graham Reynolds; Professor Edgar Rosenberg; St Louis Public Library; Union College, Schenectady; the School of Scottish Studies, Edinburgh, and Mr Alan Bruford and Mr Hamish Henderson; Mr Robert Shosteck; Professor Stuart C. Sherman; the Society of Antiquaries, London; the Society of Antiquaries, Newcastle-upon-Tyne; the Society of Authors; Dr A. W. O. Taylor; Sir Charles Tennyson; Mr A. McKinley Terhune; the late Professor Geoffrey Tillotson; Mr E. W. F. Tomlin; Mr John Wilson, Mrs Shaw Warnock.

Finally we must thank Mr Anthony Laude for help in checking; Mrs Margaret Brown for her expert typing help and much valued support; and Miss Nina Burgis, the incalculable benefit of whose regular assistance, both for this volume and the next, we have enjoyed for several years.

BIOGRAPHICAL TABLE

1842–1843

1842	2 Jan	Leaves London for Liverpool.
	4 Jan	Sails for Boston on S.S. *Britannia* with Catherine and Anne Brown.
	22 Jan–5 Feb	Boston (Speech 1 Feb).¹
	5–12 Feb	Worcester, Springfield, Hartford (Speech 8 Feb), New Haven.
	12 Feb–5 Mar	New York (Boz Ball 14 Feb; Speech 18 Feb).
	5–9 Mar	Philadelphia.
	9 Mar–1 Apr	Washington, Richmond, Baltimore; Harrisburg, Pittsburgh (by canal).
	1–26 Apr	Cincinnati, Louisville, Cairo, St Louis (by steamboat); prairie, Lebanon, Columbus, Sandusky, Buffalo.
	26 Apr–4 May	Niagara Falls.
	4–30 May	Canada: Queenstown, Toronto, Kingston, Montreal, Quebec.
	1–7 June	New York and expedition up North River.
	7 June	Sails from New York on the *George Washington*.
	29 June	Arrives in London.
	1 Aug–30 Sep	At Broadstairs with Catherine and the children.
	Early Aug	The "forged letter" published in New York.
	19 Oct	*American Notes* published.
	20 Oct	Review of Lord Londonderry's *Letter to Lord Ashley* published in the *Morning Chronicle*.
	21 Oct	Sees Longfellow off at Bristol, with Forster.
	27 Oct–4 Nov	Expedition to Cornwall with Forster, Maclise and Stanfield.
	10 Dec	Marston's *The Patrician's Daughter* performed, with Dickens's Prologue.
	31 Dec	*Martin Chuzzlewit* No. I published; continued monthly to 30 June 1844.
1843	21–24 Jan	At Bath with Catherine.
	4 Mar	"Macready as 'Benedick'" published in the *Examiner*.

By 21 Mar	Rooms taken in Cobley's Farm, Finchley, probably for the quarter.
3 June	"Report of the Commissioners appointed to inquire into the Condition of the persons variously engaged in the University of Oxford" published in the *Examiner*.
1–?18 July	At Easthorpe Hall, Yorkshire, with Catherine and Georgina, visiting the Smithsons.
?1 Aug–2 Oct	At Broadstairs, with Catherine and the children.
4–6 Oct	At Manchester, for the first Annual Soirée of the Athenaeum on 5 Oct.
8 Oct	Returns to London.
21 Oct	Review of *La Favorita* in the *Examiner*.
1 Nov	Tells Forster of his resolve to reside and travel on the continent in 1844–5.
4 Nov	"A Word in Season" published in the *Keepsake*.
19 Dec	*A Christmas Carol* published.

ABBREVIATIONS AND SYMBOLS

CD	Used throughout this edition in all references to Charles Dickens and for his name in titles of books and articles.
D	*The Dickensian; a Magazine for Dickens Lovers*, The Dickens Fellowship, 1905–.
DAB	*Dictionary of American Biography*.
DNB	*Dictionary of National Biography*.
F, 1872–4	John Forster, *The Life of Charles Dickens*, 3 vols, 1872–4.
F	John Forster, *The Life of Charles Dickens*, edited by J. W. T. Ley, 1928. Our references are to this edition unless otherwise stated.
FC	The Forster Collection, Victoria & Albert Museum, London.
Macready, *Diaries*	*The Diaries of William Charles Macready 1833–51*, edited by William Toynbee, 2 vols, 1912.
MDGH	*The Letters of Charles Dickens*, edited by his Sister-in-law and his Eldest Daughter. Vols I & II, 1880. Vol. III, 1882.
MDGH, 1882	*The Letters of Charles Dickens*, edited by his Sister-in-law and his Eldest Daughter, 2 vols, 1882.
MDGH, 1893	*The Letters of Charles Dickens*, edited by his Sister-in-law and his Eldest Daughter, 1 vol., 1893.
N	*The Letters of Charles Dickens*, edited by Walter Dexter, 3 vols, Nonesuch Press, 1938.
OED	*Oxford English Dictionary*.
To	"*To*" before a correspondent's name denotes a letter from Dickens.
[ ]	Square brackets in letter-headings enclose conjectural dates. In the text they denote words conjecturally supplied and breaks caused by damage to the MS. In footnotes they indicate editorial interpolations.
*	Asterisks in letter-headings denote letters which we believe to be hitherto unpublished. (Extracts from some of these have, however, appeared in Edgar Johnson, *Charles Dickens, his Tragedy & Triumph*, 2 vols, 1953, and in sale-catalogues.)
†	Daggers in letter-headings denote letters of which we believe part to be hitherto unpublished.

THE LETTERS
1842-1843

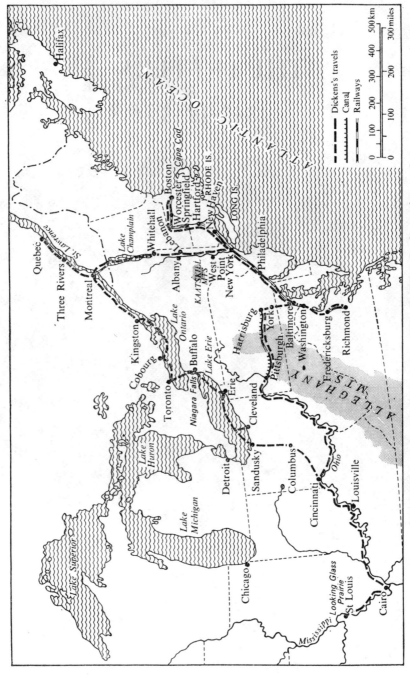

Map showing Dickens's travels in North America, 1842

To MESSRS CHAPMAN & HALL,[1] 1 JANUARY 1842†

MS Benoliel Collection.

186 Strand[2] | First January 1842.

My Dear Sirs.

In order that we may have on paper, a clear understanding of our position in reference to your advances and my receipts, on account of the American book[3] and the Monthly Work we are to commence in November,[4] I state the matter here, in regular array.

On account of the American book, I have received in all £885,[5] which is to be deducted from the first proceeds consequent on its publication.[6]

On account of the Monthly Payments agreed upon between us, in reference to the New Work, you have paid into Coutts's, the sum of £800.[7] Over and above this amount, I wish you, if you please, to make, while I am away, such payments as I have mentioned on the other side; and when I return, the balance can be struck between us.[8]

In reference to these last mentioned payments I should add that you will

---

[1] Edward Chapman (1804–80) and William Hall (?1801–47), publishers: see Vol. I, p. 128*n*.

[2] Chapman & Hall's office.

[3] The "One Volume book—such as a ten and sixpenny touch" with which CD had suggested that he might come back from America when first sounding Chapman & Hall about the visit (*To* Hall, 14 Sep 41; II, 383). *American Notes*, written on his return, was in fact published in two vols, at 10/6 each, on 19 Oct 42.

[4] See CD's Agreement with Chapman & Hall of 7 Sep 41 and the address in *Master Humphrey's Clock* (Vol. II, pp. 389*n*, 478): the first No. of the new work in monthly parts was to be published on 1 Nov 42. Meanwhile, after the completion of *Master Humphrey's Clock*, CD was to have a year's rest ("to *stop*—to write no more, not one word, for a whole year": *To* Mitton, 23 Aug 41; II, 365)—a prospect which delighted him. But within a fortnight of signing the Agreement he had decided to go to America and write a book about it. The fact that he was still, in Jan 42, envisaging the new novel as to begin the following November suggests that he expected to write *American Notes*—with the help of the diary he would be keeping and

various descriptive letters—in perhaps as little as two months. This proving impossible, publication of the opening No. of the novel (*Martin Chuzzlewit*) was postponed to 1 Jan 43.

[5] Paid by Chapman & Hall in instalments Oct–Dec 41 (Account-book, MS Messrs Coutts). A space in the MS and a couple of dots suggest that CD only filled in the figure after calculation.

[6] CD had no formal Agreement with Chapman & Hall for *American Notes*. See *To* Bradbury & Evans, 8 May 44: "I wrote them a letter giving them their share"—a quarter of the profits (N, I, 599).

[7] Credited to CD's account on 27 Dec 41 (Account-book, MS Messrs Coutts). This was £800 out of the £1800 that Chapman & Hall had agreed to advance him, in monthly instalments of £150, during his twelve months of rest and freedom: see Agreement of 7 Sep 41 (Vol. II, pp. 480–1).

[8] For the Agreement's proviso regarding liquidation of the advance, and the difficulties that ensued owing to the disappointing sales of the first six Nos of *Chuzzlewit*, see *To* Forster, 28 June 43 and *fn*. By 8 May 44 he still owed Chapman & Hall £1500 (N, I, 598).

receive, through the hands of my brother Frederick,[1] one hundred and five guineas at the end of March, and one hundred and five guineas at the end of June;[2] which you will set off against them, and duly give me credit for.

As a security for these advances, you hold three policies effected by me on my life, with the Britannia Life Assurance Company.[3]

[a]Having disposed of the business part of this letter, I should not feel at ease on leaving England, if I did not tell you once more with my whole heart, that your conduct to me, on this and on all other occasions, has ever been honorable, manly, and generous; and that I have felt it a solemn duty, in the event of any accident happening to me while I am away, to place this testimony upon record. It forms part of a Will I have made for the security of my children;—for I wish them to know it, when they are capable of understanding your worth and my appreciation of it.

Always believe me | Faithfully and truly Yours[a]
CHARLES DICKENS
(Over)

The payments referred to, to be made while I am away, are the weekly bills of my children and servants, certified as correct by my brother Frederick; ten pounds a month for the rent of their lodgings; the servants' wages; and the rent and taxes of my own house. Other payments may be rendered necessary by some omission of mine or by unlooked-for circumstances, but for whatever you pay, and for everything you pay, I request that you will take my brother Frederick's acknowledgement as mine, and that my executors and legal representatives will in every case consider it a sufficient receipt and discharge, and a proof of the correctness of your claims in these respects.

CHARLES DICKENS

To THOMAS MITTON,[4] 1 JANUARY 1842

MS Huntington Library. *Address:* Thomas Mitton Esquire (on flap of wrapper).

New Year's Day | 1842

My Dear Mitton

You will be with me at 5 of course? I merely brought these papers,[5] that you might have not[6] the inconvenience of stuffed pockets.

Faithfully Always
CD.

---

[1] Frederick William Dickens (1820–68): see Vol. I, p. 47*n*.

[2] The rent for 1 Devonshire Terrace, from Gen. Sir John Wilson (see Vol. II, p. 404*n*).

[3] For two of the Britannia policies handed over as securities by CD, see Vol. II, p. 346*n*. The third was presumably from the draft document in an unknown hand dated Dec 41, addressed to the Britannia Life Assurance Co., and numbered 524 (MS Mr C. C. Dickens).

[a-a] Extract in N, I, 371 (from MDGH); letter otherwise unpublished.

[4] Thomas Mitton (1812–78), CD's solicitor: see Vol. I, p. 35*n*.

[5] To Mitton's office, no doubt. They were presumably notes relating to his accounts with Chapman & Hall; not the bulky 1841 correspondence he deposited with Mitton before leaving for America (see Vol. I, Preface, p. xx).

[6] Thus in MS.

To DANIEL MACLISE,[1] 1 JANUARY 1842*

MS Benoliel Collection.

Devonshire Terrace | First January 1842

My Dear Maclise.

Your gloom throws a shade upon our journey in the very outset. I will say nothing of sympathy: for between such friends as we are, it is needless.[2]

I cannot go away, my dear fellow, without shaking hands with you. Between 2 and 3 to day, I *must* come and do so.

Always Your affectionate friend

Daniel Maclise Esquire CHARLES DICKENS

To EDWARD EVERETT,[3] 1 JANUARY 1842*

MS Massachusetts Historica lSociety.

Devonshire Terrace | New Year's Night | 1842.

My Dear Sir.

If I *can* thank you for your kindness and attention,[4] let me do so.

Always Yours faithfully & obliged

Edward Everett Esquire CHARLES DICKENS

[1] Daniel Maclise (?1806–70; *DNB*): see Vol. I, p. 201*n*.

[2] Maclise had written earlier on 1 Jan: "I am distressed beyond measure—my poor Mother [*Rebecca Maclise, aged 59*] is dead". She had died, he wrote, "in the most peaceful and gradual way possible with all our familiar and tearful faces round her— | Death had never been brought home to me before—and I could not have imagined the transition to be made so easy— | ... I went ... to Kensal Cemetery to-day, and chose a spot of ground the nearest I could 'tho' still far off to that spot to which a melancholy interest attaches for you— | I am gloomy beyond description—Altogether I am miserable— for your going away increases my un- happiness unspeakably—and I must aban- don the attempt to accompany you to the border of the Sea— | There is but to- morrow—and I do not like to ask you to call—and I do not intend to go out to see you— | I will not spell a blessing on you and my dear Mrs. Dickens, for I should but mar it in the expression but I will wish you all blessings *with all my heart*" (MS Huntington).

[3] Edward Everett (1794–1865; *DAB*), U.S. Minister to Great Britain 1841–5, and a leading Boston Whig. Unitarian pastor in Boston 1814–15; Professor of Greek at Harvard (Emerson a pupil) and editor of the *North American Review* 1819–24; Whig member of Congress 1825–35; Governor of Massachusetts 1836–9. Given an Honorary degree at Oxford 1843, despite Tractarian protests on the grounds of his Unitarianism. After his return from London, President of Harvard 1846–9. Devoted much of his public life to giving lectures designed to preserve the American Union.

[4] Everett had written on 30 Dec 41: "I send you a few letters for the United States. Letters are not necessary to insure you a welcome; but they may facilitate your acquaintance. I will just give you an indication of the persons written to:— | Dr Channing well known to you by reputa- tion. | Mr Ticknor a man of fortune & letters a very accomplished scholar. | Mr Bancroft one of the most eminent writers of our History of opposite politics to most people you will see in Boston. | Mr S. Brooks, my wife's brother a merchant, a real good fellow. | Mr Davis of New York: the author of Jack Downing's letters a merchant: a very ingenious, pleasant, active man, will be useful to you. | Judge Hopkinson one of the most reputable persons in Philadelphia; of slender fortune, but rich in every thing else. | Mr Gilpin of Baltimore a wealthy retired merchant; man

To LORD JEFFREY,[1] 1 JANUARY 1842

MS Free Library of Philadelphia.

Devonshire Terrace | New Year's Night 1842

My Dear Lord Jeffrey

Write you from Boston! I *think* so.[2]—I can say anything but good bye; and that, not because I have anything about me but hope and trust, but because I love my friends dearly.[3]

God bless you! | The earnest prayer of yours ever affectionately

CHARLES DICKENS

To MRS M'IAN,[4] [1 JANUARY 1842]

Text from Goodspeeds Book Shop catalogue No. 56 (1907).

My Dear Mrs. McIan

The enclosed book[5] belongs of right to you for you have beautifully per-

of taste in pictures &c. | Mr Preston, a Senator from S. Carolina. One of our most eminent men; a rich gentleman. | Col. Winthrop of the H. R. My most intimate political friend; a true-hearted man, highly accomplished in all things. | Mrs Tayloe if her recent domestic affliction permits will receive you at one of the most agreeable firesides in Washington. Her husband is a man of fortune & leisure; an excellent fellow. | Thus you see I give you the *Carte du pays*. Accept with it my best wishes for a prosperous voyage, a pleasant tour & a happy return. | I am Dear Sir, very truly yours ... | At Washington you will be able to get abundance of letters & *renseignement* for every part of the interior; & if you determine to visit any of the Indian tribes, Mr W. will put you in the way of getting proper letters to the agents of the Gov't residing among the Indians. The Sacs & Foxes one of the nearest tribes Keokuk their Head Chief will remember me as late Gov. of Massachusetts" (rough copy by Everett, MS Massachusetts Historical Society; preserved in Everett's letter-book with MS copies of his letters to all the above).

[1] Francis Jeffrey, Lord Jeffrey (1773–1850; *DNB*): see Vol. I, p. 479*n*.

[2] In the postscript to a letter of 28 Dec Jeffrey had written: "Is it very impertinent or presumptuous in me to say that I should be singularly gratified if you would send me a line or two after your arrival in America?". Earlier in his letter he referred to the "unconscionable visit" he had paid CD; accused himself of thoughtlessness for having asked CD to waste part of his "*last day*" in giving him a formal introduction to Macready; said he still hoped that CD might find a moment in which to look in on him; promised to send a "(needless) introduction to Mrs Jeffrey's family [*i.e. the Coldens*] at New York"; and sent her and his own "best love" to Catherine (MS Huntington). On Fri 31st he wrote again, sending CD two notes to deliver, expressing the hope that he might see him before he started, and ending: "*If we shall meet again, why we shall smile—if not, our last parting was well made*" (Anderson Galleries catalogue, March 1916).

[3] CD accompanied this note with an inscribed copy of *Barnaby Rudge*; now in the Widener Library.

[4] Fanny M'Ian, a painter and Jacobite like her husband Robert M'Ian (see Vol. II, p. 309*n*), her usual subjects—like his—being Highland history and life. In Oct 42 she was appointed first Superintendent of the Female School of Design, Somerset House, which the published reports show to have been quickly successful. For her giving Leech lessons in oil painting, see W. P. Frith, *John Leech*, 1891, II, 4–5.

[5] A copy of *Old Curiosity Shop*, inscribed, according to Goodspeeds Book Shop catalogue: "Mrs. McIan with the involuntary remembrances of Charles Dickens. New Years Night 1842".

petuated it.[1] You who have done so much for the love of the fiction will accept this volume I hope, for the sake of its author.

Ever believe me | Faithfully and Truly Yours

Mrs. McIan   CHARLES DICKENS

To MRS CHARLES SMITHSON,[2] 1 JANUARY 1842*

MS Mr Robert H. Taylor.

Devonshire Terrace | New Year's night 1842.
Just going.

My Dear Mrs. Smithson

God bless you—best regards to Smithson,[3] and love to the Beauteous.[4] Think of us sometimes, and accept the inclosed[5] for my poor sake.

Always Faithfully & truly Yours

Mrs. Smithson   CHARLES DICKENS

To DR SOUTHWOOD SMITH,[6] 1 JANUARY [1842]

Extract in unidentified catalogue cutting, Dickens House; *MS* 1 p.; dated Devonshire Terrace, New Year's Night—1842 on reference to the Sanatorium.

Make me a Vice President[7] and make Talfourd[8] and Macready[9] the same on my responsibility.[10] All good attend you! . . . Think of me sometimes and wish me back again.

---

[1] In her painting of Little Nell reading the inscription on the tombstone, which she presented to CD; it was exhibited at the RA 1842 under the title *Nell and the Widow*. In the sale at Christie's of 9 July 70 it fetched £44.2s (*Catalogue of the . . . Pictures . . . of CD*, ed. J. H. Stonehouse, 1935, p. 127).

[2] Elizabeth Dorothy Smithson (?1811–1860), *née* Thompson; sister of T. J. Thompson.

[3] Charles Smithson (?1804–44), formerly in partnership with Mitton: see Vol. I, p. 427*n*.

[4] Mrs Smithson's sister, Amelia Thompson (*b.* ?1809), whom CD had seen much of at Broadstairs Sep 40 (see Vol. II, p. 120*n*); called in *To* Smithson, 20 Dec 41, "beau-

teous Bill", and 10 May 43, "Beauteous Billa"—presumably corruptions, through "Milly", of Amelia.

[5] An inscribed copy of *Old Curiosity Shop*, dated New Year's Day 1842.

[6] Thomas Southwood Smith, MD (1788–1861; *DNB*), Sanitary reformer: see Vol. II, p. 164*n*.

[7] Of the Sanatorium, Devonshire Place, which was to open in April (see Vol. II, p. 165*n*).

[8] Thomas Noon Talfourd (1795–1854; *DNB*): see Vol. I, p. 290*n*.

[9] William Charles Macready (1793–1873; *DNB*): see Vol. I, p. 279*n*.

[10] Both, on CD's initiative, had become members of the Sanatorium committee in June 41 (see Vol. II, p. 293*n*).

To LORD BROUGHAM,[1] 3 JANUARY 1842*

MS Brotherton Library, Leeds.

> Adelphi Hotel Liverpool.
> Monday Third January 1842.

My Dear Lord Brougham.

I quite forgot to say to you the other day, thus much.—If any proposition for a book to be published by the Society,[2] should be made through Chapman and Hall by Mr. Hogarth (my father in law)[3] at any time during my absence, will you kindly bear in mind my having observed to you that he has written very admirable Works of Instruction in Music and History; and is a gentleman of varied and extensive information?[4] You will remember his name by the great painter's.

The Ship weighs anchor tomorrow, at Two o'Clock. That is the best excuse I have for troubling you; and I plead it in extenuation.

> Dear Lord Brougham I am always
> Yours faithfully and obliged

The Lord Brougham.   CHARLES DICKENS

To FREDERICK DICKENS, 3 JANUARY 1842*

MS Berg Collection. *Address:* Free | Frederick Dickens Esquire | Commissariat | Treasury | London.

> Adelphi Hotel. Liverpool. | Monday Third January 1842.

My Dear Fred.

We came down here in great comfort and in good spirits. We reached this house before 7. Alfred[5] we left at Birmingham.[6] He talked of coming here to dinner, but has not arrived yet. Fanny[7] came early this morning,[8] stops all night, and sees us sail tomorrow.

Tomorrow the Britannia lies a mile or so off, to be *out* of the way of the shipping, and *in* the stream. We go out to her in a small steamer, at One. She sails directly we get aboard. The passengers[9] friends accompany them in the small

---

[1] Henry Peter Brougham, 1st Baron Brougham and Vaux (1778–1868; *DNB*): see Vol. II, p. 373*n*.

[2] The Society for the Diffusion of Useful Knowledge, of which Brougham was Chairman: see Vol. II, p. 371*n*.

[3] George Hogarth (1783–1870; *DNB*): see Vol. I, p. 54*n*.

[4] Clearly CD intended to talk about publication of some work of Hogarth's during his meeting with Chapman & Hall on 23 Dec 41: hence his letter of that date urging Hogarth to come and see him next morning (Vol. II, pp. 450–1). Hogarth may have considered extending into a book his recent long article, "Music—Art of Singing", *Chambers's Information for the People*,

Edinburgh, 1841–2, II (new edn), 769–97. But the Society did not publish any book by him.

[5] Alfred Lamert Dickens (1822–60), CD's second surviving brother: see Vol. I, p. 44*n*.

[6] Where he was working as a surveyor on the railway: see *To* Beard, 11 July, *fn*.

[7] Mrs Henry Burnett, *née* Frances Elizabeth Dickens (1810–48), CD's elder sister: see Vol. I, p. 4*n*.

[8] From Manchester, where she and Burnett had settled *c.* Oct 41. They were now living at 3 Elm Terrace, Higher Ardwick, Manchester.

[9] Thus in MS.

steamer aforesaid, and return when the anchor is weighed. They talk of seventy, but I don't believe it.[1] They expect, too, a very fine passage. God send they may be right.

Our cabin is something immensely smaller than you can possibly picture to yourself. Neither of the portmanteaus could by any mechanical contrivance be got into it. When the door is open, you can't turn round. When it's shut you can't put on a clean shirt, or take off a dirty one. When its[2] day, it's dark. When it's night, it's cold. The Saloon is incredibly less than that of "The Fame. Capt. Corbyn".[3] Anyone of the beds, with pillows, sheet, and blankets complete, might be sent from one place to another through the Post Office, with only a double stamp. I believe it's the best, notwithstanding, both in respect of the motion, and its contiguity to the lady's cabin, where Anne[4] will be. That is really a comfortable room, larger than the breakfast room in Devonshire Terrace; well-lighted, sofa'd, mirrored, and so forth. From *it's*[2] door to *our* door, is literally but a step; and not a wide one either.

Captain Hewitt[5] was not on board; and all hands were very busy, stowing away meat and greens, and an enormous cow, for milk. The stewardess[6] is a Scotch woman, and has crossed the Atlantic seventeen times. She is quite young withal, and buxom enough.

Did I give you the two receipts for Sir John Wilson, with blank dates, one in March and one in June? If not, write receipts yourself at the proper time.[7]

Forster will be home early on Wednesday morning, and will give you full particulars of our departure. Kiss the dear, beloved darlings many times for Kate and me. (I needn't ask you to take care of them)—and always believe me

My Dear Fred
Your truly affectionate brother

Frederick Dickens Esquire.   CHARLES DICKENS

Kate's face is better. She is in glorious spirits.[8]
Fletcher[9] is here.
Thompson[10] has not been telegraphed, as yet.

---

[1] There were 86 (*To* Forster, 17 Jan); but the ship had accommodation for 115 (see Vol. II, p. 422*n*).

[2] Thus in MS.

[3] One of the two ships of the General Steam Navigation Co., plying between London and Ramsgate.

[4] Anne Brown, Catherine's maid: see Vol. II, p. 392*n*.

[5] John Hewitt (frequently mis-spelt "Hewett" by CD), one of the Cunard Co.'s pioneer officers, master of the *Britannia* Oct 41–Apr 47. Born *c.* 1812 in Liverpool; master of the *Royal William* 1838–9; chief officer of the *Liverpool* 1840. In *American Notes*, Ch. 1, CD described him as "a well-made, tight-built, dapper little fellow; with a ruddy face . . . and with a clear blue

honest eye, that it does one good to see one's sparkling image in". He was awarded his 1st class Master's certificate in 1850.

[6] Mrs Bean—perhaps the wife of William Bean, a customs officer of Liverpool. CD wrote of her in *American Notes*, Ch. 1: "All happiness be with her for her bright face and her pleasant Scotch tongue, which had sounds of old Home in it for my fellow traveller".

[7] Fred was then to forward the rent received to Chapman & Hall (see 1 Jan).

[8] See *To* Maclise, 3 Jan, *fn*.

[9] Angus Fletcher (1799–1862): see Vol. I, p. 514*n*, and Vol. II, *passim*.

[10] Thomas James Thompson (1812–81): see Vol. I, p. 416*n*. He is not known to have seen CD off.

Fanny stays all night, and sees us off tomorrow.

I forgot to say that I have seen Elliotson,[1] who is prepared for any summons from you, at any time of the night or day.[2] Don't trust Morgan[3] too far. You know my love for Macready. *Stick to him.* Mind nobody else.[4]

To DANIEL MACLISE, [3] JANUARY 1842*

MS Comtesse de Suzannet. *Address: Free* | Daniel Maclise Esquire. R.A. | &c &c | 14 Russell Place | Fitzroy Square | London. *Date:* Monday was 3 Jan; letter postmarked 4 Jan.

Adelphi Hotel Liverpool. | Monday Second January 1842.

My Dear Mac.

You know I try to believe that the main usefulness and purpose of Death, is to make us fonder of each other, and to bind us together the more closely during the brief term of our existence here. I never felt the Truth of this, more, than when we parted t'other day.

I shall be delighted to hear—when I *do* hear from you in those foreign latitudes —that your Home is restored to its former peace: that your father[5] has become resigned and happy: and that this shadow in a world of shadows has passed away. Omit nothing. Tell me everything you can think of.[6] Every word will be a new link to those great chain cables which moor me to the friends I love.

I wish, Mac—I wish, and I must say it, though you be never so gloomy when you get this—that you could conceive, and from personal inspection were in a condition to understand, the wild absurdity of our "cabin". I don't know what to compare it with. A small box at a coffee room is much too big. So is a hackney coach. So is a chariot cab. It is more like one of those cabs where you get in at the back;[7] but I think you could put on a shirt in one of those: and you certainly couldn't in this chamber. There are two horse-hair seats in it, fixed to the wall— one opposite the other. Either would serve for a kettle holder. The beds (one above the other of course) might both be sent to you per post, with one additional stamp. The pillows are no thicker than crumpets; and the sheets and blankets are too ridiculous to write of.

Our luggage is all aboard. They were "taking in the Milk" when we [were] there—an enormous cow! Bread, boxes, greens, and bullocks-heads for soup,

---

[1] John Elliotson, MD (1791–1868; *DNB*): see Vol. I, p. 461*n*.

[2] Elliotson had never before acted as CD's family doctor. Whether he was called in for the children during CD's and Catherine's absence is not known; but it was he who was summoned to deal with Charley's convulsions on their return (see *To* Prescott, 31 July).

[3] Presumably the children's nurse.

[4] Although the children (Charley, Mamie, Katey and Walter) were to live with Fred, Macready had enormously reassured CD and Catherine by making himself respon-

sible for them: see Vol. II, p. 390*n*. But they did not enjoy their daily visits to the Macreadys' house: see *To* Chapman, 3 Aug, *fn*.

[5] Alexander McLise (*d.* 1853), Scottish Highlander; formerly a private soldier; with his Regiment in Cork 1797, where he settled, having married Rebecca Buchanan; worked at tanning and shoe-making.

[6] An invitation to which Maclise found it impossible to respond.

[7] A hackney cabriolet (*American Notes*, Ch. 1).

were strewn about the deck. The grand impression was the smallness of the vessel. The Saloon is nothing like that of a Ramsgate boat—there!!

How often have we wished that you were here! How often shall we wish the same thing, when we all go out together tomorrow in a small steamer, to board the 'Merrikin'[1] which[2] will be then (but was not to day) lying out, a mile or so off, in the middle of the stream! When we come home again—*when* we do—if you and Forster are *only* at Liverpool, and *only* come alongside in the Pilot's boat, I shall never know greater happiness.

God bless you a hundred times. At two tomorrow, the Atlantic will be before us. Think of us then, and many times afterwards. And always believe me, My Dear Mac

Your affectionate friend
CHARLES DICKENS[3]

To MESSRS CHAPMAN & HALL, [?3 JANUARY 1842]

Mention in postscript to next. *Date:* probably 3 Jan, since not part of *To* Chapman & Hall, 1 Jan, and on 2 Jan CD was travelling to Liverpool.

[1] i.e. ship for America, not an American ship (cf. *Pickwick*, Ch. 31). Pierre Morand, a commercial traveller and amateur artist aged about 24, who was on the *Britannia* on the same crossing, besides making sketches of CD, wrote an account of the voyage, "Reminiscence of CD's First Visit to America: by a Fellow Passenger" (for text and list of his sketches of CD, see N. C. Peyrouton, "Re: Memoir of an *American Notes* Original", *Dickens Studies*, IV [1968], 23–31). Morand describes the seeing-off of CD by his friends: Catherine, it seems, had been left in the "conjugal state-room" in the morning (no doubt with Fanny for company), while CD returned to the Adelphi for a farewell celebration; and it was well after the captain came on board (cf. the different account in *American Notes*, Ch. 1) that—to Catherine's great relief—the jolly-boat carrying CD and his friends (Forster, Alfred Dickens, Fletcher, Park, perhaps Thompson, and possibly others) drew near and the "festive party stepped upon the deck, indiscriminately shaking hands all around"—the "lion of the hour alone" maintaining a "dignified composure". After a stirrup cup in the saloon with the captain, "the jovial band rowed landward, with waving hats and ebbing cheers"—to which CD responded by "raising his right hand out of his overcoat pocket in a somewhat abstract manner" (pp. 25–6).

[2] MS reads "on which".

[3] Immediately beneath CD's signature on p. 3 of a folded sheet, and running over on to the unused p. 2, is the following in Forster's hand: "I had begun a letter to you, My dear Mac, when I saw our friend begin his, and fancied this humble side would be best for me. You know that as soon as I set foot in London again, you are the first that I will see.—What is said above, is Gospel truth about the Cabin: what he has omitted was the indescribably comic shadow of momentary bafflement and discomfiture that came over *his* face when he first saw it! If I could only convey it to you!—He has quite recovered it now, you will see by the tone in which he writes of it. And the greatest source of recovery with him, from this and all other little annoyances of the hour, has been, I should not omit to say, in Mrs. D's cheerfulness about the whole thing. Never saw anything better. She deserves to be what you know she is so emphatically called—the Beloved. Even the toothache [*Catherine's: see postscript to* To *Fred Dickens, 3 Jan*], in admiration, moderates his fangs. We are as happy as we can be without you—And everything hitherto has gone as well as possible. The luggage is all aboard: and tomorrow at 2 will be the saddest good bye I have ever said in my life. But how could we bear any sadness in this world my dear Mac, if there were not in the worst of it—hope—hope—hope. Ever my dear boy with kindest regards to all at home Your affectionate John Forster. | Adelphi Hotel | Monday Night".

To THOMAS MITTON, 3 JANUARY 1842†

MS Huntington Library.

Adelphi Hotel Liverpool, | Monday Third January 1842

My Dear Mitton

This is a short note, but I will fulfil the adage, and make it a merry one.

We came down in great comfort. Our luggage is now well aboard. Anything so utterly and monstrously absurd as the size of our cabin, no gentleman of England who lives at home at ease,[1] can for a moment imagine. A water closet of that size would be something too ridiculous to think of. *Neither of the Portmanteaus would go into it.*—There!

These Cunard packets are not very large, you know, actually, but the quantity of sleeping berths makes them much smaller, so that the Saloon is not nearly as large as in one of the Ramsgate boats. The lady's cabin is so close to ours that I could knock the door open without getting off something they call my bed, but which I believe to be a muffin, beaten flat. This is a great comfort, for it is an excellent room (the only good one in the Ship); and if there be only one other lady besides Kate, as the Stewardess thinks, I hope I shall be able to sit there, very often.

They talk of seventy passengers, but I can't think there will be so many. They talk besides (which is even more to the purpose) of a very fine passage; having had a noble one, this time last year. God send it so! We are in the best spirits, and full of hope. I *was* dashed for a moment when I saw our "Cabin"; but I got over that, directly, and laughed so much at its ludicrous proportions, that you might have heard me all over the ship.

God bless you! Write to me by the first opportunity. I will do the like by you. And always believe me, your old and faithful friend

CHARLES DICKENS

*a*I have written Chapman and Hall to give you £10 for Augustus's[2] schooling,[3] on your application to them. Good bye again.*a*

To UNKNOWN CORRESPONDENT, 3 JANUARY 1842*

MS Private.

Adelphi Hotel Liverpool. | Monday Third January 1842.

My Dear Mr. [   ]

Many thanks to you for your letters. My children live at No. 25 Osnaburgh Street.

---

[1] From the 17th century ballad, "You gentlemen of England". Quoted earlier in *To* Thompson, ?9 Feb 40 (II, 22).

aa Not previously published.

[2] Augustus Newnham Dickens (1827–66), CD's youngest brother: see Vol. I, p. 485*n*.

[3] Possibly at Mount Radford College, Exeter; headmaster, the Rev. C. R. Roper, MA (Oxon); a prospectus of Mar 1828 shows the fees to have been ten guineas *p.a.* for day-boys aged 12–15. See also Vol. II, p. 289 and *n*.

Mrs. Dickens joins me in kindest regards and farewells.

Always believe me
Faithfully Yours
John [   ]¹ Esquire   CHARLES DICKENS

To MR WEBB,² 3 JANUARY 1842*

MS John Rylands Library. *Address:* Mr. Webb.

Adelphi Hotel | January Third, 1842

Mr. Charles Dickens sends his compliments to Mr. Webb; and is greatly obliged to him for his attention, and the trouble he has taken.

To JOHN FORSTER,³ [17 JANUARY 1842]

Extract in F, III, ii, 201–3. *Date:* 17 Jan according to Forster. *From* the *Britannia,* off Newfoundland.

*CD describes their stormy passage, the hurricane which blew throughout the night of Mon 10 Jan, and the steamer's behaviour in it.*⁴

For two or three hours we gave it up as a lost thing; and with many thoughts of you, and the children, and those others who are dearest to us, waited quietly for the worst. I never expected to see the day again, and resigned myself to God as well as I could.⁵ It was a great comfort to think of the earnest and devoted friends we had left behind, and to know that the darlings would not want.

We have 86 passengers; and such a strange collection of beasts never was got together upon the sea, since the days of the Ark. I have never been in the saloon since the first day; the noise, the smell, and the closeness being quite intolerable. I have only been on deck *once !*—and then I was surprised and disappointed at the smallness of the panorama. The sea, running as it does and has done, is very stupendous, and viewed from the air or some great height would be grand no doubt. But seen from the wet and rolling decks, in this weather and these circumstances, it only impresses one giddily and painfully. I was very glad to turn away, and come below again.⁶

¹ Name in both salutation and subscription has been cut out of the MS.

² Possibly W. Webb, land agent, with whom Thomas Chapman was in partnership (see Vol. II, p. 89*n*).

³ John Forster (1812–76; *DNB*): see Vol. I, p. 239*n*. The recipient of CD's longest and most detailed letters from America, written, no doubt, with the plan already in mind of retrieving them for use as a basis for *American Notes* (see F, III, viii, 279, and Preface).

⁴ Summarized by Forster because this part of CD's letter used in *American Notes,* Ch. 2.

⁵ According to Forster, the ship's chief engineer had never seen "such stress of weather"; and Capt. Hewitt later said that "nothing but a steamer, and one of that strength, could have kept her course and stood it out" (F, III, ii, 201). On CD's account in *American Notes,* Pierre Morand commented: "Granting that this war of elements was all that is claimed for it by the imaginative author, it failed to impress itself upon a majority of the passengers as a narrow escape from a watery grave" (*Dickens Studies,* IV, 29).

⁶ According to *American Notes,* during the first two full days CD was mostly in his cabin, "not ill, but going to be"; for the next three it was extremely rough, with a head wind, and—apart from one venture on deck—he lay in his bunk, "exactly in the

I have established myself, from the first, in the ladies' cabin[1]—you remember it? I'll describe its other occupants, and our way of passing the time, to you.

First, for the occupants. Kate, and I, and Anne—when she is out of bed, which is not often. A queer little Scotch body, a Mrs. P—,[2] whose husband is a silversmith in New York. He married her at Glasgow three years ago, and bolted the day after the wedding; being (which he had not told her) heavily in debt. Since then she has been living with her mother; and she is now going out under the protection of a male cousin, to give him a year's trial. If she is not comfortable at the expiration of that time, she means to go back to Scotland again. A Mrs. B—, about 20 years old, whose husband is on board with her. He is a young Englishman domiciled in New York, and by trade (as well as I can make out) a woollen-draper. They have been married a fortnight. A Mr. and Mrs. C—, marvellously fond of each other, complete the catalogue. Mrs. C— I have settled, is a publican's daughter, and Mr. C— is running away with her, the till, the time-piece off the bar mantel-shelf, the mother's gold watch from the pocket at the head of the bed; and other miscellaneous property. The women are all pretty; unusually pretty. I never saw such good faces together, anywhere.

Apropos of rolling, I have forgotten to mention that in playing whist[3] we are obliged to put the tricks in our pockets, to keep them from disappearing altogether; and that five or six times in the course of every rubber we are all flung from our seats, roll out at different doors, and keep on rolling until we are picked up by stewards. This has become such a matter of course, that we go through it with perfect gravity; and when we are bolstered up on our sofas again, resume our conversation or our game at the point where it was interrupted.

As for news, we have more of that than you would think for. One man lost fourteen pounds at vingt-un in the saloon[4] yesterday, or another got drunk

condition of the elder Mr. Willet, after the incursion of the rioters into his bar at Chigwell". The following day the hurricane started. A fellow-passenger, Antonio Gallenga, the Italian exile known as Luigi Mariotti (see *To* Mariotti, 12 Apr 43 and *fn*), who had an introduction to CD from "a mutual friend in London" (*American Notes*, Ch. 2), wrote of the voyage: "Like Dickens, I lay for nearly all the time sick to death in my berth—so sick that a shipwreck, of which we had more than one narrow escape, would have been hailed as a happy release" (*Episodes of my Second Life*, 1884, II, 118). He could not have seen much of CD on the ship, which he left at Halifax.

[1] Where, when they were able to eat again, the stewardess brought them their meals (*American Notes*, Ch. 2). "Mr. Dickens's reserve toward his fellow-passengers was a subject of general remark", wrote Morand; but "whatever may have been his reasons for this seeming exclusiveness—and they may be readily im-agined—it is doubtful whether he did not enter more intensely into the proceedings around him than he could have done had he mingled more freely with the crowd" (*Dickens Studies*, IV, 28).

[2] "The initials used here are in no case those of the real names", says Forster (F, III, ii, 202*n*).

[3] Joined by the ship's doctor, who came down to the ladies' cabin, "by special nightly invitation", to make up a rubber (*American Notes*, Ch. 2).

[4] This was Morand. He had lost nearly $75 ("almost a catastrophe for a young commercial traveler on a moderate salary") but on the following day recovered half his loss, when, at a pause in the game, he felt a touch on his shoulder, "and looking round, beheld a pair of large and wonderfully eloquent eyes beckoning [him] to come away"—and did so. Seeing CD on deck an hour later, he tried to thank him; but CD, satisfied by Morand that he did not intend to play again in that company (later

before dinner was over, or another was blinded with lobster sauce spilt over him by the steward, or another had a fall on deck and fainted. The ship's cook was drunk yesterday morning (having got at some salt-water-damaged whiskey), and the captain ordered the boatswain to play upon him with the hose of the fire engine until he roared for mercy—which he didn't get; for he was sentenced to look out, for four hours at a stretch for four nights running, without a great coat, and to have his grog stopped. Four dozen plates were broken at dinner. One steward fell down the cabin-stairs with a round of beef, and injured his foot severely. Another steward fell down after him, and cut his eye open. The baker's taken ill: so is the pastry-cook. A new man, sick to death, has been required to fill the place of the latter officer, and has been dragged out of bed and propped up in a little house upon deck, between two casks, and ordered (the captain standing over him) to make and roll out pie-crust; which he protests, with tears in his eyes, it is death to him in his bilious state to look at. Twelve dozen of bottled porter has got loose upon deck, and the bottles are rolling about distractedly, over-head. Lord Mulgrave[1] (a handsome fellow, by the bye, to look at, and nothing but a good 'un to go) laid a wager with twenty-five other men last night, whose berths, like his, are in the fore-cabin, which can only be got at by crossing the deck, that he would reach his cabin first. Watches were set by the captain's, and they sallied forth, wrapped up in coats and storm caps. The sea broke over the ship so violently, that they were *five and twenty minutes* holding on by the handrail at the starboard paddle-box, drenched to the skin by every wave, and not daring to go on or come back, lest they should be washed overboard. News! A dozen murders in town wouldn't interest us half as much.

To JOHN FORSTER, [21 JANUARY 1842]

Extract in F, III, ii, 203–5. *Date:* 21 Jan according to Forster (continuation of letter begun 17 Jan). *From the Britannia*, in the Bay of Fundy.

We were running into Halifax-harbour on Wednesday night, with little wind and a bright moon; had made the light at its outer entrance, and given the ship in charge to the pilot; were playing our rubber, all in good spirits (for it had been comparatively smooth for some days, with tolerably dry decks and other unusual comforts), when suddenly the ship STRUCK! A rush upon deck followed

recognized as sharpers), gave "a brief injunction of secrecy regarding his intervention" and "gently bowed himself away" (*Dickens Studies*, IV, 28–9).

[1] George Constantine Phipps (1819–90; *DNB*), son of the 1st Marquis of Normanby; known as the Earl of Mulgrave 1838–63, when he succeeded his father. Served in the Scots Fusilier Guards 1838–1847. Became a friend of CD's on the voyage; and was clearly one of the "three or four ... with whom", according to Morand, "he habitually conversed or walked on deck, when not engaged in solitary rambles about the ship"—an instance of "the proverbial attraction of opposites", wrote Morand (*Dickens Studies*, IV, 27, 30). (Others were probably Frederick Whitwell and Lieut. Harry Ingersoll: see 22 Jan and 6 Mar.) Mulgrave stayed with CD and Catherine at Tremont House, Boston, over the week-end of their arrival; and invited CD to produce the Montreal garrison's amateur theatricals in May. Later they visited each other in England.

of course. The men (I mean the crew! think of this) were kicking off their shoes and throwing off their jackets preparatory to swimming ashore; the pilot was beside himself; the passengers dismayed; and everything in the most intolerable confusion and hurry. Breakers were roaring ahead; the land within a couple of hundred yards; and the vessel driving upon the surf, although her paddles were worked backwards, and everything done to stay her course. It is not the custom of steamers, it seems, to have an anchor ready. An accident occurred in getting ours over the side; and for half an hour we were throwing up rockets, burning blue lights, and firing signals of distress, all of which remained unanswered, though we were so close to the shore that we could see the waving branches of the trees. All this time, as we veered about, a man was heaving the lead every two minutes; the depths of water constantly decreasing; and nobody self-possessed but Hewitt. They let go the anchor at last, got out a boat, and sent her ashore with the fourth officer, the pilot, and four men aboard, to try and find out where we were. The pilot had no idea; but Hewitt put his little finger upon a certain part of the chart, and was as confident of the exact spot (though he had never been there in his life) as if he had lived there from infancy. The boat's return about an hour afterwards proved him to be quite right.[1] We had got into a place called the Eastern-passage, in a sudden fog and through the pilot's folly. We had struck upon a mud-bank, and driven into a perfect little pond, surrounded by banks and rocks and shoals of all kinds: the only safe speck in the place. Eased by this report, and the assurance that the tide was past the ebb, we turned in at three o'clock in the morning, to lie there all night.

CD describes their landing at Halifax on 20 Jan.

Then, sir, comes a breathless man who has been already into the ship and out again, shouting my name as he tears along. I stop, arm in arm with the little doctor[2] whom I have taken ashore for oysters. The breathless man introduces

---

[1] On their last full day on board the *Britannia*, a number of the passengers (mainly English) met to record their appreciation of Hewitt's conduct of the voyage and to open a subscription "for the purchase of a piece of silver plate" as a testimonial to him. Lord Mulgrave was voted into the chair, and CD elected as secretary and treasurer. According to Morand, Mulgrave, "although endowed with an organ that could have marshalled a whole ... regiment", could on this occasion get no further than " 'Gentlemen, I—ah—awh—' " (thrice repeated); but the situation was saved by "the nimble secretary, who, gently elbowing down his honorable friend, accomplished the refractory task in his most felicitous style" (*Dickens Studies*, IV, 30). For the minutes of the meeting, dated 21 Jan 42, and the inscription decided upon (both in CD's hand), see Appx, p. 628.

On 29 Jan, on behalf of the Committee, CD presented Hewitt with the plate—a silver pitcher, salver, and goblet (a second goblet was given him later)—in the saloon of the Tremont Theatre, Boston, before a large crowd. For CD's speech, see *Speeches*, ed. K. J. Fielding, Oxford, 1960, pp. 15–17; Hewitt's reply is given in E. F. Payne, *Dickens Days in Boston*, Boston, 1927, pp. 66–7.

[2] Who had clearly become one of CD's chief ship-board friends. The *Bunker Hill Aurora and Boston Mirror* of 29 Jan, reporting that he accompanied CD, Catherine, Lord Mulgrave and Capt. Hewitt to the Tremont Theatre on 24 Jan, called him "Dr. Wiley, of the Britannia" on one page and "Dr. Witney of the Britannia" on another. Possibly he was the F. Wiley who practised in Whitby, Yorks, 1847–50 (*London and Provincial Medical Directory*).

himself as The Speaker of the house of assembly;[1] *will* drag me away to his house; and *will* have a carriage and his wife sent down for Kate, who is laid up with a hideously swoln face.[2] Then he drags me up to the Governor's house (Lord Falkland[3] is the governor), and then Heaven knows where; concluding with both houses of parliament, which happen to meet for the session that very day, and are opened by a mock speech from the throne delivered by the governor, with one of Lord Grey's sons[4] for his aide-de-camp, and a great host of officers about him. I wish you could have seen the crowds cheering the inimitable[5] in the streets. I wish you could have seen judges, law-officers, bishops, and law-makers welcoming the inimitable. I wish you could have seen the inimitable shown to a great elbow-chair by the Speaker's throne, and sitting alone in the middle of the floor of the house of commons, the observed of all observers,[6] listening with exemplary gravity to the queerest speaking possible, and breaking in spite of himself into a smile as he thought of this commencement to the Thousand and One stories in reserve for home and Lincoln's-inn fields and Jack Straw's-castle. —Ah, Forster! when I *do* come back again!——

To T. C. GRATTAN,[7] 22 JANUARY 1842†

MS Free Library of Philadelphia. *Address:* T. C. Grattan Esquire | 11 Franklin Street.

Tremont House.[8] | Saturday Night January 22nd. 1842.
My Dear Sir.

I have received your kind note with great pleasure, and shall be delighted to shake hands with you. I regret that we cannot dine with you tomorrow, for Lord

---

[1] Joseph Howe (1804–73; *DAB*), Speaker of the Nova Scotia House of Assembly 1842–3. According to G. E. Fenety, *Life and Times of the Hon. Joseph Howe* (New Brunswick, 1896, p. 180), he had met CD in England a few years before.

[2] She had had toothache before the voyage started: see *To* Fred Dickens, 3 Jan, and *To* Maclise, 3 Jan, *fn.*

[3] Lucius Bentinck Cary, 10th Viscount Falkland (1803–84), Lieut.-Governor of Nova Scotia 1840–6.

[4] Lieut.-Col. Charles Grey (1804–70; *DNB*), second surviving son of the 2nd Earl Grey. Private secretary to Prince Albert 1849–61, and to Queen Victoria 1861–70.

[5] "This word," says Forster, "applied to him by his old master, Mr. Giles [*see Vol. I, p. 429n*], was for a long time the epithet we called him by" (F, III, ii, 205n).

[6] *Hamlet*, III, i, 154.

[7] Thomas Colley Grattan (1792–1864; *DNB*), British Consul in Boston since 1839. Travel-writer and historical novelist;

best known for his *Highways and Byways* (3 series, 1823–7; dedicated to Washington Irving), describing his travels in France. Lived mainly in Brussels 1828–39, contributing frequent articles on European affairs to British and foreign journals. Contributed two articles to the *North American Review*—"Ireland" in July 40 (LI, 187), and "The Irish in America", Jan 41 (LII, 191). Chosen by both Ashburton and Webster to assist in the north-east boundary negotiations 1842. He was one of CD's escorts in Boston: on 24 Jan took him to the State Capitol, and on 3 Feb to Lowell. Spoke at the Boston Dinner to CD on 1 Feb. A friend of Mrs Trollope: for his long letter to her of 13 May 41, with description of Boston society—Channing, Bancroft, Prescott, Everett, Judge Story ("the gem of this western world"), and a "neighbouring notability", John Quincy Adams ("hard as a piece of granite, and cold as a lump of ice")—see T. A. Trollope, *What I Remember*, 2nd edn, 1887, II, 350–6. For CD's and Hood's indignation at his flattery of the

Mulgrave (who goes on to Montreal on Monday Morning to rejoin his regiment) is with us, and we have entered into a solemn league and covenant to dine alone together, after the *ªfatigues and perils of a most tempestuous passage.ª* But I hope you will give us another opportunity of enjoying your hospitality.

Mrs. Dickens begs to be commended to Mrs. Grattan. So do I. I look forward to seeing you sometime tomorrow, and am always

Faithfully Yours

T. C. Grattan Esquire.   CHARLES DICKENS

To FREDERICK A. WHITWELL,[1] 22 JANUARY [1842]*

MS Maine Historical Society. *Address:* Fredk. A. Whitwell Esquire | 48 Chesnut[2] Street. *Date:* CD's "1841" clearly written absent-mindedly.

Tremont House | Saturday Night | January Twenty Second 1841.

Dear Sir

I am exceedingly obliged to you for your polite offer[3]—the more so, because I have the greatest possible respect for Dr. Channing,[4] and hold him in the very highest estimation.

Americans in a speech, see *To* Hood, 13 Oct 42, *fn.* His *Civilized America*, 1859, was sharply critical of the country.

[8] Boston's leading hotel, opened in 1829 and then regarded as the best hotel in America. Macready, who stayed there in Sep 43, described it as "a sort of collision of tides of humanity, continual flux and reflux from all the doors, some indifferent, some staring at me, some smoking" (*Diaries*, II, 224).

ª ª Quoted in N, I, 376; letter otherwise unpublished.

[1] Frederick Augustus Whitwell (1820–1912), later a prominent Boston merchant. He had crossed with CD on the *Britannia*.

[2] Thus in MS.

[3] To take CD to hear Channing preach next morning at the First Unitarian Meeting House; Whitwell and his sister were members of Channing's congregation.

[4] William Ellery Channing, DD (1780–1842; *DAB*), Unitarian minister of the Federal Street Church, Boston, since 1803; acclaimed in both America and Europe as a man of letters and social thinker. (His *Works*, in 6 vols, Boston, 1841–3, had gone through 22 edns by 1872.) Though a semi-invalid for much of his life, became the acknowledged leader of the American Unitarians after his famous sermon at the ordination of Jared Sparks 1819. Organized the Berry Street Conference of liberal ministers from which sprang the American

Unitarian Association 1825. "No one who has not visited the United States, and witnessed the prostration even of powerful minds before public opinion, can form an adequate conception of the extent of Dr. Channing's moral courage", wrote George Combe (*Notes on the United States of North America during a Phrenological Visit in 1838-9-40*, 1841, II, 262). His denunciations of slavery had "reared up hosts of enemies against him"; later, "while the whole Union was excited with a vivid passion for war against England about the Maine boundary, ... Dr Channing again stepped forth, ... appealed to the reason of his countrymen, ... in favour of ... the interests of civilization"; financially dependent on their congregations as American ministers were, Channing as preacher had the courage to say "Ye are the men" (*op. cit.*, III, 48–9). His *Remarks on American Literature*, 1830, was an influential plea for a native literature; and Emerson, Bryant, Longfellow, Lowell, Holmes, all closely associated with the Unitarian movement, acknowledged their debt to him. In the view of Bernhard Fabian ("The Channing Revival: Remarks on Recent Publications", *Jahrbuch für Amerikastudien*, Heidelberg, II [1957], 197–212), influenced De Tocqueville, who met him in 1831; Harriet Martineau devoted a chapter of *Retrospect of Western Travel* (1838, III, 72–91) to him. Anna Jameson described him to Ottilie von

I fear, however, that after the fatigues of the Voyage we shall not be in church-going order tomorrow morning—not to mention our having no change of dress:[1] our luggage being still on board.

We are not the less indebted to you. Mrs. Dickens begs her compliments to yourself, and to your sister,[2]—in which I cordially join. I am always Dear Sir

                                                                    Faithfully Yours
Fredk. A Whitwell Esquire.   CHARLES DICKENS

To G. W. MINNS,[3] 23 JANUARY 1842

Extract from letter formerly in possession of the Philadelphia Library Company; dated Tremont House, Boston, 23 Jan 42.

I beg you to thank the Committee.[4] *Continues that he will receive them at half-past ten.*[5]

Goethe as "a very little man, with a look of feebleness and ill health, and no beauty whatever except a most beautiful expression which comes over his face when he is preaching or speaking . . . a human being more good, more wise, more pure than any other being I had ever approached" (*Letters of Anna Jameson to Ottilie von Goethe*, ed. G. H. Needler, 1939, p. 98). For CD's admiration of him, see *American Notes*, Ch. 3. Channing did not accept the invitation to the Boston Dinner; but CD and Catherine breakfasted with him on 2 Feb. For the suggestion (which CD declined) that he should write an essay on him after his death, see *To* the Rev. George Armstrong, ?5–8 Nov 42.

[1] For Samuel Warren's scorn at CD's missing hearing Channing preach for such a reason, see *To* Felton, 31 Dec 42, *fn* (but cf. Harriet Martineau in *Retrospect of Western Travel*, I, 3: "Our sea dresses . . . would not serve for a Sunday in Liverpool"). On board he had worn, according to Morand, the pea-coat ("of a coarse-haired dark brown material, and a trifle large") and cork-soled boots mentioned in *American Notes*, Ch. 2; also "a dark flat *négligé* cap" (*Dickens Studies*, IV, 27, and drawing facing p. 25). But by the Sunday afternoon, when Morand sketched him again, standing in the hotel dressed for a walk, he had changed, wrote Morand, into a "navy blue cloth coat with gilt buttons, buff casimere vest and light gray trousers . . ., and a some-what heavy looking silk hat" (drawing reproduced with description in *CD and Maria*

Beadnell, ed. G. P. Baker, privately printed, Boston, 1908, facing p. 152): but he still wore the brown pea-coat as an overcoat.

[2] Sophia L. Whitwell (*b.* 1821).

[3] George Washington Minns (1813–95), Boston lawyer and educationalist. First signatory of the invitation to CD from the "Young Men of Boston" and spoke at the Dinner (1 Feb). According to E. F. Payne (*Dickens Days in Boston*, p. 77), was presented to CD on the evening of his arrival in Boston, when CD remarked on the title of his first published Sketch—"Mr. Minns and his Cousin".

[4] Of the Young Men of Boston, appointed on 27 Nov 41 to invite CD to a public dinner. They had written to him before he left England that, in common with the whole American people, they hailed the news of his intended visit with delight. He would come to a strange land, but not among strangers; for he had long been a guest at their firesides. They were above all, they wrote, drawn to him irresistibly "by that sympathy with universal man (the concomitant only of the highest genius), which prompted you to utter the noble sentiment, that 'you were anxious to show that virtue may be found in the by-ways of the world; that it is not incompatible with poverty, or even rags; and that you wished to distil out, if you could, from evil things the soul of goodness which the Creator has put in them [*cf.* Henry V, IV, *i*, *4 and the 1841 preface to* Oliver].' " They went on to invite him to "a public dinner, or more private entertainment" at whatever time

To [HENRY DEXTER],[1] [25 JANUARY 1842]

MS Yale University Library. *Address:* Clearly to Henry Dexter since he and Alexander were the only people in America to whom CD consented to sit, and he sat to Alexander on Tues 25th. *Date:* No doubt CD had originally arranged to give first sittings to both Alexander and Dexter on the Tuesday, but to Dexter earlier in the day—at Tremont House, while he ate his breakfast.

Tremont House. | Tuesday Morning

My Dear Sir

I very much regret that I am *obliged*[2] by the pressure of correspondence, and by my late rising this morning (consequent on the fatigues of yesterday)[3] to postpone our sitting until tomorrow at the same hour.[4]

Faithfully Yours

CHARLES DICKENS

would be most agreeable to him. The letter (quoted in W. G. Wilkins, *CD in America*, 1911, pp. 19–20) was signed by the members of the Committee—Geo. Minns, Chas. H. Mills, James R. Lowell, Henry Gardner, and Samuel Parkman, Jr.

[5] Presumably that evening.

[1] Henry Dexter (1806–76; *DAB*), sculptor, self-taught; brought up in poverty; worked as a blacksmith 1822–35. In 1828 married Francis Alexander's niece. After trying portrait-painting in Providence 1836, moved in same year to Boston and, with Alexander's help, began to work on portrait-busts. Soon highly successful, his sitters including Longfellow, Louis Agassiz, Felton and CD (a commission no doubt obtained for him by Alexander). He is said to have produced nearly 200 busts in all.

[2] Underlined twice.

[3] Which included receiving callers in the morning, a visit to the Capitol in the afternoon and to the Tremont Theatre in the evening.

[4] Dexter worked, so G. W. Putnam wrote (*Atlantic Monthly*, XXVI [1870], 478), while CD "ate his breakfast, read his letters and [*after Putnam became his secretary*] dictated the answers", frequently coming over to look at him from different angles or measure bits of his face with callipers. When done, both CD and Catherine were highly pleased with the bust: CD "repeatedly alluded to it, during his stay, as a very successful work of art" (*ibid.*); and Catherine wrote to Dexter that she thought it "a beautiful likeness", would much like their English friends to see it, and hoped "for an early cast" (quoted in E. F. Payne, *Dickens Days in Boston*, p. 52). Dr Walter Channing, W. E. Channing's brother, one of a large party received by CD at Tremont House during a sitting, sent Dexter on 26 Mar an account of what he had observed: "Mr. Dickens was now speaking and now listening ... In your bust you give his expression both of feature and of feeling, just as he is about to reply to what he has heard. It is clear he has been pleased with what has been said; but at the same time along with the expression of this pleasure you gather from the bust the precise tone of his forthcoming reply" (MS Mrs Percy W. Valentine). In Nov 42 a subscription was planned by Longfellow and others "to have Dexter cut his bust of Dickens in marble, to be sent to Mrs. D." (*The Letters of H. W. Longfellow*, ed. A. Hilen, Cambridge, Mass., 1966, II, 478); but nothing came of this, and what happened to the original is not known. A cast in the possession of Dexter's grand-daughter was later given to the Boston Dickens Fellowship, who in 1962 presented it to Dickens House, Doughty Street: see frontispiece.

To MR AND MRS GEORGE BANCROFT,[1]
25 JANUARY 1842

Extract in Samuel T. Freeman & Co. catalogue, April 1937; *MS* (3rd person) 1 p.; dated Tremont House, 25 Jan 42.

Mr. & Mrs. Dickens have great pleasure in accepting Mr. & Mrs. Bancroft's[2] kind invitation for Thursday evening next.[3]

To JOSEPH M. FIELD,[4] 25 JANUARY 1842

MS Boston Public Library.

Tremont House | January Twenty Fifth | 1842.

Mr. Charles Dickens presents his compliments to Mr. Field, and is extremely obliged to him for the MS he had the goodness to send last night.[5] Though

---

[1] George Bancroft (1800–91; *DAB*), historian and diplomat; one of the very few Democrats CD met in Boston; as such, subject to Whig ostracism (see *To* Macready, 22 Mar). After four years in Europe, taught Greek at Harvard 1823, and conducted Round Hill School with J. G. Cogswell at Northampton, Mass., 1824–31. Made his reputation with the first 3 vols of his *History of the United States*, 1834–40, which, wrote Prescott, gave him a "place among the great historical writers of the age" (*North American Review*, LII [1841], 101). He and CD were in touch with each other again in 1849.

[2] *Née* Elizabeth Davis (*d.* 1866), sister of John Davis, Governor of Massachusetts, and widow of Alexander Bliss, a junior partner in Daniel Webster's law firm. Bancroft had married her in 1838, after the death of his first wife, Sarah Dwight, 1837.

[3] According to *The Journal of R. H. Dana, Jr.*, ed. R. F. Lucid, Cambridge, Mass., 1968, I, 57–9, CD dined on Thurs 27th with Francis C. Gray, a cousin of Mrs Alexander's, in Beacon Street, where the guests included, besides Dana himself, Alexander, W. H. Prescott, Sumner, C. P. Curtis, Jared Sparks, and George Ticknor (for Dana's comments on the evening, see *To* Forster, 30 Jan, *fn*); and then went with Catherine to an evening party at R. G. Shaw's. Presumably they went on afterwards to the Bancrofts. They were "constantly out two or three times in the evening" according to Catherine (see her letter to Fanny Burnett, 30 Jan 42, Appx, p. 629). In a paragraph on Boston's social customs

in *American Notes*, Ch. 3, CD explains that "the usual dinner-hour is two o'clock. A dinner party takes place at five; and at an evening party, they seldom sup later than eleven; so that it goes hard but one gets home, even from a rout, by midnight."

[4] Joseph M. Field (1810–56; *DAB*), Irish-born actor, playwright and journalist. Brought to America very young, had become a leading actor by the mid-1830s. His dramatization of *Nickleby* was performed at the Tremont Theatre in Mar 39, and the first Act revived for CD's visit there on 24 Jan: he played Mantalini and his wife Smike. The same evening he played "Boz" in his "Boz! A Masque Phrenological" (first presented at his benefit the previous Friday). On 14 Mar his *Quozziana*—a parody of the American lionizing of CD—was performed at the Tremont with great success. Field also wrote occasional verse as "Straws", and at the Boston Dinner to CD on 1 Feb sang a comic song, "The Werry Last Obserwations of Weller, Senior", composed by himself. His daughter was Kate Field, friend of Trollope, Thackeray, and the Brownings, and author of *Pen Photographs of CD's Readings*, Boston, 1868.

[5] The MS of his "Boz! | *A Masque Phrenological* | written in honour of the arrival of | CHARLES DICKENS ESQR. | Boston Jan. 22nd. | 1842" (now in the Forster Collection, V & A), in which the characters listed are Boz himself, characters from his novels, and various phrenological "faculties" ("Identity", "Mirth", "Wonder", &c). The play-bills (which gave the title

Mr. Dickens had not received any such mark of Mr. Field's courtesy and attention, he would still have felt it a pleasure and a duty to thank him for his most ingenious compliment, which afforded him very high gratification and entertainment.[1]

To CHARLES SUMNER,[2] 25 JANUARY 1842*

MS Massachusetts Historical Society.

Tremont House | January Twenty Fifth 1842.

My Dear Sir.

Many thanks to you for your note. I hoped to have seen you this morning, but I have been beset and torn to pieces all day long.[3] I shall trust myself in

as "Boz! | A Masque Phrenologic") elaborated on the faculties, as follows: "Skyblue, (a neglected genius)", "Philo progenitiveness, (as Queen Victoria)", "Self Esteem, (as a 'distinguished contributor')", "Firmness, (as General Jackson!)", "Wonder, (as a Celebrated Transcendentalist!)"—possibly Emerson; &c. The back-cloth represented State Street and the exterior of Tremont House. "Boz" spoke the final speech only: "Besides, I'm told they rather *read me* there, | For *nothing* too! yet not for that I care; | Although, no doubt, their Authors would delight | To see me paid, *so* get themselves their '*Right*'; | But pshaw! I must not quarrel with the 'Trade', | In golden smiles more richly am I paid; | Happy, when gone, if they my wish recall— | God bless their Lit'rature and bless them all!"

[1] On p. 2 of the MS of the *Masque*, Field wrote as an introduction: "Will the Author of Nicholas Nickleby permit an Actor to thank him for the compliment confer'd upon his profession in the dedication of the immortal 'Nickleby' to Wm. Macready Esqr. ? He has humbly endeavored, in his own way, to hail the arrival of Boz in America by the composition of a little piece, which, thanks to the charm which accompanies its title—'Boz', has been received with favour by the public. If the author has taken a liberty in making Boz hint at the 'International Copyright' question, he begs pardon, and would respectfully intimate, that in speaking a word for foreign writers, he is not altogether uninfluenced by a feeling for the native."

[2] Charles Sumner (1811–74; *DAB*), statesman; son of the Sheriff of Suffolk County; leader of the anti-slavery Whigs. After studying under Joseph Story at Harvard, he practised law with George S. Hillard and taught at the Harvard Law School 1835–7; travelled in England and on the Continent Dec 37–Apr 40. On his return devoted much of his energies to literary pursuits. Introducing CD and Catherine to Sumner, John Kenyon wrote: "You will have a hundred sympathies with him, and Mrs. Dickens's mild, unexacting character and manners will only make you the more disposed to be kindly and useful to her" (MS Harvard College Library). Sumner wrote to Lord Morpeth, 19 Jan: "We are on tiptoe to see who shall catch the first view of Dickens above the wave" (E. L. Pierce, *Memoir and Letters of Charles Sumner*, Boston, 1878–93, II, 201).

[3] During the morning he had sat to Francis Alexander at his studio at 41 Tremont Row, after being introduced to a large number of Alexander's friends. Going to and from the studio he had been watched by a crowd—described by G. W. Putnam as "to the last degree silent and respectful" (*Atlantic Monthly*, XXVI [1870], 477), but by Charles Parsons (quoted in E. F. Payne, *Dickens Days in Boston*, p. 36) as consisting of foolishly importunate women. His sittings to Alexander became a daily opportunity for "girls and women, who call themselves ladies" to wait for him at corners and cram Alexander's room, so that they could see CD when he came out of the studio (Mrs J. L. Motley *to* her husband, 5 Feb 42: *J. L. Motley and his Family*, ed. S. and H. St John Mildmay, 1910, p. 25).

your den[1] tomorrow, or if not tomorrow, next day. My will leads me there. My visitors keep me here. Cannot we plot to have *one* quiet day together, before I go away?[2]

Believe me ever | Faithfully Yours

Charles Sumner Esquire.　　　　　　CHARLES DICKENS

To W. W. GREENOUGH,[3] 26 JANUARY 1842*

MS Free Library of Philadelphia.

Tremont House | Twenty Sixth January 1842.

My Dear Sir.

I am truly sorry that I cannot accept the welcome Invitation you have given me on behalf of your club.[4] Pray assure the gentlemen[5] who compose it, when you thank them cordially and warmly in my name, that if I had had but one disengaged day (which I have not) I should have been proud and happy to pass it in their society.

Faithfully Yours—and theirs—

W. W. Greenough Esquire　　　　　CHARLES DICKENS

To CHESTER HARDING,[6] 26 JANUARY 1842*

Photograph, Longfellow House.

Tremont House | January Twenty Sixth 1842.

Dear Sir

I am much flattered and obliged by your request,[7] and would willingly accede

---

[1] His office at 4 Court Street, shared with George S. Hillard. Longfellow, Felton and other literary friends used it as their Boston headquarters.

[2] Sumner became CD's principal American escort in Boston. On 24 Jan he and Grattan had taken CD to the State Capitol; on the 26th he escorted him and Catherine to the ball at Papanti's Hall, after calling on him in the afternoon with Longfellow; on the 29th he and Jonathan Chapman (Mayor of Boston) took them to the Perkins Institute for the Blind (of which Sumner was a trustee) and other South Boston institutions; and on Sun 30th he and Longfellow conducted CD on a long sight-seeing walk which included Copp's Hill Burying Ground and the Bunker Hill Monument, having previously taken him to the Seamen's Bethel to hear a sermon from the famous Father Taylor (the only sermon he heard in America, as one evangelical paper indignantly pointed out: see unidentified newspaper cutting, Forster Collection, V & A). For CD's description of the sermon, see *American Notes*, Ch. 3; see also Harriet Martineau, *Retrospect of Western Travel*, III, 240f., and *Society in America*, 1837, II, 264.

[3] William Whitwell Greenough (1818–1899), Boston merchant. Graduated from Harvard 1838 and spent Dec 40 to Apr 41 in Europe. Co-founder of the American Oriental Society 1843. Later a member of the Boston Common Council.

[4] Just possibly the Wednesday Evening Club of which Greenough's grandfather had been one of the founder-members in the 1770s—though Greenough was not himself a member until 1858. Later, he supplied much of the biographical information for the club history.

[5] MS reads "gentleman".

[6] Chester Harding (1792–1866; *DAB*), portrait painter. Brought up in virtual poverty; successively a drummer in the War of 1812, a cabinet-maker, a house-decorator and sign-painter in Pittsburgh, before discovering his talent for painting portraits. Came to Boston to meet Gilbert Stuart and was soon fashionable. His sitters included Daniel Webster, Washington Allston, and Joseph Story.

[7] Clearly that CD would sit to him.

to it, if I had the time—if I could, with the slightest regard to my personal comfort, health, or exercise. But I really cannot. Believe me that I regret it very much.

Chester Harding Esquire.

Faithfully Yours
CHARLES DICKENS

To GENERAL TWIGGS,[1] 26 JANUARY 1842

MS[2] Private. *Address:* General Twigg[3] | Tremont House.

Tremont House | January 26th. 1842.

My dear Sir.
   I shall be happy to see you, and your friend at four o'clock this afternoon, if that hour will suit your convenience.

Faithfully Yours
CHARLES DICKENS[4]

To DR R. H. COLLYER,[5] 27 JANUARY 1842

Text from *Boston Morning Post*, 1 Feb 42.

Tremont House | 27 January 1842

Dear Sir,
   If we can possibly arrange it, I shall be much interested in seeing your cases,

---

[1] Presumably Colonel David Emanuel Twiggs (1790–1862; *DAB*), commanding officer of the U.S. Second Dragoons since 1836. Acting Brigadier-General during the 1836 campaign of the Second Seminole War, he apparently continued to use the title although not promoted to it till 1846. Breveted Major-General for gallantry in the Mexican War.

[2] Ending and signature are in CD's hand; the rest in Catherine's.

[3] No doubt Catherine's misreading: see her writing of the name in note below. (No General Twigg has been found.)

[4] In a note dated "Tremont House | Saturday" (clearly 29 Jan) Catherine wrote: "Mrs. Dickens presents her compliments to General Twigg's [*thus in MS*] and begs to acknowledge the receipt of the very beautiful flowers, for which she is extremely obliged."

[5] Robert Hanham Collyer, MD, physician and mesmerist; studied under Elliotson at London University 1833–5; settled in America 1836 and graduated from Berkshire Medical College, Mass., 1839. Claimed, after several successful experiments 1839–41, to be the discoverer of anaesthesia "by the inhalation of narcotic and stimulating vapours", and of "phreno-mesmerism". In June–July 41 gave demonstrations of animal magnetism before a Boston Committee "of thirty learned in law, medicine, and theology", who, if not finally convinced, were at least impressed. In the same year brought out an American edn of C. H. Townshend's *Facts in Mesmerism*, with an Appx containing the detailed report of the Boston committee, which especially mentioned Collyer's experiments on "the boy Frederick" for whom clairvoyance was claimed (cf. Townshend's own experiments on the boy Alexis: Vol. II, pp. 291–2n). Lectured in England Oct 43–Feb 44. His books include *A Manual of Phrenology*, New York, [?1835], and *Lights and Shadows of American Life*, Boston, [?1844], in which he mentions "my friend Dickens" (a claim based solely on this single exchange of letters). He also edited the *Mesmeric Magazine*, Boston, in 1842, and contributed to the *Lancet* and to Elliotson's *Zoist*. His discovery of Marryat with Mrs Collyer in their hotel bedroom at Louisville, Sep 38, caused great scandal, but a duel was averted (Marryat's *Diary in America*, ed. Jules Zanger, 1960, Introduction, pp. 23–4).

when you come to Boston.[1] With regard to my opinion on the subject of Mesmerism, I have no hesitation in saying that I have closely watched Dr. Elliotson's[2] experiments from the first[3]—that he is one of my most intimate and valued friends—that I have the utmost reliance on his honor, character, and ability, and would trust my life in his hands at any time—and that after what I have seen with my own eyes and observed with my own senses, I should be untrue both to him and myself, if I should shrink[4] for a moment from saying that I am a believer,[5] and that I became so against all my preconceived opinions.[4]

Faithfully yours,

To Dr. Collyer[4]

CHARLES DICKENS[6]

To EDMUND B. GREEN,[7] 27 JANUARY 1842

Text from *New England Weekly Review*, 5 Feb 42.

Tremont House, Boston, | Twenty Seventh January, 1842[8]

My Dear Sir,

Pray assure my friends in Hartford, that I joyfully and gladly accept their most welcome invitation—that I shall arrange to meet you at Springfield, on Monday week;[9] and that I shall have the pleasure of dining with them on

[1] Collyer had lectured in Boston on 13, 15, 20 and 22 Jan 42, but was not appearing there again until Apr; so he and CD almost certainly did not meet.

[2] The *Boston Morning Post* reads "Doct. Ellison's". But undoubtedly the text in an undated, unidentified newspaper-cutting in the BM is correct in reading "Dr. Elliotson's".

[3] For his attending experiments by Elliotson, see Vol. I, p. 461 and *n*.

[4] Text as given in BM's newspaper-cutting reads "if I shrunk, for a moment,"; "opinions and impressions"; "To Dr. Collyer, New Bedford."

[5] He demonstrated his belief by mesmerizing Catherine at Pittsburgh (see *To* Forster, 2 Apr 42).

[6] Publication of this letter aroused much newspaper comment: the *Baltimore Patriot* (25 Feb) thought CD's belief in animal magnetism should be classed as one of the "Infirmities of Genius"; but the *New World* (12 Feb) applauded the courage of a frank avowal which might detract from CD's popularity. At a lecture in Boston on 14 Apr, Collyer read his own letter to CD as well as CD's reply; and in at least one lecture in England he exhibited CD's letter (mention in BM newspaper-cutting). For a detailed discussion of Collyer, the attacks on him by the well-known phrenologist O. S. Fowler (elder brother of L. N.

Fowler, who phrenologized CD at Worcester: see *To* Forster, 17 Feb, *fn*), and the current controversy about phreno-mesmerism, see N. C. Peyrouton, "Boz and the American Phreno-Mesmerists", *Dickens Studies*, III (1967), 38–50.

[7] Edmund Brewster Green (1814–52), editor and part-proprietor of the *New England Weekly Review*, a Whig paper published at Hartford. For a time, private secretary to Henry Clay. Joined the California gold rush 1850, taking the sea route, but stopped at Panama, where he published the weekly *Panama Herald*. Father of the historian John Fiske (originally Edmund Fiske Green).

[8] Date written out thus, in full, indicates that letter was in CD's own hand (similarly, *To* Unknown Correspondent, 27 Jan): cf. Putnam's style, as secretary, in *To* Felton and *To* Roberts, 27 Jan. The writer of letters quoted from catalogue and other printed sources giving dates in abbreviated or standardized form, cannot be determined.

[9] Green was presumably one of the "deputation of two" which met CD and Catherine at Springfield on 7 Feb and took them on by steamboat to Hartford (*To* Forster, 17 Feb). He was a member of the committee of arrangements for the Hartford Dinner to CD, and one of the speakers.

Wednesday following.[1] Add that I shall ever remember my Thirtieth Birthday, (the intervening Tuesday) as the season of their kindness and congratulation, above all my other birthdays, past, present, or to come.

Faithfully yours

Edmund B. Green, Esquire.   CHARLES DICKENS

To JARED SPARKS,[2] 27 JANUARY [1842]

Mention in American Art Association catalogue, Nov 1926; *MS* 1 p.; dated Tremont House, 27 Jan.

Saying that he and Catherine intended to call on him before they left Boston.[3]

To UNKNOWN CORRESPONDENT, 27 JANUARY 1842*

MS City Library Association, Springfield, Massachusetts.

Tremont House. | January Twenty Seventh 1842.

My Dear Sir.

I am truly sorry to be obliged to refuse you, but I am so much fatigued, and have been so totally deprived of any opportunity of walking or riding, that I have resolved (among other wise resolutions) to sit no more to anyone during my stay in America.

Faithfully Yours
CHARLES DICKENS

---

[1] In three other letters (*To* Forster, 29 Jan, *To* Fred Dickens, 30 Jan, *To* Macready, 31 Jan) CD gives the day of the Hartford Dinner as a Wednesday. In fact it took place, at the City Hotel, on Tues 8 Feb (*Hartford Daily Courant*, 10 Feb). Presumably Green's invitation had mentioned 8 Feb, not the day of the week, and CD had miscalculated: cf. his not only saying in this letter that his birthday (Mon 7 Feb in 1842) was on a Tuesday, but also announcing in his Hartford speech on 8 Feb that he now had a new reason for remembering that day "which is already one of mark in my calendar, it being my birthday". The *Hartford Daily Courant* of 10 Feb described the dinner as "a grand affair—high[ly] creditable to the Young Men of Hartford". William J. Hammersley (publisher, bookseller, and local politician; later Mayor of Hartford) presided; there were

many official speeches and other toasts; and some verses, written in CD's honour by Mrs Lydia Sigourney, were recited. For CD's speech, with its allusions to international copyright, see *To* Forster, 14 Feb and *fn*, and *Speeches*, ed. K. J. Fielding, pp. 23–6 (misdated 7 Feb).

[2] Jared Sparks (1789–1866; *DAB*), historian. After a brilliant career at Harvard, was successively pastor of the First Independent (Unitarian) Church, Baltimore, 1819–23, and owner and editor of the *North American Review*, Boston, 1823–9. Thenceforth devoted himself to historical writing, editing the works of George Washington, Benjamin Franklin and other Revolutionary writers. In 1839 became McLean Professor of History at Harvard.

[3] CD met him that same evening at dinner at F. C. Gray's.

To N. P. WILLIS,[1] 27 JANUARY [1842]

Extract in Madigan's Autograph Bulletin, n.d. [?1931–2]; dated Tremont House, Boston, 27 Jan.

I am exceedingly obliged to you for your cordial welcome and shall be very glad indeed to renew our acquaintance.[2] I can scarcely hope, our movements being very rapid and uncertain, to enjoy the hospitality of your cottage,[3] but I shall look forward to seeing you at least; and to making Mrs. Dickens known to your lady.[4]

To THE NEW YORK DINNER COMMITTEE,[5] ?27 JANUARY 1842

Text from the *New York Tribune*, 9 Feb 42. *Date:* probably correct, since date in printed source is clearly based on CD's usual style. (For doubts about other 27 Jan letters, see next, *To* Alexander, *hn* and *fns*.)

Tremont House, Boston | 27th January 1842

My Dear Sirs,

I need not tell you that I accept with inexpressible pride and pleasure the invitation with which you have honored me, and I cannot tell you how much moved and gratified I have been by the terms in which it is conveyed. Your kind

---

[1] Nathaniel Parker Willis (1806–67; *DAB*), poet and journalist; published his first poems at Yale. Travelled abroad 1832–7 as correspondent of the *New York Mirror*, enjoying considerable social success in England; entertained by Lady Blessington (through whom he met Landor who entrusted him with his latest "Imaginary Conversations"—regaining them with difficulty). But the gossip and indiscretion of his *Mirror* letters (collected as *Pencillings by the Way*, 1835) infuriated many: J. G. Lockhart attacked him for "printing . . . — before your claret is dry on his lips—unrestrained *table-talk on delicate subjects, and capable of compromising individuals*" (*Quarterly*, LIV [1835], 469). Engaged Thackeray (who later parodied him as "Napoleon Putnam Wiggins" in *Fraser's*, Sep and Oct 41) to write travel letters for the *Corsair*, a New York weekly he edited 1839–40. Sympathized with CD's stand on copyright (see a long letter, mainly giving his impressions of CD at the Boz Ball, printed in *D*, XII [1916], 241–4).

[2] For his meeting with CD in Nov 35, see Vol. I, p. 88*n*.

[3] Glenmary, on Oswego Creek, New York State.

[4] An English girl, *née* Mary Stace,

daughter of General Stace, Royal Ordnance Storekeeper at Woolwich. Willis had married her 1835. She was at Glenmary when CD and Catherine were in New York and did not meet them; but Willis took Catherine sight-seeing (H. A. Beers, *N. P. Willis*, Boston, 1885, p. 264). For his asking Catherine to give him Maclise's picture of the Dickens children, see *To* Maclise, 22 Mar, *fn*.

[5] The Committee had written to CD on 24 Jan a letter of welcome congratulating him on his safe arrival and assuring him that he would find himself "no stranger" among them: "that genius", they wrote, "with which you have been so signally gifted . . . has secured to you a passport to all hearts—whilst your happy personifications, and apt illustrations—pointing at every turn, a practical & fruitful moral,— have rendered your name as familiar to us as household words." In testimony of their respect and as a tribute to his genius, they requested him to name as early a day as would be convenient for him to meet them at a public dinner. Forty-one signatures follow, including those of Irving, Bryant, Hone, Colden and Fitz-Greene Halleck (MS Forster Collection, V & A).

and earnest words have done my heart good—you have made me feel indeed that I am no stranger among you, and I have looked at your names a hundred times, as if they were the faces of old friends.

As nearly as I can guess I shall be in New-York on Saturday the 12th of February, or it may be a day earlier. Any day toward the latter end of the following week that will suit you will suit me.[1]

Be assured that you cannot name any time which will not be a bright day in the calendar of my life; and that all hours and seasons will be alike welcome to me.

Believe me, dear Sirs, with cordial and affectionate regard,

Your faithful friend,

To the Committee, &c. &c. &c., New-York.   CHARLES DICKENS[2]

To FRANCIS ALEXANDER,[3] [?27 JANUARY 1842]

MS Comtesse de Suzannet. *Date:* 26 Jan if CD's "Wednesday" correct; but according to Putnam ("Four Months with CD . . . By his Secretary", *Atlantic Monthly*, XXVI [1870], 477), himself elsewhere accurate over dates, it was in the "forenoon" of the Thursday (27 Jan) that CD mentioned to Alexander his need of

[1] CD arrived in New York on 12 Feb, and the Dinner was given on the 18th at the City Hotel, with Washington Irving in the chair.

[2] Philip Hone (see 16 Sep, *fn*) recorded in his diary, 1 Feb, that "the dinnerites" met again on 31 Jan at the Carlton House. Samuel Jones, first Chief Justice of New York City, presided, a committee of arrangement was appointed and the following officers for the dinner were selected: Washington Irving, John Duer, John A. King, Judge Betts and Hone himself (*The Diary of Philip Hone, 1828–51*, ed. Allan Nevins, new edn, New York, 1936, p. 583).

[3] Francis Alexander (1800–?81; *DAB*), portrait painter, to whom CD had promised to sit "directly on [his] arrival" in Boston (see Vol. II, p. 438 and *n*). For his boarding the *Britannia* the moment it docked, and driving CD, Catherine and Lord Mulgrave to Tremont House, see *To* Forster, 29 Jan. According to R. H. Dana, he was "thought to *toady* Dickens, & people call him 'Mr. Le Creevy'" (*The Journal of R. H. Dana, Jr.*, ed. R. F. Lucid, I, 59). But CD plainly liked him. His portrait of CD (begun Tues 25 Jan)—the only one painted of him during his visit to America—shows him with head bent forward, pen in hand, just looking up from what he has been writing. The expression is soft and lacking character, the face as a whole too smooth. The portrait is now in the Boston Museum of Fine Arts. Alexander preserved a sheet of paper on which CD had doodled and written during one of the sittings (MS Pennsylvania Historical Society). On one side are a face, a chair, perhaps a bird's wing, two asterisks, the words "Little Nell", "Charles" (with a large D-shaped scribble over the beginning of it), and various other unidentifiable marks. At the foot of the page is written: "It is a world of disappointment—often to the hopes we most cherish, and hopes that do our nature the greatest honor. | Poor Dick was dead." On the other side of the page, also in CD's hand, are three extracts from *Old Curiosity Shop*: "Oh! it is hard to take to heart the lesson that such deaths will teach . . . a way of light to Heaven!" (from Ch. 72); "Dear, gentle, patient, noble Nell was dead . . . and motionless for ever" (from Ch. 71); and Dick Swiveller's "It was always thus . . . marry a market gardener" (Ch. 56, paragraph 2, slightly altered: e.g. "young Gazelle" for "soft Gazelle"). These are followed by: " 'Oh Sammy, Sammy', said the older Mr. Weller, mournfully; 'I know'd wot u'd come o' this here vay o' doin' bisness. Vy worn't there a alleybi!'" (the final lines of *Pickwick*, Ch. 34, slightly altered); and a stanza from "The Ivy Green".

a secretary,[1] which he followed up later that day with a note, almost certainly the note below—probably written (if Thursday night 27 Jan is accepted) in the interval between his return from F. C. Gray's dinner and his departure with Catherine for two evening parties (see *To* Bancroft, 25 Jan, *fn*): see *fn*.

Tremont House. | Wednesday Night

My Dear Sir.

Will you (I forgot to ask you just now) speak to Mr. Putnam[2] for me, and bespeak his assistance[3] *during the time I am in Boston*? If I find him very useful,— then I can propose to him to travel with me, in such a manner as will not displease him.[4]

[1] A letter from Catherine to Alexander dated "Thursday Morning" (quoted in E. F. Payne, *Dickens Days in Boston*, p. 53) cancelled CD's Thursday sitting because he was "so much pressed", "had so many letters which must be written" and could not be "delayed any longer" (such as *To The New York Dinner Committee*). This was surely the immediate prelude to CD's decision to have a secretary. Catherine's "Thursday", agreeing as it does with Putnam's dating, can be more confidently accepted than CD's "Wednesday", particularly since other letters of CD's show that in the excitement of his first two weeks in America his awareness of dates was erratic.

[2] George Washington Putnam (1812–96), son of Joseph Putnam, owner of a shoe business, and Mercy Giddings Whipple, of Salem, Massachusetts. First employed at 12 as clerk in a Salem drug store; then learnt carriage and ornamental painting; but by 1841—when his picture, *The Doctor*, was exhibited in the Boston Athenaeum—had become a pupil in portrait painting of Alexander's and was writing articles on art for the *New York Herald*, *Boston Transcript*, and other newspapers. For his work for the anti-slavery cause, to which he devoted much of his life, see N. C. Peyrouton, "Mr. 'Q', CD's American Secretary", *D*, LIX (1963), 156–9. Having clearly had no success as a portrait painter, he was working as an interior decorator in Lynn, Massachusetts, when he visited CD in Boston in Nov 67.

[3] Putnam was with Alexander when CD's note arrived, and—not waiting for the following morning—they set off on the short walk to Tremont House. It was then arranged that Putnam should start work the following day; and "on Friday morning", wrote Putnam (*ibid.*), "I was there at 9 o'clock, the time appointed". Although Putnam's dating puts CD's in the wrong, there seems good reason for accepting it: since Putnam is accepted as correct in saying that CD first sat to Alexander on the Tuesday (25th), there seem no grounds for doubting his statement (on same page) that he called at Tremont House on the Thursday and began work for CD on the Friday (28th). Moreover, CD had clearly not sat to Alexander on the day he wrote this note he dated Wednesday ("just now" surely referred to the "forenoon" call, not to a morning sitting); and Catherine's letter of Thursday shows that was a day he did not sit: that he should miss sittings on two days running during his brief stay in Boston seems inconceivable. But for other dating complications, see letters that follow, and *fns*.

[4] The *Salem Observer* (quoted in the *American Traveller*, 8 Feb) announced that Putnam, Alexander's pupil, was accompanying CD "as a friend and companion in his tour". For the uses to which CD put Putnam, see *To* Alexander, 25 Feb, *fn*; references to his "Boston friend" in *American Notes* show that CD found him both efficient and an amusing companion. He was paid $10 a month (*To* Fred Dickens, 30 Jan)—later increased to $20 (*To* Mitton, 4 Apr). Towards CD Putnam felt "an ardent attachment, which has its origin not alone in the splendor of his genius, but in the daily and hourly exhibition of the finest and noblest feelings of the human heart" (letter, quoted in the *Boston Daily Evening Transcript*, 18 Mar 42). He described his experiences in "Four Months with CD. During his First Visit to America (in 1842). By his Secretary" (*Atlantic Monthly*, Oct and Nov 70, XXVI, 476–82, 591–9).

I need hardly say that if he can call upon me early tomorrow morning, he will relieve me very much.

Yours and Mrs. Alexander's[1] | Affectionately

(and pro. tem.[2] knocked up)

BOZ

To C. C. FELTON,[3] 27 JANUARY [1842]*

MS[4] Mr Noel C. Peyrouton.

Tremont House Jan 27

My dear Sir

Mrs. Dickens and myself will have great pleasure in dining with you on Tuesday next[5] at 5 o clock.

Faithfully Yours

CHARLES DICKENS

Professor Felton

To G. W. ROBERTS,[6] 27 JANUARY [1842]

MS[7] Mr Noel C. Peyrouton.

Tremont House Jan 27

Dear Sir,

I thank you for your consideration. I shall be at leisure, and glad to see you,

---

[1] *Née* Lucia Gray Swett, daughter of Col. Samuel Swett, of Boston; described by Alexander to William Dunlap as a "lady of exceptional beauty and wealth". For her later friendship with Ruskin, see 25 Feb, *fn.*

[2] Written after "temporalily" cancelled; plainly a word CD in his exhausted state could not trust himself to spell.

[3] Cornelius Conway Felton (1807–62; *DAB*), Eliot Professor of Greek Literature at Harvard since 1834; President of Harvard 1860–2. The son of poor parents, he taught at Round Hill School, Northampton, and other Massachusetts schools while at Harvard 1823–7 and for two years after graduating. Intimate at Harvard with Longfellow, Sumner, Hillard and S. G. Howe. Widely read in English literature; spoke several European languages; contributed to the *North American Review*, *Christian Examiner* and other periodicals. Described by L. G. Clark in *Harper's New Monthly*, August 62, as "one of the most kind-hearted and best of men. In person . . . very comfortably fleshy and compact; of fair complexion, and with the sweetest expression gleaming through gold spectacles from his fine blue-gray eyes." Became CD's closest American friend and

most regular correspondent. Wrote a spirited defence of *American Notes* for the *North American Review* (Jan 43): see *To* Felton, 2 Mar 43, *fn.*

[4] In Putnam's hand except for ending and signature. This letter and next, *To* Roberts, are the only known letters in Putnam's hand dated 27 Jan. It seems possible that *either* CD jotted them down on the 27th and they were the first he gave Putnam to copy when he started work on the 28th and Putnam copied the date too; *or* (more probably) that CD gave them to Putnam to write, to test his handwriting, when he and Alexander called at Tremont House on the night before he started work officially.

[5] A dating mistake: the following Tuesday (1 Feb) was the night of the Boston Dinner, beginning 5 p.m. Possibly Felton had invited CD and Catherine to dine with him before their visit to the National Theatre on the 31st (at which they arrived 6.15), mentioning date but not day, and CD had miscalculated. During the afternoon of the 31st (according to E. F. Payne, *Dickens Days in Boston*, p. 82) Felton took CD sight-seeing.

[6] George W. Roberts (1803–60), owner and publisher of the *Boston Notion* and the

at 3 o clock tomorrow.[1] In the matter of business I should add, perhaps, at once that I have no intention of writing while I remain in America, except once for the Knickerbocker;[2] and that I leave all publishing arrangements to my publishers in London.

Faithfully Yours

G. W. Roberts Esq   CHARLES DICKENS

To ROBERT H. MORRIS,[3] 28 JANUARY 1842

Text from *New York Tribune,* 3 Feb 42.

Tremont House, Boston | Jan. 28, 1842

My Dear Sir,

I beg to convey to the Committee of Gentlemen,[4] whose organ you are, my hearty and cordial thanks for their most kind congratulations; and my glad acceptance of the honor they propose to confer upon me.[5]

Boston Daily Times. In 1839 the *Notion* had serialized *Nickleby* (obviously piratically). It now not only greeted CD's arrival in America with "Welcome, loved stranger from a distand strand! | Welcome, thrice welcome to our happy land" and eulogized his characters in verse (22 Jan), but remained faithful to him when many other papers turned against him, asserting —in reply to the *Boston Courier*'s attacks— that it was "a bad return to a popular author, whose mind works for us gratis, . . . to insult him with baseless accusations of meanness and cupidity" (28 May). From Feb to Apr 42 it published a number of reports of CD's activities while in Boston.

[7] In Putnam's hand except for ending and signature. Probably written at the same time and in the same circumstances as last: see *To* Felton, *fn.*

[1] Spelt "tommorrow" by Putnam. Must refer to Fri, not Sat (when CD could not expect to be at leisure); note would be delivered by hand without delay.

[2] An intention he did not carry out.

[3] Robert Hunter Morris (1802–55), Mayor of New York City. Practised at the New York Bar from 1829 and entered politics 1833. City Recorder 1838–41 (removed by Governor Seward as a Democrat); three times Mayor 1841–3; Postmaster of the City 1845–9. As Mayor he was popular and efficient and drafted the law replacing the old watch system with a police force. Wrongly identified in *N* as Robert Morris (1818–88), author.

[4] The General Committee formed to invite CD to a public Ball in New York— dubbed "the ballites" by Philip Hone in his diary. The resolutions passed at their first meeting, at Astor House on 26 Jan, under Morris's chairmanship, are given in W. G. Wilkins, *CD in America,* pp. 105–6 (taken from the Executive Committee's Report, *Welcome to CD. The Boz Ball. . . .,* privately printed, New York, 1842). They included the resolve that ladies should participate: "for we feel assured that our countrywomen will look with little favor on any device which excludes them from joining in a Festival given in honor of him whose imagination and heart gave birth to 'little Nell' " (*Welcome to CD,* p. 2). The detailed arrangements for the Ball were entrusted to an Executive Committee of 19 (R. H. Morris Chairman, D. C. Colden and D. C. Pell Secretaries); and Philip Hone was requested to write a letter of invitation, to be delivered to CD by Colden. All present signed the letter. Details of this and subsequent meetings, and the members of both Committees, are given in Wilkins, *op. cit.,* pp. 105–12.

[5] A letter of 26 Jan, drafted by Hone, had welcomed CD, and in appreciation of the value of his "labors in the cause of humanity, & the eminently successful exercise of [his] literary talents", had requested, "in behalf of a large meeting of gentlemen convened for the purpose", his and Catherine's attendance at a public ball to be given in New York. Mr Colden, one of the Committee, would present the invitation and find out which day would suit him. 44 signatures followed (MS Forster Collection, V & A).

I have had the pleasure of seeing your agent,[1] and of explaining my movements and arrangements to that gentleman.

Rest assured, that I shall only be too proud and happy to meet you at any time you may appoint, after receiving his explanation of my engagements.[2]

With many thanks to you and the Committee, generally, I am, my dear Sir, yours, faithfully and obliged,

Robert H. Morris, Esq.   CHARLES DICKENS

To DAVID C. COLDEN,[3] 28 JANUARY 1842

Mention in Colden *to* CD, 29 Jan 42.

Referring to the Ball Committee's invitation, and evidently telling Colden that he would not be arriving in New York until the 12th.[4]

[1] David Colden (see next, *fn*) was in fact ill and had to entrust the invitation to a friend, Mr Blake. In a long letter to CD, dated 27 Jan (also delivered by Blake on 28 Jan), he explained that he had engaged to be the bearer of the invitation on the grounds that he had met CD and Catherine at the Macreadys' in Summer 1840 ("*our* friend", Macready had called him in writing to CD, 7 Dec 41: see Vol. II, p. 442*n*); also that he had learnt from his wife's sister (who was Lord Jeffrey's second wife) of the friendship that had grown up since he left England between CD's family and Lord Jeffrey's. The Committee hoped, he said, that the Ball might be arranged for 7 or 8 Feb—lest Lent, beginning the following week, kept anyone away from it. He was aware that CD had received an invitation to a dinner in New York, but the ball would not clash with this: many gentlemen were "parties to both of them". Adding "one word" for his own family—"Mrs. Colden her Mother brother sister" and himself—he said they wished CD and Catherine to take the same place among them as the Macreadys had occupied: "My wife and sister . . . will be most happy to afford Mrs. Dickens and yourself a retreat by a quiet fireside whenever you are weary of the gaieties in which I see that it is inevitable you must be involved." If CD and Catherine arrived in New York on Sat 5th, he offered them a seat in the church the family attended, where they would hear "very good preaching", and afterwards a family dinner (MS Forster Collection, V & A).

[2] This letter and *To* Colden, 28 Jan, were clearly taken back to New York by Blake; and on 29 Jan Colden wrote again on behalf of the Committee.

[3] David Cadwallader Colden (1797–1850), lawyer and philanthropist; son of C. D. Colden, Mayor of New York; grandson of Samuel Provoost (1742–1815; *DAB*), first Protestant Episcopal Bishop of New York; and great-grandson of Cadwallader Colden, botanist and loyalist Lieut-Governor of New York 1761. Admitted to the New York Bar 1819, but increasingly devoted himself to public service. Described in the *New York Historical Magazine*, Second Series, Nov 67, as a very "perfect gentleman—modest, accomplished, generous and honorable", who "mingled rarely in the mere business concerns of life, but with the advantages of fortune and position" recognized what the community owed "to talent and genius and personal distinction". He had spent Spring and Summer 1840 in England. Was Joint-Secretary of the New York Ball Committee, a member of the Dinner Committee, and one of CD's most attentive hosts in New York. They met several times again in London.

[4] Colden replied on 29 Jan that he had received CD's letter of the day before; and as CD said that he had arranged to be in New York by 12 Feb and would leave the choice of the day to the Ball Committee, they would "take the liberty of naming Monday the 14th." (MS Forster Collection, V & A).

To THE REV. H. F. [HARRINGTON],[1] 28 JANUARY [1842]*

MS[2] Longfellow House. *Address:* Subscription reads "Hannington"; presumably CD had misread Harrington's signature.

Tremont House Jan 28

Dear Sir,

I very much regret not having seen you when you did me the favor to call here. I am much gratified by the communication you have made to me from the young men of Providence, and I assure you I am unaffectedly sorry that I cannot meet them and personally reciprocate their kind feelings at present. Although the distance from Boston is so short[3] it is an almost insurmountable journey to me; every moment of my time being fully occupied and every morning and evening engaged during the whole term of my stay here.

I beg you to return my hearty thanks to those on whose behalf you have communicated with me and to say that I still look forward to meeting them when I return this way next June.[4]

I scarcely know what to say in relation to that part of your earnest letter in which you speak of the effect my books have had upon your life, but I can honestly tell you that I have never received from any quarter, public or private, any testimony of their usefulness which has impressed me more—or any encouragement to proceed in the same course which I shall longer remember.

Faithfully Yours

Rev Henry F Hannington | Providence. | R.I.   CHARLES DICKENS

To THE REV. W. E. CHANNING, 29 JANUARY 1842*

MS[5] Rhode Island Historical Society.

Tremont House | Jan 29 | 1842.

My Dear Dr. Channing,

I shall indeed be glad to shake hands with you in the free and friendly way you speak of, and if you and Mrs. Channing[6] will let us come and Breakfast with you on Wednesday morning,[7] and will let me know in one word at what hour, we shall be delighted to meet you.

[1] No doubt Henry Francis Harrington (1814–?89), of Providence; Minister at large for Unitarian societies since 1841. After graduating from Harvard 1834, taught in Boston and practised journalism for a time. Successively founded Unitarian churches in Albany, Troy, New York and Lawrence, Massachusetts.

[2] Only the ending and signature are in CD's hand; the rest in Putnam's.

[3] Approximately 40 miles.

[4] A summary of these paragraphs appeared in the *Providence Daily Journal*, 31 Jan 42. In fact CD sailed from New York, without revisiting Boston.

[5] Only the ending and signature are in CD's hand; the rest in Putnam's.

[6] *Née* Ruth Gibbs (1778–1870), daughter of George Gibbs, a well-to-do merchant of Boston and Newport, Rhode Island. She and her husband were cousins.

[7] At their house in Mount Vernon Street. They spent the summers at Oakland, the Gibbs family estate near Portsmouth, Rhode Island.

About the other engagement I am very much afraid that our time is wholly occupied, but we will settle that point, when we see each other.[1]

In the mean while I am always, believe me, with high esteem and regard,

Faithfully Yours

Rev. Dr. Channing.   CHARLES DICKENS

To RICHARD HENRY DANA, [?SR],[2] 29 JANUARY 1842

Text transcribed by Prof. Edgar Johnson from MS then in possession of H. W. L. Dana. *Address:* Since neither call nor invitation to call is mentioned in the *Journal of R. H. Dana, Jr.,* ed. R. F. Lucid, probably letter, like that of 4 Feb with similar subscription, was written to R. H. Dana, Sr.

Tremont House | Twenty Ninth January 1842

My Dear Sir,

I shall be very happy to see you at Eleven o'clock Monday Morning, if that hour will suit your convenience.

Believe me | With true regard

Faithfully Yours always

Richard Dana Esquire   CHARLES DICKENS

To MRS GEORGE HILLARD,[3] 29 JANUARY 1842

Mention, without addressee's name, in *To* Forster, 29 Jan; identified in Felton *to* Sumner, 8 Feb[4] (MS Houghton Library, Harvard).

Crying off a party at Mrs Hillard's that evening on the grounds of exhaustion.[5]

[1] No further meeting between CD and Channing is recorded.

[2] Richard Henry Dana, Sr (1787–1879; *DAB*), poet and essayist, son of Francis Dana, Revolutionary patriot and Chief Justice of Massachusetts. Early abandoned law for literature. Contributed to periodicals and published two vols of poems, 1827 and 1833; much interest was created by his public lectures on Shakespeare, given in Boston, New York, &c, 1839–40. He spoke at the Dinner to CD on 1 Feb, having probably called on him the day before it, as implied in this letter. His own letters show how captivated he was by him. To Mrs Sarah Arnold he wrote on 14 Feb: "When my eye first fell upon him I was disappointed. But the instant his face was turned towards me, there was a change. He has the finest of eyes; and his whole countenance speaks *life* and *action*—the face seems to flicker with the *heart's* and mind's activity. You cannot tell how dead the faces near him seemed" (MS Massachusetts Historical Society). To W. C. Bryant: ". . . if you do not greatly *take to* him, I am much mistaken.

He is full of life. And with him life does not appear to be according to Brunian Theory—a forced state—but a truly *natural* one. I never saw a face fuller of vivid action, or an eye fuller of light. And he is so freely animated—so unlike *our folks.* He is plainly enough a most hearty man, & a most kind hearted one. People do not seem to crowd about him as to see a lion, but from downright love of him:— As Richard said to me—you can't bear to leave him" (MS *ibid.*) And to Rufus W. Griswold: "We have had great days here with Boz; & a fine fellow he is—you can't help loving him, if you would" (MS *ibid.*).

[3] *Née* Susan Tracy Howe, daughter of Judge Samuel Howe of Northampton; wife of George Stillman Hillard (1808–79; *DAB*), lawyer, man of letters, Whig member of the State House of Representatives since 1835, and a close friend of Longfellow, Felton and Sumner (his law partner since 1834).

[4] A message condoling with Mrs Hillard "on the loss of Dickens's visit".

[5] During the morning CD, with Sumner and Jonathan Chapman, had visited the

To JOHN FORSTER, [29 JANUARY 1842]

Extract in F, III, ii, 205–7 (resumption of letter begun 17 Jan, continued 21 Jan). *Date:* "Saturday the 28th of January" according to F, III, ii, 205; but 28 Jan was Friday. Since CD refers to leaving Boston "next Saturday" he was presumably writing not on Friday 28th but on Saturday 29th—a date clinched by Forster's statement (F, III, ii, 206) that "there were but two days more before the post left for England". The *Britannia* sailed from Boston on 1 Feb. *From* Tremont House.

As the Cunard boats have a wharf of their own at the custom-house, and that a narrow one, we were a long time (an hour at least) working in. I was standing in full fig on the paddle-box beside the captain, staring about me, when suddenly, long before we were moored to the wharf, a dozen men came leaping on board at the peril of their lives, with great bundles of newspapers under their arms; worsted comforters (very much the worse for wear) round their necks; and so forth. "Aha!" says I, "this is like our London-bridge": believing of course that these visitors were news-boys. But what do you think of their being EDITORS? And what do you think of their tearing violently up to me and beginning to shake hands like madmen? Oh! If you could have seen how I wrung their wrists! And if you could but know how I hated one man in very dirty gaiters, and with very protruding upper teeth, who said to all comers after him, "So you've been introduced to our friend Dickens—eh?"[1] There was one among them, though, who really was of use; a Doctor S, editor of the ——.[2] He ran off here (two miles at least), and ordered rooms and dinner. And in course of time Kate, and I, and Lord Mulgrave (who was going back to his regiment at Montreal on Monday, and had agreed to live with us in the meanwhile) sat down in a spacious and

Perkins Institution for the Blind—the subject of a long section in *American Notes*, Ch. 3—and a number of other institutions described in the same chapter (see *To* Forster, ?4 Feb, *fn*). In the early afternoon he had presented a piece of plate to Capt. Hewitt at the Tremont Theatre, on behalf of the passengers on the *Britannia*, and made a speech. He and Catherine had had social engagements every evening throughout the week, and the evening before had met the Hillards at a large dinner party at Prescott's—the occasion on which, according to one of the guests (among whom were George Ticknor, F. C. Gray and Sumner), CD, when asked which he considered the more beautiful of the Duchess of Sutherland (Lord Morpeth's sister) and Mrs Caroline Norton, electrified the company by replying "Mrs. Norton perhaps is the most beautiful; but the duchess, to my mind, is the more kissable person" (Mrs E. Latimer, "A Girl's Recollections of Dickens", *Lippincott's Monthly Magazine*, Sep 93, VII, 339). On 19 Feb Rufus Choate wrote

to Sumner: "We hear that Mr. & Mrs. Dickens called on [the Hillards] with a significant & exclusive civility & respect" (MS Houghton Library, Harvard)—a call of apology, presumably, for the broken engagement. For Hillard's speech at the Boston Dinner, 1 Feb, see *To* Forster, 17 Feb, *fn*.

[1] E. F. Payne (*Dickens Days in Boston*, pp. 25–6) suggests that this was the editor of the *Boston Daily Mail*, who announced in his issue of 24 Jan that he had "had the honor of an introduction to this distinguished visitor, and exchanged with him the cordial grasp of hands, before he had stepped his foot upon our shores."

[2] Identified by Payne (*op. cit.*, p. 13) as Joseph Palmer, MD (1796–1871), reporter and acting editor of the *Boston Transcript*. He had an hour's interview with CD the following evening and found him "one of the most frank, sociable, noble-hearted gentlemen we ever met with, perfectly free from haughtiness or apparent self-importance" (*Boston Transcript*, 24 Jan, quoted in Payne, *op. cit.*, p. 22).

handsome room to a very handsome dinner, 'bating peculiarities of putting on table, and had forgotten the ship entirely. A Mr. Alexander, to whom I had written from England promising to sit for a portrait, was on board directly we touched the land, and brought us here in his carriage. Then, after sending a present of most beautiful flowers, he left us to ourselves, and we thanked him for it.

How can I tell you what has happened since that first day? How can I give you the faintest notion of my reception here;[1] of the crowds that pour in and out the whole day; of the people that line the streets when I go out; of the cheering when I went to the theatre;[2] of the copies of verses, letters of congratulation, welcomes of all kinds, balls, dinners, assemblies without end? There is to be a public dinner to me here in Boston, next Tuesday, and great dissatisfaction has been given to the many by the high price (three pounds sterling each) of the tickets.[3] There is to be a ball next Monday week at New York, and 150 names appear on the list of the committee. There is to be a dinner in the same place, in the same week, to which I have had an invitation with every known name in America appended to it. But what can I tell you about any of these things which will give you the slightest notion of the enthusiastic greeting they give me, or the cry that runs through the whole country! I have had deputations from the Far West, who have come from more than two thousand miles distance:[4] from the lakes, the rivers, the back-woods, the log-houses,[5] the cities, factories, villages, and towns. Authorities from nearly all the States have written to me. I have heard from the universities, congress, senate, and bodies, public and private, of every sort and kind. "It is no nonsense, and no common feeling," wrote Dr. Channing to me yesterday. "It is all heart. There never was, and never will be, such a

1 "No sooner was it known that the steamer with Dickens on board was in sight, than the Town was pouring itself out upon the wharf; and when this remarkable man reached the Boston side, the 'hacknies' were all calling out, each anxious to have the honor to carry Boz. And for days the streets were a flutter with ribbons & feathers" (R. H. Dana, Sr *to* Mrs Arnold, 14 Feb 42: MS Massachusetts Historical Society).

2 The Tremont, to see a dramatization in 3 acts of Lever's *Charles O'Malley* (its 6th performance in America), followed by Field's *Masque* and dramatization of the first act of *Nickleby* (see *To* Field, 25 Jan, *fn*)—an occasion of which Anne Warren Weston wrote to her sister Deborah: "They gave Dickens three times three & at every sound, he came forward & bowed. He is a very handsome man & will probably be followed with 'ally loo yah' (see Miggs) wherever he goes" (MS Boston Public Library).

3 A letter in the *Boston Daily Times*, 5 Feb, signed "Nicholas Nickleby", asking that a genuinely "public" dinner to Boz

should be given in Boston, obviously voiced this.

4 Presumably refers to the invitation from St Louis (see *To* Forster, 21 Mar), though no supporting evidence of "deputations" has been found.

5 Cf. CD's pleasure at being read in the "backwoods of America" (*To* Tomlin, 23 Feb 41; II, 218), in the "remote wilds of America" (Vol. II, p. 394), and reference in his Boston speech to readers "in log-houses . . ., and densest forests, and deepest solitudes of the Far West" (*Speeches*, ed. K. J. Fielding, p. 20). The thought may have first arisen from a description John Tomlin gave of himself in the letter CD answered Feb 41. In an article published in *Graham's Magazine*, Feb 42 (XX, 83), Tomlin wrote: "Dwelling in a little hamlet that is scarcely known beyond the sound of its church bell—and in a place that a few years ago, resounded only to the winds of the magic woods, or the mocassin tread of the Indian on the dry leaves,—I, a creature less known by far than my village, addressed a letter to 'Boz' [*CD's reply follows*]".

triumph." And it is a good thing, is it not, . . . to find those fancies it has given me and you the greatest satisfaction to think of, at the core of it all? It makes my heart quieter, and me a more retiring, sober, tranquil man to watch the effect of those thoughts in all this noise and hurry, even than if I sat, pen in hand, to put them down for the first time. I feel, in the best aspects of this welcome, something of the presence and influence of that spirit which directs my life, and through a heavy sorrow has pointed upwards with unchanging finger for more than four years past. And if I know my heart, not twenty times this praise would move me to an act of folly. . . .

We leave here next Saturday. We go to a place called Worcester, about 75 miles off, to the house of the governor of this place;[1] and stay with him all Sunday.[2] On Monday we go on by railroad about 50 miles further to a town called Springfield, where I am met by a "reception committee" from Hartford 20 miles further, and carried on by the multitude: I am sure I don't know how, but I shouldn't wonder if they appear with a triumphal car.[3] On Wednesday[4] I have a public dinner there. On Friday I shall be obliged to present myself in public again, at a place called Newhaven,[5] about 30 miles further. On Saturday evening I hope to be at New York; and there I shall stay ten days or a fortnight. You will suppose that I have enough to do. I am sitting for a portrait and for a bust. I have the correspondence of a secretary of state, and the engagements of a fashionable physician. I have a secretary whom I take on with me. He is a young man of the name of Q;[6] was strongly recommended to me; is most modest, obliging, silent, and willing; and does his work *well*. He boards and lodges at my expense when we travel; and his salary is ten dollars per month—about two pounds five of our English money. There will be dinners and balls at Washington, Philadelphia, Baltimore, and I believe everywhere. In Canada, I have promised to *play* at the theatre with the officers, for the benefit of a charity.[7] We are already weary, at times, past all expression; and I finish this by means of a pious fraud. We were engaged to a party, and have written to say we are both desperately ill.[8] . . . "Well," I can fancy you saying, "but about his impressions of Boston and the Americans?"—Of the latter, I will not say a word until I have seen more of them, and have gone into the interior. I will only say, now, that we have never yet been required to dine at a table d'hôte;[9] that, thus far, our rooms

---

[1] John Davis (1787–1854; *DAB*), Whig Governor of Massachusetts and a strong anti-Democrat. He and Bancroft married each other's sisters.

[2] See *To* Forster, 17 Feb, *fn*.

[3] They were met by "a deputation of two" and taken on to Hartford by steamboat (*To* Forster, 17 Feb).

[4] A mistake for Tuesday (see *To* Green, 27 Jan, *fn*).

[5] They reached New Haven, Connecticut, in the evening of 11 Feb and stayed at the Tontine Hotel, where people poured in to see him.

[6] G. W. Putnam. Forster invariably substitutes this initial for the "P" or "Putnam" used by CD.

[7] A promise given to Lord Mulgave and fulfilled on 25 May.

[8] See *To* Mrs Hillard, 29 Jan, *hn* and *fn*.

[9] i.e. at a common table in the hotel dining room—an American custom to which Mrs Trollope, for instance, conformed with much displeasure (*Domestic Manners of the Americans*, 1832, Ch. 3). The *North American Review* (July 44, LIX, 6) considered that one of the "most offensive peculiarities" of an Englishman's manners was "his horror at the idea of dining at a *table d'hote*".

are as much our own here, as they would be at the Clarendon;[1] that but for an
odd phrase now and then—such as *Snap of cold weather;* a *tongue-y man*[2] for a
talkative fellow; *Possible?* as a solitary interrogation; and *Yes?* for indeed—I
should have marked, so far, no difference whatever between the parties here and
those I have left behind. The woman are very beautiful, but they soon fade;[3]
the general breeding is neither stiff nor forward; the good nature, universal.
If you ask the way to a place—of some common waterside man, who don't
know you from Adam—he turns and goes with you. Universal deference is paid
to ladies;[4] and they walk about at all seasons, wholly unprotected . . . . This
hotel is a trifle smaller than Finsbury-square; and is made so infernally hot (I use
the expression advisedly) by means of a furnace with pipes running through the
passages, that we can hardly bear it. There are no curtains to the beds, or to the
bedroom windows. I am told there never are, hardly, all through America. The
bedrooms are indeed very bare of furniture. Ours is nearly as large as your great
room, and has a wardrobe in it of painted wood not larger (I appeal to K) than
an English watch box. I slept in this room for two nights, quite satisfied with
the belief that it was a shower bath.

To [?THE SECRETARY, BROTHERS IN UNITY], [?LATE JANUARY 1842]

Extract in the *Collector*, Dec 1894, VIII, 35; dated Tremont House, 1842—clearly
before *To* Frederick Dickens, 30 Jan, which mentions his New Haven engagement.

Pray assure the "Brothers in Unity"[5] that I accept with great pride and satisfaction the distinction they offer me.[6]

To FREDERICK DICKENS, 30 JANUARY 1842[7]*

MS Berg Collection. *Address:* By "The Britannia" Steamer. | Frederick Dickens
Esquire | Commissariat | Treasury | London | England.

My dear Fred. You were quite right, and may retire from public life upon an
honorable independence, as soon as you please. Hewett *did* stand upon the
paddle box—with a brazen speaking trumpet in his hand—wherewith he gave

---

[1] At 169 New Bond Street, "perhaps the
best hotel in London" (Peter Cunningham,
Hand-Book of London, new edn, 1850, p. 64).

[2] Cf. *Chuzzlewit,* Ch. 21: " 'You air a
tongue-y person, Gen'ral. For you talk
too much' ".

[3] See *To* Forster, 24 Feb and *fn* p. 90.

[4] To their detriment, in Harriet Martineau's view (cf. *To* Macready, 22 Mar, *fn*
p. 157).

[5] One of the two leading Yale literary
and debating societies; founded 1768, it
was the first College society to admit fresh-
men, and played a large part in Yale
intellectual life.

[6] A "public reception" according to *To*

Fred Dickens, 30 Jan. This must have
been the "engagement" at New Haven for
10 Feb which CD had to cancel on deciding
to remain at Hartford till the 11th (*To*
Forster, 17 Feb). It is not recorded in the
society's minutes.

[7] Date given by Catherine. CD's letter
starts on p. 2 of a folded sheet; p. 1 and
five-sixths of p. 2 are occupied by a letter
from Catherine, reading: "Boston | January
30th. 1842 | My dearest Frederick. It is
with great pleasure I begin our mutual
letter to you, and it will be with still greater
pleasure I read the one which I daresay you
have written me ere now and which with
others we most ardently long for. | We

his orders to the men, which were passed by sundry officers in handsome naval uniforms, from one to another, until they reached the required point. You should see the engines of one of these large vessels. There are thirty men, who attend to them alone. The sea ran so high all the way, that when we came into Boston, the funnel which was properly red, was *white* to the top, with the ocean's Salt. Such a battered looking ship as it was, you can hardly imagine. When we put into Halifax, the fragments of our broken life boat still hung upon the deck. The rumour ran from mouth to mouth, that we had picked up the wreck of one of the poor President's[1] boats at sea; and the crowd came down for splinters of it, as valuable curiosities!

I was ill for 5 days—Kate for 6. After that time we managed our knives and forks with great credit to ourselves and expense to the Cunard Company. In winter time, and with such heavy weather, it is a most miserable voyage—wretched and uncomfortable beyond all description.

I can't tell you what they do here to welcome me, or how they cheer and shout on all occasions—in the streets—in the Theatres[2]—within doors—and wherever I go. But Forster holds the papers I have sent him, in trust to communicate their news to everybody. I have only time to write one letter, which is anything like a letter. He has it, and will tell you all.

We leave here on Saturday, and go with the Governor to a place called Worcester where we stay all Sunday. On Monday we go to a place called Springfield, and there we are publicly met by the citizens of Hartford, and carried on to that place; where—on Wednesday[3]—I have a public dinner. On Thursday, I have another public reception at Newhaven. On Saturday, we reach New York. On Monday they give me a great ball there, the Committee for which, alone, is 150 strong. In the same week a great public dinner, and a[nother][4] dinner with a club.[5] I believe this is to go on all through the States. You may sup[pose][4] I have not much time to spare.

I have engaged a very good and modest secretary, who lives with us w[hen][4]

landed here after a most dreadful passage of 18 days, and have experienced all the horrors of a storm at sea, which raged frightfully for a whole night, broke our Paddle boxes and a life boat to pieces. You can imagine how relieved we were, when towards morning it lulled, and although we were tossed to and fro all day from the great swell which follows a gale, we had nothing more to fear from the wind. | I was perfectly horrified and never expected to see morning again. Another night we ran a ground owing to an unskilful pilot, which caused great consternation as we were surrounded by rocks, but we got off in a few minutes and staid there at anchor all night. | We were told afterwards that the sailors had taken off their jackets and shoes ready to swim ashore. | Charles is going to finish this so I will leave him plenty of room to tell you some more news, [*punctuated thus*]

His reception here is something beyond description as you will see by the papers sent to John Forster—How often I long to have even on[e] look at my beloved darlings, do tell me all about them when you write. | Farewell dear Fred believe me ever with true affection | Your attached sister. | CATHERINE DICKENS.

[1] The steamship *President* was lost in Atlantic gales *en route* from New York to Liverpool Mar–Apr 41. No traces of her wreckage were ever found.

[2] CD had so far only been to one—the Tremont on 24 Jan.

[3] In fact, Tuesday.

[4] Conjectural reading where triangular piece is missing from edge of paper (presumably torn by seal when letter opened).

[5] "The Novelties", a club organized chiefly by New York journalists, with some actors; its "ostensible object ... was to

we travel, and has ten dollars a month. He does his work very well, and I like him much.

God bless you and the darling children.[1] I long to be at home.

Always Your affectionate brother.
C.D.

I inclose the Giniril's receipts.[2] As Park[3] saw us on board, will you call upon him—remember me to him—say I had no time to write before the packet left—and tell him all the News? Will you do the same by Stanfield,[4] *without loss of time*?

To JOHN FORSTER, [30 JANUARY 1842]

Extracts in F, III, ii, 207–8, and F, III, i, 200 (final addition to letter begun 17 Jan, continued 21st and 29th). *Date:* According to F, III, ii, 207, the addition "bore date the 29th of January"—i.e. was written on day after portion misdated by CD 28 Jan but clearly 29 Jan (see *To* Forster, 29 Jan, *hn*).

I hardly know what to add to all this long and unconnected history. Dana,[5] the author of that *Two Years before the Mast*,[6] is a very nice fellow indeed;[7] and

render due honor to Mr. Dickens"—although it long survived his visit (P. M. Wetmore, *New York Historical Magazine*, Second Series, Aug 67). About 50 members gave CD a private dinner at Astor House on 24 Feb.

[1] On 10 Feb Macready noted in his diary: "Forster called, and, after him, F. Dickens, whom we examined and expostulated with, and whom I lectured. I sent him home to conduct himself more temperately with the servants, which he seemed to promise he would do" (*Diaries*, II, 158).

[2] Receipts from CD for the rent of 1 Devonshire Terrace, taken by General Sir John Wilson.

[3] Presumably Patric Park (1811–55; *DNB*), sculptor, to whom CD sat 1840–1: see Vol. II, pp. 138*n* and 285.

[4] Clarkson Stanfield (1793–1867; *DNB*), marine and landscape painter: see Vol. I, p. 553*n*.

[5] Richard Henry Dana, Jr (1815–82; *DAB*), son of R. H. Dana (see *To* Dana, 29 Jan); lawyer, writer, and member of an old and distinguished Boston family. Strongly Anglophile and Episcopalian, and a keen traveller. For the success of his *Two Years before the Mast*, see below. Published *The Seaman's Friend* (a manual of maritime law, of which CD later owned the English edn), 1841. Married the same year and began a highly successful legal career. A

Federalist Whig by upbringing but later drawn into alliance with the Democrats through his deep involvement in the anti-slavery movement; was a founder of the Free-Soil party and prominent in defending fugitive slaves; but did not realize his political ambitions. His *Journal*, 1841–60 (ed. R. F. Lucid, 3 vols, Cambridge, Mass., 1968, with valuable Introduction), gives probably the fullest picture known of Boston society of the period—as well as mirroring his own complex personality. Was a member of the Committee of the "Young Men of Boston" and spoke at the Dinner to CD; his journal entries show his great interest in him. On finishing *Old Curiosity Shop* in Mar 42, he wept at Nell's death (*op. cit.*, I, 64). For his comments on *American Notes*, see *To* Prescott, 15 Oct, *fn* p. 348.

[6] "A book which I had praised much to him, thinking it like De Foe", Forster interpolates. Published 1840, based on his voyage round Cape Horn as an ordinary seaman in 1834, and written in 1838 (in six months) on his return to the Harvard Law School, it was Dana's "great success". In a speech of 30 Aug 69 CD described it as "about the best sea book in the English tongue" (*Speeches*, ed. K. J. Fielding, p. 397).

[7] The change in Dana's attitude to CD can be traced clearly in his journal: from

in appearance not at all the man you would expect. He is short, mild-looking, and has a care-worn face. His father is exactly like George Cruikshank after a night's jollity—only shorter. The professors at the Cambridge university,[1] Longfellow,[2] Felton, Jared Sparks, are noble fellows. So is Kenyon's[3] friend,

social condescension typical of several patrician Bostonians to admiration. His first entry for 18 Jan, four days before CD's arrival, shows some irritation: "Nothing talked of but Dickens' arrival. The town is mad. All [will be] calling on him. I shan't go unless sent for. I can't submit to sink the equality of a gentleman by crowding after a man of note" (*Journal*, ed. R. F. Lucid, I, 56). After calling on him at CD's request on 26 Jan he recorded: "Disappointed in D.'s appearance. We have heard him called 'the handsomest man in London' &c. He is of the middle height, (under if anything) with a large expressive eye, regular nose, matted, curling, wet-looking black hair, a dissipated looking mouth with a vulgar draw to it, a muddy olive complexion, *stubby* fingers & a hand by no means patrician, a hearty, off-hand manner, far from well bred, & a rapid, dashing way of talking. He looks 'wide awake', 'up to anything', full of cleverness, with quick feelings & great ardour. You admire him, & there is a fascination about him which keeps your eyes on him, yet you cannot get over the impression that he is a low bred man. Tom Appleton [*later Longfellow's brother-in-law*] says 'Take the genius out of his face & there are a thousand young London shop-keepers, about the theaters & eating houses who look exactly like him'. He has what I suppose to be the true Cockney cut" (*op. cit.*, I, 57). But on dining with him at F. C. Gray's the following night, his verdict was entirely favourable —if a little patronizing: "Like Dickens here very much. The gentlemen are talking their best, but Dickens is perfectly natural & unpretending. He could not have behaved better. He did not say a single thing for display. I should think he had resolved to talk as he would at home, & let his reputation take care of itself. He gave a capital description of Abbotsford. It was eno' to make you cry. He described the hat Scott wore in his last illness, & the dents & bruises there were in it from his head falling against his chair when he lost the power of his muscles. It was heart-sickening. 'And to think of a man's killing himself for such a

miserable place as Abbotsford is', adds Dickens" (*ibid.*). Another example given of CD's talk was his response when the conversation turned to a lecture of Lardner's and Gray said he'd go to hear the Devil lecture if he did it well—as no doubt he would: "'He would *know a thing or two*', said Dickens, as quick as a flash" (*op. cit.*, I, 58). Dana's final analysis, recorded after calling on CD on 5 Feb, his last morning in Boston, was the most acute: "He is the *cleverest* man I ever met. I mean he impresses you more with the alertness of his various powers. His forces are all light infantry & light cavalry, & always in marching order. There are not many heavy pieces, but few *sappers* & *miners*, the scientific corps is deficient, & I fear there is no chaplain in the garrison" (*op. cit.*, I, 61).

[1] Harvard.
[2] Henry Wadsworth Longfellow (1807–1882; *DAB*) had succeeded Ticknor as Professor of Modern Languages and Belles Lettres at Harvard in 1835. Published both his prose romance, *Hyperion*, and his first book of poems, *Voices of the Night*, in 1839; and *Ballads and Other Poems* in late 1841. By Nov 41 was planning to go to Germany to take the water-cure: A. Hilen (*Letters of H. W. Longfellow*, II, 369) suggests that his purpose was also to escape the frustrations of his then unsuccessful courtship of Frances Appleton, and that his meeting CD did much to stimulate the plan. He called on CD at Tremont House on 26 Jan, with Sumner, by special arrangement; and on 30 Jan, after he and Sumner had taken CD to hear Father Taylor preach and for a 10-mile walk, wrote to his father: "Dickens ... is a glorious fellow; and the greatest possible enthusiasm exists among all classes. ... He is a gay, free and easy character; ... and withal a slight dash of the Dick Swiveller about him"; and, of Catherine: "She is a good-natured—mild, rosy young woman—not beautiful, but amiable" (*op. cit.*, II, 381). On 4 Feb CD breakfasted with him in his rooms at Craigie House, Cambridge, the other guests being Felton, Andrews Norton (Dexter

Ticknor.[1] Bancroft is a famous man; a straightforward, manly, earnest heart; and talks much of you, which is a great comfort.[2] Doctor Channing I will tell you more of, after I have breakfasted alone with him next Wednesday. . . . Sumner is of great service to me.[3] . . . The president of the Senate here[4] presides at my dinner on Tuesday. Lord Mulgrave lingered with us till last Tuesday (we had our little captain to dinner on the Monday), and then went on to Canada. Kate is quite well, and so is Anne, whose smartness surpasses belief. They yearn for home, and so do I.

Of course you will not see in the papers any true account of our voyage, for they keep the dangers of the passage, when there are any, very quiet. I observed so many perils peculiar to steamers that I am still undecided whether we shall not return by one of the New York liners.[5] On the night of the storm, I was wondering within myself where we should be, if the chimney were blown overboard: in which case, it needs no great observation to discover that the vessel must be instantly on fire from stem to stern.[6] When I went on deck next day,

Professor of Sacred Literature, Harvard, 1819–30), Sumner, Benjamin Pierce (Professor of Astronomy and Mathematics, Harvard), Samuel Ward, and Longfellow's youngest brother, Samuel. In a letter of 8 Feb to his sister, Mrs James Greenleaf, Samuel Longfellow described CD as "very animated and talkative, pleasant but not particularly humorous, with an offhand way, and the slightest tincture of rowdyism in his appearance. . . . His features are in constant play while he talks, particularly his eyebrows, giving him a French aspect. He speaks fast & rather indistinctly. . . . He talked about the literary people of England, & told us of Mrs. Norton being allowed at last to see her children [*see* To *Stanfield, 3 Feb 43*, fn]. . . . He said that Quilp was entirely a creature of the imagination[,] he had heaped together in him all possible hideousness." After breakfast CD was taken to call on Josiah Quincy, the President of Harvard; introduced to students in the Library; and shown a student's room (letter quoted by Edward Wagenknecht, "Dickens in Longfellow's Letters and Journals", *D*, LII [1955], 8–9).

[3] John Kenyon (1784–1856; *DNB*), poet and philanthropist: see Vol. I, p. 554*n*.

[1] George Ticknor (1791–1871; *DAB*), first Smith Professor of French and Spanish and of Belles Lettres at Harvard, 1819–35, where he virtually created the Department of Modern Languages. Travelled in Europe 1835–8; published his *History of Spanish Literature* 1849. A founder and considerable benefactor of the Boston Public Library. He had received letters of

introduction to CD from both Kenyon and Everett; called on him soon after his arrival, and met him at dinner at F. C. Gray's on the 27th and at W. H. Prescott's on the 28th.

[2] They had no doubt spoken of Forster's *Statesmen of the Commonwealth*; and presumably this was the book that Longfellow delivered to Bancroft on Forster's behalf after his visit to England (Longfellow *to* Forster, 15 Dec 42: *Letters*, ed. A. Hilen, II, 481).

[3] In escorting him round Boston and introducing him to his friends (see To Sumner, 25 Jan, *fn*)—a service Sumner performed for a number of people after returning from his own tour of Europe. He had devoted most of the previous month to entertaining Lord Morpeth, whom he had met in Ireland; he showed the city to Sir Charles Lyell in 1841, and to Lord Ashburton's suite in Summer 42; and similarly entertained Macready in Nov 43 (Macready, *Diaries*, II, 238–40).

[4] Josiah Quincy, Jr (1802–82), lawyer; President of the Massachusetts Senate 1842; Mayor of Boston 1846–8. CD had been introduced to him at the State Capitol on 24 Jan—when escorted there, with Lord Mulgrave and (according to Payne, *Dickens Days in Boston*, p. 29) Capt. Hewitt, by Grattan.

[5] i.e. by sailing packet—as in fact they did.

[6] This was the fear which preyed most on CD's mind: cf. *To* Forster, 24 Feb. Perhaps the 62 pages given to eye-witness accounts of the loss of American steam-

I saw that it was held up by a perfect forest of chains and ropes, which had been rigged in the night. Hewitt told me (when we were on shore, not before) that they had men lashed, hoisted up, and swinging there, all through the gale, getting these stays about it. This is not agreeable—is it?

... *"How little I thought the first time you mounted the shapeless coat, that I should have such a sad association with its back as when I saw it by the paddle-box of that small steamer."*[a]

To DANIEL MACLISE, [?30 or 31 JANUARY 1842]

Mention in Maclise *to* Forster, n.d., and in *To* Maclise, 22 Mar. *Date:* On 22 Mar CD mentions having already written Maclise two letters—one of them on 27 Feb. Almost certainly the other (untraced) was written at the end of Jan, when CD dispatched letters to Macready, Mitton, Fred Dickens and Forster, ready for mail leaving 1 Feb.[1]

To DAVID C. COLDEN, 31 JANUARY 1842*

MS Dartmouth College, New Hampshire. *Address:* David Colden Esquire | New York.

Tremont House, Boston. | January Thirty First 1842.
My Dear Sir.

I thank the Committee very much; and have booked Monday the Fourteenth for the Ball.[2] Be assured that there is no likelihood of my forming any other engagement for that Evening.[3]

boats ("by bursting of boilers, burning, wrecks, &c.") in Marryat's *Diary in America*, Part Second, 1839, I, 32–94, contributed to the fear (which Sir Charles Lyell, also on the *Britannia* in an Atlantic hurricane, did not share: see *To* Forster, 24 Feb, *fn*).

[aa] Called by Forster "the last lines of his first American letter" (F, III, i, 200). Omitted in N.

[1] In a letter on paper with a very wide black border, suggesting early days of mourning for his mother, Maclise wrote to Forster: "I'll try to write to Dickens—by the tenth, but I believe this is the 8th—Can you get for my Sis an order to see Acis & his Galatea." Macready's production of this opera at Drury Lane opened 5 Feb 42; and Maclise was probably writing on 8 Feb, before hearing from CD. In another undated letter to Forster, on paper with narrow black border, clearly written after receiving CD's first letter, Maclise wrote: "I wish I could write to Dickens—he has written a mere word to me,—nothing worth sending I mean in the way of news—I suppose I need only direct as you tell me and drop it

as usual in the post—or ought I write by Ship &c—". CD had still not heard from him on 22 Mar (*To* Maclise, that day). But Maclise was clearly going through a period of depression. His letter to Forster of ?8 Feb continued: "You [saw] Marion [*Ely:* see Vol. II, *passim*] yesterday—you have all ruined me in that quarter—and I am out of favour with Grim [*i.e. Macready*] —and I have neglected Dickens—and it is a wretched day and Im discontented." His second letter to Forster, written with a "fiery" boil on his nose, ended wistfully: "I half suspect you of leading a jolly life out there with Ainsworth at all hours—I'll engage you make now and then a descent on Macready—and I suppose you were at George Cattermole's Christening party." (MSS Forster Collection, V & A.)

[2] See Colden's letter of the 29th (*To* Colden, 28 Jan, *fn*).

[3] This was in answer to Colden's message that the Committee would "esteem it a favor if he [would] make no other engagement for the same evening".

In the matter of my first appearance before my friends in New York, I shall be so proud to avail myself of that first opportunity of meeting them, that I shall put myself wholly into the hands of the Committee, and lead quite a secluded life until they "bring me out".[1]

We shall be delighted to dine with you on the Sunday, and also to go to church with you[2]—*if* we are not too tired out by the business of the previous week, to get up early enough.

Mrs. Dickens unites with me in cordial Regards.

Always believe me | My Dear Sir
Faithfully Yours

David Colden Esquire   CHARLES DICKENS

To THOMAS MITTON, 31 JANUARY 1842

MS Huntington Library. *Address:* By the "Britannia" Steamer | Thomas Mitton Esquire | 23 Southampton Buildings | Chancery Lane | London | England.

Tremont House, Boston, | Thirty First January 1842.

My Dear Mitton.

I am so exhausted with the life I am obliged to lead here, that I have had time to write but one letter, which is at all deserving of the name, as giving any account of our movements. Forster has it, in trust to tell you all its news; and he has also some newspapers which I had an opportunity of sending him,[3] in which you will find further particulars of our progress.

---

[1] Colden had added: "As the entertainment which my friends are preparing for your reception, will be somewhat novel in its character and as they trust more than usually brilliant, they hope that you will permit this to be your first appearance in a public assemblage of our fellow citizens, and allow the Committee the honor of being the first to present you to them" (MS Forster Collection, V & A).

[2] Colden had renewed his invitation of 27 Jan (*To* Morris, 28 Jan, *fn*).

[3] These papers probably included the *Boston Daily Mail*, 24 Jan, which carried on its front page an engraving (covering two columns) of the Maclise portrait and an enthusiastic description of CD's appearance; the *Boston Daily Evening Transcript*, 24 Jan, which announced his visit to the Tremont Theatre that night with his "most beautiful and accomplished" lady; some account of his visit to the Massachusetts Legislature which, according to the *New York Express*, 29 Jan, "created quite a sensation among the members"; and the *New York Morning Courier and Enquirer*, 27 Jan, which talked of honours to come

such as "had been extended to La Fayette only". Cf. Charles Lyell, writing at Philadelphia, 1 Feb: "The newspapers are filled with accounts of the enthusiastic reception which Mr. Charles Dickens is meeting with every where. Such homage has never been paid to any foreigner since Lafayette visited the States" (*Travels in North America*, 1845, I, 199). But no American papers bearing January dates are in the Forster Collection, V & A. Evidently the papers sent were shown not merely to Mitton and to Macready (see next) but also went the round of other friends with CD's knowledge—probably in the first place lent by Forster to Talfourd, thence finding their way to Brougham, Lady Holland and Rogers (see letters of 22 Mar to these four assuming that they would have heard of his "public progress"). Doubtless Sydney Smith heard of it too; for in a letter no doubt to Carlyle he wrote: "Pray tell Dickens for me to remember that he is still but a man [*a Carlyle family joke based on an anecdote: see, e.g.,* Jane Welsh Carlyle: Letters to her Family, 1839–1863, *ed.* L. Huxley, *1924, p. 73*]—& that however

We had a dreadful passage—the worst (the officers all concur in saying) that they have ever known. We were 18 days coming; experienced a dreadful storm which swept away our paddle boxes and stove our life boats; and ran aground besides, near Halifax, among rocks and breakers, where we lay at anchor all night. After we left the English Channel,[1] we had only one fine day. And we had the additional discomfort of being 86 passengers. I was ill five days—Kate six—though indeed she had a swelled face,[2] and suffered the utmost terror all the way.[3]

I can give you no conception of my welcome here. There never was a King or Emperor upon the Earth, so cheered, and followed by crowds, and entertained in Public at splendid balls and dinners, and waited on by public bodies and deputations of all kinds. I have had one from the Far West:[4] a journey of 2,000 miles! If I go out in a carriage, the crowd surround it and escort me home. If I go to the Theatre, the whole house (crowded to the roof) rises as one man, and the timbers ring again. You cannot imagine what it is. I have 5 Great Public Dinners on hand at this moment,[5] and Invitations from every town, and village, and city, in the States.

There is a great deal afloat here, in the way of subjects for description. I keep my eyes open, pretty wide; and hope to have done so to some purpose, by the time I come home.

When you write to me again—I say again; hoping that your first letter will be soon upon its way here—direct to me to the care of David Colden Esquire, New York. He will forward all communications by the quickest conveyance, and will be perfectly acquainted with all my movements.

Always Your faithful friend

Thomas Mitton Esquire CHARLES DICKENS

To W. C. MACREADY, 31 JANUARY 1842*

MS Morgan Library. *Address:* By The "Britannia" Steamer. | W. C. Macready Esquire | Clarence Terrace | Regents Park | London | England.

Tremont House, Boston. | Thirty First January 1842.

My Dear Macready.

I have hardly time, here, to dress—undress—and go to bed. As yet, I have

---

elated by this American Deification he must return to his Anthropic State and that he will find us (you & me) good friends but bad Idolators" (MS Free Library of Philadelphia).

[1] CD clearly means St George's Channel between England and Ireland.

[2] She had had acute toothache before they left England (see *To* Maclise, 3 Jan, *fn*). On 30 Jan she wrote to Fanny Burnett, of the voyage: "We were all very sick, and to crown all my miseries, I had a most awfully swoln face, and looked quite an

object" (letter quoted in full in F. G. Kitton, *CD by Pen and Pencil*, 1890–2, I, 39: see Appx, p. 629).

[3] "I was nearly distracted with terror," wrote Catherine in another part of the same letter to Fanny, "and don't know what I should have done had it not been for the great kindness and composure of my dear Charles" (*ibid.*).

[4] From St Louis, Missouri.

[5] Besides those at Boston, Hartford and New York, he accepted only an invitation to a smaller dinner at St Louis.

had no time whatever for exercise. You may suppose I have very little for writing. This last consideration is the greatest annoyance I have.

I have, however, written one pretty long letter, and sent it to Forster—In trust to read it to you. I have penned it from time to time, and it contains some news. I have sent him at the same time a little box of letters which will interest you, I think—among them, some from David Colden[1] who is a *hearty*[2] fellow. There are Newspapers too in the same Dispatch.[3]

It is impossible to tell you what a reception I have had here. They cheer me in the Theatres;[4] in the streets; within doors; and without. I have a public dinner here tomorrow—another at Hartford on Wednesday[5]—another at New-haven on Thursday[6]—a great Ball in New York on Monday the Fourteenth—a Great Public dinner at the same place in the same week—another dinner in the same place, with a club—and entertainments of all kinds, in perspective, all through the States. Deputations and Committees wait upon me every day—some have come 2000 miles—it is nothing to say that they carry me through the country on their shoulders, or that they flock about me as if I were an Idol. Nothing will express their affectionate greeting—I only wish to God that you could see it.

I won't say a word about the Americans until I have gone further. It is enough to say, now, that they are as delicate, as considerate, as careful of giving the least offence, as the best Englishmen I ever saw.—I like their behaviour to Ladies infinitely better than that of my own countrymen; and their Institutions I reverence, love, and honor.[7]

We had a terrible passage—as you will learn from Kate's letter to Mrs. Macready. I hope to write you at greater length from New York.

How I am longing for a letter from you! How often we think of Drury Lane, and wonder what you're doing, and say 'Now the curtain's going up—now the halfprice is coming in—now they're calling for Macready'. We have agreed not to believe that there is any difference between the clocks here and those at home;[8] and we find it a marvellous satisfaction.

My Dear Macready I won't thank you for the peace of mind you have given us, and the perfect confidence we have through you in our dear children being well cared-for, and thoroughly happy.—If I could but shake hands with you, on the penalty of not saying one word—as they shewed the figures of the absent,

---

[1] Colden's two letters, of 27 and 29 Jan (see *To* Morris, 28 Jan, *fn*, and *To* Colden, 31 Jan, *fn*). Also in the "little box" he presumably sent the letters of invitation to the Boston Dinner and the New York Ball. All are now in the Forster Collection, V & A.

[2] Underlined twice.

[3] See last, *To* Mitton, *fn*.

[4] Cf. *To* Fred Dickens, 30 Jan and *fn*. Unless writing this late in the evening, he had still only been to one, though on 31 Jan he went to the National (at 6.45 p.m.) to see J. S. Jones's dramatization of Samuel

Warren's *Ten Thousand a Year*—where he was again applauded, as he entered his specially decorated box.

[5] A mistake for Tuesday (see *To* Green, 27 Jan, *fn*).

[6] This seems to have been a public reception, not a dinner (see *To* Fred Dickens, 30 Jan)—cancelled because of Catherine's swollen face (*To* Forster, 17 Feb).

[7] See *To* Forster, ?4 Feb, *fn*.

[8] Which were five hours behind American Eastern time.

in the Magic Mirror of the Fairy Tale[1]—I could express more in one squeeze than in a score of letters.

I thirst for news of Drury Lane. I don't know how we shall restrain ourselves when the time approaches for the arrival of the packet.

God bless you My Dear Macready!

Ever Your attached and most affectionate friend

W. C. Macready Esquire   CHARLES DICKENS

To LORD JEFFREY, [LATE JANUARY 1842]

Mention in *To* Colden, 4 Apr, as posted from Boston 2 Feb.

To W. W. GREENOUGH, 1 FEBRUARY 1842*

Text from copy formerly owned by Edward F. Payne.

Tremont House Feb. 1. 1842

My Dear Sir,

I shall expect the Committee[2] at the hour you mention, and have no alteration to suggest in so pleasant an arrangement. Believe me always,

Faithfully yours,

W. W. Greenough, Esq.   CHARLES DICKENS

To DR FRANCIS DANA,[3] 2 FEBRUARY [1842]*

MS[4] Longfellow House.

Tremont House Feb 2nd.

My dear Sir

In answer to your inquiry I beg to say that I know Mr. Townshend[5] well. He is a gentleman of Independent fortune and station in Society, and of very

---

[1] CD was almost certainly recalling, not a fairy tale, but Scott's story "My Aunt Margaret's Mirror" (first published in the *Keepsake*, 1829) which includes the stipulation that the watcher must remain silent, or the vision of the absent will disappear and danger may threaten the spectators.

[2] The members of the Reception Committee who were to escort him to the Dinner in Papanti's Hall that evening: George T. Bigelow, Nathan Hale, Jr, Jonathan Barrett, Theodore W. Crocket, and W. W. Story. For the Dinner, see *To* Forster, 17 Feb and *fn*.

[3] Francis Dana (1806–72), MD Harvard 1831; a Boston dentist (cousin of R. H. Dana), who employed mesmerism to anæsthetize his patients. Practised in Greenfield, Mass., 1832–41; in Boston from 1841. Secretary of the Boston Committee before which Collyer had experimented in animal magnetism that year.

[4] Only the ending, signature and subscription are in CD's hand; the rest in Putnam's.

[5] Chauncy Hare Townshend (1798–1868; *DNB*): see Vol. II, p. 110.

high and varied attainments. I need scarcely add that whatever he says is perfectly true; and that I have no doubt relative to any one of the statements contained in his Book.[1]

Doctor Dana

Dear Sir I am | Faithfully Yours
CHARLES DICKENS

To A. R. DUNTON,[2] 2 FEBRUARY 1842

Text from the *Boston Daily Mail*, 3 Mar 42.

Tremont House | Feb. 2, 1842

Dear Sir,

Mrs. Dickens and myself are exceedingly obliged for those beautiful and elegant specimens of Penmanship and Card Marking which you have done us the favor to present us with. Our friends who have seen them pronounce them equal to copper plate. We shall have pleasure in showing them in our country as a specimen of Yankee ingenuity. Hoping you will ever prosper, you will please accept our thanks, and believe me

Mr. A. R. Dunton

Faithfully yours,
CHARLES DICKENS

To MISS THEODA DAVIS FOSTER,[3] 2 FEBRUARY 1842

Text from *Memorial Sketch of Theoda Davis Foster Bush* By her Husband, Boston, 1890, p. 27.

Tremont House, Boston | 2nd February, 1842

Dear Madam,

What can I say to your very interesting letter?[4] That it has afforded me the utmost satisfaction of heart and the truest delight? You know that, I am sure, already.

---

[1] *Facts in Mesmerism, with Reasons for a Dispassionate Inquiry into It*, 1840; dedicated, with an "introductory epistle", to Elliotson. Mainly a documented account of Townshend's numerous experiments in mesmerism, both in England and on the Continent; with philosophical arguments for the existence of the mesmeric state, and a supplement of ten "testimonies". Collyer, editor of the American edn, 1841, had no doubt used some of Townshend's statements to support his own claims before the Boston Committee the previous June–July (see *To* Collyer, 27 Jan, *fn*). In Jan 42 W. C. Bryant wrote to a friend that "since the publication of the Rev. Mr. Townshend's book, animal magnetism . . . has made great progress in America. It is quite the fashion" (Parke Godwin, *A Biography of W. C. Bryant*, New York, 1883, I, 392–3).

[2] Alvin R. Dunton (1812–89), teacher of handwriting; grandson of one of the first settlers of Lincolnville, Maine. Claimed to be inventor of the "American Standard System of Penmanship", and was for many years in charge of handwriting in the Boston schools.

[3] Theoda Davis Foster (1811–88), a lifelong Unitarian. Contributor to the *Knickerbocker*, the *Garland* and the *Dew Drop*, and for several years on the staff of the *Christian Register*. Married Solon Bush, a Unitarian minister, 1849.

[4] She had written at the "urgent request" of her cousin Eddie Adams, who was ill, to say how comforted he was by CD's books —and especially by the scene of Little Nell's death, which she read to him "over and over again" (*Memorial Sketch*, p. 27).

I can but thank you, but I do so with a sincerity which may attach some value to my words; and in the same spirit I assure you, my unknown friend, that I am ever

To T. D. F.[1]

Faithfully Yours,
CHARLES DICKENS

To UNKNOWN LADIES OF PLYMOUTH, MASSACHUSETTS,[2] 2 FEBRUARY [1842]

Text from the *New York Herald*, 27 Feb 42.

Tremont House, February 2d.

My Dear Ladies,

I wish I could bring my whole head among you, but being prevented, (by reason of the arrangements I have made for going elsewhere) I confess that I am afraid to send you a lock of my hair, as the precedent would be one of a most dangerous and alarming kind, and likely to terminate before long in my total baldness.[3]

You see how very candidly I deal with you. If I had been of a deceitful nature, nothing would have been easier for me to do, than to have got a lock of hair from one of the waiters, and forwarded it to you by post.

But, as I have had much pleasure in the receipt of your letter, and feel that I may treat you with perfect confidence, I prefer even to refuse your request, and to throw myself upon your merciful consideration.

Dear Ladies, I am ever | Faithfully yours,
CHARLES DICKENS

To THE REV. MOSES STUART,[4] 2 FEBRUARY 1842*

MS[5] Northwestern Mutual Insurance Company, Seattle.

Tremont House Feb 2 1842

My dear Sir

I thank you very much for your pleasant letter. I wish I could come to see

[1] Presumably Miss Foster had signed with initials only.

[2] According to a summary of CD's letter in the *Boston Morning Post*, 11 Feb, he was replying to "three or four ladies of Plymouth".

[3] This was taken up as a joke by the newspapers. According to W. G. Wilkins, *CD in America*, pp. 160–1, the *Philadelphia Gazette* reported a party at which CD "narrowly escaped the fate of Samson", but satisfied the "bewitching ones" with "a bit of sweet poetry, or a sentiment, coupled with his autograph" instead; while an advertiser in the Philadelphia *Spirit of the Times* urged him not to be selfish about

his hair: "when it is all gone, rub your bald pate with Balm of Columbia, to be had at 71 Maiden Lane, New York". See also *To* Mrs Colden, 24 Feb, *fn*.

[4] Moses Stuart (1780–1852; *DAB*), Congregational minister and Biblical scholar; Professor of Sacred Literature at Andover Theological Seminary, Mass., 1810–48. Virtually introduced study of Hebrew and of German theological scholarship into America. Published nearly 40 books and pamphlets and was highly influential as a teacher. Strong supporter of the temperance movement.

[5] Only the ending and signature are in CD's hand; the rest in Putnam's.

you. I wish I had half an hour, or had had half an hour, during my short stay in this City.

I hope to return this way. If I do, I shall look forward to meeting you. In the mean time commend me and Mrs. Dickens to your family and believe me dear Sir | Faithfully Yours

The Rev Moses Stuart.   CHARLES DICKENS

To GEORGE TICKNOR, 2 FEBRUARY 1842†

MS Berg Collection.

Tremont House, Boston | Second February 1842.

My Dear Sir.

Thank you for your kind note.

*a*I fear (oh if you only knew the full extent of my "engagements"!)[1] that I shall not be able to accompany you until I return this way,—which I hope to do.*a* But I am not the less obliged to you, or the less desirous to avail myself of your thoughtful proffer.

Believe me always | Faithfully Yours

George Ticknor Esquire   CHARLES DICKENS

To THE EDITOR OF THE *BUNKER-HILL AURORA*,[2] [EARLY FEBRUARY 1842]

Summary from *Bunker-Hill Aurora*, 5 Feb 42.

Protesting that the sketch of his life,[3] as published in the last issue of that paper, contained statements about his birth and parentage, and that of Mrs Dickens, which were entirely new to him.[4]

aa In N, I, 381, from catalogue source; letter otherwise unpublished.

[1] He had breakfasted with Channing that morning; at some time in the day saw J. G. Maeder—one of the Boston musicians who composed "Boz Waltzes" in his honour—and gave him his autograph (John Anderson Jr. catalogue, Jan 1903); in the evening "disappointed the Paiges [*Mrs Paige was a niece of Judge Story, James W. Paige a merchant and brother-in-law of Webster*] who had prepared a magnificent dinner for him—half-an-hour after the dinner hour he sent an apology. . . . poor man, he is literally used up" (Mrs Motley *to* her husband, 5 Feb, quoted in *J. L. Motley and his Family*, ed. S. and H. St. John Mildmay, 1910, p. 24). He spent 3 Feb visiting factories at Lowell (see *To* Forster, ?4 Feb, *fn*), and apparently went to a crowded party that night at "Miss Shaw's" (possibly Elizabeth Shaw, who married Herman Melville Aug 47, though only 19 in 1842), where Julia Ward and

Fanny Appleton were among the guests (see *D*, XXXVIII [1941–2], 7). On 4 Feb he breakfasted with Longfellow and visited Harvard, and in the afternoon attended a session of the Boston court. On the 5th he left Boston.

[2] The *Bunker-Hill Aurora and Boston Mirror*, a weekly paper founded 1827, which served the Charlestown district of Boston. Its editor and proprietor was W. W. Wheildon.

[3] "Visit of 'Boz'—Sketch of his Life", *Bunker-Hill Aurora*, 29 Jan.

[4] The "Sketch" had confused the Dickens and Hogarth families. For a comparison of its text with the "Life of 'Boz' " which appeared in the *New England Weekly Review*, 12 Feb, virtually identical and clearly deriving from the same source ("one of the city papers", itself possibly abridged from a Philadelphia journal, according to the *Bunker-Hill Aurora*, 5 Feb), see *To* Green, 14 Feb, *fn*.

To RICHARD HENRY DANA,[1] 4 FEBRUARY 1842

MS Colonel Richard Gimbel. *Address:* Richard Dana Esquire | Boston.

Tremont House, Boston. | Fourth February 1842.

My Dear Sir.

I thank you most heartily, for your kind note of this morning,[2] and for the copy of Bryants[3] Poems[4] you have given me. I assure you that I shall prize it very highly for your sake; and that I attach no common value to your kind and affectionate expressions.

I shall hope to see you again, before I leave this country. But in England or America, I shall never fail to look back with pleasure to our brief intercourse, or to be with sincere regard, My Dear Sir,

Your faithful friend

Richard Dana Esquire   CHARLES DICKENS

To JAMES T. FIELDS,[5] 4 FEBRUARY [1842]*

MS[6] Mr Philo Calhoun. *Address: To* James T. Fields according to cutting from Goodspeeds Book Shop catalogue, n.d.

Tremont House Feb 4.

Dear Sir.

Not having the Book with me I really forget the date of the Publication of the

---

[1] Clearly R. H. Dana, Sr, a close friend of Bryant's, with a daughter old enough to collect leaves for Catherine (see below).

[2] Dana had written on 3 Feb: "My dear Sir— | Pray do me the kindness to take home with you this copy of my friend Bryant's Poems. And when you now & then look into it, sometimes remember me, will you ? | You have heard of our Autumn Woods; & Bryant, as you may remember, has beautifully sung them here. ... My daughter ... has slipt in a few leaves for Mrs. Dickens, only regretting that she had not a greater variety & brighter ones to send. | And you will be gone from us before they put on their Josephs again—their coats of many colors. You would hardly believe me, could I tell you how sad it makes me to think on it. ... | If you return this way I trust that you will give me an evening at my house with Allston & two or three more" (MS Colonel Richard Gimbel).

[3] Thus in MS. William Cullen Bryant: see *To* Bryant, 14 Feb, *fn.*

[4] The 6th edn, New York, 1840, of his *Poems*, 1832, inscribed to CD "with the sincere regards of Richd. H. Dana" (*Cata-*

logue of the Library of CD, ed. J. H. Stonehouse, p. 16). The volume was originally published in London (1832), with an introduction by Washington Irving, who dedicated it to Samuel Rogers.

[5] James Thomas Fields (1817–81; *DAB*), writer and publisher; clerk in a Boston book-store 1831–9; since 1839 junior partner in Ticknor, Reed & Fields (later CD's main American publishers). He wrote later that he was in the hall at Tremont House on 22 Jan when CD arrived, and described him as bounding in and shouting " 'Here we are!' "—when "several gentlemen came forward to greet him"; after CD had supped Fields and some friends followed him and Lord Mulgrave on a midnight walk in the frozen Boston streets, hearing CD keep up "one continual shout of uproarious laughter" (J. T. Fields, *Yesterdays with Authors*, 8th edn, Boston, 1874, pp. 127–30). Was at the Boston Dinner of 1 Feb, with other young men at the lower end of the table (Fields, *op. cit.*, p. 130).

[6] Only the ending and signature are in CD's hand; the rest in Putnam's.

Pickwick Papers.[1] But I think the first number appeared six years ago, come the last day of next March. Dear Sir

Faithfully Yours

CHARLES DICKENS

To JOHN FORSTER, [?4 FEBRUARY 1842]

Extract in F, III, ii, 208–9. *Date:* Though quoted by Forster as the conclusion of letter begun 17 Jan, ended 30 Jan, dispatched by the *Britannia* 1 Feb, must clearly have been written later. Muddled though he was about dates himself, CD could scarcely refer to his birthday as "next Tuesday" until Tues 1 Feb; and the only factories he is known to have visited from Boston were those at Lowell, on 3 Feb. Probably this (and more) was written shortly before he left Boston on the 5th, but instead of being posted the following Tuesday (in Hartford) it formed part of the letter posted in New York on 14 Feb—the one Forster so firmly calls CD's "second".

I wonder whether you will remember that next Tuesday is my birthday![2] This letter will leave here that morning.

On looking back through these sheets,[3] I am astonished to find how little I have told you, and how much I have, even now, in store which shall be yours by word of mouth. The American poor, the American factories,[4] the institutions of all kinds[5]—I have a book, already. There is no man in this town, or in this State

---

[1] A question surely only asked by Fields as a means of obtaining CD's autograph.

[2] His birthday was on the following Monday (cf. *To* Green, 27 Jan and *fn*).

[3] A clear indication that originally this letter contained much that appeared in *American Notes*, Ch. 3—probably, for instance, the description of Boston social customs, and of the sermon by Father Taylor, the seamen's preacher; also perhaps passages on the Transcendentalists and on church, chapel and lecture-room as the only means of excitement for women.

[4] CD had "devoted a day" to a visit to the manufacturing town of Lowell and assigned the whole of *American Notes*, Ch. 4, to the excursion. He saw several factories, and, like other English travellers, was greatly impressed by the girl mill-workers (mostly daughters of New England farmers and agricultural workers). He praised the neatness of their dress, their good health, their working conditions, and ended with three facts to "startle" his English readers: that many of their boarding-houses had pianos; that nearly all the girls subscribed to circulating libraries; and that they produced among themselves a periodical, the *Lowell Offering*. This was, Mrs Motley reported him as saying, "the happiest day he had passed in the country—he promised

to go again, and Sam Lawrence promised to give him a party, and invite 1200 girls to meet him" (*J. L. Motley and his Family*, ed. S. and H. St John Mildmay, p. 24). Harriet Martineau, who had visited Lowell with Emerson in 1834, was above all impressed by the girls' freedom from "gross immorality" (*Society in America*, 1837, II, 355); she saw the *Lowell Offering* as the victory of "MIND in a life of labour" (letter quoted in *Mind amongst the Spindles: a Selection from the Lowell Offering*, ed. Charles Knight, 1844, p. xviii). A warmly appreciative review of *American Notes* appeared in the *Lowell Offering*, Jan 43.

[5] In South Boston he had visited the State Hospital for the Insane; the House of Industry (for "old or otherwise helpless paupers", with children in an adjoining building) and the connected hospital (spoilt only for CD by a suffocating "demon of a stove"); the Boylston School for neglected boys; the House of Reformation for Juvenile Offenders; and the Massachusetts House of Correction (run on the silent system with its inmates employed on useful work instead of the treadmill—though he doubted the wisdom of this). These he described in *American Notes*, Ch. 3, and perhaps originally in this letter. All were supported, or assisted, by the State, and of

of New England, who has not a blazing fire and a meat dinner every day of his life. A flaming sword in the air would not attract so much attention as a beggar in the streets. There are no charity uniforms, no wearisome repetition of the same dull ugly dress, in that blind school.[1] All are attired after their own tastes, and every boy and girl has his or her invididuality as distinct and unimpaired as you would find it in their own homes. At the theatres, all the ladies sit in the fronts of the boxes. The gallery are as quiet as the dress circle at dear Drury-lane. A man with seven heads would be no sight at all, compared with one who couldn't read and write.

I won't speak (I say "speak"! I wish I could) about the dear precious children, because I know how much we shall hear about them when we receive those letters from home for which we long so ardently.

To WILLIAM WETMORE STORY,[2] 4 FEBRUARY [1842]

Extract in Goodspeeds Book Shop catalogue No. 174; dated Tremont House, 4 Feb, in Anderson Galleries catalogue No. 2201.

I am exceedingly obliged to you for your kind note, and for your letter of introduction, which, you may readily suppose, I shall not fail to deliver. I have already a letter and Pamphlet for your Father,[3] from Lord Brougham[4] and I shall be very happy indeed, when the opportunity presents itself to deliver them.

this CD approved, believing that, in its tendency to elevate rather than depress "the character of the industrious classes", "a Public Charity is immeasurably better than a Private Foundation, no matter how munificently the latter may be endowed". In general, he thought the institutions of Massachusetts "as nearly perfect" as wisdom, benevolence and humanity could make them.

[1] The Perkins Institution. A footnote here by Forster reads: "His description of this school, and of the case of Laura Bridgman, will be found in the *Notes*; and have therefore been, of course, omitted here." But that CD wrote anything more than the slightest of descriptions in this letter is improbable; for almost the whole of his section on Laura Bridgman in *American Notes*, Ch. 3, is taken verbatim from a pamphlet on the Perkins Institution by its Director, Dr S. G. Howe; and of this pamphlet CD sent Forster a marked copy (see *To* Felton, 1 Sep, *fn*).

[2] William Wetmore Story (1819–95; *DAB*), sculptor, essayist and poet; at this time practising law in Boston. On the Invitation Committee for the Boston Dinner to CD. A man of remarkable charm, he was described by Thomas Wentworth Higginson as "a sort of Steerforth"

to his Harvard classmates. To his father, Story wrote on 3 Feb (Henry James, *William Wetmore Story and his Friends*, 1903, I, 58): "Dickens himself is frank and hearty, and with a considerable touch of rowdyism in his manner. But his eyes are fine, and the whole muscular action of the mouth and lower part of the face beautifully free and vibratory. People *eat* him here! never was there such a revolution; Lafayette was nothing to it. But he is too strong and healthy a mind to be spoiled even by the excessive adulation and flattery that he receives." He added that CD was "now rather unwell, from excitement", he supposed, and had disappointed Mrs Paige on 2 Feb (cf. *To* Ticknor, 2 Feb, *fn*). For his later contribution of poems to *All the Year Round*, see N, III, 358.

[3] Joseph Story (1779–1845; *DAB*), Judge of the United States Supreme Court since 1811, and virtual founder of the Harvard Law School, of which he became the first Dane Professor 1829. A Unitarian and an Abolitionist: he aroused strong controversy in 1841 by his decision in the *Amistad* case to free a cargo of slaves who had seized the ship and murdered the officers. Story took particular delight in *Barnaby Rudge* (*Life and Letters of Joseph Story*, ed. W. W. Story, 1851, I, 31) and was anxious to meet

To MISS TUTHILL,[1] 7 FEBRUARY 1842*

MS Huntington Library.

City Hotel, Hertford[2] | Seventh February 1842.

Mr. Charles Dickens presents his compliments to Miss Tuthill, and begs to thank her, both for her book,[3] and her most acceptable and welcome note. Mr. Dickens has not the heart to say "Dear Madam", which has even a more formal appearance than this mode of address.—He is cordially obliged to her; and earnestly assures her that she was not mistaken in supposing that her gift would be received and acknowledged with pleasure.

To THE REV. R. C. WATERSTON,[4] 7 FEBRUARY 1842*

MS Rosenbach Foundation.

Private.   City Hotel. Hertford | Seventh February 1842.

My Dear Sir.

You have not mistaken me. I have a deep and strong interest in children, and in all creatures who appeal through their helplessness to our gentleness and mercy— in children most especially. They need more friends in England than they have.

It was not a sister of my own, I lost.[5] She was my wife's sister. God knows that no tie of blood could have bound her closer to me, or endeared her to me more. She was but seventeen when she died; and she died in one night. She lay down upon her bed in perfect health and beauty; and never rose again, but in the Spirit.

I will not tell you how sorely I was tried, four years ago last May, by this bereavement—nor how dearly I loved her; my constant affectionate, and chosen

---

CD. "When will Boz be in Washington?", he wrote to Sumner from Washington, 6 Feb; "I hope he may be here before my return home, for I have a curiosity to see him as a literary wonder" (MS Houghton Library, Harvard).

[4] Entrusted to CD on 20 Dec 41 (see Vol. II, p. 447*n*); probably *The Three Speeches of Lord Brougham upon Slavery, Negro Apprenticeship, and the Slave Trade, Delivered in the House of Lords, Jan. 29th., Feb. 20th., and March 6th., 1838*, 1838. Story admired Brougham as a lawyer, but had considerable reservations on his political judgment, and had thought him "absolutely wrong, and mischievously demolishing his high reputation" in 1838 (*Life and Letters of Joseph Story*, ed. W. W. Story, II, 299).

[1] Cornelia Louisa Tuthill (1820–70), later Mrs Pierson, eldest daughter of the Rev. Cornelius Tuthill, of New Haven, and of the authoress Louisa Tuthill. She

wrote religious and children's books, and abridged Southey's *The Book of the Church*, Boston, 1843.

[2] Mis-spelt thus by CD while staying at Hartford and afterwards, though correctly spelt before he went there. For his week-end at Worcester 5–7 Feb, see *To* Forster, 17 Feb and *fn*.

[3] No book of hers published by this date has been found.

[4] Robert Cassie Waterston (1812–93), evangelical pastor of the Pitts Street Chapel, Boston; formerly superintendent of the Bethel Sunday school under the Rev. E. T. ("Father") Taylor, the only clergyman CD heard preach in Boston (see *To* Sumner, 25 Jan, *fn*). Brought up a Unitarian. Travelled extensively in Europe and the Middle East, meeting De Quincey in Scotland. Published books on religion, and poems.

[5] As stated in the sketch of his life in the *Bunker-Hill Aurora*, 29 Jan.

companion—nor in what respects I hope this sorrow has gradually made me a better man—nor how I have learnt to look beyond the Grave—and tried, in one of my stories, to divest it of some of its terrors. It is enough to say that I *feel* what you have written and sent to me; that it touches me very much; and that I *thank* you.

I hope yet[1] to avail myself of your good company in visiting the poor of Boston.[2] In the meanwhile and always—with best wishes for yourself and your lady,[3] in which Mrs. Dickens unites—I am My Dear Sir

Faithfully Yours

The Reverend R. C. Waterston.   CHARLES DICKENS

To ARTHUR LIVERMORE,[4] 8 FEBRUARY 1842*

MS New Hampshire Historical Society.

City Hotel Hertford. | Eighth February 1842.

My Dear Sir.

I am truly obliged to you for your frank and hospitable Invitation. I fear that the course I have marked out (which is *not* restricted to highways and cities) will keep us apart;[5] but I feel equally indebted to you for your kindness.

Mrs. Dickens begs me to convey to you her best regards and thanks.

Dear Sir | Faithfully Yours

Arthur Livermore Esquire   CHARLES DICKENS

To THE YOUNG MEN'S INSTITUTE, NEW HAVEN, [?8 FEBRUARY 1842]

Mention in the *American Traveller*, Boston, 15 Feb 42. *Date:* shortly after his arrival in Hartford, where he found their letter awaiting him.

Saying in reply to an invitation to deliver a lecture before the Young Men's Institute on Thurs 10 Feb that he had never delivered a lecture in his life, but would be happy to listen to one on the evening in question.[6]

---

[1] On his then intended return to Boston.
[2] Mrs J. L. Motley was clearly mistaken when on 5 Feb she wrote to her husband from Boston: "He [CD] has been about among the poor with Waterstone [*mis-spelt thus*]" (*J. L. Motley and his Family*, ed. S. and H. St John Mildmay, p. 24).
[3] *Née* Anna Cabot Lowell Quincy (*d.* 1899), youngest daughter of Josiah Quincy, Sr, President of Harvard.
[4] Probably Arthur Livermore, Jr (1811–1905), lawyer, of Bath, New Hampshire

1839–59, rather than his father, Arthur Livermore, Sr (1766–1853), of Campton, former Chief Justice of New Hampshire Superior Court. Arthur, Jr, was American Consul in Ireland 1865–85; later practised as a solicitor in Bath, England, and died in Manchester.
[5] CD did not visit New Hampshire.
[6] Presumably CD at the time believed he could fit this in before or after his engagement of 10 Feb with the "Brothers in Unity".

To [?GEORGE] GRIFFIN,[1] [?8 FEBRUARY 1842]

Mention in next. *Date:* the day before that letter.

To MRS LYDIA SIGOURNEY,[2] [?9] FEBRUARY 1842*

MS Connecticut Historical Society. *Date:* 10 Feb was Thursday, not Wednesday, in 1842. Since Mrs Sigourney had written verses to welcome CD[3] which were recited at the Hartford Dinner on Tues 8 Feb, when no doubt she met him, it seems more likely that CD wrote to her on Wed 9th suggesting the 10th for her call than that it should be left till the 11th, his last day in Hartford, when he visited jails and asylums in the morning and left for New Haven at 5 p.m. (*To* Forster, 17 Feb).[4]

City Hotel, Hertford
Wednesday February Tenth 1842.

Dear Mrs. Sigourney.

I am very sorry to say that owing to a mistake on the part of my Secretary, Mr. Griffin's letter[5] went to New York last night by the Post.

I promise myself the pleasure of seeing you tomorrow, between twelve and two.—Mrs. Dickens is much better,[6] and sends her best regards.

Always believe me | Your friend and warm admirer

Mrs. Sigourney. CHARLES DICKENS

[1] Probably George Griffin (?1778–1860), well known New York lawyer, with whose son, according to L. G. Clark, CD dined in New York on 22 Feb (see *Harper's New Monthly*, XXV [1862], 376): a Mr Griffin had arranged many of Mrs Sigourney's contracts with publishers during her early years as a writer (Gordon S. Haight, *Mrs. Sigourney, the Sweet Singer of Hartford*, New Haven, 1930, pp. 128–9).

[2] Lydia Howard Sigourney, *née* Huntley (1791–1865; *DAB*), for 50 years the most popular poetess in America; "usually advertised, as if it were something to boast of, as the American Hemans" (*Foreign Quarterly Review*, Jan 44, XXXII, 311). Conducted schools in Norwich and Hartford 1811–19; after marriage in 1819 published numerous vols of poems and sketches, besides pious works and children's books, and contributed prolifically to magazines and annuals. In England, 1840–1, she called on Rogers, Wordsworth and the Carlyles. Mrs Carlyle described her devastatingly as "beplastered with rouge and pomatum—bare-necked at an age which had left *certainty* far behind—with long ringlets that never grew where they hung—smelling marvellously of camphor or hartshorn and oil—all glistening in black

satin as if she were an apothecary's *puff* for black *sticking-plaster*—and staring her eyes out, to give them animation" (*Jane Welsh Carlyle: Letters to her Family, 1839–1863*, ed. L. Huxley, 1924, p. 78). She was much criticized in the press for her use in *Pleasant Memories of Pleasant Lands* (1842) of a private letter from Mrs Southey about her husband's insanity: see Gordon S. Haight, *Mrs. Sigourney, the Sweet Singer of Hartford*, pp. 70–2.

[3] The first of four stanzas reads: "Welcome! o'er the ocean blue, | Welcome to the youthful West, | Ardent hearts and spirits true | Greet thee as a favour'd guest."

[4] For CD's state of confusion about the dates in this week, see *To* Green, 27 Jan, *fn.*

[5] CD's answer, presumably, to a letter from Griffin saying that he would be in Hartford during the week and hoped to see CD, but written from a New York address: hence Putnam's mistake in addressing CD's reply.

[6] For Catherine's swollen face, see *To* Mitton, 31 Jan and *fn.* By the time they reached Hartford it was so "horribly bad" that CD decided to give her a rest there, and cancelled his New Haven engagement (*To* Forster, 17 Feb).

To [?THE SECRETARY, BROTHERS IN UNITY], [?9 FEBRUARY 1842]

Mention in *To* Forster, 17 Feb. *Date:* probably the day before he had originally intended to leave for New Haven.

Cancelling his engagement for Thurs 10 Feb because his wife was unwell and needed a further day's rest at Hartford.[1]

To I. H. ADAMS,[2] 10 FEBRUARY 1842

MS Goodspeeds Book Shop. *Address:* I. H. Adams Esquire. | City Hotel.

City Hotel, Hertford. | Tenth February 1842.

My Dear Sir.

We beg to thank you (to whom we understand we are indebted for the exquisite pleasure we received last night) for your most beautiful Serenade. If you knew how much delight it afforded us, and how many thoughts of home and those who make it dearest, your charming performance awakened; you would feel how inadequate this acknowledgement is—almost as strongly as we do.

With the sincere hope that you may long live to elevate and refine the hearts of your friends by the help of such sweet sounds; and that your feeling for the tender and mournful may never have a sadder origin than in your innate power of expression and perfect appreciation of the Poet's meaning, we are

Dear Sir | Faithfully Yours
CATHERINE DICKENS

I. H. Adams Esquire   CHARLES DICKENS

I need scarcely add that we beg to include your friend Mr. Boedenhare,[3] in our grateful recollections.

To JOSEPH S. SMITH,[4] 12 FEBRUARY 1842

MS Pennsylvania Historical Society.

Private   Carlton House New York.[5] | Twelfth February 1842.

My Dear Sir

Let me say, in answer to your letter, that the wanderings, history, and death of Nell, are quite imaginary, and wholly fictitious.

---

[1] On the evening of their arrival at New Haven (8 p.m. on 11 Feb), he held a levee for "the students and professors" of Yale at his hotel, and later that night was serenaded by the college choristers (*To* Forster, 17 Feb).

[2] Isaac Hull Adams (*b.* 1813), nephew of John Quincy Adams; made his career in the Coast Survey. He had a fine tenor voice and often sang duets.

[3] The German friend referred to in *To* Forster, 17 Feb, who sang too.

[4] Identified by R. A. Hammond (*Life and Writings of CD*, Toronto, 1871, p. 197) as Joseph Stanley Smith, of Albany, New York. In 1852 he was editor of the *Albany State Register*.

[5] For CD's days at Hartford (8–11 Feb), night at New Haven (11 Feb), and arrival in New York at 2 p.m. on the 12th, see *To* Forster, 17 Feb and *fns*.

That many of the feelings which grow out of this little Story and are suggested by it, are familiar to me, I need scarcely say. The grave has closed over very deep affection and strong love of mine. So far, and no farther, there is Truth in it.

I do not usually answer questions having this reference, so freely. But yours is an honest letter, I believe. Therefore I give you an honest answer.

Your friend

Mr. Jos. S. Smith.   CHARLES DICKENS

To JONATHAN CHAPMAN,¹ [?12 FEBRUARY 1842]

Mention in Chapman *to* CD, 14 Feb.² *Date:* Chapman was clearly answering a note he had newly received from CD, probably written on 12 Feb, the day he reached New York.

Presumably thanking Chapman for his kindness in Boston and proposing that they should regard their friendship as an "alliance".

To CUTHBERT C. GORDON,³ 13 FEBRUARY [1842]

MS⁴ Princeton University Library.

Carlton House | Feby. 13th.

Dear Sir—

Your kind and welcome letter awaited me here yesterday. It did not reach Boston until after I had left.

I scarcely know how to thank you for the earnest manner in which you have conveyed to me the distinguished compliment of the directors of the Mercantile Library Association.⁵ I can only beg you to assure those gentlemen that I highly appreciate and esteem the honor they have done me, and that I shall not fail to take an early opportunity of visiting their Institution.

To you, personally, I can say no more than that you have given me unfeigned pleasure and satisfaction—that I thank you for it with all my heart—and that

I am | Dear Sir |Your friend

Cuthbert C. Gordon Esq.   CHARLES DICKENS

---

¹ Jonathan Chapman (1807–48), Whig Mayor of Boston 1840–2. Graduated from Harvard 1825; admitted to the Suffolk County bar 1828. Contributed to the *North American Review* and the *Christian Examiner*, and was an effective speaker. Received CD at the Ball at Papanti's 26 Jan; was one of his escorts on his visits to Boston institutions; and spoke at the Dinner on 1 Feb, insisting that it was to his office alone that he owed the privilege of being present—which was no doubt partly false modesty, though in fact through his family background (his father was a master-mariner, his mother the daughter of a Loyalist) he did not rank with Boston's

"aristocracy". Clearly CD soon felt much at ease with him.

² For text see *To* Chapman, 22 Feb, *fn.*

³ Cuthbert C. Gordon, Corresponding Secretary of the Mercantile Library Association, New York, since Jan 42; a member of the Board of Directors 1843.

⁴ Only the ending and signature are in CD's hand; the rest in Putnam's.

⁵ Founded 1820, its members, over 5000 in 1840, were New York merchants' clerks. It had a library of *c.* 22,000 books, and a reading-room, at Clinton Hall; and organized lectures and classes. Honorary members included Felton and Colden.

To MESSRS LEA & BLANCHARD,[1] 13 FEBRUARY 1842

Text from *Dickensian*, XI (1913), 260.

Carlton House, New York, | Thirteenth February, 1842.

My Dear Sirs,

I am cordially obliged to you for your thoughtful recollection, and for the box of books.[2] Accept my very best thanks.

I shall be exceedingly glad to know you, and shake hands with you when I come to Philadelphia, where I shall be, I hope, (though for a very few days) in a fortnight at furthest.[3]

I shall be glad to have, too—of course, between ourselves—some information on a business point which occurs to my mind just now.[4]

The intelligence of the long faces[5] had reached my ears before I received your letter. I am truly sorry for the cause of their elongation, and wish them short again with all my heart.

Dear Sirs, | Always faithfully yours,

Messrs. Lea and Blanchard.   CHARLES DICKENS

To SAMUEL WARD,[6] 13 FEBRUARY 1842*

MS Berg Collection.

Sunday. Thirteenth February | 1842.

My Dear Sir.

We are—not seven,[7] but fourteen.[8] Our whole fortnight is engaged. Wherefore, let it remain—Wednesday.[9]

[1] Originally Carey & Carey, Carey & Lea 1824, Philadelphia publishers (see Vol. I, p. 322n, and *To* Forster, 13 Mar, *fn*); the only American publishers with whom CD had had dealings (see Vol. II, p. 56n).

[2] Among these was probably William G. Simms's *Beauchampe*, published by themselves (2 vols, 1842), which Catherine later gave to Anne Brown (see *To* Neil House, ?19 Apr, *fn*). For other books possibly given by them to CD see 2 June 42.

[3] He arrived in Philadelphia on 5 Mar, and Henry C. Carey, former senior partner, entertained him on the 8th.

[4] Presumably concerning publication in America of his next novel (he would scarcely have told them of his intention to write a book about America).

[5] Of disapproval, no doubt, at his raising —in his speeches at Boston and Hartford— the subject of international copyright (see *To* Forster, 14 Feb and *fn*). For Henry Carey's attitude to the subject, see *To* Forster, 13 Mar, *fn*.

[6] Samuel Ward (1814–84; *DAB*), elder brother of Julia Ward (author of "The Battle Hymn of the Republic") who in 1843 married S. G. Howe. Studied in Europe 1831, entered his father's banking house, and in 1838 married Emily Astor, who died Feb 41. In 1849, having lost his fortune, joined the California gold rush; was successively an adventurer in the West and, during and after the Civil War, a financial lobbyist in Washington. Later "Uncle Sam" to a host of Americans.

[7] See Wordsworth's "We are Seven"— which CD thought "one of the most striking examples of his genius" (Wilkie *to* Mrs Ricketts, 14 Oct 39, after meeting CD at the *Nickleby* dinner: Sotheby's catalogue, 23 Nov 1971).

[8] Ward obviously thought CD was to spend only a week in New York. On 30 Jan Longfellow had written to him: "Dickens is a glorious fellow. You will be delighted with him; and I have promised [*thus*] him a letter to you, and want you to see him first, on his arrival in New York,—

I write this with my hands in a basin of water; being in the very act of trimming myself for going out. Mrs. D unites with me in best regards. And I am always

Faithfully Yours | (I take my shortest name)

Samuel Ward Esquire   Boz

To WILLIAM CULLEN BRYANT,[1] 14 FEBRUARY 1842

Text from Parke Godwin, *A Biography of William Cullen Bryant*, New York, 1883, I, 395.

Carlton House. | February 14, 1842.

My Dear Sir,

With one exception (and that's Irving)[2] you are the man I most wanted to see

before anyone has laid hands upon him. He will reach New York on Saturday week—that is Feb. 12. I beg you, have him and his wife to dine that day, with Irving, Halleck and Dr. Francis. And in order to secure to yourself the great pleasure of introducing to each other two such men as Irving and Dickens, write an invitation to Dickens, and inclose it to me, and I and Sumner will arrange the whole matter before hand, if you like the plan. | When shall you be here? Dickens breakfasts with me on Friday. Will you come? Let me know beforehand; for every place at table is precious;—but I shall count upon you" (*The Letters of H. W. Longfellow*, ed. A. Hilen, II, 382). None of these suggestions materialized.

⁹ On 13 Feb Felton wrote to Sumner from New York: "Next Wednesday I dine with the Dickens at the Wards—dance with ditto at ditto, in the evening. They [*the management of the Park Theatre*] also mean to repeat the ball that night; so great is the rush to get tickets that . . . now none are to be had at any price." He had called on the Wards on 12 Feb, he continued, and found them in "glorious spirits": the three girls "were writing invitations for their ball Wednesday and I lent them a helping hand, . . . they selecting all the prettiest girls of New York" (MS Harvard College Library). On 16 Feb Ward wrote to Longfellow: "We are making preparations today for the friends whom I have invited to meet Boz (who will probably be too much indisposed to attend)" (MS *ibid.*). He was proved right: CD was unable to go because he had "an inflammatory affection of the throat" (*To* Simpson, 16 Feb); and Ward wrote again to Longfellow on 18 Feb of their "Boz-*less* Ball" (MS *ibid.*). For CD's

cancelling another engagement with Ward, see 21 Feb and *fn.*

¹ William Cullen Bryant (1794–1878; *DAB*), poet and journalist. Practised law in Massachusetts 1815–25. Made his name as America's leading poet with "Thanatopsis", 1817, and *Poems*, 1821 and 1832; published further collections in 1842 and 1844. One of the very few poets praised in an article on American poetry (almost certainly by Forster: see *To* Poe, 6 Mar, *fn*) in the *Foreign Quarterly Review* (Jan 44, XXXII, 315): "When America shall have given birth to a few such poets as Bryant, she may begin to build up a national literature to the recognition of which all the world will subscribe." From 1829 editor (joint-owner 1836) of the *New York Evening Post*, which he made strongly Democratic and increasingly Abolitionist. In it on 18 Feb he wrote of CD: "He has many characteristics to interest the higher orders of mind. They are such as to recommend him peculiarly to Americans. His sympathies seek out that class with which American institutions and laws sympathize most strongly" (quoted in Godwin, *op. cit.*, I, 397). He later supported CD over international copyright. On 19 Apr 42 he wrote to R. H. Dana, Sr: "You were right in what you said of Dickens. I liked him hugely, though he was so besieged while he was here that I saw little of him—little in comparison with what I could have wished" (*op. cit.*, I, 396*n*). Later in 1842 he sent CD a copy of his *The Fountain, and Other Poems*, published that July, inscribed "from his friend and admirer | William Cullen Bryant". But he protested in the *Evening Post*, 9 Nov 42, at CD's sweeping condemnation of the American press in *American Notes*; and the

in America.[1] You have been here twice, and I have not seen you. The fault was not mine; for on the evening of my arrival committee-gentlemen were coming in and out until long after I had your card put into my hands. As I lost what I most eagerly longed for, I ask you for your sympathy, and not for your forgiveness. Now, I want to know when you will come and breakfast with me: and I don't call to leave a card at your door before asking you, because I love you too well to be ceremonious with you. I have a thumbed book at home, so well worn that it has nothing upon the back but one gilt "B," and the remotest possible traces of a "y."[2] My credentials are in my earnest admiration of its beautiful contents. Any day but next Monday or next Sunday. Time, half-past ten. Just say in writing, "My dear Dickens, such a day. Yours ever." Will you?[3]

Your faithful friend,
CHARLES DICKENS

To JOHN FORSTER, [14 FEBRUARY 1842]

Extract and summary in F, III, iii, 214, and mention in *To* Forster, 17 Feb; probably the conclusion of the letter begun ?4 Feb. *Date:* 14 Feb according to Forster. *From* the Carlton Hotel, New York.

Saying that he had spoken about international copyright twice publicly,[4] to the great indignation of some of the editors here, who are attacking me for so doing,

fact that he failed to see CD on at least four later visits to London suggests that he was among the American friends that CD lost through *Chuzzlewit*.

[2] See *To* Forster, 17 Feb and *fn* p. 70.

[1] According to Godwin (*op. cit.*, I, 395), it was reported that CD's first question on landing at Boston was "Where is Bryant?"

[2] Only the copy given him by Dana on 3 Feb was in CD's library at his death.

[3] Bryant accepted, clearly choosing 22 Feb, the day on which CD later asked Halleck to breakfast (see 17 Feb); for afterwards Felton, also a guest, wrote to him: "A breakfast with Bryant, Halleck, and Dickens, is a thing to remember forever" (*op. cit.*, I, 396). In his letter of 19 Apr Bryant told R. H. Dana, Sr: "I breakfasted with [CD] one morning, and the number of despatches that came and went made me almost think I was breakfasting with a minister of state" (*ibid.*).

[4] At the Boston Dinner of 1 Feb and the Hartford Dinner of 8 Feb. He ended his Boston speech: "You have in America great writers ... who will live in all time, and are as familiar to our lips as household words. ... I take leave to say, in the

presence of some of those gentlemen, that I hope the time is not far distant when they, in America, will receive of right some substantial profit and return in England from their labours; and when we, in England, shall receive some substantial profit and return for ours. Pray do not misunderstand me. Securing for myself from day to day the means of an honourable subsistence, I would rather have the affectionate regard of my fellow men, than I would have heaps and mines of gold. But the two things do not seem to me incompatible. ... There must be an international arrangement in this respect: England has done her part, and I am confident that the time is not far distant when America will do hers. It becomes the character of a great country; *firstly*, because it is justice; *secondly*, because without it you never can have, and keep, a literature of your own" (*Speeches*, ed. K. J. Fielding, p. 21). Winding up his Hartford speech, he said: "Gentlemen, as I have no secrets from you, in the spirit of confidence you have engendered between us, and as I have made a kind of compact with myself that I never will, while I remain in America, omit an opportunity of

right and left;[1] *that all the best men*[2] *had assured him that, if only at once followed up in England, the blow struck might bring about a change in the law; and—yielding to the agreeable delusion that the best men could be a match for the worst in such a matter—urging Forster to enlist what force was obtainable and in particular (since CD had made Scott's claim his war cry) to bring Lockhart into the field. He enclosed a newspaper and the Ball Committee's report on the Boz Ball.*[3]

referring to a topic in which I and all others of my class on both sides of the water are equally interested— . . . I would beg leave to whisper in your ear two words, International Copyright. I use them in no sordid sense, believe me, and those that know me best, best know that. For myself, I would rather that my children coming after me, trudged in the mud, and knew by the general feeling of society that their father was beloved, and had been of some use, than I would have them ride in their carriages, and know by their banker's books that he was rich. But I do not see, I confess, why one should be obliged to make the choice, or why fame, besides playing that delightful *reveille* for which she is so justly celebrated, should not blow out of her trumpet a few notes of a different kind [*cf. earlier use of this image, Vol. II, p. 416*] from those with which she has hitherto contented herself" (*op. cit.*, pp. 24–5). He then went on to "thrust . . . down [his audience's] throats" the final poverty of Scott (*To* Forster, 24 Feb and *fn*).

[1] The remarks on international copyright in his Boston speech, although reported in full in the papers, excited no immediate comment. It was the Hartford speech which precipitated attacks on him, and his remarks at the Boston Dinner were then included. The first newspaper comment, in the *Hartford Daily Times*, was stiff, but relatively mild: "Mr. Dickens alluded in his remarks to an international copyright law. In Boston he also alluded to the same subject, intimating that England had done her duty and it now remained for the United States to follow suit. It happens that we want no advice upon this subject, and it will be better for Mr. Dickens, if he refrains from introducing the matter hereafter. But it is not pleasant to pursue the question further at this time". The *New World* followed, on 12 Feb, with an attack on his remarks at the Boston Dinner ("The time, place, and occasion

taken into consideration—to us they seem to have been made in the worst taste possible"), and continued: "Has Mr. Dickens yet to learn that to the very absence of such a law as he advocates, he is mainly indebted for his widespread popularity in this country? To that class of his readers—the dwellers in log cabins [*mentioned by CD in his Boston speech*], in our back settlements—whose good opinion, he says, is dearer to him than gold, his name would hardly have been known had an international copy-right law been in existence." While probably (it went on) no more than 4000 copies were sold of his works as they originally appeared, in numbers, more than 20,000 copies "were disseminated every week, throughout the entire land, in the ample pages of the New World". This was "the secret of his wide spread fame", and the *New World* would regret any law that deprived them of the pleasure of laying his future work before its readers, while at the same time increasing his well earned fame. For the charge in the following week's *New World* which angered CD far more, see *To* Forster, 24 Feb and *fn* p. 83.

[2] Felton was not one of these; on 13 Feb he wrote to Sumner: "Some of the editors are abusing [CD] for touching up the question of copyright. I regret that he has done so; it being done, his friends ought to defend him stoutly. It would have been better had he left that topic to others. Willis fears that trouble will grow out of it; that a reaction is taking place, and that he will finally leave the country with unpleasant impressions. I do not agree with him. There will be a few growlers, but the great mass are sound-hearted, and too well disposed towards Boz to turn against him, because a few editors, disappointed at having Dickens taken out of their hands, vent their spite upon his head" (MS Houghton Library).

[3] See *To* Forster, 17 Feb, *fn*.

To EDMUND B. GREEN, 14 FEBRUARY 1842

Text from the *New World*, 26 Feb 42.

Carlton House, New York, | February 14th, 1842.

My Dear Sir,

I see you have taken my life into your paper.[1] It is so wildly imaginative, and so perfectly new to me, I could not help writing to the editor of the Bunker Hill Aurora, (in which I first saw it) to compliment him on the rich fancy of its author, whose imaginative biography, both of myself and my better half, is the most remarkable invention I ever met with.[2]

If I enter my protest against its being received as a strictly veracious account of my existence down to the present time, it is only because I may one of these days be induced to lay violent hands upon myself—in other words attempt my own life[3]—in which case, the gentleman unknown, would be quoted as authority against me.

Always faithfully Yours,

To Edmund B. Green, Esq.   CHARLES DICKENS

[1] "Life of 'Boz' " had appeared in the *New England Weekly Review* of 12 Feb.

[2] The *Bunker-Hill Aurora*'s "Visit of 'Boz'—Sketch of his Life" (see Early Feb) clearly derived from the same source as the *New England Weekly Review*'s "Life". But while the *Aurora*'s "Sketch" opened with two paragraphs of slightly qualified welcome, the introduction to the *Weekly Review*'s "Life" spoke of CD's quick success—the current of his life so "perfectly smooth" as to present "little materials for the biographer". What follows in each is virtually identical except in arrangement. An account is given of CD's publishing career: correct on a great many points, including the early attempts at dramatic composition, though wrong in dates given for *Nickleby* and *Master Humphrey* and in a few minor details concerning CD's journalism and *Sketches*. Concerning his personal life there is some confusion between the Dickens and Hogarth families—in the statements that it was John Dickens, not Hogarth, who worked on the *Morning Chronicle*; that the Miss Hogarth CD married in 1834 [in fact 1836] was "a student at the Royal Academy of Music"; that grief at the death of one of his own sisters made him "unable to carry on his professional pursuits"; but, beside this, the correct statement that one of CD's

sisters married Burnett, "the singer, of the St. James's theatre". There is confusion too, perhaps between CD and Forster, when CD is said to have been placed in the office of a barrister (Chitty, in the "Life"). But in general the account is not misleading. The final sentence in the "Life" (but not in the "Sketch") states rather grandly that there was one circumstance that could not be passed over in silence—"the care and attention paid by Mr. Dickens to his father, for whom he has purchased an estate sufficient to render him independent." The "Sketch" ends with the mention of his four children (omitted in the "Life"). The extent of knowledge shown and the introduction of such a name as Burnett's (unknown to Americans) suggest that the biography was originally written for English readers—just possibly by Shelton Mackenzie (see Vol. I, p. 367 and *n*), who was Liverpool correspondent of the *New York Union*, for a Liverpool paper. The date of the original article is proved to have been 1841 by the statement in the "Sketch" that *Barnaby Rudge* "is still in course of publication".

[3] The *New World* prefaced CD's letter with: "From the following, it would appear that our hospitable citizens, not content with making Mr. Dickens ill by their civilities, have *attempted his life*."

To LEWIS GAYLORD CLARK,[1] 15 FEBRUARY 1842*

MS Mr N. C. Peyrouton.

Carlton House | Fifteenth February 1842.

My Dear Sir

We must postpone our breakfast, I grieve to say, for a day or two. I have been in bed all day with a violent sore throat—and have been obliged to have a doctor—and am not myself by any means—though if resolutions to that effect will do it, I mean to be quite well tomorrow.

My best regards to Mrs. Clark[2]—Mrs. Dickens unites with me in all good wishes.

Faithfully Yours

[L.][3] Gaylord[4] Clark Esquire   CHARLES DICKENS

To CHARLES A. DAVIS,[5] [15 FEBRUARY 1842]

Mention in *The Diary of Philip Hone, 1828–1851*, ed. A. Nevins, New York, 1936, p. 588. *Date:* Diary entry of 16 Feb refers to CD's apology of the day before.

Apologizing for being unable to come to a dinner party at Davis's house that evening, since he was confined to his room with a sore throat and was prohibited by the doctor from going out.[6]

To UNKNOWN CORRESPONDENT, 15 FEBRUARY [1842]

Mention in C. F. Libbie catalogue, Apr 1904; *MS* 1 p.; dated 15 Feb, from New York.

A business letter.

---

[1] Lewis Gaylord Clark (1808–73; *DAB*): see Vol. 1, p. 469*n*.

[2] *Née* Ella Maria Curtis; they were married in 1834, when she was 17.

[3] Initial confused in MS: "T" seems to be intended; certainly not "L".

[4] "Gaylord" apparently altered by CD to "Garlord". He had presumably addressed his three previous letters (see Vol. II) to "The Editor of the *Knickerbocker Magazine*" and was unsure of Clark's name.

[5] Charles Augustus Davis (1795–1867), wealthy New York merchant; friend of Halleck and other *Knickerbocker* writers.

Published humorous letters in the *New York Daily Advertiser*, under the pseudonyms "Peter Scriber" and "Major Jack Downing"; and at the New York Dinner to CD read out a comic "Downing" letter. He was on the committees of both the New York Ball and New York Dinner.

[6] According to Hone, "two very good-humored notes" were received from CD; the other guests, including himself, arrived: "and so we had to perform the tragedy of 'Hamlet,' the part of Hamlet omitted" (*Diary of Philip Hone, ibid.*).

To A COMMITTEE OF GENTLEMEN OF PHILADELPHIA,[1]
[?15 FEBRUARY 1842]

Mention in *Philadelphia Gazette*, Wednesday Afternoon, 16 Feb, quoting a report in the *Chronicle* of that morning. *Date:* more likely to have been written on the 15th when exhausted by the Boz Ball and ill with his sore throat (see *To* Forster, 17 Feb) than on the day of the Ball itself.

Declining a public dinner offered him by a Committee of Gentlemen of Philadelphia, and saying that his stay would be short and he wished to see the people.[2]

To THE YOUNG MEN OF BALTIMORE,[3]
[?15 FEBRUARY 1842]

Mention in *To* Forster, 24 Feb. *Date:* On 10 Feb, after CD had left Boston, Dana recorded in his journal: "Letter to Dickens upon business confided to me from Baltimore. Wm. Watson to take it, as a letter of introduction" (*The Journal of R. H. Dana, Jr.*, ed. R. F. Lucid, I, 61). Watson, a New York lawyer, presumably delivered the letter shortly after CD's arrival in New York, and CD's refusal was perhaps written on the day he declined the Philadelphia dinner.

Declining their invitation to a Public Dinner.[4]

To CHARLES H. DELAVAN,[5] 16 FEBRUARY [1842]

Text from *New York Tribune*, 23 Feb 42.

Carlton House, February 16

Dear Sir,

I very much regret, and so does Mrs. Dickens, that in consequence of the numerous engagements which we have made, it is not in our power to accept

[1] One of them was probably Ingersoll, whom CD already knew (see 6 Mar and *fn*).

[2] "Sensible man, this Boz, if left to act on his own responsibility", commented the *Gazette*. Before CD's arrival in Philadelphia on 5 Mar, it made two further announcements to the same effect—on 24 Feb, "Mr. Dickens . . . wisely declines all dinners, balls, parades, shows, junketings . . ., preferring to meet with such private, unostentatious hospitalities as a courteous people would extend to any gentleman and stranger"; and on 1 Mar, "he declines all public entertainments. Personal civilities and private hospitality, of course, he cheerfully receives". For the *Gazette*'s regret and indignation when things fell out otherwise, see *To* Maull, 10 Mar, *fn*.

[3] On 5 Feb William F. Frick, a Baltimore lawyer, had written to R. H. Dana, Jr, enclosing an invitation "from some 20 or 30 young men of our City (Members of the Bar & others of literary taste,)—asking to have the pleasure of a social dinner with

Mr Dickens, in case he should pass any time in Baltimore, on his way to Washington & the Southern States" (MS Massachusetts Historical Society).

[4] Although he had not until the end of the week reached the state of desperation in which he wrote to Chapman on 22 Feb, he must already—after cutting short his visit to New Haven to give Catherine a longer rest at Hartford—have foreseen the impracticability of tying himself down to social functions far in advance. In the event, although at first expecting to reach Baltimore on 4 Mar, he did not arrive there until the 21st.

[5] Mis-spelt "Delevan" in the *Tribune*. Charles H. Delavan (1810–92), son of General Daniel Delavan, a friend of Washington and Lafayette. Appointed U.S. Consul to Sydney, Nova Scotia, in Autumn 1842. Cousin of E. C. Delavan (1793–1871; *DAB*), co-founder of the New York State Temperance Society.

the welcome invitation of the New York Mechanics' Institute.[1] And I assure you that I regret this the more because I have formed the very highest respect for the object which brings them together on the anniversary of Washington's birthday, and for its great influence upon the most valuable portions of society.[2]

I am, dear sir, yours faithfully and obliged,

Charles H. Delevan, Esq.   CHARLES DICKENS

To [WILLIAM] MITCHELL,[3] 16 FEBRUARY [1842]*

MS[4] Benoliel Collection. *Address:* Undoubtedly to William Mitchell, but "J B" in subscription shows that CD had forgotten his first name (cf. subscription "R. Mitchell Esquire" in letter of 30 Apr).

Carlton House Feby. 16th.

My dear Sir.

I am really obliged to you for your frank and courteous letter. If, during our short and hurried stay, Mrs. Dickens and I can make but one escape to your pleasant Theatre,[5] trust me that we shall only be too happy to do so,[6] as[7] the Drama is one of our most constant amusements in London and some of our dearest friends are intimately connected with it.

For myself I have perhaps a stronger interest in you than you suspect. I was a very staunch admirer of yours (and I paid in those days) at the Queens[8]

[1] Founded in Winter 1830–1; incorporated 1833. By 1849 its original 45 members had become over 3000; its library contained 3000 books; lectures, meetings and debates were held at least twice a week in winter; and its school had *c.* 300 pupils of both sexes.

[2] The invitation was to hear Delavan lecture on Temperance at the Hall of the New York Society Library on 22 Feb. According to the *New York Tribune* of 23 Feb (quoted in W. G. Wilkins, *CD in America*, p. 118), "He divided the subject into four parts or classifications: economy, health and mental capacity, laws of decorum, and patriotism; which he forcibly illustrated by the retrospective and concurrent effects of intemperance." Before his lecture Delavan read out CD's letter. On 26 Feb the *New World* parodied the invitation to show the exploitation of CD's name.

[3] William Mitchell (1798–1856; *DAB*), English-born actor, dramatist, stage manager. First appeared on the stage at Newcastle-on-Tyne; at the Strand Theatre, London, 1831; actor and stage manager, Coburg Theatre, London, 1834; fined £50 for acting in *A Roland for an Oliver* at the New Strand Theatre, 5 Jan 35, without a licence from the Lord Chamberlain. Migrated to New York Aug 36 and became actor-manager successively of the National Theatre and (from 1839) the Olympic Theatre, Broadway. His comic parts at the National included Sam Weller and Squeers; at the Olympic, Tom Sparks in *The Strange Gentleman*, Crummles in two extravaganzas (see Malcolm Morley, "Early Dickens Drama in America", *D*, XLIV [1948], 155–6), and Sam Weller in *Boz*, a satire on the lionizing of CD in New York (see *To* Mitchell, 30 Apr, *fn*).

[4] Only the ending and signature are in CD's hand; the rest in Putnam's.

[5] CD described the Olympic in *American Notes*, Ch. 6, as "a tiny show-box for vaudevilles and burlesques. . . singularly well-conducted by Mr. Mitchell, a comic actor of great quiet humour and originality, who is well remembered and esteemed by London playgoers."

[6] No record of their managing to do so has been found. CD's description of the theatre was perhaps written from hearsay, out of sympathy for Mitchell.

[7] MS reads "As".

[8] Thus in MS.

Theatre in the remote times of the "wandering minstrel",[1] and the "revolt of the Workhouse".[2] I was constantly with you at the Strand Theatre, both before and after that time. I followed you to Covent Garden when you did very good things in a very bad part in "His first Campaign".[3] Thence I tracked you to Brahams[4] and lost you thereabouts to find you at the Ball the other night.

I am truly glad to hear on all sides that you are meeting with the success you deserve; and I hope it may be prolonged and increased until you see fit to come back to England again, a rich man.[5]

Always believe me | Faithfully Yours

J. B. Mitchell Esq.   CHARLES DICKENS

To EDMUND S. SIMPSON,[6] 16 FEBRUARY 1842*

MS Free Library of Philadelphia.

Carlton House. | Sixteenth February 1842.

Dear Sir.

I write to you from my bed; and I am truly sorry to say that I do so for the purpose of informing you that I cannot attend the Ball tonight,[7] owing to an inflammatory affection of the throat which confined me to the house during the whole of yesterday, and obliges me to keep my room to day.

I am sure I need not tell you how very much I regret this disappointment, or how great an effort I would make to come to the Theatre, if I could do so with any degree of prudence. But you will see by the inclosed[8] that my doctor

[1] A burletta by Henry Mayhew, first performed at the Royal Fitzroy Theatre (later the Queen's) 16 Jan 34. Mitchell played Jim Baggs.

[2] A "burlesque ballad opera" by Gilbert à Beckett, first performed 24 Feb 34, with Mitchell as Moll Chubb. See *Oliver Twist*, ed. K. Tillotson, Oxford, 1966, p. xviin.

[3] A military spectacle by J. R. Planché, first produced at Covent Garden 1 Oct 32; founded on an incident in the early life of the 1st Duke of Marlborough. Mitchell had a low comic part—an Irish sutler, Mrs Branagan.

[4] Thus in MS. St James's Theatre, owned by John Braham (?1774–1856; *DNB*): see Vol. I, p. 118n. Mitchell's parts there between Dec 35 and Mar 36 included Corney Callaghan in J. T. Haines's farce, *A House Divided*; Tag in *The Spoiled Child*, by Mrs Jordan; Benjamin Bunting in the burletta, *The Rejected Addresses*; and Leopold in J. Cobb's comic opera, *The Siege of Belgrade*. He had left England before rehearsals of CD's *The Strange Gentleman* and *The Village Coquettes* began at the St James's (Sep 36).

[5] Mitchell ran the Olympic with immense success until 1850; but afterwards lost money and died in New York in poverty.

[6] Edmund Shaw Simpson (1784–1848; *DAB*), English-born actor and manager, lessee of the Park Theatre, New York, since 1840. Widely esteemed, he struggled against the financial difficulties of his managership till 1848.

[7] It was to be a "repeat performance" of the Boz Ball of 14 Feb (see *To* Forster, 17 Feb and *fns*), with tickets at half the original price. CD had apparently intended to put in an appearance after dining and dancing at the Wards (see *To* Ward, 13 Feb, *fn*).

[8] A letter from Dr George Wilkes, Mrs Colden's brother, who was treating him, which read: "February 16, 1842. | My Dear Sir, | Mr Colden suggests, in case Mr. Simpson is called upon by any of his friends to account for your non-attendance to night, that I had better state it, as my opinion, that it would be highly improper for you to expose yourself to the night air, while laboring under the inflammatory affection of the throat, with which I find you. With great respect, | Your's most truly, | Geo. Wilkes."

expressly forbids it; and if you could see me, you would be at no loss to discover the soundness of his reasons for doing so.[1]

I am Dear Sir Faithfully Yours
— Simpson Esquire   CHARLES DICKENS

To JOHN FORSTER, 17 FEBRUARY 1842

Extract in F, III, iii, 214-18.

Carlton-house, New York: Thursday, February Seventeenth, 1842

As there is a sailing-packet from here to England to-morrow which is warranted (by the owners) to be a marvellous fast sailer, and as it appears most probable that she will reach home (I write the word with a pang) before the Cunard steamer of next month, I indite this letter.[2] And lest this letter should reach you before another letter which I dispatched from here last Monday, let me say in the first place that I *did* dispatch a brief epistle to you on that day, together with a newspaper,[3] and a pamphlet touching the Boz ball;[4] and that I put in the post-office at Boston another newspaper for you containing an account of the dinner,[5] which was just about to come off, you remember, when I wrote to you from that city.

[1] Although Wilkes's letter had been Colden's idea and supplied voluntarily by CD, its publication in the *New York Herald* and other papers on 17 Feb aroused great indignation against the management of the Park Theatre. *"Poor Dickens"*, commented the *Boston Press and Post* on 22 Feb; "The New Yorkers have made him sick—he couldn't attend the second ball in consequence of having a sore throat. What gives the affair a very vulgar appearance is the fact that one of the managers thought it necessary that Mr. Dickens's physician should furnish a *written certificate of his patient's illness, to satisfy the gentlemen and ladies attending the ball that Mr D. was positively unable to perform that eve!* and thereby preventing the aforesaid ladies and gentlemen from kicking up a row!" On 26 Feb *Brother Jonathan* declared that it had "never heard of a more disgraceful insult than this to such a man". The *Boston Morning Post* had previously (18 Feb) suggested that the managers of the Park Theatre should "engage Dickens for six or seven nights, he draws so well", and protested that the repetition converted "an act of courtesy to a private gentleman into a raree-show"; and the *Onondaga Standard* (Syracuse, N.Y.), 2 Mar, felt that the result would be CD's declining any such future invitations. According to the New York *Albion*, 19 Feb, at the repetition on 16 Feb, the Ball "was announced to take place

again"—for the third time—on the 18th; but no more was heard of this.

[2] For his missing the "fast sailer" from New York, see continuation of this letter on 24 Feb.

[3] Probably the *New England Weekly Review*, Hartford, of which the portion describing the Hartford Dinner (7½ columns) is now in the Forster Collection, V & A, with date of issue missing. The same issue contains the "Life of 'Boz'", of which CD had complained to the editor (*To* Green, 14 Feb).

[4] The Ball Committee's report, *Welcome to Charles Dickens. The Boz Ball. To be Given under the Direction of a Committee of Citizens of New York, at the Park Theatre, on the Evening of the Fourteenth of February Next*, New York 1842 (now in the Forster Collection, V & A). Eight pages long, the pamphlet gives the full history of the Ball arrangements, the names of the 87 members of the "General Committee", and the resolutions and reports of the "Committee of Arrangements". For the invitation to CD and further details, see *To* Morris, 28 Jan and *fn*.

[5] At Papanti's Hall on 1 Feb. Clearly CD had sent the copy of the *Boston Semi-Weekly Advertiser* of 5 Feb now in the Forster Collection, V & A. Its account, filling the front page and 2½ columns of the next, was reprinted, in part, by several New York papers.

It was a most superb affair; and the speaking *admirable*.[1] Indeed the general talent for public speaking here, is one of the most striking of the things that force themselves upon an Englishman's notice. As every man looks on to being a member of Congress, every man prepares himself for it; and the result is quite surprising. You will observe one odd custom—the drinking of sentiments. It is quite extinct with us, but here everybody is expected to be prepared with an epigram as a matter of course.[2]

We left Boston on the fifth, and went away with the governor of the city to stay till Monday at his house at Worcester.[3] He married a sister of Bancroft's,[4]

[1] A full account of the Dinner, including texts of all the speeches, was published in a pamphlet, *Report of the Dinner Given to Charles Dickens, in Boston, February 1, 1842*, by Thomas Gill and William English, reporters of the *Boston Morning Post*. According to the title-page, "most of the speeches" were "revised by their authors". W. G. Wilkins, *CD in America*, pp. 23–87, reprints the account given in the *Advertiser*. For CD's own speech, see *Speeches*, ed. K. J. Fielding, pp. 18–22. R. H. Dana commented on it: "Dickens spoke excellently. I never heard a speech wh. went off better. He speaks naturally, with a good voice, beautiful intonations, & an ardent, generous manner. It is the speaking of a man who is no orator, but says what he wishes to say in a manner natural & unpracticed" (*The Journal of R. H. Dana, Jr.*, ed. R. F. Lucid. I, 59–60). The Dinner lasted from 5 p.m. until nearly 1 a.m., and the speakers included Josiah Quincy, Jr, who presided, and his father, President of Harvard, T. C. Grattan, the R. H. Danas, father and son, Washington Allston, George S. Hillard, George Bancroft, Jonathan Chapman, and Dr Bigelow. Oliver Wendell Holmes sang some verses of his own, and J. M. Field one of his comic songs. Between speeches the President—who, according to *Brother Jonathan* (20 May), had previously been "wholly unacquainted with the works of Boz"—kept up a running commentary of quotations from Sam Weller, fed to him by "another gentleman" at appropriate moments. George Hillard's speech (he gave the toast, "*The gifted minds of England—Hers by birth; ours by adoption*") was regarded especially highly: "It is the admired speech of the occasion", Sumner wrote; "Ld Morpeth writes me that it is unsurpassed 'for exquisite feeling & consummate taste', & that he 'read it twice over, word for word, & cried over it each time'"

(Sumner *to* Francis Lieber, 24 Feb 42, MS Huntington).

[2] R. H. Dana, Jr, for instance, proposed: "*The Columbus of modern literature*—We welcome him to the new world, who has himself opened new worlds to us."

[3] On the day of his arrival there, he was phrenologized by L. N. Fowler (whose phrenological reading of his head is reproduced in *Dickens Studies*, III [1967], facing p. 41). That evening, John Davis, the Governor, held a levee for him "at which", wrote Felton to Sumner, 8 Feb, "the aristocracy and the Learned Blacksmith [*Elihu Burritt (1810–79; DAB)*] were present. All were delighted, charmed, fascinated" (MS Houghton Library). On Sunday Davis had a private dinner party for CD (mentioned by Felton in the same letter). Possibly at one of these functions CD met Dr Pliny Earle (1809–92; *DAB*), Quaker and Abolitionist, then on the staff of the Friends' Hospital for the Insane at Frankford, Philadelphia, whose parents lived at Worcester, and who was himself phrenologized there by Fowler in early 1842: he dined with CD at Devonshire Terrace on 5 July 49 (*Memoirs of Pliny Earle, M.D., with Extracts from his Diary and Letters (1830–1892)* . . . , ed. F. B. Sanborn, Boston, 1898, p. 150). The Worcester Asylum made preparations for a visit from CD which he was unable to pay (*Bunker-Hill Aurora*, 26 Feb). On 9 Feb a detailed description of his personal appearance was printed in the *Worcester Aegis* (quoted in Paul B. Davis, "Dickens and the American Press, 1842", *Dickens Studies*, IV [1968], 58–61). Its writer urged that all known prints of CD should be discounted; for none showed the deeply marked lines, or the strongly developed muscles "arching the eyebrows in conversation" and giving the whole face "motion and variety of expression". He

and another sister of Bancroft's[1] went down with us. The village of Worcester is one of the prettiest in New England.[2] ... On Monday morning at nine o'clock we started again by railroad and went on to Springfield, where a deputation of two were waiting, and everything was in readiness that the utmost attention could suggest. Owing to the mildness of the weather, the Connecticut river was "open," videlicet not frozen, and they had a steamboat[3] ready to carry us on to Hartford; thus saving a land-journey of only twenty-five miles, but on such roads at this time of year that it takes nearly twelve hours to accomplish! The boat was very small, the river full of floating blocks of ice, and the depth where we went (to avoid the ice and the current) not more than a few inches. After two hours and a half of this queer travelling we got to Hartford. There, there was quite an English inn;[4] except in respect of the bed-rooms, which are always uncomfortable; and the best committee of management that has yet presented itself. They kept us more quiet, and were more considerate and thoughtful, even to their own exclusion, than any I have yet had to deal with. Kate's face being horribly bad, I determined to give her a rest here; and accordingly wrote to get rid of my engagement at Newhaven,[5] on that plea. We remained in this town until the eleventh: holding a formal levee every day for two hours, and receiving on each from two hundred to three hundred people. At five o'clock on the afternoon of the eleventh, we set off (still by railroad) for Newhaven, which we reached about eight o'clock. The moment we had had tea, we were forced to open another levee for the students and professors of the college[6] (the largest in the States), and the townspeople. I suppose we shook hands, before going to bed, with considerably more than five hundred people; and I stood, as a matter of course, the whole time.[7] ...

noted (among much else) that the region about CD's eyes was "prominent"—the eyeballs completely filling their sockets; that when speaking, "the facial muscles occasionally [drew] the upper lip most strongly on the left side" (cf. Dana's description in *To* Forster, 30 Jan, *fn* p. 39). Inevitably CD's clothes were also described (for the coat which had replaced his ship-board pea-coat, see *To* Maclise, 22 Mar and *fn*). This article was reprinted (usually only in part) by newspapers in nearly every city CD visited, and may well have contributed, Paul Davis suggests, to the irritation shown in *To* Forster, 15 Apr. A week later the *Aegis* apologized for the article.

4 Eliza Bancroft (1791–1872).

1 Lucretia Bancroft (*b.* 1803); married Welcome Farnum 1845. On 6 Feb CD copied out and signed for her the two passages from *Old Curiosity Shop*, Ch. 71, which he usually chose when giving Americans his autograph: "Dear, gentle, patient, noble Nell was dead...." and "Oh it is

hard to take to heart the lessons that such Deaths ..." (MS Mr Justin Turner).

2 See *American Notes*, Ch. 5.

3 According to C. E. Crane, *Let Me Show You Vermont* (New York, 1937, p. 78), the *Massachusetts*, the only steamboat running on the Upper Connecticut River in 1842.

4 The City Hotel.

5 See *To* "Brothers in Unity", Late Jan and ?9 Feb and *fns*.

6 Yale College—as it was called until 1887.

7 They stayed at the Tontine Hotel. Felton called between 9 and 10 that night and described the scene in a letter to Sumner of 13 Feb: "The excitement in New Haven was immense. The Tontine Hotel was besieged by the whole population of the town.... | People were pouring in, a constant stream introduced by a red-headed young Irishman who called himself the Lion-Keeper;—much to the annoyance of the respectable citizens and their wives. [*Professor*] Woolsey & I stood aside, and saw the whole host as it filed before

Now, the deputation of two had come on with us from Hartford; and at New-haven there was another committee; and the immense fatigue and worry of all this, no words can exaggerate. We had been in the morning over jails and deaf and dumb asylums;[1] had stopped on the journey at a place called Wallingford, where a whole town had turned out to see me, and to gratify whose curiosity the train stopped expressly; had had a day of great excitement and exertion on the Thursday (this being Friday); and were inexpressibly worn out. And when at last we got to bed and were "going" to fall asleep, the choristers of the college turned out in a body, under the window, and serenaded us! We had had, by the bye, another serenade at Hartford, from a Mr. Adams[2] (a nephew of John Quincey Adams)[3] and a German friend. *They* were most beautiful singers: and when they began, in the dead of the night, in a long, musical, echoing pas-sage outside our chamber door; singing, in low voices to guitars, about home and absent friends and other topics that they knew would interest us; we were more moved than I can tell you.[4] In the midst of my sentimentality though, a thought occurred to me which made me laugh so immoderately that I was obliged to cover my face with the bedclothes. "Good Heavens!" I said to Kate, "what a monstrously ridiculous and commonplace appearance my boots must have, outside the door!" I never *was* so impressed with a sense of the absurdity of boots, in all my life.

The Newhaven serenade was not so good; though there were a great many voices, and a "reg'lar" band. It hadn't the heart of the other. Before it was six hours old, we were dressing with might and main, and making ready for our departure: it being a drive of twenty minutes to the steamboat, and the hour of sailing nine o'clock. After a hasty breakfast we started off; and after another levee on the deck (actually on the deck), and "three times three for Dickens," moved towards New York.

I was delighted to find on board a Mr. Felton whom I had known at Boston. He is the Greek professor at Cambridge, and was going on to the ball and dinner. Like most men of his class whom I have seen, he is a most delightful fellow—unaffected, hearty, genial, jolly; quite an Englishman of the best sort. We drank all the porter on board, ate all the cold pork and cheese, and were very merry indeed.[5] I should have told you, in its proper place, that both at Hartford and

---

Dickens, and passed out at the door. It was infinitely amusing. Woolsey, being with me saw much more of Dickens than any one else and was *very much* pleased with his manner and conversation and his cordial, hearty way" (MS Houghton Lib-rary). For another account of the evening see G. W. Putnam in the *Atlantic Monthly*, xxvi (1870), 479.

[1] CD found both the Insane Asylum and the Institution for the Deaf and Dumb "admirably conducted", the New Con-necticut State prison "very well-ordered", and the jail for untried offenders "the best ... in the world" (*American Notes*, Ch. 5).

[2] Isaac Hull Adams (see 10 Feb).

[3] See *To* Adams, 10 or 11 Mar and *fn*. (Mis-spelt "Quincey" in both F, III, iii, 216, and CD's MS letter to Fonblanque, 12 Mar.)

[4] Cf. Fanny Butler at Baltimore (1 Jan 33): "This very romantic piece of gallantry ... is very common in this country" (*Journal*, 1835, II, 108n).

[5] Felton thus described the journey in his letter of 13 Feb to Sumner: "We were nearly six hours and I had an uninterrupted talk with D & his wife. How much I en-joyed that passage—one of the most de-lightful passages in my life—how many good things he said—how we had a Pickwickian

Newhaven a regular bank was subscribed, by these committees, for *all* my expenses. No bill was to be got at the bar, and everything was paid for. But as I would on no account suffer this to be done, I stoutly and positively refused to budge an inch until Mr. Q should have received the bills from the landlord's own hands, and paid them to the last farthing. Finding it impossible to move me, they suffered me, most unwillingly, to carry the point.

About half past 2, we arrived here. In half an hour more, we reached this hotel, where a very splendid suite of rooms was prepared for us;[1] and where everything is very comfortable, and no doubt (as at Boston) *enormously* dear.[2] Just as we sat down to dinner, David Colden made his appearance; and when he had gone, and we were taking our wine, Washington Irving[3] came in alone, with open arms. And here he stopped, until ten o'clock at night.[4] Having got so far,

luncheon on cold punch and bread and cheese—how we drank the last bottle of porter, and the last three bottles of beer— on board the boat—how people strained to see him eating, drinking, and [jollifying], in the after deck making a table of the bottom of the deck boat—how the crowd, on the wharves welcomed Boz—what perils we encountered from the press of coachmen and drays—how we got through the press of people at the landing—how the Captain safely piloted Mrs. D. through the crowd— while I rendered the same service to Mr. D. —how the coachmen rushed up to shake hands with him—behold. All these things are not yet written. | You will receive a Herald containing a very good description of Boz's arrival—the 'friend' was myself, and 'Mr. Colden' was the Captain—all the rest is true to nature. The Captain says, as the boat was approaching the wharf, he heard a fellow saying, 'Which is he—the one with spectacles?' So you see I have actually been taken for Boz—almost,—. Tomorrow I am going to take a stroll with Dickens over to Jersey City . . . I shall go to the ball. | Tickets are selling for 45 to 50 dollars and now there are none to be had at any price. | I think people here are quite as enthusiastic as in Boston and the mania is spreading and intensifying. I don't know what it will end in" (MS Houghton Library).

[1] At the Carlton House Hotel, Broadway. Their suite consisted of a parlour, drawing-room, and two bedrooms overlooking Broadway and Leonard Street.

[2] The price of board at the Carlton House in 1846 was $2 a day (J. Doggett, *The Great Metropolis; a Guide to New-York for 1846*, New York). The Astor was the same price, and the most expensive hotel $2.50.

[3] Washington Irving (1783–1859; *DAB*): see Vol. II, p. 55*n*.

[4] After their very warm correspondence in 1841 (see Vol. II), both men clearly expected much of the meeting. But according to Maunsell B. Field (*Memories of Many Men and Some Women*, New York, 1874, p. 31), Irving later in Madrid (i.e. in 1843 or 44) gave him an indignant account of it: CD's first salutation, as he jumped up from the table, was apparently, "Irving, I am delighted to see you! What will you drink, a mint julep or a gin cocktail?"; and he found CD "outrageously vulgar—in dress, manners, and mind". This story has been adduced to explain why CD and Irving never met in England and corresponded only once after his return, but is quite inconsistent with what is known of their relations during the American visit, which developed into all that CD could have wished. Felton, who spent much time with them in New York, recorded their "cordial intercourse" (P. M. Irving, *Life and Letters of W. Irving*, 1863, III, 145); G. W. Putnam described them as being "greatly delighted with each other" (*Atlantic Monthly*, XXVI [1870], 480); L. G. Clark spoke of their "mutual regard and affection" and conviviality as his fellow-guests at dinner (*Harper's*, XXV [1862], 376). Moreover (strongest indication of all), Irving, having said goodbye to CD at Washington, unexpectedly followed him to Baltimore for a long evening's final leave-taking. Clearly Irving, when talking to M. B. Field of his relations with CD, antedated the strong disapproval he felt after publication of *American Notes* and *Chuzzlewit*, and Field (himself prejudiced against CD) in his turn probably exaggerated. But how decisive the change in Irving's attitude to CD was,

I shall divide my discourse into four points. First, the ball. Secondly, some slight specimens of a certain phase of character in the Americans. Thirdly, international copyright. Fourthly, my life here, and projects to be carried out while I remain.

Firstly, the ball. It came off last Monday (vide pamphlet). "At a quarter past 9, exactly," (I quote the printed order of proceeding), we were waited upon by "David Colden, Esquire, and General George Morris;"[1] habited, the former in full ball costume, the latter in the full dress uniform of Heaven knows what regiment of militia. The general took Kate, Colden gave his arm to me, and we proceeded downstairs to a carriage at the door, which took us to the stage door of the theatre: greatly to the disappointment of an enormous crowd who were besetting the main door, and making a most tremendous hullaballoo. The scene on our entrance was very striking. There were three thousand people present in full dress; from the roof to the floor, the theatre was decorated magnificently;[2] and the light, glitter, glare, show, noise, and cheering, baffle my descriptive powers. We were walked in through the centre of the centre dress-box, the front whereof was taken out for the occasion; so to the back of the stage, where the mayor and other dignitaries received us; and we were then paraded all round the enormous ball-room, twice, for the gratification of the many-headed. That done, we began to dance—Heaven knows how we did it, for there was no room.[3] And we continued dancing until, being no longer able even to stand, we slipped away quietly, and came back to the hotel. All the documents connected with this extraordinary festival (quite unparalleled here) we have preserved;[4] so

is shown in two diary entries of 1859, one by E. A. Duyckinck, the other by P. M. Irving, quoted in W. C. D. Pacey, "Washington Irving and CD", *American Literature*, XVI (1945), 332–9.

[1] George Pope Morris (1802–64; *DAB*), journalist and poet. Brigadier-General in the New York State Militia since 1837. Since 1824 had edited the *New York Mirror* (of which he was a co-founder 1823) with Bryant, Halleck and N. P. Willis among the contributors. During the 1840s was associated with Willis in editing the *New Mirror*, the *Evening Mirror*, and from 1846 the *Home Journal*. Published many sentimental lyrics: his "Woodman, Spare that Tree" was highly regarded by Poe, and his songs described as "nearly faultless" by Griswold. CD gave him inscribed copies of the American edn of *Old Curiosity Shop* and *Barnaby* on 1 June (Suzannet collection; see *D*, xxx [1934], 114).

[2] Beneath chandeliers and festoons of bunting, the walls, white muslin-draped, were decorated with medallions representing CD's works, interspersed with rosettes and silver stars, and in the centre a portrait of CD, surmounted by an eagle holding a laurel crown in its beak. For a detailed description, see Edgar Johnson, *CD, his Tragedy and Triumph*, 1953, I, 385–6.

[3] The ballroom, 150 feet by 70, had been made by extending the stage to cover the entire theatre pit; between dances, *tableaux vivants* of scenes in CD's novels were shown on a platform at one end of it (see Ada Nisbet, "The Boz Ball", *American Heritage*, IX [1957], 11).

[4] The main document was no doubt *The Extra Boz Herald* of 15 Feb, a special number of the *New York Herald* devoted to the Ball: CD's copy is in the Forster Collection, V & A—endorsed in an unknown hand: "A splendid affair and upwards of 4000 persons clearing to the Park Theatre at least $6000!!!!!!". It includes a two-page description of the scene, illustrated by engravings of the interior of the Park Theatre, of 12 of the medallions decorating it, and by a poor engraving of Laurence's portrait of CD. The description begins: "This most extraordinary, brilliant, fashionable, humorous, Sam Wellerish, singular, superb, delightful, and astonishing affair 'came off' (as the horse jockeys say)

you may suppose that on this head alone we shall have enough to show you when we come home. The bill of fare for supper, is, in its amount and extent, quite a curiosity.[1]

Now, the phase of character in the Americans which amuses me most, was put before me in its most amusing shape by the circumstances attending this affair. I had noticed it before, and have since, but I cannot better illustrate it than by reference to this theme. Of course I can do nothing but in some shape or other it gets into the newspapers. All manner of lies get there, and occasionally a truth so twisted and distorted that it has as much resemblance to the real fact as Quilp's leg to Taglioni's.[2] But with this ball to come off, the newspapers were if possible unusually loquacious; and in their accounts of me, and my seeings, sayings, and doings on the Saturday night and Sunday before, they describe my manner, mode of speaking, dressing, and so forth.[3] In doing this, they report that I am a very charming fellow (of course), and have a very free and easy way with me; "which," say they, "at first amused a few fashionables;" but soon pleased them exceedingly. Another paper, coming after the ball, dwells upon its splendour and brilliancy; hugs itself and its readers upon all that Dickens saw;[4] and winds up by gravely expressing its conviction, that Dickens was never in such society in England as he has seen in New York,[5] and that its

last night, and nothing ever seen, heard, or told of in this world before, ever went off with such indescribable *eclat*". Two later paragraphs read: "As for Dickens, himself, he danced in half a dozen quadrilles, and was so overpowered and excited by his reception, that he retired about half past 12 o' clock; with a sore throat, and quite used up; perfectly bored to death, by a few fools, during the dancing, and drinking . . . Altogether, it was a perfect *olla podrida* —prudery, distinctions and cliques were forgotten; the *recherché* lady was *vis-a-vis* to her maid; the *parvenu* to the scion of the *noblesse*. Boz was particularly pleased—his lady was up for several quadrilles."

    [1] This CD sent to Maclise: see 27 Feb.
    [2] Marie Taglioni (1804–84), Italian-Swedish ballet-dancer. She had appeared frequently in England since 1830.
    [3] There had certainly been a great to-do about the Boz Ball and the papers had reported it and the preparations for it very fully. But before his arrival in New York a note of warning against over-enthusiasm had already been sounded in the press: on 5 Feb *Brother Jonathan* had pleaded that CD should be treated with dignity and that "toadyism and ridiculous man-worship be sedulously avoided"; and on 11 Feb the *New Haven Commercial Advertiser* hoped "our folks will treat him like a gentleman, and not like a show." On his arrival in New

York, according to the *New York Tribune* of Mon 14 Feb, he "was allowed with very little annoyance to proceed to his rooms at the Carlton House" and spent the Saturday evening and Sunday undisturbed. Probably one of the papers CD now chiefly had in mind was the *New York Aurora* which on Mon 14 Feb had published a parody of the extravagances in earlier accounts of his sayings and doings.

    [4] CD appears to have accepted the Ball in his honour—and even its successor (see To Simpson, 16 Feb)—unquestioningly and uncritically . But privately many Americans were embarrassed. In a letter to R. H. Dana of 16 Feb, W. Watson, for instance, wrote: "This ball was got up by some of the small fry in the literary world. At the instance of some nincompoop he was received at the entrance to the ball room with cheers & paraded around to the tune of God save the queen . . . The whole transaction was such an offence against the laws of decorum that I felt in common with many others the blood tingling in my cheeks" (MS Massachusetts Historical Society).

    [5] Cf. the *New York Aurora*, concerning a dinner party Colden was giving for CD (probably on Thurs 17th): "It will doubtless be an elegant affair, and the quiet family party, which Mr. Dickens insists upon, will be made up of the élite of the

high and striking tone cannot fail to make an indelible impression on his mind! For the same reason I am always represented, whenever I appear in public, as being "very pale;" "apparently thunderstruck;" and utterly confounded by all I see.[1] ... You recognize the queer vanity which is at the root of all this? I have plenty of stories in connection with it to amuse you with when I return.

To FITZ-GREENE HALLECK,[2] 17 FEBRUARY 1842

MS Professor Ronald Paulson.

Carlton House. | Seventeenth February 1842

My Dear Sir

Will you come and breakfast with me on Tuesday the Twenty Second, at half

ancient régime. Indeed, it is probable that Mr. Dickens was never, in England, admitted into such really good society, as since he landed in this country. He has seen and will see more aristocracy in Boston and New York than he has ever seen, and probably ever will see, in his native land." The piece was reprinted in the *Aurora* "Extra", together with the paper's "Welcome to Thee, Charles Dickens!" of 12 Feb (which contained "We glory that thou art one of us ... thy father an honest haberdasher"—probably one of the "lies" CD mentions), "Scenes at the Carlton" of 14 Feb, and description of "The Great Boz Ball", 15 Feb. All are included in *Account of the Ball Given in Honor of CD in New York City ... from the New York Aurora—Extra*, privately printed, Cedar Rapids, Iowa, 1908, with an Introduction by W. P. Beazell—who argues that all are satiric but "satire of so rare a sort" that CD "missed the point of it all" and took it seriously. That he could have taken "Scenes at the Carlton" as anything but parody is inconceivable. But the passage about "really good society", untrue though it was, seems to have been read by CD as "gravely" meant; and, in fact, was taken up as a charge by other American papers when, later, they turned against him. In an unidentified newspaper cutting in the Forster Collection (V & A), for instance, he is described as in no way "conversant with the habits, thoughts, feelings, or intercourse of gentlemen"; he knows only what he picked up as a "Hash Reporter".

[1] "Boz looked pale and thunderstruck—his charming wife was completely overpowered" (*Extra Boz Herald*, 15 Feb).

[2] Fitz-Greene Halleck (1790–1867; *DAB*), poet. Born in Connecticut, he was employ-

ed much of his life by John Jacob Astor; visited Europe 1822; first Vice-President of the Authors' Club 1837, and original trustee of the Astor Library. His poems, "Marco Bozzaris" (1825) in particular, were praised in the *Foreign Quarterly Review* (Jan 44, XXXII, 313) for showing "a knowledge as complete, as it is rare among his contemporaries, of the musical mysteries of his art". He was at the Boz Ball; was one of the Committee for the New York Dinner to CD; and was present at the Novelties Club dinner at the Astor House on 24 Feb. On 8 Mar he wrote to a friend: "I am quite delighted with [Dickens]. He is a thorough good fellow, with nothing of the author about him but the reputation, and goes through his task as Lion with exemplary grace, patience, and good nature" (N. F. Adkins, *Fitz-Greene Halleck, an Early Knickerbocker Wit and Poet*, New Haven, 1930, p. 295). On 6 June he gave CD his *Alnwick Castle* (1827), inscribed "from his friend and admirer" (*Catalogue of the Library of CD*, ed. J. H. Stonehouse, p. 54). In an article, "An Hour with Halleck" (quoted in N. F. Adkins, *op. cit.*, p. 293), he is reported as saying later: "I for one was greatly pained at reading Martin Chuzzlewit, but trust in my heart Mr. Dickens will apologize for it before he dies, for the sake of his fame among so many warm friends here. I believe he will yet do so from the depths of his charitable nature." He and CD looked forward to meeting again on CD's second visit to America (see CD *to* Gen. J. G. Wilson, 11 Jan 68: J. G. Wilson, *Life and Letters of Fitz-Greene Halleck*, New York, 1869, p. 439), but Halleck died on 19 Nov 67, the day CD landed at Boston.

past ten? Say yes.[1] I should have been truly delighted to have a talk with you tonight (being quite alone) but the Doctor says that if I talk to man, woman, or child this Evening, I shall be dumb tomorrow.

Believe me with true regard
Faithfully | Your friend

Fitzgreene Halleck Esquire   CHARLES DICKENS

To THE EDITOR OF THE *NEW YORK HERALD*,[2]
19 FEBRUARY 1842

Summary in *New York Herald*, 20 Feb 42.

Returning the draft report of his speech at the New York Dinner, the evening before, and expressing "his highest encomiums at its remarkable accuracy".[3]

To J. P. GEBLER,[4] J. M. DAVIS,[5] T. B. FLORENCE,[6]
J. G. BRESLEY,[7] 20 FEBRUARY [1842]

Text from *Philadelphia Public Ledger*, 23 Feb 42.

Carlton House, Feb 20th.

Dear Sirs,

I thank you for your letter.[8] No man subscribes more heartily to the sentiments you express in reference to the worth of that class of society which you represent,[9] than I do; and I unaffectedly assure you that I am proud of your good opinion.

I have already[10] declined various invitations to a public reception in Phila-

[1] This was no doubt the breakfast party at which Bryant and Felton were fellow-guests: see *To* Bryant, 14 Feb, *fn.*

[2] J. G. Bennett: see *To* Forster, 24 Feb, *fn* p. 84.

[3] According to the *New York Herald*, "only a few verbal alterations, of no importance," were made by CD to its verbatim report.

[4] Printer, of 9 North 13th Street, Philadelphia.

[5] Bookbinder, of 201 Chestnut Street, Philadelphia.

[6] Thomas Birch Florence (1812–75; *DAB*), Philadelphia journalist and politician; Colonel in the State militia. Owned a hat business 1833–41; on its failure, became Secretary to the Board of Comptrollers, Philadelphia public schools, 1842–9. CD described him to Putnam in a letter of 24

July 51 as "a little hatter with black whiskers".

[7] Probably a mis-spelling of John Breslaw, of 11 Prosperous Alley, Philadelphia.

[8] According to the *Philadelphia Gazette* of 9 Mar, the letter included the following: "It is needless to ask you whether you intend visiting Philadelphia. Doubtless you have determined this in your mind already; and, without doubt, many of the *soi disant* magnates of our city have conceived a multitude of plans for the *monopoly* of '*Boz*,' and it is of this that we complain; for we cannot conceive why you should be the *exclusive property* of a self delegated clique, who may claim to be all in all, to the extinction of all others."

[9] Presumably journalists and printers.

[10] See ?15 Feb.

delphia, but I shall be exceedingly glad to shake hands with you when I arrive there, and shall hope that you will give me an opportunity of doing so.[1]

I remain, gentlemen, faithfully yours,

To John P. Gebler, James M. Davis,   CHARLES DICKENS
Thomas B. Florence, John G. Bresley, Esqrs.

To SAMUEL WARD, 21 FEBRUARY 1842*

MS Berg Collection.

To Samuel Ward Esquire

Carlton House. | Twenty First February 1842

God forgive me! I was already engaged for Sunday.[2] I thought it could scarcely be that I—I, the devoted one; the sacrifice—could have a morning to myself. Pity and pardon the miserable, but not impenitent

BOZ.

Ask me to breakfast when I return here—do.[3]

---

[1] On the strength of this—and in spite of CD's writing a second letter (*To* Florence, 24 Feb), protesting that his first had been misunderstood—the following notice, obviously inserted by Florence and his friends, appeared in the *Philadelphia Public Ledger* on the morning of Tues 8 Mar: "*Mr. Dickens.*—This gentleman will, we understand, be gratified to shake hands with his friends between the hours of half-past ten and half-past eleven o'clock. He leaves for the South to-morrow." This led to CD's having, against his will, to hold a public reception in his room at the United States Hotel, during which Florence introduced some 500 strangers to him. According to Putnam (*Atlantic Monthly*, XXVI, 481), the landlord had told CD that his refusal to receive the people "would doubtless create a riot"; and when at last he consented, for "two mortal hours or more the crowd poured in, and he shook hands and exchanged words with all, while the dapper little author of the scene stood smiling by, giving hundreds and thousands of introductions". The press sympathized with CD: the *Philadelphia Gazette* of 9 Mar protested against the unauthorized use made of his letter, and praised his acting "with the complaisance of a gentleman"; and the *Public Ledger* gave a sarcastic account of Florence's introductions (quoted in W. G. Wilkins, *CD in America*, pp. 157–8). Clearly the reception forced on Martin by Captain Kedgick in *Chuzzlewit*, Ch. 22, was based partly on this experience.

[2] Sun 27th, the day on which CD, when visiting Ward at his office on the 21st, had promised to breakfast with him.

[3] Ward wrote to Longfellow on the 22nd: "Flying images of Boz and rumors of his presence and sayings—the triumphant Boast of those who have seen him and the despairing sorrow of those to whom that pleasure has been denied and must remain so—all this has turned the head of our fashionables. Not on my own account but for the sake of my sisters . . . and several others who did not go to either Ball or Dinner, I regret he did not come to our home [*see* 16 Feb, fn]. Now, he is so persecuted that he will run into misanthropy or Americano-phobia. I saw a manifest wildness in his eye yesterday—when he was kind enough to pay me a visit at the office. . . . Yesterday he promised to breakfast with me next Sunday. I had hardly made the fact known . . . when I received a note from him written in a fit of desperation—He was already engaged for Sunday. I have done. He ought to have bestowed a month upon New York" (MS Harvard College Library). Ward followed this up with another letter to Longfellow, on 25 Feb: "I am not altogether delighted with Dickens. I know that the persecutions to which he is a martyr justify him in his defensive system. But there was infinitely more satisfaction in dealing with Morpeth than I find with Dickens. However, he is a lion"; and on 15 June, after CD's brief return to New York, he wrote to Longfellow: "he did not

To M. F. WHITTIER,[1] 21 FEBRUARY [1842]

Mention in John Anderson Jr. catalogue No. 152 and George D. Smith catalogue, n.d. [?1907]; *MS* 1 p.; dated Carlton House, 21 Feb.

Acknowledging a letter. Faithfully yours, CHARLES DICKENS[2]

To JONATHAN CHAPMAN, 22 FEBRUARY 1842

MS Comtesse de Suzannet.

Carlton House, New York. | Twenty Second February 1842.

My Dear Friend.

Here's my hand.—Our alliance is complete.[3] Let the Sea rise never so high between us, we will rise higher. And when you come to England, we will have such walks and talks together, as shall indemnify us for years of separation.[4]

I am sick to death of the life I have been leading here—worn out in mind and body—and quite weary and distressed. I have declined all future Invitations of a public nature; and mean to be resolute from this time forth. I am a splendid illustration of the wisdom of the fable concerning the old man and his ass. Half the population take it ill if I *do* go where I am asked; and the other half take it ill if I *don't*. So I mean, in future, to consult my own wishes,—and those of no other person in this Hemisphere.

I have never in my life been so shocked and disgusted, or made so sick and sore at heart, as I have been by the treatment I have received here (in America I mean), in reference to the International Copyright question. I,—the greatest loser by[5] the existing Law, alive,—say in perfect good humour and disinterestedness (for God knows that I have little hope of its ever being changed in my time) that I hope the day will come when Writers will be justly treated; and straightway there fall upon me scores of your newspapers; imputing motives to me, the

call on me, and if he were Emperor of Russia instead of Grub Street I should insist upon being civilly treated" (M. H. Elliott, *Uncle Sam Ward and his Circle*, New York, 1938, pp. 340, 352).

[1] Matthew Franklin Whittier (1812–83), younger brother of the poet John Greenleaf Whittier; like him, a Quaker and strong Abolitionist. Published satirical anti-slavery letters, as "Ethan Spike of Hornby", in the *Portland Transcript*, 1860–1.

[2] Only the ending and signature are in CD's hand, according to catalogues.

[3] In a long letter to CD, Chapman had written (on 14 Feb, the night of the Boz Ball): "My dear Friend, | Nothing, I am sure, but the delight of writing those pleasant words 'My Dear Friend' as applied to you, could make me so crazy as to write you a letter, when I know that amidst balls and dinners and attentions of a thousand kinds, you not only can have no time to answer

but hardly any to read it; I know all this, and yet, after reading to-night your note to me, for the twentieth time—I, in my quiet study, whilst you are in the mazy dance, it speaks to me so like the voice of one long sought, though newly found, yet an old and familiar friend—that I am impelled by an irresistible impulse to say a word to you. Cold and calculating reason may forbid, but the heart will not." He assured CD of his "prompt and devoted entrance" into the "alliance" CD's note had proposed, and continued: "I feel as if Providence had marked us as friends. I seemed to read it in your face the first moment I looked upon it". (For full text see *D*, XXXVIII [1942], 8.)

[4] Chapman in fact never came to England.

[5] N, I, 391, reads "I, the greatest cock of".

very suggestion of which turns my blood to gall; and attacking me in such terms of vagabond scurrility as they would denounce no murderer with.[1] I vow to Heaven that the scorn and indignation I have felt under this unmanly and ungenerous treatment has been to me an amount of agony such as I never experienced since my birth. But it has had the one good effect of making me iron upon this theme; and iron I will be, here and at home, by word of mouth and in writing, as long as I can articulate a syllable, or hold a pen.

I open my whole heart to you, you see! I write in such a spirit of confidence that I pour out all I have felt upon this subject,—though I have said nothing in reference to it, even to my wife.[2] This is a foretaste of what you have brought upon yourself.

I shall be in Washington, about the sixth or seventh of March.[3] While I am there, I will write to you again; and I shall hope to see your handwriting before I go further South. How I wish that you were not Mayor of Boston, and would join us there, and travel with us until the end of May![4]

Always Your faithful | And affectionate friend

Jonathan Chapman Esquire   CHARLES DICKENS

To CHARLES WILSON PEALE,[5] 22 FEBRUARY [1842]

Extract in Dodd, Mead Company catalogue No. 90; *MS* 1 p.; dated Carlton House, 22 Feb.

I beg to acknowledge your invitation to visit your store. I am sorry to add, however, that as every "moment" of my time is engaged during the whole of the remainder of my short stay in the City, I cannot have an opportunity of doing so.[6]

To MRS MARY GRIFFITH,[7] 23 FEBRUARY [1842]*

MS[8] Mr N. C. Peyrouton.

Carlton House Feby. 23rd.

My dear Madam.

Let me thank you heartily for your kind and interesting letter and for the books[9] which accompanied it.

[1] For some of these atttacks, see *To* Forster, 14 Feb, *fn*.

[2] To no other American friend did CD write about America so freely. But he did not answer Chapman's reply to this letter (see *To* Chapman, 2 June); and their correspondence did not extend beyond the end of 1842.

[3] Because of Catherine's illness (see *To* Putnam, 1 and 2 Mar), they did not reach Washington until the 9th.

[4] Their next meeting was when Chapman joined the party which saw CD and Catherine off on the *George Washington*.

[5] Probably Charles Wilson Peale, owner of a "curiosity shop", 468½ Broadway, New York; apparently not related to the portrait painter and naturalist Charles Willson Peale (1741-1827; *DAB*).

[6] Signed by CD according to catalogue; the text no doubt in Putnam's hand.

[7] Probably Mrs Mary Griffith of New York, miscellaneous writer. Her books included *Our Neighbourhood*, New York, 1831; *Camperdown*, Philadelphia, 1836; and *The Two Defaulters*, New York, 1842. She also wrote for periodicals.

[8] Only the ending and signature are in CD's hand; the rest in Putnam's.

[9] Presumably her own, though none were in the Gad's Hill library at CD's death.

I wish it were in my power to come to see you, but I have no leisure for anything I wish to do; and can only thank you on that head also.

And lastly, let me thank you for the letter of introduction to your daughter.[1] But I shall only be three days at Philda., and I greatly fear that I may never deliver it.

Rest assured that if I can, I will, and

Believe me | Faithfully Your friend

Mrs. Mary Griffith.   CHARLES DICKENS

To HENRY WADSWORTH LONGFELLOW, 23 FEBRUARY 1842*

MS Free Library of Philadelphia.

Carlton House. | Twenty Third February 1842.

My Dear Longfellow.

You are coming to England, you know.—Now, listen to me. When you return to London, I shall be there, Please God. Write to me from the Continent, and tell me when to expect you. We live quietly—not uncomfortably—and among people whom I am sure you would like to know; as much as they would like to know you. Have no home but mine—see nothing in town on your way towards Germany—and let me be your London host and cicerone.[2] Is this a bargain?

Always | Faithfully | Your friend

Professor Longfellow.   CHARLES DICKENS

To UNKNOWN BOOKSELLER, [23 FEBRUARY 1842]

Mention in *To* Forster, 24 Feb 42.[3]

Refusing him financial help.

---

[1] Unidentified.

[2] On 27 Feb Longfellow wrote to his father, quoting CD's letter and adding: "So hearty an invitation as this I shall not hesitate to accept, if he is in London when I am there. It will render my visit very agreeable" (*The Letters of H. W. Longfellow*, ed. A. Hilen, II, 388). For his stay at 1 Devonshire Terrace see Oct 42. CD's letter was brought to Longfellow by Felton, fresh from his "*roistering and oystering*" (as Hillard called it) in New York; and Longfellow enclosed his answer in a letter to Ward of 27 Feb, asking him to hand it to CD if he had not already left New York and—if he had—to give it to Colden, "who is his agent—or what not" (*ibid.*). But Ward did not see CD again (see 21 Feb, *fn*).

[3] See also next and *fn*.

To JOHN S. BARTLETT,[1] 24 FEBRUARY 1842

MS Doheny Memorial Library, California.

Private and Confidential

Carlton House. | Twenty Fourth February 1842.

My Dear Sir.

Our friend Clark[2] has shewn me your letter. It is so very generous and manly, and is couched in so true a spirit, that I cannot help inflicting this note upon you, in reply.

I do not expect that any alteration will take place in the Law of International Copyright, until I am past the sense of Justice or Injustice, and my children are fighting their own way in the World. Until the Law is altered nothing can be done through the General Honesty and Good Feeling. The absence of all Generosity, Honor, or Truth which distinguishes the gross assaults that have been made upon me, here, for alluding to the subject, sufficiently assures me of *that*.

I thank you, nevertheless, for your frank note; and hold the feeling which dictated it, in unaffected respect.[3]

I have just received a communication, which is such an exquisite satire upon some of the loudest upholders of the existing system, that I cannot forbear sending it to you—with full permission to print it, if you like.[4] The circumstances of its receipt are these.—A man came here the day before yesterday, and demanded—not besought—demanded pecuniary assistance from the gentleman who acts as my secretary: on the ground that he was an itinerant vendor of books, and had earned his living by selling mine. As his manner was extremely offensive and bullying, and as I really did not recognize the validity of his *claim*, I begged the gentleman aforesaid, to write him a note to the effect that I every day received a vast number of similar applications (which I need scarcely say is the Truth)—that if I were a man of large fortune, I could not assist all those who appealed to me—and that I regretted the not being able to assist him. Upon the receipt of this epistle, he sent me the inclosed. Will you return it to me by

---

[1] John Sherren Bartlett (1790–1863; *DAB*), editor of the *Albion, or British, Colonial, and Foreign Weekly Gazette*: see Vol. II, p. 421*n*.

[2] Lewis Gaylord Clark, with whom CD and Catherine had dined the previous evening, as recalled in *To* Clark, 2 Mar 43. According to an article by Clark in *Harper's New Monthly*, Aug 62 (xxv, 377), the other guests included Irving, Bryant, Halleck, Henry Brevoort, Henry Inman the portrait painter, Bishop Wainwright (to whom CD had a letter of introduction from Harness),

and Felton (called "Mr. D——" in Clark's account, but easily identifiable). The conversation, as retailed by Clark, turned largely on various criminal cases.

[3] Bartlett had presumably written to Clark asking him to convey to CD an apology for having earlier pirated his *Sketches*, and his sympathy with him in his stand on international copyright. His paper gave CD generous attention throughout his American visit.

[4] Bartlett did not do so.

post in the course of tomorrow, as I wish to save it for England? It is much too good to be lost.[1]

My Dear Sir, I am always,
Faithfully | Your friend
John. S. Bartlett Esquire   CHARLES DICKENS

To WILLIAM C. BARTON,[2] 24 FEBRUARY [1842]*

MS[3] Dr Noël J. Cortés.

Carlton House February 24
Dear Sir
I have read your letter with much pleasure and cordially thank you for it.
I am a little surprised by the question you ask, as the whole meaning and purpose of the story pointed to that end or none. I am not aware that I can give you any better reason for Nell's death than you will find in the last paragraph of page 352 of Lea and Blanchards American Edition of the tale.[4]

I am Dear Sir | Faithfully Yours
Wm. C. Barton Esq.   CHARLES DICKENS

To MRS DAVID C. COLDEN,[5] 24 FEBRUARY 1842

MS Colonel Richard Gimbel. *Address:* With a small parcel.[6] | Mrs. Colden | 28 Laight Street | Hudson Square.

Carlton House. | Twenty Fourth February 1842.
My Dear Mrs. Colden.
Kate told me when I had my hair docked t'other day,[7] that you wanted some of it to give away. I am so desirous to live in your recollection, and in that of your good husband and esteemed family, that I have been vain enough to have a very small specimen of my head, set in the accompanying little brooch; of

---

[1] For a summary of the man's letter, see *To* Forster, 24 Feb. Putnam gives an account of the same incident, describing the man as an "Irish book-pedler" who wanted money from CD to set up a book store (*Atlantic Monthly*, XXVI, 480).

[2] William Paul Crillon Barton (1786–1856; *DAB*), botanist and naval surgeon; Professor of Botany, University of Pennsylvania, 1815; first Chief of the Bureau of Medicine and Surgery, U. S. Navy, 1842–4. Resigned after attacks on his attempted reforms in naval sanitation and temperance. His publications include *Flora of North America*, 1821–3.

[3] Only the ending and signature are in CD's hand; the rest in Putnam's.

[4] The paragraph in Ch. 72 beginning, "Oh! It is hard to take to heart the lesson that such deaths will teach". Barton is one of the few Americans known to have questioned the necessity of Nell's death.

[5] *Née* Frances Wilkes (*b.* ?1796), daughter of Charles Wilkes, banker, of New York, and great-niece of the famous John Wilkes; married Colden 1819 (see also *To* Morris, 28 Jan, *fn*). One of the party of ladies who, with Catherine, came to hear the speeches at the New York Dinner to CD.

[6] "'(a brooch with Mr. Dickens's hair)" is written beneath, in an unknown hand.

[7] By Martelle of Maiden Lane, a well-known New York barber. According to the *Bay State Democrat*, 25 Feb, he was besieged by ladies asking for locks: "Martelle could have sold the hair for 1000 shares of U.S. Bank stock, but he preferred presenting it gratis to his numerous fair customers."

which, with more good wishes than I can express, and a sincerer meaning than I can convey to you, I entreat your acceptance.[1]

To THOMAS B. FLORENCE, 24 FEBRUARY [1842]

Text from American Art Association catalogue, Nov 1924; *MS* 2 pp.

Carlton House | February 24

I beg to refer you again to my former letter[2] which you seem to have misunderstood. I wished and still wish to respectfully decline any Public reception or recognition of any kind; and I beg most earnestly to repeat this desire.

Faithfully | your friend
CHARLES DICKENS[3]

To THE REV. W. B. SPRAGUE,[4] 24 FEBRUARY [1842]

Mention in Anderson Galleries catalogue No. 2029 (1926); *MS* 2 pp.; dated Carlton House, 24 Feb.

Saying that he expects to be in Albany before June.[5]

To JOHN FORSTER, 24 FEBRUARY [1842]

Extract in F, III, iii, 218–23 (continuation of letter begun 17 Feb).

Twenty-fourth February

It is unnecessary to say . . . that this letter *didn't* come by the sailing packet, and *will* come by the Cunard boat.[6] After the ball I was laid up with a very bad sore throat, which confined me to the house four whole days; and as I was unable to write, or indeed to do anything but doze and drink lemonade, I missed the ship. . . . I have still a horrible cold, and so has Kate, but in other respects we are all right. I proceed to my third head: the international copyright question.

I believe there is no country, on the face of the earth, where there is less freedom of opinion on any subject in reference to which there is a broad difference of opinion, than in this.[7]—There!—I write the words with reluctance,

[1] Endorsed in pencil, "Signature torn off".

[2] *To* Gebler, Florence & Others, 20 Feb.

[3] Only the signature is in CD's hand according to Goodspeeds Book Shop catalogue No. 396.

[4] William Buell Sprague (1795–1876; *DAB*), Congregationalist minister, prolific writer and avid autograph collector. Left *c.* 40,000 autographs at his death, reputed the largest and most valuable collection in America.

[5] Possibly at the same time refusing an invitation: see *To* Forster, 24 Feb.

[6] See beginning of this letter (17 Feb). The completed letter must have gone to Boston, thence on 1 Mar by the *Unicorn* to Halifax, where the mail was transferred to the Cunard *Acadia* sailing for Liverpool 11 Mar.

[7] The complexities of opinion on the issue of international copyright were much greater than CD realized. Opposition was to be expected from the book trade and from most of the new "mammoth" papers, which were making large profits from piracy. But American writers and editors, especially in New York, were themselves divided. L. G. Clark, leader of the Whig, Anglophile *Knickerbocker* group, supported international copyright because, like CD, he held that an author's works were, in

disappointment, and sorrow; but I believe it from the bottom of my soul. I spoke, as you know, of international copyright, at Boston; and I spoke of it again at Hartford.[1] My friends were paralysed with wonder at such audacious daring. The notion that I, a man alone by himself, in America, should venture to suggest to the Americans that there was one point on which they were neither just to their own countrymen nor to us, actually struck the boldest dumb! Washington Irving, Prescott, Hoffman,[2] Bryant, Halleck, Dana, Washington Allston[3]—every man who writes in this country is devoted to the question, and not one of them *dares* to raise his voice and complain of the atrocious state of the law.[4] It is nothing that of all men living I am the greatest loser by it. It is nothing that I have a claim to speak and be heard. The wonder is that a breathing man can be found with temerity enough to suggest to the Americans the possibility of their having done wrong. I wish you could have seen the faces that I saw, down both

justice, his sacred property. Cornelius Mathews and Evert Duyckinck, leaders of the Democratic "Young America" circle, supported it also—not to protect British authors, but to encourage the growth of a native American literature. On the other hand, Bancroft, the Democrats' chief intellectual spokesman, declared that there could be no exclusive right to creations of the mind; while the *Democratic Review* argued against international copyright as an interference with free trade. These differences of attitude help to explain the inconsistency of some of the editors of the "mammoth" papers, several of whom, including R. W. Griswold, Horace Greeley and H. Hastings Weld, supported international copyright by petitions or editorials, while at the same time pirating on a large scale (see L. H. Houtchens, *American Literature*, XIII [1941], 18–28).

[1] See *To* Forster, 14 Feb, *fn.* For a long passage on Scott which followed in his Hartford speech, see below.

[2] Charles Fenno Hoffman (1806–84; *DAB*), poet, novelist, and first editor of the *Knickerbocker* 1833; contributed to several New York literary magazines 1835–48; worked in the New York Customs Office 1841–4; went insane in 1849 and spent his last 35 years in an asylum. Griswold's *Poets and Poetry of America*, 1842, contained 45 of his poems; and several of his songs became very popular. "No American", said Griswold, "is comparable to him as a song-writer"; on which the *Foreign Quarterly Review* (Jan 44, XXXII, 323) commented: "We are not surprised at the fact, considering the magnitude of his obligations to Moore.

Hoffman is Moore hocused for the American market." A strong supporter of international copyright, he discussed it with CD the day before his return to England and told him he ought to meet Griswold, who was coming out in its favour in *Graham's Magazine* (Hoffman *to* R. W. Griswold, 28 June 42, quoted in H. F. Barnes, *C. F. Hoffman*, New York, 1930, p. 224).

[3] Washington Allston (1779–1843; *DAB*), better known as a painter than a writer. Studied 1801–3 at the Royal Academy, London, under Benjamin West; in Italy, 1804–8, formed close friendships with Irving and with Coleridge, who wrote to him from Florence, 17 June 1806: ". . . had I not known the Wordsworths, [I] should have loved & esteemed you *first* and *most* and as [it] is, next to them I love and honor you" (*Collected Letters of S. T. Coleridge*, ed. E. L. Griggs, Oxford, 1956–71, II, 1173). His portrait of Coleridge is now in the National Portrait Gallery. His first wife was W. E. Channing's sister; his second, Dana's.

[4] Many Americans CD met had worked for the movement since 1837: Clay, Francis Lieber, L. G. Clark, Bryant, and, behind the scenes, the expatriate Frederick Saunders. But no one had spoken out so publicly for a change in the law—or demanded it so uncompromisingly as a *right*—as CD had done. Most American writers were fully aware of the intense opposition to the movement in the book trade—and of its power in taming even as popular a writer as James Fenimore Cooper when he attempted to be his own publisher.

sides of the table at Hartford, when I began to talk about Scott.[1] I wish you could have heard how I gave it out. My blood so boiled as I thought of the monstrous injustice that I felt as if I were twelve feet high when I thrust it down their throats.

I had no sooner made that second speech than such an outcry began (for the purpose of deterring me from doing the like in this city) as an Englishman can form no notion of.[2] Anonymous letters; verbal dissuasions; newspaper attacks making Colt (a murderer who is attracting great attention here)[3] an angel by comparison with me; assertions that I was no gentleman, but a mere mercenary scoundrel; coupled with the most monstrous mis-representations relative to my design and purpose in visiting the United States;[4] came pouring in upon me every day. The dinner committee here (composed of the first gentlemen in America, remember that) were so dismayed, that they besought me[5] not to pursue the subject *although they every one agreed with me*. I answered that I would. That nothing should deter me. . . . That the shame was theirs, not mine; and that as I would not spare them when I got home, I would not be silenced here. Accordingly, when the night came, I asserted my right, with all the means I could command to give it dignity, in face, manner, or words;[6] and

[1] CD had pictured for his audience Scott on his death-bed, "crushed both in mind and body by his honourable struggle", while the characters from his books hovered round him, "hanging down their heads in shame and sorrow that, from all those lands into which they had carried gladness, instruction, and delight for millions, they had brought him not one friendly hand to help to raise him from that sad, sad bed. No, nor brought him from that land in which his own language was spoken, and in every house and hut of which his own books were read in his own tongue, one grateful dollar-piece to buy a garland for his grave" (*Speeches*, ed. K. J. Fielding, p. 25). For the partial injustice of this, see *To* Forster, 13 Mar, *fn*.

[2] See instances in *To* Forster, 14 Feb, *fn*.

[3] John Caldwell Colt (1810–42), found guilty in Jan 42 of the murder of Samuel Adams. The *New York Herald's* description of the proceedings at his trial is quoted at length in Forster's "The Newspaper Literature of America", *Foreign Quarterly Review*, Oct 42, xxx, 208n–210n, as an example of "filthy" reporting.

[4] "His *business* in visiting the United States at this season of the year—a season not usually chosen by travellers for pleasure—is to procure, or to assist in procuring, the passage, by Congress, of an International Copy-right Law", announced the *New World*, 19 Feb. CD was vulnerable here: see his reference in his Hartford speech to the "compact" he had made with himself (*To* Forster, 14 Feb, *fn*). This interpretation of his motives was what angered him most in the *Edinburgh's* review of *American Notes* (see *To The Times*, 15 Jan 43 and *fn*, and *To* Napier, 21 Jan 43).

[5] Probably through Colden, the member of the committee with whom CD was most closely in touch.

[6] With considerable restraint, and with the dignity at which he aimed, CD, while appealing for international copyright, made a bid to redress the antagonism his Hartford speech had aroused. "Gentlemen", he said, " . . . I came here in an open, honest, and confiding spirit, if ever man did, and because I heartily inclined toward you; had I felt otherwise I should have kept away. As I came here, and *am* here, without the least admixture of the hundredth portion of a grain of base alloy, without the faintest unworthy reference to self in any word I have ever addressed to you, . . . I assert my right tonight, in regard to the past for the last time, . . . to appeal to you, as I have done on two former occasions, on a question of universal literary interest in both countries. And, gentlemen, I claim this justice: that I have made the appeal as one who has a most righteous claim to speak and to be heard; and that I have done so in a frank, and courteous, and good-

I believe that if you could have seen and heard me, you would have loved me better for it than ever you did in your life.[1]

The *New York Herald,* which you will receive with this,[2] is the *Satirist*[3] of America;[4] but having a great circulation (on account of its commercial intelligence and early news) it can afford to secure the best reporters.[5] . . . My speech is done, upon the whole, with remarkable accuracy. There are a great many typographical errors in it; and by the omission of one or two words, or the substitution of one word for another, it is often materially weakened. Thus I did not say that I "claimed" my right, but that I "asserted" it; and I did not say

humoured spirit of deference to those who frankly, courteously, and good humouredly differed from me in any or every respect. For myself, gentlemen, I have only to add that I will ever be as true to you as you have been to me" (*Speeches*, ed. K. J. Fielding, p. 28). This being loudly cheered, he spoke of his audience's "enthusiastic approval" of his creations, his own care for "the common good", and then hurried on to the longest section of his speech—praise of Washington Irving's work (*op. cit.*, pp. 29–31), of which he showed intimate knowledge (cf. *To Irving*, 21 Apr 41; II, 267–8).

[1] CD implies, through silence about the other speakers, that—as at the Boston and Hartford Dinners—he alone spoke on the subject. But, perhaps as an act of courtesy, the committee had arranged it otherwise. Irving, from the Chair, gave a toast to "International Copyright"; and, in reply, Cornelius Mathews (see 28 Dec 42, *fn*) made a long and fervent plea in its support (quoted in W. G. Wilkins, *CD in America*, pp. 139–47). What hope, he asked, was there for the native author while domestic literature was borne down by unrestrained republication of foreign work; the "enormous fraud practised upon their British brethren" had so operated against American writers as to "blight their hopes and darken their fair fame". Moreover, public taste was affected by indiscriminate republication of the good and the bad, till the general reader was unable to choose between CD and Ainsworth, between Talfourd and Boucicault. "Surprise" had been felt in some quarters that CD, a British writer, should himself have "addressed the American people on the subject of Copyright"; but he could imagine what must have been CD's feelings about the "hand stretched stealthily towards the MS. on his desk, to snatch it away ere it was dry, and blazon it

throughout the whole New World, as an acquisition honestly made". The speech ended with a passionate plea that the "great rights of Thought" should be regarded as sacred property. CD had himself made the point about American literature in the final sentence of his judicious reference to copyright at the Boston Dinner—as well as in a letter of 1840 to L. G. Clark, who had published the passage in the *Knickerbocker* (see Vol. II, pp. 55*n* and 56).

[2] The portion of the *Herald*, 20 Feb, reporting the New York Dinner, is now in the Forster Collection, V & A.

[3] The *Satirist, or Censor of the Times*, a London weekly owned and edited (1831–49) by Barnard Gregory (see *To Forster*, 14 Feb 43), was notorious for its scurrility.

[4] Marryat, who must have suffered from the *Herald* himself, considered it of all papers "the most remarkable . . . for its obscenity, and total disregard for all decency and truth in its personal attacks" (*Diary in America*, Second Part, 1839, I, 171). Its editor and founder, James Gordon Bennett (1795–1872; *DAB*), violently attacked and virtually ostracized for sensationalism, was on 15 Feb 42 fined \$350 for libels on two New York judges.

[5] Founded in 1835, the *Herald* had the most comprehensive news service in the country and a circulation approaching 30,000. It was the first American paper to give stock exchange prices, and had boats patrolling outside New York to obtain early transatlantic news. Forster commented in the *Foreign Quarterly Review*, Oct 42, on the "superior excellence of its commercial news" (XXX, 199) but attacked it vehemently as a paper "read by every one, quoted by every one, patronised by the President, in favour with his Government, patted gently by the Judges—rampant, reckless, triumphant, without one restraint to its unbridled villany" (XXX, 216).

that I had "some claim," but that I had "a most righteous claim," to speak. But altogether it is very correct.[1,2]

The effect of all this copyright agitation at least has been to awaken a great sensation on both sides of the subject; the respectable newspapers and reviews taking up the cudgels as strongly in my favour,[3] as the others have done against me. Some of the vagabonds take great credit to themselves (grant us patience!) for having made me popular by publishing my books in newspapers:[4] as if there were no England, no Scotland,[5] no Germany,[6] no place but America in the whole world. A splendid satire upon this kind of trash has just occurred. A man came here yesterday, and demanded, not besought but demanded, pecuniary assistance; and fairly bullied Mr. Q for money. When I came home, I dictated a letter to this effect—that such applications reached me in vast numbers every day; that if I were a man of fortune, I could not render assistance to all who sought it; and that, depending on my own exertion for all the help I could give, I regretted to say I could afford him none. Upon this, my gentleman sits down and writes me that he is an itinerant bookseller; that he is the first man who sold my books in New York; that he is distressed in the city where I am revelling in luxury; that he thinks it rather strange that the man who wrote *Nickleby* should be utterly destitute of feeling; and that he would have me "take care I don't repent it." What do you think of *that*?[7]—as Mac would say. I thought it such a good

---

[1] A later note in the same issue of the paper claimed that their report of CD's speech was the best published: see *To* the Editor of the *New York Herald*, 19 Feb, and *fn*. The report in the *New York American*, 19 Feb, was in fact as accurate (*Speeches*, ed. K. J. Fielding, p. 425).

[2] Here Forster interrupts the letter with an account (imparted to him by Felton) of Irving's dread that he would break down in his speech as chairman; and how in fact he did break down (F, III, iii, 219–20). After speaking of his pride at witnessing—in a country accused of being "sordid and mercenary"—the spontaneous "burst of enthusiasm . . . to welcome a mere literary visitor", the "scene of homage paid to intellect", he ended: "Gentlemen, it is impossible for me to proceed", and gave the toast "Charles Dickens, the Literary Guest of the Nation" (quoted by J. W. T. Ley in F, III, iii, 229, *n* 209).

[3] CD's most conspicuous supporter was Horace Greeley's *Tribune*, which published two editorials urging international copyright, probably written by Greeley himself. The first, 14 Feb 42, demanded it on the grounds of personal justice to CD: "He ought to speak out on this matter, for who shall protest against robbery if those who

are robbed may not?" The second, 21 Feb, written in support of Mathews's speech at the New York Dinner, added justice to American writers to the demand for abstract justice. Texts of both editorials are given in W. G. Wilkins, *CD in America*, pp. 242–5. The *New York Mirror*, 14 Feb, reprinted an article from Mathews's own paper, *Arcturus*, welcoming CD and calling for action on international copyright as a "proper tribute" to him.

[4] See, for instance, the *New World*, 12 Feb (*To* Forster, 14 Feb, *fn*).

[5] Where he had been enthusiastically acclaimed at the Edinburgh Dinner in his honour, 25 June 41 (see Vol. II).

[6] For CD's immediate and widespread popularity in Germany, see E. N. Gummer, *Dickens' Works in Germany*, Oxford, 1940. In 1839 his "Complete Works" in English had been advertised by F. Fleischer of Leipzig. By 1844 his books had all been translated at least three times (*op. cit.*, pp. 8–9).

[7] Repeated in *To* Maclise, 22 Mar, *To* Mitton, 22 Mar, *To* Colden, 29 Apr. A catch phrase; cf. "What d'ye think of that, my Cat? | What d'ye think of that, my Dog?", the refrain of Hood's poem "The Bachelor's Dream".

commentary, that I dispatched the letter to the editor of the only English news-paper here,[1] and told him he might print it if he liked.

I will tell you what *I* should like, my dear friend, always supposing that your judgment concurs with mine; and that you would take the trouble to get such a document. I should like to have a short letter addressed to me,[2] by the principal English authors who signed the international copyright petition,[3] expressive of their sense that I have done my duty to the cause. I am sure I deserve it, but I don't wish it on that ground. It is because its publication in the best journals here would unquestionably do great good. As the gauntlet is down, let us go on. Clay[4] has already sent a gentleman to me express from Washington (where I shall be on the 6th or 7th of next month) to declare his strong interest in the matter, his cordial approval of the "manly" course I have held in reference to it, and his desire to stir in it if possible.[5] I have lighted up such a blaze[6] that a meeting of

[1] The *Albion*: see *To* Bartlett, 24 Feb.

[2] Forster, with Bulwer's aid, procured for CD the letter he requested, signed by 12 British writers, together with a memorial on international copyright addressed to "the American People", similarly signed, and a separate letter from Carlyle. See *To* Felton, 29 Apr; and, for texts, Appx, pp. 621-4.

[3] The petition presented to the Senate by Henry Clay on 2 Feb 37, signed by 56 British authors, headed by Thomas Moore, praying Congress to grant to them the exclusive benefit of their writings within the United States (*Senate Documents*, 24th Congress, 2nd Session, 1837, Doc. 134). The signatories (only six of whom, besides Carlyle, signed the memorial sent to CD) included Lady Blessington, Bulwer, Campbell, Disraeli, Maria Edgeworth, Hallam, Harriet Martineau, Milman, Rogers, Southey and Talfourd. It was prepared—probably jointly—by Harriet Martineau and her publishers, Saunders & Otley, and sent to Clay (a personal friend of hers) through the American explorer Capt. Charles Wilkes (Arno L. Bader, "Frederick Saunders and the Early History of the International Copyright Movement in America", *Library Quarterly*, VIII [1938], 34; Parke Godwin, *W. C. Bryant*, I, 315). Harriet Martineau herself sent copies of it, with letters in support, to influential American friends. To Everett she wrote on 8 Nov 36 complaining of "the late shameless aggressions of Messrs. Harper of New York on the property of Messrs. Saunders & Otley". "Every author of note is signing", she said; "the Americans in London are confident that we shall obtain

a Copyright Law, this very Session: & indeed I believe every American (not a bookseller) is willing to do us justice" (MS Massachusetts Historical Society; abbreviations expanded by us here and in letter below). To Dr James Rush, of Philadelphia, she wrote on the same day: "Now will you,—*not go to anybody in the trade,* (for they live upon our unpaid labours, & in return cut up our works,)—but take steps to have Congress memorialized by American authors, [to] obtain a Copyright Law for us; you will thus have done a good deed, & deserve the gratitude of both nations" (quoted by Arno L. Bader, p. 33). Bader mentions similar letters to J. Q. Adams and Judge Wayne.

[4] Henry Clay (1777–1852; *DAB*), Senator from Kentucky, Whig leader and the strongest advocate of international copyright in Congress. Bitter opponent of Jackson; Secretary of State under Adams 1824–8; three times unsuccessful candidate for the Presidency (1824, 1832, 1844); since 1840 leader of the Whig Administration. A strong nationalist and Unionist, and founder of the "American system" of protective tariffs, he resigned from the Senate 31 Mar 42 on Tyler's vetoing his chief resolutions. Famous for his Compromise Bills of 1833 (in the Nullification crisis) and 1850 (in an attempt to prevent civil war). His remarkable powers of oratory excited both the strongest support and enmity. For CD's impression of him when they met in Washington on 10 Mar, see *To* Fonblanque, 12 Mar.

[5] Clay had first introduced his Bill to change the international copyright law in Feb 37. He had submitted it four times

the foremost people on the other side (very respectfully and properly conducted in reference to me, personally, I am bound to say) was held in this town 'tother[1] night.[2] And it would be a thousand pities if we did not strike as hard as we can, now that the iron is so hot.

I have come at last, and it is time I did, to my life here, and intentions for the future. I can do nothing that I want to do, go nowhere where I want to go, and see nothing that I want to see. If I turn into the street, I am followed by a multitude. If I stay at home, the house becomes, with callers, like a fair. If I visit a public institution, with only one friend, the directors come down incontinently, waylay me in the yard, and address me in a long speech. I go to a party in the evening, and am so inclosed and hemmed about by people, stand where I will, that I am exhausted for want of air. I dine out, and have to talk about everything, to everybody. I go to church for quiet, and there is a violent rush to the neighbourhood of the pew I sit in, and the clergyman preaches *at* me. I take my seat in a railroad car, and the very conductor won't leave me alone. I get out at a station, and can't drink a glass of water, without having a hundred people looking down my throat when I open my mouth to swallow.[3] Conceive what all this is! Then by every post, letters on letters arrive, all about nothing, and all demanding an immediate answer. This man is offended because I won't live in his house; and that man is thoroughly disgusted because I won't go out more than four times in one evening. I have no rest or peace, and am in a perpetual worry.

Under these febrile circumstances, which this climate especially favors, I have come to the resolution that I will not (so far as my will has anything to do with the matter) accept any more public entertainments or public recognitions of any kind, during my stay in the United States;[4] and in pursuance of this determination I have refused invitations from Philadelphia, Baltimore, Washington,

since, in Dec 37, Dec 38, Jan 40 and Jan 42, without success, and had presented numerous petitions. For the petition of American writers handed to him by CD in Mar, see *To* Forster, 27 Feb, *fn.*

[6] Cf. Bishop Latimer: "We shall this day light such a candle . . ." (Foxe's *Actes and Monuments*, 1570).

[1] Thus in F, 1872–4, I, 305.

[2] Clearly the meeting of the Home League on 10 Feb, reported in the *New York Evening Post* of 11 Feb. The League accepted the fears of its paper-maker members that an international copyright law might reduce the demand for paper, and undertook to address a memorial to Congress against it. In its editorial the *Evening Post* insisted on the justice of copyright against the League's view, and assured the paper-makers that, whatever course Congress might adopt, they "need not fear that the world will cease to read, or that they will be thrown out of business".

[3] Cf. Martin's experiences at the "lĕ— vēe" he is forced to hold at the "National Hotel" (*Chuzzlewit*, Ch. 22). When he opens his mouth to speak, a gentleman is "on one knee before him, looking in at his teeth, with the nice scrutiny of a dentist".

[4] He had announced this publicly in his speech at the New York Dinner, 18 Feb: "Remembering the short time I have before me in this land of mighty interest, . . . I have felt it almost a duty to decline the honours which my generous friends elsewhere would heap upon me, and henceforth to pass through the country more quietly. Argus himself, though he had but one mouth for his hundred eyes, would have found the reception of a public entertainment once a week somewhat relaxing to his vigilance and activity. [*Great laughter and applause.*] And . . . I have resolved . . . for the future to shake hands with Americans not at parties, but at home. [*Long*

Virginia, Albany, and Providence.[1] Heaven knows whether this will be effectual, but I shall soon see, for on Monday morning the 28th we leave for Philadelphia.[2] There, I shall only stay three days. Thence we go to Baltimore, and *there* I shall only stay three days. Thence to Washington, where we may stay perhaps ten days; perhaps not so long. Thence to Virginia, where we may halt for one day; and thence to Charleston[3], where we may pass a week perhaps; and where we shall very likely remain until your March letters reach us, through David Colden. I had a design of going from Charleston to Columbia in South Carolina, and there engaging a carriage, a baggage-tender and negro boy to guard the same, and a saddle-horse for myself—with which caravan I intended going "right away," as they say here, into the west, through the wilds of Kentucky and Tennessee, across the Alleghany-mountains, and so on until we should strike the lakes and could get to Canada.[4] But it has been represented to me that this is a track only known to travelling merchants; that the roads are bad[5], the country a tremendous waste, the inns log-houses, and the journey one that would play the very devil with Kate. I am staggered, but not deterred. If I find it possible to be done in the time, I mean to do it; being quite satisfied that without some such dash, I can never be a free agent, or see anything worth the telling.

We mean to return home in a packet-ship—not a steamer. Her name is the George Washington, and she will sail from here, for Liverpool, on the seventh of June. At that season of the year, they are seldom more than three weeks making the voyage; and I never will trust myself upon the wide ocean, if it please Heaven, in a steamer again.[6] When I tell you all that I observed on board that Britannia, I shall astonish you. Meanwhile, consider two of their dangers. First, that if the funnel were blown overboard, the vessel must instantly be on fire,

---

continued cheering.]" (*Speeches*, ed. K. J. Fielding, pp. 27–8). Whatever disappointment this may have caused, CD's decision was thoroughly approved of by his more discriminating admirers. Catherine M. Sedgwick, for example, spoke of his "discretion and good sense" in this. "It is a proof of his power that he has stood as steadily in this focus of sunbeams as if he were in the cool shade of private life" (*Life and Letters of Catherine M. Sedgwick*, ed. Mary E. Dewey, New York, 1871, p. 280). The newspapers which had already protested against the prevalent "Boz mania" also sympathized with CD's decision. The *New World*, for example, thought he had acted "with excellent judgment . . . He will now be able to study the American character 'at home', with its genuine and native traits" (26 Feb).

[1] Independent evidence for these refusals has been found for only Philadelphia (?15 Feb), Baltimore (?15 Feb) and possibly Albany (24 Feb).

[2] His refusal was not effectual there: see *To* Gebler and Others, 20 Feb, *fn*.

[3] This was as far south as the endorsement (dated 4 Jan 42) of his policy of 17 July 38 with the Britannia Life Assurance Co. permitted him to go (see Vol. II, p. 414*n*). In the event, he went no further south than Richmond, Virginia (see *To* Forster, 13 Mar).

[4] Instead of going overland through Kentucky and Tennessee, they went mainly by canal-boat and steamer.

[5] The only good national highway to the West in 1842 was the National Pike to Vandalia (Illinois).

[6] According to the *New World*, 5 Mar, CD's reason for deciding to return by packet-boat had nothing to do with safety. "Mr. Dickens," it announced with satisfaction, "like all those with whom we have conversed, . . . is loud in his complaints of the accommodations furnished to passengers on board the Cunard line of steamers. He will take passage home in one of our packets, the comforts and accommodations of which for travellers, far surpass those of the best Atlantic steamships."

from stem to stern:[1] to comprehend which consequence, you have only to understand that the funnel is more than 40 feet high, and that at night you see the solid fire two or three feet above its top. Imagine this swept down by a strong wind, and picture to yourself the amount of flame on deck; and that a strong wind is likely to sweep it down you soon learn, from the precautions taken to keep it up in a storm, when it is the first thing thought of.[2] Secondly, each of these boats consumes between London and Halifax 700 tons of coals;[3] and it is pretty clear, from this enormous difference of weight in a ship of only 1200 tons burden in all, that she must either be too heavy when she comes out of port, or too light when she goes in. The daily difference in her rolling, as she burns the coals out, is something absolutely fearful.[4] Add to all this, that by day and night she is full of fire and people, that she has no boats, and that the struggling of that enormous machinery in a heavy sea seems as though it would rend her into fragments—and you may have a pretty con-siderable damned good sort of a feeble notion that it don't fit nohow; and that it a'nt calculated[5] to make you smart, overmuch; and that you don't feel 'special bright; and by no means first rate; and not at all tonguey (or disposed for conversation);[6] and that however rowdy[7] you may be by

[1] In *To* Forster, 30 Jan, CD had expressed the same fear in the same words.

[2] For another description of the *Britannia* in an Atlantic hurricane, Sep 45, see Lyell, *Second Visit to the United States*, 1849, I, Ch. I. Some "experienced American sea-captains" on board watched "with professional interest the Britannia's behaviour in the storm" and concluded that she was safer than any sailing-packet. Lyell visited the engine room and was filled with admiration of all he saw in it. He returned to England also on the *Britannia*, and on this voyage the chief hazard was icebergs (of thrilling interest to him as a geologist). He recorded that an officer on board considered icebergs the probable cause of the loss of the *President*.

[3] Probably an over-estimate: see Vol. II, p. 422*n*.

[4] What struck Lyell was that with the increase of speed as she got lighter, the vibration caused by the machinery increased too, "much to the discomfort of the passengers" (*op. cit.*, I, 10).

[5] Mrs Trollope recorded a conversation on a canal boat between two Yankees, one of whom used the word "calculate" in five sentences out of eight (*Domestic Manners of the Americans*, 1832, p. 309). Cf. Fanny Kemble: "By the by, of Mr. ——, while he was speaking, he came to the word *calculate*, and stopping half way, substituted another for it, which made me laugh internally. Mercy on me! how sore all these people are about Mrs. Trollope's book, and how glad I am I did not read it" (*Journal*, I, 67). In an imaginary scene from American family life, broadly caricatured, Mrs Trollope produced, besides "calculate", "oblivate", "eventuate" and "dubiate" (*Domestic Manners*, pp. 270–76). *Pickwick in America!*, edited by "Bos", 1840, added "imaginate" (p. 18).

[6] Probably an interpolation by Forster, and an inept one: cf. CD's explanation of the word on 29 Jan.

[7] Rowdy, rowdyism, or rowdyish, appear in many descriptions of CD: his dress had "rather a rowdy aspect" (*Worcester Aegis*, 16 Feb); his hair was "long and dark, and had a 'rowdyish' appearance" (Philadelphia *Spirit of the Times*, 9 Mar); S. Longfellow and W. W. Story wrote of rowdyism in his appearance or manner (*To* Forster, 30 Jan, *fn*, and *To* Story, 4 Feb, *fn*). Here the meaning has clearly been extended to "loud", flashy, or slightly vulgar. In *To* Forster, 6 Mar (*American Notes*, Ch. 6), CD has the "keeper" at the Tombs admitting that, for a boy detained there as a witness, "it a'nt a very rowdy life, and *that's* a fact"—the sense here being "lively", or "riotous". In *Chuzzlewit*, the *Rowdy Journal* (doubtless the *New York Herald*) is blackguardly and pugnacious as well as vulgar.

natur', it does use you up com-plete, and that's a fact; and makes you quake considerable, and disposed toe damn the ĕngīne!—All of which phrases, I beg to add, are pure Americanisms of the first water.[1]

When we reach Baltimore, we are in the regions of slavery. It exists there, in its least shocking and most mitigated form; but there it is. They whisper, here (they dare only whisper, you know, and that below their breaths), that in that place, and all through the South, there is a dull gloomy cloud on which the very word seems written. I shall be able to say, one of these days, that I accepted no public mark of respect in any place where slavery was; —and that's something.

The ladies of America are decidedly and unquestionably beautiful. Their complexions are not so good as those of Englishwomen; their beauty does not last so long; and their figures are very inferior. But they are most beautiful.[2] I still reserve my opinion of the national character—just whispering that I tremble for a radical coming here, unless he is a radical on principle, by reason and reflection, and from the sense of right.[3] I fear that if he were anything else, he would return home a tory. . . . I say no more on that head for two months from this time, save that I do fear that the heaviest blow ever dealt at liberty will be dealt by this country, in the failure of its example to the earth. The scenes that are passing in Congress now, all tending to the separation of the States,[4] fill one with such a deep disgust that I dislike the very name of Washington (meaning the place, not the man), and am repelled by the mere thought of approaching it.

To FRANCIS ALEXANDER, 25 FEBRUARY 1842

MS Mr Charles Hamilton.

Carlton House, New York. | Twenty Fifth February 1842.
My Dear Mr. Alexander.
Your beautiful and welcome present,[5] arrived safely to day. I will hang it in my own room at home, please God—and you shall see it there.

---

[1] Most of these phrases are given in J. R. Bartlett, *Dictionary of Americanisms*, New York, 1848.

[2] Nearly all English travellers remarked on this; many added that their beauty faded quickly—a fact usually attributed to the climate (e.g. by Marryat in *Diary in America*, Part Second, II, 2), but by some to their unhealthy lives (see, e.g., Fanny Kemble, *Journal*, II, 97 and I, 312, 105*n*, and Harriet Martineau, *Society in America*, 1837, III, 71).

[3] CD almost certainly had in mind Harriet Martineau, who remained determinedly optimistic about the future of American democracy (see *To* Macready, 22 Mar, *fn* p. 15). What happened to his own views can be seen on page after page of *Chuzzlewit*.

[4] The major separatist issue was slavery.

CD was no doubt referring to the fierce debate in the House of Representatives following J. Q. Adams's presentation of a petition on 24 Jan "to dissolve the Union" (see *To* Fonblanque, 12 Mar, *fn*) which had continued till 7 Feb. Lord Morpeth, who had heard some of it, commented: "One is tempted to think that the Union must break up next morning; but the flame appeared generally to smoulder almost as quickly as it ignited" (*Travels in America*, p. 32).

[5] Perhaps the picture *Fame*, recorded as "Presented by an artist during Mr. Dickens's first visit to America", painter unknown, in Christie's catalogue, 9 July 70 (see *Catalogue of the . . . Pictures, . . . of CD*, ed. J. H. Stonehouse, 1935, p. 126).

Yes. I *have* kept the Total Abstinence Pledge.[1] And I mean to keep it, unbroken, to the last.

Mr. P though no longer a new broom, sweeps clean still. He does what he has to do, well,—and always with a ready, cheerful will.[2]

For him, and much more—thank you!

Always believe me | Faithfully, | Your friend

Francis Alexander Esquire   CHARLES DICKENS

over[3]

To MRS ALEXANDER, 25 FEBRUARY 1842

MS Mr Charles Hamilton.

Carlton House, New York. | Twenty Fifth February 1842.

My Dear Mrs. Alexander.

I have received your beautiful book[4] with exceeding pleasure, and will always preserve it carefully, for your sake. I have scarcely the heart to rob you of such beautiful triumphs,—and yet I would not be without them for a great deal.[5]

Mrs. Dickens has a very bad cold, but she sends a host of very warm messages and loves. She begs you to kiss "Fan"[6] in her name. If you will ask Fan to kiss you in mine (when Mr. Alexander is looking another way) I shall be even more indebted to you than I am already.

Ever believe me | Faithfully Yours

CHARLES DICKENS

[1] Probably his decision, just announced to Forster, to accept no more public invitations during his stay in America.

[2] Relatively few letters in Putnam's hand survive (many people may have simply cut off and preserved CD's signature, but destroyed the rest), and fewer than ever after Feb. Clearly by then Putnam had become less a secretary and more a courier and guardian; but he came into his own as secretary when making copies of the copyright documents to be sent to four American newspapers (see 27 Apr and *fn*).

[3] CD wrote this letter on p. 1 of a folded sheet; on p. 3 he wrote *To* Mrs Alexander, 25 Feb (see next).

[4] A small book of Mrs Alexander's miniature etchings (see L. G. Swett, *John Ruskin's Letters to Francesca and Memoirs of the Alexanders*, Boston, [1931], p. 218).

[5] In a letter of condolence to Catherine after CD's death, Mrs Alexander evidently wrote that she would be glad to have the book back. Catherine replied on 22 Aug 70: "I quite recollect the little Book of drawings you allude to, but I need not tell you, that unhappily for the last twelve years, I was separated from my late Husband, and consequently do not know where the Book in question is to be found"; CD's Library, left by his Will to Charley, was now in packing-cases, she said; but she had written Charley a description of the book and asked him to look out for it when the books were unpacked. (Since not listed in the *Catalogue of the Library of CD*, ed. J. H. Stonehouse, it was perhaps found and returned.) Catherine added: "It took me back to much happier days receiving *your* letter dear Mrs Alexander, and I can assure you, I have never forgotten, the great kindness we received from your Husband and yourself at Boston" (MS University of Rochester).

[6] The Alexanders' daughter, Esther Francesca (1837–1917); later a protégée of Ruskin's. After meeting her and her mother in Florence Oct 82, he recorded in his diary: "I never knew such vivid goodness and innocence in any living creatures" (*The Works of John Ruskin*, ed. E. T. Cook and A. Wedderburn, 1903–12, XXXII, xxii); he lectured on her pen and ink drawings at Oxford 1883.

To GEORGE C. BAKER,[1] 27 FEBRUARY 1842

Mention in Dodd, Mead & Co. catalogue, Nov 1901; *MS* 1 p.; dated Carlton House, New York, 27 Feb 42.

To JOHN FORSTER, 27 FEBRUARY [1842]

Extract in F, III, iii, 224 (end of letter begun 17 Feb, continued 24 Feb). *From* New York.

Twenty-seventh February. Sunday.

There begins to be great consternation here, in reference to the Cunard packet[2] which (we suppose) left Liverpool on the fourth. She has not yet arrived. We scarcely know what to do with ourselves in our extreme anxiety to get letters from home. I have really had serious thoughts of going back to Boston, alone, to be nearer news. We have determined to remain here until Tuesday afternoon, if she should not arrive before, and to send Mr. Q and the luggage on to Philadelphia to-morrow morning. God grant she may not have gone down: but every ship that comes in brings intelligence of a terrible gale (which indeed was felt ashore here) on the night of the fourteenth; and the sea-captains swear (not without some prejudice of course) that no steamer could have lived through it, supposing her to have been in its full fury. As there is no steam packet to go to England, supposing the Caledonia not to arrive, we are obliged to send our letters by the Garrick ship, which sails early to-morrow morning. Consequently I must huddle this up, and dispatch it to the post-office with all speed. I have so much to say that I could fill quires of paper, which renders this sudden pull-up[3] the more provoking.

I have in my portmanteau a petition for an international copyright law, signed by all the best American writers with Washington Irving at their head.[4] They have requested me to hand it to Clay for presentation,[5] and to back it with any remarks I may think proper to offer. So "Hoo-roar for the principle, as the money-lender said, ven he vouldn't renoo the bill."[6]

God bless you. . . . You know what I would say about home and the darlings.

---

[1] Probably George C. Baker, bookseller, 158 Pearl Street, New York.

[2] The *Caledonia*, sister ship of the *Britannia*, *Acadia* and *Columbia*.

[3] "That's rayther a sudden pull up, ain't it, Sammy?" (*Pickwick*, Ch. 33).

[4] Its 25 signatories included—besides Irving—Hoffman, Bryant, Griswold, L. G. Clark, Willis and Fitz-Greene Halleck (for the full list and text, see L. H. Houtchens, "CD and International Copyright", *American Literature*, XIII [1941], 19–21). The author was almost certainly Frederick Saunders (see 16 Mar, *fn*), who himself handed it over to CD; he had presented at least six such petitions to Congress, of which Marryat had taken charge of one and G. P. R. James of another ("A Reminiscence in Copyright History", *Publishers' Weekly*, June 88, XXXIII, 988). Houtchens argues for CD's authorship, mainly from a comparison of the petition with his speeches at Boston and Hartford and letters to Forster and others; but its arguments had already been used—e.g., in the Clay Bill on copyright presented to the Senate in Feb 37, the petition of American authors presented by Clay the same month, and the petition of Citizens of Boston, Apr 38.

[5] See *To* Forster, 15 Mar.

[6] *Pickwick*, Ch. 35.

A hundred times God bless you. . . . Fears are entertained for Lord Ashburton[1] also. Nothing has been heard of him.[2]

To DANIEL MACLISE, 27 FEBRUARY 1842†

MS Comtesse de Suzannet. *Address:* By Packet Ship "Garrick" from N. York. | Daniel Maclise Esquire.R.A. | 14 Russell Place | Fitzroy Square | London | England.

Carlton House, New York. | February The Twenty Seventh 1842.

My Dear Mac. Don't blame me for writing a short letter.—I am obliged, most unexpectedly to despatch it by a Sailing Ship tomorrow, instead of having until Tuesday or Wednesday; for the Caledonia Steamer which left Liverpool on the Fourth, *has not yet arrived*, and terrible apprehensions are beginning to be entertained for her safety,[3] as there was an awful gale on the night of the Fourteenth, and the coast hereabouts is strewn with wrecks. God knows, dear Mac, whether your hand-writing is not now at the bottom of the deep Sea. When I think of the passengers, and the fine fellows in command of the vessel, and how recently we have been exposed to the same dangers, my heart grows sick and faint within me.

I *did* intend leaving here for Philadelphia, tomorrow. But I have resolved to send my secretary and baggage on, and to linger behind until Tuesday afternoon, in the hope that the poor steamer may yet arrive in safety. It is worth remarking that I "registered a vow"[4] soon after we came ashore, not to return in a steamer; having observed on our passage many dangers to which those demons are peculiarly liable. Indeed, the wonder with me, is, how they get across in heavy weather, as they have done. Instead of riding on the tops of the waves as ships do, they cleave their passage through them, and are under water the whole time. I wish you could once—only once—hear the noise of the sea upon her deck, and feel how she stops and quivers. Oh! It is a most damnable invention out upon the wide ocean; by the ghosts of all those who went down in the President it is.

[1] Alexander Baring, 1st Baron Ashburton (1774–1848; *DNB*), financier and statesman; son of Sir Francis Baring, founder of Baring Brothers; while working in America to extend the firm's operations, was involved in the handling of the Louisiana Purchase; married the daughter of William Bingham, Senator from Philadelphia. President, Board of Trade, in Peel's first Govt 1834–5; raised to the peerage 1835. Now at sea on his way to America as English Commissioner to settle the north-east boundary dispute between Canada and America. He and Webster signed the Ashburton Treaty on 9 Aug. For the favourable impression he created, see *To* Forster, 4 Apr, *fn.*

[2] Ashburton had left Portsmouth on 10 Feb on the steam frigate *Warspite*. It had had to put back to the Isle of Wight in a gale and, after heavy weather, did not reach America until 2 Apr.

[3] She was seriously damaged by storms and forced to return to Cork, where passengers and mail were transferred to the *Acadia*.

[4] O'Connell's phrase: see Vol. II, p. 443 and *n*.

[a]We purpose returning in a Ship—the George Washington—which is advertized to sail from here, on the Seventh of June. We were going on, South, tomorrow, but have decided to remain here until Tuesday afternoon, in the hope of yet getting letters from dear, old, hearty home.

I send you with this, a newspaper (the Satirist of America,[1] but the best paper here) containing an account of the Dinner. It is impossible to describe the Ball. I will only tell you that there were Three Thousand People present, and that it was the most splendid, gorgeous, brilliant affair you—yes, even you, Mac—and Good God my dear Dan, what an eye you have[2]—can possibly conceive.

Oh for Jack Straw's! Oh for Jack![3] oh for Topping![4]—oh for Charley, Mamey, Katey[5]—the study, the Sunday's dinner, the anything and everything connected with our life at Home! How cheerfully would I turn from this land of freedom and spittoons—of crowds, and noise, and endless rush of strangers—of everything public, and nothing private—of endless rounds of entertainments, and daily levees to receive 500 people—to the lightest, least-prized pleasure of "Den'ner Terrace"![6] I turn my eyes towards the picture[7] (which is always set out in great state, wherever we are) and yearn for Home, three thousand miles away. Oh Mac, Mac!

Exchange news with Forster—I say "exchange", for I send you herewith, a document of which he knows *nothing*.[8] The Bill of Fare, at the Ball Supper.[9] God bless you. Ever believe me, My Dear Mac,[a]

Your affectionate and attached friend

CD.

[aa] Not previously published.

[1] The *New York Herald*: see *To* Forster, 24 Feb and *fn*.

[2] Ejaculation repeated in *To* Maclise, 22 Mar—almost certainly a parody of Forster (himself perhaps echoing Pope, *Epistle to Arbuthnot*, l. 118).

[3] i.e. Forster; the first (possibly only) time CD is known to have called him this.

[4] William Topping, CD's groom: see Vol. II, p. 42*n*.

[5] Charles Culliford Boz (1837–96), Mary (1838–96) and Kate Macready (1839–1929), CD's three elder children.

[6] The Dickens children's name for Devonshire Terrace.

[7] Maclise's crayon drawing of the four Dickens children, with the raven, which he had done at Catherine's request the previous autumn. For his letter to Catherine agreeing to do it "With all my heart", see Vol. II, p. 393*n*.

[8] Underlined twice.

[9] Beneath his signed initials, CD pasted on to the letter some newspaper cuttings concerning the Boz Ball, from the *Extra Boz Herald*. One gave the Bill of Fare, which included: 50,000 oysters, 10,000 sandwiches, 40 hams, 76 tongues, 50 rounds of beef, 50 jellied turkeys, 50 pairs of chickens and 25 of ducks; also "2,000 fried Mutton Chops—cold" and "12 Floating Swans, a new device". For sweets there were: 350 quarts of jelly and blanc mange, 300 quarts of ice cream, "300 pound of Mottoes", "2,000 Kisses", "25 Pyramids—one cost $30, and had the 'Curiosity Shop' on the top", besides almonds, raisins, apples, oranges, cakes and "Ladies Fingers in thousands". For drinks: 2 hogsheads of Lemonade, 60 gallons of tea, 1½ barrels of Port, 150 gallons of Madeira, unspecified quantities of Claret and coffee. Other cuttings described the Ball arrangements and decorations and include a limpid-eyed woodcut ostensibly of Catherine (but probably from the newspaper's stock: see W. P. Beazell's Introduction to *Account of the Ball . . .*, p. 17), under which CD put eight exclamation marks. Below them he wrote: "All this information is exclusive." He had mentioned the Bill of Fare to Forster on 17 Feb, but did not send him it.

To THOMAS MITTON, 27 FEBRUARY 1842

MS Huntington Library.

Carlton House, New York | Twenty Seventh February 1842.
My Dear Friend.

I have but a moment for writing to you; all my plans of correspondence this month, being sadly deranged by the non-arrival of the Caledonia, which, it is much feared has gone down at Sea. She *may* arrive, yet; but if she left England to her time, she has been out 23 days.

You will receive a newspaper from me by a Sailing packet which sailed from here this morning. By the April steamer I will write you at length.[1]

Always Yours faithfully
Thomas Mitton Esquire   CD.

To JOHN FORSTER, 28 FEBRUARY 1842

Extract in F, III, iii, 224–6.[2]

Carlton-house, New York, | February twenty-eighth, 1842.

The Caledonia, I grieve and regret to say, has not arrived. If she left England to her time, she has been four and twenty days at sea. There is no news of her; and on the nights of the fourteenth and eighteenth it blew a terrible gale, which almost justifies the worst suspicions. For myself, I have hardly any hope of her; having seen enough, in our passage out, to convince me that steaming across the ocean in heavy weather is as yet an experiment of the utmost hazard.

As it was supposed that there would be no steamer whatever for England this month (since in ordinary course the Caledonia would have returned with the mails on the 2nd of March), I hastily got the letters ready yesterday and sent them by the Garrick; which may perhaps be three weeks out, but is not very likely to be longer. But belonging to the Cunard company is a boat called the Unicorn,[3] which in the summer time plies up the St. Lawrence, and brings passengers from Canada to join the British and North American steamers at Halifax. In the winter she lies at the last-mentioned place; from which news has come this morning that they have sent her on to Boston for the mails; and, rather than interrupt the communication, mean to dispatch her to England in lieu of the poor Caledonia. This in itself, by the way, is a daring deed; for she was originally built to run between Liverpool and Glasgow, and is no more designed for the Atlantic than a Calais packet-boat; though she once crossed it, in the summer season.

You may judge, therefore, what the owners think of the probability of the Caledonia's arrival. How slight an alteration in our plans would have made us passengers on board of her!

---

[1] He wrote him a long letter on 22 Mar.
[2] Described by Forster as a brief letter sent "by the minister's bag".
[3] A steam coaster, built in Glasgow 1836, bought by the Cunard Co. for the St Lawrence River mail from Picton to Quebec; had made her first run to Halifax and Boston on 16 May 1840.

It would be difficult to tell you, my dear fellow, what an impression this has made upon our minds, or with what intense anxiety and suspense we have been waiting for your letters from home. We were to have gone South to-day, but linger here until to-morrow afternoon (having sent the secretary and luggage forward) for one more chance of news. Love to dear Macready, and to dear Mac, and every one we care for. It's useless to speak of the dear children. It seems now as though we should never hear of them. . . .

P.S. Washington Irving is *a great* fellow. We have laughed most heartily together. He is just the man he ought to be. So is Doctor Channing, with whom I have had an interesting correspondence since I saw him last at Boston.[1] Halleck is a merry little man. Bryant a sad one, and very reserved. Washington Allston the painter (who wrote *Monaldi*)[2] is a fine specimen of a glorious old genius.[3] Longfellow, whose volume of poems[4] I have got for you, is a frank accomplished man as well as a fine writer, and will be in town "next fall." Tell Macready that I suspect prices here must have rather altered since his time. I paid our fortnight's bill here, last night. We have dined out every day (except when I was laid up with a sore throat), and only had in all four bottles of wine. The bill was 70*l.* English!!!

You will see, by my other letter, how we have been fêted and feasted; and how there is war to the knife about the international copyright; and how I *will* speak about it, and decline to be put down. . . .

Oh for news from home! I think of your letters so full of heart and friendship, with perhaps a little scrawl of Charley's or Mamey's, lying at the bottom of the deep sea; and am as full of sorrow as if they had once been living creatures.— Well! they *may* come, yet.

To MISS SARAH MOORE,[5] 28 FEBRUARY 1842*

MS[6] Dunedin Public Library.

Carlton House Feby. 28th. 1842.

Mr. Charles Dickens presents his Compliments to Miss Sarah Moore, and in forwarding the enclosed letter of Introduction, begs to say, that he defered[7] doing so until he left the City[8] as every moment of his time was occupied during the whole period of his stay, and he did not wish to trouble Miss M. unnescessarily.[7]

---

[1] Apparently only *To* Channing, 29 Jan, has survived, and the original of no letter from him to CD.

[2] *Monaldi: a Tale*; a Gothic romance set in Italy, published 1841, but written by 1822. A copy is listed in the inventory of his books CD made before leaving for Italy 1844.

[3] Cf. R. H. Dana's veneration for him: *Journal*, ed. R. F. Lucid, Vol. I, *passim*.

[4] Probably *Ballads and Other Poems*, Cambridge, Mass., 1841, his most recent volume.

[5] Unidentified.

[6] In Putnam's hand.

[7] Thus in MS. CD evidently did not correct his secretary's spelling mistakes.

[8] Which implies that he was leaving on the day he wrote this, as first intended, though in fact he and Catherine lay low in New York until 5 Mar (see *To* Putnam, 4 Mar and *fn*).

To THE REV. JOHN McVICKAR,[1] 28 FEBRUARY 1842

Text from John Brett Longstaff, *The Enterprising Life: John McVickar, 1787–1868*, New York, 1961, p. 272.

Carlton House | 28 February 1842

Mr. Charles Dickens presents his compliments to the Reverend Professor McVickar, and in forwarding the enclosed letter of Introduction begs to say that he deferred doing so until he left the city as every moment of his time was fully occupied during the whole period of his stay, and he did not wish to trouble Mr. McVickar unnecessarily.

To GEORGE W. PUTNAM, 1 MARCH 1842*

MS Columbia University Libraries.

Carlton House, New York | First of March 1842.

Dear Mr. Putnam

Mrs. Dickens is so very unwell with a bad sore throat, that I am constrained to remain here until tomorrow. I hope to come, either with or without her, by the train which leaves here at five o'Clock tomorrow afternoon.[2]

If you see Mr. Ingersoll[3] in the meanwhile, make my best regards to him[4]— I have only just found that there was some writing on this sheet of paper. This is the cause of the unseemly lining-out, which gives the foregoing handsome appearance to this note.

Faithfully Yours

G. W. Putnam Esquire   CD.

To GEORGE W. PUTNAM, 2 MARCH 1842*

MS Berg Collection. *Address:* G. W. Putnam Esquire United States Hotel | Philadelphia.

Carlton House. | March The Second 1842

Dear Mr. Putnam.

As the doctor forbids Mrs. Dickens' getting up; and as I fear that if I left her here, alone in sickness at such a great distance from Home, she would feel distressed after I had gone; I have determined to remain here until she can come on with me. I hope she will be able to travel, by the day after tomorrow; but I will write to you again tomorrow, and tell you.[5]

---

[1] John McVickar (1787–1868; *DAB*), prominent Episcopal clergyman and economist. Professor of Moral Philosophy, Columbia, 1817–57.

[2] For his change of plan, see next and *fn.*

[3] See *To* Ingersoll, 6 Mar, *fn.*

[4] At this point a line and a half, unconnected with this letter, are heavily cancelled.

[5] CD had originally planned to leave New York for Philadelphia on Mon 28 Feb (*To* Forster, 24 Feb), but sent Putnam ahead with the luggage on that day, intending to follow on Tues 1 Mar (*To* Forster, 27 Feb).

She has an ulcerated sore throat. It is not *very* bad. But she is subject to an attack of this kind every Spring; and on that account the doctor is more cautious than he would otherwise be.

There is no news of the Caledonia—except that the Unicorn has cruised out to look for her. A fisherman has reported at Boston that being out in his boat some mornings ago, he saw in a certain latitude not very far from Halifax, a large steam vessel quite disabled;[1] being under no sail and having no smoke issuing from her funnel; and tossing about at the mercy of the sea. Whether this appearance had its sole existence in the fisherman's brain, or whether it was some other ship, or whether (as in the case of the poor President) men's fancies have begun to float about flying-Dutchman[2]-wise, on the ocean, I can't say.

After this detention, I shall limit my stay at Philadelphia to *two* days—knock off Baltimore in one—and dispose of Washington in a week.

Faithfully Yours

CD.

To THOMAS S. GIBBS,[3] 3 MARCH 1842

Extract in Sotheby's catalogue, Apr 1968; *MS* 1 p.; dated New York, 3 Mar 42.

Thanking him for his invitation, but regretting that he is engaged for the whole of the next day even if he remains in New York so long which I am by no means sure of doing.

To GEORGE W. PUTNAM, 4 MARCH 1842*

Text from transcript by Mr Walter Dexter.

Carlton House, New York | Fourth of March 1842

Dear Mr. Putnam,

Mrs. Dickens is better; and we shall come on—without fail, I hope—by the 5 o'Clock train tomorrow (Saturday).

Pray *do not on any account* lead anyone to suppose that I shall remain in Philadelphia more than two days.[4] We cannot mark time, and must go forward. I do not think now, that I shall make any halt in Baltimore; as I am assured by those who know the place, that if we do not proceed to Charleston with all possible despatch, we shall find the heat most oppressive and uncomfortable.[5] Do not talk about our movements, except so far as Philadelphia is concerned, to anybody. I have so much enjoyed the quiet I have had here for the last two or

---

[1] Not the *Caledonia*, which had put back to Cork.

[2] A spectral ship, it or its captain (in some versions called Vanderdecken) doomed to range the seas for ever, usually in the region of the Cape of Good Hope; to see it was thought unlucky. The story, widely current, was brought into recent prominence by Marryat's novel *The Phantom Ship*, 1839; see also a poem of the same title in *Bentley's Miscellany*, Nov 38, IV, 433.

[3] Probably Thomas Gibbs, merchant, of 28 South Street, New York.

[4] He stayed there from 5 Mar to early on the 9th.

[5] In fact they stayed at Baltimore and did not go on to Charleston.

three days (owing to its having been generally supposed that I left New York on Monday), that I am more anxious than ever, to travel peaceably.[1]

I received your letter this morning.

They have moved us into a room looking upon Broadway, which is more cheerful and gay than our old one; to say nothing of its having a decent chimney, which the smoke goes up, instead of coming down.

You had better give our Philadelphia landlord notice of our movements—I mean of our intention to leave on Wednesday morning. Don't let our coming be buzzed about—so that there may be no more people at the depot than there usually are.[2]

Faithfully yours,
CHARLES DICKENS

To ASBURY DICKENS,[3] 6 MARCH 1842

Mention in John Anderson Jr. catalogue No. 297; *MS* 1 p.; dated Philadelphia, 6 Mar 42.

To JOHN FORSTER, 6 MARCH 1842

Extract in F, III, iv, 230–5.

United-states-hotel Philadelphia, | Sunday, sixth March, 1842

As this is likely to be the only quiet day I shall have for a long time, I devote it to writing to you. We have heard nothing from you*[4] yet, and only have for our consolation the reflection that the Columbia[5] is now on her way out. No news had been heard of the Caledonia yesterday afternoon, when we left New York. We *were* to have quitted that place last Tuesday, but have been detained there

---

[1] CD's one really exhausting day in Philadelphia was on Tues 8th, when Isaac Lea called on him at 10 a.m.; he then "shook hands with 500 people" at the reception forced on him by J. P. Gebler, T. B. Florence and others (see 20 Feb, *fn*, and *To* Forster, 13 Mar); next, paid a long visit to the Eastern Penitentiary, where he dined; afterwards went to a party at H. C. Carey's. At some point in the morning, Lucretia Mott (1793–1880; *DAB*), the Quaker campaigner against slavery, on whom CD had left a letter of introduction from Mrs E. J. Reid, called on him with her husband and daughter, and later wrote of the visit: "Jas. Mott talked to him about his travels in the south and hoped he would not be deceived by the outside appearance—but try to get a peep behind the scenes. I too said a word or two on the same subject" (Otelia Cromwell,

Lucretia Mott, Cambridge, Mass., 1958, p. 104).

[2] In fact his arrival on 5 Mar seems to have been achieved without any public knowledge of it: on 7 Mar the *Philadelphia Gazette* announced that he had arrived from New York "yesterday afternoon".

[3] Asbury Dickens (1773–1861), Secretary to the Senate 1836 to his death. Born in North Carolina; spent some years in Europe; in U.S. Treasury Dept 1831–4; Chief Clerk in the State Dept under Van Buren 1835–6. It was probably he who had sent CD the invitations to visit the President and the Senate on 10 Mar: see *To* Colden, that day.

[4] For the postcript linked to this statement by asterisk in F, see 15 Mar, *aa*.

[5] "The ship next in rotation to the *Caledonia* from Liverpool" (F, III, iv, 230*n*).

all the week by Kate having so bad a sore throat that she was obliged to keep her
bed. We left yesterday afternoon at five o'clock, and arrived here at eleven last
night. Let me say, by the way, that this is a very trying climate.

I have often asked Americans in London which were the better railroads—ours
or theirs? They have taken time for reflection, and generally replied on mature
consideration that they rather thought we excelled; in respect of the punctuality
with which we arrived at our stations, and the smoothness of our travelling. I
wish you could see what an American railroad is, in some parts where I now have
seen them.[1] I won't say I wish you could feel what it is, because that would be an
unchristian and savage aspiration. It is never inclosed, or warded off. You walk
down the main street of a large town: and, slap-dash, headlong, pell-mell, down
the middle of the street; with pigs burrowing, and boys flying kites and playing
marbles, and men smoking, and women talking, and children crawling, close to
the very rails; there comes tearing along a mad locomotive with its train of cars,
scattering a red-hot shower of sparks (from its *wood* fire) in all directions;
screeching, hissing, yelling, and panting; and nobody one atom more concerned
than if it were a hundred miles away. You cross a turnpike-road; and there is
no gate, no policeman, no signal—nothing to keep the wayfarer or quiet traveller
out of the way, but a wooden arch on which is written in great letters "Look out
for the locomotive." And if any man, woman, or child, don't look out, why it's
his or her fault, and there's an end of it.

The cars are like very shabby omnibuses—only larger; holding sixty or
seventy people. The seats, instead of being placed long ways, are put cross-wise,
back to front. Each holds two. There is a long row of these on each side of the
caravan, and a narrow passage up the centre. The windows are usually all closed,
and there is very often, in addition, a hot, close, most intolerable charcoal stove
in a red-hot glow. The heat and closeness are quite insupportable. But this is the
characteristic of all American houses, of all the public institutions, chapels,
theatres, and prisons. From the constant use of the hard anthracite coal in these
beastly furnaces, a perfectly new class of diseases is springing up in the country.
Their effect upon an Englishman is briefly told. He is always very sick and very
faint; and has an intolerable headache, morning, noon, and night.[2]

In the ladies' car, there is no smoking of tobacco allowed. All gentlemen who
have ladies with them, sit in this car; and it is usually very full. Before it, is the
gentlemen's car; which is something narrower. As I had a window close to me
yesterday which commanded this gentlemen's car, I looked at it pretty often,
perforce. The flashes of saliva flew so perpetually and incessantly out of the
windows all the way, that it looked as though they were ripping open feather-
beds inside, and letting the wind dispose of the feathers.[3] But this spitting is
universal. In the courts of law, the judge has his spittoon on the bench, the
counsel have theirs, the witness has his, the prisoner his, and the crier his.
The jury are accommodated at the rate of three men to a spittoon (or spit-box

[1] The description which follows, with
further detail, is used in *American Notes*,
Ch. 4, but of the journey from Boston to
Lowell.

[2] Other English travellers made the same
complaint: see, for instance, T. C. Grattan,
Civilized America, I, 105, and Harriet
Martineau, *Society in America*, III, 155.

[3] This image is repeated in *American
Notes*, Ch. 7.

as they call it here); and the spectators in the gallery are provided for, as so many men who in the course of nature expectorate without cessation. There are spit-boxes in every steamboat, bar-room, public dining-room, house of office, and place of general resort, no matter what it be. In the hospitals, the students are requested, by placard, to use the boxes provided for them, and not to spit upon the stairs. I have twice seen gentlemen, at evening parties in New York, turn aside when they were not engaged in conversation, and spit upon the drawing-room carpet. And in every bar-room and hotel passage the stone floor looks as if it were paved with open oysters—from the quantity of this kind of deposit which tesselates it all over.[1] . . .

The institutions at Boston,[2] and at Hartford, are most admirable. It would be very difficult indeed to improve upon them. But this is not so at New York; where there is an ill-managed lunatic asylum,[3] a bad jail,[4] a dismal workhouse,[5] and a perfectly intolerable place of police-imprisonment.[6] A man is found drunk in the streets, and is thrown into a cell[7] below the surface of the earth; profoundly dark; so full of noisome vapours that when you enter it with a candle you see a ring about the light, like that which surrounds the moon in wet and cloudy weather; and so offensive and disgusting in its filthy odours, that you *cannot bear* its stench. He is shut up within an iron door, in a series of vaulted passages where no one stays; has no drop of water, or ray of light, or visitor, or help of any

---

[1] All English travellers mentioned the spitting, some with greater disgust than others: see, for instance, Mrs Trollope on the spitting in a Mississippi steamboat (*Domestic Manners of the Americans*, 5th edn, 1839, pp. 11–12). R. H. Dana, Jr, wrote in his journal (27 Feb 44), during his first journey south of Philadelphia: "One thing only disgusted me, . . . & that did really so, & to no small degree. I had read in the works of British travelers about the American habits of spitting, & supposed it an exaggeration, for I knew that although we in N. Eng. spit more than the English, yet we did not do it eno' to justify so much fault as the English found. But in the cars between Balt. & Philad., & at Balt., it was disgusting even to a New Englander [*a detailed description follows*]" (*Journal*, ed. R. F. Lucid, I, 237). Harriet Martineau treated the "nauseous subject" only briefly (*Society in America*, III, 71).

[2] See *To* Forster, ?4 Feb, *fn.*

[3] "On Long Island", says CD in *American Notes*, Ch. 6; in fact Blackwell's Island (off Long Island); erected 1839 by New York County as the first State hospital for insane paupers. Everything in it, according to CD, "had a lounging, listless, madhouse air, which was very painful". He was shocked that its governorship was a political appointment (*ibid.*).

LCD III—E

[4] The City Penitentiary on Blackwell's Island, which he visited on the same day (27 Feb) as the asylum and the workhouse. He was rowed out to all three by Penitentiary prisoners (*American Notes*, Ch. 6). His description of the jail in *American Notes* is virtually the same as the description later in this letter.

[5] The Bellevue Almshouse, on the East River, 1¼ miles from Blackwell's Island; built after the Yates Report on poor relief of 1824 as the County workhouse. CD describes it in *American Notes*, Ch. 6, as "badly ventilated, and badly lighted"; it was also, no doubt—as an Assembly Committee reported of all the County workhouses—appallingly overcrowded (*History of the State of New York*, ed. A. C. Flick, New York, 1933–7, VIII, 309–10).

[6] With the exception of the City watch-house, George Combe visited all these institutions in Nov 38 and found them equally unsatisfactory. The chief reasons, he was told, were the distance from the City centre, the political wisdom—for the Party in power—of economizing, lack of influential advocates, and the unpopularity of exposing the imperfections of any American institutions (*Notes on the United States of North America during a Phrenological Visit in 1838-9-40*, 1841, I, 226–7).

[7] Of the City watch-house.

kind; and there he remains until the magistrate's arrival. If he die (as one man did not long ago) he is half eaten by the rats in an hour's time (as this man was). I expressed, on seeing these places the other night, the disgust I felt, and which it would be impossible to repress. "Well; I don't know," said the night constable— that's a national answer by the bye—"Well; I don't know. I've had six and twenty young women locked up here together, and beautiful ones too, and that's a fact." The cell was certainly no larger than the wine-cellar in Devonshire-terrace; at least three feet lower; and stunk like a common sewer. There was one woman in it, then. The magistrate begins his examinations at five o'clock in the morning; the watch is set at seven at night; if the prisoners have been given in charge by an officer, they are not taken out before nine or ten; and in the interval they remain in these places, where they could no more be heard to cry for help, in case of a fit or swoon among them, than a man's voice could be heard after he was coffined up in his grave.

There is a prison[1] in the same city, and indeed in the same building, where prisoners for grave offences await their trial, and to which they are sent back when under remand. It sometimes happens that a man or woman will remain here for twelve months, waiting the result of motions for new trial, and in arrest of judgment, and what not. I went into it the other day: without any notice or preparation, otherwise I find it difficult to catch them in their work-a-day aspect. I stood in a long, high, narrow building, consisting of four galleries one above the other, with a bridge across each, on which sat a turnkey, sleeping or reading as the case might be. From the roof, a couple of windsails dangled and drooped, limp and useless; the skylight being fast closed, and they only designed for summer use. In the centre of the building was the eternal stove; and along both sides of every gallery was a long row of iron doors—looking like furnace doors, being very small, but black and cold as if the fires within had gone out.

A man with keys appears, to show us round. A good-looking fellow, and, in his way, civil and obliging.[2]

"Suppose a man's here for twelve months. Do you mean to say he never comes out of that little iron door."

"He *may* walk some, perhaps—not much."

"Will you show me a few of them?"

"Ah! All, if you like."

He threw open a door, and I looked in. An old man was sitting on his bed, reading. The light came in through a small chink, very high up in the wall. Across the room ran a thick iron pipe to carry off filth; this was bored for the reception of something like a big funnel in shape; and over the funnel was a watercock. This was his washing apparatus and water-closet. It was not savoury,

[1] The Tombs, the New York House of Detention, visited by CD on 2 Mar; built in 1838, it was modelled on an Egyptian royal burial-place. The descriptions of the watch-house and the Tombs are substantially the same in *American Notes*, Ch. 6; but their order is reversed—possibly so that the climax could be the eating of the dead prisoner by rats.

[2] Here Forster inserts the statement that he is omitting a dialogue given in *American Notes* and printing "only that which appears for the first time here"; yet the passages following are, in fact, in *American Notes*, though rearranged.

but not very offensive. He looked up at me; gave himself an odd, dogged kind of shake; and fixed his eyes on his book again. I came out, and the door was shut and locked. He had been there a month, and would have to wait another month for his trial. "Has he ever walked out now, for instance?" "No." . . .

"In England, if a man is under sentence of death even, he has a yard to walk in at certain times."

"Possible?"

. . . Making me this answer with a coolness which is perfectly untranslateable and inexpressible, and which is quite peculiar to the soil, he took me to the women's side; telling me, upon the way, all about this man, who, it seems, murdered his wife, and will certainly be hanged. The women's doors have a small square aperture in them; I looked through one, and saw a pretty boy about ten or twelve years old, who seemed lonely and miserable enough—as well he might.[1] "What's *he* been doing?" says I. "Nothing" says my friend. "Nothing!" says I. "No," says he. "He's here for safe keeping. He saw his father kill his mother, and is detained to give evidence against him—that was his father, you saw just now." "But that's rather hard treatment for a witness, isn't it?"—"Well! I don't know. It a'nt a very rowdy life, and *that's* a fact." So my friend, who was an excellent fellow in his way, and very obliging, and a handsome young man to boot, took me off to show me some more curiosities; and I was very much obliged to him,[2] for the place was so hot, and I so giddy, that I could scarcely stand. . . .

When a man is hanged in New York, he is walked out of one of these cells, without any condemned sermon or other religious formalities, straight into the narrow jail yard, which may be about the width of Cranbourn-alley. There, a gibbet is erected, which is of curious construction; for the culprit stands on the earth with the rope about his neck, which passes through a pulley in the top of the "Tree" (see *Newgate Calendar* passim),[3] and is attached to a weight something heavier than the man. This weight being suddenly let go, drags the rope down with it, and sends the criminal flying up fourteen feet into the air; while the judge, and jury, and five and twenty citizens (whose presence is required by the

[1] There was virtually no segregation of children in prisons: in 1846, 282 children under 10 were committed to the Tombs, and *c.* 4000 between 10 and 20 (P. Klein, *Prison Methods in New York State*, New York, 1920, p. 74). The same year two blind boys of seven and nine, who had strayed from the Blind Asylum, spent two days in a cell with a corpse and some abandoned criminals (*ibid.*).

[2] The Keeper, identified by W. H. Seward (Governor of New York) as a Colonel Jones, who "had done his best to be courteous to the distinguished author", was "distressed to find himself presented in quite another light" in *American Notes* (in which these final lines of praise do not appear). On 18 Nov 42 Seward wrote to a friend that the faults in the New York House of Detention were not exaggerated in *American Notes*, "nor the dialogue untrue"; but CD had unintentionally given a wrong idea of the keeper—"one of the most candid of men", who "told the truth in a homely way"; Seward recognized some of Jones's "customary expressions". "But Dickens so turns the dialogue as to make Jones appear bold, swaggering, and rowdyish. On the contrary, notwithstanding his vulgar forms of speech, he is gentle, modest, and respectful, and it would be easy for one who knew him to discover, by his answers, that he was abashed" (*Autobiography of W. H. Seward . . . With a Memoir of his Life, and Selections from his Letters from 1836 to 1846 by F. W. Seward*, New York, 1877, p. 627).

[3] These four words obviously interpolated by Forster.

law), stand by, that they may afterwards certify to the fact. This yard is a very dismal place; and when I looked at it, I thought the practice infinitely superior to ours: much more solemn, and far less degrading and indecent.

There is another prison[1] near New York which is a house of correction. The convicts labour in stone-quarries near at hand, but the jail has no covered yards or shops, so that when the weather is wet (as it was when I was there) each man is shut up in his own little cell, all the live-long day. These cells, in all the correction-houses I have seen, are on one uniform plan—thus:

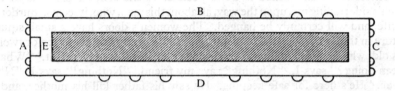

A, B, C, and D, are the walls of the building with windows in them, high up in the wall. The shaded place in the centre represents four tiers of cells, one above the other, with doors of grated iron, and a light grated gallery to each tier. Four tiers front to B, and four to D, so that by this means you may be said, in walking round, to see eight tiers in all. The intermediate blank space you walk in, looking up at these galleries; so that, coming in at the door E, and going either to the right or left till you come back to the door again, you see all the cells under one roof and in one high room.[2] Imagine them in number 400,[3] and in every one a man locked up; this one with his hands through the bars of his grate, this one in bed (in the middle of the day, remember), and this one flung down in a heap upon the ground with his head against the bars like a wild beast. Make the rain pour down in torrents outside. Put the everlasting stove in the midst; hot, suffocating, and vaporous, as a witch's cauldron. Add a smell like that of a thousand old mildewed umbrellas wet through, and a thousand dirty clothes-bags musty, moist, and fusty, and you will have some idea—a very feeble one, my dear friend, on my word—of this place yesterday week. You know of course that we adopted our improvements in prison-discipline from the American pattern;[4] but I am confident that the writers who have the most lustily lauded the American prisons, have never seen Chesterton's[5] domain or Tracey's.[6] There is no more comparison between these two prisons of ours, and any I have seen here YET,

---

[1] The Penitentiary on Blackwell's Island.

[2] Both plan and description of it are omitted in *American Notes*.

[3] "Some two or three hundred" in *American Notes*. CD was presumably including the women, whom he mentions there. Combe noted that in 1839 the Male Penitentiary contained 232 prisoners, and the Female 224 (*Notes on the United States of North America*, III, 35).

[4] CD is referring here to the "Auburn" or "Silent Associated" system. For

T. B. L. Baker's pointing out to him that it was itself copied from the Gloucester Penitentiary in England, see *To* Baker, 3 Feb 43, *fn*.

[5] George Laval Chesterton (*d.* 1868), Governor of the Middlesex House of Correction, Coldbath Fields: see Vol. I, p. 101*n*.

[6] Lieut. Augustus Frederick Tracey, RN (1798–1878), Governor of the Westminster House of Correction, Tothill Fields: see Vol. II, p. 270*n*.

than there is between the keepers here,[1] and those two gentlemen. Putting out of sight the difficulty we have in England of finding *useful* labour for the prisoners (which of course arises from our being an older country, and having vast numbers of artizans unemployed),[2] our system is more complete, more impressive, and more satisfactory in every respect. It is very possible that I have not come to the best, not having yet seen Mount Auburn.[3] I will tell you when I have. And also when I have come to those inns, mentioned—vaguely rather—by Miss Martineau, where they undercharge literary people for the love the landlords bear them.[4] My experience, so far, has been of establishments where (perhaps for the same reason) they very monstrously and violently overcharge a man whose position forbids remonstrance.[5]

[1] The best known Governor of the Auburn system prisons was their virtual creator, Capt. Elam Lynds (1784–1855; *DAB*), twice Warden of Auburn and Sing Sing since 1821. After two resignations, following charges of over-severity, he was finally removed in 1844 on charges of cruelty and misappropriation of State property. De Tocqueville, who had two long conversations with him in 1831, found him intelligent and "singularly energetic", but vulgar in looks and speech (*Journey to America*, transl. G. Lawrence, ed. J. P. Mayer, 1959, p. 23). On his visit to the Eastern Penitentiary, Philadephia, CD met and liked the former Warden, Samuel R. Wood, a Quaker.

[2] A point made by CD in *American Notes*, Ch. 3. But there he also questioned the wisdom of employing prisoners on ordinary productive work—both because rigid silence was difficult to enforce against the noise of the loom, the forge, the hammer, the saw, and more particularly because he felt prison labour should be of a punitive kind, like the treadmill and oakum-picking, "marked and degraded everywhere as belonging only to felons in jails." Over this, as in his dealing with the Eastern Penitentiary in *American Notes*, Ch. 7, CD's view had become more positive in the time between his initial letter to Forster and its use in the book.

[3] i.e. Auburn State prison in Cayuga County, New York (mistakenly called "Mount Auburn" in *American Notes*, Ch. 6, too, though corrected in later edns). Opened in 1819, it soon adopted the "Auburn" or "Silent Associated" system of congregate work by day and separation by night, with silence enforced by severe corporal discipline. The system impressed

many penologists and prison reformers (such as Louis Dwight); but, among travellers, CD was unusual in preferring it to the Philadelphia Separate system. He saw it in operation in the House of Correction in Boston (see *American Notes*, Ch. 3), and in the New Connecticut State Prison, outside Hartford (*To Forster, 17 Feb and fn p. 69*), though not at either Auburn itself nor at Sing Sing. De Tocqueville, who visited both these last in 1831, considered such severe discipline dangerous and not likely to result in reformation (*Journey to America*, pp. 203, 205); Harriet Martineau felt the punishment (particularly stocks for the women), and the herding together of prisoners, must kill self-respect (*Retrospect of Western Travel*, I, 202–3), and disliked the imposition of silence: "They ought to talk; and they do, in spite of spies, governor, and the whip" (*Society in America*, III, 186).

[4] Harriet Martineau gives an instance of undercharging at an inn at Elbridge, New York State, where a large breakfast for her whole party of six cost "only two dollars and a quarter" (*Society in America*, III, 88); but she says nothing about "literary people". CD may perhaps have had partly in mind Marryat's experience of various inns where the innkeeper was regarded as your host and with his wife sat "at the head of the *table-d'hôte*", the continual stream of travellers which poured through the country enabling him "to abstain from excessive charges": "no more is charged to the President of the United States than to other people" (*Diary in America*, Part Second, I, 95, 97).

[5] But see CD's happy experience at Harrisburg (*To Forster, 28 Mar and fn*).

To HARRY INGERSOLL,[1] 6 MARCH 1842*

MS Isabella Stewart Gardner Museum, Boston. *Address:* Harry Ingersoll Esquire.

United States Hotel [2]| Sunday Morning March Sixth 1842.

My Dear Sir

Mrs. Dickens *is* with me;[3] and we shall both be very happy to dine with you tomorrow, as you so kindly propose.

If you be disengaged, I should be glad to plan some lion-inspecting[4] expedition for tomorrow morning, but of that we can speak, when I have the pleasure of seeing you.—I go on to Washington next Wednesday without fail.

Always Believe me | My Dear Sir | Faithfully Yours

CHARLES DICKENS

We are most comfortably bestowed here, and owe you many thanks for your good offices.

To EDGAR ALLAN POE,[5] 6 MARCH 1842*

MS Berg Collection.

Private

United States Hotel | Sixth March 1842.

My Dear Sir

I shall be very glad to see you, whenever you will do me the favor to call.[6]

---

[1] Harry Ingersoll (1809–86), Lieut. U.S. Navy; member of a well-known Philadelphia family. Fellow-passenger of CD's on the *Britannia*, presumably returning on leave from the Mediterranean where he had been serving.

[2] In Chestnut Street.

[3] For CD's earlier uncertainty about this, see *To* Putnam, 1 Mar.

[4] i.e. sight-seeing.

[5] Edgar Allan Poe (1809–49; *DAB*) had already published three vols of poems and *Tales of the Grotesque and Arabesque* (2 vols, 1840), besides many of his later best known separate tales (including "The Fall of the House of Usher", "William Wilson", "Morella") and numerous critical articles. "The Fall of the House of Usher" and two other tales were reprinted in *Bentley's Miscellany*, July, Oct and Dec 1840 (pirated). Wrote for and edited the *Southern Literary Messenger*, Richmond, Dec 35 to Jan 37; *Burton's Gentleman's Magazine* 1839–40; and *Graham's Magazine*, Philadelphia, Jan 41–May 42—increasing its circulation from 6000 to 40,000 and making it the most popular literary journal in America. Probably the first American critic to see CD's true importance, he used him in his articles, from 1841, as a model by which to judge other writers, and almost certainly gained ideas from him (for instance, from the story in *Master Humphrey's Clock*, No 3, and "A Madman's Manuscript", *Pickwick*, Ch.11) for his own tales and poems. For Poe's asking CD's help in finding him an English publisher, see *To* Poe, 27 Nov 42.

[6] He and CD had two long interviews in the course of which they discussed American poetry, Poe told J. R. Lowell, in a letter of 2 July 44 written after he had read in the *Foreign Quarterly Review*, Jan 44 (XXXII, 291–324), an article on "American Poetry" of which he said he was convinced that CD was the author. The article, which named at its head R. W. Griswold's *Poets and Poetry of America*, Philadelphia, 1842, Longfellow's *Voices of the Night*, 1843, Bryant's *Poems*, and two other recent publications, was a devastating attack: "All the poetasters who could be scrambled together are crammed into [Griswold's] volume", the review remarked, and proceeded to go through them with damaging (and often laughable) quotations. Only Longfellow ("unquestionably the first of her poets"), Bryant, Emerson and—to a lesser extent—

I think I am more likely to be in the way between half past eleven and twelve, than at any other time.

I have glanced over the books you have been so kind as to send me;[1] and more particularly at the papers to which you called my attention.[2] I have the greater pleasure in expressing my desire to see you, on their account.

Apropos of the "construction" of Caleb Williams.[3] Do you know that Godwin wrote it *backwards*—the last Volume first—and that when he had produced the hunting-down of Caleb, and the Catastrophe, he waited for months, casting about for a means of accounting for what he had done?[4]

Faithfully Yours always

Edgar. A. Poe Esquire.   CHARLES DICKENS

Halleck, came in for any praise. Poe (and this clearly infuriated him) won praise only in a context illustrating how imitative American poetry was: "Poe is a capital artist after the manner of Tennyson". In a letter to Lowell of 30 Mar 44, Poe claimed indignantly that he had published the poems "long before Tennyson was heard of" (but see *To* Forster, 3 May, *fn*); also that he was sure on "strong internal evidence" that CD wrote the review—his reason, given on 2 July, being that the review repeated "nearly every thing" that he or CD had said during their two meetings, and even quoted "To the Humble Bee" which Poe had read to CD (*Letters of E. A. Poe*, ed. J. W. Ostrom, Cambridge, Mass., 1948, I, 246, 254, 258). But Lowell had not shared Poe's view: on 27 June he had written that he was sure the author was not CD but "a friend of his named *Forster* (or Foster) ... Dickens may have given him hints. Forster is a friend of some of the Longfellow clique here which perhaps accounts for his putting L. at the top of our Parnassus" (H. F. Barnes, *C. F. Hoffman*, p. 146). There seems indeed no doubt (though the article is not in any volume of cuttings in the Forster Collection, V & A) that Lowell was right. This is supported by comparison with Forster's second article on the American press (*Foreign Quarterly*, Apr 43), from which the Poetry article (p. 295) contains one direct quotation; but above all by the following, in a letter from Longfellow to Forster, 8 May 45: "I have never yet thanked you, directly, though I have commissioned Felton to do it, for the cordial praise of me in the Foreign Quarterly, which I am confident you had a hand in, and for which I beg you now to receive my warmest thanks" (MS V A &).

[1] Probably his most recently published work, the two volumes of *Tales*; but only his *Poetical Works*, 1853, was in CD's library at his death.

[2] CD's final paragraph shows that one of these was Poe's recent review of *Barnaby* in *Graham's Magazine*, Feb 42 (reprinted in *The Book of Poe*, ed. Addison Hibbard, New York, 1929, pp. 97–115). No doubt Poe had also sent his review of *Old Curiosity Shop* (*Graham's*, May 41), which he had ardently praised for its "chaste, vigorous, and glorious *imagination*", only regretting Nell's death as leaving "too painful an impression" (see Preface to Vol. II, p. x). Perhaps he sent the "prospective review" of *Barnaby* (*Saturday Evening Post*, Philadelphia, 1 May 41; reprinted in *D*, IX [1913], 174–8), which he had written after publication of only four chapters of the book—though this seems less certain, since apart from identifying "the stranger" as Rudge and the murderer, his predictions were wide of the mark.

[3] Godwin's best known novel, *Things as They Are; or, The Adventures of Caleb Williams*, 3 vols, 1794. Poe's review of *Barnaby* in *Graham's Magazine* had concluded: "*Caleb Williams* is a far less noble work than *The Old Curiosity Shop*; but Mr. Dickens could no more have *constructed* the one than Mr. Godwin could have dreamed of the other."

[4] Godwin gave an account of his construction of the novel in the Preface to the 1832 edition of *Fleetwood*: in planning it ("putting down hints for my story"), he began with the third volume and worked backwards. But his diary (quoted from MS Abinger Papers in *Caleb Williams*, ed. D. McCracken, 1970, p. xin) shows that the novel itself was written in the natural order. In "A Chapter of Suggestions"

To ISAAC LEA,[1] 7 MARCH 1842*

MS Mr Henry Lea Hudson.

U.S. Hotel. | Seventh March 1842.

My Dear Sir.

I am very much obliged to you for your note. I have no occasion to trouble you, for you have anticipated all my wants, but I shall be happy to see you—and as I leave on Wednesday morning, and am engaged nearly all day tomorrow, I would say ten o'clock tomorrow morning, if it will not be inconvenient to you to shake hands with me at that hour.

Dear Sir | Faithfully Yours

Isaac Lea Esquire   CHARLES DICKENS

To JOHN M. PATTON AND OTHERS,[2] 7 MARCH [1842]

Text from the *Richmond Enquirer*, 19 Mar 42.

United States Hotel, March 7

Gentlemen,

I am truly obliged to you for your most kind and friendly invitation to a public dinner in Richmond.[3]

I regret to say, however, that I have found it necessary, (putting a strong restraint upon my inclination,) to form a resolution not to accept any more public entertainments, during my short stay in this country. Upon the faith of this decision, I have already, most unwillingly, declined the proffered hospitality of many generous friends in other places; and no alternative is left me but to do the like by you.[4]

Believe me that I am not the less sensible of your kindness, and that I am always,

Faithfully, your friend,

To John M. Patton, Esq, &c., &c.   CHARLES DICKENS

(*The Opal*, 1845), Poe paraphrased this remark of CD's, without acknowledgement, in the course of criticism of CD's plots; and he paraphrased it again, though professing to be quoting it, in the opening paragraph of "The Philosophy of Composition" (*Graham's Magazine*, Apr 46).

[1] Isaac Lea (1792–1886; *DAB*), publisher and scientist; son-in-law of Mathew Carey, in whose publishing house he worked. President, Academy of Natural Sciences of Philadelphia, 1858–63; and of the American Association for the Advancement of Science 1860.

[2] John Mercer Patton (1797–1858;*DAB*), lawyer and politician. Member of Congress 1830–8, as a Democrat; senior member of

Virginia Executive Council and briefly Acting Governor 1841. Afterwards left politics to become leader of the Richmond bar.

[3] The invitation, dated 25 Feb and signed by 12 Committee members, spoke of the "great satisfaction" CD's acceptance would give to Richmond admirers of his "character and genius", who sincerely desired to welcome him as a friend "to the hospitality of the 'Ancient Dominion' " (*Richmond Enquirer*, 19 Mar).

[4] On his arrival in Richmond, 17 Mar, CD did, however, accept the Committee's invitation to a "social supper" that evening (see *To* Forster, 21 Mar, *fn*).

To PETER RICHINGS,[1] 7 MARCH 1842

Extract in John Anderson Jr. catalogue No. 141 (1902); dated 7 Mar 42.

I must decline to make any public visits to the theatre.[2]

Faithfully yours

CHARLES DICKENS

To JOSEPH STORY, 9 MARCH 1842*

MS University of Texas.

Fuller's Hotel[3] | Wednesday Ninth March 1842.

Mr. Charles Dickens presents his compliments to Mr. Justice Story, and begs to forward the accompanying letters; one of which (Lord Brougham's) was accidentally unsealed, when it was detached from an outer envelope. And Mr. Dickens is extremely sorry to add that a pamphlet[4] which Lord Brougham begged him to deliver to Mr. Justice Story, has been most unfortunately left behind, with some other papers, at New York. He earnestly hopes that Mr. Justice Story will not be inconvenienced by a few weeks' delay.

To DAVID C. COLDEN, 10 MARCH 1842

MS Free Library of Philadelphia. *Address:* David C. Colden Esquire | 28 Laight Street | Hudson Square | New York.

Fuller's Hotel Washington | March The Tenth 1842.

My Dear Colden.

We reached this place safely last night: having sustained no more damage by the way, than the presence of a miraculously fractious child in the railroad Car from Philadelphia to Baltimore; who, leaving us at the last-named place, was relieved by another child in the same frame of mind,—in whose cheerful company we arrived here. He (it was a boy) set in so very heavily at Baltimore that I thought it impossible he could last; especially as his friends tempted him from time to time with a tin mug of milk and water, and other refreshment, from a basket. But contrary to my expectations, he cried the whole forty miles

---

[1] Peter Richings, originally Puget (1798–1871; *DAB*), actor, singer and theatre manager. Of English birth—almost certainly the son of Capt. (later Rear-Admiral) Peter Puget, after whom Puget Sound was named. Educated at Charterhouse and Pembroke, Oxford. Migrated to New York 1821 and had great success at the Park Theatre 1821–34, his subsequent parts

including Bill Sikes. Moved to Philadelphia 1840, acting at the National Theatre and managing the Walnut Street and Chestnut Street Theatres.

[2] Text in Putnam's hand according to catalogue.

[3] In Washington; described in *American Notes*, Ch. 8.

[4] See *To* W. W. Story, 4 Feb, *fn*.

through; and when he was taken out at the station, the crown of his head was covered with crimson pimples—the consequence of his supernatural exertion.[1]

We were very comfortably lodged at Philadelphia—and indeed we deserved to be; for the landlord not only charged us half rent for the rooms during the time he had expected us (which was quite right) but charged us also—when I say us, I mean Kate, her maid, and I—for board during the whole of the same period. As I could not help regarding the statement that he had paid for our food while we were paying for it at New York, in the light of a pleasant fiction, or ingenious jest, I *did* suggest through my factotum the slightest possible insinuation to that effect. It appeared, however, that it was "the custom"; and as strangers in Rome do as they do in Rome, I bowed to the custom, and paid.

I passed a whole day in the Penitentiary[2]—where, as you know, the principle of Solitary confinement is observed, in the strictest manner, in every case. It is inexpressibly painful to see so many of the prisoners as I did, and to converse with them;[3] but I fear that to a certain extent the system is a good one. I use the expression "I fear", because it is dreadful to believe that it is ever necessary to impose such a torture of the mind upon our fellow creatures. But it seems, from all one can learn, to do good:[4] and now and then to effect that reclamation which gives joy in heaven.[5] In the case of a very long term of imprisonment, however, I cannot but think it cruel, though I know it is mercifully and well intended. One man had been shut up by himself in the same Cell, for nearly twelve years.[6] His time is just expiring. I asked him how he felt at the prospect of release,—and he answered—plucking in a strange way at his fingers, and looking restlessly about the walls and floor—that he didn't care; that it was all the same to him now; that he had looked forward to it once, but that was so long ago, that

---

[1] Other details of the journey are given in *American Notes*, Ch. 8. They left Philadelphia at 6 a.m. by boat—on which they breakfasted; at 9 a.m. transferred to the railway; at noon crossed "a wide river [*the Susquehanna*] in another steamboat" and got into another train, which took them to Baltimore, where they dined ("waited on, for the first time, by slaves"). Thence they went by rail to Washington, which they reached at 6.30.

[2] The famous Eastern Penitentiary near Philadelphia, run on the Philadelphia (or Separate) System, based on the belief that reformation of prisoners was only possible if they were separated from criminal companions. Considerable pride was felt in it by Philadelphians and most English travellers were taken to see it. Opened in 1830, the prison was the first in America to be built with the façade of a vast mediæval castle; for its striking plan with seven long wings radiating from a central tower, see drawing by the architect John Haviland

(1792–1852) in the V & A's Dickens commemorative catalogue (1970), plate 32.

[3] See *To* Forster, 13 Mar and *fn*.

[4] Besides no doubt hearing the Penitentiary praised in Philadelphia, CD was aware of Harriet Martineau's approval of the system: "the criminals of the United States", she pointed out, "are rarely the depraved, brutish creatures that fill the prisons of the old world" (*Society in America*, III, 184)—a fact which no doubt contributed to CD's fears for them, but to her suggested that they could best be reclaimed when treated as individuals. Marryat, too, had on the whole approved of the prison (*Diary in America*, II, 266–80). But both these visitors stressed the necessity that solitude should be accompanied by labour—or the punishment was "too horrible and unjust to be thought of" (H. Martineau, *Retrospect of Western Travel*, I, 207–8).

[5] *St Luke*, XV, 7.

[6] The sailor: see *American Notes*, Ch. 7.

he had come to have no regard for anything. And so, with a heavy sigh, he went about his work,[1] and would say no more. We are accustomed to hear it said sometimes that such a person must have felt in a minute, a year of suffering. But if ever twelve years of the most intense mental anguish were written in the small compass of one face, I saw it in this prisoner's. Indeed the men, however unlike naturally, become alike, and strikingly alike, in this place. There is the same bright eye, and haggard look, in them all; and an indescribable something —distantly resembling the attentive and sorrowful expression you see in the blind—which is never to be forgotten. The women bear it better, and acquire a patient and subdued look, that makes you very sad, but not distressingly so. Each of them seems a better creature than one feels one's-self to be, and that's a comfort. The prison is beautifully—exquisitely—kept, and thoroughly well managed: but I never in my life was more affected by anything which was not strictly my own grief, than I was by this sight. It will live in my recollection always. When I come to tell you something of my brief experience there, you will often think of it too.

We have been to both Houses of the Legislature to-day,[2] and have seen many of the Lions, both living and stuffed. I think of going every day while I remain here.

I went to the Presidents,[3] too, this morning, in company with a namesake who is Secretary to the Senate.[4] He has a good face, (I mean the President) and his manners are very mild and gentlemanly.[5] He expressed great surprise at my being so young. I would have returned the compliment; but he looked so jaded, that it stuck in my throat like Macbeth's amen.

Some twenty gentlemen were waiting in a lower room, for audiences. There is no denying that they *did* expectorate considerably. They wrought a complete change in the pattern of the carpet, even while I was there.—Before I forget it, let me ask you at what annual salary in Dollars, you would hold that office? Would you do it cheap—or dear?

---

[1] Weaving and shoe-making were the trades most commonly learnt in the Penitentiary.

[2] See *To* Fonblanque, 12 Mar, and *American Notes*, Ch. 8.

[3] Thus in MS. John Tyler (1790–1862; *DAB*), former Governor of Virginia. Vice-President under William Henry Harrison, he became President 4 Apr 41 on Harrison's death after one month in office. Carried through the Webster–Ashburton Treaty of Aug 42 and the annexation of Texas 1844. For his difficulties as President, see *To* Forster, 15 Mar, *fn*.

[4] Asbury Dickens: see 6 Mar, *fn*. On 12 Mar Catherine wrote to him: "My dear Mr. Dickens. | Charles has just shown me your kind note, and he begs me to say that he agrees with me in thinking we had better dine quietly here on Wednesday [*the day they left for Richmond*], as we have to get our English dispatches ready, and all the paying and packing to do previous to our departure. We have already refused two invitations for that day, but we will do ourselves the pleasure of calling in the course of the morning. | With kind regards to all your circle in which my husband joins | Believe me My dear Mr. Dickens | Yours very truly | Catherine Dickens" (MS Maine Historical Society).

[5] According to W. O. Stoddard, *William H. Harrison, John Tyler, and James K. Polk* (New York, 1888, p. 55), Tyler was "approachable and courteous in his official intercourse", with a "notable faculty . . . for telling a good story, and for making keen conversational hits"—hardly the impression gained from CD's account of this meeting in *To* Fonblanque, 12 Mar.

We start for Charleston on Wednesday next.[1] In the meanwhile if any news should reach you of the poor Caledonia, or our letters, I need not say how glad we shall be to receive it; or how happy we shall be to hear from you at all times and seasons. Those very small darlings we have left behind, hold Giants' places in our hearts; and that's the reason I suppose, why they are always full when we think of home.

We mean to wait at Charleston for the other letters you will send us, and which are now upon their way to you in the March Steamer from Liverpool. As we shall make no halt to speak of, between this place and Charleston, will you write to us, after we move from here, at

PAGE'S HOTEL, CHARLESTON, S.C.

Our route after that—whether it shall be back to New York, and so into Canada, or back to Baltimore, or back to Philadelphia, and thence to Pittsburgh and thereabout—I have not decided. But from Charleston, I will write to you again when I have received your packet there; with full and particular details.

God bless you. Give our united loves to Mrs. Colden and to Mrs. Wilkes,[2] and to "Mrs. S",[3] and Doctor Wilkes, and all friends—not forgetting the dear children and Nela Gibbs,[4] to whom I beg my especial regards. We often talk of you and yours, and devoutly wish you lived at Charleston as well as New York, and could be there when we are. But if our wishes could take effect, you would be very Jactars[5] in roving, so it's well they are nothing but affectionate breath. Ever my dear Colden

Faithfully Your friend
CHARLES DICKENS

To JOHN T. MAULL,[6] 10 MARCH 1842*

MS Colonel Richard Gimbel. *Address:*[7] John T. Maull | 83 Pine St | Philadelphia.

Washington | Tenth March 1842.

Dear Sir.

I am much obliged to you for the note you wrote me at Philadelphia, which place I left so hastily that I could not send you an earlier acknowledgment.[8] I had great pleasure, I assure you, in its Receipt.

Faithfully Yours

John. T. Maull Esquire   CHARLES DICKENS

---

[1] They in fact changed their plans and went to Richmond instead: see *To* Forster, 13 Mar.

[2] Mrs Colden's sister-in-law.

[3] Possibly Mrs Charles Sedgwick: see *To* Colden, 29 Apr.

[4] Unidentified; perhaps daughter of Thomas S. Gibbs (see 3 Mar).

[5] A joke form of Jack Tars.

[6] John Troubat Maull (1817–92), Philadelphia attorney.

[7] In Putnam's hand, written on outside of the folded sheet.

[8] They had left on the morning of the 9th, after a visit—so far as the public knew—of only two full days (*To* Putnam, 4 Mar, *fn*). The day he left, the *Philadelphia Gazette* commented: "It will be a matter of deep regret, if the presence of this distinguished private gentleman in this city should give rise to heart burnings and criminations among any portion of the

To UNKNOWN CORRESPONDENT, 10 MARCH 1842

Mention in John Heise catalogue, Dec 1943; dated Fuller's Hotel, 10 Mar 42.

Regretting that he cannot accept an invitation.

To JOHN QUINCY ADAMS,[1] [10 or 11 MARCH 1842]

Mention in Robert C. Winthrop,[2] *Reminiscences of Foreign Travel*, privately printed, [Boston], 1894, p. 62. *Date:* Adams had received the letter by Saturday 12th (see *fn*).

Refusing an invitation to dinner, but saying that he wished to have the privilege of coming, with his wife, to luncheon on Sunday.[3]

citizens of Philadelphia"—and then went on to its attack on the intrusion on CD's privacy organized by Gebler, Florence and others (see 20 Feb and *fn*), ending: "it is positively rude, if not exceedingly impertinent, for people promiscuously to trespass upon either the time or attention of private gentlemen, merely to gratify their vague, if not idle curiosity."

[1] John Quincy Adams (1767–1848; *DAB*), sixth American President 1825–9; son of John Adams, second President. From 1831 to his death served in the House of Representatives, where his political experience, integrity, fearlessness in debate and lack of Party allegiance made him a formidable figure. Although not an Abolitionist, he became the House's main channel for anti-slavery petitions, and fought the "Gag Rule" of 1836, which sought to prevent their discussion, against violent opposition and censure from Southern members, till it was at last rescinded in 1844. For CD's description of him, see *To* Fonblanque, 12 Mar. According to Robert C. Winthrop (*op. cit.*, p. 62), Adams did not appreciate CD's writings: he had read some of *Pickwick*, he said, but "could not get beyond a few chapters"; CD had "a wonderful faculty of description", he added, "but the difficulty is, the things are not worth describing!" There is, however, among his Papers (MS Massachusetts Historical Society) a gallant poem addressed to Catherine Dickens: "There is a greeting of the heart | Which words cannot reveal— | How, Lady, shall I then impart | The sentiment I feel. | How in one word combine the spell | Of joy and

sorrow too; | And mark the bosom's mingled swell | Of welcome!—and Adieu!"

[2] Robert Charles Winthrop (1809–94; *DAB*), Whig Representative from Massachusetts 1840–50; Everett's "most intimate political friend" (see *To* Everett, 1 Jan, *fn*).

[3] According to Winthrop, Adams told him of CD's letter on Sat 12 Mar and added: "Now, I have no idea of meeting him alone, and I want you and Mr. Saltonstall to come to my aid". Both went. CD and Catherine arrived late and left before the elaborate luncheon was over, to dress for dinner at 5.30 p.m. with Robert Greenhow, a translator in the State Dept (for CD's own reference to this engagement, see *To* Macready, 22 Mar). Winthrop, obviously rather shocked, continues: "and the table of the Ex-President was broken up accordingly! It was a curious instance of the infelicity of the 'previous engagements' into which Mr. Dickens had been betrayed by officious friends. He seemed rather to prefer dining with reporters and newspaper men than with persons in official position, and he occasionally exhibited a *brusquerie* and waywardness— perhaps resulting from the flattery he had received at Boston and New York—which led him to put on airs in the company of men entitled to his respect" (R. C. Winthrop, *op. cit.*, pp. 62–3). Philip Hone, another luncheon-guest, was similarly surprised: "A most particularly funny idea to leave the table of John Quincy Adams to dress for a dinner at Robert Greenhow's!" (*Diary of Philip Hone, 1828–51*, ed. B. Tuckerman, New York, 1889, II, 120).

To H. D. GILPIN,[1] 11 MARCH 1842*

MS Colonel Richard Gimbel.

Fuller's Hotel, Washington | Eleventh March 1842.

My Dear Sir

I thank you heartily for the letters;[2] and for your own kind epistle, which I have received with great pleasure.

I wish I could have remained longer in Philadelphia, but I am forced onward by my poverty of time—not by my will[3]—and in some sort following the example of that renowned Sultan to whose despotism we are indebted for so much delight, must go on making friendships over-night, and cutting their heads off, every morning.[4]

If the sharp and rapid severance of our pleasant intercourse should leave you any future opportunity of remembering me, I shall be glad to live in your recollection, and will honestly return the compliment.

Mrs. Dickens begs her kindest regards to yourself and Mrs. Gilpin[5]—in which I join—and I am always My Dear Sir

Faithfully Yours
CHARLES DICKENS

To MRS S. J. HALE,[6] 11 MARCH 1842

MS Huntington Library.

Private.   Fuller's Hotel, Washington | Eleventh of March 1842.
My Dear Madam.

I left Philadelphia so hurriedly, that I had not time to reply to your earnest and gratifying letter.

---

[1] Henry Dilworth Gilpin (1801–60; *DAB*), Philadelphia lawyer and politician. Born in England and spent four years at school there; brother of William Gilpin, first territorial Governor of Colorado. A Jacksonian Democrat, had ended his political career as Attorney-General (1840–1) in Van Buren's Administration. Argued and lost the *Amistad* negro slave case against J. Q. Adams (see *To* W. W. Story, 4 Feb, *fn*). Published *The Papers of James Madison*, 3 vols, 1840; and *The Opinions of the Attorneys-General of the United States*, 1841. From 1842 devoted himself to literary pursuits and classical scholarship. President of the Pennsylvania Academy of Fine Arts, Trustee of the University of Pennsylvania, and member of the Athenæum of Philadelphia—to which he introduced CD on 7 Mar (MS Visitors Register, Athenæum).

[2] Probably letters of introduction to Gilpin's Washington friends.

[3] Cf. *Romeo and Juliet*, v, i, 75: "My poverty, but not my will, consents".

[4] An allusion to the introductory section of *The Arabian Nights' Entertainments*; repeated by CD three days later in his speech at the dinner given by the Alleghany Club, and again in his speech at the Richmond "social supper", 18 Mar (see *Speeches*, ed. K. J. Fielding, pp. 33 and 35).

[5] *Née* Eliza Sibley, of N. Carolina; widow of Senator Josiah S. Johnston, of Louisiana. A well-known hostess.

[6] Sarah Josepha Hale, *née* Buell (1788–1879; *DAB*), literary editor of *Godey's Lady's Book*, Philadelphia, 1837–77. Had previously edited the *Ladies' Magazine*, Boston. Left a widow with five young children in 1822, she became a prolific writer of verse, essays and sketches, and a passionate advocate of women's education. Her books included *Woman's Record, or Sketches of Distinguished Women*, 1853 (a collection of 1500 biographies); and she

Believe me, that I did not read your beautiful lines unmoved; and that you could not have devised a mode of pleasing me more, than by the production of such a tribute.[1] I scarcely know how to thank you for it. As I am in that condition, however, wherein we are apt to feel that we cannot say enough, but in which a very little may be very expressive, I will only add that I thank you with my whole heart.

—On second thoughts though, I must couple with these latter words, one assurance, no less truthful and sincere. It is, that you will never find me departing from those sympathies which we cherish in common, and which have won me your esteem and approval.[2]

Mrs. Dickens unites with me in cordial regards and best wishes. And I am always

Dear Madam | Faithfully | Your friend

Mrs. S. J. Hale.   CHARLES DICKENS

To DAVID C. COLDEN, 12 MARCH 1842

Mention in unidentified catalogue, 4 Apr; *MS* 1 p.; dated Washington, 12 Mar 42.[3]

To ALBANY FONBLANQUE,[4] 12 [and ?21] MARCH 1842

MS Berg Collection. *Date:* for the finishing of letter on ?21 Mar, see *fn* p. 120. Like *To* Mitton, 22 Mar, it bears an English postmark of 21 Apr 42. *Address:* Albany Fonblanque Esquire | Connaught Square | Edgeware Road | London | England.

Washington (Fuller's Hotel) | Twelfth March 1842.

My Dear Fonblanque. I have reserved my fire upon you until I came to this place, thinking you would best like to know something about the political oddities of this land. No doubt you have heard the leading points in my adventures —as how we had a bad passage out, of 18 days—how I have been dined, and balled (there were 3000 people at the ball) and feted in all directions—and how I can't stir, without a great crowd at my heels—and am by no means in my element, in consequence. I shall therefore spare you these experiences, whereof Forster is a living chronicle; and carry you straightway to the President's house.[5]

It's a good house to look at, but—to follow out the common saying—an

considerably influenced Matthew Vassar, founder of Vassar College. She had met CD at the ball given for him in Boston (Diary of T. W. Higginson, quoted in E. F. Payne, *Dickens Days in Boston*, p. 48).

[1] Her verses, "The Welcome of Philadelphia to Charles Dickens", dated 22 Feb 42, are reprinted in *D*, XI (1915), 155.

[2] Perhaps refers to stanza 4: "For thou has[t] raised the lowly, | And made the wicked yield, | And wakened feelings holy, | The orphan poor to shield; . . ."

[3] Probably asking that their letters should be forwarded to Richmond, not to Charleston as arranged in *To* Colden, 10 Mar. For this change of plan, see *To* Forster, 13 Mar.

[4] Albany Fonblanque (1793–1872; *DNB*), editor of the *Examiner*: see Vol. I, p. 205*n*.

[5] While writing his chapter "Washington. The Legislature. And the President's House" for *American Notes* (Ch. 8), CD borrowed this letter from Fonblanque (see 26 Aug) and drew on it extensively.

uncommon bad 'un to go; at least I should think so. I arrived here on Wednesday night; and on Thursday morning was taken there by the Secretary to the
Senate: a namesake of mine, whom "John Tyler" had despatched to carry me
to him for a private interview which is considered a greater compliment than
the public audience. *a*We entered a large hall, and rang a large bell—if I may
judge from the size of the handle. Nobody answering the bell,[1] we walked about
on our own account, as divers other gentlemen (mostly with their hats on, and
their hands in their pockets) were doing, very leisurely. Some of them had
ladies with them to whom they were shewing the premises; others were lounging on the chairs and sofas; others, yawning and picking their teeth. The greater
part of this assemblage were rather asserting their supremacy than doing anything else; as they had no particular business there, that anybody knew of. A
few were eyeing the moveables as if to make quite sure that the President (who
is not popular)[2] hadn't made away with any of the furniture, or sold the fixtures
for his private benefit.

After glancing at these loungers who were scattered over a pretty drawing
room, furnished with blue and silver, opening upon a terrace with a beautiful
prospect of the Potomac River and adjacent country—and a larger state room,
not unlike the dining room at the Athenæum—we went up stairs into another
chamber, where were the more favored visitors who were waiting for audiences.
At sight of my conductor, a black in plain clothes and yellow slippers, who was
moving noiselessly about, and whispering messages in the ears of the more
impatient, made a sign of recognition and glided off to announce us.

There were some twenty men in the room. One, a tall, wiry, muscular old
man from the West, sunburnt and swarthy,—with a brown white hat and a giant
umbrella, who sat bolt upright in his chair, frowning steadily at the carpet, as
if he had made up his mind that he was going to "fix" the President in what he
had to say, and wouldn't bate him a grain. Another, a Kentucky farmer nearly
seven feet high, with his hat on, and his hands under his coat tails, who leaned
against the wall, and kicked the floor with his heel, as though he had Time's head
under his shoe, and were literally "killing" him. A third, a short, round-faced
man with sleek black hair cropped close, and whiskers and beard shaved down
into blue dots, who sucked the head of a big stick, and from time to time took
it out of his mouth to see how it was getting on. A fourth did nothing but
whistle.*a* The rest balanced themselves, now on one leg, and now on the other,
and chewed mighty quids of tobacco—such mighty quids, that they all looked
as if their faces were swoln with erisypelas. They all constantly squirted forth
upon the carpet, a yellow saliva which quite altered its pattern; and even the few
who did not indulge in this recreation, expectorated abundantly.

In five minutes time, the black in yellow slippers came back, and led us into
an upper room—a kind of office—where, by the side of a hot stove, though it was

aa Used nearly verbatim towards the end
of *American Notes*, Ch. 8.
[1] Cf. Dana's experience when he called
with Rufus Griswold at the President's
house and rang the bell (*Journal of R. H.
Dana, Jr.*, ed. R. F. Lucid, I, 242; entry

for 28 Feb 44): the door was opened by
"a clownish Irish servant ... shabbily
dressed, with dirty linen ... & an impudent,
sleepy expression".
[2] See *To* Forster, 15 Mar, *fn.*

a very hot day, sat the President—all alone; and close to him a great spit box, which is an indispensable article of furniture here. In the private sitting room in which I am writing this, there are two; one on each side of the fire place. They are made of brass, to match the fender and fire irons; and are as bright as decanter stands.—But I am wandering from the President. Well! The President got up, and said, "Is *this* Mr. Dickens?"—"Sir", returned Mr. Dickens—"it is". "I am astonished to see so young a man Sir", said the President. Mr. Dickens smiled, and thought of returning the compliment—but he didn't; for the President looked too worn and tired, to justify it. "I am happy to join with my fellow citizens in welcoming you, warmly, to this country", said the President. Mr. Dickens thanked him, and shook hands. Then the other Mr. Dickens, the secretary, asked the President to come to his house that night, which the President said he should be glad to do, but for the pressure of business, and measles. Then the President And the two Mr. Dickenses sat and looked at each other, until Mr. Dickens of London observed that no doubt the President's time was fully occupied, and he and the other Mr. Dickens had better go. Upon that they all rose up; and the President invited Mr. Dickens (of London) to come again, which he said he would. And that was the end of the conference.

From the President's house, I went up to the Capitol, and visited both the Senate, and the House of Representatives, which, as I dare say you know are under one roof. Both are of the amphitheatre form, and very tastefully fitted up; with large galleries for ladies, and for the public generally. In the Senate, which is much the smaller of the two, I made the acquaintance of everybody in the first quarter of an hour—among the rest of Clay, who is one of the most agreeable and fascinating men I ever saw. He is tall and slim, with long, limp, gray hair —a good head[1]—refined features—a bright eye—a good voice—and a manner more frank and captivating than I ever saw in any man, at all advanced in life. I was perfectly charmed with him.[2] In the other house, John Quincey Adams interested me very much. He is something like Rogers,[3] but not so infirm; is very accomplished; and perfectly "game".[4] The rest were in appearance a

---

[1] Cf. CD's mocking disclaimer in *American Notes* (Ch. 8), when asked whether he "had not been very much impressed by the *heads* of the lawmakers at Washington; meaning not their chiefs and leaders, but literally their . . . personal heads, whereon their hair grew"—a phrenological question by which he refused to be drawn. For George Combe's analysis of Clay's personality after studying his head on a visit to Congress, see his *Notes on the United States of North America during a Phrenological Visit in 1838-9-40*, II, 96.

[2] Harriet Martineau, who knew Clay well, commented: "His mode of talking, deliberate and somewhat formal, including sometimes a grave humour, and sometimes a gentle sentiment, very touching from the lips of a sagacious man of ambition, has but one fault,—its obvious adaptation to the supposed state of mind of the person to whom it is addressed" (*Retrospect of Western Travel*, I, 290-1).

[3] Samuel Rogers (1763-1855; *DNB*): see Vol. I, p. 602n. Cf. Dr Pliny Earle, who found Rogers "much resembling the late John Quincy Adams", on meeting him at a dinner party of CD's, 5 July 49: *Memoirs of Pliny Earle, M.D., with Extracts from his Diary and Letters (1830-1892)*, ed. F. B. Sanborn, p. 290.

[4] "He put one in mind of a fine old gamecock", said Lord Morpeth, who had heard him defend the right of petition in the House a short time before (*Travels in America*: see below)—though Philip Hone recorded that his manner of doing so was "equally calculated to disgust his friends and exasperate his enemies, and . . . alienate the respect which all are disposed

good deal like our own members—some of them very bilious-looking, some very rough, some heartily good natured, and some very coarse. I asked which was Mr. Wyse,[1] who lives in my mind, from the circumstance of his having made a very violent speech about England t'other day,[2] which he emphasized (with great gentlemanly feeling and good taste) by pointing, as he spoke, at Lord Morpeth[3] who happened to be present.[4] They pointed out a wild looking, evil-visaged man, something like Roebuck,[5] but much more savage, with a great ball of tobacco in his left cheek.[6] I was quite satisfied.

I didn't see the honorable member who on being called to order by another honorable member some three weeks since, said "Damn your eyes Sir, if you presume to call *me* to order, I'll cut your damnation throat from ear to ear";— he wasn't there—but they shewed me the honorable member to whom he addressed this rather strong Parliamentary language; and I was obliged to content myself with him.[7]

to render to his consummate learning and admirable talents" (*Diary*, ed. A. Nevins, p. 581). The struggle had reached a climax in Jan in a motion to censure the 73-year-old Adams for presenting a petition "to dissolve the Union"; but on 7 Feb Adams emerged triumphant over his Southern pro-slavery opponents, and presented nearly 200 more petitions before the House adjourned.

[1] Mis-spelt by CD. Henry Alexander Wise (1806–76; *DAB*), of an old Virginia family. Representative from Virginia 1833–44. Close friend of Tyler's and leader of his supporters in Congress. An aggressive defender of Southern rights and slavery, he was J. Q. Adams's chief opponent on anti-slavery petitions—attacking him, wrote Hone, "in language which the veriest demagogue of a porterhouse would blush to use to his vulgar associates" (*Diary*, ed. A. Nevins, p. 581). Democratic Governor of Virginia 1856–60; Confederate General 1861. Published *Seven Decades of the Union*, 1872, mostly a review and eulogy of Tyler's life.

[2] During the debate on the petition "to dissolve the Union" in Jan, Wise had, in an abusive attack, accused Adams of belonging to an English party in the U.S.A. which wanted to destroy American institutions.

[3] George William Frederick Howard, Viscount Morpeth, later 7th Earl of Carlisle (1802–64; *DNB*): see Vol. II, p. 447 and *n*. Whig MP 1826 until the Govt's defeat in 1841; now spending a year in America and Canada. A close friend of Sumner's, he met most of CD's hosts; was

publicly entertained in New York; and travelled through 22 of the 26 States (see *To* Lady Holland, 22 Mar, *fn*). An abhorrer of slavery, he paid particular respect to leading Abolitionists (see O. Cromwell, *Lucretia Mott*, p. 105). Kept a journal during his visit on which he based a lecture (mainly appreciative, apart from an attack on slavery) to the Leeds Mechanics' Institute in Dec 50, published in his *Two Lectures on the Poetry of Pope, and . . . Travels in America*, Leeds, 1851.

[4] Cf. the *New York American*, quoted in Forster's "The Newspaper Literature of America", *Foreign Quarterly Review*, Oct 42, XXX, 220: "Lord Morpeth . . . was apparently the person to whom Wise directed all his swaggering, bullying abuse of the British nation and government. Whenever he said any thing abusive, he always turned to the Viscount, and pointed significantly at him, apparently delighted to insult a stranger and a lord, without the possibility of a reply."

[5] John Arthur Roebuck (1801–79; *DNB*), outspoken Radical, friend of J. S. Mill, and Independent MP for Bath 1832–7, 1841–7, later for Sheffield; attacked all who disagreed with him so vehemently as to earn for himself the nickname "Tear 'em". For his connection with the *Westminster Review*, see *To* Sumner, 13 Mar and *fn*.

[6] Wise is described by the Congress reporter B. P. Poore as having "a complexion saffron-hued, from his inordinate use of tobacco, and coarse, long hair, brushed back from his low forehead" (*Perley's Reminiscences*, Philadelphia, [1886], I, 278).

[7] According to Forster's "The News-

Yesterday, I went there again. A debate was in progress concerning the removal of a certain postmaster, charged with mal-practises, and with having interfered in elections.[1] The speaking I heard, was partly what they call "Stump Oratory"—meaning that kind of eloquence which is delivered in the West, from that natural rostrum[2]—and partly, a dry and prosy chopping of very small logic into very small mincemeat. It was no worse than ours, and no better. One gentleman being interrupted by a laugh from the opposition, mimicked the laugh, as a child would in quarrelling with another child, and said that "before he had done he'd make honorable members sing out, a little more on the other side of their mouths". This was the most remarkable sentiment I heard, in the course of a couple of hours.

I said something just now, about the prevalence of spit-boxes. They are everywhere. In hospitals, prisons, watch-houses, and courts of law—on the bench, in the witness box, in the jury box, and in the gallery; in the stage coach, the steam boat, the rail road car, the hotel, the hall of a private gentleman, and the chamber of Congress; where every two men have one of these conveniences between them—and very unnecessarily, for they flood the carpet, while they talk to you. Of all things in this country, this practice is to me the most insufferable. I can bear anything but filth. I would be content even to live in an atmosphere of spit, if they would but *spit clean*; but when every man ejects from his mouth that odious, most disgusting, compound of saliva and tobacco, I vow that my stomach revolts, and I cannot endure it. The marble stairs and passages of every handsome public building are polluted with these abominable stains; they are squirted about the base of every column that supports the roof; and they make the floors brown, despite the printed entreaty that visitors will not disfigure them with "tobacco spittle". It is the most sickening, beastly, and abominable custom that ever civilization saw.

When an American gentleman is polished, he *is* a perfect gentleman. Coupled with all the good qualities that such an Englishman possesses, he has a warmth of heart and an earnestness, to which I render up myself hand and heart. Indeed the whole people have most affectionate and generous impulses. I have not travelled anywhere, yet, without making upon the road a pleasant acquaintance

paper Literature of America", *Foreign Quarterly Review*, XXX, 221, the speaker was General Dawson of Louisiana; the man addressed, Mr Arnold of Tennessee. CD refers to the incident in *American Notes*, Ch. 8. Forster had possibly derived the information from CD's diary (he gives no source).

[1] This is not recorded in the *Congressional Globe* for 11 Mar. CD seems to have misunderstood the subject: most of the day's acrimonious debate arose from a proposal to withhold the salary of the First Auditor of the Treasury, charged with gross neglect of duty over the misappropriation by Samuel Swartwout, Collector of the Port of New York 1829–38, of a million dollars.

The proposal was obviously a political attack on Tyler's Administration. See CD's reference in *Chuzzlewit*, Ch. 34, to "a western postmaster, who, being a public defaulter not very long before (a character not at all uncommon in America), had been removed from office"; on whose behalf Elijah Pogram had thundered a defence, "from his seat in Congress, at the head of an unpopular President."

[2] Explained by CD as if an Americanism unfamiliar in England. In *OED* given as originally *U.S.*; first example Jefferson 1813; not necessarily derogatory. The term was popularized in England as a Yankeeism by Carlyle's *Latter-Day Pamphlets*, 1850.

who has gone out of his way to serve and assist me. I have never met with any common man who would not have been hurt and offended if I had offered him money, for any trifling service he has been able to render me. Gallantry and deference to females are universal. No man wod. retain his seat in a public conveyance to the exclusion of a lady, or hesitate for an instant in exchanging places with her, however much to his discomfort, if the wish were but remotely hinted. They are generous, hospitable, affectionate, and kind. I have been obliged to throw open my doors at a certain hour, in every place I have visited, and receive from 300 to 7 or 800 people; but I have never once been asked a rude or impertinent question, except by an Englishman—and when an Englishman has been settled here for ten or twelve years, he is worse than the Devil.[1] [2]

For all this, I would not live here two years—no, not for any gift they could bestow upon me. Apart from my natural desire to be among my friends and to be at home again, I have a yearning after our English Customs and english[3] manners, such as you cannot conceive. It would be impossible to say, in this compass, in what respects America differs from my preconceived opinion of it, but between you and me—privately and confidentially—I shall be truly glad to leave it, though I have formed a perfect attachment to many people here, and have a public progress through the Land, such as it never saw, except in the case of Lafayette.[4] I am going away, now, into the Far West. A public entertainment has been arranged in every town I have visited; but I found it absolutely necessary to decline them—with one reservation.—I am going now, to meet a whole people of my readers in the Far West—two thousand miles from N. York—on the borders of the Indian Territory!

Since I wrote the inclosed sheet,[5] I have had an Invitation from the President

---

[1] Repeated in *To* Forster, 15 Mar. Cf. Harriet Martineau: "One of the first impressions of a foreigner in New York is of the extreme insolence and vulgarity of certain young Englishmen, who thus make themselves very conspicuous. Well-mannered Englishmen are scarcely distinguishable from the natives, and thus escape observation" (*Retrospect of Western Travel*, I, 54).

[2] Either at this point in the letter (the bottom of p. 4 of a folded quarto sheet) or —less probably—at the end of the previous paragraph, CD clearly set the letter aside, unfinished. No change in ink or handwriting is evident, but several statements in the paragraphs which follow could only have been written at a later date. Probably he completed the letter on the morning of 21 Mar, at Washington (to which he had returned from Richmond on the evening of the 20th and which he left for Baltimore in the afternoon of the 21st). Cf. his first dated reference to his decision to go "two thousand miles" west of New York, to the "confines of the Indian territory", in *To*

Forster, 21 Mar ("At Washington again").

[3] Thus, with a small "e", in MS.

[4] Marie Joseph Paul Roch Yves Gilbert Motier, Marquis de La Fayette (1757–1834), "the hero of two worlds", had visited America four times: see *A Pilgrimage of Liberty: a Contemporary Account of the Triumphal Tour of General Lafayette through the Southern and Western States in 1825, as Reported by the Local Newspapers*, ed. Edgar E. Brandon, Ohio, 1944. Of CD, Ticknor wrote to Kenyon: "A triumph has been prepared for him in which the whole country will join. He will have a progress through the States unequalled since Lafayette's" (F, III, ii, 210). See also Lyell's journal entry, 1 Feb (*To* Mitton, 31 Jan, *fn*). The comparison was frequently made in newspapers, though in fact as early as 27 Jan, the *New York Morning Courier* had feared the Americans would make themselves ridiculous by honouring CD to that extent. For one disadvantage to CD himself, see *To* Forster, 13 Mar.

[5] He was now writing on the inside of the cover-sheet which bore the address.

to dinner. I couldn't go: being obliged to leave Washington before the day he named.[1] But Mrs. Dickens and I went to the public drawing room[2] where pretty nearly all the natives go, who choose. It was most remarkable and most striking to see the perfect order observed—without one soldier, sailor, constable, or policeman in attendance, within the house or without; though the crowd was immense.

I have been as far South, as Richmond in Virginia.[3]—I needn't say how odious the sight of Slavery is,[4] or how frantic the holders are in their wrath against England, because of this Creole business.[5]—If you see Forster soon, ask him how the Negroes drive in rough roads.[6]

And if you should ever have time to scratch a few lines to a poor transported man, address them to the care of David Colden Esquire 28 Laight Street, Hudson Square, New York. He will forward them to me wherever I be. You must do on your side, what I can't do on this—pay the postage—or your letter will come back to you.

How long will the Tory Ministry last?[7] Say six months, and receive my blessing.

Mrs. Dickens unites with me in best regards to Mrs. Fonblanque[8] and her sister.[9] And I am always, My Dear Fonblanque

Faithfully Your friend

CHARLES DICKENS

[1] He left on the 16th.

[2] On 15 Mar (*To* Forster, that day)—the last levee of the season, attended by the Cabinet, several Foreign Ministers, Judges, Senators, and over 50 Representatives. CD and Irving (in Washington to receive his instructions before leaving for Spain) were treated as the chief of the 1500 guests present. Both the *New York Express* and the *Baltimore Patriot* described CD as the greatest lion there, and B. P. Poore wrote that he "totally eclipsed" Irving (*Perley's Reminiscences*, I, 298); but, according to Hone, "Irving out-bozzed Boz" (*Diary*, ed. A. Nevins, p. 591). Mrs Robert Tyler, the President's daughter-in-law, wrote, after meeting CD at the levee: "He is not at all romantic looking, is rather thick set, and wears entirely too much jewelry, very English in his appearance, and not the best English. He was accompanied by his wife, quite a sweet-looking, plump woman, tastelessly dressed, and more English looking than Boz himself. Poor fellow, he seemed horribly bored by the crowd pressing around" (E. T. Coleman, *Priscilla Cooper Tyler and the American Scene 1816–1889*, Alabama, 1955, pp. 96–7). As they left, the coloured drivers shouted: "Lord Boz's carriage! Lord Boz's carriage!" (Robert C. Winthrop, *Reminiscences of Foreign Travel*, p. 61).

[3] He arrived there 17 Mar.

[4] See *To* Forster, 21 Mar.

[5] One of the outstanding causes of the Southern States' hatred of Britain. In the previous Nov slaves on the *Creole*, an American ship sailing from Hampton Roads, Virginia, to New Orleans, had overpowered the crew, killed one of their owners, and put into the British port of Nassau. The British freed all except those charged with the murder, and refused to surrender them to the American authorities. The affair caused intense controversy. As Secretary of State, Webster wrote a strong and carefully argued protest against the English Govt's action, answered by Channing in a pamphlet, *The Duty of the Free States* (2 parts, May and June 42)—of which Sumner and Hillard revised the proofs (E. L. Pierce, *Memoir and Letters of Charles Sumner*, II, 194). Britain finally paid an indemnity of $110,000 in 1853.

[6] Described by CD in his letter to Forster of 17 Mar, but omitted in F, III, iv, 239, because used in *American Notes*, Ch. 9.

[7] Peel's ministry, in office since Aug 41. It lasted until June 1846.

[8] Daughter of Capt. Keane, of Meath, Ireland.

[9] Nothing is known of her.

To CHARLES MURRAY,[1] JAMES HOBAN,[2] AND PHILLIP ENNIS,[3] 12 MARCH 1842

Text from the *National Intelligencer*, 23 Mar 42.

Washington, March 12, 1842

Gentlemen,

I am truly obliged to you for your kind and flattering invitation.[4] It would have afforded me the greatest pleasure to accept it, but I regret to say that I leave this city on the 16th, and have made arrangements for doing so, which I cannot depart from.

Accept my cordial thanks, and believe me, gentlemen, yours, faithfully and obliged,

CHARLES DICKENS

To J. G. TOTTEN,[5] 12 MARCH 1842*

MS Berg Collection.

Washington | Twelfth March 1842.

Mr. Charles Dickens presents his compts. to Colonel Totten; and thanking him exceedingly for his kind note, very much regrets that both himself and Mrs. Dickens are engaged for every day during their short sojourn in Washington. Under more fortunate circumstances, it would have afforded them sincere pleasure to have accepted Colonel Totten's hospitable offer, and to have "named the day".

To GEORGE WATTERSTON,[6] 12 MARCH 1842*

MS Huntington Library.

Fuller's Hotel, Washington | Twelfth March 1842.

My Dear Sir

I am truly obliged to you for the interesting book[7] you have been good enough

---

[1] Perhaps Charles Murray of Washington, Navy purser from Mar 43.

[2] James Hoban (1809–46), U.S. District Attorney for Columbia; son of James Hoban, the Irish-born architect of the White House.

[3] Perhaps Philip Ennis of Washington, "meat cellar" according to directory.

[4] To a St Patrick's Day dinner at Fuller's Hotel, Washington. Philip Ennis was one of the Vice-Presidents. John Tyler and J. Q. Adams also declined invitations.

[5] Colonel Joseph Gilbert Totten (1788–1864; *DAB*), Chief Engineer of the U.S. Army and Inspector of the U.S. Military Academy, West Point since 1838. Brig.-Gen. 1863. Fort Totten in New York harbour was named after him.

[6] George Watterston (1783–1854; *DAB*), of Scottish descent; novelist, librarian and journalist; editor of the *Washington National Journal* since 1830. Librarian of Congress 1815–29, when summarily displaced by President Jackson. Secretary of the Washington National Monument Society 1833 to his death. Besides novels, published numerous guide-books, biographical sketches and text-books.

[7] Probably Watterston's *A Picture of Washington*, Washington, 1840.

to send me; and for the kind and gratifying expressions with which you have accompanied it. Accept my sincere thanks; and believe me, dear Sir

Faithfully Yours

George Watterston Esquire   CHARLES DICKENS

To JOHN FORSTER, 13 MARCH 1842

Extract in F, III, iv, 235–7 (continuation of letter of 6 Mar).

Washington, Sunday, March the Thirteenth 1842.

In allusion to the last sentence,[1] my dear friend, I must tell you a slight experience I had in Philadelphia. My rooms had been ordered for a week, but, in consequence of Kate's illness, only Mr. Q and the luggage had gone on. Mr. Q always lives at the table d'hôte, so that while we were in New York our rooms were empty. The landlord not only charged me half the full rent for the time during which the rooms were reserved for us (which was quite right), but charged me also *for board for myself and Kate and Anne, at the rate of nine dollars per day* for the same period, when we were actually living, at the same expense, in New York!!! I *did* remonstrate upon this head; but was coolly told it was the custom (which I have since been assured is a lie), and had nothing for it but to pay the amount. What else could I do? I was going away by the steamboat at five o'clock in the morning; and the landlord knew perfectly well that my disputing an item of his bill would draw down upon me the sacred wrath of the newspapers, which would one and all demand in capitals if THIS was the gratitude of the man whom America had received as she had never received any other man but La Fayette?

I went last Tuesday to the Eastern Penitentiary near Philadelphia,[2] which is the only prison in the States, or I believe in the world, on the principle of hopeless, strict, and unrelaxed solitary confinement, during the whole term of the sentence. It is wonderfully kept, but a most dreadful, fearful place. The inspectors, immediately on my arrival in Philadelphia, invited me to pass the day in the jail, and to dine with them when I had finished my inspection, that they might hear my opinion of the system. Accordingly I passed the whole day in going from cell to cell, and conversing with the prisoners.[3] Every facility was given me, and no constraint whatever imposed upon any man's free speech. If I were to write you a letter of twenty sheets, I could not tell you this one day's work; so I will reserve it until that happy time when we shall sit round the table at Jack Straw's—you, and I, and Mac—and go over my diary.[4] I never shall

---

[1] Concerning overcharging at hotels.

[2] See *To* Colden, 10 Mar and *fn.*

[3] For descriptions of the prisoners he talked with, see *American Notes*, Ch. 6, and for his description of one, a sailor, *To* Colden, 10 Mar.

[4] See *To* Forster, 22 Sep 41; II, 388. The diary has apparently not survived, but was still in CD's possession in 1850 when he drew on it in a long footnote to "Pet

Prisoners" (*Household Words*, I, 100; *Miscellaneous Papers*, ed. B. W. Matz, 1914), in commenting on and correcting at several points the Rev. J. Field's attack on his account of the Penitentiary. For instance, Field had quoted a Philadelphia paper's statement that CD had spent only two hours there, but CD had at the time recorded in his diary that he left his hotel for the prison at noon, "being waited on,

be able to dismiss from my mind, the impressions of that day. Making notes of them, as I have done, is an absurdity, for they are written, beyond all power of erasure, in my brain. I saw men who had been there, five years, six years, eleven years, two years, two months, two days; some whose term was nearly over, and some whose term had only just begun. Women too, under the same variety of circumstances. Every prisoner who comes into the jail, comes at night; is put into a bath, and dressed in the prison garb; and then a black hood is drawn over his face and head, and he is led to the cell from which he never stirs again until his whole period of confinement has expired. I looked at some of them with the same awe as I should have looked at men who had been buried alive, and dug up again.

We dined in the jail: and I told them after dinner how much the sight had affected me, and what an awful punishment it was. I dwelt upon this; for, although the inspectors are extremely kind and benevolent men, I question whether they are sufficiently acquainted with the human mind to know what it is they are doing.[1] Indeed, I am sure they do not know. I bore testimony, as every one who sees it must, to the admirable government of the institution (Stanfield[2] is the keeper: grown a little younger, that's all); but added that nothing could justify such a punishment, but its working a reformation in the prisoners. That for short terms—say two years for the maximum[3]—I conceived, especially after what they had told me of its good effects in certain cases, it might perhaps be highly beneficial,[4] but that, carried to so great an extent, I thought it cruel and unjustifiable; and further, that their sentences for small offences were very rigorous, not to say savage. All this, they took like men who were really anxious to have one's free opinion, and to do right. And we were very much pleased with each other, and parted in the friendliest way.[5]

by appointment, by the gentlemen who showed it to him", and returned between 7 and 8 p.m.—i.e. virtually spent the "whole day" there.

[1] Cf. *American Notes*, Ch. 7: "I hold this slow and daily tampering with the mysteries of the brain, to be immeasurably worse than any torture of the body".

[2] A man resembling Clarkson Stanfield.

[3] Cf. Pentonville, opened Dec 42, a small-scale experiment on the separate system, where the maximum term of imprisonment was 18 months—regarded as a period of probation in which prisoners could be taught trades before transportation.

[4] See the view he expressed in *To* Colden, 10 Mar. But cf. *American Notes*, Ch. 7: "I hesitated once, debating with myself, whether, if I had the power of saying 'Yes' or 'No,' I would allow it to be tried in certain cases, where the terms of imprisonment were short; but now, I solemnly declare, that with no rewards or honours could I walk a happy man . . . with the consciousness that one human creature, for any length of time, . . . lay suffering this unknown punishment in his silent cell". (By 1850 he had thought of many objections to the system other than the prisoners' suffering: see "Pet Prisoners".)

[5] That CD and his hosts had parted thus, no-one has disputed; but what criticisms he made of the Penitentiary, at the time, seem to have gone unnoticed. Samuel R. Wood (a former Warden), for instance, wrote: "I met CD, by invitation, at the Eastern Penitentiary, . . . and was with him most of the time; and . . . I heard the remarks he made before he left. We again met at *Harrisburg* and visited the *Dauphin County* Prison, then nearly completed, but not occupied. And on these occasions he said much in favour of both prisons, *but not one word against the system of Separate Confinement*" (*Pennsylvania Journal of Prison Discipline*, I [1845], 204). The publication of the account in *American Notes* came therefore as a shock to supporters of

They sent me back to Philadelphia in a carriage they had sent for me in the morning; and then I had to dress in a hurry, and follow Kate to Cary's[1] the bookseller's, where there was a party. He married a sister[2] of Leslie's.[3] There are three Miss Leslies[4] here, very accomplished; and one of them has copied all her brother's principal pictures.[5] These copies hang about the room. We got away from this as soon as we could; and next morning had to turn out at five. In the morning I had received and shaken hands with five hundred people,[6] so

the Philadelphia system, and the fact that the Boston Prison Discipline Society—which favoured the Auburn system—appended CD's account to its Annual Report, 1843, made matters worse. A vehement attack on its use of CD's "pathetic remarks . . . all addressed to the feelings, and not to the understanding" was published in the *Report of a Minority of the Special Committee of the Boston Prison Discipline Society, Appointed at the Annual Meeting, May 27, 1845*, Boston, 1846, pp. 12–13. Earlier, a refutation by Francis Lieber of CD's description of the sobbing girl had appeared in the *Philadelphia Inquirer and National Gazette* (15 Nov 43). At the request of the Philadelphia Prison Society, William Peter, British Consul-General in the city, investigated the history of each prisoner CD had described, and published his findings in a letter dated 25 Jan 45 in the *Pennsylvania Journal of Prison Discipline* (I, 86–8): with one exception ("the black burglar") each of them, after discharge, was known to be "doing well". Criticism of CD became increasingly bitter. The *Pennsylvania Journal*, I (1845), 48, attacked his "sickly fancy" which worked up the material furnished "into ghosts and hobgoblins, for the entertainment of his credulous admirers". In *Prisons and Prisoners*, 1845, Joseph Adshead (an Englishman) denounced him as "this fugacious prison inspector . . . with an effrontery unwarranted by his age or experience"; and the Rev. J. Field, in *Prison Discipline. The Advantages of the Separate System of Imprisonment*, 1846, p. 93, declared that "shameful advantage [had] been taken of the general want of information" on a subject "of by far too serious a nature for discussion in a mere volume of amusement" (a description derided by CD in his footnote to "Pet Prisoners").

[1] Thus in F. Henry Charles Carey (1793–1879; *DAB*), publisher and political economist; head (1825–34) of Carey & Lea, Philadelphia—founded by his father, an Irish political refugee. Though opposed to international copyright, one of the first American publishers to pay royalties to British authors: to Scott, for instance, an average of £75 for each of the *Waverley* novels, and £295 ($1475) for his *Life of Napoleon Buonaparte* (see David Kaser, *Messrs. Carey & Lea of Philadelphia*, Philadelphia, 1957). Since 1837 Carey had virtually retired from the firm, devoting himself to research in social science and to business ventures. Originally an advocate of free trade, he became the acknowledged leader of the American protectionist school. Paid three visits to Europe, but disliked England.

[2] Martha Leslie *d.* 1847); they had married 1819.

[3] Charles Robert Leslie (1794–1859; *DNB*, *DAB*), painter: see Vol. II, p. 395*n*. He had given CD a letter of introduction to the Careys (E. P. Oberholtzer, *Literary History of Philadelphia*, Philadelphia, 1906, p. 345).

[4] CD was presumably including Mrs Carey, as Leslie had only two other sisters, Eliza and Anne. Eliza Leslie (1787–1858; *DAB*) wrote cookery books, books on domestic economy and children's stories; was a frequent contributor to *Graham's Magazine* and *Godey's Lady's Book*; and edited *The Gift*, an Annual. Her *Domestic Cookery Book*, 1837, had run to 41 editions by 1851. Anne Leslie painted portraits; she had lived with her brother Charles in London during 1824, and many of his letters printed in *Autobiographical Recollections* (ed. Tom Taylor, 2 vols, 1860) are addressed to her.

[5] Clearly Anne. Most of Leslie's original pictures are in England, many in the Victoria & Albert Museum.

[6] At the reception presided over by T. B. Florence: see *To* Gebler and Others, 20 Feb, *fn*.

you may suppose that I was pretty well tired. Indeed I am obliged to be very careful of myself; to avoid smoking and drinking; to get to bed soon; and to be particular in respect of what I eat. . . . You cannot think how bilious and trying the climate is. One day it is hot summer, without a breath of air; the next, twenty degrees below freezing, with a wind blowing that cuts your skin like steel. These changes have occurred here several times since last Wednesday night.

I have altered my route, and don't mean to go to Charleston. The country, all the way from here, is nothing but a dismal swamp; there is a bad night of sea-coasting in the journey; the equinoctial gales are blowing hard; and Clay (a most *charming* fellow, by the bye), whom I have consulted, strongly dissuades me. The weather is intensely hot there; the spring fever is coming on; and there is very little to see, after all. We therefore go next Wednesday night to Richmond, which we shall reach on Thursday. There, we shall stop three days; my object being to see some tobacco plantations. Then we shall go by James river back to Baltimore,[1] which we have already passed through,[2] and where we shall stay two days. Then we shall go West at once, straight through the most gigantic part of this continent: across the Alleghany-mountains, and over a prairie.

To CHARLES SUMNER, 13 MARCH 1842

MS Harvard College Library.

Washington. | Thirteenth March 1842.—Sunday.
My Dear Sumner.

Hood says of a man in a quandary, in one of his books, that he could no more collect himself than the Irish Tithes.[3] I was really in this plight, when I opened your hundred times welcome letter last night. I thought the hand writing looked reproachfully at me; reminding me of solemn promises to correspond, all violated—and of a hundred good intentions unfulfilled. But I know you will forgive me. I do a good deal of work as a Paviour in Hell, in common with most men; but I keep many pledges too. And I would have kept these, religiously (and interestedly, too, for the pleasure of hearing from you) if I had had but time—which is one of the few good things your countrymen don't give me.

You cannot think how glad we are to know that you have thought about us, and our letters, and that poor Caledonia which I have quite given over. Her non-arrival has been, of course, a sad disappointment, and has filled us with weary longings for news of home. It is a strange feeling to think of some odd little blotted scrawl which one of our small toddlers believed to be a letter, lying at the bottom of the deep sea, among drowned men, and fragments of fine Ships, and such serious, uncongenial company; but when I think how easily we might have been ourselves in that dread plight, and how strange, it seems that we, who have so many friends about us, should not have deferred our departure until

[1] They in fact stayed a night at Washington on their way to Baltimore.

[2] On their way to Washington (see *To* Colden, 10 Mar, *fn*).

[3] Quotation untraced.

February, that we might have had our Christmas Time at home, unbroken, I thank God we are here, and am ashamed that a thought of those pieces of paper —packages of love and affection though they be—should mingle with our anxiety for the poor passengers, and their friends and children in such desolate expectation.

As to the agent,[1] he is paid for his faith; and I no more believe in it, than I do in that of a bishopric-aspiring parson.

I have seen no place, yet, that I like so well as Boston. I hope I may be able to return there, but I fear not. We are now in the regions of slavery, spittoons, and senators—all three are evils in all countries, but the spittoon is the worst. I don't see the use of it, either. If it be in deference to the opinion of society, I, for one, would rather not be obliged to imagine constantly what may be inside that circular orifice. I prefer the box of sand which is a candid piece of furniture and invites contemplation. But why one should be troubled with either, when everybody uses the carpet, is not satisfactorily proved to me by any means.

There are many men in both houses with whom I am greatly taken, but I confess a wild attachment to Clay. He is a fine fellow, and has won my heart. —Did John Quincey[2] Adams ever remind you of Rogers? When the President speaks to you, he curls up his legs as I thought nobody but Talfourd could. Mr. Wyse[2] is like Roebuck of the Westminster Review[3]—or like what Roebuck would have been, if he had been suckled, Romulus-like, by a wolf and had been savage all his boyhood.

We have altered our route, and don't mean to go to Charleston. We leave here on Wednesday Night for Richmond, where we shall stop three days. On Monday, we shall go down James River to Baltimore, where we shall stay two days. Then we shall proceed along the line of internal improvement,[4] over the Mountains, to Pittsburgh, which is a three days halting place; thence into Kentucky, to Lexington, Louisville, and so forth: then down the lakes to Buffalo where we shall arrive, please God, upon the Thirtieth of April or the first of May. And after some days at Niagara, we shall run into Canada. We embark in a packet ship from New York, on the Seventh of June.—There are our plans. All correspondence will be gratefully received, and thankfully acknowledged.

I miss Felton sadly.[5] Half the pleasure of my world, as Charles Lamb says,

---

[1] The Cunard Co.'s agent in Boston.

[2] Mis-spelt thus in MS, as elsewhere.

[3] John Bowring (see 15 July 43, *fn*), first editor of the *Westminster Review*, later recalled "the exceedingly pungent articles which emanated from the pens" of James Mill, W. J. Fox, Grote, Roebuck, and many others "who came forward in the van" of the philosophical radicals writing for the *Review* (*Autobiographical Recollections*, 1877, p. 67). He described Roebuck himself as "an able but unmanageable man, sharp, severe", but his articles as "all remarkable for their soundness of view and clearness of expression. He brought as much common sense into his writings as ever did Cobbett,

and far more of instruction—the result of study and reflection" (pp. 75, 76).

[4] i.e. on the Baltimore and Ohio Railroad (opened 1830) as far as York; thence by road to Harrisburg; thence to Pittsburgh, 350 miles due West, by the Main Line Canal (opened 1834). The canal, whose boats crossed the Alleghany Mountains by means of the Portage Railroad (see *To* Forster, 28 Mar), was the most impressive of Pennsylvania's internal improvements.

[5] CD had been with him constantly in New York. On 22 Feb Samuel Ward wrote to Longfellow: "One thing that will give you satisfaction is Felton's having seen him

has gone with him.¹ I used to remonstrate with him on his eating so many oysters—at such a distance from home.² He commonly took them fried. Perhaps that saved him. I would give—I hardly know what I would not give—to have him at No 1 Devonshire Terrace, York Gate Regents Park, London; for I have a sincere affection for him.

Don't you think you could come to Buffalo—stay at Niagara with us—and run into Canada to see some of the pleasant Englishmen there about?³ Think of it —Do—You know what became of that young man (*he* was a lawyer, I have no doubt) who was always at work, and never at play; he was a dull dog at last. Be wise in time. You ask me what you can do for me—this.

Always believe me, My Dear Sumner,

(with my wife's best regards)

Faithfully and cordially Your friend

Charles Sumner Esquire   CHARLES DICKENS

Remember me to Mr. and Mrs. Hillard, and Bancroft, and Prescott,⁴ and all friends. I don't like Mrs. Governor Davis. She is too good a housekeeper, and has a hungry eye.⁵ The papers say that Govr. Seward⁶ and some other men are invited to pay a visit there. If you care for anybody that's asked, write him an anonymous letter & tell him Not to go on any Terms.⁷

To JOHN BARNEY,⁸ 14 MARCH [1842]

Extract in Anderson Galleries catalogue, May 1913; dated Fuller's Hotel, 14 Mar.

I shall probably be in Baltimore on Monday Night. I shall remain there two

daily and almost hourly. They have walked, laughed, talked, eaten oysters and drunk champagne together—in fact, nothing but the interference of Madame D—— prevented their being attached to each other like the Siamese twins, *a volume of 'Pickwick' serving as connecting membrane.* Imagine their swinging up Broadway, the grave Eliot-Professor, and the swelling, theatrical Boz" (M. H. Elliott, *Uncle Sam Ward and his Circle*, p. 337).

¹ Cf. Lamb on James White at end of "The Praise of Chimney Sweepers" (*Essays of Elia*). CD quotes from the same passage in writing to Edward Dubois about Thomas Hill (see Vol. II, p. 250 and *n*).

² i.e. from Boston.

³ Sumner did not join them.

⁴ Sumner sent the letter on to Prescott, who replied the same month: "Thank you for the Boz letter—very characteristic—& caustic—in the right place, I suppose, though I think you are right not to show it to many—unless you can abstract the P.S. which is a stinger. . . . When you write to Dickens please to give my cordial regards

& good wishes to him—& advise him to take out a drawing of a spittoon for Cruikshank's next" (MS Houghton Library, Harvard).

⁵ Prescott wrote to his wife 5 June 42 that CD "laughed about the short commons at the Governor's, where I believe they got tea and roast apples, and Dickens is a great trencher-man" (*Correspondence of W. H. Prescott*, ed. R. Wolcott, Cambridge, Mass., 1925, p. 310). For their stay with John Davis at Worcester, see *To* Forster, 17 Feb.

⁶ William Henry Seward (1801–72; *DAB*), Whig Governor of New York 1839–42; Secretary of State under Lincoln. CD is not known to have met him. For his comment on *American Notes*, see *To* Forster, 6 Mar, *fn*.

⁷ These six words written larger than the rest for emphasis.

⁸ John Barney (1785–1857), son of Joshua Barney, naval officer. Federalist member of Congress 1825–9; previously Asst District Quartermaster General in the U.S. Army 1814–5. From 1829 devoted himself to literary pursuits.

days. I shall devote an hour each day to receiving any friends who may do me the favor of a call.[1]

To C. C. FELTON, 14 MARCH 1842†

Text from James T. Fields, "Our Whispering Gallery, VI", *Atlantic Monthly*, XXVII (1871), 765.[2]

Fuller's Hotel, Washington, Monday, March 14, 1842.

My dear Felton,

I was more delighted than I can possibly tell you to receive (last Saturday night) your welcome letter. We and the oysters missed you terribly in New York. You carried away with you more than half the delight and pleasure of my New World;[3] and I heartily wish you could bring it back again.

There are very interesting men in this place,—highly interesting, of course, —but it's not a comfortable place; is it? If spittle could wait at table we should be nobly attended, but as that property has not been imparted to it in the present state of mechanical science, we are rather lonely and orphan-like, in respect of "being looked arter." A blithe black was introduced on our arrival, as our peculiar and especial attendant. He is the only gentleman in the town who has a peculiar delicacy in intruding upon my valuable time. It usually takes seven rings and a threatening message from ———[4] to produce him; and when he comes he goes to fetch something, and, forgetting it by the way, comes back no more.

We have been in great distress, really in distress, at the non-arrival of the Caledonia. You may conceive what our joy was, when, while we were dining out yesterday, Putnam[5] arrived with the joyful intelligence of her safety. The very news of her having really arrived seemed to diminish the distance between ourselves and home, by one half at least.

And this morning (though we have not yet received our heap of despatches, for which we are looking eagerly forward to this night's mail),—this morning there reached us unexpectedly, through the government bag (Heaven knows how they came there), two of our many and long-looked-for letters, wherein was a circumstantial account of the whole conduct and behavior of our pets; with marvellous narrations of Charley's precocity at a Twelfth Night juvenile party

---

[1] *The Baltimore Patriot and Commercial Gazette*, 14 Feb, had announced that the first step towards the reception of CD in Baltimore had been taken by the Baltimore Lyceum in appointing a committee of five to discuss with the city's Literary Societies appropriate arrangements for the occasion. Clearly CD declined whatever proposal was made to him—as he had also declined an independent invitation to a public dinner (see *To* The Young Men of Baltimore ?15 Feb 42).

[2] CD's letters to Felton were published by Fields in the *Atlantic Monthly* (reprinted in *Yesterdays with Authors*, 1871); those of which we have seen the MSS show that in many he made cuts or omitted names, probably as a result of consultation with Georgina Hogarth. Later editions have almost invariably followed Fields's text.

[3] Cf. *To* Sumner, 13 Mar and *fn*.

[4] Perhaps Catherine's maid, Anne Brown. Presumably not Putnam, or MDGH would have restored the name: see next note.

[5] *Atlantic Monthly* reads "H."; MDGH follows. MDGH 1882 and 1893 replace the initial with "Putnam"—though possibly not correctly: the "H." may have stood for the nickname "Hamlet" (see *To* Felton, 29 Apr).

at Macready's; and tremendous predictions of the governess, dimly suggesting his having got out of pot-hooks and hangers, and darkly insinuating the possibility of his writing us a letter before long; and many other workings of the same prophetic spirit, in reference to him and his sisters, very gladdening to their mother's heart, and not at all depressing to their father's. There was, also, the doctor's report, which was a clean bill; and the nurse's report, which was perfectly electrifying; showing as it did how Master Walter had been weaned, and had cut a double tooth, and done many other extraordinary things, quite worthy of his high descent. In short, we were made very happy and grateful; and felt as if the prodigal father and mother had got home again.

What do you think of this incendiary card being left at my door last night? "General G.[1] sends compliments to Mr. Dickens, and called with two literary ladies.[2] As the two L. L.'s are ambitious of the honor of a personal introduction to Mr. D., General G. requests the honor of an appointment for to-morrow." I draw a veil over my sufferings. They are sacred.

[a]We have altered our route, and don't mean to go to Charleston, for I want to see the West, and have taken it into my head that as I am not obliged to go to Charleston, and don't exactly know why I should go there, I need do no violence to my own inclinations. My route is of Mr. Clay's designing, and I think it a very good one. We go on Wednesday night to Richmond in Virginia. On Monday we return to Baltimore for two days. On Thursday morning we start for Pittsburg, and so go by the Ohio to Cincinnati, Louisville, Kentucky, Lexington, St. Louis; and either down the Lakes to Buffalo, or back to Philadelphia, and by New York to that place, where we shall stay a week, and then make a hasty trip into Canada.[a] We shall be in Buffalo, please Heaven, on the 30th of April. If I don't find a letter from you in the care of the postmaster at that place, I'll never write to you from England.

But if I *do* find one, my right hand shall forget its cunning,[3] before I forget to be your truthful and constant correspondent; not, dear Felton, because I promised it, nor because I have a natural tendency to correspond (which is far from being the case), nor because I am truly grateful to you for, and have been made truly proud by, that affectionate and elegant tribute which ——[4] sent me, but because you are a man after my own heart, and I love you *well*. And for the

[1] Clearly General Edmund Pendleton Gaines (1777–1849; *DAB*); mis-spelt "Ganes" by CD in *To* Felton, 29 Apr, where again Fields's printed text gives only the initial "G". Had been promoted Brig.-General after defending Fort Erie against the British in the War of 1812. Preoccupied in the 1840s with preparations for the defence of America in the event of war with Mexico or England (either or both of which he considered likely); advocated short-line railroads and steam warships to be used as floating batteries, and had recently come to Washington to present his proposals to the Secretary of War. Of a fiery and violent nature, he constantly quarrelled with the War Dept; and at the beginning of the Mexican War (1846–7) was court-martialled for raising volunteers without authority (though proceedings were stopped). Possibly contributed some touches to General Cyrus Choke in *Chuzzlewit*, Ch. 21.

[2] A phrase which perhaps gained currency from Maria Edgeworth's *Letters for Literary Ladies* (1795). In *Chuzzlewit*, Ch. 34, "two literary ladies" or "L.L.'s" who are "Transcendental" send a note begging to be introduced by Mrs Hominy to Elijah Pogram.

[a][a] Omitted in earlier printed texts.

[3] Cf. *Psalms*, cxxxvii, 5.

[4] What name omitted is not known.

love I bear you, and the pleasure with which I shall always think of you, and the glow I shall feel when I see your handwriting in my own home, I hereby enter into a solemn league and covenant to write as many letters to you as you write to me, at least. Amen.

Come to England! Come to England! Our oysters are small I know; they are said by Americans to be coppery, but our hearts are of the largest size. We are thought to excel in shrimps, to be far from despicable in point of lobsters, and in periwinkles are considered to challenge the universe. Our oysters, small though they be, are not devoid of the refreshing influence which that species of fish is supposed to exercise in these latitudes.[1] Try them and compare.[2]

Affectionately yours,
CHARLES DICKENS

To UNKNOWN CORRESPONDENT, 14 MARCH 1842

Mention in Chicago Book & Art Auction catalogue No. 2; *MS*[3] 2 pp.; dated 14 Mar 42.

Declining further engagements in Baltimore.

Yours faithfully and obliged
CHARLES DICKENS

To JOHN FORSTER, [15 MARCH 1842]

Extracts in F, III, iv, 230*n* and 237-9 (resumption of letter begun on 6 Mar, continued 13 Mar).

[a]*Read on. We *have* your precious letters, but you'll think, at first, we have not. C.D.[a]

Still at Washington, Fifteenth March, 1842. . . . It is impossible, my dear friend, to tell you what we felt, when Mr. Q (who is a fearfully sentimental genius, but heartily interested in all that concerns us) came to where we were dining last Sunday,[4] and sent in a note to the effect that the Caledonia had arrived![5] Being really assured of her safety, we felt as if the distance between

---

[1] i.e., presumably, as an aphrodisiac: hence the long-windedness of this sentence. For CD's awareness of the oyster's reputation, see his sketch "Love and Oysters" (*Bell's Life in London*, 25 Oct 35), renamed "Misplaced Attachment of Mr. John Dounce" for *Sketches by Boz*.

[2] Felton did not visit CD in England until May 53; but Longfellow, after his visit of Autumn 42, tried to disillusion him: "He swears", wrote Felton to Henry R. Cleveland, 28 Nov 42, "the London oyster is not to be eaten as long as the memory of the New York dwells upon the palate" (MS Longfellow House).

[3] Only ending and signature are in CD's hand according to catalogue; the rest presumably in Putnam's.

[a] Written at the top of letter of 6 Mar "above the address and date", according to F, III, iv, 230*n*; linked by an asterisk to "We have heard nothing from you"; clearly not written until the 15th. Omitted in N.

[4] At Robert Greenhow's (see *To* J. Q. Adams, 10 or 11 Mar, *fn*).

[5] In fact the *Acadia* with the *Caledonia* mails.

us and home were diminished by at least one half. There was great joy everywhere here, for she had been quite despaired of, but *our* joy was beyond all
telling. This news came on by express. Last night your letters reached us. I
was dining with a club[1] (for I can't avoid a dinner of that sort, now and then),
and Kate sent me a note about nine o'clock to say they were here.[2] But she didn't
open them—which I consider heroic—until I came home. That was about half
past ten; and we read them until nearly two in the morning.

I won't say a word about your letters; except that Kate and I have come to
a conclusion which makes me tremble in my shoes, for we decide that humourous
narrative is your forte, and not statesmen of the commonwealth.[3] I won't say
a word about your news; for how could I in that case, while you want to hear
what we are doing, resist the temptation of expending pages on those darling
children. . . .

I have the privilege of appearing on the floor of both houses here, and go to
them every day.[4] They are very handsome and commodious. There is a great
deal of bad speaking, but there are a great many very remarkable men, in the
legislature: such as John Quincey[5] Adams, Clay, Preston,[6] Calhoun,[7] and others:

[1] The Alleghany Club. The dinner was held at Boulanger's, with George M. Keim, U.S. Marshal for East Pennsylvania, in the chair, and J. Q. Adams a fellow-guest. Eight of the 28 present were members of the House of Representatives. As a private dinner, it was apparently not reported by the press; but an account of it is quoted, from a diary kept by Benjamin B. French, in R. S. Mackenzie, *Life of CD*, Philadelphia [1870], pp. 139–42 (drawn on for *Speeches*, ed. K. J. Fielding, pp. 32–4). There were speeches and songs; and in reply to the Chairman's toast of "Philanthropy and Genius, and a representative of both, now our guest in Washington, whom Washington himself would have rejoiced to welcome", CD made a short speech bringing into it the *Arabian Nights* allusion made in *To* Gilpin, 11 Mar. Later, after other toasts, he said: "Allow me to assume the character of Mr. Pickwick, and in that character to give you 'The President of the United States' "—possibly, as K. J. Fielding suggests (*op. cit.*, p. 33), having mounted on his chair, to stand, with one hand behind his coat tails and the other waving in the air, as shown in Seymour's first illustration to *Pickwick*. French summed up in his diary: "Dickens, by his modesty, his social powers, and his eloquence, has added to the high esteem in which I was previously induced to hold him. I believe every person present was delighted" (R. S. Mackenzie, *op. cit.*, p. 140).

[2] About 11 p.m., "in the most feelingly beautiful manner possible", CD said good-night, announcing that his letters from England had arrived at last and the company would understand his anxiety to read them, and ending with the assurance: "this has been the most pleasant evening I have passed in the United States" (R. S. Mackenzie, *op. cit.*, pp. 140, 142).

[3] An allusion to Forster's *Statesmen of the Commonwealth*, 5 vols, 1840, reprinted from contributions to Lardner's *Cabinet Cyclopædia*.

[4] Throughout the period 10–16 Mar, the Senate debated Clay's proposals for increased taxation and economies to meet Govt expenditure, and the House of Representatives debated the General Appropriation Bill. On 14 Mar Clay presented several petitions to the Senate complaining of its ineffectiveness: one protested at the time "consumed in personal invective", which lost it "the respect of the country and the civilized world" (*Congressional Globe*, 14 Mar).

[5] Mis-spelt in F, III, iv, 237, no doubt following a mis-spelling by CD.

[6] William Campbell Preston (1794–1860; *DAB*), lawyer, orator, supporter of Nullification, and strong defender of slavery. Senator from South Carolina since 1833; succeeded Clay as Whig leader in the Senate 1842, but soon broke with Van Buren and Calhoun and resigned rather than obey instructions from the Legislature.

[7] John Caldwell Calhoun (1782–1850;

with whom I need scarcely add I have been placed in the friendliest relations. Adams is a fine old fellow—seventy-six years old, but with most surprising vigour, memory, readiness, and pluck. Clay is perfectly enchanting; an irresistible man. There are some very noble specimens, too, out of the West. Splendid men to look at, hard to deceive, prompt to act, lions in energy, Crichtons in varied accomplishments, Indians in quickness of eye and gesture, Americans in affectionate and generous impulse. It would be difficult to exaggerate the nobility of some of these glorious fellows.

When Clay retires, as he does this month, Preston will become the leader of the whig party. He so solemnly assures me that the international copyright shall and will be passed, that I almost begin to hope;[1] and I shall be entitled to say, if it be, that I have brought it about.[2] You have no idea how universal the discussion of its merits and demerits has become; or how eager for the change I have made a portion of the people.

You remember what Webster[3] was, in England.[4] If you *could* but see him

DAB), Senator from South Carolina. Graduate of Yale; elected to Congress 1811; Vice-President 1824–5 and 1828–32; resigned after supporting States' rights in the Nullification controversy; as Senator, became the chief defender of slavery. On 20 Mar 42 he wrote to his daughter Mrs Clemson: "[CD] brought me letters and I saw a good deal of both of them. He is rather good looking; but not strikingly so; young, fair complexion and a pleasant countenance, with easy simple manners. Not very marked for anything, that I could see, but nothing in the slightest degree offensive . . . His Lady is quite homely and somewhat countrified in her manners, but I would say amiable and sensible, of which I think she gave proof by continuing at her needle all the time, when I visited them in the morning, except when she took part in the conversation" ("Correspondence of John C. Calhoun", ed. J. F. Jameson, *Annual Report of the American Historical Association*, 1899, II, 506).

[1] Preston had been on Clay's committee Feb 37, and had since corresponded on the subject with Francis Lieber, who had sent him, for his use in debate, the MS of his *On International Copyright, in a Letter to the Hon. William C. Preston* (New York, 1840)—a pamphlet which, though rejected by six publishers, helped to "revive waning interest" (see F. Freidel, *Francis Lieber*, Louisiana, 1947, pp. 188–9). But it was a little naïve of CD to imagine that Preston could have achieved anything unless he gained more support in the Senate.

[2] To some it seemed that CD had, if

anything, delayed the passage of the Bill, through the anger aroused by his interference. But though Clay had introduced it in Jan 42, the Kennedy committee (see last paragraph of letter) would probably not have been set up had CD not brought the petition to Washington. He did at least help to keep the subject alive.

[3] Name replaced by a dash in F, 1872–4, I, 330; restored in F, 1876. Daniel Webster (1782–1852; *DAB*), brilliant lawyer and orator and probably the most controversial statesman of his time. Whig Senator for Massachusetts 1827–41 and 1845–50; Secretary of State 1841–3. Negotiated with Lord Ashburton the Treaty of Aug 42 settling the Canadian boundary dispute with England. He disapproved of slavery and opposed Nullification, but in 1850 supported the Compromise with its fugitive slave law. Webster asked Irving to bring CD to dine with him at his house in Washington (*Records of the Columbia Historical Society*, XIX [1916], 33); but since CD does not here mention such a visit it is improbable that he was able to go.

[4] Webster had paid a private visit to England with his family June–Oct 39. Nicknamed the "Great Western", he had been lionized and widely entertained, meeting the Queen, statesmen of both parties, and all the leading men of letters. He had met CD at dinner at John Kenyon's on 11 June 39 (*Diary, Reminiscences, and Correspondence of Henry Crabb Robinson*, ed. T. Sadler, 1869, III, 176), and had described him in a letter as "rather small, light complexion, and a good deal of hair,

here! If you could only have seen him when he called on us the other day—feigning abstraction in the dreadful pressure of affairs of state;[1] rubbing his forehead as one who was a-weary of the world;[2] and exhibiting a sublime caricature of Lord Burleigh.[3] He is the only thoroughly unreal man I have seen, on this side the ocean.[4] Heaven help the President! All parties are against him, and he appears truly wretched.[5] We go to a levee at his house to-night.[6] He has invited me to dinner on Friday, but I am obliged to decline; for we leave, per steamboat, to-morrow night.

I said I wouldn't write anything more concerning the American people, for two months. Second thoughts are best. I shall not change, and may as well speak out—to *you*. They are friendly, earnest, hospitable, kind, frank, very often accomplished, far less prejudiced than you would suppose, warm-hearted, fervent, and enthusiastic. They are chivalrous in their universal politeness to women, courteous, obliging, disinterested; and, when they conceive a perfect affection for a man (as I may venture to say of myself), entirely devoted to him. I have received thousands of people of all ranks and grades, and have never once been asked an offensive or unpolite question—except by Englishmen, who, when

shows none of his peculiar humor in conversation, and is rather shy and retiring" (*Writings and Speeches*, Boston, 1903, XVI, 309). His own magnificent head had made a great impression: best known is Carlyle's description to Emerson: "The tanned complexion, that amorphous crag-like face; the dull black eyes under their precipice of brows, like dull anthracite furnaces, needing only to be *blown*; the mastiff-mouth, accurately closed:—I have not traced as much of *silent Berserkir-rage*, that I remember of, in any other man" (*Correspondence of Emerson and Carlyle*, ed. J. Slater, 1964, p. 240).

[1] Webster had every reason to feel such pressure. Since Mar 41 he had had to deal, as Secretary of State, with three incidents which might have brought England and America to the brink of war: the Canadian destruction of the American steamboat *Caroline*; arising out of it, the trial in New York of Alexander McLeod, a Canadian, for murder (see Vol. II, p. 405n); and, most recently, the *Creole* affair (see To Fonblanque, 12 Mar, *fn*). As the only member of Tyler's original Cabinet not to resign on the U.S. Bank issue, he was subjected to constant criticism by Clay's supporters in Congress and the Whig press; also to a systematic slander campaign. This he felt deeply; and Emerson, in Oct 41, found him changed —"black as a thunder cloud, & care worn" (*Journals and Miscellaneous Notebooks of R. W. Emerson*, ed. W. H.

Gilman and J. E. Parsons, Cambridge, Mass., VIII [1970], 111).

[2] Cassius in *Julius Caesar*, IV, iii, 94.

[3] In Sheridan's *The Critic*; for the same allusion, see Vol. II, p. 249, and *American Notes*, Ch. I.

[4] Harriet Martineau (on hearing him in the Supreme Court or Senate) was fascinated: "Seeing one so dreamy and *nonchalant* roused into strong excitement" seemed to her "like having a curtain lifted up, . . . like hearing autobiographical secrets. . . . These are the moments", she wrote, "when it becomes clear that this pleasure-loving man works for his honours and his gains" (*Retrospect of Western Travel*, I, 277).

[5] Relations between Tyler's new Cabinet and Congress were virtually at a deadlock throughout 1842; he had been formally expelled by the Whigs (Sep 41) and was distrusted by the Democrats. The climax came with a Whig resolution for his impeachment, moved by J. M. Botts on 10 July (defeated 10 Jan 43): "Because I will not go with [Clay], I am abused, in Congress and out, as man never was before—assailed as a traitor", he wrote that day (L. G. Tyler, *Letters and Times of the Tylers*, Richmond, Va, 1885, II, 173). For the charge that he used the scurrilous *New York Herald* as the Govt's mouthpiece, see Forster's second article on the American Press (*Foreign Quarterly*, Apr 43).

[6] See To Fonblanque, 12 Mar, *fn*.

they have been "located"[1] here for some years, are worse than the devil in his blackest painting. The State is a parent to its people; has a parental care and watch over all poor children, women labouring of child, sick persons, and captives.[2] The common men render you assistance in the streets, and would revolt from the offer of a piece of money. The desire to oblige is universal; and I have never once travelled in a public conveyance, without making some generous acquaintance whom I have been sorry to part from, and who has in many cases come on miles, to see us again. But I don't like the country. I would not live here, on any consideration. It goes against the grain with me. It would with you. I think it impossible, utterly impossible, for any Englishman to live here, and be happy. I have a confidence that I must be right, because I have everything, God knows, to lead me to the opposite conclusion: and yet I cannot resist coming to this one. As to the causes, they are too many to enter upon here. . . .

One of two petitions for an international copyright which I brought here from American authors, with Irving at their head,[3] has been presented to the house of representatives.[4] Clay retains the other for presentation to the senate after I have left Washington.[5] The presented one has been referred to a committee;[6] the Speaker[7] has nominated as its chairman Mr. Kennedy, member for Baltimore, who is himself an author[8] and notoriously favourable to such a law; and I am going to assist him in his report.[9]

---

[1] For this and other Americanisms, see *To* Forster, 24 Feb.

[2] Litany, *Book of Common Prayer*.

[3] See *To* Forster, 27 Feb and *fn*.

[4] On 14 Mar, by Edward Stanley, Representative from North Carolina. It was identical with that presented to the Senate by Clay.

[5] He presented it on 30 Mar. It was referred to the Committee on the Judiciary for a report. On 11 May Preston was told that this was ready, but that Clay had asked that it be retained for additional information. Moreover, the Committee were opposed to an international copyright bill (*Niles' National Register*, 14 May 1842, LXII, 175, quoted by L. H. Houtchens, *American Literature*, XIII [1941], 21). No report was submitted, and this was apparently the last mention of the petition in the Senate.

[6] Consisting of J. P. Kennedy, Robert C. Winthrop, John H. Brockway, John McKeon, and Benjamin G. Shields (T. Solberg, *Copyright in Congress, 1789–1904*, Washington, 1905, pp. 158–9).

[7] John White, Representative from Kentucky.

[8] John Pendleton Kennedy (1795–1870; *DAB*), Whig politician and writer, son of a Northern Irish merchant settled in Baltimore. Member of the House of Representatives 1838–44. Published *A Defence of the Whigs*, 1844, denouncing Tyler's defection from Whig principles. His best known books were *Swallow Barn*, 1832, sketches of life in post-Revolution Virginia, and *Horse-Shoe Robinson*, a novel about the Battle of King's Mountain, 1835—both written under the pseudonym "Mark Littleton". Some contemporary critics classed him with Fenimore Cooper and Irving. He wrote other novels, sketches and political pamphlets, and contributed to the *National Intelligencer*.

[9] CD did not in fact help him: for his reasons, see *To* Kennedy, 30 Apr 42. Kennedy drafted a bill—criticized by N. P. Willis as too detailed and liable to "embarrass the muddy wits of some of our geese of the Capitol" (Willis *to* Kennedy, n.d., quoted in C. H. Bohner, *J. P. Kennedy, Gentleman from Baltimore*, Baltimore, 1961, p. 157)—but, as with the Senate petition, the Committee submitted no report. In addition to the expected opposition, there were political difficulties: the Democrats opposed any pro-English bill on principle, and Kennedy, as a Whig, could not afford to demonstrate his evident anglophilism by a too vigorous support (*op. cit.*, p. 158).

To WASHINGTON IRVING, 15 MARCH 1842*

MS Berg Collection.

Fuller's | Fifteenth March 1842.

My Dear Irving.

We leave here tomorrow night.—Say that you will come and dine with us tomorrow—inviolably alone—at 4. Don't refuse, if you love me. It may be a very long time before we dine together again.[1]

I am glad to say that I have a[2] brother to whose memory we can drink a glass of wine—he died in his infancy some nine and twenty years ago.[3] He wasn't a twin, but we must make the best of him.[4]

Heartily | Your friend

Washington Irving Esquire   CHARLES DICKENS

To ROBERT GILMOR,[5] 16 MARCH 1842

MS Historical Society of Pennsylvania. *Address:* Paid | R. Gilmour[6] Esquire | Messrs. R. Gilmour & Sons | Baltimore.

Washington. | Sixteenth March 1842.

My Dear Sir.

I hope to be in Baltimore on Monday night, and to remain there *two days*, before going West—in the course of which brief stay, I shall rob you of certain large sums in Gold and Silver to carry into those remote parts. Meanwhile let me advise you that as Coutts's house[7] by some strange mistake directed my letter of credit to a gentleman, formerly of this place, who has been dead some six years,[8] I have been obliged to draw Fifty Pounds from the Metropolis

---

[1] It was not: see *To* Irving, 21 Mar, *fn.*

[2] Written over "no" cancelled. CD must have originally intended to write "no brother who has died".

[3] Alfred, the John Dickenses' second son, *b.* 1813.

[4] Six of Irving's seven brothers were dead: three had died in infancy—none of them a twin. Possibly the suggested toast arose from the fact that L. G. Clark (a friend of them both) had had a twin, Willis, *d.* June 1841.

[5] Robert Gilmor (1774–1848), Baltimore banker and merchant. Retired from active partnership in Robert Gilmor & Sons 1830 and devoted his time to patronage of the arts, collecting, and the many learned societies to which he belonged. President, Maryland Academy of Science and Literature, 1822; a founder of the Maryland Historical Society. Lived at 57 Lombard Street, a house which was the centre of social activity in Baltimore.

[6] Mis-spelt thus by CD.

[7] Where Edward Marjoribanks, a partner, was arranging credit for him: see *To* Marjoribanks, 11 Dec 41 (II, 442–3). CD had then asked for a letter of credit on Coutts's correspondent in New York for £800—an amount advanced by Edward Chapman and credited to CD's account on 27 Dec 41 (Account-book, MS Messrs Coutts). The sum represented £50 more than the payment due for the five months Jan to May 42 (for Chapman & Hall's agreement that CD should have £150 a month throughout the year in which he was not engaged on a book, see Vol. II, p. 372). His account-book (MS Messrs Coutts) shows payments direct to Gilmor & Sons of £50 and £400 on 18 June 42.

[8] Unidentified. Cf. *To* Miss Coutts, 22 Mar.

Bank, and have given them a draft on you to that amount. I should have written to you for a supply, but it did not occur to me to enquire after the deceased Agent until last night (though I thought it odd not to have heard of him)— and tonight I leave this City, for Richmond.

Dear Sir | Faithfully Yours

R. Gilmour Esquire   CHARLES DICKENS

To FREDERICK SAUNDERS,[1] 16 MARCH 1842*

MS Fales Collection, New York University Library.

Private   Washington | Sixteenth March 1842

Dear Sir

I have but a moment, before leaving here, to acknowledge the receipt of your communication. It is, I fear, too late to add the signatures you have sent me, for I confided both the petitions to Mr. Clay's charge some days since, and one— that to the house of Representatives—has been presented.

That petition, you will be glad to hear, has been referred to a Committee, of which Mr. Kennedy from Baltimore (himself an Author) is apppointed chairman. I augur *good*[2] results from his report.[3]

Faithfully Yours

F. Saunders Esquire   CHARLES DICKENS

To W. W. SEATON,[4] 16 MARCH 1842

Text from [Josephine Seaton], *William Winston Seaton of the "National Intelligencer." A Biographical Sketch. With Passing Notices of his Associates and Friends*, [Boston], 1871, p. 272.

Washington | March 16, 1842

My dear Sir,

I am truly obliged to you for your kind note. I am so constantly engaged,

---

[1] Frederick Saunders (1807–1902; *DAB*), son of William Saunders, the senior partner of Saunders & Otley, London publishers. Set up a branch of the firm in New York 1836 to stop American piracies, particularly by Harper & Brothers; unsuccessful, he remained as a pioneer worker for international copyright and helped to prepare many petitions to Congress. Founded a bookshop; became a friend of Irving and Bryant; and was for a time city editor of the latter's *New York Evening Post*. Published several collections of essays—*Salad for the Solitary*, 1853, the best known. For his work for copyright and his early struggle with Harper's see Arno L. Bader, "Frederick Saunders and the Early History of the International Copyright Movement in America", *Library Quarterly*, Chicago, VIII (1938), 25–39.

[2] Underlined twice.

[3] See *To* Forster, 15 Mar, *fn*.

[4] William Winston Seaton (1785–1866; *DAB*), of an old Virginia family, co-editor of the *National Intelligencer*, Washington, with his brother-in-law Joseph Gales, the younger; Mayor of Washington 1840–50. A progressive Whig, he developed local education, favoured gradual emancipation of slaves and freed his own, but opposed the total Abolitionists. He and Gales were the exclusive shorthand reporters of Congress 1812–29. Seaton became a warm supporter of CD's efforts for international copyright. Genial and popular, he was a friend of Daniel Webster and of leading Southern politicians.

however, that I think I *must* deny myself the pleasure of making an appointment with you, which I could scarcely keep without making a most uncomfortable scramble of it. I will report my knowledge of the lions to you, and you shall judge how I have been shown about.

In case I should forget it when we meet to-night,[1] may I venture to ask two favors of you,—or rather one favor with two heads.

It is that you will kindly (if you see no objection) let my friends here know through that channel which is open to you, and over which you so ably preside, that whenever I make an appointment I keep it; and that it gives me great uneasiness and pain to be placarded all over the town as intending to make a visit to the theatre, when I have given no authority whatever to any person to publish such an announcement; and secondly, that travelling as we do, we can never return the calls of our friends, in consequence of their immense number, and our very limited stay in any one place.[2]

Let me take this opportunity of thanking you, most heartily and earnestly, for the exceedingly kind attention I have received at your hands, and the pleasure I have enjoyed in your society and in that of your family.[3] I need scarcely say that Mrs. Dickens desires me to say as much for her.

I am, my dear sir, with true regard, faithfully yours,

W. W. Seaton, Esq.   CHARLES DICKENS

To JOHN FORSTER, 17 MARCH [1842]

Extracts in F, III, iv, 239 (resumption of letter begun 6 Mar, continued 13th and 15th).

Richmond, in Virginia. Thursday Night, March 17.

Irving was with me at Washington yesterday, and *wept heartily* at parting. He is a fine fellow, when you know him well; and you would relish him, my dear friend, of all things. We have laughed together at some absurdities we have encountered in company, quite in my vociferous Devonshire-terrace style. The

---

[1] The night they left (by steamboat) for Richmond. They had dined with the Seatons the previous night, before the President's reception, when Mrs Madison, Clay, Webster and Robert C. Winthrop were among the guests (R. C. Winthrop, *Reminiscences of Foreign Travel*, p. 62).

[2] A paragraph on p. 1 of the *National Intelligencer* of 19 Mar announced that CD and Catherine had left Washington on the 16th, sketched their future plans, mentioned the cordiality with which "these interesting strangers . . . received and appreciated the respectful attentions which were so extensively shown them", and stated that the paper was requested "by a friend" to express CD's and Catherine's

regret at having been unable to return the numerous calls they had received, and that, "as the arrangements of Mr. D. for his departure on Wednesday evening would have prevented his attending the theatre, the annunciation that he would do so was made without his authority."

[3] Seaton's wife, Sarah, was the daughter of Joseph Gales, the elder, founder and editor of the Jeffersonian *Raleigh Register*, North Carolina. They were married in 1809. She translated Spanish documents for him for the *National Intelligencer*, and was a well-known Washington hostess. Their living children were Gales (1817–57), Josephine (*b.* 1822), Caroline (1824–55) and Malcolm (1829–1904).

"Merrikin" government have treated him, he says, most liberally and handsomely in every respect.[1] He thinks of sailing for Liverpool on the 7th of April;[2] passing a short time in London;[3] and then going to Paris.[4] Perhaps you may meet him.[5] If you do, he will know that you are my dearest friend, and will open his whole heart to you at once. His secretary of legation, Mr. Coggleswell,[6] is a man of very remarkable information, a great traveller, a good talker, and a scholar.[7]

I am going to sketch you our trip here from Washington, as it involves nine miles of a "Virginny Road."[8] That done, I must be brief, good brother. . . .

[1] Irving had been appointed American Minister to Spain in Feb: a popular choice in both countries. "The appointment, he says, was altogether unexpected to him", Philip Hone recorded; "but I have no doubt from his manner of speaking of it that he is pleased" (*Diary*, ed. A. Nevins, p. 585).

[2] He did so, on the *Independence*.

[3] He spent 1–22 May mainly in London, living in the Little Cloisters, Westminster Abbey. He renewed his friendships with Moore, Rogers and Leslie; attended a levée at Buckingham Palace and a fancy dress ball given by the Queen; was toasted at the Literary Fund dinner on 12 May; dined at Lady Holland's; and met Wordsworth twice (see G. S. Hellman, *Washington Irving Esquire*, 1925, pp. 259–61).

[4] Where he stayed 25 May to 11 July; was presented to King Louis Philippe and entertained widely by the diplomatic corps (including Bulwer's brother Henry, British Chargé d'Affaires). He reached Madrid on 25 July.

[5] There is no evidence that Forster did.

[6] Mis-spelt thus in F. Joseph Green Cogswell (1786–1871; *DAB*), teacher and librarian. Spent 1815–20 mainly in Europe; was one of the first Americans to study in Germany (at Göttingen 1817), where he knew and corresponded with Goethe. Librarian of Harvard 1820–3; joint founder with Bancroft of the Round Hill School, Northampton, Mass., 1823; editor and proprietor of the *New York Review* 1839–42. Lived with Samuel Ward 1836–8 and tutored his children. Although appointed as Irving's Secretary, was persuaded by J. J. Astor to remain in New York as a Trustee of his Library Fund (and subsequently Librarian), and Alexander Hamilton, of New York, was appointed instead.

[7] Cogswell did not think so highly of CD. On 28 Feb he had written to George Ticknor: "I have seen a good deal of Dickens during his visit here, although I attended none of the public festivities in honor of him. He does not please me over-much as a man, although I am a very warm admirer of his writings. I do not see that he does anything particularly well, except writing 'Pickwick Stories'. His dinner speeches, his answers to letters, and the like are generally artificial and commonplace. In society he is quite natural enough, and careless enough too, to please any Dick Swiveller, and a good deal too much so, I confess, to please me" ([A. E. Ticknor], *The Life of J. G. Cogswell as Sketched in his Letters*, Cambridge, Mass., 1874, pp. 229–30).

[8] "The humorous descriptions of the night steamer on the Potomac, and of the black driver over the Virginia-road" were both in this letter, says Forster (F, III, iv, 239), but omitted here because given in *American Notes*. J. R. Godley, who was in America from July 1842, travelled by stage from Potomac Creek to Fredericksburg, over the very road "celebrated by Dickens" and noted: "The 'black driver,' whom he describes, is highly indignant at the part he is made to play as hero in the scene, and strongly denies the truth of the representation" (*Letters from America*, 1844, II, 192). CD's reference to "that *Virginia road*" in his speech at the Richmond supper (*To* Forster, 21 Mar) aroused "laughter and cheering" and the exclamation from the President, "No more of that, Hal, an you love me" (W. G. Wilkins, *CD in America*, p. 187).

To MISS EMMA MORDECAI,[1] 19 MARCH 1842*

MS Colonel Richard Gimbel.

Richmond. Virginia | Nineteenth March 1842.

My Dear Dreamer.

I have received the southern flowers most joyfully—though I need nothing to remind me of *you*, believe me. I shall place them on my pillow tonight, and trust to their influence for some sweet visions in which you may be the chief actor.

Believe me
(Sleeping or waking)

Faithfully Yours

Miss Emma Mordecai   CHARLES DICKENS

To JOHN FORSTER, 21 MARCH [1842]

Extract in F, IV, iii, 239–41 (continuation of letter begun 6 Mar).

At Washington again, Monday, March the twenty-first.

We had intended to go to Baltimore from Richmond, by a place called Norfolk: but one of the boats being under repair, I found we should probably be detained at this Norfolk two days. Therefore we came back here yesterday, by the road we had travelled before;[2] lay here last night; and go on to Baltimore this afternoon, at four o'clock. It is a journey of only two hours and a half. Richmond is a prettily situated town;[3] but, like other towns in slave districts (as the planters themselves admit), has an aspect of decay and gloom which to an unaccustomed eye is *most* distressing. In the black car (for they don't let them sit with the whites), on the railroad as we went there, were a mother and family, whom the [?owner][4] was conveying away, to sell; retaining the man (the husband and father I mean) on his plantation. The children cried the whole way. Yesterday, on board the boat, a slave owner and two constables were our fellow-passengers. They were coming here in search of two negroes who had run away on the previous day. On the bridge at Richmond there is a notice against fast driving over it, as it is rotten and crazy: penalty—for whites, five dollars; for slaves, fifteen stripes. My heart is lightened as if a great load had

[1] Emma Mordecai (1812–1906), one of the 13 children of Jacob Mordecai (1762–1838), Hebrew scholar and founder 1809 of Warrenton Academy, Virginia, the first girls' boarding-school in the South. Devoted much of her life to education; by 1847 Superintendent of the Hebrew School, Richmond. Her sister Rachel, assistant at Warrenton, had corresponded for several years with Maria Edgeworth. CD may have been introduced to Emma by Gales

Seaton (see *To* W. W. Seaton, 16 Mar, *fn*), who took him to Church Hill, where the Mordecais lived.

[2] i.e. by rail to Fredericksburg, thence by coach to Potomac Creek, and to Washington by steamboat (*American Notes*, Ch. 9).

[3] "On eight hills, overhanging James River; a sparkling stream . . ." (*American Notes*, Ch. 9).

[4] F reads "steamer", clearly in error; "owner" seems likely.

been taken from it, when I think that we are turning our backs on this accursed and detested system. I really don't think I could have borne it any longer. It is all very well to say "be silent on the subject." They won't let you be silent. They *will* ask you what you think of it; and *will* expatiate on slavery as if it were one of the greatest blessings of mankind. "It's not," said a hard, bad-looking fellow to me the other day, "it's not the interest of a man to use his slaves ill. It's damned nonsense that you hear in England."—I told him quietly that it was not a man's interest to get drunk, or to steal, or to game, or to indulge in any other vice, but he *did* indulge in it for all that. That cruelty, and the abuse of irresponsible power, were two of the bad passions of human nature, with the gratification of which, considerations of interest or of ruin had nothing whatever to do; and that, while every candid man must admit that even a slave might be happy enough with a good master, all human beings knew that bad masters, cruel masters, and masters who disgraced the form they bore, were matters of experience and history, whose existence was as undisputed as that of slaves themselves.[1] He was a little taken aback by this, and asked me if I believed in the bible. Yes, I said, but if any man could prove to me that it sanctioned slavery, I would place no further credence in it. "Well then," he said, "by God, sir, the niggers must be kept down, and the whites have put down the coloured people wherever they have found them." "That's the whole question" said I. "Yes, and by God," says he, "the British had better not stand out on that point when Lord Ashburton comes over, for I never felt so warlike as I do now,—and that's a fact." I was obliged to accept a public supper in this Richmond,[2] and I

---

[1] Cf., in Theodore D. Weld's highly important anti-slavery pamphlet *American Slavery as It Is: Testimony of a Thousand Witnesses*, New York, 1839, p. 132, the opening paragraph of section headed "*Objections Considered*—Interest of Masters. Objection V.—'It is for the interest of the masters to treat their slaves well.' " The pamphlet was in CD's library at his death, and he quoted from it verbatim when writing his chapter on slavery for *American Notes* (see *To* Chapman, 16 Sep, *fn*). Whether he had read it before his visit to Virginia is uncertain; but his reply to the slave-owner follows closely Weld's opening argument. Weld went on to discuss "the *pecuniary* interests of masters to treat their slaves well", and after enumerating the large classes of slaves unprofitable to their owners—old, worn out, diseased, incorrigible, &c—concluded: "It is for the interest of slaveholders, upon their own principles, and by their own showing, TO TREAT CRUELLY the great body of their slaves." Weld had been in Washington while CD was there, acting as adviser to the Abolitionist group in Congress; but it seems clear that they did not meet.

[2] He had already declined an invitation to a public dinner; but on a deputation's renewing its request the day after his arrival, he accepted an invitation to a "social supper" that evening (Fri 18th). This was given at the Exchange Hotel, where he was staying; Thomas Ritchie, editor of the *Richmond Enquirer*, was in the chair; and there were nearly 100 present. For the report in the *Richmond Enquirer* of 24 Mar, see W. G. Wilkins, *CD in America*, pp. 181–90; see also *Speeches*, ed. K. J. Fielding, pp. 35–6. Ritchie's speech of welcome to CD included, after praise of his books, a passage which seems curious in the light of CD's now widely publicized views on the piracy of his work: "Let us not forget, too, how much we are deeply indebted to that 'miraculous organ' the Press for the communication of these pleasures. No sooner is thought conceived and transferred to Mr. Dickens's paper from his brain, in his solitary chamber in distant England, than it is transmitted by the Press, across the broad Atlantic, with the rapidity of electricity" (contrast Mathews's speech at the New York Dinner: see *To* Forster, 24 Feb,

saw plainly enough, there, that the hatred which these Southern States bear to us as a nation has been fanned up and revived again by this Creole business,[1] and can scarcely be exaggerated. . . . We were desperately tired at Richmond, as we went to a great many places,[2] and received a very great number of visitors. We appoint usually two hours in every day for this latter purpose, and have our room so full at that period that it is difficult to move or breathe. Before we left Richmond, a gentleman told me, when I really was so exhausted that I could hardly stand, that "three people of great fashion" were much offended by having been told, when they called last evening, that I was tired and not visible, then, but would be "at home" from twelve to two next day![3] Another gentleman (no doubt of great fashion also) sent a letter to me two hours after I had gone to bed, preparatory to rising at four next morning, with instructions to the slave who brought it to knock me up and wait for an answer!

I am going to break my resolution of accepting no more public entertainments, in favour of the originators of the printed document overleaf.[4] They live upon the confines of the Indian territory, some two thousand miles or more west of New York! Think of my dining there! And yet, please God, the festival will come off—I should say about the 12th or [13th][5] of next month.[6]

---

fn. p. 84). He went on to beg CD not to let success turn his head or paralyse his pen. CD replied with a good-humoured speech; "He was . . . very happy", Gales Seaton reported to his father on 21 Mar, " and every one else very insipid in their efforts, except Mr. Ritchie, with whom [CD] was greatly pleased" ([Josephine Seaton], *W. W. Seaton of the "National Intelligencer"*, p. 275).

[1] Although no hint of this hatred appears in the published account of the supper, CD may well have overheard hostile remarks and could not fail to be aware of the general feeling in the South. Hostility towards England had been expressed at its strongest by J. C. Calhoun, the leading defender of slavery, in a speech to the Senate on 13 Mar 40 (later widely circulated as a pamphlet): he charged England with having been "the greatest slave dealer on earth" in the past; even now she held "hundreds of thousands of slaves in the most wretched condition" in India; the conditions of the poor in Ireland and England itself showed up the flagrant hypocrisy of her attacks on American slavery (*Congressional Globe*, VIII [1839–40], Appx, pp. 266–70). For the violent attacks

of H. A. Wise, Representative from Virginia, see *To* Fonblanque, 12 Mar and *fn*; and for the anger engendered by the *Creole* affair, *To* Brougham, 22 Mar.

[2] The Capitol, the public library, a tobacco factory where the workmen were all slaves, a plantation, and the planter's house (see *American Notes*, Ch. 9). With Gales Seaton he walked to French Gardens (see *To* W. W. Seaton, 21 Mar, *fn*). They also went to the theatre to see *Ion* (see *To* Talfourd, 22 Mar).

[3] The familiar complaint that invitations for the supper had been circulated only "among a select few", as self-appointed representatives of the city, was voiced in the *Richmond Star*, 21 Mar.

[4] A series of resolutions by the leading citizens of St Louis, Missouri, inviting him to their city, "eulogising his genius, and tendering to him their warmest hospitalities" (F, III, iv, 241). The document is not in the Forster Collection, V & A.

[5] F reads "15th", surely a misreading of "13th", or a printer's error.

[6] It came off on the 13th: but a soirée and ball, not a dinner (*To* Forster, 15 Apr).

To ROBERT GILMOR, 21 MARCH [1842]

MS Historical Society of Pennsylvania. *Address:* Robert Gilmor[1] Esquire | Exchange Place.

Barnum's Hotel[2] | Monday Evening Twenty First March.
My Dear Sir
I am greatly obliged to you for your kind letter.—I should have come to you today, beyond all doubt if I had been here; but I have only just now (past 6 O'Clock) arrived.[3] I will call on you tomorrow at eleven, and shall hope to find you as much better as in these sudden changes of temperature, may be reasonably expected.

Faithfully Yours

Robert Gilmour[1] Esquire   CHARLES DICKENS

To WASHINGTON IRVING, 21 MARCH 1842

MS Yale University Library. *Address:* Washington Irving Esquire | at Brown's.

Washington. | Monday afternoon. March Twenty First. | 1842
My Dear Irving.
We passed through—literally passed through—this place, again to day. I did not come to see you, for I really have not the heart to say "good bye" again, and felt more than I can tell you when we shook hands last Wednesday.

You will not be at Baltimore, I fear? I thought at the time[4] that you only said you might be there, to make our parting the gayer.[5]

Wherever you go, God bless you! What pleasure I have had in seeing and talking with you, I will not attempt to say. I shall never forget it as long as I live. What *would* I give, if we could have but a quiet week together!

Spain is a lazy place, and its climate an indolent one. But if you have ever leisure under its sunny skies to think of a man who loves you, and holds communion with your spirit, oftener perhaps than any other person alive—leisure

---

[1] Spelt correctly on outside of letter, incorrectly in subscription.

[2] At Baltimore. Described by CD as the most comfortable of all the hotels he stayed in: "where the English traveller will find curtains to his bed, for the first and probably the last time, in America; and where he will be likely to have enough water for washing himself, which is not at all a common case" (*American Notes*, Ch. 9). "It had the appearance of a large private house," wrote R. H. Dana, Jr; "the walls were covered with paper representing scenes from the classic history or mythology, in the old fashioned style, & there was a prodigality of room in the entries & passage ways"; but—as was typical of the South—"things wh. had

broken had been left unrepaired in the yard of this large & fashionable hotel, a piece of rope took the place of a broken door handle", and so on (*Journal*, ed. R. F. Lucid, I, 237).

[3] After one night in Washington on their way from Richmond.

[4] Of their dining together on 16 Mar (see *To* Irving, 15 Mar).

[5] Irving came to Baltimore, in fact, and met CD twice: on the 22nd Robert Gilmor took them both to dine with his friend Jonathan Meredith, where Hone was a fellow-guest (*Diary of Philip Hone*, ed. A. Nevins, p. 592); and on the evening of the 23rd they dined together and drank a mint julep (*To* Guy, 23 Mar and *fn*).

from listlessness, I mean—and will write to me in London, you will give me an inexpressible amount of pleasure.[1]

Your affectionate friend

Washington Irving Esquire   CHARLES DICKENS[2]

To W. W. SEATON, 21 MARCH 1842*

MS Benoliel Collection. *Address:* W. W. Seaton Esquire.

Washington | Monday afternoon. March Twenty First | 1842.

My Dear Sir.

This will reach you when we have gone on to Baltimore; and will tell you that we came back here last night, and left this morning. It is such a hard thing, that saying good b'ye, when one has no time to say anything besides, that we resolved to write it. Here it is—and with it our best regards to Mrs. Seaton and your family, whom we shall not easily forget.

Your son shewed us every attention, in Richmond. You were a false prophet in respect of his requiring to be drawn out. We were friends directly.[3]

With many thanks to you for your hospitality and kindness, believe me ever

Faithfully Yours

W. W. Seaton Esquire   CHARLES DICKENS

To LORD BROUGHAM, 22 MARCH 1842*

MS The Hon. Mrs John Mildmay-White. *Address:* The Right Honorable | The Lord Brougham | Grafton Street | London | England.

Baltimore. United States. | Twenty Second March 1842.

Dear Lord Brougham.

As you were so kind as to express some interest in my movements, I cannot resist the temptation I feel to write and tell you that I have seen Judge Story, and

---

[1] Only one later letter (dated 5 July 56: MDGH, III, 178) from CD to Irving is known (see *To* Forster, 17 Feb, *fn*).

[2] Letter is endorsed "Baltimore March 21—1842": perhaps a note made by Irving of CD's movements. CD would have reached Baltimore at about 6.30 that evening.

[3] Seaton's elder son, Gales, had called on CD the morning after his arrival in Richmond, and on 20 Mar described his experiences in a letter to his father: "Entering the room with somewhat of a tremor, . . . I was seized by the hand and almost *slung* [*thus: see To Seaton, 30 Apr*, fn] across the room, and a dozen remarks and questions addressed to me in a breath. For he was entirely alone and writing. In

reply, I at first could only gasp, without much power of articulation; for I suppose few persons feel with more devotion the homage due to the majesty of genius than I. He proposed a walk, and we went to French Gardens. I need not say that I was delighted with his affable, cordial, frank, and conversible manner, a strong proof of which is, that in ten minutes I nearly forgot his distinction as an author, and conversed with him on a variety of topics as they naturally arose." He went on to mention CD's numerous later visitors and a further meeting at the levee CD held on 19 Mar (see [Josephine Seaton], *W. W. Seaton of the "National Intelligencer"*, pp. 274-6).

executed your commission;[1] and that if there be anything I can possibly do for you before I return on the 7th. of June, I shall be truly proud and glad to do it. Is there nothing I can bring back for you—animate or inanimate? Have you no fancy for any American reprint of any book? Cannot you invent a desire which I may be the means of gratifying? If you can, and will write to me, to the care of David Colden Esquire, 28 Laight Street, Hudson Square, New York, your letter will be safely sent on to me, wherever I may be.

You may perhaps have heard that they do me great honor here, and that I can't help making a public progress through the land—sorely against my own habits and inclinations. As they purposed getting up a public entertainment in every town I passed through, I was obliged to diffuse public notice that I would not accept any festivals after leaving New York. But I have made an exception in favor of one body of readers in the Far West. They reside at St. Louis, which is two thousand miles from here, and on the confines of the Indian Territory. I am going there—to dinner—and start the day after tomorrow.

I have been South as far as Richmond in Virginia; but the weather becoming prematurely hot; and the sight of Slavery, and the mere fact of living in a town where it exists being positive misery to me; I turned back. The Southerners are perfectly frantic on the subject of your speech in reference to the Creole affair.[2] I know you are not sorry, my Lord, to hear *that*.

I have done, and am doing, my best to shame the Americans into the passing of an International Copyright Law with England. Mr. Preston who will be the leader of the Whig party on Mr. Clay's retirement gives me such positive assurances, that I almost begin to hope it may be brought about. The system, as it stands, is most iniquitous and disgraceful. A writer not only gets nothing for his labours, though they are diffused all over this enormous Continent, but cannot even choose his company. Any wretched halfpenny newspaper can print him at its pleasure—place him side by side with productions which disgust his common sense—and by means of the companionship in which it constantly shews him, engenders a feeling of association in the minds of a large class of readers, from which he would revolt, and to avoid which he would pay almost any price.[3]

I have some scruples of conscience whether a letter so brief and so devoid of interest be worth the sending; but I give myself the benefit of the doubt on the chance of being useful to you. And I am always My Lord

Yours faithfully and obliged

CHARLES DICKENS

The Right Honorable | The Lord Brougham.

---

[1] See *To* W. W. Story, 4 Feb and *fn.*

[2] See *To* Fonblanque, 12 (and ?21) Mar. In the House of Lords on 14 Feb Brougham had argued that, since the slaves' alleged offence had been committed on "American territory" (the ship), there was no provision under English law either for their detention or their delivery to the American Govt.

[3] For CD's more passionate outburst on the subject, see *To* Austin, 1 May and *fn.*

To MISS BURDETT COUTTS,[1] 22 MARCH 1842

MS Morgan Library. *Address:* Miss Burdett Coutts | Stratton Street | Piccadilly | London | England.

Baltimore. United States. | Twenty Second March 1842.

Dear Miss Coutts.

You have long ago discharged from your mind any favorable opinion you may ever have entertained of me—and have set me down, I know, as a neglectful, erratic, promise-breaking, and most unworthy person.

And yet I have not forgotten the book you asked me to bring home for you— nor the pebble I am to gather for Lady Burdett[2] at Niagara—nor the something unstipulated[3] which I am to put in my portmanteau for Miss Meredith.[4] The truth is that they give me everything here, but Time. That they never will leave me alone. That I shake hands every day when I am not travelling, with five or six hundred people. That Mrs. Dickens and I hold a formal Levee in every town we come to, and usually faint away (from fatigue) every day while dressing for dinner.—In a word, that we devoutly long for Home, and look forward to the seventh of next June when we sail, please God, from New York—most ardently.

I have sent you some newspapers; and I hope they have reached you. They gave me a ball at New York, at which Three Thousand people were present—and a public dinner besides—and another in Boston—and another in a place called Hertford. Others were projected, literally all through the States, but I gave public notice, that I couldn't accept them: being of mere flesh and blood, and having only mortal powers of digestion. But I have made an exception in favor of one body of readers at St. Louis—a town in the Far West, on the confines of the Indian territory. I am going there to dinner—it's only two thousand miles from here—and start the day after tomorrow.

I look forward to making such an impression on you with the store of anecdote and description with which I shall return, that I can't find it in my Heart to open it—on paper. I don't see how I shall ever get rid of my gatherings. It seems to me, at present, that when I come home I must take a cottage on Putney Heath, or Richmond Green, or some other wild and desolate place, and talk to myself for a month or two, until I have sobered down a little, and am quiet again. A prophetic feeling comes upon me sometimes, and hints that I shall return, a bore—.[5]

We had a terrible passage out, and mean to return in a sailing ship. Can you

---

[1] Angela Georgina Burdett Coutts (1814–1906; *DNB*), later Baroness Burdett-Coutts: see Vol. I, p. 559*n*.

[2] Miss Coutts's mother, formerly Sophia Coutts (1775–1844), one of the three daughters of Thomas Coutts the banker— nicknamed "the three Graces". She married Sir Francis Burdett 1793; their early married life was unhappy, and she was an invalid for many years before her death. Lived abroad for some time and kept up an intimate correspondence with Adelaide d'Orléans, Louis Philippe's sister. Like her sister Lady Guilford, quarrelled bitterly with her father after his second marriage, to Harriet Mellon, within a fortnight of her mother's death (Jan 1815); but was eventually reconciled.

[3] For the various mementoes promised, see Vol. II, p. 444, and for those he brought back, 2 July 42.

[4] Hannah Meredith (*d.* 1878), Miss Coutts's companion: see Vol. II, p. 168*n*.

[5] CD's expressed fear on his return from Scotland: see Vol. II, p. 335.

think of anything I can bring back for you? If you can possibly commission me to bring you any article whatever from the New Country, I need scarcely say how proud and glad you will make me. Any letter addressed to me to the care of David Colden Esquire 28 Laight Street Hudson Square New York, would be forwarded to me wheresoever I might chance to be at the time of its receipt.

May I ask you when you next see Mr. Marjoribanks[1] to tell him, with my best regards, that I thank him very much for his letters,[2] and have received the greatest attention from all his correspondents—except the poor gentleman at Washington —who has been dead six years. Not finding him readily (no wonder!) I went into a bank to ask for him. I happened to make the enquiry of a very old clerk, who staggered to a stool and fell into a cold perspiration, as if he had seen a spectre. Being feeble, and the shock being very great, he took to his bed—but he has since recovered: to the great joy of his wife and family.

With every good and cordial wish for your health and happiness—many messages of regard to Miss Meredith—and very many scruples of conscience in sending you so poor a letter from so long a distance—I am always, Dear Miss Coutts,

With true regard | Faithfully Your obliged friend
CHARLES DICKENS

P.S. I forgot to say that I have been at Washington (which is beyond here) and as far beyond that, again, as Richmond in Virginia. But the prematurely hot weather, and the sight of slaves, turned me back.

To GEORGE D'ALMAINE,[3] [?22 MARCH 1842]

Mention in next. *Date:* CD received a letter from D'Almaine in Philadelphia, 5–9 Mar (*To* Forster, 1 Apr); by 13 Mar he had decided to break his journey West at Pittsburgh (*To* Sumner, that day); but he probably answered D'Almaine's letter only when he knew which day he could be expected.

Asking him to meet their canal boat at Pittsburgh and secure rooms for them at a hotel there.

To FREDERICK DICKENS, 22 MARCH 1842*

MS Berg Collection.

Baltimore. United States. | Twenty Second March 1842.

My Dear Fred.

You must take the will for the deed in my case, and not measure the length of your letters, by the length of mine. Although I have declined, and constantly

---

[1] Edward Marjoribanks (1776–1868), senior partner in Coutts's Bank: see Vol. I, p. 527*n*.

[2] Arranging credit for CD in the cities he visited.

[3] George D'Almaine (?1808–93), portrait-painter, whom CD had known before he migrated to America *c.* 1840 (see *To* Forster, 1 Apr 42). He had settled in Pittsburgh by 1841; did some painting in New York and Boston; and lived 1853–84 in Baltimore, where he is said to have always kept a British flag in his house (*250 Years of Painting in Maryland*, Baltimore, 1945, p. 59).

decline, all public entertainments, our life is a very fatiguing one. In every place we come to, we hold regular Levees or drawing rooms, and receive immense crowds of people. This, and constant engagements morning, noon, and night (to say nothing of the fatigues of travelling by railroad, stage, & steam boat, and getting up at four or five o'Clock in the morning for that purpose) occasionally quite wear us out; and at the best leave very little leisure, as you may suppose, for writing.

The Secretary continues to do very well—Kate of course don't like him. He is sentimental certainly—has a languishing air—and is a cross between Burnett[1] and Hartland.[2] He sings too—and tells marvellous lies concerning his past life— in both of which aspects of his character, you will detect a resemblance to one of the gentlemen I have likened him to.[3] But he is of great use. If it were for nothing else but paying the bills, and collecting the luggage, he would be, like the soothing Syrup, "A real blessing"—As to the baggage, its amount is fearful to behold. We are going into the Far West, the day after tomorrow; and as we shall have to cross Mountains, Forests, and Prairies, we are packing a quantity of it off to New York, and cutting ourselves down to the smallest amount of necessaries. Anne is a very good land traveller; but at sea she is the dismallest of the dismal.

We have struck Charleston out of our trip, as the weather South, is intensely and prematurely hot. We have been as far as Richmond, and, even under more favorable circumstances, would certainly not have been tempted by the sight of Slavery, to proceed. I have made one exception in my determination, and accepted a public entertainment at St. Louis, where they had a meeting and passed certain resolutions which I have sent to Forster. It is on the borders of the Indian Territory—only two thousand miles from here—and, as one may say, almost next door.

Do you remember little George D'Almaine? He is a portrait painter at a Western town on the Ohio, called Pittsburgh. We shall be there next Sunday;[4] and as he wrote me a very good letter, I have written to beg him to secure rooms for us at the Hotel[5] (whatever it may be) and to meet us at the Canal boat. Fancy us on board a canal boat—walking on the towing path whenever we feel disposed for a change—and having four days and nights of it! We go from Pittsburgh to Cincinnati—to Louisville—to St. Louis—back to Louisville—across the Great Prairie to Chicago[6]—then down the lakes to Buffalo—by railroad to Niagara, where we stay a week. From thence we run into Canada, and so return to New York. We have arranged to embark from New York for England in the George Washington Packet Ship, on the 7th. of June. We shall count the days until that blessed time arrives.

We had your first letter—the Caledonia one—at Washington, & it is impossible

---

[1] Henry Burnett (1811–93), CD's brother-in-law: see Vol. I, p. 342*n*, and *To* Burnett, 25 Nov 42, *fn*.

[2] H. G. Hartland, an acquaintance of CD's reporting days: see Vol. I, p. 10.

[3] Probably Burnett, a professional singer.

[4] They arrived there on the Monday evening.

[5] D'Almaine booked rooms for them at the Exchange Hotel and dined with them on the three days they were in Pittsburgh.

[6] They in fact cut out Chicago and went to Buffalo *via* Cincinnati and Columbus.

to say with what joy we sat up half the night, and read that, and the whole packetfull.[1] Your second letter awaited us here last night, together with Forster's Ontario[2] epistle. I can't make out how that second letter of yours, came. You have marked it by the Acadia—not the steam packet surely?[3]

Forrest[4] breakfasted with us at Richmond (Richmond is in Virginia, among the tobacco manufactories) last Saturday. He appears to be a very amiable fellow—has a charming wife[5]—and spoke most gratefully of Macready's kindness to him when he was in London.[6] All manner of Theatricals are at the lowest possible ebb here. The Southern people are perfectly frantic about the Creole business. Lord Ashburton is looked for every day. We were at a drawing room at the Presidents, and were invited to dinner besides, but couldn't wait. Kate's face swells every other day. My hair is terribly long, & I am afraid, to have it cut, lest the barber (bribed by admirers) should clip it all off for presents.[7] And I think that's all our personal news. I have told a very few of our adventures to Forster, who will tell them to you. But I reserve my great effects (including some brilliant stories, illustrations, imitations &c) until I come home.

*a*I can't tell you, Fred, how very much pleased I have been with your letters, or truly gratified by your affectionate care of our dear darlings. But I shall never forget your brotherly regard, or cease to place the most implicit and unhesitating reliance in all you say and do in reference to what is dear to Kate and me.*a*

Always Your loving brother

CHARLES DICKENS

Write long letters—long letters—full, true, and particular accounts—and always direct to the care of David Colden—who is as prompt and anxious as if they were his letters; not ours.[8]

---

[1] Thus in MS.

[2] The packet-boat *Ontario I*, of the Red Swallowtail Line, London, one of the fastest transatlantic packets.

[3] CD presumably supposed that a letter coming by the *Acadia* would have reached him on 13 Mar when he received the *Caledonia* mail which the *Acadia* had carried besides its own, and was puzzled by the letter's arrival a week later. But probably the *Acadia* had given the delayed *Caledonia* mail priority.

[4] Edwin Forrest (1806–72; *DAB*), the first major American-born actor. Made his début in Philadelphia 1820; played Othello in New York 1826; and by 1830 was the leading American tragic actor. He had immense vigour and a dominating presence. Acted with great success in London 1836–7, when CD (and perhaps Fred too) may well have seen him.

[5] *Née* Catherine Norton Sinclair, daughter of the singer and composer John Sinclair (1791–1857; *DNB*). They were

married in England in June 37—and divorced in 1852 after a notorious trial.

[6] See *To* Macready, 22 Mar, *fn*.

[7] See *To* Mrs Colden, 24 Feb, *fn*.

aa A thick wavy line has been drawn down the margin beside this paragraph—possibly by Fred, either on first reading the letter or (perhaps more probably) on a rereading in 1857 when CD had refused to help him with his debts. Fred then bitterly reminded him of his "protestations of affection & regard . . . in years gone by" (5 Feb 57: MS Huntington).

[8] CD's letter occupies 2⅓ pp. of a folded sheet. On the remaining 1⅔ pp. (one of them crossed) Catherine added: "Many thanks my dearest Fred for your most kind and thrice welcome letter which I received last night most unexpectedly on arriving at this place. | Its contents were delightful and satisfactory to me and it is impossible to feel anxious about my darlings, when they have such a kind and anxious friend in you. I am as well as

To LADY HOLLAND,[1] 22 MARCH 1842†

MS The Earl of Ilchester. *Address:* The Right Honorable | The Lady Holland |
South Street. Grosvenor Square | London | England.

Baltimore. United States. | Twenty Second March 1842.
Dear Lady Holland.

*a*I know I am not mistaken in thinking that you would like to hear from my
own lips that I am well; not at all spoiled (you remember that you thought I
should be?); and longing, in common with my wife, to be again in our dear old
home, and among our friends and children. You will have smiled, before getting
so far, at my using the word "lips";—but my pen has so long supplied the place
of a voice, that the expression comes quite naturally to me.*a*

Perhaps you know something of the Public Progress I am obliged to make in
this country—of the ball (attended by three thousand people) which they gave me
at New York—and of the festivals of all kinds with which they have received me.
Public entertainments were proposed in every town I intended to visit—but I
gave public notice that I could not possibly bear it, and have refused all those in
contemplation, except one. This originates with the people of St. Louis; a town
in the Far West, near the Indian territory. It is only two thousand miles from
here—quite next door, as one may say—and I am going there to dinner. We
start the day after tomorrow.

It was a great delight to me to see Irving, for whom I have conceived a perfect
affection. He talks of leaving here for Liverpool on the 7th. of next month—
when I say, here, I mean New York. He goes on to London of course. We spoke
very much of you—and with a grateful pleasure that had at least the merit of
being perfectly sincere.[2]

Charles deeply grateful to you, for your
attention to them dear Fred. | We are
thankful to get away from the South—the
heat is already intense and to us unbearable.
the other day at Richmond we could
hardly breathe, and I daresay you can
hardly realize (a favourite expression here)
seeing Peach trees in full blossom in March,
but so it is. As you may imagine the sight
of the slavery was most painful to us and
we were most happy to turn our backs upon
it, however we are still in a slave state and
shall be until Thursday morning, when we
go West, yet we dont see it here, and there
are none in the Hotel. Thank God, they
are all white, we are quite tired of black
faces. We were much amused by Forster's
account of Topping and Blackie. I think
Sir John [*Wilson*] must be a little bit mean
to make such a fuss about sixpence a week.
Will you give my best regards to Harriet,
Charlotte and St[?ockhausen]. The latter's
wages now from the time Walter was
weaned are at the rate of ten guineas a
year. The others I think you have a correct

list of. We are now anxiously looking for
the Columbia when I hope to receive another long letter from you. In the meantime as Charles is hurrying me and wishes
to put up the Packet of Letters I will only
add with thousands of loves and kisses to
my most beloved children that I am My
dearest Fred | Your sincerely attached
sister | CATHERINE DICKENS | I am so glad
to hear dear Mamma has been out and
that she has seen the children. I have
written a long letter to Georgina by this
Packet. What a strange coincidence that
young Power should have been in the
Caledonia—how could he venture in a
Steamer [*his father, Tyrone Power, having
been drowned in the* President *1841*]."

[1] Elizabeth Vassall Fox (1770–1845;
DNB), wife of the 3rd Baron Holland: see
Vol. I, p. 412*n*.

aa Not previously published.

[2] Irving had been entertained at Holland
House several times on his former stay in
London. He dined with Lady Holland
again, in South Street, on 4 May 42.

*a*Mrs. Dickens remains well in this very trying climate, and begs me to thank your Ladyship for the kind message you sent her, when I came to take leave of you. We are obliged to hold a Levee for all comers, every day when we are not travelling—and labour very hard indeed, I do assure you. The Queen and Prince Albert can scarcely be more tired—for ours is a perpetual Drawing Room. Our crown, too, is not a Golden one, except in opinion.*a*

We have been to Boston, Worcester, Hertford, New Haven, New York, Philadelphia, Washington, and Richmond in Virginia. We originally intended to have gone as far South as Charleston, but the prematurely hot weather, and the sight of slavery, turned us back.[1] We are now on our way to the Forests, Mountains, and Prairies of the West; and have taken our passage in a sailing ship which leaves New York for England on the 7th. of June.

I have made *some* observations, of course. They are not all favorable, for I love England better than I did when I left her. But I am bound to say that travellers have grossly exaggerated Amcrican rudeness and obtrusion.[2] Among all the thousands whom I have seen, within doors and without (and they are so many that I have almost paralyzed my right arm by constantly shaking hands) I have never once encountered a man, woman, or child, who has asked me a rude question, or made a rude remark. The best and only passports needed in this country, are frankness and good humour. This is not the opinion of a man who has been conciliated by flattery or attention. I have much to say on the other side of the question. But the people are naturally courteous, good-tempered, generous, warmhearted, and obliging. That is a matter of fact, and not of opinion.

I have been a week or so behind Lord Morpeth everywhere. He is now in the South,[3] but if the rumoured account of his movements be correct, I still hope to fall in with him, westward.[4] Wherever he has been, he has won the hearts of all kinds of people. They quite love him; and as I truly respect his character, I am proud and glad to hear his praises.[5]

---

aa Not previously published.

[1] For Lady Holland's belief that one of CD's main purposes in going to America was "to ascertain by personal inspection the condition of the poor slaves", see Vol. II, p. 447*n*.

[2] It was only when he went further West that he experienced this—e.g. on the canal boat from Harrisburg (*American Notes*, Ch. 10) and at Cleveland on Lake Erie (*To Forster*, 26 Apr and *fn*).

[3] After leaving Washington, Morpeth had gone by steamboat and railroad to Charleston; thence by mail-packet (2–14 Mar) to Cuba. While on board he noted in his diary: "I thought it a still higher compliment to Dickens than all the public demonstrations he has received that almost every one of the motley crew I have enumerated were engaged in reading one or other of his novels" (MS Mr George Howard).

[4] They did not meet, but missed each other narrowly in Louisville, where CD stayed a night for the second time, on his return from St Louis on 17 Apr, and Lord Morpeth arrived a few days later from New Orleans. By early May CD had crossed into Canada, while Morpeth was in Virginia again, after a visit to Henry Clay in Ashland, Kentucky. Morpeth then travelled to Canada through Cincinnati (which CD had left on 20 Apr), St Louis, Chicago and the Great Lakes.

[5] Sumner wrote to Morpeth on 28 Dec 41: "[Prescott's] heart was full of you, and I was delighted to find such sympathy for my own feelings. . . . Believe me, everybody feels most kindly to you" (E. L. Pierce, *Memoir and Letters of Charles Sumner*, II, 189). Philip Hone, who had given a dinner party for him in New York in Dec 41, recorded: "Lord Morpeth grows upon us amazingly"

*a*This is a poor letter to send you, Lady Holland, from so great a distance; but if it were only because it is a gratification of heart to me to wish you peace of mind, health, and happiness—if I had not the selfish desire to live in your remembrance—I should be tempted to inflict it upon you. If you can charge me with any commission, great or small, I need scarcely say it would be a real pleasure to me to execute it. Any letter addressed to me, to the care of David Colden Esquire 28 Laight Street Hudson Square New York, would be sure to reach me.

I am always
Yours faithfully, and truly obliged

The Lady Holland.   CHARLES DICKENS

I beg to be kindly remembered to Mr. Allen.[1]
We carry with us, a sketch of our darlings, by Maclise. It is a great [comfort.][2] We unpack it every night, if we be on a journey; and make as [?much of t][3]his little Household God, as though it were alive.*a*

To LORD JEFFREY, [?22 MARCH 1842]

Mention in *To* Colden, 4 Apr. *Date:* sent by the steamer leaving Boston on 2 Apr; probably written on 22 Mar, the day CD wrote to other English friends.

To DANIEL MACLISE, 22 MARCH 1842

MS Comtesse de Suzannet. *Address:* Daniel Maclise Esquire. R.A. | 14 Russell Place | Fitzroy Square | London | England.

Baltimore. | Twenty Second March 1842.

My very dear Mac.
From the depths of the Far West, whither we are now going—from the heights of

<hr>

(*Diary*, ed. B. Tuckerman, II, 103). Several newspaper reports contrasted his aristocratic bearing with CD's. Dana recorded that he "preferred Lord Morpeth"—who was "well educated, well bred, high minded, agreeable", although lacking CD's genius and "native cleverness" (*Journal*, ed. R. F. Lucid, I, 59). For Ward's comparison, see 21 Feb, *fn.*

aa Not previously published.

[1] John Allen (1771–1843; *DNB*), MD Edinburgh 1791; Whig scholar and historical writer; contributor to the *Edinburgh Review*. Physician and secretary to Lord Holland in Spain 1801–5 and 1808–9, and thereafter lived at Holland House as librarian and one of the family; meanwhile Warden of Dulwich College

1811–20 and Master 1820 to his death. A man of great learning and general information, "indispensable at every Holland House entertainment" (*Elizabeth, Lady Holland to her Son*, ed. the Earl of Ilchester, 1946, p. viii); known as "Lady Holland's atheist", and the subject of numerous affectionate jokes in Sydney Smith's letters to her. She described herself as "like a fish out of water when Allen is absent" (*op. cit.*, p. 47).

[2] Tear in paper at seal has removed word of about 7 letters, but tops of last 4 are just visible: "comfort" seems certain.

[3] Words of about 10 letters (including spaces between words) missing through hole at seal: "much of t" seems probable.

the Alleghanny[1] Mountains which we are about to ascend—from the small cabin of the canal boat in which we embark—from the surface of the Lakes we have yet to traverse—and amidst the silence of the broad Prairies we shall shortly cross—nay from the gloom of the Great Mammoth Cave in Kentucky,[2] and high above the roar and spray of dread Niagara—my voice shall be heard, cursing the Academy. I will call down imprecations on the head of Martin Archer Shee[3] from the solitudes where the Indians used to roam, and from which the white man has driven everything but the red sun which lingers there every evening as it did of yore—(oh beautiful, beautiful!)[4] I will Anathematize the Green table and *un* holy water bottles[5] in the splendour of early morning, and the softened beauty of the night. I will spit upon Trafalgar Square,[6] and set my heel upon the Council Chamber. The aged and staggering associates shall dwindle peak and pine,[7] beneath my withering blight—and the ranks of R.A's shall be thinned by me.

And could you—*could* you, Mac— lose the recollection of us, in the crownĕd presence of the King of Prussia?[8] Was Devonshire Terrace forgotten, in the Monarch's state? Was it a necessary consequence of being out of your sight (and good God my dear boy, what an eye you have)[9] that we should be out of your mind, likewise? Oh Mac, Mac. The Caledonia, having no letter from you on board, was ashamed of her mission, and put back. The very ocean rebelled at the enormity. How it must have gone to your heart—what coals of fire were heaped upon your head—when you had those two letters from me; and especially that one with the ball bill of fare, and Kate's portrait![10]—You were penitent *then*. I know you were.[11]

---

[1] Thus in MS.

[2] Discovered 1809, near Green River, south of Louisville. Called by Harriet Martineau, who made a coach-journey of two nights and a day to reach it from Nashville, "the largest explored cave in the world"; "All the lords and lights of England had been to see [it], except the king", the guide told her (see *Society in America*, I, 227–35). An article in the *New World*, 6 Aug 42, by J. C. Zabriskie (who had visited it that year), described the "main Cave" as seven miles long, with 159 branches, the extent to which anyone had "groped through" them being 70 miles. Though CD changed boats at Louisville twice, he clearly had no time for an extra expedition by coach.

[3] Sir Martin Archer Shee (1769–1850; *DNB*), PRA: see Vol. II, p. 262n.

[4] Evidently a private joke between CD, Maclise and Forster (perhaps at Forster's expense): cf. *To* Maclise, 25 Nov 40 (II, 157); Maclise *to* CD, of *Ethelstan*, "very, very beautiful!!" (II, 209n); and *To* Forster, 28 Mar.

[5] Of the RA Committee room: cf. Vol. II, p. 209.

[6] The site of the Royal Academy 1836 to 1868, when it moved to Burlington House, Piccadilly.

[7] *Macbeth*, I, iii, 23.

[8] King Frederick of Prussia had paid a State visit to England 22 Jan–4 Feb for the christening of the Prince of Wales, his godson. He visited the National Gallery with Peel on 28 Jan, and was received by Shee and several Trustees of the RA. Detailed accounts of his movements appeared in the newspapers (and were parodied in *Punch*, Feb 42, II, 76–7).

[9] Clearly a private joke: cf. *To* Maclise, 27 Feb and *fn*.

[10] The ridiculous woodcut in the *Extra Boz Herald*: see *To* Maclise, 27 Feb, *fn*.

[11] Maclise had wanted to write, but had not managed it: see *To* Maclise, ?30 or 31 Jan, *fn*. But CD received a letter from him later: see *To* Forster, 26 May.

We have been travelling a great deal. Forster has a few scraps of description—in trust, as usual. As to Scenery, we really have seen very little as yet. It is the same thing over and over again. The railroads go through the low grounds and swamps, and it is all one eternal forest, with fallen trees mouldering away in stagnant water and decayed vegetable matter—and heaps of timber in every aspect of decay and utter ruin. I dress up imaginary tribes of Indians, as we rattle on, and scatter them among the trees as they used to be—sleeping in their blankets, cleaning their arms, nursing brown children, and so forth. But saving an occasional log hut, with children at the door, or a slave house, or a white man with an axe and a great dog, long miles and miles are wholly destitute of life, or change of any kind.

You will be familiar, very likely on the day this reaches you, with all that I have written to Forster. I will let it have the freshness of novelty, and spare you its repetition. He tells me great things of your Hamlet.[1] What would I give to see it! But we shall be home, please God, before the exhibition closes; and thats[2] a comfort.[3]

Do you feel as though you would like some summer rides, some summer walks, some dinners, strolls at night, and minor theatre visitations? Do you feel as if, when we come home, you would like us, even better than the Academy, for a few weeks? For myself, if Shee stood bodily upon the pier of Liverpool when I leaped ashore, I would forget the past, and shake hands with him.— Yes.—I would.

Imagine Kate and I—a kind of Queen and Albert—holding a Levee every day (proclaimed and placarded in newspapers) and receiving all who choose to come. Imagine—but you can't imagine, without seeing them—how now and then a republican boy, of surpassing and indescribable free and easiness comes in among the company, and keeping his cap upon his head, inspects me at his leisure. We had one the other day who remained two hours, and took no other refreshment during the whole time than an occasional pick at his nose, or survey of the street from the open window, whence he invited other boys to come up, and do the like. Imagine, when I landed from a steam boat in New York, in a dense crowd, some twenty or thirty people, screwing small dabs of fur out of the back of that costly great coat I bought in Regent Street![4] Imagine these public receptions occurring *every day*, and how I feel towards the people who come in, fresh, and full of speech and questioning, when I am quite tired out! Every railroad car is like a great omnibus. Whenever we come to a town station, the crowd surround it, let down all the windows, thrust in their heads, stare at me, and compare notes respecting my appearance, with as much coolness as if I

---

[1] *The Play Scene in Hamlet*: see *To Forster*, 22–23 Mar, *fn.*
[2] Thus in MS.
[3] CD saw the picture on 23 July.
[4] Described by the *Worcester Aegis* (9 Feb) as "a shaggy coat of bear or buffalo skin that would excite the admiration of a Kentucky huntsman"; by the *Extra Boz Herald* (15 Feb) as "about three times as shaggy as the hide of a Siberian bear". It evidently contrasted strongly with CD's waistcoats and cravats which were often considered "flash".

were a Marble image. What do you think of *that*—as you would say, your-self.

Ever My Dear Mac
Your Faithful (though unacademic) friend
CHARLES DICKENS

My best regards to all your house.[1]

To W. C. MACREADY, 22 MARCH 1842†

MS Morgan Library. *Address:* W. C. Macready Esquire | 5 Clarence Terrace | York Gate Regents Park | London | England.

Baltimore. Twenty Second March 1842.

My Dear Friend.

I beg your pardon—but you were speaking of rash leaps at hasty conclusions. Are you quite sure you designed that remark for me? Have you not, in the hurry of correspondence, slipped a paragraph into my letter, which belongs of right to somebody else?[2] When did you ever know me leap at a *wrong* conclusion? I pause for a reply.[3] Pray Sir did you ever find me admiring Mr. Bryden?[4] On the contrary, did you never hear of my protesting through good, better, and best report, that he was not an open or a candid man and would one day *beyond all doubt* displease you by not being so. I pause again for a reply.

Are you quite sure, Mr. Macready,—and I address myself to you with the sternness of a man in the pit—are you quite sure Sir, that you do not view America through the pleasant mirage which often surrounds a thing that has been, but not a thing that is. Are you quite sure that when you were here,[5] you relished it as well as you do now, when you look back upon it. The early spring birds, Mr. Macready, *do* sing in the groves, that you were very often not over well pleased with many of the new Country's social aspects. Are the birds[6] to be trusted? Again I pause for a reply.

My dear Macready, I desire to be so honest and just to those who have so

---

[1] Catherine added the following on p. 3 of CD's letter (words or parts of words missing through hole torn at seal are given here in square brackets; "Marion" was clearly Marion Ely: see Vol. II, p. 79*n*): "Dear Mr. Maclise | I only add a word to put you in mind there is such a being in existence which I fear you have forgotten unless that heavenly portrait [*a joke: see above*] has awakened some dormant recollections. Pray write to us, you do not know what a delight it is to receive letters from our friends in this distant [land]. Does Marion still reign paramou[nt] in your heart or has some [other] bright being taken her place? It is just dinner time so [I] only add that I am alway[s] | Your very sincere frie[nd] | CATHERINE DICKENS | My beautiful sketch of our dar[lings] is more admired than I can possibly describe. It is in great demand wherever we go and Willis, the author actually asked me to give it to him imagine such impudence! and audacity!"

[2] Presumably CD was commenting on Macready's letter to him of 30 Jan (written while Forster was writing on his behalf to *The Times*: see *Diaries*, II, 155)—at last received at Washington on 13 Mar (*To* Forster, 15 Mar). Macready's next letter reached CD at Pittsburgh on 1 Apr.

[3] Brutus to Plebeians, *Julius Caesar*, III, ii, 34.

[4] i.e. Brydone, Macready's business-manager (see Vol. II, p. 72*n*). For Mac-ready's enraged outburst of 2 Jan 42 at Brydone's inefficiency, see *Diaries*, II, 153.

[5] On an eight-months' tour 1826–7.

[6] No doubt the Coldens, who had seen much of Macready at the time.

enthusiastically and earnestly welcomed me, that I burned the last letter I wrote to you[1]—even to *you* to whom I would speak as to myself—rather than let it come with anything that might seem like an ill-considered word of disappointment. I preferred that you should think me neglectful (if you could imagine anything so wild) rather than I should do wrong in this respect.—Still it is of no use. I *am* disappointed. This is not the Republic I came to see. This is not the Republic of my imagination. I infinitely prefer a liberal Monarchy—even with its sickening accompaniments of Court Circulars, and Kings of Prussia[2]—to such a Government as this. *a*In every respect but that of National Education,[3] the Country disappoints me.*a* The more I think of its youth and strength, the poorer and more trifling in a thousand respects, it appears in my eyes. In everything of which it has made a boast—excepting its education of the people, and its care for poor children[4]—it sinks immeasurably below the level I had placed it upon. And England, even England, bad and faulty as the old land is, and miserable as millions of her people are, rises in the comparison. *b*Strike down the established church,[5] and I would take her to my heart for better or worse, and reject this new love without a pang or moment's hesitation.*b*

You live here, Macready, as I have sometimes heard you imagining! *You!* Loving you with all my heart and soul, *c*and knowing what your disposition

[1] Probably on 27 Feb—the day CD wrote to his other English friends.

[2] See *To* Maclise, 22 Mar, *fn.*

aa; bb Omitted in MDGH and subsequent editions.

[3] An exception made in most other English travellers' criticisms. See for instance Lord Morpeth, *Travels in America*, 1851, p. 23: "It would be uncandid if I did not state that the universality of the instruction, and the excellence of what fell under my own observation, presented to my mind some mortifying points of contrast with what we have hitherto effected at home." In *Chuzzlewit* (Ch. 17) the good Mr Bevan replies to Martin's question about American education: "Pretty well on that head, . . . still no mighty matter to boast of . . . We shine out brightly in comparison with England, certainly, but hers is a very extreme case." To a more conservative mind such as Lyell's, America's universal education was "the only good result" tending to counterbalance the evils of universal suffrage (*Travels in North America*, I, 120).

[4] CD had visited five institutions which cared for poor children. In Boston he had seen the Perkins Institution (see *To* Felton, 1 Sep, *fn*); the Boylston school for neglected and indigent boys, who "appeared exceedingly well-taught, and not better taught than fed"; the House of

Reformation for Juvenile Offenders, designed to be "a place of purification and improvement, not of demoralisation and corruption"; and the orphans' and young children's section of the House of Industry, where—for the very small children—Lilliputian stairs fitted "their tiny strides", the seats looked like "articles of furniture for a pauper doll's-house", and CD imagined to himself how the English Poor Law Commissioners would laugh at "the notion of these seats having arms and backs" (*American Notes*, Ch. 3). In New York he visited the Refuge for the Destitute, an institution to reclaim youthful offenders, black and white, and teach them trades (*op. cit.*, Ch. 6).

[5] Macready would have understood what CD meant. On 20 Aug 40 he recorded in his diary: "Talked much with Dickens, whose views on politics and religion seem very much to square with mine" (*Diaries*, II, 75). To both, the English Church had become politically, through its dependence on the State, a bastion of reactionary Toryism and bigotry—from which Macready disassociated himself, "being, or professing to be, a *Christian*" (*op. cit.*, II, 223).

cc Added over a caret in same ink as final paragraph of letter; clearly an afterthought.

really is,*c* I would not condemn you to a year's residence on this side of the Atlantic, for any money.[1] Freedom of opinion! Where is it? I see a press more mean and paltry and silly and disgraceful than any country ever knew,—if that be its standard, here it is. But I speak of Bancroft, and am advised to be silent on that subject, for he is "a black sheep—a democrat".[2] I speak of Bryant, and am entreated to be more careful—for the same reason.[3] I speak of International copyright, and am implored not to ruin myself outright. I speak of Miss Martineau, and all parties—slave upholders and abolitionists; Whigs, Tyler Whigs, and Democrats, shower down upon her[4] a perfect cataract of abuse. "But what has she done? Surely she praised America enough!"[5]—"Yes, but she told us of some of our faults,[6] and Americans can't bear to be told of their faults. Don't split on that

[1] During his second American tour (Sep 43–Oct 44) Macready did not change his mind about the country. He had disliked both the style and matter of *American Notes*, and on 12 Mar 44 (while at Mobile, Alabama) wrote: "Dickens's misjudgment is as clear to me as the noon-day sun, and much is to be said in explanation and excuse, but Dickens is a man who fills such a place in the world's opinion, the people cannot think that he ought to need an excuse—alas! the greatest man is but a man!" (*Diaries*, II, 266).

[2] As a leading Democrat, Bancroft was strongly opposed by his own friends and relations in Boston—virtually all Whigs: e.g. by his brother-in-law, Governor John Davis, and by his old friend Edward Everett, who cut him during the 1839 Governorship election (R. B. Nye, *George Bancroft, Brahmin Rebel*, New York, 1945, p. 121).

[3] As editor of the *New York Evening Post* since 1829, Bryant had consistently supported the Democrats.

[4] This word is bracketed in the MS in pencil, and "me" substituted for it in MDGH. The passages omitted from the letter are similarly bracketed.

[5] Harriet Martineau had arrived in the country, she wrote, with "a strong disposition to admire democratic institutions", and the aim of seeing how far the Americans "lived up to . . . their own theory" as laid down in the Declaration of Rights. She was greatly struck by the absence of poverty, of illiteracy, of "all servility" (no "badge of menial service [was] to be met with . . . except in the houses of the foreign ambassadors at Washington"). The "stout-souled, full-grown, original men" who formed the Senate inspired "a deep, involuntary respect" in her (cf. *To* Fon-

blanque, 12 Mar and *fn*). She praised "the provisions made for every class of unfortunates"; "by a happy coincidence of outward plenty with liberal institutions", there was "a smaller amount of crime . . . than [had] ever been known in any society". She was delighted with the kindliness she had found in American private life; and, unlike most other travellers, approved of the freedom of manners of the many American children whose parents had made them "friends from the very beginning". Finally, she proclaimed that, whatever evils remained, the means of remedy were in the hands of the whole people—who had "the glorious certainty that time and exertion [would] infallibly secure all wisely desired objects." (*Society in America*, I, x, 27; III, 54, 144, 168, 259, 297–8; *Retrospect of Western Travel*, I, 301–2.) All this must have much appealed to CD when reading her books before his visit.

[6] Naturally the outstanding fault in Harriet Martineau's eyes was the American tolerance of slavery, that "deadly sin against their own principles", with its accompanying horrors. "Fear of opinion" (an American characteristic she deplored above all others), fanned by an infamous newspaper press, often took the form "of an almost insane dread of responsibility" keeping many good men out of public life. She protested at the violence which broke out against Abolitionists: "mobbing" was the act not of paupers—for there were no paupers in the States—but of "gentlemen", who habitually escaped prosecution. On the "degradation" of American women she had much to say: "While woman's intellect is confined, her morals crushed, her health ruined, her weaknesses encouraged, . . . she is told that her lot is cast in the

rock, Mr. Dickens, don't write about America—we are so very suspicious."[1]—
Freedom of opinion! Macready, if I had been born here, and had written my
books in this country,—producing them with no stamp of approval from any
other land—it is my solemn belief that I should have lived and died, poor,
unnoticed, and "a black sheep"[2]—to boot. I never was more convinced of
anything than I am of that.

The people are affectionate, generous, open-hearted, hospitable, enthusiastic,
good humoured, polite to women, frank and cordial to all strangers; anxious to
oblige; far less prejudiced than they have been described to be; frequently
polished and refined, very seldom rude or disagreeable. I have made a great many
friends here, even in public conveyances, whom I have been truly sorry to part
from. In the towns, I have formed perfect attachments. I have seen none of that
greediness and indecorum on which travellers have laid so much emphasis.
I have returned frankness with frankness—met questions not intended to be rude,
with answers meant to be satisfactory—and have not spoken to one man, woman,
or child of any degree, who has not grown positively affectionate before we parted.
In the respects[3] of not being left alone, and of being horribly disgusted by tobacco
chewing and tobacco spittle, I have suffered considerably. The sight of Slavery
in Virginia; the hatred of British feeling upon that subject; and the miserable
hints of the impotent indignation of the South, have pained me very much—on
the last head, of course, I have felt nothing but a mingled pity and amusement;
on the others, sheer distress. But however much I like the ingredients of this
great dish, I cannot but come back to the point from which I started, and say
that the dish itself goes against the grain with me, and that I don't like it.

You know that I am, *truly*, a Liberal. I believe I have as little Pride as most
men; and I am conscious of not the smallest annoyance from being hail fellow
well met, with everybody. I have not had greater pleasure in the company of
any set of men among the thousands whom I have received (I hold a regular
Levee every day, you know, which is duly heralded and proclaimed in the
Newspapers) than in that of the Carmen of Hertford,[4] who presented themselves

paradise of women: and there is . . .
much boasting of the 'chivalrous' treatment she enjoys. That is to say,—she
has the best place in stage-coaches" (a
passage Marryat quoted with approval:
Diary in America, Part Second, II, 21).
Spitting, bragging and smart dealing she
dealt with lightly. Summing up, she posed
the questions: whether the kindness of
the American people generally was attribut-
able to their republicanism; and "how far
their republicanism [was] answerable for
their greatest fault,—their deficiency of
moral independence." (*Society in America*,
I, 147, 160, 164, 180; II, 108 ff.; III, 106,
300.)

[1] Cf. Forster in the *Foreign Quarterly
Review*, Oct 42 (XXX, 213): "The ruling
maxim of the life of Mr. Sampson Brass's
father, *Suspect Every Body*, is now the

dominant fashion of the Republic". And
see Marryat: "Defamation . . . is a disease
which pervades the land; which renders
every man suspicious and cautious of his
neighbour" (*Diary in America*, Part Second,
I, 181). With his usual Tory bias, Marryat
saw this state of affairs as a natural result
of "a free and enlightened people govern-
ing themselves" (*op. cit.*, I, 186).

[2] To Harriet Martineau's mind, if a real
"native genius" had appeared in America,
he would have won his way; and piracy of
English books could not be held responsible
for the lack of first class work (*Society in
America*, III, 217–18).

[3] "In respect of" written first; then
"the" squeezed in before "respect" and
an "s" added.

[4] No report mentioning these has been
found.

in a body in their blue frocks, among a crowd of well-dressed ladies and gentlemen, and bad me welcome through their spokesmen. They had all read my books, and all perfectly understood them. It is not these things I have in my mind when I say that the man who comes to this Country a Radical and goes home again with his old opinions unchanged, must be a Radical on reason, sympathy, and reflection, and one who has so well considered the subject, that he has no chance of wavering.[1]

We have been to Boston, Worcester, Hertford, New Haven, New York, Philadelphia, Baltimore, Washington, Fredericksburgh, Richmond, and back to Washington again. The premature heat of the weather (it was 80 yesterday in the shade) and Clay's advice—how you would like Clay![2]—made me determine not to go to Charleston; but having got to Richmond, I think I should have turned back, under any circumstances. We remain at Baltimore for two days, of which this is one. Then we go to Harrisburgh. Then by the Canal boat and the Railroad over the Alleghany Mountains, to Pittsburgh. Then down the Ohio to Cincinnati; then to Louisville, and then to St. Louis. I have been invited to a public entertainment in every town I have entered, and have refused them; but I have excepted St. Louis, as the farthest point of my travels. My friends there have passed some resolutions which Forster has, and will shew you. From St. Louis we cross to Chicago, traversing immense prairies. Thence by the lakes and Detroit to Buffalo, and so to Niagara. A run into Canada follows of course, and then—let me write the blessed word in capitals—we turn towards H O M E .[3]

Kate has written to Mrs. Macready,[4] and it is useless for me to thank you my dearest friend, or her, for your care of our dear children, which is our constant theme of discourse. Forster has gladdened our hearts with his account of the triumph of Acis and Galatea,[5]—and I am anxiously looking for news of the Tragedy.[6]—Forrest breakfasted with us at Richmond last Saturday—he was acting there, and I invited him—and he spoke very gratefully and very like a man, of your kindness to him when he was in London.[7]

[1] i.e. someone like Harriet Martineau.

[2] Macready had already met him, in 1827. Meeting him again in 1844 in New Orleans, he found him "most kind, urbane and cheerful", though naturally lacking "the vivacity and great animal spirits" of 17 years before (*Diaries*, II, 261).

[3] Written in large Gothic capitals.

[4] *Née* Catherine Frances Atkins (1805–52): see Vol. II, p. 149*n*.

[5] An opera adapted from Handel's serenata (libretto by Gay), which Macready had produced at Drury Lane on 5 Feb, with notable scenery by Stanfield. In a letter to Frederic Tennyson of 6 Feb, Edward FitzGerald described it: "the drop scene rises, and there is the sea-shore, a long curling bay: the sea heaving under the moon, and breaking upon the beach, and rolling the surf down—the stage! This is

really capitally done" (*Letters of Edward Fitzgerald*, ed. W. A. Wright, 1894, I, 102–3). Marston recorded that when the curtain rose the sea "was ecstatically applauded . . . as though it had been a distinguished actor" (*Our Recent Actors*, 1888, I, 63). Macready had recorded in his diary the night before: "have never seen anything of the kind in my life so perfectly beautiful. . . . At the conclusion was called for and most enthusiastically received . . . Too much excited to think of sleeping" (*Diaries*, II, 157).

[6] Gerald Griffin's *Gisippus*, produced 23 Feb, which CD and others had heard Macready read on 17 Oct 40 (see Vol. II, p. 138 and *n*).

[7] On first meeting Forrest in Oct 36 Macready recorded: "Liked him much—a noble appearance, and a manly, mild, and

David Colden is as good a fellow as ever lived; and I am deeply in love with his wife. Indeed we have received the greatest and most earnest and zealous kindness from the whole family, and quite love them all. Do you remember one Greenhow,[1] whom you invited to pass some days with you at the hotel on the Kaatskill Mountains ?[2] He is translator to the State Office at Washington— has a very pretty wife[3]—and a little girl of five years old. We dined with them, and had a very pleasant day. The President invited me to dinner, but I couldn't stay for it. I had a private audience, however, and we attended the Public drawing room besides.

Now don't you rush at the quick conclusion, that *I* have rushed at a quick conclusion. Pray be upon your guard. If you can by any process estimate the extent of my affectionate regard for you, and the rush I shall make when I reach London to take you by your true right hand, I don't object. But let me entreat you to be very careful how you come down upon the sharp-sighted Individual who pens these words, which you seem to me to have done in what Willmott wod. call "one of Mr. Macready's rushes"—As my pen is getting past its work I have taken a new one to say, that I am ever, My Dear Macready your faithful friend.   CD.

To THOMAS MITTON, 22 MARCH 1842

MS Huntington Library. *Address:* Thomas Mitton Esquire | 23 Southampton Buildings. | Chancery Lane | London England.

Baltimore—United States | Twenty Second March 1842.
My Dear friend.

We have been as far South as Richmond in Virginia (where they grow and manufacture Tobacco; and where the labour is all performed by Slaves) but the Season in those latitudes is so intensely and prematurely hot, that it was considered a matter of doubtful expediency to go on to Charleston. *[a]*For this unexpected reason; and because the country between Richmond and Charleston is but a desolate swamp the whole way; and because Slavery is anything but a cheerful thing to live amidst, I have altered my route by the advice of Mr. Clay (the great political leader in this country) and have returned here, previous to diving into the Far West.*[a]* We start for that part of the country—which includes

interesting demeanour" (*Diaries*, I, 349), and he went out of his way to welcome and entertain him—though Forrest's performing at Covent Garden parallel roles to his own at Drury Lane piqued and worried him; and he suffered similar annoyance during his own American tour of 1843–4. For their later relations, culminating in the violent riots in Astor Place, New York, in 1849, see *Diaries*, II, and A. S. Downer, *The Eminent Tragedian*, 1966, Ch. 7.

[1] Robert Greenhow (1800–54; *DAB*), translator to the State Department 1828–50; especially proficient in French and Spanish. Published *The History and Present Condi-*

tion of Tripoli, 1835, and *The History of Oregon and California*, 1844.

[2] Spelt thus in the 18th century and in *Rip Van Winkle*, but "Catskill" in maps since the 1830s; in New York State, *c.* 100 miles north of New York.

[3] *Née* Rose O'Neale, of Maryland (*d.* 1864). Imprisoned Aug 61—May 62 as a secret agent of the Confederate Govt, she described her experiences in *My Imprisonment and the First Year of Abolition Rule at Washington*, 1863.

[aa; bb; cc; dd; ee] Passages published in MDGH 1880, but omitted in later editions, including N.

mountain travelling, and Lake travelling, and Prairie travelling—the day after tomorrow at 8 o'Clock in the Morning; and shall be in the west, and from there going Northward again, until the 30th. of April or 1st. of May, when we shall halt for a week at Niagara, before going further into Canada. We have taken our passage Home (God bless the word) in the George Washington Packet Ship from New York. She sails on the 7th. of June.

I have departed from my resolution not to accept any more public entertainments—they have been proposed in every town I have visited—in favor of the people of St. Louis—my utmost Western point. That town is on the borders of the Indian territory—a trifling distance from this place—only 2000[1] miles! At my second halting place I shall be able to write on to fix the day. I suppose it will be somewhere about the 12th. of April. Think of my going so far towards the setting Sun, to dinner!

In every town where we stay, though it be only for a day, we hold a regular levee or drawing room, where I shake hands, on an average with five or six hundred people, who pass on from me to Kate, and are shaken again by her. Maclise's picture of our darlings stands upon a table or sideboard the while; and my "travelling Secretary", assisted very often by a committee belonging to the place, presents the people in due form. Think of two hours of this, every day,— and the people coming in by hundreds—all fresh, and piping hot, and full of questions—when we are literally exhausted, and can hardly stand. I *really do believe* that if I had not had a lady with me, I should have been obliged to leave the country and go back to England. But for her, they never would leave me alone by day or night; and as it is, a Slave comes to me now and then *in the middle of the night* with a letter—and waits at the bedroom door for an answer!

It was so hot at Richmond that we could scarcely breathe,—and the Peach and other Fruit trees were in full blossom. It was so cold at Washington next day, that we were shivering! But even in the same town you might often wear nothing but a shirt and trousers in the morning, and two Great coats at night— the thermometer very frequently taking a little trip of 30 degrees between sunrise and sunset.

They *do* lay it on at the Hotels, in such style! They charge by the day; so that whether one dines out or dines at home, makes no manner of difference. T'other day, I wrote to order our rooms at Philadelphia to be ready on a certain day, and was detained a week longer than I expected in New York. The Philadelphia landlord not only charged me half rent for the rooms during the whole of that time, but board for myself, and Kate, and Anne during the whole time too, though we were actually boarding at the same expense during the same time, in New York!—What do you say to *that*? If I remonstrated, the whole virtue of the newspapers would be aroused directly.

*b*We were at the President's drawing room while we were in Washington. I had a private audience besides, and was asked to dinner, but couldn't stay.*b*

Parties—parties—parties—of course, every day and night. But it's not all parties. I go into the prisons, the police offices, the watch-houses, the hospitals, the workhouses. I was out half the night in New York with two of their most

---

[1] Written large.

famous constables[1]—started at midnight—and went into every brothel, thieves' house, murdering hovel, sailors dancing place, and abode of villainny,[2] both black and white, in the town. I went incog behind the scenes to the little Theatre where Mitchell is making a fortune. He has been rearing a little dog for me, and has called him "Boz".[3] I am going to bring him home.—In a word I go everywhere, and a hard life it is. *But I am careful to drink hardly anything, and not to smoke at all. I have recourse to my medicine chest whenever I feel at all bilious; and am, thank God, thoroughly well.*

When I next write to you, I shall have begun, I hope, to turn my face homeward. I have a great store of oddity and whimsicality, and am going now into the oddest and most characteristic part of this most queer country.[4]

*Always direct to the care of David Colden Esqre. 28 Laight Street Hudson Square New York. I received your Caledonia letter with the greatest joy.

Kate sends her best remembrances.* And I am always,

[   ]

[CHARLES DICKENS][5]

P.S. Richmond was my extreme southern point; and I turn from the South altogether, the day after tomorrow. Will you let the Britannia know of this change[6]—if needful ?

To SAMUEL ROGERS, 22 MARCH 1842

MS Professor E. S. Pearson. *Address:* Samuel Rogers Esquire | 22 Saint James's Place | London | England.

Baltimore. United States. | Twenty Second March 1842.

My Dear Mr. Rogers.

I know you will be glad to hear, under my own hand, that we are both well, —though very anxious to get back to dear old home, our friends, and darling children. I am obliged to make, as perhaps you have heard, a kind of Public Progress through this Country; and have been so oppressed with Festivals given in my honor, that I have found it necessary to notify my disinclination, to accept any more; or I should rather say my determination not to lead such a trying life. I have made one departure from this rule, and that is in the case of a body of readers in the Far West—at a town called St. Louis, on the confines of the

---

[1] The New York Police Dept was in process of being organized during the early 1840s, the old watch system being replaced by a regular police force.

[2] Thus in MS.

[3] A "white Havana spaniel" according to MDGH, I, 67*n*; but described by Forster as "a small white shaggy terrier, who bore at first the imposing name of Timber Doodle" (F, III, viii, 279–80). This was changed to Snittle Timbery, after one of the actors in Crummles's company (*To* Forster, 11 Aug 42), and later shortened to Timber.

[4] The common image of the West which Irving and other Easterners had no doubt given him.

[5] Ending and signature cut away, presumably for an autograph collector.

[6] That he was not going as far south as Charleston, although the endorsement of his policy with the Britannia Insurance Co. (see Vol. II, p. 414*n*) permitted him to do so. His statement about drinking and smoking may also have been intended for the Britannia, "if needful".

Indian Territory. I am going there to dinner (it is only two thousand miles off) —and start the day after tomorrow.

If you ever have leisure to write a line, saying that you have received this, and are well, I shall be truly delighted to hear from you. Any letter addressed to me, to the care of David Colden Esquire, 28 Laight Street Hudson Square New York, will be forwarded to me without delay.

They give me everything here, but Time. If they had added that to the long catalogue of their hospitalities, I should certainly have inflicted a long letter upon you, which would have wandered into it's impossible to say how long a description of our[1] travels and adventures. So you may consider yourself very fortunate.

I hope you are as well as ever, and as great a walker as ever, and as good a talker as ever—in short as perfect and complete a Samuel Rogers as ever— which I don't doubt in the least. I have made great exertions here in behalf of an International Copyright law,[2] and almost begin to hope, from the assurance the leaders of the different parties at Washington have given me, that it may be brought about.

We have arranged to sail from New York for England, on the 7th. of June, in the George Washington Packet Ship. We had so bad a voyage out, that I have eschewed ocean steamers for ever.

The peace and quiet of Broadstairs never seemed so great as now. I could hug Miss Collins the Bather,[3] as though she were a very Venus.

Believe me—here and everywhere—
Faithfully | Your friend

Samuel Rogers Esquire   CHARLES DICKENS[4]

To T. N. TALFOURD, 22 MARCH 1842*

MS Free Library of Philadelphia. *Address:* Mr. Serjeant Talfourd | Serjeant's Inn Chancery Lane | London | England.

Baltimore, United States | Twenty Second March 1842.

My Dear Talfourd.

I am not going to inflict a long letter upon you. Nor am I going to weary you

---

[1] "wanderings" cancelled here.

[2] Rogers had signed the petition presented to the Senate on 2 Feb 37: see *To* Forster, 24 Feb, *fn.* He was also one of the 12 signatories to the memorial sent to CD in Apr.

[3] A Broadstairs joke: see Vol. II, p. 123. Described in a paragraph on Broadstairs in the *Age*, 11 Sep 42, as "the pretty and obliging chatterbox ... presiding at the bathing machines".

[4] Catherine added the following on p. 3 of CD's letter: "My dear Mr. Rogers. | I must add one line to remind you of your kind promise to me, the last time we saw you before we left home, that when you wrote to Charles, you would also send me a few words of remembrance. I need not say what pride and pleasure it would give me. | We are both anxiously looking forward to the 7th. of June when we sail on our return to dear England. You may easily imagine how often our thoughts turn in that direction, and how often we long to see those dear little ones, who I almost fear will have forgotten their truant parents before we get back to them. My impatient husband is hurrying me as he wishes to put up the parcel. Therefore I can only add that I am dear Mr. Rogers | Your affectionate friend | C. DICKENS."

with any account of the Public Progress they oblige me to make through this country. I dare say you will have heard enough of that.

My purposes are threefold—first to tell you that we are safe and well—secondly to ask you to bear me in mind sometimes—thirdly, to add that if you can ever find time to write to me, it will give me true delight to recognize your familiar hand at this long—long—distance from dear old Home. Any letter addressed to me, to the care of David Colden Esquire 28 Laight Street Hudson Square New York, will be forwarded to me wherever I may be.

We have been as far South, as Richmond in Virginia; and are now going into the Far West. The first thing I saw in Richmond was a Play bill, whereon was I O N[1] in enormous capitals. One Mrs. Shaw[2] from New York (a very handsome woman and a good actress) played Ion—very well she played it too, I assure you; and the piece was applauded to the echoe.[3]

I have exerted myself very much in the way of remonstrance, private influence, and public speeches, to advance the International Copyright question. And I have received such strong assurances from the party leaders at Washington, that I almost begin to hope something will be done at last. I dare say Forster will have seen you on this subject, in compliance with my request, however.[4]

The day after tomorrow, we start for the Mountains, Forests, and Prairies. Towards the end of April we shall go round by the lakes to Niagara—then run into Canada—and return, please God, on the 7th. of June by the George Washington Packet Ship from New York.

I need scarcely say that as you were one of the last friends I saw before leaving England, you will be one of the first whom I hope to see on my return. Mrs. Dickens unites with me in cordial remembrances to yourself, Mrs. Talfourd, Miss Ely, Frank, Mary,[5] and all the children. And I am ever My Dear Talfourd

Faithfully | Your Friend

Mr. Serjeant Talfourd.   CHARLES DICKENS

---

[1] Talfourd's tragedy, first performed 1835; the word itself written here in enormous capitals. Probably a letter from Talfourd crossed this from CD; for on 30 Apr CD asked Lea & Blanchard to let him have "any and every edition" of *Ion* that they could lay hands on. Talfourd's pride in his own works was regarded by his friends as something of a joke (see *To* Rogers, 26 Sep, *fn*).

[2] Eliza Mary Ann Shaw, *née* Trewar. Her husband, Thomas S. Hamblin (1800–53; *DAB*), was manager of the Bowery Theatre, New York, 1830 to his death. She made her début in New York July 36 and played several times with Edwin Forrest, her parts including Desdemona and Cordelia. On 19 Feb CD saw her play at the Bowery in *The Love Chase*. She was in New York for much of March and had presumably gone to Richmond for a short engagement.

[3] Thus in MS. Cf. *Macbeth*, v, iii, 53.

[4] Talfourd signed the memorial on international copyright, which CD had asked Forster to procure (*To* Forster, 24 Feb).

[5] Mrs Talfourd, *née* Rachel Rutt (see Vol. I, p. 315*n*); Marion Ely, Mrs Talfourd's niece; Frank, Talfourd's eldest son (1828–62; *DNB*), a schoolboy at Eton; Mary, one of Talfourd's two daughters (see Vol. II, p. 446 and *n*).

To JOHN FORSTER, 22–23 MARCH [1842]

Extract in F, III, iv, 241–2 (final addition to letter begun 6 Mar, continued 13th, 17th and 21st).

Baltimore,[1] | Tuesday, March 22nd.

I have a great diffidence in running counter to any impression formed by a man of Maclise's genius, on a subject he has fully considered. But I quite agree with you, about the King in *Hamlet*.[2] Talking of Hamlet, I constantly carry in my great-coat pocket the *Shakespeare* you bought for me in Liverpool. What an unspeakable source of delight that book is to me!

Your Ontario letter, I found here to-night: sent on by the vigilant and faithful Colden, who makes every thing having reference to us, or our affairs, a labour of the heartiest love. We devoured its contents, greedily. Good Heaven, my dear fellow, how I miss you! and how I count the time 'twixt this and coming home again. Shall I ever forget the day of our parting at Liverpool! when even ——[3] became jolly and radiant in his sympathy with our separation! Never, never shall I forget that time. Ah! how seriously I thought then, and how seriously I have thought many, many times since, of the terrible folly of ever quarrelling with a true friend, on good for nothing trifles! Every little hasty word that has ever passed between us, rose up before me like a reproachful ghost. At this great distance, I seem to look back upon any miserable small interruption of our affectionate intercourse, though only for the instant it has never outlived, with a sort of pity for myself as if I were another creature.[4]

I have bought another accordion.[5] The steward[6] lent me one, on the passage

---

[1] Apparently CD absent-mindedly dated this letter "Richmond", and Forster followed without noticing the mistake till after he had passed the final proofs of the *Life*, Vol. I; for on 12 Nov 71 he wrote to John Bradbury, praising the almost faultless printing (he had found only two minor errors of punctuation), but continuing: "There are three—not errata but corrigenda—which I must ask you kindly *to stop the working for, and correct at once.* ... I was misled by Dickens himself dating 'Richmond' instead of 'Baltimore' . . . How can you forgive me! *Because I must impose upon you the further trouble of sending* THIS *correction to America*" (extract in Sotheran catalogue, 1902).

[2] Unexplained; but other criticism of the picture is implied in a letter from Maclise to Forster dated "Monday Night" (?4 Apr 42): "I have made Hamlet handsome and I am sure taken every vestige of Keanism out of him"; and in a letter of 5 Apr: "Macready called today and really seemed most highly pleased. He did not I am happy to inform you see the least shadow of a shade of resemblance to the Haymarket Hamlet remaining" (MSV & A).

[3] Name omitted by Forster; identity unknown.

[4] For an apparent reference to hasty words, see Vol. I, p. 503 and *n*; for the one major recorded quarrel before this date, Vol. II, p. 116 and *n*; and for an instance of CD's irritation with Forster, Vol. II, pp. 158–9 and *n*.

[5] On the return voyage on the *George Washington* he played it "perpetually" (*To* Mrs Colden, 15 July), accompanied by other passengers on the violin and the key-bugle: "the combined effect . . ., when they all played different tunes, in different parts of the ship, at the same time ... was sublimely hideous" (*American Notes*, Ch. 16). J. T. Lightwood, *CD and Music*, 1912, Ch. 1, writes of CD's unsuccessful piano and violin lessons at Wellington House, and calls the accordion playing "his third and last attempt to become an instrumentalist".

[6] Presumably the chief steward, Mr Orme, highly praised by the passengers (*Bunker-Hill Aurora*, 29 Jan 42).

out, and I regaled the ladies' cabin with my performances. You can't think with what feeling I play *Home Sweet Home*[1] every night, or how pleasantly sad it makes us. . . . And so God bless you. . . . I leave space for a short postscript before sealing this, but it will probably contain nothing. The dear, dear children! what a happiness it is to know that they are in such hands.[2]

P.S. Twenty-third March, 1842. Nothing new. And all well. I have no heard that the Columbia is in, but she is hourly expected. Washington Irving has come on for another leave-taking, and dines with me to-day. We start for the West, at half after eight to-morrow morning. I send you a newspaper, the most respectable in the States, with a very just copyright article.[3]

To WILLIAM [GUY],[4] 23 MARCH 1842

MS Harvard University Library.

Barnum's Hotel. | Twenty Third March 1842

My Dear Sir

I am truly obliged to you for the beautiful and delicious mint julep you have so kindly sent me.[5] It's quite a mercy that I knew what it was.[6] I have tasted it, but reserve further proceedings until the arrival of Washington Irving whom I expect to dine with me, tete a tete;[7] and who will help me to drink your health, with many thanks to you.[8]

Dear Sir | Faithfully Yours

— Gay[9] Esquire   CHARLES DICKENS

[1] From John Howard Payne's *Clari; or, The Maid of Milan*, 1823, the opera CD had produced in Bentinck Street in Apr 33 (see Vol. I, pp. 18–21).

[2] Macready's.

[3] Presumably the long paragraph, no doubt by W. W. Seaton, which had appeared in the Washington *National Intelligencer*, 19 Mar, in CD's defence. "Mr. Dickens", it declared, "has been roughly handled in two or three papers, because on about as many occasions he made public allusion to the propriety of passing an international copy-right law." His reference had been considered "indelicate and obtrusive"; and there would be ground for the charge if he had spoken on his own behalf in particular instead of touching on the subject of justice to foreign authors in general. It was true that he was himself one of these, but "only one of a great mass, the representative of future generations of writers as well as the present. Warmed by the welcome he had received, he naturally took an occasion . . . to mention the wrongs which genius suffered". If he had been "in any degree culpable for the introduc-

tion of this subject, while standing in the position of an honored guest, in what light", the paper asked, "do those appear who think that they have settled in full the claims of a living author . . . by the mere breath of their applause, or the smile of their favor!"

[4] William Guy, proprietor of Monument House, a hotel at the corner of Fayette Street and Monument Square.

[5] Writing to Charles Lanman on 5 Feb 68, CD described it as "a most enormous mint julep, wreathed with flowers".

[6] Marryat, who found it "with the thermometer at 100°, one of the most delightful and insinuating potations that ever was invented", gave a recipe (*Diary in America*, Part Second, I, 117–18). Macready found it "the most deliciously cunning compound that ever I tasted; nectar could not stand before it; Jupiter would have hobnobbed in it" (*Diaries*, II, 267).

[7] Thus in MS.

[8] The julep lasted them, CD told Lanman, "far into the night" (N, III, 616–17).

[9] Mis-spelt thus in MS.

To UNKNOWN CORRESPONDENT, 23 MARCH 1842

Text from Goodspeeds Book Shop catalogue No. 169; *MS* 1 p.; dated Baltimore, 23 Mar 42.

My dear young friend.

I have had great satisfaction in the receipt of your letter; and am truly glad to know that I have given you so much pleasure. It will be my endeavour when I go home to England, to enlarge your stock of amusement and happiness—and I shall always be,

Very faithfully yours,
CHARLES DICKENS

To JOHN FORSTER, 28 MARCH 1842

Extract in F, III, v, 246–51.

On board the canal boat.[1] Going to Pittsburgh.
Monday, March twenty-eighth, 1842.

We left Baltimore last Thursday the twenty-fourth at half-past eight in the morning, by railroad; and got to a place called York,[2] about twelve. There we dined, and took a stage-coach for Harrisburgh;[3] twenty-five miles further. This stage-coach was like nothing so much as the body of one of the swings you see at a fair set upon four wheels and roofed and covered at the sides with painted canvas. There were twelve *inside*! I, thank my stars, was on the box. The luggage was on the roof; among it, a good-sized dining table, and a big rocking-chair. We also took up an intoxicated gentleman, who sat for ten miles between me and the coachman; and another intoxicated gentleman who got up behind, but in the course of a mile or two fell off without hurting himself, and was seen in the distant perspective reeling back to the grog-shop where we had found him. There were four horses to this land-ark,[4] of course; but we did not perform the journey until after half-past six o'clock that night. . . . The first half of the journey was tame enough, but the second lay through the valley of the Susquehanah[5] (I think I spell it right, but I haven't that American Geography at hand)[6] which is very beautiful. . . .

---

[1] Forster prefaces the travel-letters, of which this was the first, with a repetition of his "rule" (already frequently broken) not to quote in the *Life* passages which had appeared in *American Notes*. The difficulty had been great; for the "freshness of first impressions" was "in the letters alone", and the passages CD had amplified for the book had not been improved. He mentions several omissions which he had felt bound to make. Concerning the MSS of the letters themselves, he adds: "Written amid such distraction, fatigue, and weariness as they describe, amid the jarring noises of hotels and streets, aboard steamers, on canal boats, and in log huts, there is not an erasure in

them" (F, III, v, 244–6). (As against this, the MS of the parallel chapters in *American Notes* is heavily corrected.)

[2] About 60 miles north of Baltimore, in Pennsylvania.

[3] i.e. Harrisburg—where they stayed the night at the Eagle Hotel, kept by Henry Buehler (W. G. Wilkins, *CD in America* p. 196).

[4] In *American Notes*, "barge on wheels".

[5] i.e. Susquehanna.

[6] In an inventory of his books made before leaving for Italy 1844, CD noted one Geography of America and 27 American Guide Books (MS Major Philip Dickens).

I think I formerly made a casual remark to you touching the precocity of the youth of this country.[1] When we changed horses on this journey I got down to stretch my legs, refresh myself with a glass of whiskey and water, and shake the wet off my great coat—for it was raining very heavily, and continued to do so, all night. Mounting to my seat again, I observed something lying on the roof of the coach, which I took to be a rather large fiddle in a brown bag. In the course of ten miles or so, however, I discovered that it had a pair of dirty shoes at one end, and a glazed cap at the other; and further observation demonstrated it to be a small boy, in a snuff-coloured coat, with his arms quite pinioned to his sides by deep forcing into his pockets. He was, I presume, a relative or friend of the coachman's, as he lay a-top of the luggage, with his face towards the rain; and, except when a change of position brought his shoes in contact with my hat, he appeared to be asleep. Sir, when we stopped to water the horses, about two miles from Harrisburgh, this thing slowly upreared itself to the height of three foot eight, and fixing its eyes on me with a mingled expression of complacency, patronage, national independence, and sympathy for all outer barbarians and foreigners, said, in shrill piping accents, "Well now, stranger, I guess you find this, a'most like an English a'ternoon,—hey?" It is unnecessary to add that I thirsted for his blood. . . .

We had all next morning in Harrisburgh, as the canal-boat was not to start until three o'clock in the afternoon. The officials called upon me before I had finished breakfast; and as the town is the seat of the Pennsylvanian legislature, I went up to the capitol.[2] I was very much interested in looking over a number of treaties made with the poor Indians,[3] their signatures being rough drawings of the creatures or weapons they are called after; and the extraordinary drawing of these emblems, showing the queer, unused, shaky manner in which each man has held the pen, struck me very much.[4]

You know my small respect for our house of commons. These local legisla-

---

[1] T. C. Grattan also commented on the precocity of American boys: "they run through their boyhood with marvellous rapidity. As soon as they can read they begin to study the public papers . . . They enter at once into public life. They, in fact, do almost everything which is unbecoming to their early years, and very little, and that very imperfectly, which would give a grace to them" (*Civilized America*, 1859, II, 318).

[2] A "dignified, comfortable and rather quaint structure", dating from 1819–22, with "a portico upheld by sandstone pillars, opening into a rotunda" (*King's Handbook of the United States*, Buffalo, N.Y., 1891). Harrisburg replaced Lancaster as capital of Pennsylvania in 1812.

[3] Pennsylvania's Indian Deeds (of which *c*. 30 are still preserved in Harrisburg) consist of surrenders of land claims throughout Pennsylvania by Delaware, Susquehannock, Iroquois and other Indian tribes. They date from 15 July 1682 to 3 Feb 1791. CD would almost certainly have been shown the widely known "Walking Purchase" of 1737, which completed the sale of the Delaware lands. (Information kindly given by Mr William A. Hunter of the Pennsylvania Historical and Museum Commission, Harrisburg.)

[4] The signatures to the "Walking Purchase" include a turtle and a turkey track. There seems no doubt that CD also saw the Iroquois Deed of 11 Oct 1736, with signatures, clearly identifiable, of a "Great Turtle", war hatchets, arrows and scalps (see *American Notes*, Ch. 9), besides two human figures, two quadrupeds lying on their backs (?buffaloes), and a bird. Signatures to the majority of the Deeds are crosses and unidentifiable marks. Most are crudely and, as CD says, shakily formed.

tures are too insufferably apish of mighty legislation, to be seen without bile; for which reason, and because a great crowd of senators and ladies had assembled in both houses to behold the inimitable, and had already begun to pour in upon him even in the secretary's private room, I went back to the hotel, with all speed.[1] The members of both branches of the legislature followed me there, however, so we had to hold the usual levee before our half-past one o'clock dinner. We received a great number of them. Pretty nearly every man spat upon the carpet, as usual; and one blew his nose with his fingers—also on the carpet, which was a very neat one, the room given up to us being the private parlor of the landlord's wife. This has become so common since, however, that it scarcely seems worth mentioning. Please to observe that the gentleman in question was a member of the senate, which answers (as they very often tell me) to our house of lords.

The innkeeper was the most attentive, civil, and obliging person I ever saw in my life. On being asked for his bill, he said there was no bill: the honor and pleasure &c. being more than sufficient.[2] I did not permit this, of course; and begged Mr. Q to explain to him, that, travelling four strong, I could not hear of it on any account.

And now I come to the Canal Boat. Bless your heart and soul, my dear fellow,—if you could only see us on board the canal boat! Let me think, for a moment, at what time of the day or night I should best like you to see us. In the morning? Between five and six in the morning, shall I say? Well! you *would* like to see me, standing on the deck, fishing the dirty water out of the canal with a tin ladle chained to the boat by a long chain; pouring the same into a tin-basin (also chained up in like manner); and scrubbing my face with the jack towel. At night, shall I say? I don't know that you *would* like to look into the cabin at night, only to see me lying on a temporary shelf exactly the width of this sheet of paper when it's open (*I measured it this morning*),[3] with one man above me, and another below; and, in all, eight and twenty in a low cabin, which you can't stand upright in with your hat on. I don't think you would like to look in at breakfast time either, for then these shelves have only just been taken down and put away, and the atmosphere of the place is, as you may suppose, by no means fresh; though there *are* upon the table tea and coffee, and bread and

---

[1] At some point in the morning CD was shown Harrisburg's newly built "model prison on the solitary system" (*American Notes*, Ch. 9)—presumably by Samuel R. Wood, Warden of the Eastern Penitentiary, Philadelphia (the "friendly Quaker", no doubt, whom CD had invited to call at his hotel: see *To* Felton, 29 Apr). Wood was later found talking to CD and Catherine on the Williamsport canal boat by Ellis Lewis, Chief Justice of Philadelphia. Lewis had gone to the canal boat to escape the crowds, and during the conversation obtained CD's autograph for his young daughter (account by Lewis quoted in R. S. Mackenzie, *Life of CD*, pp. 147–8).

[2] A footnote by Forster (F, 1872, I, 346)

reads: "Miss Martineau was perhaps partly right then ?", and refers back to CD's letter of 6 Mar. Ley (F, III, v, 248) replaces the query by an exclamation-mark.

[3] "16 inches exactly", according to Forster. Philip Hone, who made the same journey in June 47, found it "pleasant enough in the daytime, but the sleeping is awful . . . [in the men's cabin] the sleepers are packed away on narrow shelves, fastened to the sides of the boat, like dead pigs in a Cincinnati pork warehouse. We go to bed at nine o'clock, and rise when we are told in the morning; for the bedsteads are formed of the seats and the tables" (*Diary of Philip Hone*, ed. A. Nevins, p. 804).

butter, and salmon, and shad, and liver, and steak, and potatoes, and pickles, and ham, and pudding,[1] and sausages; and three and thirty people sitting round it, eating and drinking; and savoury bottles of gin, and whiskey, and brandy, and rum, in the bar hard by; and seven and twenty out of the eight and twenty men, in foul linen, with yellow streams from half-chewed tobacco trickling down their chins. Perhaps the best time for you to take a peep would be the present: eleven o'clock in the forenoon: when the barber is at his shaving, and the gentlemen are lounging about the stove waiting for their turns, and not more than seventeen are spitting in concert, and two or three are walking overhead (lying down on the luggage every time the man at the helm calls "Bridge!"), and I am writing this in the ladies'-cabin, which is a part of the gentlemen's, and only screened off by a red curtain. Indeed it exactly resembles the dwarf's private apartment in a caravan at a fair; and the gentlemen, generally, represent the spectators at a penny-a-head. The place is just as clean and just as large as that caravan you and I were in at Greenwich-fair last past. Outside, it is exactly like any canal-boat you have seen near the Regent's-park, or elsewhere.

You never can conceive what the hawking and spitting is, the whole night through. Last night was the worst. *Upon my honor and word* I was obliged, this morning, to lay my fur-coat on the deck, and wipe the half dried flakes of spittle from it with my handkerchief: and the only surprise seemed to be, that I should consider it necessary to do so. When I turned in last night, I put it on a stool beside me, and there it lay, under a cross fire from five men—three opposite; one above; and one below. I make no complaints, and shew no disgust. I am looked upon as highly facetious at night, for I crack jokes with everybody near me until we fall asleep.[2] I am considered very hardy in the morning, for I run up, bare-necked, and plunge my head into the half-frozen water, by half past five o'clock. I am respected for my activity, inasmuch as I jump from the boat to the towing-path, and walk five or six miles before breakfast; keeping up with the horses all the time. In a word, they are quite astonished to find a sedentary Englishman roughing it so well, and taking so much exercise; and question me very much on that head. The greater part of the men will sit and shiver round the stove all day, rather than put one foot before the other. As to having a window open, that's not to be thought of.

We expect to reach Pittsburgh to-night, between eight and nine o'clock; and there we ardently hope to find your March letters awaiting us. We have had, with the exception of Friday afternoon, exquisite weather, but cold. Clear starlight and moonlight nights. The canal has run, for the most part, by the side of the Susquehanah and Iwanata[3] rivers; and has been carried through tremendous

---

[1] "black-puddings" in *American Notes*, Ch. 10.

[2] Basil Hall, an experienced traveller, exclaimed of a similar journey: "Oh, the misery of a long night on board of a crowded steam-boat!" The red-hot stove blazing or smoking in the middle of the cabin, the "steaming and breathing of brandy, gin, and tobacco", the "half-whispered prosings" of berthless passengers, brought him to "a most distracting pitch of restlessness" (*Travels in North America*, 1829, II, 382). But for CD, even such "oddities" had "a humour of their own" and he enjoyed them (*American Notes*, Ch. 10).

[3] i.e. Juniata. The Pennsylvania Canal followed the river most of the way to Hollidaysburg, at the foot of the Alleghany Mountains.

obstacles. Yesterday, we crossed the mountain.[1] This is done *by railroad. . . .*[2] You dine at an inn upon the mountain; and, including the half hour allowed for the meal, are rather more than five hours performing this strange part of the journey. The people north and "down east" have terrible legends of its danger; but they appear to be exceedingly careful, and don't go to work at all wildly. There are some queer precipices close to the rails, certainly; but every precaution is taken, I am inclined to think, that such difficulties, and such a vast work, will admit of.

The scenery, before you reach the mountains, and when you are on them, and after you have left them, is very grand and fine; and the canal winds its way through some deep, sullen gorges, which, seen by moonlight, are very impressive:[3] though immeasurably inferior to Glencoe, to whose terrors I have not seen the smallest *approach.* We have passed, both in the mountains and elsewhere, a great number of new settlements, and detached log-houses. Their utterly forlorn and miserable appearance baffles all description. I have not seen six cabins out of six hundred, where the windows have been whole. Old hats, old clothes, old boards, old fragments of blanket and paper, are stuffed into the broken glass; and their air is misery and desolation.[4] It pains the eye to see the stumps of great trees thickly strewn in every field of wheat; and never to lose the eternal swamp and dull morass, with hundreds of rotten trunks, of elm and pine and sycamore and logwood, steeped in its unwholesome water; where the frogs so croak at night that after dark there is an incessant sound as if millions of phantom teams, with bells, were travelling through the upper air, at an enormous distance off. It is quite an oppressive circumstance, too, to *come* upon great tracks, where settlers have been burning down the trees; and where their wounded bodies lie about, like those of murdered creatures; while here and there some charred and blackened giant rears two bare arms aloft, and seems to curse his enemies.[5] The prettiest sight I have seen was yesterday, when we— on the heights of the mountain, and in a keen wind—looked down into a valley full of light and softness: catching glimpses of scattered cabins; children running to the doors; dogs bursting out to bark; pigs scampering home, like so many prodigal sons; families sitting out in their gardens; cows gazing upward, with a stupid indifference; men in their shirt-sleeves, looking on at their unfinished houses, and planning work for to-morrow;—and the train riding on, high above them, like a storm. But I know this is beautiful—very—very beautiful![6]

[1] Blair's Gap Summit, 1378 feet.

[2] Here CD had described the method by which the railway (opened 1833) made the 36 mile journey over the mountain (see *American Notes*, Ch. 10). A more detailed but less vivid description is given in *Society in America*, II, 190–2.

[3] After Johnstown, the canal ran beside the Conemaugh, Kiskiminetas and Alleghany rivers for the 172 miles to Pittsburgh.

[4] Cf. Harriet Martineau on the broken windows "throughout the entire country, (out of the cities)" (*Society in America*, II, 204).

[5] Cf. Basil Hall's horror (while travelling through New York State) at the "great black stumps" and "tall scorched, branchless stems of trees, which had undergone the barbarous operation known by the name of girdling"; their destruction "being accelerated by the action of fire, these wretched trunks in a year or two present the most miserable objects of decrepitude that can be conceived" (*op. cit.*, I, 128–9). The whole passage is recalled in *Chuzzlewit*, Ch. 23.

[6] Private joke: see *To* Maclise, 22 Mar and *fn.*

... I wonder whether you and Mac mean to go to Greenwich-fair! Perhaps you dine at the Crown-and-sceptre to-day, for it's Easter-Monday—who knows! I wish you drank punch, dear Forster. It's a shabby thing, not to be able to picture you with that cool green glass. ...

I told you of the many uses of the word "fix."[1] I ask Mr. Q on board a steamboat if breakfast be nearly ready, and he tells me yes he should think so, for when he was last below the steward was "fixing the tables"—in other words, laying the cloth. When we have been writing, and I beg him (do you remember anything of my love of order, at this distance of time?) to collect our papers, he answers that he'll "fix 'em presently." So when a man's dressing he's "fixing" himself, and when you put yourself under a doctor he "fixes" you in no time. T'other night, before we came on board here, when I had ordered a bottle of mulled claret and waited some time for it, it was put on table with an apology from the landlord (a lieutenant-colonel)[2] that "he feared it wasn't fixed properly." And here, on Saturday morning, a Western man, handing the potatoes to Mr. Q at breakfast, enquired if he wouldn't take some of "these fixings" with his meat. I remained as grave as a judge. I catch them looking at me sometimes, and feel that they think I don't take any notice. Politics are very high here; dreadfully strong; handbills, denunciations, invectives, threats, and quarrels. The question is, who shall be the next President.[3] The election comes off in *three years and a half* from this time.

To JOHN PENDLETON KENNEDY, [LATE MARCH 1842]

Mention in *To* Kennedy, 30 Apr 42.[4] *Date:* since according to CD written from Pittsburgh, one of the last three days in Mar.

Saying that, after many attempts to write a memorandum for Kennedy's Committee on international copyright, he had found he could not do so, and giving his reasons.

---

[1] "The Caleb Quotem [*the jack-of-all-trades character in George Colman the Younger's farce*, The Review] of the American vocabulary" (*American Notes*, Ch. 10). Cf. Marryat's *Diary in America*, II, 228: "Shall I *fix* your coat or your breakfast first?"

[2] Obviously in the State militia, like Colonel Diver, Major Pawkins, General Fladdock, General Choke in *Chuzzlewit*: military officers, says Martin, "spring up in every field"; "As thick as scarecrows in England, sir", Mark interposes (Ch. 21). Cf. the "gentlemen in the cabin" whom Mrs Trollope heard addressed as general,

colonel and major on her journey up the Mississippi (*Domestic Manners of the Americans*, 5th edn, 1839, p. 13).

[3] Tyler had no chance of being re-nominated, much less re-elected. The Democrats finally nominated a dark horse candidate, James K. Polk, who won the election, defeating Clay, the Whig candidate.

[4] When CD had discovered that an earlier letter he had written to Kennedy had accidentally gone to England in a packet of other letters.

To W. C. MACREADY, 1 APRIL 1842

MS Morgan Library. *Address*: W. C. Macready Esquire | 5 Clarence Terrace | York Gate Regents Park | London | England.

On Board the Steamboat | From Pittsburgh to Cincinnati
Friday Night April The First 1842.
(which will account for tremulous writing)

My Dear Macready. But that I know from constant experience that there are seasons, and many seasons, in a life of excitement and hard work, when a man needs all the manhood he has in him, *not* to give in—and to keep up—doing the labour he has to do in this doing world—and facing the weather, whatever it be, bravely—I should quarrel with you for your despondent letter in which I do fear certain rotten sins called Sunday Newspapers, and certain rotten creatures with mens'[1] forms and devils' hearts (serving the demoniac ability) called writers, have greater part and share than they should.[2] I have been thinking all day, as we have been skimming down this beautiful Ohio, its wooded heights all radiant in the sunlight,[3] how *can* a man like Macready fret, and fume, and chafe himself for such lice of literature as these! You may say that they are like lice, for another reason besides their meanness—because they live in peoples'[1] heads. I don't believe it. I have no faith in their influence, good or bad. I put no trust in them, for good or evil. Associating you with my recollections and meditations in this, and all other journeys, and becoming more and more mindful at such times, if that can be, of the images with which you have stored my brain, and the human

---

[1] Thus in MS.

[2] Macready's return to the management of Drury Lane, triumphal opening on 27 Dec 41, and brilliant success with *Acis and Galatea* (5 Feb) had been marred for him by vicious attacks in the Sunday papers sparked off by his letter to *The Times* of 31 Jan defending his new moral policy (see Vol. II, p. 454n). On 6 Feb the *Sunday Times* accused him of "Managerial Humbug"; the *Weekly Dispatch* of a gross violation of good faith with the public; while the *Satirist*, referring to him as "that obtrusive mountebank" and to his "ridiculous egotism", accused him of making up for failure on the stage by disguising himself "as a moral reformer". The following Sunday both the *Weekly Dispatch* and the *Satirist* printed a letter from Benjamin Webster (read with indignation by Macready on 22 Feb: see *Diaries*, II, 158), accusing Macready of announcing a "Mr Webster" in his *corps de ballet* deliberately to mislead the public and to annoy him; Macready had taken Drury Lane, the letter went on, not for the advancement of the drama, but solely to revenge himself on Charles Mathews and Webster himself (for Macready's "release from the fangs of

Webster", see Vol. II, p. 436 and *n*). The *Satirist* again poured scorn on "Macready's Morality Process" on 20 Feb.

[3] In *American Notes* CD awards the Ohio no higher praise than that it was "a fine broad river" (Ch. 11) and "sparkling neighbour" of the "intolerable" Mississippi (Ch. 14). Cf. Mrs Trollope's delight in its "sweet scenery"; in her party's eagerness to be on deck, "we almost learnt", she wrote, "to rival our neighbours at table in their voracious rapidity of swallowing, . . . lest we might lose sight of the beauty that was passing away from us" (*Domestic Manners of the Americans*, p. 25). But CD's mood was disenchanted, as he watched from the little stern-gallery (having escaped from his fellow-passengers between the meals they bolted in "gloomy silence": "Undertakers on duty would be sprightly beside them"). He saw in human terms what he was passing: the very occasional log cabin in its little clearing, with a poor field of wheat beside it and a settler watching the boat wistfully; and "the same, eternal foreground", with stately trees fallen into the stream and become "mere dry grizzly skeletons"—by which their unwieldy boat took "its hoarse sullen way" (Ch. 11).

energies and great passions you have set before me, and remembering the stamp and substance you have impressed on unsubstantial thoughts,—I have wondered a hundred times how things so mean and small—so wholly unconnected with your image, and utterly separated from the exercise of your genius, in its effects on all men—can, for an instant, disturb you. Fine talking, you will say,—and so it is. For I know the vague desire to take somebody by the throat, which is consequent upon the discharge of these pigmy arrows. But it is not the more rational because I have felt it also; and I vow to try and overcome it, and gain the victory by being indifferent, and feeling my own worth, and bidding them whistle on.

The theatre, Forster tells me, is doing well. Everybody tells me it is doing well. You yourself don't say that it is doing ill. In the joint names of Hercules and the Waggoner, cheer up then! The work will not always be so hard. You won't always take it so much to heart.—My mind misgives me that you have been living too long on chops—and that you don't take enough "rosy"[1] to drink—and that you are altogether in what Beau Tibbs,[2] with another meaning in his mind, would call "a horrid low way".—But if Elliotson be the man I take him to be (and if he be not, the whole human race wear masks and dominoes) he will already have administered, the necessary restoratives. He will have said that you must, and shall, have regular dinner times. He will have spoken emphatically of nourishing meats; generous drinks; and healths five fathoms deep, to the distant Dickens. He will have created a new office in the Theatre, and appointed to it a strictly virtuous female, whose function is, to come upon the stage at 12 at noon, bearing in her hand a tumbler-glass, containing the yolk of a new laid egg, discreetly mixed with Golden Sherry,[3] concerning which, the stage direction shall be "Macready drinks, smacks his lips, and becomes refreshed."

Seriously, my dear Macready, no man can work in mind and body, long, unless he uses a dining table as christians should. I have always thoroughly abominated and abjured those chops——those nasty Hemming chops.[4] Old Parr[5] never dined off chops, or in his dressing room. Chops and Cheerfulness are impossible of connection, but Joints and joy are clearly related; and Port and peace go hand in hand. *Do*[6] say in your next that you have left off eating with your fingers on week days, and have taken to knives and forks again. *Do* say that you are better, and healthfully disposed—but not unless you really are so. And never acknowledge to yourself (so shall your affectionate confidence have no occasion to acknowledge to me) that in the smallest angle of your heart, you ever framed that wish or thought twice—that thought, which seriously entertained for but one moment's space—would give pain, in Heaven, to the Spirit of your own child.[7]

---

[1] Wine (slang).

[2] The shabby aspirant to fashionable society in Goldsmith's *The Citizen of the World*.

[3] This was the drink CD himself took before Readings and in the intervals during his second American tour.

[4] Chops provided at the Wrekin Tavern (proprietor Henry Hemming), 22 Broad Court, Drury Lane.

[5] Thomas Parr (?1483–1635; *DNB*), husbandman of Shropshire; proverbial for his extreme and possibly legendary longevity.

[6] Underlined twice.

[7] Joan, died 25 Nov 40 (see Vol. II, p. 158*n*).

We received your letter, and that of your dear wife and sister,[1] with all our other epistolary treasures this morning—most fortunately and opportunely just before we left Pittsburgh. We have been looking for them painfully, these many days; and if they had arrived but four and twenty hours later, would have gone on our way with heavy hearts. The steamer that brought them had a terrible passage.[2] Her engine was disabled, and she came on with her sails (they carry but two; and neither is larger than a T.R.D.L. flat[3]—I mean one of a pair). She staggered into Halifax, and the stationary steamer[4] brought on her Mails and passengers.

I will not tell you of our route; for I have written at some length to Forster, and he will, no doubt, read my letter to you. Nor will I tell you (for the same reason) of my extraordinary success in magnetizing Kate. I hope you will be a witness of that, many, many, many happy times.

I have not changed—I cannot change, my dear Macready—my secret opinion of this country; its follies, vices, grievous disappointments. I have said to Forster that I believe the heaviest blow ever dealt at Liberty's Head, will be dealt by this nation in the ultimate failure of its example to the Earth.[5] See what is passing now—Look at the exhausted Treasury;[6] the paralyzed government; the unworthy representatives of a free people; the desperate contests between the North and the South; the iron curb and brazen muzzle[7] fastened upon every man who speaks his mind, even in that Republican Hall, to which Republican men are sent by a Republican people to speak Republican Truths[8]—the stabbings, and shootings,[9]

[1] Letitia Margaret Macready (1794–1858), who lived with them.

[2] The *Columbia*: see *To* Mitton, 4 Apr.

[3] A piece of scenery at the Theatre Royal, Drury Lane.

[4] The *Acadia*.

[5] Cf. *To* Forster, 24 Feb.

[6] Throughout 1841 the American Treasury had had acute difficulty in finding the money for the daily expense of government. In July 41 it had raised a loan of $12 million; and the Treasury Note Bill of Jan 42 authorized the immediate issue of $5 million of Treasury notes. During most of March the Senate debated Clay's resolutions for retrenchment and economy, to prevent further loans or issues of Treasury notes; while the House of Representatives debated a proposed Loan Bill to extend the loan of 1841 by adding to it the $5 million Treasury notes issued in Jan. The *Examiner*, 23 Apr (reporting American news to 1 Apr), announced that American finances were "in a deplorable state. The Treasury of the nation is bankrupt", and its 6 per cent. notes were being "hawked about at a depreciation varying from 3 to 6 per cent. discount."

[7] Cf. "iron muzzle disguised beneath a flower or two" in the suppressed Introduc-

tory chapter of *American Notes* (*To* Forster, 20 Sep, *fn*).

[8] This clearly refers to the notorious "Gag Rule" of the House of Representatives: see *To* J. Q. Adams, 10 or 11 Mar, *fn*.

[9] J. H. Franklin (*The Militant South, 1800–61*, Cambridge, Mass., 1956) gives frequent examples of street-fights with knives or guns, shootings during elections, and duels. Introducing a Bill to prohibit duelling in Columbia in 1838—following the fatal outcome of the duel between Jonathan Cilley and William Graves (Representatives from Maine and Kentucky)—Samuel Prentiss spoke of the "spirit of insubordination and lawless violence which is abroad in the land, infecting and pervading, it would seem entire communities . . . which, if not checked and subdued, will . . . sooner or later, overthrow all law and all government, and open the way to brutal anarchy and misrule" (*Congressional Globe*, 25th Congress, 2nd Session, 2 Mar 38, p. 207, quoted in J. H. Franklin, *op. cit.*, p. 52). Harriet Martineau described Southern society as the most savage in the world (*Society in America*, II, 329).

and coarse and brutal threatenings exchanged between Senators under the very Senate's roof[1]—the intrusion of the most pitiful, mean, malicious, creeping, crawling, sneaking party spirit, into all transactions of life[2]—even into the appointments of physicians to pauper madhouses[3]—the silly, drivelling, slanderous, wicked, monstrous Party Press.[4] I say nothing of the egotism which makes of Lord Ashburton's appointment, the conciliatory act of a frightened Government; nothing of the boastful, vain-glorious spirit which dictates a million of such absurdities; and which is *not English*. I love and honor very many of the people here—but *"the Mass"* (to use our monarchical term) are miserably dependent in great things, and miserably independent in small ones. That's a Truth, and you will find it so. The Nation is a body without a head; and the arms and legs, are occupied in quarrelling with the trunk and each other, and exchanging bruises at random.

God bless you my dearest friend. A hundred times God bless you. I will not thank you (how *can* I thank you!) for your care of our dear children: but I will ever be, heart and soul, your faithful friend

CHARLES DICKENS

P.S. I need not say that I have many pleasant things to say of America. God forbid that it should be otherwise. I speak to you, as I would to myself. I am a Lover of Freedom, disappointed—That's all. I am carrying this letter on to Cincinnati, to send to Boston from there.[5]

To JOHN FORSTER, 1, 2, 3 and 4 APRIL 1842

Extracts in F, III, v, 251–6 (continuation and conclusion of letter begun 28 Mar).

On board the steam boat from Pittsburgh to Cincinnati, April the first, 1842. A very tremulous steam boat, which makes my hand shake.[6] This morning, my

---

[1] Cf. the examples given in *To* Fonblanque, 12 Mar, repeated in *American Notes*, Ch. 8. Another example is given by Forster in the *Foreign Quarterly Review* (Oct 42, XXX, 220)—possibly drawing on CD's note book, since source unnamed (only outlined in *American Notes*): during an altercation in the Senate, late Feb 42, T. H. Benton ("the fiercest tiger in the den": Hone, *Diary*, ed. A. Nevins, p. 150), when reproved by Clay for calling N. P. Tallmadge a liar, threatened Clay with*"action"*; yet, commented Forster, "No one took the least notice of this gross insult to by far the ablest . . . of all the American statesmen."

[2] For an account of the "spoils system" under both Democratic and Whig administrations, see L. D. White, *The Jacksonians*, New York, 1963. J. Q. Adams referred (Mar 41) to "the numberless office-hunters blockading the President's house and all the Executive departments of the Government —famished for place" (*Memoirs*, ed. C. F.

Adams, Philadelphia, 1874–7, X, 447–8); and later (May 42) called them the "wolves of the antechamber, prowling for offices" (*op. cit.*, XI, 156). Appointments to every kind of executive office were given for political services.

[3] Probably a reference to the Governor of the lunatic asylum on Blackwell's Island, New York (see *To* Forster, 6 Mar, *fn*).

[4] The two words written large. See CD on "the vicious character of these infamous journals" in *American Notes*, Ch. 18; also Forster's article in the *Foreign Quarterly Review*, Oct 42.

[5] It must have gone on the mail-steamer leaving Boston on 1 May.

[6] The *Messenger* (see illustration in W. G. Wilkins, *CD in America*, facing p. 204). This must have been one of the steamboats, with pilot-house "all glass and 'gingerbread'" and "gorgeous" paddle-boxes, whose arrival in the upper reaches of the Mississippi Mark Twain (aged 7 in 1842)

dear friend, this very morning, which, passing by without bringing news from England, would have seen us on our way to St. Louis (viâ Cincinnati and Louisville) with sad hearts and dejected countenances, and the prospect of remaining for at least three weeks longer without any intelligence of those so inexpressibly dear to us—this very morning, bright and lucky morning that it was, a great packet was brought to our bed-room door, from HOME. How I have read and re-read your affectionate, hearty, interesting, funny, serious, delightful, and thoroughly Forsterian Columbia letter, I will not attempt to tell you; or how glad I am that you liked my first; or how afraid I am that my second was not written in such good spirits as it should have been; or how glad I am again to think that my third *was*; or how I hope you will find some amusement from my fourth: this present missive.[1] All this, and more affectionate and earnest words than the post office would convey at any price, though they have no sharp edges to hurt the stamping-clerk—you will understand, I know, without expression, or attempt at expression. So having got over the first agitation of so much pleasure; and having walked the deck; and being now in the cabin, where one party are playing at chess, and another party are asleep, and another are talking round the stove, and all are spitting; and a persevering bore of a horrible New Englander[2] with a droning voice like a gigantic bee *will* sit down beside me, though I am writing, and talk incessantly, in my very car, to Kate;—here goes again.

Let me see. I should tell you, first, that we got to Pittsburgh between eight and nine o'clock of the evening of the day on which I left off at the top of this sheet; and were there received by a little man (a very little man) whom I knew years ago in London. He rejoiceth in the name of [George D'Almaine];[3] and, when I knew him, was in partnership with his father on the stock-exchange, and lived handsomely at Dalston. They failed in business soon afterwards, and then this little man began to turn to account what had previously been his amusement and accomplishment, by painting little subjects for the fancy shops. So I lost sight of him, nearly ten years ago; and here he turned up 'tother day, as a portrait painter in Pittsburgh! He had previously written me a letter which moved me a good deal, by a kind of quiet independence and contentment it breathed, and still a painful sense of being alone, so very far from home. I received it in Philadelphia, and answered it. He dined with us every day of our stay in Pittsburgh (they were only three), and was truly gratified and delighted to find me unchanged— more so than I can tell you. I am very glad to-night to think how much happiness we have fortunately been able to give him.

Pittsburgh is like Birmingham—at least its townsfolks say so; and I didn't

watched with such excitement (see *Life on the Mississippi*, 1883, p. 4). "Mr. Dickens", Twain commented (p. 354), "declined to agree that the Mississippi steamboats were 'magnificent,' or that they were 'floating palaces,'—... terms which did not over-express the admiration with which the people viewed them". The only American steamboat CD dignified with the term "floating palace" was the *Burlington*, on which he spent a night on his way back from Canada to New York (see *To* Kennedy, 2 June, *fn*; and *American Notes*, Ch. 15).

[1] CD had completed letters to Forster on 30 Jan, 14, 27, 28 Feb, and 22 Mar; so this was in fact his sixth.

[2] See *To* Forster, 2 Apr, *fn*.

[3] F reads "D G", obviously as a disguise: see *To* Fred Dickens, 22 Mar and *fn*.

contradict them. It is, in one respect. There is a great deal of smoke in it.[1] I quite offended a man at our yesterday's levee, who supposed I was "now quite at home," by telling him that the notion of London being so dark a place was a popular mistake. We had very queer customers at our receptions,[2] I do assure you. Not least among them, a gentleman with his inexpressibles[3] imperfectly buttoned and his waistband resting on his thighs, who stood behind the half-opened door, and could by no temptation or inducement be prevailed upon to come out. There was also another gentleman, with one eye and one fixed goose-berry, who stood in a corner, motionless like an eight-day clock, and glared upon me, as I courteously received the Pittsburgians. There were also two red-headed brothers—boys—young dragons rather—who hovered about Kate, and wouldn't go. A great crowd they were, for three days; and a very queer one.

Still in the same Boat. April the Second, 1842.

Many, many, happy returns of the day.[4] It's only eight o'clock in the morning now, but we mean to drink your health after dinner, in a bumper; and scores of Richmond dinners to us![5] We have some wine (a present sent on board by our Pittsburgh landlord) in our own cabin; and we shall tap it to good purpose, I assure you; wishing you all manner and kinds of happiness, and a long life to ourselves that we may be partakers of it. We have wondered a hundred times already, whether you and Mac will dine anywhere together, in honour of the day. I say yes, but Kate says no. She predicts that you'll ask Mac, and he won't go. I have not yet heard from him.[6]

We have a better cabin here, than we had on board the Britannia; the berths being much wider, and the den having two doors: one opening on the ladies'

---

[1] Hone recorded his arrival at Pittsburgh, after the same journey on 15 June 47, thus: "We arrived at 'the Birmingham of America' at eleven o'clock this evening . . . its appearance was quite a novelty: bright flames issuing from foundries, glass and gas works, and rolling-mills, steam-engines puffing like broken-winded horses, and heavy clouds of smoke making the night's darkness darker, gave us a grand entrée to Pittsburgh" (*Diary*, ed. A. Nevins, p. 805).

[2] The *Pittsburgh Morning Chronicle*, 2 Apr, prided itself on "the quiet hospitality" the city offered to CD, as against the more flamboyant welcomes of the East. "He was not bespattered with that fulsome praise with which he was bedaubed in the East, and which, we have not the least doubt, was as disagreeable to himself as it was sickening to all sensible men" (quoted in Wilkins, *CD in America*, p. 201). Among those who planned to call on him at the Monongahela House on 31 Mar were William Barclay Foster (1779–1855), Mayor of Allegheny

since Dec 41, and his son Stephen (1826–64; *DAB*), the folk-song composer (J. T. Howard, *Stephen Foster, America's Troubadour*, New York, 1934, p. 113). Apparently CD was unwell while in Pittsburgh, and was attended by Dr Andrew N. McDowell, Stephen Foster's future father-in-law (*op. cit.*, p. 157). Charles B. Scully, a prominent Pittsburgh lawyer, recorded calling on CD on 29 Mar and advising Catherine to take a steamboat equipped with Evans's safety valves, as a precaution against boiler explosions (diary entry, quoted in Wilkins, *op. cit.*, pp. 202–3).

[3] Colloquialism first noted in *OED* from Wolcot's *A Roland for an Oliver*, 1790.

[4] Forster's 30th birthday.

[5] It was also CD's and Catherine's wedding anniversary: they usually celebrated both together at the Star and Garter, Richmond.

[6] Maclise apparently wrote only once—a letter CD received on 25 May (*To* Forster, 26 May).

cabin, and one upon a little gallery in the stern of the boat.[1] We expect to be at Cincinnati some time on Monday morning, and we carry about fifty passengers. The cabin for meals goes right through the boat, from the prow to the stern, and is very long; only a small portion of it being divided off, by a partition of wood and ground-glass, for the ladies. We breakfast at half after seven, dine at one, and sup at six. Nobody will sit down to any one of these meals, though the dishes are smoking on the board, until the ladies have appeared, and taken their chairs. It was the same in the canal boat.

The washing department is a little more civilized than it was on the canal, but bad is the best. Indeed the Americans when they are travelling, as Miss Martineau seems disposed to admit, are exceedingly negligent: not to say dirty. To the best of my making out, the ladies, under most circumstances, are content with smearing their hands and faces in a very small quantity of water.[2] So are the men; who superadd to that mode of ablution, a hasty use of the common brush and comb.[3] It is quite a practice, too, to wear but one cotton shirt a week, and three or four fine linen *fronts*. Anne reports that this is Mr. Q's course of proceeding: and my portrait-painting friend[4] told me that it was the case with pretty nearly all his sitters; so that when he bought a piece of cloth not long ago, and instructed the sempstress to make it *all* into shirts, not fronts, she thought him deranged.

My friend the New Englander, of whom I wrote last night, is perhaps the most intolerable bore on this vast continent. He drones, and snuffles, and writes poems, and talks small philosophy and metaphysics, and never *will* be quiet, under any circumstances. He is going to a great temperance convention at Cincinnati;[5] along with a doctor of whom I saw something at Pittsburgh.[6] The doctor, in addition to being everything that the New Englander is, is a phrenologist besides. I dodge them about the boat. Whenever I appear on deck, I see them bearing down upon me—and fly. The New Englander was very anxious last night that he and I should "form a magnetic chain," and magnetize the doctor, for the benefit of all incredulous passengers; but I declined, on the plea of tremendous occupation in the way of letter-writing.

[1] They had been "very gravely recommended to keep as far aft as possible, 'because the steamboats generally blew up forward'" (*American Notes*, Ch. 11).

[2] Cf. Harriet Martineau, *Society in America*, III, 151: "In steam-boats, the accommodations for washing are limited in the extreme . . . How ladies of the cabin can expect to enjoy any degree of vigour and cheerfulness during a voyage of four or five days, during which they wash merely their faces and hands, I cannot imagine."

[3] Marryat refers to the "very unpleasant cutaneous diseases to which the Americans are subject" from its use. "They are certainly", he adds, "very unrefined in the toilet as yet" (*Diary in America*, Part Second, 1, 103*n*). "Of course, a common comb and hair-brush in the saloon, which all used", Macready recorded on the Alabama River, 1 Feb 44 (*Diaries*, II, 260).

[4] George D'Almaine.

[5] This may well have been William H. Burleigh (1812–71; *DAB*), editor of the *Washington Banner*, Allegheny, and former public lecturer. He was born in Woodstock, Connecticut; had published a vol. of poems 1840; was a temperance advocate; and, according to Celia Burleigh (*Poems by W. H. Burleigh, with a Sketch of his Life*, New York, 1871, p. vii), "enjoyed a short but pleasant intimacy" with CD on his visit to America. He had formerly edited the *Christian Witness*, Pittsburgh, was an Abolitionist, and supported female suffrage.

[6] Perhaps Dr Andrew McDowell: see *To Forster*, 1 Apr, *fn*.

And speaking of magnetism, let me tell you that the other night at Pittsburgh, there being present only Mr. Q and the portrait-painter, Kate sat down, laughing, for me to try my hand upon her. I had been holding forth upon the subject rather luminously, and asserting that I thought I could exercise the influence, but had never tried. In six minutes, I magnetized her into hysterics, and then into the magnetic sleep. I tried again next night, and she fell into the slumber in little more than two minutes. . . . I can wake her with perfect ease; but I confess (not being prepared for anything so sudden and complete), I was on the first occasion rather alarmed. . . . The Western parts being sometimes hazardous,[1] I have fitted out the whole of my little company with LIFE PRESERVERS, which I inflate with great solemnity when we get aboard any boat, and keep, as Mrs. Cluppins did her umbrella in the court of common pleas, ready for use upon a moment's notice.[2] . . .

Sunday, April the third

Besides the doctor and the dread New Englander, we have on board that valiant general[3] who wrote to me about the "two LL's."[4] He is an old, old man with a weazen face, and the remains of a pigeon-breast in his military surtout. He is acutely gentlemanly and officer-like. The breast has so subsided, and the face has become so strongly marked, that he seems, like a pigeon-pie, to show only the feet of the bird outside, and to keep the rest to himself. He is perhaps *the* most horrible bore in this country. And I am quite serious when I say that I do not believe there are, on the whole earth besides, so many intensified bores as in these United States. No man can form an adequate idea of the real meaning of the word, without coming here.[5] There are no particular characters on board, with

[1] Largely through the dangers of striking wrecks or snags—or through fires (see *To* Forster, 30 Jan, *fn*). But an additional hazard came for a time from steamboats racing each other. The *Moselle*, for instance, made the run of 141 miles in 12 hours in 1837, but in the same year exploded (Marryat gives an eye-witness account: see *Diary in America*, Part Second, 1, 77–86). But "Racing was royal fun", wrote Mark Twain, recalling his early days; "The public always had an idea that racing was dangerous", but that was before laws were passed "which restricted each boat to just so many pounds of steam to the square inch"; no engineer, he added, "was ever sleepy or careless when his heart was in a race. . . . The dangerous place was on slow, plodding boats"—one was so slow that "when she finally sunk in Madrid Bend, it was five years before the owners heard of it" (*Life on the Mississippi*, 1883, pp. 162, 169).

[2] See *Pickwick*, Ch. 34: in fact it was Mrs Sanders who, while Mrs Cluppins was in the witness-box, kept "her right thumb pressed on the spring" of a large umbrella, "as if she were fully prepared to put it up at a moment's notice."

[3] General Gaines: see *To* Felton, 14 Mar, *fn*.

[4] The two "literary ladies" for whom Gaines had requested an introduction to CD next day.

[5] Cf. Harriet Martineau, *Society in America*, III, 77. She describes American conversation as "prosy, but withal rich and droll". For some weeks she found it difficult to keep awake during the entire reply to any question she happened to ask. "The person questioned seemed to feel himself put upon his conscience to give a full, true, and particular reply; and so he went back as near to the Deluge as the subject would admit, and forward to the millennium, taking care to omit nothing of consequence in the interval". But she "presently found the information [she] obtained . . . so full, impartial, and accurate, and the shrewdness and drollery with which it was conveyed so amusing that [she] became a great admirer of the American way of talking before six months were over".

these three exceptions. Indeed I seldom see the passengers but at meal-times, as I read and write in our own little state room. . . . I have smuggled two chairs into our crib; and write this on a book upon my knee. Everything is in the neatest order, of course; and my shaving tackle, dressing case, brushes, books, and papers, are arranged with as much precision as if we were going to remain here a month. Thank God we are not.

The average width of the river rather exceeds that of the Thames at Greenwich. In parts it is much broader; and then there is usually a green island, covered with trees, dividing it into two streams. Occasionally we stop for a few minutes at a small town, or village (I ought to say city, everything is a city here); but the banks are for the most part deep solitudes, overgrown with trees, which, in these western latitudes, are already in leaf, and very green . . .

All this I see, as I write, from the little door into the stern-gallery which I mentioned just now. It don't happen six times in a day that any other passenger comes near it; and, as the weather is amply warm enough to admit of our sitting with it open, here we remain from morning until night: reading, writing, talking. What our theme of conversation is, I need not tell you. No beauty or variety makes us weary less for home. We count the days, and say, "When May comes, and we can say—*next month*—the time will seem almost gone." We are never tired of imagining what you are all about. I allow of no calculation for the difference of clocks, but insist on a corresponding minute in London. It is much the shortest way, and best. . . . Yesterday, we drank your health and many happy returns—in wine, after dinner; in a small milk-pot jug of gin-punch, at night. And when I made a temporary table, to hold the little candlestick, of one of my dressing-case trays; cunningly inserted under the mattress of my berth with a weight a-top of it to keep it in its place, so that it made a perfectly exquisite bracket; we agreed, that, please God, this should be a joke at the Star-and-garter on the second of April eighteen hundred and forty-three.[1] If your blank *can* be surpassed . . . believe me ours transcends it. My heart gets, sometimes, SORE for home.

At Pittsburgh I saw another solitary confinement prison:[2] Pittsburgh being also in Pennsylvania. A horrible thought occurred to me when I was recalling all I had seen, that night. *What if ghosts be one of the terrors of these jails?* I have pondered on it often, since then. The utter solitude by day and night; the many hours of darkness; the silence of death; the mind for ever brooding on melancholy themes, and having no relief; sometimes an evil conscience very busy; imagine a prisoner covering up his head in the bedclothes and looking out from time to time, with a ghastly dread of some inexplicable silent figure that always sits upon his bed, or stands (if a thing can be said to stand, that never walks as men do) in the same corner of his cell. The more I think of it, the more certain I feel that not a few of these men (during a portion of their imprisonment at least) are nightly visited by spectres. I did ask one man in this last jail, if he dreamed much. He gave me a most extraordinary look, and said—under his breath—in a whisper—"No." . . .

[1] When they had their usual celebration: see *To* Beard, 31 Mar 43.
[2] The Western Penitentiary, less than a third of the size of the Eastern Penitentiary, but built on the same plan (not mentioned in *American Notes*).

Cincinnati. Fourth April, 1842.

We arrived here this morning; about three o'clock, I believe, but I was fast asleep in my berth. I turned out soon after six, dressed, and breakfasted on board. About half after eight,[1] we came ashore and drove to the hotel,[2] to which we had written on from Pittsburgh ordering rooms; and which is within a stone's throw of the boat wharf. Before I had issued an official notification that we were "not at home," two Judges called, on the part of the inhabitants, to know when we would receive the townspeople. We appointed to-morrow morning, from half-past eleven to one,[3] arranged to go out, with these two gentlemen, to see the town, *at* one; and were fixed for an evening party to-morrow night at the house of one of them.[4] On Wednesday morning we go on by the mail-boat to Louisville, a trip of fourteen hours; and from that place proceed in the next good boat to St. Louis, which is a voyage of four days. Finding from my judicial friends (well-informed and most agreeable gentlemen) this morning, that the prairie travel to Chicago is a very fatiguing one, and that the lakes are stormy, sea-sicky, and not over-safe at this season, I wrote by our captain to St. Louis (for the boat that brought us here goes on there) to the effect that I should not take the lake route, but should come back here; and should visit the prairies, which are within thirty miles of St. Louis, immediately on my arrival there. . . .

I have walked to the window, since I turned this page, to see what aspect the town wears. We are in a wide street: paved in the carriage way with small white stones, and in the footway with small red tiles. The houses are for the most part one story high; some are of wood; others of a clean white brick. Nearly all have green blinds outside every window. The principal shops over the way, are, according to the inscriptions over them, a Large Bread Bakery; a Book Bindery; a Dry Goods Store; and a Carriage Repository; the last named establishment looking very like an exceedingly small retail coal-shed. On the pavement under our window, a black man is chopping wood; and another black man is talking (confidentially) to a pig.[5] The public table, at this hotel and at the hotel opposite, has just now finished dinner. The diners are collected on the pavement, on both sides of the way, picking their teeth, and talking. The day being warm, some of them have brought chairs into the street. Some are on three chairs; some on two; and some, in defiance of all known laws of gravity, are sitting quite comfortably

[1] An Americanism CD had picked up.

[2] The Broadway Hotel.

[3] Announced by the *Cincinnati Daily Republican*, 5 Apr, as from 11 a.m. until 3. Other Cincinnati papers reported CD's and Catherine's arrival, but made no mention of a reception (W. G. Wilkins, *CD in America*, p. 206).

[4] Judge Timothy Walker (see *To* Forster, 15 Apr, *fn*). Walker recorded in his diary on 5 Apr: "Had a visit from Charles Dickens and Lady. Rode with them about the city and gave them a party in the evening. Liked them much. Have read all his works and with great interest. Felt acquainted with him before I saw him. Like

him still better now" (MS Cincinnati Historical Society). For CD's description of the party, see *To* Forster, 15 Apr.

[5] CD, having described the pigs in *American Notes*, Ch. 6, at New York, omits them at Cincinnati where other travellers usually commented on them—Mrs Trollope with some disgust, Charles Lyell with amusement at their walking "at large about the streets, as if they owned the town": "It is a favourite amusement of the boys", he wrote, "to ride upon the pigs, and we were shown one sagacious old hog, who was in the habit of lying down as soon as a boy came in sight" (*Travels in America*, II, 72-3).

on one: with three of the chair's legs, and their own two, high up in the air. The loungers, underneath our window, are talking of a great Temperance convention which comes off here to-morrow.[1] Others, about me. Others, about England. Sir Robert Peel is popular here, with everybody.[2] ...

To DAVID C. COLDEN, 4 APRIL 1842*

MS Free Library of Philadelphia. *Address: Paid.* | David. C. Colden Esquire | 28 Laight Street | Hudson Square | New York City.

Cincinnati. Ohio. | Monday Fourth April 1842.

My Dear Friend.

We arrived here this morning, safe and sound, and not materially the worse for wear; although the Pittsburgh Levees *were* rather hard work, & although certain gaunt and grim Pittsburghians *did* stand behind the door and in remote corners of the reception chamber by the hour together; and resist all temptations to come forth, or to be seduced into conversation.[3] Mrs. Colden (the beloved Mrs. Colden, if I may make so bold as to trust that expression to your keeping) complimented me, before I left New York, on my feats of sleight of hand. I am improving very much; and expect to be able in a short time to swallow a black-handled dinner knife, and reproduce it at pleasure. I have not yet passed the ferrule, but I am getting on by degrees. Necessity and two-pronged forks[4] are the mothers of invention.

Our letters, thank God, brought none but the best and most cheerful and cheering news. We are entrusted with more kind remembrances and messages to you, than the Post Office at this place will undertake to forward on any terms. The Theatre flourishes nobly, but Macready has been very hard-worked and is not quite well, wherefore he writes in low Spirits. I have returned his shuttle-cock more lightly than it came, and hope the match will be played out, merrily, on both sides.

Did you ever pass a night on board a canal boat? Did you ever pass a morning on board a canal boat? Did you ever find yourself on board a canal boat under any circumstances when washing and dressing were necessary? If not, I exult in the consciousness of my immeasurable superiority. When I think of the cold mornings whereon I scooped the dirty water out of the canal with a tin ladle chained to the boat, and having so filled a tin basin also chained to the boat, plunged my face into the same, and wiped it into a kind of damp and slimy dryness on *the* jack towel, I feel something between Robinson Crusoe and Philip

---

[1] Described in *To* Forster, 15 Apr.

[2] Peel's ministry, which had replaced Melbourne's in Aug 41, had shown itself much better disposed towards America. Lord Aberdeen, the new Foreign Secretary, was anxious to calm relations disturbed by the *Creole* and *Caroline* affairs; and there was considerable good-will in America towards the Ashburton mission. On 6 Sep Sumner wrote to Morpeth: "Lord Ashburton and his suite spread a social charm over Washington, and filled everybody with friendly feelings toward England" (E. L. Pierce, *Memoir and Letters of Sumner,* II, 225). Peel's movement towards free trade was also very popular.

[3] See *To* Forster, 1 Apr.

[4] Cf. Fanny Kemble: "the wretched two-pronged iron implements furnished us by our host were any thing but ... convenient" (*Journal,* 1835, II, 267).

Quarll,[1] with a dash of Sinbad the Sailor—and think of leaving off ordinary clothes, and going clad, for the future, in skins and furs; with a gun on each shoulder, and two axes in a belt round my middle.

We are not quite clear whether we shall cross to Chicago from St. Louis, and so get to Buffaloe[2] by the Lakes; or whether we shall return to Pittsburgh by steamboat, and go from that place to Erie, and so to Buffaloe. Some wise men of the West have told me that the Grand Prairie will be too wet for comfortable travelling until May; and other wise men report that its present state is nothing less than perfection. In like manner, some authorities are of opinion that it takes four days and nights to cross the Prairies; and others know for a certainty that the journey can be accomplished in four and twenty hours.[3] Upon the whole— though I shall not finally decide until I have consulted the St. Louis people—I think it most likely that we shall eschew the Lakes, and avoid sea-sickness.[4] Sich (as Miggs[5] would say) is Mrs. D desires; and as my wishes is to please her inclinations, it will be my endeavours to make myself conformable to her dispositions, though I *am* but a husband.

In either case, will you in your kindness, send any letters, you may have for us, —addressed to the care of the Postmaster at Buffaloe, up to the twenty fourth of this month. I calculate that on the night of the twenty fourth we shall sleep in that town;[6] and you may be sure that on our arrival, I shall not be slow to send to the Post Office. Whatever you receive for us in the meanwhile, please to keep in your counting house until the time arrives for sending them to Buffaloe with a view to their receipt by us on that date. From that town, we shall go straight to the hotel at Niagara, *on the English side*, where we purpose remaining a week, at least, and where you may safely address any later despatches. But directly we arrive there, I will write to you again.

In the matter of the George Washington, we trust ourselves entirely in your hands for the choice of our State Room. If there should be any larger or family one, which possesses *decided* advantages, I should be very glad to pay extra for it;[7] our object being to be comfortable—if I may use a word so wildly and preposterously impossible of connection with all Christian peoples' experience of a Ship. In a word, and to copy the phraseology of the advertisements in our English Newspapers "Wages is not so much an object as a comfortable situation". But whatever you do, will be right; and will be certain to please us.

---

[1] The hero of Peter Longueville's *The Hermit: or, the Unparalleled Sufferings and Surprising Adventures of Mr. Philip Quarll*, 1727: 13 editions by 1800, and frequently adapted for children. Dramatized also as *Philip Quarll, the English Hermit*, and most recently performed at the Olympic 1840. Mentioned again by CD in *Chuzzlewit*: see John Westlock on the furnishing of his chambers: "nothing but a few little bachelor contrivances! the sort of impromptu arrangements that might have suggested themselves to Philip Quarll or Robinson Crusoe: that's all!" (Ch. 36).

[2] Thus in MS.

[3] For CD's expedition from St Louis, solely to the Looking-Glass Prairie, see *To Forster*, 16 Apr.

[4] Which they did.

[5] In *Barnaby Rudge*. CD again adopts Miggs's style in *To* Colden, 21 May.

[6] In fact they did not reach Buffalo till the 26th, and spent only three hours there.

[7] The normal passage to England on the *George Washington* was $100 "without wines or liquors".

If paper could blush; this, for the trouble it gives you, would be rose-colored by the time of its arrival in New York. You see what you have brought upon yourself by making us regard you and yours in the light of dear old friends! Take warning from this sad experience, and make that house in Laight Street a disagreeable and repulsive one from this time.

But as you never can make it so to us, who are in the secret, give our joint loves and affectionate regards to all who are in it. And believe me My Dear friend
Always Faithfully | And cordially Yours
David. C. Colden. Esquire.   CHARLES DICKENS

P.S. I wrote to Lord Jeffrey by the Steamer from Boston on the Second.

To CHARLES A. DAVIS, 4 APRIL 1842*

MS Mr John J. Emery. *Address*: Charles Augustus Davis Esquire | Broadway | New York City.
Cincinnati. Ohio. | Monday, Fourth April 1842.
My Dear Davis.

Please to turn back to your daily memorandum book, and to erase that leaf whereon you have written down my name as a thoughtless and unmindful Vagabond. And substitute in its place another entry, doing full justice to my virtues and captiwations—inadwertent, or otherwise.

It is so long since I saw a fork with three prongs, that I shall be greatly disconcerted by their use, when I get back to New York. I don't often wash myself in these parts; and as to shaving—but that's a weakness; not the more defensible because of its being commonly entertained.

Perhaps you never made your toilette on board a canal boat? If you never did —don't. Perhaps you never slept on a perch, like a Canary Bird? I have. It's not so hard to hold on as you would suppose, after the first two or three nights. Travel from Baltimore to Pittsburgh (by way of the Canal) and try.

We are on our way now—or shall be, the day after tomorrow—to Saint Louis, whence I make a day's journey into the Prairies. Then we purpose returning here, and going by two places (one is Columbus, and the other sounds like Sandisky[1]—it ought to be in Poland) to Buffaloe. So to Niagara.

I have put that cotton of yours in my pipe, and smoked it carefully. The idea is an exceedingly good one, and *might* be made very striking. I am not so sure that it falls in my path. I have not made up my mind yet, even, to write anything about America, and my wanderings in it.[2] Nous verrons.

John Quincey Adams is as like your sketch of him[3] as he is like the John Quincey Adams in his bedroom Mirror. What a fine fellow he is! I saw him several times. We dined there one day; and another day I met him at a Club of gentlemen who invited me to dinner.[4] There he ate, and drunk, and made a

---

[1] Sandusky.

[2] This is disingenuous: before he set out, he had virtually agreed with Chapman & Hall to write about his American experiences: see Vol. II, p. 388.

[3] Presumably in conversation or a letter: Adams does not appear in Davis's *Letters of J. Downing, Major* (New York, 1834).

[4] The Alleghany Club, Washington (see *To* Forster, 15 Mar and *fn*).

speech, and talked, and perfectly astonished me by his memory, freshness, vigour, and intellect. I delivered the greater part of your letters, and had abundant reason to thank you for your friendly precaution, in giving them to me. We enjoyed Washington very much. As to Mr. Clay—he is perfectly enchanting.

We went from Washington to Richmond. But finding the time melting away, I acted on Mr. Clay's advice, and went no further South—returned to Baltimore for two days—and here we are.

This is an intolerably stupid letter, I know. But I am fain to send it, and to wait no longer for time to write anything of interest to you—otherwise the chances are, that I should arrive in New York before my autograph.

Mrs. Dickens unites with me in best regards to Mrs. Davis[1] (concerning whom I grieve to say I have dreamed no dreams lately)—and to your daughter—and I am always

| | My Dear Davis \| Faithfully Yours |
| Charles Augustus Davis Esquire | CHARLES DICKENS |

To DR F. H. DEANE,[2] 4 APRIL 1842

MS Rosenbach Foundation. *Address:* Dr. F. H. Deane | Richmond | Virginia.

Cincinnati. Ohio. Fourth April 1842.

My Dear Sir.

I have not been unmindful of your request, for a moment; but have not been able to think of it until now. I hope my good friends (for whose Christian names I have left blanks in the Epitaph)[3] may like what I have written; and that they will take comfort, and be happy again.[4] I sail on the Seventh of June, [a]nd purpose being at the Carlton House New York, about the first. It will make me easy to know that this [let]ter[5] has reached you.

| | Faithfully Yours |
| Doctor F. H. Deane | CHARLES DICKENS |

---

[1] Daughter (?or niece) of Mrs Harriet Howell, with whom the Davises lived.

[2] Francis H. Deane, MD (1810–70), born at Juverna, Cumberland County; graduated MD University of Pennsylvania 1832; practised in Richmond, Virginia, 1834 to his death. Whether CD met him at the Richmond "social supper" on 18 Mar or as one of the callers at the Exchange Hotel on the following day is not known.

[3] See below. They were Anthony and Mary Jane Thornton (*née* Irving; said, "on good authority", to be a distant cousin of Washington Irving), of South Second Street, Richmond; married 1839.

[4] Their first child had died shortly before CD's arrival in Richmond, and appears to have been widely mourned: the *Richmond Whig and Public Advertiser* of 18 Mar announced CD's arrival in four lines, but devoted 21 to the baby's obituary. He was buried near Cumberland Court House at "Oak Hill", the estate of Capt. William Mynn Thornton, his paternal grandfather.

[5] Paper defaced and only part of word legible.

[1]This is the Grave
of
A Little Child,
Whom God in his goodness
Called to a Bright Eternity,
When he was very young.
Hard as it is
For Human Affection
To reconcile itself
To Death,
In any shape;
(And most of all, perhaps,
At First,
In This)
His parents
Can even now believe
That it will be a consolation to them,
Throughout Their Lives,
And when they shall have grown old
And grey,
always to think of him
As a Child,
In Heaven.[2]

———————

"And Jesus called a little child unto
him, and set him in the midst of them."

———————

He was the son of A   and M   Thornton.
Christened[3] CHARLES IRVING[4]
He was born on the 20th. day of January 1841,
And he died on the 12th. day of March 1842.
Having lived only Thirteen Months, and nine[3] days.

---

[1] The epitaph is written on a separate page. It was used by the Thorntons with only slight alterations to capitals and punctuation, and the change of two words (see below). The stone still stands, "though somewhat forlornly, in what is now part of a state forest". For this and the other details in these notes we are indebted to Mr Randolph W. Church's article, "Charles Dickens Sends his Sympathy", *Virginia Cavalcade*, Summer 1971, pp. 42–7, which contains a photograph of the tombstone—the epitaph clearly legible.

[2] Written larger than the rest.

[3] "Christened" altered on tombstone to "Called", and "nine" to "19".

[4] N (from MDGH) mistakenly reads as "Jerking".

To FREDERICK DICKENS, 4 APRIL 1842*

MS Berg Collection. *Address:* Frederick Dickens Esquire | Commissariat | Treasury | London | England.

Cincinnati. Ohio. Monday Fourth April 1842.

My Dear Fred. After a long delay (for the steamer had, again, a terrible voyage) we received our welcome and most ardently looked-for packet of letters, at Pittsburgh last Friday Morning, the First,—just before embarking in the Steamboat for this place, which is more than Five Hundred Miles from it. You may conceive how delighted we were to get the long-expected news from Home; and with what heartfelt pleasure we read your account of our dear darlings, whom we so long to see, that twenty times a day we count the days between this, and our return.

The steamer in which we came here, is called the Messenger; and has far better accommodations than the Britannia. There is one enormous Cabin, running all through the boat; and opening from it, little state rooms with two berths in each. Those which are set apart for married folks have each another little door opening on a light gallery at the stern; and here we sat very comfortably: looking at the prospect on the banks of the river, where there are great solitudes for many long miles together—only broken by log-houses where the new settlers live in the roughest and most desolate fashion you can well imagine.[1] Think what rivers are, in this country! The Ohio is 900 miles long;[2] and usually as broad as the Thames at Greenwich—very often much wider. We are going down to its mouth, and then 200 miles up the Mississippi, as you will see if you look for St. Louis on the map. We leave here on Wednesday; and intend halting at Louisville for a day.—I have been told that the Prairies are too wet to be easily crossed at this season of the year. If this should prove to be so,[3] we shall return to Pittsburgh from St. Louis (very likely by the same boat that brought us here)—and get to Buffaloe from there, by the way of Erie. This will still bring us to Niagara by the twenty fourth or twenty fifth.

I have only had time to write one letter on board;[4] and that I have sent to Forster, who will make you acquainted with its contents. I would not therefore tell you anything about the Canal boat or other modes of conveyance, even if I had the time; as I have described them to him.

We have not heard from Alfred,[5] nor have we written to him, for we have both forgotten his address. I wish you would do so. I need not say what delight it gives me to hear that Fanny is doing so well,[6] nor how sure I feel that she will yet

[1] In *American Notes*, Ch. 11, CD put this more strongly: "For miles, and miles, and miles, these solitudes are unbroken by any sign of human life or trace of human footstep". Six years later the Ohio's banks were well populated: see Archibald Prentice, *A Tour of the United States*, 1848, p. 45.

[2] In fact 981.

[3] It did not: see *To* Forster, 16 Apr.

[4] Not true; he had written one to Macready.

[5] Alfred Lamert Dickens (1822–60), CD's second-eldest surviving brother: see Vol. I, p. 44n. He was working as a surveyor on the Birmingham and Derby Railway (see Vol. II, p. 223n).

[6] The Burnetts first appeared in Manchester at a public concert in Feb 42. They sang a "duetto" from Rossini's *La Serenata* (*Musical World*, 24 Feb); see also *To* Burnett, 25 Nov, *fn*.

do much better. I suppose Burnett has become quite an aristocrat[1]—and that he rides to give lessons[2] on a thorough-bred Hunter?

You will wonder to see this lined paper, but the Immortal Secretary being absent, looking after the luggage, I am obliged to use the writing-materials of the Hotel; and in this part of the Globe they are much given to this uncomfortable paper.—What do you think of my having magnetized Kate, with amazing success? She will rather astonish you, when we come home, I can tell you.

I should think Sir John Wilson, having had so little enjoyment out of the house,[3] would consider it dear at any price. The very walls must wonder at its being so dull; and what the bitter beer can assign in its own mind as the reason of its not being tapped, I am at a loss to conceive. By the bye,—on the first of June will you get Sir John's permission to have two strong men in, to roll the casks out, and stand them on the horse in the old place? Otherwise, it will not be in drinking trim when we arrive. I think you have the key of the Wine cellar?

Remember me, kindly and heartily, to Chapman and Hall; from whom I have not yet heard once. And will you do so, too, to Beard? And will you tell him that I have only time, in the multiplicity of my engagements, to write more than one letter containing anything like an account of our proceedings—and that Forster will be pleased to shew these documents to him, if he has sufficient interest in them to give him a call.

Our hearts ache for home. It is impossible to say how we long to see the dear children. God bless you and them!

Always Your affectionate brother
CHARLES DICKENS[4]

To THOMAS MITTON, 4 APRIL 1842

MS Huntington Library.

In Haste[5]

Cincinnati. Ohio. | April The Fourth 1842.

My Dear friend.

I received yours with great delight and pleasure. It was very late, as the Columbia had a bad passage, and broke her engine by the way. We got our

---

[1] Having retired from the stage by 1841.

[2] Singing lessons in Manchester.

[3] 1 Devonshire Terrace.

[4] In the space remaining on p. 1 of a folded sheet, Catherine wrote: "Dearest Fred. Charles has not left me too much paper I find, therefore I shall only be able to add a very few lines to his epistle to say how delighted we were to receive our long wished for letters ([very] behindhand as the Columbia had a drea[dful] passage) and how easy and happy we feel about our treasures as we hear from all such accounts of their health and happiness. God grant it may be so till we return. The time will soon be here—dont forget dear Fred to drink my health on the 19th. of May which is my birthday—You may be sure we did not forget the 2d. of April which festival we held in our Stateroom on board the Steamer. I see from Charles and Mr. Forster's letters you are to get all the news, & I will not therefore inflict any upon you. | I am so glad to hear that you go out sometimes to see them at Kensington as I am sure it must do Mama much good. I am looking for a long letter from you by the next parcel. God bless you dearest Fred. | Believe me ever Your truly attached sister | KATE". (Two words uncertain where paper torn at seal.)

[5] Ink and writing suggest written after finishing letter.

letters from England, most opportunely on the very morning we left Pittsburgh, and within a very few hours of the boat's starting. If they had missed us there, we should in all probability not have received them for weeks, through being constantly before the Mail.

Ever since, and including, the day of their receipt, we have been coming here by Steamboat; along the Ohio River. This River is 900 Miles in length (think of that!) and we have travelled about 550 miles upon it: stopping at a great many intermediate places. On Wednesday morning we start again; and changing boats, and perhaps stoppi[ng? two days][1] at Louisville; go down to its mouth, and two hundred [miles up the] Mississippi river, to get to St. Louis. Since we left [Baltimore,[2] we have] travelled upwards of a hundred miles by railroad and [stage-coach], and 250 miles by canal, besides.

Forster has the best journal I have had time to keep in these conveyances, of our adventures. He will be glad to shew, or read it to you. I think you will be amused by it.

I was greatly pained to find that you had misconstrued that passage in my first letter, in which I made allusion to our darlings.[3] I put it there, because it naturally fell there; and my account of the gale brought me to it. But if you think that in saying it was a consolation to me to reflect upon the friends they would have, I for an instant lost sight of you, my old and familiar friend, in whom I repose so much and such implicit confidence, I can hardly say which you wrong most—yourself or me.[4]

I am glad to hear that the business goes on bravely—You know that you yourself are not more interested in its success than I am.[5] The anxious time, in everything, is the first part of the struggle. That over, the path is smooth and straight.

I shall have so much to tell and talk about when I come home, that I am half afraid I may return a Bore.[6] But for the pleasure of being at home again, I will consent even to that.

We count the days; and long, and yearn, for Home. Kate is very well, and

---

[1] Triangular pieces are missing at left and right edges of both pages of the MS, presumably torn away at the seal when letter was opened. Conjectures here and below are based on space and probable substance. In fact they only stayed one night at Louisville; but it was not until they discovered that the city presented "no objects of . . . interest" that they "resolved to proceed next day" (*American Notes*, Ch. 12).

[2] CD's last letter to Mitton had been from Baltimore.

[3] See extract from CD's description of the storm at beginning of *To* Forster, 17 Jan (presumably seen by Mitton). The

names of "devoted friends" the Dickens children would have if orphaned were presumably given in the MS (though omitted in F), and Mitton's not among them.

[4] For Mitton's undoubted jealousy of Forster, see *To* Mitton, 11 July, *fn.*

[5] Mitton, having broken away from Smithson (see Vol. II, pp. 152 and *n*, and 414), was practising on his own at Isleworth 1842–4 (W. J. Carlton, "The Strange Story of Thomas Mitton", *D*, LVI [1960], p. 144). CD's "interest" was partly financial: see *To* Mitton, 17 Sep 43.

[6] Written large.

sends her best regards to you. Anne is a very good traveller; and the Secretary (whose wages I have "ris" to twenty dollars a month) takes such care of the luggage and all other matters, that I walk into and out of every coach, car, wagon, boat, and barge, as if I had nothing with me but one shirt, and that were [in] my pocket.

I am vexed to hear that that father of mine [is "in trou]ble"—again.[1] How long he is, growing up to be a m[an!]

I am always My dear friend | Faithfully and truly Yours

CHARLES DICKENS

Did you remember that last Saturday, the First, was our Wedding-Day?[2]

To UNKNOWN CORRESPONDENT, [?4–6 APRIL] 1842

Extract in Bangs & Co. catalogue No. 2341 (1886); *MS* 1 p.; dated 1842. *Date:* clearly after meeting Gilmor on 22 Mar; perhaps in Cincinnati where he stayed 4–6 Apr.

Mr. Gilmor, of Baltimore, gave me a letter to you, begging your advice in the matter of getting cashed any drafts I might draw upon his house. But after doing so he gave me a letter to a Banker in this city[3] for the same purpose; therefore I will not trouble you with the communication—which is a mere business one, rendered quite unnecessary.

---

[1] i.e. again in money difficulties. On 12 Feb John Dickens had applied to Macready for a loan of £20 which, after consulting with Forster, Macready sent him, "desiring him not to mention it to his son" (*Diaries*, II, 158). His application on 24 Mar to "Miss Coutts & Co." was refused (MSS Morgan). CD's accounts (MS Messrs Coutts) Jan to June 42 show no direct payments to him or to Mitton as intermediary; but two lump sums paid to Barclay & Co.—£100 on 29 Mar and £175 on 7 July—may have covered some arrangement for their paying him an allowance in CD's absence. £100 to Mitton on 3 Sep and another £100 to him on 31 Oct were almost certainly for John Dickens.

[2] He meant "last Saturday the Second".

[3] The following, from Sir Charles Lyell to Sumner, Cincinnati, 25 May 42, suggests that the city may have been Cincinnati: "We hear much of your friend Mr Dickens here—He was kept a long time waiting in a banking house here while they were cashing a bill & one Mr Longstreet a rich man of this place, but one who dressed shabbily, entered into a long conversation with him. He was asked afterwards what notion he had formed of the person with whom he had talked. He said he was a shrewd & rich man which last he had inferred merely from the satisfied tone of Mr L." (MS Houghton Library, Harvard).

To WILLIAM C. KINNEY,¹ 14 APRIL 1842

Text from the *Belleville Weekly Advocate*, 21 Apr 42.

Planters' House,² St. Louis | Fourteenth April 1842.
My Dear Sir,
I am truly obliged to you for your letter of welcome and congratulation,³
which has given me real pleasure. Accept my cordial thanks, and believe me,
Faithfully yours,
CHARLES DICKENS

To JOHN FORSTER, 15, 16 and [17] APRIL 1842

Extracts in F, III, vi, 257–65.

On board the Messenger again. Going from St. Louis back to Cincinnati.
Friday, fifteenth April, 1842.

We remained in Cincinnati one whole day after the date of my last, and left
on Wednesday morning the 6th.⁴ We reached Louisville soon after midnight on
the same night;⁵ and slept there.⁶ Next day at one o'clock we put ourselves on
board another steamer,⁷ and travelled on until last Sunday evening the tenth;
when we reached St. Louis at about nine o'clock. The next day we devoted to
seeing the city. Next day, Tuesday the twelfth, I started off with a party of men
(we were fourteen in all) to see a prairie;⁸ returned to St. Louis about noon on

---

¹ William C. Kinney (1781–1843), born
in Kentucky, settled in St Clair Co.,
Illinois, where he became a large land-
owner. A talented man of little education
(taught to read by his wife), he was at
various times a Baptist preacher, stump
orator, storekeeper, and finally politician
(an ardent Jacksonian democrat). Served
in the Illinois State Senate, and as the
State's Internal Improvement Commissioner. Lieut. Governor 1826–30. Greatly
angered by *American Notes*, he issued from
Belleville a printed pamphlet attacking both
CD and England. "It was like firing a pop-
gun against a first-class iron-clad. . . . The
pamphlet was a terrible failure" (*Memoirs
of Gustav Koerner, 1809–1896*, ed. T. J.
McCormack, Cedar Rapids, 1909, I, 475).

² See *To* Forster, 17 Apr.

³ In it, according to the *Advocate*, Kinney
had enclosed a specimen of his own writing
—ignored by CD.

⁴ "In the Pike steam-boat, which, carrying the mails, was a packet of a much better
class than that in which we had come from
Pittsburg" (*American Notes*, Ch. 12).

⁵ There had been on board, besides "the
usual dreary crowd of passengers", Pitchlynn, an Indian chief: see *ibid.* and *To* Miss
Hutton, 23 Dec.

⁶ At the Galt House—"a splendid hotel",
where they were "as handsomely lodged as
though [they] had been in Paris, rather than
hundreds of miles beyond the Alleghanies"
(*American Notes*, Ch. 12). But they found
the city of little interest.

⁷ The *Fulton*, which they boarded at
Portland, a suburb of Louisville; joined on
it by a 7 ft 8 Kentucky Giant (*ibid.*).

⁸ The Looking-Glass Prairie, St Clair
County (see *To* Forster, 16 Apr).

the thirteenth; attended a soirée and ball[1]—not a dinner—given in my honor that night; and yesterday afternoon at four o'clock we turned our faces homewards. Thank Heaven!

Cincinnati is only fifty years old, but is a very beautiful city:[2] I think the prettiest place I have seen here, except Boston. It has risen out of the forest like an Arabian-night city; is well laid out; ornamented in the suburbs with pretty villas; and above all, for this is a very rare feature in America, has smooth turf-plots and well kept gardens. There happened to be a great temperance festival; and[3] the procession mustered under, and passed, our windows early in the morning. I suppose they were twenty thousand strong, at least. Some of the banners were quaint and odd enough. The ship-carpenters, for instance, displayed on one side of their flag, the good Ship Temperance in full sail; on the other, the Steamer Alcohol blowing up sky-high. The Irishmen[4] had a portrait of Father Mathew,[5] you may be sure. And Washington's broad lower jaw (by the bye, Washington had not a pleasant face)[6] figured in all parts of the ranks. In a kind of square at one outskirt of the city, they divided into bodies, and were addressed by different speakers. Drier speaking I never heard. I own that I felt quite uncomfortable to think they could take the taste of it out of their mouths with nothing better than water.

[1] An announcement in the *St. Louis Republican* of 12 Apr stated that a soirée would be given in preference to a ball, so as not to "interfere with the scruples of propriety of any" (quoted in W. G. Wilkins, *CD in America*, p. 217). But the *St. Louis People's Organ* of 15 Apr reported the occasion as being both: "The Grand Boz Ball—the splendid Soirée—the great *omnium gatherum* of gentility and civility ... The magnificent bombshell, rammed full of pride, aristocracy, ... soft soap, curiosity, folly, ...", "the great farce". On 16 Apr it described the event in detail: "Some stood with their *mouths* and eyes wide open! Would to heaven Cruikshank could have seen them! What a picture they would have made! ... Boz bore it as long as possible, answered pleasantly all questions addressed to him, and then broke the ice by offering his arm to the amiable and lovely Mrs. E****, and joining the promenaders." Finally there was dancing until 2 a.m., in which CD and Catherine did not join, but slipped away at about midnight.

[2] "One of the much-cried-up wonders of the West, and not without reason" (Basil Hall, *Travels in North America*, III, 388).

[3] Described in fuller detail in *American Notes*, Ch. 11. It consisted of members of various "Washington Auxiliary Temperance Societies".

[4] Described in *American Notes* as forming "a distinct society among themselves ...

They looked as jolly and good-humoured as ever; and, working the hardest for their living ..., were the most independent fellows there, I thought" (Ch. 11).

[5] Theobald Mathew (1790–1856; *DNB*), the much loved and honoured Irish Catholic friar and temperance preacher. After signing the pledge in 1838, preached temperance with remarkable success throughout Ireland, in London 1843, and in the principal American cities 1849–51. Numerous American temperance societies were named after him.

[6] The portrait reproduced was no doubt one of the many variants of Gilbert Stuart's "Athenaeum Head" (1796), used on stamps and paper money and hung in public places. Washington, from his early forties, had had to wear uncouth false teeth with which he had constant difficulty. "His mouth was like no other that I ever saw", recorded an English traveller in 1790; "the lips firm and the under jaw seemed to grasp the upper with force, as if its muscles were in full action when he sat still" (J. H. Morgan and M. Fielding, *The Life Portraits of Washington*, Philadelphia, 1931, p. xix). Stuart, for his portrait, tried to "soften the protrusion of the lower teeth by getting Washington to put rolls of cotton in his mouth": hence the plumpness. (John Woodforde, *The Strange Story of False Teeth*, 1968, p. 107).

In the evening[1] we went to a party at Judge Walker's,[2] and were introduced to at least one hundred and fifty first-rate bores, separately and singly. I was required to sit down by the greater part of them, and talk![3] In the night we were serenaded (as we usually are in every place we come to), and very well serenaded, I assure you. But we were very much knocked up. I really think my face has acquired a fixed expression of sadness from the constant and unmitigated boring I endure. The LL's[4] have carried away all my cheerfulness. There is a line in my chin (on the right side of the under-lip), indelibly fixed there by the New-Englander I told you of in my last. I have the print of a crow's foot on the outside of my left eye, which I attribute to the literary characters of small towns. A dimple has vanished from my cheek which I felt myself robbed of at the time by a wise legislator.[5] But on the other hand I am really indebted for a good broad grin to P..E..,[6] literary critic of Philadelphia, and sole proprietor of the English language in its grammatical and idiomatical purity; to P. .E.., with the shiny straight hair and turned-down shirt collar, who taketh all of us English men of letters to task in print, roundly and uncompromisingly,[7] but told me, at the same time, that I had "awakened a new era" in his mind....[8]

The last 200 miles of the voyage from Cincinnati to St. Louis are upon the Mississippi, for you come down the Ohio to its mouth. It is well for society that this Mississippi, the renowned father of waters, had no children who take after him. It is the beastliest river in the world....[9]

[1] Of 5 Apr.

[2] Timothy Walker (1802–56; *DAB*), lawyer and legal writer; descended from William Brewster, Elder of the *Mayflower* pilgrims. After graduating from Harvard and teaching at Round Hill School, practised law in Cincinnati from 1831; established the Cincinnati Law School 1833, and founded the Cincinnati Young Men's Mercantile Library. His *Introduction to American Law*, 1837, went through 11 editions. Appointed a circuit judge in Mar 42, and later introduced many reforms in the South Ohio courts. For CD's liking him very much, see *To* Felton, 29 Apr; and for Walker's liking of CD, *To* Forster, 4 Apr, *fn*.

[3] A long and ingenuous account of the final phase of this party, written by a young lady guest, is quoted in F, III, vi, 258–9*n*, from "one of the American memoirs" (in fact from R. S. Mackenzie, *Life of CD*, pp. 145–7). She arrived with other late-comers as CD was about to leave, and he was persuaded to sit down again for their "gratification". Forster's comment is, "This appalling picture supplements and very sufficiently explains the mournful passage in the text."

[4] Literary Ladies.

[5] No doubt one of the Judges described in *American Notes*, Ch. 11, as "gentlemen of high character and attainments"; CD visited one of the courts "for a few minutes".

[6] Thus in F, as a disguise for Poe. CD's mention of him here suggests that Poe's reviews were one of the topics raised by the "LL's".

[7] The reference is almost certainly to Poe's remarking, in his second review of *Barnaby Rudge* (*Graham's Magazine*, Feb 42), that though CD's English was "usually pure", he (and Bulwer too) made the "remarkable error ... of employing the adverb 'directly' in the sense of 'as soon as' " —"a gross imitation of what, itself, is a gross imitation. We mean the manner of Lamb—a manner based on the Latin construction."

[8] In his first review of *Barnaby* (*Saturday Evening Post*, May 41), Poe had described CD's books as having "formed an era in the reading of every man of genius".

[9] For the two-day journey toiling up the Mississippi ("an enormous ditch ... running liquid mud, ... its strong and frothy current choked and obstructed everywhere by huge logs and whole forest trees") see *American Notes*, Ch. 12. Cf. Marryat's "I hate the Mississippi" (*Diary in America*, II, 143).

Conceive the pleasure of rushing down this stream by night (as we did last night) at the rate of fifteen miles an hour; striking against floating blocks of timber every instant; and dreading some infernal blow at every bump.[1] The helmsman in these boats is in a little glass-house upon the roof. In the Mississippi, another man stands in the very head of the vessel, listening and watching intently; listening, because they can tell in dark nights by the noise when any great obstruction is at hand. This man holds the rope of a large bell which hangs close to the wheel-house, and whenever he pulls it, the engine is to stop directly, and not to stir until he rings again. Last night, this bell rang at least once in every five minutes; and at each alarm there was a concussion which nearly flung one out of bed. . . . While I have been writing this account, we have shot out of that hideous river, thanks be to God;[2] never to see it again, I hope, but in a nightmare. We are now on the smooth Ohio, and the change is like the transition from pain to perfect ease.[3]

We had a very crowded levee in St. Louis. Of course the paper had an account of it.[4] If I were to drop a letter in the street, it would be in the newspaper next day,[5] and nobody would think its publication an outrage. The editor objected to my hair, as not curling sufficiently.[6] He admitted an eye;[7] but objected again to dress,[8] as being somewhat foppish, "and indeed perhaps rather flash."—"But such," he benevolently adds, "are the differences between American and English taste—rendered more apparent, perhaps, by all the other gentlemen present being dressed in black."[9] Oh, that you could have seen the other gentlemen! . . .

[1] Presumably CD's boat was equipped, like the one on which Basil Hall travelled up the Mississippi, with a watertight "snag-chamber" at the front, "cut off as entirely from the rest of the hold, as if it belonged to another boat". It was this, then, that would be pierced, harmlessly, yet the warning given (see Hall's detailed account of navigation of the river, *Travels in America*, III, 357–69).

[2] They shot out of it at Cairo, the "Eden" of *Chuzzlewit*, described in *American Notes*, Ch. 12, where, on this return journey, they stopped to take in wood (Ch. 14). There is no evidence to support the legend that CD had speculated in the Cairo venture: see Vol. II, p. 160n.

[3] Typically, Harriet Martineau, after nine days on the river, wrote: "We sighed to think how soon our wonderful voyage would be over" (*Retrospect of Western Travel*, II, 194).

[4] The *Republican*, 15 Apr, simply stated that a large number of ladies and gentlemen paid their respects to Mr Dickens and lady at a soirée given at the Planter's House on 13 Apr; but the *St. Louis People's Organ* published two highly satirical accounts of it (15 and 16 Apr: see above, p. 193, *fn*).

[5] Cf. *Chuzzlewit*, Ch. 22. In fact, since leaving Richmond CD had no longer been to the same extent "news"; nor, since leaving Philadelphia, had he had to put up with detailed (or facetious) accounts of his doings: the *People's Organ* seems to have been an exception.

[6] "His hair has been described as very fine. We did not find it remarkably so; it is slightly waxy, and has a glossy, soft texture. It is very long, with unequivocal soap-locks, which to our eye looked badly. We had thought from his portraits that it was thick, but did not find it so" (*St. Louis People's Organ*, 12 Apr, reporting a call on CD on the day after his arrival).

[7] "His eye is, to our perception, *blue, dark blue,* and full; it stands out slightly, and is handsome,—very beautiful. It is the *striking* feature of his physiognomy" (*ibid.*).

[8] Beneath a black dress coat CD wore a "satin vest with very gay and variegated colors, light colored pantaloons, and boots polished to a fault" (*ibid.*).

[9] "His whole appearance is foppish, and partakes of the flash order [*a phrase used by the* Worcester Aegis: *see* To *Forster, 17 Feb,* fn]. To our American taste it was decidedly

A St. Louis lady complimented Kate upon her voice and manner of speaking: assuring her that she should never have suspected her of being Scotch, or even English. She was so obliging as to add that she would have taken her for an American, anywhere: which she (Kate) was no doubt aware was a very great compliment, as the Americans were admitted on all hands to have greatly refined upon the English language! I need not tell you that out of Boston and New York a nasal drawl is universal,[1] but I may as well hint that the prevailing grammar is also more than doubtful; that the oddest vulgarisms are received idioms; that all the women who have been bred in slave-states speak more or less like negroes, from having been constantly in their childhood with black nurses; and that the most fashionable and aristocratic (these are two words in great use), instead of asking you in what place you were born, enquire where you "hail from?"!![2]

Lord Ashburton arrived at Annapolis t'other day,[3] after a voyage of forty odd days in heavy weather. Straightway the newspapers state, on the authority of a correspondent who "rowed round the ship" (I leave you to fancy her condition), that America need fear no superiority from England, in respect of her wooden walls. The same correspondent is "quite pleased" with the frank manner of the English officers; and patronizes them as being, for John Bulls, quite refined. My face, like Haji Baba's, turns upside down, and my liver is changed to water,[4] when I come upon such things, and think who writes and who read them. . . .

They won't let me alone about slavery. A certain Judge in St. Louis went so far yesterday, that I fell upon him (to the indescribable horror of the man who brought him) and told him a piece of my mind.[5] I said that I was very averse to speaking on the subject here, and always forbore, if possible: but when he pitied our national ignorance of the truths of slavery, I must remind him that we went upon indisputable records, obtained after many years of careful investigation, and at all sorts of self-sacrifice; and that I believed we were much more competent to judge of its atrocity and horror, than he who had been brought up in the midst of

so; especially as most gentlemen in the room were dressed chiefly in black" (*ibid.*). Cf. the *Quarterly* (LXIV [1839], 310), reviewing C. A. Murray's *Travels in North America*: "We must remember . . . that this was probably the first genuine specimen of the modern dandy genus that had been exhibited in those regions, and therefore allow for the natural influence . . . of blue satin and French polish, suddenly outshining stiff frills and Day and Martin".

[1] The *Quarterly* caustically suggested that this was "an accent clearly traceable to the drawling whine and snuffle of the old conventicle preachers" (LXIV, 313).

[2] The first example given in *OED* is from George Catlin, *Letters and Notes on the . . . North American Indians*, 1841. The phrase was not understood by Martin when Mrs Hominy asked where he hailed from (*Chuzzlewit*, Ch. 22).

[3] On 2 Apr: see *To* Forster, 27 Feb, *fn*.

[4] Cf. J. J. Morier's *The Adventures of Hajji Baba of Ispahan in England*, 1828: "The ambassador's face was thrown upside down; the hairs of his beard became distended; and he oozed at every pore" (Ch. 21); ". . . to throw my heart upside down, and to turn my liver into water" (Ch. 17); &c. See also *To* Beard, 8 Sep.

[5] Possibly this was Judge Breese who when asked if he would invite CD to take a seat on the bench in his court replied, "Don't talk to me of this! He is one of those puffed up Englishmen, who, when they get home, use their pens only to ridicule and traduce us. He can come in like any other mortal" (*Memoirs of Gustav Koerner*, 1, 475).

it. I told him that I could sympathise with men who admitted it to be a dreadful evil, but frankly confessed their inability to devise a means of getting rid of it: but that men who spoke of it as a blessing, as a matter of course, as a state of things to be desired, were out of the pale of reason; and that for them to speak of ignorance or prejudice was an absurdity too ridiculous to be combated. . . .

It is not six years ago, since a slave in this very same St. Louis, being arrested (I forget for what), and knowing he had no chance of a fair trial, be his offence what it might, drew his bowie knife and ripped the constable across the body. A scuffle ensuing, the desperate negro stabbed two others with the same weapon. The mob who gathered round (among whom were men of mark, wealth, and influence in the place) overpowered him by numbers; carried him away to a piece of open ground beyond the city; *and burned him alive*. This, I say, was done within six years in broad day; in a city with its courts, lawyers, tipstaffs, judges, jails, and hangman; and not a hair on the head of one of those men has been hurt to this day.[1] And it is, believe me, it is the miserable, wretched independence in small things; the paltry republicanism which recoils from honest service to an honest man, but does not shrink from every trick, artifice, and knavery in business; that makes these slaves necessary, and will render them so, until the indignation of other countries sets them free.

They say the slaves are fond of their masters. Look at this pretty vignette[2] (part of the stock-in-trade of a newspaper), and judge how you would feel, when men, looking in your face, told you such tales with the newspaper lying on the table. In all the slave districts, advertisements for runaways are as much matters

---

[1] The incident, which took place on 28 Apr 36, is described by Harriet Martineau with greater detail and more knowledge of the facts. A free negro (a citizen of Philadelphia called Mackintosh, who was steward on a steam-boat then at St Louis) rescued a slave who had been arrested, was consequently arrested himself, and on his way to gaol killed one peace-officer and wounded another. The citizens of St Louis collected round the gaol and demanded the prisoner, who was given up to them. They took him to the woods, tied him to a tree and burnt him. Between two and three thousand people witnessed the act in silence. Harriet Martineau saw the first report of this incident in the St Louis papers. It stated that the burning was an unjustifiable act and to be regretted, but hoped that the veil of oblivion would be drawn over it. Newspapers of the Union in general followed this lead. When the case was heard, the judge told the jury that a bad and lamentable deed had been committed, and that if it were proved to have been the act of a few, they must be punished; but if it were the act of "the many, incited by that electric and metaphysical influence which

occasionally carries on a multitude to do deeds above and beyond the law, it was no affair for a jury to interfere in. He spoke of Mackintosh as connected with the body of abolitionists [*on the ground that he had prayed or sung hymns while he was burning*]. Of course, the affair was found to be electric and metaphysical, and all proceedings were dropped" (*Retrospect of Western Travel*, II, 206–9). Lurid details of the burning are given in [T. D. Weld], *American Slavery as It Is: Testimony of a Thousand Witnesses*, New York, 1839, pp. 156–7.

[2] An advertisement enclosed by CD, headed "Runaway Negro in Jail". It "had a woodcut of master and slave in its corner, and announced that Wilford Garner, Sheriff and Jailor, of Chicot County, Arkansas, requested owner to come and prove property—or—" (F, III, vi, 261*n*; not found in any volume of cuttings in the Forster Collection, V & A). Cf. Harriet Martineau, *Society in America*, II, 121: "Everybody who has been in America is familiar with the little newspaper picture of a black man, hieing with his stick and bundle, which is prefixed to the advertisements of runaways."

of course as the announcement of the play for the evening with us.[1] The poor creatures themselves fairly worship English people: they would do anything for them. They are perfectly acquainted with all that takes place in reference to emancipation; and *of course* their attachment to us grows out of their deep devotion to their owners. I cut this illustration out of a newspaper which had a leader in reference to *the abominable and hellish doctrine of Abolition—repugnant alike to every law of God and Nature.* "I know something" said a Dr. Bartlett[2] (a very accomplished man), late a fellow-passenger of ours: "I know something of their fondness for their masters. I live in Kentucky; and I can assert upon my honour, that, in my neighbourhood, it is as common for a runaway slave, retaken, to draw his bowie knife and rip his owner's bowels open, as it is for you to see a drunken fight in London."

Same Boat, Saturday, Sixteenth April, 1842.

Let me tell you, my dear Forster, before I forget it, a pretty little scene we had on board the boat between Louisville and St. Louis, as we were going to the latter place. It is not much to tell, but it was very pleasant and interesting to witness.[3]

There was a little woman on board, with a little baby; and both little woman and little child were cheerful, good-looking, bright-eyed, and fair to see. The little woman had been passing a long time with a sick mother in New York, and had left her home in St. Louis in that condition in which ladies who truly love their lords desire to be.[4] The baby had been born in her mother's house, and she had not seen her husband (to whom she was now returning) for twelve months: having left him a month or two after their marriage. Well, to be sure, there never was a little woman so full of hope, and tenderness, and love, and anxiety, as this little woman was: and there she was, all the livelong day, wondering whether "he" would be at the wharf; and whether "he" had got her letter;

---

[1] For CD's quoting 44 of such advertisements in *American Notes*, Ch. 17, see To Edward Chapman, 16 Sep, *fn*.

[2] Elisha Bartlett, MD (1804–55; *DAB*), of a Quaker family, distinguished physician and writer. Studied at Brown University, Providence, and in France; began practice in the textile village of Lowell, Mass., and became its first Mayor 1836. Held various University and Medical School professorships 1832–54; when CD met him (possibly on his journey to or from Lowell, 3 Feb), was Professor of Medicine, Transylvania University, Lexington, Kentucky. His best known books are the standard *Fevers in the United States*, 1842, and his *Essay on the Philosophy of Medicine*, 1844. His broad outlook on medicine and medical education put him much in advance of his age. He gave CD an inscribed copy of his pamphlet *A Vindication of the Character and Condition of the Females Employed in the Lowell Mills*,

Lowell, 1841, and was in touch with him again in 1850.

[3] The incident that follows, Forster admits, had appeared in *American Notes* (Ch. 12) and therefore "ought not" to be included in the *Life,* according to his "rule". He includes it under the pretext that the printed version had suffered "by the alteration of some touches and the omission of others"; but both were in fact so slight that it seems certain that he quoted the passage in full not for its divergences but because he considered it "one of the most charming soul-felt pictures of character and emotion that ever warmed the heart in fact or fiction" (F, III, vi, 262); also because he knew Jeffrey had greatly admired it (see To Felton, 31 Dec, *fn*). N omits the whole passage, as if it were an actual quotation from *American Notes*.

[4] Cf. John Home, *Douglas*, I, i: "As women wish to be who love their lords" (a frequent allusion of CD's).

and whether, if she sent the baby on shore by somebody else, *"he" would know it, meeting it in the street:* which, seeing that he had never set eyes upon it in his life, was not very likely in the abstract, but was probable enough to the young mother. She was such an artless little creature; and was in such a sunny, beaming, hopeful state; and let out all this matter, clinging close about her heart, so freely; that all the other lady passengers entered into the spirit of it as much as she: and the captain (who heard all about it from his wife) was wondrous sly, I promise you: enquiring, every time we met at table, whether she expected anybody to meet her at St. Louis, and supposing she wouldn't want to go ashore the night we reached it, and cutting many other dry jokes which convulsed all his hearers, but especially the ladies. There was one little, weazen, dried-apple old woman among them, who took occasion to doubt the constancy of husbands under such circumstances of bereavement; and there was another lady (with a lap dog), old enough to moralize on the lightness of human affections, and yet not so old that she could help nursing the baby now and then, or laughing with the rest when the little woman called it by its father's name, and asked it all manner of fantastic questions concerning him, in the joy of her heart. It was something of a blow to the little woman, that when we were within twenty miles of our destination, it became clearly necessary to put the baby to bed; but she got over that with the same good humour, tied a little handkerchief over her little head, and came out into the gallery with the rest. Then, such an oracle as she became in reference to the localities! and such facetiousness as was displayed by the married ladies! and such sympathy as was shown by the single ones! and such peals of laughter as the little woman herself (who would just as soon have cried) greeted every jest with! At last, there were the lights of St. Louis—and here was the wharf—and those were the steps—and the little woman, covering her face with her hands, and laughing, or seeming to laugh, more than ever, ran into her own cabin, and shut herself up tight. I have no doubt, that, in the charming inconsistency of such excitement, she stopped her ears lest she should hear "him" asking for her; but I didn't see her do it. Then a great crowd of people rushed on board, though the boat was not yet made fast, and was staggering about among the other boats to find a landing-place; and everybody looked for the husband, and nobody saw him; when all of a sudden, right in the midst of them—God knows how she ever got there—there was the little woman hugging with both arms round the neck of a fine, good-looking, sturdy fellow! And in a moment afterwards, there she was again, dragging him through the small door of her small cabin, to look at the baby as he lay asleep!—What a good thing it is to know that so many of us would have been quite downhearted and sorry if that husband had failed to come.

But about the Prairie—it is not, I must confess, so good in its way as this; but I'll tell you all about that too, and leave you to judge for yourself.[1] Tuesday the

---

[1] For a detailed description of the trip, see "A Jaunt to the Looking-Glass Prairie and Back" which occupies the whole of *American Notes*, Ch. 13. It includes CD's conversation in the inn at Belleville with "Doctor Crocus" (a slang term for a quack doctor), a Scotsman lecturing that night on phrenology—described, and identified as "an adventurer calling himself Dr. Angus Melrose—perhaps an assumed name", by an eye-witness, Dr J. F. Snyder, then a boy (*Journal of the Illinois State Historical Society*, III [1910], 7–22).

12th was the day fixed; and we were to start at five in the morning—sharp. I turned out at four; shaved and dressed; got some bread and milk; and throwing up the window, looked down into the street. Deuce a coach was there, nor did anybody seem to be stirring in the house. I waited until half-past five; but no preparations being visible even then, I left Mr. Q to look out, and lay down upon the bed again. There I slept until nearly seven, when I was called. . . . Exclusive of Mr. Q and myself, there were twelve of my committee[1] in the party: all lawyers except one.[2] He was an intelligent, mild, well-informed gentleman of my own age—the unitarian minister of the place.[3] With him, and two other companions, I got into the first coach.[4] . . .

We halted at so good an inn at Lebanon[5] that we resolved to return there at night, if possible. One would scarcely find a better village alehouse of a homely kind in England. During our halt I walked into the village, and met a *dwelling-house* coming down-hill at a good round trot, drawn by some twenty oxen! We resumed our journey as soon as possible, and got upon the looking-glass prairie at sunset. We halted near a solitary log-house for the sake of its water; unpacked the baskets; formed an encampment with the carriages; and dined.

Now, a prairie is undoubtedly worth seeing—but more, that one may say one has seen it, than for any sublimity it possesses in itself. Like most things, great or small, in this country, you hear of it with considerable exaggerations. Basil Hall was really quite right in depreciating the general character of the scenery.[6] The widely-famed Far West is not to be compared with even the tamest portions of Scotland or Wales. You stand upon the prairie, and see the unbroken horizon all round you. You are on a great plain, which is like a sea without water.[7] I am exceedingly fond of wild and lonely scenery, and believe

[1] The Committee which had invited him to St Louis.

[2] According to J. F. Snyder the party included John J. Anderson, a banker, and George Knapp, of the *Missouri Republican*.

[3] William Greenleaf Eliot (1811–87; *DAB*), minister of the St Louis First Congregational Church 1835–70; founder of Eliot Seminary, St Louis (later Washington University) 1853. A political and philosophical liberal, he favoured gradual emancipation of the slaves and worked strenuously for it.

[4] The first of four. The procession crossed the Mississippi by ferry-boat and went forward, with a rider on horseback ahead, "through mud and mire, and damp, and festering heat . . . attended always by the music of the frogs and pigs", to Belleville where they halted for lunch. They reached Lebanon at 3 p.m. (*American Notes*, Ch. 13).

[5] The Mermaid Hotel, owned by Capt. Lyman Adams, a retired New England sea captain, according to J. F. Snyder.

[6] In talk presumably, on some occasion when Forster was present. In *Travels in North America* (III, 385) he scarcely "depreciates" the prairies; but he treats them a little perfunctorily, explaining that he has not room (he was now near the end of his book as of his travels) to describe his adventures on them more fully. He singles out the Looking-Glass Prairie as being "particularly beautiful of its kind".

[7] Cf. Hall (*ibid.*): "The resemblance to the sea, which some of the Prairies exhibited, was really most singular. I had heard of this before, but always supposed the account exaggerated. There is one spot in particular . . . where . . . the similarity was so very striking, that I almost forgot where I was. This deception was heightened by . . . the appearance of the distant insulated trees . . . so exactly like strange sails heaving in sight". See also Marryat, *Diary in America*, II, 132: "Look round in every quarter of the compass, and there you are as if on the ocean—not a landmark, not a vestige of any thing human but yourself. Instead of sky and water, it is one vast field, bounded only by the horizon, its surface

that I have the faculty of being as much impressed by it as any man living. But the prairie fell, by far, short of my preconceived idea. I felt no such emotions as I do in crossing Salisbury plain. The excessive flatness of the scene makes it dreary, but tame. Grandeur is certainly not its characteristic. I retired from the rest of the party, to understand my own feelings the better; and looked all round, again and again. It was fine. It was worth the ride. The sun was going down, very red and bright; and the prospect looked like that ruddy sketch of Catlin's,[1] which attracted our attention (you remember?); except that there was not so much ground as he represents, between the spectator and the horizon.[2] But to say (as the fashion is, here) that the sight is a landmark in one's existence, and awakens a new set of sensations, is sheer gammon. I would say to every man who can't see a prairie—go to Salisbury plain, Marlborough downs, or any of the broad, high, open lands near the sea. Many of them are fully as impressive; and Salisbury plain is *decidedly* more so.[3]

We had brought roast fowls, buffalo's tongue, ham, bread, cheese, butter, biscuits, sherry, champagne, lemons and sugar for punch, and abundance of ice. It was a delicious meal: and as they were most anxious that I should be pleased, I warmed myself into a state of surpassing jollity; proposed toasts from the coach-box (which was the chair); ate and drank with the best; and made, I believe, an excellent companion to a very friendly companionable party. In an hour or so, we packed up, and drove back to the inn at Lebanon. While supper was preparing, I took a pleasant walk with my unitarian friend; and when it was over (we drank nothing with it but tea and coffee) we went to bed. The clergyman and I had an exquisitely clean little chamber of our own: and the rest of the party were quartered overhead. . . .

We got back to St. Louis[4] soon after twelve at noon; and I rested during the

gently undulating like the waves of the ocean; and as the wind . . . bows down the heads of the high grass, it gives you the idea of a running swell".

[1] George Catlin (1796–1872; *DAB*): see Vol. II, p. 438n. They had no doubt seen the exhibition of Catlin's "Indian Gallery" at the Egyptian Hall, Piccadilly, in 1840.

[2] Cf. *American Notes*, Ch. 13: "Looking towards the setting sun, there lay . . . a vast expanse of level ground; unbroken . . . until it met the glowing sky". In its notice of the book on 24 Nov 42, the *Belleville Weekly Advocate* commented that if the sun was setting on the opposite side of the prairie, it was doing so "upon that particular evening, . . . in the north-east", and concluded that CD must have been "decidedly drunk". Perhaps when writing up for *American Notes* the description he had given, not incorrectly, to Forster, CD had Catlin's sketch more clearly in mind than the prairie itself.

[3] CD's description of the prairie in *American Notes* ends: "It is not a scene to

be forgotten, but it is scarcely one, I think (at all events, as I saw it), to remember with much pleasure, or to covet the looking-on again, in after life." But he no doubt gave a more favourable impression to his hosts; for the *Belleville Weekly Advocate*, 21 Apr, stated: "We understand that Boz . . . was much enraptured with the scenery which this short romantic tour opened to his view"; and a letter in the same issue reported that he had "intimated an intention on his return to his native country, to give a picturesque view of the novelty, real beauty and sublimity of our whole prairie system". This discrepancy doubtless contributed to Governor Kinney's anger with *American Notes* (*To* Kinney, 14 Apr, *fn*).

[4] By a different route, passing an encampment of German immigrants, an Indian burial-place where once had stood a Trappist monastery, and (when finally recrossing the Mississippi) "Bloody Island, the duelling-ground of St. Louis" (see next)—CD surmising that neither monks

remainder of the day. The soirée came off at night, in a very good ball-room at our inn—the Planter's-house.[1] The whole of the guests were introduced to us, singly. We were glad enough, you may believe, to come away at midnight; and were very tired. Yesterday, I wore a blouse.[2] To-day, a fur-coat. Trying changes!

In the same Boat, | Sunday, Sixteenth[3] April, 1842.

The inns in these outlandish corners of the world would astonish you by their goodness. The Planter's-house[4] is as large as the Middlesex-hospital and built very much on our hospital plan, with long wards abundantly ventilated, and plain whitewashed walls. They had a famous notion of sending up at breakfast-time large glasses of new milk with blocks of ice in them as clear as crystal. Our table was abundantly supplied indeed at every meal. One day when Kate and I were dining alone together, in our own room, we counted sixteen dishes on the table at the same time.

The society is pretty rough, and intolerably conceited. All the inhabitants are young. *I didn't see one grey head in St. Louis.* There is an island close by, called bloody island. It is the duelling ground of St. Louis; and is so called from the last fatal duel which was fought there.[5] It was a pistol duel, breast to breast, and both parties fell dead at the same time. One of our prairie party (a young man) had acted as second there, in several encounters. The last occasion was a duel with rifles, at forty paces; and coming home he told us how he had bought his man a coat of green linen to fight in, woollen being usually fatal to rifle wounds. Prairie is variously called (on the refinement principle I suppose) Para*a*rer; par*e*arer; and par*o*arer.[6] I am afraid, my dear fellow, you will have had great difficulty in reading all the foregoing text. I have written it, very laboriously, on my knee; and the engine throbs and starts as if the boat were possessed with a devil.

To DR STEPHEN COLLINS,[7] 19 APRIL 1842*

MS Fales Collection, New York University Library.

Cincinnati. | Nineteenth April 1842.

My Dear Sir.

We have been on to Saint Louis, and are now returning through this place and by way of Columbus to Buffalo.

nor duellists had been any "great loss to the community" (*American Notes*, Ch. 13).

[1] Thus in F.

[2] Also "a great straw hat, with a green ribbon, and no gloves" (*American Notes*).

[3] Misdated; Sunday was 17 Apr.

[4] Described by J. F. Snyder as "then by far the finest hotel west of the Mississippi" (*Journal of the Illinois State Historical Society*, III [1910], pp. 7–8). It was their headquarters 10 to 14 Apr.

[5] American duelling, a result of the failure of the law to give adequate protection against defamation of character, was notorious, particularly in the South.

[6] "Perearers" was CD's choice for Elijah Pogram in *Chuzzlewit*, Ch. 34.

[7] Stephen Collins, MD (1797–1871); practised medicine in Washington 1823–32, then in Baltimore. Elected to Maryland House of Delegates as a Whig 1838. An active Elder of the Presbyterian Church, he wrote a religious *Autobiography*, published posthumously, Philadelphia, 1872, besides a volume of essays.

I gladly embrace this—really the *first*—opportunity I have had since I left Baltimore to thank you, heartily and cordially, for your kind letter, and for its most gratifying and welcome enclosures.[1] I have read your criticisms[2] with the sincerest pleasure, I do earnestly assure you.

My address in London, is No. 1 Devonshire Terrace, York Gate, Regents Park. It will give me great satisfaction to hear from you at any time.

Dear Sir Believe me | Faithfully Yours

Dr. Stephen Collins.   CHARLES DICKENS

To THE PROPRIETOR OF THE NEIL HOUSE, COLUMBUS,[3]
[?19 APRIL 1842]

MS[4] Cornell University Library. *Date:* Since the coach for Columbus left Cincinnati at 8 a.m. on Wed 20 Apr and CD had arrived in Cincinnati only at 1 a.m. on Tues 19th, letter must have been dispatched on 19 Apr—though CD could have drafted it (see *fn*) on 18 Apr, while on the *Benjamin Franklin*.

Sir

I am requested by Mr. Charles Dickens to inform you that he is coming to Columbus by the Coach which leaves this City on Wednesday Morning next,[5] and reaches your town on Thursday—and that he purposes resting that day, and night, at your house; preparatory to going on to Sandusky on Friday morning.

He will be greatly obliged to you if you will have the goodness to prepare comfortable quarters for him;[6] and if you will have the kindness to say (in case any enquiries should be made on the subject) that he will not be able to have the pleasure of receiving any visitors in Columbus,[7] as his short stay is one of *rest*: of which both himself and Mrs. Dickens stand in need,—as they have for some weeks been constantly travelling.

The accommodation we shall require, are a comfortable private parlor and bedroom adjoining—or as near to it as convenient—another sleeping chamber for myself—and another for Mrs. Dickens' Maid.

---

[1] Probably proof-copies or earlier magazine publication of portions of his *Miscellanies*, Philadelphia, 1842 (Preface dated 1 Oct): the first essay (pp. 9–33) was on CD.

[2] The essay on CD was entirely eulogistic and ended: "He confers honor on his country and his species; and every admirer of genius in union with virtue, will wish that he may live to erect—if he have not already accomplished the work—an imperishable literary monument for England."

[3] R. B. Cowles.

[4] Written in pencil on the fly-leaf of Vol. 1 of William G. Simms's *Beauchampe*,

2 vols, Lea & Blanchard, 1842; presumably a draft for Putnam's use. On the second fly-leaf is written: "Ann Brown from Catherine Dickens, New York".

[5] They changed coaches twice between Cincinnati and Columbus.

[6] The rooms prepared for him (in the very large, unfinished, hotel) were "excellent", richly fitted in black walnut and opening on a portico and stone verandah "like rooms in some Italian mansion" (*American Notes*, Ch. 14).

[7] In the event, they "held a levee for half an hour" (*To* Forster, 24 Apr).

To MRS R. S. NICHOLS,[1] 19 APRIL 1842*

MS Berg Collection.

Cincinnati. | Nineteenth April 1842.

My Dear Madam

I am very much obliged to you for your beautiful lines upon the death of Nell;[2] which I have read with great interest and pleasure.

Believe me | Faithfully Yours

Mrs. R. S. Nichols.   CHARLES DICKENS

To JOHN FORSTER, 24 and 26 APRIL 1842

Extracts in F, III, vi, 265–71 (continuation and conclusion of letter of 15, 16 and [17] Apr).

Sandusky | Sunday, Twenty-fourth April, 1842.

We went ashore at Louisville this night week, where I left off, two lines above; and slept at the hotel, in which we had put up before. The Messenger being abominably slow, we got our luggage out next morning, and started on again at eleven o'clock in the Benjamin Franklin mail boat: a splendid vessel with a cabin more than two hundred feet long, and little state-rooms affording proportionate conveniences. She got in at Cincinnati by one o'clock next morning, when we landed in the dark and went back to our old hotel.[3] As we made our way on foot over the broken pavement, Anne measured her length upon the ground, but didn't hurt herself. I say nothing of Kate's troubles—but you recollect her propensity? She falls into, or out of, every coach or boat we enter; scrapes the skin off her legs; brings great sores and swellings on her feet; chips large fragments out of her ankle-bones; and makes herself blue with bruises. She really has, however, since we got over the first trial of being among circumstances so new and so fatiguing, made a *most admirable* traveller in every respect. She has never screamed or expressed alarm under circumstances that would have fully justified her in doing so, even in my eyes; has never given way to despondency or fatigue, though we have now been travelling incessantly, through a very rough country, for more than a month, and have been at times, as you may readily suppose, most thoroughly tired; has always accommodated

---

[1] Rebecca S. Nichols, *née* Reed (1819–1903), poet and song-writer, then living in Cincinnati. Contributed during the 1840s to the *Knickerbocker*, *Graham's Magazine* and several mid-Western periodicals; her books included *Bernice, or the Curse of Minna, and Other Poems*, 1844.

[2] A three-stanza poem commemorating Nell in Spring, Summer and Autumn. It began: "Spring, with breezes cool and airy, | Opened on a little fairy; | Ever restless, making merry, | She, with pouting lips of cherry, | Lisped the words she could not master, | Vexed that she might speak no faster— ... | Full of baby-mirth and glee, | It was a joyous sight to see | Sweet Little Nell!" It closed: "And a little grave they made her, | In the churchyard cold they laid her— | Laid her softly down to rest, | With a white rose on her breast— | Poor Little Nell!" The poem was included in *The Female Poets of America*, ed. R. W. Griswold, Philadelphia, 1849.

[3] The Broadway.

herself, well and cheerfully, to everything; and has pleased me very much, and proved herself perfectly game.[1]

We remained at Cincinnati, all Tuesday the nineteenth, and all that night. At eight o'clock on Wednesday morning the twentieth, we left in the mail stage for Columbus: Anne, Kate, and Mr. Q inside; I on the box.[2] The distance is a hundred and twenty miles; the road macadamized; and for an American road, very good. We were three and twenty hours performing the journey. We travelled all night;[3] reached Columbus at seven in the morning; breakfasted; and went to bed until dinner time. At night we held a levee for half an hour, and the people poured in as they always do: each gentleman with a lady on each arm, exactly like the Chorus to God Save the Queen.[4] I wish you could see them, that you might know what a splendid comparison this is. They wear their clothes, precisely as the chorus people do; and stand—supposing Kate and me to be in the centre of the stage, with our backs to the footlights—just as the company would, on the first night of the season. They shake hands exactly after the manner of the guests at a ball at the Adelphi or the Haymarket; receive any facetiousness on my part, as if there were a stage direction "all laugh;" and have rather more difficulty in "getting off" than the last gentlemen, in white pantaloons, polished boots, and berlins,[5] usually display, under the most trying circumstances.

Next morning, that is to say on Friday the 22nd at seven o'clock exactly, we resumed our journey.[6] The stage from Columbus to this place only running thrice a week, and not on that day, I bargained for an "exclusive extra" with four horses, for which I paid forty dollars, or eight pounds English: the horses changing, as they would if it were the regular stage. To ensure our getting on properly, the proprietors sent an agent on the box; and, with no other company but him and a hamper full of eatables and drinkables, we went upon our way. It is impossible to convey an adequate idea to you of the kind of road over which we travelled. I can only say that it was, at the best, but a track through the wild forest, and among the swamps, bogs, and morasses of the withered bush. A great portion of it was what is called a "corduroy road:" which is made by throwing round logs or whole trees into a swamp, and leaving them to settle there. Good Heaven! if you only felt one of the least of the jolts with which the coach falls from log to log! It is like nothing but going up a steep flight of stairs

---

[1] Putnam thus describes CD's attempts to help Catherine during their coach-journey from Columbus to Sandusky later that week: "Mrs. Dickens had the back seat to herself; as the terrible jolting increased, Mr. Dickens, taking two handkerchiefs, tied the ends of them to the door-posts on each side, and the other ends Mrs. Dickens wound around her wrists and hands. This contrivance, to which was added the utmost bracing of the feet, enabled the kind and patient lady to endure the torture of the 'corduroy' [road]" (*Atlantic Monthly*, XXVI, 596).

[2] His favourite seat.

[3] They stopped for supper at the Mansion House hotel, Marion (*D*, XXVII [1941], 170).

[4] i.e. the line-up of the chorus for the national anthem.

[5] Short for "Berlin Gloves"; knitted gloves, of Berlin wool.

[6] There is a vivid account of it in *American Notes*, Ch. 14; and Putnam (*Atlantic Monthly*, XXVI, 595–8) gives many further details.

in an omnibus.[1] Now the coach flung us in a heap on its floor, and now crushed our heads against its roof. Now one side of it was deep in the mire, and we were holding on to the other. Now it was lying on the horses' tails, and now again upon its back. But it never, never, was in any position, attitude, or kind of motion, to which we are accustomed in coaches; or made the smallest approach to our experience of the proceedings of any sort of vehicle that goes on wheels. Still, the day was beautiful, the air delicious, and we were *alone:* with no tobacco spittle, or eternal prosy conversation about dollars and politics (the only two subjects they ever converse about, or can converse upon) to bore us. We really enjoyed it; made a joke of the being knocked about; and were quite merry. At two o'clock we stopped in the wood to open our hamper and dine;[2] and we drank to our darlings and all friends at home. Then we started again and went on until ten o'clock at night: when we reached a place called Lower Sandusky,[3] sixty-two miles from our starting point. The last three hours of the journey were not very pleasant, for it lightened—awfully: every flash very vivid, very blue, and very long: and, the wood being so dense that the branches on *either* side of the track rattled and broke *against* the coach, it was rather a dangerous neighbourhood for a thunder storm.

The inn at which we halted was a rough log-house. The people were all abed, and we had to knock them up. We had the queerest sleeping room,[4] with two doors, one opposite the other; both opening directly on the wild black country, and neither having any lock or bolt. The effect of these opposite doors was, that one was always blowing the other open: an ingenuity in the art of building, which I don't remember to have met with before. You should have seen me, in my shirt, blockading them with portmanteaus, and desperately endeavouring to make the room tidy! But the blockading was really needful, for in my dressing case I have about 250*l.* in gold; and for the amount of the middle figure in that scarce metal, there are not a few men in the West who would murder their fathers. Apropos of this golden store, consider at your leisure the strange state of things in this country. It has no money; really *no money.*[5] The bank paper won't pass;[6] the newspapers are full of advertisements from

---

[1] "attempting to go up to the top of Saint Paul's in an omnibus" (*American Notes*, Ch. 14).

[2] Putnam relates how, before doing so, CD asked him to take a large quantity of dessert, with wine, to the driver and agent, who had already dined. "It was a little incident; but it was characteristic of that man throughout life to *remember others*" (*Atlantic Monthly*, XXVI, 596).

[3] In fact, Upper Sandusky (correctly named in *American Notes*), a settlement of the Wyandot Indians.

[4] Described in *American Notes* as "a large, low, ghostly room".

[5] Pennsylvania was the State in worst trouble, its debt amounting to about £8,000,000. See CD's cursory, and rather flippant, reference in *American Notes*, Ch. 7.

[6] Lyell recounted an occasion in a Philadelphia circulating library when, before acceptance of the dollars he offered as deposit, reference had to be made to a pamphlet detailing which banks in the Union were solvent and which not, and giving a description of "spurious notes". Later, in Apr 42, the driver of the carriage which had taken him to Harper's Ferry, Virginia, told him that one of the dollar notes he offered in payment "was bad, 'a mere personal note' ", and that "he had issued such notes himself. 'A friend of mine at Baltimore', he said, 'who kept an oyster store, once proposed to me to sign twenty-five such notes, promising that if I would eat out their value in oysters, he would circulate them. They all passed, and we never heard of them again' "

tradesmen who sell by barter; and American gold is not to be had, or purchased. I bought sovereigns, English sovereigns at first: but as I could get none of them at Cincinnati to this day, I have had to purchase French gold; 20-franc pieces; with which I am travelling as if I were in Paris!

But let's go back to Lower Sandusky. Mr. Q went to bed up in the roof of the log-house somewhere, but was so beset by bugs[1] that he got up after an hour and *lay in the coach*[2] . . . where he was obliged to wait till breakfast time. We breakfasted, driver and all, in the one common room. It was papered with news-papers, and was as rough a place as need be. At half past seven we started again, and we reached Sandusky at six o'clock yesterday afternoon.[3] It is on Lake Erie, twenty-four hours' journey by steam boat from Buffalo. We found no boat here, nor has there been one, since. We are waiting, with every thing packed up, ready to start on the shortest notice; and are anxiously looking out for smoke in the distance.

There was an old gentleman in the Log inn at Lower Sandusky who treats with the Indians on the part of the American government,[4] and has just con-cluded a treaty with the Wyandot Indians at that place to remove next year to some land provided for them west of the Mississippi: a little way beyond St. Louis.[5] He described his negotiation to me, and their reluctance to go,[6] exceed-ingly well. They are a fine people, but degraded and broken down.[7] If you could see any of their men and women on a race-course in England, you would not know them from gipsies.

We are in a small house here,[8] but a very comfortable one, and the people are exceedingly obliging. Their demeanour in these country parts is invariably morose, sullen, clownish, and repulsive. I should think there is not, on the face of the earth, a people so entirely destitute of humour, vivacity, or the capacity of enjoyment. It is most remarkable. I am quite serious when I say that I have not

(*Travels in North America*, I, 215; II, 7–8). Clearly the full title of CD's book—*American Notes for General Circulation*—was a pun on the American monetary situation, with perhaps a secondary reference to the kind of circulation the book could expect, thanks to lack of an inter-national copyright.

[1] Catherine too, she told Putnam, was "almost devoured by the bugs!" (*Atlantic Monthly*, XXVI, 597).

[2] From which he was afraid to come out again because of the pigs, who looked "upon the coach as a kind of pie with some manner of meat inside", and "grunted round it . . . hideously" (*American Notes*, Ch. 14).

[3] They did the last four hours of the journey, from Tiffin to Sandusky, by rail.

[4] Colonel John Johnston (Indian agent in Ohio for many years), appointed in Mar 40 to negotiate with the Wyandot Indians, the only tribe which remained in Ohio.

[5] On 17 Mar 42 Henry Jacques and other Wyandot chiefs had agreed, in return for 148,000 acres west of the Mississippi and $10,000 for migration expenses, to release all their remaining land (109,144 acres) in Crawford County. The last 674 of them finally left on 12 July 43 (John Johnston, *Recollections of Sixty Years*, Dayton, Ohio, 1915, p. 47).

[6] "The night they agreed to give it up, many of the chiefs shed tears" (*ibid.*).

[7] Marryat, who had made a point (having enough time) of going out to Indian reserva-tions, saw for the first time Indians in their primitive state, not "debased by intercourse with the whites, and the use of spirituous liquors", when he visited the Sioux of the North West Territory (*Diary in America*, II, 81).

[8] The Steamboat Hotel.

heard a hearty laugh these six weeks, except my own; nor have I seen a merry face on any shoulders but a black man's. Lounging listlessly about; idling in bar-rooms; smoking; spitting; and lolling on the pavement in rocking-chairs,[1] outside the shop doors; are the only recreations. I don't think the national shrewdness extends beyond the Yankees;[2] that is, the Eastern men. The rest are heavy, dull, and ignorant. Our landlord here[3] is from the East. He is a handsome, obliging, civil fellow. He comes into the room with his hat on; spits in the fire place as he talks; sits down on the sofa with his hat on; pulls out his newspaper, and reads; but to all this I am accustomed. He is anxious to please—and that is enough.[4]

We are wishing very much for a boat; for we hope to find our letters at Buffalo. It is half past one; and as there is no boat in sight, we are fain (sorely against our wills) to order an early dinner.

Tuesday, April Twenty-sixth, 1842.
NIAGARA FALLS!!! (upon the *English*[5] Side).

I don't know at what length I might have written you from Sandusky, my beloved friend, if a steamer had not come in sight just as I finished the last unintelligible sheet (oh! the ink in these parts!): whereupon I was obliged to pack up bag and baggage, to swallow a hasty apology for a dinner, and to hurry my train on board with all the speed I might. She was a fine steamship, four hundred tons burden, name the Constitution, had very few passengers on board, and had bountiful and handsome accommodation. It's all very fine talking about Lake Erie, but it won't do for persons who are liable to sea-sickness. We were all sick. It's almost as bad in that respect as the Atlantic. The waves are very short, and horribly constant. We reached Buffalo at six this morning; went ashore to breakfast; sent to the post-office forthwith; and received—oh! who or what can

---

[1] To Harriet Martineau the "disagreeable practice of rocking in the chair" was almost as bad as tobacco chewing. "How this lazy and ungraceful indulgence ever became general, I cannot imagine", she wrote (*Retrospect of Western Travel*, I, 108). Lyell remarked on how singular it was "that this luxury, after being popular for ages all over Lancashire, required transplantation to the New World before it could be improved and become fashionable, so as to be reimported into its native land" (*Travels in North America*, I, 141–2). CD brought one back to England for Miss Coutts: see 2 July.

[2] Originally used by both Dutch and English as a nickname for New Englanders; this usage general in USA throughout the 19th century, but by 1784 generally used in England to mean any American.

[3] Hewson L. Peeke (*Ohio State Archaeological and Historical Quarterly*, XXVIII

[1919], 79) identifies him as a Colonel R. E. Colt, landlord of Colt's Exchange.

[4] Cf. *American Notes*, Ch. 14, where "to all this I am accustomed" becomes "I merely mention these traits as characteristic of the country; not at all as being matter of complaint". In England, where they were not the custom, CD continues, they would be "impertinencies"; but he had no more right to measure the manners of this good-natured landlord by English standards than to quarrel with him for not being the height to qualify for the Grenadier Guards. This passage was quoted in the *Boston Courier*, 15 Nov 42, with the approving comment: "This is frank and honest acknowledgement, and as unlike as possible any thing that ever came from an English traveler before."

[5] "Ten dashes underneath the word" according to F.

say with how much pleasure and what unspeakable delight!—our English letters!

We lay all Sunday night, at a town (and a beautiful town too) called Cleveland; on Lake Erie. The people poured on board, in crowds, by six on Monday morning, to see me; and a party of "gentlemen" actually planted themselves before our little cabin, and stared in at the door and windows *while I was washing,* and *Kate lay in bed.*[1] I was so incensed at this, and at a certain newspaper published in that town which I had accidentally seen in Sandusky (advocating war with England to the death,[2] saying that Britain must be "whipped again," and promising all true Americans that within two years they should sing Yankee-doodle in Hyde-park and Hail Columbia in the courts of Westminster),[3] that when the mayor[4] came on board to present himself to me, according to custom, I refused to see him, and bade Mr. Q tell him why and wherefore. His honor took it very coolly, and retired to the top of the wharf, with a big stick and a whittling knife, with which he worked so lustily (staring at the closed door of our cabin all the time) that long before the boat left the big stick was no bigger than a cribbage peg![5]

[1] Six years earlier, Harriet Martineau had made the Journey from Chicago to Buffalo by Lakes Michigan, Huron and Erie by "sailing vessel, the only one on the Lakes, and now on her first trip". "This ship", she recorded, "was the only place in America where I saw a prevalence of bad manners. ... None of us had ever before seen, in America, a disregard of women. The swearing was incessant; and the spitting such as to amaze my American companions as much as myself" (*Society in America,* II, 2–3).

[2] The newly established *Cleveland Plain Dealer,* which on 13 Apr had reprinted from an editorial in the Alexandria, D.C., *Index* of 12 Mar, with acknowledgment, a bellicose, violently anti-English article, "War with England", inspired by Lord Ashburton's recent arrival in Washington. "England", it declared, "must conquer the United States of America or she must sink into the grave of nations. Statesmen and diplomats may dream of peace, but the enemy's cannon will ere long arouse them with a thunder note, and then a war of extermination will commence in earnest." Ten reasons for war were given, beginning with the English claim to search vessels at sea and her interference with American slaves. The article is quoted ostensibly in full by W. J. Roffey in *D,* XXV (Winter 1928–9), 45–6, though Webster and Ashburton, mentioned in CD's summary of the article in *American Notes,* Ch. 14, do not appear in it except by implication.

[3] "The people demand war! Our country is insulted and her glory is dimmed by the insolence of England. ... We whipped England when we were in our infancy; we thrashed her again when we arrived at the age of manhood; and with the blessing of God we can, in a short time, sing 'Jefferson and Liberty' in Hyde Park, and 'Hail Columbia' in the scarlet courts of Westminster." After reading *American Notes,* the editor of the *Plain Dealer* (described by CD as "no doubt ... a prodigious man in his way") commented in the paper: "That immortalizes us ... But for a vagrant copy of 'The Plain Dealer,' ... we might have lived and died in comparative obscurity" (*D,* XXV, 44).

[4] Joshua Mills, an eminent physician according to Arthur A. Adrian, "Dickens in Cleveland, Ohio", *D,* XLIV (Winter 1947–8), 48–50.

[5] In *American Notes,* Ch. 14, it is the boat's captain who "whittles", while talking. Allowing for some exaggeration, cf. Marryat on whittling: "It is a habit, arising from the natural restlessness of the American when he is not employed, of cutting a piece of stick, or any thing else, with his knife. ... A yankee shewn into a room to await the arrival of another, has been known to whittle away nearly the whole of the mantle-piece. Lawyers in court whittle away at the table before them; and judges will cut through their own bench. In some courts, they put sticks before noted whittlers to save the furniture" (*Diary in America,* I, 236).

I never in my life was in such a state of excitement as coming from Buffalo here, this morning.[1] You come by railroad; and are nigh two hours upon the way. I looked out for the spray, and listened for the roar, as far beyond the bounds of possibility, as though, landing in Liverpool, I were to listen for the music of your pleasant voice in Lincoln's-inn-fields. At last, when the train stopped, I saw two great white clouds rising up from the depths of the earth—nothing more. They rose up slowly, gently, majestically, into the air. I dragged Kate down a deep and slippery path leading to the ferry boat; bullied Anne for not coming fast enough; perspired at every pore; and felt, it is impossible to say how, as the sound grew louder and louder in my ears, and yet nothing could be seen for the mist.[2]

There were two English officers with us (ah! what *gentlemen*, what noblemen of nature they seemed), and they hurried off with me; leaving Kate and Anne on a crag of ice; and clambered after me over the rocks at the foot of the small Fall,[3] while the ferryman was getting the boat ready. I was not disappointed, —but I could make out nothing. In an instant, I was blinded by the spray, and wet to the skin. I saw the water tearing madly down from some immense height, but could get no idea of shape, or situation, or anything but vague immensity. But when we were seated in the boat, and crossing at the very foot of the cataract—then I began to feel what it was.[4] Directly I had changed my clothes at the inn I went out again, taking Kate with me; and hurried to the Horse-shoe-fall.[5] I went down alone, into the very basin. It would be hard for a man to stand nearer God than he does there. There was a bright rainbow at my feet; and from that I looked up to—great Heaven! to *what* a fall of bright green water! The broad, deep, mighty stream seems to die in the act of falling; and, from its unfathomable grave arises that tremendous ghost of spray and mist

[1] Basil Hall likened his own feelings on coming within hearing of Niagara to those he had experienced at St Helena "when waiting in Napoleon's outer room", hearing his tread, and conscious that he "was separated from this astonishing person, only by a door, which was just about to open" (*Travels in North America*, I, 181).

[2] CD's description of Niagara in *American Notes*, Ch. 14, is largely based on this paragraph and the two following. But in *American Notes* he describes himself as standing on Table Rock looking, "—Great Heaven, on what a fall of bright green water!—", when Niagara's "full might and majesty" came on him; and it is the moment of standing on Table Rock that is stressed in *To* Sumner, 16 May, too. But clearly the greatest moment for CD was when he stood in the basin, looking up. In *American Notes* he "made the description very brief (as it should be)" (*To* Forster, 14 Sep), but nevertheless brought Mary

Hogarth into it ("when I felt how near to my Creator I was standing, the first effect . . . was Peace . . . Calm recollections of the Dead . . ."—a passage mocked by Samuel Warren in *Blackwood's*, Dec 42), and followed this with three paragraphs of heightened poetic prose. In fact, all English travellers were encouraged to put their emotions on seeing Niagara into words. "Did you not", an American woman asked Harriet Martineau, "long to throw yourself down, and mingle with your mother earth?"—"No", replied H. M. (*Society in America*, III, 81).

[3] In fact, the fall on the American side is the higher of the two, but narrower.

[4] According to Putnam, as they were midway over, CD "said, solemnly, as if to himself: 'Great God! How can any man be disappointed at this!'" (*Atlantic Monthly*, XXVI, 598).

[5] The Canadian fall, 158 ft high.

which is never laid, and has been haunting this place with the same dread solemnity—perhaps from the creation of the world.[1]

We purpose remaining here a week.[2] In my next I will try to give you some idea of my impressions, and to tell you how they change with every day. At present it is impossible. I can only say that the first effect of this tremendous spectacle on me, was peace of mind—tranquillity—great thoughts of eternal rest and happiness—nothing of terror. I can shudder at the recollection of Glencoe[3] (dear friend, with Heaven's leave we must see Glencoe together), but whenever I think of Niagara, I shall think of its beauty.

If you could hear the roar that is in my ears as I write this. Both Falls are under our windows. From our sitting-room and bed-room we look down straight upon them. There is not a soul in the house but ourselves. What would I give if you and Mac were here, to share the sensations of this time! I was going to add, what would I give if the dear girl whose ashes lie in Kensal-green, had lived to come so far along with us—but she has been here many times, I doubt not, since her sweet face faded from my earthly sight.

One word on the precious letters[4] before I close. You are right, my dear fellow, about the papers; and you are right (I grieve to say) about the people. *Am I right?* quoth the conjuror. *Yes!* from gallery, pit, and boxes. I *did* let out those things, at first, against my will,[5] but when I come to tell you all—well; only wait—only wait—till the end of July.[6] I say no more.

I do perceive a perplexingly divided and subdivided duty,[7] in the matter of the book of travels. Oh! the sublimated essence of comicality that I *could* distil, from the materials I have! . . . You are a part, and an essential part, of our home, dear friend, and I exhaust my imagination in picturing the circumstances under which I shall surprise you by walking into 58, Lincoln's-inn fields. We are truly grateful to God for the health and happiness of our inexpressibly dear children and all our friends. But one letter more—only one. . . . I don't seem to have been half affectionate enough, but there *are* thoughts, you know, that lie too deep for words.[8]

---

[1] This is elaborated in the final sentence of *American Notes*, Ch. 14. Cf. Byron, *Childe Harold's Pilgrimage*, IV, 182 (on the sea), "Such as creation's dawn beheld, thou rollest now".

[2] They stayed for ten days, at the Clifton House Hotel.

[3] See Vol. II, p. 324.

[4] Among the mail they found awaiting them at Buffalo were the letters on international copyright CD had asked for (see *To* Forster, 14 Feb, *fn*, and 24 Feb; and *To* Felton, 29 Apr, *fn*).

[5] Here the implication may be that Forster had thought CD had gone too far in his pugnacious remarks about copyright to the New York Dinner Committee ("That the shame was theirs, not mine" &c: see 24 Feb).

[6] Presumably Forster's misreading of June (CD arrived in London on 29 June). For the ease with which a final "e" could be misread as "ly" in this period, see "Terrace" in facsimile of *To* Owen, 27 Dec 41; Vol. II, facing p. xiii.

[7] Cf. *Othello*, I, iii, 181.

[8] Cf. Wordsworth's *Ode on Intimations of Immortality*, last line.

To THOMAS MITTON, 26 APRIL 1842

MS Huntington Library.

Niagara Falls | (Upon the English Side)
April The Twenty Sixth 1842 (at night)

My Dear Friend.

I have time for but six words. Coming here only today from a Month's hard travelling in the Far West, we have lost the Great Western,[1] and have to make up a packet for the Cunard Boat, as though it were tea and sugar, or yellow soap, or anything else that can be tied up and dispatched by mere handicraft.

We are in good health, and tip top spirits. For now home, [?sweet][2] Home [?, begins] to look near. Forster has some scraps from my Journal [?, and will give you] such details of our proceedings as I have made h[?im acquainted with.]

This place is the most wonderful and beautiful in the w[? orld. We have it a]ll to ourselves, and by the next boat I will tell you more [abou]t it.

I made no question about the Packet Ship; knowing that it is esteemed much safer. I had your affectionate letter this morning, and read it with surpassing pleasure.—You won't be surprised if I rush into your bedroom early one morning, about the end of June?

Kate (who has proved herself an out and outer to travel)[3] unites with me in best regards. And I am, and always will be,

Your staunch and faithful friend

Thomas Mitton Esquire.   CHARLES DICKENS

To THE EDITORS OF FOUR AMERICAN NEWSPAPERS,[4] 27 APRIL 1842

MS Berg Collection. *Date:* written 27th April, the day after receiving Forster's letter and accompanying documents, but date changed to 30 April on copies sent to the Press (see below).

To the Editor &c[5]

Niagara Falls | Twenty Seventh April 1842.

Sir

I found, awaiting me[6] at the Post Office in Buffalo, certain letters from England, of which the following are copies.[7] I ask the favor of you that you will

---

[1] Designed by I. K. Brunel as a continuation of his Great Western Railway from Bristol to New York, and built at Bristol 1836–7. Made her maiden voyage to New York Apr 38 in 15 days, and over 60 crossings on the same route during the next eight years.

[2] Triangular pieces are missing at the left and right edges of the page, clearly torn away near the seal through careless opening. Conjectural readings are based on the probable number of letters missing.

[3] i.e. a perfect traveller (cf. *To* Forster, 24 Apr).

[4] The *Boston Advertiser, New York Evening Post, New York Herald,* and Washington *National Intelligencer,* but copied in many others (see *To* Felton, 29 Apr and *fn*).

[5] Underlined by CD with short double strokes to indicate capitals.

[6] "yesterday" cancelled here because of change of date on copies made for publication.

[7] Copies made by Putnam of the memorial on international copyright signed by 12 British authors (requested in *To* Forster, 24 Feb), their joint letter to CD and a separate letter to him from Carlyle (for

publish them in your columns; and I do so, in order that the People of America may understand that the sentiments I have expressed on all public occasions since I have been in these United States, in reference to a law of International Copyright, are not merely my individual sentiments, but are, without any qualification, abatement or reserve, the opinions of the great body of British Authors—represented by the distinguished men whose signatures are attached to these documents.[1]

That they are also the opinions of the Native Writers of America, they have sufficiently shewn in their earnest petitions to the Legislature upon this subject.[2]

I would beg to lay particular stress upon the letter from Mr. Carlyle,[3] not only because the plain and manly Truth it speaks is calculated, I should conceive, to arrest attention and respect in any country, and most of all in this; but because his creed in this respect is, without the abatement of one jot or[4] atom, mine; and because I never have considered and never will consider this question in any other light than as one of plain Right or Wrong—Justice or Injustice.

I am Sir | Your faithful Servant

CHARLES DICKENS[5]

texts, see Appx, pp. 621–4). With them went Putnam's copy of this covering letter, signed by CD.

[1] Bulwer, Thomas Campbell, Tennyson, Talfourd, Hood, Hunt, Henry Hallam, Sydney Smith, Henry Milman, Rogers, Forster, Barry Cornwall and Carlyle. Of these the *New World* (14 May) claimed that many were virtually unknown in America. The inclusion of Moore, Marryat, Basil Hall, Harriet Martineau and Mrs Trollope would have "imparted a value to it", to Americans; but "Tennyson is wholly unknown here, except by a few of his pretty poetical conceits, which have found their way into the newspapers; Hood has long ceased to be popular; Hunt is known only as an agreeable writer of casual magazine articles and a traducer of Lord Byron; Forster is not known at all, and it may therefore be well for us to assure people that he is a man of talent, the literary editor of the London Examiner, the toady of Sir E. L. Bulwer and Mr. Macready; and, as for Barry Cornwall, we will be bound to say that the republisher of his poems will be glad to transmit to him all the profits of the edition, if he will give good security to pay the losses".

[2] See *To* Forster, 24 Feb, *fns.* Between Feb 37 and Apr 42 eight American petitions in favour of international copyright are recorded—and 20 against (T. Solberg, *Copyright in Congress, 1789–1904*, Washington, 1905, pp. 148–59). Those in favour were presented to the Senate by Clay, and to the House of Representatives usually by C. C. Cambreleng, Chairman of the Committee on Ways and Means.

[3] Enclosing this letter to Forster on 26 Mar, Carlyle wrote: "The Inclosed I have written in the greatest haste, without time to make a rough draught or any copy of it: judge you whether it should go to its address or not. Dickens deserves praise and support: but the claims of Authors seem to me so infinitely beyond what anybody rates them at, or what any Congress will hear of, that I can seldom speak of them without either getting into banter, or a tone inconveniently *loud*, which is worse. Congress will evidently throw out this proposal, and the next, and the next, and babble of the thing for many years,—and then do it. We are all right to shorten the *years* as we can" (MS Forster Collection, V & A).

[4] "tittle" cancelled here.

[5] Immediately after his signature on p. 2 of this letter, CD himself copied out the documents for publication, and it was from this copy that Putnam's were made for the four papers. CD's original letter and master-copy of the documents, he presented to Putnam, who in 1886 sold them, through a Mr A. F. Houghton, with a statement on how they came into his hands (MS Berg).

To C. C. FELTON, 29 APRIL 1842

MS Huntington Library.

Clifton House. | Niagara Falls. | Twenty Ninth April 1842.

My Dear Felton.

Before I go any further, let me explain to you what these great Inclosures portend; lest—supposing them part and parcel of my letter, and asking to be read—you shall fall into fits, from which recovery might be doubtful.

They are, as you will see, four copies of the same thing.[1] The nature of the Document, you will discover at a glance. As I hoped and believed, the best of the British brotherhood took fire at my being attacked because I spoke my mind and theirs on the subject of an International Copyright; and with all good speed, and hearty private letters,[2] transmitted to me this small parcel of gauntlets for immediate casting down.[3]

Now, my first idea was—publicity being the object—to send one copy to you for a Boston newspaper[4]—another to Bryant for his paper[5]—a third to the New York Herald (because of its large circulation)—and a fourth to a highly respectable journal at Washington (the property of a gentleman, and a fine fellow named Seaton,[6] whom I knew there) which I think is called The Intelligencer. Then the Knickerbocker[7] stepped into my mind—and then it occurred to me that possibly the North American Review[8] might be the best Organ after all, because indisputably the most respectable and honorable; and the most concerned in the Rights of Literature.[9]

---

[1] The memorial on copyright and accompanying letters, with CD's covering letter (see last).

[2] The only private letters of encouragement known, through CD's answers to them, were from Forster and Austin (answered on 26 Apr and 1 May).

[3] CD did not tell any of his American friends that he had himself asked Forster to procure the memorial for him. It was drawn up in fact by Bulwer, who on 24 Mar 42 wrote to Forster: "Agreeably to your wish I send you a memorial signed— If presented as a petition—it should be properly headed.—Your suggestions are so loosely formed that I know not if you desired merely a letter to Dickens, or a Petition to Congress. I send the latter as more really useful, & using those arguments which I consider the most dignified from Englishmen, & the most pertinent to Americans. | Dickens is very right to jeopardize an idler popularity for the probability of advancing a cause which may put so many dollars into his pocket" (MS Lytton Papers). Although the author of the memorial, Bulwer was not himself enthusiastic: "After all little is to be

gained, I fancy, except by Dickens & Ainsworth, to whom we benevolently purvey—even if the Yankees yield", he wrote to Forster on 2 Apr (*ibid.*).

[4] Felton sent it to the *Boston Daily Advertiser*.

[5] The *New York Evening Post*.

[6] To whom CD wrote separately: see 30 Apr.

[7] The memorial did not appear there.

[8] Founded in Boston 1815 by William Tudor as a bi-monthly; became a quarterly 1818. Dignified and respected, its contributors included most New Englanders prominent in literature and public affairs. Under J. G. Palfrey, Professor of Sacred Literature at Harvard, editor 1836–42, it somewhat declined. His successor, Francis Bowen, was a strong supporter of international copyright.

[9] The memorial did not appear in the *North American Review*; but in July the *Review* reprinted, from Boston papers, a petition of 4 June from citizens of "Boston and its Vicinity" to Congress, for the passing of an international copyright law (LV, 245–64). They were, they stated, influenced solely by the palpable merits of

Whether to limit its publication to one journal, or to extend it to several, is a question so very difficult of decision to a stranger, that I have finally resolved to send these papers to you, and ask you (mindful of the conversation we had on this head one day, in that renowned oyster Cellar) to resolve the point for me. You need feel no weighty sense of responsibility, my dear Felton, for whatever you do, is *sure* to please me. If you see Sumner, take him into our councils.[1] The only two things to be borne in mind, are,—first, that if they be published in several quarters, they must be published in all, *simultaneously*.[2] Secondly, that I hold them in trust, to put them before The People.

I fear this is imposing a heavy tax upon your friendship; and I don't fear it the less, by reason of being well assured that it is one you will most readily pay.— I shall be in Montreal about the 11th. of May. Will you write to me there, to the care of the Earl of Mulgrave, and tell me what you have done?

So much for that. Bis'ness first, pleasure artervards, as King Richard the Third said ven he stabbed the t'other King in The Tower, afore he murdered the babbies.[3]

I have long suspected that oysters have a rheumatic tendency. Their feet are always wet; and so much damp company in a man's inside, cannot contribute to his peace.—But whatever the cause of your indisposition, we are truly grieved and pained to hear of it—and should be more so, but that we hope from your account of that Farewell Dinner,[4] that you are all Right again. I *did* receive Longfellow's note.[5] Sumner I have not yet heard from—for which reason I am constantly bringing Telescopes to bear on the Ferry Boat, in hopes to see him coming over, accompanied by a modest portmanteau.[6]

the case—not by "the late representations of some British writers, though not a whit more highly colored, in our opinion, than justice calls for". The writings of Leigh Hunt and Tennyson "and such like"—and of Bulwer—they virtually dismissed. CD they used to illustrate the working of competition: "Dickens, for instance, is almost a necessary of life to some people. He is, to us. But if Dickens should put himself too high, there are those who would make shift to live upon D'Israeli, James, Lover, Ainsworth, and so down through the different qualities of fare; till at last Dickens . . . would find it worth while to come down in his demand" (p. 251).

[1] This Felton did (see *To* Sumner, 16 May).

[2] Felton, Sumner, and Seaton too, clearly agreed to help: the memorial and letters appeared within three days of each other (8–10 May) in the *Boston Daily Advertiser, New York Evening Post, New York Herald,* and Washington *National Intelligencer.* They were reprinted widely —for instance in the *Bay State Democrat,* 9 May, the *Boston Weekly Messenger* and the

Baltimore Patriot on 11 May, and the *Albion,* 14 May. Editorial comment was mixed. The *Evening Post* contained a strong supporting editorial (see *To* Kennedy, 30 Apr, *fn*); the *Boston Weekly Messenger* referred to "the impressive manner in which this subject has been brought to the attention of the public"; the *Albion* was, as to be expected, strongly in support, but not hopeful about changes in the law. But many papers attacked: the *Bay State Democrat,* for instance, criticized CD for the comparison—made by Carlyle —between the American Govt and people and a band of marauders; and "Americus" in the *Boston Courier,* 12 May, accused CD of being the paid agent of British authors— "They cry stealing! and he, of course, barks louder than ever".

[3] Cf. *Pickwick,* Ch. 25.

[4] Presumably to Longfellow, on his departure for Germany.

[5] This has not survived.

[6] For CD's lighthearted suggestion that Sumner should join him somewhere during his travels, see 13 Mar.

To say anything about this wonderful place, would be sheer nonsense. It far exceeds my most sanguine expectations,—though the impression on my mind has been, from the first, nothing but Beauty and Peace. I haven't drunk the water. Bearing in mind your caution, I have devoted myself to Beer, whereof there is an exceedingly pretty Fall in this house.

One of the noble hearts who sat for the Cheeryble Brothers, is dead.[1] If I had been in England, I would certainly have gone into mourning, for the loss of such a Glorious Life. His brother is not expected to survive him.[2] I am told that it appears from a memorandum found among the papers of the deceased, that in his life time he gave away in charity £600,000, or Three Millions of Dollars!

What do you say to my *acting* at the Montreal Theatre?—I am an old hand at such matters, and am going to join the Officers of the Garrison in a public representation for the benefit of a Local Charity. We shall have a Good House, they say. I am going to enact one Mr. Snobbington in a funny farce called a Good Night's rest.[3] I shall want a Flaxen Wig and Eyebrows; and my nightly rest is broken by visions of there being no such commodities in Canada. I wake in the dead of night in a cold perspiration, surrounded by imaginary barbers all denying the existence or possibility of obtaining such articles.[4] If Hamlet[5] had a Flaxen Head, I would certainly have it shaved, and get a wig and eyebrows out of him, for a small pecuniary compensation.

[1] William Grant (?1769–1842), whom CD had met, with his brother Daniel, in Manchester at a dinner-party given by Gilbert Winter Nov 38 (see Vol. I, p. 471*n*). Son of a Scottish cattle-dealer who with his wife and seven children had migrated to Lancashire (1783) in search of work. First employed at a calico-printing and manufacturing works at Hampson Mills, near Bury; set up his own calico-printing business, assisted by his brothers Daniel, John and Charles, ?1800; after moving to Manchester, they bought the printworks belonging to Sir Robert Peel at Ramsbottom 1806, and the Nuttall Mill 1812. The firm, William Grant & Brothers, managed by William and Daniel, prospered, and the two brothers became renowned for their charity and care for their employees. Their life-story is given as an example of successful thrift and industry by Samuel Smiles in *Self-Help*, 1860 edn, Ch. 13. William had died on 28 Feb. In CD's Preface to the first edn of *Nickleby*, he unguardedly announced that "the BROTHERS CHEERYBLE live; that their liberal charity . . . and their unbounded benevolence, are no creations of the Author's brain"—and as a result, according to his Preface to the Cheap Edn, 1848, received "hundreds upon hundreds" of begging letters, "from all sorts of people in all sorts of climates", who had seen "this unlucky paragraph" and requested him to forward their applications to the Brothers Cheeryble "(with whom [*he now wrote*] I never interchanged any communication in my life)".

[2] Daniel Grant, *b.* ?1780, lived until 12 Mar 55. W. H. Elliot, with knowledge of the brothers' characteristics presumably gained in Manchester, argues that CD united in Brother Charles the appearance of the 69-year-old William with the buoyant speech of the younger Daniel, and made Brother Ned speak in the tranquil and self-controlled manner of William (*The Story of the "Cheeryble" Grants*, 1906, pp. 221–35).

[3] See *To* Forster, 12 and 26 May, and *fns*.

[4] For his writing to William Mitchell for the wig, see 30 Apr.

[5] i.e. Putnam. Earlier printed texts, deriving from J. T. Fields, *Atlantic Monthly*, XXVII (1871), 768, substitute a dash, and in following paragraph for "Hamlet" read "H". The Putnam/Hamlet joke (see also *To* Felton, 14 Mar, *fn*) must have originally been made in conversation with Felton—and probably by Felton himself, not CD; for Forster knew nothing of it until CD's letter of 3 May told him quite flatly that Putnam wore a cloak, "like Hamlet".

By the bye, if you could only have seen the Prince[1] at Harrisburgh, crushing a friendly Quaker[2] in the Parlour Door!—It was the greatest sight I ever saw. I had told him not to admit anybody whatever—forgetting that I had previously given this honest Quaker a special invitation to come. The Quaker would not be denied, and Hamlet was staunch. When I came upon them, the Quaker was black in the face, and Hamlet was administering the final squeeze. The Quaker was still rubbing his waistcoat with an expression of acute inward suffering, when I left the town. I have been looking for his Death in the Newspapers, almost daily.

Do you know one General Ganes?[3] He is a weazen-faced Warrior—and in his dotage. I had him for a fellow passenger on board a steamboat.[4] I had also a statistical Colonel with me, outside the coach from Cincinnati to Columbus. A New England Poet[5] buzzed about me on the Ohio, like a gigantic Bee—A mesmeric Doctor, of an impossibly great age, gave me pamphlets at Louisville[6] —I have suffered much—very much.

If I could get beyond New York to see anybody, it would be (as you know) to see *you*. But I do not expect to reach the Carlton until the last day of May —and then we are going with the Coldens, somewhere on the banks of the North River for a couple of days.[7] So you see we shall not have much leisure for our Voyaging preparations.

You and Doctor Howe[8] (to whom my Love) *must*[9] come to New York. On the Sixth of June, you must engage yourselves to dine with us at the Carlton;[10] and if we don't make a merry evening of it, the fault shall not be in us.

Mrs. Dickens unites with me in best regards to Mrs. Felton and your little daughter.[11] And I am always My Dear Felton

Affectionately Your friend
CHARLES DICKENS

---

[1] Earlier printed texts read "the man".

[2] No doubt Samuel R. Wood (see *To* Forster, 28 Mar, *fn*).

[3] i.e. General Gaines (see *To* Felton, 14 Mar, *fn*). Earlier printed texts read "General G."

[4] See *To* Forster, 3 Apr.

[5] Perhaps William H. Burleigh: see *To* Forster, 2 Apr, *fn*.

[6] Clearly Charles Caldwell, MD (1772–1853; *DAB*), first Professor of Medicine, Louisville Medical Institute, 1837–49. Practised mesmerism and phrenology and believed in spontaneous generation. Author of over 200 books and pamphlets, including *Thoughts and Experiments on Mesmerism*, 1842, and an autobiography, published 1855.

[7] They spent five days on the trip, 2–6 June (see *To* Granville, 2 June, *fn*).

[8] Samuel Gridley Howe (1801–76; *DAB*), Director of the Perkins Institution and Massachusetts Asylum for the Blind, near Boston, 1832 to his death. The fifth (after Cleveland's death) in the "Five of Clubs", with Felton, Longfellow, Sumner and Hillard. MD Harvard 1824; surgeon to the Greek Independence Forces 1824–30; for some weeks of 1832, imprisoned in Prussia for assisting the Poles against Russian rule. ("From this, judge what a chivalrous youth he is", wrote Longfellow—who often addressed him as "Chevalier": *Letters of H. W. Longfellow*, ed. A. Hilen, II, 532.) On his return, opened the Perkins Institution; campaigned for better education, prison reform, aid to discharged convicts, care of the insane. Corresponding secretary of the Boston Phrenological Society during the early 1840s. An active Abolitionist.

[9] Underlined twice.

[10] For this farewell dinner party, attended by both Felton and Howe, see *To* Granville, 2 June, *fn*.

[11] Mary Sullivan Felton, *b.* 30 Apr 39.

I saw a good deal of Walker[1] at Cincinnati. I like him very much. We took to him mightily at first, because he resembled you in face and figure, we thought. —You will be glad to hear that our news from home is cheering from first to last—all well, happy, and loving—My friend Forster says in his last letter that he "wants to know Felton"—and looks forward to Longfellow—

To MRS CHARLES SEDGWICK,[2] [?29 APRIL 1842]

Mention in next. *Date:* probably written the same day.

To DAVID C. COLDEN, 29 APRIL 1842

Photograph Dickens House.

                                    Clifton House, Niagara Falls. | Twenty Ninth April 1842.
My Dear Friend.

Again let me thank you heartily for our letters,[3] and for your note,—over which, I assure you, we were very merry. You will be glad to hear that nothing can be more cheering or happy than all our news from Home; and that we have not one speck or dot of uneasiness or regret.

There is no company here—to our unspeakable delight. We have the Falls to ourselves; ramble about, all day long; do just as we please; play cribbage o'nights; dine at two in the day; wear our oldest clothes; walk ankle-deep in the mud; and thoroughly enjoy ourselves. We have left corduroy roads, high pressure steamboats, seventeen-inside stage coaches, two-pronged pocket pitchforks, and crooked knives with both sides of the blade alike, far—far—behind us. New York is before us—beyond that home—and (as Mr. Brass observes) "the still small voice is a singing comic songs within us, and all is happiness and peace."[4]

Will you send the next packet of letters to Montreal, addressed to the care of The Earl of Mulgrave?—I am going to *act* at the Montreal Theatre, with him and the officers of the Garrison, for the benefit of a local charity.—What do you think of that?—I can't get the books I wanted, and cannot therefore play any of the parts I should have liked best. I am going to do Mr. Snobbington (a priggish bank clerk of the most tidy habits possible) in a piece called A Good Night's Rest.[5] It is funny enough. I would give fifty pounds if you were all coming from Laight Street to see it.

I don't expect that we shall be at the Carlton before the Thirtieth or the Thirty First of May. The day after our arrival, I should like to devote to leaving

---

[1] Judge Timothy Walker (see *To* Forster, 15 Apr, *fn*).

[2] *Née* Elizabeth Buckminster Dwight (1801–64), teacher and writer of educational and pious books; sister-in-law of Catharine M. Sedgwick, author of *The Linwoods*.

From 1828 kept a girls' school at Lenox, Mass. Friend of Fanny Kemble.

[3] Forwarded by Colden from New York throughout their journey.

[4] Cf. *Old Curiosity Shop*, Ch. 57.

[5] See *To* Forster, 12 and 26 May, *fns*.

cards at divers street doors. After that, I wish to Heaven you would lay an embargo on us, and bear us off. Bespeak us—lay claim to us—let everybody know that we are not to be had—leave me no possibility of being persuaded, over-powered, or induced by any coaxings or threatenings to do violence to my own wishes, by going anywhere else. Put it in my power to say to all comers— "En-gaged—bespoke—fully occupied, and tightly bound"—Take the bill down, and come into possession of us 'till we go on board the George Washington. I was under a kind of promise to go and see Mrs. Charles Sedgwick, but I have written her that it is impossible, and have pleaded prior engagements with you. We therefore resign ourselves, fully and unconditionally, into your hands— reserving only Monday June the Sixth, on which day we beseech your company to dinner at the Carlton House. I must ask Mr. and Mrs. Davis[1]—and I think Professor Felton from Cambridge, and Dr. Howe from Boston, will be of the party likewise.

At Cleveland on Lake Erie, our steamboat lay all night. At 6 in the morning a party of gentlemen planted themselves opposite our little State room (it was an uncommonly tight fit, even for a State room) and stared in at the door and windows while I was washing, and Kate lay in bed. I was so incensed at this, that I straightway went to bed, and when the Mayor came, refused to see him. His Honor planted himself on the Wharf with a big stick, and a whittling knife, with which, after receiving my refusal, he worked so lustily that when the boat left, the stick which was at first a trifle bigger than a wooden leg, was shaved down to a small-sized cribbage peg.

We are charged in all our letters with all manner of loves to you and yours. We add our own to the number, and look forward to meeting you again (*we* count the days too) with inexpressible pleasure.

                    Always My Dear Friend | Faithfully Yours
David. C. Colden Esquire   CHARLES DICKENS

You will most likely see by the publication of some documents which I have sent to Boston for that purpose, that the Greatest Writers in England have taken fire at my being misrepresented in the International Copyright matter, and have flung their gauntlets down atop of mine, nobly.

To MRS DAVID C. COLDEN, 29 APRIL 1842

Photograph Dickens House.

                    Clifton House, Niagara Falls. | Twenty Ninth April 1842.
My better Angel.

If this should meet **HIS**[2] eye, I trust to you to throw dust into the same. **HIS** suspicions must not be aroused.

HE says that I have applied tender epithets to a certain Mrs. D. I repel the charge with indignation. Alas his motive is but too apparent! He conceives that by piquing you, and rousing your—forgive me for the application of such

---

[1] Whose dinner-party CD had had to cry off owing to his sore throat (*To* Davis, 15 Feb).

[2] The words written in huge capitals are also underlined.

a term to your ethereal[1] nature—your vanity, he will disrupt that bond between us, which nothing but that (and Death) can ever sever. **HE IS A SERPENT.**[2] You are the Bride of a Scorpion—Like the (I forget the animal's name, but you will find it in any book of Natural History, dearest)—his sting is in his Tale—this tale—which I pronounce to be base and calumnious.

And could you?—but no—no—I am sure you couldn't!

I have thrown my feelings into verse; you will find it neatly copied on the other side. Forgive my presumption. I scarcely know what I write. It is difficult to be coherent, with a bosom full of arrows. Inclosed is a groan. I shall not miss it. I have a great many left.

Take no heed of **HIM** or **HIS** reports. Be true to me, and we may defy **HIS** malice.—When I think of **HIS** futile attempts to tear two hearts asunder that are so closely knit together, I laugh like a Fiend.

Ha! ha! ha!

CupiD

LOVE SONG.[3]

Air—"*London now is out of Town.*"

Sweet Woman is of many kinds;
She sometimes is propi-tious;
She sometimes has a Thousand minds;
Sometimes is rayther wi-cious.
Above her sex, my love doth shine,
Though by no means a bold 'un,
"I'd crowns resign, to call her mine"
—Her name is Missis . . . . . .

—Poor Frankenstein, that Prince of fools
Why grim male monster made he,
When with the self-same clay and tools
He might have built a Lady!
How wealthy in the Worlds effects,
If he had made and sold 'un,
So wery prime in all respects
As charming Missis . . . . . . !

But vain reflection! who could rear,
On scaffold, pier, or starling,
A creetur half so bright or dear,
As my unmentioned Darling!
No artist in the World's broad ways
Could ever carve or mould 'un,
That might aspire to lace the stays
Of charming Mrs. . . . . . .

---

[1] MS shows uncertainty over spelling; CD first ended the word "ial", then altered the "i" to "e" but left the dot.

[2] Cf. Pott to Winkle, *Pickwick*, Ch. 18.
[3] The song is written on p. 3 of a folded sheet.

To ASBURY DICKENS, 30 APRIL 1842

Extract in Anderson Galleries catalogue No. 297 (1904); *MS* 2 pp.; dated Niagara Falls, 30 Apr 42.

We have reached this wonderful place in safety. We often speak of you and your kindness in Washington. I say that you can't be a relation, however distant—if you were we never could have been on such good terms.

To JOHN PENDLETON KENNEDY, 30 APRIL 1842*

MS Peabody Institute, Maryland.

Niagara Falls | Thirtieth April 1842.

My Dear Sir

I am truly vexed to discover, by a mere accident, that a letter I wrote to you from Pittsburgh a month ago, *went to England* in a packet with others! The mistake is so ridiculous that I can hardly offer a serious apology to you for it, although it has annoyed me, inexpressibly.

I told you in that letter (it will come back to you, I dare say, one of these days) that on consideration, and on sitting down to the task, I found I could not write anything which was at all likely to prove of service to you in the matter of your report.[1] That I have always felt, and do always feel, so keenly, the outrage which the existing Piracy inflicts upon writers—the flagrant injustice which Law Makers suffer to be committed upon them as though the exercise of the highest gifts of the Creator, of right entailed upon a man, heavy pains and penalties, and put him beyond the pale of Congressional and Senatorial sympathies—that I *cannot*, though I try ever so hard, discuss the question as one of expediency, or reason it as one of National profit and loss.[2] Again and again, I put pen to paper, agreeably to the promise I made you; and again and again I threw it down in disgust. When Miss Martineau came to me to sign the petition which was presented to the American Legislature a few years ago, I said, then, that I had an invincible repugnance to ask humbly for what I had as clear a right to, as the coat upon my back; and that I could not bring myself to sue to a Body which had so long sanctioned such a Monstrous and Wholesale Injustice, as if, in seeking its correction, I asked a favor at their hands. I was persuaded to sign that petition, and did so.[3] I have always regretted it since. And now, if I begin

---

[1] See *To* Forster, 15 Mar (last paragraph).

[2] The argument adopted by many American supporters of international copyright. The *New York Evening Post* of 9 May, e.g., which published the memorial and letters to CD, carried an editorial, probably by Bryant, arguing that American writers would in future years stand to gain more from a copyright law than their British counterparts did now. It claimed that within the last year more American books had been successfully republished in Britain than foreign works in America,

among them J. L. Stephens's *Incidents of Travel in Central America*, Catlin's *Letters and Notes on the . . . North American Indians*, Fenimore Cooper's *The Deerslayer*, and Vol. III of Bancroft's *History of the United States*: "We should be puzzled to find an equivalent in works written in England within the same time and republished here" (quoted in W. G. Wilkins, *CD in America*, pp. 255–7).

[3] This can only refer to the British Authors' petition of 2 Feb 37, prepared by Harriet Martineau (see *To* Forster, 24 Feb, *fn*): but CD was not one of the 56

to write upon the subject, the old fit comes upon me, and I get (as Carlyle says of himself in the same matter) "inconveniently loud".[1]—I made a few sketches for your report, clearly shewing—as all we authors know perfectly well—that under an International Copyright Law, popular books would be no dearer than they are now. Then I bethought myself that I had always said, and always intended to say, that the question was one of Plain Right and Wrong, and was not to be considered, honestly, in any other Light. So down went my pen, at the thought that if I went on with what I was doing, I could not reiterate that opinion, and say that much for myself, in writing on the subject when I got home. All this, I wrote to tell you: and all this is wandering about England at this moment.

I found the documents of which the inclosed are copies, awaiting me at Buffalo a day or two since. You will see that they are signed by the first writers in England; and that their object (as they have taken fire at my being misrepresented on such a matter) is *Publicity*. Not being very well able, as a stranger, to decide whether it would be best to publish these letters and the memorial, in a literary journal, or, in the newspapers, I have sent them to some friends in Boston; begging them to decide, and to do with them what they shall conclude right. I have added a few lines from myself—also for publication—stating that Mr. Carlyle's creed is mine.

I expect to be in New York, on the Thirtieth or Thirty First of March.[2]— May I hope to hear from you?

Faithfully Yours always | My Dear Sir

The Honorable | — Kennedy.   CHARLES DICKENS

To MESSRS LEA & BLANCHARD, 30 APRIL 1842*

MS Messrs Lea & Febiger. *Address:* Paid | Messrs. Lea and Blanchard | Booksellers | Philadelphia.

Niagara Falls. | Thirtieth April 1842.

My Dear Sirs.

Availing myself of your kind offers of service, I am going to trouble you with a few troublesome commissions. If you will execute them for me, between this time, and the end of May, and will send me to New York, at the same time, a note of the amount you have expended for me in so doing, you will very much oblige me.

1st.—Can you get me a good copy of a Book called "History of the Indian Tribes of North America, with biographical sketches and anecdotes of the Principal Chiefs &c 120 portraits. By Thomas. L. Mc Kenny and James Hall.

signatories to the document as sent to Congress (*Senate Documents*, 24th Congress, 2nd Session, 1837, Doc. 134); nor does his name appear on the supplementary list. Moreover, it seems strange that CD nowhere else refers to having been visited by Harriet Martineau as early as Oct or Nov 36.

[1] A phrase from Carlyle's letter to Forster of 26 Mar (see *To* Editors of Four American Newspapers, 27 Apr, *fn*), no doubt quoted by Forster in the letter CD received with the memorial &c at Buffalo.

[2] "May" plainly intended.

Published in Philadelphia. By C. Biddle."? If it be not very expensive,[1] and is easily obtained, I should like two copies.

2ndly. Will you send me one complete set of my books?[2]

3rdly. Did you republish an English Book, called "Lives of the Statesmen of the Commonwealth. By John Forster of the Middle Temple, London"?[3]—If so, will you send me a Copy?

4thly.—Will you send me any and every edition of Mr. Talfourd's Tragedy of "Ion",[4] that you can possibly lay your hands on?

There—that's modest. I have quite done.

Faithfully Yours always

Messrs. Lea and Blanchard   CHARLES DICKENS

To WILLIAM MITCHELL, 30 APRIL 1842*

MS Mrs A. M. Stern.

Private.   Niagara Falls. | Thirtieth April 1842.

My Dear Sir

I write to ask a favor of you, which is quite in your way, and in which the exercise of your discretion will be of material assistance to me.

I am going to act at Montreal in some Private Theatricals, with the officers there—and I want a good, *comical*, flaxen wig; such as a priggish, tidy, bachelor clerk in the Bank would wear—if with a little bit of whisker, about half way down the cheek, so much the better. Now, I fear I should not be able to get such a commodity in Montreal; you have the size of my head, in virtue of the possession of that old hat; you no doubt know where to get such a thing; and if you will kindly try to procure it (within two days from the receipt of this, if possible) and will send it by the quickest conveyance, addressed to me at Montreal to the care of The Earl of Mulgrave, you will oblige me very much.

I hope to be in New York on the Thirtieth or Thirty First of May—and I need not add that I shall be happy to pay all expenses then.[5]

[1] The set of 3 folio vols, 1836–44, each lavishly illustrated, cost $120. *To* Lea & Blanchard, 2 Apr 44, shows that he received them.

[2] The 1844 inventory of CD's books lists "Various Amer. copies of Mr. Dickens' works 16"—the complete set up to, though not later than, *Barnaby*, presumably.

[3] The first American edn was published by Harper's, New York, 1846.

[4] The only known American edn by this date was published by Dearborn, New York, 1837.

[5] Mitchell clearly already owned a suitable wig: the bill made out for "Flaxen dress wig & whiskers $15", "Bought of Vair Clirehugh", is dated 4 Apr 42; its envelope reads: "Dickens | Bill | Not paid | W Mitchell" (MSS Mrs A. M. Stern).

I hear that you have "got me up" with great effect.[1]—I hope I am putting money in your purse?[2]

Always believe me | Faithfully Yours

R.[3] Mitchell Esquire   CHARLES DICKENS

To W. W. SEATON, 30 APRIL 1842

Text from [Josephine Seaton], *William Winston Seaton of the "National Intelli-gencer"*, [Boston], 1871, p. 274.

Niagara Falls, 30th April, 1842.

My dear Sir,

You will be glad, I know, to receive my hasty report of our safe arrival at this scene of beauty and wonder,—of our being off Western waters and corduroy roads,—and of our looking forward with great pleasure and delight to home. We are perfectly well, and not at all tired by our long journey.

I have received some documents from the greatest writers of England, relative to the International Copyright, which they call upon me to make public immediately. They have taken fire at my being misrepresented in such a matter, and have acted as such men should.

They consist of two letters, and a memorial to the American people, signed by Bulwer, Rogers, Hallam, Talfourd, Sydney Smith, and so forth. Not very well knowing, as a stranger, whether it would be best to publish them in newspapers, or in a literary journal, I have sent them to some gentlemen in Boston, and have begged them to decide. In the event of their recommending the first-mentioned course, I have begged them to send a manuscript copy to you immediately.[4]

We often speak of you and your family, I assure you; and entertain a lively recollection of your great kindness, and the pleasant hours we passed in your society. Mrs. Dickens unites with me in cordial regards to Mrs. Seaton and your family. And I am always, my dear sir,

Faithfully yours,
CHARLES DICKENS

[1] *Boz*, described on the play-bill (reproduced in *D*, XLIV [1948], 192) as "An entirely original Novelty . . . abounding in Fun, Facetiæ, Flights of Fancy and Far Fetched Funniment, Sentiment and Sam Wellerisms" and as a "Quizzical and Satirical Extravaganza", had opened at the Olympic, New York, on 11 Apr. Henry Horncastle played Mr Boz, "the literary Lion, who crossed the Atlantic and got over bored", and Mitchell Sam Weller, "borrowed from Mr. Pickwick for the occasion attending Mr. Boz as his valet". Among other characters were Ergo Nobody Chisel, "a Sculptor and amateur Writer— a man who would be great if every body else was little", Mr Lionize, "showman to the Lion", and Mrs Novelgobble. Scene I was at the Dock, showing "what befel the Lion when he landed", Scene 2 "The Lion at the Carlton", Scene 3 "The Lion Besieged", and so on. It was a success and ran for 34 nights. The *Albion* reviewer, however (30 Apr), found it distasteful; and Longfellow, though praising Horncastle's performance as CD, wrote to Sumner on 26 Apr: "I tried exceedingly hard to amuse myself; but found it rather dull" (*Letters of H. W. Longfellow*, ed. A. Hilen, II, 404).

[2] *Othello*, I, iii, 338.

[3] Thus in MS; cf. a different mistake over Mitchell's initials in letter of 16 Feb.

[4] The memorial and letters were published in the *National Intelligencer* on 10 May.

P.S. I enclose your son's pleasant and capital letter.[1] Tell him that if he should ever come to London I will "swing" him about *that city* to some purpose,—being an indifferent good showman of the lions thereof.[2]

To N. P. WILLIS, 30 APRIL 1842

Summary in H. A. Beers, *Nathaniel Parker Willis*, Boston, 1885, pp. 264-5; dated 30 Apr 42.

Regretting that he has not time to accept Willis's invitation to visit him at Oswego.

To THOMAS BEARD,[3] 1 MAY 1842

MS Comtesse de Suzannet. *Address*: Per Steam ship "Unicorn", by way of Halifax. | Thomas Beard Esquire | 42 Portman Place | Edgeware Road | London | England.

Niagara Falls (Upon the *English* Side)
First of May—Sunday—1842.

My Dear Beard.

This letter will not be as old a one when it comes to you,—as (observing this date) you will at first suppose it. I write it now: thinking it very probable that if I don't, I may be again disappointed in my endeavours to find time for that purpose. But I shall be obliged, for steamboat purposes, to carry it on to Montreal; and before I post it, I will add a line or two with the Latest Intelligence of our health and spirits.

I dare say you have long ago set me down as a forgetful, unmindful, discourteous, unfriendly—and not to say utterly profligate and abandoned villain. But we have been travelling so far and so constantly—have been, if I may be allowed the expression, such perfect Pashanger-Marjits[4]—and have been, moreover, so beset, waylaid, hustled, set upon, beaten about, trampled down, mashed, bruised, and pounded, by crowds, that I never knew less of myself in all my life, or had less time for those confidential Interviews with myself whereby I earn my bread, than in these United States of America. But all our journeyings by Land and Water; by coach and steamer; wagon, railway, prairie, lake and river, shall be yours anon; and I will not be tempted to take the edge off that hearty laughter we shall raise (please God) in Number One,[5] over its not despicable vintages, before we are many weeks older, by launching into present description. We have been into the Far West—into the Bush—the Forest—the log cabin—the swamp—the Black Hollow—and out upon the open Prairies.

---

[1] Seaton had clearly sent CD his son Gales's letter of 20 Mar, describing his meeting with CD at Richmond (see *To* Seaton, 21 Mar, *fn*).

[2] In his letter Gales Seaton had confessed his fear of being placed "rather more in the attitude of a lion-hunter" than he liked; and had described himself, according to *W. W. Seaton*, p. 274, as being "almost *slung* across the room" when CD seized his hand in greeting ("slung" perhaps a misreading of "swung": cf. CD's "swing").

[3] Thomas Beard (1807-91): see Vol. I, p. 3*n*.

[4] "Passengers to Margate", a recurrent joke in letters to Beard.

[5] 1 Devonshire Terrace.

By the time we reach home, we shall have travelled Ten thousand miles or more. I have a horrible fear that I shall return "a bore"—not to anticipate which dire consummation, I will only add, on this head, that we sail from New York, per George Washington Packet *Ship* (none of your steamers) on Tuesday the Seventh of June. Hoo — ray — ay — ay — ay — ay — ay — ay — ay!!!!!

You will naturally enquire about the Medicine chest[1]—Oh! Shade of Sir Humphrey Davy![2]—if you could only have seen me, Beard, endeavouring (with that impossible pair of scales, and those weights, invisible to the naked eye) to make up pills in heavy weather, on the rolling Atlantic! If you could only have seen me,—when Kate and Anne were deadly fearful of Shipwreck,—bent on raising their spirits by means of calomel, and ringing the changes on all the bottles in that Mahogany box, to restore their peace of mind! Anne struck at last. She objected to take any more pills, powders, or mixtures, "unless she knew what was inside of 'em". This stipulation did not please me by any means for two reasons —firstly, because it implied the absence of that blind reliance and faith which are essential to all great cures; and secondly, because I didn't always know, myself. She made distant allusions, too, to having her wages "ris"—and to physic not being in her articles of engagement. I therefore stopped short; but sometimes, in that unsettled state of body which fast travelling engenders, she *asks* for physic —and then—then—I give it her. No half measures. Strong, and plenty of it.

This is the only place we have had to ourselves, since we left home. We came here last Tuesday; and stay until next Wednesday Morning. Directly I arrived, I yearned to come over to the English Side, and ordered the Ferryman out, in a pouring rain, for that purpose. It fortunately happens that there really is no point of view to see the Falls from, properly, but this. They are under our windows. But in any case I should have come here. You cannot conceive with what transports of joy, I beheld an English Sentinel—though he didn't look much like one, I confess, with his boots outside his trousers, and a great fur cap on his head. I was taken dreadfully loyal after dinner, and drank the Queen's health in a bumper—in Port too, and by no means bad Port—the first I had put to my lips, since leaving home.

I was not sick for more than five or six days coming out. We had a terrible passage—had our paddle boxes torn off, and life boats broken to pieces—and were under water; wet; and leaky through every seam and crevice; the whole time. The agent at Liverpool came on board with me, and politely begged, on the part of the owners, that I would live in the Ladies' Cabin, which was the best on board. As there were only four ladies in all, we were very comfortable. I ordered dinner, and carved in great state every day. At night, we always had a rubber— Love points; half crown bets. We had the doctor down to play, regularly. And every night the captain appeared at half after ten, and we drank mulled wine together very jovially. I effected various improvements in the cabin; made it very tidy; invented new drinks; suggested the introduction of hot collops for lunch; and was admitted, even by the initiated stewardess, to be a great acquisition to her society.

[1] Made up for him, presumably, by   [2] The distinguished chemist.
Beard's brother, Frank.

*a*I only recollect one amusing circumstance in my sickness. One day—it's impossible to say how I got there—I found myself on deck—the ship, now on the top of a mountain; now in the bottom of a deep valley. It was blowing hard; and I was holding on to something—I don't know what. I think it was a pump— or a man—or the cow.[1] I can't say for certain, which. My stomach, with its contents, appeared to be in my forehead. I couldn't understand which was the sea and which the sky; and was endeavouring to form an opinion, or a thought, or to get some distant glimmering of anything approaching to an idea, when I beheld, standing before me, a small figure with a speaking trumpet. It waved, and fluctuated, and came and went, as if smoke were passing between it and me, but I knew, by its very good-natured face, that it was the captain. It waved its trumpet, moved its Jaws, and evidently spoke very loud. I no more heard it, than if it had been a dumb man, but I *felt* that it remonstrated with me for standing up to my knees in water.—I was, in fact, doing so. Of course I don't know why. Sir, I tried to smile. Yes.—Such is the affability of my disposition, that even in that moment I tried to smile. Not being able to do so, and being perfectly sensible that the attempt had faded into a sickly hiccough, I tried to speak—to jest—at all events to explain. But I could only get out two words. They bore reference to the kind of boots I wore, and were these—"Cork soles".— I repeated, in the feeblest of voices, and with my body all limp and helpless,— "Cork Soles",—perhaps a hundred times (for I couldn't stop; it was a part of the disease)—The captain, seeing that I was quite childish, and for the time a maniac, had me taken below to my berth. And when consciousness returned I was still saying to myself, in a voice that might have melted a heart of sheer steel— "Cork Soles—Cork Soles!"—

Soon after this, we had a terrible gale at night. Indeed, I believe that gale drove my sickness away. At all events, there were, in the Ladies Cabin (which adjoined our little state room, the size whereof was something smaller than one of those Cabs with the door behind) Kate, Anne, and a little Scotch Lady—all in their night dresses, and all nearly mad with terror. It was blowing great guns; the ship was rolling from side to side with her masts in the water at every plunge; and the lightning streamed through the skylight, awfully. I could do no less, of course, than try to comfort them: and the first thing that occurred to me was Brandy and Water. Now all along this cabin was a great fixed sofa—built so as to form a part of it; and running the whole length. They were all three heaped together at one end of this sofa, when I appeared with the Jorum of Grog in my hand. Just as I was administering it to the lady who happened to be at the top of the live bundle, the vessel rolled, and to my horror and astonishment they all went to the other end of the couch. By the time I staggered to that end, there came another roll, and they all tumbled back to the other—as if they were in an otherwise empty omnibus, and two Giants were tilting it by turns at either end. I dodged them, perhaps for half an hour, without catching them once—with nothing on but a pair of rough trousers, and that blue jacket I used to wear at

aa CD evidently borrowed this letter from Beard when writing *American Notes*. These two paragraphs appear, substantially the same but slightly toned down, in Ch. 2.

[1] Taken on board for milk.

Petersham.[1] And in all the misery of the time, I had a keen sense of the absurdity of my position which I cannot, even now, surpass.[a]

We gave the Captain some Plate[2] afterwards: and he well deserved it. I presented it, in the Saloon of the Boston Theatre—and thought of Stone and the snuff box.[3]—Look over leaf for the PS—Remember me, heartily, (and Kate who, in getting in and out of coaches and boats has fallen down, per register, three hundred and forty seven times)[4] to Catherine[5] and your other sisters—and to Frank[6] and Will[7]—and to your father and mother.[8] And ever believe me My Dear Beard Your old and faithful friend

Thomas Beard Esquire.   CHARLES DICKENS[9]

To HENRY AUSTIN,[10] 1 MAY 1842

Facsimile in A Reference Catalogue of British and Foreign Autographs and Manuscripts *Edited by Thomas J. Wise—Part III. The Autographs of Charles Dickens. . . . London, 1894. Address: Per Unicorn Steam Ship by way of Halifax. | Henry Austin Esquire. | 87 Hatton Garden. | London | England.*

Niagara Falls. (English side) | Sunday First of May 1842.

My Dear Henry.

Although I date this letter as above, it will not be so old a one as at first sight it would appear to be when it reaches you. I shall carry it on with me to Montreal and dispatch it from there, by the steamer which goes to Halifax to meet the Cunard boat at that place with Canadian Letters and Passengers. Before I finally close it, I will add a short Postscript; so that it will contain the Latest Intelligence.

We have had a blessed Interval of quiet in this beautiful place, of which, as you may suppose, we stood greatly in need; not only by reason of our hard travelling for a long time, but on account of the incessant persecution of the people, by land and water; on stage coach, railway car, and steamer; which exceeds anything you can picture to yourself by the utmost stretch of your imagination.

---

[1] "formerly admired upon the Thames at Richmond" (*American Notes*, Ch. 2). For CD's months at Petersham in 1836 and 1839, see Vol. I.

[2] See *To* Forster, 21 Jan, *fn*.

[3] Presented to Frank Stone, as Honorary Secretary of the Shakespeare Club, by his fellow-members—probably in 1839, on the Club's coming to an end. His son Marcus described it as a "very precious piece of Louis XV goldsmith's work", with "a generous appreciation" of Stone's efficiency inscribed on its lid. See *D*, XLI (1944–5), 40.

[4] In *To* Austin, 1 May, Kate is said to have fallen down 743 times—i.e., with the same numbers reversed. The smaller estimate seems likely to have been written first.

[5] Catherine Charlotte Beard (1809–93), the eldest of Beard's five sisters.

[6] Francis Carr Beard (1814–93): see Vol. I, p. 40*n*.

[7] William Beard (1812–1905): see Vol. I, p. 51*n*.

[8] Nathaniel (1776–1855) and Catherine Beard: see Vol. I, p. 50*n*.

[9] For postscript to letter, see 12 May.

[10] Henry Austin (?1812–61), CD's brother-in-law: see Vol. I, p. 21*n*.

So far, we have had this Hotel nearly to ourselves. It is a large square house standing on a bold height, with over-hanging eaves like a Swiss Cottage; and a wide, handsome gallery, outside every story. These Colonnades make it look so very light, that it has exactly the appearance of a house built with a pack of cards; and I live in bodily terror, lest any man should venture to step out of a little observatory on the roof, and crush the whole structure with one stamp of his foot.[1]

Our sittingroom (which is large and low, like a Nursery) is on the second floor, and is so close to the Falls that the windows are always wet and dim with Spray. Two bedrooms open out of it; one our own; one Anne's.—The Secretary slumbers near at hand, but without these sacred precincts. From these three chambers, or any part of them, you can see the Falls rolling and tumbling, and roaring and leaping, all day long—with bright rainbows making fairy arches, down a hundred feet below us. When the Sun is on them they shine and glow like molten gold. *a*When the day is gloomy, the water falls like snow—or sometimes it seems to crumble away like the face of a great chalk Cliff—or sometimes again, to roll along the front of the rock like white smoke.*a* But at all seasons, gay or gloomy, dark or light, by sun or moon; from the bottom of both falls, there is always rising up a solemn ghostly cloud,[2] which hides the boiling cauldron from human sight, and makes it, in its mystery, a hundred times more grand than if you could see all the secrets that lie hidden in its tremendous depth.—One Fall is as close to us, as York Gate is to No. 1 Devonshire Terrace. The other (the great Horse-Shoe Fall) may be perhaps about half as far off as "Cready's".[3] One circumstance in connexion with them, is, in all the accounts, absurdly exaggerated;—I mean the noise. Last night was perfectly still. Kate and I *could just hear them* at the quiet time of Sunset, a mile off. Whereas, believing the statements I heard, I began putting my ear to the ground, like a Savage or a Bandit in a ballet, thirty miles off, when we were coming here from Buffalo!

I was delighted to receive your famous letter, and to read your account of our darlings; whom we long to see, with an intensity it is impossible to shadow forth, ever so faintly. I do believe, though I say it as shouldn't, that they *are* good 'uns—both to look at, and to go.[4] I roared out this morning, as soon as I was awake, "Next Month",[5]—which we have been longing to be able to say, ever since we have been here: I really do not know how we shall ever knock at the door, when that slowest of all impossibly slow hackney Coaches shall pull up—at Home.

I am glad you exult in the fight I have made about the copyright. If you knew how they tried to stop me, you would have a still greater interest in it. The Greatest Men in England have sent me out, through Forster, a very manly and becoming, and spirited, Memorial and address, backing me in all I have done.

---

[1] This description is used in *American Notes*, Ch. 4, not of the Niagara hotel but of one in Lowell, Massachusetts.

aa On 6 Sep, before writing his Niagara passage for *American Notes*, CD asked Austin for the loan of this letter. These two sentences he used almost verbatim in the last paragraph of Ch. 14.

[2] "that tremendous ghost of spray and mist which is never laid", in *American Notes*.

[3] The Dickens children's name for Macready's.

[4] Cf. *To* Forster, 17 Jan (of Lord Mulgrave).

[5] Written larger than the rest.

I have dispatched it to Boston for publication, and am coolly prepared for the storm it will raise. But my best rod is in pickle.[1]

Is it not a horrible thing that scoundrel-booksellers should grow rich here from publishing books, the authors of which do not reap one farthing from their issue, by scores of thousands ?[2] And that every vile, blackguard, and detestable news-paper,—so filthy and so bestial that no honest man would admit one into his house, for a water-closet door-mat—should be able to publish those same writings, side by side, cheek by jowl, with the coarsest and most obscene compan-ions, with which they *must* become connected in course of time, in people's minds ?[3] Is it tolerable that besides being robbed and rifled, an author should be *forced* to appear in any form —in any vulgar dress[4]—in any atrocious company—that he should have no choice of his audience—no controul over his own distorted text[5]—and that he should be compelled to jostle out of the course, the best men in this country who only ask to *live*, by writing ? I vow before High Heaven that my blood so boils at these enormities, that when I speak about them, I seem to grow twenty feet high, and to swell out in proportion.[6] "Robbers that ye are"— I think to myself, when I get upon my legs—"Here goes!—"[7]

The places we have lodged in; the roads we have gone over; the company we

[1] He was presumably already planning his letter of 7 July addressed to British Authors. Cf. *To* Felton, 16 May.

[2] CD probably had Harper & Brothers in mind.

[3] Unidentified; but—since it did not publish fiction—not the *New York Herald*, the paper so violently attacked by Forster as a "foul mass of positive obscenity", in his first article on the American press (*Foreign Quarterly Review*, Oct 42, xxx, 199). For the same indignant charge, see *To* Brougham, 22 Mar.

[4] Possibly a reference to the "mammoth" weekly papers, *Brother Jonathan* and the *New World*: see *To* British Authors, 7 July and *fn*.

[5] For one kind of distortion, see Marryat, who drew attention to the "dishonest practice" whereby standard religious works by English authors were republished in America "with whole pages altered, ad-vantage being taken of the great reputation of the orthodox writers, to disseminate Unitarian and Socinian principles" (*Diary in America*, Part Second, I, 242–3).

[6] Cf. "My blood so boiled . . . that I felt as if I were twelve feet high", in *To* Forster, 24 Feb.

[7] CD was no doubt particularly galled by the fact that three of the "robbers", Gris-wold, Weld and Greeley, while taking full advantage of the absence of a copyright law, professed themselves believers in it and had even signed Irving's petition (see

To Forster, 27 Feb and *fn*). Greeleys' attitude to CD in fact changed radically during his visit. His editorial in the *New York Tribune* of 27 Jan urged support for Clay's international copyright bill: "For the want of such a law Mr. Dickens has lost $100,000—the fair and honest net proceeds of the sale of his works in this country. . . . Before we make a parade of honoring, would it not be well to cease plundering him ?"; an editorial on 14 Feb, after CD's Hartford speech, still supported him ("Good reader! if you think our guest ought to be enabled to live by and enjoy the fruits of his talents and toil, just put your names to a petition for an International Copyright Law, and then you can take his hand heartily . . . and say . . . 'I have done what is in my power to protect you from robbery!' "). But after publication of the memorial and letters to CD, a *Tribune* editorial claimed defensively that the reprinting of material already published was permissible—though "an intimation from [CD] that he deemed himself in any way injured or aggrieved, under the circumstances actually existing, by such reprint as ours, would have prevented any such publication on our part". This change of attitude is grist to the mill of those who believe that without CD's intervention the copyright bill might well have gone through in the course of 1842—instead of, finally, in 1891.

have been among; the tobacco spittle we have wallowed in; the strange customs we have complied with; the packing cases in which we have travelled; the woods, swamps, rivers, prairies, lakes, and mountains, we have crossed; are all subjects for legend and tale at home. Quires—reams—wouldn't hold them. In landing and going aboard, and getting in and out of coaches, Kate has fallen down (per register) seven hundred and forty three times. Once in going over a corduroy road—which is made by throwing trunks of trees into a marsh—she very nearly had her head taken off. It was a very hot day. She was lying in a languishing manner with her neck upon the open window—B[um]p![1]—Crash!—it's a little on one side to this hour. I don't think Anne has so much as seen an American Tree. She never looks at a prospect by any chance, or displays the smallest emotion at any sight whatever. She objects to Niagara that "its[2] nothing but water", and considers that "there is too much of that"!!!

I suppose you have heard that I am going to act at the Montreal Theatre, with the officers? Farce books being scarce, and choice consequently limited I have selected Keeley's[3] part in Two O'Clock in The Morning. I wrote yesterday to Mitchell, the actor and Manager at New York, to get and send me, a comic wig—light flaxen, with a small whisker halfway down the cheek. Over this, I mean to wear two nightcaps; one with a tassel, and one of flannel. A Flannel wrapper, drab tights, and slippers, will complete the costume.

I am very sorry to hear that business[4] is so flat, but the Proverb says it never rains but it pours; and it may be remarked with equal Truth upon the other side, that it never *don't* rain, but it holds up very much indeed. You will be busy again, long before we come home, I have no doubt.

We purpose leaving here on Wednesday Morning.—Give my love to Letitia[5] and to mother. Also my affectionate and most devoted regards to Mr. Bremner.[6]

And always Believe me | My Dear Henry | Affectionately Yours

CHARLES DICKENS[7]

To JOHN FORSTER, 3 MAY 1842

Extract in F, III, vii, 272–4.

Niagara Falls. | Tuesday, Third May, 1842

I'll tell you what the two obstacles to the passing of an international copyright law with England, are: firstly, the national love of "doing" a man in any bargain or matter of business; secondly, the national vanity.[8] Both these characteristics prevail to an extent which no stranger can possibly estimate.

With regard to the first, I seriously believe that it is an essential part of the

[1] Middle of word illegible; letter worn at fold.

[2] Thus in MS.

[3] See *To* Forster, 26 May, *fn*.

[4] His practice as an architect and civil engineer.

[5] CD's sister, Letitia Mary (1816–93), Austin's wife: see Vol. I, p. 34*n*.

[6] Presumably a joke—probably referring either to John Bremner, baker, of 203 Piccadilly, or to Bremner & Till, tobacco brokers, 148 Fenchurch Street.

[7] For postscript to letter, see 12 May.

[8] First commented on by CD in *To* Forster, 17 Feb; also remarked on by most English visitors. T. C. Grattan devoted a section of his *Civilized America* to "the National Conceit encouraged by Leading Public Men"—mainly in bombastic speeches (II, 81–4).

pleasure derived from the perusal of a popular English book, that the author gets nothing for it. It is so dar-nation 'cute—so knowing in Jonathan to get his reading on those terms. He has the Englishmen so regularly on the hip that his eye twinkles with slyness, cunning, and delight; and he chuckles over the humour of the page with an appreciation of it, quite inconsistent with, and apart from, its honest purchase. The raven hasn't more joy in eating a stolen piece of meat, than the American has in reading the English book which he gets for nothing.[1]

With regard to the second, it reconciles that better and more elevated class who are above this sort of satisfaction, with surprising ease. The man's read in America! The Americans like him! They are glad to see him when he comes here! They flock about him, and tell him that they are grateful to him for spirits in sickness; for many hours of delight in health; for a hundred fanciful associations which are constantly interchanged between themselves, and their wives and children at home! It is nothing that all this takes place in countries where he is *paid:* it is nothing that he has won fame for himself elsewhere, and profit too. The Americans read him; the free, enlightened, independent Americans; and what more *would* he have? Here's reward enough for any man. The national vanity swallows up all other countries on the face of the earth, and leaves but this above the ocean. Now, mark what the real value of this American reading is. Find me in the whole range of literature one single solitary English book which becomes popular with them,[a] before, by going through the ordeal at home and becoming popular there, it has forced itself on their attention[2]—[a]and I am content that the law should remain as it is, for ever and a day. I must make one exception. There *are* some mawkish tales of fashionable life before which crowds fall down as they were gilded calves, which have been snugly enshrined in circulating libraries at home, from the date of their publication.[3]

[1] As far as piracy in magazines went, American writers themselves had been receiving nothing, or little. From their beginning American magazines had been eclectic; until the Revolution they were "British magazines published in the Colonies" and it was as natural for them to lift material from English magazines as for one English magazine to do so from another. The *North American Review* in the 1820s was the first magazine of importance to begin to achieve a "national" outlook. Payment for original contributions was practically unknown until 1819; and in the next two decades infrequent (e.g. the *Knickerbocker* in the 1830s only paid for "such contributions as we consider best"). Not until 1842—the year of CD's visit—did payment for original contributions become usual and, through the example set by *Graham's* and *Godey's*, more liberal. See F. L. Mott, *A History of American Magazines, 1741–1850*, 1930.

[a][a] First edition reading. Since not very clear, wording re-ordered by Forster in F, III, vii, 273.

[2] Obvious examples were Carlyle's *Sartor Resartus* and Tennyson's early poems, 1830 and 1833 (two little volumes referred to as "the darling of the young" for "ten years back" in the *Dial*, July 41). For James Spedding's statement that "the miscellaneous writings of Mr Carlyle had been collected and printed in America, before his name was generally known in England", see his review of *American Notes* in the *Edinburgh*, Jan 43 (LXXVI, 518).

[3] CD doubtless had in mind some of the high-life romances pirated by *Brother Jonathan* and the *New World*, as well as by Harper's and other American publishers. But most of the authors (chiefly women: Lady Blessington, Mrs Gore, Lady Charlotte Bury) were equally popular in England and America. F. L. Mott, *Golden Multitudes*, New York, 1947, gives figures of best-sellers in America during the period.

As to telling them, they will have no literature of their own, the universal answer (out of Boston) is, "We don't want one. Why should we pay for one when we can get it for nothing? Our people don't think of poetry, sir. Dollars, banks, and cotton are *our* books, sir." And they certainly are in one sense; for a lower average of general information than exists in this country on all other topics, it would be very hard to find. So much, at present, for international copyright.

[1]One of the most amusing phrases in use all through the country, for its constant repetition, and adaptation to every emergency is "Yes, Sir." Let me give you a specimen.[2] . . . I am not joking, upon my word. This is exactly the dialogue. Nothing else occurring to me at this moment, let me give you the secretary's portrait. Shall I?

He is of a sentimental turn—strongly sentimental; and tells Anne as June approaches that he hopes "we shall sometimes think of him" in our own country. He wears a cloak, like Hamlet;[3] and a very tall, big, limp, dusty black hat, which he exchanges on long journeys for a cap like Harlequin's. . . . He sings; and in some of our quarters, when his bedroom has been near ours, we have heard him grunting bass notes through the keyhole of his door, to attract our attention. His desire that I should formally ask him to sing, and his devices to make me do so, are irresistibly absurd. There was a piano in our room at Hartford (you recollect our being there, early in February?)—and he asked me one night, when we were alone, if "Mrs. D" played. "Yes, Mr. Q." "Oh indeed Sir! *I* sing: so whenever you want *a little soothing*—" You may imagine how hastily I left the room, on some false pretence, without hearing more.

He paints.[4] . . . An enormous box of oil colours is the main part of his luggage: and with these he blazes away, in his own room, for hours together. Anne got hold of some big-headed, pot-bellied sketches he made of the passengers on board the canal-boat (including me in my fur-coat), the recollection of which brings the tears into my eyes at this minute. He painted the Falls, at Niagara, superbly; and is supposed now to be engaged on a full-length representation of me: waiters having reported that chamber-maids have said that there is a picture in his room which has a great deal of hair. One girl opined that it was "the beginning of the King's-arms"; but I am pretty sure that the Lion is myself.[5] . . .

Sometimes, but not often, he commences a conversation. That usually occurs when we are walking the deck after dark; or when we are alone together in a coach. It is his practice at such times to relate the most notorious and patriarchial[6] Joe Miller,[7] as something that occurred in his own family. When travelling by

[1] In the following paragraph, says Forster, CD kept the promise made in his previous letter to send one or two more sketches of character.

[2] The specimen, Forster interpolates, was the dialogue used in *American Notes* (Ch. 14) between "Straw Hat" and "Brown Hat" during the coach-journey to Sandusky.

[3] Hence Putnam's occasional appearance in CD's letters as "Hamlet" or "the Prince".

[4] He was studying portrait painting under Francis Alexander when CD first employed him: see *To* Alexander, ?27 Jan, *fn*.

[5] Unfortunately, neither sketch nor supposed portrait has been discovered.

[6] Thus in MS.

[7] i.e. chestnut. So called after the well known jest book.

coach, he is particularly fond of imitating cows and pigs;[1] and nearly challenged a fellow passenger the other day, who had been moved by the display of this accomplishment into telling him that he was "a Perfect Calf." He thinks it an indispensable act of politeness and attention to enquire constantly whether we're not sleepy, or, to use his own words, whether we don't "suffer for sleep." If we have taken a long nap of fourteen hours or so, after a long journey, he is sure to meet me at the bedroom door when I turn out in the morning, with this enquiry. But apart from the amusement he gives us, I could not by possibility have lighted on any one who would have suited my purpose so well. I have raised his ten dollars per month to twenty; and mean to make it up for six months.

To THE EARL OF MULGRAVE, [7 MAY 1842]

Extract in unidentified catalogue, Eastgate House, Rochester. *Date:* written from Kingston where they arrived 7 May.[2]

Expect us at [Lachine][3] on Wednesday afternoon,[4] and we shall count on your escort to Montreal.[5] The School for Scandal is usually considered the most impracticable and difficult play in the whole Theatrical Calendar, the parts being without a single exception "characters", which require very delicate manipulation. . . . I have heard so much of the fame of your Montreal Amateurs, since I have been in Canada, with considerable and becoming diffidence.

To B. J. TAYLOR,[6] 11 MAY 1842*

MS The Marquis of Normanby.

Montreal. | Wednesday Eleventh May 1842.

My Dear Sir.

Don't be alarmed at my troubling you so soon—but will you allow your Servant to enquire at Lord Mulgrave's (they don't know, here,[7] where he lives)

---

[1] Cf. Putnam's own description of how, when dawn broke after his frozen night in the coach at Upper Sandusky, he " 'crowed' very loudly several times, hoping that the old darky who did the chores would think it was morning and get up and light the fires. But the ruse didn't succeed, though the 'crowing' was very well done indeed" (*Atlantic Monthly*, XXVI, 597).

[2] Leaving Niagara Falls on 4 May, they had crossed Lake Ontario by steamboat and the same evening reached Toronto, where they stayed two nights; re-embarking at noon on the 6th, and spending that night on the boat, they had reached Kingston at 8 a.m. on the 7th.

[3] Misread as "Luchini" in catalogue.

[4] They left Kingston at 9.30 a.m. on the 10th, by steamboat (the *Gildersleeve*)

on the St Lawrence—much struck by its beauty; changed to stage-coach at 7 p.m. to avoid the rapids; embarked on another steamboat at 10 p.m. and slept on board; transferred to a stage-coach next morning at 8 a.m.; boarded another steamboat on the St Lawrence at noon, and reached Lachine (9 miles from Montreal) at 3 p.m. on Wed 11th.

[5] See *To* Forster, 12 May. During their stay in Montreal, 11–30 May, Mulgrave showed them every kindness, and accompanied them on a visit to Quebec 26–27 May (*Quebec Mercury*, 28 May).

[6] Brook John Taylor (1810–81), Capt. 85th Foot Regt; Military Secretary to Sir Richard Jackson in Montreal since Aug 41; General 1877.

[7] Rasco's Hotel, St Paul Street.

whether there are not some *more* letters for me? Those we expected from home are not among the number received just now; and Mrs. Dickens is consequently in the last extremity of wonderment and complicated disappointment.

Believe me | Faithfully Yours

Captain Taylor.   CHARLES DICKENS

To HENRY AUSTIN, 12 MAY 1842

Facsimile in *A Reference Catalogue* . . . Edited by T. J. Wise . . . (conclusion of letter begun 1 May).

Montreal, Canada. Twelfth May, 1842—All well, though (with the exception of one from Fred) we have received *no letters whatever* by the Caledonia. We have experienced impossible-to-be-described attentions in Canada. Everybody's carriages and horses are at our disposal; and everybody's servants; and all the Government boats and boats crews. We shall play between the 20th. and the 25th.[1]—A Roland for an Oliver—Two o'Clock in the Morning—and Deaf as a Post.

To THOMAS BEARD, 12 MAY 1842

MS Comtesse de Suzannet (conclusion of letter begun 1 May).

Montreal—Canada. May Twelfth 1842—All well, and looking forward to home. We have been to Toronto and to Kingston—have had everybodys[2] carriages and horses at our disposal—and all the Govt boats, boats' crews, officers, and steamers. Derbishire[3] (you remember him?) is a Member of Parliament at Kingston—holds a good sinecure office; Lord Sydenham's[4] gift; and is quite a great man.—

To JOHN FORSTER, 12 MAY [1842]

Extract in F, III, vii, 274–5 (conclusion of letter begun 3 May).

Montreal, Thursday twelfth May

This will be a very short and stupid letter, my dear friend; for the post leaves here much earlier than I expected, and all my grand designs for being unusually brilliant fall to the ground. I will write you *one line* by the next Cunard boat—reserving all else until our happy and long long looked-for meeting.

---

[1] On the 25th and 28th, in fact.

[2] Thus in MS.

[3] Stewart Derbishire (?1797–1863), born in London; barrister (Gray's Inn) 1821. Went to Canada as attaché to Lord Durham 1838; appointed Queen's printer in Canada 1841; member of the Legislative Assembly of United Canada 1841–4. On 9 May he gave CD a copy, inscribed "a Canadian Present from an old Country Friend"

(*Catalogue of the Library of CD*, ed. J. H. Stonehouse, p. 84), of *Memoirs of the Life of the late John Mytton, Esq., of Halston, Shropshire . . . with Notices of his Hunting, Shooting, Driving, Racing, Eccentric and Extravagant Exploits.* By Nimrod [C. J. Apperley], 1835.

[4] Charles Edward Poulett Thomson, Baron Sydenham (1799–1841; *DNB*), Governor-General of Canada 1839–41.

We have been to Toronto,[1] and Kingston;[2] experiencing attentions at each which I should have difficulty in describing. The wild and rabid toryism of Toronto, is, I speak seriously, *appalling*.[3] English kindness is very different from American. People send their horses and carriages for your use, but they don't exact as payment the right of being always under your nose.[4] We had no less than *five* carriages at Kingston waiting our pleasure at one time;[5] not to mention the commodore's[6] barge and crew, and a beautiful government steamer.[7] We dined with Sir Charles Bagot[8] last Sunday. Lord Mulgrave was to have met us yesterday at Lachine; but as he was wind-bound in his yacht and couldn't get in, Sir Richard Jackson[9] sent his drag four-in-hand, with two other young fellows who are also his aides, and in we came in grand style.

The Theatricals (I think I told you I had been invited to play with the officers of the Coldstream guards[10] here) are, *A Roland for an Oliver; Two o'clock in the*

---

[1] Capital of the Province of Upper Canada until the Union of Feb 41 (population then 14,000). According to the *Toronto Patriot*, 6 May, "every attention that individuals could offer" was paid them there.

[2] First capital of the United Province of Canada (population 6,000). They stayed at Daley's British American Hotel; visited the Penitentiary, the Fort, and Dock Yard; and made excursions to Kingston Mills and the neighbouring countryside. According to the *Kingston Chronicle & Gazette*, 11 May, CD praised the Penitentiary highly, and gave it "in most respects the preference over all others of the kind he had seen, either at home or in foreign countries" (see his praise in *American Notes*, Ch. 15, which apparently extended even to the prisoners' being employed on useful work: cf. To Forster, 6 Mar, *fn*, for his opposite view when visiting American prisons). The newspaper report added: "Of the condition and prospects of this Country, the grandeur and beauty of its scenery, and extensive water communication, Mr. Dickens spoke with the warmth and admiration of a Canadian."

[3] Tory adherents of the old provincial oligarchy, the "Family Compact"—vehemently supported by Orangemen—were still struggling, despite union, to keep the "British connexion"; and violence between them and the French in the 1841 elections had led to several deaths—including that of one man (James Dunn) shot in Toronto, according to *American Notes*, Ch. 15, from a window, by an Orangeman. The *Toronto Herald*, 21 Nov 42, protested violently at CD's account, "founded upon no better evidence than the dark whisperings of political bigotry, or the false witness of a venal and party-coloured commission". It went on to give its own account of the shooting, apparently "*in a riot*", and of the subsequent trial; and ended with the accusation that CD's condemnation of the city had held it up "to public censure, as a place unfit for the abode of civilized man".

[4] The *Kingston Chronicle*, 11 May, claimed that in Canada he had "not been hunted down as a Lion"; and the *Montreal Transcript*, 14 May, commented: "Mr. Dickens must be heartily tired of the endless calls and fêtes with which he was greeted by our neighbours, and must be anxious for that repose which, however anxious our citizens may be to see him, will most probably be afforded him."

[5] The *Kingston Chronicle & Gazette*, 11 May, mentioned Major Wright, the Commandant of the Fort, and Mr and Mrs Smith of the Penitentiary, as paying attentions to CD, besides Commodore Sandom and Capt. Harper (see below).

[6] Williams Sandom, RN (?1788–1858), Commander-in-Chief, Naval Forces on the Canadian Lakes, 1838–43. Rear-Admiral 1854.

[7] Presumably the *Traveller* (under Capt. Harper).

[8] Sir Charles Bagot (1781–1843; *DNB*), Governor-General of Canada since 1841: see Vol. II, p. 450*n*.

[9] Lieut.-General Sir Richard Downes Jackson(1777–1845),Commander-in-Chief, British Forces in North America, from 1839; Govt administrator in Lower Canada 1839–40.

[10] CD was mistaken: the Montreal Garrison was made up of the 23rd (Royal Welch Fusiliers) and 85th Foot Regts. The Coldstream Guards were stationed at Quebec.

Morning;[1] and either the *Young Widow*,[2] or *Deaf as a Post*.[3] Ladies (unprofessional)[4] are going to play, for the first time.[5] I wrote to Mitchell at New York for a wig for Mr. Snobbington, which has arrived, and is brilliant. If they had done *Love, Law, and Physick*,[6] as at first proposed, I was already "up" in Flexible, having played it of old, before my authorship days;[7] but if it should be Splash[8] in the *Young Widow*, you will have to do me the favor to imagine me in a smart livery-coat, shiny black hat and cockade, white knee-cords, white top-boots, blue stock, small whip, red cheeks and dark eyebrows. Conceive Topping's state of mind if I bring this dress home and put it on unexpectedly ! . . . God bless you, dear friend. I can say nothing about the seventh, the day on which we sail. It is impossible. Words cannot express what we feel now that the time is so near.

To [?DAVID C. COLDEN], 13 MAY 1842

Extract in unidentified New York catalogue, Apr 1939; *MS* 2 pp.; dated Montreal, Canada, 13 May 42. *Address:* almost certainly to Colden with whom CD had promised to make an expedition up the North River after his return to New York (*To* Felton, 29 Apr).

Your plans are mine, to a T. I particularly want to visit the scene of Rip Van Winkle's game at nine pins.[9]

[1] A comic interlude adapted from Etienne Arnal's *Passé Minuit*. Since CD earlier refers to it as *A Good Night's Rest* (*To* Colden and *To* Felton, 29 Apr) and calls the bank clerk (to be played by himself) Snobbington, the version chosen seems likely to have been Mrs Gore's *A Good Night's Rest; or, Two in the Morning* (Strand, Aug 39). But that there was uncertainty about the title is shown by the playbills: for the private performance of 25 May (see *To* Forster, 26 May) it was billed as *Past Two o'Clock in the Morning*; for the public performance of 28 May as *Two o'Clock in the Morning*. In neither is the adapter's name mentioned. Malcolm Morley (in "Theatre Royal, Montreal", *D*, xLV [Winter 1948/9], 43) implies, on evidence unknown, that the adaptation chosen was Charles Mathews's (see *To* Forster, 26 May, *fn*), and suggests that CD "tinkered with the piece", substituting the name Snobbington, from Mrs Gore's version, for Mathews's Newpenny; but this seems unlikely.

[2] By J. T. G. Rodwell, first produced 1824.

[3] *Deaf as a Post* was chosen: see *To* Forster, 26 May, *fn*.

[4] Among them Catherine (see *To* Forster, 26 May).

[5] The private performance on 25 May.

[6] A farce by James Kenney, first produced at Covent Garden 1812, with Charles Mathews as Flexible.

[7] No family (or school) performance of the farce is recorded, or seems likely. Perhaps, then, CD had played Flexible in one of the private theatres—"in Catherine Street, Strand, the purlieus of the city, the neighbourhood of Gray's Inn Lane, or the vicinity of Sadler's Wells", among whose patrons he ironically lists "low copying-clerks in attorneys' offices" ("Private Theatres", *Sketches by Boz*). Cf. the statement of Edward Blackmore (of Ellis & Blackmore, attorneys, for whom he worked 1827–8), quoted in F, I, iii, 46: "[CD's] taste for theatricals was much promoted by a fellow-clerk named Potter, since dead, with whom he chiefly associated. They took every opportunity, then unknown to me, of going together to a minor theatre, where (I afterwards heard) they not unfrequently engaged in parts." Alternatively, by "played" CD may well have meant practised the part to himself: see letter of 1845, F, v, i, 380.

[8] The high-spirited, intriguing valet, played in the first production by Benjamin Wrench.

[9] The Kaatskill Mountains. He merely saw them, towering "in the blue distance, like stately clouds", on a 30-mile drive (with the Coldens) from Hudson to Lebanon Springs (*American Notes*, Ch. 15).

To C. C. FELTON, 16 MAY 1842*

Typescript Harvard College Library.

Montreal. | Sixteenth May 1842.

My Dear Felton.

A hundred thousand thanks for your ready and most friendly kindness in the matter of the International copyright. It would have been impossible to have taken a better or a more judicious course.[1]

I shall bear the Bostonians and their Memorial in loving remembrance.[2] I am steeping a little rod in strong Pickle, expressly on their account.[3]

I have but a moment to add my best regards and Kate's to Mrs. Felton and my dear little friend.[4] On the Sixth, we shall expect you, with Dr. Howe under your arm.[5]

The play comes off on the Twenty Fifth. The wig and whiskers have arrived.

[   ]

[CHARLES DICKENS][6]

To CHARLES SUMNER, 16 MAY 1842*

MS Maine Historical Society. *Address: Paid* | Charles Sumner Esquire | 4 Court Street | Boston.

Montreal—Canada. | Monday Sixteenth May 1842.

My Dear Sumner.

I received your last, at Niagara; where we enjoyed nine days of perfect repose; and where we were most comfortable and happy.

Directly we arrived at the end of the Railroad[7] I hurried off: bearing Kate with me, as though General Swett were behind us[8]—ran down the slope (it was

---

[1] See *To* Felton, 29 Apr and *fn.*

[2] A memorial against international copyright had been forwarded to Congress by a convention of printers, publishers and others engaged in the book trade, after a meeting in Boston on 26 Apr—held, according to CD, "to counter any effect" pryduced by the American authors' petition (*To* British Authors, 7 July 42). The memorial asked for a change in the mode of levying duties on foreign books and remonstrated against an international copyright law. Several times longer than the American authors' petition, it concluded with statistics showing that 41,000 people were employed in the American book trade and that the capital invested was almost 15 million dollars. CD was particularly angry that Samuel Goodrich ("Peter Parley"), who had discussed the problem with him sympathetically in Washington, acted as Chairman; and that one of the memorial's arguments against international copyright was that, if granted, it would prevent American editors from adapting English books to their wants (see *To* Hood,

13 Oct 42). The memorial (*Senate Documents*, 1841–2, IV, No. 323) was presented to the Senate on 13 June, on the same day as two similar petitions, by printers and booksellers from Philadelphia, were presented to the House of Representatives. No action was taken on them.

[3] The circular letter, 7 July 42, which he addressed to British authors and newspapers on his return.

[4] Felton's daughter, Mary.

[5] At the dinner CD gave at the Carlton House, New York (see *To* Granville, 2 June, *fn*).

[6] Ending and signature missing, but probably no more.

[7] From Buffalo to Niagara.

[8] The allusion is probably to Samuel Swett (1782–1866), Colonel in the Volunteers and first Commander of the New England Guards, whom CD had no doubt met with his daughter Mrs Alexander. The joke presumably refers to Swett's *Sketch of the Bunker Hill Battle*, 1818, which describes the British retreat from Bunker Hill (visited by CD with Sumner 30 Jan).

raining hard, and was very slippery) ordered out the Ferryman—got into the boat—and crossed straightway; previously, I should have said, getting wet through, to the skin, by clambering over the rocks under the American Fall. I had a vague sense of the greatness of the scene, as we crossed; but it was not until I got upon Table Rock, that I was able to comprehend it—for I was in a kind of whirl up to that time, and should have been rather at a loss if I had been suddenly called upon to state what part of me I regarded as my head, and what as my heels. But when I had looked at the Great Horse Shoe Fall for a few minutes, from this point, I comprehended the whole scene.

I was never for a moment disappointed in any respect, except in the noise, which is preposterously exaggerated, and which really did not strike me at any time as being very loud,—except when one stands *in* the basin, and upon a level with the river, in front of the Horse Shoe Fall. Every other expectation I had formed, was fully and entirely realized. From the first, the impression on my mind was one of Beauty, unmixed with any sense of Terror. In the Vale of Glencoe in the Highlands of Scotland, I lost all count of time, and was exalted above every other reflection in the tremendous gloom and horror of the place, which filled me with the grandest sensations I have ever known.[1] At Niagara, I never for a moment forgot that I *was* at Niagara, although from the first to the last of my stay there, I never looked at the Falling Water, without having the same train of thought awakened by it. It was always Peaceful Eternity; without the least admixture of trouble or commotion.

We idled about this Great Place, as I have said, for nine days—morning, noon, and night. And I think it would be difficult for any visitors to contemplate it under better circumstances than we did.

My wrath is kindled, past all human powers of extinction, by the disgusting entries in the books which are kept at the Guide's house;[2] and which, made in such a spot, and preserved afterwards, are a disgrace and degradation to our nature. If I were a despot, I would force these Hogs to live for the rest of their lives on all Fours, and to wallow in filth expressly provided for them by Scavengers who should be maintained at the Public expence. Their drink should be the stagnant ditch, and their food the rankest garbage; and every morning they should each receive as many stripes as there are letters in their detestable obscenities.

I don't quite know what I would do with Mr. James Silk Buckingham,[3] who

[1] See Vol. II, p. 324.

[2] On Table Rock. In *American Notes*, Ch. 15, he describes the entries as "the vilest and the filthiest ribaldry that ever human hogs delighted in", and protested that they were "a disgrace to the English language . . ., and a reproach to the English side"—though he hoped few of the entries had been made by Englishmen. J. S. Buckingham (see below) merely found them "frivolous and contemptible in the extreme" (*America: Historical, Statistic, and Descriptive*, 1841, II, 512).

[3] James Silk Buckingham (1786–1855; *DNB*), author, traveller, and lecturer.

Established the *Calcutta Journal* 1818 (whose censure of governmental abuses led to his expulsion from India 1823); the *Oriental Herald & Colonial Review* (1824–9); the weekly *Sphinx* (1827–9); and the *Athenæum* 1828—which he soon relinquished to John Sterling. Published 1822–30 four books on his travels in the Middle East. Radical MP for Sheffield 1832–7. Toured America 1837–40, lecturing as he went on temperance and other reforms, and was warmly received by religious bodies and temperance societies. By the end of 1842 had published three detailed and unbiased books on America—

writes blank verse in praise of the scene, and has it hung up framed and glazed, in the same chamber.[1] Solitary confinement; lukewarm milk and water; very damp, clammy sop; and his own books to read; would perhaps be a sufficient punishment.

The extraordinary kindness and attention we experience here, in Canada, no words can express. I believe all the carriages, horses, boats, yachts, boats crews, and servants, in the Colony (whether belonging to Government or Private Individuals) are, or have been, at our disposal.

Let me thank you heartily, for the consultation you held with Felton about the copyright matter. *It was impossible to take a more judicious course.*

I am afraid and ashamed to give you trouble, but with regard to those books and things which were left in your charge at Boston.—My factotum reports that at the Dry Goods Stores there are old boxes to be bought for five and twenty cents or so, one of which wod. be a Masterpiece of art to pack them in. May I ask you to send them to New York, in such a Package, directed to me at the Carlton? And as soon as you please?—If I thought you would ever retaliate on me, I would invent fifty useless commissions for you to discharge, that I might have the pleasure of doing something for you.

Kate sends her best regards. And I am always (with cordiall[2] remembrances to all friends)

Affectionately Yours | My Dear Sumner
CHARLES DICKENS

I was quite charmed with Hillard's lines on Longfellow's departure.[3] Their Music is of the heart, and it goes to mine.[4]

I shall walk into the Bostonians when I get home, for their precious Memorial, and its extravagant dishonesty. I have thought of a rod with tingling ends; and have put it in Pickle.

America: Historical, Statistic, and Descriptive, 3 vols, 1841, *The Slave States of America*, 2 vols, 1842, and *The Eastern and Western States of America*, 3 vols, 1842. Had married Elizabeth Jennings 1806; their youngest son, Leicester Silk Buckingham, became a dramatist. Buckingham was active and benevolent, but vain and self-important and undertook many more schemes than he could carry through.

[1] Buckingham, who had spent five days at Niagara, devoted a chapter of his *America*, Vol. II, to its description and praise (pp. 498–514), and in an Appendix included a poem of 10 stanzas, written "at the first sight of its Falls—August 12th, 1838"; but it is in fourteeners, not blank verse. It begins: "Hail! Sovereign of the World of Floods!—whose majesty and might | First dazzles—then enraptures— then o'erawes the aching sight".

[2] Thus (or "cordiale") in MS.
[3] "Lines Addressed to the Ship Ville de Lyons, which Sails from New York for Havre, Tomorrow, April 24th"; published in the *Boston Daily Advertiser*, 23 Apr (the sailing was in fact delayed until the 27th, owing to head-winds). Longfellow was leaving for Marienberg, to take the waters. Sumner wrote to him on the 23rd: "[The lines] excite universal admiration. Judge Story, Quincy, Prescott, Greenleaf, all admire them" (E. L. Pierce, *Memoir and Letters of Charles Sumner*, II, 206).
[4] The first stanza (out of seven) begins: "O, ship, beneath whose cleaving prow | The deep sea soon shall roar, | Were wishes winds, how soon thy keel | Would graze thy destined shore."

To [HUGH SIBBALD],[1] 17 MAY 1842

Text from *Leisure Hour*, 1876, pp. 63–4, with emendations and additions from text provided by F. P. Hett in *D*, xxxiii (1937), 162.[2] *Address:* recipient identified as Hugh Sibbald by Hett.

[*Private*][3]   [Rasco's][4] Hotel, Montreal, | Seventeenth May, 1842
Dear Sir,

I am much indebted to you for your gratifying and welcome letter,[5] and am proud to know that you have conferred[6] my name on your child in recollection of my writings.

That he may become all you wish him to be, and that he may in his [turn][7] derive some entertainment and instruction from my endeavours[8] to beguile the leisure time of children of a larger growth, is my sincere and earnest wish. If I could ever learn that I had happily been the means of awakening within him any new love of his fellow-creatures, and desire to help and assist them with his sympathy, I should [gain][9] much pleasure from the knowledge.

Believe me, faithfully yours,

[Mr. Andrew Hughes][10]   CHARLES DICKENS

---

[1] Hugh Sibbald, one of the 11 children of Colonel William Sibbald, 15th Foot Regt, and Susan Sibbald. After his father's death, taken to Canada by his mother 1835, and brought up at Eildon Hall, Lake Simcoe, 50 miles from Toronto. Settled in India by Dec 48 and highly recommended to the Governor-General by G. P. R. James, a close family friend (*Memoirs of Susan Sibbald*, ed. F. P. Hett, 1926, p. xviii). Owned and developed a plantation of 33,000 acres in Bengal, according to *Leisure Hour*, No. 1256 (1876), 64. Was "in his teens" when, during CD's visit to Montreal, he "hit upon a clever idea for enlisting [his] sympathy" and "securing a much desired autograph letter" (*D*, xxxiii [1937], 162).

[2] Clearly both texts derive direct from a family source: *Leisure Hour*'s anonymously; that in *D*, xxxiii, 162, from F. P. Hett, Sibbald's great-nephew. The *Leisure Hour* text is accepted here as on the whole the better; readings from Hett's text where preferable are footnoted.

[3] Omitted in *Leisure Hour*.

[4] Correct in Hett; mis-spelt "Roscoe's" in *Leisure Hour*.

[5] The letter read, in Hett's version (not so grossly illiterate as the version given in *Leisure Hour*, *loc. cit.*) as follows: "A.D. 1842 | Mr. Dickens, Sir. | Me and my wifes got a boy and we has a heard tell a deal about the beautiful books you've a writ and the deal of good you try to do for us poor folks. Now we was a thinkin that if it is not takin too much of a liberty we should like to call our lad Charles Dickens for we be told that Charles is your christened name. We be no scholars ourselves but we hope if he and we be spared as wage is good and eddication is cheap and larning plenty he shall one day read the books you have writ for hisself. Hoping that this will find you well and happy as you diserve and if so as you will allow of our request please direct to Andrew Hughes, Montreal, P.O. | Yr. sarvants to command | Andrew Hughes | Mary Hughes." CD may not have been deceived.

[6] Hett's reading "bestowed" could be correct.

[7] *Leisure Hour* reads "time".

[8] *Leisure Hour*, surely mistakenly, reads "my poor endeavours".

[9] *Leisure Hour* reads "feel".

[10] Subscription is given by Hett but omitted in *Leisure Hour*.

To DAVID C. COLDEN, 21 MAY 1842

Photograph Dickens House.

Rasco's Hotel, Montreal
(which, by the bye, is the worst
in the whole wide World)[1] | 21st. May. 1842.

My Dear Friend.

I received your kind letter yesterday; and am truly grateful to you for the trouble you have taken, in the matter of the George Washington. The *two* state rooms decidedly—and as they offer to open a door of communication, please let them do so. It will be a great comfort and convenience to us.

My Bostonian factotum will come on to New York a day before us, with the baggage—I mean the trunks; not Kate. I will instruct him to call in Laight Street and give you timely notice of our movements. We are becoming very impatient to move, I assure you.

The young woman as formerly waited on G Warsen[2] and wife, begs me to say that her name was at that time Miggs—*not* "Moggs".[3] She considers that though she is but a servant, and her stations is humble and her fortunes lowly,[4] no gentleman as can lay any claims to sich a title, has a rights to call her out of her name. Her name is but a short one, but she considers that it come direct from Evins, and was there invented for her ancestors' use and distinction. She thanks her blessed Stars that she has no shame in connections with her name, and has no call to disguise it; and she is of opinion that it hill becomes a 'Publican and Sinner (she is supposed to mean *R*epublican) to miscall his feller creeturs as isn't clothed in purple through no faults of their own, but may fly equally up'ards ven the time comes, in calico, notwithstanding.

Kate sends her best love to all. I join her heartily; and looking forward to our speedy meeting, am always My Dear friend

Faithfully Yours
CHARLES DICKENS

^a *P.S.*

I inclose one tear for you ... my soul – one out of many,

wrung from me by the hand of cruel Destiny. It is not so large as I could wish, but you will take the will for the deed.^a

---

[1] Opened in 1836, it was the leading hotel in Montreal in 1842 and held 150 guests.

[2] Thus, unmistakably, in MS.

[3] Colden apparently did not know his *Barnaby* and had misread "Miggs" in CD's letter of 4 Apr.

[4] Cf. Miggs in *Barnaby*, Ch. 71: "'Ho yes! My situations is lowly, and my capacities is limited, and my duties is to humble myself . . .'".

^aa Perhaps intended for Mrs Colden.

To C. C. FELTON, 21 MAY 1842†

MS Carl H. Pforzheimer Library. *Address:* Professor Felton | Cambridge | Massachusetts | U.S.

Montreal. | Saturday Twenty First May 1842.

My Dear Felton.

I was delighted to receive your letter, yesterday; and was well pleased with its contents. I anticipated objection to Carlyle's Letter.[1] I called particular attention to it for three reasons. Firstly, because he boldly *said* what all the others *think*; and therefore deserved to be manfully supported. Secondly, because it is my deliberate opinion that I have been assailed on this subject in a manner in which no man with any pretensions to public respect, or with the remotest right to express an opinion on a subject of universal literary interest, would be assailed in any other country *ᵃ*on the face of the Earth.[2] Thirdly, because I have seen enough to be assured that it is of no use to clutch these robbers in any other part of their ungodly persons but the throat. And Fourthly (I will add a fourth reason) because, meaning to let my indignation loose when I get home, I do not choose to curb it here, when I have an opportunity of giving it vent.*ᵃ*

I really cannot sufficiently thank you, dear Felton, for your warm and hearty interest in these proceedings. But it would be idle to pursue that theme, so let it pass.

The wig and whiskers are in a state of the highest preservation. The play comes off, next Wednesday night, the Twenty Fifth. What would I give to see you in the front row of the centre box—your spectacles gleaming not unlike those of my dear friend Pickwick—your face radiant with as broad a grin as a staid Professor may indulge in—and your very coat, waistcoat, and shoulders, expressive of *ᵇ*the rum and water we should drink*ᵇ* together, when the performance was over! I would give something (not so much, but still a good round sum) if you could only stumble into that very dark and dusty Theatre in the day time (at any minute between 12 and 3) and see me, with my coat off, the Stage Manager and Universal Director, urging impracticable ladies and impossible gentlemen on to the very confines of insanity—shouting and driving about, in my own person, to an extent which would justify any philanthropic stranger in clapping me into a strait waistcoat without further enquiry— endeavouring to goad Hamlet into some dim and faint understanding of a

---

[1] On international copyright (see *To* Felton, 29 Apr, *fn*, and Appx, p. 623). Carlyle's comparison of American pirates of English books with Rob Roy and his cattle-thieves not unnaturally aroused furious resentment in some American papers. Reviewing the controversy later, Samuel Goodrich ("Peter Parley") accused the whole British press of backing CD up "with the cry of thief, robber, pirate", because the Americans "did precisely what was then and had been done everywhere"

(*Recollections of a Lifetime*, New York and Auburn, 1857, II, 358).

ᵃᵃ Not previously published.

[2] The *Montreal Gazette* had just reprinted CD's letter of 30 Apr to the American newspapers, with the memorial and accompanying letters, and had given his struggle its full support (18 and 19 May).

ᵇᵇ MDGH alters to "what we should take together".

prompter's duties—and struggling in such a vortex of noise, dirt, bustle, confusion, and inextricable entanglement of speech and action, as you would grow giddy in contemplating. We perform a Roland for an Oliver—A Good Night's Rest—and Deaf as a Post. This kind of voluntary hard labour used to be my great delight. The furor has come strong upon me again; and I begin to be once more of opinion that nature intended me for the Lessee of a National Theatre —and that pen ink and paper have spoiled a Manager.

Oh! How I look forward across that rolling water to Home, and its small tenantry! How I busy myself in thinking how my books look; and where the tables are; and in what positions the chairs stand, relatively to the other furniture; and whether we shall get there in the night, or in the morning, or in the afternoon—and whether we shall be able to surprise them—or whether they will be too sharply looking out for us—and what our pets will say—and how they'll look—and who will be the first to come and shake hands—and so forth! If I could but tell you how I have set my heart on rushing into Forster's study (Forster is my great friend, and writes at the bottom of all his letters—"My Love to Felton") and into Maclise's painting room, and into Macready's managerial ditto, without a moment's warning—and how I picture every little trait and circumstance of our arrival to myself, down to the very colour of the bow on the cook's cap—you would almost think I had changed places with my eldest son, and was still in pantaloons of the thinnest texture. I left all these things—God only knows what a love I have for them—as coolly and calmly as any animated cucumber; but when I come upon them again I shall have lost all power of self-restraint, and shall as certainly make a fool of myself (in the popular meaning of that expression) as ever Grimaldi[1] did in his way, or George The Third in his.

And not the less so, dear Felton, for having found some warm hearts, and left some instalments of earnest and sincere affection, behind me on this continent. And whenever I turn my mental telescope hitherward, trust me that one of the first figures it will descry will wear spectacles so like yours that the maker couldn't tell the difference, and shall address a Greek class in such an exact imitation of your voice, that the very students, hearing it, should cry "That's he! Three cheers for Felton Hoo—ray—ay—ay—ay—ay!"

—About those joints of yours—I think you are mistaken. They *can't* be stiff. At the worst, they merely want the air of New York, which, being impregnated with the flavor of last year's oysters, has a surprising effect in rendering the human frame supple and flexible, in all cases of rust.

A terrible idea occurred to me, as I wrote those words—The oyster cellars —what do they do, when oysters are not in season? Is pickled salmon vended there—do they sell crabs, shrimps, winkles, herrings?—The oyster openers, what do *they* do? Do they commit suicide in despair, or wrench open tight drawers and cupboards and hermetically-sealed bottles—for practice? Perhaps they are dentists out of the oyster season. Who knows!

---

[1] Joseph Grimaldi (1779-1837; *DNB*), the clown, whose memoirs CD had edited in 1838.

^cKate sends her love to you, and Mrs. Felton, and your little girl—in which I join with all my heart. Being ever my dear Felton^c

[   ]

[CHARLES DICKENS]¹

To DAVID C. COLDEN, 25 MAY 1842

Mention in unidentified catalogue, 4 Apr, n.y.; dated Montreal, 25 May 42.

To JOHN FORSTER, 26 MAY [1842]

Extract in F, III, vii, 275–7.

[Rasco's]² Hotel, Montreal, Canada, twenty-sixth of May
This, like my last, will be a stupid letter, because both Kate and I are thrown into such a state of excitement by the near approach of the seventh of June, that we can do nothing, and think of nothing.

The play came off last night.³ The audience, between five and six hundred strong, were invited as to a party; a regular table with refreshments being spread in the lobby and saloon. We had the band of the twenty-third⁴ (one of the finest in the service) in the orchestra, the theatre was lighted with gas, the scenery was excellent, and the properties were all brought from private houses. Sir Charles Bagot, Sir Richard Jackson, and their staffs were present; and as the military portion of the audience were all in full uniform, it was really a splendid scene.

We "went" also splendidly; though with nothing very remarkable in the acting way. We had for Sir Mark Chase⁵ a genuine odd fish,⁶ with plenty of humour; but our Tristram Sappy⁷ was not up to the marvellous reputation he has somehow or other acquired here. I am not however, let me tell you, placarded as stage-manager for nothing. Everybody was told they would have to submit to the most iron despotism; and didn't I come Macready over them?

---

^{cc} Not previously published.

¹ Ending and signature cut away.

² F reads "Peasco's", a not surprising misreading of CD's curious "R" in an unfamiliar word.

³ The Garrison Amateurs, with amateur actresses (including Catherine), performed three plays on 25 May, in all of which CD appeared. He played Alfred Highflier in Thomas Morton's comedy *A Roland for an Oliver*, Mr Snobbington in the interlude (see *To* Forster, 12 May, *fn*) and Gallop in John Poole's farce *Deaf as a Post*. See the playbill facing page 246. For this private performance, the Theatre Royal was designated the Queen's Theatre; a

public performance followed on the 28th. For notices in Montreal papers, see *D*, XLV (Winter, 1948–9), 39–44, and *D*, XXXVIII (1942), 72–4.

⁴ The 23rd Royal Welch Fusiliers.

⁵ In *A Roland for an Oliver*.

⁶ The Hon. Frederick Methuen (1818–91), Lieut. 71st Foot Regt, singled out for special praise by the *Montreal Gazette* 30 May; the *Montreal Herald* named him and CD as apparently "no strangers to the boards".

⁷ In *Deaf as a Post*; played by Dr George Griffin, surgeon, 85th Foot Regt. According to the *Montreal Transcript*, he "was far from doing himself justice" (*D*, XLV, 42).

Oh no. By no means. Certainly not.[1] The pains I have taken with them, and the perspiration I have expended, during the last ten days, exceed in amount anything you can imagine. I had regular plots of the scenery made out, and lists of the properties wanted; and had them nailed up by the prompter's chair. Every letter that was to be delivered, was written; every piece of money that had to be given, provided; and not a single thing lost sight of.[2] I prompted, myself, when I was not on; when I was, I made the regular prompter of the theatre my deputy; and I never saw anything so perfectly touch and go, as the first two pieces.[3] The bedroom scene in the interlude was as well furnished as Vestris had it;[4] with a "practicable" fireplace blazing away like mad, and everything in a concatenation accordingly.[5] I really do believe that I was very funny:[6] at least I know that I laughed heartily at myself, and made the part a character, such as you and I know very well: a mixture of T——,[7] Harley,[8]

[1] Cf. the Artful Dodger, of Fagin: "And don't he know me? Oh, no! Not in the least! By no means. Certainly not!" (*Oliver Twist*, Ch. 8).

[2] CD himself drafted the invitation card. It read:

"PRIVATE THEATRICALS.
COMMITTEE

Mrs. Torrens | Mrs. Perry
Colonel Ermatinger | Captain Torrens
The Earl of Mulgrave.

The Committee request the pleasure of company at the Queen's Theatre, Montreal, on Wednesday Evening the Twenty Fifth of May, at half past Seven oClock precisely. It is to be expressly understood that this is a card of Invitation, and not a ticket of admission; and is therefore not transferable. To ensure a strict observance of this understanding, it will be required to be presented at the door" (MS Benoliel Collection; another copy in CD's hand is in the possession of the Comtesse de Suzannet). William C. Ermatinger ("Colonel" is cancelled in the MS and "Wm." and "Esq." supplied in an unknown hand), the son of a fur-trader and an Indian woman, was a civilian and afterwards police magistrate of Montreal. Arthur Wellesley Torrens (1809–55; *DNB*), 23rd Royal Welch Fusiliers, was promoted Major-General and knighted 1854, after distinguished service n the Crimean War. Mrs Perry was probably the wife of one of the Garrison officers.

[3] CD's Highflyer was considered "a spirited performance" by the *Gazette*, and "in that part where the expression of his madness bordered on the tragic . . . peculiarly happy" by the *Transcript*.

[4] Madame Vestris had produced at Covent Garden, 3 Oct 40, a new version of the interlude, by Charles Mathews, entitled *Two in the Morning*. It was performed by Mathews and Keeley. The notice in the *Morning Post*, 5 Oct, mentioned the realistic set (in that production spring-rollers for the blinds and a copper coal-scuttle); cf. Douglas Jerrold *to* CD, 13 June 43: "Madame Vestris . . . fears that her judgment would be somewhat warped by any comedy not susceptible of upholstery" (MS Mr Douglas Jerrold).

[5] Goldsmith, *She Stoops to Conquer*, Act I (cf. *To Beard*, 24 Apr 40; II, 62).

[6] The *Montreal Gazette*, 30 May, found the interlude "the gem of the evening . . . most mirth-provoking" . . . "The helpless, hypochondriacal Cockney, fond of his little creature comforts, methodical as a Quaker, and regular as the Horse Guards lick, who is disturbed in his night's rest, and put to all kinds of shifts and inconveniences by the boisterous inroad of the Tom-and-Jerry sort of a stranger . . . was performed to the life by Mr. Dickens. His style is a sort of mixture of the late Charles Mathews and Mr. Buckstone's, and would do no discredit to either of those eminent performers" (quoted in *D*, XXXVIII, 73–4).

[7] Clearly someone, other than an actor, known to both CD and Forster. Just possibly Talfourd, and the use of his real initial one of the "exceptions" Forster made to his general rule of changing initials in order to disguise names (see F, III, ii, 202n).

[8] John Pritt Harley (1786–1858; *DNB*), comic actor: see Vol. I, p. 167n.

Private Theatricals.

COMMITTEE.

Mrs. TORRENS.	Mrs. PERRY.
W. C. ERMATINGER, Esq.	Captain TORRENS.

THE EARL OF MULGRAVE.

STAGE MANAGER—MR. CHARLES DICKENS.

QUEEN'S THEATRE, MONTREAL.

ON WEDNESDAY EVENING, MAY 25TH, 1842,

WILL BE PERFORMED,

A ROLAND FOR AN OLIVER.

MRS. SELBORNE.	*Mrs Torrens*
MARIA DARLINGTON.	*Miss Griffin*
MRS. FIXTURE.	*Miss Ermatinger.*
MR. SELBORNE.	*Lord Mulgrave*
ALFRED HIGHFLYER.	*Mr Charles Dickens*
SIR MARK CHASE.	*Honoble Mr Mathew*
FIXTURE.	*Captain Willoughby.*
GAMEKEEPER.	*Captain Granville*

AFTER WHICH, AN INTERLUDE IN ONE SCENE, (FROM THE FRENCH,) CALLED

Past Two o'Clock in the Morning.

THE STRANGER.	*Captain Granville*
MR. SNOBBINGTON.	*Mr Charles Dickens*

TO CONCLUDE WITH THE FARCE, IN ONE ACT, ENTITLED

DEAF AS A POST.

MRS. PLUMPLEY.	*Mrs Torrens*
AMY TEMPLETON.	*Mrs Charles Dickens!!!!!!!!*
SOPHY WALTON.	*Mrs Perry.*
SALLY MAGGS.	*Miss Griffin*
CAPTAIN TEMPLETON.	*Captain Torrens*
MR. WALTON.	*Captain Willoughby.*
TRISTRAM SAPPY.	*Doctor Griffin*
CRUPPER.	*Lord Mulgrave*
GALLOP.	*Mr Charles Dickens.*

MONTREAL, May 24, 1842.   GAZETTE OFFICE,

Playbill of the Private Theatricals
Montreal, 25 May 1842

Theatre Royal.

FOR THIS NIGHT ONLY.

The Manager has the honor to announce a Performance, in which

CHARLES DICKENS, ESQ.

Together with the distinguished

GARRISON AMATEURS,

Whose successful performance on Wednesday last, created such unbounded admiration, will appear.

THIS EVENING, SATURDAY, MAY 28, 1842,

The Performances will commence with a

ROLAND FOR AN OLIVER.

Sir Mark Chase,	The Hon. P. Methuen.
Alfred Highflyer,	Mr. Charles Dickens
Mr. Selbourne,	The Earl of Mulgrave.
Fixture,	Captain Willoughby.
GAME-KEEPERS, &c. &c	
Maria Darlington,	Mrs. A. W. Penson.
Mrs. Selbourne,	Mrs. Brown.
Mrs. Fixture,	Mrs. Henry.

AFTER WHICH,

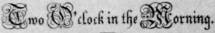

Two O'clock in the Morning.

Snobbington,	Mr. Charles Dickens.
The Stranger,	Capt. Granville, 23d Regt.

TO CONCLUDE WITH,

HIGH LIFE
BELOW STAIRS.

My Lord Duke,	Dr. Griffin, 85th Regt.
Sir Harry,	Capt. Willoughby, 23d Regt.
Lovel,	Capt. Torrens. do
Coachman,	Capt. Granville, 23d Regt.
Freeman,	Earl of Mulgrave.
Phillip,	Mr. Charles Dickens.
Kingston,	Mr. Thomas.
Tom,	Mr. Hughes.
Mrs. Kitty,	Mrs. A. W. Penson.
Lady Bab,	Mrs. Henry.
Lady Charlotte,	Mrs. Brown.
Chloe,	Miss Heath.

The Performance to commence at half-past Seven.

ON MONDAY EVENING,

MRS. AND MR. SLOMAN'S
THIRD APPEARANCE.

Montreal, May 28, 1842. GAZETTE OFFICE.

Playbill of the Public Theatricals
Montreal, 28 May 1842

Yates,[1] Keeley,[2] and Jerry Sneak.[3] It went with a roar, all through; and, as I am closing this, they have told me I was so well made up that Sir Charles Bagot, who sat in the stage box, had no idea who played Mr. Snobbington, until the piece was over.[4]

But only think of Kate playing! and playing devilish well, I assure you! All the ladies were capital, and we had no wait or hitch for an instant.[5] You may suppose this, when I tell you that we began at eight, and had the curtain down at eleven. It is their custom here, to prevent heartburnings in a very heartburning town, whenever they have played in private, to repeat the performance in public.[6] So, on Saturday (substituting, of course, real actresses[7] for the ladies), we repeat the two first pieces to a paying audience,[8] for the manager's[9] benefit. . . .

I send you a bill,[10] to which I have appended a key.[11]

I have not told you half enough. But I promise you I shall make you shake your sides about this play. Wasn't it worthy of Crummles that when Lord Mulgrave and I went out to the door to receive the Governor-general, the regular prompter followed us in agony with four tall candlesticks with wax

---

[1] Frederick Henry Yates (1797–1842; *DNB*), actor-manager: see Vol. II, p.10*n*.

[2] Robert Keeley (1793–1869; *DNB*), comic actor; a protégé of Elliston's from 1817; played at all the main London theatres 1819–42. Numerous parts were written for him by R. B. Peake and Planché. Married Mary Ann Goward 1829, and they frequently played together. According to Thomas Marshall (*Lives of the Most Celebrated Actors and Actresses*, [1848], p. 101) his performance at Covent Garden under Mathews Oct 40 as Diego in Beaumont and Fletcher's *Spanish Curate* had removed all doubt of his "capabilities for the legitimate drama". For CD's admiration of his acting, see Vol. II, p. 455 and *n*. Talfourd considered him "the most genuine comedian who [had] made his appearance for years" (quoted in *Representative Actors*, ed. W. Clark Russell, n.d., p. 373).

[3] A hen-pecked husband in Samuel Foote's *The Mayor of Garratt* (1764). It was Samuel Russell's great part, and contemporaries considered that Keeley's whole "style of acting" was influenced by it (Thomas Marshall, *op. cit.*, p. 100).

[4] The players' names were omitted in the playbill of the private performance. Consequently the *Montreal Transcript* praised CD as the Stranger and Capt. Granville as Mr Snobbington.

[5] Cf. CD's reference to the Montreal theatricals in his speech at the Royal General Theatrical Fund dinner, 4 Apr 63: since "no ladies were to be found", "young and newly caught officers" were brought in to "supply their places"; but "in order that they might acquire something of the feminine walk it was found absolutely necessary to tie their legs" (*Speeches*, ed. K. J. Fielding, p. 318). This obviously was pure fantasy.

[6] A number of amateur companies performed at the Theatre Royal, where the professional seasons were irregular; among them the Garrison Amateurs were the most long-lived; officers had in fact performed in Montreal long before the first theatre was built there in 1804 (*D*, XLV, 40).

[7] Mrs A. W. Penson, Mrs Brown, Mrs Henry and Miss Heath (see playbill for 28 May, on page facing).

[8] Instead of the third, *Deaf as a Post*, they played James Townley's *High Life below Stairs*, with CD as Philip.

[9] Henry Tuthill, who had recently taken the lease of the Theatre Royal; in the course of his present two months' season, close on 50 plays were put on at the Theatre (*D*, XLV, 39, 43).

[10] The playbill for the performance of 25 May, doubtless issued privately by the Committee.

[11] See playbill of the performance, facing page 246.

candles in them, and besought us with a bleeding heart to carry two apiece, in accordance with all the precedents? . . .

I have hardly spoken of our letters, which reached us yesterday, shortly before the play began. A hundred thousand thanks for your delightful main-sail¹ of that gallant little packet. I read it again and again; and had it all over again at breakfast time this morning. I heard also, by the same ship, from Talfourd, Miss Coutts, Brougham, Rogers, and others. A delicious letter from Mac too, as good as his painting I swear. Give my hearty love to him. . . . God bless you, my dear friend. As the time draws nearer, we get FEVERED with anxiety for home. . . . Kiss our darlings for us. We shall soon meet, please God, and be happier and merrier than ever we were, in all our lives. . . . Oh home—home—home—home—home—home—HOME ! ! ! ! ! ! ! ! ! ! !

To JONATHAN CHAPMAN, 2 JUNE 1842

MS Comtesse de Suzannet. *Address:* Private. | The Honorable Jonathan Chapman Boston | Mass.

Carlton House, New York. | Second June 1842.

My Dear Friend.

I am going up the Hudson, for rest; and shall not return here until Monday. Though I have but a minute to spare, I cannot choose but answer your affectionate and warmly-welcomed letter.

I *did* receive that other communication from you,² of which you speak. I am not ashamed to own it, although I have not written. I answered a great many other letters. They were mere things of course. But I always laid yours aside, and said "This is quite another matter. I won't write *him* a traveller's hurried, common-place note. I will wait"—Well! You know what waiting comes to, under such circumstances as these?

Besides, I have always said to my wife, "He'll come over to New York. I feel confident that he will dine with us, on Monday The Sixth."—When your letter was brought in, I plumed myself very much (before opening it) on being so accurate. And I do assure you that for a moment I was quite sorry and disappointed.³ But to connect any such feelings with such a letter, long, was out of the question; so I brightened up again, very soon, and am now quite radiant.

The ocean can no more divide you and me, than darkness can shut out Heaven from a blind man. Were it twenty times as broad as it is, we could send a warm pressure of the hand, across it. And I feel, besides, an inexpressible confidence that, on one side of it, or the other, we shall meet again.⁴

God bless you, my dear fellow. In the happiness of Home, I shall only remember you the more earnestly, heartily, and affectionately. I don't know

---

¹ i.e. covering letter to the copyright MSS.

² Neither of the letters mentioned here appears with Chapman's others to CD in *D*, xxxviii, Winter 1941/2. Presumably he kept no copies. The "other communica-tion" must have been in answer to CD's bitter outburst of 22 Feb.

³ Chapman did in fact see CD off at New York (*Diary of Philip Hone*, ed. B. Tucker-man, II, 132).

⁴ They did not.

how extravagantly I shall feel, or what extravagant things I shall do, in the joy of heart with which I shall first stand among my household Deities again. But, I will tell you all about it, from the midst of them, with God's leave.

—I write God bless you, once more, as if that were a satisfaction. Who that has ever reflected on the enormous and vast amount of leave-taking there is in this Life, can ever have doubted the existence of another!

I have more than half a mind to write those three words of farewell, again. —But let this go without, for you know that it comes from Yours with all his heart

CHARLES DICKENS

The Honorable Jonathan Chapman.

I cannot tell you how often I feel grieved at our not having dined together, alone, on that day when we went to South Boston.[1] And now, it really weighs upon me, quite heavily.

To JOHN PENDLETON KENNEDY, 2 JUNE 1842*

MS Peabody Institute, Baltimore.

In Haste.

Carlton House, New York.
Second of June 1842.

My Dear Sir

I am going on a short excursion up the Hudson, and shall not return until the day of Sailing. I have been here but a few hours,[2] and have barely time to acknowledge the receipt of your very welcome and interesting letter.

My address in London is No. 1 Devonshire Terrace, York Gate, Regents Park. Command me, at all times and seasons, in the International Copyright matter. And trust me that I will leave no stone unturned which human levers can uproot. Bulwer, Hallam,[3] and all the signers of that letter (with many more behind) will help me cordially.[4] Whatever you have need of, ask for. I will communicate your letter to them all, immediately on my arrival in England.[5]

My first step shall be, to *stop*[6] the sale of early proofs to any Newspaper in

---

[1] On 29 Jan, to see the South Boston institutions.

[2] They had left Montreal on 30 May by steamboat across the St Lawrence; gone by rail via St John's to Lake Champlain and boarded an American vessel (described by CD as a "floating palace"), on which they spent the night; disembarked at Whitehall, and gone on by stage-coach to Albany; thence by a crowded North River steamboat, which brought them to New York at 5 a.m. on 2 June (*American Notes*, Ch. 15).

[3] Henry Hallam (1777–1859; *DNB*), Whig historian; father of Tennyson's friend, Arthur Henry Hallam.

[4] Although Bulwer had both drafted and signed the copyright memorial, he gave CD no further support: see *To* Marryat, 21 Jan 43.

[5] CD's circular letter of 7 July mentions the copyright committee of which Kennedy was chairman, but not his letter.

[6] Very heavily underlined.

the United States.[1] We will deprive them of *that* interest in the present Robbery, at any rate.

I inclose you Carlyle's autograph communication.[2] And am always

Faithfully Yours

The Honorable J. P. Kennedy.   CHARLES DICKENS

To MESSRS LEA & BLANCHARD, 2 JUNE 1842

MS Messrs Lea & Febiger. *Address:* Paid | Messrs. Lea and Blanchard | Philadelphia.

Carlton House. New York. | Second of June 1842.

My Dear Sirs

I thank you, very sincerely, for your kind letter, and your handsome Present of Books. I shall carry them all home, and put them beside your other contributions to my shelves.[3]

My inclination would lead me, with a silken cord, to Philadelphia. But, I am weary of travelling, and am going to lie in the shade of some Trees on the bank of the North River until Tuesday comes—that bright day in my Calendar when I turn towards Home and England.

Good b'ye. | Always Believe me
Faithfully Your friend

Messrs. Lea and Blanchard.   CHARLES DICKENS

To FREDERICK GRANVILLE,[4] 2 JUNE 1842*

MS Benoliel Collection.

Carlton House. | Thursday Second June 1842.

My Dear Granville.

I have taken a State room for you & Captain Woodhouse,[5] on board the George Washington.[6] It is just amidships, where there is least motion; and is

---

[1] For his attempt to do this, see *To British Authors*, 7 July.

[2] A copy of Carlyle's letter of 26 Mar: see Appx, p. 623.

[3] Besides a "complete set" of their edns of his books (of which he inscribed *Old Curiosity Shop* and *Barnaby Rudge* to George Morris, New York, 1 June), asked for by CD on 30 Apr, Lea & Blanchard may well have given him now or on his arrival in New York (see 13 Feb) some of the following, published by themselves and listed in CD's 1844 inventory: Mathew Carey's *Essays on Political Economy*, 1822; *The American Museum*, 1787–1792, ed. Mathew Carey; *Encyclopaedia Americana*, ed. Francis Lieber and E. Wigglesworth, 13 vols, 1829–42; Fenimore Cooper's *Novels and Tales*, 40 vols in 20, 1841–2; J. P. Kennedy's *Swallow Barn*, 1832.

[4] Frederick Granville (1810–85), Capt.

23rd Foot Regt; Major 1846. Commanded the 2nd Warwick Militia 1858; its Colonel from 1878. A distinguished shot. In the Montreal theatricals he played the Gamekeeper in *A Roland for an Oliver*; and his performance as the Stranger in *Past Two o'Clock in the Morning* was, according to the *Montreal Gazette*, "exactly what was wanted—a forcible contrast, in its turbulent, fiery, and destructive character" to CD's "quiet, placid, and conservative lodger on the second floor front" (quoted in *D*, xxxviii, 74).

[5] Possibly Robert Woodhouse, Capt. 38th Foot Regt.

[6] A sailing packet of just over 600 tons, built in New Bedford 1832; she ran in the Blue Swallowtail Line between New York and Liverpool until 1845, when converted to a whaler.

2 June 1842   251

next door to ours. She is not full; and promises, I hope, to be exceedingly comfortable.[1]

Our goods and chattels will go on board at 9 o'Clock on Monday Morning. Mrs. Dickens's maid and Mr. Putnam are going down with them. They will stow your things, if you please, at the same time; and will observe any directions you may give them.

I am just starting on a short excursion up the Hudson.[2] It is not very likely that we shall return before Monday. Will you be in the way between 11 and 1 on that morning? I have not paid for your passage, or my own: the owners[3] begging me not to do so, until the day before sailing. We will call upon them together, and settle.

In the mean time, pray make use of our sitting room. And pray beg Captain Woodhouse, in my name, to dine with us on Monday at 6.[4]

Always Faithfully Yours
CHARLES DICKENS

[1] There were only 15 cabin-passengers, the majority from Canada; and the passage home—helped by good weather—was clearly immeasurably more comfortable than the passage out. They were constantly on deck; had "no lack of music" (CD playing the accordion); "had chess for those who played it, whist, cribbage, books, backgammon, and shovelboard"; and at dinner formed a "jovial" and "select" association, of which CD was president. A different "source of interest" was what they saw on looking down at the deck occupied by the steerage passengers (nearly 100 of them: "a little world of poverty"), whose histories they enquired of the ship's carpenter (*American Notes*, Ch. 16). On this CD later drew for Martin's and Mark's steerage-passage to America (*Chuzzlewit*, Ch. 15).

[2] See *American Notes*, Ch. 15. With the Coldens and Miss Wilkes, they went up the North River as far as Hudson, thence by hired vehicle to Lebanon Springs where they met Prescott and the Ticknors and spent the night of 3 June. Next day they drove to the Shaker Village, hoping—like other visitors—to see the Shaker worship, but found the chapel closed to the public, owing to "unseemly interruptions". (For the curious dances and singing which formed a large part of every Shaker service, see, among others, Marryat, *Diary in America*, I, 118–121, Fanny Appleton's Journal, 15 Sep 39, quoted in *Mrs. Long-fellow, Selected Letters and Journals . . .* ed. E. Wagenknecht, 1959, pp. 61–3, and *The Dial*, Oct 43: CD's account in *Ameri-*

can Notes was merely from hearsay.) While CD conceded the apparent success of their economy and communal way of life, their particular piety was inevitably distasteful to him, and he left the village, he wrote, "with a hearty dislike of the old Shakers, and a hearty pity for the young ones". Ticknor described him rather maliciously as "much grieved that the Shakers were so insensible to his wide-spread merit, and so little respecters of persons, as to refuse to show him any of their mysteries, or managements touching men and beasts" (letter to H. S. Legaré, 9 June 42, quoted in *Life, Letters, and Journals of George Ticknor*, Boston, 1876, II, 207). The party returned by the same route, staying the nights of 4 and 5 June at West Point.

[3] Grinnell, Minturn & Co., of New York. They invited a large party of CD's American friends, including Jonathan Chapman, Colden, Dr Wilkes and Philip Hone, to accompany him, by steamboat from Jersey City, on to the *George Washington*. There, after a "cold collation" and champagne, there were speeches and toasts; Hone gave "Charles Dickens: the welcome acquired by literary reputation has been confirmed and justified by personal inter-course". The guests then returned to their steamer which towed the *George Washington* to a point off Sandy Hook, whence it sailed (*Diary of Philip Hone*, ed. A. Nevins, pp. 605–6).

[4] The dinner was given at the Carlton House, New York, the guests being the Coldens, Dr and Miss Wilkes, Dr Howe,

To WILLIAM MITCHELL, 6 JUNE 1842*

MS Mrs A. M. Stern.

Carlton House. | Monday Evening | Sixth June 1842.

My Dear Sir.

I am more sorry than I can tell you, to find that I am bound, in pursuance of a very old engagement, to go out to breakfast tomorrow Morning.[1] You will believe, readily, that on the eve of going back to the old country, I regret this, sincerely, for the sake of past times. But I have just been reminded of this promise, and cannot choose but fulfil it, for many reasons—not least among them, for the sake of my best friends on this side.[2]

I shall send you from England, please God, English copies of my books.[3] If you receive them in the spirit in which I send them, the Olympic will prosper more and more; for I wish you more than well—not merely by reason of your extraordinary *quiet*, rich, comic humour (which I never saw exceeded) but in recollection of the gentlemanly and considerate spirit you have shewn in every pleasant communication we have had together.

The dog[4] is in a superb state; & is already deeply attached to my Wife's maid.

Always believe me | Faithfully Yours

CHARLES DICKENS

To A. H. BURROWS,[5] [?28 JUNE 1842]

Mention in *Boston Daily Evening Transcript*, 21 July 42. *Date:* They landed at Liverpool early on Wed 29 June; letter was probably written the day before.

A letter of thanks to the Captain of the George Washington *for the comfort they had experienced and the attention they had received, signed by all the passengers.*

Capt. Granville, Capt. Woodhouse, Mr and Mrs C. A. Davis, Felton, Halleck and Bryant (CD's list, MS Houghton Library, Harvard).

[1] The day of his departure. The engagement seems unlikely to have been "very old", since Philip Hone received his invitation only on the morning of the breakfast party.

[2] The party was given by James G. King (one of the New York Dinner Committee) and his wife at Highwood, their country house outside New York. Hone and his wife arrived at 10 a.m. and found there, besides "the Boz and Bozess", Mr and Mrs Archibald Gracie, Dr and Miss Wilkes, the Coldens, and Julia Ward. "We had a breakfast worthy of the entertainers and the entertained", he recorded in his diary; "and such strawberries and cream! The house and the grounds and the view and the libraries and the conservatory were all more beautiful than I have ever seen

them" (*Diary of Philip Hone*, ed. A. Nevins p. 605).

[3] Which Mitchell, as an expatriate, would have appreciated more than the American editions.

[4] See *To* Mitton, 22 Mar and *fn*.

[5] Ambrose Hilliard Burrows, Jr (?1813–43), of Connecticut, Master of the *George Washington*. When he died (on board his ship), he had crossed the Atlantic 66 times and had made two voyages to China (Carl C. Cutler, *Queens of the Western Ocean: the Story of America's Mail and Passenger Sailing Lines*, Annapolis, 1961, p. 256). Described by CD in *American Notes*, Ch. 16, as "an honest, manly-hearted captain". According to J. Stonehouse of Liverpool, Burrows told him that he read *Old Curiosity Shop* on this voyage and was so upset by the death of Little Nell, that he threw the book into the sea (unidentified cutting from Liverpool paper).

To ALBANY FONBLANQUE, 1 JULY 1842*

MS Southeast Missouri State College.

Devonshire Terrace. | First July 1842.

My Dear Fonblanque.

Many thanks for your kind note and welcome.

We should have been truly delighted to have dined with you to day, had we not previously pledged ourselves to regale with Forster. I should have written to tell you this, yesterday afternoon, but the happy hurry of getting into my home again,[1] made me oblivious.

In haste | Believe me ever

Heartily Yours

Albany Fonblanque Esquire   CHARLES DICKENS

To THOMAS LONGMAN,[2] [1 JULY 1842]

Text from MDGH, I, 73. *Date:* clearly the day after the meeting of 30 June chaired by Longman.

Athenæum, Friday Afternoon.

My dear Sir,

If I could possibly have attended the meeting yesterday[3] I would most gladly have done so. But I [had][4] been up the whole night, and was too much exhausted even to write and say so before the proceedings came on.

[1] He clearly reached London a day before he was expected (for his arrival surprised both Macready and Forster: see *To* Chapman, 3 Aug and *fns*); and presumably with Catherine spent the night of the 29th with the children at 25 Osnaburgh Street. Mamie Dickens later described their arrival thus: "One evening, after dark, we were hurried to the gate, a cab was driving up to the door, or, rather, as it would then have been called, a hackney-coach; before it could stop, a figure jumped out, some one lifted me up in their arms, and I was kissing my father through the bars of the gate. *How* all this happened, and why the gate was shut I am unable to explain" (*CD by his Eldest Daughter*, 1911 edn, p. 80). They all moved back into 1 Devonshire Terrace on 30 June.

[2] Thomas Longman (1804–79; *DNB*), publisher: see Vol. I, p. 578n. Succeeded as head of the firm after his father's death on 29 Aug 42.

[3] A public meeting of authors and publishers, held at the Freemasons' Tavern, to consider "the enormous and increasing evil of the foreign piracy of British literary works", and to adopt measures to end it. G. P. R. James (see 26 July, *fn*) made the main speech, pointing out that publishers, besides authors, were hit by the import into England of cheap pirated books printed abroad; and that the Govt lost a considerable duty on paper. There was immense piracy of British books in France and Germany (380 works in France alone according to James), besides America—whose "mammoths" circulated freely in Canada and other British colonies. The International Copyright Act, 1838, which allowed mutual copyright treaties, had not been carried out. James, seconded by Horace Smith, moved a resolution "that a right of property in literary productions ought to be recognized by all civilized nations." Similar resolutions—mostly demanding mutual treaties—were moved and seconded by Lord William Lennox, Sir Charles Morgan, Longman, Blackwood, Colburn, Hood, J. S. Buckingham, and others. Letters were read from Bulwer, Talfourd and Samuel Warren in support. It was resolved to forward the resolutions to the Govt; and a memorial in favour of international copyright was sent to the Board of Trade.

[4] MDGH reads "have", clearly in error.

I have fought the fight across the Atlantic with the utmost energy I could command; have never been turned aside by any consideration for an instant; am fresher for the fray than ever; will battle it to the death, and die game to the last.

I am happy to say that my boy is quite well again. From being in perfect health he fell into alarming convulsions with the surprise and joy of our return.[1]

I beg my regards to Mrs. Longman,[2]

And am always, | Faithfully yours

[CHARLES DICKENS]

To MISS BURDETT COUTTS, 2 JULY 1842

MS Morgan Library. *Address:* Miss Coutts | Stratton Street.

Devonshire Terrace.

Saturday Evening | Second July 1842

My Dear Miss Coutts.

I beg to report myself arrived and well—and in proof of the fact, to send you the Rocking Chair.[3] Let me also ask your acceptance of some specimens of American Poetry,[4] which I forward at the same time.

I send for Miss Meredith, an Eagle's feather.[5] Its rightful owner fell over the great fall at Niagara last winter (or, I should rather say, was carried over by the strong current) and was picked up, dead, some miles down the river.

I did not forget Lady Burdett's request. A piece of rock from the cave behind the great sheet of water is slumbering ignominiously in the Custom House, among some other contraband articles. As soon as the chest comes to hand, I shall have the pleasure of redeeming my vow.[6]

Believe me always

Yours faithfully and obliged

Miss Burdett Coutts   CHARLES DICKENS

---

[1] See *To* Prescott, 31 July, for a fuller account of Charley's "disorder".

[2] *Née* Georgina Townsend: see Vol. I, p. 578*n*.

[3] Apparently he brought one for himself as well. In "Personal Reminiscences of my Father" (supplement to the *Windsor Magazine*, Christmas 1934) Charley Dickens wrote: "My first really clear recollection of [my father] is in connection with a certain American rocking-chair, which I presume he had brought back with him from the States, and in which he often used to sit of an evening, singing comic songs to a wondering and delighted audience consisting of myself and my two sisters. The Loving Ballad of Lord Bateman . . . was one of these ditties". Catherine had brought back with her an "old Fan with Chinese Figures, and Musical Instruments in the Sticks", given her in America—by whom is not known. (She left it in her Will, 31 Jan 78, to Mamie.)

[4] Probably Rufus Griswold's *Poets and Poetry of America*, Philadelphia, 1842. Cf. *To* Lady Holland, 11 July and *fn*.

[5] Cf. *To* Miss Coutts, 22 Mar; and, for the gift of a similar feather, *To* Lady Holland, 11 July.

[6] He did so on 13 Jan 43 (*To* Lady Burdett, that day).

To CHARLES MACKAY,[1] [?EARLY JULY 1842]

Extract in Walpole Galleries catalogue No. 132; *MS* 2 pp. *Date:* probably not long after 30 June 42, date of publication of *The Salamandrine* (see *fn*).

My Dear Sir,

I have read your "wild poem"[2] with great pleasure and delight . . .

Faithfully Yours

CHARLES DICKENS

To DANIEL MACLISE, 4 JULY 1842

Mention in N, I, 461.

To MRS MACREADY, 4 JULY 1842*

MS Morgan Library.

Devonshire Terrace.
Monday Evening | Fourth July 1842.

My Dear Mrs. Macready.

As we never can thank you enough in all our lives for your most kind and zealous friendship,[3] let me ask you to accept the accompanying little token of our love[4]—to the end that whenever you look upon it, you may remember how powerless we were to express our grateful feeling to you on coming home from America, and how much we should have said, if we could have found words in our full hearts.

Ever Your affectionate friend

Mrs. Macready.   CHARLES DICKENS

To DAVID BARNES,[5] 6 JULY 1842*

MS Messrs Chas J. Sawyer Ltd.

1 Devonshire Terrace. | York Gate Regents Park.
Wednesday Sixth July 1842.

Dear Mr. Barnes.

We should like to get a house at Broadstairs this year, for the Months of August and September; and I shall be glad to hear from you, at your leisure, on the subject.

We wish it to be on the Terrace—and it must have a Water Closet.

---

[1] Charles Mackay (1814–89; *DNB*), poet and journalist: see Vol. I, p. 485*n*.

[2] *The Salamandrine; or, Love and Immortality*, a long poem in irregular ballad metre, inspired by a passage in the Rosicrucian romance, *Le Comte de Gabalis*, by the Abbé de Villars, 1670. The story, somewhat similar to that of *Undine*, is of a fire spirit falling in love with a human being. In his Preface, Mackay calls it "wild and fantastic".

[3] In assuming responsibility for the children during CD's and Catherine's absence.

[4] What the present was is not known.

[5] David Barnes, Albion Street, Broadstairs, house agent: see Vol. II, p. 77*n*.

I think of bringing my carriage (which is a one-horse Phaeton) down with me, but my Groom I shall be obliged to leave in town, to take care of the house, as I don't like to trust it to a stranger. Can you let me know whether I could get stabling &c in Broadstairs, and what it would cost—including, of course, the keep of the horse, and keeping the carriage and harness clean for daily use?

                                                    Faithfully Yours
Mr. Barnes.   CHARLES DICKENS

To W. HARRISON AINSWORTH,[1] 7 JULY 1842

MS Brotherton Library, Leeds.

                                   Devonshire Terrace. | Seventh July 1842.
My Dear Ainsworth.

I turned back t'other day, directly Maclise called out to me that you had passed—and turned back up Portland Place yesterday, after an imaginary William Harrison—but it was no go on either occasion.

Will you dine with me at 6, next Saturday Week? I give you so long a notice —not because of any great party or mighty preparations, but in the hope of finding you disengaged.

My love to Mrs. Touchett[2] and Miss Buckley[3]—and to the Misses Ainsworth,[4] with whom I am afraid (for I know what women they are by this time) of being too tender, lest they should erect their heads and wither me with a look.

                                            Always My Dear Ainsworth
                                                    Faithfully Yours
William Harrison Ainsworth Esquire.   CHARLES DICKENS

To BRITISH AUTHORS AND JOURNALS, 7 JULY 1842

Text from printed Circular.[5]

                          1, Devonshire Terrace, York Gate, Regent's Park,
                                                    Seventh July, 1842.
[My Dear   ]

You may perhaps be aware that during my stay in America, I lost no opportunity of endeavouring to awaken the public mind to a sense of the unjust and

---

[1] William Harrison Ainsworth (1805–82; *DNB*), novelist: see Vol. I, p. 115n. CD's last recorded meeting with him was in May 41 (Vol. II, p. 274).

[2] Mis-spelt in MS. Eliza Touchet (1792–1869), Ainsworth's cousin by marriage: see Vol. I, p. 277n, and Vol. II, p. 274n.

[3] Anne Buckley, Mrs Touchet's younger sister.

[4] Ainsworth's three daughters—Fanny (1827–1908) and Emily (1829–1885), who both died unmarried, and Anne Blanche (1830–1908), who married (1861) Capt. Francis Swanson. They had been living with their father since 1841.

[5] Among friends and acquaintances to whom CD sent this printed circular, adding salutations and subscriptions in MS, were Lady Blessington (printed in *The Collection of Autograph Letters and Historical Documents Formed . . . by Alfred Morrison . . . The Blessington Papers*, privately printed, 1895, pp. 42–3); Dyce (MS V & A); Hallam (see *To* Fred Dickens, 7 Aug); Harness (MS Mrs E. Duncan-Jones); Fanny Kemble (see *Records of Later Life*, 1882, II, 267); Monckton Milnes (MS Trinity College, Cambridge); John Murray (MS Sir John Murray); William Pickering (MS Mrs A. M. Stern); and Thackeray (see *The Letters and Private*

iniquitous state of the law in that country, in reference to the wholesale piracy of British works.

Having been successful in making the subject one of general discussion in the United States, I carried to Washington, for presentation to Congress by Mr. Clay, a petition from the whole body of American authors, earnestly praying for the enactment of an International Copyright Law. It was signed by Mr. Washington Irving, Mr. Prescott, Mr. Cooper,[1] and every man who has distinguished himself in the literature of America; and has since been referred to a Select Committee of the House of Representatives.[2]

To counter any effect which might be produced by that petition, a meeting was held in Boston—which you will remember is the seat and stronghold of Learning and Letters in the United States—at which a memorial against any change in the existing state of things in this respect was agreed to,[3] with but one dissentient voice.[4] This document, which, incredible as it may appear to you, was actually forwarded to Congress, and received, deliberately stated that if English authors were invested with any controul over the republication of their own books, it would be no longer possible for American authors to alter and adapt them (as they do now) to the American taste![5]

Papers of W. M. Thackeray, ed. G. N. Ray, 1945, II, 66). The circular appeared in the *Morning Chronicle*, 14 July; the *Examiner*, *Athenæum* and *Literary Gazette*, 16 July; the *New Monthly* (as addressed to Hood); the *United Services Journal*, and other journals.

[1] James Fenimore Cooper (1789–1851; *DAB*) had already published most of his novels (*The Deerslayer*, 1841, most recently), and as the most popular in England of all American writers had, like CD, suffered severely from lack of an international copyright (11 of his books had by this time appeared in Bentley's Standard Novels). Of CD's circular letter he wrote (6 Aug) to the *New York Evening Post* (11 Aug): "I see, by an extract in your paper, that, in a letter recently published in England, Mr. Dickens names me as one of those writers who have petitioned Congress to pass an 'International copy-right law.' . . . Mr. Dickens is in error. . . . I have never even seen the petition in question". Had he done so, he was "far from certain" that he would have signed it: "I wish for no *international* legislation on any subject; and least of all with England." He accepted CD's "general argument" as "unanswerably true"; but argued on higher grounds that, since the rights of property (God-ordained) were seen, as nations "advanced in civilisation", to include the products of the human mind, America (whatever might be the practice of other countries) should do that which brought her legislature "up to the level of the progress of the age, and to the revealed law of God".

[2] See *To* Forster, 27 Feb, *fn.*

[3] For the memorial against international copyright drawn up by the Boston book trade convention, see *To* Felton, 16 May, *fn.*

[4] That of Francis Bowen (see *To* Prescott, 31 July, *fn*), whose objection to the memorial, "as embracing two subjects not necessarily connected with each other, viz. Protection to American Industry and International Copyright", led to a long debate. Another objector—unnamed in the report—moved that the part of the memorial relating to international copyright be struck out (*Boston Mercantile Journal*, 27 Apr 42; quoted in W. G. Wilkins, *CD in America*, p. 247).

[5] The sentence in question read: "If English authors obtain copyrights upon their works here, and our markets are supplied with them, it is apparent that, having no power to adapt them to our wants, our institutions, and our state of society, we must permit their circulation as they are" (*Senate Documents*, 1841–2, IV, p. 3). The *American Traveller*, 26 Aug, in a furious attack on CD's circular, argued that adaptation was necessary because all British writing was "tinged with monarchism". After various charges of corrupt

This memorial was, without loss of time, replied to by Mr. Prescott,[1] who commented, with the natural indignation of a gentleman, and a Man of Letters, upon its extraordinary dishonesty. I am satisfied that this brief mention of its tone and spirit, is sufficient to impress you with the conviction that it becomes all those who are in any way connected with the Literature of England, to take that high stand, to which the nature of their pursuits, and the extent of their sphere of usefulness, justly entitle them; to discourage the upholders of such doctrines by every means in their power; and to hold themselves aloof from the remotest participation in a system, from which the moral sense and honourable feeling of all just men must instinctively recoil.

For myself, I have resolved that I will never from this time enter into any negociation with any person for the transmission, across the Atlantic, of early proofs of any thing I may write;[2] and that I will forego all profit derivable from such a source. I do not venture to urge this line of proceeding upon you, but I would beg to suggest, and to lay great stress upon the necessity of observing, one other course of action: to which I cannot too emphatically call your attention.

The persons who exert themselves to mislead the American public on this question; to put down its discussion; and to suppress and distort the truth, in reference to it, in every possible way; are (as you may easily suppose) those who have a strong interest in the existing system of piracy and plunder; inasmuch as, so long as it continues, they can gain a very comfortable living out of the brains of other men, while they would find it very difficult to earn bread by the exercise of their own. These are the editors and proprietors of newspapers almost exclusively devoted to the republication of popular English works.[3] They

despotism against British publishers (e.g. that they had hired Sir Walter Scott to slander Napoleon), it turned to CD: "Mr. Dickens would have our people so instructed with 'unaltered' English books, that they might tamely submit to the same horrible oppression. And, because they calmly and with dignity decline it, he gets in a towering passion, and calls them thieves, pirates, soulless money-getters, and brutal robbers. Yes,—Mr. Dickens, who receives some forty thousand guineas per annum for his works in England, opens upon us in his foulest billingsgate because we will not permit him to double the sum out of our own pockets." For Marryat on the American adaptation of texts, see *To* Austin, 1 May, *fn.*

[1] Prescott headed the signatories to the counter-memorial, but its author was Francis Bowen, as CD realized later: see *To* Prescott, 31 July.

[2] CD held to this for 10 years. (For his later negotiations with Harper & Brothers, see W. G. Wilkins, *First and Early American Editions of the Works of CD*, privately printed, Cedar Rapids, Iowa, 1910.)

[3] This must refer to Park Benjamin's and R. W. Griswold's "mammoth" weekly papers, *Brother Jonathan* (launched July 39 and later edited by H. H. Weld and John Neal successively) and the *New World* (launched Oct 39, edited by Benjamin himself). They were "mammoth" in size; the *New World*'s pages, for instance, were about four feet long and eleven columns wide—though in 1840 a 4to edn of the *New World* appeared also, which *Brother Jonathan* later copied. Both papers relied principally on reprinting English works. *Brother Jonathan* pirated to a very large extent stories from *Fraser's*, *Tait's*, the *New Monthly*, *Blackwood's*, *Ainsworth's*, and *Bentley's*, although including some American contributions (e.g. Cornelius Mathews's *Puffer Hopkins*). But the *New World* concentrated largely on serialization of English novels, CD's among them, and must have, far more than *Brother Jonathan*, aroused CD's ire. *Old Curiosity Shop*, for instance, ran serially in the *New World*, Vol. 1, from 6 June 40, side by side with Ainsworth's *Tower of London* and *Guy Fawkes*, Warren's *Ten Thousand a Year*,

are, for the most part, men of very low attainments and of more than indifferent reputation;[1] and I have frequently seen them, in the same sheet in which they boast of the rapid sale of many thousand copies of an English reprint, coarsely and insolently attacking the author of that very book, and heaping scurrility and slander upon his head.[2]

I would therefore entreat you, in the name of the honourable pursuit with which you are so intimately connected, never to hold correspondence with any of these men, and never to negociate with them for the sale of early proofs of any work over which you have control; but to treat, on all occasions, with some respectable American publishing house, and with such an establishment only.[3]

Our common interest in this subject, and my advocacy of it, single-handed,[4] on every occasion that has presented itself during my absence from Europe, form my excuse for addressing you.

And I am,

Faithfully yours,

CHARLES DICKENS[5]

and Marryat's *Poor Jack*; Vols II and III, 1841, after completing *Old Curiosity Shop*, pirated *Barnaby Rudge* and *The Pic Nic Papers*; for the plans the *New World* announced in May 42, see *To* Mackenzie, 1 Sep, *fn.* Having soon found serial publication too slow, and keen to have complete novels in print ahead of pirating firms such as Harper & Brothers, the *New World* (and to a lesser extent *Brother Jonathan*, e.g. with Bulwer's *Zanoni*) issued them as "Extras", consisting of 16, 32 or 48 closely printed 4to pages (often at as little as ten cents a copy, thus easily underselling Harper's dollar edns). For the speed with which the *New World* produced *American Notes*, see *To* Chapman, 15 Oct, *fn.* The craze for these papers was at its height at the time of CD's visit; their speedy decline began in 1843, when the postal authorities imposed pamphlet rates on the "Extras".

[1] Doubtless CD had Park Benjamin (see *To* Forster, ?30 or 31 Aug) most in mind.

[2] See, for instance, the *New World*, 12 Feb (*To* Forster, 14 Feb, *fn*).

[3] Thackeray, in the postscript of a letter to Chapman & Hall of 23 July 42, wrote: "I have received Dickens' suckular and shall be delighted to act against the Americans in any way he thinks fit" (*Letters and Private Papers of W. M. Thackeray*, ed. G. N. Ray, II, 66). But by 19 Jan 43 CD apparently did not know that he had gained even one English writer's support (*To* Mrs Trollope, that day). He himself took the extreme course of not dealing even with his "respectable" publishers Lea & Blan-

chard (see 28 Dec)—and was given credit for his consistency in the *New World*, 19 Nov.

[4] CD is forgetting, it seems, Cornelius Mathews's impassioned plea for international copyright in his speech at the New York Dinner (see *To* Forster, 24 Feb, *fn* p. 84).

[5] The reception of this circular in England was favourable. The *Examiner*, *Literary Gazette* and *New Monthly* supported it; the *Morning Chronicle* found the "pretence" of the Boston Convention that English books had to be revised, in order to modify any non-American sentiments, "unrivalled in the annals of hypocrisy". The *Athenæum* approved of CD's "straightforward and hearty" opposition to "the disgraceful practice" of the American pirates, though it did not see clearly "the good that would result even from a general adoption of the proposed measures". American comment was mainly hostile. J. S. Bartlett (an Englishman) showed his approval of the circular in the *Albion* (see 6 Sep); but the *New World*, recognizing the references to itself, was incensed (see *To* Forster, ?30 or 31 Aug and *fn*); the *Boston Courier* (2 Aug) hoped "that the two countries will not become involved in a bloody war on this subject"; the *Boston Atlas* (quoted in the *New World*, 13 Aug) thought CD's letter "impolitic, in bad taste and bad temper, and will do more to injure both Mr. Dickens and his cause, than anything he has ever done"; for the view of the *American Traveller*, see p. 257. In

To [W. C. MACREADY], 7 JULY 1842*

MS Morgan Library. Endorsed on outside in CD's hand: "Affidavit | of | Charles
Dickens. *Address:* Both tone of letter and Macready's diary entry for 9 July, "A
very amusing letter from Dickens" (*Diaries*, II, 179), point to him, not his wife, as
recipient.

*a*Charles Dickens*a* of No. 1 Devonshire Terrace York Gate Regents Park in
the County of Middlesex Gentleman, Maketh oath and saith, That this Deponent
hath been for many years last past in the custom and habit of making certain
annual visits (to wit in the months of August, September and October) to a
certain seaside dipping, bathing, or watering-place, much frequented by individuals of a lone and quiet temper, and by certain virtuous and monastic fishermen; as also by a gloomy and thoughtful race much given to contemplation and
retirement, and commonly known as The Preventive Service[1]—to wit, the
Port, Landing, Village, hamlet, or town of Broadstairs in the County of Kent.
And this Deponent saith that the said Port, Landing, Village, hamlet, or town of
Broadstairs in the said county, was and is, and to the best of this Deponent's
judgment and belief will always be, the chosen resort and retreat of jaded intellect and exhausted nature; being, as this Deponent further saith it is, far removed
from the sights and noises of the busy world,[2] and filled with the delicious mur-
mur and repose of the broad ocean; the said broad ocean being (as this Deponent
further saith and fearlessly asserteth) the finest feature (when you are off it) in
the whole creation.

And this Deponent further saith That he has been informed and verily
believes that there are, roaming the world, and in particular the dominions of
her Gracious Majesty Victoria, By the Grace of God, Queen Defender of the
Faith and so forth; certain persons who by reason of their inability to appreciate
the many excellencies and unequalled beauties of the said Port, landing, village,
hamlet, or town of Broadstairs, do falsely and heretically decry the same; and
do annually repair to a certain sty, hole, den, and sink of deep disgust called
Eastbourne,[3] which, as this Deponent hath been informed and verily believes

several papers comment was confused
through the association with CD's text of
various forged paragraphs (see *To* Forster,
?30 or 31 Aug, *fn*). R. H. Dana, meditating,
after the publication of *American Notes*, on
CD's whole management of the international copyright question, considered it
"ill judged" and his letters on the subject
"careless, pretentious, & |with a kind of
off-hand, slang-ey, defying tone, which a
man with a well-balanced mind & the
delicate perceptions & self respect of a
gentleman could not fall into" (*Journal*, ed.
R. F. Lucid, I, 103).

aa Written larger than the rest.

[1] i.e. coastguards.

[2] Perhaps an echo of Tennyson, "The
Gardener's Daughter", "Not wholly in the
busy world". Broadstairs, although less
than two miles from Ramsgate, and from

Margate, had remained a quiet, secluded
village. Its population in 1841 was 1,500.
"Punch's Guide to the Watering Places"
(*Punch*, 30 July 42) described it as "a
shrine to which certain fashionable people
make a yearly pilgrimage, in order to do
penance"; "originally colonized by genteel
emigrants from Margate, who were driven
thither by the migratory hordes from
Tooley Street. | Its principal attractions
consist of a black wooden pier with white
rails [*the pier Prout was sketching in Sep 40:
see Vol. II, p. 123*], and a solitary pony."
(For CD's numerous visits, see Vol. I, p.
303*n*).

[3] The Macreadys' favourite seaside
place. Macready joined his wife and children there for three short spells during the
month 6 July to 6 Aug 42.

is a desolate and desert place, inhabited by gulls and sea-Mews, and excessively geological—in points of flints and chalk. And this Deponent further saith that the aforesaid sty, hole, den, and sink of deep disgust called Eastbourne, is, and was, and to the best of this Deponent's judgment and belief will always be, a kind of English Saint Helena, to which stern husbands banish their unwilling and reluctant wives. And that so great and manifold are the horrors of the aforesaid sty, hole, den, and sink of deep disgust called Eastbourne, that persons there confined grow desperate, as was distinctly proved not long ago (to wit last year) in a case which came within the observation and happened within the knowledge of this Deponent (to wit, the case of Catherine Macready) who being tolerably lodged therein, and furthermore supplied with meat, and drink, and clothes, did nevertheless grow weary of her life,[1] and being frantic did indite and send strange letters to her Lord and Master, to wit, threatening and Swing-like[2] letters, demanding her release on pain of Death and Suicide. And this Deponent further saith that he distinctly remembereth having heard the aforesaid Catherine vehemently protest that if she had not been brought up to London, she would have come without being sent for; and that if there had been no boat, or coach, or other carriage, she would have walked on foot; with other strong and terrible expressions, whereat the hair of this Deponent stood on end, and all bystanders shuddered. Wherefore this Deponent Saith—That the aforesaid sty, hole, den, and sink of deep disgust called Eastbourne, is in no wise comparable, and can by no credible and reasoning persons be likened unto, the delightful and un-equalled Port, landing, village, hamlet or town of Broadstairs, which this Deponent doth assert to be (in the words of Thryza to Isambiel) *a*"A token and a tone"*a*—for evermore.[3]

CHARLES DICKENS

Sworn before me, at the
Mansion House, London, this
Seventh day of July, in the
year of our Lord one thousand
eight hundred and forty Two
John Pirie[4] Mayor

[1] During Mrs Macready's 1841 visit to Eastbourne Macready seems only to have been free to join her once—20–23 June (*Reminiscences*, ed. F. Pollock, 1875, II, 179).

[2] Threatening desperate action (derived from the fictitious Captain Swing: *OED*). Also used by CD in *To* Landor, 26 July 40 (II, 106).

[3] In a case recently heard before the Marlborough Street magistrates, and reported at length in the *Morning Chronicle* of 1 July, Frederick Isambiel, former valet to Lord Littleton, had brought a summons against Miss Thyrza (mis-spelt "Thryza" by CD) Sumner for "having torn his coat" (when attempting to kiss him), and for

having "so beset him with her matrimonial advances, as to render it necessary for him to seek the protection of the law". He produced three letters from her—two of them almost worthy of Fanny Squeers. The second (containing the words here quoted by CD) declared: "Dearest, dearest Isambiel—My spirits are now at the warmest ebb. This always occurs at the sound of thy sweet and lovely name. . . . I see thee not—I hear thee not—yet now I am so rapt up in thee, thou art my only — — . . . My voice shall with thy future vision blend, and reach into thy heart when mine is cold, a token and a tone. I should very much like to be mistress of an hotel. The only man in business I should like to

To LADY HOLLAND, 8 JULY 1842*

MS The Earl of Ilchester.

Private and Confidential.   1 Devonshire Terrace. | Eighth July 1842.

Dear Lady Holland.

You will, I know, forgive me for writing, before coming to see you; as the subject on which I am going to beg your kind influence, is one which admits of no delay.

Pehaps you are aware that the Courier Newspaper (formerly on the Whig side, and recently Conservative)[1] is just now dead, and incorporated with the Globe.[2] If I had been aware of its condition (which my absence from Europe prevented) I should have put myself into instant communication with the leaders of the Liberal party, and made proposals to them for saving the Paper—nailing the true colours to the mast—and fighting the battle staunchly, and to the Death. I need scarcely say, that if I threw my small person into the breach, and wrote for the paper (literary articles as well as political) I could command immediate attention; while the influence I have with Booksellers and Authors would give me a better chance of stamping it with a new character, and securing for it, after a reasonable trial, good advertisements, than almost any other man could possess.

I am assured, beyond all doubt, that the premises and types and so forth, are still to be disposed of—and I am strongly inclined to establish a new evening paper, on the right side, in its place. But of course it would be impossible for me to do this, unless I were assured of the countenance, and could receive direct pecuniary assistance from the Members of the late Government or from the Reform Club.[3] It has occurred to me that the only straight-forward and

marry is one who keeps an hotel. I am fit for it, I can assure you. . . . | Thyrza Sumner". Replying, Isambiel reproached her for her "indelicate hint" that they should keep a hotel together. She answered sternly: "Isambiel—For defamation of character duty and aunt require you to make an apology. . . . I have a gentleman who will meet you in honour of my character . . .—in a duel. If you do not recal what you have said about me, my friend will meet you, and you will receive the death-blow, or he does. . . . Thyrza". The case was dismissed.

[4] John Pirie (1781–1851), a merchant ship-broker and ship owner; made a baronet 13 Apr 42 because a Prince of Wales was born while he was Lord Mayor.

[1] The *Courier*, an evening paper, had had a chequered political career. Founded in 1792, to popularize the "Ideas of 1789", it was originally Whig, but thereafter generally associated with the Govt in

power. After a long Tory allegiance 1807–30, it came virtually into Brougham's hands with the accession of the Whigs in 1830. S. L. Blanchard, editor 1837–9, a strong Whig, resigned when, after a change of proprietors, it became Conservative. Its last issue was on 6 July 42.

[2] Also an evening paper, founded 1813, and avowedly Whig since 1830, when Palmerston became its special patron. During the 1820s it had absorbed the *Traveller, Statesman, Evening Chronicle, Nation,* and *Argus;* but there is no further evidence of its now absorbing the *Courier.* Its editor was E. R. Moran (see Vol. I, p. 185*n*).

[3] Founded in 1836. Several of the founder-members had held office in Whig Govts, the Trustees including the Earl of Mulgrave, the Earl of Durham and Richard Ellice the elder; and the Committee, Edward Stanley and Daniel O'Connell.

short course of proceeding (and despatch is of great importance, as the things are about to be put up to auction, which I would prevent, if possible) is, to ascertain the sentiments of the leading members of the party, with as little delay as possible—and that, through you, if you would kindly make known the contents of this note—say to Lord Melbourne and Lord Lansdowne.[1] With the latter I would communicate myself,[2] and with Mr. Stanley[3] and one or two more, did I not feel that, asking your kind interposition at all, I had better leave the matter entirely in your hands.

I feel a perfect confidence that I could establish an organ for the party which would do good service, and which would have the inestimable advantage of taking a certain position at once, instead of struggling for years before it became known. Knowing how strongly you sympathize with the views I am so earnestly desirous of advocating, I can scarcely think that I need offer you any lengthened apology—even for this long trespass on your time and patience.

Always Dear Lady Holland
Yours faithfully and obliged

The Lady Holland. CHARLES DICKENS

To SIR JOHN EASTHOPE,[4] [JULY 1842]

Mention in next.

To THOMAS BEARD, 11 JULY 1842

MS Dickens House. *Address:* Thomas Beard Esquire | 42 Portman Place | Edgeware Road.

Devonshire Terrace. | Eleventh July 1842.

My Dear Beard.

Alfred has written me to say that the Line of Railway he is employed on, being nearly finished,[5] the Head thereof[6] (under whom he has been some Years) has

---

[1] The leaders of the Whig Opposition. Henry Petty-Fitzmaurice, 3rd Marquess of Lansdowne (1780–1863; *DNB*), had been President of the Council through most of the previous ministry.

[2] CD had met Lord Lansdowne when he first dined at Holland House, on 12 Aug 38 (Holland House Dinner Book, MS BM); and on 6 Dec 41 a visit to Bowood, Lansdowne's house, had been suggested by Rogers, but CD evidently declined (MS Huntington). He had met Melbourne at a dinner party of Lady Holland's in South Street on 22 May 41 (MS *ibid.*).

[3] Edward John Stanley (1802–69; *DNB*), afterwards 2nd Baron Stanley of Alderley. Under-Secretary to the Home Department during the previous Whig Ministry 1834–41. For his earlier help to CD, see Vol. I, pp. 451 and 533; and for Mrs Stanley's inviting CD to dinner, Vol. II, p. 284.

[4] Sir John Easthope (1784–1865; *DNB*), proprietor of the *Morning Chronicle*, from which CD had resigned Nov 36: see Vol. I, pp. 123*n* and 196. Made a baronet in Aug 41 for services to the Liberal party and for advocacy of a war policy in Syria.

[5] The track of the Birmingham and Derby Junction between Whitacre and Birmingham, on which Alfred was working, had been opened on 10 Feb; the goods station and connecting branch were still incomplete.

[6] The chief engineer was John Cass Birkinshaw (1811–67), Robert Stephenson's first articled pupil at Newcastle; engineer of the London end of the London and Birmingham line 1835, of the Birmingham and Derby line 1837–42, and of many other railways projected but not made.

given him a letter of Introduction to Mr. Locke:[1] engineer of the Southampton —Havre and Rouen—and divers other works. He has it in his head (with some reason I dare say) that a word from Sir John Easthope would do his business— and has written to me for a Letter of Introduction to the Baronet; which I have given him.[2]

If it comes in your way, to help him or keep him in mind at the right time, I know you will do so.

You are acquainted with the business that kept me away from the Chronicle last Saturday.[3]—George Cruikshank came home in my phaeton, on his head— to the great delight of the loose Midnight Loungers in Regent Street. He was last seen, taking Gin with a Waterman.

Faithfully Yours always

Thomas Beard Esquire   CHARLES DICKENS

P.S. Directly I have concluded the Broadstairs arrangements, I will send you timely notice. Prepare the Baronet for an enormous[4] absence. No half measures.

---

[1] Joseph Locke (1805–60; *DNB*), distinguished railway engineer. Articled to George Stephenson 1823 and helped him construct the Manchester and Liverpool line (opened 1830). Constructed the London and Southampton line 1836–40, besides other lines in Britain; the Paris and Rouen line 1841–3; Rouen and Le Havre 1843; and lines in Spain and Germany. FRS 1838. MP Honiton, Devon, 1847–60. President of the Institution of Civil Engineers 1858 and 1859. Designed the "Crewe engine". *The Times* obituary, 21 Sep 60, bracketed him with Stephenson and Brunel.

[2] Easthope was a Director of the London and South Western Railway: hence Alfred's request.

[3] The dinner at Greenwich on 9 July, organized by Forster, to celebrate CD's return. Hood described it on 11 July in a letter to Mrs Elliot (wife of William Elliot, MD, the Hoods' doctor since 1835). He was to have taken the chair, but was not well enough, and Marryat presided; Jerdan was vice-chairman, and the 27 present included Forster, Ainsworth, Maclise, Stanfield, Cruikshank, Cattermole, Elliotson, Milnes, Procter, Barham, Mahony, Charles and Tom Landseer, and Dr Quin. Barham sang a Robin Hood ballad and Cruikshank a "Burlesque Ballad of Lord H——". "Well," Hood went on, "we drank 'the Boz,' with a delectable clatter, which drew from him a good warm hearted speech, in which he hinted the great advantage of going to America for the pleasure of coming back again—& pleasantly described the embarrassing attentions of the Transatlantickers, who made his private house & private cabin particularly public. He looked very well" (MS Yale; *Letters of Thomas Hood*, ed. Peter Morgan, Toronto, 1973, p. 486). Thackeray had been invited, but was in Ireland at the time. Edwin Landseer had been invited too, and wrote to Maclise on 5 July: "I have unfortunately lost Forster's Card. Will you see him and pray express my sorrow at not being able to accompany you to Whitebait and Dickens. . . . (Between you and I) let me propose another welcome home to Boz, with this difference—we will take some Women with us. Mrs. N [*Caroline Norton*] and perhaps another to meet Mrs. Boz as well as *C.D.* C.N. tells me she shall be charmed to go—and I will ask dear old Rogers to be of our party" (MS Private). Hood wrote to CD on 11 July with the further suggestion: "Mrs. Hood thinks there ought to be a Ladies' Dinner to Mrs. Dickens— I think *she* wants to go to Greenwich seeing how much good it has done me" (MS Huntington; *Letters of Thomas Hood*, ed. P. Morgan, p. 490).

[4] Written three times as large as the rest.

To MESSRS JOSEPH ELLIS & SON,[1] 11 JULY 1842*

MS Free Library of Philadelphia.

Devonshire Terrace | Eleventh July 1842.

Gentlemen.

If you will have the goodness to send me your last year's Bill, I shall be glad to settle it.[2]

And let me have, if you please, four dozen of Sparkling Champagne, and six dozen of the Metternich Hock—three dozen yellow seal, and three red. I have a dinner party on Saturday,[3] and am out of both Wines. I want them, therefore, with all speed.

Faithfully Yours

Messrs. Ellis and Son.   CHARLES DICKENS

To LADY HOLLAND, 11 JULY 1842*

MS The Earl of Ilchester.

Devonshire Terrace. | Eleventh July 1842.

Dear Lady Holland.

I cannot tell you how very much obliged to you I feel, for your kindness and interest in the matter in which I sought your valuable aid. Nor can I thank you sufficiently, believe me.

I think it very possible that Mr. Stanley is right[4]—though we must not forget that in such questions, the Liberal party have very seldom made a mistake on the Bold side.

You embolden me to ask another favor of you. It is, that whenever you happen to see those with whom you spoke, again, you will give them to understand (if they do not already know) that my idea originated in no thought of personal advantage; and that at the very best, I should have been, in a pecuniary sense, a loser for many years;—besides undertaking a very serious amount of mental labour, as I could not have afforded to desist from my other pursuits. I should not have hinted at this fact while there remained any chance of trying the project, but there being none, I feel it but justice to myself to say that much.

The notion of this newspaper was bred in me by my old training—I was as

---

[1] Wine Merchants, of Hill Street, Richmond (founded 1831 by Joseph Ellis, proprietor of the Star & Garter Hotel, Richmond); later, Charles Ellis & Co., of Brickhill Lane, London. For CD's subsequent relations with Joseph Ellis's two sons, Joseph and Charles, see N. C. Peyrouton in *D*, LVII (1961), 105–111.

[2] There appears to have been no bill to settle. CD's account-book (MS Messrs Coutts) shows a payment of £75.8.8 to Ellis & Sons in July 40, and of £74.2.11 in Aug 41. The next payments to them were £33.2.6 in Jan 43 and £4 in Feb 43—fol-

lowed by £104 in June 44. (Some of these amounts probably covered CD's Star & Garter entertaining.) Meanwhile he was dealing with another wine merchant, D. Macfarlane of 13 Cecil Street, Strand, to whom he paid £81.13.0 in Sep 41, £59.12.0 in Jan 42, and, between Mar 43 and Apr 44, about £125 in four payments.

[3] His guests included Ainsworth (invited 7 July) and Marryat (see 16 July).

[4] Stanley had clearly said that the *Courier* could not rely on Liberal financial support: see *To* Mitton, 11 July, postscript.

well acquainted with the management of one,[1] some years ago, as an Engineer is, with the Steam engine. And I always feel when I take up a paper now (which is not often) that the subjects which all the writers leave unhandled (except Fonblanque, who is another Swift)[2] are exactly the questions which interest the people, and concern their business and bosoms,[3] most.

I shall have the pleasure of calling in South Street on Thursday Morning.[4] Meantime Mrs. Dickens begs me "to thank Lady Holland for her kind remembrance of her, and to say how happy she feels, now that she is at home again." —We found our children, thank God, quite well; but the eldest fell into convulsions soon after our arrival—from being, as he said, "too glad"—and was in a dangerous state all that night. He has since quite recovered.

Dear Lady Holland. Yours always faithfully
And Truly obliged

The Lady Holland.   CHARLES DICKENS

[a]P.S. I send with this—I brought them home from America, for the purpose—a book of American Poetry, in which Mr. Longfellow's pieces are very good,[5] and an Eagle's Feather from the Great Falls at Niagara.—I hope the regard and respect which accompany them, may give them a value they have not in themselves.[a]

To MISS C. LE GRAND,[6] 11 JULY 1842

Text from N, 1, 462.

London, 1 Devonshire Terrace, York Gate, Regent's Park
Monday, Eleventh July, 1842

Mr. Charles Dickens presents his compliments to Miss Le Grand, and begs to assure her that he is much flattered and pleased by her obliging note; and that it will afford him much pleasure to accept the Dedication she does him the honor to offer.

---

[1] Probably not the *Morning Chronicle* but the *Mirror of Parliament*, edited by his uncle, J. H. Barrow, on whose staff he had worked for about four years in the early 30s.

[2] He was noted for his brilliant satirical wit. In his *Examiner* leaders 1841-2, he poured scorn on Peel, his Corn Law policy, and the Tories.

[3] Cf. Dedication to Bacon's *Essays*.

[4] This call was shortly followed by an invitation to dinner; the Holland House Dinner Book (MS BM) shows that CD dined there on 22 July, with the Duke and Duchess of Sutherland and their daughter Lady Elizabeth Leveson Gower, Lord Lansdowne, Lord Melbourne, "Mr Ponsonby" (a son of the Earl of Bessborough), "Mr Parker" (probably John Parker, a Whig and MP for Sheffield), Lady Caroline Barrington (daughter of Lord Grey) and her daughter Mary, and Henry Luttrell.

[a][a] Written at the top of first page above the address.

[5] Presumably Rufus Griswold's *Poets and Poetry of America*, 1842, which included, among other poems of Longfellow's, "The Village Blacksmith" (1841) and "Excelsior" (1842). For Forster's review of the volume, see *To* Poe, 6 Mar, *fn.*

[6] Unidentified.

To THOMAS MITTON, 11 JULY 1842

MS Huntington Library.

Devonshire Terrace. | Monday Eleventh July | 1842.

My Dear Mitton

Have you had the counterpart of the Inclosed ?[1]—I have not given it the most absorbing attention possible, certainly; but I can't understand it for the Life of me.

I will come to you on Thursday between One and Two, if that will suit you.

Always Faithfully
CD.

Thomas Mitton Esquire.

(Over)

They can't stand the Money for the Newspaper. I will shew you the letters thereanent.—Before I go to Broadstairs, I should like (if your household arrangements should be completed before I leave town) to have a chop in the swell first floor.[2]

[1] Not identified; but just possibly connected with the following extraordinary letter from Mitton to Forster of 6 July 42: "Sir | I can scarce bring myself to a state sufficiently calm to enable me to put to paper those sentiments by which I am actuated in now addressing you and unfortunately the conduct you have been guilty of toward me being (as I am fully persuaded) only part and parcel of your regular course I cannot help feeling that little or no impression is to be made upon you by any thing which may now be said by me—Nevertheless with this conviction before me I cannot pass over without one word of complaint or remonstrance the injuries you have *endeavoured* to inflict upon me because in giving vent to my indignation I do to a certain extent relieve my bosom of part of the weight with which it is now encumbered—That you should have tried to injure me with one for whom (as I will emphatically assert you well knew) I entertain the most sincere friendship that one man can do toward another and that too by the meanest and most despicable of systems I cannot refrain from denouncing as an Act unworthy of any being save such as yourself—which to my humble opinion is saying as much as Language can convey.— | From all I have ever heard and what little I have ever seen of you I cannot but regret most fervently that any Friend of mine should have had the misfortune to make such an acquaintance but the time may still come and I sincerely hope and trust most speedily when the Eyes of that friend shall be open and he be enabled to read your true Character—that he should not have done so long ago is a circumstance quite marvelous [*thus*] to many who enjoy Mr. Dickens' friendship as well as myself. | I am above—in my own Opinion—(beneath perhaps in yours) the ridiculous absurdity of requiring satisfaction in the mode in which that term is now (mis)-understood and certainly as none such would be afforded me by such a sanguinary farce I shall for the present put up with the Annoyance you have occasioned me—and shall be pleased if chance never throws [me] in your way— | Thomas Mitton | J. Forster Esq." (MS Huntington). As CD's solicitor, Mitton may frequently have resented the important part Forster played (probably rather ostentatiously) in business matters with CD's publishers; that he was jealous and touchy in other contexts can be inferred from *To* Mitton, 4 Apr 42. But the immediate cause of this outburst is unknown.

[2] CD's letter seems to have been written at three different times (first paragraph and postscript with a thick nib; what comes between with a thin).

To JOHN OVERS,[1] 11 JULY 1842*

Text from typescript, Huntington Library.

Devonshire Terrace, | Eleventh July 1842.

Dear Mr. Overs,

I am truly glad to hear that you are so much better; and am rejoiced (though not surprised) by this new instance of Dr Elliotson's kindness, and surpassing goodness of heart.[2]

I shall not fail to tell Mr Ainsworth that you mentioned his very considerate reply to your note,[3] and I shall add that I feel personally obliged to him for it.

I am usually at home every day between 11 and 12; and on Sunday, as of old, am almost always visible at that time. I shall be very glad to see you whenever you like to come.

Always faithfully yours,

Mr J. A. Overs.   CHARLES DICKENS

To H. P. SMITH,[4] 11 JULY 1842*

MS Miss Mabel Hodge.

Devonshire Terrace. | Eleventh July 1842.

My Dear Smith.

I hoped to have been able to come to you today, with Mrs. Dickens, who bears this. But the correspondence I have to get through just now (to say nothing of any American Sketches that may be just shaping themselves in my head) is so preposterously enormous that even on this sunny day I am forced to stay at home until dinner time—though by Noon I was in the desperate condition of Jack in the spelling book, who was also a Martyr to all work and no play.

I was home within the half Year. Is it necessary for me to make any formal application to the Directors for the return of the balance of the sum paid for extra premium[5]—or is this note to you enough?

If it will be necessary for me to come to the office, I am ready.

Always My Dear Smith | Cordially Yours

H. P. Smith Esquire   CHARLES DICKENS

---

[1] John A. Overs (1808–44), cabinet maker: see Vol. I, p. 504*n*.

[2] For Elliotson's treating Overs in Aug 41 at CD's request, see Vol. II, pp. 362, 368, 369.

[3] Possibly the reply (undated) quoted in S. M. Ellis, *W. H. Ainsworth and his Friends*, 1911, I, 393: "If I can strike out some plan, by which I can avail myself of your talents, I will gladly do so . . . I hope to use some of the shorter papers, and in earnest of my good wishes and intentions

send you the enclosed". *Ainsworths Magazine* was launched Feb 42; but nothing by Overs has been found in it.

[4] Henry Porter Smith (1797–1880), actuary of the Eagle Life Assurance Co.: see Vol. II, p. 251*n*.

[5] Payment of an additional premium of £30 on 4 Jan 42 covered CD's trip to America "for a term not exceeding Twelve Calendar Months" (endorsement of his original Eagle policy of 17 July 38: MS Mr C. C. Dickens).

To R. MONCKTON MILNES, 13 JULY 1842*

MS Private.

Devonshire Terrace | Thirteenth July 1842.

My Dear Milnes

Do you dine with me on Saturday at 6,—or are you otherwise engaged?
A word in answer.

Always Faithfully Yours

Richard Monckton Milnes Esquire   CHARLES DICKENS

To H. P. SMITH, 13 JULY 1842

Extract in Maggs Bros catalogue No. 486 (1926); *MS* 1 p.; dated Devonshire
Terrace, 13 July 42.

My rates and taxes being all paid, I beg to vote for Richmond—a Plumper.[1]
Richmond, Rustic Refreshment, and the rippling river!

I have already begun working like a dray-horse;[2] to the great astonishment of
my red face,[3] which is turning white with wonder.

To T. J. THOMPSON, 13 JULY 1842

Mention in list of letters from CD to Thompson made by his son-in-law Wilfrid
Meynell; *MS* 1 p.; from Devonshire Terrace, 13 July 42.[4]

---

[1] Vote given solely to one candidate, instead of to two or more (*OED*).

[2] He had probably already written his Introductory Chapter (see p. 270) and was now working on *American Notes*, Ch. 1 (by 19 July Ch. 2 was finished: see *To* Beard, that day). Before starting work on the main book he no doubt reclaimed from Forster the letters on which the book was to be largely based. A number of people had heard Forster read these letters aloud —or seen them. Crabb Robinson noted in his diary, 20 June 42: "I went after breakfasting with my brother, self-invited, to Forster's to hear him read to Kenyon etc., some of Dickens's letters from America —better letters I never heard read. The descriptions most animated, satire and sublime painting admirably intermixed. I was gratified by finding that he had not been deceived by the gross flattery of the people; he sees through them. He confirms my dislike of the people. Their want of honesty is not so flagrant as their grossness of manners, but it is as certain. . . . These letters must form the nucleus of a work on America which might be one of the most efficient ever written" (*H. C. Robinson on Books and their Writers*, ed. E. J. Morley, 1938, II, 618). On 18 Aug 42, almost certainly as a result of letters shown him earlier by Forster, D'Orsay wrote to Lord Lichfield: "You are soon going to have Dickens' work on America it will probably be the best book he has written, to judge from his letters which I have read" (W. Connely, *Count D'Orsay*, 1952, p. 377). Harriet Martineau apparently heard about the letters from Crabb Robinson, and clearly did not wholly approve: on the publication of *American Notes* she was "rejoiced" to find its tone more moderate than "his speeches, and conversation, and letters" (*to* Crabb Robinson, 29 Oct 42; MS Dr Williams's Library).

[3] Sunburnt from the voyage home, no doubt.

[4] Presumably this was one of several of CD's letters known to have been lost in 1947 at the time of the Exhibition celebrating the centenary of Alice Meynell's birth.

To LORD BROUGHAM, 14 JULY 1842*

MS Brotherton Library, Leeds.

Devonshire Terrace. | Fourteenth July 1842.

Dear Lord Brougham.

In reply to your kind note, let me say, that I shall be disengaged next Saturday Week, or on the Wednesday following that Saturday. I need scarcely add that I shall be delighted to have an opportunity of seeing you before you leave town.—I go to the seaside on the First of August.

Faithfully Yours always

The Lord Brougham.   CHARLES DICKENS

To H. P. SMITH, 14 JULY 1842

MS Huntington Library.

Devonshire Terrace. | Thursday Fourteenth July 1842.

My Dear Smith.

The cheque safely received.[1] As you say—it would be cheap at any money. My devotion to the fine arts renders it impossible for me to cash it. I have therefore ordered it to be framed and glazed.[2]

I am really grateful to you for the interest you take in my proceedings. Next time I come into the City, I will shew you my introductory chapter to the American book.[3] It may seem to prepare the reader for a much greater amount of slaughter than he will meet with; but it is *honest* and *true*.[4] Therefore my hand does not shake.

[1] A refund on his premium to the Eagle Assurance Co. (see 11 July).

[2] Smith, when lending this letter to Mamie and Georgina, explained this as an allusion "to the stamp of the office upon the cheque, which was . . . 'almost a work of art'—a truculent-looking eagle seated on a rock and scattering rays over the whole sheet" (1842 "Narrative", MDGH, I, 54).

[3] The chapter quoted in F, III, viii, 284–6, but not included in *American Notes*. The MS, headed by CD "CHAPTER THE FIRST | INTRODUCTORY. | AND NECESSARY TO BE READ", survives in the Forster Collection (V & A), bound in with the MS of *American Notes* as Ch. 1. On 29 July CD showed the chapter to Macready, who wrote in his diary: "*I do not like it*" (*Diaries*, II, 181). On 14 Sep, when nearing the end of the book, CD began to think it over (*To* Forster, that day). At a conference with Forster in Oct, he reluctantly agreed to omit it (*To* Forster, 10 Oct, *fn*). For the omission's upsetting his chapter numbers, see *To* Mitton, 4 Sep, *fn*. We follow throughout the numbering of the printed text in one-volume edns, unless otherwise stated.

[4] It opened militantly: "I have placed the foregoing title at the head of this page, because I challenge and deny the right of any person to pass judgment on this book, or to arrive at any reasonable conclusion in reference to it, without first being at the trouble of becoming acquainted with its design and purpose." It was simply a record of "impressions", with "not a grain of any political ingredient in its whole composition". He knew that it would offend the many Americans "so tenderly and delicately constituted, that they [could not] bear the truth in any form"; and he did not need the "gift of prophecy" to foretell that those "aptest to detect malice" and lack of gratitude for the welcome he had received would be "certain native journalists, veracious and gentlemanly, who were at great pains to prove to [him] . . . that the aforesaid welcome was utterly worthless". But of the view of "intelligent, reflecting, and educated Americans" he had no fear. He had gone to America resolved "to do

Best loves and regards—"Certainly" to the Richmondian intentions.[1]

Always Faithfully Your friend

H. P. Smith Esquire

CD.

To MRS DAVID C. COLDEN, 15 JULY 1842

Photograph Dickens House. *Address:* By The Cunard Steamboat Viâ Halifax | Mrs. Colden | 28 Laight Street | Hudson Square | New York | U.S.

Fifteenth July 1842.

My Dear Mrs. Colden.

It is more clear to me than ever that Kate is as near being a Donkey, as one of that sex whose luminary and sun you are, *can* be. You will immediately recall, when I express this—not strong, but merely expressive opinion,—that she has written about Great Westerns sailing on Fourteenths, and other impossibilities, when all reasoning beings know that this letter will come by the Cunard boat, and that the sixteenth is its day—at least I *think* it is: and any impression of mine is, I need not say, much better than a fact.[2]

We ought to have written you by the last boat,[3] and fully intended to have done so; but the thick throng of occupations which has continually beset me, has really, so far as I am concerned, deprived me of leisure to do anything I should have liked to do. And even now, in this Preface or Prologue to our future correspondence (in which I mean to shine very much) I have only time to be dull, and inclination to be bright.

How we enjoy our own home, and revel in everything connected wi[th][4] it; and how I every day resolve to go dreadfully to work directly after breakfas[t and][4] break my resolution in favor of some gentlemanly piece of vagabondism wit[h][4] Maclise and Forster (who, by the bye, are madly delighted with, and grateful for, th[e][4] Shaker Pipes)[5] or some most riotous game at trapbat and ball[6] in the Garden with the children—and how I played the accordion[7]

justice to the country", and expecting "greater things" than he found. Coming home "with a corrected and sober judgment", he felt "no less bound to do justice" to what he believed was "the truth". See also 20 Sep and 10 Oct, *fns*. (Emerson, after reading *American Notes*, commented in his journal, 25 Nov: "Truth is not his object for a single instant . . . As an account of America it is not [to] be considered for a moment . . . We can hear throughout every page the dialogue between the author and his publisher, 'Mr Dickens the book must be entertaining,—that is the essential point. Truth! damn truth' ": *Journals of R. W. Emerson*, ed. W. H. Gilman and J. E. Parsons, VIII, 222.)

[1] The trip to Richmond proposed to Smith on 13 July.

[2] It was the *Great Western* which sailed for New York on the 16th; no Cunard boat left that day. So CD was wrong too.

[3] The *Southerner* had left Liverpool for New York on 13 July; the *Palmyra* and the *Columbus* both on 11 July.

[4] Final letters are missing in 4 lines through tear at seal.

[5] Presumably some of the "trifling purchases of Shaker goods" made by CD when he visited the Shaker colony: see *To Granville, 2 June, fn*, and *American Notes*, Ch. 15.

[6] Trap-ball (a game dating from the early 14th century) was played with up to six or eight players a side. The ball was released to the batsman when a mechanism (the "trap") was struck by a bludgeon. He scored if he hit the ball between two boundaries; otherwise he was out. He could also be caught out, or got out by the return of the ball to the trap.

[7] See *To* Forster, 22 Mar.

perpetually on board ship (as I write the words, and remember that you never heard me perform on that instrument, my soul is filled with grief)—and established a select dinner party of four at the bottom of the table all the way home, who were called The United Vagabonds, of which honorable Society I was President[1]—are topics which I shall handle in my next. At present I will only add; hearing the Bellman[2] (an English Institution connected with the Post office, sweet Foreigner); that I wish you would come and live next door; for the best part of my heart is in Laight Street, and I find it difficult to get on without it.

God bless you—and—yes—and even—*Him*.[3] And *Them* too, for I never loved any people better. For which reason I am half mournfully, and wholly faithfully

Yours | Always | My Dear Mrs. Colden
CHARLES DICKENS

To GEORGE W. PUTNAM, [15 JULY 1842]

Extract in Putnam *to* Charles Sumner, 4 Aug 42 (MS Houghton Library, Harvard). *Date:* 15 July according to Putnam.

Asking Putnam to tell Sumner that he could rely on hearing from him in August;[4] *that they were* perfectly happy; *that he had not a moment for correspondence; and that Sumner was not to be alarmed at his silence. He had* found his children and friends quite well—thank God.[5]

To FREDERICK MARRYAT, 16 JULY 1842

MS Free Library of Philadelphia.

Devonshire Terrace | Sixteenth July 1842.

My Dear Marryatt.

Most unquestionably and undoubtedly I expect you at 6 to day—to dinner.[6] I should have sent you a reminder, but when the Invitation has been given at dinner time,[7] I have a delicacy in doing so, lest it should seem to intimate a suspicion that the Invited One was drunk!

Faithfully Yours always
CHARLES DICKENS

I think I can give you some Hock today[8] which will do your Leg good.

---

[1] For the voyage, see *To* Granville, 2 June, *fn*, and *American Notes*, Ch. 16.

[2] Letter-carriers ringing bells went on their rounds in London in the late afternoon, collecting letters at a penny more than the price of a letter posted at a Receiving Office.

[3] Written large.

[4] CD wrote to Sumner on 31 July.

[5] Though this was all that Putnam was instructed to tell Sumner, it seems more than likely that CD gave him some account of his homecoming. On 1 Aug a paragraph in the *Boston Daily Evening Transcript*, headed "Return of Boz: Dangerous excess of joy", gave news, supplied by "a friend" (who else if not Putnam?), of Charley's "transport of delight", his "delirium", and the calling in of "several physicians ... almost despairing of his recovery". For the only known accounts in CD's hand, see *To* Prescott, 31 July, and *To* Chapman, 3 Aug.

[6] Ainsworth had been invited too (see 7 July).

[7] Presumably at the Greenwich dinner, 9 July.

[8] Cf. his order to Ellis & Son, 11 July.

To THOMAS BEARD, 19 JULY 1842

MS Dickens House. *Address:* Thomas Beard Esquire | 42 Portman Place | Edgeware Road.

Devonshire Terrace. | Nineteenth July 1842

My Dear Beard.

I have been thinking about a breast of Venison next Sunday at half past 5 —and about making the Falstaffic F, read, in the evening,[1] our passage out,[2] which I have just finished writing—What do you say?

Kate begs her love to your sister Catherine, and desires me to say, that she counts upon seeing her, along with you. Mind you give that Message.

I have, at present, some Port Wine, called "Croft's London Particular".[3] It is worthy of notice.

The Broadstairs arrangements being now concluded, I beg to give you notice that I have taken last Year's house at Broadstairs,[4] for the months of August and September. Make your arrangements accordingly; but don't chip such a small piece as a week out of the Baronet. Cut a slice from him.

Always My Dear Beard | Heartily Yours

Thomas Beard Esquire.   CHARLES DICKENS

To LEIGH HUNT,[5] 19 JULY 1842

Facsimile *D*, XII (1916), 41.

Devonshire Terrace. | Nineteenth July 1842.

My Dear Hunt.

I don't know your friend—but to the best of my belief he is *not* a bookseller;[6] and therefore comes within the pale of human sympathies.

Although you didn't send me the Florentine Legend,[7] nor the Palfrey,[8] I have them both; and when that leg of Mutton *does* come off (Good God, how long it has been unamputated!) you shall write your name in them, for the sake of my Lawful Heir.

Your paper for Mrs. Macrone's book[9] was sent by me to Mr. Colburn, for

---

[1] According to Mrs Bridell Fox, Forster was "without exception the very best reader" she ever heard: "His voice was rich and melodious, and full of varied intonations. If any author was anxious to make a particularly good impression with his new play or poem on a select audience, it was Mr Fo[r]ster who was begged to read it aloud. He used no action whatever in his reading, and, with the exception of his eyes, which flashed and glowed under heavy beetling brows, he depended entirely on the modulation of his voice. This was quite different from Macready, whose manner of reading was emphatically that of the actor" (Richard and Edward Garnett, *Life of W. J. Fox*, 1910, p. 200).

[2] *American Notes*, Ch. 2—written, no doubt, with his letter to Forster of 17–30 Jan beside him.

[3] "London Particular" was normally a Madeira, not a Port (cf. *All the Year Round*, XII [1864], 153). The phrase was also commonly used of the thick dirty fog peculiar to London.

[4] 37 Albion Street, the house next to Barnes's Library.

[5] James Henry Leigh Hunt (1784–1859; *DNB*): see Vol. I, p. 341*n*.

[6] i.e. publisher.

[7] *A Legend of Florence*, 1840, produced at Covent Garden 7 Feb 40.

[8] *The Palfrey: a Love-Story of Old Times*, 1842.

[9] *The Pic Nic Papers*, edited by CD, and at last published Aug 41.

the Printer. Mr. Colburn exercised my duties, and accepted and rejected Papers at his most literary will and pleasure. I resisted this monstrous indecency in Mr. Colburn for a whole year; and then wrote him[1] that as it was a work of charity, and I wanted his money for Mrs. Macrone, I would give him his own way—which, if it were my own case, and I wanted bread, I would never do. I damned his eyes (by implication and construction) at the same time; and declined to hold any further correspondence with him, on any subject.

But if you wish me to apply to him, or any of his Myrmidons, for this particular paper, I will do so. We fell out about a paper of Landor's,[2] which he said "his literary friend had told him *wasnt Protestant*" ! ! ! ! ! ! ! ! ! !

Leigh Hunt Esquire

Faithfully Yours always
CHARLES DICKENS

To MISS JULIA PARDOE,[3] 19 JULY 1842

MS Harvard College Library.

1 Devonshire Terrace | York Gate Regents Park.
Nineteenth July 1842.

Dear Madam.

I beg to set you right on one point, in reference to the American Robbers, which perhaps you do not quite understand.

The existing law allows them to reprint any English book, without any communication whatever—with the author, or anybody else. My books have all been reprinted on these agreeable terms.—But *sometimes* when expectation is awakened there, about a book, before its publication, one firm of Pirates will pay a trifle to procure early proofs of it,[4] and get so much the start of the rest, as they can obtain by the time necessarily consumed in printing it. Directly it is printed, it is common property; and may be reprinted a thousand times.[5]

My circular only referred to such bargains as these.

I should add that I have no hope of the States doing Justice in this dishonest

---

[1] On 1 Apr 41: see Vol. II, p. 247.

[2] The main subject of CD's outburst of 1 Apr 41.

[3] Julia Pardoe (1806–62; *DNB*), travel-writer, popular historian and novelist. Author of a volume of poems at 13. Travelled abroad for her health, and had already published five successful books on Portugal, Turkey, Hungary and France 1836–9, besides tales and novels. Her historical books were mainly condensations of French memoirs. Granted a Civil List pension 1860.

[4] As Lea & Blanchard (whom CD now seems to be classing among the pirates) had done for *Oliver Twist*, *Old Curiosity Shop* and *Barnaby*.

[5] Probably Julia Pardoe had received some payment from Carey & Lea, and in response to CD's circular letter of 7 July had written to tell him so. They had published her *Traits and Traditions of Portugal*, 1834 (750 copies printed), *The Mardens, and the Daventrys, Tales*, 1835, and *The City of the Sultan*, 1838 (1000 of each printed): see *The Cost Book of Cary & Lea 1825–1838*, ed. David Kaser, Philadelphia, 1963. Yet it is less likely that she was paid for her novel *Speculation*, published by Harper & Brothers in 1834; and now *Brother Jonathan* was pirating her works: her poem "Blue-Stockings" on 23 Apr, "The Fatal Jest" on 28 May (both lifted from *Ainsworth's Magazine*); and *Hungarian Tales and Legends* appeared in a *Brother Jonathan* "Extra" on 17 Aug 42.

respect, and therefore do not expect to overtake these fellows—but we may cry "Stop Thief" nevertheless—especially as they wince and smart under it.

Faithfully Yours always

Miss Pardoe.   CHARLES DICKENS

To HORACE SMITH,[1] 19 JULY 1842*

MS Free Library of Philadelphia.

Devonshire Terrace | York Gate Regents Park.
Nineteenth July 1842.

My Dear Sir.

I am happy in the receipt of your kind note; and am very glad that we have become better acquainted through crying Stop Thief, together, in a crowd.

I believe there are hopes of throttling the continental Brigands.[2] I have no hope, whatever, of stopping American Piracy in this Generation.[3] But we may just as well serve the next, and assert our wrongs; and I *know* it galls them, and they wince.[4]—That should be a comfort to us. It is a very great one to me.

I am very glad to read that passage in your letter, wherein you say that you have nearly run your literary career. For as all rich men complain of being poor, I trust I may discern in this, the promise of a great many more books from your Pen.[5]

Believe me My Dear Sir

Very faithfully | Your friend

Horace Smith Esquire.   CHARLES DICKENS

---

[1] Horatio Smith, always known as Horace (1779–1849; *DNB*), poet and novelist, co-author with his brother James of *Rejected Addresses* 1812. Had met Keats, and his friends included Shelley, Leigh Hunt and Cobden. Settled in Brighton 1826 and entertained widely. CD may have met him through Miss Coutts or Rogers. On his death, Thackeray (who named Laura Pendennis after his youngest daughter) wrote of him as "that good serene old man who went out of the world in charity with all in it, . . . a true loyal Xtian man" (*to* Mrs Brookfield, 13 July 49: *Letters and Private Papers of W. M. Thackeray,* ed. G. N. Ray, II, 563).

[2] The meeting of 30 June led to no immediate legislation. But, under a new Act of 1844, a reciprocal copyright convention was signed with Prussia (1846); and, under an Act of 1852, with France (1852), and Belgium (1855), Spain (1857), and Sardinia (1861). Most European countries, including Britain, adopted the Berne copyright convention of 1887.

[3] CD's pessimism was more than justified. Considerable pressure for reciprocal copyright with Britain was exerted by American authors and publishers over the next 48 years: 12 bills were presented to Congress; numerous petitions signed; and several associations formed, of which the foremost was G. P. Putnam's American Publishers' Copyright League. But no legislation was passed until the Chase Copyright Act of 1891.

[4] Cf. *Hamlet,* II, iii, 237.

[5] *Rejected Addresses* had reached its 20th edn in 1841. Smith had also published 11 novels (of which *Brambletye House,* 1826, was the most popular and *Masaniello, an Historical Romance,* 1842, the latest), a collection of essays and verse, *Gaieties and Gravities,* 3 vols, 1825, and minor works. After July 42 he published three more novels, contributed two self-parodies to *Imitations of Celebrated Authors,* [ed. P. G. Patmore], 1844, and his *Poetical Works,* 2 vols, appeared in 1846.

To CHARLES SWAIN,[1] 20 JULY 1842*

MS Manchester Public Libraries.

London. 1 Devonshire Terrace.
York Gate, Regents Park.
Twentieth July 1842.

My Dear Sir.

Let me thank you with unaffected cordiality, for your beautiful book.[2] I have read it with great pleasure; and have derived many interesting and instructive thoughts from its teeming pages.[3]

For this, and for the valuable and welcome terms of your note, I am very much your debtor.

Always believe me | Faithfully Your friend

Charles Swain Esquire   CHARLES DICKENS

To THOMAS BEARD, 21 JULY 1842

MS Dickens House. *Address:* Thomas Beard Esquire | 42 Portman Place | Edgeware Road.

Devonshire Terrace. | Twenty First July 1842.

My Dear Beard.

I have consulted Mr. Groves of Charing Cross.[4] His suggestive mind gave birth to this remarkable expression—"then why not consider this here breast o' wenson, off—and let me git another prime 'un in good eatin' order for you, for Sunday week? What"—continued Mr. Groves—"is the hodds to a day?"

Mr. Groves slapped a piece of venison[5] as he spoke, with the palm of his hand; and plainly signified, by his manner no less than by his words, that this was wisdom. What do you say to it?—And what your sister?

Faithfully Always

CHARLES DICKENS

If I don't swim, this Autumn, may I—but we will not anticipate.

To DANIEL MACLISE, [24] JULY 1842*

MS Messrs Henry Sotheran Ltd. *Date:* Sunday was 24 July in 1842.

Devonshire Terrace
Sunday Twenty Third July | 1842.

My Dear Mac.

I only heard from Forster yesterday Evening that you were still unwell;[6] and

---

[1] Charles Swain (1801–74; *DNB*), poet. Began work at 15 as clerk in a dye-house; from *c.* 1830 an engraver in Manchester. Published *Metrical Essays*, 1827, *The Mind, and Other Poems*—his most ambitious work—1832, and several other vols of poems. Many of his songs were set to music.

[2] Almost certainly the illustrated edn (1841) of *The Mind, and Other Poems.*

[3] It is over 300 pages long and includes notes; "The Mind" itself, a long philosophical poem, has, besides notes, an "analysis" of each of its four Parts.

[4] Thomas Grove, 33 Charing Cross, fishmonger and venison dealer.

[5] Written "vension".

[6] For Maclise's depression and ill health earlier in the year, see *To* Maclise, ?30 or 31 Jan, *fn.*

had (with a tardy but most commendable wisdom) called in Blue Beard.[1]—
Send me word how you are, preparatory to my coming to see you between
2 and 4.

I say Seaside. So will Elliotson if you ask him. Tomorrow week, we shall
go down by way of Rochester and Canterbury. That's *your* road, if you be wise.

We were at the Exhibition yesterday.[2] Nothing is to be said of the Hamlet,
but *Wonderful*.[3] You know what I honestly think of your extraordinary powers;
and how much in earnest I am when I say that it amazed, even me.

Faithfully Always

Daniel Maclise Esquire.   CD.

To LADY HOLLAND, [?18–25 JULY 1842]

Extract in Charles De F. Burns catalogue, May 1883; *MS* 1 p. *Date:* 1842
according to catalogue; since the conjuror was no doubt Döbler—to whom CD
wrote on 26 Apr 44 that he had seen him perform "on the last occasion"
of his being in London, and Döbler was not in England in 1843—CD was presumably writing on or soon after 18 July 42 (see *fn*) but before Döbler's final 1842
performance on 25 July.

I had engaged to carry a whole bevy of young people to see the conjuror[4]
tonight.[5]

[1] Dr Elliotson (see Vol. II, pp. 330 and 331*n*).

[2] The day the RA Summer Exhibition closed.

[3] The picture had excited great interest. The *Examiner* (3 May) thought it the finest work Maclise had yet exhibited; the *Art Union* for June pronounced it "in all respects, a *chef-d'oeuvre* of the British school"; the *Athenæum* devoted over a column to its praise, finding only one fault in it—the inaccuracy of the murderer's "menacing and doom-like shadow" (cf. CD's, Thackeray's and *Blackwood's* view in *To* Sumner, 31 July and *fn*). The *Times* (3 May) described it as "the lion of the gallery", but criticized the "unnatural colour", the "marvellous resemblance in all the countenances", and the lack of perspective; it found Ophelia "somewhat vulgarized" (*Blackwood's*, July 42, called her "little better than a barmaid"). As a result of adverse criticisms, particularly of the Ophelia, Maclise—before allowing the painting to be engraved for the *Art Journal* (1862)—"went over the entire work again. The figure of Ophelia was repainted" (W. J. O'Driscoll, *Daniel Maclise*, 1871, p. 79*n*). The picture is now in the Tate Gallery.

[4] Ludwig Döbler (1801–64), "Meister der natürlichen Magic", son of a Viennese engraver; referred to in *To* Mitton, 6 Feb 43. He performed at St James's Theatre 12 Apr–25 July 42, and at Windsor Castle; on his return to England Apr 44 he announced himself as "Artist in Natural Philosophy to His Majesty the King of Prussia", claiming to have appeared "at the several courts of Europe, Vienna, St. Petersburg, Berlin", besides before the Queen and Prince Albert (Playbill, BM). The *Morning Chronicle*, 13 Apr 42, reviewed him enthusiastically: he "achieves [his feats] with the entire ease and perfection of a master"; *Punch* remarked on 9 July: "The phenomenon of the candles . . . is supposed to be the result of a private understanding between the Herr and the *wicked* one!" His tricks are described in Thomas Frost's *Lives of the Conjurors*, 1876. On his retirement 1847, he took up engraving and became Burgomaster of Eschenau.

[5] CD was perhaps declining a last minute invitation from Lady Holland—possibly to the dinner party she gave on 18 July, or for some later after-dinner call; she herself dined out all nights 12–17 July (Holland House Dinner Book, MS BM).

To OCTAVIAN BLEWITT,[1] 25 JULY 1842

MS Royal Literary Fund.

Devonshire Terrace | Twenty Fifth July 1842

My Dear Sir.

I am exceedingly anxious to procure some assistance from the Literary Fund for Mr. W. A. Chatto,[2] author of the History of Wood Engraving[3] (published by Charles Knight)—Rambles on the Scottish Border[4]—the History of Fly-fishing[5]—and various works of research, and patient investigation. He is reduced by various causes, to a state of the most extreme temporary distress; and is, I earnestly assure you, a most fit and proper subject for immediate relief.

In addition to my personal certificate and assurance that this is the case, he has the strongest recommendation to the Committee from Messrs. Chapman and Hall, booksellers, who are well acquainted with his situation, and have already assisted him themselves.[6]

Pray, my dear Sir, do all you can in this matter,[7] and oblige

Yours always Faithfully

CHARLES DICKENS

O. Blewitt Esquire

I should have addressed the Committee without delay, but having only just now returned home from America, I do not know whether they are sitting or no.

To THE EDITOR OF THE *MORNING CHRONICLE,* 25 JULY 1842

Text from the *Morning Chronicle,* 25 July 42; signed "B."[8]

Monday morning, July 25, 1842

Sir,

As the Mines and Collieries Bill[9] will be committed in the House of Lords to-night; or, in other words, as it will arrive to-night at that stage in which the tender mercies of the Colliery Lords will so distort and maim it, that its

[1] Octavian Blewitt (1810–84; *DNB*), Secretary of the Literary Fund: see Vol. 1, p. 602*n*.

[2] William Andrew Chatto (1799–1864; *DNB*), miscellaneous writer; born at Newcastle-on-Tyne. Tea-dealer in London 1830–4; then gave up business to devote himself to writing. Besides the books listed by CD, he published *The Angler's Souvenir by Payne Fisher,* 1835; *A Paper:—of Tobacco by 'Joseph Fume'* (illustrated by H. K. Browne), 1838; and *The History and Art of Wood Engraving,* 1848. Edited the *New Sporting Magazine,* 1839–41, and *Puck,* 1844. His son Andrew was joint founder of the publishing firm Chatto & Windus.

[3] *A Treatise on Wood Engraving, Historical and Practical,* illustrated by J. Jackson, 1839.

[4] *Rambles in Northumberland and on the Scottish Border,* 1835, under the pseudonym "Stephen Oliver".

[5] *Scenes and Recollections of Fly-fishing in Northumberland, Cumberland, and Westmorland,* 1834, under the pseudonym "Stephen Oliver the Younger".

[6] Chapman & Hall, who had published Chatto's first book, had that morning told CD of his condition. They wrote a supporting letter to Blewitt, enclosing CD's, and stating that recent illness had prevented Chatto's finishing a new book for them (MS Royal Literary Fund).

[7] Blewitt at once saw Chatto, but found that he had decided not to apply after all. He was granted £50 after an application in 1848, and helped again in 1852 (MS *ibid.*).

[8] On 29 July Macready recorded in his diary: "Read Dickens's letter on the mines

relations and friends elsewhere will be sorely puzzled to know it again when it is returned to them, I venture to trouble you with a few remarks upon the subject. From its first public exposition it has had such ready sympathy from you, and has received such able and manly support in your journal,[1] that I offer no apology for this intrusion on your time and space.

That for very many years these mines and all belonging to them, as they have been out[2] of sight in the dark earth, have been utterly out of legislative mind; that for so many years all considerations of humanity, policy, social virtue, and common decency, have been left rotting at the pit's mouth, with other disregarded dunghill matter from which lordly colliers could extract no money; that for very many years, a state of things has existed in these places, in the heart and core of a Christian country, which, if it had been discovered by mariners or missionaries in the Sandwich Islands,[3] would have made the fortune of two quarto volumes, filled the whole bench of bishops with emotion,[4] and nerved to new and mighty projects the Society for the Propagation of the

and collieries, which I like very much" (*Diaries*, II, 181). Doubtless the letter was to the *Morning Chronicle* (see CD's offer to the editor, John Black, on 15 Aug)—a paper which strongly supported Lord Ashley's Bill on Mines and Collieries. The signature "B" could well stand for "Boz". In his letters to the *Chronicle* about the Courvoisier trial in June 40 (see Vol. II, p. 86 and *n*, and p. 90) CD had chosen to write anonymously—perhaps to hoodwink Easthope. His choosing to do so for a letter on Ashley's Bill may have had as contributory reason the wish that Napier, to whom he had promised, but never supplied, an article on children in mines for the *Edinburgh*, should be unaware of his authorship. (For his possible reasons for not writing the *Edinburgh* article, see *To* Napier, 26 July and *fn*.) Whether he post-dated his letter, or wrote it in the early hours of Monday 25th and dispatched it at once by hand, having asked Black to be ready for it, is not certainly known; but it was imperative that it should appear on the 25th, the day when the Mines and Collieries Bill was to be considered in Committee by the House of Lords, having failed to obtain there the Govt support promised in the Commons.

9 "An Act to prohibit the Employment of Women and Girls in Mines and Collieries, to regulate the Employment of Boys, and make Provisions for the Safety of Persons working therein", moved by Lord Ashley on 7 June. Besides excluding from the pits all women and girls, all boys under 13 and parish apprentices, it was to

restrict enginemen (often young boys) to men between 21 and 50. For CD's support of the Children's Employment Commission, whose Report led to the Bill, see Vol. II, p. 165.

1 For instance, in editorials of 29 June (urging a large Commons majority for the Bill), 7 July (warning its readers of "the sinister interest of a clique of mine-owners", who would obstruct the Bill in the Lords), and 14 July (castigating the mine-owners' support of "the principle of the 'freedom of labour' " as "all sheer cant"). On 14 May Ashley had recorded in his diary: "Wrote pointedly to thank the editor of the *Morning Chronicle* for his support, *which is most effective*" (E. Hodder, *Life and Work of the Seventh Earl of Shaftesbury, K. G.*, 1886, I, 418).

2 *Chronicle* reads "out out". For CD's reference to the misprints in this letter, see *To* Mackay, 19 Oct.

3 CD was probably referring to the Sandwich Islands as typically far-off and exotic; American missionaries had in fact been there since 1819. The previous King and Queen, Kamehameha II and Kamamalu, had both died of measles on a visit to England in 1824; and the Islands were in the news again in Feb 43 when Kamehameha III offered—unsuccessfully—to cede them to England.

4 On 26 July Ashley recorded: "Three bishops only present", when the Bill passed through the Lords Committee (E. Hodder, *op. cit.*, I, 431).

Gospel in Foreign Parts,[1] is well known to every one. That the evidence taken by the commissioners wrought (as well it might) an extraordinary impression on the public mind, from the first moment of its diffusion;[2] that the bill founded upon it, passed the House of Commons with the hearty consent of all parties, and the ready union of all interests;[3] that the people of every class, and their representatives of every class, were no sooner made acquainted with the evil, than they hastened to apply the remedy, are recent and notorious facts. It was reserved for the House of Lords alone to discover that this kind of legislation was very bad and odious, and would never do.[4] Let us see on what grounds.

It is an interference with the rights of labour, because it proposes to banish women from the mines.[5] It proceeds on insufficient evidence, because the witnesses were not upon oath. The sub-commissioners who examined the witnesses did so improperly. Nobody knows how or why—but somebody says so. To these formidable heads of objection Lord Londonderry[6] adds (with true Lord Londonderry *naïveté*) that the prints upon their lordships' table[7] are

[1] Founded 1701.

[2] For the findings of the Commission's first Report of May 42, and the disgust they aroused, see Vol. II, p. 354*n*. Peel himself referred to these "mining abominations" (letter of 16 June 42, MS BM; quoted in G. F. A. Best, *Shaftesbury*, 1964, p. 105). Ashley's two-hour speech of 7 June, setting out the evidence, had an overwhelming effect: "Many men, I hear, shed tears", he recorded. "It has given me hopes for the Empire, hopes for its permanence, hopes for its service in the purposes of the Messiah. God prosper the issue!" (E. Hodder, *op. cit.*, I, 422).

[3] The Bill had passed its first and second readings in the Commons, on 7 and 15 June, unchallenged; and, despite an attempt to adjourn the third reading on 1 July, it was passed on 5 July—"amid cheers", Ashley recorded (*op. cit.*, I, 429)—practically unaltered although the minimum age for working in the mines was changed from 13 to ten. Both Peel and Palmerston voted in its favour, and Sir James Graham, the Home Secretary, promised Govt support.

[4] The Lords, with a powerful section of mine-owning peers, were expectedly hostile to the Bill. Ashley had, after difficulty, found only Lord Devon to sponsor it. Nevertheless, its first and second readings were passed on 7 and 14 July, after a motion to delay it; and its third reading on 1 Aug, after considerable amendments. It received the Royal Assent on 10 Aug. The main opponent was Lord Londonderry, who attacked

Ashley and the Report, accused the Sub-Commissioners of having "got up evidence by underhand means", and charged the Bill's sponsors with "working upon the cant of hypocritical humanity, which was now so much in vogue". The Lords' hostility drove Ashley to near-despair. On 13 July he recorded in his diary: "Now then I am impotent—nothing remains (humanly speaking) but public opinion—were it not for this I should not be able to carry *one* particle of the Bill"; and on the 26th, after the Committee stage: "Never have I seen such a display of selfishness, frigidity to every human sentiment, such ready and happy self-delusion" (E. Hodder, *op. cit.*, I, 430, 431).

[5] Fear of loss of the women's wages was naturally encouraged by the owners; but exclusion of women was in fact the least contested of the proposed reforms, since the Bill's most powerful opponents did not themselves employ women. The women turned out under the Act—especially those in Scotland—suffered serious distress (see J. L. and Barbara Hammond, *Lord Shaftesbury*, 1923, pp. 80–2).

[6] Charles William Vane, formerly Stewart (1778–1854; *DNB*), 3rd Marquis of Londonderry; half-brother of Viscount Castlereagh. He and his wife owned vast coalfields at Seaham, Durham.

[7] Prints (often reproduced) from drawings of women and children at work in the mines (done on the spot, at Southwood Smith's instigation: see Vol. II, p. 165*n*), with which the Commissioners' Report was illustrated.

excessively disgusting. Wherefore, he argues, (with true Lord Londonderry logic) that the parties who originated them are excessively hypocritical.[1]

In addition to these grounds of opposition, it was stoutly contended by their collier lordships that there are no grievances, no discomforts, no miseries whatever, in the mines; that all labourers in mines are perpetually singing and dancing, and festively enjoying themselves; in a word, that they lead such rollicking and roystering lives that it is well they work below the surface of the earth, or society would be deafened by their shouts of merriment. This is humorous, but not new. Exactly the same things have been said of slavery, factory-work, Irish destitution, and every other grade of poverty, neglect, oppression, and distress. There is a kind of opposition to truth, which may be called the out-and-out, or whole-hog opposition. It stops at nothing, and recognises no middle course. Show beyond all dispute, and the remotest possibility of doubt, that any class of persons are in especial need of legislative protection and assistance, and opponents of this stamp will instantly arise, and meet you with the assertion, not that that class are moderately well off, or have an average amount of comfort; but that of all earthly ranks and conditions, theirs is the most surpassingly and exquisitely desirable. Now, happiness capers and sings on a slave plantation, making it an Eden of ebony. Now, she dwelleth in a roofless cabin, with potatoes thrice a week, buttermilk o' Sundays, a pig in the parlour, a fever in the dungheap, seven naked children on the damp earth-floor, and a wife newly delivered of an eighth, upon a door, brought from the nearest hut that boasts one—five miles off. Now, she rambles through a refreshing grove of steam engines, at midnight, with a Manchester child, patting him occasionally on the head with a billy-roller.[2] And now she sits down in the dark, a thousand feet below the level of the sea, passing the livelong day beside a little trapper six years old.[3] If I were not this great peer, quoth Lord Londonderry, I would be that small trapper. If I were not a lord, doomed unhappily in my high place to preserve a solemn bearing, for the wonder and admiration of mankind, and hold myself aloof from innocent sports, I would be a jolly little trapper. Oh, for the cindery days of trapper infancy! The babes in the wood had a rich and cruel uncle. When were the children in the coals ever murdered for their inheritance? Jolly, jolly trappers![4]

---

[1] Londonderry had attacked the prints on 24 June as "pictorial representations of the most disgusting and obscene character", and on 14 July explained that the charge he had just made of hypocrisy applied to "those who were guilty of inflaming the minds of the public" through "the circulation of the disgusting prints on their lordships' table."

[2] Earlier in the century "much talked of in the controversies between the operatives and masters in the cotton factories, as an instrument of cruel punishment to children" (*Ure's Dictionary of Arts, Manufactures, and Mines*, 6th edn, 1867, III, 1103).

[3] The youngest children were employed as "trappers", to open and shut the numerous doors or traps for the coal-carriages. They sat alone by their doors, in the dark, for 12 hours or more a day.

[4] CD clearly based this paragraph on the *Morning Chronicle* report, 25 June, of Londonderry's speech of the 24th: "He contended that the labour of boys in the collieries was not nearly so hard labour as that of sailor boys. The truth was, the boys engaged in the collieries were as happy as the day was long, and they sat at their little trap doors amusing themselves cutting out figures. No young class of workpeople were so jolly and joyous [*a*

It is an interference with the rights of labour to exclude women from the mines—women who work by the side of naked men—(daughters often do this beside their own fathers)—and harnessed to carts in a most revolting and disgusting fashion, by iron chains. Is it among the rights of labour to blot out from that sex all form and stamp, and character of womanhood—to predestine their neglected offspring, from the hour of their conception in the womb, to lives of certain sin and suffering, misery and crime—to divest them of all knowledge of home, and all chance of womanly influence in the humble sphere of a poor peasant's hearth—to make them but so many weaker men, saving in respect of their more rapid and irresistible opportunities of being brutalised themselves, and of brutalizing others; and their capacity of breeding for the scaffold and the gaol? When we talk of "rights of labour," do we picture to ourselves a hideous phantom whispering discontent in the depths of pits and mines, sharpening the Chartist's[1] pike by stealth, and skulking from the farmer's rickyard? Or are we men, possessing the common average of reason bestowed by God upon the descendants of Adam, who well know that what these lords proclaim to be the rights of labour are its wrongs? Who well know that the opposition to this vital clause originates with men who stand, it may be almost said, upon their trial—who in any other tribunal would be heard with caution and distrust; and could not sit upon the jury, far less carry in their pockets friendly verdicts from absent jurymen, by the score! To speak more plainly yet, do we not know, right well, that the real leader of the opposition to this very clause is himself the owner of the worst-conducted mine in that worst district of Scotland; who has at this moment 400 women in his weekly pay and service?[2] And is there a man alive (out of the House of Lords) who does not read in this phrase "rights of labour," fears of possible claims for higher wages from the men, when the women no longer prostitute all the faculties of their minds and bodies to the degrading work they have pursued too long? Who does not see upon its face distinctly pictured apprehensions of a louder cry for bread? The mining labourers, with no complaint or hope of change, are bound to work, from year to year, and from age to age, their fingers to the bone; to turn their women into men, and children into devils; and do all this to live. These are the "rights of labour" with your collier lords!

The evidence is insufficient, because not taken upon oath. It was well

laugh]." In fact, these contentions—fairly reported in themselves—were made, not by Londonderry, but in a petition against the Bill from colliery owners of Northumberland and Durham, presented by Londonderry (*Hansard*, House of Lords, 24 June).

[1] *Chronicle* reads "Chartists' ".

[2] Although Lord Londonderry had declared in the Lords on 25 July that he "represented" the coal-owners, he himself owned no mine in Scotland, and no women were employed in his and his wife's collieries in Durham. CD may have been referring to Sir John Hope, Bt (1781– 1853): he employed 194 women in his three collieries in Midlothian (the highest number employed by any mine-owner); the proportion of women to men (one to three) working in Midlothian and East Lothian mines was the highest reported by the Commissioners; and there was a great deal of drunkenness at Inveresk, the site of New Craighall, Hope's largest colliery (*Report from Commissioners: 1842: Children's Employment*, XVI, 401). CD was in any event exaggerating, since the total number of women and girls employed in all Midlothian collieries was 341.

observed in your journal some days since, that this was made no ground of objection to the Poor Law Bill upon its introduction; and that it arises for the first time.[1] But why this extraordinary distinction between the Poor Law Act, and that for the better regulation of mines and collieries? Simply, because in the one case property sought protection against poverty; and in the other, poverty seeks protection against property. "A man may see how this world goes, with no eyes. Look with thine ears; see how yon justice rails upon yon simple thief. Hark in thine ear: change places: and handy-dandy, which is the justice, which is the thief?"[2]

Abuse of the sub-commissioners is a very fruitful theme, and it daily grows in favour with these lords. Now, the sub-commissioners were chosen from among barristers, medical gentlemen, and civil engineers.[3] I have examined the result of their labours, very attentively;[4] and I honestly believe that a more impartial, able, and carefully-conducted investigation never was pursued. I believe that is the almost universal opinion; and I only concur with every friend of humanity, when I express my gratitude to these gentlemen, for the extraordinary pains they have taken to arrive at the truth; and the luminous manner in which they have stated it. But they by no means please the collier lords. I should be greatly surprised if they did. Barristers are not so liable as other men to be easily imposed on by false statements; surgeons cannot be blinded to the present and probable effects of a pernicious atmosphere, and the work of beasts of burden, on tender years and frames. Civil engineers are well acquainted with the dangers that lurk in ill-conducted pits, where no provision is made for the safety of the labourers. Lord Littleton's[5] valet, Lord Londonderry's butler, and any steward or overseer of the Duke of Hamilton[6] would have known better. They would have made an excellent commission. With three such sub-commissioners (one to form a quorum) the collier lords would have got on briskly. Jolly little trappers would have been quoted against us by the dozen, and not a whisper would have been heard about their jolly little affidavits.

It is something so new for a rational being to agree with Lord Londonderry on any subject, that I am happy to be enabled to lay claim to that distinction.

---

[1] Referring to the Poor Law Amendment Bill, the editorial in the *Morning Chronicle* of 21 July had said: "Upon the unsworn testimony of adults the screw was turned upon pauperism; but not the unsworn testimony of children incapable of successful deception is to prevent the turning of the proprietary screw on the most helpless class of labourers."

[2] *King Lear*, IV, vi, 150–4.

[3] The 20 Sub-Commissioners (ten of them concerned with mines) included three barristers, two doctors, a clergyman and the writer R. H. Horne; most of the others were presumably engineers.

[4] Southwood Smith had apparently sent him early confidential copies of the Report and evidence: see Vol. II, p. 353.

[5] Clearly Edward John Littleton, 1st Baron Hatherton since 1835 (1791–1863; *DNB*), who had taken up the case of the Staffordshire mine-owners in the Lords; he had given notice to move for a Select Committee on the Bill's second reading (14 July)—supported by the Duke of Wellington—but withdrew it, to Londonderry's chagrin.

[6] Alexander Hamilton Douglas, 10th Duke of Hamilton (1767–1852; *DNB*), premier Scottish peer. His colliery at Polmont, Stirlingshire, employed 127 women. In a speech on 19 July, he had criticized the Bill as "most objectionable in principle and detail".

The pictures on the table of the House of Lords are unquestionably disgusting. They exhibit human beings in a condition which it is horrible to contemplate —which is disgraceful to the country, dangerous to the community, repulsive and offensive to all right-thinking persons, in the highest degree. But Lord Londonderry's objection is not to the existence of this deplorable state of society; it is confined to the naughty pictures that set it forth and illustrate it; "Keep it in the mines," says he, "but don't lay it on the table. Preserve it, but don't paint it. I equally protest against legislation and lithograph." In like manner the delicacy of the distillers of Hogarth's time was grievously outraged by the print of "Gin Lane,"[1] and nearly all the stout landladies[2] dwelling about Covent-garden voted "The Harlot's Progress"[3] indecent and immoral.

Without taking up your time by following Lord Londonderry into his acute deduction before mentioned, that because these prints disgust him, therefore the gentlemen with whom they originated are of necessity hypocrites, I would beg, in conclusion, earnestly to impress on your readers that these are the only objections which have been urged against the Mines and Collieries Bill; and that these are the men who will to-night, by motions for delay, and other means, so pare, and cut, and fritter it away, as to reduce it to the very ghost and shadow of its former self, and to a mere absurd nonentity.[4] Of the few petitions which have been presented against it by these same hands, purporting to come from the labourers in mines, I say nothing,[5] as it is not very difficult to understand how signatures are procured to them, and as Lord Londonderry himself admitted a few nights ago, in his usually happy manner, on presenting one of these very documents, that the prospect of this relief "had thrown them into a fever."[6]

[1] For CD's comments on "Gin Lane" (familiar to him in the print-shops from an early date), see letter to Forster of *c.* Summer 1848 quoted in F, VI, iii, 491; the Hogarth picture forced attention not, he pointed out, on drunkenness alone but on the "abject condition of life" that caused it.

[2] *Chronicle* reads "landlady's".

[3] Published 1732; the first of Hogarth's "Progresses".

[4] The Lords made numerous amendments. They cancelled a previous agreement that boys between ten and 13 should only work on alternate days; sanctioned the employment of boys as enginemen at 15; allowed existing apprenticeship indentures to remain; postponed the exclusion of women until Mar 43. But on 1 Aug the Bill was passed in substance and was still one of Ashley's greatest achievements. All females and boys under 10 were barred from working underground; parish apprentices could not be bound beyond 18; safety regulations were enforced and inspectors appointed. Ashley was bitter about the changes made: "Strange to say

of so great a man," he recorded in his diary, "but never did impudence go beyond that of the Duke of Wellington [*who had spoken against the Bill*] who expressed a belief to me that 'I was satisfied with what has been done to my bill in the H. of Lords.' I told him, 'just the reverse'" (1 Aug 42; quoted in G. F. A. Best *Shaftesbury*, p. 105).

[5] A large number of petitions both for and against the Bill had been presented to the Lords. Those against included many from both men and women mine-workers who clearly feared unemployment or loss of wages as a consequence of the Bill. Several mine-owners contended that the expense of employing men rather than women would lead to closure of the smaller pits, unemployment and the workhouse.

[6] "Hitherto", Londonderry had said in his speech of 14 July, the great body of miners had been "contented, quiet, and happy. But the promoters of this Bill had managed to work up a state of fever among them, which it would be found very difficult to set at rest" (*Morning Chronicle*, 15 July).

In these times, when so wide a gulf has opened between the rich and poor, which, instead of narrowing, as all good men would have it, grows broader daily; it is most important that all ranks and degrees of people should understand whose hands are stretched out to separate these two great divisions of society each of whom, for its strength and happiness, and the future existence of this country, as a great and powerful nation, is dependent on the other. Therefore it is that I implore your readers closely to watch the fate of this measure, which has for its sole object the improvement of the condition and character of one great class of hewers of wood and drawars[1] of water,[2] whose lives, at the very best, must be fraught with danger, toil, and hardship; to compare the fate of this bill in the House of Lords, with its reception by the country,[3] and its progress through the House of Commons, and to bestow their best attention on the debate of this night.   B.

To FREDERICK DICKENS, 26 JULY 1842

MS John Rylands Library.

Devonshire Terrace | Twenty Sixth July 1842

My Dear Fred.

It has occurred to me that Mitton (having, I know, some unexamined papers of father's in his desk, and being necessarily absent from business just now) would wish him to know of the Death in his family.[4] Will you write and tell him?[5]

Don't forget Mister Groves[6]—The battledores have arrived. They are brilliant—but the Shuttlecocks are not big enough.

Affy. Always

Frederick Dickens Esquire   CD.

To G. P. R. JAMES,[7] 26 JULY 1842*

MS Haverford College, Pennsylvania.

Devonshire Terrace | Twenty Sixth July 1842.

My Dear Sir.

I am happy to acknowledge the receipt of your letter.[8]

---

[1] Thus in *Chronicle*.

[2] *Joshua*, 9, *v.* 21.

[3] Prince Albert, to whom Ashley had sent his speech of 7 June, had written privately to him on the 23rd: "I have no doubt but that the whole country must be with you—at all events, I can assure you that the Queen is, whom your statements have filled with the deepest sympathy. . . . Believe me, with my best wishes for your *total* success . . ." (E. Hodder, *op. cit.*, I, 428).

[4] See *To* Mitton, 26 July.

[5] That he would not himself write this letter shows how completely CD had at

this time cut himself off from direct communication with John Dickens on matters even remotely connected with business.

[6] See *To* Beard, 21 July.

[7] George Payne Rainsford James (1801–60; *DNB*), prolific writer of historical novels and popular histories, now at the height of his success; by the end of 1842 had published 43 out of the final total of 91 works listed in S. M. Ellis, *The Solitary Horseman*, 1927. His novels were parodied by Thackeray in the series "Punch's Prize Novelists" (*Punch*, July 1847; reprinted in "Novels by Eminent Hands", *Works*, 1879, Vol. xv). Landor, who had tried to

You are perfectly right, no doubt, in thinking that even in respect of the price of books, the American people would suffer very little (if at all) by being honest. I am well assured that they would have as cheap books as they have now; and would have them much more correctly[1] and creditably printed.

With regard to the question of a corrupted Text, I fancy there is very little danger of that, in your case, or mine,[2] or any such instance. I put forth that plea of the Pirates,[3] rather as a proof of the amazing obtuseness of their moral sense, than as a reason for any serious alarm in the breasts of Writers of Fiction.

I fully agree with you that one can expect but little in this respect from a people who have shewn themselves so shamelessly dishonest in the plain question of repaying or with-holding borrowed money.[4] But we can at least shew them that we, the robbed, entertain for them, the robbers, a very disdainful and contemptuous disgust. And I rather think that this, in the slow fulness of Time, will move them more, than all the considerations of abstract Justice that will have been spread abroad, between the first hour of the creation, and the last of the Day of Judgment, would be likely to do, if they could be all arrayed together and brought to bear against them.

Always Believe me | Faithfully Yours

G. P. R. James Esquire.   CHARLES DICKENS

---

arrange a meeting between him and CD in 1840 (see Vol. II, p. 23*n*), was a close friend of his and godfather of his first child. His activities (since 1840) in the campaign against Continental piracy of books (see *To* Marryat, 21 Jan 43) gained public acknowledgment from Ainsworth in a Dedicatory Letter prefixed to *Saint James's, or the Court of Queen Anne*, 1844: "Your brother writers owe you a debt of gratitude, though I fear it has been but imperfectly paid. It is mainly, if not entirely, to your influence and exertions, that Continental Piracy has received a check, and that unauthorized foreign reprints of English works have been kept out of the market" (quoted in Ellis, *op. cit.*, pp. 102–3).

[8] No doubt in reply to CD's circular letter to British Authors of 7 July. James, who had made the chief speech at the public meeting on international copyright of 30 June (see *To* Longman, 1 July, *fn*), had been one of the greatest sufferers from piracy. According to R. H. Horne (*A New Spirit of the Age*, 1844), 21 "substantial three-volumed novels" by him were listed by Baudry of Paris, 1841, in a catalogue of works pirated from English authors.

[1] Written above "cheaply" cancelled.

[2] CD's novels may have been safe from adaptation, but American editors were quite ready to "improve" *American Notes*. *Brother Jonathan*, 24 Sep, announcing its forthcoming publication, declared: "We are ready to read, and make whatever improvement of the matter the work may permit".

[3] See his circular letter to British Authors, 7 July and *fn*.

[4] The financial panic of 1837 and its aftermath led to several State Governments and Corporations being unable to repay capital raised in London. As late as 1845 interest was still suspended on the bonds of seven States, and two—Michigan and Mississippi—had repudiated their bonds. In his petition to Congress, 7 Mar 43, later published in the *Morning Chronicle*, 18 May 43, Sydney Smith, who had lost money through Pennsylvania's suspension of interest, inveighed against "a nation with whom no contract can be made because none will be kept" (see *Letters of Sydney Smith*, ed. Nowell C. Smith, Oxford, 1953, II, 807*n*). On reading *American Notes*, Crabb Robinson was "angry" at CD's neglecting to "show up" repudiation as he had shown up slavery (MS Diary, 27 Oct, Dr Williams's Library).

To CHARLES MACKAY, 26 JULY 1842†

MS Berg Collection. Endorsed, probably by Mackay: "Chas. Dickens | In reference to the proposed establishment of a Literary Club".

Devonshire Terrace. | Twenty Sixth July 1842.

My Dear Sir.

In the *principle* of your note, I heartily concur. Of the chances that hang about its successful reduction into practice, I am somewhat doubtful. These experiments have been very often tried; and have, almost as often, failed.[1]

Nevertheless I shall be exceedingly glad to talk with you upon the subject; and any morning this week that may be convenient to you, I shall be happy to see you. About one o'Clock is usually the best time for such a purpose with me—but chuse your own time, and I will make it mine.

*a*Don't ask if I am at home, but say, magisterially, to the servant as you give him your card—"Take that to Mr. Dickens, and tell him I am waiting."*a*

Faithfully Yours always

Charles Mackay Esquire.   CHARLES DICKENS

To DANIEL MACLISE, 26 JULY 1842

MS Colonel Richard Gimbel.

Twenty Sixth July 1842.

My Dear Mac

How are you?

Well enough to dine with us (inviolably alone) at 5—before the evening ride? If so, say Yes.

Dieted at all? If so, say on what.[2]

Yours

Sutherland.[3]

---

[1] Mackay's scheme was for a "Union or Institute", with writing-room, reading-room and library—not primarily a club, but an association of men of letters for "mutual support and assistance"; to be called the Milton Institute, Milton being "the greatest professional man of letters" (C. Mackay, *Forty Years' Recollections*, 1877, I, 168–70; for later developments see *To* Mackay, 19 Oct 42 and 17 Feb 43). Two earlier experiments must have been known to CD. Campbell's "Literary Union Club" (described by the *Athenæum*, 20 Mar 30, as "anything but Literary or United") held a public meeting on 15 Mar 31, its original object being to raise capital so that members could co-operate in publishing their own works; but it soon ran into financial difficulties (W. Jerdan, *Illustrations of the Plan of a National Association for the Encouragement and Protection of Authors, and Men of Talent*

and Genius, 1839, pp. 18–28), and continued mainly as a social meeting-place, "the Clarence Club" in Waterloo Place (C. Redding, *Fifty Years' Recollections, with Observations on Men and Things*, 1858, III, 10–15). Jerdan himself issued the prospectus of a "National Association" for the "Encouragement and Protection of Authors" on 1 May 38, along similar lines, his committee including Lord Nugent, Emerson Tennent, G. P. R. James, and Samuel Lover (Jerdan, *op. cit.*, pp. 29–46); but no more is known of its activities.

aa Not previously published.

[2] It was probably on receiving this letter that Maclise wrote to Forster: "I am better, but very very weak—I am going to crawl up to Dickens for the purpose you invite [*slip for "he invites"*?] me—having ordered him to get *two* chops (small) and *well done*—at 5. I'll tell him now that you will drop in" (MS Forster Collection,

To THOMAS MITTON, 26 JULY 1842

MS Free Library of Philadelphia.

Devonshire Terrace. | Twenty Sixth July 1842.

My Dear Mitton

I am heartily sorry to hear of your poor father's death;[1] though it is a very great comfort to hear of any death, that it was unaccompanied by Pain. It is a real happiness, too, to know that for many years past, he has lived respectably and happily, which he never could have done but for your arrangements and care.

I should have written to you, directly on the receipt of this sad intelligence; but taking it for granted that you would be out of town, and would have many things to attend to, I deemed it best to wait a little. I did not yield to my first impulse, which was to write and tell you that I should be glad to attend the Funeral, if you desired it, because a moment's reflection assured me that if you had any such wish, you would have summoned me without hesitation.

Remember me with all the kindness possible, to your mother and sister.[2] And believe me, in this trouble, as in all others, and at all times

Faithfully | Your friend

Thomas Mitton Esquire.   CHARLES DICKENS

To MACVEY NAPIER, 26 JULY 1842

MS British Museum.

Devonshire Terrace. | Twenty Sixth July 1842.

My Dear Sir.

In thanking you for your last letter, let me thank you also for your last but one,[3] which reached me shortly before I left England, and which I did religiously intend to answer. The thousand and one preparations for my American journey, alone prevented me from doing so.

I am happy to say that both Mrs. Dickens and I are in the highest health and greatest force—very happy, too, to be at home again, as you may readily suppose.

Before I heard from you, this last time, I had begun to fear that our subject[4]

V & A; undated, but, since on mourning paper, 1842).

[3] A joke perhaps referring to the Duke of Sutherland, a patron of art and owner of the great collection of paintings at Stafford House. CD had met him at Holland House on 22 July.

[1] Thomas Mitton, senior (?1773–1842), one-time publican of Saffron Hill and Battle Bridge, London, and possibly for a time a near neighbour of the Dickenses (see Vol. I, p. 35*n*), had died 22 July 42 from a stroke, at Isleworth (where his son was living).

[2] Mary Ann Mitton (?1815–1913); married John Cartwright Cooper, a market gardener, and lived at Southgate where she

was known as Mrs Strawberry Cooper. Notorious locally for her eccentric clothes (e.g. a dress trimmed with bells, in which she went to church until requested not to). In her 90s gave a number of interviews to newspapers, describing herself as a childhood playmate of CD's, who—she averred —called her "Little Dorrit". See W. J. Carlton, "The Strange Story of Thomas Mitton", *D*, LVI (1960), 141–6.

[3] Presumably Napier's letter of 26 Oct 41: see Vol. II, p. 406*n*.

[4] The employment of children in mines —on which CD had first promised Napier an article for the *Edinburgh Review* when they met in June 41 (see Vol. II, p. 317).

was too stale.[1] You see that I was not mistaken in supposing it would create a very strong and very general sensation, on the publication of the evidence.

I have resolved to describe my American journies, in a couple of volumes;[2] and am consequently, just now, very closely engaged. I fear I shall not have anything for your October No., therefore; but I am really desirous to "come out" in the Edinburgh, and hope to do so, in the number following. I will keep the matter in my thoughts, and consult you, without loss of time, in reference to any subject that may occur to me.[3]

Mrs. Dickens begs her best regards. And I am always

My Dear Sir | Faithfully Yours
Professor Napier   CHARLES DICKENS

To LADY HOLLAND, [27] JULY 1842*

MS The Earl of Ilchester. *Date:* 26 July 42 was Tuesday; doubtless CD was writing on the 27th. This misdating raises the possibility that last six letters, all dated 26 July 42 but without day of the week, were also written on the 27th.

Devonshire Terrace. | Wednesday Twenty Sixth July | 1842.

Dear Lady Holland

Pray do not suppose that I have ever forgotten my pledge[4] to send you the

---

[1] The handling of it suggested by Napier ("more *descriptive* than speculative": see Vol. II, p. 354*n*) would certainly be stale by the time the next number of the *Edinburgh* came out (October), so much having appeared in the press since publication of the Commissioners' First Report on 7 May 42. With *Barnaby* on his hands when he made his promise to Napier, followed by his own illness and preparations for America, it is scarcely surprising that he had found no time for the article. But now (perhaps on thinking over Napier's latest reminder) he no doubt saw that he must publish something on the subject at once, if at all. In fact to write a vehement letter to the *Chronicle* at a crucial moment in the passage of Ashley's Bill must have come far more naturally to him than would producing a serious article (more than a year after his promise) for the *Edinburgh*. But that he wrote to Napier a day after the appearance of his letter to the *Chronicle*, without mentioning it, suggests a distinctly uneasy conscience.

[2] Not only was this already generally known, but on 20 July Macaulay reported to Napier that he had been told CD's book would give more offence to the Americans than "all the Fearons, Trollopes, Marryats, and Martineaus together", and on 25 July asked Napier to keep the book for him to review: "Of course I shall be courteous

to Dickens whom I know, and whom I think both a man of genius and a good-hearted man, in spite of some faults of taste." But on 19 Oct he wrote: "I have now read [*American Notes*]. It is impossible for me to review it ... I cannot praise it; and I will not cut it up. ... It is written like the worst parts of Humphrey's Clock. What is meant to be easy and sprightly is vulgar and flippant, as in the first two pages. What is meant to be fine is a great deal to[o] fine for me, as the description of the fall of Niagara"; for amusement, a reader had better go to Mrs Trollope, "coarse and malignant as she is"; for information, "even to so poor a creature as Buckingham": "In short I pronounce the book, in spite of some gleams of genius, at once frivolous and dull." (MSS BM.) Napier then offered the book to James Spedding for review, and he accepted: see *To The Times*, 15 Jan 43, *fn*.

[3] Macaulay desired this for CD too, and as his final reason for refusing to attack *American Notes* wrote to Napier, 19 Oct: "I wish to see him inrolled in our blue and yellow corps, where he may do excellent service as a skirmisher and sharpshooter" (MS BM). But in spite of promises CD never contributed to the *Edinburgh*.

[4] Perhaps made during his call of 14 July (*To* Lady Holland, 11 July and *fn*).

inclosed books.[1] The truth is that I found my own first copy so blotted and defaced by scoring and underlining, that you would have found it quite a Nuisance. I therefore sent for another; and did not get it until yesterday.

You must not suppose, either, that I have marked in the index to each volume the only pieces I think worth reading. On the contrary I really believe them to be nearly all equally good. I can only say of those I have marked, that they are good things to begin with.[2]

Always Dear Lady Holland
Yours faithfully and obliged

The Lady Holland   CHARLES DICKENS

To THOMAS MITTON, 29 JULY 1842

MS Huntington Library.

Devonshire Terrace | Twenty Ninth July 1842. | Friday.

My Dear Mitton

I will call on you tonight at 8 OClock, punctually.—I shall be writing all day.[3]

To DAVID C. COLDEN, 31 JULY 1842

Photograph Dickens House. *Address:* By The Cunard Steam Packet viâ Liverpool. | David. C. Colden Esquire | 28 Laight Street | Hudson Square | New York | United States.

London 1 Devonshire Terrace
York Gate Regents Park. | Thirty First July 1842.

My Dear Friend.

Just to shew that I am a good boy, and not unmindful, being at home, of those to whom I am indebted for so much delight abroad, I write to say—all well—and Mrs. D *going* to write, next time. We move off to the Seaside to-morrow morning, and I write this in the agonies of packing, with nothing (except the carpet) in its usual place.

You remember our talking about a certain bust—of *Maclise*[4]—done by a man in Howland Street,[5] who forces folks into his sitting chair. It is in the Exhibition

---

[1] Probably Longfellow's first two books of poems, *Voices of the Night*, 1839, and *Ballads and Other Poems*, late 1841. Samuel Longfellow described CD as leaving his brother's breakfast party on 4 Feb "in a carriage with . . . Sumner, an umbrella, a bear skin coat, & two octavo volumes of Longfellow's poems" (quoted by Edward Wagenknecht, "Dickens in Longfellow's Letters and Journals", *D*, LII [1955], 9).

[2] *Voices of the Night* includes "A Psalm of Life" ("Tell me not, in mournful numbers . . ."); *Ballads and Other Poems*, "The Wreck of the Hesperus", "The Village Blacksmith" and "Excelsior".

[3] He had no doubt already finished his long Ch. 3, "Boston" (probably begun on 20 July, the day after he finished Ch. 2: see *To* Beard, 19 July) and was now working on his much shorter Ch. 4, apparently completed by 31 July (see *To* Felton, that day, *fn*). The rest of the page has been cut away. It may well have contained some reference to John Dickens, besides the ending and signature.

[4] Underlined twice.

[5] The bust was of Colden himself—its fancied likeness to Maclise being obviously an earlier joke of CD's. The sculptor was Christopher Moore, of 23 Howland Street, who exhibited over 130 pieces at the RA 1821–60, mainly portrait busts. His sitters included Thomas Moore, Daniel O'Connell, Lord Stanley, Lord Brougham and George Stephenson.

this year, and is certainly not a striking success. I don't think I should have recognized it in a room, but I certainly did not in the Academy without referring to the Catalogue; though I was looking hard in its face.—He says he don't exactly know what to do in the matter, and would like to know. It has good points. If I were he, I should give instructions for having it forwarded.

"Nothing is stirring but stagnation."[1] I thank God that Peel continues hideously unpopular. Our united loves to all at home, beginning with H E R.[2]

Always My Dear friend | Yours with Sincere regard

Bully and Meek.[3]

To C. C. FELTON, 31 JULY 1842†

MS Berg Collection. *Address:* [By The][4] Cunard Packet viâ Liverpool | Professor Felton | Cambridge | Massachusetts | United States.

London. 1 Devonshire Terrace. | York Gate Regents Park.

Sunday Thirty First July 1842.

My Dear Felton.

Of all the monstrous and incalculable amount of occupation that ever beset one unfortunate man, mine has been the most stupendous since I came home. The dinners I have had to eat, the places I have had to go to, the letters I have had to answer, the sea of business of business and business of pleasure in which I have been plunged,—not even the genius of an L.L.[5] or the pen of a Putnam[6] could describe.

Wherefore I indite a monstrously short, and wildly uninteresting epistle to the American Dando—but perhaps you don't know who Dando was ?[7] He was an oyster eater, my dear Felton. He used to go into oyster shops, without a farthing of money, and stand at the counter, eating Natives, until the man who opened them grew pale, cast down his knife, staggered backward, struck his white forehead with his open hand, and cried "You are Dando! ! !"—He has been known to eat twenty dozen at one sitting; and would have eaten forty, if the truth had not flashed upon the shop-keeper.[8] For these offences he was

---

[1] Perhaps a quotation, but untraced.

[2] Written in large ornate capitals.

[3] i.e. CD himself and Catherine.

[4] A hole here in the paper, made by the removal of CD's signature on other side. "By The" seems probable: see address of last.

[5] "Literary Lady" (see *To* Forster, 3 Apr, *fn*). Initials omitted in previous editions.

[6] As CD's secretary. Name omitted in previous editions.

[7] John Dando, subject of many caricatures and of a play by Edward Stirling, 1838. Macaulay, after playing with his niece Alice in Apr 50, recorded: "I was Dando at a pastry-cook's, and then at an oyster-shop" (G. O. Trevelyan, *Life and Letters of Lord Macaulay*, 1876, II, 276);

Trevelyan described him as "the 'bouncing, seedy, swell'; hero of a hundred ballads; who was at least twice in every month brought before the magistrates for having refused to settle his bill after over-eating himself in an oyster-shop" (*op. cit.*, II, 276*n*). He died in Clerkenwell Gaol. In CD's sketch "The River" (*Evening Chronicle*, 6 June 35), a Thames boatman is described as a man who "shares with the defunct oyster-swallower the celebrated name of Dando".

[8] In Aug 1830, for instance, he was sued for eating 11 dozen of the largest oysters, without payment. He was discharged, but the oysterman threw a bucket of water at him and thrashed him afterwards (*The Times*, 20 Aug 1830).

constantly committed to the House of Correction. During his last imprison-ment, he was taken ill—got worse and worse—and at last began knocking violent double knocks at Death's Door. The Doctor stood beside his bed, with his fingers on his pulse. "He is going"—says the Doctor. "I see it in his eye. There is only one thing that would keep life in him for another hour, and that is —oysters." They were immediately brought. Dando swallowed eight, and feebly took a ninth. He held it in his mouth, and looked round the bed, strangely. "Not a bad one, is it?" says the doctor. The patient shook his head, rubbed his trembling hand upon his stomach, bolted the oyster, and fell back—Dead. They buried him in the Prison Yard, and paved his Grave with oyster shells.

We are all well and hearty, and have already begun to wonder what time next year you and Mrs. Felton[1] and Doctor Howe, will come across the briny sea together.[2] Tomorrow we go to the Seaside for two months. I am looking out for news of Longfellow, and shall be delighted when I know that he is on his way to London and this house.[3]

I am bent upon striking at the Piratical newspapers[4] with the sharpest edge I can put upon my small axe; and hope in the next session of Parliament to stop their entrance into Canada.[5] For the first time within the memory of man, the professors of English Literature seem disposed to act together, upon this question.[6] It is a good thing to aggravate a scoundrel if one can do nothing else— and I think we *can* make them smart a little in this way. *In a circular letter which I have addressed to every person connected with letters, I have (of course by mistake) given Prescott the credit of the Counter Memorial drawn by Mr. Bowen.[7] I will take the earliest opportunity of doing Mr. Bowen justice.*

I wish you had been at Greenwich the other day,[8] where a party of friends gave me a private dinner—public ones, I have refused. George Cruikshank[9] was perfectly wild at the reunion; and after singing all manner of maniac[10] songs, wound up the entertainment by coming home (six miles) in a little open phaeton of mine, *on his head*—to the mingled delight and indignation of the Metropolitan Police. We were very jovial, indeed; and I assure you that I drank your health with fearful vigor and energy.

[1] *Née* Mary Whitney; had married Felton 1838; died 1845.

[2] Howe and his wife came in 1843 (see *To* Howe, 19 May 43). But Felton did not come until 1853.

[3] For his arrival, see *To* Mitton, 6 Oct.

[4] i.e. *Brother Jonathan* and the other American "mammoths".

[5] Although the Copyright Amendment Act of 1 July 42—revised by the Customs and Excise Act of 9 July—prohibited the import of pirated works into the Colonies and authorized their seizure, Canada and the West Indies, in particular, found loopholes in the drafting and constantly evaded the law. In Mar 43 the London Post Office declared both *Brother Jonathan* and the *New World* contraband, under the Act: they could henceforward pass no British frontier, except in a cover and with letter postage (Washington *National Intelligencer*, 28 Mar 43).

[6] Individual petitioners to Parliament for the Copyright Bill, 1842, included Thomas Arnold, Carlyle, Wordsworth, Cobbett, Hood and Hartley Coleridge; joint petitions from British authors and publishers were also presented. Monckton Milnes had supported the Bill in a long and striking speech on 6 Apr. See also *To* Longman, 1 July, and *To* Murray, 2 Aug, and *fns.*

a Not previously published.

[7] See next *To* Prescott, *fn.*

[8] 9 July: see *To* Beard, 11 July.

[9] Name omitted in previous editions.

[10] MDGH and later editions mis-read as "marine".

On board that ship coming home, I established a club, called The United Vagabonds, to the huge amusement of the rest of the passengers. This Holy Brotherhood committed all kinds of absurdities, and dined always, with a variety of solemn forms, at one end of the table, below the mast, away from the rest. The Captain being ill when we were three or four days out, I produced my medicine chest, and recovered him. We had a few more sick men after that; and I went round "the wards" every day, in great state, accompanied by two Vagabonds, habited as Ben Allen and Bob Sawyer, bearing enormous rolls of plaister, and huge pairs of scissors. We were really very merry, all the way— breakfasted in one party at Liverpool—shook hands—and parted most cordially.

*a*God bless you my dear Felton. Commend me heartily to Mrs. Felton, and to your pretty little daughter, to whom our small fry send all manner of loves. Kate is—it is impossible to say how earnest in her messages. And I am always*a*

Affectionately | Your faithful friend
[CHARLES DICKENS][1]

I have looked over my Journal; and have decided to produce my American Trip in two Volumes. I have written about half the first,[2] since I came home; and hope to be out in October.—This is "exclusive news"—to be communicated to any friends to whom you may like to intrust it,[3] my dear F.

To THE EARL OF MULGRAVE, 31 JULY 1842*

Extract in unidentified bookseller's catalogue, n.d., Eastgate House, Rochester; dated 31 July 42.

What a villain you must suppose me to be! as to Sir Richard[4] he has blotted me out of the Calendar of his affections altogether I know. . . . Good God, what

---

aa Not previously published.
[1] Signature cut away, removing part of address on outside.
[2] At the end of his Ch. 10, "A Night Steamer on the Potomac River" (Ch. 9 in the printed text), CD wrote "END OF THE FIRST VOLUME", having then completed 160 slips. He had doubtless now just finished his short Ch. 4, "An American Railroad. Lowell and its Factory System", which ended on the 78th slip of his MS. For the later decision to end the first volume one chapter earlier, see *To* Mitton, 4 Sep and *fn*.
[3] Some of CD's American friends already knew that he was going to write a book about his visit. Sumner, for instance, had written to Channing on 23 June: "Dickens will write a series of graphic sketches on our country,—one on 'International Copyright;' another, I think, on 'Slavery,' with the first sentence from the Declaration of Independence for his motto" (*Memoir and*

Letters of Sumner, ed. E. L. Pierce, II, 212). Fanny Appleton (later Longfellow's wife) had written to her brother Thomas on 14 June: "This book will apparently be far from what is expected jocose & good natured, but is to lash our backs again about copyright & slavery. He meant, what would have been far wiser, only to introduce his American experiences to spice his future sketches of humanity, but his friends choose to expect a book about us which is very stupid of them, I think, for it is a thrice told tale & not in his line" (quoted in Edward Wagenknecht, "Dickens in Longfellow's Letters and Journals", *D*, LII [1955], 11). Speculation about his intentions was widespread after publication in early Aug of the forged *Morning Chronicle* letter (see *To* Forster, ?30 or 31 Aug and *fn*).
[4] Sir Richard Jackson (see *To* Forster, 12 May and *fn*).

a dream that play[1] appears; I can hardly believe that Mister Latham[2] had any material existence; Mr Whats-his-name in the Mackintosh, who puts our wigs on, I look upon as a mere fancy of my own brain.

To W. H. PRESCOTT, 31 JULY 1842*

MS Massachusetts Historical Society. *Address:* (By The Cunard Steam Packet, vîa Liverpool) | W. H. Prescott Esquire | Boston | United States.

London. 1 Devonshire Terrace | York Gate Regents Park.
Sunday Thirty First July 1842

My Dear Prescott.

I seize upon a few spare minutes which present themselves before I leave town for the seaside (which I do, tomorrow morning) to acknowledge the receipt of your welcome letter, and to thank you for it, heartily. I was most delighted by its receipt, and read it with an unusual amount of eagerness, I assure you.

I have been stirring up our English Writers, in the matter of the International Copyright; and have other measures brewing. In a circular letter which I addressed to the whole Literature of England (you may perhaps have seen it)[3] I gave you the credit of drawing up the Counter-Memorial. For although Felton had written me at Niagara a faithful account of Mr. Bowen's[4] gallantry,[5] I understood you to say, at Lebanon,[6] that you were the author of that Document. I see clearly, from your letter[7] that I was led into this mistake by your having

[1] *A Roland for an Oliver*: see *To* Forster, 26 May, *fn*.

[2] Perhaps W. H. Latham, comic actor, who had moved from London to New York in 1834; stage manager, National Theatre, New York, 1840–1; in 1843 acting at Mitchell's Olympic Theatre. Possibly he had brought CD's wig to Montreal from Mitchell.

[3] It, or extracts from it, appeared in a number of American papers on 6 Aug.

[4] Francis Bowen (1811–90; *DAB*), philosopher and political economist; protectionist and anti-British. Tutor at Harvard 1835; travelled in Europe 1839–41; proprietor and editor of the *North American Review* 1843–53; Alvord Professor of Natural Religion, Harvard, 1853–89. Wrote biographies and philosophical works besides numerous articles and reviews. Author, in collaboration with Felton (according to F. L. Mott, *A History of American Magazines 1741–1850*, p. 394), of "The Morals, Manners, and Poetry of England", *North American Review*, July 44 (LIX, 1–44), an article replying to "The Poets and Poetry of America",

Foreign Quarterly Review, Jan 44 (see *To* Poe, 6 Mar 42, *fn*)—his share in the article undoubtedly being the vitriolic attack on the English character for its "essential brutality and licentiousness", extensively citing as evidence the more discreditable details of English history, among them the employment of women and children in mines and collieries (sections from the 1842 report quoted). Felton may have been responsible for the first four pages about early Britain ("fruitful in barbarians, tin, and lead"), and was perhaps again involved in the final 12 pages which demonstrated that the English ("universal plagiarists") wholly lacked a "national" literature—clearly a parody of the *Foreign Quarterly*'s article.

[5] Clearly in the letter CD answered on 16 May. In *To* British Authors, 7 July, *fn*, CD referred to Bowen's as the "one dissentient voice".

[6] Where Prescott and CD had last met (see *To* Granville, 2 June, *fn*).

[7] Not published in *The Correspondence of W. H. Prescott 1833–1847*, ed. Roger Wolcott, 1925.

been the first signer.[1] Whenever you come across Mr. Bowen, pray tell him that I am exceedingly sorry to have made this error, and will do him justice.[2]

We found our Darlings (thank God) quite well, and most rejoiced to see us. Charley, our eldest, told his mother he was "too glad", and fell, soon afterwards, into very alarming convulsions. We were obliged, besides having our regular apothecary,[3] to call up Dr. Elliotson in the middle of the night, who said that joy had quite overthrown his system; and that he had never seen such a case before. I am happy to say the disorder took a favorable turn in a few hours, and he very soon recovered. He—that is, Charley—had previously confided to a confidential friend of his (a washerwoman) that he was afraid that when we *did* come home, he should "shake very much". He is a very queer fellow.[4]

Everything here is proceeding in the usual track. Peel is desperately unpopular; and the labouring classes are badly off and worse disposed. There is no doubt of this, although their condition is stated in the Newspapers with Newspaper exaggeration.[5]

I think it better to have the gratification of writing you a stupid letter, rather than none at all. Therefore, my dear Prescott, I hope you will receive this infliction, as having within it, a warm and lively assurance of my sincere regard. Remember me particularly to your father and mother, and all your house—and

[1] On 3 Aug Prescott wrote to Sumner: "You see Dickens has made mention of our giving no credit for Bowen's work—which I am sorry for, as B . . . deserves honourable mention" (MS Houghton Library).

[2] No public correction of the mistake has been found.

[3] Dr F. P. B. Pickthorn: see Vol. i, p. 390*n*.

[4] "I was much obliged by your friendly letter", wrote Prescott on 31 Aug; "Your account of your little boy's illness on your arrival is very touching. He has a stock of real sensibility, which may make him very happy or miserable in life, according to circumstances. I should love that chap very much, though with some trembling. Such fine spirits are not made for the rough and tumble of this coarse world." He continued: "I am delighted to hear you are getting on so rapidly with the Travels. You saw Brother Jonathan in rather a peculiar aspect,—his anxious visage relaxed into a broad grin the whole time, with a double dose of impertinent curiosity—and yet that curiosity was a compliment. The copyright I see sticks in your throat. It has stuck long in mine, but a Yankee who really loves his country may find worse things to stick there of late. *Go ahead* is our motto, but we have been doing it the last four or five years, as a

Paddy might say, stern foremost" (*Correspondence of W. H. Prescott 1833–1847*, p. 316).

[5] Both social and economic conditions had deteriorated badly throughout the year. Working-class anger was directed against the Corn Laws, the factory system and the New Poor Law; and there were disorders in the manufacturing areas. Peel was seen as the great criminal. He was burned in effigy in several provincial towns, there were rumours of plans to assassinate him, and posters put up by the Anti-Corn Law League in Manchester proclaimed him as responsible for the crisis. The Radical press was highly critical of him: the *Morning Chronicle*, 12 July, declared: "Sir Robert Peel is pre-eminently and in every way responsible for the present condition of the people"; the *Examiner*, 23 July, painted a picture of the Govt's looking forward to their shooting and hunting in the autumn, "and a turn out with the yeomanry if the people should not starve peaceably". But CD was probably right in his criticism of the press: cf. G. Kitson Clark, "Hunger and Politics in 1842", *Journal of Modern History*, xxv (1953), 370: "The evidence does not point to a real danger to the state . . . but it does point to a very serious fissure in the community".

then to all friends. Mrs. Dickens adds her love. For the love of you, I waive
considerations of jealousy, and forward it.

Ever believe me | Faithfully Your friend

W. H. Prescott Esquire   CHARLES DICKENS

P.S. There is a very general interest and curiosity here, to know what you are
doing.—I hope you are getting on bravely with your new book.[1]

To CHARLES SUMNER, 31 JULY 1842

MS Harvard College Library. *Address:* By The Cunard Steam Packet via Liver-
pool | Charles Sumner Esquire | Boston | Massachusetts | United States.

London 1 Devonshire Terrace | York Gate Regents Park.

Sunday Thirty First July 1842.

My Dear Sumner.

Here I am—at home again. Here I am in my own old room, with my books,
and pen and ink and paper,—battledores and shuttlecocks—bats and balls—
dumbbells—dog—and Raven. The Raven, I am sorry to say, has become a
Maniac. He falls into fits periodically; throws himself wildly on his back; and
plucks his own feathers up, by the roots. Nothing can be more unravenlike than
that. To hurt anybody else would have been quite in character, but to hurt
himself—Insanity in its most hopeless aspect.

I have had a medical gentleman who looks after the queen's birds,[2] to see him.
He says if it an't the weather, he don't know what it is. My man says its "aggera-
wation". The medical gentleman retorts that there is no such disorder in the
books. *I* suspect poison.[3] A malicious butcher was heard to threaten, some
months since. He said that "he worn't a goin to have pieces took out of his leg
ev'ry time he come down them Mews, at no price. And that if the wery dove as
come out o' the Hark interfered with him, he wished he might be busted, if he
wouldn't scrag him."—which looks alarming, I think?

Lady Holland has fitted up some of the lower rooms at Holland House, and
there are dinners there, as of yore. But the old rooms she has never entered.[4] I

---

[1] *A History of the Conquest of Mexico,*
which at their meeting at Lebanon Springs
CD had "offered to take charge of" in
London (*Correspondence of W. H. Prescott,*
p. 310). See 15 Oct and *fn.* Prescott commented on this letter to Sumner: "Dickens
is very lively & literary—I got a letter
from him also—but it contained nothing
of interest or I would send it to you. Do
you think he wrote the pieces attributed to
him in the papers? [*see ?30 or 31 Aug,* fn]
No—" (MS Houghton Library). He gave
CD's letter away to Mrs T. C. Cary, on 9
Nov 42 (MS Massachusetts Historical
Society).

[2] Presumably William Herring, dealer
in birds and live animals, the "medical

gentleman" who is mentioned as attending
Grip, the original raven, in all CD's
accounts of his death (see Vol. II, p. 231
and *n*).

[3] In this and what follows, CD either
repeats verbatim what he had written in
letters of 1841 about the death of Grip I, or
embroiders on it.

[4] Since Lord Holland's death, Lady
Holland had paid brief visits to Holland
House in Apr and Sep 41. But in June 42
some of the ground-floor rooms were
altered for her, and she stayed there inter-
mittently until late Oct, entertaining much
as before. In Nov, when she had returned
to 31 South Street, Sydney Smith wrote:
"The Widow Holland is remarkably well,

dined there, a week ago,[1] and had a strange sense of their being dark and vacant, overhead.[2] Sydney Smith is in greater force than ever, though waxing gouty. Talfourd has just now printed privately, and circulated among his friends, a little book (in prose) called "Recollections of a Visit to the Alps in 1841".[3] Here is the Dedication—Some folks think it uxorious.

To

H E R[4]

Whose Image Endears The Recollections

Of a Delightful Tour,

As it cheers and graces

The journey of life,

These "trivial, fond records"

Printed only for partial eyes,

Are Inscribed

By

A grateful and admiring husband

Well, after writing it out, I *do* think it is rather Adam-and-Evey.[5]

Brougham is in good health and spirits. Lyndhurst[6] has been ill, but is recovering. Jeffrey is much better, and sits in his Court again.[7] Rogers[8] is a thought more deaf than he was eight months ago. Tom Moore ages. Mrs. Norton[9] and Lady Seymour[10] are both sights for the Gods, as they always have

has changed her lacrymal habits and gives herself up to dining" (*The Letters of Sydney Smith*, ed. Nowell C. Smith, II, 770). After John Allen's death in Apr 43, she never stayed in Holland House again.

[1] See *To* Lady Holland, 11 July, *fn.*

[2] After her week's stay in the ground-floor rooms in Sep 41, Lady Holland had written of "a *stillness* that strikes to the heart, and drives me away" (Lord Ilchester, *Chronicles of Holland House*, 1937, p. 294).

[3] *Recollections of a First Visit to the Alps, in August and September, 1841*, printed for private circulation. A copy was in the Gad's Hill library at CD's death.

[4] Written large, in ornate capitals.

[5] Cf. Talfourd's speech at the supper on the first night of *Ion* (26 May 36), ascribing to his wife, in "lively vein", what amounted to "the whole merit of the production" (Macready, *Diaries*, I, 319). Several entries in Macready's diaries suggest that Mrs Talfourd (see Vol. I, p. 315*n*) was a woman to be reckoned with in her husband's affairs, and could be tiresome.

[6] John Singleton Copley, Baron Lyndhurst (1772–1863; *DNB*); son of John Singleton Copley, the elder (1737–1815; *DNB*), Boston portrait-painter; was Lord

Chancellor for the third time 1841–5. Sumner had met him in Feb 39, at a dinner-party given by Brougham (*Memoir and Letters of Charles Sumner*, ed. E. L. Pierce, II, 66); CD also had met him at Brougham's, 20 Dec 41 (Vol. II, p. 447*n*).

[7] He had had a bad fainting-fit in court in June 41, followed by a long illness. He resumed sitting in May 42, but gave his judgments in writing. In Nov 42 he was moved to the First Division of the Court of Session, where he sat with three colleagues.

[8] CD and Catherine apparently had dined with him on 7 July: see below.

[9] Caroline Elizabeth Sarah Norton (1808–77; *DNB*): see Vol. I, p. 302*n*. A letter from Rogers to Mrs Norton, saying "Please dine with me on Thursday next the 7th.—at 7 oClock to meet Dickens (Boz) & sundry others, skilful in pen & pencil" (facsimile in F. G. Kitton, *CD by Pen & Pencil*, 1890–92, III, facing p. 32), was probably an invitation for Thurs 7 July 42; for Mrs Norton later wrote to Catherine (in early Aug, presumably): "Dear Madam, | I trust to your recollecting our meeting and introduction at Mr. Rogers', to excuse my writing to beg of you to join a party, now concocting, to Rich-

been. Poor Southey's case is quite hopeless.[1] Landor is like forty lions concentrated into one Poet. D'Orsay is confined at home by bailiffs,[2] but is not an atom the worse in temper, health, looks, or spirits. Lady Blessington[3] wears brilliantly, and has the gloss upon her, yet. Bulwer is out of town, and I have not yet seen him. Edwin Landseer has thoroughly recovered.[4] Macready is

mond on Monday 15th. A *Hindoo* gentleman who rejoices in the name of *Dwarkananth Tagore*, is at present staying in England and has been staying with the Queen at Windsor [*in July 42*], and otherwise much fêted here. A few evenings since, he came to my house, and he asked which of the company (there were a *very* few friends and relations with me) was Mr. T. Moore—which was Mr. Rogers—which Mr. Dickens? You may conceive my shame at finding he expected to meet at my house all persons distinguished for talent, or remarkable in literature. I said 'give me another chance Sir, and I will collect a few of those you desire to see'. | This [is] the history of my excuse to you. He immediately said he would give a dinner at Richmond, and leave me to fulfil my promise as to company. He is full of Mr. Dickens' praise and says no English author is so generally known. Pray persuade Mr. Dickens to come and also, if agreeable, your pretty sister, and *any one* you consider an addition to the party. | If Monday the 15th suits you, and fortunately finds you disengaged, I will forthwith send word of our arrangements. We have a little steamer of our own to go down the river. | Yours dear Madam | Very truly, | Caroline Norton" (quoted in Alice Acland, *Caroline Norton*, 1948, pp. 129–30). But on 15 Aug CD and Catherine were at Broadstairs.
[10] Mrs Norton's younger sister, Jane Georgiana Sheridan (1809–84), married in 1830 to Lord Edward Seymour, later 12th Duke of Somerset. The Queen of Beauty at the "Eglinton Tournament" 1839.
[1] Robert Southey (1774–1843; *DNB*), the poet laureate, died the following March after a long mental illness.
[2] As he had been throughout 1841 (see Vol II, p. 291*n*).
[3] Marguerite, Countess of Blessington (1789–1849; *DNB*): see Vol. II, p. 58*n*.
[4] Edwin Henry Landseer, Edwin John on death certificate (1802–1873; *DNB*), animal painter, third and youngest son of John Landseer; brother of Thomas, en-

graver, and Charles, historical painter (see Vol. I, p. 566 and *n*, p. 601 and *n*). His precocious genius was encouraged by his family and by Haydon; began to exhibit at the Society of Arts 1813 and at the Royal Academy 1815; entered its schools as "a pretty little curly-headed boy", wrote Leslie (*Autobiographical Recollections*, ed. Tom Taylor, 1860, I, 39) who accompanied him on the first of many annual visits to Scotland 1824 when he drew Scott and his dogs at Abbotsford. Elected ARA 1826 at earliest possible age; RA 1831; and exhibited annually to 1850, except in 1841. Had evidently met CD well before 11 May 40 (see Vol. II, p. 65), but was less in literary circles than his brothers, and more in fashionable high society through his portrait painting. Was intimate with the whole family of the Russells and particularly Georgiana, wife of John, sixth Duke of Bedford (1766–1839), who, though twenty years older than himself, with ten children, was strikingly handsome and vivacious. According to a tradition in the family (John Woodward, Introduction to *Catalogue of the Royal Academy Landseer Exhibition*, 1961), concealed by all his early biographers, Landseer proposed to her in 1839 or 1840 and was rejected—possibly the cause of his mental breakdown in 1840. For Lord Holland's note on the advice he had given the Duchess of Bedford "relating to the *marrying Edwin Landseer*", see The Diary of B. R. Haydon, ed. W. B. Pope, 1960–3, V, 452. Elizabeth Barrett on 11 Jan 42 had just heard a "dreadful story" of his "cruel agitations through an attachment to the Duchess of Bedford—that they were secretly married"; and she is one source for the further story that Landseer was employed by the Duchess to paint a portrait of Lord William Russell after his murder by Courvoisier in Apr 40—"he, and *the Duchess only*, were shut up with the murdered man ... the artist overcome by a dreadful complexity of feeling and emotion went mad at his task and has never recovered his mind from that ... day to this" (*Elizabeth Barrett to Miss*

making great preparations for his next season at Drury Lane.[1] Ditto the Kembles for theirs at Covent Garden.[2] Forster is still uproarious with the joy of our return. Everybody else the same as usual.[3]

Maclise's picture from Hamlet[4] is a *tremendous* production. There are things in it, which in their powerful thought, exceed anything I have ever beheld in painting. You know the subject?—The play scene in Hamlet. The murderer is just pouring the poison into the ear of the mimic King. But what a notion is that, which hoods this murderer's head, as who should say to the real King—"*You*[5] know what face is under that!" What an extraordinary fellow he must be, who so manages the lights in this picture, that on the scene behind, is an enormous shadow of this groupe—as if the real murder were being done again by phantoms! And what a carrying-out of the prevailing idea, it is, to paint the very proscenium of the little stage with stories of Sin and Blood—the first temptation—Cain and Abel—and such like subjects—crying Murder! from the very walls.[6]

Mitford, ed. Betty Miller, 1954, p. 99). Landseer was certainly afflicted by mental depression ("full of terror & horror, expecting an assassin to destroy him", wrote Lady Holland, 22 May 40: *Elizabeth, Lady Holland to her Son, 1821–1845*, 1946, pp. 184–5), and went abroad with his old friend and business manager Jacob Bell from Aug to Dec 40, exhibiting nothing in 1841; the Duchess was much concerned and they remained close friends until her death in 1853. In Autumn 41 visited Scotland and was painting again; exhibited as usual 1842, including *Otter and Salmon* and *The Sanctuary*. Mrs Trollope's novel, *The Blue Belles of England*, published 1842, perhaps revived the rumours by her caricature of him as Bradley ("of diminutive form", "eccentrically familiar" towards ladies, with "a patent privilege . . . for falling in love with every face he paints" and "wild and whimsical bursts of mingled folly and cleverness"). He was much favoured by the Queen, had already painted several royal portraits, had taught her and Prince Albert etching; and received from them (as Maclise had too: see *To* Felton, 1 Sep 43) private commissions for surprise birthday presents to each other; he was an obvious choice for the fresco decoration of the royal summer-house in 1843 (see *To* Maclise, 6 July 43). In 1842 he was offered a knighthood, but refused.

[1] The season opened on 1 Oct with an outstanding *As You Like It* (Macready as Jaques, Louisa Nisbett as Rosalind; scenery by Charles Marshall—not, as often stated, by Stanfield). The second major revival was *King John*. See *To* Forster, 22 Sep.

[2] Charles Kemble had recently taken over the management of Covent Garden from Madame Vestris, and was preparing for *Norma* and Douglas Jerrold's *Gertrude's Cherries*. Owing to the last-minute illness of Adelaide Kemble, who was singing Norma, his opening had to be postponed from 2 to 9 Sep.

[3] Of the friends of whom CD was giving news, Sumner is known to have met Rogers, Landor, D'Orsay, Lady Blessington, Bulwer, Macready, Forster and Fanny Kemble during his visit to England of 1838–9.

[4] Which CD had been to see on 23 July (*To* Maclise, 24 July).

[5] Underlined twice.

[6] In a description of the picture in *Ainsworth's Magazine*, June 42, I, 321 ("An Exhibition Gossip" by M. A. Titmarsh), Thackeray had emphasized the same points: "Fancy, in the little theatre, the king asleep; a lamp in front casts a huge forked fantastic shadow over the scene—a shadow that looks like a horrible devil in the background that is grinning and aping the murder. Fancy ghastly flickering tapestries of Cain and Abel on the walls, . . ." The reviewer in the July *Blackwood's* (LII, 28) was similarly struck: "The light of a lamp is intercepted, by the hand pouring the poison into the sleeping king's ear, and there is the large shadow of the transaction awfully depicted on the wall. Mr. Maclise had no precedent for this—it is original, and evinces great

He is a great fellow, and I wish you knew him. I meant to write a long letter, and I wish you knew *that*, but you never will, for I am called away by invaders, and must finish this before I go, or lose the steamer. Remember me to all friends, beginning with Mr. and Mrs. Hillard.[1] Accept all imaginable regards from Kate,—and always believe me

My Dear Sumner | Faithfully | Your friend

CHARLES DICKENS

Lord Morpeth has written home, strong praise of Prescott. But not more than he deserves.

To GEORGE W. PUTNAM, [?JULY 1842]

Mention in *To* Putnam, 18 Oct 42. *Date:* while "the large Packing Case" sent by Putnam from New York in June was still in the English Customs.

Asking Putnam to send him the books collected on his visit to America.[2]

To JOHN MURRAY, 2 AUGUST 1842*

MS Sir John Murray.

Broadstairs | Tuesday Evening | August The Second 1842

My Dear Sir

On coming here an hour ago[3] (it is just now, post time) I found your note. If any conveyance *but* tonight's Mail could have brought me to town in sufficient time to join the Deputation who wait on Mr. Gladstone,[4] I should unquestionably have been a member of it.[5]

But as it would have been necessary for me,—even to get a place in this Mail, —to have started off to Ramsgate immediately on my arrival, in a most dilapidated and dusty condition, I have no alternative but to write to you,—assuring you that if I had been fortunate enough to have seen you on Sunday, or to have received your note two hours earlier, I would have sacrificed any consideration of convenience or personal comfort, for the lightest feather of a cause in which I have taken, and shall ever take, such an earnest interest.

I send you a letter, just received, and a newspaper.[6] They shew what the

---

genius." About the picture's "faults and merits", wrote Thackeray (*Ainsworth's*, 1, 320), there had been "some loud controversies" (see 24 July, *fn*); "but in every Exhibition for the last five years, if you saw a crowd before a picture, it was sure to be before [Maclise's]", and his *Hamlet*, Thackeray thought, was the best he had ever painted.

[1] Written over "Hillier" cancelled.

[2] These Putnam had already sent: see 18 Oct.

[3] Slightly disingenuous in implying that he had only just arrived in Broadstairs

though he had almost certainly arrived the day before as planned (*To* Colden, 31 July).

[4] William Ewart Gladstone (1809–98; *DNB*).

[5] The deputation was no doubt concerned with the import of pirated books into the Colonies, prohibited in recent Acts (see *To* Felton, 31 July, *fn*). Gladstone, as President of the Board of Trade, was responsible for their implementation.

[6] Not in the archives of John Murray Ltd. They had probably come from America on the *Caledonia*, which arrived 29 July.

scoundrels are doing; and point out a new feature in their frauds which I think is *most important*[1] Mr. Gladstone should understand.

If, at your convenience, you will write me a very brief account of what passed between the Deputation and Mr. Gladstone,[2] I shall be truly obliged to you. And if any other deputation, or any other meeting or discussion of any kind should ensue, pray give me such notice as will enable me to be present.

In great haste to save the post,

Always Believe Me | Faithfully Yours

John Murray Esquire   CHARLES DICKENS

To JONATHAN CHAPMAN, 3 AUGUST 1842

Text from *Massachusetts Historical Society Proceedings*, Boston, 1922, LIV, 153.[3]

Broadstairs, Kent | Wednesday, August the Third, 1842.

My dear Friend,

I date this letter from a little fishing town on the sea coast, whither we have retired (according to our annual custom) for a couple of months. It is a very delicious place; and I wish I could meet you on the beach in one of my long walks hereabouts.

The receipt of your letter gave me inexpressible pleasure. I have read the lines in which you recall our parting—many times[4]—always with new interest, and a still more eager looking forward to that bright day when we shall meet again on this side of the ocean. For I make a point of taking it for granted that that day is to come, and is to come moderately soon. There is nothing like assuming a fact stoutly in such a case as this. The comfort is unspeakable.

When we sat down in our own dear old home again, we did just as you have[5] imagined. I never in my life felt so keenly as on the night of our reaching it. When we had expended ourselves upon the children, I hurried away to see

---

[1] Underlined four times.

[2] Not discovered, if written.

[3] This text seems preferable to that in *D*, VI (1910), 214, though doubtful at two points noted below.

[4] Chapman had written to CD on 1 July: "As I cannot look upon your face or hear your voice or speak to you with mine, I seize my pen to write down my thoughts and send them to you as they rise. I was bitterly saddened at parting with you in the bay. I was not ready for it. The delightful day I spent with you in New York, by making me better acquainted with you, only made me the more unwilling to part, and after we cut loose from you, I gazed upon your ship until every vestige of her disappeared and I could not really say in my heart 'Good bye' until the last line

vanished. I had a gloomy sail back, and will you believe it, my thoughts involuntarily took the following form. It is not often, I assure you, that I am seduced from the plain path of prose, and it must be strong emotion indeed which could make me halt in verse; but as you inspired the verse, and as no one knows better than you how to appreciate hearty feeling even behind a ragged garment, I will tell them to you" (*D*, XXXVIII [Winter 1941/2], 11). Six stanzas follow, of which the first reads: "Farewell my Friend, I own the spell | Thy presence flung o'er me— | That as we part, my feelings swell | So lovingly to thee".

[5] *D* reads "would have". If "have" is correct, the reference must be to a lost part of Chapman's letter.

Macready who had had charge of them in our absence.[1] He was sitting in a dark room by an open window, and had no idea who it was, until I laid my hand upon his sleeve and spoke. Such a scene as we had then![2] I hustled[3] off to see another most intimate friend. He was dining out. Thereupon I drove to the place where he was dining; and admonishing the servant not to say who it was, told him to carry in the message that a gentleman wanted to speak to him. Guessing directly what it was, he came flying out of the house, got into the carriage, pulled up the window and began to cry. We had gone a couple of miles before he remembered he had left his hat behind him![4]

It would have been worth going anywhere—far less going where I have gained such friends as you—to feel the affection and attachment I have been made sensible of in ten thousand quiet ways, since I came home. As to the pleasures of home itself; they are unspeakable.

We found our darlings heartily well; and delighted beyond all telling to see us. They were in bed, but we very quickly had them up, you may believe. Charley (our eldest boy) told his mother that he was "too glad," as indeed he was, for he soon afterwards fell into violent convulsions. Dr. Elliotson told us afterwards that the sudden joy had perfectly turned his brain and overthrown his system, and that he had never seen the like in a child. Thank God he soon got well again. I can see him now, from the window at which I am writing, digging up the sand on the shore with a very small spade, and compressing it into a perfectly impossible wheelbarrow. The cliffs being high and the sea pretty cold, he looks a mere dot in creation. It is extraordinary how many hopes and affections we may pile up on such a speck; small as it is.

I have decided on writing an account of my journeyings in America[5] and am at this moment busily engaged upon the book. It will be published in a couple of volumes, either in October (I hope) or November next.

[1] According to Mamie, they had not been "very happy" during their parents' absence; for the Macreadys, at whose house they spent their days, "although the very kindest of the kind, brought up their own children with much more severity and seriousness than the little Dickens babies had ever been used to, and they were all certainly most miserable in the prim, gloomy, unjoyful house. And the youngest girl would cry and sob . . . the whole time she was being dressed, declaring over and over again that she would 'not doe'" (*CD by his Eldest Daughter*, p. 68).

[2] "I was lying on the sofa", Macready recorded in his diary, 30 June, "when a person entered abruptly, whom I glanced at as Forster?—*no*. Jonathan Bucknill?—*no*. Who was it but dear Dickens holding me in his arms in a transport of joy. God bless him!" (*Diaries*, II, 178).

[3] *D* reads "bustled".

[4] This was plainly Forster. According to F, III, viii, 278, what CD "had planned

before sailing as the way [they] should meet, received literal fulfilment"; cf., in *To* Forster, 26 Apr, "I shall surprise you by walking into 58, Lincoln's-inn fields". The plan before sailing must simply have been that CD would descend on Forster— wherever he might be—unannounced. Forster recalls (F, VI, iii, 506) that the "first book [CD] placed in [his] hands on his return from America, with reiterated injunctions to read it", was Hawthorne's *Mosses from an Old Manse*; but since this was not published until 1846, CD perhaps simply gave him a copy of the *Boston Miscellany*, May 1842, which contained "A Virtuoso's Collection" (referring to Barnaby Rudge's raven), one of the magazine stories afterwards collected in *Mosses*; alternatively, and more probably, the gift was Hawthorne's *Twice Told Tales*, second series, published Boston early in 1842.

[5] A decision made in Sep 41 and part and parcel of his plan to go to America (see Vol. II, p. 388).

I shall be very curious and eager to get your first letter after reading it.[1] As I fear I may miss the next packet even at the best, I must make this a very short epistle. But as I never should feel, though I made it a mile long, that I had said anything I want to say, I have the less scruple in closing it. Mrs. Dickens desires her best regards to yourself and Mrs. Chapman. The children, hearing us speak of you look very hard at this sheet of paper, and repeat the message. So I will add Mary's love and Katey's and Walter's, and take upon myself the responsibility of sending Charley's also.

God bless you, ever believe me, affectionately your friend,

CHARLES DICKENS

To JOHN FORSTER, [EARLY AUGUST 1842]

Extract in F, III, viii, 279. *Date:* one of CD's "first announcements" from Broadstairs according to Forster, who dates it 18 July—mistakenly (the Broadstairs visit began 1 Aug).[2] CD was clearly replying to a letter from Forster presumably written shortly after the departure for Broadstairs, since proofs of the Boston chapter (finished before 29 July: see *To* Mitton, 29 July, *fn*) could soon be expected.

The subjects at the beginning of the book are of that kind that I can't *dash* at them, and now and then they fret me in consequence.[3] When I come to Washington, I am all right. The solitary prison at Philadelphia is a good subject, though; I forgot that for the moment. Have you seen the Boston chapter yet? . . . I have never been in Cornwall either.[4] A mine certainly; and a letter for that purpose shall be got from Southwood Smith.[5] I have some notion of opening the new book in the lantern of a lighthouse![6]

[1] In reply to this letter, Chapman wrote of his fears about the coming book: see 15 Oct, *fn*.

[2] Forster makes a second mistake when introducing the extract: CD's house, he says, was "still in the occupation of Sir John Wilson" (see Vol. II, p. 404*n*)—and therefore he went to Broadstairs.

[3] He had probably now begun Ch. 5 ("Worcester. The Connecticut River. Hartford. New Haven to New York")—a short chapter (11 slips) like Ch. 4 (10 slips), but containing much factual detail. He "got to New York" (Ch. 6) on 10 Aug (*To* Forster, 11 Aug).

[4] As a special celebration of CD's homecoming, wrote Forster, "by way of challenge to what he had seen while abroad", a journey was to be arranged— for CD, Maclise, Stanfield and Forster himself—"into such of the most striking scenes of a picturesque English county as the majority of us might not before have visited: Cornwall being ultimately chosen" (F, III, viii, 278). Stanfield had been there before and painted St Michael's Mount.

[5] Thomas Southwood Smith, MD (1788–1861; *DNB*), physician, sanitary reformer and one of the four Infant Labour Commissioners to enquire into conditions in mines: see Vol. II, p. 164*n*. CD wrote on 22 Oct to ask his help in going down a Cornish mine.

[6] See *To* Southwood Smith, 22 Oct, *fn*. This idea was not finally abandoned until after his return from Cornwall (see *To* Forster, 12 Nov, *fn*).

To THOMAS BEARD, 4 AUGUST 1842

MS Dickens House. *Address:* Thomas Beard Esquire | 42 Portman Place | Edgeware Road | London.

Broadstairs | Thursday Fourth August 1842.

My Dear Beard.

Thank you heartily for your thoughtfulness and consideration in the matter of Alfred.[1] I have sent your note to him, by this Post.

I am looking out anxiously for your definite notice about that Month's holiday—for I say a Month, and down with the Baronet. This place is most beautiful just now: the weather being past all descriptive powers. Heavens, how crisp the water is—I bathed yesterday.

Ballard[2] too has got me some Port Wine which is quite remarkable—for a place like this, really astonishing.

Regards from all | Faithfully Yours always

Thomas Beard Esquire   CHARLES DICKENS

To COUNT D'ORSAY, 5 AUGUST 1842*

MS Comte de Gramont.

Broadstairs, Kent. | Fifth August 1842.

My Dear Count D'Orsay.

That fatal direction over your name—or I should rather say that fatal address[3] —includes my answer to your kind and welcome note. A Tiger with such a name as Dwarkanaught Tagore,[4] is not an everyday animal. Can a pinch of salt be dropped upon his tail?

I seem to think that I have seen puppet-shows in the Streets, placarding the Drama of Dwarkanaught Tagore—I half remember having seen him at Astleys, clad in a Leopard Skin with Salmon-colored arms and legs, throwing summersets in the Ring, and performing such feats of strength as amazed everybody but that misbelieving clown. I in part believe that I have seen him made up in a very small parcel with his heels very close together, and his card on his breast, at the Egyptian Room in the British Museum. And again my treacherous memory conjures up his portrait in colours, cut from a sheet of Theatrical Characters, and pasted on the lamp of a baked potatoe[5] stand, in the public street at night.

Dwarkanaught Tagore! What does the postman think of him—what does a long-stage coachman say, when he has him on the Waybill—what does his

---

[1] See *To* Beard, 11 July.

[2] James Ballard (?1806–74), landlord of the Albion Hotel: see Vol. I, p. 303*n*.

[3] i.e. "Broadstairs, Kent".

[4] Dwarkanath (mis-spelt by CD) Tagore (1794–1846), Calcutta merchant and philanthropist, now on his first visit to England. He had arrived 9 June; was presented to the Queen 16 June and later dined with her; met Peel, Palmerston and Brougham; and on 23 Aug received the Freedom of the

City of Edinburgh "as a Native Merchant in our Indian Empire". For his desire to meet CD and other English writers, see Caroline Norton *to* Catherine (*To* Sumner, 31 July, *fn*). CD called on him shortly before his departure on 15 Oct (Kissory Chand Mittra, *Memoir of Dwarkanath Tagore*, Calcutta, 1870, p. 103). He died during his second visit to England.

[5] Thus in MS.

washerwoman call him, when she mentions him to her friends—who gave him that name[1]—had he godfathers and godmothers—or did some old Maniac of a Brahmin, drunk with the spirit of Rice, invent it? Sometimes I think he is that grizzly Bear you spoke of—but then I remember that *he* came from America—not India. I have spelt it backwards, but it makes no less tremendous nonsense that way. He is a live hieroglyphic. I give him up.

I have hardly strength, after the exhaustion of this man, to beg my regards to Lady Blessington, and to Miss Power—and to say how very sorry I am—and how busy I am—for I have got into the very heart of my American Book, and night and day wish myself well through it.

Always Believe Me | Dear Count D'Orsay | Faithfully Yours
CHARLES DICKENS

To [HENRY] HALLAM,[2] [?7 AUGUST 1842]

Mention in next.

To FREDERICK DICKENS, 7 AUGUST 1842*

MS Mr Robert H. Taylor.

Broadstairs | Sunday Seventh August 1842.

My Dear Fred.

We shall find somebody or other, soon, to bring down the Accordion,[3] I dare say.—By the bye, if you should see or hear from Fletcher, tell him I shall be very glad to see him in these Latitudes.[4]

Let me have any Income Tax notices that may be left,[5]—with all convenient speed.

Tell Topping that Mr. Handisyde[6] has instructions to go into the dining

---

[1] Cf. *Book of Common Prayer*, Catechism.
[2] No doubt Henry Hallam (1777–1859; *DNB*), historian.
[3] See *To* Mrs Colden, 15 July and *fn*.
[4] For Fletcher's visit to Broadstairs in 1840 and the jokes about his eccentricities, see Vol. II, pp. 122–3 and *n*, 127 and *n*, and 129.
[5] Income Tax had been introduced while CD was in America. On 11 Mar 42, Peel announced a tax of 7d. in the pound on incomes of £150 *p.a.* and over, for a trial period of three years. The immediate outcry against the tax had been impassioned: it was described in the press as "pernicious", "monstrous", "inquisitorial", a "revolting injustice", an "obnoxious expedient"; the *Examiner* (26 Mar) denounced it as "the offspring of the Corn Monopoly" and execrated Peel (9 and 23 Apr) as "The Deceiver General". Protests had continued sporadically throughout the summer; but the tax was now becoming the subject of jokes. Forms were distributed in Aug, with 21 days allowed for their completion. *Punch*, on 13 Aug, remarked that as the greater part of its own assets had been "collected in a hat", the assessor must be a "clever fellow if he ever finds out what it comes to". But in the Lyceum's current production of *Bluebeard*, "some chance attempts at a joke about the Income Tax" were received with a "kind of shriek or howl—it was not laughter certainly", which was "mournfully instructive" (*Examiner*, 13 Aug).
[6] Probably of Thomas Handisyde & Son, upholsterers: see Vol. I, p. 242n. CD's accounts (MS Messrs Coutts) show a payment to them of £12.10.0 on 24 Aug 42. On 15 July 39 he had paid the firm £50.14.6; on 9 Sep 40, £102.15.0; and on 28 Oct 41, £28.15.6.

room whenever he pleases. And in case Hewett *should* call, and leave his card, I know I may rely on your going to see him forthwith, and directly writing to me. I would come to town immediately, for the pleasure of meeting him.[1]

I inclose a note for Mr. Hallam, to whom one of those pamphlets[2] I spoke to you about sending, was addressed. Let Topping take it.

And at your leisure will you call at that big floorcloth place in the Strand (near St. Clements)[3] and make an appointment with somebody to meet you in Devonshire Terrace. I want to know whether the floorcloth in the Hall, be worth new-painting. If so, they may take it up and do it. If not, let them state the cost of a new one of the same Pattern.

Has Maclise's framer[4] sent for the picture and prints in the little room? If not, let Topping take them. Maclise will give you the address.

One more commission—Will you tell Chapman and Hall (at any time that may suit you) that I want to know what it would cost to have gas carried into the Hall, and to have the Hall Lamp altered, for burning it.[5] Their gas-fitter wod. perhaps be the best workman to survey the job, and tell me.

All wcll,—with loves | Affy. always
CD.

To JOHN FORSTER, [7 AUGUST 1842]

Extract in F, III, viii, 280. *Date:* 7 Aug according to Forster.

I have been reading Tennyson[6] all this morning on the seashore. Among other trifling effects, the waters have dried up as they did of old, and shown me

[1] No doubt CD was referring to Capt. John Hewitt of the *Britannia* (see *To* Fred Dickens, 3 Jan, *fn*). But the call could not have taken place, for on 5 Aug the *Britannia* sailed from Liverpool for Boston. For his stay at Devonshire Terrace in Feb 43, see *To* Felton, 2 Mar.

[2] i.e. *To* British Authors, 7 July.

[3] Probably John Wilson, floorcloth manufacturer, 253 Strand (north side). St Clement's (on the same side) was listed in directories as between Nos 263 and 264.

[4] In 1844 this was Joseph Green of 14 Charles Street.

[5] Gas-lighting had been first publicly exhibited by Philippe Lebon (1767–1804) in Paris 1801 and by William Murdock (1754–1839; *DNB*) in London 1802. Gas was quickly used to light streets and, by 1825, large buildings (including *The Times* printing office and Drury Lane Theatre); but imperfect purification, leaky joints and blackened ceilings made its use in private houses uncommon till the invention of the atmospheric burner *c.* 1840. Scott introduced it at Abbotsford in 1823; the "reservoir gasometer" was filled about

twice a week, and produced "a great profusion of light" at small expense, but "his family heartily wished it had never been thought of", owing to the intense glare and unpleasant odour (Lockhart, *Life of Sir Walter Scott*, 1837–8, V, 266–8).

[6] See *To* Tennyson, 9 Mar 43, *fn*. *Poems*, in two vols (the first chiefly poems published 1830 and 1833, though often revised), had been published by Moxon on 14 May 42; by August widely and favourably reviewed, in contrast to earlier vols (E. F. Shannon, *Tennyson and the Reviewers*, Cambridge, Mass., 1952, pp. 60–81); Tennyson was now regarded as a poet of the first rank. On 8 Sep 42 he wrote to Edmund Lushington: "500 of my books are sold: according to Moxon's brother I have made a sensation!" (the 1833 volume had taken two years to sell 300). Forster's enthusiastic review (four columns) in the *Examiner* of 28 May was perhaps the earliest; he was also very probably the fervent reviewer of *Poems*, 1833, in the *True Sun*, 19 Jan 33 (E. F. Shannon, *op. cit.*, p. 18). The volumes were much talked of: Elizabeth Barrett

all the mermen and mermaids, at the bottom of the ocean;[1] together with millions of queer creatures, half-fish and half-fungus, looking down into all manner of coral caves and seaweed conservatories; and staring in with their great dull eyes at every open nook and loophole.[2] Who else, too, could conjure up such a close to the extraordinary and as Landor would say "most woonderful" series of pictures in the "dream of fair women," as—

> Squadrons and squares of men in brazen plates,
> Scaffolds, still sheets of water, divers woes,
> Ranges of glimmering vaults with iron grates,
> And hushed seraglios![3]

I am getting on pretty well, but it was so glittering and sunshiny yesterday that I was forced to make holiday.

To FREDERICK DICKENS, 10 AUGUST 1842

MS Benoliel Collection.

Broadstairs. | Wednesday Tenth August 1842.

My Dear Fred.

In consequence of a letter I have had from Alfred, I expect him down here by Monday's boat. I wish you would write to him by Thursday's post (the day you receive this) at Birmingham, and tell him that Topping will bring Georgina's[4] parcel to him, on board the 9 o'Clock Ramsgate Boat. And I wish Topping would take "Belle"[5] down too. I should like to have her here.

The accordion, *and* Kate's parcel, both arrived safely.

Love from all.

Have you got your leave yet?

Affecy. Always

Frederick Dickens Esquire.   CHARLES DICKENS

To JOHN FORSTER, [11 AUGUST 1842]

Extract in F, III, viii, 280. *Date:* four days later than letter of 7 Aug according to Forster.

I have not written a word this blessed day. I got to New York yesterday,[6]

on 21 May said they had "rapt [her] in Elysium" (*Elizabeth Barrett to Miss Mitford*, ed. Betty Miller, 1954, p. 117); Carlyle wrote to Tennyson, 7 Dec, that it was long since he had felt in an English book "the pulse of a real man's heart . . . strong as a lion's, yet gentle, loving and full of music . . . a genuine singer's heart! there are tones as of the nightingale" (*Alfred Lord Tennyson, a Memoir*, by his Son, 1897, I, 213), and he used his authority to spread his view abroad: see for instance his letter to Jane Wilson, 9 Dec 42 (*Nineteenth Century*, LXXXIX [1921], 811).

[1] *Poems*, 1842, included "The Merman" and "The Mermaid" (first published 1830).

[2] Cf., in "The Mermaid", the great snake who would "look in at the gate | With his large calm eyes"; and, in "The Merman", "the pale-green sea-groves straight and high".

[3] Stanza ix of "A Dream of Fair Women" (first published 1832).

[4] Georgina Hogarth (1827–1917), Catherine's younger sister. See *To* Longfellow, 29 Dec, *fn*.

[5] An animal not elsewhere mentioned.

[6] i.e. he had begun *American Notes*, Ch. 6.

and think it goes as it should . . . . Little doggy[1] improves rapidly, and now jumps over my stick at the word of command. I have changed his name to Snittle Timbery, as more sonorous and expressive. He unites with the rest of the family in cordial regards and loves. *Nota Bene.* The Margate theatre is open every evening,[2] and the Four Patagonians[3] (see Goldsmith's *Essays*)[4] are performing thrice a week at Ranelagh.[5]

To DANIEL MACLISE, 14 AUGUST 1842*

MS Private; seen before partial destruction in Prestwick air-crash Dec 1954; fragments (*aa, bb*) MS Colonel Richard Gimbel.

Broadstairs | Sunday Fourteenth August 42.

My Dear Mac

At the risk of awakening that suspicious resentment which always appears to fire your bosom when I give you an Invitation, I ask, I implore, I *recommend*[6] you to come *a*down here. The beauty of the weather, the delicacy of the bathing, the crispness of the sea, and the charms of the Screamer,[7] all cry "Come!"*a* Her swelling bosom and swelling other B invite you. Come! come! come! Had I three mouths I'd ask you.[8]

*b*I want to know (with a view to the accuracy of a passage in*b* the Book I am writing) what an old Irishwoman would call a Burying Ground at home. Would she call that place in which the bones of her kindred lie—a Burying Ground— a Chapel Yard—or what. Mrs. Hall[9] would call it a Cushla Ma Cree or a Ma Vourneen or an Obedadsir[10]—but that's not what I mean, at all.[11]

Tell me—and come.

Faithfully Ever
CHARLES DICKENS

[1] Given him in America by William Mitchell: see *To* Mitton, 22 Mar and *fn.*

[2] The Theatre Royal, closed and used as a chapel for a year, after J. S. Faucit's managership 1820–40, had re-opened on 23 July under the management of J. D. Robson, proprietor of the Royal Hotel (Malcolm Morley, *Margate and its Theatres*, 1966, pp. 50–8). Its opening plays were *The Hypocrite* (a version of *Tartuffe*) and Planché's *The Loan of a Lover*, followed by *Hamlet*.

[3] A group of tumblers; reviewed in the *Kent Herald*, 4 Aug, as "the celebrated four Patagonians, Messrs Ethair, Lesage, Bartini, and Laflar", who performed "astonishing feats . . . pyramids and equilibriums, classical delineations, tending to display the first principles of mathematics".

[4] No doubt a reference to "the giant fair ones of Patagonia" in Letter CXIV of *The Citizen of the World* ("Against the Marriage Act. A Fable"; reprinted as "The Genius of Love" in *Essays*, 1765).

[5] Peter's Gardens, Margate, a diminutive replica of the Tivoli Gardens (see *To* Mitton, 21 Sep, *fn*), had taken the name Ranelagh. It ceased to be used for performances after the "Patagonians" had left (M. Morley, *op. cit.*, p. 57).

[6] Underlined twice.

[7] Perhaps Miss Collins or Miss Strivens: see Vol. II, p. 123 and *n.*

[8] Cf. *Macbeth*, IV, i, 78: "Had I three ears, I'ld hear thee".

[9] Anna Maria Hall (1800–81; *DNB*), writer, wife of S. C. Hall: see Vol. I, p. 481*n.*

[10] "Cushla" and "Mavourneen" both appear as terms of endearment in Mrs Hall's *Lights and Shadows of Irish Life*, 1838, for instance. "Obedadsir" is obviously CD's invention.

[11] Maclise apparently recommended "graveyard": see *American Notes*, Ch. 6.

To JOHN BLACK,[1] 15 AUGUST 1842

Extract in John Heise catalogue No. 744 (1927); *MS* 1 p.; dated Broadstairs, Kent, Monday Fifteenth August 1842.

I see that Lord Londonderry advertizes a letter to Lord Ashley on the subject of mines and collieries.[2] If you would like to have it noticed, and will send it to me, HERE, when it comes out, I shall be happy to review it.[3] Faithfully yours always, My dear Sir

[CHARLES DICKENS]

To W. H. MAXWELL,[4] 15 AUGUST [1842]*

Text from transcript by Mr Walter Dexter. *Date:* 15 Aug was Monday in 1842.

Broadstairs | Monday Fifteenth August

My Dear Sir,

I was engaged to go to *Minster*[5] early this morning[6]—and I regret to say that in the hurry of getting away, I forgot to write to you. Pray excuse me.

I shall be at home to-morrow at half past one. If I should not see you then, I will do myself the pleasure of calling on you.

Faithfully yours,
CHARLES DICKENS

To GEORGE CRUIKSHANK, 20 AUGUST 1842

MS Colonel Richard Gimbel.

Broadstairs, Twentieth August 1842.

My Dear George

Don't be much after 10 O'Clock. I'll tell you why.—We will dine late, and make a Morning at Minster, where there is a good old Church.[7] We will send

---

[1] John Black (1783–1855; *DNB*), editor of the *Morning Chronicle*: see Vol. I, p. 83*n*.

[2] *A Letter to Lord Ashley, M.P., On the Mines and Collieries Bill*, by C. W. Vane, Marquess of Londonderry, G.C.B.; advertised by Colburn in the *Morning Chronicle*, 13 Aug, and *The Times*, 15 Aug, as to be published "in a few days". A pamphlet of 145 pages, it did not in fact appear until October.

[3] For the pamphlet and CD's review in the *Chronicle*, see *To* Mackay, 19 Oct, *fn*.

[4] William Hamilton Maxwell (1792–1850; *DNB*), novelist: see Vol. I, p. 354*n*, and (for CD's disapproval of two of his contributions to *Bentley's Miscellany*) Vol. I, pp. 236 and 307. CD had included his "Expedition of Major Ap Owen to the Lakes of Killarney" in *The Pic Nic Papers*, 1841. His *Rambling Recollections of a Soldier of Fortune* was published Dublin, 1842.

[5] A village (now a small town) 4½ miles west of Ramsgate and 5½ south-west of Broadstairs.

[6] Perhaps with a view to arranging an expedition there: see next.

[7] Mainly late Norman and Early English, and one of the finest churches in Kent; close to the ruined Augustinian Abbey.

the Ladies there in a Fly—leaving them to start at a quarter before 12—and you, Maclise, Forster,[1] and I, will start forthwith, to walk.

Always Faithfully Yours

BOZ

All manner of loves to Mrs. C—including mine.

To JOHN FORSTER, [?25 AUGUST 1842]

Extract in F, III, viii, 283; wrongly given as part of letter of 25 Sep. *Date: American Notes* was first advertised on Tues 30 Aug as to be published "in October next, in 2 vols" (*Morning Chronicle*); CD presumably suggested the title to Forster a few days before (see *fn*).

What do you think of this for my title—*American Notes for General Circulation;* and of this motto?

"In reply to a question from the Bench, the Solicitor for the Bank observed, that this kind of notes circulated the most extensively, in those parts of the world where they were stolen and forged.[2] *Old Bailey Report*."[3]

To ALBANY FONBLANQUE, 26 AUGUST 1842

Summary in Parke-Bernet Galleries catalogue, Jan 1941; *MS* 1 p.; dated Broadstairs, Kent, 26 Aug 42. *Address* (envelope, MS Sotheby's, June 1962): Albany Fonblanque Esquire | 48 Connaught Square | Edgeware Road | London; PM 27 Aug 42 (clearly day of receipt).

Asking if he might borrow the letter he had written Fonblanque from Washington[4] to save himself the trouble of describing the scenes again.[5]

---

[1] Forster had probably come down the evening before (a Friday), after seeing the week's *Examiner* to the press, and possibly Maclise came with him. *To* Forster, 11 Aug (holding out the Margate theatre and the Patagonians as bait) shows no expectation of a visit then; and there is no hint in *To* Fred Dickens, 7 Aug, that Maclise would shortly be leaving London.

[2] Possibly title and motto came to CD's mind while writing his Philadelphia chapter (finished 24 Aug: see *To* Forster, ?30 or 31 Aug, *fn*), which mentioned the stoppage of the United States Bank, "with all its ruinous consequences". He may well have sent the idea to Forster on 25 Aug, before embarking on his Washington chapter.

[3] Not found. "The motto was omitted, objection being made to it", says Forster (F, III, viii, 283)—himself doubtless the objector.

[4] *To* Fonblanque, 12 Mar 42.

[5] CD had already written 13 slips of his Washington chapter when he made this request to Fonblanque, and had pencilled at the foot of the 13th the message to his printer, "more of this Chapter to come" (MS V & A). In the remaining six slips of the chapter, he used from his letter to Fonblanque the description of the President's house and two anecdotes about debates in the Senate, virtually verbatim.

To JOHN FORSTER, [?30 or 31 AUGUST 1842]

Extract in F, III, viii, 281. *Date:* "the opening of September" according to Forster;
but news of the forged letter must have been sent to Forster before CD wrote about
it to Felton and others on 1 Sep—on which day, moreover, he was in London, seeing
Forster (*To* Felton, 1 Sep), and had no need to write. The *Emerald* from New York
and *Columbia* from Boston both arrived at Liverpool 29 Aug, and mail should have
reached Broadstairs on the 30th or 31st. Proofs of *American Notes*, Ch. 7, would
almost certainly have arrived by 30 Aug (see *fn*).

The Philadelphia chapter I think very good,[1] but I am sorry to say it has not
made as much in print as I hoped.[2] . . . In America they have forged a letter
with my signature, which they coolly declare appeared in the *Chronicle* with
the copyright circular;[3] and in which I express myself in such terms as you
may imagine, in reference to the dinners and so forth. It has been widely distributed all over the States;[4] and the felon who invented it is a "smart man" of

[1] Ch. 7, "Philadelphia, and its Solitary
Prison", seemed to Lord Jeffrey "as
pathetic and powerful a piece of writing"
as he had ever seen (letter to CD: see *To*
Felton, 31 Dec, *fn*), and a number of English reviewers picked it out for praise.
The *Morning Chronicle* thought its "appalling disclosures" would be read with
"deep interest". But to those who had
accompanied CD on his visit to the Penitentiary (8 Mar) and had believed that he
approved of it, and to many others who
were proud both of the prison and its
system, CD's account in *American Notes*
came as a great shock, and it was bitterly
attacked (see *To* Forster, 13 Mar, *fn*).

[2] On the likely assumption that he wrote
a chapter a week at this stage of the book,
he would have finished Ch. 7 on 24 Aug.
He had begun Ch. 6 on 10 Aug (*To* Forster, 11 Aug); and on the 26th was concerned with Ch. 8 (see last).

[3] The full text of the forged letter appeared in one paper only—the *New York
Evening Tattler* of 11 Aug (of which the
only copy found is in the Union College,
Schenectady, N.Y.). See Appx, pp. 625-7.

[4] The facts, taken from sample papers,
seem to have been these.—Clearly on 2 or 3
Aug, the *Evening Tattler* (as quoted in the
New Haven Daily Herald, 4 Aug) had
announced that it had found, "with no
small regret", in different numbers of the
Morning Chronicle, two letters from CD to
the editor "which cast several very ungenerous flings at the American people";
it quoted part of paragraph 6 of the authentic circular letter of 7 July ("The persons
who exert themselves to mislead the

American public . . . men of . . . more than
indifferent reputation"), and followed it
with three paragraphs which were pure
invention—aimed to show CD's attitude
as one of ingratitude, superiority, and dislike (see Appx, pp. 626-7, paragraphs 4, 6,
10). Many papers besides the *New Haven
Daily Herald* reprinted the paragraphs
(e.g. the *Boston Courier*, 6 Aug, copied in
the *Hartford Daily Courant*, 11 Aug),
inevitably fusing the spurious with the
genuine, or—if they had doubts—uncertain which was which. Thus on 6 Aug the
*Philadelphia North American and Daily
Advertiser* announced that a "mean forgery" was going the rounds of the newspapers "in the shape of a letter" from CD,
yet quoted paragraph 10 of the forgery.
On 12 Aug the *New Haven Daily Herald*
stated that the opinion was "gaining
ground" that most of the extracts were
forgeries, and quoted the *Evening Tattler's*
response of 10 Aug to the challenge: their
publication of the four paragraphs having
aroused, the *Tattler* said, "a good deal of
misconception", they must emphasize that
there were "*two* letters"—one of them CD's
circular; the other they would print in full
on the following day: "We don't believe
another office in the city has the London
paper containing it". To their original
three forged paragraphs they now gaily
added another ten, and on 11 Aug the
whole was duly published as "To the
Editor of the Morning Chronicle, Devonshire Terrace, Parkgate [*thus*], July 15th,
1842", signed "Charles Dickens". The
New England Weekly Review, now sure
that the letter was not authentic, yet still

course. You are to understand that it is not done as a joke, and is scurrilously reviewed.[1] Mr. Park Benjamin[2] begins a lucubration upon it with these capitals, DICKENS IS A FOOL, AND A LIAR. . . .[3] I have a new protégé, in the person of a wretched deaf and dumb boy whom I found upon the sands the other day, half dead, and have got (for the present) into the union infirmary at Minster. A most deplorable case.

believing it to have originated in the *Morning Chronicle*, attributed it to "some jackass of an American, residing in London". Some papers (e.g. the *Boston Transcript*, 16 Aug) continued to quote from the forged paragraphs; but several had from the beginning refused to believe that CD was the author of anything but the circular. One, for instance, wrote: "When the recent forged letter was published, so gross, that on the very first day of its publication we did not hesitate to pronounce it a base and malicious libel; so transparent, that the publishers of it themselves came speedily forward and acknowledged it was a forgery, impudently laughing at the few gudgeons they had caught with it—when this appeared, there were not wanting newspapers to copy it with inflammatory comments, and procure its circulation in parts of the country where it was less liable to detection" (unidentified newspaper cutting, Forster Collection, V & A). Almost certainly CD had seen only the original three forged paragraphs; among these, his reference is clearly to "I did not seek their attentions, their dinners, and their balls. On the contrary, these things were forced upon me . . ." (paragraph 6).

[1] The *Tattler* (as quoted in the *New Haven Daily Herald*, 4 Aug) commented sharply on its own invention: "Thank you, Mr. Boz. The next time you or any other 'well bred' book makers from foreign parts, come to this country, . . . you will be spared the opportunity of witnessing the 'glaring faults' of American society"; and ended, "We have heard of cool insolence before, but we think this goes beyond the limit". The *Boston Courier*, as quoted in the Worcester *Massachusetts Spy* of 17 Aug, thought CD's ingratitude for kindnesses done him could only be viewed with "indignation and contempt"; "prate" as he might of good breeding, he had exhibited "*baseness of heart*" (for this and other attacks in the *Spy*, see Paul B. Davis, "Dickens and the American Press, 1842", *Dickens Studies*, IV [1968], 33–4). But

many papers slanted their criticism as much against the "American aristocracy" as against CD himself (see the *Tattler*'s own comment, Appx, pp. 625–6). Thus the *Boston Courier*, 6 Aug (quoted in the *Hartford Daily Courant*, 11 Aug) introduced the three forged paragraphs with: "When the *first people* of our good city of Boston . . . abstracted ten dollars apiece from their overflowing purses to enable them to give a magnificent illustration of their own aristocratic folly . . . they played into [Boz's] hands . . . as appears by the following extracts"; and then reprinted from the *New York Express*, under the heading "The Toasters and Feasters of Boz": "We are happy to see that the sycophants of Dickens, and the numerous toadies that thronged his chambers, night and day, are to be well *Trollopized* before they escape from his claws. . . . We hope to have a book now from Dickens before he has done."

[2] Park Benjamin (1809–64; *DAB*), founder and editor of the weekly *New World* (1839–45) and virtual father of the "mammoth" papers; in 1839 had founded *Brother Jonathan*, and the *Evening Tattler*, from both of which he withdrew after a few months. For his piracies of CD's works in the *New World*, see To British Authors, 7 July and *fn*. Benjamin also throve on sensationalism, defamation and abuse of rival editors; he wrote verse and much caustic criticism, and frequently quarrelled with his associates. Although he and L. G. Clark were described as "endeavouring to put themselves forward & do the honors for [CD] when he comes" (John McCracken *to* Sumner, 21 Dec 41, MS Houghton Library, Harvard), he wrote to Irving on 20 Feb 42: "I did not attend the festival to Mr. Dickens, because I could not do so consistently with my disapproval of the rendition of any such public honors to any English author. Apart from the fact that their aggravated praise will recoil upon the object of them, and thus people will punish him for their

To MESSRS THOMAS BARGE JUNR & BROS,[1]
1 SEPTEMBER 1842*

MS Dr Gordon N. Ray.

1 Devonshire Terrace, York Gate | Regents Park London.
First September 1842.

Gentlemen.

I am much indebted to you for your obliging letter (which I should have acknowledged sooner, but that I have been absent from town)—and for its most ingenious inclosure.

I assure you that I shall be proud and happy to accept your proposed present. And that I am always

Yours faithfully and obliged
CHARLES DICKENS

Messrs. Thomas Barge Junr. and Brothers.

---

own folly, I deplore the ready sycophancy of Americans toward foreigners" (MS Columbia University Library). For early newspaper warnings against over-lionizing CD, see *To* Forster, 17 Feb, *fn* p. 72.

[3] In fact the article in the *New World* of 6 Aug to which CD is obviously referring was a comment not on the forged letter but on his circular to British Authors of 7 July, which it quoted in full from the *Literary Gazette*, under the heading "The Copyright Fever". "The writer", it ran, "is either a fool or a knave [*not a "Liar", though "malicious lie" comes in text below—and not in capitals*]. That he is not a fool, we know; he is a man of extraordinary genius, who has written works that have delighted the age. We conclude, therefore, that he is a knave; for he has been guilty of gross falsehood and a gross endeavor to deceive and mislead the British public. . . . He betrays, moreover, a very insolent and malignant spirit. He was terribly disappointed, no doubt, in failing to accomplish the object of his mission to the United States; but this does not justify his abuse of gentlemen, whose rank in society is quite as high as that of the writer's former employers and masters, when he was a reporter and penny-a-liner for the London press. But this species of abuse we look upon as but the beginning of the end.

We have, from the first, expected from Mr. Dickens a book ridiculing the Americans, and showing up the silly people, who shouted in his footsteps as if he had been a demi-god. | Our own paper is one of those which republish English books, and we therefore consider ourselves *blackguarded* with the rest—although, if Mr. Dickens dares to assert that the New World ever attacked the English author of a book, of the rapid sale of which we boasted [*see To British Authors, 7 July*], he dares utter a paltry and malicious lie, for which it would be difficult to find an excuse, either in his ignorance or his ill temper." The editorial went on to apologize for having previously published "one or two articles outrageously laudatory of Mr. Dickens"; but these were inserted solely "at the earnest solicitation of an old and valued friend . . . We disapproved entirely of the miserable adulation with which this young man was followed; and we refused, on every occasion, to join with the senseless rabble. The consequences we feared, are already upon us, in the slanders of the foregoing letter". Finally the editorial quoted an "excellent article" from the *New York Sun* on the beneficial effects of "cheap books for the people".

[1] Merchants, of Dickinson Street, Manchester.

To JOHN JAY,[1] 1 SEPTEMBER 1842

Text from the *New York Independent*, 25 Dec 1879.

Devonshire Terrace, York Gate, | Regent's Park, London,
[Private]   First Sept., 1842

My Dear Sir,
    I am greatly obliged to you for your letter and for the newspapers which accompanied it.[2]
    You know what the American press is. I need scarcely add that these passages purporting to have been written by me, to which you call my attention, are forgeries as false as our felons swing for. I have not contradicted them publicly, nor shall I do so. I had not been many weeks in America (no stranger can be) before I was amazed and repelled beyond expression by these instruments of public degradation. No deed of their doing would surprise me and no falsehood of their telling would move me into communication with them for an instant.

I am, my dear sir, faithfully yours,
CHARLES DICKENS

To LEWIS GAYLORD CLARK, [? 1 SEPTEMBER 1842]

Extract quoted in Clark *to* Robert Balmanno, [Oct 42], *Letters of Willis Gaylord Clark and Lewis Gaylord Clark*, ed. L. W. Dunlap, New York, 1940, p. 137 (*aa*); and extract in *Knickerbocker Magazine*, Oct 42, xx, 395 (*bb*). *Date:* Subject and wording point to same day as last.

*a*You know what the American papers are. Is it necessary for me to say that the passages which have been published in my name are lies and forgeries? I have not contradicted them publicly, nor do I mean to do so. When I enter the lists of literature with such adversaries, I shall have left my self-respect without the Barrier.*a*3

[1] John Jay (1817–94; *DAB*), American lawyer, historian and diplomat; son of Judge William Jay and grandson of Chief Justice John Jay. Practised law in New York City 1839–58; advocated international copyright, and published *International Copyright: Memorials of John Jay and of William C. Bryant and others*, . . . New York, 1848. Prominent in the anti-slavery movement, acting as counsel for negro fugitives under the Fugitive Slave Law, 1850. CD owned his pamphlet, *The Progress and Results of Emancipation in the English West Indies*, New York, 1842.

[2] Newspapers containing parts of the forged letter; possibly the first copies CD saw.

[3] After the quotation, Clark comments: "His allusion is to the 'papers in question',

and not intended to be so broad as to include the American press *proper* but rather *improper*". The *Knickerbocker* of Sep 42 contained the following comment: "Some of the daily and weekly journals have published a letter purporting to come from MR. DICKENS, speaking in disrespectful terms of the people of this country, and of the attentions which were shown him in his progress through the Union. We have good reasons for stating, that only *one* letter from MR. DICKENS has appeared since his return home, and that was in relation to the International Copy-right question, in which no more was stated, save a clause reflecting in too unmeasured terms upon the mammoth weekly journals, than the writer publicly avowed while in this country."

*b*I have not forgotten my promise[1] nor your patience. I *will* not forget either.*b*

To C. C. FELTON, 1 SEPTEMBER 1842†

MS (incomplete) Yale University Library; missing passage (*aa*) from typescript Harvard College Library. *Address:* By The Great Wester[n Steamer vïa Bristol] | Professor Fel[ton] | Ca[mbridge | Massachusetts | United States.]

1 Devonshire Terrace, York Gate | Regents Park London
First September 1842

My Dear Felton

Of course[2] that letter in the Papers was as foul a forgery as ever felon swung for. *b*You know what the American Press is, and are as little surprised as I am.*b*

I have not contradicted it publicly, nor shall I.[3] When I tilt at such wringings-out of the dirtiest mortality, I shall be another man indeed—almost the creature they would make me.

I gave your message to Forster, who sends a despatch-box full of kind remembrances in return. He is in a great state of delight with the first Volume of my American Book (which I have just finished)[4]—and swears loudly by it. It is *True*, and Honorable, *b*but they will like it the less for having those two obnoxious properties,*b* I know. I shall hope to send it you, complete, by the First Steamer in November.

Your description of the Porter and the carpet bags,[5] prepares me for a first-rate facetious Novel, brim full of the richest humour, on which I have no doubt you are engaged. What is it called?—Sometimes I imagine the title-page thus:

OYSTERS

IN

EVERY STYLE

OR

OPENINGS

OF

LIFE.

BY

YOUNG DANDO[6]

bb Not previously published.

[1] To write for the *Knickerbocker*: see Vol. II, p. 55 and *n*.

[2] Written very large and underlined with emphatic short double strokes.

[3] CD held to this intention; but in fact a denial in his own words did appear in the American press, sent by Hone: see 16 Sep, *fn*.

[4] i.e. he had now finished Ch. 10, "A Night Steamer on the Potomac River" (Ch. 9 in the printed text), and written "END OF THE FIRST VOLUME". This chapter

must have been written fairly quickly; for on 26 Aug he still had the previous chapter ("Washington") on his hands—though probably with little left to do to it beyond adding from his letter to Fonblanque of 12 Mar (see 26 Aug and *fn*), and while awaiting this he may well have started his Ch. 10. For the decision to end the volume after all with his Washington chapter, see *To* Mitton, 4 Sep and *fn*.

[5] "On board the packet ship [*in New York harbour*] Felton accidentally met with his carpet bag which, it seems, had

As to the man putting the luggage on his head, as a sort of sign—I adopt it from this hour.

I date this from London, where I have come, as a good profligate, graceless bachelor, for a day or two—leaving my wife and babbies at the Seaside, *b*just as you leave Mrs. Felton and that pretty little daughter in the academic Groves of Cambridge, while you gallivant about New York.*b* Heavens! If you were but here, at this minute! A piece of Salmon and a Steak are cooking in the kitchen—it's a very wet day, and I have had a fire lighted—the Wine sparkles on a side table—the room looks the more snug from being the only *un*dismantled one in the house[1]—plates are warming for Forster and Maclise whose knock I am momentarily expecting—that groom I told you of,[2] who never comes into the house, except when we are all out of town—is walking about, in his shirt sleeves, without the smallest consciousness of impropriety[3]—and a great mound of proofs are waiting to be read aloud,[4] after dinner. With what a shout I would clap you down into the easiest chair, my genial Felton, if you could but appear—and order you a pair of slippers instantly!—

Since I have written this, the aforesaid groom—a very small man (as the fashion is) with fiery red hair (as the fashion is *not*) has looked very hard at me, and fluttered about me at the same time, like a giant butterfly. After a pause, he says, in a Sam-Wellerish kind of way—"I vent to the Club this mornin' Sir. There vorn't no letters Sir"—"Very good, Topping"—"How's Missis Sir?"—"Pretty well, Topping"—"Glad to hear it Sir. *My* Missis an't wery vell Sir"—"No!"—"No Sir—She's a goin', Sir, to have a hin-crease[5] wery soon, and it makes her rather nervous Sir; and ven a young 'ooman gets at all down upon her luck at sich a time Sir, she goes down wery deep Sir"—To this sentiment, I reply affirmatively. And then he adds, as he stirs the fire (as if he were thinking out loud) "Wot a mystery it is! Wot a go is Natur!"—with which scrap of philosophy, he gradually gets nearer to the door, and so fades out of the room.

This same man asked me one day, soon after I came home, [wh]at[6] Sir John Wilson was. This is a friend of mine, who took our house *a*and servants, and everything as it stood, during our absence in America. I told him, an officer —"A wot Sir?"—"an officer"—and then, for fear he should think I meant a Police officer, I added—"an officer in the army". "I beg your pardon Sir", he said touching his hat, "but the club as I always drove him to, wos the United Servants".

The real name of this club is the United Service, but I have no doubt he

taken a liking to Dickens' luggage and bewitched the porter who had been charged to carry it on board the Providence steamer, into placing it along with the 'Boz baggage' " (Samuel Ward *to* Longfellow, 15 June 42, quoted in *The Letters of H. W. Longfellow*, ed. A. Hilen, II, 455*n*).

[6] See *To* Felton, 31 July and *fn*.
[1] For work being done on the house in his absence, see *To* Fred Dickens, 7 Aug.
[2] Topping.

[3] A detail calculated to appeal to an American, presumably.
[4] Perhaps by Forster: see *To* Beard, 19 July.
[5] A daughter, Mary Keziah Topping, born 2 Nov 42.
[6] Beginning of word torn away at corner of page.

thought it was a High Life Below Stairs[1] kind of resort, and that this gentleman was a retired Butler, or superannuated Footman.[a]

[c]There's the knock—and the Great Western sails—or steams rather—tomorrow. Write soon again dear Felton, and ever believe me, [b]with best regards from Kate to yourself and Mrs. Felton, in which I heartily join[b]

Your Affectionate friend
CHARLES DICKENS[c]

All good Angels prosper Dr. Howe's Courtship![2] He, at least, will not like me the less, I hope, for what I shall say of Laura.[3]

To T. C. GRATTAN, 1 SEPTEMBER 1842

Extract in Parke-Bernet Galleries catalogue No. 1583; *MS* 1 p.; dated London, 1 Sep 42.

Everybody is cursing the Income Tax,[4] except the men to whom it gives places . . . You will have seen that I have followed up the International Copyright question, and that they have forged a letter under my hand in the American

---

[1] James Townley's farce, 1759.

[cc] This passage is written in pencil in an unknown hand on p. 3 of the MS with the note "(cut out for an autograph)". Above it, in CD's own hand, is "All good Angels . . . Laura", which J. T. Fields (*Atlantic Monthly*, XXVIII, 107), MDGH and later editions give, no doubt correctly, as a postscript. On the reverse of p. 3 the address to Felton is cut in half vertically.

[2] Of Julia Ward, to whom he became engaged in Feb 43 and married on 26 Apr 43. On 15 June 42 Felton, who had been visiting New York with Howe, had written to Longfellow: "Julia is the most remarkable person I ever knew. Every time I see her, some new power or attraction strikes me; and I am astounded that all the unmarried men are not piled up at her feet" (see *Letters of Longfellow*, ed. A. Hilen, II, 443n).

[3] Laura Bridgman, one of Howe's deaf, dumb and blind patients at the Perkins Institution. Most of the description of her in the Boston chapter of *American Notes* comes direct from the pamphlet *The Perkins Institution and Massachusetts Asylum for the Blind*, Howe's Report, as Secretary, for 1841. A long Appendix gives her history, from birth (in New Hampshire Dec 1829) to 1840 when she had spent three years in the Institution. Clearly CD had two copies of the pamphlet. In the margins of one (afterwards sent to Forster and now in the

V & A) he wrote three notes, presumably soon after his visit to the Institution. Two of them (the passage about the doll round whose eyes Laura had bound a green ribbon such as she wore round her own, and his comment on the brightness of the school which made him feel "a strange kind of sorrow . . . that it should be so very light" while its inmates were blind) he used in *American Notes*. The third, not used, reads as follows: "Dr. Howe, riding through Boston, got his leg crushed, not long ago. Laura asking why he didn't come to her, was told of the accident. Instead of being much grieved, as they expected, (for she perfectly doats upon him) she burst into a violent fit of laughter, and signed with her fingers—'Why, doctor *can see*. Doctor can see *his* way!' " At the end of this copy CD wrote: "I send you her name. She wrote it while I was there." Her signature, in pencil, is on a scrap of paper pasted below. The other copy of the pamphlet CD cut up, and pasted the pages he wished to use in *American Notes* into his MS, writing in instructions such as: "*To the Printer.* | When you get to the bottom of this printed slip, turn to the other side of it, and print that also | CD." (Slips 42, 43, 44, 45, 48, and 49 of his MS consist almost wholly of pages from Howe's pamphlet.)

[4] See *To* Fred Dickens, 7 Aug, *fn.*

papers—which does not startle me in the least. Nothing but Honesty or common sense would startle me, from such a quarter.

To JACOB HARVEY,[1] 1 SEPTEMBER 1842

Text from Harry B. Smith, *A Sentimental Library*, privately printed, [New York], 1914, p. 88.

Says that he received Harvey's letter just before he embarked for England.

I always seek, in drawing characters, for a mixture of Good and Evil, as the Almighty has created human character after that fashion. It is commonly one of the weaknesses of my characters that they drink spirituous liquors—just because that is one of the weaknesses of real men. They do not prosper in their fortunes *because* of this taste (far from it), but in spite of it, through their better natures. I certainly do not advocate Temperance Doctrines, and on this plain ground: my reason and sense of justice are not at all convinced that men who can drink without abuse and excess should be deprived of the enjoyment of drinking in moderation because there are a vast number of men in the world who do not know what moderation is. A great many good qualities and a great many genial feelings are brought out in good men by a cheerful glass. I think Temperance may be as immoderate and irrational in its way as abuse is in *its* way; and what is called Total Abstinence is, in my opinion, a good thing ridden to death—just as Drunkenness is. . . . I learn that the New York newspapers have been forging some passages under my hand. Nothing that American newspapers can do (unless they should chance on something honest or becoming a decent state of society) would surprise me in the least.

To R. SHELTON MACKENZIE,[2] 1 SEPTEMBER 1842

Extract in R. S. Mackenzie, *Life of CD*, Philadelphia, [1870], p. 219; dated "First September, 1842".

I am greatly obliged to you for your note and its accompanying Paper,[3] which is indeed a phenomenon. The announcement[4] you allude to had attracted

---

[1] Jacob Harvey (1797–1848), Irish-born New York merchant; former Quaker. Friend and correspondent of Charles Sumner. His wife was the daughter of the well-known New York doctor and botanist, David Hosack.

[2] Robert Shelton Mackenzie (1809–80; *DNB*): see Vol. I, p. 367*n*.

[3] One of the American "mammoths", "either the *New World*—or an enormous *Brother Jonathan*", according to Mackenzie; but no doubt the *New World* (see below).

[4] "in America, of a new work by Mr. Dickens, which he had neither written nor intended to write", Mackenzie interjects— clearly a reference to the announcement in the *New World* of 28 May that in future there would be fewer continued works in their pages, though monthly serials such as *Handy Andy*, *Our Mess*, and *The Miser's Daughter* would be continued, "*together with the new novel by Dickens (Boz), to be published in monthly numbers, the first of which may be expected to reach us in July, as it undoubtedly will appear in a week after he gets back to England*" (an announcement CD had doubtless seen or heard of before he left America). It went on: "We shall also republish in our regular edition his travels in America, if they appear in numbers, as they probably will". As Liverpool correspondent of the *New York*

my attention. We shall see a hundred others of the same family, and we shall
continue to see them until we die.

To DANIEL MACLISE, 1 SEPTEMBER 1842

MS Dickens House.

Devonshire Terrace | Thursday First September 1842.

My Dear Mac
    Come here at a quarter before 3 tomorrow, to meet John Forster and
                                            Yours ever faithfully
                                                CHARLES DICKENS

To THOMAS MITTON, 4 SEPTEMBER 1842

MS Huntington Library.

Broadstairs | Fourth September 1842 | Sunday.

My Dear Mitton
    I quite forgot yesterday, to bring down some money with me. Will you get
a bank-note for the inclosed,[1] and send it me by Post?
    I am happy to say that Chapman and Hall, and Bradbury and Evans opine
that I was doing too much for the money—so that the first Volume will end
with Washington, and the second begin with the black driver[2]—which is a
great help.

                                            Faithfully Always
                                                CD.

I am very unwell with a disordered stomach and a Beastly sickness.

Union, Mackenzie had denied that CD
would publish any work on America (reported in the *Boston Evening Transcript*, 25
Aug); but now, drawing on the announcement in the *Morning Chronicle* of 30 Aug,
and on CD's letter, he sent a correction:
"Charles Dickens *is* writing a work on
America! He will *certainly* bring it out
in November, and is now at Broadstairs
writing it"; the title in full followed this,
with the forecast that the book would be
"*dreadfully satirical*" (report copied in
Boston Transcript, 21 Sep). Mackenzie's
"November" is curious, but was perhaps
his estimate of when the book would reach
America.
    [1] Presumably the cheque for £50 en-
tered in CD's account-book (MS Messrs
Coutts) on 7 Sep as to "House" (i.e. for
house-keeping expenses). Registered post
had come in in 1841; previously the Post
Office had advised senders of bank notes
to cut them in half and send the halves at
different times.

[2] The volume which his publishers and
printers considered "too much for the
money" was up to this time to have con-
sisted of ten chapters—including not only
"A Night Steamer on the Potomac River.
A Virginia Road, and a Black Driver . . .",
but his Introductory "CHAPTER THE
FIRST" (see *To* Smith, 14 July, *fn*) as well.
With the decision to end the volume with
the Washington chapter (beneath which
CD now wrote again "END OF VOLUME
THE FIRST", forgetting to cancel the words
after the "black driver" chapter—so that
they appear twice in the MS), followed in
Oct by the decision to suppress Ch. 1 (*To*
Forster, 10 Oct, *fn*), the volume was
reduced to eight chapters. The omission of
Ch. 1 naturally upset the chapter-num-
bering of the volume.

To ALBANY FONBLANQUE, 5 SEPTEMBER 1842*

MS University of Iowa Libraries. *Address:* Albany Fonblanque Esquire | 48 Connaught Square, Edgeware Road, London.

Broadstairs | Fifth September 1842.

My Dear Fonblanque

Many thanks for the inclosed.[1] I shall hope to send you my book, pretty early in October.

Always Faithfully Yours | My Dear Fonblanque

Albany Fonblanque Esquire.   CHARLES DICKENS

To HENRY AUSTIN, 6 SEPTEMBER 1842*

MS Morgan Library.

Broadstairs | Tuesday Sixth September | 1842.

My Dear Henry.

Do you happen to have by you, in a semi-tindery state, the letter I wrote you from Niagara?[2] I know it is not at all likely that you have, but *if*[3] you have, will you lend it me? I should like to refer to it, when I come to that part of my "Voyages and Travels".[4]

With love to Letitia, in which Kate and all the babbies join,

Believe me always | Affectionately Yours

Henry Austin Esquire   CHARLES DICKENS

To JOHN S. BARTLETT, 6 SEPTEMBER 1842*

MS Doheny Memorial Library, California. *Address:* By the British Queen Steam Packet. | Doctor Bartlett | Office of | The Albion Newspaper | New York | United States | Private.

Private.[5]   1 Devonshire Terrace, York Gate | Regents Park London.[6]

Sixth September 1842.

My Dear Sir

I am greatly indebted to you for your letter,[7] which does honor to yourself and to the Proprietors of the Journal over which you preside. I beg you to thank them in my name, and to assure them of my respect and obligation.

---

[1] Doubtless CD was returning his letter about Washington: see *To* Fonblanque, 26 Aug.

[2] On 1 May 42.

[3] Underlined three times.

[4] CD used three sentences from his letter to Austin nearly word for word (see 1 May, *fn*). Some other passages he elaborated: for instance, "bright rainbows making fiery arches" became "gorgeous arches which the changing rainbows made" in the exclamatory passage, "what Heavenly promise glistened in those angels' tears" (*American Notes*, Ch. 14). Cf. his

treatment of his letter from Niagara to Forster (26 Apr, *fns*).

[5] Underlined twice.

[6] In fact written at Broadstairs: postmarked Ramsgate.

[7] Bartlett had consistently supported CD's stand on international copyright in the *Albion*, and had probably now written in approval of his circular letter to British Authors of 7 July. The *Albion* had published it on 6 Aug, together with the following letter to the Editors of the *Journal of Commerce*: "Messrs Editors:—I think you are not doing justice to Charles

I cannot, however, enter into any such arrangement as that which you propose; nor can I submit it to other English Authors.

I decline to do so, simply because so long as the Law remains in its present state (and it will outlast our time) I shall rigidly abide by the determination I have publicly expressed,[1] never to enter into any negociation for the transmission across the Atlantic, of early Proofs of anything I may write—because I object to addressing any book of mine to the American people, or recognizing them as Patrons of Literature, while they cling to the present system—and because I will not make an appeal to them, which I believe, with a penny's-weight in the other scale, they would certainly reject.

I am not the less obliged to you for this honorable and worthy carrying-out of the spirit you manifested in our first communication. And I am

My Dear Sir | Yours faithfully and obliged

Doctor Bartlett.   CHARLES DICKENS

To THOMAS BEARD, 8 SEPTEMBER 1842

MS Dickens House. *Address:* Thomas Beard Esquire | 42 Portman Place | Edgeware Road | London.

Broadstairs | Thursday Eighth September 1842

My Dear Beard

When is that jolly old Baronet (may Jackasses sit upon his Grandfather's grave!)[2] coming home? Here is the bathing, in a most unprecedented state—the Punch, toothsome beyond description—the Ranelagh Gardens[3] exulting in the Proprietorship of a family of Tumblers, called "The Five Patagonians"—the Theatre open at Margate—all manner of breeziness, freshness, and waviness going on—and no Beard! Again I ask, when does Fir Grove[4] come on to Dunsinane?—and pause for a reply.

Faithfully Yours ever

Thomas Beard Esquire   CHARLES DICKENS

Dickens; he speaks as every one is apt to do under the impression that an injury is inflicted upon him: whether that impression is right or wrong is another thing. Mr. Cooper, Mr. Irving and Mr. Any-body-else, can go to England and sell the copyright of any work there for a large and remunerating sum; all the rights invested in a British subject are ceded to the citizen of 'Our Republic' without a question; while here, such right of preserving *his own* is denied him, and the very penny papers who have fattened upon his attractions, call him a meddling fool, and boast they have increased his popularity *by their circulation*! Where would their papers have been now but for such aid? | I do not look at the Copyright law,—I merely ask to have the complaints of Dickens, Carlyle and others, read with allowance and consideration. When a stranger treads upon our corns, we are apt to lose temper. | Yours, respectfully, Bob Short".

[1] In *To* British Authors, 7 July.

[2] Type of curse common in Morier's two *Hajji Baba* books; e.g., "May his father's grave be polluted" (*The Adventures of Hajji Baba*, 1894 edn, Ch. 70). CD's "Jackasses" may have been inspired by "I will defile the grave of '*dam's*' [*the much-used British swear-word*] father. I will do whatever an ass can do to his mother, sister, wife, and all his ancestry" (*Hajji Baba . . . in England*, 1, Ch. 21).

[3] See *To* Forster, 11 Aug, *fn.*

[4] The name of Easthope's house near Weybridge.

To G. L. CHESTERTON, 11 SEPTEMBER 1842

MS Comtesse de Suzannet. *Address: Private* | —Chesterton Esquire | Middlesex House of Correction | Coldbath Fields | London.

Private.   Broadstairs, Kent. | Sunday Eleventh September | 1842.

My Dear Sir

In my Book on America, I purpose introducing this note.[1] Please to tell me in one line (directed here, where I am enjoying myself quietly, until the end of the Month) whether there is anything in it, you would desire to be altered or omitted.

Faithfully Yours
— Chesterton Esquire   CHARLES DICKENS

To AUGUSTUS TRACEY, 11 SEPTEMBER 1842*

MS University of Texas.

Private.

Broadstairs, Kent. | Sunday Eleventh September | 1842.
My Dear Sir.

In my book on America, I purpose introducing this note.[2] Please to inform me, in one line (directed here, where I am staying quietly, until the end of the Month) whether there is anything in it, you would wish altered or omitted.

Faithfully Yours
— Tracey Esquire   CHARLES DICKENS

To FREDERICK DICKENS, 12 SEPTEMBER 1842

Mention in American Art Association catalogue No. 3891; dated Broadstairs, 12 Sep 42; signed initials.

---

[1] The following footnote to Ch. 3 appeared in the 1st edn of *American Notes* (I, 121–2), reappeared in the Cheap edn (1850) and the Library edn (1859), but was omitted in the Charles Dickens edn (1868) and its later reprints: "Apart from profit made by the useful labour of prisoners, which we can never hope to realize to any great extent, and which it is perhaps not expedient for us to try to gain, there are two prisons in London, in all respects equal, and in some decidedly superior, to any I saw or have ever heard or read of in America. One is the Tothill Fields Bridewell, conducted by Lieutenant A. F. Tracey, R.N.; the other the Middlesex House of Correction, superintended by Mr. Chesterton. This gentleman also holds an appointment in the Public Service. Both are enlightened and superior men: and it would be as difficult to find persons better qualified for the functions they discharge with firmness, zeal, intelligence, and humanity, as it would be to exceed the perfect order and arrangement of the institutions they govern." See Vol. II, p. 270*n*; and for a discussion of the two prisons, Philip Collins, *Dickens and Crime*, 1962, Ch. 3.

[2] See last, *fn.*

To W. HARRISON AINSWORTH, 14 SEPTEMBER 1842

MS Huntington Library.

Broadstairs, Kent. | Fourteenth September 1842.

My Dear Ainsworth.

The inclosed has been sent to me by a young gentleman in Devonshire[1] (of whom I know no more than that I have occasionally, at his request, read, and suggested amendments in, some of his writings) with a special petition that I would recommend it to you for insertion in your Magazine.

I think it very pretty, and I have no doubt you will also. But it is Poetry, and may be too long.

He is a very modest young fellow, and has decided ability.

I hope when I come home at the end of the Month, we shall foregather more frequently. Of course you are working, tooth and nail;[2] and of course I am.

Kate joins me in best regards to yourself, and all your house (not forgetting, but especially remembering my old friend Mrs. Touchett).[3] And I am always

My Dear Ainsworth
Heartily Yours

William Harrison Ainsworth Esquire   CHARLES DICKENS

To JOHN FORSTER, [14 SEPTEMBER 1842]

Extract in F, III, viii, 281. *Date:* 14 Sep according to Forster. *From* Broadstairs.

I have pleased myself very much to-day in the matter of Niagara.[4] I have made the description very brief (as it should be), but I fancy it is good.[5] I am beginning to think over the introductory chapter,[6] and it has meanwhile occurred to me that I should like, at the beginning of the volumes, to put what follows on a blank page. *I dedicate this Book to those friends of mine in America, who, loving their country, can bear the truth, when it is written good humouredly and in a kind spirit.* What do you think? Do you see any objection?[7]

---

[1] R. S. Horrell: see 2 Dec 42 and *fn*.

[2] Besides editing *Ainsworth's Magazine*, Ainsworth was writing two novels concurrently, each first published in monthly instalments in his own magazine: *The Miser's Daughter* (Jan–Nov 42) and *Windsor Forest* (July 42–June 43).

[3] Mis-spelt by CD—as in *To* Ainsworth, 7 July.

[4] With which *American Notes*, Ch. 14, ends.

[5] For his use of two letters written from Niagara, see *To* Forster, 26 Apr, *fns*, and *To* Austin, 1 May and 6 Sep, *fns*. Forster justly remarks that although "so much is made in the book" of the description of Niagara, "the first vividness is in his letter. . . . The instant impression we find to be worth more than the eloquent recollection" (F, III, vi, 257).

[6] See *To* H. P. Smith, 14 July, *fn*.

[7] "My reply", says Forster, "is to be inferred from what he sent back on the 20th".

To EDWARD CHAPMAN, 16 SEPTEMBER 1842

MS Comtesse de Suzannet.

Broadstairs | Sixteenth September 1842.

My Dear Sir

All right. That is the kind of extract I want.[1] Mr. Forster seems to have got it into his head (and the quantity of hair he wears, probably prevents its coming out again) that I mean to use them for a separate chapter, and that they are not strong enough for such a purpose. Whereas I want them for the chapter on Slavery, as an Illustration of the State of Society in the Slave Districts.[2]

Read the inclosed Letter from Mr. Prescott.[3] I think it probable that a book of which *he* speaks so highly, is likely to be a creditable work. What do you say to it?[4]

Summer is come again. Such a day as it is is here, this blessed sixteenth of September!

I suppose the Co. are tremendously busy, furnishing that house.[5] Let them

---

[1] Extracts from American newspapers reporting crimes of violence by slave owners against each other, their characters (as he wrote in *American Notes*, Ch. 17) "formed in slave districts" and "brutalised by slave customs".

[2] Seven out of the 12 extracts quoted by CD towards the end of Ch. 17 ("Horrible Tragedy", "The Wisconsin Tragedy", &c) were apparently collected by Chapman: they are in the hand of a copying-clerk, and pasted on to blank pages in CD's MS (V & A), with their sources cancelled by CD, and the passages to be italicized indicated by his underlinings. The other five are in his own hand. Shortly before these extracts, CD quoted 44 advertisements for runaway slaves, clearly taken direct from the section headed "Advertisements for Fugitive Slaves: Brandings, maimings, and gunshot wounds" in the American Anti-Slavery Society's pamphlet, *American Slavery as It Is: Testimony of a Thousand Witnesses* (see *To* Forster, 21 Mar, *fn*).

[3] Prescott had written to CD on 31 Aug: "I hope you will not say on receiving this letter 'here are some of the precious fruits of a visit to those troublesome Yankees.' But I am going to ask a favour. A friend of mine, Madame Calderón de la Barca, is about publishing an account of a two years' residence in Mexico and Cuba, in a series of letters addressed to different friends. . . . She is a woman of much talent and her descriptions of that pic-

turesque country and society are so spirited, and she had such numerous opportunities for observation, that I urged her to collect her scattered letters and print them. She finds they will make about two volumes 12mo" (*Correspondence of W. H. Prescott, 1833–1847*, ed. R. Wolcott, p. 315). Madame Calderón (1804–82), *née* Fanny Erskine Inglis, was a Scot who had married Don Angel Calderón de la Barca, then Spanish Minister in Washington, in 1838; he was sent to Mexico to arrange a treaty and they lived there till 1841, and, wrote Prescott, "saw society in a way in which no foreigner has seen it". Prescott asked if he might send the MS of the book for CD to offer to a responsible publisher on the best possible terms, "to appear simultaneously with its publication here . . . probably by January or February" (*op. cit.*, p. 316). He himself showed his good opinion of the work by writing a Preface to it, and also by reviewing it in the *North American Review*, Jan 43.

[4] For Chapman & Hall's acceptance of the book and Prescott's further letters about it, see *To* Prescott, 15 Oct and *fn*. It was rare for CD to recommend a book to his publishers (see Vol. II, pp. 145 and 420); but he was naturally anxious to preserve the goodwill of an American he respected.

[5] Clareville Cottage, Old Brompton, into which the Chapmans moved that autumn.

be careful, for we will be down upon them in the way of criticism (you and I, I mean) when the Warming comes off.

How is Mrs. Chapman? Tell her with my love, that I have ordered a Mug, and should be glad to know whether it is to be engraved for a Boy or a Girl.[1] *I* say, a boy. Sometimes I think of twins, in which case there must be two mugs.

At the end of the month we had better advertize, I suppose, for the 20th. of October.[2] There is no doubt, please God, of our being punctual to that day, easily.

Faithfully Yours always

Edward Chapman Esquire   CHARLES DICKENS

To JOHN FORSTER, [16 SEPTEMBER 1842]

Extract in F, III, viii, 281 (*aa*), written "before the end of the month",[3] and extract in F, III, viii, 279 (*bb*), dated 16 Sep according to Forster. *From* Broadstairs.

*a*For the last two or three days I have been rather slack in point of work; not being in the vein.[4] To-day I had not written twenty lines before I rushed out (the weather being gorgeous) to bathe. And when I have done that, it is all up with me in the way of authorship until to-morrow. The little dog is in the highest spirits; and jumps, as Mr. Kenwigs would say, perpetivally.[5] I have had letters by the Britannia from Felton, Prescott, Mr. Q., and others, all very earnest and kind. I think you will like what I have written on the poor emigrants and their ways as I literally and truly saw them on the boat from Quebec to Montreal.*a*[6]

*b*At the Isle of Thanet races yesterday I saw—oh! who shall say what an immense amount of character in the way of inconceivable villainy and black-guardism! I even got some new wrinkles in the way of showmen, conjurors, pea-and-thimblers,[7] and trampers generally. I think of opening my new book

---

[1] A daughter, christened Meta (later Mrs Gaye) was born to Mrs Chapman on 23 Nov. She recorded her memories of her father and his friends for Arthur Waugh's *A Hundred Years of Publishing*, 1930.

[2] *American Notes* was in fact published on 19 Oct. It was advertised in *The Times*, 1 Oct, as to be published "early in October"; but in *The Times* and *Morning Chronicle*, 6 Oct, and in subsequent advertisements, the day of publication was given as the 19th.

[3] And doubtless part of his letter of 16 Sep—the day on which he wrote to both Philip Hone and Edward Chapman mentioning letters just received from America (one of them from Prescott). References to the weather in this and *To* Chapman, 16 Sep, agree; his day at the Isle of Thanet races (held on 14 and 15 Sep) would have been one of those on which he was "rather

slack in point of work". (The extract Forster explicitly dates 16 Sep is quoted by him earlier in the *Life* in order to link it with CD's reference to Cornwall of 18 July.)

[4] Having finished Ch. 14 (with Niagara as its climax) by 14 Sep, he now, for Ch. 15, had to write of Canada.

[5] Mr Kenwigs in fact pronounces "v"s as "w"s, but not "w"s as "v"s.

[6] *American Notes*, Ch. 15. Forster did like it, and quoted CD's reflections on the theme "it is very much harder for the poor to be virtuous than it is for the rich" at length in a footnote (F, III, viii, 282). See also Lord Jeffrey's praise in *To* Felton, 31 Dec, *fn*.

[7] i.e. thimbleriggers—sharpers who played a sleight-of-hand trick with three thimbles and a pea, challenging bystanders to guess under which thimble the pea lay (*OED*). Cf. *Chuzzlewit*, Ch. 37.

on the coast of Cornwall, in some terribly dreary iron-bound spot.[1] I hope to have finished the American book before the end of next month;[2] and we will then together fly down into that desolate region.[b]

To PHILIP HONE,[3] 16 SEPTEMBER 1842

MS Comtesse de Suzannet. *Address:* By Steam Packet. | Philip Hone Esquire | New York | United States.

Broadstairs, Kent. England. | Sixteenth September 1842.
My Dear Sir
I am very much obliged to you for your friendly letter, which I have received with real pleasure.[4] It reached me last night, being forwarded from London

---

[1] Cf. *To* Forster, Early Aug.

[2] Given the strong probability that Forster's dating of this extract is correct, he must surely have meddled here with the text: cf. *To* Chapman, 16 Sep, where CD anticipates actual publication of *American Notes* on 20 Oct.

[3] Philip Hone (1780–1851; *DAB*), diarist. Son of a joiner; made his fortune in an auction business and retired 1821. Became one of New York's most prominent citizens; Mayor 1825–6, when he represented New York at the reception of Lafayette; patron of numerous institutions; an active Whig, intimate with Webster, Clay, J. Q. Adams and Seward; friend of Irving. Lost heavily in the 1837 financial panic and in 1843 re-entered business as President of the newly formed American Mutual Insurance Co. His Diary, 1828–51 (28 quarto vols, MS New York Historical Society), gives the best surviving picture of social life in New York during the period. A great admirer of CD's writings, he was a Vice-President of the New York Dinner, and drafted the invitation to him to the Boz Ball, at which he was Chairman of the Reception Committee. Of the Ball arrangements he commented: "This is all very well, but there is danger of overdoing the matter and making our well-meant hospitalities oppressive to the recipient" (*Diary*, ed. A. Nevins, p. 582). On 15 Feb he described CD as "a small, bright-eyed, intelligent-looking young fellow . . . somewhat of a dandy in his dress, . . . brisk in his manner and of a lively conversation"; and Catherine as "a little, fat, English-looking woman, of an agreeable countenance, and, I should think, a 'nice person'" (*op. cit.*, p. 588). CD's speech at the New York Dinner he described as "excellent

. . . delivered with great animation and characterized by good taste and warm feeling" (p. 589). Gave one of the toasts at the farewell party for CD on the *George Washington*, 7 June.

[4] After reading the forged anti-American letter which purported to be CD's (see Appx, pp. 626–7), Hone had copied paragraphs 6 and 10 into his diary (17 Aug), recording before the first of them: "I have written him a letter calling for his avowal or denial of this unworthy piece of splenetic impudence, . . . and he must stand or fall in my estimation by his answer, if he chooses to make one. If the following sentiments are indeed Mr Dickens' he has proved himself a slanderer more vile than any of his predecessors, in the disreputable trade of misrepresenting the United States and their people"; and, before the second extract, he wrote: "The following is . . . so arrogant and so ungrateful, that I am led to hope the whole may be a forgery" (MS New York Historical Society). In his letter to CD he clearly wrote as if assuming that it was, wholly or partly, a forgery, and on receiving his reply accepted his assurance and sent the text of the second paragraph minus its last sentence (misdated 30 Sep), to the *New York American*—from which it was copied in the *Boston Daily Evening Transcript*, 11 Oct. After seeing *American Notes*, he doubted whether "any writer [had] been more unfairly treated by my countrymen". "Lies were circulated in advance; sentiments were attributed to him which he never uttered. His name was forged to papers which he never saw; his distinct and indignant disavowal was refused the publicity which was accorded with satisfaction to the slanders regarding the unworthy

to this sea-side Fishing town, where we are enjoying ourselves quietly, until the end of the month. I answer it without an hour's delay, though I fear my reply may lie at the Post office some days, before it finds a Steampacket to convey it across the ocean.

The letter to which you refer, is, from beginning to end, in every word and syllable, the cross of every t, and the dot of every i, a most wicked and nefarious Forgery. I have never published one word or line in reference to America, in any quarter whatever, except the Copyright Circular. And the unhung Scoundrel who invented that astounding Lie, knew this as well as I do.

It has caused me more pain, and more of a vague desire to take somebody by the throat, than such an act should, perhaps, have awakened in any honorable man. But I have not contradicted it publicly: deeming that it would not become my character or elevate me in my own self-respect, to do so.

I shall hope to send for your acceptance next month, my "American Notes".[1] Meanwhile and always, and with cordial remembrances to all friends, I am My Dear Sir

Faithfully Yours

Philip Hone Esquire.   CHARLES DICKENS

To JOHN FORSTER, [20 SEPTEMBER 1842]

Extract in F, III, viii, 281. *Date:* 20 Sep according to Forster. *From* Broadstairs.

I don't quite see my way towards an expression in the dedication of any feeling in reference to the American reception.[2] Of course I have always intended to glance at it, gratefully, in the end of the book; and it will have its place in the introductory chapter, if we decide for that.[3] Would it do to put in,

character of the present work. These slanders have been refuted by the appearance of the book itself" (*Diary*, 14 Nov 42, ed. A. Nevins, p. 632). He was treated like this, Hone added, because some Americans had "made a little too much fuss about him", but "more especially because [he] saw with an unprejudiced eye the horrible licentiousness of the daily press in this country, and uttered in the language of truth his denunciation of the stupendous evil, and would fain assist in wiping out the foul blot from our national escutcheon!"

[1] Hone found *American Notes* "very fair and impartial", though somewhat dull; "his sketches are slightly drawn from hasty observation . . . But the public institutions of the country, its manufacturing establishments, hospitals, prisons, courts, and colleges are praised or censured with equal justice and impartiality, and not unfrequently most favorably contrasted with similar institutions in his own country" (*op. cit.*, 14 Nov, p. 633). The American chapters in *Chuzzlewit*, however, made him very bitter (see *To* Forster, 15 Aug 43, *fn*).

[2] For his proposed dedication, on which Forster had now commented, see 14 Sep.

[3] The Introductory Chapter skates over his gratitude for the welcome he had received— though implies it in the reference to "certain native journalists" (see *To* Smith, 14 July, *fn*). But it dwells on the Americans who had "crowded round" him —"old readers, over-grateful and over-partial perhaps"— in whose "hospitable hands" he had seen "a home-made wreath of laurel; and not an iron muzzle disguised beneath a flower or two". The final sentence of the published book, evidently written when the Introductory Chapter had been scrapped (see *To* Forster, 10 Oct, *fn*), echoes this, making what seems chilly acknowledgment to those "partial readers" of his former books, who met him "with an open hand, and not with one that closed upon an iron muzzle."

after "friends in America," *who giving me a welcome I must ever gratefully and proudly remember, left my judgment free, and* who, loving, &c. If so, so be it.[1]

To THOMAS MITTON, 21 SEPTEMBER 1842†

MS Huntington Library.

Broadstairs | Twenty First September 1842.

My Dear Mitton

I am very glad indeed to have heard from you, for I began to wonder where you were, and whether some country practitioner on whom you called with a large sum of money in your pocket-book, could possibly have laid violent hands on you in his Private Office.

[a]Emma Picken (as wos)[2] and her husband[3] are here, as you have heard.[4] But [   ] no more. But Fred,[5] I believe has seen something of them, and danced with her in her Honey Moon Hops[6] at the Ranelagh Gardens.[7a]

---

[1] This was the final form the dedication took.

[aa] Not previously published. Heavily cancelled in ink (presumably by Georgina Hogarth: see Vol. I, Preface, p. xx), and recovered only with the aid of infra-red photography. After "But", in second sentence, about seven lines have been cut clean away.

[2] Eleanor Emma Picken (?1820–98), elder daughter of Andrew Picken (1788–1833; *DNB*), Scottish novelist, best known for his *The Dominie's Legacy* (1830) and his posthumous *The Black Watch* (1834). His early death left his wife and six children in grave financial difficulties for many years. The eldest, Andrew (1815–45; *DNB*), earned a reputation as an excellent draughtsman and lithographer; Thomas and James became lithographers too; and Emma shared the family talent. She won the Society of Arts silver Isis medal 1837; had ten portraits exhibited in the RA 1843–7 and another in 1854. On 7 Sep 42, after a long engagement, she married Edward Christian. For her first meeting with CD, her flirtatious acquaintance with him at Broadstairs in Sep 40, and his later coldness, see Vol. II, pp. 119*n*, 120*n*, and 173*n*. All are described in considerable (though not always reliable) detail in her "Reminiscences of CD", *Englishwoman's Domestic Magazine*, June 1871, x, 336–344, and "Recollections of CD", *Temple Bar*, LXXXII [1888], 481–506—the first signed "E.E.C.", the second "Eleanor E. Christian". For further biographical details, see W. J. Carlton, "Who Was the Lady?", *D*, LX (1964), 68–77.

[3] Edward Christian (?1815–1903), officer in the Merchant Navy, risen from ship's boy. Became first officer in the P. & O. liner, the *Tiber*, 1846, and served on several other of the company's ships, including the *Syria* 1867 and the *Sumatra* 1874–5. Later became a Principal Officer of the Board of Trade for the South of Ireland District. His sister had been T. J. Thompson's first wife.

[4] Mrs Christian insists that she had not expected CD to be at Broadstairs, "as it was late in the season". But since it was in Sep that she had met him there in 1840 (he was again there in Sep 41), this may be taken with a grain of salt.

[5] Fred Dickens remained a friend of Emma's, and in time became a distant connection through his marriage to Anna Weller, the sister of T. J. Thompson's second wife, Christiana.

[6] Cf. Mrs Christian on this Broadstairs visit: "Fred, who was a great friend of my husband, soon found us out, and we were constantly together; but I kept aloof from his brother, and only spoke to him on one occasion during our stay, which was when we went, accompanied by Fred, to the Tivoli Gardens, and Mr. Dickens and his party were there. If I remember rightly, Miss Hogarth danced with my husband and I with Fred, in a few quadrilles made up with their set. Mr[s]. Dickens was as kind as ever, and 'Boz' danced with her and her sister alternately, with as much enjoyment of the fun as any of us" ("Reminiscences of CD", *loc. cit.*, p. 343).

[7] See *To* Forster, 11 Aug, *fn*. Presumably it was after this letter was written that

I am going on rarely I hope. We intend to publish on the Twentieth of next month, please God. There is great curiosity afloat in all directions, about the book. I have made no arrangement in reference to it,[1] nor shall I; but I think in all these matters, their[2] interests and mine must be *a little* more identified than you think.

All well and hearty—A regatta here today, and a great flying of bright flags —let me know when you return to town.

Always Faithfully

Thomas Mitton Esquire   CHARLES DICKENS

To JOHN FORSTER, [22 SEPTEMBER 1842]

Extract in F, III, viii, 282. *Date:* in the last week of Sep according to Forster; but clearly the day after the Broadstairs regatta (see last).

I send you proofs as far as Niagara. . . . I am rather holiday-making this week . . . taking principal part in a regatta here yesterday, very pretty and gay indeed. We think of coming up in time for Macready's opening,[3] when perhaps you will give us a chop; and of course you and Mac will dine with *us* the next day? I shall leave nothing of the book to do after coming home, please God, but the two chapters on slavery and the people[4] which I could manage easily in a week, if need were.[5] . . . The policeman who supposed the Duke of Brunswick[6] to be

CD "and his party" coincided with Emma and her husband at the Tivoli Gardens, half a mile from Margate, which, besides lake, vista, bowling green and maze, had, in front of the hotel, "a monster Platform, level with the turf, for 'dancing on the green' ", and "a large Building, in which concerts and balls took place every evening during the season" (*Handbook of the Isle of Thanet*, 1859).

[1] i.e. no formal Agreement.

[2] Chapman & Hall's.

[3] Of his second season at Drury Lane, with *As You Like It*, on 1 Oct. Macready played Jaques. For the care he took over every detail of the production, his restoration of the original text, and the dramatic and pictorial use he made of supers, see A. S. Downer, *The Eminent Tragedian*, 1966, pp. 215–16 and 243–4. But Macready recorded in his diary the following day: "In a state of very uneasy doubt as to the effect of the play last night from the circumstance of not having heard anything of Forster. Mrs. Dickens and Georgina called; stayed a short time with them. Forster called. He, as Mrs. Dickens had done, expressed himself *delighted* with the play . . . Dickens called—in the same tone" (*Diaries*, II, 184–5). In his *Examiner* review, 8 Oct, Forster gave the production

high praise: the play "was a succession of pictures: from which nothing seemed to have been omitted, how minute soever, that could give beauty to the imagination in them, or life to their reality". The staging was described by a prompter in his copy of the Drury Lane master-text as "the most wonderfully perfect representation of court and pastoral life ever witnessed on the English stage" (quoted in Downer, *op. cit.*, p. 243, from copy in the Folger Shakespeare Library).

[4] Chs 17 and 18. Therefore in his remaining eight days at Broadstairs he had to write Ch. 16 ("The Passage Home"). He possibly also had to finish Ch. 15— somewhat neglected, it seems; for since 14 Sep he had been first "rather slack" (*To* Forster, 16 Sep) and in the present week was "rather holiday-making".

[5] Ch. 17, in particular, would not take long to write, since a large part of it (in the event, more than half) was to consist of extracts from newspapers, at least some of which CD already had by him (see *To* Chapman, 16 Sep and *fn*). He finished it at midnight on 4 Oct (*To* Forster, 5 Oct).

[6] Charles Frederick August William (1804–73), nephew of King George IV. Deposed as reigning Duke during the 1830 Revolution in France; spent his exile

one of the swell mob,[1] ought instantly to be made an inspector.[2] The suspicion reflects the highest credit (I seriously think) on his penetration and judgment.

To HENRY AUSTIN, 25 SEPTEMBER 1842

Text from Goodspeeds Book Shop monthly bulletin, n.d.

Broadstairs, | Sunday, twenty-fifth September, 1842

My Dear Henry,

I inclose you the Niagara letter,[3] with many thanks for the loan of it.

Pray tell Mr. Chadwick[4] that I am greatly obliged to him for his remembrance of me, and that I heartily concur with him in the great importance and interest of the subject[5]—though I do differ from him, to the death, on his crack topic, the new Poor Law.[6]

I had been turning my thoughts to this very item in the condition of American

mainly in Paris, where he lived a fashionable life and collected diamonds. In 1845 lent Louis Napoleon £6000 to aid his escape from Ham, on a pledge—never honoured by the Emperor—of mutual help in the restoration of their territories.

[1] "A class of pickpockets who assume the dress and manners of respectable people in order to escape detection" (*slang: OED*).

[2] The Duke had been mistakenly arrested at Preston, Lancs, on 15 Sep. The *Morning Chronicle*, 20 Sep, under the heading "*An Awkward Mistake*—Arrest of the ex-Duke of Brunswick on Suspicion of being one of the Swell Mob", gave a full account of the incident, taken from the *Lancaster Guardian*. Following a £2000 bank robbery the week before, a suspicious hotel proprietor had sent for a policeman when "a dashingly-attired foreigner" tendered a £5 note for a bottle of wine. Despite the Duke's protestations, the policeman took him forcibly to the police-station, where he proved his identity. The *Chronicle* quoted the *Lancaster Guardian*'s comment: "The festival of the guild exhibited many sights worthy of special commemoration; but the spectacle of a deposed ruler, allied to the most illustrious reigning families of Europe, being dragged to a police-office on a charge of pocket-picking, is, we may safely assert, without parallel".

[3] His letter to Austin of 1 May, asked for by CD on 6 Sep.

[4] Edwin Chadwick (1800–90; *DNB*), social reformer: see Vol. I, p. 545*n*.

[5] Chadwick had written to Austin on 7 Sep, asking him to give CD a copy of his *Report on the Sanitary Condition of the Labouring Population*, 1842, as a mark of his respect. He had seen it announced in the papers that CD was preparing *American Notes* and believed that the conclusions of his Report were *a fortiori* applicable to American towns. Lack of drainage and proper privies were the causes of fever in America too, he wrote: "Men in high practice are too busy to develope these causes & the sawbones whom Mr. Dickens has so admirably developed are the last people who would do so. . . . I should suppose the structural arrangements of the American towns could scarcely have escaped so able an observer. . . . I hope he who has so well exposed parochial administration will do something better than that inaccurate observer, & rash generaliser de Tocqueville. . . . Mr. Dickens will have possession of the ear not only of America but of Europe & whatever he may say on the importance of a better & scientific attention to the structural arrangements for promoting the health & pleasure & moral improvement of the population cannot fail to produce extensively beneficial effects" (MS University College, London).

[6] Chadwick was Secretary to the New Poor Law Commission 1834 and one of those mainly responsible for the Poor Law Amendment Act of that year. For CD's hostility to the New Poor Law, see Vol. I, p. 231*n*.

towns, and have put their present defects strongly before the American people.[1]
Therefore I shall read his report with the greater interest and attention.

We return next Saturday night. If you will dine with us next day, or any day
in that week, we shall be truly glad and delighted to see you.

Let me know here, what day you will come.

I need scarcely say that I shall joyfully talk with you about the Metropolitan
Improvement Society,[2] then, or at any time—and with love to Letitia in which
Kate and the babies join, I am always

My dear Henry, | Affectionately Yours,
CHARLES DICKENS

The childrens'[3] present names are as follows:

Katey (from a lurking propensity to fiery-ness)	Lucifer Box
Mamey (as generally descriptive of her bearing)	Mild Gloster
Charley (as a corruption of Master Toby)	Flaster Floby
Walter (suggested by his high cheek bones)	Young Skull

Each is pronounced with a peculiar howl, which I shall have great pleasure in
illustrating.

---

[1] He had not in fact yet written this passage. It appears in the final paragraph of his reflexions on America in Ch. 18—one of the chapters to be written after his return to London (see last and *fn*). In the MS of *American Notes*, it begins on a scrap of paper pasted on to the penultimate slip, and continues on the final slip—in ink and handwriting identical with what follows (the book's three closing paragraphs), probably written 10 Oct: see *To* Forster, that day, *fn*. It reads: "Above all, in public institutions, and throughout the whole of every town and city, the system of ventilation, and drainage, and removal of impurities, requires to be thoroughly revised. There is no local Legislature in America which may not study Mr. Chadwick's excellent Report upon the Sanitary Condition of our Labouring Classes, with immense advantage."

[2] Founded at a public meeting on 29 Jan 42, held with a view to forming "an association to watch, on the part of the public, the improvements now in progress, and to urge upon the government the importance of preparing some general and comprehensive plan, embracing the interests of the whole metropolis" (*Examiner*, 7 Feb). C. W. Dilke was in the chair. Austin was soon afterwards appointed Hon. Secretary and the Society's programme clearly owed much to his stimulus: following a long article, "Metropolitan Improve-ments", in the *Westminster Review*, Oct 41, signed "L.-H." (reprinted as a pamphlet Jan 42), he addressed a signed letter to the Editor (Jan 42, XXXVII, 241–4), stressing the need for co-ordination of plans for metropolitan improvement and for accurate and informed surveys. The first general meeting was held on 30 July 42 at the Society's office, 20 Bedford Street, Covent Garden, and the following subjects discussed: smoke abatement, burial grounds, sanitation, water supply, the formation of a library of plans and maps of London, and Chadwick's *Report on the Sanitary Condition of the Labouring Population*. A deputation from the Society, led by Lord Robert Grosvenor, had on 15 June urged the Govt to prepare "a general plan of metropolitan improvement . . . with a view not merely to ornamental embellishment, but to the sanatory state of the poorer districts" (*Morning Chronicle*, 8 Aug). The first provisional General Committee, of 45 members, included Chadwick, Southwood Smith, Dilke, Lord Robert Grosvenor, Bulwer, Elliotson, W. E. Hickson (editor of the *Westminster Review*); William Lindley, civil engineer, acted as temporary Treasurer, and E. Clarkson as Hon. Secretary—before Austin's appointment. CD joined the Committee in Nov 42. (The last Annual Report found is the fourth, published July 45.)

[3] Thus in MS.

To JOHN FORSTER, [25 SEPTEMBER 1842]

Extract in F, III, viii, 283. *Date:* three days later than letter of 22 Sep according to Forster.

For the last two days we have had gales blowing from the north-east, and seas rolling on us that drown the pier. To-day it is tremendous. Such a sea was never known here at this season, and it is running in at this moment in waves of twelve feet high. You would hardly know the place. But we shall be punctual to your dinner hour on Saturday.[1] If the wind should hold in the same quarter, we may be obliged to come up by land; and in that case I should start the caravan at six in the morning.[2]

To SAMUEL ROGERS, 26 SEPTEMBER 1842

MS Mrs A. M. Stern.

Broadstairs | Twenty Sixth September 1842

My Dear Mr. Rogers.

May I appoint tomorrow evening instead of tonight, for the pleasure of seeing you and Mr. Maltby?[3] If I may, I pledge myself to walk eight miles tonight; detect Talfourd ensconced in fancied security in the Margate Theatre to see the Athenian Captive[4] (at least, I fondly hope so); and report fully to you tomorrow, over our tea table.

It would be a brilliant thing to take him in the act; and it is well worth the effort. Is it not?[5]

Faithfully Yours Ever

Samuel Rogers Esquire.   CHARLES DICKENS

---

[1] i.e. for the "chop": see 22 Sep.

[2] At this point, following dots, F, III, viii, 283 appends CD's announcement of the title he proposed for *American Notes*— but clearly in error: the book had been advertised with this title as early as 30 Aug (see *To* Forster, ?25 Aug).

[3] William Maltby (1763–1854; *DNB*): see Vol. I, p. 643*n*.

[4] On its first night in Henry Betty's new season at Margate. (For its original production 4 Aug 38 at the Haymarket, see Vol. I, p. 355*n*.)

[5] Probably CD did not "take [Talfourd] in the act", since there is no mention of it in *To* Forster, 27 Sep. But in a notice of Henry Betty's performances as Melmotte in *The Lady of Lyons* and Thoas in *The Athenian Captive*, the *Observer*, 9 Oct, reported: "The celebrated and talented author Mr. Serjeant Talfourd came down purposely to witness Mr. Betty's representation of Thoas, which appeared to agree perfectly with his conception, as he joined constantly in the applause which resounded on all sides". Talfourd's attendance at performances of his own plays was a joke among his friends. See A. G. L'Estrange, *The Literary Life of the Rev. William Harness*, 1871, p. 166: "On one occasion, when Dickens was calling on Rogers at Broadstairs, he observed, 'We shall have Talfourd here to-night.' 'Shall we?' returned the Poet; 'I am rejoiced to hear it . . . but how do you know he is coming?' 'Because "Ion" is to be acted at Margate, and he is never absent from any of its representations.' "

To JOHN FORSTER, [27 SEPTEMBER 1842]

Extract in F, III, viii, 280. *Date:* Forster implies that this was written in Aug; but since Betty's first performance in *The Athenian Captive* in this Margate season was on 26 Sep, CD must have been writing the day after the planned visit mentioned in *To* Rogers, 26 Sep.

Now you really must come. Seeing only is believing, very often isn't that, and even Being the thing falls a long way short of believing it. Mrs Nickleby[1] herself once asked me, as you know, if I really believed there ever was such a woman; but there'll be no more belief, either in me or my descriptions, after what I have to tell of our excellent friend's tragedy, if you don't come and have it played again for yourself "by particular desire." We saw it last night, and oh! if you had but been with us! Young Betty,[2] doing what the mind of man without my help never *can* conceive, with his legs like padded boot-trees wrapped up in faded yellow drawers, was the hero. The comic man of the company enveloped in a white sheet, with his head tied with red tape like a brief and greeted with yells of laughter whenever he appeared, was the venerable priest.[3] A poor toothless old idiot at whom the very gallery roared with contempt when he was called a tyrant, was the remorseless and aged Creon. And Ismene, being arrayed in spangled muslin trowsers very loose in the legs and very tight in the ankles, such as Fatima would wear in *Blue Beard*, was at her appearance immediately called upon for a song. After this, can you longer . . . ?

To HENRY AUSTIN, 28 SEPTEMBER 1842*

MS Morgan Library.

Broadstairs | Twenty Eighth September 1842.

My Dear Henry

Young Methusaleh[4] will put the initiatory dish on, at half past five, sharp.[5]

Faithfully Always

Henry Austin Esquire   CHARLES DICKENS

[1] i.e. CD's mother (see F, VI, vii, 151).

[2] Henry Thomas Betty (1819–97), only son of the one-time boy-actor, the "Young Roscius", W. H. W. Betty (1791–1874; *DNB*). First appeared on the stage Oct 35 at Gravesend; acted in the provinces 1838–43 and in London 1844–54 (first as Hamlet, at Covent Garden Dec 44). Talfourd, in his 1844 preface to *The Athenian Captive*, wrote of Betty's responsibility for numerous provincial performances of the tragedy—in which he played Macready's original part, Thoas, "with energy and grace, which all who recollect the brilliant passages of his father's youth, or who are acquainted with his own modest worth, will rejoice to find ensuring the best rewards which the present condition of the stage allows to its professors." He joined his father in retirement 1854, yet at his death left over £56,000—£10,000 of it to the Royal General Theatrical Fund; the residue, after various bequests, to establish a "Betty Fund" for the relief of poor actors and actresses. But this—an attempt to "salvage something of the Betty name and fame"—was voided in the Court of Probate (see Giles Playfair, *The Prodigy*, 1967, pp. 177–8).

[3] Iphetus, Priest of the Temple of Jupiter the Avenger at Corinth.

[4] Possibly Tom, the servant who had accompanied CD and Catherine to Scotland (see Vol. II, p. 322 and *n*)—or a new servant.

[5] See CD's invitation of 25 Sep.

To HENRY WADSWORTH LONGFELLOW,
28 SEPTEMBER 1842

MS Longfellow House, Cambridge, Massachusetts. *Address:* M: W. H. Long-fellow | Poste Restante | Bruges.

Broadstairs, Kent.
Twenty Eighth September Eighteen Forty Two.

My Dear Longfellow.

How stands it about your visit, do you say?[1] Thus.—Your bed is waiting to be slept in, the door is gaping hospitably to receive you, I am ready to spring towards it with open arms at the first indication of a Longfellow knock or ring; and the door, the bed, I, and everybody else who is in the secret, have been expecting you for the last month.

The tortures of the mind that I have undergone—and all along of you—since I have been down here; a term of nine weeks!—The imaginings I have had of the possibility of your knocking at my door in London without notice, and finding nobody there, but an old woman who is remarkable for nothing but a face of unchangeable dirtiness—the misgivings that have come across me of your being, successively, in every foreign steamer that has passed these windows, homeward bound, since the first of last month—the horrible possibilities that have flashed across me of your shipping yourself aboard a Cunard Packet in gloomy desperation, and steaming back to Boston—the hideous train of Fancies from which your letter has relieved me, baffle all description.

My address in town (I shall be there, please God, next Saturday) is No. 1 Devonshire Terrace York Gate Regents Park. But if you can manage to write and tell me when you will arrive in London, and by what conveyance, I will be there to meet you. This will be by far the best plan, so arrange it in that way, if you can. If you cannot, I shall look for you at home, and be ready for you.[2]

I send you the circular you speak of. I addressed it to every person connected with Literature, who is at all known in England. It has made a great noise here, and will strip the Privateers of all *exclusive* profit in time to come. The forged letter of which Felton speaks, was published in the New York Papers, with a statement that I had addressed it to the Editor of the London Morning Chron-icle, who had published it in his columns. I disparaged America very much in this production, and girded at my own reception. You know what the Ameri-can Press is, and will be, I dare say, as little surprised at this outrage as I was. Still, it exasperated me (I am of rather a fierce turn, at times) very much; and I walked about for a week or two, with a vague desire to take somebody by the throat and shake him—which was rather feverish.

I have decided (perhaps you know this?) to publish my American Visit. By

---

[1] Longfellow had clearly written to ask when CD was expecting him at Devon-shire Terrace, and given the address at which letters would reach him on his travels between Marienberg (left on 18 Sep) and England.

[2] Longfellow received CD's letter at Malines on 3 Oct, and noted in his Journal under that date: "Letter from Dickens. He is expecting me. I shall start for London to-morrow" (H. W. L. Dana, "Long-fellow and Dickens", *Cambridge Historical Society Publications*, XXVIII [1942], 71). He turned up unexpectedly at Devonshire Terrace on 5 Oct (*To* Mitton, 6 Oct), and stayed until the 20th.

the time you come to me, I hope I shall have finished writing it.[1] I have spoken very honestly and fairly; and I know that those in America for whom I care, will like me the better for the book. A great many people, I dare say, will like me infinitely the worse, and make a Devil of me, straightway.[2]

Rogers is staying here, and begs me to commend him to you, and to say that he has made me pledge myself, on pain of non forgiveness ever afterwards, to carry you to see him without loss of time, when you come among us.[3] Among other pleasant enjoyments we shall have together, and to which I look eagerly forward, I think I can promise you that we shall see Shakespeare on the stage as never he was seen before.[4]

Mrs. Dickens unites with me in cordial remembrances to you. And I am always

My Dear Longfellow | Faithfully | Your friend

CHARLES DICKENS

P.S. I have heard thrice from Felton, whom I love; and once from Prescott. I am sorry to see that Sumner, in the North American, speaks slightingly of

[1] Longfellow read it while he was staying with CD and in a letter to Sumner of 16 Oct (written in CD's study, "the focus from which so many luminous things have radiated") described it as "jovial and good-natured, and at times very severe. You will read it with delight, and for the most part approbation. He has a grand chapter on Slavery. *Spitting* and *politics* at Washington are the other topics of censure. Both you and I would censure them with equal severity to say the least"; and he quoted its affectionate reference to Felton, "heartiest of Greek Professors!", and praise of Howe (*Letters of Longfellow*, ed. A. Hilen, II, 473–4). Felton, on 28 Nov, wrote to a friend: "Opinions are various, but we agree pretty well here, in thinking it a capital book, lively spirited, true and good humored. He has made a few mistakes, but they are trifling. Spitting and Slavery, are the two things he tilts against most vigorously" (photograph, Longfellow House).

[2] For the opinions of other American friends, including attacks and adverse views, see *To* Prescott, 15 Oct, *fns*.

[3] According to P. W. Clayden (*Rogers and his Contemporaries*, 1889, II, 167), Rogers's "youthful recollections of the struggle for American independence, of his father's good wishes for its success, of Dr. Priestley's going forth from Rogers's own house to his American exile ... made Rogers more than usually friendly to Americans who came to see him." He was,

moreover, gratified by American admiration of his poetry. Rogers called on CD on 16 Oct, the day after his return to London, and spent half an hour with Longfellow. CD and Longfellow breakfasted with him on the 18th and dined with him on the 19th; Longfellow wrote in Jan 43 that he had "met at his table Tom Campbell, and Mr. Moxon the publisher and Sonneteer" (*Letters of Longfellow*, ed. A. Hilen, II, 496).

[4] CD took Longfellow to *As You Like It* on 6 Oct; and with Forster and Maclise they called on Macready in his dressing-room afterwards. On 9 Oct he met Macready and Maclise again, also Stanfield, Forster and Harley, at a dinner given by CD; and with CD dined at Macready's on 18 Oct in the company of "Quin, the Butlers, Mr. Sartoris . . . and Carlyle" (*Macready's Reminiscences*, ed. Sir Frederick Pollock, 1875, II, 203). He also met Cruikshank at CD's house: "We had very pleasant dinners," he wrote to Freiligrath in Jan 43, "drank Schloss-Johannisberger, and *cold punch*, (the same article that got Mr. Pickwick into the Pound) and led a life like the monks of old"; Catherine he described as "a most kind, amiable person, and his four children beautiful in the extreme" (*op. cit.*, II, 495). Later, in a letter to Forster of 8 May 45 (when they were both "invalids"), he recalled how they had been "the jolliest of all the youths at Dickens's table in the autumn of '42" (MS V & A).

Tennyson.[1] Good God how strange it seems to me that anyone can do that—though many do.

To THOMAS MITTON, 28 SEPTEMBER 1842*

MS University of Texas. *Address:* Thomas Mitton Esquire | 23 Southampton Buildings | Chancery Lane | London.

Broadstairs | Twenty Eighth September 1842.
My Dear Mitton

I suppose it will be best to let him[2] have the Cheque.[3]—He has been living, it seems, in a cottage adjoining the old one,[4] which he rented, furnished, at Twelve Shillings Pr. week.

I will call upon you on Monday—either between four and five, or between Seven and Eight.

Faithfully Yours always
Thomas Mitton Esquire   CHARLES DICKENS

To JOHN FORSTER, [29 SEPTEMBER 1842]

Extract in F, III, viii, 283. *Date:* Forster makes two contradictory statements—that this letter was written on 25 Sep, and that he received it "on the last day of the month". The second is obviously correct: CD was writing the day before he left Broadstairs, and was leaving on Fri 30 Sep instead of Sat 1 Oct.

Strange as it may appear to you, the sea is running so high that we have no choice but to return by land. No steamer can come out of Ramsgate, and the Margate boat lay out all night on Wednesday with all her passengers on board. You may be sure of us therefore on Saturday at 5, for I have determined to

[1] For the *North American Review*'s only recent reference to Tennyson, see *To* Felton, 29 Apr, *fn.* CD must be referring to this, although the review is indexed as by J. G. Palfrey, not Sumner.

[2] John Dickens, without doubt.

[3] On 3 Sep CD had paid Mitton £100 (Account-book, MS Messrs Coutts)—a sum probably to reimburse him for money paid to John Dickens while he himself was in America. Whether enough of this sum remained to pay the cheque now demanded is not known; but CD's accounts show another payment of £100 to Mitton on 31 Oct. For his earlier quarterly allowance to his father, paid through Mitton, see Vol. II, p. 226n.

[4] John Dickens had announced to CD as early as May 41 that it "would not be possible for him to stay more than another year in Devonshire" (Vol. II, p. 289). In Mar 42 he had written to "Miss Coutts & Co." that his term in the Alphington cottage expired on 31 July and he would be returning to London. His "preparatory demonstrations of migration", he said, had led to "what may be considered a vote of 'want of confidence'," which tended "very much to the embarrassment of [his] financial arrangements", and he asked for £25, on his own security because he knew how indignant his son would be if he heard of the request—which was naturally not granted (MS Morgan). In June and July 42, he presented pages of the MS of CD's *O'Thello* to friends—surely as a *quid pro quo*. He had probably now moved temporarily, with his wife and Augustus, into the cottage next door, belonging to his landlady Mrs Pannell (see Vol. I, pp. 517–19). For their subsequent movements, see *To* Mitton, 7 Dec and *fn*, and *To* Marryat, 21 Jan 43, *fn.*

leave here to-morrow, as we could not otherwise manage it in time; and have engaged an omnibus to bring the whole caravan by the overland route.[1] . . . We cannot open a window, or a door; legs are of no use on the terrace; and the Margate boats can only take people aboard at Herne Bay!

To JOHN FORSTER, [5 OCTOBER 1842]

Extract in F, III, viii, 283. *Date:* 5 Oct according to Forster.

I want you very much to come and dine to-day that we may repair to Drury-lane together;[2] and let us say half-past four, or there is no time to be comfortable. I am going out to Tottenham this morning, on a cheerless mission I would willingly have avoided. Hone, of the *Every Day Book*,[3] is dying;[4] and sent Cruikshank yesterday to beg me to go and see him, as, having read no books but mine of late, he wanted to see and shake hands with me before (as George said) "he went". There is no help for it, of course; so to Tottenham I repair,[5]

[1] A topical reference to the overland route to India, first attempted by Lieut. Thomas Waghorn, RN, in 1829; the normal route for ordinary travellers as well as mails since 1841. Waghorn had established a service first of caravans, later of English carriages, vans and horses instead of camels, across the desert between Cairo and Suez. The route was in 1842 still something of a novelty: cf. newspapers with news from the East headed "Arrival of the Overland Mail", &c.

[2] To see Byron's *Marino Faliero*, with Macready as the Doge. (For Macready's innovation at the play's end, see A. S. Downer, *The Eminent Tragedian*, p. 250.) It was followed by J. R. Planché's *The Follies of a Night* and J. M. Morton's *The Attic Story*.

[3] William Hone (1780–1842; *DNB*), Radical author, publisher and bookseller. Tried for blasphemy three times in 1817 for his political pamphlets, but defended himself successfully; helped by public subscription to set up as a publisher and bookseller at 45 Ludgate Hill. Collaborated with the young George Cruikshank in a series of brilliant political satires published in cheap pamphlet form; *The Political House that Jack Built*, 1819, *The Queen's Matrimonial Ladder*, 1820, and *The Political Showman*, 1821, were more effective than any newspaper in their denunciation of the King and the Ministry, and made Cruikshank's name. Hone turned from politics to popular antiquarian miscellanies, including *The Every-Day Book* (with Cruikshank as one of the illustrators) in threepenny weekly numbers (1825–6), and *The Table Book* (1827–8); Lamb was a contributor and the two became firm friends. Despite the success of these Hone was in constant financial difficulties. In 1832 he was converted from free-thinking by hearing a sermon by Thomas Binney (see *To* Felton, 2 Mar 43), and he and all his family were admitted members of the Weigh House Chapel 1834. Worked as sub-editor of the *Patriot* 1832–40, when ill health compelled him to retire and the family moved to Tottenham. *The Early Life and Conversion of William Hone, by Himself* was edited by his son in 1841.

[4] Hone died at Tottenham on 6 Nov. For CD's account of the funeral, see *To* Felton, 2 Mar 43.

[5] Mrs Hone recorded in the family diary on 6 Oct: "George Cruikshank and Charles Dickens were here yesterday. Father was greatly delighted to see them; they speak of calling again" (F. W. Hackwood, *William Hone: his Life and Times*, 1912, p. 345). She also wrote to her son Alfred the same day that Hone wished her to tell him "that he has had another visit from George Cruikshank, and with him Charles Dickens, with whom father was greatly pleased. Mr. Woollaston begged we would not hurry them; they were with him about half an hour; he held George's hand the whole time. They promised to come again soon" (*op. cit.*, p. 346). This meeting with Cruikshank was a reconciliation after 15 years' estrangement.

this morning. I worked all day, and till midnight; and finished the slavery chapter[1] yesterday.

To THOMAS MITTON, [6 OCTOBER 1842]*

MS University of Texas. *Date:* On Thurs 6 Oct CD took Longfellow to Drury Lane to see *As You Like It* (Macready, *Diaries,* II, 185); Longfellow had evidently arrived the night before, having left Belgium on 4 Oct (see *To* Longfellow, 28 Sep, *fn*). *Address:* Thomas Mitton Esquire.

Devonshire Terrace. | Thursday Morning
My Dear Mitton
I am paralyzed by having to tell you, that the American Professor whom I expected on the 10th. suddenly made his appearance here, last night. Hence I am captive today—in which light I would have considered myself on no less compulsion, as you will readily suppose.

Faithfully Always
Thomas Mitton Esquire   CD.

To A[NDREW] B[ELL], [9] OCTOBER 1842*

MS Mrs A. M. Stern. *Address:* To | A. B.[2] *Date:* Sunday was 9 Oct in 1842.

Sunday Morning | October the Eighth. Forty two.
Dear Sir
I was aware of the *cause* of the preponderance in the representation, possessed by the Slave owners. But as it has its origin in the principle of representing Property (which finds favor here) I thought it would, with some persons, weaken the case, to state it.[3]

---

[1] Ch. 17, begun after his return from London on 30 Sep.

[2] Almost certainly Andrew Bell: see Vol. II, p.254*n*, with its suggestion that Bell was a printer by trade, and recently employed by Bradbury & Evans. As printer he would have seen CD's slavery chapter while it was still in proof; and this letter, folded and addressed on the outside simply "To A.B.", was presumably either attached by CD to the proofs mentioned in *To* ?Hall, 8 Oct, or enclosed in that letter. Bell had spent a year in America, and CD had read and commented on his *Men and Things in America,* 1838 (see Vol. II, p. 402).

[3] Bell had obviously commented on a passage (in Ch. 17) in which CD, inveighing against "public opinion" as stronghold of the maintenance of slavery, asks: "what class of men have an immense preponderance over the rest of the community, in their power of representing public opinion in the legislature? the slave owners. They send from their twelve States one hundred members, while the fourteen free States, with a free population nearly double, return but a hundred and forty-two." In *Men and Things in America,* Bell had himself remarked on the "strange law" in some slave States which allowed a slave-holder additional votes in right of his slaves; and sarcastically suggested that proponents of universal suffrage in England "might take a hint" from this and "let every costermonger have a vote for his donkey" (p. 179).

I have called the drivers "Coachmen", simply because I know it will annoy them;[1] and they deserve[2] to be annoyed for such absurdities.

You will see that I have made an insertion relative to their sleeping in Iron Collars[3]—though that was expressed in their wearing them, as it is not a kind of hosiery which is easily put on and taken off, or frequently sent to the Wash.

I am much obliged to you for your suggestions.

Faithfully Yours

To A.B.   CHARLES DICKENS

To [?WILLIAM HALL], [?9] OCTOBER 1842

Extract in John Waller catalogue No. 142 (1884); dated 8 Oct 42; signed "D" according to catalogue, but presumably "CD". *Address:* since the visit was to return proofs and dining had been suggested, probably to William Hall, the partner in Chapman & Hall usually concerned with business arrangements (see references to dining with him in Vol. II, pp. 50 and 97). *Date:* probably 9 not 8 Oct (see last).

My American friend is going out on Monday evening.[4] I can't dine with you; but I will be with you laden with proofs, at 7 exactly.

Faithfully yours ever

[CD.]

To MISS C. LE GRAND, 9 OCTOBER 1842

Mention in American Art Association catalogue No. 3823; *MS* 1 p., 3rd person; dated London, 9 Oct 42.

Acknowledging the receipt of her work, and thanking her for the compliment of her dedication.

To UNKNOWN CORRESPONDENT, 9 OCTOBER 1842

Extract in S. J. Davey catalogue No. 6336 (1893); *MS* 1 p.; dated 9 Oct 42.

I have looked over your sketches with very great pleasure; and have been quite charmed with their fidelity and their artistical merits.

To JOHN FORSTER, [10 OCTOBER 1842]

Mention in F, III, viii, 283–4.[5]

[1] i.e. annoy the slave-owners. (But in Ch. 9 CD does in fact refer to the "black driver".)

[2] Written "deseve".

[3] In the passage "To make them wear iron collars by day and night" (in an interpolation after 31 of the quoted advertisements for runaway slaves), "and night" is added in the MS over a caret.

[4] Perhaps to Macready's *Hamlet*: see *To* Longfellow, 28 Sep, *fn.*

[5] "On the 10th of October", says Forster, "I heard from him that the chapter intended to be introductory to the *Notes* was written, and waiting our conference whether or not it should be printed." In fact the Introductory Chapter was in existence as early as July (see *To* H. P. Smith, 14 July), and was evidently the first CD wrote when settling down to *American Notes*. Writing the *Life* nearly 30 years later, and apparently having no

To LADY BLESSINGTON, [13 OCTOBER 1842]*

Photograph, Longfellow House. *Date:* Letter is endorsed "October 13, 1842", a Thursday.

Devonshire Terrace. | Thursday Morning

Dear Lady Blessington

Professor Longfellow, the best of the American Poets, (and a gentleman also, which latter recommendation it may be well to add), is staying with me on his way home from the Continent of Europe; and is very desirous to have the honor of being presented to you. May I bring him to Gore House some morning, for that purpose ?[1] *I warrant him, not a Penciller by the way.*[2]

I beg my best regards to Miss Power[3] and to Count D'Orsay. And am always

Dear Lady Blessington
Faithfully Yours
CHARLES DICKENS

The | Countess of Blessington.

July letter from CD that mentioned his working on the chapter, Forster was obviously misled by the references to it in CD's letters to him of 14 and 20 Sep, taking them as evidence of its being the last, not first, chapter written. At their meeting in Oct to consider whether it should be printed, they decided against it—though CD "so reluctantly" that Forster had to undertake to publish it "when a more fitting time should come" (and did so in Vol. II of the *Life*, 1873: see F, III, viii, 284–6). His counsel had certainly been wise: such an introductory chapter would immediately have antagonized American readers. Macready had disliked it (see *To Smith,* 14 July, *fn*); and CD's letters to Forster of 14 and 20 Sep show that he was himself uncertain of it. On deciding to omit it, CD (very probably at or immediately after his meeting with Forster of 10 Oct) wrote, to replace it, the three short paragraphs with which he closed the book.

[1] Recalling this visit, Longfellow wrote to Freiligrath, 6 Jan 43: "Lady Blessington . . . cheered my eyes by her fair presence; —a lady *well preserved,* but rather *deep zoned,* as the Greeks would say;— in St. Goar [*where Freiligrath lived*] we should say *stoutish.* Count D'Orsay was in attendance being confined to the house by a severe attack of the *bum-bailiffs*; he only ventures

out on Sundays" (*Letters of Longfellow,* ed. A. Hilen, II, 496). In a long letter to Lord Lichfield, begun 12 Oct and continued at least to the 19th, D'Orsay wrote, rather spitefully: "Yesterday Dickens brought an American professor, Mr Longfellow, who has returned cured of his rheumatism. He is going back in triumph to Boston. He was delighted with my condescension towards him—the fool did not know I was cross-examining him in your interests [*Lichfield, a martyr to rheumatism, was in Italy taking a succession of cures*]" (quoted in Willard Connely, *Count D'Orsay,* 1952, p. 379).

[2] i.e. not one to accept hospitality and then exploit it in articles or a book, as N. P. Willis had done in *Pencillings by the Way,* 1835 (see 27 Jan 42, *fn*). But Lady Blessington probably did not need this assurance: if at all annoyed by Willis's earlier abuse of her hospitality, she had not shown it—perhaps because she knew that Willis had made both her and D'Orsay "widely talked about, and, favourably, in America" (W. Connely, *op. cit.,* p. 231).

[3] Lady Blessington's niece Marguerite Power (1815–67; *DNB*), who had lived at Gore House since Sep 39—an arrangement no doubt first made for the sake of appearances when D'Orsay moved there.

To THOMAS HOOD, 13 OCTOBER 1842*

MS Mrs A. M. Stern.

Devonshire Terrace. | Thirteenth October 1842.

My Dear Hood.

I can (and will) give you a copy of the American book, next Monday.[1] It will not be in the hands of any other friend I have, until Tuesday night.

I will bring it myself about noon on Monday; and with it, if you will let me, Professor Longfellow of Boston (whose poetry you may have seen) who, admiring you as all good and true men do, wants to know you.[2]

Peter Parley[3] is a scoundrel and a Liar; and if he would present himself at my door, he would, as he very well knows, be summarily pitched into the street.[4] That fellow, Hood, came to me at Washington, at his own request;[5] brought papers and documents, and many dismal lamentations on the International robbery; got at my views on the subject, and heard me speak in full frankness and confidence; and then—went away to Boston, *ªand presided at that Meeting,*[6] *where the Resolution was passed, that the Law must not be changed, for if it were, American Editors could not alter English books.*[7ª] I was immediately informed of this, by Mr. Felton, Greek Professor at the American

---

[1] On 12 Oct Hood had written: "Can you let me have an early Copy of the American Notes, so that I may review it in the New Monthly?—Is it really likely to be ready as advertised?" He ended his letter with the following postscript: "Do you want a motto for your Book?—Coleridge in his Pantisocracy days used frequently to exclaim in soliloquy—'I wish I was in A-me-ri-ca!' Perhaps you might find something in the advertisements of Oldridge's *Balm of Columbia* or the American Soothing Syrup. Qy. Gin twist?" (MS Huntington; *Letters of Thomas Hood*, ed. P. Morgan, Toronto, 1973, pp. 497–8). For his review of *American Notes* in the November *New Monthly*, see *To* Hood, 12 Nov, *fn.*

[2] J. T. Fields later recorded Longfellow's description of Hood on this visit as "a small, thin man, looking very pale and worn, not saying much himself, but listening to Dickens with evident affection and interest" (see *Some Noted Princes, Authors, and Statesmen of Our Time*, ed. James Parton, Norwich, Conn., 1885, p. 153, quoted by Alvin Whitley, "Hood and Dickens: Some New Letters", *Huntington Library Quarterly*, XIV [1951], 388). For Longfellow's letter to Hood's family in 1852, recalling the visit, see *Memorials of Thomas Hood*, ed. [Mrs F. F. Broderip and T. Hood, Jr], 1860, II, 275.

[3] Samuel Griswold Goodrich (1793–1860; *DAB*), publisher, and writer of

children's books, best known by his pen name "Peter Parley". Member of a well-known Connecticut family of clergymen and lawyers; began publishing in 1816; travelled in Britain 1823–4 and met Scott, Jeffrey, Lockhart, and Hannah More, who is said to have suggested the Peter Parley books. Brought out *The Tales of Peter Parley about America*, 1827—the first of a series of over 100 Parley books which he claimed to have either written or edited himself. According to his *Recollections of a Lifetime*, New York, 1857, approximately seven million copies of his books had been sold by 1856. Numerous Parley books sprang up in imitation of his in both England and America—including *Parley's Penny Library* (see *To* Talfourd, 30 Dec 42).

[4] Hood had written in his letter of 12 Oct: "I have had Mr. Goderich [*thus*] (Peter Parley) here disclaiming the American right to alter English works, and denying the practice. He is to address a letter to me—but I doubt whether he *can* get over the Boston Petition & Mathews's comment."

[5] Nothing is known of this visit.

ªª "and presided at that Meeting" underlined twice; the rest once.

[6] The Convention of the Book Trade, held on 26 Apr: see *To* Felton, 16 May 42, *fn.*

[7] For this passage in the Boston Memorial, see *To* British Authors, 7 July 42, *fn.*

Cambridge, and the best fellow in the States. I was so astonished at Parley's baseness (though before God, it was very American and tradesmen-like) that I wrote back to Felton, and besought him to be quite sure that there was no mistake.[1] He returned for answer that the only gentleman[2] present, who had spirit enough to protest against the proceedings, assured him, upon his honor, that he stood on Parley's right hand, and Parley filled the chair. Wherefore I will ever proclaim said Parley to be a Scoundrel.[3]

I saw Grattan's speech.[4] He is a very false and time-serving fellow. He lives by those qualities, and is worth nothing but contempt.[5]

Ever since we have been at home, my other half has been gradually filtering away, through the medium of a cold in her head. Directly she has anything solid about her, she is coming to make friends with Mrs. Hood. I hope it may be on Monday. The sooner the better, *she* says. And so do I, with all my heart.

My Dear Hood | Always Heartily Yours

Thomas Hood Esquire   CHARLES DICKENS

To FREDERICK MARRYAT, 13 OCTOBER 1842

MS Harvard College Library.

Devonshire Terrace | Thirteenth October 1842

My Dear Marryatt

Many thanks for your famous book;[6] over which I have been chuckling, and

[1] CD's reply (16 May) to the letter from Felton telling him of the Boston Memorial contained no mention of Goodrich and asked no question; nor is there any hint in *To* Felton, 21 May, of an intermediate exchange of letters on the subject. Perhaps CD is recounting the gist of a later conversation.

[2] Presumably Bowen: see *To* British Authors, 7 July, *fn*.

[3] Goodrich gave his views on CD's American visit and on international copyright at length in *Recollections of a Lifetime*, II, pp. 355–78. He attacked CD's crusading and the petition he organized, and saw *American Notes* as his revenge for failure to obtain a copyright law. He himself, with his paramount desire to protect the "American book producers", rejected the "absolute right" claimed by CD, though accepting an author's claim to some compensation; but his attitude was in general ambiguous.

[4] "[Goodrich] came to me", wrote Hood in the same letter, "with an introduction from Grattan, once a *Colley*flower of literature, now our consul at Boston. Did you notice Grattan's speech at the Ashburton Dinner when his health was drunk as the Representative of English Literature —whereupon he so handsomely dropped all allusion to Authors & Authorship & played the Diplomatic? He deserves I think an American Note?" The dinner to Lord Ashburton, held in New York on 1 Sep, was reported in *The Times* of 26 Sep. Grattan, answering the toast of "The British Representative (on this occasion) of the dominion of Letters", chose conciliation between England and America as the theme of his speech, and made a passing reference to international copyright merely to play it down: "If . . . no disturbance on questions of political right is to be feared, we may still look out for some on questions of international copyright. (Laughter and cheers). But I shall not dwell on that subject. In the words of a distinguished countryman of mine, Sir Lucius O'Trigger [*a character in* The Rivals], 'it is a very pretty quarrel as it stands'. (Renewed laughter). But we, gentlemen, can have no dread of any serious issue to those inevitable discussions of right or wrong."

[5] Forster's first article on the American press in the *Foreign Quarterly* (Oct 42, xxx, 218–19n) described Grattan's speech as "in the most execrable bad taste", in its flattery of the Americans and appeal to popular applause.

[6] Presumably *Percival Keene*, 3 vols, published 1 Sep 42. There is plenty in it

grinning, and clenching my fists, and becoming warlike, for three whole days last past.

I have delayed acknowledging its receipt, that I might send you, at the same time, my American Volumes. But as I shall not be able to do so, I find, until Tuesday, I despatch this Thankful and Congratulatory Epistle first.

Believe me always | Faithfully Yours
CHARLES DICKENS

Stanfield tells me you have taken to drinking Cold Water in the morning. So have I. One of our pumps is dry, and the other drying, I drink so much of it.

To UNKNOWN CORRESPONDENT, 13 OCTOBER 1842

Extract from unidentified source; dated 13 Oct 42.

Longfellow is with us; we have taken many Expeditions; to Rochester: to the prisons: among tramps and thieves in the Mint lodging houses.[1]

To HENRY AUSTIN, 14 OCTOBER 1842*

MS Morgan Library.

Devonshire Terrace | Saturday October Fourteenth | Forty Two.
My Dear Henry.

Here are a plump brace of partridges and a stewed steak, on table today at half past five—and nobody to partake of them but the phlegmatic Poet. Can you come and assist?[2]

Affectionately Always
CD.

Henry Austin Esquire

Love to Tish.[3]

---

to amuse CD and make him feel "warlike": particularly the hero's escapades as a boy (blowing up a tyrannical schoolmaster with fireworks, scattering sneezing-powder at the opera) and in the Navy (fighting the French, as captain of a naval sloop); he eventually inherits a fortune as the natural son of a nobleman.

[1] Cf. F, III, viii, 278–9. During his visit to England of 1868, Longfellow reminded Forster of two experiences of 1842: their day at Rochester, and their night—under police protection afforded by Chesterton and Tracey—in "the worst haunts of the most dangerous classes". Maclise was with them on the second of these expeditions and "was struck with such sickness on entering the first of the Mint lodging-houses in the borough, that he had to remain, for the time [they] were in them, under guardianship of the police outside" (F, III, viii, 279). For CD's later visit to the Old Mint, when he found it "infinitely quieter and more subdued", see "On Duty with Inspector Field", *Household Words*, 14 June 51, III, 265–70, and *Reprinted Pieces*.

[2] Question-mark written very large.

[3] Letitia Austin.

To MRS HENRY BURNETT, [?14 OCTOBER 1842]†

MS Dickens House. *Date:* during the week before publication of *American Notes.*
Envelope (MS Private), postmarked Manchester 15 Oct 42 (day of receipt),
presumably belongs with this letter. *Address:* Mrs. Henry Burnett | 3 Elm Terrace |
Higher Ardwick | Manchester.

. . .¹ *ᵃworking people living in it. He² seems to be somewhat of that opinion
himself . . .
. . . to you all.ᵃ*
I don't think it probable that I shall have a copy of my American book until
Tuesday. On Tuesday night, I will send you, by the Mail train, a Parcel containing its two volumes, and Barnaby. The orders for it from the trade already,
are much larger than have ever been known since Scott's time—taking off
3000 copies in two days, a week before its publication.
Make our affectionate remembrance to Burnett, and the children.—Harry,³
I suppose, is almost marriageable by this time.

Your affectionate brother
CHARLES DICKENS

Why don't you put your address in your letters?

To EDWARD JESSE,⁴ 14 OCTOBER 1842

Mention in Sotheby's catalogue, July 1909; *MS* 1 p.; dated 14 Oct 42.

To MISS [THOMASINA] ROSS,⁵ 14 OCTOBER 1842

Mention in N, I, 482.

To JONATHAN CHAPMAN, 15 OCTOBER 1842

MS Comtesse de Suzannet. *Address:* By Mail Steamer. | The Honorable Jonathan
Chapman | Boston | Massachusetts | United States.

1 Devonshire Terrace | York Gate Regents Park.
Fifteenth October 1842.

My Dear Friend.
I was heartily glad to see your hand-writing when the Cunard Boat which
brought your letter, came in. And I was heartily glad to read it—not the less

---

¹ The whole of first page of a folded
sheet, except for 2 lines at the bottom of
side one, and 3 words on its reverse, is
missing. A pencil note in an unknown
hand (possibly F. G. Kitton's) reads: "this
part entirely irrecoverable. taken probably
(says Burnett) to light a candle."
ᵃᵃ Not previously published.
² Perhaps John Dickens, and CD's first
page reported on an exchange of letters
about finding a house for him in London
when he left Alphington (see *To* Mitton,
7 Dec and *fn*). If so, the destruction of

p. 1 was probably not only to "light a
candle", but part of the family's policy of
suppressing references to John Dickens's
money affairs.
³ Henry Augustus, her first child, born
Nov 39; a cripple, died Jan 49. See
To Mrs Burnett, 24 Sep 43.
⁴ Edward Jesse (1780–1868; *DNB*),
Surveyor of Royal Parks and Palaces: see
Vol. II, p. 430*n*.
⁵ Clearly Thomasina Ross: see *To*
Chapman & Hall, 20 Oct and *fn*.

so, because it led me to the belief that your tenderness for me was keener and less bold[1] than any anxiety you would ever entertain for yourself.[2]

In lieu of the American people (or the worst among them) as a mass, consider them, for a moment, as a man. If you could only retain the friendship of an Individual by the sacrifice of everything which elevates you in your own respect —by fearing to speak the Truth—by keeping a timid silence—by debating within yourself at every turn, as though he were a rich relation, "will he like this; will he be angry if I say that; will he find out that I am but a toy for his amusement, if I do the other"—would you seek to hold it, for a day? If I know you, No. Neither would I. And because I claim to have been kindly received in America, by reason of something I had done to amuse its people and pre-possess them in my favor; and not with reference to something I was not to do; therefore I write about its people, and write freely. And as I have never been deterred by hopes of promotion or visions of greatness, from pointing out abuses at home, so no amount of popular breath shall blow me from my purpose, if I see fit to point out what in my judgment are abuses abroad. And if my being an honest man, bring down caprice, and weathercock fickleness, and the falsest kind of insult on my head, what matters it to me—or to you—or to any man who is worth the name, and, being right, can look down on the crowd, and whistle while they hiss?

What is to prevent my writing? The certainty of not pleasing them. How does the certainty appear? By every claim I have upon them being disregarded and cast ruthlessly aside, at the printed bidding of some abandoned fellow; and aspersions being greedily believed which make me out a lying adventurer.[3] My dear Chapman, if we yielded to such reasons or such men as these; in five year's[4] time there would be no such thing as Truth in the world; and from that hour downward, her cause would be a hopeless, desperate venture.

---

[1] i.e. more gentle.

[2] In answering CD's letter of 3 Aug, Chapman (according to *D*, xxxviii [Winter 1941/2], 12) told him candidly of the "journalistic mud" that was being "flung at him since his departure", and continued: "Yes, my dear Friend, with my feelings toward you unchanged I have the inexpressible bitterness of reading and hearing the evidence of this change of general feeling toward you, caused in the manner I have told you. You said in one of your letters to me [*22 Feb 42*], 'I open my whole heart to you, you see; I write in such a spirit of confidence that I pour out all that I have felt upon this subject.' Rejoicing to have you do so, I have done likewise. . . . You, I know will appreciate my purpose." He then asked: "Can you wonder that I look with some apprehension for the appearance here of your book on America? Knowing, as I do, how difficult, if not impossible it is to write a book about us under present circumstances which shall place you before our people in the position which you have heretofore held and which I so long to have you occupy, can you wonder at my wish, that instead of writing directly or formally upon the country, you had worked up scenes and characters you met incidentally and in the same way in which you have them which you found elsewhere. However, I presume not to advise you. Your plans are made, and perhaps 'ere this reaches you the sheets will be printed. I need not say that I shall look for it with the deepest interest, and from the bottom of my heart I trust that it may disabuse the public mind here of all the aspersions which have been thrown upon you, and present you in your true light and as such as I know you to be."

[3] Presumably refers to the forged letter: see *To* Forster, ?30 or 31 Aug.

[4] Thus in MS.

I am well convinced that in your heart of hearts, you think and feel with me. I am well convinced that there is not, in my book, one solitary line in which you, and such as you, will not most thoroughly concur. I dispassionately believe that in the slow fulness of time, what I have written, will have some effect in purging your community of evils which threaten its very existence. And I know that it is written kindly and good-humouredly; and that I have never, for an instant, suffered myself to be betrayed into a hasty or unfair expression, or one I shall, at any time, regret.[1] Believe me, my dear friend, the fact is literally so; and that you will find it so, to your entire contentment. And when you meet with evidences of a change in the popular opinion towards me, is it not enough to say within yourself, "if he had not brought about that change himself, he would not be the man who is my friend, but would be some other fellow whom I could hear dispraised with supreme indifference"?

Longfellow from Cambridge is staying with us just now, and will return, I believe, by the Great Western next Saturday. I shall charge him with a copy of my book for you. I have caused my publishers to take such precautions as will prevent (I hope) its reaching America by the Steamer which will bring you this letter.[2]

[1] CD stood by this statement until 1859. In his Preface to the Cheap edn of *American Notes*, 1850, he still insisted that he had "nothing to defend, or to explain away. The truth is the truth"; but this assertion was omitted in his Preface to the Library edn, 1859 (written while he was first considering a reading tour in America), and the whole tone made less pugnacious. However, in his "The Young Man from the Country" (*All the Year Round*, 1 Mar 62; *Miscellaneous Papers*, ed. B. W. Matz, 1914), written during the American Civil War, he reprinted most of his 1850 Preface, including "I have nothing to defend . . . The truth is the truth"; and added to it his attack on the House of Representatives from *American Notes*, Ch. 8, and on "Universal Distrust", " 'smart' dealing", and the Press, from Ch. 18. For his admission in 1868 that his earlier impressions might have been "extreme", see *Speeches*, ed. K. J. Fielding, pp. 380–1, and the Postscript appended to this book and *Chuzzlewit* in the Charles Dickens edn of 1868.

[2] The *Caledonia*, which sailed from Liverpool to Boston on 20 Oct, arriving 2 Nov. CD's precautions were apparently successful, for on Sat 5 Nov *Brother Jonathan* announced that it would "positively receive" the sheets of *American Notes* "by the *Great Western*, either today or Monday". They arrived on Sunday even-

ing, 6 Nov. Both *Brother Jonathan* and the *New World* published the entire book on Monday 7th at 12½ cents—*Brother Jonathan* in an "Extra" (of 46 pp., small 4to, double column), headed "First American Edition"; the *New World* (which had advertised that morning for "thirty compositors" to whom it offered "full cases and extra pay") in a "double extra number" (33 pp., 3 columns) at 1 p.m., selling within 24 hours 24,000 copies. The same morning the *New York Herald* published what it described as "the principal passages—those containing [CD's] most racy and bitter opinions of society in the United States" (Peter Bracher, "The New York *Herald* and *American Notes*", *Dickens Studies*, V [1969], 82). Harpers, according to the *New World*, brought out a book-sized edn (92 pp., double column, at 1/–) 25 hours later. By 9 Nov Lea & Blanchard had an edition of 5,000 copies available in Philadelphia, published, with portrait, as "Boz's Works—No. 21" (i.e. as part of their 1842 reissued series of CD), at 25 cents; this was followed 10 Nov by what was advertised as a 2nd "edition", without portrait, at 12½ cents; faulty pagination, irregularity of size of both page and type, and unusual employment of six printers, show it was prepared with great haste (P. Bracher, *The Lea & Blanchard Edition of Dickens's American Notes, 1842, Papers of the Bibliographical Society of*

Our darlings are all well, and send all manner of messages in broken English, to yours. Mrs. Dickens joins me in cordial and sincere remembrances to yourself, and to Mrs. Chapman.[1] And I am always—stay; not always—conditionally—conditionally on your not, at any future time, talking about the length of your letters, or committing any such monstrous absurdity—Your faithful friend

CHARLES DICKENS

To W. H. PRESCOTT, 15 OCTOBER 1842†

MS Berg Collection. *Address:* By Mail Steamer | W. H. Prescott Esquire | Boston | Massachusetts | United States.

Devonshire Terrace | York Gate Regents Park London
Fifteenth October 1842.

My Dear Prescott.

My publishers, Messrs. Chapman and Hall, will be happy to republish that book of which you speak: requiring no better commendation of it, than your description of its merits.[2] *a* They are exceedingly anxious to treat with you for the purchase of your new history; and I can distinctly say, from every day's knowledge and experience, that they are perfectly truthful, reliable, and honorable men in all their dealings.

Perhaps you don't know—if you do not, it is right you should—that Bentley advertizes himself as the Publisher, on this side, of the History aforesaid.[3] But if he have done so, without authority, do not be disturbed; for the bookseller, whomsoever he may prove, to whom you send early proofs, will anticipate and stop him, beyond all kind of question.[4a]

America, LXIII [1969], 296–300). For the story that Isaac C. Pray, former editor of the *Boston Pearl*—then editing a Radical London evening paper—bribed a pressman in Bradbury & Evans's printing house for proof sheets and sent them to Boston in advance of the legitimate proofs, see W. G. Wilkins, *First and Early American Editions of the Works of CD*, privately printed, Cedar Rapids, 1910, pp. 22–4.

[1] *Née* Lucinda Dwight, daughter of the Hon. Timothy Dwight, of Springfield, Mass. She had married Chapman in Apr 32.

[2] See *To* Edward Chapman, 16 Sep, *fn.* For the book's publication by Chapman & Hall, with the title *Life in Mexico*, see *To* Prescott, 2 Mar 43, *fn.*

aa; bb Not previously published.

[3] In the earliest advertisement yet found, *Bentley's Advertiser* for Nov, Bentley listed as "In the Press", "The Discovery and Conquest of Mexico. By W. H.

Prescott, Esq. . . . 3 vols. 8vo. With Portraits". This misleading and premature announcement was Bentley's attempt, as the publisher of the English edition of Prescott's *History of the Reign of Ferdinand and Isabella* in 1838, to stake his claim against other English publishers, such as Longmans who had advertised *The Conquest of Mexico* as in the press in a catalogue received by Prescott on 27 June 42 (*The Literary Memoranda of W. H. Prescott*, ed. C. Harvey Gardiner, Oklahoma, 1961, II, 89–90). Prescott took Bentley's advertisement into account in their negotiations, saying "he has asserted, by advertising it, his right to the new work" (*Correspondence of W. H. Prescott 1833–1847*, ed. R. Wolcott, p. 344). For Prescott's letter to Bentley of 31 Dec and his negotiations with other publishers, see *To* Prescott, 2 Mar 43 and *fn.*

[4] See *To* Prescott, 10 Nov 43 and *fn.*

Longfellow is staying with me; and has been for some days. He thinks of returning by the Great Western on this day week. I shall charge him with a copy of my American Notes for you.[1] I have no fear but they will find favor in your eyes, though they may not in those of the mass.[2]

[1] This (published 19 Oct) he inscribed to Prescott "From his friend | Charles Dickens | October Nineteenth 1842" (Suzannet Collection). Presumably Prescott wrote CD a note of thanks; but the only reference to *American Notes* in his published *Correspondence* (p. 323) is the following, dated 1 Dec 42: "Your own book has risen to the honour of the press under the Harpers, who are obliged to sell or rather sacrifice it at the ninepenny price of Bagmen's editions.... Your friend, the learned Grecian [*Felton*] is to *fix* you I understand in the 'North American' [*of Jan 43*]. It is well you are not handed over to one of the gentlemen of the far West, who *chaw* and salivate so vigorously. Your gabardine would carry off a sample of it, I fancy." But Dana, who dined at Ticknor's on 11 Nov (Prescott and Longfellow being among the guests), recorded in his journal: "All think Dickens' book entertaining & clever". On finishing it himself, however, though conceding various merits, he considered that "whenever he comes to abstractions or to generalising, or indeed to any deductions or reflections of his own, he is below par. His style then becomes swollen & vaporous.... The book will make him unpopular without adding to his reputation. He is not a gentleman, & his genius is in a narrow line. In that line he is insurpassable, to be sure. His journey to America has been a Moscow expedition for his fame" (*Journal*, ed. R. F. Lucid, I, 102–3).

[2] The most serious and thoughtful attacks on the book came from the champions of the Philadelphia "separate system", described by CD after his visit to the Eastern Penitentiary: see *To* Forster, 13 Mar, *fn*. As was to be expected, the *New York Herald* was abusive, but in general terms: the book was the product of "the most coarse, vulgar, impudent, and superficial" mind "that ever had the courage to write about ... this original and remarkable country" (quoted in P. Bracher, "The New York *Herald* and *American Notes*", *Dickens Studies*, V [1969], 82). For other extracts see Ada B. Nisbet, "The Mystery

of *Martin Chuzzlewit*" (*Essays Critical and Historical, Dedicated to Lily B. Campbell*, 1950, p. 213). The *New Englander* (Jan 43, I, 64–84) was filled with "contempt for such a compound of egotism, coxcombry, and cockneyism", and regretted the whole publication, which bore the "marks of hasty composition", and exhibited CD's "moral character in a most undesirable light" (especially his enjoyment of drinking: cf. the impression made on Emerson of CD as "a gourmand & a great lover of wines and brandies", who sentimentalized "on every prison & orphan asylum, until ... the great hour of Dinner": *Journals of R. W. Emerson*, ed. W. H. Gilman and J. E. Parsons, VIII, 222); one good result of an international copyright law, the *New Englander* concluded, would be to limit the circulation of CD's books in America. Poe, in the *Southern Literary Messenger* (Jan 43, IX, 60), called the book "one of the most suicidal productions, ever deliberately published by an author, who had the least reputation to lose". But CD had his defenders: the *Boston Daily Evening Transcript* (ed. Cornelia W. Walter, who succeeded her brother L. M. Walter as editor 24 July) thought well of the book on its first quick reading (8 Nov); on 10 Nov, it quoted briefly a defence that had appeared in the *New York Union*, and then gave its own more considered view: the book had been "written easily, and with a quick observation, without great depth, if any depth at all" and was "meant in good humor"; the erudite might call it superficial, yet it was simply what its title claimed for it—"Notes", which would certainly be circulated "without incurring for its author, any ill will amongst liberal people"; it was "as amusing as the 'last new novel' used to be". The paper returned to the subject on 12 Nov in a long editorial headed "YANKEE LOVE OF EXCITEMENT: CHARLES DICKENS": "We all liked Boz—there was such a love of humanity ... that we could not help it; he touched our hearts ... We told him so ... And, now how very foolish it is for more than half of us 'to get mad,' and dart right off to the other

*b*With best regards to your father[1] and mother,[2] and to all friends. Believe me My Dear Prescott,

Always Faithfully Yours

W. H. Prescott Esquire. CHARLES DICKENS*b*

To AUGUSTUS TRACEY, 15 OCTOBER [1842]*

MS University of Texas. *Date:* 15 Oct was Saturday in 1842; handwriting supports that year.

Devonshire Terrace. | Saturday Fifteenth Octr.

My Dear Sir

Our letters crossed.—For Heaven's sake, put the virtuous boy between those dismal blinkers, instantly.

We will carry you home in a hackney Coach on Monday Evening, and take up our friend, the Warden, in the same conveyance. Nothing can do better.

Faithfully Yours always

Lieutenant Tracey CHARLES DICKENS
&c &c &c

To EDWARD MOXON,[3] 17 OCTOBER [1842]

MS copy, Massachusetts Historical Society. *Address:* Edward Moxon Esquire | Dover Street | Piccadilly; postmark 17 Oct 42.

Devonshire Terrace | Monday Seventeenth October

My Dear Sir.

Mr. Longfellow, the best of the American Poets, (as I have no doubt you know) is staying with me and wishes to see you on the subject of republishing his verses.[4]

We breakfast with Mr. Rogers tomorrow morning, and will call upon you, if convenient to yourself, when we leave his house.

Faithfully yours

Edward Moxon Esquire CHARLES DICKENS

extreme, and hate and blame as violently as we loved and praised. And, why? Because, forsooth, he has spoken his free opinion of the worst part of the newspaper press, and laughed honestly at some of our little foibles! . . . For the life of us, we cannot discover any 'shocking injustice,' any 'deep wrong,' any 'terrible insult,' or any 'unthankful spirit' in the late work, which has called up so much newspaper invective against the 'Notes' and their author."

[1] Judge William Prescott, of Boston, son of Col. William Prescott, hero of the Battle of Bunker Hill.

[2] Catherine Greene Prescott, daughter of Thomas Hickling, U.S. Consul at St Michael's in the Azores. CD had met them both in June at Lebanon Springs.

[3] Edward Moxon (1801–58; *DNB*), publisher: see Vol. II, p. 64*n*.

[4] See *To* Moxon, 17 Nov, *fn*.

To MRS HENRY BURNETT, 18 OCTOBER 1842*

MS Free Library of Philadelphia.

In great haste
Devonshire Terrace | Eighteenth October 42.

Dear Fanny

I send you the books by tonights[1] Mail. As I have made great efforts to baulk the American Pirates by not suffering the American Volumes to go out by tomorrow's boat,[2] be very careful to keep them strictly to yourself and Henry until Thursday.

Affy. always
CD.

To THE EARL OF MULGRAVE, 18 OCTOBER 1842

Extract in unidentified bookseller's catalogue, n.d., Eastgate House, Rochester; dated 18 Oct 42.

Since I received your letter Mrs Dickens wrote to W. Patison's Hotel[3] begging Miss Fisher[4] to come and stay here. . . . Joe Miller[5] whom you ask about was a Canadian dyspeptic who was ill the whole way home, and who, in the midst of apparently strong health, would suddenly fall head first into a bucket on deck and be horribly sick.

To GEORGE W. PUTNAM, 18 OCTOBER 1842*

MS Free Library of Philadelphia. *Address:* By Mail Steamer. | Mr. George. W. Putnam | Salem | Massachusetts | United States.

1 Devonshire Terrace | York Gate Regents Park London
Eighteenth October 1842.

Dear Mr. Putnam

I received the parcel you sent me by the hands of Captain Hewett,[6] quite safely. The papers, according to my old custom, I put in the fire without opening; but I was not the less obliged to you for sending them to me, as I know you did so, with the best intentions.

The truth is, that you so anticipated all my wants when we left New York, that I had no occasion for that parcel after all. When I wrote to you, to send me what books you had; the large Packing Case was still at the Custom House, and I was ignorant of its miscellaneous contents. But long before your last arrived, it came home; and I found in it, everything I could possibly require.

---

[1] Thus in MS.

[2] The *Caledonia*, which sailed on the 20th: see *To* Chapman, 15 Oct, *fn.*

[3] Probably Patterson's Hotel, 48 Brook Street, London.

[4] A friend made in Canada or on the *George Washington*, presumably: see *To* Capt. Granville, 20 Oct.

[5] Possibly a nickname (inspired by *Joe Miller's Jest Book*) given to some fellow-passenger on the *George Washington*.

[6] Capt. Hewitt of the *Britannia*, which had arrived in Liverpool 10 Sep.

I send you, by the hands of Mr. Longfellow who has been staying with me for a week or two, and returns in *The Great Western*, a copy of a book I have just published, containing an account of our wanderings.[1] Mr. Sumner of Boston will give it to you, or to anybody whom you may authorize to receive it.

Being in doubt where to address this, I send it to Salem: relying on its reaching you, through some of your friends. I have taken it into my head that you *must* be painting the portraits of the Factory Young Ladies at Lowell.[2] If so,—make them very handsome, and the demand is certain to be brisk. The skilful introduction of a gold-watch occasionally, would be very judicious: and if you can counterfeit satin to the life,[3] your fortune is made.[4]

If I could make it, I would: for my recollection of your zealous and faithful services does not weaken with time or distance. Being no wizard however, [and][5] having no aunt or grandmother who is a fairy (as the good people in the story books always have) I can only send you, across the Atlantic, my best and heartiest wishes.

Mrs. Dickens joins in them, she says, most sincerely: and desires all manner of kind remembrances to you. Anne (who is very blooming, but still a spinster) does the like. And the children, who are quite well and very happy, send their loves.

Remember me to Julia,[6] and to all your family.[7] And believe me, however much you may see me abused (it will not be seldom or sparingly) still Faithfully

Your friend

Mr. George. W. Putnam.   CHARLES DICKENS

To CHARLES MACKAY, [19 OCTOBER 1842]

MS John Rylands Library. *Date:* CD's review appeared in the *Morning Chronicle* of Thurs 20 Oct. *Address:* Charles Mackay Esquire.

MC Office | Wednesday Night

My Dear Sir

Here is a review I promised to write (sub rosâ) of Lord Londonderry's Letter,[8]

---

[1] Longfellow also took copies for Felton, Sumner, the elder Dana, Allston, Bancroft and Jonathan Chapman (H. W. L. Dana, "Longfellow and Dickens", *Cambridge Historical Society Publications*, XXVIII [1942], 75), besides a copy for Putnam.

[2] See *To* Forster, ?4 Feb, *fn*.

[3] Like A. E. Chalon (see Vol. II, p. 201*n*).

[4] Most English travellers commented on the Lowell girls' dress. Marryat recorded a clergyman's surprise at seeing them appear "in *silks*, with *scarfs*, *veils*, and *parasols*" (*Diary in America*, Part Second, II, 50). The Lowell girls had such a reputation for "gentility of manner and dress" that Charles Lyell thought it should be impressed on any foreigner who visited the mills that he had been seeing factories "on

a great scale . . . so managed as to yield high profits", not simply a set of "gentlemen and ladies, playing at factory for their amusement" (*Travels in North America*, 1845, I, 118).

[5] Word missing through hole at fold.

[6] Presumably Julia Amanda Putnam (*b*. 1813), perhaps a cousin, whom he married in Aug 44.

[7] His father was Joseph Putnam (1777–1859), a shoe-manufacturer and inventor; his mother, *née* Mercy Giddings Whipple (1779–1859); there were six other children. A cousin was Edwin Whipple (1819–86; *DAB*), essayist and lecturer, whom CD met in Boston 1867–8 (see N. C. Peyrouton, "Mr. 'Q,' Dickens's American Secretary", *D*, LIX [1963], 156 and *n*).

[8] See *To* Black, 15 Aug, *fn*. The MS of

just now published.[1] Will you kindly ask Hogarth,[2] for me, to read the proof very carefully; as the Printers (unmindful of our old acquaintance)[3] maimed my last communication, most surgically.[4]

I have been *going*, every day, to write you about the Miltonians.[5] I will, in a day or two. I cannot make up my mind that the thing would do—not by reason of any defects of its own, but because of its jarring materials.[6]

Faithfully Yours always

Charles Mackay Esquire   CHARLES DICKENS

To THOMAS CAMPBELL,[7] OCTOBER 1842

Mention in Stan Henkels catalogue No. 1337 (1923); dated Devonshire Terrace, Oct 42 (clearly before leaving for Cornwall).

To [EDWARD CHAPMAN], 20 OCTOBER 1842*

MS Berg Collection. *Address:* clearly to Edward Chapman: see reference to Mrs Chapman's expected baby in letter of 16 Sep.

Thursday | Twentieth October 1842.

My Dear Sir

Here is Mrs. Chapman's Autograph[8]—the gratification of her wish—"a real blessing to mothers"[9]—in perspective.

Faithfully Always

CD.

CD's review is in the John Rylands Library, Manchester; for the text with footnotes giving his MS corrections, see the *Bulletin of the John Rylands Library*, XVIII (1934), 182–91. Almost two columns long in the *Chronicle*, it pilloried Londonderry's literary style and tastelessness with contemptuous sarcasm; and ended with the suggestion that since, out of the Letter's 145 pages, 131 simply recapitulated discussions in the Lords, these could be jettisoned and the remaining 14 "original" pages published cheaply on very small sheets under the title, "The New Polite Letter Writer, or Noble Scholar's Companion"—with an appropriate vignette by "H.B." (the great caricaturist, John Doyle). Of Londonderry's charges against Ashley and the Bill it said virtually nothing, presumably implying that they were beneath notice.

[1] *A Letter to Lord Ashley, M.P., on the Mines and Collieries Bill*. By C. W. Vane, Marquess of Londonderry, G.C.B., &c. Colburn, 1842. It set out to show that the Bill had been carried "by manœuvres, chicanery, and misrepresentations"; and that, for the sake of "mistaken humanity . . . general education and overstrained

morality", the national interest was being ignored. It attacked the characters of the Commissioners and Sub-Commissioners, "the exaggerated Report . . . and the disgusting pictorial woodcuts"; quoted statistics to show the relative health, prosperity and lawfulness of colliers; and ended with a final attack on Ashley's "overflowing haste" in pushing forward his "absurd mania" and with a threat to resist his future measures.

[2] George Hogarth, CD's father-in-law.

[3] CD had been a reporter on the *Chronicle* Sep 34–Nov 36. See Vol. I.

[4] For misprints in his letter on Ashley's Mines and Collieries Bill, see *To* the *Morning Chronicle*, 25 July, *fns*. The printed text also shows a number of slipped letters at the ends of lines.

[5] See *To* Mackay, 26 July and *fn*.

[6] Among those who promised support were Dr Beattie, John Britton, Thomas Campbell, and John Robertson.

[7] CD was probably writing about the Milton Institute; see last.

[8] CD's note is written on p. 3 of a folded sheet; on p. 1 are stanzas 8 and 9 of Longfellow's "The Beleaguered City" ("En-

To MESSRS CHAPMAN & HALL, 20 OCTOBER 1842*

MS Mr W. J. Goddard.

Devonshire Terrace | Twentieth October 1842

My Dear Sirs

I have given the lady who wrote the enclosed note,[1] a letter of Introduction to you. There is no doubt whatever, of her ability as a translatress; and her credentials, as you will see, are of the best kind.

If you can avail yourselves of her services, I shall be particularly glad. For she is most deserving and reliable (though not beautiful); and it will be a high satisfaction to me, to have been instrumental in serving her. For this reason I write you privately; that you may know I really am interested in her.[2]

Faithfully Yours always

Messrs. | Chapman and Hall.   CHARLES DICKENS

To MESSRS CHAPMAN & HALL, 20 OCTOBER 1842

Text from N, I, 485.

1 Devonshire Terrace York Gate, Regents Park
Twentieth October 1842

Dear Sirs,

This will introduce you to Miss Ross; the lady in reference to whom I have already written you. I need say no more to secure to her your ready attention.

Faithfully yours always

[CHARLES DICKENS]

To MISS THOMASINA ROSS, 20 OCTOBER 1842*

MS Huntington Library.

Devonshire Terrace | Twentieth October 1842.

My Dear Miss Ross.

I have been very closely engaged since I received your note, or I would have answered it, sooner.

---

camped beside Life's rushing stream . . ." and "Upon its midnight battleground . . ."), signed by Longfellow and dated 20 Oct 42.

[9] The claim in the advertisements of "Mrs Johnson's Soothing Syrup", for "relieving children when suffering from painful dentition", prepared by Barclay & Sons, 95 Farringdon Street.

[1] A letter which CD had presumably encouraged her, on 14 Oct, to write. Thomasina Muir Ross (?1796–1875), author and translator; eldest of eight children of William Ross (1764–1852), linguist and contributor to *The Times*. Assisted Jerdan on the *Literary Gazette* 1817, and he found her a "ready and ex-

cellent translator" (*Autobiography*, 1852, II, 178). A number of her translations appeared in the *Polytechnic Journal* 1840–2 and in *Bentley's Miscellany* 1848. Five volumes translated by her from French, German and Spanish appeared in the mid and late 40s. For her contributions to *Household Words*, her other work, and Civil List pension, see later vols.

[2] CD was interested in the whole family. Thomasina was sister of his aunt Janet Barrow (see Vol. I, p. 49*n*), of Georgina (Vol. I, p. 7*n*), of Charles, Francis and John (Vol. I, pp. 7, 85, 248 and *nn*). See W. J. Carlton, "Dickens and the Ross Family", *D*, LI (1955), 58–66.

To Chapman and Hall I have written very strongly, to the effect you desire; and I have urged the matter on them as one personally interesting to myself. This is the reason why I send you so brief a note of introduction as the Enclosed.[1] Such a communication as I have made to them in private, will have fifty times the weight of any letter I could give you; and I can confidently depend on their attending to it.[2]

If, either now or at any other time, you desire me to do more, or to render you further assistance, trust me that I will promptly meet your wishes, and that I shall have real pleasure in doing so.

Mrs. Dickens begs me to send you her kind regards. And I am always, believe me,

	Faithfully Yours
Miss Ross.	CHARLES DICKENS

To FREDERICK GRANVILLE, 20 OCTOBER 1842*

MS Benoliel Collection.

1 Devonshire Terrace | York Gate Regents Park.
Twentieth October 1842.

My Dear Granville

It gave me very great pleasure this morning to hear from you; for I began to think—either that you had over-eaten yourself under the parental gooseberry bushes (as you threatened to do, aboard ship),[3] or had been violently married by some Warwickshire beauty.[4]

Of course there is no place like old England. There never was, and never will be. What has a rational man to do with Canada? Nothing at all. Nobody who "calls himself a gentleman"—here I quote our Theatricals,[5] which have come to be like a dream—has anything in common with such outlandish parts.

Anything in the way of Game, is always acceptable. So shall anything in the shape of Granville, be, whenever it presents itself in these Latitudes.

Mrs. Dickens sends her best regards. Little Miss Fisher, of Muffin Memory, is in town, and coming to stay here. We had a letter from Mulgrave, commending her to our protecting care.[6]

	Always Believe me	Faithfully Yours
Captain Granville	CHARLES DICKENS

---

[1] See last.

[2] No record of her having translated anything for Chapman & Hall has been found.

[3] On the *George Washington*, returning from America.

[4] Granville, who came from a Warwickshire family, married Isabel Sheldon, of Brailes House, Shipston-on-Stour, Warwickshire, in June 54.

[5] His own part, Snobbington, in *A Good Night's Rest*: "Pray, Sir, do you call this behaving like a gentleman? I say, Sir, do you call this behaving like a gentleman?"

[6] See *To* Mulgrave, 18 Oct.

To LEIGH HUNT, 20 OCTOBER 1842

MS British Museum.

> 1 Devonshire Terrace | York Gate Regents Park
> Twentieth October 1842.

My Dear Hunt.

Many thanks to you for your note. I saw the Rustic Walk and Dinner in the old Monthly;[1] and had so much pleasure in seeing it, that I never once bethought myself of having had any other share in it, at any time, than that intimate one which all its readers may claim.[2] You have apostrophized me and all true men in the cheese,[3] the salad,[4] the chairs, the view, the walk, and everything else. What more would a reasonable creature, such as I claim to be, have!

Trust me, that if you knew all, you would better like to have your Palfrey[5] cantering, at your expense,[6] through the whole American territory, wide as it is, than you would relish being there yourself.

> Always My Dear Hunt | Faithfully Yours

Leigh Hunt Esquire
> CHARLES DICKENS

To FREDERICK SALMON,[7] 22 OCTOBER 1842*

MS Berg Collection.

> 1 Devonshire Terrace | York Gate Regents Park.
> Twenty Second October 1842.

My Dear Salmon.

Binding these Volumes[8] to match the others,[9] has occasioned a delay of two or three days, or you would have received them sooner.[10]

God bless you, and yours.

> Always Faithfully | Your friend

Frederick Salmon Esquire
> CHARLES DICKENS

[1] Hunt's poem in two parts, "The Walk" and "The Dinner", had appeared in the *Monthly Magazine*, Sep and Oct 42.

[2] In May 40 Hunt had sent CD the poem in MS, no doubt because it celebrated an actual walk and dinner with him as companion (see Vol. II, p. 66). Now, possibly, Hunt—having hoped for a letter of appreciation from CD, since he had been so closely involved—had written (to prick him into some response) a letter asking whether he should have made CD's connection with the poem explicit by including him in the apostrophe (see II, 66n).

[3] "also the old cheese, | The right rich crumble, betwixt dry and moist."

[4] "and the crisp salad cold | And it's in basins;—deep;—we fork it up, | Like haycocks; . . ."

[5] See *To* Hunt, 19 July, *fn.*

[6] i.e. pirated.

[7] Frederick Salmon (1796–1868), the surgeon who had operated on CD in Oct 41: see Vol. II, p. 404n.

[8] Of *American Notes* (now in the Berg Collection).

[9] He had already given Salmon inscribed copies of *Pickwick, Nickleby, Oliver,* and *Master Humphrey* (see Vol. II, pp. 409 and *n,* 456 and *n*).

[10] Since publication day, 19th, CD had, moreover (with Forster: *Letters of H. W. Longfellow,* ed. A. Hilen, II, 475n), accompanied Longfellow to Bath to see Landor (on 20th) and next day seen him on to the *Great Western* at Bristol.

To DR SOUTHWOOD SMITH, 22 OCTOBER 1842

Text from Mrs C. L. Lewes, *Dr Southwood Smith*, 1898, p. 87.

Devonshire Terrace, | Saturday, October Twenty-second, 1842.
My dear Sir,

I have an expedition afoot in which I think you can assist me.

I want to see the very dreariest and most desolate portion of the sea-coast of Cornwall; and start next Thursday,[1] with a couple of friends,[2] for St. Michael's Mount.[3] Can you tell me of your own knowledge, or through the information of any of the Mining Sub-Commissioners,[4] what is the next best bleak and barren part? And can you, furthermore, while I am in those regions, help me down a mine?[5]

I ought to make many apologies for troubling you, but somehow or other I don't—which is your fault and not mine.

Always believe me faithfully your friend,

Dr Southwood Smith.   CHARLES DICKENS

To THOMAS CARLYLE, 26 OCTOBER 1842*

MS Berg Collection.

Devonshire Terrace | October Twenty Sixth 1842.
My Dear Carlyle.

I have been truly delighted by the receipt of your most welcome letter. You will believe me, I know, when I tell you that having always held you in high

[1] On "Thursday morning" (27 Oct) Catherine wrote to Beard that "Charles who has gone to Cornwall this morning" had asked her to send Beard a copy of the 2nd edn of *American Notes* (*Dickens to his Oldest Friend*, ed. W. Dexter, 1932, p. 271). *Wolmer's Exeter Gazette*, 4 Nov 42, reported: "Mr. Charles Dickens, after paying a visit to Walter Savage Landor, Esq. . . . at St. James's Square, Bath, arrived with some friends at the New London Inn, in this city, on Saturday evening [*29 Oct*]; and after visiting his father at Alphington, set off for Plymouth on an excursion to the Eddystone and the Land's End. Mr. Dickens is probably in search of materials for his new tale of English Life and Manners, the first number of which is announced to appear on the 1st. January next." For CD's probable route, see *To* Felton, 31 Dec, *fn*.

[2] Three in fact: Forster, Maclise and Stanfield.

[3] The starting-point for this was Marazion. According to a local story, a solicitor, Richard Tippett, knowing that CD was to dine there, served the party as a waiter; but after correcting a Latin quotation, he had to explain himself and was invited to join them at dessert (G. C. Boase, *Collectanea Cornubiensia*, Truro, 1890, col. 995).

[4] The officials appointed by the four Infant Labour Commissioners (of whom Southwood Smith was one) to enquire into conditions in mines in various parts of the country. Charles Barham, MD, was sub-commissioner for the mining districts of Devon and Cornwall. The great age of mining (chiefly for tin and copper) in Cornwall was from the 1840s to '80s; in 1842 more than 200 mines were being worked, of which only two survive. The working conditions in the four main mining districts (Callington, St Austell, Gwennap and Land's End) are very fully described in the 1842 Report of the Commissioners.

[5] According to F, IV, i, 288, they "descended into several mines". See *To* Felton, 31 Dec and *fn*.

regard for the manliness and honesty with which you have exercised your great abilities, there are very few men in the world whose commendation, so expressed, would so well please me.[1]

I am going down into Cornwall for a few days. When I return, I shall come to Chelsea and report myself. For as we are to know each other *well* (which I take to be clearly recognized as a fact in perspective, by both of us) the sooner we begin, the better.

Ever believe me | Heartily Yours
CHARLES DICKENS

To T. L. CUYLER,[2] 26 OCTOBER 1842

Text from T. L. Cuyler, *Recollections of a Long Life: an Autobiography*, 1902, p. 21.

1 Devonshire Terrace, | Regents Park, Oct. 26th, 1842.

My Dear Sir,

I am heartily obliged to you for your frank and manly letter.[3] I shall always remember it in connection with my American book; and never—believe me—save in the foremost rank of its pleasant and honorable associations.

Let me subscribe myself, as I really am

Faithfully your Friend,

Mr. Theodore Ledyard Cuyler. CHARLES DICKENS

---

[1] What Carlyle wrote in praise of *American Notes* (of which CD had sent him an inscribed copy on 19 Oct) is not known. But in *Past and Present*, 1843 (II, 3), he referred to the American reception of CD: "Oh, if all Yankee-land follow a small good 'Schnüspel the distinguished Novelist' [*CD*] with blazing torches, dinner-invitations, universal hep-hep-hurrah, feeling that he, though small, *is* something; how might all Angel-land once follow a hero-martyr and great true Son of Heaven!" And 29 years later, after reading Vol. I of Forster's *Life*, he commented in a letter to Gavan Duffy: "Me nothing in it so surprises as these two American explosions around poor Dickens, *all* Yankee-doodle-dom, blazing up like one universal soda-water bottle round so very measurable a phenomenon" (Sir C. G. Duffy, *Conversations with Carlyle*, 1892, p. 245).

[2] Theodore Ledyard Cuyler (1822–1909; *DAB*), later a Presbyterian minister. Graduated from Princeton 1841, met CD

for a short time in Philadelphia Mar 42, and called on him in London that summer. Ordained 1848; minister in New York 1853–60, in Brooklyn 1860–90. Well-known evangelical preacher, devotional writer and temperance advocate. An intense admirer of CD's works, on 11 Mar 42 he sent his aunt, Charlotte Morrell, an enthusiastic account of meeting him in Philadelphia (MS New York Historical Society). In his *Recollections of a Long Life*, pp. 20–22, he described his visit to Devonshire Terrace; as he was leaving, CD, he says, called out: "If you see Mrs. Lucretia Mott tell her that I have not forgotten the slave". His account ends with disappointment that CD did not support temperance and "could utterly ignore" Christianity in his novels.

[3] In which (according to his *Recollections*, p. 21) he thanked CD for "some things" in *American Notes*—which he nevertheless described as "that hasty and faulty volume".

To DR SOUTHWOOD SMITH, 26 OCTOBER 1842*

MS Yale University Library.

Devonshire Terrace | Twenty Sixth October 1842.
My Dear Dr. Smith

Many thanks for your kind communication.[1] I will bear all your hints in mind, and attend to them as promptly and faithfully, as though I were (which Heaven forbid!) in a high fever.

Believe me | Always Your friend
Dr. Southwood Smith.   CHARLES DICKENS

To JOHN LEECH,[2] 5 NOVEMBER 1842

MS Comtesse de Suzannet. *Address:* John Leech Esquire | 9 Powis Place | Queen Square.

Private   1 Devonshire Terrace | York Gate Regents Park
                                 Saturday Evening Fifth November | 1842.
My Dear Sir.

I have had great pleasure in the receipt of your manly note; which I should have answered sooner, but that I have been in Cornwall for some days, and am only just now returned.[3]

[1] Southwood Smith had replied to CD's first letter on 25 Oct, recommending the coast about Land's End as "incomparably more dreary" than St Michael's Mount. "But the place above all for dreariness is Tintagel (King Arthur's) Castle, near Camelford. There shall you see nothing but bleak-looking rocks and an everlastingly boisterous sea, both in much the same state as when good King Arthur reigned." He enclosed an introduction to Dr Barham of Truro who was "thoroughly acquainted with every nook in Cornwall and known to every mine. . . . But pray do not forget that a Cornish mine is quite different from a coal-mine: while much less disagreeable to the senses, far more fatal in its effects upon the men and boys (they have no women)" (quoted in Mrs C. L. Lewes, *Dr Southwood Smith*, 1898, pp. 88–9). They did not use the introduction: see *To* Southwood Smith, 8 Nov.

[2] John Leech (1817–64; *DNB*), comic artist: see Vol. I, p. 168*n*. His career up to 1840 had progressed slowly; his first success was with illustrations to Percival Leigh's *Comic Latin Grammar* and *Comic English Grammar* (both 1840); also collaborated with Leigh in *Children of the Mobility*, 1841 (see Vol. II, p. 201 and *n*). His regular work for *Bentley's Miscellany*

began with the "Ingoldsby Legends" in 1840; his first drawing for *Punch* was published 7 Aug 41, and from 4 Mar 43 he was its chief cartoonist; also contributed to Hood's *Comic Annual*, 1842, the *New Monthly* and Jerrold's *Illuminated Magazine*. Henceforth he was prosperous, but often troubled, like CD, by his father's financial importunities. In 1843 married Ann Eaton, with whom he had fallen in love on seeing her in the street: "following her home, he noted the number of the house, looked out the name, obtained an introduction" (F. G. Kitton, *John Leech*, 1884 edn, p. 79). Mark Lemon recalled long afterwards "those dear old days when Leech first married" and "how delightful were the little homely banquets [*at Rose Cottage, Brook Green*] of mutton and gin and water" to which they entertained *Punch* friends (MS Silver Diary). For his illustrating the *Carol*, see *To* Leech, 14 Dec 43 and *fn*.

[3] Forster mistakenly says that the Cornish trip extended well into their "third week of absence" (F, IV, i, 288); in fact they were away for only eight or nine days. They left London on Thurs 27 Oct (*To* Southwood Smith, 22 Oct and *fn*), passed through Exeter on their way back on 3 Nov, and presumably reached London on Fri 4

I had quite forgotten the circumstance to which you refer, and have never blamed you in the smallest degree.[1] But I have never forgotten the having seen you some years ago,[2] or ceased to watch your progress with much interest and satisfaction. I congratulate you heartily on your success; and myself on having had my eye upon the means by which you have obtained it.[3]

If it can possibly be arranged, consistently with that regard which I feel bound to pay to Mr. Browne,[4] I shall be truly happy to avail myself of your genius in my forthcoming Monthly Work. Until I have communicated with him (which I will do immediately) in reference to a project which has occurred to me, I cannot well explain myself further.[5] But I will write to you again, in the course of next week; and will tell you exactly how my arrangements stand.

In the mean time let me say with perfect sincerity, that I shall hope, in any case, to improve your acquaintance, and not to lose sight of you any more.

My Dear Sir believe me | Faithfully Yours

John Leech Esquire   CHARLES DICKENS

To MESSRS THOMAS BARGE JUNR & BROS, 5 NOVEMBER 1842*

MS Dr Gordon Ray.

1 Devonshire Terrace | York Gate Regents Park
Fifth November 1842.

Dear Sirs.

Accept my cordial thanks for the two pieces of Nickleby furniture you have so kindly sent me. They are in course of conversion into Nursery bed curtains for my smallest Works; to the noisy delight of all the Four Volumes.[6]

Faithfully Yours

Messrs. Thomas Barge Junr. and Brothers.   CHARLES DICKENS

To THOMAS BEARD, 5 NOVEMBER [1842]

MS Dickens House. *Address:* Thomas Beard Esquire | 42 Portman Place | Edgeware Road.

Devonshire Terrace | Saturday Fifth November

My Dear Beard

If you are not at the Barrow Knight's[7] tomorrow, or otherwise better engaged,

Nov. For CD's account of the holiday, and a later account by Maclise, see *To* Felton, 31 Dec and *fn*.

[1] For what, is not certainly known. But it seems possible that Leech had been invited to the Greenwich dinner of 9 July by Forster, and had for some reason excused himself from coming.

[2] Presumably in Summer 1836 (see Vol. I, p. 168).

[3] Probably refers to CD's enjoyment in watching 1841–2 the success of Leech's work in *Punch*.

[4] Hablot Knight Browne, "Phiz" (1815–1882; *DNB*): see Vol. I, p. 163*n*.

[5] CD was presumably considering whether once again to employ two illustrators (the *Chuzzlewit* advertisements of 29 Oct had not named the illustrator, so he was still uncommitted). But Browne evidently objected: see 7 Nov and *fn*.

[6] i.e. his four children.

[7] i.e. Baronet's—Sir John Easthope's.

there is a Leg of delicate Welsh Mutton in the Pantry (to be served up at half past five) which deserves attention.

Always Faithfully Yours

Thomas Beard Esquire   CHARLES DICKENS

To JOHN HILLARD,[1] 5 NOVEMBER 1842*

MS Berg Collection.

1 Devonshire Terrace | York Gate Regents Park.
Fifth November 1842.

Dear Sir

I have been out of town for some days and have only just now returned home, or I would have sent you an earlier acknowledgement of the safe receipt of your enclosure of Ten Pounds on account of our friend Longfellow—who I fear has been most piteously tossed about, on that maddest of Oceans, during the last fortnight.[2]

Faithfully Yours

John Hillard Esquire   CHARLES DICKENS

To G. JOY,[3] 5 NOVEMBER 1842*

MS Dr De Coursey Fales. *Address:* G. Joy according to contemporary endorsement.

Devonshire Terrace | York Gate Regents Park.
Fifth November 1842.

Mr. Charles Dickens presents his compliments to Mr. Joy, and begs to acknowledge the receipt of his obliging letter. He grieves to add, that there are but too many such instances as that which Mr. Joy cites, of the strange halting of Law and Equity.—He wishes he had the reforming of them.

To COUNT D'ORSAY, 7 NOVEMBER 1842*

MS Comte de Gramont.

1 Devonshire Terrace | Seventh November 1842.

My Dear Count D'Orsay.

You would make me very glad, if you would come and dine with me next Sunday Week (I name that distant day, to give myself the better chance of laying

---

[1] Brother of George Hillard (see *To Mrs George Hillard*, 29 Jan, *fn*); connected with Coates & Co., America Merchants, 13 Bread Street, Cheapside. Longfellow's letters from Europe to America, July–Nov 42, were forwarded through him (*Letters*, ed. Hilen, II, 435*n*).

[2] On the *Great Western*, which reached New York 6 Nov. Longfellow wrote to Freiligrath on 6 Jan 43: "We sailed (or rather paddled) out in the very teeth of a violent West-wind, which blew for a week . . . I was not out of my berth more than twelve hours for the first twelve days. I was in the forward part of the vessel, where all the great waves struck and broke with voices of thunder" (*Letters of H. W. Longfellow*, ed. A. Hilen, II, 496). Nevertheless he wrote his Slavery poems on the voyage: see *To Longfellow*, 29 Dec, *fn*.

[3] Unidentified.

violent hands upon you) at seven o'Clock.[1] If this should find you able and willing, I will ask Fonblanque and Maclise, and perhaps Elliotson,—whom I know you like,—to meet you.

Always believe me | Faithfully Yours

Le Comte D'Orsay.   CHARLES DICKENS

To JOHN LEECH, 7 NOVEMBER [1842]

MS Comtesse de Suzannet. *Address:* Private | John Leech Esquire | Powis Place.

Private

1 Devonshire Terrace | Monday Seventh November

My Dear Sir.

I find that there are so many mechanical difficulties, complications, entanglements, and impossibilities, in the way of the project I was revolving in my mind when I wrote to you last,[2] as to render it quite impracticable. I perceive that it could not be satisfactory to you, as giving you no fair opportunity; and that it would, in practice, be irksome and distressing to me.[3] I am therefore compelled to relinquish the idea, and for the present to deny myself the advantage of your valuable assistance.

But as I desire, notwithstanding, to lay a small quantity of salt on the tail of your private and personal coat, will you give me the means of doing so, by joining our family dinner table next Sunday at half past five?

Faithfully Yours

John Leech Esquire.   CHARLES DICKENS

To CLARKSON STANFIELD, 7 NOVEMBER 1842

MS University of Kentucky.

Devonshire Terrace | Monday Seventh November | 1842

My Dear Stanfield

On making up our travelling accounts, I find that the total Expences were £88,[4] and the stock purse £90. This leaves me with £2 in hand, one fourth of which, I now inclose you.

Always my Dear Stanfield | Heartily Yours

Clarkson Stanfield Esquire   CHARLES DICKENS

---

[1] D'Orsay replied from Gore House on 8 Nov that he would be "perfectly delighted" to come (MS Morgan).

[2] See 5 Nov.

[3] Browne's evident unwillingness to accept Leech as co-illustrator is understandable. He had apparently collaborated happily with Cattermole—a considerably older man and an established artist for whom CD had usually chosen architectural subjects, in which he was an expert. But Leech's illustrations would have trespassed too much on Browne's own ground; he had already taken Browne's place as illustrator of the *New Monthly*, and could be seen as a rival.

[4] For the Cornish trip. For an expedition of eight days for four persons the amount seems high, but post-horses and potations doubtless account for it.

To THE REV. GEORGE ARMSTRONG,[1]
[?5–8 NOVEMBER 1842]

Mention in Robert Henderson, *A Memoir of the Late Rev. George Armstrong, Formerly Incumbent of Bangor in the Diocese of Down, and Latterly One of the Ministers of Lewin's-Mead Chapel, Bristol. With Extracts from his Journals and Correspondence,* 1859, p. 150. *Date:* early Nov according to *Memoir.*

Declining Armstrong's suggestion that he should write an essay on W. E. Channing, but expressing a deep interest in him.[2]

To ALBANY FONBLANQUE, 8 NOVEMBER 1842†

MS Free Library of Philadelphia.

Devonshire Terrace | Eighth November 1842.

My Dear Fonblanque.

^aWill you dine with me on Sunday Week, the Twentieth, at seven o'Clock? I name that distant day because D'Orsay dines with me then, and I know you and he have a great liking for each other.^{3a}

I was very sorry to see in the Postscript to the last Examiner, something that careless readers (a large class) will easily twist into a comparison between

---

¹ The Rev. George Armstrong (1792–1857); born at Drogheda, Ireland; graduate of Trinity College, Dublin. Ordained in the Church of England 1815, but resigned his Orders and became an active champion of Unitarianism. Settled in Bristol 1838.

² Armstrong had written a long letter the day after reading of Channing's death in the London papers (1 Nov), giving as explanation of the liberty he was taking in addressing CD the joy he had had on reading the passages on Channing in *American Notes*; he went on to urge CD "to seize this opportunity . . . for fixing the attention of the reading world, on both sides of the Atlantic, on . . . that . . . most gifted of Christian teachers". "What a ferment in the literary world", he wrote, "would be the announcement of 'An Essay on the Character, Genius and Writings of the late William Ellery Channing, D.D., by Charles Dickens, Esq., Author of the Notes on America, &c. &c.' Undertake it, and thousands upon thousands living and to come will bless you for the deed!" He described the profound influence on himself of Channing's Baltimore sermon of 1819; mentioned various eulogies of him in the press (e.g. in the *Athenæum*, 3 Jan 35, and the *Monthly Repository*, June 30);

declared that the honour of making him known to posterity could not be slight; and ended, "May that honour be yours" (R. Henderson, *op. cit.*, pp. 146–50). Replying to CD's refusal, Armstrong regretfully admitted its force, but asked whether he might prefix to a discourse on Channing he had just given, which was to be printed, the expression of "deep interest" in him conveyed in CD's note. No such expression appeared, however, in *A Discourse, Delivered in Lewin's Mead Chapel, Bristol, on . . . November 6th, 1842,* 1842.

^{aa} Not previously published.

³ Fonblanque had been for some years a friend of both D'Orsay's and Lady Blessington's. He was a member of the 1840 Commission which had recommended abolition of imprisonment for debt; and in 1842 D'Orsay had enlisted his support in the *Examiner* for a bill giving effect to this (see *Examiner,* 9 Apr, 23 July 42). On 10 Aug the Insolvent Debtors' Bill, backed by both Brougham and Lord Lyndhurst, went through both Houses unopposed. In his articles Fonblanque frequently made use of D'Orsay's anecdotes (*Life and Labours of Albany Fonblanque,* ed. E. B. de Fonblanque, 1874, p. 41*n*).

the English and American Newspapers.[1] Bad as many of our journals are, Heaven knows, they cannot be set against each other for a moment; and Decency is not befriended by any effort to excuse the Transatlantic Blackguardism, which is so intense that I seriously believe words cannot describe it.[2]

My Dear Fonblanque
Always Faithfully Yours
Albany Fonblanque Esquire   CHARLES DICKENS

[1] CD is clearly referring to a paragraph that appeared only in the latest edn of the *Examiner* of 5 Nov under the heading "Court and Aristocracy". After exposing as groundless "a malignant tale of calumny" about one of the Queen's Ladies in Waiting that was newly going the round of the English papers, it went on: "Our press is just now ringing with attacks on the Americans for supporting a trade in slander, and with what consistency can we throw the stone at this vulgar vice, the foul appetite of the emptiest minds, while so much of it exists in our own community. It is as much the policy of society to protect the reputations of its members as to protect their lives, their persons, and their properties."

[2] Attacking the popular American press (a "monster of depravity") in his "Concluding Remarks" to *American Notes* (Ch. 18), CD declared that he had "neither space nor inclination to convey an adequate idea of this frightful engine in America", and in a footnote referred those who desired confirmation to the unsigned article "Newspaper Literature of America" (now known to have been by Forster: his marked proofs are in the Forster Collection, V & A), which had appeared in the current *Foreign Quarterly Review* (Oct 42, XXX, 197–222), describing it as "an able, and perfectly truthful article" to which his attention had "been attracted" while *American Notes* was passing through the press. In fact the article, no doubt with CD's concurrence, is a lengthy and detailed supplement to parts of *American Notes* and such of CD's letters from America as Forster had access to: besides repeating CD's two instances of "disgraceful personal encounters" in the House (see *To* Fonblanque, 12 Mar 42, *fn* p. 118), it added two others, supplying for one of them the source; and it elaborated on other themes of CD's, such as "Universal Distrust" (*loc. cit.*, p. 215, and *American Notes*, Ch. 18). J. R. Godley

described it as "forcibly and severely written", but with "a tendency to degenerate in many places into the faults which it condemns" (*Letters from America*, II, 107). Its attack was particularly aimed at J. G. Bennett's *New York Herald*—a "broadsheet of lies and filth", the only word for whose tone was *"blackguardism"* (pp. 198, 199). Sections of the American press were outraged by the article; not surprisingly several newspapers (the *New York Morning Courier* apparently in the vanguard) attributed it (as did most people: see Godley, *ibid.*) to CD—though speculation later shifted to Fenimore Cooper, to Dionysius Lardner, and to others: see Forster's second article on the American press (*Foreign Quarterly*, Apr 43, XXXI, 256, 268–72). This article was in the main a comment on the *New York Herald*'s abuse of Forster's first article (five pages were devoted to extracts from it) and a reply to a notice of *American Notes* in the *Westminster Review* of Feb 43, which had gone even further than the paragraph CD had objected to in the *Examiner*, by defending the American press as in its moral tone not so low as the English ("with honorable exceptions"): "We make this statement deliberately, and after the careful examination of a file of the 'New York Herald,' the paper especially referred to by Mr. Dickens and the Foreign Quarterly Review, as the worst in the United States"; the *Herald*, bad as it was, was "freer from gross obscenities and ribald jests" than either the *Age* or the *Satirist*, it declared (XXXIX, 156–7). The comparison was inept, as Forster pointed out; for while the *Herald* was a daily with a vast circulation (because of its "early commercial intelligence"), which won government approval, the *Age* and *Satirist*, though infamous indeed, were mere weekly scandal-sheets of no influence or political import. Forster then recounted, in veiled terms (p. 164), the direct action recently taken by "some

To THE REV. WILLIAM HARNESS,[1]
8 NOVEMBER 1842

Text from MDGH, I, 76.

Devonshire Terrace, November 8th, 1842.

My dear Harness,

Some time ago, you sent me a note from a friend of yours, a barrister,[2] I think, begging me to forward to him any letters I might receive from a deranged nephew of his, at Newcastle. In the midst of a most bewildering correspondence with unknown people, on every possible and impossible subject, I have forgotten this gentleman's name,[3] though I have a kind of hazy remembrance that he lived near Russell Square. As the Post Office would be rather puzzled, perhaps, to identify him by such an address, may I ask the favour of you to hand him the enclosed, and to say that it is the second I have received since I returned from America? The last, I think, was a defiance to mortal combat.[4] With best remembrances to your sister,[5] in which Mrs. Dickens joins, believe me, my dear Harness,

Always faithfully yours
[CHARLES DICKENS]

To T. J. OUSELEY,[6] 8 NOVEMBER 1842*

MS Berg Collection.

Devonshire Terrace | Eighth November 1842.

My Dear Sir

I am greatly obliged to you for your note, and shall be truly glad to comply with your request:[7] which I will do with the first opportunity of safe conveyance.

I had heard of the Fraser Article,[8] and I know the Writer[9]—to whom, I need scarcely add, I have ever been kind and considerate. It is of no moment.

Faithfully Yours always
T. J. Ouseley Esquire   CHARLES DICKENS

---

hundreds, representing the good old hearty English feeling", against Gregory, editor of the *Satirist* (see *To* Forster, 14 Feb 43 and *fn*). (That Forster was author of both articles on the American press is confirmed by his reference in a letter to Napier, 12 Feb 44, to efforts he had made "some months ago, by articles in the *Foreign Quarterly*, to direct attention to the abuses of the American Newspaper Press": MS BM.)

[1] William Harness (1790–1869; *DNB*): see Vol. II, p. 178*n*.

[2] Nathaniel Ellison (*b*. ?1786): see Vol. II, p. 202*n*.

[3] Nathaniel Bates (see *ibid*.).

[4] See *ibid*.; also Vol. II, p. 211*n*.

[5] Mary Harness (*b*. 1801), Harness's only sister, who kept house for him; Nelson's god-daughter; close friend of Mary Russell Mitford.

[6] Thomas John Ouseley (*d*. 1874), minor poet: see Vol. I, p. 526*n*.

[7] Presumably to inscribe a copy of *American Notes* for him.

[8] Clearly the anonymous review of *American Notes* in *Fraser's*, Nov 42 (XXVI, 617–29); it was as unremittingly offensive as any that CD had. "Surely", it protested, "a little reflection might have taught [CD] that a very different order of qualifications, natural and acquired, from those which enabled him to please the town with his monthly and weekly effusions touching Cockneys and the peculiar regions, physical and moral, in which they flourish, was required for the author of a work on the

To CHARLES BARHAM,[1] [?8 NOVEMBER 1842]

Mention in next. *Date:* probably written the same day.

To DR SOUTHWOOD SMITH, 8 NOVEMBER 1842

Text from Mrs C. L. Lewes, *Dr Southwood Smith*, 1898, p. 89.

1 Devonshire Terrace, | York Gate, Eighth November 1842.

My dear Sir,

I have just come home from Cornwall. I did not, after all, deliver your letter. Having Stanfield and Maclise and another friend[2] with me, I determined not to do so, unless I found it absolutely necessary; lest the unfortunate Doctor should consider himself in a state of siege.

I saw all I wanted to see, and a noble coast it is. I have sent your letter to Dr Barham with a line or two from myself; and am as much obliged to you as though I had driven him wild with trouble.

Always faithfully yours,

Dr Southwood Smith.   CHARLES DICKENS

United States of America." It would have been different if he had covered new ground, gone to the Far West, faced dangers; but travelling with his wife "on the old highways, high-roads, canals, rail-roads ... [he] appeals in vain to our sympathies touching his sufferings". Over three pages of the review are then given to the findings of earlier travellers (listed)—leading up to: "Mr. Dickens has given us a small *réchauffé* of all those matters we were so familiarly acquainted with before"; all that is new is that "every thing is made to wear a new face from the way in which it is painted, and patched, and frizzed, and powdered, before it is brought upon the stage. Every thing is made to wear Boz's peculiar colours". Like Warren in his review in *Blackwood's*, Dec 42 (see *To* Felton, 31 Dec, *fn*), the reviewer deplored CD's slighting references to the British Houses of Parliament and constitution, and his invidious comparisons of English universities with Cambridge, Massachusetts ("Does Mr. Dickens know any thing of our universities?"). For other English reviews of *American Notes*, see *To* Felton, 31 Dec, *fn*.

[9] Described in *To* Felton, 31 Dec, as "a miserable creature; a disappointed man in great poverty", he has never been identi-fied; but the field seems relatively small. Among lesser Fraserians to whom CD might feel he had been "kind" were P. W. Banks, Maclise's brother-in-law (1805–50: see Vol. I, p. 160*n*), and perhaps E. V. Kenealy (1819–80; *DNB*: see Vol. I, p. 337*n*), who—a struggling, rather pushful writer 1841–3, a friend of Maginn, and on the fringe of CD's acquaintance—seems a quite possible candidate. The "kindness" may have been in accepting verses for *Bentley's Miscellany* (unidentified, though Kenealy's name is in the *List* for 1837); Kenealy wrote satirical verses on *Chuzzlewit* which Ainsworth (to whose *Magazine* he contributed) declined (S. M. Ellis, *W. H. Ainsworth and his Friends*, 1911, II, 68–9).

[1] Charles Foster Barham (1804–84; *DNB*), of Truro, senior physician to the Royal Cornwall Infirmary 1837–73. Published *Report on the Sanitary State of the Labouring Classes in the Town of Truro*, [1840]. See *To* Southwood Smith, 22 and 26 Oct, *fns*.

[2] The omission of Forster's name is curious; see also CD's statement in *To* Southwood Smith, 22 Oct, that he was going to Cornwall with "a couple of friends".

To DANIEL MACLISE, 9 NOVEMBER 1842*

MS Benoliel Collection.

Ninth November 1842. Wednesday

My Dear Mac

It's a holiday—Lord Mayor's Day. We pledged ourselves to keep it. Do you remember? Shave. I'll come down, directly.

Faithfully Always
CD.

To THE GENERAL COMMITTEE OF THE LITERARY FUND,[1] 12 NOVEMBER 1842*

MS Royal Literary Fund.

1 Devonshire Terrace | York Gate Regents Park
Twelfth November 1842

Gentlemen.

As one of a Committee[2] of Gentlemen who are exerting themselves for the relief of the Destitute widow and children of the late Mr. Hone, the author of The Every Day Book and other works of the same character which are well known to you, I beg to submit their hard case to your favorable consideration.

I am aware that Mr. Hone himself was more than once assisted by the excellent Institution whose affairs you administer.[3] Nevertheless, I am well assured that the claims of his Widow[4] and Family[5] are not weakened in your opinion by that circumstance; and that you will feel, with me, that his contributions to the stock of cheerful blameless Literature, are deserving of remembrance in their afflicted persons.

I may be permitted to add, on behalf of myself and those other gentlemen who act with me in this matter, that the best use will be made of any sum of money you may be pleased to bestow on Mrs. Hone;[6] and that in its appropriation, the strictest regard will be had to its being of lasting benefit and service to her, if possible.

I am Gentlemen | With great respect
Your faithful friend and Servant
CHARLES DICKENS

To | The General Committee of The Literary Fund.

---

[1] See Vol. I, p. 283*n*.

[2] Clearly Cruikshank was also a member, but nothing is known of the others.

[3] He had been granted £30 in Feb 34 and £40 in Dec 40 (MSS Royal Literary Fund).

[4] *Née* Sarah Johnson (1781–1864); married Hone July 1800, and had 12 children.

[5] There were nine surviving children, two daughters entirely dependent on Mrs Hone (MS *ibid.*). The obituary in the *Morning Chronicle*, 9 Nov, said that they were left "almost wholly unprovided for", but that "some kind friends of the deceased purpose using their endeavours to influence the generous feelings of the benevolent".

[6] She was given £50 (*To* Blewitt, 15 Dec).

To OCTAVIAN BLEWITT, 12 NOVEMBER 1842*

MS Royal Literary Fund.

Devonshire Terrace | Twelfth November 1842.

My Dear Sir

Will you do me the favor to lay the enclosed before the Committee at their next Meeting; and to communicate the result to me?

Always My Dear Sir | Faithfully Yours

O. Blewitt Esquire   CHARLES DICKENS

To MISS BURDETT COUTTS, 12 NOVEMBER 1842

MS Morgan Library.

Devonshire Terrace | Twelfth November 1842.

My Dear Miss Coutts.

Your most kind note found me in the agonies of plotting and contriving[1] a new book;[2] in which stage of the tremendous process, I am accustomed to walk up and down the house, smiting my forehead dejectedly; and to be so horribly cross and surly, that the boldest fly at my approach. At such times, even the Postman knocks at the door with a mild feebleness, and my publishers always come two together, lest I should fall upon a single invader and do murder on his intrusive body.

I am afraid if I came to see you under such circumstances, you would be very glad to be rid of me in two hours at the most; but I would risk even that disgrace, in my desire to accept your kind Invitation, if it were not indispensable just now, that I should be always in the way.[3] In starting a work which is to last for twenty months, there are so many little things to attend to, which require my personal superintendence, that I am obliged to be constantly on the watch; and I may add, seriously, that unless I were to shut myself up, obstinately and sullenly in my own room for a great many days without writing a word, I don't think I ever should make a beginning.

For these reasons, I am fain to be resolute and virtuous, and to deny myself and Mrs. Dickens the great pleasure you offer us. I have not answered your letter until now, because I have really been tempted and hesitating. But the lapse of every new day, only gives me a stronger reason for being perseveringly uncomfortable, that out of my gloom and solitude, something comical (or meant to be) may straightway grow up.

[1] He had allowed himself a break of nearly a month since finishing *American Notes* (probably on 10 Oct: see *To* Forster, that day, *fn*) before settling to *Chuzzlewit*. He had not finished No. 1 by 8 Dec (*To* Forster, that day).

[2] The book (its title still not finally chosen: see next and *fn*) had been advertised in *American Notes*, 1st edn, and in the *Athenæum*, 29 Oct, in almost identical terms, as follows: "NEW WORK BY MR. DICKENS. | On the 1st of January, 1843, will be published, price ONE SHILLING, | THE FIRST NUMBER OF | A NEW TALE | OF | ENGLISH LIFE AND MANNERS. | By "Boz". | To be completed in Twenty Monthly Numbers, and illustrated with Two etchings on Steel." The emphasis on "English Life and Manners" was to preclude expectations of an American scene. In the event, the public got both.

[3] Within reach or call (*OED*).

If you should still be in your present retreat when I have got my first number written (after which, I go on with great nonchalance) we shall be more than glad to come to you for one or two days. In the meantime Mrs. Dickens begs me to add her best remembrances to my own; and to say that if you can oblige her with your box at Covent Garden on any of Miss Kemble's nights,[1] she will be very thankful.

I am always Dear Miss Coutts

Yours faithfully and obliged
CHARLES DICKENS

It is impossible for me to say how I should argue with Miss Meredith, under existing circumstances.[2]

To JOHN FORSTER, [12 NOVEMBER 1842]

Extract in F, IV, i, 290. *Date:* 12 Nov according to Forster.

Behold finally the title of the new book[;][3] don't lose it, for I have no copy. "The Life and Adventures of Martin Chuzzlewig,[4] his family, friends, and enemies. Comprising all his wills and his ways. With an historical record of what he did and what he didn't. The whole forming a complete key to the house of Chuzzlewig."[5]

To THOMAS HOOD, 12 NOVEMBER 1842†

MS Yale University Library.

Devonshire Terrace | Twelfth November 1842.

My Dear Hood

*a*What *could* I be, but delighted with the New Monthly Notice?[6] What

---

[1] Adelaide Kemble was appearing concurrently in the English versions of Rossini's *Semiramide* and Cimarosa's *Il Matrimonio Segreto.*

[2] His arguments with Miss Meredith became a standing joke in letters to Miss Coutts (see Vol. II, p. 168*n*).

[3] This was CD's first note to him after their return from Cornwall, says Forster: "Title and even story had been undetermined while we travelled, from the lingering wish he still had to begin it among those Cornish scenes [*see* To *Forster, Early Aug and 16 Sep*]; but this intention had now been finally abandoned, and the reader lost nothing by his substitution, for the lighthouse or mine in Cornwall, of the Wiltshire-village forge" (F, IV, i, 290).

[4] Though CD had had no doubts about "Martin", he had earlier jotted down on small slips several ideas for the surname—among them Chubblewig, Chuzzlebog and

Sweezleback (for the full list, see F, *ibid.*)—Chuzzlewig and Chuzzlewit being the final choices. In the MS of the novel itself, there is no hesitation over the name; the heading on p. 1 has "Martin Chuzzlewit" from the start. (Both the slips with trial names and the trial title-pages are now at the beginning of the MS of the novel in the V & A.)

[5] From 26 Nov (in the *Athenæum*) onwards, it was advertised almost exactly in these words, though with the alteration to "Chuzzlewit", and "showing, moreover, | WHO INHERITED THE FAMILY PLATE, | WHO CAME IN FOR THE SILVER SPOONS, | AND WHO FOR THE WOODEN LADLES" inserted before the last sentence.

aa; bb Not previously published.

[6] Hood had written that he had recently called at Devonshire Terrace to congratulate CD on the success of *American Notes*, of which he had heard the highest com-

can I say in reference to the Pirates,[1] but demnition seize 'em; and that my blunt[2] and my sharpness (such as they are) are both ready for the service of the association you suggest.[3] Any set of men, but authors, would have had such an Institution long ago.*a*

I can't state in figures (not very well remembering how to get beyond a Million) the number of Candidates for the Sanatorium Matronship, but if you will ask your little boy[4] to trace figures in the beds of your garden, beginning at the front wall, going down to the cricket ground,[5] coming back to the wall again, and "carrying over" to the next door; and will then set a skilful accountant to add up the whole; the product, as the Tutors assistants say, will give you the amount required.—I have pledged myself (being assured of her capability) to support a near relation of Miss Edgeworth's.[6] Otherwise I need not say how glad I should have been to forward any wish of yours.[7]

We shall be more than glad to come to you on any Evening you may name.[8] *b* I am in the agonics of new harness just now, and walk up and down the house smiting my forehead dejectedly, to the unspeakable consternation of my wife and children, and the great uneasiness of a very small dog.*b*

Always My Dear Hood | Heartily Yours

Thomas Hood Esquire   CHARLES DICKENS

mendations. He added: "I hope you did not dislike the notice in the N.M.M." In fact the review must have given CD great pleasure. It described the public's keen curiosity on seeing announcements of the book: "Numerous had been the writers on the land of the stars and stripes—a host of travelled ladies and gentlemen, liberals and illiberals, utilitarians and inutilitarians—human bowls of every bias had trundled over the United States without hitting, or in the opinion of the natives, even coming near the jack"; hence the eagerness on both sides of the Atlantic to read the opinions of a writer who had proved "that his heart was in the right place, that his head was not in the wrong one, and that his hand was a good hand at description. One thing at least was certain, that nothing would be set down in malice". The book (from which the review quoted at length) would, wrote Hood, "bring no disappointment to such as can be luxuriously content with good sense, good feeling, good fun, and good writing" (*New Monthly*, LXVI, 396–406).

[1] Hood had mentioned "American Notes by Buz advertised from Holywell Street—of course a piracy".

[2] i.e. blunt sword, punning slang for ready money (*OED* gives examples from both CD and Hood).

[3] In his postscript Hood had suggested that there "ought to be a Literary Association for the Suppression of Piracy—a fund subscribed by Authors Booksellers & friends to Letters" organized to take immediate legal proceedings against offenders, and on 11 Nov 42 "sounded one or two Booksellers . . . about the association". He found that G. P. R. James had already proposed it to Longman, who had drawn up a plan; whereupon he gave his and CD's views and "offered to cooperate". (MSS Huntington; *Letters of Thomas Hood*, ed. P. Morgan, pp. 506, 509–10.)

[4] Thomas Hood, the younger (1835–74).

[5] Lord's. Hood was now living at 17 Elm Tree Road, St John's Wood, which overlooked it.

[6] Her niece, Mrs Gibbons (see *To* Mitton, 18 Nov, *fn*).

[7] Hood had asked for CD's "voice and interest", if "not otherwise bespoke", in support of the candidature of "Mrs. K."— a friend of his friend and physician William Elliot (*op. cit.*, p. 505).

[8] In the same letter, Hood had asked if CD and Catherine could spend an evening with him to meet the Elliots "& a few friends, The Dilkes &c &c." The visit was fixed for 6 Dec (see *To* Hood, 30 Nov, *fn*).

To W. C. MACREADY, 12 NOVEMBER 1842

MS Morgan Library.

Devonshire Terrace | Saturday Twelfth Novr. 1842.

My Dear Macready

You pass this house every day, on your way to, or from, the Theatre. I wish you would call once as you go by—and soon, that you may have plenty of time to deliberate on what I wish to suggest to you. The more I think of Marston's[1] Play,[2] the more sure I feel that a Prologue, to the purpose, would help it materially,[3] and almost decide the fate of any ticklish point on the first night.[4] Now I have an idea (not easily explainable in writing, but told in five words) which would take the prologue out of the conventional dress of prologues— quite—get the curtain up with a dash—and begin the play with a sledge hammer

---

[1] John Westland Marston (1819–90; *DNB*), poet and dramatist; for many years one of the mainstays of poetic drama on the English stage. His 14 plays, performed 1842–69 (most of them published in his *Dramatic and Poetical Works*, 2 vols, 1876), included seven tragedies and historical dramas in verse.

[2] *The Patrician's Daughter*, Marston's first play, a verse tragedy in 5 Acts, published 1841, with dedication to Macready; republished, "enlarged and adapted for representation", 1842. In his Preface to the 1st edn Marston said that his intention was to "write a Tragedy entirely indebted for its incident, and passion, to the habits and spirit of the age". The play is set in 1842, and its plot is very simple: Mordaunt, the hero, a successful politician of low birth, obtains the hand of Lady Mabel Lynterne, only to repudiate her before her assembled family and friends, to avenge an earlier slight engineered by her maiden aunt, Lady Lydia. Mabel dies brokenhearted. Macready on first reading it, Oct 41, thought it "most powerful", and on rereading it, Aug 42, "most interesting and touching . . . I will act it, if I am prosperous" (*Diaries*, II, 145, 182). In production, according to Marston, he "was anxious—perhaps more anxious than the author—to invest the action with every detail of the most modern realism"— including in one Act, since the season was summer, parasols for the actresses. "'Blank verse and parasols,' said Mrs Warner [*who was playing Lady Lydia*] . . . 'Is not that quite a new combination?'" (*Our Recent Actors*, II, 285–6). CD ob-

viously heard much of the venture from Forster or Macready himself; moreover Marston had dedicated to him his *Gerald, and Other Poems*, published Oct 42. The play (the first new play of Macready's season) was given 11 performances at Drury Lane between 10 Dec and 20 Jan 43.

[3] By preparing the audience for the play's contemporary setting.

[4] The play was well received by the audience, and most of the reviews were favourable. *The Times* and *Morning Chronicle* (both 12 Dec) praised the contemporary setting and mentioned the prologue with approval, the *Chronicle* linking Marston's experiment with "the change which, as to poetry generally, has been achieved by Wordsworth and his coadjutors". The *Examiner*'s notice of 17 Dec (probably by Forster) gave great praise to the production, décor and acting, and considered that the prologue, by "impressing the audience strongly with the scope and purpose of what they had come to see, thoroughly prepared them for welcome and applause". But the *Morning Post* attacked both the play (in which it saw Whig or Radical propaganda) and CD's prologue ("milk and water"; "doubtless a very pretty academical exercise"). For the *Monthly Magazine*'s criticism, see *To* Macready, 25 Nov (afternoon), *fn*. The play when performed at the Theatre Royal, Edinburgh, in Dec 43, was a great success and a triumph for Helen Faucit; the *Theatrical Journal*, 9 Dec, felt that justice had not been done to it in London.

blow. If, on consideration, you should think with me, I will write the Prologue, heartily.[1]

Faithfully Yours ever

W. C. Macready Esquire   CHARLES DICKENS

To MRS PAYNTER,[2] 12 NOVEMBER 1842

Text from *Sketches from the Diaries of Rose Lady Graves Sawle 1833–1896*, privately printed, 1908, p. 54.

Devonshire Terrace, York Gate, | Regent's Park.
Twelfth November, 1842.

My dear Mrs. Paynter,

Many thanks to you for your kind letter and for its enclosure from Lord A.,[3] which I beg to return to you. The monument of which I make mention in my "Notes," is that which is raised to Wolfe and Montcalm[4] jointly; and I call it worthy of two great nations, because it was created by subscriptions of the French and English.[5] I do not enter into Canadian topics, or desire to make any extended mention of them, for the reason I have given in my book;[6] and therefore I have no use for any information, highly valuable although it could not fail to be, which your kindness would procure for me from your brother.

I am afraid that the preparations for my new book will put a padlock on my locomotive powers, and keep me fast at home for some time. But, if I should get to Bath, rest assured that I have too pleasant a recollection of our old evenings there, and too earnest a desire to see you and Miss Paynter[7] again, not

---

[1] A remarkable offer in the light of what CD wrote about his work to Miss Coutts the same day; but in the course of the next fortnight he produced a first draft. Three versions in his hand are known: the MS of this preliminary draft (now in the Morgan Library), a corrected version (photostat in the Morgan Library), and the MS of a later fair-copy (MS Morgan). The preliminary draft is printed in MDGH, I, 77–8, and reprinted in F. G. Kitton, *The Poems and Verses of CD*, 1903, with the mistaken statement by Georgina Hogarth that this was "the revised and only correct version". The prologue consists of 48 lines in heroic couplets.

[2] Sophia Paynter (1790–1873): see Vol. II, p. 107*n*.

[3] Matthew Whitworth-Aylmer, 5th Lord Aylmer (1775–1850), Mrs Paynter's half-brother. Governor-General of Canada 1830–5; Colonel 18th Foot 1832; General 1841.

[4] Louis Joseph, Marquis de Montcalm (1712–59); military commander of Canada from 1756. Fell, as Wolfe did, at Quebec.

[5] The monument commemorating the battle of the Plains of Abraham, outside Quebec (mentioned in *American Notes*, Ch. 15).

[6] That he wished to avoid making any comparison between "the social features" of America and Canada, and would therefore confine himself to "a very brief account" of his Canadian journeyings (Ch. 15). His account was indeed brief. But in his summing-up he could not resist what, after his strictures on America, amounted to comparisons: public feeling, for instance, he described as in a "wholesome state", and he was impressed by the "respectability and character of the public journals". See, however, *To Forster*, 12 May, for his comment on Toronto's "wild and rabid toryism".

[7] Rose Caroline Paynter (*b.* 1818): see Vol. II, p. 106*n*.

to come very quickly up that inaccessible hill, and inflict a cheery double knock upon your door, to which the street shall ring again.[1]

Mrs Dickens begs me to say all that is loving and kind;[2] and, venturing to add similar remembrances to Miss Paynter on my own account,

I am, always faithfully yours,

CHARLES DICKENS

To MRS [A. T.] THOMSON,[3] 12 NOVEMBER 1842*

MS Winifred A. Myers (Autographs) Ltd.

Devonshire Terrace | Saturday Twelfth November | 1842.

Dear Mrs. Thomson.

It would have given me great pleasure to vote for the lady in whom you are interested, if I had not already pledged myself (being assured of her capability) to support another candidate who is a near relation of Miss Edgeworth's, and who, therefore, has a strong claim on my attention and regard.

Believe me | Faithfully Yours

Mrs. Thomson   CHARLES DICKENS

To THOMAS BEARD, 15 NOVEMBER 1842

MS Dickens House. *Address:* Thomas Beard Esquire | 42 Portman Place | Edgeware Road.

Devonshire Terrace | Fifteenth November 1842.

My Dear Beard.

I should have been truly glad (I need not tell you) to serve any friend of yours,[4] if my sympathy and interest had not been strongly enlisted beforehand, in behalf of a Niece of Miss Edgeworth, whose testimonials are immeasurably better than those of any other Candidate; and who has learned tenderness and patience, in the bitterest of schools.

I shall expect to see you towards the close of the week, if the Barrow Knight acts up to his title, and gives you leisure.

Best Regards and loves from everybody to everybody else.

I am working away upon my new book, like—like a brick. I don't know why it is, but that popular simile *seems* a good one.

Always Faithfully | Your friend

Thomas Beard Esquire   CHARLES DICKENS

---

[1] Cf. Rose Paynter's "the usually quiet streets of Bath rang with their inextinguishable laughter", of CD's and Forster's visit in 1840 (Vol. II, p. 37n). CD noticeably makes no reference to their two Bath visits of Oct (see *To* Salmon and *To* Southwood Smith, 22 Oct, *fns*).

[2] She had presumably met Mrs Paynter during one of the Paynter family's visits to London (see *Sketches from the Diaries*,

p. 55); for she had not accompanied CD to Bath in Feb 40.

[3] Presumably Katherine Thomson (1798–1862; *DNB*): see Vol. II, p. 39 and *n*.

[4] According to Walter Dexter's note (*Dickens to his Oldest Friend*, p. 76) Beard had sent CD a letter from W. G. Greenhill asking him to obtain CD's help on behalf of a Miss Gilbeck's application.

To JOHN BLACK, 15 NOVEMBER 1842

MS National Library of Scotland.

Devonshire Terrace | Fifteenth[1] November 1842.

My Dear Sir

If an advertizement should come to the Chronicle from a Committee (to which I belong) who are trying to raise a little money for the Wife and Family of poor Hone of the Every Day Book, will you, if you see no objection, call attention to it, by a line in the Paper?[2] They are very poor, and he was not a common man.

John Black Esquire

Faithfully Yours always

CHARLES DICKENS

To W. P. FRITH,[3] 15 NOVEMBER 1842

MS Victoria & Albert Museum.

1 Devonshire Terrace | York Gate Regents Park.
Fifteenth November 1842.

My Dear Sir.

I shall be very glad if you will do me the favor to paint me two little companion pictures; one, a Dolly Varden (whom you have so exquisitely done already), the other a Kate Nickleby.[4]

Faithfully Yours always

CHARLES DICKENS

P.S. I take it for granted that the original picture of Dolly with the Bracelet, is sold?[5]

---

[1] Apparently written over "Fourteenth".

[2] No notice from the Committee appeared in the *Morning Chronicle* or in *The Times* or the *Patriot* (on which Hone had worked), and the result of the appeal is not known: for one donation, see *To* Ablett, 19 Jan 43.

[3] William Powell Frith (1819–1909; *DNB*), painter. Born of parents in domestic service and sent to a school at Knaresborough, "more or less of the 'Dotheboys Hall' pattern" (*My Autobiography and Reminiscences*, 1887, I, 3). Studied art at the RA schools. Exhibited at the British Institution 1839; at the Royal Academy 1840; ARA 1845; RA 1853. He had read CD's novels with delight and in the hope of finding subjects in them. At last, in *Barnaby Rudge*, he saw that his opportunity had come with Dolly Varden. Having found a "capital model", he painted her as Dolly "in a variety of attitudes" (*op. cit.*, I, 102), and on 9 Aug 41 wrote to CD: "Sir | Having painted 2 Pictures from

'Barnaby Rudge' which a great many of my artist friends tell me are successful, . . . I am naturally most anxious to hear yr. opinion . . . —and this must be my excuse for troubling you with this note— | The subject in each picture is that exquisite creation Dolly Varden—, one when she is *admiring the Bracelet*—the other when she is leaning laughing against the Tree". H. K. Browne, he went on, although a stranger to him, had called to see the pictures, had greatly approved, and it was on his encouragement that Frith was writing to ask CD if he might show him them in the course of the week, when he gathered from Browne that CD might be in London (MS Huntington). However, CD's next visits to London were purely for business; and he neither saw Frith, nor apparently answered his letter.

[4] In response to this request, Frith painted Kate Nickleby working at Madame Mantalini's—"at the moment when her thoughts wander from her work, as she sits

To DANIEL MACLISE, 15 NOVEMBER 1842*

MS Benoliel Collection.

Tuesday Fifteenth November 1842.

My Dear Mac

Will you put the No on the enclosed, that John may take it?—I have asked him[1] to paint for me, two little companion pictures. One, a Dolly Varden. One, a Kate Nickleby.

I have been working feebly all day; and between that and the weather, am damnably hipped.[2] Shall we repair to some Saloon tonight? If so, I'll call on you, about half past seven.

Faithfully Yours always
CD.

To THOMAS MITTON, 15 NOVEMBER 1842

MS Huntington Library.

Devonshire Terrace. | Fifteenth November 1842

My Dear Mitton

I am sorry to say, I couldn't help Mrs. Stevens.[3] I was, and am, strongly interested in another Candidate, who is immeasurably the best among them. And besides, I had already, as a principle, strongly objected to their electing anybody who had been, or had sought to be, connected as Matron with any *charity*. It would have been destructive of the whole spirit and object of the Sanatorium, which heals and shelters those, who are above the receipt of charitable aid.

I am very much engaged—but will come to you on Thursday, at about 4 O'Clock.

Always Faithfully

Thomas Mitton Esquire   CHARLES DICKENS

Wednesday. I open this again to say—Friday, instead of Thursday.

---

sewing a ball-dress spread upon her knees" —and Dolly "tripping through the woods, and looking back saucily at her lover" (*op. cit.*, I, 104). CD came to see the pictures, and relieved the "agony of mind" with which Frith awaited his verdict with the words: "All I can say is, they are exactly what I meant" (*ibid.*); a few days later he brought Catherine and Georgina to see them. He paid Frith £40, though not until 8 Aug 43 (Account-book, MS Messrs Coutts). The pictures were sold for £1360 at Christie's on 9 July 70 (*Cata-*

logue of the Pictures ... Belonging to CD, ed. J. H. Stonehouse, p. 127). "Kate Nickleby" was later engraved, but not the "Dolly Varden".

[5] By Nov 42 CD had presumably seen "Dolly with the Bracelet" at some London gallery (though not the RA), and a proof of "the laughing Dolly": see 17 Nov and *fn.*

[1] Frith: see last. His address was 11 Osnaburgh Street, Regent's Park.

[2] i.e. depressed.

[3] Unidentified.

To GEORGE CRUIKSHANK, 17 NOVEMBER 1842

MS Colonel Richard Gimbel. *Address:* George Cruikshank Esquire | Amwell Street | Pentonville.

Devonshire Terrace. | Seventeenth November 1842.

My Dear George.

I want to ask you a question,[1] when you next happen to be passing this way.

Faithfully Yours

George Cruikshank Esquire   CHARLES DICKENS

To W. P. FRITH, 17 NOVEMBER 1842

MS Victoria & Albert Museum.

Devonshire Terrace | Seventeenth November 1842

My Dear Sir

Pray consult your own convenience, in the matter of my little commission. Whatever suits your engagements and prospects, will best suit me.

I saw an unfinished proof of Dolly,[2] at Mitchell's,[3] some two or three months ago. I thought she was proceeding excellently well, *then*. It will give me great pleasure to see her when completed.

Faithfully Yours

H.[4] P. Frith Esquire   CHARLES DICKENS

To EDWARD MOXON, 17 NOVEMBER 1842

Extract in American Art Association catalogue, Jan 1935; *MS* 1 p.; dated Devonshire Terrace, 17 Nov 42.

Concerning the proposed publication of an American poet in England.[5]

Pray write me such a reply as I can send to the author of the volumes; and to get absolution for my conscience in this matter.

---

[1] Probably connected with the subscription to help Hone's family (see *To* Black, 15 Nov, and *To* Cruikshank, 24 Nov).

[2] Presumably of " the laughing Dolly"— the only Dolly picture that Frith mentions as being engraved (*My Autobiography and Reminiscences*, 1, 102).

[3] More likely to be James Mitchell (1791–1852; *DNB*), line-engraver, than his son Robert (1820–73; *DNB*), also an engraver, whose main work was done during the 1850s. James's two best known works were engravings after paintings by Wilkie; he also did six illustrations for the Author's edn of the *Waverley Novels*, 1830–34. His studio was in Bond Street.

[4] Thus in MS.

[5] Longfellow, according to catalogue, but possibly a mistaken inference. See *To*

Poe, 27 Nov, forwarding an answer from Moxon to a suggestion that he should publish a book of Poe's. Since Moxon and Longfellow had met and discussed business in Oct, there seems no reason for CD's writing to Moxon in Nov, with a bad conscience, to request a letter for Longfellow—though every reason for a bad conscience with regard to Poe. The reference to "volumes", however, unless the plural was the cataloguer's misreading, seems to point to Longfellow's work rather than Poe's. Moxon did not, in fact, publish a book of Poe's; but he had 250 copies of Longfellow's *Ballads* and of his *The Spanish Student* (a 3-Act verse comedy) printed for him in America for English publication 1843.

To THOMAS BEARD, 18 NOVEMBER 1842

MS Dickens House. *Address:* Thomas Beard Esquire | 42 Portman Place | Edgeware Road,

Devonshire Terrace | Eighteenth November 1842.

My Dear Beard

I quite forgot yesterday, that I am engaged tomorrow. Wherefore, let our Prison trip[1] stand over until your next Day of leisure.

Faithfully Yours always

Thomas Beard Esquire   CHARLES DICKENS

To NAHUM CAPEN,[2] 18 NOVEMBER 1842

MS Mr Robert H. Taylor. *Address:* By The Britannia Steam Ship | Mr. Nahum Capen | Boston | United States.

London. 1 Devonshire Terrace | York Gate Regents Park
Eighteenth November 1842.

Dear Sir

I beg to acknowledge the receipt of your obliging letter, and to express my general concurrence in its contents. It is exactly because I think the subject[3] is not understood, or sufficiently discussed by those who are bound to bring it forward, that I have always, without fear or favor, expressed my opinion in reference to it, whenever I have had an opportunity of doing so. At the same time, I have always considered Justice in this respect, as pertaining only to a very advanced state of society; and that it will not be rendered until you and I have been many years in our graves.

Have the goodness to present my compliments and regards to your Partner. And believe me Dear Sir

Faithfully Yours

Mr. Nahum Capen   CHARLES DICKENS

To FREDERICK DICKENS, 18 NOVEMBER 1842*

MS Free Library of Philadelphia.

Devonshire Terrace | Eighteenth November 1842.

My Dear Fred

As I am engaged on Sunday, I wish you would call upon me, if you can,

---

[1] Probably to Coldbath Fields or Tothill Fields.

[2] Nahum Capen (1804–86; *DAB*), of William B. Fowle and Nahum Capen, Boston publishers. An early supporter of international copyright; signed several copyright petitions to Congress and wrote memorials to Webster and Clay. Asked by Hawthorne to read his first book, *Fanshawe*, published anonymously 1828. Edited *The*

Phrenological Library, 1835; his later books included *Reminiscences of Dr Spurzheim and George Combe*, 1881. Spent 1835–6 in Europe, visiting hospitals, schools, asylums and institutions for the blind, deaf, dumb, and delinquent; on his return, worked for popular education. Helped to found the Massachusetts State Board of Education.

[3] Obviously international copyright.

on Tuesday. I will tell you then what I shall have determined on, in reference to the Alphington Removal.[1]

Frederick Dickens Esquire

Affy. Always
CD.

To L. HOSKINS,[2] 18 NOVEMBER 1842

Mention in N, I, 490.

To THOMAS MITTON, 18 NOVEMBER 1842*

MS University of Texas. *Address:* Thomas Mitton Esquire | Southampton Buildings.

Devonshire Terrace. | Eighteenth November 1842.

My Dear Mitton

The meeting at the Sanatorium, which *was* to have taken place yesterday, is postponed until today.[3] I must therefore (as no doubt you go out of town tomorrow afternoon), defer our appointment until Monday.

Thomas Mitton Esquire

Faithfully Always
CHARLES DICKENS

To MESSRS BRADBURY & EVANS, 19 NOVEMBER 1842*

MS Library of Congress.

Devonshire Terrace | Nineteenth November | 1842.

Dear Sirs

I wish you would send me by the Bearer, if you please, a dozen of the Chuzzle-wit bills.[4]

Messrs. Bradbury and Evans.

Faithfully Yours
CHARLES DICKENS

To W. C. MACREADY, 22 NOVEMBER 1842*

MS Morgan Library.

Devonshire Terrace
Tuesday November Twenty Second | 1842.

My Dear Macready

Don't fire such blunt arrows into my premises, but enlighten me like a Christian (not Pagan) manager, on two points; in respect of which I must know something, or I can't get my mind upon the subject.[5] Firstly, what scene do you mean to have?[6] Secondly, when do you propose to shew it?

---

[1] That this was imminent, see *To* Mrs Burnett, ?14 Oct and *fn*; and for plans for the move to London, *To* Mitton, 7 Dec and *fn*.

[2] Unidentified.

[3] Out of nearly 100 applicants the Committee unanimously selected Maria Edgeworth's niece, Mrs Gibbons: see *To* Thomas Chapman, 27 Dec.

[4] i.e. handbills.

[5] Of the Prologue to *The Patrician's Daughter* (see *To* Macready, 12 Nov and *fn*).

[6] The play opens in the library at Lynterne Castle.

At my cue in the Prologue,[1] or when Anderson[2] comes on?[3] If your Hall
Cerberus hadn't clean forgotten me during my absence in America, I would
have come down and asked you these questions. As it is, I wait by proxy,
in top boots;[4] and demand to be instantly satisfied.

                                                            Indignantly Always
W. C. Macready Esquire   CHARLES DICKENS

To GEORGE CRUIKSHANK, [24 NOVEMBER 1842]*

MS Benoliel Collection. *Date:* Written across the top of the page is the following
note in Cruikshank's hand: "My Dear Sir | I have just received this note from
Mr. Dickens—| Yours truly | Geo Cruikshank | Nov. 24 | 42 | 8 oCk. | Dr. West".

                                          Devonshire Terrace. | Thursday Evening
My Dear George.
    I only received Coutts's answer this Afternoon; and was just about to send
to you.—They will be happy to receive Subscriptions.[5]

                                                            Faithfully Yours always
George Cruikshank Esquire   CHARLES DICKENS

[1] i.e. at some telling moment in the course of it. This is clearly what Macready chose. In the preliminary Morgan version CD broke the line beginning "Awake the Present!" on the phrase's first occurrence, wrote "(*Picture discovered*)" on the line beneath, and continued below with "Though the steel-clad age". But he also, between the second "Awake the Present!" (eight lines further on) and "What The Past has Sown", pencilled in a caret with above it "qy.—discover tableau here." In the later fair-copy (MS Morgan), "(*tableau discovered*)" appears in the position indicated by CD's query.

[2] James Robertson Anderson (1811–95; *DNB*): see Vol. I, p. 475*n*. At this date CD apparently expected him to play Mordaunt, the hero. But Marston, given by Macready the choice between Anderson (the much younger man) and himself for the part, unhesitatingly chose Macready (J. W. Marston, *Our Recent Actors*, I, 57–8). Anderson was bitter about it, and wrote: "Macready played the hero . . . and I was left out in the cold. Charles Dickens wrote a charming prologue to the play, which I was to have spoken; but the mana-

ger, eager to have the lion's share, changed his mind, and spoke it himself" (*An Actor's Life*, 1902, p. 114). But this does not quite square with Macready's diary entries, which suggest that Anderson, presumably after having been deprived of the hero's part, refused to speak the Prologue, so Macready had to learn it himself (*Diaries*, II, 188).

[3] i.e. at the beginning of the play itself. This choice would have meant that the curtain rose immediately after the final line of the Prologue: "Yourselves the Actors, and Your Homes the scene" (fair-copy, MS Morgan). This line, rejected as the Prologue's climax, CD later thought of using as a motto for *Chuzzlewit*, altered to "*Your* homes the scene. *Your-selves* the actors, here", and jotted it down at the foot of one of the pages of rough notes for names (see *To* Forster, 12 Nov, *fn*). But Forster dissuaded him from its use (F, IV, ii, 311).

[4] i.e. Topping, the groom, was taking the note, with instructions to wait for an answer.

[5] For the fund for Mrs Hone: see *To* Black, 15 Nov.

To HENRY BURNETT, [25 NOVEMBER 1842]

Mention in Henry Burnett *to* F. G. Kitton, 19 Dec 88 (MS Huntington). *Date:* given by Burnett.

Telling Burnett that he had received the Bill he had put his hand to on Burnett's behalf.[1]

To W. C. MACREADY, [25 NOVEMBER 1842]*

MS Morgan Library. *Date:* clearly written on the Friday after hearing from Macready what the first scene was to be and when he proposed to "shew it" (questions asked in *To* Macready, 22 Nov).

Devonshire Terrace | Friday Morning

My Dear Macready

I have made some verbal alterations in the enclosed, and substituted three new lines after the disclosure of the Library; in lieu of the three I first wrote.[2] And I think it is improved.

Is it too late for me to say, that after considering the idea of the Allegorical Picture, I wish you would reconsider it also? Suppose the frame had, at first, merely some dim ground within it, like black glass—

Faithfully Always

CD.

[1] When sending this, with other letters he and Fanny had received from CD, to Kitton for his *CD, his Life, Writings, and Personality*, 1902, Burnett explained the circumstances. He had decided to give up the stage (see Vol. II, p. 37n) and to move to Manchester where there seemed to be a good opening for a teacher of singing. "But the removal and interval of work", he wrote, "involved expence. Dickens offered to lend me a hundred pounds. But found it would suit him best to put his hand to a Bill for six months [*clearly an undated Bill, made out before CD left for America*]." He had arrived in Manchester in 1841 and was now launched on his new career as a teacher of singing. Since the summer he had been conducting, at the Manchester Athenæum and the Mechanics Institution, "Vocal Music Classes" (based on "Wilhelm's Method of Teaching Singing"), and on 26 Oct began at the Athenæum a second course "for the practice of *Part Music*, and for the acquisition of a thorough knowledge of the Clefs". He also sang, sometimes with Fanny, at public concerts in Peter Street. Before the end of 1842, he and Fanny had become members of the Congregational Chapel, Rusholme Road, under the Rev. James Griffin (1805–98).

[2] To his preliminary draft, CD made such verbal changes as "Harp" to "song", "strains" to "chords"; transposed "breeds" and "engenders" to make line 37 read, "How Pride engenders Pride, and Wrong breeds Wrong"; and substituted, for "Read in the Volume, Mirth has held so long: | Assur'd that where Life's flowers freshest blow, | The sharpest thorns and keenest briars grow", the following three new lines: "And Truth, and Falsehood, hand in hand along | High Places walk, in Monster-like embrace: | The modern Janus with the twofold face".

To W. C. MACREADY, [25 NOVEMBER 1842]*

MS Morgan Library. *Date:* no doubt the same day as last; Macready received and answered CD's morning letter (both letter and answer clearly being sent by hand) before going out (*Diaries*, II, 188); the "veiled picture" of the afternoon letter must have been what CD in his morning letter had suggested as an alternative to "the Allegorical Picture". By the following Friday Anderson was no longer involved with the Prologue.

Devonshire Terrace. | Friday afternoon

My Dear Macready

I am *very glad* you like the Prologue; and also that you like the idea of the veiled picture first. I think I see it, as a good, mysterious thing, and simple too, as becomes the subject.

"Clangour" is an infinitely better word. Strange enough, I thought so, today.[1]

I will come down to the Theatre once or twice (when you tell me it is time to do so), and hear and see the thing. If any word sound harshly then, or seem in Anderson's way, I need not say that as I write to please you and not myself, I will most gladly alter it.

Marston called on me yesterday, and asked 'if he were free to use my name as the author of the Prologue?'—I told him 'yes, provided he had a desire to do so'—He then asked 'if he were free to publish it, with the altered Edition of the Play?' And again I told him 'Yes'.—But both these matters are dependent on your opinions and wishes, for they are mine. *a*It might be judicious to keep the Prologue fresh, and out of the book,[2] and to say nothing of it but in the Bills of the Day? Eh?*a*

Faithfully Always
CD.

[1] In line 3, "clangour" is written faintly in pencil over "clamour"—probably by Macready after receiving CD's agreement, though in the fair-copy (MS Morgan) the word remains "clamour". However, the text of the Prologue as published in the *Sunday Times*, 11 Dec, has "clangor" (presumably from Macready's copy).

[2] In the three 1842 edns, the first of which appeared on 9 Dec, the day before the first performance, Marston thanked CD for his "spontaneous kindness" in writing the Prologue, but the Prologue itself was not printed. Its absence drew unfavourable comment from the *Monthly Magazine*, Jan 43. After castigating Marston's servility to Macready, shown in the dedication, the review continued:

"The same symptoms of a patronizing air peep out, in Mr. Dickens's refusal to print the prologue, a thing unprecedented in theatrical annals". It then accused the *Examiner*—which in its notice of 17 Dec had referred to CD's "good-nature" in writing a prologue—of showing "the same illiberal spirit" by suggesting "condescension on the part of Mr. Dickens". After criticizing the play as "on a level with those sentimental novels, that some years since deluged the circulating libraries", it reprinted CD's prologue in full. Unusually the Lord Chamberlain's MS (in BM) does not include the Prologue.

aa Squeezed in at end of paragraph, clearly as an afterthought.

To JOHN FORSTER, [25 NOVEMBER 1842]

Extract in F, IV, i, 291. *Date:* 25 Nov according to Forster, confirmed by *To* Maclise, 26 Nov.

Browning's play[1] has thrown me into a perfect passion of sorrow. To say that there is anything in its subject save what is lovely, true, deeply affecting, full of the best emotion, the most earnest feeling, and the most true and tender source of interest, is to say that there is no light in the sun, and no heat in blood. It is full of genius, natural and great thoughts, profound, and yet simple and beautiful in its vigour.[2] I know nothing that is so affecting, nothing in any book I have ever read, as Mildred's recurrence to that "I was so young —I had no mother."[3] I know no love like it, no passion like it, no moulding of a splendid thing after its conception, like it. And I swear it is a tragedy

[1] *A Blot in the 'Scutcheon,* the fourth play of Robert Browning (1812–89; *DNB*). Macready and Forster, early admirers of his *Paracelsus,* 1835, had met him in that year through W. J. Fox, and encouraged him to write *Strafford*—eventually produced at Covent Garden 2 May 37, after many doubts and delays on Macready's part, and performed five times. His next two plays in 1839–40 were refused, and published in *Bells and Pomegranates,* his "dramatic" series of shilling pamphlets (Nos II and IV, Mar 42 and Jan 43). Forster, chief among Browning's early defenders, continued to review his work enthusiastically (except for *Sordello*) in the *Examiner;* and "importuned" by him, Macready glanced over the new tragedy in Sep 41 (*Diaries,* II, 143), but set it aside for his first Drury Lane season 1841–2, reserving it as a possibility for the second; in Apr 42 Browning wrote—from "Forster's Rooms"—asking for a decision (*New Letters of Robert Browning,* ed. W. C. DeVane and K. L. Knickerbocker, 1951, pp. 25–6), and perhaps by Nov the play was being reluctantly reconsidered. Forster, whose warm review of *Dramatic Lyrics* was published in the same week (*Examiner,* 26 Nov) had privately lent CD the MS of *A Blot,* probably hoping for his support in resolving Macready's natural doubts about its "dangerous" subject.

[2] CD's fervent response does no more than justice to this moving play. Thorold, Lord Tresham, head of an ancient house, is first seen formally accepting the bashful young Henry, Lord Mertoun as a suitor for the hand of his beloved 14-year-old sister Mildred. The true situation is then grad-

ually revealed, but only to the reader: irresistibly attracted, the two (innocent and ignorant) have already become secret lovers, but Mildred is now torn between conviction that their love is right, and an increasing sense of guilt because of the need to dissemble to her brother. Meanwhile Mertoun has been seen but not recognized on his nightly visits by an "old servant"; Mildred's silence under accusation and Thorold's passionate pride of race precipitate the catastrophe. Mertoun's dying words are "Leave | Their honourable world to them—for God | We're good enough, tho' the world casts us out!"

[3] The words "I was so young—I loved him so—I had | No mother—God forgot me—and I fell" originally appeared four times (with slight variations)—twice in the soliloquy that closes Act I, and twice in Act II; three times in the published text (*Bells and Pomegranates,* No. v); but only once (in Act II) in the text as cut for performance and approved by the Lord Chamberlain (MS BM) and then with "Heaven" substituted for "God". Though Mildred's youth is still emphasized, Macready had changed her age to eighteen. Lines and phrases suggesting that Mertoun was a mere boy were modified, and several references to the lovers' "sin" were cut. Joseph W. Reed's account of the transcript (called by Browning the "stage-copy") now at Yale, in "Browning and Macready: the Final Quarrel", *Publications of the Modern Language Association of America,* LXXV (1960), 597–603, includes details of all changes made at that stage— but Reed was unaware of the later stage represented by MS BM.

that MUST be played; and must be played, moreover, by Macready.[1] There are some things I would have changed if I could (they are very slight, mostly broken lines); and I assuredly would have the old servant[2] *begin his tale upon the scene*; and be taken by the throat, or drawn upon, by his master, in its commencement. But the tragedy I never shall forget, or less vividly remember than I do now. And if you tell Browning that I have seen it,[3] tell him that

[1] Macready had by 13 Dec committed himself to producing the play, but put off having it read to the Drury Lane cast until 28 Jan—and then, to its detriment, by Willmott, the head prompter (Sir T. Martin, *Helena Faucit*, 1900, p. 104). For the events of the next fortnight, Macready's decision that Phelps instead of himself should play Tresham (a part obviously written with Macready in mind), and his eleventh-hour change of mind, see Macready, *Diaries*, II, 194–6; Browning defied him and insisted on Phelps—"all this in face of a whole green-room. You imagine the fury . . . of our managerial wrath" (Joseph Arnould *to* Alfred Domett, *c.* 15 May, *Robert Browning and Alfred Domett*, ed. F. G. Kenyon, 1906, p. 64). Macready's proposed change at the close, omitting Tresham's death, was rejected and the cuts in the final acting version were less extensive than originally suggested; but one major change (besides Mildred's age) was accepted—Tresham's recognition of Mertoun comes after the fatal wound. (Browning published the play in time to be sold at the theatre on the day of performance, 11 Feb 43, so that it might be judged independently.) But on the first night the play triumphed over all difficulties; with Helen Faucit a Mildred of "overwhelming power and beauty" and Macready's absence from the cast "as little regretted as it possibly could be" (*Theatrical Journal*, 18 Feb), its reception, according to Arnould, was "magnificent . . . a triumph" (p. 65). John Kenyon told Miss Barrett of "the tears upon stedfast faces, the silence and applause not offered but compelled" (*Elizabeth Barrett to Miss Mitford*, ed. Betty Miller, 1954, p. 171). It closed, however, after two further nights, 15 and 17 Feb (with dwindling audiences); Browning and his partisans suspected Macready's influence on the critics; but the fullest unfavourable comments, in the weeklies on 18 Feb, came too late to affect the play's fortunes. These emphasized

faults in construction and probability, and the unpleasantness of the subject; only the *Examiner* (obviously Forster) accorded fully with CD's view—"unutterably tender, passionate and true"—and defended the play against conventional criticisms, while tactfully omitting almost all reference to the performance. In Browning's lasting breach with Macready, CD and Forster were not implicated; but CD was evidently not at the first night (see *To* Forster, 12 Feb) and perhaps absented himself deliberately.

[2] Gerard. The scene (II, i) was (rightly) not altered as CD suggests; Tresham begins by cross-examining him on the tale which he has only half heard and partly grasped.

[3] Evidently Forster did not, perhaps not wishing to risk exacerbating the differences between Macready and Browning. Browning saw the extract from the letter in 1872 and resented not being told of it earlier (*Diary of Alfred Domett, 1872–1885*, ed. E. A. Horsman, 1953, p. 68; letter to Frank Hill, 15 Dec 1884, in Mrs Sutherland Orr, *Life and Letters of Robert Browning*, ed. F. G. Kenyon, 1908, p. 111). One of the many inaccuracies in his account is that CD's letter was "directed by him to be shown to myself". But Forster can have had no ungenerous motive for withholding it; he was always eager for the success of the play and wrote by far the most favourable notice. CD's high opinion did become generally known at least by 1848, when it was cited in reviews of Phelps's successful production at Sadler's Wells: see Gertrude Reese, "Robert Browning and *A Blot in the 'Scutcheon*", *Modern Language Notes*, LXIII (1948), 237–40. Forster and Browning remained on good terms—apart from a temporary breach when Forster wrote an unfavourable review of *Colombe's Birthday* in 1844 —for the next twenty-five years; and in the small volume of *Selections* which Forster edited with Procter (anonymously but with

I believe from my soul there is no man living (and not many dead) who could produce such a work.—Macready likes the altered prologue[1] very much.

To WILLIAM MARTIN,[2] 25 NOVEMBER 1842

Extract in N, 1, 491, from catalogue source; dated 25 Nov 42.

I sincerely regret to say, that I cannot comply with the request you prefer to me, on behalf of Miss Isaacs,[3] not, believe me, from any indifference to that young lady's position, or to her honorable exertions; but because I am, I may almost say every day and hour, *forced*, to convey a refusal to similar applicants; which is scarcely less painful to them, than it is to me.

To DANIEL MACLISE, 26 NOVEMBER 1842*

MS Private (destroyed in Prestwick air-crash, Dec 1954).

Saturday Morning | Twenty Sixth November 1842

My Dear Mac

I wonder when *you* would look up No 1 Devonshire Terrace, if No 1 Devonshire Terrace didn't look up you.

I dined out yesterday, and stayed at home the day before.

The Beloved and Co[4] (indignant, as I suspect, at my not reviving the subject of Love for Love)[5] immolate themselves tonight on Mrs. Macready's Private Altar. What do we do? Do you dine here at 5, or do we dine elsewhere at 5? Will you call here, or I shall[6] call there? Did I see on your chimney piece t'other day, a summons for tonight to that Tomb of Good Fellowship in Trafalgar Square,[7] or was I deceived? Tell me. Lead on. I'll follow.

How do you get on with the charming picture?[8]

Always and Ever

CD

I gasp to write it—we go to Fonblanque's tomorrow.[9] No such luck as meeting you there, I suppose?

[a] P.S I do not hesitate to say that Browning's Tragedy could have been written by no other man living; and by very few dead. It is at once the most tender and the most terrible story I ever read. It made my eyes so red and dim, in the perusal, that I thought they would never sparkle (hem!) any more.[a]

Browning's sanction) in 1863, an entire scene from *A Blot* was included. But after a personal quarrel in about 1867 they were never really reconciled, and this no doubt affected Browning's resentment.

[1] To *The Patrician's Daughter*; see last two letters.

[2] Unidentified.

[3] Unidentified; she had probably wanted CD to read a MS.

[4] Catherine (cf. *To* Maclise, 3 Jan 42, *fn*) and Georgina.

[5] Congreve's play, revived by Macready on 19 Nov.

[6] Thus in MS.

[7] The Royal Academy.

[8] *A Girl at a Waterfall* (see *To* Beard, 18 Dec and *fn*).

[9] "gasp" presumably because it would be only a week since Fonblanque dined with CD at Devonshire Terrace.

[aa] Written by itself on p. 2 of a folded sheet, in very short lines, in a column, with "P.S." at top centre as heading.

To THOMAS CHAPMAN,[1] 27 NOVEMBER 1842*

MS Free Library of Philadelphia.

Devonshire Terrace | Sunday Twenty Seventh Novr. | 1842

My Dear Sir

Agreeably to your wish, I send you a sketch of what I shod. recommend for insertion in the Newspapers; relative to the Prince and the Sanatorium.[2] I have been particularly mindful of the great desideratum in such a case, which is to say as little in relation to space, and as much in relation to purpose, as possible.

I think two letters (I have marked them in Pencil) are quite enough to publish. But if your opinion should differ from mine, I beg you to act upon it without ceremony, as we have but one object.

Always Believe me | Faithfully Yours

Thomas Chapman Esquire   CHARLES DICKENS

To EDGAR ALLAN POE, 27 NOVEMBER 1842

Text from the *Century Magazine*, New Series, XXVI (1894), 730.

London, 1 Devonshire Terrace, | York Gate, Regent's Park, November 27, 1842.

Dear Sir,

By some strange accident (I presume it must have been through some mistake on the part of Mr. Putnam in the great quantity of business he had to arrange for me), I have never been able to find among my papers, since I came to England, the letter you wrote to me at New York. But I read it there, and think I am correct in believing that it charged me with no other mission than that which you had already entrusted to me by word of mouth.[3] Believe me that it

---

[1] Thomas Chapman (1798–1885), senior partner in John Chapman & Co., merchants, of 2 Leadenhall Street, Chairman of Lloyds Register of Shipping; and now Chairman of the Sanatorium Committee.

[2] Prince Albert had just consented to become President of the Sanatorium, Devonshire House. Publishing his letter of consent of 22 Nov and Chapman's reply of 24 Nov, the *Morning Chronicle*, 29 Nov, after compliments to the Prince, added the following (presumably from CD's MS: see *To* Chapman, 27 Dec, *fn*): "Let it never be forgotten, that the Sanatorium is not a charity, to which persons of independent and honourable feeling would be naturally most unwilling to apply for help. It is a self-supporting institution, where, in consideration of an annual subscription of one guinea in time of health, and the most moderate and economical weekly charge possible in time of sickness, any of that large and most respectable class of persons who are seeking a subsistence in the metropolis at a distance from their friends can, being stricken ill, repair as to a home. | Private, cheerful, and wholesome rooms, the first medical advice, the most delicate and unremitting attention; the best provision that can possibly be made for tranquillity, rest, and mental ease, at a time when they are most important and indispensable;—these are the advantages yielded by the Sanatorium. | It furnishes them to its members and their nominees as a matter of right, and not as a matter of favour; and the more genteelly bred, the more sensitive and delicate-minded the patient, whether male or female, the more distinct and peculiar the advantages of the Sanatorium."

[3] When they met at Philadelphia (see 6 Mar and *fn*).

never, for a moment, escaped my recollection; and that I have done all in my power to bring it to a successful issue—I regret to say, in vain.

I should have forwarded you the accompanying letter from Mr. Moxon[1] before now, but that I have delayed doing so in the hope that some other channel for the publication of [y]our book[2] on this side of the water would present itself to me. I am, however, unable to report any success. I have mentioned it to publishers with whom I have influence, but they have, one and all, declined the venture.[3] And the only consolation I can give you is that I do not believe any collection of detached pieces by an unknown writer, even though he were an Englishman, would be at all likely to find a publisher in this metropolis just now.

Do not for a moment suppose that I have ever thought of you but with a pleasant recollection; and that I am not at all times prepared to forward your views in this country if I can.

Faithfully yours,
CHARLES DICKENS.

To THOMAS MITTON, 28 NOVEMBER [1842]

MS Huntington Library. *Date:* 1842 on handwriting; confirmed by reference to Greenwich in *To* Mitton, 1 Dec.

Devonshire Terrace. | Twenty Eighth November

My Dear Mitton

I have just received from Talfourd, a vexatious reminder of a solemn promise I had utterly forgotten—to dine with him in his Chambers tomorrow. Will you write and tell me, whether Friday or Saturday would suit you for the Greenwich Expedition?

I have heard from the Govr.,[4] who professes peace.[5]

Faithfully Ever

Thos Mitton Esquire
CD.

To COUNT D'ORSAY, 30 NOVEMBER 1842*

MS Comte de Gramont.

Devonshire Terrace. |Thirtieth November 1842

My Dear Count D'Orsay

We shall all three[6] be delighted to dine at Gore House on Friday; and,

---

[1] Just possibly Moxon's response to CD's letter to him of 17 Nov.

[2] *Tales of the Grotesque and Arabesque,* Philadelphia, 1840.

[3] Wiley & Putnam published an English edn of Poe's *Tales* in 1845; but they were not published by an English firm until 1852.

[4] N, mistakenly, reads "hero".

[5] Perhaps John Dickens had earlier protested at some suggestion of CD's about his move to London (see *To* Mrs Burnett, ?14 Oct, *fn*).

[6] i.e., no doubt, Forster, Maclise and himself, as in *To* Maclise, 27 Dec.

(as you do not mention the hour) we shall take it for granted that you dine at Half past Seven, unless we hear to the contrary.

Always Believe me | Faithfully Yours
CHARLES DICKENS

To THOMAS HOOD, 30 NOVEMBER 1842

Text from *Memorials of Thomas Hood*, ed. [Mrs F. F. Broderip and T. Hood, Jr], 1860, II, 146–7.

Devonshire Terrace, November 30th, 1842.

My dear Hood,

In asking your and Mrs. Hood's leave to bring Mrs. D.'s sister (who stays with us) on Tuesday,[1] let me add that I should very much like to bring at the same time a very unaffected and ardent admirer of your genius, who has no small portion of that commodity in his own right, and is a very dear friend of mine and a very famous fellow; to wit, Maclise, the painter, who would be glad (as he has often told me) to know you better, and would be much pleased, I know, if I could say to him, "Hood wants me to bring you."

I use so little ceremony with you, in the conviction that you will use as little with me, and say, "My dear D.—Convenient;" or, "My dear D.—Ill-convenient," (as the popular phrase is), just as the case may be. Of course, I have said nothing to him.[2]

Always heartily yours,
BOZ

[1] For Hood's invitation to CD and Catherine, see 12 Nov, *fn.*

[2] Hood replied the following day: " 'The more the merrier'—which I suppose is the reason of such a mob of mourners at an Irish Funeral. | Many thanks therefore for your friendly additions to our little edition of a party. We shall be most happy to see Mrs. Dickens's sister (who will perhaps kindly forego the formality of a previous call from Mrs. Hood) and as to Maclise I would rather be introduced to him—in spite of Mason on Self Knowledge [*a treatise by John Mason (1706–63*; DNB), *Nonconformist minister*; *published 1745*]—than to myself. Pray tell him so much—& give him the 'Meet'. | I fancied one day that I saw coming out of your house a younger Brother who dined with us at Greenwich [*no doubt Fred*]—would he object to come with you?—but I will not suggest, Mrs. Hood having just desired me to send you the enclosed, which you must consider, on both sides, to comprehend" (MS Huntington; *Letters of Thomas Hood*, ed. P. Morgan, p. 513). A footnote in *Memorials*, II, 147, reads: "I do not know what the enclosure was, but I remember on one side my father painted a white vehicle on a black ground, thus giving Mr. Dickens a *carte blanche* to bring whom he pleased." Other guests who accepted included Forster, Ainsworth, Julia Pardoe and Manley Hopkins (the father of Gerard); R. H. Barham, B. W. Procter, Lady Morgan and John Poole were expected (Hood *to* Dr Elliot, ?2 Dec 42, quoted in W. G. Lane, "A Chord in Melancholy: Hood's Last Years", *Keats-Shelley Journal*, XIII [1964], 51).

To DANIEL MACLISE, 30 NOVEMBER 1842*

MS Benoliel Collection.

Devonshire Terrace. | Thirtieth November 1842

My Dear Mac.

You shall decide. Shall we go to Dulwich, and stroll and dine pictorially?[1] Or to Richmond, and stroll and dine aquatically?[2] (in either of which cases I will call for you at 1) Or take an afternoon's walk about the streets contemplatively, and afterwards dine Athenæumatively (in which case I will call between two and three)?

Decide. And I am ready.

I have said nothing to my Venuses,[3] nor will I unless our arrangements include them; the which I mention,[4]

To THOMAS MITTON, 1 DECEMBER 1842

MS Huntington Library.

Devonshire Terrace | First December 1842.

My Dear Mitton

I am under an old engagement to *dine* with D'Orsay tomorrow, at ½ past 7. I don't like our only lunching at Greenwich, but if the day particularly suit you, I will be with you at 11.

If, like me, you would prefer our having a whole day, what say you to next Tuesday?

Faithfully Always

Thomas Mitton Esquire   CD.

I have an immense No of letters from America.[5] The effect of the book on the better orders, is *decidedly favorable*.

[1] i.e., and visit the Dulwich Picture Gallery. This, founded by Sir Francis Bourgeois, who bequeathed his collection of 354 pictures to Dulwich College in 1811, with funds to erect a gallery, was built by Soane, 1812; described by Hazlitt in his *Sketches of the Principal Picture-galleries in England* (1824, collected in *Criticisms on Art*, 2 vols, 1843–4). Referred to by CD in 1856 as "a charming gallery of interesting pictures—very freely and laudably open to the public—which pictures are seen with an unusual absence of glare and bustle, with pleasant gardens outside and a beautiful country" (*Speeches*, ed. K. J. Fielding, p. 215). Mary Cowden Clarke wrote of it: "What an exquisite place is that Dulwich gallery, in the midst of a garden, set in the midst of a lovely English village! Many a

charming dreamy day have Charles and I spent there together" (*Letters to an Enthusiast*, ed. A. U. Nettleton, Chicago, 1902, p. 95). Especially valued for its examples of Dutch and Flemish painting, the collection also included Murillo, Velasquez, Poussin, Gainsborough, and Reynolds. Frequented by Ruskin, Browning, and George Eliot, and also by Mr Pickwick in his retirement (*Pickwick Papers*, Ch. 57).

[2] i.e. at the Star & Garter, whose garden ran down to the river.

[3] Catherine and Georgina.

[4] End of letter torn off.

[5] Among them were doubtless letters from some of those who had received copies of *American Notes* through Longfellow: see *To* Putnam, 18 Oct, *fn*.

To GEORGE CATTERMOLE,[1] 2 DECEMBER 1842*

MS Berg Collection.

Devonshire Terrace
Friday Evening | Second December 1842.

My Dear Cattermole

I have delayed writing to you, until I saw how this day's work turned out—much or little. I am sorry to say that it is as little a one as I would desire to see; and, consequently, that I must stay at home tomorrow.

Best loves and regards.

Faithfully Yours always
George Cattermole Esqre.   CHARLES DICKENS

To R. S. HORRELL,[2] 2 DECEMBER 1842

MS Public Library of Victoria, Melbourne.

Devonshire Terrace. | Second December 1842.

My Dear Sir

I write in haste to you to say that I no sooner received your two pieces, than I sent them to Mr. Ainsworth[3] (previously speaking to him on the subject), who returned me a favorable and hopeful answer. But since then, I have not seen *him*,[4] or heard of *them*.

I think the best thing you can do, if you see no objection, will be to leave them where they are: resting assured that I will be their faithful guardian during your absence.[5]

I should have written to you before, but I have been expecting every day to have some good news for you.

With best wishes for your restoration to health,

Believe me always | Faithfully Yours
R. S. Horrell Esquire   CHARLES DICKENS

To W. C. MACREADY, 4 DECEMBER 1842*

MS Morgan Library.

Devonshire Terrace | Fourth December 1842

My Dear Macready

Here are three Income Tax notions.[6] Two of them I mentioned to you,

---

[1] George Cattermole (1800–68; *DNB*), painter: see Vol. I, p. 277*n*.

[2] Robert Sydney Horrell (pseud. S. Harford), solicitor's clerk at Exeter, who had first written to CD for literary advice in Oct 40: see Vol. II, p. 135*n*. CD had gone to considerable trouble to help him with criticism (see, e.g., his long letter of 25 Nov 40; II, 154–7).

[3] See *To* Ainsworth, 14 Sep.

[4] But an enthusiastic review of *American Notes* had appeared in the Nov number of *Ainsworth's Magazine* (II, 470–4), under the name "Uncle Sam" (i.e. G. P. Payne: see Vol. I, p. 247*n*).

[5] Presumably in Australia, where Horrell died of consumption not long after receiving this letter.

[6] On 27 July Macready had recorded in his diary: "Tried to understand the Income Tax paper, which perplexed and annoyed me." Although assessment forms were not distributed till Aug, tax was deducted in July from dividends on Govt Stocks. Mac-

and one I didn't. If there be anything else I can do; you know how truly delighted I shall be to do it.

—— gather'd, stored, and grown
I think you made that alteration ?[1]

It might be well to counsel Marston to burn his copy of the prologue, pro tem: in order that he may be enabled to say, if applied to by any of the papers, that he hasn't got it—If you think so, pour that wholesome medicine in his ear.[2]

And if you have a Private Box to spare on *the* night,[3] remember the truly Inimitable; so shall he ever pray &c.

Faithfully Always
W. C. Macready Esquire   CD.

To OCTAVIAN BLEWITT, 7 DECEMBER 1842*

Text from transcript by Mr Walter Dexter.

Devonshire Terrace | Seventh December 1842
My Dear Sir,

Can you tell me (in a word) whether Mr. Davis the writer of the letter I enclose, states the Truth ?[4] He mentions the Literary Fund; and perhaps you may know something of his case.

I have not known Mrs. Hone, save by report, until very lately; and therefore do not think (do you ?) that I can very well sign the enclosed form.[5] Perhaps my letter[6] will serve the purpose as well.

I shall be glad to be at the Board of the Literary Fund once more, if its members, having an opportunity of summoning me thither, should desire to avail themselves of it.[7]

My Dear Sir, | Faithfully Yours
Octavian Blewitt Esquire.   CHARLES DICKENS

ready recorded this deduction on 11 July, with the comment: "Bear on, ye free people, enslaved to the worst cant that ever stultified mankind." (*Diaries*, 11, 179, 181.)

[1] This alteration, from "garner'd, reap'd, and grown" in the original draft, is roughly written in by Macready on the copy sent him on 25 Nov. But probably it was later withdrawn; for in the fair-copy, "garner'd, reap'd, and grown" still stands.

[2] The Prologue was, in fact, printed in full in the *Theatrical Journal*, 17 Dec, besides the *Sunday Times*, 11 Dec. Macready may well have forgotten what CD asked; for on 5 Dec he was chiefly concerned with the question whether the play might not be better if Marston changed the ending to a happy one. Forster agreed that

this was advisable, but later—perhaps having found CD strongly against it—came with him and Maclise to dissuade Macready from pursuing this (*Diaries*, 11, 188–9).

[3] Sat 10 Dec, the first night of *The Patrician's Daughter*.

[4] Unidentified; not the recipient of a Literary Fund grant in this period.

[5] Her application form to the Fund: CD did not sign as one of her two sponsors.

[6] Of 12 Nov.

[7] CD had been a member of the General Committee since Mar 39, but he was not present at any of the Committee meetings in 1842 or 1843 (Minute Book, MS Royal Literary Fund).

_To_ RICHARD KING,¹ 7 DECEMBER 1842

Text from typescript, Huntington Library.

1 Devonshire Terrace, | York Gate Regents Park.
Seventh December 1842.

Dear Sir,

I am much obliged to you for your note, and its accompanying Prospectus;² and I beg to assure you that I am strongly impressed with a sense of the great importance and value of such a society as that whose objects it developes. But I regret to add that I cannot become a member of it at this time; being already connected with so many Institutions, that if I were free of half of them for evermore, I should still be encumbered by the number of the rest.

Faithfully yours,

Richard King Esquire.   CHARLES DICKENS

_To_ MRS JOHN DICKENS, [DECEMBER 1842]

Mention in next.

_To_ THOMAS MITTON, 7 DECEMBER 1842

MS Huntington Library.

Devonshire Terrace | Seventh December 1842 | Wednesday Night.

My Dear Mitton

I have been so busy and so full of complicated thoughts to day, that I could not get to my Mother in person.³ But I have written to her, and shall be glad if you will make the Seventy Pound offer for that little house on Blackheath.⁴

I inclose a cheque for the Pensioner—four and twenty pounds.⁵

¹ Richard King (?1811–76; _DNB_), MRCS, Arctic traveller and ethnologist. Surgeon to Sir George Back's expedition to the Great Fish River 1833–5, his account of which he published as _Narrative of a Journey to the Shore of the Arctic Ocean, under Command of Captain Back_, 1836. Surgeon to the expedition to find Franklin 1850, which he criticized to the Admiralty —correctly—as an impossible task (Noel Wright, _Quest for Franklin_, 1959, p. 117). Awarded the Arctic Medal 1857. Wrote works on the Eskimos and Laplanders; also contributed frequently to the _Medical Times_, of which he was for some time editor. Member of the General Council of the British Association.

² Issued by King on 20 July 42, on the founding of the Ethnological Society, of which he was first Secretary. Both it and its successor, the Anthropological Society,

were in 1870 merged in the Anthropological Institute of Great Britain.

³ She was clearly already in London, possibly staying with the Austins.

⁴ He had seen his father on his way to Cornwall at the end of Oct (_To_ Southwood Smith, 22 Oct, _fn_) and no doubt plans for the move were then discussed. Perhaps nothing came of the offer CD is suggesting; but their address is known to have been the Manor House, Lewisham, in Feb and July 43, and probably earlier and later too (see _To_ Mitton, 28 Sep 43, _fn_).

⁵ Made payable, as usual, to Mitton (Account-book, MS Messrs Coutts). In the period since his return from America, CD's accounts show payments to Mitton (obviously for John Dickens) of £45 on 15 July, £100 on 3 Sep, and another £100 on 31 Oct.

A party and some hot Punch—made hotter inside of me by dancing, last night¹—has rather impaired my memory today. Did you say you would like to go on Saturday, *if* I could get a newspaper order, or how was it?

Faithfully Yours ever

Thomas Mitton Esquire   CD.

To T. J. PETTIGREW,² 7 DECEMBER 1842

Text from N, I, 493.

Devonshire Terrace | December Seventh 1842

My Dear Pettigrew,

I shall be delighted³—and was coming, myself,⁴ this morning to tell you so.

Faithfully yours always

[CHARLES DICKENS]

To JOHN FORSTER, [8 DECEMBER 1842]

Extract in F, IV, i, 290. *Date:* 8 Dec according to Forster.

The *Chuzzlewit* copy makes so much more than I supposed,⁵ that the number is nearly done. Thank God!

---

¹ At the Hoods' (see *To* Hood, 30 Nov).

² Thomas Joseph Pettigrew (1791–1865; *DNB*), FRCS, FRS, FSA; surgeon of Charing Cross Hospital until 1835 and to the Dukes of Kent and Sussex; librarian to the Duke of Sussex; treasurer, British Archaeological Association, 1843. A prominent Egyptologist; unrolled and gave demonstrations on a large number of mummies; his *History of Egyptian Mummies*, partly illustrated by Cruikshank, 1834, was in the Gad's Hill library at CD's death. Published *Encyclopaedia Aegyptica; or Dictionary of Egyptian Antiquities*, No. 1, 1842, also several works of medical history and biography, and a life of Nelson, 1849 (the first to establish the nature of his relationship with Lady Hamilton); see also *To* Pettigrew, 22 Dec 43. Interested in the condition of pauper children and in 1836 (i.e. in the *Oliver* period) wrote a letter to

Lord John Russell on the sick children returned from Norwood to their parishes; since Russell did not answer, he published it in the *Morning Chronicle*, 12 Mar 36, and as a pamphlet, *The Pauper Farming System*, 19 Apr; the scandal was covered up, but conditions improved. He was an intimate friend of Ainsworth and Cruikshank (through whom CD may have met him), and responsible for their reconciliation and agreement to work together again (see Blanchard Jerrold, *The Life of George Cruikshank*, 1882, I, 281–2).

³ To accept an invitation for 14 Dec (see *To* Pettigrew, that day).

⁴ Pettigrew lived at 8 Savile Row, Piccadilly.

⁵ Clearly CD had had the earlier chapters of No. 1 set up in proof. (The proofs of Chs 1–3 are in the Forster Collection, V & A.)

To SAMUEL PHILLIPS,[1] [?8 DECEMBER 1842]

Extract in Mrs Oliphant, *Annals of a Publishing House*: *William Blackwood and his Sons*, 1897, II, 306. *Date:* probably received by Phillips on 9 Dec (see below).

Having begun your story[2] I cannot resist telling you at once that I think it *excellent*, and of *great* merit, and that next week I promise myself the pleasure of writing you again, and giving you my opinion more in detail.[3]

To W. C. MACREADY, [10 DECEMBER 1842]†

MS Morgan Library. *Date:* clearly a last minute suggestion for *The Patrician's Daughter;* could scarcely have been written on Sat 3rd, or *To* Macready, 4 Dec, would have contained some reference to Macready's response.

Saturday Morning

My Dear Macready

One suggestion, though it be a late one. *Do* have upon the table in the opening scene of the second act, something in a velvet case or frame that may look like a large Miniature of Mabel[4]—such as one of Ross's;[5] and eschew that Picture.[6] It haunts me with a sense of danger. Even a titter at that critical time[7] with the whole of that act before you, would be a fatal thing. The picture

---

[1] Samuel Phillips (1814–54; *DNB*), journalist; a *Blackwood's* protégé of Jewish "Cockney" origin. His first literary venture, *Caleb Stukely*, appeared in *Blackwood's* Feb 42–May 43, and in 3 vols, anon., 1844. Contributed stories and reviews to the magazine until in 1846 his connection with it lapsed on his becoming leader-writer for the *Morning Herald* and a powerful (often hotly resented) literary reviewer for *The Times*. On 4 Dec he had written to Alexander Blackwood applauding Samuel Warren's review of *American Notes* in the December *Blackwood's* (see *To* Felton, 31 Dec, *fn*) and predicting that the close of CD's literary career would be "as full of useful warning as his rise was sudden and astounding" (cf. the *Quarterly's* "rocket, and . . . stick"; quoted Vol. I, p. 316n). He added the opinion of a friend of his (on the *Morning Post*) that CD spoilt "what might be good, by straining after effect, and mounting into the *falsetto* of exaggerated description, or inappropriate reflection"; his work suggested "a want of literary education" (MS National Library of Scotland). Such criticism of CD's work was not unpleasing to the Blackwoods.

[2] *Caleb Stukely*.

[3] This letter (to a stranger, about an uncompleted story, with the promise to write about it again) is curious and unusual enough to suggest that CD's motive in

writing may have been to show a member of the *Blackwood's* team that Warren's review had left him unruffled. Phillips followed up his letter to Alexander Blackwood of 4 Dec with another on the 9th, quoting this passage from what he described as CD's "very flattering epistle", and ending: "I think I must retract all that I said to you against Boz in my last" (MS *ibid.*). But his hostility to CD's work seems to have continued (see *To* Beard, 22 Mar 47; N, II, 20).

[4] CD's suggestion was apparently adopted: Act II, Sc. i, the Drawing-Room at Lynterne Castle, begins with the stage-direction: "Mordaunt discovered, seated at table, gazing on a miniature of Mabel" (1842 edn).

[5] Presumably Sir William Charles Ross (1794–1860; *DNB*), the leading Victorian miniaturist; RA 1843; knighted June 42. His sitters included the Queen, Prince Albert and the royal children.

[6] Presumably the "Allegorical Picture" which Macready had agreed should earlier be veiled (see 25 Nov, afternoon).

[7] Act II, Sc. i, begins with a long dialogue between Mordaunt and Lady Mabel, revealing her romantic idealism and their love for each other. Mabel's aunt, Lady Lydia, then enters and makes clear her intention to separate them.

is bad in itself, bad in its effect upon the beautiful room, bad in all its associations with the house. In case of your having nothing at hand, I send you by Bearer what would be a Million times better.

Always My Dear Macready | Faithfully Yours
CHARLES DICKENS

I need not remind you how common it is, to have such pictures in cases, lying about elegant rooms: *a*and what a frightful phenomonon[1] such a work of art as that Portrait and its stand would be in real life.*a*

To T. J. PETTIGREW, 14 DECEMBER 1842

Facsimile in Ralph Straus, *Dickens: a Portrait in Pencil*, 1928, facing p. 72.

Devonshire Terrace | Fourteenth December 1842

My Dear Pettigrew.

I cannot tell you how much I regret the being obliged to say that I have received letters this morning which oblige me to leave town by Railroad immediately on some family business[2] (not the most pleasant in its nature), which will detain me until tomorrow.[3]

In haste | Believe me
Always Faithfully Yours

T. J. Pettigrew Esquire

CHARLES DICKENS

To OCTAVIAN BLEWITT, 15 DECEMBER 1842*

MS Royal Literary Fund.

Devonshire Terrace | Thursday Evening | Fifteenth December 1842

My Dear Sir

I beg to acknowledge, with very many thanks, the safe receipt of a donation of £50 from the Literary Fund, for Mrs. Hone. And I entreat you to present her most grateful thanks to the Committee of that estimable Society for their liberal gift.[4]

Dear Sir | Faithfully Yours always

Octavian Blewitt Esquire

CHARLES DICKENS

---

aa Not previously published.

[1] Thus in MS.

[2] Possibly connected with the removal from Alphington, and fresh debts incurred by John Dickens.

[3] He had accepted an invitation from Pettigrew for the 14th on 7 Dec.

[4] Thanking Blewitt herself on 19 Dec, Mrs Hone wrote: "The munificence of the sum . . . exceeds my highest expectations" (MS Royal Literary Fund).

To [THOMAS] COOKE,[1] 15 DECEMBER 1842

MS John Rylands Library.

Devonshire Terrace | Thursday Evening | Fifteenth December 1842

My Dear Cooke

I am most unfeignedly and heartily obliged to you for your kind remembrance of me. I don't *begin* in Cornwall,[2] though it is possible I may come there, in course of time. If you can get the dialect book without inconvenience, I shall be very glad to see it.[3]

Mrs. D desires her best regards to Mrs. Cooke. And I am always

Hers and Yours | Faithfully
CHARLES DICKENS

I want to improve the acquaintance of your "little boy"; and I wish you would give me his address.

To GEORGE CRUIKSHANK, 16 DECEMBER 1842

Text from N, I, 494.

Devonshire Terrace | Sixteenth December 1842

My Dear George,

I am happy to say that I received the enclosed last night from the Secretary of the Literary Fund, and that I have a fifty pound note to hand over to anyone authorised to receive it on behalf of the committee.

Always believe me | Heartily Yours
[CHARLES DICKENS]

To DANIEL MACLISE, [?16 DECEMBER 1842]*

MS Colonel Richard Gimbel. *Date:* late 1842 on handwriting, and paper watermarked 1842. The first number was "nearly done" on 8 Dec (*To* Forster, that day); but working time would have been lost on 9th–10th through *The Patrician's Daughter* and on 14th–15th by the unexpected journey on family business.

Devonshire Terrace | Friday

My Dear Mac

Let our engagement for tonight, stand for *tomorrow* instead; will you? I am afraid to go out this evening: having pledged myself to the Printer, that I will finish tomorrow morning.[4]

Faithfully Always
CD.

---

[1] Almost certainly Thomas Cooke (*b.* 1762); MA Oxon. 1786; admitted Gray's Inn 1788; Fellow of the Society of Antiquaries 1790; name removed 1845 for being six years in arrears with subscriptions (information from Society of Antiquaries).

[2] See *To* Forster, early Aug and 16 Sep.

[3] An extract from an undated note from T. Cooke to William Sandys (an authority on dialects: see *To* Sandys, 13 June 43, *fn*) in Maggs Bros. catalogue No. 104 (Apr 1896), "Boz will be thankful for the loan of the Dialogues and Glossary", suggests that Cooke was acting as an intermediary.

[4] As soon as he had completed it, CD "was so eager to try the effect of Pecksniff and Pinch" that he read it aloud to Forster, who was ill, in his rooms (F, IV, i, 291).

To MRS FRANCES TROLLOPE,[1] 16 DECEMBER 1842

MS Berg Collection.

1 Devonshire Terrace | York Gate, Regents Park
Sixteenth December 1842

My Dear Mrs. Trollope

Let me thank you most cordially for your kind note in reference to *my* Notes; which has given me true pleasure and gratification.

As I never scrupled to say in America, so I can have no delicacy in saying to you, that allowing for the change you worked in many social features of American Society, and for the time that has passed since you wrote of the Country,[2] I am convinced that there is no Writer who has so well and accurately (I need not add, so entertainingly) described it, in many of its aspects, as you have done;[3] and this renders your praise the more valuable to me.

I do not recollect ever to have heard or seen the charge of exaggeration made against a feeble performance, though, in its feebleness, it may have been most untrue. It seems to me essentially natural, and quite inevitable, that common

---

[1] Frances Trollope (1780–1863; *DNB*): see Vol. I, p. 499n, and Vol. II, p. 402 and *n*.

[2] It was ten years since publication of *Domestic Manners of the Americans*, a book widely read on both sides of the Atlantic, enraging the Americans more than any other about their country by an English author. In her Preface to the 5th edn, 1839, Mrs Trollope declared that, though "very considerable changes" had taken place in the interval, on both sides of the Atlantic, there were few points on which she had altered her opinion. In footnotes she questioned whether some matters were not now as bad, or even worse, in England than in America—e.g. the licentiousness of the press (Ch. 10), and the attitude towards religious worship (Ch. 12); but she saw one change in America for the better—the improved behaviour of theatre audiences (Ch. 13)—for which she could well have been held responsible. Donald Smalley, in a footnote to his edn of *Domestic Manners* (1949; Vintage Paperbacks, 1960, p. 134), quotes the *New York Mirror*'s statement (12 Jan 33) that her name was already a "by-word in taverns and in the pit of the theatres... She has, nevertheless, although in a most ungracious way, 'done the state some service.' Spitters and chewers, look to it; and ye indolent beings, who lounge on two chairs with your feet on the mantelpiece, ... be no more guilty of a *Trollope*!" After *Domestic Manners*, Mrs Trollope continued to use her American experiences in

novels, and in *The Old World and the New*, 1849, implied improvements, and even noted the wish of some Americans to improve their English as a sign of grace.

[3] Except to a few selected friends, CD would surely have "scrupled" to say this in America in 1842. But in later years Americans marvelled at the fury Mrs Trollope's book had aroused. "Certainly no country ever rendered itself more ridiculous than did ours, when it made the welkin ring with cries of indignation", wrote Kate Field on *Domestic Manners* in 1864 (*Atlantic Monthly*, XIV, 668). "Poor candid Mrs. Trollope ... so handsomely cursed and reviled by this nation ... was merely telling the truth", said Mark Twain; "She was painting a state of things which did not disappear at once. It lasted to well along in my youth, and I remember it.... Of all those tourists I like Dame Trollope best.... She knew her subject well, and she set it forth fairly and squarely" (suppressed passages from *Life on the Mississippi*, quoted in *Domestic Manners*, ed. D. Smalley, Vintage Paperbacks, p. v). But the faults in *Domestic Manners* were clear. Thomas Adolphus Trollope insisted on the accuracy of his mother's book— nothing was "intentionally caricatured or exaggerated"; but "the tone ... was unfriendly, ... the result of offended taste rather than of well-weighed opinion", and the observations were gathered "almost entirely in what was then the Far West" (*What I Remember*, 1887, I, 233–4).

observers should accuse an uncommon one of this fault. And I have no doubt
that you were long ago of this opinion; very much to your comfort.[1]

Mrs. Dickens begs me to thank you for your kind remembrance of her:
and to convey to you, her best regards.

                                    Always believe me | Faithfully Yours
Mrs. Trollope.   CHARLES DICKENS

To THOMAS BEARD, 18 DECEMBER [1842]

MS Dickens House. *Address:* Wait | Thomas Beard Esquire | 42 Portman Place |
Edgeware Road.

                                    Eighteenth December | Sunday
My Dear Beard

I want your help in a pious fraud—such a pious one, that I have no doubt
you will give it me.

I am very anxious for many reasons, to possess a little picture which Maclise
is at this minute painting;[2] and I know very well, that if I were to say so, he
would either insist upon giving it to me, or would set some preposterous price
upon it, which he can by no means afford to take. Now, I think I may purchase
it without his knowing I am the purchaser; and if I can, he is a cleverer fellow
than I take him to be (highly as I estimate his abilities), if he can ever return
the money to me afterwards.

Behold my project.

I want you to write him a note, and say that Mr. So and So of such and such
a place in Sussex—one of your country friends—is enthusiastic in his admiration
of him, and is very anxious to possess a small picture (he can't afford a large
one) of his painting. That he has commissioned you to ask him what he has
now by him, and has empowered you to purchase any subject, with *one*[3] figure
in it. That you have spoken to me on the subject, and I have mentioned privately
to you, his having a most charming picture of a girl at a Waterfall. That you
wish to buy the girl at the Waterfall, forthwith. That you will take it as a
personal favor, if he will sell you the girl at the Waterfall. And that you are
prepared to give him the money *down*, for the girl at the Waterfall, if he will

---

[1] Mrs Trollope may not have cared for
CD's assumption that exaggeration had
been a part of her stock-in-trade (see above).
But it was the charge frequently laid
against CD himself. The *New York
Mirror* of 19 Nov, for instance, considered
the "chief merits and faults" of *American
Notes* to be "the developments of one
principle—*humorous exaggeration*". The
Lowell Offering defended him in Jan 43:
"There is evidently a style of exaggeration
in his descriptions; but no false impression
will be conveyed to those accustomed to

the author's usual manner of narration".
Emerson, in a letter of 25 Nov, referred to
him as "the slight, the exaggerating, the
fabulous man" (*Letters*, ed. R. L. Rusk,
Columbia, 1939, III, 100).

[2] *A Girl at a Waterfall*, with background
from the sketch Maclise had made of the
waterfall of St Nighton during the recent
trip to Cornwall, and in the foreground a
girl bearing a pitcher on her shoulder, for
which the model had been Georgina
Hogarth.

[3] Written larger than the rest.

let you know what sum you shall forward to him as her ransom from his damned uncomfortable studio.[1]

A hundred, or a hundred and fifty Guineas, will most likely be the mark. If you can only buy it, I will give you the needful instantly wherewith to close the bargain;[2] and a hundred and fifty thousand thanks, *in*.

All minor points I leave to your discretion.—I suppose you *an't* at home, and *couldn't* dine here today at half past five—could you?

Always Faithfully
CD.

Thomas Beard Esquire

To GEORGE CATTERMOLE, 20 DECEMBER 1842†

MS Berg Collection. *Address:* George Cattermole Esquire.

Devonshire Terrace | Twentieth December 1842

My Dear George

It is impossible for me to tell you how greatly I am charmed with those beautiful pictures,[3] in which the whole feeling and thought and expression of the little story is rendered to the gratification of my inmost heart; and on

---

[1] Richard Redgrave recounted the sequel, as "a most amusing story of Maclise", in a letter to a friend (ostensibly written in 1842, but showing signs of revision for publication in F. M. Redgrave, *Richard Redgrave, C.B., R.A., a Memoir, Compiled from his Diary*, 1891, pp. 314–15). In Redgrave's version (embellished, no doubt, but to what extent is not known), CD, after a preliminary call on Maclise by Beard, himself wrote to him in the "feeble old hand" and "garrulous strain" of "an old gentleman in the country", speaking rapturously of his work, and asking the price of the picture. Maclise, delighted with the letter (conceivably written by Beard, to whom CD had left "all minor points"), hurried off to show it to Dickens, saying that it had pleased him so much that he would name a low price. "'Oh, no, by no means,' said Dickens, 'you would be very wrong; it is evidently from some rich old enthusiast who can afford to pay well.'" After arguing the point, Maclise was persuaded to put his best price on the work; the "first agent" called again, brought the money and arranged for the picture's dispatch. "A week or two after, at Christmas", according to Redgrave, a large party was invited to dine with CD, among them Maclise—who at the last minute, however,

pleaded illness and did not come. Consequently CD unveiled the picture "to the admiring eyes of his friends", but unaccompanied by Maclise's "wondering astonishment".

[2] The "pious fraud", however conducted, was successful. CD's account-book (MS Messrs Coutts) shows a payment to Beard of 100 guineas on 24 Dec. (For Maclise's objection, see *To* Maclise, ?Late Dec and *fns*.) The picture was exhibited at the RA 1843, and the figure of "the girl" much admired (the *Art Journal* saw her as an Irish maiden, "no vulgar rustic" but "a lovely specimen of Nature's aristocracy"). On CD's death it was bought by Forster for £640.10.0 (*Catalogue of the . . . Pictures . . . of CD*, ed. J. H. Stonehouse, p. 127). It is now in the Forster Collection, V & A.

[3] Watercolour drawings of two of Cattermole's illustrations to *Old Curiosity Shop*—commissioned by CD (see MDGH, I, 55), though curiously no payment to Cattermole appears in CD's accounts of the following 18 months. One, of Nell's grave, bought by Forster at the Christie's sale of CD's pictures, 9 July 70, is now in the Forster Collection, V & A; the other, of the interior of the Curiosity Shop, is in Dickens House.

which you have lavished those amazing resources of yours with a power, at which I fairly wondered when I sat down yesterday before them.[1]

I took them to Mac, straightway, in a cab—and it would have done you good if you could have seen and heard him. You can't think how moved he was by the old man in the church, or how proud *I* was to have chosen it, before he saw the drawings.

You are such a queer fellow, and hold yourself so much aloof, that I am afraid to say half I would say, touching my grateful admiration. So you shall imagine the rest.

a I enclose a note from Kate; to which I hope you will bring the only one acceptable reply.*a* Always

My Dear Cattermole | Faithfully Yours

George Cattermole Esquire   CHARLES DICKENS

To LEIGH HUNT, 20 DECEMBER 1842

MS Iowa University Libraries.

Devonshire Terrace | Twentieth December 1842.

My Dear Hunt.

I have received your letter—and read it with some pain. In Heaven's name, don't imagine there is any man alive from whom you could possibly, if you knew his heart, accept a "favor"[2] with less reason for feeling it a burden or a cause of uneasiness, than

Your faithful friend

Leigh Hunt Esquire   CHARLES DICKENS

To THOMAS BEARD, 22 DECEMBER 1842

MS Dickens House. *Address:* Thomas Beard Esquire | 42 Portman Place | Edgeware Road.

Devonshire Terrace | Twenty Second December | 1842.

My Dear Beard.

I have a few people coming to dine here tomorrow at a quarter past Six, on a short notice, to meet a gentlemanly bore from Quebec[3] from whom I received some attentions, who is going away directly. Join us at that hour, and try the Wintages.

Ever Faithfully

Thomas Beard Esquire   CD.

[1] Cattermole's watercolour drawings show various departures from his original woodcuts. In the church containing Nell's grave he changed the glimpse of a Norman aisle to a Gothic, and introduced in each of a series of niches above the central (now highly elaborate) arch a young female figure (see commemorative catalogue of the V & A Exhibition, 1970, plate 45). To the Shop, while elaborating the lumber, he made two striking additions: on the stacked table at the back, a bust of Shakespeare; and on the ceiling above the door, a head of Christ, with small cross (see *D*, LXI [1965], p. 130).

aa Not previously published.

[2] Presumably a loan—but a small one, since not shown in CD's accounts.

[3] Unidentified.

To ALBANY FONBLANQUE, 22 DECEMBER [1842]

Extract in Chas J. Sawyer catalogue, 1939; *MS* 1 p.; dated Devonshire Terrace, 22 Dec (1842 on evidence of CD's article).

As I haven't had time to do that "Snoring for the Million"[1] yet, and shall not have until tomorrow, I will tell Forster to send a boy here for it tomorrow afternoon; and will despatch it straight to the Printers.

To LADY HOLLAND, 23 DECEMBER 1842*

MS The Earl of Ilchester.

Devonshire Terrace | Twenty Third December 1842

Dear Lady Holland.

I return you, with this, the French Papers you kindly lent me.[2] And I send, at the same time, Kohl's[3] book on Russia;[4] and a queer old book for Mr. Allan,[5] which he and I were talking of t'other night.[6]

[1] A short, sarcastic article published in the *Examiner*, 24 Dec, not previously attributed to CD. On the analogy of "singing for the million" ("the great reform of the nineteenth century"), CD suggested "a system of Snoring for the Million", with instruction to be provided in Exeter Hall. The system would enable persons of quality to be oblivious of the Reform Bill, and the middle classes of the Income Tax and the Prime Minister. "But it is, in its effects upon the lower classes; upon the million; the labourers and artizans; the vulgar men of toil and sweat, and want and rags; that this system has peculiar claims upon the present Administration. No more complaints of hunger, when the starving poor may sleep and dream of loaves at will! No more pinching of the Landed Interest's corn in its good old gouty shoe! The ravelled sleeve of Care which flutters in the murky streets of our manufacturing towns, shadowing strange shapes in its dreary gambols, will be sewn up by the quickest process in the world. ... all will be peace and comfort: there will be forgetfulness for those who have nothing, and undisturbed enjoyment for those who have everything".

[2] Perhaps these included the *Journal des Débats*, 31 Jan 42, which contained Jules Janin's onslaught on *Nicholas Nickleby* and on CD himself, following a melodramatized performance of *Nickleby* at the Ambigu-Comique. Thackeray, in *Fraser's*, Mar 42 (xxv, 342–52), gave a rollicking account of the Paris performance, and followed it with a witheringly sarcastic answer to Janin's "most stern and ferocious criticism" of both the French *Nickleby* and CD himself —making much of the fact that Janin knew no English and had clearly based his view on this grotesque adaptation. Although CD was away in America when the *Fraser's* article appeared, Forster probably sent it to him, and he may well have expressed to Lady Holland a curiosity to see Janin's attack. (For her lending him other French papers, see 28 Feb 43.) Possibly Thackeray's article was what made CD "very happy once, a long way from home": see *To* Rogers, 17 Dec 43, *fn*.

[3] Johann Georg Kohl (1808–78), distinguished travel-writer and geographer. During 1841 had published *Petersburg in Bildern und Skizzen; Reisen in Südrussland;* and *Reisen im Inneren von Russland und Poland.*

[4] Kohl's *Russia*, 1842, was in the Gad's Hill library at CD's death. It is quoted extensively in "Common-sense on Wheels", *Household Words*, 12 Apr 51, written by Wills, Grenville Murray and CD according to the Contributors Book.

[5] Thus in MS. Clearly John Allen.

[6] CD had dined with Lady Holland at South Street on 21 Dec; the other guests were Lord Shelburne, Henry Wood and his wife Lady Mary Wood, Sir Benjamin Brodie, Sir Stephen Hammick, Charles Buller, Charles Gore, and "Mr Wickham" (Holland House Dinner Book, MS BM).

I will make an early report to you, touching Bulwer.[1] And am always
                    Dear Lady Holland | Yours faithfully and obliged
The Lady Holland.   CHARLES DICKENS

To MISS CATHERINE HUTTON,[2] 23 DECEMBER 1842

Text from Catherine H. Beale, *Reminiscences of a Gentlewoman of the Last Century*, 1891, p. 210.

                                1, Devonshire Terrace, | York Gate, Regent's Park,
                                                        Twenty-third December, 1842.

Dear Miss Hutton,

I am very glad to have heard from you again, and to have such evidence of your good health and spirits as I find in your letter; though I cannot agree with you on the subject of your penmanship, which, in its marvellous plainness, so puts mine to the blush that I should not be at all surprised if, by the time this reaches you, it seems to have been written in red ink.

It gave me a great shock at the time, and I am very unwilling to tell you now, that my friend Pitch[lynn]'s[3] card is *printed*.[4] If it had been written, I would have sent it to you.

I am the worst correspondent in the known world, for when I have been writing (as I have this morning), I am as anxious to get the pen out of my hand, as a school-boy is. But if you will only imagine what I would say to you, and will lay great stress on my assurance that I have committed the offending picture[5] (it *was* a bad one) to the flames, you will forgive me readily, for this short infliction.

                                Always believe me, faithfully yours,
Miss Hutton.   CHARLES DICKENS

---

[1] Probably concerning his health, after consulting Forster who was in frequent touch with him. On 10 Nov Bulwer had written to Forster: "I have suffered much pain & am still suffering—. . . & as it affects my head, have been disabled from writing . . . I am unequal to any thing—save doctoring my self & counting the hours" (MS Lytton Papers). Since losing his seat in Parliament in the General Election of June 41, his literary exertions had brought much exhaustion. In Feb 42 he published his first occult novel, *Zanoni* (applauded by Harriet Martineau and Carlyle), the one of his works he himself later said he liked best (T. H. S. Escott, *Edward Bulwer*, 1910, p. 253); in May a little volume, *Eva and Other Poems*; in July, in the *Foreign Quarterly* (XXIX, 275–308), "The Reign of Terror"; and he then began *The Last of the Barons*—as a novel, because Macready did not see it as a play (Macready, *Diaries*, II, 180).

[2] Catherine Hutton (1756–1846; *DNB*),

writer, who in 1841 had sent CD her "father's biography", and later a purse she had netted for him (one of her main marks of favour): see Vol. II, pp. 259*n*, 260, 451 and *n*. On 24 Dec 42 Macready recorded in his diary: "Received a note and purse from a lady signing herself Catherine" (*Diaries*, II, 190).

[3] Misread "Pitchgan" in *Reminiscences*; described in *American Notes*, Ch. 12, as "a chief of the Choctaw tribe of Indians, who *sent in his card*" to CD on board the steamboat from Cincinnati to Louisville, and conversed with him about Scott's poetry, Catlin's Indian Collection and Fenimore Cooper.

[4] i.e. not signed in the Indian way with a symbol.

[5] No doubt the lithographed portrait of himself which Pitchlynn sent CD soon after meeting him. CD describes it in *American Notes* as "very like, though scarcely handsome enough", adding that he had "carefully preserved" it in memory of

To UNKNOWN CORRESPONDENT, 23 DECEMBER 1842

Mention in Anderson Galleries catalogue No. 1143 (1915); dated Devonshire Terrace, 23 Dec 42; signed initials.

Mentions that he is writing an article[1] *for Fonblanque, who is ill.*

To THOMAS MITTON, 24 DECEMBER [1842]*

MS University of Texas. *Date:* Christmas Eve was Saturday in 1842; handwriting supports that year.

Saturday Mg. Xmas Eve | 9 o'Clock

My Dear Mitton

I am reminded of my promise to see to the Pantomime,[2] and am called out at this unholy hour. I shall hope to be in time to see you before you leave. I have not more than £20 at Coutts's, in all.[3]

Faithfully Always
CD

To COUNT D'ORSAY, [26 DECEMBER 1842]*

MS Comte de Gramont. *Date:* Maclise had sat to D'Orsay on Tues 20 Dec 42;[4] doubtless CD was writing the following Monday. He, Maclise and Forster dined at Gore House on Wed 28 Dec (see *To* Maclise, 27 Dec).

Devonshire Terrace | Monday Evening

My Dear Count D'Orsay.

I think Maclise's profile, *most excellent.* I should have recognized it instantly, though I had seen it pasted on the wooden leg of a Greenwich Pensioner,[5]

their brief acquaintance. Presumably Catherine Hutton had written that she would like to see both it and the card, and had asked questions CD had no time or inclination to answer.

[1] "Snoring for the Million" (see *To* Fonblanque, 22 Dec).

[2] *Harlequin and William Tell, or, The Genius of the Ribstone Pippin*, put on by Macready at Drury Lane. CD saw its rehearsal that morning (Macready, *Diaries*, II, 190); and "see to" suggests that he wrote the *Examiner* notice of 31 Dec. This declared: "It is the best we have had for years", and, describing a fight between "Liberty" and "Slavery", referred to "hordes of full-grown lubberly slave-drivers, in which a marvellously small boatswain, with enormous whiskers, and a whistle as big as himself, behaves with unparalleled bravery".

[3] On 1 Dec he had received from Chapman & Hall his last monthly payment of £150 (see *To* Chapman & Hall, 1 Jan, *fn*). On 23 Dec he received from them £100 (the first instalment of the £200 due for *Chuzzlewit* on 1 Jan 43: see Agreement of 7 Sep 41; Vol. II, p. 478). His accounts (MS Messrs Coutts) show that without this sum he would not have been able to send 100 guineas to Beard for the Maclise picture (see *To* Beard, 18 Dec, *fn*).

[4] See chronology of D'Orsay's drawings in Willard Connely, *Count D'Orsay*, 1952, p. 570.

[5] Notorious among London beggars; other crippled beggars often carried a "pad" (with description or illustration) attached to their persons.

or in any other equally unexpected place. It is a very striking likeness; and is full of character.

I shall be rejoiced to dine at Gore House on Wednesday. Pray convey my best regards, with all the good wishes of the Season, to Lady Blessington and the Miss Powers—I can't say "the Misses Power", for it looks so like the blue board at the Gate of a Ladies' Seminary.[1]

Always Believe me | Faithfully Yours
CHARLES DICKENS

My Wife has just come in, and is delighted with Maclise's likeness, which, she says, he couldn't have done better, if he had done it himself.

To THOMAS CHAPMAN, 27 DECEMBER 1842

Extract in American Art Association catalogue, Feb 1922; *MS* 3 pp.; dated Devonshire Terrace, 27 Dec 42.[2]

About the Sanatorium.

There is a natural repugnance on the part of most people to be in the society or neighborhood of madmen. . . . Touching Mrs. Gibbons[3] she appears rather to have gone into the matter as if the patients were, by the ordinary and established laws of nature, her natural enemies—as if she were a warranted mouser and they all mice.

To DANIEL MACLISE, 27 DECEMBER 1842*

MS Benoliel Collection.

Devonshire Terrace | Twenty Seventh December 1842
My Dear Mac
I received yours, this morning.

I have had a Note from D'Orsay asking me to dine there, tomorrow. I can't make out from its contents whether you are already invited or I am to invite you; for he says "you, Maclise, and Forster, en famille". How is it? Do you go? *I* will.

Faithfully Always

Daniel Maclise Esquire   CD.

[1] Cf. "The Miss Crumptons, or to quote the authority of the inscription on the garden-gate of Minerva House, Hammersmith, 'The Misses Crumpton' " ("Sentiment", in *Sketches by Boz*). Thackeray's "The Professor" (*Bentley's Miscellany*, Sep 37) refers to the "ensign of blue and gold" on the gate of "Bulgaria House, Seminary for Young Ladies", kept by "the Misses Pidge".

[2] Accompanying the letter, according to catalogue, was "a manuscript about [the Sanatorium]"—clearly the MS CD had sent Thomas Chapman on 27 Nov, separated from the letter with which it belonged (see *To* Chapman, that day, and *fn*).

[3] Mrs Emmeline Gibbons, the newly elected Matron of the Sanatorium, Devonshire House (see *To* Mitton, 18 Nov, *fn*); daughter of a distinguished surgeon, John King, and Emmeline Edgeworth, and widow of a Richmond doctor. CD had previously been convinced of her suitability for the post (*To* Beard and *To* Mitton, 15 Nov).

To JOHN FORSTER, [?27 DECEMBER 1842]*

MS Victoria & Albert Museum (FC). *Date:* Handwriting suggests late 1842; possibly "the Notice" was his *Examiner* review of Macready's pantomime (see *To* Mitton, 24 Dec and *fn*). *Address:* John Forster Esqre.

Devonshire Terrace | Tuesday Evg.

My Dear F.

Here is the Notice.—I will come down at about 12 tomorrow, to correct the proof, if you can have it by that time.

Faithfully Always
CD.

To MRS LYDIA MARIA CHILD,[1] 28 DECEMBER 1842*

MS Boston Public Library. *Address:* [By M]ail Steamer | [Mrs. Lydia] M. Child | [Ne]w York | United States.[2]

1 Devonshire Terrace, York Gate, Regents Park.
Twenty Eighth December 1842.

My Dear Madam.

Let me thank you for your earnest and interesting letter; and pray do not estimate the amount of pleasure I have had in it, by the length of my reply: which has reference only to the extent of my correspondence and the nature of my avocations.

You hardly give me credit, I think, for being as good a friend to Temperance as I really am.[3] As to denying myself my cheerful glass of wine because other men get drunk, I see no more reason for doing so, than I do for recognizing no distinction between Use and Abuse in any other commodity, temporal or

---

[1] Lydia Maria Child, *née* Francis (1802–80; *DAB*), writer and reformer. Her *Appeal in Favour of that Class of Americans Called Africans*, 1833, was the first work in America to advocate the immediate emancipation of slaves. In a review of her *Letters from New York*, 1843, the *Examiner* (30 Sep 43) described her as seeming "to belong to the ultra-sentimental or transcendental school", and criticized her for sentimentality over capital punishment. Frederika Bremer, visiting America in 1849–51, thought her "a beautiful soul, but too angular to be happy" (*The Homes of the New World*, 1853, I, 16). According to her biographer Helen G. Baer (*The Heart is Like Heaven*, Philadelphia, 1964, p. 153), her "heart warmed toward Dickens for his exposé of Five Points" (the New York slum quarter mentioned in *American Notes*, Ch. 6): "When a cartoonist sketched Boz dancing at the Points with, as the caption read, a 'great, splay-footed nigger,' she

and Dickens were both pleased" because it showed CD's criticism had gone home. Edited 1841–9, with her husband's assistance, the *National Anti-Slavery Standard*, a New York weekly paper. Also wrote on religion, and on household and child management.

[2] The bottom third of sides 3–4 of a folded sheet has been cut away, removing from side 3 probably no more than the ending, signature and subscription, and from side 4 parts of the address.

[3] Mrs Child had presumably written to comment on CD's description of the Temperance Convention at Cincinnati (*American Notes*, Ch. 11). He in fact described it quite kindly, except for remarking that the speeches "were certainly adapted to the occasion, as having that degree of relationship to cold water which wet blankets may claim". Several of her stories show her support of Temperance.

spiritual. I am a great friend to Temperance, and a great foe to Abstinence. The more stoutly that Abstinence is insisted upon now, the more clearly I can foresee, I think, that the next age will run riot in Drunkenness. For all history and experience warn us that of one violent extreme, its opposite has always sprung.

Besides which, there is an immense amount of ignorance and folly and false reasoning, constantly broached by the Abstinence Disseminators. The position that Drunkenness is the cause of all other passions, is one of the most monstrous in the world. You will almost invariably find that some other passion has been the cause of Drunkenness; and that that vice is the coping on the top of most of the Devil's Edifices—not the foundation stone, as your mole-eyed enquirers into Human Nature would have us believe.

The man who cannot drink without drinking too much for his Soul and Body, should be urged to abstinence by all manner of means. But the man who can, should be left alone. If I walk among honest men with my hand kerchief hanging out of my pocket, I am guilty of throwing no temptation in their way, but if I do the like among thieves I am very culpable indeed.

To STEPHEN COLLINS, 28 DECEMBER 1842*

MS New York University Library. *Address:* By Mail Steamer | Stephen Collins Esquire | Baltimore | United States.

1 Devonshire Terrace, York Gate, Regents Park.
Twenty Eighth December 1842

Dear Sir.

I have duly received your letter and your book;[1] for both of which, I beg to thank you cordially.

Mrs. Dickens (who, with our children, is quite well and happy) begs to be kindly remembered to you.

I am always, Dear Sir
Yours faithfully and obliged

Stephen Collins Esquire.   CHARLES DICKENS

To MESSRS LEA & BLANCHARD, 28 DECEMBER 1842

MS Messrs Lea & Febiger. *Address:* Private. By Mail Steamer. | Messrs. Lea and Blanchard. | Philadelphia. | United States.

1 Devonshire Terrace, York Gate, Regents Park.
Twenty Eighth December 1842.

Dear Sirs

Rest assured that if any personal or private feeling were intermixed with the resolution at which I arrived when I came home in reference to American republications of my books,[2] it would have great weight in *your* favor. I formed

---

[1] *Miscellanies*, Philadelphia, 1842 (see   [2] See *To* British Authors, 7 July.
To Collins, 19 Apr, *fn*).

it, on principle. Disgusted with the infamous state of the Law in respect of Copyright, and confirmed in the opinion I have always held that there is no reasonable ray of hope of its being changed for very many years to come, I determined that so far as I was concerned the American people should have the full pride, honor, glory, and profit of it; that I would be no party to its evasion; and that I would have nothing blown to me by a side-wind, which the dishonest breath of the popular legislature with-held.

I hope that the more you see of this plunder, and the dirty hands into which it goes; the more you will feel and advocate the necessity of a change.[1]

Always Believe me | Faithfully Yours

Messrs. Lea and Blanchard.   CHARLES DICKENS

To CORNELIUS MATHEWS,[2] 28 DECEMBER 1842†

MS Berg Collection. *Address:* By Mail Steamer. | Cornelius Mathews Esquire | 14 Pine Street | New York | United States.

1 Devonshire Terrace, York Gate, Regents Park.
Twenty Eighth December 1842

My Dear Sir

I was very glad to receive your letter, and to read your remarks on the spirit of my American book. I know it deserves them for its good intentions.

[1] Lea & Blanchard were well acquainted with the business methods of one of the chief culprits, Park Benjamin, who on 26 Aug 41 had tried to strike a bargain with them. If, wrote Benjamin, they would send him a copy of each Part of *Barnaby Rudge* as soon as they received it, so that the *New World* could publish on the same day as they did, he would himself have the wood-cuts for it engraved within two days (and "done much better than those you publish"), thus saving them the expense: "If you will consider, a moment, gentlemen, this arrangement must be advantageous, since we certainly cannot interfere with you more than the Tribune which publishes each part of Barnaby for a cent and sells it directly it reaches the city". If they agreed, Benjamin pledged his honour not to publish ahead of them, unless he had obtained his copy independently from England: "But whether it comes from England or not, the cuts shall be your's; because it will be an advantage to us to publish with cuts on the same day that others publish without" (MS Columbia University Libraries).

[2] Cornelius Mathews (1817–89; *DAB*), New York journalist and writer and passionate advocate of a native American literature. As leaders of the "Young Ameri-

cans", he and his friend Evert Duyckinck (1816–78; *DAB*) were in continual conflict with L. G. Clark and the "anglophile" *Knickerbocker*: see Perry Miller, *The Raven and the Whale*, New York, 1956. With Duyckinck, founded and edited *Arcturus* (1840–2). Also wrote romances, plays, criticism and poetry; best known probably for his *Poems on Man in his Various Aspects under the American Republic*, 1843—of which Elizabeth Barrett wrote to R. H. Horne on 20 Feb 44: "He has no ordinary degree of mental power, . . . and he is no imitator of English models—which is remarkable. Moreover, I believe him to be full of genial kindness and generosity, upright and warm-hearted, and so, for the best reasons, well worth serving" (*Letters Addressed to R. H. Horne, ed.* S. R. Townshend Mayer, 1877, I, 247). Helped to publish Elizabeth Barrett Browning in America. In Jan 42 became a fervent advocate of international copyright and presented CD (whom he much admired) with a copy of his pamphlet, *An Appeal to American Authors and the American Press*; for his speech on copyright at the New York Dinner, see *To* Forster, 24 Feb, *fn*. His enemies' nickname for him—earned by his domineering manner—was "the Centurion" (P. Miller, *op. cit.*, p. 80).

Do not suppose, I beg you, that I for a moment misunderstood your suggestions in reference to the want of an International Copyright, or that I conceived it possible you had any personal or private interest to serve, in making them. I simply intended to convey to you my rooted and decided objection to get the better of *a*the nefarious system which now exists*a* (and will, long after you and I are dead) by an *evasion*, or to take anything from the American People which they will not give me honestly and openly. So far as I am concerned, your[1] intensely intelligent and respectable newspapers[2] shall have the full credit and profit of the present state of things. And perhaps, in time, your publishers may begin to see that it is their interest to have some Law besides the Law of Plunder.

I have to thank you for the Copy of Puffer Hopkins[3] you have kindly sent me for myself; and to acknowledge the receipt of those other sheets of the same work which you sent me at the same time, for a purpose to which, I am sorry to say, I cannot put them. I know of no publisher here, who is at all disposed to reprint an American book unless it have attached to it, some name which is already well known on this side of the water. Since I came home, I have, in the discharge of other commissions to the same effect, several times offered American books (on any terms) to Mr. Moxon,[4] the most likely bookseller for the purpose; but always with the same result.

In the matter of the Brother Jonathan, I would certainly recommend you to take charge of that Journal, if you can do so with profit and advantage.[5] As to your using the works of British Authors, there can be no doubt that you would be justified in doing so, while matters remain as they are; and that the best return you could make, would be the advocacy of an honorable and honest change. At the same time, I am quite certain in my own mind that such an advocacy would be prejudicial to the interest of the paper, and would seriously affect its circulation, when opposed to the *b*free and independent doctrines of Mr. Benjamin; which are popular and patriotic.*b*

My Dear Sir | Faithfully Yours

Cornelius Mathews Esquire   CHARLES DICKENS

To FRANK STONE,[6] 28 DECEMBER 1842*

MS Mr David Borowitz.

1 Devonshire Terrace, York Gate
Twenty Eighth December 1842

My Dear Stone

All manner of childish entertainments are coming off here on Twelfth Night, in honor of my eldest son attaining the tremendous age of six years. It has

---

aa; bb These words appear in N, I, 496 from a catalogue source; letter otherwise unpublished.

[1] i.e. America's.

[2] Sarcastic: the reference is to the pirating "mammoths".

[3] *The Career of Puffer Hopkins*, 1842, a novel satirizing political electioneering and the sensationalist "mammoth" newspapers; first published serially in *Arcturus*, June 41–May 42.

[4] Poe's, for instance: see 27 Nov.

[5] These negotiations came to nothing.

[6] Frank Stone (1800–59; *DNB*), painter: see Vol. I, p. 487*n*.

occurred to me that a few older boys and girls (all of whom you know) might protract the festivities on their own account, and make a merry evening of it. Come and try—as early as between 7 and 8. I have asked Charles Landseer[1] to join us, also.

Faithfully Yours always

Frank Stone Esquire. CHARLES DICKENS

To HENRY WADSWORTH LONGFELLOW, 29 DECEMBER 1842

MS Princeton University Library.

London. 1 Devonshire Terrace | York Gate Regents Park
Twenty Ninth December 1842.

My Dear Longfellow.

I was delighted to receive your assurance of your safe arrival among our hearty friends, and to think of your sitting down in your own comfortable rooms[2] after all your cold watering[3] (and Good God what a quantity of water you had in that halfyear, counting the two passages!) safe and sound again. I was but poorly received when I came home from Bristol that night,[4] in consequence of my inability to report that I had left you actually on board the Great Western; and that I had seen the chimney smoking. But I have got over this .. gradually; and am again respected.

I have been blazing away at my new book, whereof the first Number will probably be published under the black flag,[5] almost as soon as you receive this. The Notes had an enormous sale;[6] and I trust the Chuzzlewit (so I call this new baby) will go and do likewise. I quite agree with you that we shall never live to see the passing of an International Law. I have always held the same opinion. But we may sow the seed, and leave the gathering of the fruit to others.

Heaven speed your Slavery poems![7] They will be manful, vigorous, and

[1] Charles Landseer (1799–1879; *DNB*), painter: see Vol. I, p. 566*n*.

[2] At Craigie House, "so well adapted to enjoyment and to labor", so comfortable that his friends tended to fall asleep in them (*Letters of H. W. Longfellow*, ed. A. Hilen, II, 458, 477, 489).

[3] In Aug, wrote Longfellow to Samuel Ward from Marienberg, he was taking six baths a day (*op. cit.*, II, 453).

[4] 21 Oct, the night before Longfellow sailed.

[5] i.e. pirated.

[6] "I suppose more than a hundred thousand copies have been sold", wrote Felton to Cleveland, 28 Nov 42 (MS Longfellow House), of America.

[7] *Poems on Slavery*, dedicated to Channing, published Cambridge, Mass., Dec

42. The last of the eight poems, "The Warning", prophesies the slaves' rebelling, "Till the vast Temple of our liberties | A shapeless mass of wreck and rubbish lies". Longfellow, earlier urged to write anti-slavery poems by Sumner, composed seven of them on the *Great Western* when returning home in Oct 42: ("I meditated upon them in the stormy, sleepless nights, and wrote them down with a pencil in the morning": *Letters of H. W. Longfellow*, ed. A. Hilen, II, 496). The first is about Channing, written before hearing of his death on 2 Oct. Sending a copy to Forster on 15 Dec, he wrote of the poems: "They are written in a kindly—not a vindictive spirit. Humanity is the chord to be touched. Denunciation of Slaveholders would do more harm than good; besides,

full of indig nant Truth, I know. I am looking for them eagerly. By the way I have been somewhat shocked to find that Everett[1] plays fast and loose in our English Society on that question; and says, as any trimming counting-house porter might, "that it is easy to find fault with the system, and not so easy to propound a remedy"[2]—as if any man with a head on his shoulders fit for anything but a block to put his hat on, did not know perfectly well that it is only after many years of strong denouncement that any remedy in such a case has birth! But here is another instance of the discordant materials he represents. He is the Minister of the Federal Government; and the Federal Government upholds Slavery—wherefore the man of Massachusetts goes to the wall and Freedom with him.

There is nothing new here. A tragedy of the present day has been played at Drury Lane, for which I wrote a Prologue which was spoken by Macready. It has been excellently received, but has not drawn money. He is quite well. Mrs. Macready has just presented him with a little girl,[3] with whose coming (having an indifferent good stock already) they would perhaps have dispensed if they could have done so, conveniently.[4] Forster thinks he is hard at work; in which delusion he has been plunged for the last six years.[5] Rogers has appeared at a Police Office, after threshing divers frail ladies (his former con-cubines) with a big umbrella.[6] Talfourd—who much regrets not having seen

that is not my vein. I leave that to more ferocious natures" (*op. cit.*, II, 481). Forster, reviewing them in the *Examiner* (8 Apr 43), paid tribute to Longfellow's "courage and humanity", but devoted most of his space to an exposure of the atrocities committed by Southern slaveholders. Seven of the poems were reprinted by the New England Anti-Slavery Tract Association (Boston, 1842).

[1] See 1 Jan 42, *fn*.

[2] Presumably in conversation, or as reported to CD; no reference to slavery in a public speech has been found. Everett was regarded as a compromiser by the abolitionists. C. F. Adams, his connexion by marriage, described him as "stuff not good enough to wear in rainy weather, though bright enough in sunshine" (E. L. Pierce, *Memoir and Letters of Charles Sumner*, III, 369–70).

[3] Lydia Jane, *b.* 26 Dec.

[4] She was Macready's seventh child and fourth daughter.

[5] In which period he had produced his five-volume *Statesmen of the Common-wealth* (a copy of which he had given Longfellow in Oct: *Letters of H. W. Long-fellow*, ed. A. Hilen, II, 475), had been dramatic critic of the *Examiner* (since 1833), and had for two years edited and written for the *Foreign Quarterly Review*.

[6] Five middle-aged females were charged at Marlborough Street Police Court on 2 Nov (reported in *The Times*, 3 Nov) with "annoying and victimizing" Rogers under the pretence that he had seduced them in their youth; he had, it was stated, been frequently annoyed by such females, had lodged a complaint at Vine Street police station without result, and had appealed to the Mendicity officers. One of these, Horsford, gave evidence that he had seen the prisoners follow Rogers from his house to the Athenæum and keep watch until he left the club and proceeded into St James's Park where he "was instantly surrounded by the whole of the party. He tried to beat them off with his umbrella, but they still continued to annoy him, until he (Horsford), having obtained assistance, took the whole party into custody". One of them claimed "that she had known Mr. Rogers for upwards of 40 years, and that for some years he had allowed her 10s per week, and that she had merely stopped him to ask for her money"; she appealed to the chief usher of the court to confirm that she had received such payments, and when the magistrate asked what they were for, replied "Oh! spare me the recollection of my juvenile indiscretions". They were each sentenced to a month's imprisonment with hard labour. "A Blotted Leaf from

you[1]—is in rude health and high spirits, in consequence of the Tragedy before-mentioned, not having proved attractive.[2] George Cruikshank got rather drunk here, last Friday night, and declined to go away until Four in the morning, when he went—I don't know where, but certainly not home.[3] D'Orsay was in great force yesterday, when I dined at Gore House;[4] and Lady Blessington asked kindly after you. Maclise is painting wonderful pictures.[5] And the Cornwall expedition was the greatest success ever known in this country.

After you left us, Charley invented and rehearsed with his sisters a dramatic scene in your honor, which is still occasionally enacted. It commences with expressive pantomime, and begins immediately after the ceremony of drinking healths. The three small glasses are all raised together, and they look at each other very hard. Then Charley cries "Mr. Longfellow! Hoo —ra — a — a — a — a — a — e!". Two other shrill voices repeat the sentiment, and the little glasses are drained to the bottom. The whole concludes with a violent rapping of the table, and a hideous barking from the little dog, who wakes up for the purpose.

They all send their loves to you, in which Kate joins very earnestly. I wish you had seen her sister who is usually with us, as she is now;[6] but was with her mother when you were here. There *was*[7] another when we were first married, but She has been my better Angel six long years.

Ever My Dear Longfellow Faithfully Your friend

CHARLES DICKENS

---

the Pleasures of Memory" is the title of a coloured sketch issued in Nov by "H.B.", and the incident was also the subject of various quips in the *Satirist*, 6 Nov, with the same inevitable allusions to Rogers's poem. That his unregenerate youth had been the subject of popular gossip is shown in *To John Overs*, 27 Oct 40 (II, 140–1).

[1] He was one of the people Longfellow was particularly sorry not to have met in England; others were Kenyon, Tennyson and Milnes—also Westland Marston and Meadows Taylor (*Letters of H. W. Longfellow*, ed. A. Hilen, II, 496, 510).

[2] Cf. Macready's amusement (20 Sep 40) at "the frank declaration of Mrs. Talfourd, that she could not wish any play to succeed now" (*Diaries*, II, 82).

[3] Cf. *To Beard*, 11 July 42. Blanchard Jerrold (*The Life of George Cruikshank*, 1882, II 49) describes occasional wild nights during the time that CD knew him, when Cruickshank returned to his early haunts "among humble boon companions". Earlier in 1842 his set of four etchings to John O'Neill's poem *The Drunkard* had appeared.

[4] According to Willard Connely (*Count D'Orsay*, p. 384), it was on 28 Dec that CD sat to D'Orsay for the second time (for the first, see Vol. II, p. 426*n*).

[5] Maclise exhibited two pictures at the RA the following summer: *The Actor's Reception of the Author.—Scene from Gil Blas* and *A Girl at a Waterfall* (see *To* Beard, 18 Dec, *fn*).

[6] Commenting on CD's mention of Georgina in his letter of 12 Feb 43, Forster describes her as "since his return from America, having become part of his household". She was staying at 1 Devonshire Terrace on 12 July when CD mesmerized her and Catherine at an evening party (Macready, *Diaries*, II, 180); is known to have been with the family in late Nov (see *To* Hood and *To* Maclise, 30 Nov); and by 29 Dec had probably been a permanency for some time. (In the "Violated Letter" of 25 May 58 CD describes her as having "from the age of 15 . . . devoted herself to our house and our children": she was 16 in Jan 43).

[7] Underlined twice.

P.S. Mc Dowall the boo[t] Maker,[1] Beale the Hosier,[2] Laffin the Trousers Maker,[3] and Blackmore the Coat Cutter,[4] have all been at the point of death, but have slowly recovered. The medical gentlemen agreed that it was exhaustion, occasioned by early rising—to wait upon you, at those unholy hours.[5]

To T. N. TALFOURD, 30 DECEMBER [1842]*

MS Free Library of Philadelphia. *Date:* 30 Dec was Friday in 1842; handwriting supports that year.

Devonshire Terrace | Friday Night Thirtieth Decr.

My Dear Talfourd.

My attention was attracted to the *book* in the accompanying parcel, by an advertisement in the Papers the other day, which announced for eighteen pence Such and such a Volume of "Parley's Library. Containing every incident in The Old Curiosity Shop and Barnaby Rudge".[6] The yellow pamphlets (Nos. of the same publication)[7] contain a great amount of Extract from the

---

[1] MS reads "book Maker", an easy error; John McDowall was "Bootmaker to the Queen & Duke of Cambridge", at 14 Regent Street.

[2] James Beale, hosier & glover, 131 New Bond Street.

[3] Laffin, Butler & Laffin, tailors, 17 Princes Street, Hanover Square.

[4] Presumably C. Blackmore & Co., tailors, 10 Cork Street, Burlington Gardens.

[5] CD himself dealt with them all: with McDowall from Mar 40, with Beale from Nov 41, with Laffin from May 40, with C. Blackmore from May 43 (Account-book, MS Messrs Coutts). Felton wrote of Longfellow to his friend Cleveland on 28 Nov: "He dresses less tight, having refitted his wardrobe in England. He weareth also stouter boots" (MS Longfellow House).

[6] Hood had written to CD on 26 Dec: "As you are so busy the following advt. in todays Herald may escape your notice. | Now Ready. Tenth Edition 1ˢ/. | Parley's Library Vol I. contains every incident in Master Humphrey's Clock—the whole of the Curiosity Shop & Barnaby Rudge. | Cleave Shoe Lane Fleet Street Lee & Haddock printers Craven Yard Drury Lane" (MS Huntington; *Letters of Thomas Hood*, ed. P. Morgan, p. 517). The *Herald's* advertisement also included, after the price, "or handsomely bound for 1s 6d", and, after the contents, "with 71 other

articles of value, and 96 engravings. The Sixth Volume of Parley's Library is nearly ready, and all the back numbers are reprinted". *Parley's Penny Library; or, Treasury of Knowledge, Entertainment, and Delight* was a weekly periodical representing the doings of the Parley family, the parents didactically retailing instructive anecdotes and instalments of fiction to their four children. Vol. I (Dec 41) was dedicated by the "editors" to CD, "with sincerest admiration and esteem", as "the living Shakespeare | . . . the last and best creation of whose genius | Master Humphrey's Clock, | is herein analytically reproduced". *The Old Curiosity Shop*, *Barnaby Rudge*, and "The Lamplighter's Story" from *The Pic Nic Papers* occupied about a quarter of the volume—the first quite skilfully condensed into 56 pages; but for *Barnaby Rudge*, the abridgment of Chs 1–32 extended to about 80 pages, with the events of the rest of the novel hastily summarized in a mere eight. Vol. I also contained a crudely re-drawn head from Maclise's portrait, and some discussion on CD's decision to discontinue the *Clock*, with critical comments.

[7] Weekly Numbers, of 24 or 32 12mo pages, sold at a penny; these were collected into volumes about every three months, the series being completed in 9 vols by Dec 43, when it was succeeded by *Parley's Illuminated Library*.

American Book.[1] The fellow who publishes these Piracies hasn't a penny in the World; but I shall be glad to know, at your convenience, whether the Law gives us any means of stopping him short.[2]

If you will tell me in one line, when and where I can see you, I will come, and be much obliged to you.

My Dear Talfourd | Always Faithfully Yours
CHARLES DICKENS

To C. C. FELTON, 31 DECEMBER 1842†

MS Huntington Library. *Address:* By Mail Steamer. | Professor Felton | Cambridge | Massachusetts | United States.

London. 1 Devonshire Terrace, York Gate, Regents Park
Thirty First December 1842

My dear Felton. Many and many happy New Years to you and yours! As many happy children as may be quite convenient, (no more); and as many happy meetings between them and our children and between you and us, as the kind Fates in their utmost kindness shall favorably decree!

The American book (to begin with that), has been a most complete and thorough-going success—Four large Editions have now been sold *and paid for*;[3] and it has won golden opinions from all sorts of men[4]—except our friend in

[1] The Nos of Oct–Dec 42 included a total of 50 pages of verbatim extracts, mainly from the first 11 chapters of *American Notes*, strung on a thread of commentary, some of it unfavourable.

[2] The name of "Cleave, Shoe-lane, Fleet-street" (John Cleave, radical journalist and publisher of the *London Satirist*, *Penny Gazette*, and similar journals) appeared on the title-page; but CD probably guessed that the "fellow" mainly responsible was R[ichard] E[gan] Lee, named as printer of most vols of *Parley's* ("Lee & Haddock" in Vols v–ix). For his action in Jan 44 against all three, and three other booksellers, over the still more flagrant piracy of *A Christmas Carol*, see Vol. IV, and E. T. Jaques, *CD in Chancery*, 1914. These proceedings identify the "editor" who "analytically reproduced" or "reoriginated" CD's work as Henry Hewitt. Lee claimed that before Christmas 1841 he sent CD an inscribed copy of Vol. I, which he accepted; this is unlikely, but CD in his affidavit of 17 Jan 44 also denied "to the best of his recollection and belief" that he had "at any time seen or read any copy of the said volume . . . or any part thereof". The present

letter shows that he had at least seen it; presumably Talfourd thought that nothing could be done, and in 1844 advised him to suppress any earlier knowledge of the publication.

[3] A 2nd edn was published by 27 Oct (see *To* Southwood Smith, 22 Oct, *fn*). *The Times* had advertised the 3rd edn on 18 Nov, and a 4th on 24 Nov.

[4] For instance, from Carlyle (see 26 Oct), Mrs Trollope (see 16 Dec), and Lord Jeffrey—who had declared: "I think that you have perfectly accomplished all that you profess or undertake to do, and that the world has never yet seen a more faithful, graphic, amusing, kind-hearted narrative" (quoted by Forster—who thought the book "thoroughly deserved" this estimate—in F, III, viii, 286). Jeffrey particularly admired CD's account of the Pennsylvania solitary prison, and his "sweet airy little snatch of the happy little woman, taking her new babe home to her young husband"; while his "manly and feeling appeal in behalf of the poor Irish" was a reminder that "we have still among us the creator of Nelly, and Smike, and the schoolmaster, and his dying pupil, &c." (Jeffrey *to* CD, 16 Oct 4?, quoted in

Fraser,[1] who is a miserable creature; a disappointed man in great poverty, to whom I have ever been most kind and considerate (I need scarcely say that); and another friend in Blackwood[2]—no less a person than an illustrious gentleman named Warren,[3] who wrote a story called Ten Thousand a Year.[4] They have done no harm, and have fallen short of their mark, which, of course, was

Cockburn, *Life of Lord Jeffrey*, 1852, II, 373). CD may well have learnt from Forster of the high approval of Crabb Robinson, who had been enthusiastic on hearing his letters from America read aloud by Forster (see *To H. P. Smith*, 13 July, *fn*) and was equally pleased with *American Notes*: "Nothing", he wrote in his diary (22 Oct), "can exceed his power of description of manners. It is in his highest style of humour. I am equally delighted with the view he takes of *Slavery*. . . . There are also serious passages of great worth. His argument against solitary imprisonment, and his acct. of a blind deaf & dumb child are affecting. Equally excellent is his summary of the national character" (MS Dr Williams's Library). The majority of reviews so far were favourable. For instance, *The Times* (25 Oct) approved CD's satire as having "a moral, not a tainting effect", and praised his sensibility in the serious passages—particularly in his descriptions of the Perkins Institution, the Massachusetts Asylum, the Lowell Factories, and above all the Philadelphia solitary prison. The *Morning Chronicle* (21 and 22 Oct) found it "an impartial book . . . not the indiscriminate outpourings of personal petulance, or national prejudice"; "he never twaddles . . . but, which is better praise, he never *Trollopizes*". Like *The Times*, it picked out his serious comments on institutions for special praise, and ended with extended quotations from, and a strong endorsement of, the chapter on slavery. Forster in the *Examiner* (22 Oct) praised in particular the book's liveliness: "Its own vitality would have given the subject old acquaintance and engrossing interest, if it had been about a people in the moon." This sentence he repeated almost word for word in F, III, v, 246; and on p. 245 much else from the review reappeared, verbatim or in paraphrase—as was his practice in other parts of the *Life*.
    [1] Earlier printed texts, deriving from J. T. Fields in *Atlantic Monthly*, XXVIII,

107–9, substitute "F—". For the review of *American Notes* in *Fraser's*, see *To Ouseley*, 8 Nov, *fn*.
    [2] Earlier printed texts read "B—".
    [3] Name omitted in earlier printed texts. Samuel Warren (1807–77; *DNB*), lawyer and author; studied medicine at Edinburgh 1826–7 (hence his *Passages from the Diary of a Late Physician*, *Blackwood's*, 1830–7: see Vol. I, p. 410*n*); called to the Bar 1837; QC 1851; Recorder of Hull 1852–74; Tory MP for Midhurst 1856–9, when appointed Master in Lunacy—"himself little better than a lunatic, although a clever one" (Serjeant Ballantine, *Some Experiences of a Barrister's Life*, 6th edn, 1882, p. 57). Notorious for his vanity. Author of miscellaneous articles and reviews in *Blackwood's* and of several tracts and legal manuals; but his literary fame rested on his *Ten Thousand a-Year*, serialized in *Blackwood's* Oct 39 to Aug 41 and published in 3 vols, anon., 1841.
    [4] Title previously omitted. The novel had been immensely popular. In Lockhart's opinion, it "beat Boz hollow—anyway, was fully his match" (Mrs Oliphant, *Annals of a Publishing House*, 1897, II, 218). On 28 Oct 42 Warren wrote to Alexander Blackwood: "What say you to a Review by me of Dicken's [*thus*] new book on America?—A *fair, prudent*, and *real* review?—bearing in mind my own position as a sort of *honourable yet fearless rival* of his, & your position with reference to the Edinburgh affair [*the fêting of CD, June 41, in which the Blackwoods had joined*]?" He had read the first 40 pages, and found in them CD's "*peculiar excellencies* & faults"—"palpable *genius* . . . real humour . . . *exaggeration*; glaring but unconscious egotism & vanity, glympses of *under-breeding*": these last he would "touch on in a manly and delicate & generous spirit." "I will do him good", he exulted, "and will make him self acknowledge me a high-minded rival, *a real friend*. (Don't think me drunk.)" (MS National Library of Scotland). Clearly, as K. J. Fielding has said, Warren was one of the critics "lying in

to annoy me. Now I am perfectly free from any diseased curiosity in such respects, and whenever I hear of a notice of this kind, I never read it. Whereby I always conceive (don't you?) that I get the Victory. With regard to your Slave owners, they may cry, 'till they are as black in the face as their own Slaves, that Dickens lies. Dickens does not write for their satisfaction, and Dickens will not explain for their comfort. Dickens has[1] the name and date of every newspaper in which every one of those advertisements[2] appeared;—as they know perfectly well; but Dickens does not choose to give them, and will not, at any time between this and the Day of Judgment. *a*Neither will Dickens correct, to the joy of the Republican Free (and Easy) Newspapers, any little local errors into which he has fallen—not even that of Brock's Monument,[3] which is a misprint[4]—but he will leave the book with all its imperfections on its head,[5] just as it first came out, and alter nothing.*a*

I have been hard at work on my new book, of which the first Number has just appeared.[6] The Paul Jones's[7] who pursue Happiness—and Profit—at other

wait" for the book, ready to "jump on [CD] as fair game the moment he ventured outside fiction" (*"American Notes* and Some English Reviewers", *Modern Language Review*, LIX [1964], 529). The Blackwoods and John Wilson were uneasy at the thought of publishing an unsigned attack on CD, lest it should be taken to be by Wilson. The review therefore appeared in the December *Blackwood's* (LII, 783–801) as by "Q.Q.Q.", and, as might be expected, its tone was patronizing rather than openly hostile. Warren commented on CD's sudden rise to fame—from what background and with what education no-one knew, and it would be "impertinent" to ask; applauded his skill in drawing, with "Hogarth-like pencil", the Cockney, but found each work of CD's "inferior to its predecessor". Coming at last to *American Notes*, he disputed CD's decision to include no sketches of eminent people; chid "dear Boz" for missing hearing Channing preach because (newly arrived in Boston) he had no change of clothes; disliked the impression the book gave of "perpetual and . . . unpleasant locomotion" and its "sickening details . . . of the filthy habits of the inferior Americans"; groaned at its descriptions of prisons and lunatic asylums, which seemed to be CD's "first and anxious object on arriving at any new town"; pilloried the passages on Niagara (see *To* Forster, 26 Apr, *fn*). He approved of Ch. 2 ("The Voyage Out"), of the pages on Dr Howe and Laura Bridgman and description of the poor settlers in Ch. 11.

But altogether the book was a "very flimsy" performance; its intrusion of politics a mistake; and its style slipshod.

[1] Written over "I have" cancelled.

[2] The advertisements for runaway slaves quoted in *American Notes*, Ch. 17 (see *To* Edward Chapman, 16 Sep, *fn*).

aa Not previously published.

[3] The monument in memory of Major-Gen. Sir Isaac Brock (1769–1812; *DNB*), British Commander in Upper Canada in the American War of 1812. Erected by the Provincial Legislature on Queenston Heights, where he was killed 13 Oct 1812, it was blown up in 1840 by a Canadian rebel, who had seceded to America. CD in Ch. 15 describes it as "now a melancholy ruin", protesting that it should be repaired at the public cost. A mass public meeting in July 40 had in fact resolved to restore the monument. £5000 was raised; and a new monument and statue were completed in 1856.

[4] The "local error" complained of was presumably CD's statement that Brock was killed "after having won the victory". In fact, the British force attempting to take Queenston Heights retreated on his death; the Americans proclaimed their success; and the British victory came only after the arrival of reinforcements.

[5] Cf. *Hamlet*, I, v, 79.

[6] The first No. of *Martin Chuzzlewit* had appeared that day.

[7] Thus in MS. John Paul Jones (1747–92; *DNB*), naval adventurer, smuggler and plunderer.

mens'[1] cost, will no doubt enable you to read it, almost as soon as you receive this. I hope you will like it. And I particularly commend, my dear Felton, one Mr. Pecksniff and his daughters, to your tender regard.[2] I have a kind of liking for them, myself.

Blessed star of morning, such a trip as[3] we had into Cornwall, just after Longfellow went away! The "we", means Forster, Maclise, Stanfield (the renowned Marine Painter) and the Inimitable Boz. We went down into Devonshire by the Railroad, and there we hired an open carriage[4] from an Innkeeper, patriotic in all Pickwick matters; and went on with Post Horses. Sometimes we travelled all night; sometimes all day; sometimes both.[5] I kept the joint stock purse; ordered all the dinners and drinks;[6] paid all the turnpikes; conducted facetious conversations with the postboys; and regulated the pace at which we travelled. Stanfield (an old sailor) consulted an enormous map on all disputed points of wayfaring: and referred moreover to a pocket compass and other scientific Instruments. The luggage was in Forster's department; and Maclise, having nothing particular to do, sang songs. Heavens! If you could have seen the necks of bottles—distracting in their immense varieties of shape —peering out of the carriage pockets! If you could have witnessed the deep devotion of the post boys—the wild attachment of the Hostlers—the maniac glee of the waiters. If you could have followed us into the earthy old Churches we visited, and into the strange caverns on the gloomy seashore, and down into the depths of Mines,[7] and up to the tops of giddy heights[8] where the

---

[1] Thus in MS.

[2] "Pecksniff and his daughters, and Pinch, are admirable,—quite first-rate painting, such as no one but yourself can execute", wrote Sydney Smith to CD on 6 Jan 43 (*Letters of Sydney Smith*, ed. Nowell C. Smith, Oxford, 1953, II, 776).

[3] MS reads "such as a trip as".

[4] The four of them, seated in a carriage with labelled luggage attached behind, are shown in a sketch once thought to be by Maclise but more probably by Thackeray— who, according to F, IV, i, 289, celebrated the trip (at some date unmentioned) "in one of his pen-and-ink pleasantries". F. G. Kitton, after showing the sketch to Anne Thackeray Ritchie, who "immediately recognised something of her father's touch in it", reproduced it in *CD by Pen & Pencil*, 1890–2 (III, 67) as "a supposed sketch" by Thackeray; B. W. Matz, reproducing it in his edn of Forster's *Life*, 1911, attributed it to Thackeray; and the style indeed seems far closer to Thackeray's than to Maclise's. It is now in the Forster Collection, V & A.

[5] CD's few references to places visited, supplemented by Maclise's (see below), and the local papers (see *To* Southwood Smith, 22 Oct), make it possible, with the help of contemporary guidebooks, to work out a conjectural route. On either Saturday night (29 Oct) or Sunday morning they went from Exeter to Plymouth (43 miles), with the intention of visiting the Eddystone Lighthouse; from there they went to Marazion for St Michael's Mount, probably through Liskeard, Bodmin and Truro (where they omitted to call on Dr Barham), a total of about 110 miles; thence to Land's End (10 miles) and probably St Just-in-Penwith, arriving there late on Monday night (31 Oct). Their return journey to Exeter included a sightseeing detour to Tintagel and St Nighton's Kieve and was accomplished in two days (about 160 miles), since they passed through Exeter on Thurs 3 Nov (*Wolmer's Exeter Gazette*, 4 Nov).

[6] "and drinks" previously omitted.

[7] They could have visited several mines near Land's End; one was certainly the famous Botallack Mine, to which Wilkie Collins, in his *Rambles beyond Railways*, 1851, devoted a whole chapter; CD recalled it in *A Child's History of England*, Ch. 1 (*Household Words*, 25 Jan 51), when referring to the Phoenicians: "The most

unspeakably green water was roaring I dont know how many hundred feet below! If you could have seen but one gleam of the bright fires by which we sat in the big rooms of ancient Inns at night, until long after the small hours had come and gone—or smelt but one steam of the *hot*[1] Punch (not white, dear Felton, like that amazing compound I sent you a taste of, but a rich, genial, glowing brown) which came in every evening in a huge broad china Bowl! I never laughed in my life as I did on this journey. It would have done you good to hear me. I was choaking and gasping and bursting the buckle off the back of my stock, all the way. And Stanfield (who is very much of your figure and temperament, but fifteen years older) got into such apoplectic entanglements that we were often obliged to beat him on the back with Portmanteaus before we could recover him. Seriously, I do believe there never was such a trip.[2] And they made such sketches, those two men, in the most romantic of our halting places,[3] that you would have sworn we had the Spirit of Beauty with

celebrated tin mines in Cornwall are, still, close to the sea. One of them, which I have seen, is so close to it that it is hollowed out underneath the ocean; and the miners say that, in stormy weather, when they are at work down in that deep place, they can hear the . . . waves, thundering above their heads." Cyrus Redding, in his *Illustrated History of the County of Cornwall*, published Apr 42, had described it as "an astonishing undertaking on the very edge of the sea"; it was "seventy fathoms under the most tempestuous sea . . . where the workmen . . . hear the waves thundering over their heads"—words which CD evidently remembered.

[8] Written after "precipices" cancelled.

[1] Underlined twice.

[2] One experience of the trip later found its way into "The Holly-Tree Inn" (*Household Words*, Christmas No., 1855); recalling various inns, CD there described an occasion "in the remotest part of Cornwall", when the inn was full: "A great annual Miners' Feast was being holden at the Inn, when I and my travelling companions presented ourselves at night among the wild crowd that were dancing before it by torchlight. We had had a break-down in the dark, on a stony morass some miles away; and I had the honor of leading one of the unharnessed post-horses." Since the inn was "full, and twenty times full", and only the post-horse could be received, the travellers debated how to pass the night and part of next day until "the jovial blacksmith and the jovial wheelwright" were "in a condition to go out on the morass and mend the coach"; eventually

they were housed by a local chairmaker. The "remotest part" was surely Land's End; and the only recorded miners' feast anywhere in Cornwall which fell at this season was at St Just, near Cape Cornwall, about six miles from Land's End; this annual feast, beginning on the Sunday nearest to All Saints' Day, was "kept up with more revelry than almost any other"; "on the Monday . . . much beer and 'moonshine' . . . were drunk" and a fair was held in the streets in the evening (M. A. Courtney, *Cornish Feasts and Folk-Lore*, Penzance, 1890, pp. 3–4). The *Penzance Gazette* of 9 Nov 42 reported that the feast had been "kept up with the usual degree of spirit"; hundreds paraded the street, and there were bands of music. The travellers' late arrival accords with Forster's reference (F, IV, i, 288) to the sunset seen from Land's End before they reached their inn. Cyrus Redding, who stayed there at "a comfortable country inn", described St Just as "situated on one of the most naked spots we ever beheld"; there were several mines, worked through granite; "a wilder country we never saw" (*op. cit.*, p. 174). On the basis of CD's description in "The Holly-Tree Inn", though without reference to the feast, Walter Dexter proposed St Just as a place CD visited (*The England of Dickens*, 1925, p. 131).

[3] One of Maclise's was of the waterfall of St Nighton, used later for the setting of his painting of Georgina Hogarth (see *To Beard*, 18 Dec, and *fn*). Stanfield's were of the Logan Rock with Forster perched on top of it (see plate 49 in V & A Dickens commemorative catalogue), of Land's End,

us, as well as the Spirit of Fun.—But stop 'till you come to England—I say no more—.

The actuary of the National Debt couldn't calculate the number of children who are coming here on Twelfth Night, in honor of Charley's birthday, for which occasion I have provided a Magic Lantern and divers other tremendous engines of that nature. But the best of it, is, that Forster and I have purchased between us the entire stock in trade of a conjurer,[1] the practice and display whereof is entrusted to me. And oh my dear eyes, Felton, if you could see me conjuring the company's watches into impossible tea caddies, and causing pieces of money to fly, and burning pocket handkerchiefs without hurting 'em,—and practising in my own room, without anybody to admire—you would never forget it as long as you live. In those tricks which require a confederate I am assisted (by reason of his imperturbable good humour) by Stanfield, who always does his part exactly the wrong way: to the unspeakable delight of all beholders. We come out on a small scale tonight, at Forster's, where we see the Old Year out and the New One in. Particulars *b*of Success*b* shall be forwarded in my next.

I have quite made up my mind that Forster[2] really belie[ves][3] he *does* know you personally, and has, all his life. He talks to me about you with such gravity that I am afraid to grin; and feel it necessary to look quite serious. Sometimes he *tells* me things about you—doesn't ask me, you know—so that I am, occasionally perplexed beyond all telling, and begin to think it was he, and not I, who went to America. It's the queerest thing in the World.

The book I was to have given Longfellow for you, is not worth sending by

<hr>

and possibly of the Eddystone Lighthouse (later perhaps used as the basis for the drop-curtain of *The Lighthouse* at the Tavistock House private theatricals June 55). Maclise recalled all this to Forster in a letter of 13 Oct 68: "Don't I know you of old—need I mention the Logan Stone—you perched on the giddy top, we rocking it on its pivot . . . don't I see you again sitting on the tip top stone of the cradle turret high up over the topmost battlements of the Castle of St Michael's Mount —your legs dependent over the side and not a ledge projection or coign of vantage 'twixt you and the depths below? This you did at the instigation of the legend attached to the feat no doubt with an eye to possible marital tyranny [*According to the legend, the first to sit in "St Michael's Chair" after marriage gained the mastery.*] —But let that pass. Last do I forget your clambering up the Goat Path to King Arthurs Castle of Tintagel—where in my vain wish to follow I grovelled & clung to the soil like a Caliban & you in the manner of a tricksy spirit & stout Ariel actually

danced up & down before me" (MS Forster Collection, V & A). Cf. Forster's version of this letter in F, IV, i, 289, with its several alterations—e.g. omission of the legend about "marital tyranny", and introduction of the sentence, "Should I ever have blundered on the waterfall of St. Wighton [*thus in F, 1872–4*], if you had not piloted the way?" The waterfall, in Trevillet Glen, a few miles from Tintagel, had already been the subject of several pictures and poems, of which Forster at least is likely to have known Letitia Landon's poem "St Knighton's Kieve", written to accompany an engraving of Thomas Allom's drawing for *Fisher's Drawing-Room Scrap-Book* (1835), an annual she edited 1831–38.

[1] Clearly from Hamley's; see *To* Mitton, 6 Feb 43.

bb Not previously published.

[2] MDGH follows Fields in *Atlantic Monthly* in substituting "F—"; but MDGH, 1882, boldly prints "Forster", and later edns follow.

[3] End of word torn away at seal.

itself: being only a Barnaby. But I will look up some Manuscript for you (I think I have that of the American Notes complete)[1] and will try to make the parcel better worth its long conveyance. With regard to Maclise's pictures, you certainly are quite right in your impression of them; but he is "such a discursive devil", (as he says of himself) and flies off at such odd tangents that I feel it difficult to convey to you any general notion of his purpose. I will try to do so, when I write again.[2]

I want very much to know about Howe[3] and that charming girl;[4] *cand to hear whether he has got as far as the finger (or squeezing) language yet.[5]c Give me full particulars. Will you remember me cordially to Sumner, and say I thank him for his welcome letter? The like to Hillard, with many regards to himself and *dmost sensibled* wife, with whom I had one night a little conversation which I shall not readily forget.[6] The like to Washington Allston, and all friends who care for me, and have outlived my book. *eKate joins me in earnest and affectionate remembrances to yourself and Mrs. Felton and your little daughters. So does Charley. So does Mary. So does Kate. So does Walter.e* Always My Dear Felton

> With true regard and affection Yours
> CHARLES DICKENS

To W. H. PRESCOTT, [28–31 DECEMBER 1842]

Mention in Prescott *to* CD, 30 Jan 43. *Date:* received by Prescott "by the last steamer", i.e. the *Caledonia*, which had sailed from Liverpool 4 Jan and arrived in Boston 25 Jan; CD clearly intended his other American letters of 28–31 Dec for the same boat.

About arrangements for the publication of Mme Calderón's book, and stating the amount Chapman & Hall proposed to advance.[7]

[1] If CD sent any MS pages of *American Notes* to Felton, he must have copied them specially; for the MS in the Forster Collection, V & A, is complete.

[2] See *To* Felton, 2 Mar 43, which virtually repeats this description.

[3] Name previously omitted.

[4] Julia Ward (see *To* Felton, 1 Sep 42, *fn*).

cc; dd; ee Not previously published.

[5] A joke referring to Howe's work with the deaf and dumb.

[6] CD was reported to have said that he liked Mrs Hillard better than any American lady he had met (S. I. Lesley, *Recollections of my Mother, Mrs. A. J. Lyman*, Boston, 1899, p. 378).

[7] "I received your note by the last steamer, and am much obliged by your kindness in taking charge of my protégé. Your publishers do not advance a very startling amount for the work", replied Prescott (*Correspondence of W. H. Prescott, 1833–1847*, ed. R. Wolcott, p. 329). See also *To* Prescott, 2 Mar 43. Prescott had already (15 Dec) thanked CD for the trouble he had taken over Mme Calderón's book, and in the same letter told him of the progress of his own work, *The Conquest of Mexico*: "I am hammering away on my old Aztecs and have nearly knocked their capital about their ears. They die game certainly, and one can't help feeling a sympathy for them, though they did occasionally fricassee a Christian or two,—'A slice of cold clergyman,' as Sydney Smith says" (*Correspondence, ibid.*).

To DANIEL MACLISE, [?LATE DECEMBER 1842]

Text from W. Justin O'Driscoll, *A Memoir of Daniel Maclise, R.A.*, 1871, p. 67.
Date: clearly soon after the "device" (see *To* Beard, 18 Dec and *fn*) was revealed to
Maclise, which must have been not long after the payment of the cheque to Beard
on 24 Dec, but later than *To* Maclise, 27 Dec, where the matter is not mentioned.

Do not be offended. I quite appreciate the feeling which induced you to
return what I sent you;[1] notwithstanding, I *must* ask you to take it back again.
If I could have contemplated for an instant the selfish engrossment of so much
of your time and extraordinary powers, I should have had no need (knowing you,
I knew that well) to resort to the little device[2] I played off. I will take anything
else from you at any time that you will give me, any scrap from your hand; but
I entreat you not to disturb this matter.[3] I am willing to be your debtor for
anything else in the whole wide range of your art, as you shall very readily find
whenever you put me to the proof.

To CLARKSON STANFIELD, [?1842]

Extract in Walter M. Hill catalogue No. 50 (1914); from Devonshire Terrace.
Date: Probably CD's thanks were for one (or both) of Stanfield's watercolour
drawings, *Land's End* and *The Logan Rock*,[4] done during the trip to Cornwall
Oct–Nov 42 (see *To* Felton, 31 Dec, *fn* p. 415).

My dear Stanfield
Many thanks for your most beautiful present, which I shall frame conspicuously, and prize, most highly.
Mrs. Dickens sends her best regards to Mrs. Stanfield and hopes she is
getting on well,

[1] Maclise had written: "My dear
Dickens, | How could *you* think of sending
me a cheque for what was to me a matter of
gratification? I am almost inclined to be
offended with you. May I not be permitted
to give some proof of the value I attach to
your friendship? I return the cheque, and
regret that you should have thought it
necessary to send it to yours faithfully, |
Daniel Maclise"(W. J. O'Driscoll, *A Memoir
of Daniel Maclise, R.A.*, pp. 66–7). According to O'Driscoll, the incident was concerned with the Nickleby portrait in 1839,
and his view was accepted by us in Vol. I,
p. 577 and *n*, where both letters are placed,
against the testimony of Forster (F, IV, i,
290 and *n*) who relates them to *A Girl at a
Waterfall*. But since it is known that
Chapman & Hall commissioned the
Nickleby portrait and gave it to CD
(*Catalogue of the . . . Pictures . . . of CD*,
ed. J. H. Stonehouse, p. 128, and cf. Kate
Perugini, "CD, as a Lover of Art and

Artists", *Magazine of Art*, Jan 1903, pp
127–9), Forster must be right.
[2] The letter, and Maclise's reply, are
also given in an article by J. W. T. Ley, *D*,
x (1914), 285–9; his source appears to be
O'Driscoll, but he gives "artifice" for
"device" (perhaps from the account in F,
IV, i, 290) and has other minor variants.
[3] Forster says CD "steadily refused to
take back the money which on discovery of
the artifice Maclise pressed upon him".
He accepted the pencil sketch of himself,
Catherine and Georgina made by Maclise
in Feb 43 (see *To* Forster, 12 Feb, *fn*), and
the "voluntary offering" of a portrait of
Catherine painted (according to Forster)
"four years later" (exhibited RA 1848).
The tone of both notes suggests that
Maclise was rather hurt by the whole
episode.
[4] See *Catalogue of the . . . Pictures . . .
of CD*, ed. J. H. Stonehouse, p. 125.

To COUNT D'ORSAY, 2 JANUARY 1843*

MS Comte de Gramont.

Devonshire Terrace | Second January 1843.
My Dear Count D'Orsay

Mrs. Dickens thinks the portrait,[1] "capital", and so do divers other domestic authorities who have seen it—though some protest that the lower part of the face is susceptible of improvement.

I have kept it thus long, to collect opinions.

Always Believe me | Faithfully Yours
Le Comte D'Orsay. CHARLES DICKENS

To FRANK STONE, 2 JANUARY [1843]*

MS Benoliel Collection. *Date:* 1842 impossible; clearly CD's error for 1843. Handwriting supports.

Devonshire Terrace | Second January 1842
My Dear Stone

Did you get a letter I wrote to you t'other day,[2] and forwarded Per Post, touching the next Twelfth Night as ever comes? If 'yes', well and good. If 'no', learn that you are expected here, *early* on that Evening.

Faithfully Yours always
Frank Stone Esquire CHARLES DICKENS

To LEIGH HUNT, 3 JANUARY 1843

MS Brotherton Library, Leeds.

1 Devonshire Terrace. | Third January 1843.
My Dear Hunt.

Next Friday—Twelfth Night—is the Anniversary of my Son and Heir's birthday; on which occasion, a Magic Lantern and divers other engines are going to be let off on these premises.

I have asked some children of a larger growth (all of whom you know)[3] to come and make merry on their own account. If you be well enough to join us, and

---

[1] The second of two profile portraits of CD by D'Orsay now in the Suzannet Collection at Dickens House; for the first, see Vol. II, p. 426*n.* A pencil drawing, half length, in profile to the left, signed by the artist and endorsed by him "the Best of the two"; dated 28 Dec 42 (reproduced in catalogue of centenary loan exhibition "Treasures from the Suzannet Collection" at Dickens House, 1970). The lower part of the face is still "susceptible of improvement".

[2] *To* Stone, 28 Dec.

[3] On the same day Catherine wrote to "My dear Mrs. Blanchard", inviting the Blanchards and their daughter (Lavinia, afterwards Mrs Blanchard Jerrold) at "about seven. We meet at that early hour, as Charles is going to exhibit a magic lantern for the amusement of the children" (MS Mr Douglas Jerrold).

will do so by half past seven, you will give my Wife and myself great pleasure, and (I think I may predict) Leigh Hunt no pain.

Always Faithfully Your friend

Leigh Hunt Esquire   CHARLES DICKENS

To FREDERICK MARRYAT, 3 JANUARY [1843]

Text from *Life and Letters of Captain Marryat*, ed. Florence Marryat, 1872, II, 118–9. *Date:* 6 Jan was Friday in 1843; and see *To* Hunt, above, and next. Misdated 1849 in N, II, 141.

Devonshire Terrace | January 3

My Dear Marryat,

Friday next—twelfth night—is the anniversary of my son and heir's birthday; on which occasion I am going to let off a magic lantern and other strong engines.

I have asked some children of a larger growth (nearly all of whom you know) to come and make merry. If you are in town, and will join us as early as half-past seven or so, you will give us *very great* pleasure.

Faithfully yours always,

CHARLES DICKENS

To FREDERICK MARRYAT, 3 JANUARY 1843*

MS Colegate University Library, New York.

Devonshire Terrace | Third January 1843

My Dear Marryat

As we old girls and boys will muster in sufficient strength to defend ourselves, on Friday; I can safely promise to give you some Supper. But I think it *would* be prudent if you were to dine before you come.

My son and heir is not (being of very tender years) a fast-goer in the reading way, yet: and consequently is not in the possession of Masterman Ready.[1] But I will undertake for his being very proud of the book as your gift, when he is much older. And if he be not Delighted with its contents, he is no son of mine —which, at present, I believe him to be. So don't forget it, please.

I will immediately remedy that dire mistake, concerning the American Notes.[2] I cannot conceive how it has arisen, but I am as much vexed, as if it were my own fault.

They sent *me* that Christian Book[3] too. Setting aside the incidental cant, I thought it a good article.

Always Faithfully Yours

Captain Marryat.   CHARLES DICKENS

---

[1] Vol. III was published on 22 Dec 42, completing the novel.
[2] Presumably Chapman & Hall had omitted to send Marryat a copy as directed: see *To* Marryat, 13 Oct 42.
[3] Unidentified.

To MISS BURDETT COUTTS, 6 JANUARY 1843*

MS Morgan Library. *Address:* Miss B Coutts (in Mrs Dickens's hand).

Devonshire Terrace | Friday Sixth January | 1843

Dear Miss Coutts

I shall be delighted to dine with you on Wednesday next—always supposing that the fatality which seems to have attended all my recent chances of seeing you, should so far relent, as to allow me to enjoy that pleasure.

Always Yours | Faithfully and obliged

Miss Coutts.   CHARLES DICKENS

To JOHN FORSTER, [8 JANUARY 1843]

Extract in F, IV, i, 292. *Date:* 8 Jan according to Forster.

I hope the number[1] will be very good. I have been hammering away, and at home all day. Ditto yesterday; except for two hours in the afternoon, when I ploughed through snow half a foot deep, round about the wilds of Willesden.

To [LADY BURDETT], 13 JANUARY 1843*

MS Chicago University Library.

1 Devonshire Terrace | Thirteenth January 1843.

Mr. Charles Dickens presents his compliments to [Lady Burdett][2] and begs to express (with Compliments to [Sir Francis])[3] the great regret it gives him to be already engaged on Monday, and therefore unable to dine in [Saint James's Place].[4]

Mr. Dickens begs, at the same time, to forward to [Lady Burdett], two very small Mineral Specimens from America, which he brought home expressly for [her]. The yellow piece, is Virginia Marble;[5] and the dark piece is from Niagara.[6] He brought it away from behind the Great Horse Shoe Fall, where it formed a portion of the cavern worn into the Rock by the mere spray of the Cascade in tumbling over from the height above. It has been saturated in its dismal home, for Ages.

To MISS HANNAH MEREDITH, 13 JANUARY 1843

MS Morgan Library.

1 Devonshire Terrace | Thirteenth Jany. 1843

Dear Miss Meredith

Pray thank Miss Coutts from me, for her kindness in respect of the box.

I am sorry I was not at home, and able to answer your note yesterday. I was

---

[1] *Chuzzlewit*, No. II: see *To* Miss Meredith, 13 Jan.

[2] See next; the name has been cut out.

[3] Name cut out.

[4] About 20 letters cut out.

[5] Small amounts of marble were found in Virginia.

[6] See *To* Miss Coutts, 2 July 42.

ploughing at a tremendous pace through the snow near Harrow, with Mr. Pinch on my right hand and the Pecksniffs on my left.[1]

To day I have sent Lady Burdett a piece (a very small one) of Niagara, and also a tiny scrap of Virginia Marble. As ill-luck would have it, I was already engaged for Monday.

Mrs. Dickens begs me to add her Compliments.

Always Believe Me

> (with the firm conviction that you will shortly dote
> (dramatically speaking) on Anderson)[2]

Faithfully Yours

Miss Meredith   CHARLES DICKENS

To JOHN TOMLIN,[3] 13 JANUARY 1843

Text from N, I, 503.

1 Devonshire Terrace, York Gate, Regent's Park, London
January 13, 1843.

Dear Sir,

I am much flattered by your having inscribed to me your very beautiful lines to Shelley's memory.[4] I have read them with very great pleasure, and like them exceedingly. I regret, however, that I cannot undertake to procure their insertion in a London Magazine, as I have no connection with any of them, and am obliged to make a rule never to address their Editors on behalf of other writers. If I did, I assure you they would have no rest; and I should be suffocated by favours of their conferring.

Always your faithful and obliged,

[CHARLES DICKENS]

To THE EDITOR OF *THE TIMES*, 15 JANUARY 1843

Text from *The Times*, 16 Jan 43.

1, Devonshire-Terrace, Sunday, Jan. 15.

Sir,

In your paper of Saturday you thought it worth while to refer to an article

---

[1] Both Pecksniff and Tom Pinch appear in Ch. 5 of No. II (Chs 4–5) with Martin's arrival as Pecksniff's pupil.

[2] At Drury Lane during Jan he was playing Faulconbridge in *King John*, Cassio in *Othello*, Posthumus in *Cymbeline* and Orlando in *As You Like It*.

[3] John Tomlin (1806–50), American autograph collector: see Vol. II, p. 217*n*.

[4] The poem, in 13 stanzas and with no dedication to CD, was published in the Washington *National Intelligencer* of 22 July 43 and subsequently in *Shelley's Grave, and Other Poems*, privately printed, 1845, and noticed in the *Broadway Journal*, New York, 12 Apr 45. Presumably Tomlin wished the poem, if published in an English magazine, to be inscribed to CD as another defender of liberty.

on my *American Notes* published in the recent number of the *Edinburgh Review*,[1] for the purpose of commenting on a statement of the reviewer's in reference to the English and American press, with which I have no further concern than that I know it to be a monstrous likening of unlike things.[2]

I am anxious to give another misrepresentation made by the same writer, whosoever he may be,—which *is* personal to myself,—the most public and positive contradiction in my power; and I shall be really obliged to you if you will allow me to do this through the medium of your columns.

He asserts "That if he be rightly informed, I went to America as a kind of missionary in the cause of international copyright."[3] I deny it wholly. He is wrongly informed; and reports, without inquiry, a piece of information which I could only characterize by using one of the shortest and strongest words in the language. Upon my honour the assertion is destitute of any particle, aspect, or colouring of truth.

[1] The review in the January number (CLIV, 497–522) by James Spedding (1808–81; *DNB*), formerly at the Colonial Office, friend of Thackeray, Tennyson, Carlyle, and Milnes, and editor of Bacon. Collected with a few revisions in his *Reviews and Discussions*, 1879, with a long note recounting the resultant controversy; extracts from his correspondence with Napier; and a defence of his position using passages from CD's letters in Forster's *Life*. Spedding, who had been a contributor since 1836, wrote it at short notice "by the editor's express desire" (*Reviews*, p. 270): see *To* Napier, 26 July 42, *fn*. His obvious qualification was his recent experience of America as secretary to Lord Ashburton's boundary mission (see *To* Forster, 27 Feb 42, *fn*). The review was less favourable than Napier expected, and some of the severer passages were struck out, but it remained disparaging or at best patronizing almost throughout; began by emphasizing CD's "considerable disadvantages" in his "desultory education", and his satiric and fanciful bent; the book lacked sound knowledge, was the result of hurried and superficial observation, and showed CD's "habitual exaggeration". Samuel Warren classed this review with Croker's in the *Quarterly* (Mar 43) and that in *Fraser's* (Nov 42; see *To* Ouseley, 8 Nov, *fn*): "three such reviews . . . must do Dickens tremendous mischief" (MS letter, 12 Mar 43; quoted in K. J. Fielding, "*American Notes* and some English Reviewers", *Modern Language Review*, LIX [1964], 527–37, the fullest discussion of the whole matter).

[2] Spedding declined to comment on the justice of CD's censures of the American press, "not having ourselves gone through the nauseous course of reading by which he has qualified himself to speak", but argued at some length that slander and misrepresentation were also common in the English press, and that readers were to blame: "We cannot but regard the condition of our own Daily Press, as a morning and evening witness against the moral character of the people". The *Times* leader of 14 Jan, over a column long, opened its defence by quoting this sentence, and suggested that such a view did not come well from the *Edinburgh*. See *To* Brougham, 25 Jan, and *To* Felton, 2 Mar and *fn*.

[3] See *Edinburgh Review*, CLIV, 500; to Spedding, this was another of CD's disqualifications—"the study of America does not appear to have been his primary object in going, nor his main business while there". The cause of International Copyright "must be presumed . . . to have chiefly occupied his thoughts", and in this "he decidedly failed"; to which Spedding attributed the omission of all reference to the matter in *American Notes*. CD's own account is confirmed by his earlier letters; but he had laid himself open to misconstruction by a passage in his Hartford speech (see *To* Forster, 24 Feb, *fn*). What Spedding claimed that he originally wrote, and restored when he collected the review, was a shade less objectionable: "He is understood to have gone out as a kind of missionary" instead of "He went out, if we are rightly informed, . . ."

It occurred to me to speak (as other English travellers connected with literature have done before me) of the existing laws—or rather want of laws—on the subject of international copyright, when I found myself in America, simply because I had never hesitated to denounce their injustice while at home; because I thought it a duty to English writers, that their case should be fairly represented; and because, inexperienced at that time in the American people, I believed that they would listen to the truth, even from one presumed to have an interest in stating it, and would no longer refuse to recognize a principle of common honesty, even though it happened to clash with a miserably short-sighted view of their own profit and advantage.

I am, Sir, your obliged servant

CHARLES DICKENS

To MISS BURDETT COUTTS, 16 JANUARY 1843†

MS Morgan Library.

Devonshire Terrace | Monday Sixteenth Jany. | 1843.

Dear Miss Coutts

I am very sorry to say that we, only yesterday, made an engagement for Wednesday. I was not much disposed to contemplate it with satisfaction then; but now I hate it.

Mr. Penn[1] made an engagement to call on me on Wednesday Morning, "to talk about America". I find I shall not have finished my Number by that time, and must put him off. As I don't know his address, if Miss Meredith would kindly convey this piece of information to him on my behalf, per post—adding that I shall be glad to see him any day next week he may appoint—she would bind me to her for ever.

Your note finds me in Mr. Pinch's society. He seems comfortable and in good spirits: having a holiday.[2]

Always believe me | Dear Miss Coutts | Faithfully Yours

Miss Coutts   CHARLES DICKENS

P.S. Mrs. Dickens begs me to present her compliments, and to express her regrets.

To MRS M'IAN, 16 JANUARY 1843*

MS Private.

Devonshire Terrace | Monday Sixteenth Jany. | 1843.

Dear Mrs. Mc Ian

I am greatly obliged to you for your kind Note, and will certainly do myself the pleasure of calling tomorrow.

---

[1] Probably Richard Penn (1784–1863; *DNB*), a civil servant in the Colonial Office, and author of *Maxims and Hints for an Angler* (1833, reprinted 1839), illustrated by Seymour, and of other works; a cousin of Granville Penn, of Stoke Park, and descended from William Penn, founder of Pennsylvania; known to Crabb Robinson (MS Diary, Dr Williams's Library).

[2] In Ch. 5, Tom Pinch goes to Salisbury to meet Martin.

I hope your face is better.

Always believe me | Faithfully Yours

Mrs. Mc Ian CHARLES DICKENS

To HENRY AUSTIN, 17 JANUARY 1843*

MS Morgan Library.

Devonshire Terrace | Tuesday Seventeenth Jany. 1843

My Dear Henry

Mitton is going to dine with me at the Jack Straw's Castle at Hampstead, on Friday next, when I shall most likely have the new No. in my pocket. Will you be my only other guest? If so, let us meet at his place in Southampton Buildings at 3, and I will drive you up there.

With love to Letitia, | Always Affectionately

Henry Austin Esquire CD.

To R. R. M'IAN,[1] 17 JANUARY 1843*

MS Huntington Library.

Devonshire Terrace. | Seventeenth January 1843

My Dear Sir

I am perfectly *delighted* with the Sketches[2] you have so kindly sent me. I will swear to their truthfulness, at all times and seasons, and am proud to possess them. Thank you, heartily.

There seems to be some spell against my calling in Coram Street,[3] for I have twice been kept in double irons at home, when I have been coming to you. Will you and Mrs. Mc Ian reverse the venture, and promise to come to us next Wednesday at Six exactly? That is our dinner-hour. We have either no party at all, or a very, very, small one.

Always Faithfully Yours

R. R. Mc Ian Esquire. CHARLES DICKENS

---

[1] Robert Ronald M'Ian (1803–56; *DNB*), actor and painter: see Vol. II, p. 309*n*. Last recorded as acting in Aug 42 in Murray's company at Edinburgh, where he played Dougal in *Rob Roy* (J. C. Dibdin, *Annals of the Edinburgh Stage*, Edinburgh, 1888, p. 384). One of his paintings from Highland history was exhibited at the RA 1843; *The Clans of the Scottish Highlands*, illustrated from his original sketches, was published 1845; toured Scotland with the Samuel Carter Halls in 1845–6 for a projected book, never published (S. C. Hall, *Retrospect of a Long Life*, 1883, II, 268–91).

[2] Presumably of Scotland.

[3] The M'Ians lived at 9 Great Coram Street.

To THOMAS MITTON, [17 JANUARY 1843]*

MS Huntington Library. *Date:* the Tuesday before Fri 20 Jan 43; see *fn.*
Handwriting supports.

Devonshire Terrace | Tuesday Morning
My Dear Mitton
Unless Friday will be too late for Parbury purposes,[1] I should like to appoint that morning at your own hour. If Thursday would be better, I *can* (but not so conveniently) make it that day instead.

Faithfully Always

Thomas Mitton Esquire   CD

To [JOSEPH] ABLETT,[2] 19 JANUARY 1843*

MS Yale University Library.

1 Devonshire Terrace. | York Gate Regents Park
Nineteenth Jany. 1843.

Mr. Charles Dickens presents his compliments to Mr. Ablett, and begs, with many thanks, to acknowledge the receipt of his kind cheque on the London and Westminster for Two Pounds, in aid of the Subscription for the Widow and family[3] of the late Mr. Hone.

---

[1] J. W. Parbury (of Parbury, Thacker & Co., East India agents, 41 Threadneedle Street) had evidently been consulted by Mitton about a legal representative in Calcutta to prevent the infringement of copyright of *Chuzzlewit*; his letter of 19 Jan, addressed to "Chapman and Hall *or* Messrs Smithson and Mitton" (MS Mrs D. Danby), proposed the name of "Mr. Philip Peard—he being the partner, and now only representative of the firm employed by the Booksellers of Calcutta to move in the matter of copyright in the year 1837". It was necessary for CD to execute a "Deed or Letter of Attorney" in favour of Peard, accompanied by a "Declaration verifying copy of registration of proprietorship of Copyright of Book and also of due execution of Power of Attorney". Drafts of both documents survive (MSS Mrs D. Danby), accompanied by a draft letter of Attorney for use in the Dominions which Chapman & Hall had had drawn up (apparently for any of their books) and on which they obtained counsel's opinion from James Bacon, dated 27 Dec 42; Bacon had advised that a Declaration would be necessary, verified "by some

person whose signature is known in the Colony". A receipted bill, dated 20 Jan, which includes the item "East India Secretary's legality and fee 8.0", and a pencilled annotation "George Parbury" on the draft Deed, shows that one of the firm verified CD's Declaration. CD and Chapman & Hall, as joint proprietors of the copyright (see Vol. II, p. 480), hoped to prevent the printing of unauthorized Indian editions such as had been common for his earlier novels (Arents Collection, New York Public Library, has *The New Series. Sketches by Boz*, Calcutta, Published by the Booksellers, 1837).

[2] Probably Joseph Ablett of Llanbedr Hall, Denbigh (*d.* 1848), editor of the privately printed *Literary Hours: by Various Friends*, 1837, containing work by Landor, a lifelong friend who spoke highly of his great kindness and generosity; known also to Forster since about 1836.

[3] Ablett had presumably received a personal letter or printed circular from the appeal committee formed shortly after Hone's death: see *To* Committee of the Literary Fund, 12 Nov 42; *To* Black, 15 Nov 42 and *fn.*

To WILLIAM DAY,[1] 19 JANUARY 1843†

MS Benoliel Collection.

Private

1 Devonshire Terrace | York Gate Regents Park
Nineteenth January 1843

My Dear Sir.

Let me thank you for the proof of the letter you have addressed to me;[2] which I received, by your favor, this morning. I have read it with the greatest satisfaction. And though I cannot lay claim to the merit you would give me; for doing so slight a thing as denouncing Slavery on any terms, but especially in co-existence with that monstrous Lie, the declaration of American Independence; still I cannot but feel proud of your approval and Good opinion.

Faithfully Yours

William Day Esquire   CHARLES DICKENS

To MRS FRANCES TROLLOPE, 19 JANUARY 1843†

MS Berg Collection.

Devonshire Terrace | York Gate Regents Park
Nineteenth Jany. 1843

My Dear Mrs. Trollope.

Do, in the name of all the live physic[3] in the World, read *my* letter from your esteemed correspondent! And when you have done so, kindly send it back to me: for it is too good to be lost.

What do you suppose the delicate readers of books (whose ears, as Mrs. Slipslop[4] says, are the delicatest parts about them) would have said, if you had imagined such a case as this, in your Domestic Manners?

I am much pleased by your communicating the matter to me: and can only feel gratified by your making any mention of me you please, to this, or any other skulker under the Black Flag of Literature.

But it is right I should tell you, at the same time, that I have not yet learned that there is any *general* intention of abstaining from the custom of selling early

---

[1] William Day, miscellaneous writer, of Exeter; formerly editor of *The Christian's Friend* and the *Jersey Argus*. Author of a pamphlet, *Slavery in America Shown to be Peculiarly Abominable*, 1841 (2nd edn, 1857), dedicated to Thomas Clarkson; a copy was given to CD "with the Author's respectful compliments" (*Catalogue of the Library of CD*, ed. J. H. Stonehouse, p. 88).

[2] His letter to CD appeared in the *Western Times* of 28 Jan 43, dated 17 Jan from New North Road, Exeter; beginning by referring to "the fashion among some people to think that whatever passes under the *name* of freedom must be deserving of admiration" and to their defence of slavery, he congratulated CD on the courage and independence of his "manly observations" in *American Notes* and quoted from it at length; he rejoiced in the extensive circulation of CD's work in America, and hoped some of the slave-owners might be converted.

[3] Probably leeches, in reference to the bloodsucking habits of American publishers.

[4] In *Joseph Andrews*, Book I, Ch. 9, Mrs Slipslop says "people's ears are sometimes the nicest part about them".

proofs when they are asked for, on the other side. Indeed I know of nobody save myself who has come to that resolution.

Always Believe me | Dear Mrs. Trollope
Faithfully Yours

Mrs. Trollope.   CHARLES DICKENS

P.S. I have sent Mr. T. J. Marshall,[1] this letter from my Solicitors.

Sir

We are requested by our client, Mr. Charles Dickens, to inform you, that having had an opportunity of comparing your letter to him of the 13th. Instant, with another (to a similar purpose, but couched in a very different tone) which you addressed elsewhere on the very next day; he would consider himself degraded by holding any communication with you.

We have it further in request from Mr. Dickens, to acquaint you, that if you address him again, your letter will be returned, unopened, to the Post Office; and that your letter of the 13th. would have been sent back to you herewith, but that it is probable Mr. Dickens may want it for reference hereafter.

Smithson and Mitton
23 Southampton Buildings.

To SIR ROBERT INGLIS,[2] 21 JANUARY 1843

Mention in Stan Henkels catalogue No. 1297 (1922); dated Devonshire Terrace, 21 Jan 43.

Regretting his inability to accept an invitation.

To FREDERICK MARRYAT, 21 JANUARY 1843*

Facsimile, Nicolas Rauch S.A. Geneva (Auction catalogue No. 13).

1 Devonshire Terrace | Twenty First Jany. 1843

My Dear Marryat.

I have always been on friendly terms with Bulwer, but I am by no means pleased with his having taken no notice of my International Copyright letter. I held my Gauntlet somewhat toughly to Jonathan's nose, and should have deserved better of the Baronet though I had been a stranger.

---

[1] Untraced; probably the London agent of an American publisher, who had perhaps threatened Mrs Trollope with reprisals if she did not supply early proofs of *The Barnabys in America*, serialized in the *New Monthly* Apr 42 to Sep 43, or of *Jessie Phillips*, of which the first monthly No. had appeared 31 Dec 42.

[2] Sir Robert Harry Inglis (1786–1855; *DNB*), politician: see Vol. II, p. 167*n*. Held breakfasts and weekly conversaziones, to which he invited many literary and scientific figures, including Babbage (Frederick Pollock, *Personal Remembrances*, 1887, I, 187; letter of 25 Nov 41).

Therefore I will not sign his paper;[1] the rather as it seems to me to be an unnecessary kind of flourish, importing that we mean to do, what we can do very well, without blast of trumpet.

Mrs. Dickens and her sister beg to be well remembered to you. We are going to Bath[2] today, but shall be home again in the middle of the week.

Always My Dear Marryat | Faithfully Yours

CHARLES DICKENS

To MACVEY NAPIER, 21 JANUARY 1843

MS British Museum.

London. 1 Devonshire Terrace | York Gate Regents Park.
Twenty First January 1843.

My Dear Sir.

In acknowledging the receipt of your two letters, let me hasten to say, in the fullest and most explicit manner, that you have acted a most honorable, open, fair, and manly part in the matter of my complaint;[3] for which I beg you to accept my best thanks, and the assurance of my friendship and regard.

---

[1] A notice prepared by Bulwer and G. P. R. James, informing circulating libraries that, if they continued to stock and hire out foreign reprints of English copyright books, they would be liable under Section 17 of the Customs and Excise Act of 9 July (see *To* Murray, 2 Aug 42, *fn*). Bulwer and James had enlisted the support of Marryat. (Information kindly given by Mr James J. Barnes; for further details see his forthcoming *Authors, Publishers, and Politicians: The Quest for an Anglo-American Copyright Agreement, 1815–54*). James must have been well up in the subject; his article "Some Observations on the Book Trade, as Connected with Literature, in England", which appeared the following month (*Journal of the Royal Statistical Society*, VI, 50–60), illustrated the harm done to sales of English works both in England and the colonies, especially from French reprints—Baudry and Galignani of Paris had depots at Calais and Boulogne, advertised delivery to England and paid travellers to take books in.

[2] See *To* Smale, 3 Feb. The nature of his unexpected business is not known; possibly connected with John Dickens, whose movements since Oct 42 are obscure (*To* Mitton, 7 Dec 42 and *fn*). It must have been urgent for them to miss Georgina's 16th birthday on 22 Jan. Two Bath weeklies, the *Bath and Cheltenham Gazette* (24 Jan) and the *Bath Chronicle* (25 Jan),

noted "Mr. and Mrs. Charles Dickens" among the arrivals at York House. They returned on 24 Jan (see *To* Brougham, 25 Jan).

[3] Napier had evidently written to CD immediately on seeing his letter to *The Times* (16 Jan) and again on hearing from Spedding who wrote to him the same day. Spedding declined to retract, but said he had not suspected that CD "should be so angry"; he offered to let Napier mention him as responsible "if it would be any satisfaction to you or tend to set your relations with him on a comfortable footing again". His defence was that "in America at least, there was a very general impression that he came chiefly to urge the cause of international copyright" and he distinctly remembered "the word 'mission' somewhere applied to his visit". He also cited a letter written by CD "to a Washington paper before he left America" (Napier papers, MS BM)—presumably the *National Intelligencer*, 10 May. In answering, Napier said that as Spedding spoke "without any *direct* authority", CD had "good reason to complain", and that Napier had offered "for *publication*, if he thinks it worth while, a *retractation* of the offensive statement"; he had not given CD Spedding's name, but had "quoted what you urge to me as the grounds of belief". For Spedding's further letter, saying that he did not regard "Missionary" as a disparag-

I would on no account, publish the letter you have sent me for that purpose; as I conceive that doing so, I should not reciprocate the spirit in which you have written to me privately. But if you should, upon consideration, think it not inexpedient to set the Review right in regard to this point of fact, by a note in the next number,[1] I should be glad to see it there.

In reference to the article itself (which I consider now, as I need hardly say, quite apart from you) it did, by repeating this statement, hurt my feelings excessively; and is, in this respect, I still conceive, most unworthy of its author. I am at no loss to divine who its author is.[2] I _know_ he read in some cut-throat American paper, this and other monstrous statements, which I could at any time have converted into sickening praise by the payment of some fifty dollars. I know that he is perfectly aware that his statement in the Review, in corroboration of these Lies, will be disseminated through the whole of the United States; and that my contradiction will never be heard of. And though I care very little for the opinion of any person who will set the statement of an American Editor (almost invariably an atrocious scoundrel) against my character and conduct, such as they may be; still, my sense of Justice does revolt from this most cavalier and careless exhibition of me to a whole people, as a traveller under false pretences, and a disappointed intriguer.

The better the acquaintance with America, the more defenceless and more inexcusable such conduct is. For I solemnly declare (and appeal to any man, but the Writer of this Paper, who has travelled in that country; for confirmation of my statement) that the source from which he drew the "Information" so recklessly put forth again in England, is infinitely more obscene, disgusting, and brutal, than the very worst Sunday newspaper that has ever been printed in Great Britain.—Conceive the Edinburgh Review, quoting "The Satirist", or "The Man about Town", as an authority against a man with one grain of honor or feather-weight of reputation!

With regard to yourself, let me say again that I thank you with all sincerity and heartiness; and fully acquit you of everything but kind and generous intentions towards me. In proof of which, I do assure you that I am even more

---

ing term, and his later defence of his sources in "the general conversation of Washington", see _Reviews and Discussions_, 1879, pp. 271–6, where extracts from the correspondence are given, those from Spedding's letters being from his own drafts.

[1] As there was an extra number of the _Edinburgh_ in Feb, the note appeared very soon: "NOTE _to the Article on_ Mr DICKENS'S '_American Notes,' in No._ 154. | In the above article we happened to state that Mr Dickens went to America as a 'Missionary in the cause of International Copyright.' We have since found that we were misinformed in saying so. We had no intention, however, to disparage a gentleman whose character and genius we alike esteem, by that statement. We thought the cause a good cause, and that we had sufficient authority for what was stated. But as it would be very wrong to ascribe Mr Dickens's visit to America to an erroneous cause, we willingly retract the statement, and regret that it was made" (CLV, 301).

[2] He was convinced it was Lord Morpeth (_To_ Brougham, 25 Jan), who had been in North America for a year, from Autumn 1841. Napier had evidently referred to the author's recent extended visit, and CD, who had been hoping to meet Morpeth there (see _To_ Lady Holland, 17 Dec 41), drew the wrong conclusion.

desirous than before, to write for the Review, and to find some topic which would at once please me, and you.

My Dear Sir I am always | Faithfully Yours

Professor Napier CHARLES DICKENS[1]

To LORD BROUGHAM, 25 JANUARY 1843*

MS Brotherton Library, Leeds.

1 Devonshire Terrace | York Gate Regents Park
Twenty Fifth January 1843.

Dear Lord Brougham.

I have been passing a few days at Bath; on my return from which place, last night, I found your kind letter.[2] I address my answer to your town residence: hoping, from what you tell me of your movements, that you are already on your way home.

The first information I had of that mighty cool and reckless statement in the Edinburgh review (taken, by the bye, from the most atrocious of the American Newspapers;[3] which I could have silenced at any time by the payment of a pound or two; or by consenting—which I never would—to receive the Editor) was brought to me last Saturday Week. I immediately wrote a letter to the Times, giving it the flattest and strongest contradiction I could put into words. I did not write to Napier, because I knew; having always been on friendly terms with him; that he was kindly disposed towards me. And I was apprehensive that by doing so, I might occasion some difference between him and Jeffrey, who, I also knew, was very favourable to the book, in his affectionate regard for me.

But the next Post brought me a long, and very honorable letter, from Napier himself: giving me the whole history of the Notice (except the Writer's name) and expressing his very great regret. He enclosed a second letter; for publication if I desired; retracting the assertion most explicitly and fully. I wrote him back, that I would on no account publish it, as I did not think I should, in doing so, respond to the manly spirit in which he had written to me. But that if he thought it not inexpedient to correct the statement by a note in the next No. of the review, I should be glad to see it there.

I have not the least doubt of the review having been written by Lord Morpeth.[4] Not the slightest in the world.

[1] Thomas Longman, publisher of the *Edinburgh*, who had thought CD's letter to *The Times* "petulant" and "bombastic", was shown the present letter, and agreed that it "does him great credit. He is no doubt a good-hearted fellow" (Longman *to* Napier, 17 and 30 Jan 43; MSS BM).

[2] Brougham wrote to Napier from Paris on 22 Jan, expressing sympathy with CD: "I can take upon me to say he had no kind of mission—and you should correct this next No—as he will be much vexed" (MS BM), and presumably wrote to CD at about the same time.

[3] Probably the notorious *New York Herald*, edited by James Gordon Bennett (see *To* Forster, 24 Feb 42 and *fn* p. 84), the *Rowdy Journal* of *Chuzzlewit*, Ch. 16.

[4] For CD's discovery that this was not so, see *To* Lady Holland, 28 Feb.

The English Press[1] is bad enough—a great part of it, very bad—but it can no more be compared with the American Journalism, than a silver fork can be likened to a bowie knife, or a gold bracelet to an iron handcuff. I firmly believe it has no parallel in the history of the World. And I hope to God it never may have.

I quite agree with you in your estimate of the power of newspapers at home, in the long run. But in the short run—the trot of the day—they can be Angel or Devil—as the humour seizes them—with vast effect, I think.

I am always | My Dear Lord
Yours faithfully and obliged

The Lord Brougham.   CHARLES DICKENS

To ALBANY FONBLANQUE, 25 JANUARY 1843

Mention in unidentified catalogue, New York Public Library, and in N, 1, 505; *MS* 1 p.; dated Devonshire Terrace, 25 Jan 43 (date in N); signed initials.

Bitterly attacking Lord Morpeth for writing a review.

To W. M. THACKERAY,[2] 26 JANUARY 1843

MS Comtesse de Suzannet.

Devonshire Terrace | Twenty Sixth January 1843.

My Dear Thackeray
    I have been at Bath for some few days.—Remember, that I expect you to dinner on Sunday, at Six, sharp. No party.

Faithfully Yours
CHARLES DICKENS

---

[1] Brougham approved the reviewer's strictures on the English press, "tho' only 1/100 of the truth", and thought CD's one error was "not looking to the *moat* in our own eye—because the Yankees have a beam" (Brougham *to* Napier, MS BM).

[2] William Makepeace Thackeray (1811–63; *DNB*): see Vol. I, p. 305*n*. He had just returned from a visit to his family in Paris, and was leading a bachelor life owing to his wife's mental breakdown in 1840, while maintaining himself by literary journalism. Had gained some reputation with *The Paris Sketch Book*, July 40, followed by the less successful *Second Funeral of Napoleon*, Jan 41, and his two volumes of *Comic Tales & Sketches*, Apr 41; was writing stories, reviews, and art criticisms for *Fraser's*, several papers for the *Foreign Quarterly Review* under Forster's editorship in 1842–4, and in June 1842 began contributing to *Punch*. By March he was "making lots of drawings and the Punch people are beginning at last to find out that they are good" (*Letters and Private Papers*, ed. G. N. Ray, II, 97). As yet there were no signs of disagreement with CD, despite some critical references to *Oliver Twist* in *Catherine* (1839–40); he had regretted his inability to be one of "the welcomers" on CD's return from America, as he was on his way to Ireland, where he toured for four months and wrote *The Irish Sketch Book*, published May 1843 (see *To* Thackeray, 6–18 May 43). For his sketch of the expedition to Cornwall, see *To* Felton, 31 Dec 42, *fn*.

To RICHARD LANE,[1] 30 JANUARY 1843*

MS Birthplace Museum, Portsmouth.

Monday Morng | January 30th. | 1843

My Dear Sir

Tomorrow at eleven will suit me excellently well.

I am very sorry that "Mercy"[2] arrived when I was dressing; and that I could not therefore have the pleasure of becoming personally acquainted with her. But I count on having that gratification before long.

My Dear Sir | Faithfully Yours

Richard Lane Esquire   CHARLES DICKENS

To CLARKSON STANFIELD, 30 JANUARY [1843]

MS Chas J. Sawyer Ltd. *Date:* 1843 on handwriting.

Victoria By The Grace of God Queen Defender of The Faith, to her trusty subjects John Forster and Charles Dickens, Greeting.

This is to will and require you, the said John Forster and Charles Dickens to have in your safe keeping, at No 1 Devonshire Terrace on this present Thirtieth day of January at half past five exactly, the body of Clarkson Stanfield, Royal Academician, and him in safe Custody to keep and hold, until the said Clarkson has taken his fill of certain Meat, to wit hashed Venison from America, and has washed down the same with certain liquors, to wit fermented liquors, provided at the said Charles Dickens' proper cost and charge.

Herein fail not at your peril.

Countersigned   Victoria.

CHARLES DICKENS
JOHN FORSTER

To RICHARD LANE, 31 JANUARY 1843*

MS Mr L. C. Hopkins.

Devonshire Terrace | Thirty First January 1843

My Dear Sir

I am obliged to be the postponer, this morning. In the hurry of writing

---

[1] Richard James Lane (1800–1872; *DNB*), line-engraver and lithographer, brother of Edward Lane (translator of the *Arabian Nights*) and great-uncle of Gerard Manley Hopkins. Articled to Charles Heath; ARA 1827; lithographer to the Queen 1837; best known for his chalk portraits, including one of Queen Victoria, aged 10, and others of the Royal Family; also for his numerous lithographs for well-known artists, including Leslie and Landseer. Married Sophia Hodges 1825 and in 1843 was living at 11 Chester Place, Regent's Park; a friend of Macready and of D'Orsay. According to Leonardo Catter-

mole (F. G. Kitton, *CD by Pen & Pencil*, 1, 36), met CD at George Cattermole's house on various "convivial occasions" and was inspired by the idea of "taking his portrait". This was exhibited at the RA 1843; purchased by Cattermole, and after CD's death, on Lytton's suggestion, offered to the Queen; now in the Royal collection at Windsor. For reproductions see B. W. Matz's edition of Forster's *Life*, 1911, 1, 170, and *D*, xv (1919) and xliv (1948).

[2] Possibly someone thought to resemble Mercy Pecksniff, described in detail in *Chuzzlewit*, Ch. 2.

to you yesterday, I forgot an engagement which compels me to ask whether tomorrow at the same hour will suit you instead of today.

Faithfully Yours

Richard. J. Lane Esquire   CHARLES DICKENS

To ANDREW BELL, 1 FEBRUARY 1843*

MS Morgan Library. *Address:* Andrew Bell Esquire | 23 Liverpool Terrace | Islington.

1 Devonshire Terrace, | York Gate Regents Park
First February 1843

My Dear Sir

I thank you for your gratifying letter; and for the loan of the enclosed sketches.[1] They have pleased me very much. I know something of Coal Heavers, and of the hostelry you mention in that paper. There is another in Milbank[2]—not very far from Abingdon Street; on the left hand side of the way, as you go towards Vauxhall Bridge. It is a famous house.[3] There is a heaver who uses it, who, in his sober moments is a merry fellow, but who, after his eighth or ninth pot (I am not sure which) becomes rather maudlin and Byronical. You will find him in this state any night when the clock strikes Twelve, staggering past the great lamp-post in the Strand, opposite Northumberland House, and crying "I'm a bloody orphan!" in accents full of grief. This is really a fact. He never says more, and never less; is a sturdy, broad-shouldered, honest fellow; fifty years old, or more; sensitive to a fault in porter, but quite a plain man out of it.

I owe you an apology for having thought you hard on the Americans.[4] Accept it from me, in my improved and clearer sight. Your dedication to Peel stuck in my throat; and I thought (perhaps still think) that you lost sight of the fact that the Republic had its growth—not in liberal principles, but in the wrongest-headed Toryism and the obstinacy of that swine-headed anointed of the Lord—his Majesty King George The Third. But for him it might have been a very different place at this hour.

The note you are free to use.[5] I wish it were better worth your using. Such as it is, it is heartily at your service.

Faithfully Yours always

Andrew Bell Esquire   CHARLES DICKENS

---

[1] Not identified.

[2] Thus in MS.

[3] There were many public-houses in Millbank, four of which were close to the coal-heavers' wharves. There is a description of a coal-heaver in "a water-side tap-room" by Thomas Miller in *Gavarni in London*, ed. Albert Smith, 1849.

[4] In *Men and Things in America*, 1838: see *To* Bell, 12 Oct 41 and *n* (II, 402).

[5] Possibly a note to a publisher or editor on behalf of Bell's sketches.

To W. CARPENTER,[1] 1 FEBRUARY 1843

Mention in Waller catalogue No. 124 (1879); dated Devonshire Terrace, 1 Feb 43.

Declining the Presidentship of the Literary and Dramatic Fund.[2]

To JOHN DE GEX,[3] 1 FEBRUARY 1843

MS Bernard Quaritch Ltd. *Address:* John De Gex Esquire| 5 New Square | Lincolns Inn.

Devonshire Terrace. | First February 1843.

My Dear De Gex.

I am very sorry I missed you t'other day.

You have done quite right, I think, in deciding to run the hazard of the die.[4] I need not say that I shall drop my white ball into the box,[5] vigorously.

I never ask men to vote for a friend, when the voting is by ballot, nor do I ever respond to those who ask that favor of me: as I hold it to be inconsistent with the ballot to have any negociation on such a subject. But if anybody ask me whether I know you, I will give that report of you which dwelleth within me.

Always Believe me | Faithfully Yours

John De Gex Esquire.   CHARLES DICKENS

To DR SOUTHWOOD SMITH, 1 FEBRUARY 1843

MS Boston Public Library.

Devonshire Terrace | First February 1843

My Dear Dr. Smith

I have read the enclosed with great pain, and with a foreknowledge of its entire Truth.

I fear, however, that I cannot take up the subject.[6] Firstly and mainly, because I am fully engaged in doing my best for similar objects by different means.[7] And secondly, because this question involves the whole subject of the

---

[1] William Carpenter (1797–1874; *DNB*), miscellaneous writer; interested in political reform and imprisoned for his unstamped *Political Letters* 1831; edited various periodicals including the *Railway Observer* 1843, *Lloyd's Weekly News* 1844, and the *Court Journal* 1848.

[2] The Literary and Dramatic Fund Association, a benevolent fund established late in 1842, held its first meeting on 6 June 43; Benjamin Bond Cabbell was President; and the vice-presidents included T. S. Duncombe, MP, Sheridan Knowles and Douglas Jerrold (*Court Journal*, 10 June 43). Carpenter was secretary.

[3] John Peter De Gex (1809–87), barrister and law reporter: see Vol. II, p. 423*n*.

[4] "And I will stand the hazard of the die" (*Richard III*, v, iv, 9).

[5] Possibly for the Athenæum; but De Gex was not one of the three new members elected. The other possibility is the Parthenon, of which little is known (see Vol. I, p. 380*n*).

[6] The Second Report of the Children's Employment Commission (see *To* Southwood Smith, 6 Mar) was completed by 30 Jan, but not published until the end of Feb. The summary, of which a copy was in the Gad's Hill library at CD's death, was presumably published at the same time and can hardly be referred to here. Southwood Smith had probably communicated his conclusions to CD in the hope that he would write an article or pamphlet after the Report was published.

[7] Not clear what this refers to, as *Chuzzlewit* does not bear on the subject.

condition of the mass of people in this country. And I greatly fear that until Governments are honest, and Parliaments pure, and Great men less considered, and small men more so, it is almost a Cruelty to limit, even the dreadful hours and ways[1] of Labor which at this time prevail. Want is so general, distress so great, and Poverty so rampant—it is, in a word, so hard for the Million to live by any means—that I scarcely know how we can step between them, and one weekly farthing. The necessity of a mighty change, I clearly see; and yet I cannot reconcile it to myself to reduce the earnings of any family—their means of existence being now so very scant and spare.

I shall be very glad to see the evidence,[2] and to have an opportunity of studying it. It will not fall on rocky ground if you send it here, I think.

Always Faithfully Yours

Dr. Southwood Smith   CHARLES DICKENS

To T. B. L. BAKER,[3] 3 FEBRUARY 1843*

MS Miss Olive K. Lloyd-Baker. *Address:* T. B. G.[4] Baker Esquire | Hardwicke Court.

Private.   London. 1 Devonshire Terrace | York Gate Regents Park.

Third February 1843

Dear Sir.

I am much indebted to you for your interesting note.[5] The Gloucestershire facts were quite unknown to me. The sad history of Captain Brenton and his Institution,[6] I was perfectly acquainted with. But I feared to make any

---

[1] N, 1, 505 misreads as "wages".

[2] Contained in the long Appendix to the Report.

[3] Thomas Barwick Lloyd Baker (1807–86; *DNB*), one of the founders of the reformatory school system; lived at Hardwicke Court, Gloucester; magistrate, and visiting justice at Gloucester prison. His school at Hardwicke was opened Mar 52, two years before the first Reformatory Schools Act. His writings were collected, with a memoir, in *War with Crime*, ed. H. Philips and E. Verney, 1886.

[4] Thus in MS.

[5] Baker's letter commented on two points in *American Notes*: he quoted from CD's note that the Boston House of Correction used "the improved system which we have imported into England", and showed that this was anticipated by the reforms instigated by George Onesiphorus Paul (1746–1820; *DNB*), high sheriff of Gloucestershire, in the new gaol and penitentiary at Gloucester, opened 1791; he believed this was "what the Americans copied", since Commissioners from America inspected the penitentiary "about 1810". He re-

called that after Commissioners had been sent to America (including William Crawford, whose official report on "Penitentiaries of the United States" was published in 1834), Lord John Russell "sent orders to us at Gloucester to entirely remodel our whole prison . . . his new rules were precisely the same wh. we had followed for the last 40 years—with one or two exceptions". He also referred ironically to recent comments in *The Times* on Gloucester magistrates as "a low & vulgar set of people besides being atrociously cruel" (i.e. *The Times's* campaign in Oct–Dec 42 against Northleach and other prisons in Gloucestershire).

[6] Mentioned by Baker as a parallel to the Boylston School in Boston, visited by CD. Capt. Edward Pelham Brenton (1774–1839; *DNB*) established the Children's Friend Society (see his *The Bible and Spade*, 1837, and Sophia Elizabeth De Morgan, *Reminiscences*, 1895, pp. 192–204); its management was severely and, as both Baker and CD thought, unfairly criticized: "the Virtuous Times . . . laid bare the enormity of separating juvenile pick-

allusion to it in my book, lest some Samaritan should be sickened and put out of heart, and his good deeds throttled in their birth.

I thank you cordially, for your obliging favor. And am

Faithfully Yours

T. B. G. Baker Esquire CHARLES DICKENS

To H. SMALE,[1] 3 FEBRUARY 1843

Extract in N, I, 506.

Devonshire Terrace | Third February, 1843

The months come round so fast. . . .

. . . I shall not be able to have the pleasure of coming to dine with you until my February work has had its throat cut: which laudable deed I shall perform with all convenient despatch.

I was hurried away unexpectedly to Bath, in the beginning of my January leisure, and have since been reposing on some rheumatic laurels gathered on the railway.

To CLARKSON STANFIELD, 3 [FEBRUARY] 1843

MS University of Kentucky. *Date:* "January" clearly an error; 3 Feb 43 was a Friday, and 4 Feb Ainsworth's birthday.

Devonshire Terrace | Friday Morning | Third January 1843.

My Dear Stanfield.

Landseer[2] has spread such exciting reports of the conjurations we performed on Twelfth Night,[3] that I have been fain to promise Mrs. Norton they shall come off for the behoof of her boys on Monday.[4]

pockets from their parents . . . and sending them to the Cape . . . where they were sold for slaves (i.e. apprenticed on far more favourable terms to themselves than they cd. obtain in England) where some few— turned out ill (more have gone on well) and one who ran away—got back to England and told the Times all about it". *The Times* denounced Brenton "as a monster who trafficked in slaves"; their charges were later disproved, but by then Brenton was dead. (Draft, Baker *to* CD: MS Miss Olive K. Lloyd-Baker). Baker was referring to *The Times*'s attacks on the Society in 1838, its prominent reports of the complaints of boys and their parents at Marylebone Police Court in 1839, and especially to its leading article of 5 Apr 39, which called the Society the "children's kidnapping society". The Society came to an end shortly after Brenton's death.

[1] Henry Lewis Smale, proctor and notary; practised at 3 Dean's Court, Doctors' Commons, 1812–58. One of the original subscribers to the *Mirror of Parliament* in 1828, he had occasionally employed CD to report cases in the ecclesiastical courts at Doctors' Commons (see W. J. Carlton, *CD, Shorthand Writer*, 1926, p. 55*n*). Director of Britannia Life Assurance Co. 1841–56.

[2] Charles Landseer: see *To* Stone, 28 Dec 42.

[3] For details, see *To* Felton, 31 Dec 42. This was clearly the first of a long series of Twelfth Night parties with conjuring; Mamie (now nearly five), recalled 40 years later how her father "would very often, dressed as a magician, give a conjuring entertainment, when a little figure, which appeared from a wonderful and mysterious bag, and which was supposed to be a personal friend of the conjurer, would greatly delight the audience by his funny stories, his eccentric voice and way of speaking, and by his miraculous appearances and disappearances. Of course, a plum-pudding was made in a hat, and was

I have some new tricks, and some improvements on the old, which require an exact knowledge on the part of Ivory.[1] And as I hear you are going to Mrs. Norton's on Monday, will you be here at 5—not later—that we may have time to go over them? Do you dine at Ainsworth's tomorrow? In the event of such extraordinary good luck, will you come here *tomorrow* at 5?

A word in answer.

Faithfully Always

Clarkson Stanfield Esquire   CD.

To W. HARRISON AINSWORTH,
[?EARLY FEBRUARY 1843]

MS Morgan Library. *Date:* Handwriting points to early 43; probably soon after seeing Ainsworth on 4 Feb.

My Dear Ainsworth.

Relying on auld acquaintance, I had made exactly the arrangement you propose; and shall send the Carriage back in the Evening for my small relation.[2] Many thanks for the Magazine.[3]

Always Heartily

CD.

To THOMAS MITTON, 6 FEBRUARY 1843

Text from J. B. Findlay, *Charles Dickens and his Magic,* privately printed, Shanklin, 1962. *Address:* Thomas Mitton Esquire, | 23 Southampton Buildings.

Devonshire Terrace. | Monday, Sixth February, 1843.

My Dear Mitton,

I am greatly obliged to you for the trouble you have taken in relation to the turn-out.[4] I had already told the coachmaker to put all possible strength into the splinter-bar, and to make as stout a job of it as he really could.

always one of the great successes of the evening" ("Dickens with his children", *Some Noted Princes, Authors, and Statesmen of our Time,* ed. J. Parton, New York, [1885], p. 33).

[4] In Oct 42 Mrs Norton had succeeded in persuading her husband to allow her to have her children with her for half the year; they were Fletcher (*b.* 1829) and Thomas Brinsley (*b.* 1831), William (*b.* 1833) having died in a riding accident in Sep 42. They spent Christmas together at her brother's at Frampton. CD had given Samuel Longfellow in Feb 42 a sympathetic account of her distress over her separation from them; "she said that every morning when she woke she felt that they were one day nearer forgetting their mother for ever" (see *To* Forster, 30 Jan 42, *fn*).

[1] i.e. Stanfield. Possibly "Ivory" was the name of an actual conjuror's assistant—but not of any well-known conjuror; perhaps the man whose stock CD had purchased. A James Ivory, scientist, died at Hampstead 8 Oct 42.

[2] Georgina, who in her old age recalled the parties at Ainsworth's as among the most pleasant remembrances of her girlhood (S. M. Ellis, *W. H. Ainsworth and his Friends,* II, 37).

[3] *Ainsworth's Magazine,* Feb. 43, includes an article by "Uncle Sam" (G. P. Payne) describing the arrival in America of an English Marquis, besieged by "News Collectors".

[4] "A driving equipage" (*OED*).

You will be delighted to hear that my Mother is formally "bespoke" for the Easthorpe[1] Park delivery!!![2]

I have made a most splendid trick of that apparatus which Hamley[3] couldn't manage: by the addition of one or two simple contrivances. It is better than the Northern Wizard[4] and as good as Doebler.

Faithfully Always,

CD.

To GEORGE STEVENSON,[5] 6 FEBRUARY 1843

Mention in Autograph Prices Current, *v, 1919–21;* MS *2 pp.; dated 6 Feb 43; signed initials.*

Referring to repairs to a coach.

To MESSRS CHAPMAN & HALL, 7 FEBRUARY 1843

MS Brotherton Library, Leeds.

Devonshire Terrace | Seventh February 1843.

Dear Sirs

I wrote to Mr. Browne yesterday morning, and told him he should have both subjects by the Tenth. In the meantime, I asked him to make and send me, a sketch of Mark, who will appear in the first.[6]

Faithfully Yours always

CHARLES DICKENS

Messrs. Chapman and Hall

---

[1] Text reads "Easthope". For a description of the house, see *To* Maclise, 6 July 43, *fn.*

[2] i.e. to assist at Mrs Smithson's confinement, as she had with Catherine and Fanny, and perhaps on other occasions; "formally" doubtless implies a fee, which would help the parental finances. The baby was born on 16 Mar.

[3] W. Hamley, Noah's Ark Toy Warehouse, 231 High Holborn; CD had paid him £2.8.0 on 2 Jan (Account-book, MS Messrs Coutts).

[4] John Henry Anderson (1815–74; *DNB*), who was then appearing at the Adelphi; a Scot, he toured Scotland with his performance in 1837–9 and first appeared in London 1840, at the Strand and then at St James's Bazaar; at the Adelphi 1841 and 1843–4; last appeared in London at Covent Garden 1846, but was less successful. Among his famous tricks were Pluto's Bottle, Flora's Bouquet, and the Cabinet of Confucius (Thomas Frost, *Lives of the Conjurers*, 1876). The *Examiner* noticed him favourably 17 June 43, as "a clever well-mannered man" who "boils fowls back into wings and feathers, scatters abroad inexhaustible nosegays, and is as amazing as the renowned Döbler himself".

[5] Possibly George Stephens, coach smith, 36 Brownlow St, Drury Lane.

[6] Mark appears in the second illustration, "Mark begins to be jolly under creditable circumstances", in Ch. 7 of the March No., the first being "Mr Pinch and the new pupil, on a social occasion"; but he had been described in Ch. 5 of the Feb No.

To JOHN FORSTER, [12 FEBRUARY 1843]

Extract in F, IV, i, 292. *Date:* 12 Feb according to Forster.

I am in a difficulty, and am coming down to you some time to-day or to-night. I couldn't write a line yesterday; not a word, though I really tried hard. In a kind of despair I started off at half-past two with my pair of petti-coats[1] to Richmond; and dined there!![2] Oh what a lovely day it was in those parts.

To DR JOHN ELLIOTSON, 13 FEBRUARY 1843*

MS Colonel Richard Gimbel.

Devonshire Terrace | Thirteenth February 1843

My Dear Elliotson.

I am much indebted to you for the loan of the enclosed.[3] The letter has particularly interested me: being very womanly and tender.

But I fear—I greatly fear—that in that place, which is the very last resort of the most hardened crime, we must be stern.

Always Faithfully Yours

Dr. Elliotson.   CHARLES DICKENS

To JOHN FORSTER, [14 FEBRUARY 1843]

Extract in F, IV, i, 293, dated by Forster two days after letter of 12 Feb.

Send me word how you are.[4] But not so much for that I now write, as to tell you, peremptorily, that I insist on your wrapping yourself up and coming

---

[1] Catherine and Georgina. Forster says that "not many days after", Maclise made the pencil drawing of the three of them in profile now in the Forster collection (re-produced in F. G. Kitton, *CD by Pen and Pencil*, facing p. 49, and elsewhere). "The likenesses of all are excellent", wrote Forster; "nothing ever done of Dickens himself has conveyed more vividly his look and bearing at this yet youthful time. He is in his most pleasing aspect; flattered, if you will; but nothing that is known to me gives a general impression so lifelike and true of the then frank, eager, handsome face" (F, IV, i, 293).

[2] This was the first night of *A Blot in the 'Scutcheon.*

[3] Nothing is known of the enclosure; perhaps some plea on behalf of a con-demned man. Elliotson was interested in the physiognomy of criminals; the first number of his monthly periodical, *The Zoist* (Apr 43), included a report of his address to the Phrenological Society, delivered 21 Nov 42, in which he referred

to CD ("pardon me the vanity of saying *my friend* Charles Dickens") and, discuss-ing the appearance of murderers, recalled CD's observations on Nancy's humanity in the 1841 Preface to *Oliver Twist*.

[4] Forster (F, IV, i, 293) says "It was a year of much illness with me, which had ever helpful and active sympathy from him". Longfellow by 21 Mar had heard of his "violent *rheumatic fever*" (Longfellow *to* Catherine Norton, *Letters of Henry Wadsworth Longfellow*, ed. A. Hilen, II, 521). Jane Carlyle was also moved by the plight of the solitary bachelor: "Forster ... is ill—all that prodigious 'Brummigam enthusiasm' and foaming vitality bottled up in a sick arm chair—very deplorable to see! for I actually went to see him. One is so sorry for a man *ill* with only a tiger to look after him—tho' *his* is the pink of Tigers!" (*Letters to her Family, 1839–1863*, ed. L. Huxley, 1924, p. 91; letter of 2 Mar). He did not however accept CD's invitation to Devonshire Terrace.

here in a hackney-coach, with a big portmanteau, to-morrow. It surely is better to be unwell with a Quick and Cheerful (and Co.) in the neighbourhood, than in the dreary vastness of Lincolns-inn-fields. Here is the snuggest tent-bedstead in the world, and there you are with the drawing-room for your workshop, the Q and C for your pal, and 'everythink in a concatenation accordingly.' I begin to have hopes of the regeneration of mankind after the reception of Gregory[1] last night, though I have none of the *Chronicle*[2] for not denouncing the villain. Have you seen the note touching my *Notes* in the blue and yellow?[3]

To JOHN FORSTER, [?MID-FEBRUARY 1843]

Extract in F, IV, ii, 311. *Date:* probably while writing the March No. (Chs 6–8); see below.

As to the way in which these characters have opened out,[4] that is, to me, one of the most surprising processes of the mind in this sort of invention. Given what one knows, what one does not know springs up; and I am as absolutely certain of its being true, as I am of the law of gravitation—if such a thing be possible, more so.

---

[1] Barnard Gregory (1796–1852; *DNB*), journalist; proprietor and editor of the *Satirist* from its inception in 1831 to its suppression in 1849. Constantly involved in libel actions and several times imprisoned; exposed by Renton Nicholson in the *Town* (28 July 38); but continued his attacks, especially on the Duke of Brunswick. Had some experience as a Shakespearian actor, and on 13 Feb appeared as Hamlet at Covent Garden, but was hissed from the stage, in what the *Theatrical Journal* (18 Feb 43) called "the most violently uproarious row . . . since the famous O.P. riots". A placard was put out by the *Punch* contributors; Leech was one of those who attended in order to protest and sat with W. J. Linton in a front row: "so soon as Hamlet made his appearance, an outcry, a burst of execration . . . hisses and hootings, cries of 'Off! off! Blackguard! Scoundrel!'" arose; "Leech was hoarse for days" (W. J. Linton, *Memories*, 1895, pp. 199–200). A protest had also been concerted beforehand by the Duke of Brunswick and his supporters; Gregory claimed that they had hired "ruffians" to fill the gallery, "sub-marshalled by a low public-house keeper". The *Satirist* was filled with letters in his defence and protests against the action of Bartley, the stage-manager, who also played Polonius, in stopping the performance after an act

and a half in dumb show. The general view, however, was that "it was the burst of popular indignation at the effrontery of a person connected with so obscene a publication appearing before a respectable audience" (*Theatrical Journal*). Gregory brought an action against the Duke, but lost; he was later found guilty of libelling the Duke and though he fled in disguise was eventually captured and imprisoned.

[2] Macready on 19 Feb was "dissatisfied with the silence of the *Examiner* (Fonblanque) upon the disgraceful wretch who was allowed to insult decency by coming from his lurking-place . . . and braving public indignation—the vile emulator of the wretch Bunn, Mr. Gregory" (*Diaries*, II, 196).

[3] See *To* Napier, 21 Jan 43, *fn*.

[4] Forster refers this to the "two most prominent figures" in *Chuzzlewit*, "as soon as all their capabilities were revealed to him"; to CD the "most prominent" would be Pecksniff and Tom Pinch, whose "capabilities" and interrelation have "opened out" in Ch. 6, while Mr Pecksniff is further developed in Ch. 8 where he takes his daughters to Todgers's. In this section of Forster's chapter he also discusses Jonas and Mrs Gamp as prominent figures; if either of these is meant, the letter would be some months later. But this seems unlikely.

To EBENEZER JOHNSTON,[1] 15 FEBRUARY 1843*

MS Dickens House.

Devonshire Terrace | Fifteenth February 1843

My Dear Sir

I have been waiting to answer your note, until now, simply because Mrs. Dickens has been exceedingly unwell, ever since your daughters[2] did her the favor to call here (when she had already been in bed two or three days), and is only just now recovering. Though greatly better, she is afraid to encounter the night air,—nor do I think, though generally on the bold side in such matters, that it would be well for her to do so, for some few days longer.

For myself, I am in agonies peculiar to February—a month which, by reason of its shortness, ought to be blotted out of the almanacks—and although, if she had been able to come to you on Friday, I would have made a dash and accompanied her; still, now that I have the opportunity of consideration which her staying at home gives me, I decide in behalf of Virtue and Constancy, and remain at home to finish.[3]

Mrs. Dickens begs her compliments to your daughters, and looks forward to returning their visit, very soon.

Faithfully Yours

Ebenezer Johnstone Esquire   CHARLES DICKENS

P.S. Not being quite certain of your address, I despatch this to the root and branch in Fenchurch Street.[4]

To CHARLES MACKAY, 17 FEBRUARY 1843

Text from Charles Mackay, *Forty Years' Recollections*, 1877, I, 172.

Devonshire Terrace | Seventeenth February 1843

My dear Mackay,

I have such strong reasons to doubt the easy working of your project,[5] and to fear it will end in disappointment, that I "cannot"—as the honest, and I am

---

[1] Ebenezer Johnston (1789–1850); a Unitarian and prominent member of the Gravel Pit Chapel, Hackney; member of the Ironmongers' Company; from 1846 a trustee of Dr Williams's Library with Henry Crabb Robinson (Crabb Robinson MS Diary, Dr Williams's Library, and Walter D. Jeremy, *The Presbyterian Fund and Dr. Daniel Williams's Trust*, 1885).

[2] Nothing is known of them, except that one had married a surgeon called Jones by Oct 48 (Crabb Robinson MS Diary).

[3] He finished his number on Sat 18 Feb (see *To* Mitton, 20 Feb).

[4] Probably an error for Gracechurch Street, where Robert Johnston & Co. were wholesale ironmongers at No. 63. "Ebenezer Johnston" is named as "ironmonger,

7 Bishopsgate Without" in the Directory of 1842, but not later.

[5] The proposed Society of British Authors, which according to Mackay (*Forty Years' Recollections*, I, 168f.) had developed from the "Milton Institute" projected in 1842 (see *To* Mackay, 26 July and 19 Oct 42). Sir Walter Besant, in "The First Society of British Authors" (*Contemporary Review*, July 1889, collected in *Essays and Historiettes*, 1903)—based on original papers, an early version of the Prospectus, and letters to Robertson, none of which can now be traced—regarded it as a new project; they first met, he wrote, "in some informal preliminary manner, of which no record has been kept": it was no doubt to this that CD's letter refers. The

sorry to add, very heavy servant in "High Life below Stairs,"[1] says,—"make one among you." Some of these weighty arguments shall be yours when I see you next.

Faithfully yours,

Charles Mackay, Esquire CHARLES DICKENS

To THOMAS MITTON, 17 FEBRUARY 1843

MS Huntington Library.

Devonshire Terrace | Seventeenth Feby. | 1843.

My Dear Mitton

If I bring the carriage down on Tuesday, at what time shall I come?

Shall we make a day of it, somewhere? I shall most likely have the No.[2] in my pocket.

Until that day, will you stave off the mischievous lunatic[3] (on the best terms you can) whose letter I enclose? And will you tell the man, Reeves,[4] under Grays Inn archway who has sent me in *for the second time* a bill which I think is Frederick's, that the papers[5] never came to me, and I know nothing about 'em?

In haste | Always Faithfully
CD.

To LORD BROUGHAM, 20 FEBRUARY 1843*

MS Brotherton Library, Leeds.

Devonshire Terrace | Twentieth February 1843

Dear Lord Brougham.

Thank you for your kind note. I was misled by Napier's letter; which seemed strongly to point to Lord Morpeth; and did indeed admit, as I thought, of no other construction than that which I put upon it. Except to you, I had only mentioned my impression to one friend, however: and therefore I have done him but little injustice beyond the compass of my own thoughts.

original group included Mackay, John Robertson, John Britton and G. L. Craik; by 19 Mar they had persuaded Carlyle to join them at a further informal meeting on 21 Mar, when resolutions were passed which were sanctioned at the first formal meeting on 25 Mar at the British Hotel, Cockspur Street, with Thomas Campbell in the chair. The speakers are said to have included Carlyle, Bulwer, Poole, and Westland Marston (for Carlyle's impressions, see *To* Babbage, 27 Apr, *fn*). The general objects as set out in the proof of the Prospectus (Free Library of Philadelphia) were "to facilitate the labours, and protect the rights of authors"; it was proposed, for example, "to register the names and works of all the authors in the British Empire" so as to encourage contact among them, to form a library where new books might be read, and to arrange "annual or occasional discourses". A draft prospectus was drawn up and a sub-committee appointed to consider and revise it. Between this date and 8 Apr CD was persuaded to join: see *To* Britton, 2 Mar, and *To* Beard, 7 Apr.

[1] Tom, in Act II.

[2] The proof; N reads "MS", in error.

[3] Probably a creditor of John Dickens: see *To* Mitton, 20 Feb.

[4] Perhaps Charles Reeves, Dining rooms, 58 Grays Inn Lane.

[5] Possibly advertisements.

I know the Writer's name now.[1]

You saw how the town took the law into their own hands in the case of a scoundrel Editor who appeared, the other night, as an Actor at Covent Garden ?[2] It is as good a sign of the popular detestation of printed stabs, as I have seen, I think.

Always Faithfully Yours

The Lord Brougham.   CHARLES DICKENS

To EDWIN LANDSEER, 20 FEBRUARY 1843*

MS Mrs Joan Stern.

Devonshire Terrace | Monday Twentieth February | 1843.

My Dear Landseer

Have you anything better to do, than to dine here next Wednesday at 6—sharp—precise—exact ? We have no party, saving Mc Ian and his wife; and may be two others whom you know.

Faithfully Yours always

Edwin Landseer Esquire.   CHARLES DICKENS

To THOMAS MITTON, 20 FEBRUARY 1843

MS Huntington Library.

Devonshire Terrace | Twentieth February 1843.

My Dear Mitton

I quite agree in opinion with you, touching my father[3] who I really believe, as Sam Weller says of some one in Pickwick, "has gone ravin' mad with conscious willany".[4] The thought of him besets me, night and day; and I really do not know what is to be done with him. It is quite clear that the more we do, the more outrageous and audacious he becomes.

Perhaps we cannot do better tomorrow than go to Dulwich where there is an interesting Picture Gallery, which I think you never saw. I will be with you at one. If the day be anything short of cats, dogs, and pitchforks, in its dampness, I will send Topping on, by buss, in order that you may the better see (from the

---

[1] Clearly Brougham had told him only that it was not Morpeth; but CD had already learnt the author's name, perhaps from Fonblanque (see *To* Fonblanque, 25 Jan).

[2] See *To* Forster, 14 Feb 43 and *fn*.

[3] These two words heavily deleted in blue ink, but legible under infra-red.

[4] CD is confusing a speech from his *Is She his Wife?* (Sc. ii) with *Pickwick*, Ch. 23, where Sam Weller says to Job Trotter, "What are you melting vith now —the consciousness o' willainy?"

box seat), the performance of the horses. I have to go to a party at night,[1] but not until late.

Faithfully Yours always

Thomas Mitton Esquire   CHARLES DICKENS

P.S. I finished on Saturday Night, last.

To T. PRICE,[2] 24 FEBRUARY 1843*

MS Chas J. Sawyer Ltd. *Address:* T. Price Esquire | 95 Islington | Birmingham.

Private.   London. 1 Devonshire Terrace | York Gate Regents Park
                                                    Twenty Fourth February 1843
Sir.

I am much obliged to you for your good-humoured note. The sheets to which you allude, are merely (as I conceive) impressions of some detached tales published in the commencement of the clock:[3] which I have had cancelled, at some loss, merely because I considered that they injured the effect of the two long stories, which are now published in separate Volumes, without those interruptions. They *sold* as well as the rest, but they did not please me; and therefore I disposed of them to the four Winds.

Faithfully Yours

T. Price Esquire   CHARLES DICKENS

To H. P. SMITH, 24 FEBRUARY 1843*

MS Miss Mabel Hodge.

Devonshire Terrace | Twenty Fourth February 1843
My Dear Smith.

We rejoice in your being out of quarantine at last; and congratulate you, heartily, thereupon.

On Tuesday, we shall be very glad indeed, to dine with you. I should have written you as much yesterday, but that I was from home all day.

Faithfully Yours

H. P. Smith Esquire   CHARLES DICKENS

[1] Almost certainly the ball at the Procters', referred to on 27 Mar by Jane Carlyle (who was unable to go) as "some month ago" (*Letters to her Family*, p. 105); Thackeray saw CD and Catherine there, and told his wife "how splendid Mrs. Dickens was in pink satin and Mr. Dickens in geranium and ringlets" (*Letters and Private*

Papers of W. M. Thackeray, ed. G. N. Ray, II, 110).

[2] Possibly the Mr Price mentioned in Ainsworth *to* CD, 15 Feb 41 (Vol. II, p. 212*n*), as having sent him a critical notice of the *Clock*.

[3] See Vol. II, p. 453*n*.

To CLARKSON STANFIELD, 27 FEBRUARY 1843*

MS University of Kentucky.

Devonshire Terrace | Twenty Seventh February | 1843.

My Dear Stanfield

My Missis says that we dine at 5, not half past—otherwise it is such a struggle and bustle to reach the Theatre[1] in time. Of course I understand that you will come or not, just as suits your convenience.

Faithfully always

Clarkson Stanfield Esquire   CD

To T. E. WELLER,[2] 27 FEBRUARY 1843*

MS Mrs Sowerby.

1 Devonshire Terrace | York Gate Regents Park.
Twenty Seventh February 1843

Dear Sir.

I am obliged to you for your good-humoured letter; and I beg you to present my regards to your accomplished daughter,[3] together with this autograph,[4]

---

[1] Probably Drury Lane for Macready's *Hamlet*.

[2] Thomas Edmund Weller (1799–1884), father of Christiana, was the son of Thomas and Lucy Weller of Mayfield, Sussex, where his father kept a private school. Married Betty Dixon Southerden of Rye 1822; they lived for many years in Cheltenham, where T. E. Weller, an amateur architect, had built the "Literary Saloon" (a library and concert room). He contributed musical and dramatic criticisms to various local papers, and was employed as secretary of the Cheltenham Protector Coal Company; in 1829 his wife set up a high-class school at Bath Villa. In 1838 the family moved to Liverpool, where Weller was clerk in the City of Dublin Steam Packet Company, whose marine manager, James Crescent Shaw, married his eldest daughter, Betsy, in 1840. In 1839 the Wellers were living at Spring Bank Villa, Walton Breck, where Mrs Weller opened another school, but in 1843 their home was at the more humble Hillside Terrace, 43 Breck Road, and her mother also lived with them. Through his employment, Weller knew Captain Hewitt, who was staying at Devonshire Terrace in the latter part of Feb (see *To* Felton, 2 Mar) and may have brought Weller's letter to CD and carried back the reply. (Information mainly from family papers in possession of Mrs Sowerby, and from local press.)

[3] Christiana Jane (1825–1910), Weller's second daughter, already a concert pianist; taught by her mother (a pupil of Pio Cianchettini), she and her elder sister first appeared in public as child prodigies in 1834. On 8 Dec 42 she had appeared with Thalberg at the Rotunda in Dublin and won great acclaim for her "brilliancy of execution" in playing with him his celebrated duet for two pianos from *Norma*; Thalberg forecast a great future for her; press reports also referred to her "highly prepossessing appearance" and "ease and freedom from affectation". By Apr 43 the *Court Journal* had heard that she was "shortly to appear in the metropolis". (For CD's meeting with her at Liverpool in 1844 and her marriage to T. J. Thompson in 1845, see next vol.) The other daughter at home was Anna Delancey (*b.* 1830), who married Fred Dickens in 1849.

[4] On 1 Mar Christiana wrote in her pocket diary (MS Mrs Sowerby), "Papa brought home with him a beautiful note from CHARLES DICKENS" (with 19 exclamation marks). Another entry shows that she was reading the numbers of *Chuzzlewit* as they appeared.

which must be understood to include all manner of good wishes for her, and you, and the Wellers generally.[1]

Faithfully Yours

T. E. Weller Esquire   CHARLES DICKENS

To MISS BURDETT COUTTS, 28 FEBRUARY 1843

MS Morgan Library.

Devonshire Terrace | Twenty Eighth February 1843

Dear Miss Coutts.

I don't know whether you may happen to remember that there was a Public Subscription some two or three years ago, for the purchase of a Testimonial to Macready, in honor of his exertions to elevate the National Drama. However, there *was*: a handsome piece of plate was designed and made;[2] and is at last[3] to be presented by the Duke of Sussex[4] in the course of the ensuing month.[5]

But the failure of Hammersley's Bank, and the consequent loss of a part of the money, has rendered a second Subscription necessary. Being a Member of the Committee, and casting about to whom it would be right to apply, I have naturally thought of you. Firstly, because I know you are attached to the most rational of all amusements. And secondly, because in the horrible indifference to it which prevails among people of influence and station, any support from you, cannot fail to be at once most valuable to the cause, and most gratifying and cheering to Macready himself.

Therefore, if you see no objection to aiding the object (a much higher one than the froth of the World suppose) I shall be most proud and glad to act as your Secretary or steward in the matter. Lord Lansdowne is one of the very few men in high places, who have dealt with it as they should. There be some (whose titles would startle you) who have put down their names with round sums attached, but have not put down their money; in consequence of which, I am in danger of turning misanthropical, Byronic, and devilish.

I hope you liked the Much Ado—and the Comus[6]—and that you will go to

---

[1] Weller had probably made some jocular reference to his namesakes in *Pickwick*.

[2] A committee for the testimonial was appointed in 1839: see Vol. II, p. 2*n*. The piece of plate, valued at £500, was a design showing Macready studying a play and surrounded by the Arts and Muses. For the inscription, see *To* Major Stephens, 12 June 43.

[3] Correspondence between Forster and Bulwer shows a series of postponements in 1842–3 (see *Bulwer and Macready*, ed. C. H. Shattuck, Illinois, 1958, pp. 215–6): Oct 42, when the presentation might have been of practical benefit to Macready's forthcoming season, was impossible because no one had been found to officiate; later,

the ill-health of the Duke of Sussex led to further delays.

[4] Augustus Frederick, Duke of Sussex (1773–1843; *DNB*), sixth son of George III.

[5] The ceremony was expected to take place on 15 Mar, but that date failed too and the Duke may have withdrawn altogether.

[6] Produced at Drury Lane on Fri 24 Feb, for Macready's benefit; he played Benedick and Comus. CD went on the first night and wrote on "Macready as 'Benedick'" in the *Examiner*, 4 Mar 43, "in calm reflection, and not in the excitement of having recently witnessed it". Macready was pleased with his reception on the first night ("The audience went with the play",

see Virginius[1] next Monday. If you were not pleased last Friday, I shall certainly carry my misanthropical impulses into effect, and leave off my neck cloth[2] without further notice.

Dear Miss Coutts | Always Yours faithfully
CHARLES DICKENS

To LADY HOLLAND, 28 FEBRUARY 1843*

MS The Earl of Ilchester.

Devonshire Terrace. | Twenty Eighth February 1843

Dear Lady Holland.

I beg to return you the French newspapers, with many thanks. I shall hope to have the pleasure of coming to see you when the middle of next month is past. My plan now, is, to keep myself strictly at home (with the exception of a long country walk or ride every day) during one half of the month; and I find it a capital one, both for health, and pleasant authorship.

Let me thank you too, for your kind Message, touching the Edinburgh Review. Napier's private letters to me, seemed to point so plainly at Lord Morpeth, that I fell into that mistake against my will and desire: which were, and always have been, to consider him incapable of any but good actions. Saving to Fonblanque, I only mentioned my suspicion to one other person. That was Lord Brougham; who immediately corrected it, and set me right.

I hope you are in such health and spirits as I would have you enjoy. And I am always

Dear Lady Holland
Yours faithfully and truly obliged

The Lady Holland.   CHARLES DICKENS

Diaries, II, 197); it was repeated eleven times with remarkable success; critics were generally favourable, despite a preconception that Macready was unsuited to comedy. CD's *Examiner* article referred to this: "Some people are rather disposed to take it ill that he should make them laugh who has so often made them cry", adding (with a fellow-feeling?) that there is "a very general feeling . . . that the path which a man has trodden for many years . . . must be of necessity his allotted one, and . . . the only one in which he is qualified to walk". In CD's view Macready triumphed over all difficulties: on the first night, "before his very first scene was over, the whole house felt . . . a presentment of the character so fresh, distinct, vigorous, and enjoyable, as they could not choose but relish, and go along with". The

arbor scene is particularly praised, and the whole seen as "a finished and exquisite performance" (*Miscellaneous Papers*, ed. B. W. Matz, 1914). Many years later CD recalled Keeley's performance as Verges: "he threw Dogberry into the shade . . . so lost in admiration of that portentous jackass . . . as he became more ridiculous, that he in a manner appropriated Dogberry to himself" (*To* Herman Merivale, 3 Mar 69; N, III, 709).

[1] Mon 6 Mar, with Macready in the title role.

[2] i.e. like Byron; a common association. "Despair, Madam, is the word—Byronish —I hate mankind, and wear my shirt collars turned down" (Thackeray *to* Mrs Procter, 1841, *Letters and Private Papers*, ed. G. N. Ray, II, 22).

To D. M. MOIR,[1] [JANUARY–FEBRUARY 1843]

Mention in letter from Moir to Aird, quoted in *The Poetical Works of David Macbeth Moir*, ed. Thomas Aird, 1852, p. lxv. *Date:* according to Moir, "a few months" before he wrote the Preface to the edition published 18 May,[2] but not before Jan 43.

Encouraging him to publish his Domestic Verses *circulated privately early in 1843.*[3]

To THE REV. EDWARD TAGART,[4]
[?DECEMBER 1842–FEBRUARY 1843]

Extract from unidentified newspaper cutting about a Dickens exhibition, in possession of Mr W. J. Carlton. *Date:* clearly at least some weeks after CD first heard Tagart in Nov 42 (see *To* Felton, 2 Mar 43, *fn*), but tone suggests early in their acquaintance, and the "discourse" may have been in Feb; see below.

As one of your congregation[5] I cannot resist the opportunity of conveying to you my earnest and grateful feelings for your eloquent and charming discourse of last Sunday.[6] It made more impression upon me than any sermon I have ever yet heard—even from your lips.[7]

---

[1] David Macbeth Moir (1798–1851; *DNB*), physician and author: see Vol. II, p. 440*n*.

[2] See *To* Moir, 19 May 43.

[3] The title-page read: "Domestic Verses by △ Not Published Edinburgh 1843", and the contents were seven poems on the deaths of four of Moir's children. According to Aird's quotation, many other writers, including Wordsworth, Tennyson, Warren, and most decisively, Jeffrey, gave similar encouragement; none of these letters appear to have survived. By 12 Mar, Moir was discussing the publication of an enlarged volume and selecting "lyrics of a congenial character, which would harmonize with the others" (Moir *to* Blackwood, MS National Library of Scotland).

[4] Edward Tagart (1804–58; *DNB*), Unitarian minister, first at Octagon Chapel, Norwich, then (1828) at York Street, St James's Square, and from 1833 at Little Portland Street. Secretary of Unitarian Association 1841. Married 1828 Helen, daughter of Joseph Bourne and widow of Dr Thomas Martineau, eldest brother of Harriet; had two daughters, Helen and Emily; Mrs Gaskell disliked "the rude quarrelsome tone" in the family and their "frightful bonnets" (*Letters of Mrs. Gaskell*, ed. J. Chapple and A. Pollard, 1966, pp. 145, 213, 216). Sympathetic to various liberal and philanthropic enter-prises; interested in literature, philosophy and science, and a member of the Society of Antiquaries; "proprietor" of University College and a member of the Council of University Hall. Attracted a distinguished congregation; but some Unitarians thought his manner cold and patronizing. Crabb Robinson thought him "a commonplace dogmatist" (MS Diary, 21 July 47, Dr Williams's Library).

[5] See *To* Felton, 2 Mar and *fn*.

[6] Extract reads "discourses". In Feb–Mar 43 Tagart was repeating his "Discourses on the Reformers" published Apr 43 as *Sketches of the Lives and Characters of the Leading Reformers* (he gave CD a copy "with the Author's kind respects"); but on 19 Feb the discourse was on "the Doctrine and present Social Position of Unitarian Christianity" (advertised *Morning Chronicle*, 18 Feb)—possibly the one referred to by CD.

[7] Though Tagart did not preach extempore, he was "composed and easy, earnest without being noisy, his voice was deep and rich . . . He did not habitually indulge his taste for metaphysical speculations" but kept to "scriptural or practical topics" and "asserted Unitarian doctrines with simplicity and fervour" ("Memoir of the late Rev. Edward Tagart", *Christian Reformer*, Feb 1859, xv, 65–85).

To JOHN BRITTON,[1] 2 MARCH 1843*

MS Mrs S. S. Clephan.

Devonshire Terrace | Thursday Evening | Second March 1843

Dear Sir.

Nobody who knows me, will, I am certain, consider me supine when the interests of Literature or any of its Professors are in question. I have always done my duty in upholding it and them to the utmost extent of my power. And if, in my business transactions I had had less regard to its honor, and more to my own profit, I might have been by this time—almost as rich a man as you take me for.

But I am not by any means clear that the Society[2] you propose *will* tend to its advancement. Nor can I exercise that right of private judgment in such a matter which unquestionably belongs to me, until I know of whom it is composed, and what it is to do. Until I have reasonable information on these heads from its own proceedings, I must, in all good humour, decline to add another to my already long list of Clubs and Societies. In the meantime, pray rest assured that the Pursuit of Literature as a Profession shall suffer no greater disparagement in my person, than I can possibly help.

Faithfully Yours

John Britton Esquire.   CHARLES DICKENS

To [MESSRS CHAPMAN & HALL], 2 MARCH 1843*

MS Dr Peter Beattie.

Devonshire Terrace | Second March 1843

Dear Sirs

I enclose you Mr. Prescott's letter.[3]

I shall be glad to hear of any improvement in Chuzzlewit.[4] Please to take care that Mrs. Hogarth has the No. every month.

Faithfully Yours

CHARLES DICKENS

To LEWIS GAYLORD CLARK, 2 MARCH 1843

MS Berg Collection.

London. 1 Devonshire Terrace | York Gate Regents Park.
Second March 1843.

My Dear Clark

Let us lay a wager upon that Copyright business. What impossible odds shall

---

[1] John Britton (1777–1857; *DNB*), antiquarian; had employed Cattermole. CD bought his *Beauties of England and Wales* in 1839: see Vol. I, p. 621.

[2] Both were on the sub-committee for considering and revising the Prospectus of the Society of Authors, with Carlyle, Campbell, Bulwer, Robert Bell, and John Robertson (W. Besant, *Essays and Historiettes*, pp. 276–7).

[3] The letter of 30 Jan: see *To* Prescott, 2 Mar.

[4] The earliest reference to the disappointing sales, a little over 20,000; cf. F, IV, ii, 302, clearly referring to the first three numbers. See *To* Forster, 28 June 43 and *fn*.

I set against some piece of property of yours, that we shall be in our graves and out of them again in particles of dust, impalpable, before those honest men at Washington, in their earthy riots, care one miserable damn for Mind?

You will not take it ill when I tell you that the last-sent Nicks[1] remain uncut. When I resolved on shipboard coming home, to write upon America, I solemnly determined with myself that I would never read an American Criticism on the book. Innumerable newspapers have been sent to me across the Atlantic since its publication. If there were anything to pay, they have gone back to the Post Office; if nothing, they have gone, unopened, into the fire. I have never once departed from my resolution in the least degree. And I feel the wisdom of it, in my good spirits and good humour.[2]

I don't think you will like Chuzzlewit less, as it goes on. I particularly commend Mr. Pinch, and a sister of his who will one day appear upon the scene,[3] to your favorable consideration.

Ah! That unfulfilled promise! If I ever have a scene of Chuzzlewit written early enough to send to you—but I will not lay down any more pieces of stone in the Infernal Pavement. Nous verrons.

Mrs. Dickens sends her best regards to yourself and Mrs. Clark; in which I cordially join.—Last Thursday twelvemonth, we dined at your house.[4]

Always Faithfully Yours

L. Gaylord Clark Esquire.   CHARLES DICKENS

To C. C. FELTON, 2 MARCH 1843†

MS Berg Collection. *Address:* By Mail Steamer | Professor Felton | Cambridge | Massachusetts | United States.

1 Devonshire Terrace York Gate Regents Park London
Second March 1843.

My Dear Felton.

I don't know where to begin, but plunge headlong with a terrible splash into this letter, on the chance of turning up somewhere.

Hurrah! Up like a Cork again—with the North American Review[5] in my

---

[1] Copies of the *Knickerbocker Magazine*, edited by Clark. The issue of Feb 43 contained an article "Boz at Idelberg", a fanciful account of CD's reception. There was a short and not very favourable notice of *American Notes*, and comments on the October *Foreign Quarterly*'s attack on the American press (see *To* Fonblanque, 8 Nov 42, *fn*) in the issue of Dec 42.

[2] Clark quoted most of this paragraph in the June No.

[3] Ruth Pinch first appears in Ch. 9 in the April No.

[4] See *To* Bartlett, 24 Feb 42, *fn*. When quoting this sentence in *Harper's New Monthly*, Aug 1862 (xxv, 376), Clark calls

it a postscript, and turns it into "This day twelvemonth I dined at your house; the pleasantest dinner I enjoyed in America. What a company!" Elsewhere in the article he gives pointlessly garbled versions of other parts of the same letter, misdating one of them 1849.

[5] "Charles Dickens; his Genius and Style" in the Jan number; a 25-page article, the latter half on *American Notes*. CD would have valued especially Felton's public support of his views on international copyright, and his rebuttal of the common charge ("unjust, false, virulent and vulgar") of being a hired agent of English publishers and authors. Felton

hand. Like you, my dear Felton. And I can say no more in praise of it, though I go on to the end of the sheet. You cannot think how much notice it has attracted here. Brougham called the other day with the No. (thinking I might not have seen it) and I being out at the time, he left a note, speaking of it, and of the writer, in terms that warmed my heart. Lord Ashburton (one of whose people wrote a Notice in the Edinburgh, which they have since publicly contradicted)[1] also wrote to me about it in just the same strain. And many others have done the like.

I am in great health and spirits, and powdering away at Chuzzlewit, with all manner of facetiousness rising up before me as I go on. As to news, I have really none, saving that Forster (who never took any exercise in his life) has been laid up with the rheumatism for weeks past, but is now, I hope, getting better. My little captain,[2] as I call him—he who took me out, I mean, and with whom I had that adventure of the cork soles[3]—has been in London too, and seeing all the lions under my escort. Good Heavens! I wish you could have seen certain other mahogany faced men (also Captains) who used to call here for him in the morning, and bear him off to Docks and Rivers and all sorts of queer places, whence he always returned late at night, with rum and water tear-drops in his eyes, and a complication of Punchy smells in his mouth! He was better than a Comedy to us—having marvellous ways of tying his pocket hand kerchief round his neck at dinner time in a kind of jolly embarrasment[4]—and then forgetting what he had done with it. Also of singing songs to wrong tunes, and calling land objects by sea names, and never knowing what o'Clock it was, but taking midnight for seven in the evening; with many other sailor oddities, all full of honesty, manliness, and good temper. We took him to Drury Lane Theatre to see Much Ado About Nothing.[5] But I never could find out what he meant by turning round to Kate after he had watched the first two scenes with great attention; and enquiring "whether it was a Polish piece?"!

[a]Forster must make haste and get well, for this day month, the second of April, is our wedding day and his birthday; on which high festival, we always go down in great state to Richmond (an exquisite place upon the River Thames: some twelve miles off) and hold a solemn dinner, whereat we empty our glasses, you may believe.[a] On the fourth, I am going to preside at a Public Dinner for

also admitted some justice in CD's attack on American newspapers, though thinking it exaggerated (see *To* Mrs Trollope, 16 Dec 42) and denying their power and influence; "the honorable and high-minded man" had nothing to fear from them. CD's book, "scattered all over the country by the penny press", had been read "with general approbation"; its pictures were the humorous scenes of a creative artist, not satires on American civilization; the style was free, graphic and flowing, the general tone frank, honest and manly, steering clear of personalities. The review contained long quotations of the less controversial passages—e.g. the voyage, the Lowell Institution, Niagara, the pigs in New York (compared with a passage in Head's *Bubbles from the Brunnens of Nassau*). Felton's general survey of CD's career and achievement, also highly favourable, compared his correction of "ancient abuses" with Channing's.

[1] See *To* the Editor of *The Times*, 15 Jan and *fn*.

[2] Hewitt; he had evidently left Devonshire Terrace, but did not sail again until 4 Apr.

[3] See *To* Beard, 1 May 42.

[4] Thus in MS.

[5] On 24 Feb.

[aa] Not previously published.

the benefit of the Printers;[1] and if you were a guest at that table, wouldn't I smite you on the shoulder, harder than ever I rapped the well-beloved back of Washington Irving at the City Hotel in New York![2]

You were asking me—I love to say, asking—as if we could talk together—about Maclise. He is such a discursive fellow, and so eccentric in his might, that on a mental review of his pictures I can hardly tell you of them as leading to any one strong purpose. But the Annual Exhibition at the Royal Academy comes off in May,[3] and then I will endeavour to give you some notion of him. He is a tremendous creature, and might do anything. But like all tremendous creatures, he takes his own way, and flies off at unexpected breaches in the conventional wall.

You know Hone's[4] Every Day Book, I dare say. Ah! I saw a scene of mingled comicality and seriousness at his funeral some weeks ago,[5] which has choked me at dinner-time ever since. George Cruikshank and I, went as Mourners;[6] and as he lived, poor fellow, five miles out of town, I drove George down. It was such a day as I hope for the credit of Nature is seldom seen in any parts but these—muddy, foggy, wet, dark, cold, and unutterably wretched in every possible respect. Now, George has enormous whiskers which straggle all down his throat in such weather, and stick out in front of him, like a partially unravelled bird's-nest; so that he looks queer enough at the best, but when he is very wet, and in a state between jollity (he is always very jolly with me) and the deepest gravity (going to a funeral, you know) it is utterly impossible to resist him: especially as he makes the strangest remarks the mind of man can conceive, without any intention of being funny, but rather meaning to be philosophical. I really cried with an irresistible sense of his comicality, all the way, but when he was drest out in a black cloak and a very long black hatband by an undertaker, who (as he whispered me with tears in his eyes—for he had known Hone many years—was "a character, and he would like to sketch him") I thought I should have been obliged to go away. However, we went into a little parlor where the funeral party was, and God knows it was miserable enough, for the

---

[1] The anniversary festival of the Printers' Pension Society, held at the London Tavern: see *Speeches*, ed. K. J. Fielding, pp 36–40. CD again referred to Spedding's comments on the American and English press in the *Edinburgh Review*. Forster, Jerrold, Stanfield, Tom Landseer, M'Ian, Bell and Hood were also present and the last two spoke. CD's accountbook (MS Messrs Coutts) shows a payment of £7.5s to the Society on 14 June. The annual meeting the following year referred to the appeal at this dinner as having "produced to the charity the net sum of £250, the largest amount ever collected on any similar occasion" (*The Age*, 9 Mar 44).

[2] i.e., presumably, at the Dinner to CD on 18 Feb at which Irving presided (see *To* Forster, 24 Feb, *fn*).

[3] Besides *The Waterfall at St. Nightons' Kieve* (see *To* Felton, 31 Dec 42 and *fns*) Maclise exhibited *The Actors' Reception of the Author* (Gil Blas); Thackeray was struck by his "extraordinary power of minute presentation" in both pictures (*Pictorial Times*, 6 May 43). CD did not write to Felton in May, as promised, and has left no record of his visit to the Academy.

[4] For Hone, and CD's last visit, see *To* Forster, 5 Oct 42.

[5] On 11 Nov 42, at Abney Park cemetery, Stoke Newington.

[6] The *Nonconformist*, 23 Nov, noted the presence of "a few friends only" besides the family, and named Binney, Cruikshank, and CD.

widow and children were crying bitterly in one corner, and the other mourners —mere people of ceremony, who cared no more for the Dead Man than the hearse did—were talking quite coolly and carelessly together in another; and the contrast was as painful and distressing as anything I ever saw. There was an Independent clergyman[1] present, with his bands on and a bible under his arm who as soon as we were seated, addressed George thus, in a loud emphatic voice—"Mr. Cruikshank. Have you seen a paragraph respecting our departed friend, which has gone the round of the morning papers?"[2]—"Yes Sir", says George, "I have"—looking very hard at me the while, for he had told me with some pride, coming down, that it was his composition. "Oh!" said the clergyman. "Then you will agree with me Mr. Cruikshank that it is not only an insult to me who am the servant of the Almighty, but an insult to the Almighty whose servant I am"—"How's that Sir?" says George. "It is stated, Mr. Cruikshank, in that paragraph", says the Minister, "that when Mr. Hone failed in business as a bookseller, he was persuaded by *me* to try the Pulpit, which is false, incorrect, unchristian, in a manner blasphemous, and in all respects contemptible. Let us pray." With which, my dear Felton—and in the same breath I give you my word—he knelt down, as we all did, and began a very miserable [jumble][3] of an extemporary prayer. I was really penetrated with sorrow for the family, but when George (upon his knees, and sobbing for the loss of an old friend) whispered me "that if that wasn't a clergyman, and it wasn't a funeral, he'd have punched his head", I felt as if nothing but convulsions could possibly relieve me.[4]

[1] The Rev. Thomas Binney (1798–1874; *DNB*), nonconformist divine, the most eminent in his generation; known as "the great Dissenting bishop", he regarded the Established Church as a national evil. For 40 years Independent |minister at Weigh House Chapel (in Eastcheap to 1834, then demolished and re-erected in Fish Street Hill), where he drew large congregations. Very tall and of striking appearance, he was an effective but at times an eccentric preacher, "a man around whom all kinds of legends developed" (E. Kaye, *History of the King's Weigh House Church*, 1968, p. 62).

[2] The obituary of Hone in the *Morning Herald* (9 Nov) had stated that after the failure of his business Hone had become acquainted with Binney who "persuaded him to try his powers in the pulpit, and he frequently preached in the Weigh-house Chapel, Eastcheap"; two days later a correction was inserted, saying that "Mr. Hone was for some years a member of the Weigh House, but he never preached either in that or in any chapel".

[3] Only the dot of the "j", the "m", and final "le" are visible.

[4] The description of Hone's funeral was quoted by Forster in his 2nd volume (F, 1872–4, II, 11–13) from the text of the letter given by James T. Fields (*Atlantic Monthly*, July 1871, XXVIII, 110–111); in his next volume Forster published an extract from Binney's "counter-statement" in the *Evangelical Magazine* of Jan 73, though without naming Binney (F, III, 520–1), and in the next edn (1876) omitted the description of the funeral altogether. According to W. Robertson Nicoll (*Dickens's Own Story*, 1923, pp. 147–70) who quotes the whole of Binney's letter, he was assisted in the rebuttal by the Rev. Joshua C. Harrison and by Cruikshank. Cruikshank had also written a letter to the *Daily Telegraph* (23 Nov 72) making similar corrections, and saying that he had disclaimed the "offensive" part of the notice in the *Herald* of 9 Nov 42, which had been added by Captain Barker. The corrections are matters of detail; Forster's comment is "The reader must be left to judge between what is said of the incident in the text and these recollections of it after thirty years". According to Hone's biographer, F. W. Hackwood, Hone's daughter (Mrs Burn) "denied the

*b*Tell Longfellow that I can't find that book of his, but that I have some others from the Shakespeare Society[1] for him; and that I want to know whether I shall send them to Hillard.[2] Remember me heartily to *our* Hillard, and to Sumner, and all friends. We have been greatly concerned at Mrs. Felton's not being well,[3] but hope your next accounts will be more favorable. Our united loves to her. Tell me something in your next, about Dr. Channing's family. Disgusted with our Established Church, and its Puseyisms,[4] and daily outrages on common sense and humanity, I have carried into effect an old idea of mine, and joined the Unitarians,[5] who *would* do something for human improvement,

misstatements in Forster's Life as soon as they appeared in 1872", and pointed out that of the 24 people present at the funeral all except CD were either relatives or intimate friends (*William Hone, his Life and Times*, 1912, p. 354). Blanchard Jerrold (*Life of George Cruikshank*, new edn, 1894, p. 72) says that CD "used to describe a serio-comic scene with Mrs. Cruikshank at the time, who implored him to intercede, not only because she feared George might be indiscreet and get into trouble, but because she could not bear 'those horrid Miss Hones' ". CD giving an outsider's impression and may have improved on the incident a little for Felton's benefit.

bb Not previously published.

[1] See Vol. II, p. 462*n*; CD was about to become one of the five new members of the Council of 21, elected 26 Apr (*Athenæum*, 29 Apr 43); the five retiring members were Craik, Harness, Macready, Milman and Oxenford; CD retired in 44. On 18 Apr 43 he was one of the auditors of the accounts, with Charles Purton Cooper, the antiquary and barrister, and Henry Crabb Robinson (*Report of the 2nd Annual Meeting*, 1843); Crabb Robinson refers to "Dickens the romance writer" and adds "I was the man of business" (MS Diary, Dr Williams's Library). The seven publications of the year ending 31 Dec 42, whose editors included Peter Cunningham, David Laing, Dyce and Collier, were presumably the books to be sent to Longfellow. (He lent nine vols to Emerson in Dec 45; *Journals*, ed. Gilman and Parsons, IX, 567*n*.) Forty-nine vols of publications from 1841 to 1853 were in CD's library at his death (*Catalogue of the Library of CD*, ed. J. H. Stonehouse, p. 101).

[2] John Hillard, the American merchant (see 5 Nov 42, *fn*), as distinct from his brother George, Longfellow's friend.

[3] Longfellow in a letter to Forster on 28 Feb (*Letters of Henry Wadsworth Longfellow*, ed. A. Hilen, II, 509) reported that "Felton's wife is very ill,—dangerously ill", having fallen downstairs before her confinement; he feared "still worse news", but Mrs Felton lived till 12 Apr 45.

[4] For CD's published attack on them, see *To* Thompson, 26 May 43, *fn*.

[5] According to Clement E. Pike, "CD and Unitarianism" (*Unitarian Monthly*, Feb 1912, p. 18), CD began to attend at Essex Street Chapel after his return from America, and then, "learning that a funeral sermon on Dr. Channing . . . was to be preached by the Rev. Edward Tagart, at the Unitarian Chapel in Little Portland Street, on November 20 [1842], he resolved to hear it. After the service he had some talk with Mr. Tagart, and finding that they each held similar views of religious truths he took sittings in the chapel for himself and his family" (CD's Accounts, MS Messrs Coutts, show a payment of £7 for "Pew-rent" on 8 Jan 44). The sermon, published in 1842, praised Channing's views on slavery, and said that his qualities counteracted the painful impressions of America "which reach us from so many quarters", instancing the "hard and selfish spirit of social competition" and the "monstrous and disgusting licentiousness of the public press". The minister at Essex Street was Thomas Madge (William J. Roffey, "Essex Street Chapel", *D*, XXII [1926], 187). The family continued to attend regularly at Little Portland Street whenever they were in England until 1847 (according to Pike's information from Tagart's daughters) and CD afterwards occasionally attended alone. If Pike's information is correct it is surprising that there is no reference in *To* Felton, 31 Dec 42. See also *To* Tagart, ?Dec 42–Feb 43.

if they could; and who practise Charity and Toleration. The Tories will love me better than ever, if this gets wind. My children shall return the compliment, please God!*b*

Faithfully Always My Dear Felton

CD.

To W. H. PRESCOTT, 2 MARCH 1843

MS Comtesse de Suzannet. *Address:* By Mail Steamer | W. H. Prescott Esquire | Boston | Massachusetts | United States.

London. 1 Devonshire Terrace | York Gate Regents Park

Second March 1843.

My Dear Prescott.

You are playing at blindmans buff with International copyrights, I see. In the existing state of the law (whereof the folks at Washington have the full credit) no transmission of early copies, secures a copyright in this country. All you gain is priority of publication; and at this moment anybody who thought it worth his while could print Madame de Calderon's book,[1] or yours, on his own account, without paying the author one sixpence. Therefore what you have to consider in the disposal of your own wares, is, who will give you the most, for the desperate chance he purchases.[2]

[1] See *To* Prescott, 15 Oct 42. Prescott had sent the MS for CD to forward to Chapman & Hall in instalments during Dec. It was published in two parts, 21 Jan and 4 Feb, as *Life in Mexico, during a Residence of Two Years in that Country. By Madame C— de la B—. With a Preface by W. H. Prescott.* Prescott explained that initials should be used because of her position as an ambassador's wife, although her name was given in full in Chapman & Hall's advertisements. Reviews were good and the book sold well, though with no profit to the author. (*Correspondence of W. H. Prescott,* ed. R. Wolcott, Boston, 1925, pp. 322–3, 328–9, 369, and *The Papers of W. H. Prescott,* ed. C. Harvey Gardiner, Urbana, 1964, pp. 196–7.)

[2] CD was answering Prescott's letter of 30 Jan 43 (*Correspondence,* pp. 329–30) in which he had said, in connection with Mme Calderón's book, "Doesn't the purchase of a copyright protect the English publishers? If not how can I dispose of my own wares? It would be better for me in that case to publish for half profits as I do with Bentley now [i.e. *Ferdinand and Isabella*]. I am in somewhat of a puzzle". Prescott had written to Bentley on 31 Dec

42 (*Correspondence,* p. 328) in doubt about disposing of "half the copyright, as before", or "of the whole for a round sum at once", because of the low returns on his earlier book; his letter to Colonel T. Aspinwall, his London agent, of 30 Jan 43 (*Correspondence,* pp. 330–1) shows that he was also influenced by advice given independently by Charles Lyell and CD to sell the copyright outright, both considering that "the work ought to bring five or six hundred pounds". In his letter to Bentley Prescott had mentioned his intention of entrusting the negotiations to Aspinwall: "As my intercourse with you has been so agreeable to me, I shall desire, as he will understand, to give you the preference". He also gave Bentley particulars of the proposed length of the book. His letter to Aspinwall makes it clear that Bentley was to have the preference, despite the limited returns on *Ferdinand and Isabella,* and his action in advertising the *Conquest* without authority; but other possibilities were to be explored: "Dickens offered to make an arrangement for me with his publishers. As I shall leave the matter to you, you will do as you please about it when the time comes".

Chapman and Hall are going to write you by this packet;[1] and therefore I will leave business matters to them. We are all well, and unite in cordial regards to yourself, and Mrs. Prescott, and all your house.

As to the Pirates, let them wave their black flag, and rob under it, and stab into the bargain, until the crack of doom. I should hardly be comfortable if I knew they *bought* the right of blackguarding me in the Model Republic; but while they steal it, I am happy.[2] So hurrah for Spring; which, I hope, by the time you get this, will be drawing upon us in England; and may we all enjoy what Leigh Hunt calls "the leafy greenery"[3] as much as Heaven meant us to, in sending it!

Faithfully your friend My Dear Prescott

W. H. Prescott Esquire.   CHARLES DICKENS

To GEORGE W. PUTNAM, 2 MARCH 1843*

MS New York Public Library. *Address:* By Mail Steamer. | Mr. G. W. Putnam | *Nashua* | New Haven | United States.

London. 1 Devonshire Terrace, York Gate, Regents Park.
Second March 1843.

Dear Mr. Putnam.

I was very glad indeed to receive your letter dated on the First of January; for, from your long silence, we began to fear you were not well; and to wonder, if you were, what on earth had become of you. I hope you will not only put counterfeit gold into the portraits,[4] but will put the real metal into your own

---

[1] Chapman & Hall on 3 Mar sent Prescott £25 for Mme Calderón, and asked for another work from her, and for an opportunity to publish Prescott in England (C. Harvey Gardiner, "William Hickling Prescott: Author's Agent", *Mid-America*, Apr 1959, XXXI, 70–1). Prescott commented, "I have had a letter from Mr. Dickens's publishers asking me to let them have the book. But I do not think they have a standing that would give éclat to it, and they write as if there were no validity in a copyright. But if they offer you a good sum one might waive other scruples" (Prescott *to* Aspinwall, 1 Apr 43, *Correspondence*, p. 344). Prescott had evidently been unconvinced by CD's explanation of the copyright position; he thought the position had recently deteriorated as a result of "the conduct of our publishers" and that "the rights of foreigners are now regarded more with jealousy and distrust . . . I suspect something of this feeling may be traced to Dickens himself, who feels very sore at the piratical usage he has met with here" (Prescott *to* Edward Everett, 30 Apr 43, *Correspondence*, p. 351). After further pro-longed negotiations with Murray, Longman, and Bentley, the copyright was sold outright to Bentley in June for £650; the agreement was signed 17 Aug (*op. cit.,* pp. 344–83; text of Agreement in C. Harvey Gardiner, *Prescott and his Publishers*, Southern Illinois, 1959, Appx E). For the publication, see *To* Prescott, 10 Nov and *fn*.

[2] Prescott had written "Your friend the Greek professor dined with me *tête à tête* today. We discussed you over our claret, and did justice to both, I assure you. We heard an anecdote the other day which we agreed one, perhaps both of us, will tell you. A friend of ours walking on the streets of New York saw a boy hawking one of your last immortals, Barnaby I think, and offering it at sixpence! 'What?' said our friend, 'Can you offer it so cheap, my boy?' 'Oh yes, Sir,' said the *varmint*, 'Dickens is fell now!' You see how the bloody pirates run you down".

[3] Both words, especially "leafy", are characteristic of Hunt's writings, but the actual phrase has not been found.

[4] Cf. *To* Putnam, 18 Oct 42.

pockets. For I know you deserve it, and should be better pleased to hear of your well-doing than I can easily tell you.

You write of the American newspapers, and cause me to smile afresh as I turn once more to your letter. If you could see me in my quiet study at home here, you would begin to know how little they trouble me, I fancy. You remember my old way of not reading them? Well! Since I came home, and the book was published, I have received some bushels of them by post. If there were anything to pay, they went back to the post office; if nothing, they went, with their covers on them, into the fire. And to this hour I have not seen one line of their producing, but am in glorious health and glorious spirits, and writing merrily at my new story.

Mrs. Dickens is quite well, and desires to be cordially remembered to you. So does Anne, who brightened up very much on the receipt of your message, and says she wouldn't mind travelling over all that land and water, again. As to Kate, she holds her old opinion on this point—which perhaps you recollect? The children are mightily red in the face and very fat; and if we tell them we are going to America again, they all roar lustily.

Captain Hewitt has been in town here, and I have shewn him all the Lions; as I should very much like to do for you. Perhaps I shall, one of these days. In the meantime, and ever, believe in the assurance of my true regard, and always reckon me

Faithfully Your friend
CHARLES DICKENS

Mrs. Dickens says I have "forgotten Julia"; to which *I* say "No. For she is understood, like a latin pronoun, though not expressed."—We went to Bath (a hundred miles or so) the other day, with one of the renowned boys, which made us talk of you more than once, upon the road.[1]

To LADY LOVELACE,[2] 4 MARCH 1843*

MS Estate of Mary Lady Lovelace.

Devonshire Terrace | Fourth March 1843

Mr. Charles Dickens presents his compliments to Lady Lovelace, and in acknowledging the receipt of her kind answer to his note, begs to say that he will be very happy to call in St. James's Square at ten o'Clock on Tuesday morning.

He is not aware that the subscription list[3] has ever been printed, or that any

[1] See *To* Marryat, 21 Jan. They returned by railway.

[2] Ada, Countess of Lovelace (1815–52), Byron's daughter; married the Earl of Lovelace 1835; Lady George Murray described her in 1836 as "very fond of mathematics, astronomy, and music, but possesses no soul for poetry" (Caroline Fox, *Memories of Old Friends*, 1882, I, 14–15). Friend of Babbage, and translated Mena-

brea's *Notices* on his calculating machine; also of Mrs Somerville and Augustus De Morgan, who said she could have been a Senior Wrangler; later took to gambling on horse-racing and pawned the family jewels.

[3] Must refer to the subscription list for Macready's testimonial (see *To* Miss Coutts, 8 Feb 43).

copy of it is in existence, save that which has been most desperately thumbed by a persevering collector.[1] But he will procure it, such as it is, and bring it with him on Tuesday.

He may be permitted to add that he is too well assured of the interest felt by Lady Lovelace in all that concerns the improvement and happiness of the people, to have ever entertained the idea of addressing her on this subject, *merely* as the daughter of Lord Byron.[2] He intended to urge that circumstance, only as an apology for what, under other circumstances, might have seemed an unwarrantable intrusion.

To DR SOUTHWOOD SMITH, 6 MARCH 1843

MS Mr W. A. Foyle. *Address:* Dr. Southwood Smith | New Broad Street | City.

Private

Devonshire Terrace | Sixth March 1843.

My Dear Dr. Smith

I sent a message across the way today, begging you, in case you should come to the Sanatorium, to call on me, if convenient. My reason was this;—

I am so perfectly stricken down by the blue book[3] you have sent me, that I think (as soon as I shall have done my month's work) of writing, and bringing out, a very cheap pamphlet, called "An appeal to the People of England, on behalf of the Poor Man's Child"—with my name attached, of course. I should

[1] i.e. his own list, thumbed by Forster (Vol. II, p. 2n).

[2] There is no evidence that Lady Lovelace ever shared any of her mother's and husband's philanthropical interests and special concern for the education of the poor; but CD might not know this, and would think of Macready's labours for the drama as conducing to the "improvement and happiness" of the people. He had presumably mentioned Byron because *Werner* was one of Macready's successes.

[3] The Second Report of the Children's Employment Commission, published at the end of Feb, was concerned particularly with "Trades and Manufactures", as the First Report had been with "Mines and Collieries"; but also with the general condition of all child employees, the Commissioners' conclusions on "The Moral Condition of the whole youthful population" occupying pp. 141–204. Two volumes of "Appendix" set out the evidence drawn from hundreds of interviews, and by this any reader would be "perfectly stricken". Southwood Smith was one of the four Commissioners (see Vol. II, p. 165n), the others being Thomas Tooke, Leonard Horner, and Robert John Saunders. R. H. Horne, as one of the many sub-commissioners, was responsible for collecting evidence in the Wolverhampton district in 1841. The Report made a great impression; it inspired Elizabeth Barrett's "The Cry of the Children" (*Blackwood's*, Aug 1843; see *Letters of Elizabeth Barrett Browning to R. H. Horne*, ed. S. R. Townshend Mayer, 1877, I, 80), and was heavily drawn upon by Disraeli in *Sybil*, 1845 (Sheila M. Smith, "Willenhall and Wodgate: Disraeli's use of Blue Book Evidence", *Review of English Studies*, new series, XIII [1962], 368–84). Extracts from the Report and comments upon it were given in the press. It had not been generally realized in how many trades children began work under seven years of age and worked 10–12 hours, without legal protection; the most striking and painful revelations were of their physical state, their ignorance and complete moral and educational neglect. On 28 Feb Lord Ashley moved the Address to the Crown for the education of the working classes and on 8 Mar the Factory Education Bill was laid before the House, only to break down a few months later on the clauses on religious education (see *To* Napier, 16 Sep, *fn*).

be very glad to take counsel with you in the matter, and to receive any suggestions from you, in reference to it. Suppose I were to call on you one evening in the course of ten days or so, what would be the most likely hour to find you at home?

In haste | Always Faithfully | Your friend

Dr. Southwood Smith   CHARLES DICKENS

To ALFRED TENNYSON,[1] 9 MARCH 1843

MS Yale University Library. *Address:* Alfred Tennyson Esquire.

Devonshire Terrace | Ninth March 1843.

My Dear Tennyson.

For the love I bear you, as a man whose writings enlist my whole heart and nature in admiration of their Truth and Beauty, set these books upon your shelves[2]; believing that you have no more earnest and sincere homage than mine.[3]

Faithfully | and Gratefully | Your friend

Alfred Tennyson Esquire   CHARLES DICKENS

[1] Alfred Tennyson (1809–92; *DNB*), poet, *b.* at Somersby, Lincs, his home until 1837; was living with his mother and sisters near Maidstone, but in 1840s frequently in London, often visiting his Cambridge friend James Spedding, Thackeray, and the Carlyles. Carlyle, in a letter of 5 Sep 40 (when Tennyson was "still new to Jane"), described him as "shaggyheaded . . . dusty, smoky, free and easy: who swims, outwardly and inwardly, with great composure in an inarticulate element as of tranquil chaos and tobacco smoke; great now and then where he does emerge; a most restful, brotherly, solidhearted man" (*Alfred Lord Tennyson, a Memoir*, by his Son, 1897, I, 187*n*; text here corrected from original MS as quoted in C. R. Sanders, "Carlyle and Tennyson", *Publications of the Modern Language Association of America*, LXXVI, 1961, 82–97). Thackeray too found his conversation "delightful . . . full of breadth manliness and humour" (*Letters and Private Papers*, ed. G. N. Ray, II, 26). In 1843 a recent financial disaster and increased ill-health had deepened both his melancholy and his friends' protective affection; attempts to obtain the laureateship after Southey's death in Mar were not successful, but Carlyle was active in obtaining for him through Milnes a Civil List pension 1845. He was less often in London in 1843. When he and CD first met is not known; the present letter does not suggest personal familiarity, and it was perhaps CD's admiration for the 1842 volumes (see *To* Forster, 7 Aug 42) that led him to seek Tennyson's acquaintance through Forster or Thackeray. But within a few weeks, almost certainly on 27 Apr 43, CD entertained him, with Thackeray and FitzGerald (as the latter's guest), to dinner at Devonshire Terrace, after a drive together; FitzGerald, whose brief reference is the only surviving contemporary record, found "Boz . . . unaffected and hospitable" (Thomas Wright, *Life of Edward Fitz-Gerald*, 1904, I, 171; correction of Wright's misdating confirmed by information kindly supplied by Mr A. McKinley Terhune). But as his sole meeting with CD it was long remembered, and revived by reading Forster's *Life* in 1872–3; he mentions again CD's "unaffectedness" despite his "American Triumph", "seeming to wish anyone to show off rather than himself", and recalls that they "talked of Crabbe" and had "a round game at cards and mulled claret in the evening" (FitzGerald *to* Mrs Tennyson [Dec 72], quoted in *Tennyson and his Friends*, ed. Hallam, Lord Tennyson, 1911, pp. 112–3; further information from Mr McKinley Terhune).

[2] No early editions of CD's works survive in the residue of Tennyson's library at the Tennyson Research Centre, Lincoln.

[3] This is manifest not only in CD's letter to Forster, 7 Aug 42, but in echoes

To MR LOVE,[1] 10 MARCH 1843

Mention in Samuel T. Freeman & Co. catalogue, Apr 1917; *MS* 1 p. (3rd person); dated Devonshire Terrace, 10 Mar 43.

To DR SOUTHWOOD SMITH, 10 MARCH 1843

MS Mr W. A. Foyle. *Address:* Dr. Southwood Smith | 36 New Broad Street | City.

Devonshire Terrace | Tenth March 1843.

My Dear Dr. Smith

Don't be frightened when I tell you, that since I wrote to you last, reasons have presented themselves for deferring the production of that pamphlet, until the end of the year. I am not at liberty to explain them further, just now; but *rest assured* that when you know them, and see what I do, and where, and how, you will certainly feel that a Sledge hammer has come down with twenty times the force—twenty thousand times the force—I could exert by following out my first idea. Even so recently as when I wrote to you the other day, I had not contemplated the means I shall now, please God, use. But they have been suggested to me, and I have girded myself for their seizure—as you shall see in due time.[2]

If you will allow our tete a tete, and projected conversation on the subject, still to come off, I will write to you, as soon as I see my way to the end of my Month's work.

Always Faithfully Yours

Dr. Southwood Smith   CHARLES DICKENS

---

of "Locksley Hall" in *To* Babbage, 27 Apr 43, of "Lady Clara Vere de Vere" in his Manchester speech in Oct (*Speeches*, ed. K. J. Fielding, p. 56), and of "Mariana" in Stave II of the *Carol* (description of the deserted schoolhouse).

  [1] Unidentified.

  [2] The reference to "the end of the year" indicates that CD had already thought of relating his appeal on behalf of the poor man's child to the Christmas season, though not necessarily in fictional form. Perhaps he meant to insert a small pamphlet in the December No. of *Chuzzlewit*; the essence of this would be surprise, which would account for his keeping it secret from Southwood Smith. It can hardly have been the *Edinburgh Review* article, first thought of in 1841 after the First Report; Southwood Smith knew about that, and an anonymous article in

the *Edinburgh* would not have the exceptional impact which CD anticipates. In the event, the idea was merged in *A Christmas Carol*; the early germination of this first notion is compatible with Forster's statement that the "fancy" first occurred to him in October. In the *Carol*, CD's response to the Second Report is most evident at the end of Stave III where Scrooge is shown the two wretched children under the robes of the Spirit of Christmas Present: "Yellow, meagre, ragged, scowling, wolfish . . . where angels might have sat enthroned, devils lurked, and glared out menacing . . . 'They are Man's,' said the Spirit . . . 'This boy is Ignorance. This girl is Want. Beware them both, and all of their degree, but most of all beware this boy, for on his brow I see that written which is Doom, unless the writing be erased.' "

To T. J. THOMPSON, 10 MARCH 1843

MS Huntington Library.

Devonshire Terrace. | Tenth March 1843

My Dear Thompson.

When you said t'other day that you had forgotten how much you gave to the Macready Testimonial, I told you I thought it was five guineas. Now, how I got that idea into my mind, I don't know—perhaps I had a confused remembrance of your giving that sum to the Minor Theatrical Fund[1]—but however that may be, I think it right to tell you that I have looked at the Subscription List, and find *you didn't give anything*!

Will you like to remedy this defect, and taking up the stone you have laid down in the infernal pavement, replace it with precious metal? You can tell me on Sunday.

Always Faithfully Yours

T. J. Thompson Esquire   CHARLES DICKENS

To ALBANY FONBLANQUE, 13 MARCH 1843*

MS Berg Collection.

Devonshire Terrace | Thirteenth March 1843.

My Dear Fonblanque

I plainly see, by your treatment of that order, that you are going over to the Tories. You stand by your order[2] too long and too much.—If you don't take the Examiner with you, leave it to me, and I'll be your Shadow; undoubtedly faint; but warranted fierce.

The Drury Lane Order for next Saturday would purge me of a promise,[3] made in an unthinking hour. I say no more.

I have been expecting to see or hear from you, all the week. Forster told me you had found a mote in Pecksniff's eye;[4] and I see too much brightness in yours, to render me indifferent to the knowledge of it, or anything but anxious that you should freely point it out to me.

I find that I am getting horribly bitter about Puseyism. Good God to talk in these times of most untimely ignorance among the people, about what Priests shall wear, and whither they shall turn[5] when they say their prayers.—They

---

[1] The General Theatrical Fund, as distinct from the special funds for Drury Lane and Covent Garden.

[2] A stock phrase in Tory oratory.

[3] See next; CD had evidently promised Beard an order for Drury Lane. *Much Ado* was played on the following Saturday, 18 Mar.

[4] Pecksniff appears in Chs 6 and 8 of the March No. It is not known what Fonblanque's "mote" was, and no revision was made in later editions.

[5] The *Examiner* (13 Oct 42), quoting the *Morning Chronicle*, had made fun of the Bishop of London's Charge and its "compromises—after the Peel fashion" with Puseyism, particularly over the wearing of surplice or gown, and turning to the east. Some of CD's "bitterness" was expressed in his *Examiner* article of 3 June: see *To* Thompson, 26 May, *fn.*

had best not discuss the latter question too long, or I shrewdly suspect they will turn to the right about: not easily to come back again.

Always Heartily Yours

CHARLES DICKENS

To THOMAS BEARD, 13 MARCH 1843

MS Dickens House. *Address:* Thomas Beard Esquire | 42 Portman Place | Edgeware Road.

Devonshire Terrace | Thirteenth March 1843

My Dear Beard.

Coming on, in due course, for the first vacant Saturday, I send you the unforgotten Drury Lane Order.

Always Faithfully Yours

Thomas Beard Esquire CHARLES DICKENS

To THOMAS MITTON, [13 MARCH 1843]

Mention in next.

To THOMAS MITTON, 14 MARCH 1843

MS Huntington Library.

Devonshire Terrace | Tuesday, Fourteenth March 1843

My Dear Mitton

When I wrote to you last night, I had not received your letter. All I meant by "deferring the consideration" of the freehold project, was, that I had received C and H's account; and that the balance being still heavy against me,[1] I wished to be careful.

It must be something highly advantageous (don't you think?) which would render it desirable to borrow any part of the purchase money? And I fear that Highgate, though a place I like of all things, would be too dear. But I shall be guided, very much, by your enquiries and advice.[2]

Hertfordshire—some twelve or thirteen miles from town, in the direction of Rickmansworth &c—is the cheapest neighbourhood I know of.

Write me again if you have time—supposing, that is, that I don't come to you this evening before 8.

I inclose a cheque for £15[3]

Faithfully Ever

Thomas Mitton Esquire CD.

---

[1] For the advances made under the Agreement of 7 Sep 41, see *To* Chapman & Hall, 1 Jan 42, *fn.* His accounts (MS Messrs Coutts) show that he was spending most of the £200 each month; for the state of CD's bank balance near the end of 1842, see *To* Mitton, 24 Dec 42 and *fn.*

[2] CD had presumably thought of buying a house or cottage out of town; instead he rented rooms at a farmhouse at Finchley (see *To* Beard, 21 Mar).

[3] One of several payments ranging from £6 to £50 made to Mitton in the course of 1843.

To T. J. THOMPSON, 15 MARCH 1843*

MS Mrs Sowerby.

Devonshire Terrace | Fifteenth March 1843.

My Dear Thompson

Second sight no doubt—caught (I see it all), from Donald what's his name, who came bock agen to that unspellable Glen, and published the news of his arrival so extensively.[1]

Next time you send to your bankers, if you will let them have a cheque for the money, payable to Coutts & Co. on account of the Macready Testimonial; you will receive the hearty thanks of the committee, and all other privileges and gratifications to which the subscription entitles you.

I shall very likely see you, sometime next week.

Always Faithfully Yours

T. J. Thompson Esquire   CHARLES DICKENS

To FRANCIS ROSS,[2] 16 MARCH 1843*

MS The Rev. Charles T. Mentzer.

Devonshire Terrace | Sixteenth March 1843

My Dear Frank

I am truly sorry that I missed you again, last Sunday. And therefore I write to give you notice that I have altered my former arrangements for that day; and that a quarter before Two, is the time to have me on the hip.[3]

Faithfully Yours

Francis Ross Esquire   CHARLES DICKENS

To SAMUEL ROGERS, 20 MARCH 1843

Text from P. W. Clayden, *Rogers and his Contemporaries*, 1889, II, 231.

Devonshire Terrace: | Twentieth March, 1843.

My dear Mr. Rogers,

If I am not at your house at seven next Wednesday, write me down an ass.[4]

Faithfully yours always,

CHARLES DICKENS

---

[1] This seems to be a confused recollection of Scott's poem "Donald Caird's come again"; part of the refrain is "Tell the news in brugh and glen". "Second sight" is perhaps attributed by CD to all Highlanders. An anonymous patriotic song "Back Again" of *c.* 1801 (C. Mackay, *Songs of Scotland*, 1857), in which one verse refers to "Donald" (but none to second sight or a glen), is another possibility. "Bock agen" was evidently a catch phrase, not necessarily connected with "Donald"; it is found in Cruikshank's *Illustrations of Time*, 1827: one plate shows a gardener and

a man at a broken fence with the dialogue: "[Gardener] Hollo! you sir, where are you going to? [Man] Bock o'gen!" Its familiarity is shown by references in *Punch* in Mar 48 and Aug 61.

[2] Francis Ross (*b.* 1804), Parliamentary reporter: see Vol. I, p. 85*n*, Vol. II, p. 436*n*. In 1843 published anonymously *Sir Robert Peel and his Era*; his authorship is given by Charles Mackay in *Forty Years' Recollections*, I, 135.

[3] Cf. *Merchant of Venice*, IV, i, 330.

[4] *Much Ado*, III, v, 80.

To THOMAS BEARD, 21 MARCH 1843

MS Dickens House. *Address:* Thomas Beard Esquire | 42 Portman Place | Edgeware Road.

Devonshire Terrace | Twenty First March 1843

My Dear Beard.

I write to you with mingled feelings of Pride and Shame—of honest pride, for that I have discovered a sequestered Farm House at Finchley,[1] five miles and a half from the Regents Park, whereat I do beseech the honor of your company to dinner, next Sunday; and to which retreat I will myself conduct you, if you will be *here* at a quarter before Two. Beds on the premises, or close at hand.

Now for the bitter, bitter shame.

I don't know whether I mentioned to you at the Theatre,[2] that a Finchley Postman, meeting me in the road accompanied by an animal I brought from America, made proposals of marriage, having reference to that creature—in short, to Timber; for I must write his name, sooner or later. Having my doubts on certain points of consummation, I avoided the subject (ran away, in fact) but yesterday, of all evil days in the year, I met this demon Postman in a solitary lane. Again he proposed; and I think I saw distinctly, something fiendish in his face. The result was, that the settlements (involving all possible contingencies of probable puppies) were arranged; and Timber was taken by Topping to the demon's cave; I dining meanwhile, at a rural tavern in the neighbourhood.

The female appeared to be of his own breed—in the full glow of youth and passion—and in every point of view, in the highest state of perfection.

He was absent one hour and a half.

He returned, covered with disgrace and mortification. He had done *nothing*. The official report was, that he had tried, but was considered to be weak in his loins.

I am in a distracted frame of mind. Dreadful thoughts come over me at times, of taking his life. At other times I think of only taking his—but I will

---

[1] Cobley's Farm, where CD rented rooms probably for the second quarter of the year; Forster, who called it "a cottage", where he joined CD (see *To* Pichot, 7 June), says (F, IV, i, 294) that "in the green lanes as the midsummer months were coming on", CD devised Mrs Gamp, who first appears in the Aug No. (Ch. 19). Correspondence and notes in the *Finchley Press* on 6, 13 May, 3, 10, 17 June 1927 and an article, "Dickens's Arcadian Retreat", 20 May, with a sketch, show that it was quite a large farmhouse formerly called Fallow Farm, in Bow Lane, North Finchley, said to have been owned by Richard Cobley (the 1845 Directory shows only "Cobley, William, farmer"). There is a photograph in B. W. Matz's edition of Forster's *Life*, I, 294. The house was on the site of what is now 70 Queen's Avenue, which bears a tablet; a neighbouring road is named Dickens Avenue (*D*, XXIII [1927], 28, and XXIV [1928], 96). Finchley at that date was completely rural, consisting of three hamlets, Church End, North End, and East End, and Finchley Common, traces of which still remain as open ground here and there. CD's route, riding or walking, would be by what is now Finchley Road, from which a turning led to East End and Bow Lane, which joins the Great North Road. Omnibuses ran to London from the Five Bells, East End, three times daily, taking three hours.

[2] See *To* Fonblanque, 13 Mar and *fn*.

not anticipate. Heaven send him a safe deliverance. He is at present in a basket on the top of the bookcase, pending the decision of the particular kind of Torture to which he shall be exposed.

Yours despondingly
CHARLES DICKENS

To MISS BURDETT COUTTS, 21 MARCH 1843

MS Morgan Library. *Address:* Miss Coutts.

Devonshire Terrace | Twenty First March 1843

Dear Miss Coutts.

I hope you have by this time got the better of your cold. I speak feelingly, having had a tremendous one of my own, besides the pleasure of six weeks contemplation of another in my wife. I have discovered a lonely Farm House at Finchley; and am going to bury myself there for at least a month to come; visiting this City at rare Intervals[1]—and immersing myself in my story. But it is not so far off that I shall have any difficulty in reaching this place "for a consideration"[2]—and if you will give me that kind and valuable one which will lie in a favorable answer to the enclosed, I shall be delighted.

Macready has been so much pleased by your approval and support;[3] and is a man who while he courts nobody, feels such encouragement with great keenness; that I shall be glad to present him to you, if you will dine here.[4] I know you will like him, as a private gentleman, exceedingly.

With best regards to Miss Meredith

Believe me always
Yours faithfully and obliged

Miss Coutts.   CHARLES DICKENS

P.S. I return the enclosed with many thanks, and I need hardly say that it was most gratifying to all of us—but especially so to the party chiefly interested.

To THOMAS MITTON, 22 MARCH 1843

Text from N, 1, 514.

Devonshire Terrace | Twenty-Second March 1843

My Dear Mitton,

I enclose you the accounts. If you see either of the firm, say nothing to them of what I am about in the writing way.[5] I am bent on its coming (if it come at all) a surprise.

Faithfully always,
[CHARLES DICKENS]

---

[1] The intervals were less rare than CD hoped, chiefly because of Society of Authors' business; but clearly Cobley's Farm was his base for some weeks, and extra engagements were avoided: see *To* Lane, 2 Apr, and *To* Mariotti, 12 Apr.

[2] A favourite phrase of Trapbois the usurer in Scott, *The Fortunes of Nigel*, 1822, Ch. 22.

[3] In subscribing to his testimonial.

[4] See *To* Macready, 2 Apr.

[5] Probably sending Martin to America: this "desperate resolution" is formed in Ch. 12, at the end of the May No. which CD had perhaps begun; he goes in Ch. 15 (finished by the end of Apr). Conceivably CD may have been working out his plan for a "sledgehammer blow" at the end of

To THOMAS MITTON, 28 MARCH 1843

Mention in Hodgson & Co. catalogue, May 1903; dated 28 Mar 43.

To JOHN DE GEX, 30 MARCH 1843

Extract in Hodgson & Co. catalogue, June 1914; *MS* 2pp; dated Devonshire Terrace, 30 Mar 1843.

Accepting an invitation.[1] If the devil could be got to dine at the Freemasons' through one season, I think he'd die; and then the world would come all right again.

To E. W. ELTON,[2] 30 MARCH 1843

MS Duke University Library.

Devonshire Terrace
Thursday Morning | March Thirtieth 1843

My Dear Sir
I beg to enclose you the Fund Document,[3] duly executed and attested.

Faithfully Yours
E. W. Elton Esquire CHARLES DICKENS

To THOMAS BEARD, 31 MARCH 1843

MS Dickens House.

Finchley | Friday Thirty First March | 1843

My Dear Beard
I find that the wedding feast at Richmond,[4] *does* come off on Sunday. *Tomorrow week*, therefore, I shall expect you here, as early as you can come. The green man[5] will receive you with open arms. So will the flesh-colored one.

Faithfully Always
CD.

I am happy to report that Timber runs into a corner and stands on 2 legs, at the word of command.

the year: cf. *To* Southwood Smith, 10 Mar and *fn*.

[1] No advertisement or report of the many public dinners at the Freemasons' Tavern (or elsewhere) in the next two months shows De Gex and CD present; possibly a semi-private dinner, and perhaps the same as seems to be referred to in *To* De Gex, 18 Apr.

[2] Edward William Elton, formerly Elt (1794–1843; *DNB*): see *To* Miss Coutts, 26 July 43. Actor in Macready's company; during Lent was acting at City Theatre on Wednesdays and Fridays, appearing as Brutus in *Julius Caesar* with great success. Chairman and Treasurer of the General Theatrical Fund (for the minor theatres), founded 1839. On his wife's death in 1840,

Elton was offered assistance from the Fund for his large family, but had refused it.

[3] The rules were amended at a meeting on 13 June, according to a pamphlet, *Rules and Regulations of the General Theatrical Fund* (1847), and this amendment was doubtless the "Fund Document". CD was a trustee, with Talfourd and Benjamin Cabbell.

[4] The usual celebration on 2 Apr, which was also Forster's birthday.

[5] The Green Man, on the Great North Road on Finchley Common, kept by Charles Spelt; the present public house of the same name, 394 High Road, was built in 1932; the old inn on the same site was small, with stables, and a forge adjoining.

To RICHARD LANE, 2 APRIL 1843†

MS Dr De Coursey Fales.

Devonshire Terrace | Sunday Second April | 1843.

My Dear Sir

I am sorry to say that I cannot sit to you any morning next week, for my whole time is disposed of. If I could have anticipated your request, I would have arranged to meet it; but I had a notion in my head (Heaven knows how it came there), that the Drawing was done.

Faithfully Yours

Richard Lane Esquire   CHARLES DICKENS

To W. C. MACREADY, [2 APRIL 1843]

Mention in Macready, *Diaries,* II, 201.

About dining with Miss Coutts on Friday.[1]

To OCTAVIAN BLEWITT, 6 APRIL 1843*

MS Royal Literary Fund.

Devonshire Terrace | York Gate Regents Park
Sixth April 1843

My Dear Sir

I beg you to thank the Vice Presidents and other officers of the Literary Fund, on my behalf, for the Invitation to the Anniversary Dinner with which they have honored me, and which I am most happy to accept.[2]

Always Faithfully Yours

Octavian Blewitt Esquire   CHARLES DICKENS

To J. P. HARLEY, 6 APRIL 1843*

MS Dickens House.

Devonshire Terrace | Sixth April 1843

My Dear Harley

Thank you very much for consulting me in the matter of our friend's[3] note. He must be rather a rum customer, I take it, for he *had* written to me before, forwarding a book of Poems (?) of his writing: the which I graciously acknowledged. Therefore I should have thought he needed no other Introduction. Whatever you desire to do in the matter—do—and be assured it will please me.

always Faithfully Your friend

J. P. Harley Esquire.   CHARLES DICKENS

[1] This plan came to nothing, and Miss Coutts did not meet Macready until 1845.
[2] Reports of the dinner on 10 May do not include CD's name, though some give lists of guests; the Duke of Sutherland was in the chair and Charles Lever replied for the novelists. See *To* Leeks, 10 May.
[3] Not identified.

To THE REV. WILLIAM HARNESS, 6 APRIL 1843*

MS The Frank Hollings Bookshop. *Address:* The Reverend William Harness |
Heathcoate Street | Mecklenburg Square.

Devonshire Terrace | Sixth April 1843

My Dear Harness.

I can never be sufficiently grateful to you for that amazing and stupendous
circular. You have conferred an obligation on me which is as enduring in its
character as Humbug itself.

I must ask your leave (and that of Miss Harness) to retain it—at all events for
a short time. I have thought of certain weekly squibbers who ought to know of it.
For it is a noble thing.[1]

Always Faithfully Yours

The Reverend William Harness.   CHARLES DICKENS

To MARK LEMON,[2] 6 APRIL 1843*

MS Birthplace Museum, Portsmouth.

1 Devonshire Terrace | York Gate Regents Park
Sixth April 1843.

My Dear Sir

Don't forget that you dine with me next Wednesday (with as little botheration

[1] CD sent the circular to *Punch*, where
it was published—his only known communication—on 15 Apr under the heading
"Punch's Police. Literary Mendicity.—
Begging Letters". The literary beggar was
Edward West, who is represented as
dropping his letter into a pint of beer
carried by a small boy. It announced a
periodical of "a *correct* and *moral* tendency [Punch *deliberately omits the name*]
designed to be completed in 52 weekly
(3d) numbers", beginning on 31 Dec 42,
and asks "the *Ladies of the Metropolis*" to
support him by filling in the enclosed
form. *Chronicles of the Careworn; or, Walks
and Wanderings* by Edward West, printer,
dedicated by permission to Lord Ashley,
was published in 1843; according to
Punch, 13 May 43, West was "Secretary of
the Shipwrecked Fishermen and Mariners'
Benevolent Society, 26 Bucklersbury" and
continued to send out advertisements of
his periodical along with the society's
prospectus.

[2] Mark Lemon (1809–1870; *DNB*),
playwright and editor of *Punch* 1841–70.
Spent his early years at Hendon and at
Cheam School; then, when the family

fortunes deteriorated, in his uncle's hops
business in Lincs. By 1836 was living in
London, from 1837 employed at a brewery,
and in 1840 at Shakespeare's Head
Tavern, Wych Street, which became the
resort of theatrical and literary men—
probably he met Jerrold and Thackeray at
this time. Contributed to *New Sporting
Magazine*, 1834–7, and *Bentley's Miscellany*, 1837–8 (but not apparently then
known to CD) and was writing for the
stage—his first piece being a farce, *The
P.L., or, 30, Strand* (25 Apr 36). Collaborated in his first opera, *Rob of the Fen*
(1838), with Frank Romer, actor and
composer, whose sister Nelly he married
in 1839. The turning-point of his career
was the launching of *Punch* in July 41,
with Henry Mayhew and Ebenezer Lan-
dells, the engraver; shared editorship at
first with Mayhew and Stirling Coyne,
but became sole editor in 1842. Had kept
Punch going with income from his plays
until Bradbury & Evans took it over in
1842, Evans later recalling that it was
Lemon's "eloquence alone that induced
us to buy *Punch*", and Lemon that "I was
made for *Punch* and *Punch* for me".

about it, in the way of ceremony as may be) at a quarter before 6 for 6 *sharp*—not a blunt half after.

Faithfully Yours

Mark Lemon Esquire   CHARLES DICKENS

To THOMAS BEARD, 7 APRIL 1843

MS Dickens House.

Devonshire Terrace | Friday. Seventh April 1843

My Dear Beard

As I am obliged to attend a Meeting of Authors[1] in town tomorrow, at 2 o'Clock, wouldn't it be as well for us to dine somewhere, and walk out afterwards ? If you will call on me as you go by in the morning, we can arrange in a second, about place and time.

Faithfully Ever

CD.

According to Joseph Hatton, *With a Show in the North*, 1871, p. 1, "he believed in one God, in one woman, in one publication"; "His system is to let each man write what he likes, subject to M.L.'s supervision. 'All cleverer fellows than I am'" (MS Silver Diary). For some time he continued to write for theatre and other periodicals, assisting Ingram on the *Illustrated London News*, and contributing "The Boys of London" to Jerrold's *Illuminated Magazine* in May 43; was author of over 30 plays, mainly farces, burlettas, and melodramas. (Wrote so many theatrical pieces that *The Times* in 1840 said "It is impossible that anything less than a bundle of quills could write so many".) Most recently, his burlesque of 1841, *Ils Amores da Gileso Scroggini e Molli Brownini*, had been put on at the Olympic (27 Mar 43), and he also wrote the libretto for the English version of Rossini's *La Donna del Lago*, well received at Covent Garden in Feb. By this date had two children and had moved to The Lodge, 2 Brook Green, Hammersmith. There is no evidence of meeting CD before 1843; probably introduced by Jerrold, they soon became friends, having in common a love of good fellowship and a strong social conscience. For Lemon's dramatization of *The Chimes*, theatricals, and *Daily News*, see next vol. Lemon appears in Mrs Gamp's 1847 account (F, VI, i, 462) as "a fat gentleman with curly black hair and a merry face . . . rubbing his two hands over one another, as if he were washing on 'em, and shaking his head and shoulders very much". The fullest account of his career and character is Arthur A. Adrian, *Mark Lemon, First Editor of Punch*, 1966.

[1] The second meeting, at which CD took the chair. Besant (*Essays and Historiettes*, p. 277) gives the names of the 19 who were present, who included Forster, Blanchard, Shelton Mackenzie, Mackay, Westland Marston, Silk Buckingham, S. C. Hall, and Thackeray. The result was the printing of the "Proposed Prospectus", which was then circulated "to the principal writers of the country, asking for suggestions, and for co-operation with the movement" (see *To* Mackay, 17 Feb). Robertson was named as honorary secretary and the committee included Bulwer, G. P. R. James, Westland Marston, Marryat, Augustus De Morgan and Horace Smith. There is also a list of authors "who have already signified their adhesion to the Society"; over 100 in number, but not including Carlyle, CD, Forster, Browning, or Tennyson.

To W. C. MACREADY, 7 APRIL 1843*

MS Morgan Library.

Devonshire Terrace | Friday Evening | Seventh April 1843.
My Dear Macready

Forster is here; and we are all very anxious to know what kind of house there was, on the Third Night of our friend of the Italian Academies.[1] If you are at home, tell us.

T'other night, at the Printers' Dinner, I asked Jerrold,[2] and Mr. Lemon of Punch (in return for his kindly inviting us to the Palace)[3] to dine with me next Wednesday at a quarter before 6 for 6 exactly. Will you come? If you can—do.[4] I have since asked Serle.[5]

Affectionately always
W. C. Macready.[6]
Over[7]

[1] Clara Novello, later Countess Gigliucci (1818–1908; *DNB*), singer, daughter of Vincent Novello and sister of Mrs Mary Cowden Clarke; made her Italian début in opera July 40, and sang principal roles at most of the opera-houses in Italy, at Bologna, Genoa, and Rome, 1840–3; returned to England Mar 43. As one of her successes had been in Giovanni Pacini's *Saffo* in 1842, T. J. Serle, her brother-in-law, had arranged for her to sing in his translation, *Sappho*, at Drury Lane; her meeting with Macready on 20 Mar was not propitious: "Serle . . . brought in Miss Clara Novello. She is handsome but not winning—much assumption, some affectation, and evidently a *great* opinion of herself. She did not prepossess me. She gave me a shock and a fright in wishing to be announced 'Clara Novello' with all her *titles* from the various foreign academies, etc. Serle and I combated it to the utmost, but not with much effect" (*Diaries*, II, 199). Miss Novello was not impressed with Macready: "What a stilted conceit-concrete was he!" (*Clara Novello's Reminiscences*, with a memoir by A. D. Coleridge, 1910, p. 118). Next day at the rehearsal Macready thought "she made herself conspicuously ridiculous" and was "still stubborn" on the announcements. "She agreed to refer it to Dickens and Jerrold" (*Diaries*, II, 199)—who apparently persuaded her to accept Macready's judgment, since the bill for the first performance (Enthoven Collection, V & A) announced her simply as "From the principal Theatres in Italy". CD was present at the first night (1 Apr) when the

opera was well received by the critics, although Macready recorded, "Miss Novello was very good. The house in amount was below even my calculations. In spirit, it was an assemblage of brutes" (*Diaries*, II, 201). J. R. Anderson described Macready as "*broken-hearted*. He told us he was thoroughly sick of the whole affair, and longed to get the season over" (*Newcastle Weekly Chronicle*, 9 Apr 87; not included in *An Actor's Life*). A verse account of the opera ran through three issues of *Punch* (22, 29 Apr, 6 May).

[2] Douglas William Jerrold (1803–57; *DNB*), writer and wit: see Vol. I, p. 192*n*.

[3] "Punch's Court Circular", *Punch*, 25 Feb 43, pretended that "distinguished members of literature, art and science" were invited to court banquets, including "Charles Dickens Esq" and "William Charles Macready Esq".

[4] Macready's diary for 12 Apr has "Dined with Dickens. Met Stanfield, Serle, Jerrold, Mark Lemon, Forster, Blanchard. A very cheerful day" (*Diaries*, II, 203). Macready had little sympathy with *Punch*, having been sent in Feb 42 "a volume . . . containing copious abuse of myself" and "made angry by a paltry impertinence" in Sep (*Diaries*, II, 158, 183) and by a take-off in *Punch's Pantomime, or Harlequin King John* (Dec 42).

[5] Thomas James Serle (1798–1889), actor and dramatist: see Vol. I, p. 355*n*, Vol. II, p. 151*n*.

[6] The name is scrawled and occupies (presumably in error) the place of CD's signature, instead of being placed bottom left as usual.

To LUIGI MARIOTTI,[1] 12 APRIL 1843*

MS Free Library of Philadelphia.

Devonshire Terrace | April Twelfth 1843.

Dear Sir.

I am at present staying out of town, that I may the better get through certain labours in which I am engaged. I am only here today for a few hours: and contemplate retiring to my Cave[2] again, this evening. But on Sunday *Week* (not Sunday next) I shall be visible here, between two o'Clock and half past. I contemplate making a longer stay than the Comet did;[3] for after that time, I have no idea of being out of my sphere (supposing this place to be my proper orbit) for some months.

I have not forgotten our "Merry Meeting" on board of that accursed Craft, wherein we crossed the damnable Atlantic Ocean. In grateful recollection of the Mustard poultice, I shall be truly glad to see you.[4]

Believe me | Faithfully yours

— Mariotti Esquire   CHARLES DICKENS

[7] On the reverse is a note from Catherine to Mrs Macready: "My dear Mrs Macready | Will you also give us the pleasure of seeing you with your husband on Wednesday. | With affectionate love to all | Believe me always | Your attached friend | Catherine Dickens".

[1] The name assumed in 1833 by Antonio Carlo Napoleone Gallenga (1810–95; *DNB*), author and Italian refugee; in America 1836–9, helped by Edward Everett and by Longfellow; taught at a Harvard young ladies' academy; his friends were mostly Unitarians. In England 1839–42 (with an interval at Florence), introduced by Catherine Sedgwick to John Kenyon, through whom he met Landor, Rogers, Milnes; contributed to *Foreign Quarterly*, *Metropolitan Magazine* and *Westminster Review*. Published his *Metropolitan* articles with others in *Italy* (1841, repr. 1846) which increased his literary acquaintance; he met Lady Morgan, Lady Blessington, Hunt, Hood, Thackeray, Ainsworth and Carlyle. Professor of Modern Languages at Windsor, Nova Scotia 1842, returning to England Spring 1843. He was teaching Italian in London 1843–8; in 1846 went to Manchester to lecture on Dante where, as Espinasse records, "he found more than an audience for his lectures", for here he married Juliet Schunck, daughter of one of the wealthiest German merchant families, whom he met through his fellow countryman, Gambardella, "and the struggling

Italian exile was a made man for life" (*Literary Recollections and Sketches*, 1893, pp. 167–8). After his marriage in Apr 47 he was naturalized and resumed his own name, except on his books.

[2] i.e. to the farmhouse at Finchley.

[3] A supposed comet seen in England, America and elsewhere on the evening of 16 Mar 43 was described by Sir John Herschel as "a comet of first class magnitude or, if not a comet, some phenomenon beyond the earth's atmosphere of a nature even yet more remarkable" (*Companion to the British Almanac for 1844*, p. 246); it was seen only as "a dim oval nebula" and appeared to be "receding with great velocity" (*Annual Register*).

[4] See *To* Forster, 17 Jan 42, *fn*. According to *American Notes*, Ch. 2, CD "was long troubled with the idea that he [*Mariotti*] might be up, and well, and a hundred times a day expecting me to call upon him in the saloon . . . I don't think I ever felt such perfect gratification and gratitude of heart, as I did when I heard from the ship's doctor that he had been obliged to put a large mustard poultice on this very gentleman's stomach. I date my recovery from the receipt of that intelligence". Mariotti was to become a frequent visitor to Devonshire Terrace during 1843–4 when he gave CD and Catherine lessons in Italian; he recalled CD as "a bright-eyed, ready-witted, somewhat gushing, happy man, cheered by the world's applause, equally idolised

To THOMAS MITTON, 13 APRIL 1843*

MS Yale University Library. *Address:* Thomas Mitton Esquire | 23 Southampton Buildings.

Devonshire Terrace. | Thursday | April Thirteenth 1843

My Dear Mitton

I will call on you tomorrow, between five and a quarter past; I am forced to go to Chelsea[1] to day.

In haste

                                                        Faithfully Always

Thomas Mitton Esquire   CHARLES DICKENS

To THOMAS CARLYLE, 18 APRIL 1843[2]

MS Historical Society of Pennsylvania. *Address:* Thomas Carlyle Esquire | 5 Cheyne Row | Chelsea.

Devonshire Terrace | Eighteenth April 1843

My Dear Carlyle

In the multitude of our unmentioned Wrongs under the Black Flag of Literature, I don't think Mr. Ticknor's case deserving of especial mention;[3] and I have therefore returned it, as you requested, to the Geologist.[4] I am the less

by his wife, by his children, by every member of his family, while as yet not even the shadow of a cloud had risen to darken the light of his household" (A. Gallenga, *Episodes of my Second Life*, 1884, II, 372–3).

[1] Presumably to see Carlyle; see next.

[2] Carlyle and CD had planned to meet this month, for pleasure rather than Society of Authors' business: a visit to Horton had been proposed by Carlyle to Forster—postponed in a letter of 19 Apr on account of "Doctor's devilry in my interior", but with the suggestion that when it did take place it should be "a right Literary Party ... Perhaps Dickens would go, and other chosen men. And then ought not as in the case of the Todgers people 'our rugged natures to be softened' (probably) 'by the presence of lovely woman' on such an occasion?" (Carlyle *to* Forster, MS V & A). Carlyle's health evidently prevented it; on 24 Apr he wrote to Catherine Dickens saying that he and his wife were "poor sickly creatures" and must deny themselves the pleasure of dining out, "even that of dining out at your house on Saturday,—one of the agreeablest dinners that human ingenuity could provide for us!" (MS Morgan). In the matter of the present letter, Carlyle was a natural intermediary: he had met

Ticknor in 1838, and was attending lectures by "the Geologist".

[3] Clearly, an instance of some supposed wrong done by English publishers to an American author; unlikely to be Ticknor himself. George Ticknor, friend of Prescott and Lyell, had published only minor works, not apparently reprinted in England, until his *History of Spanish Literature*, 1849—John Murray was responsible for its English edition. For Ticknor's liberal and well-reasoned views on international copyright in a paper sent to Daniel Webster in 1852, see *Life, Letters and Journals of George Ticknor*, 1876, II, 278–80; there is no evidence of active earlier interest.

[4] (Sir) Charles Lyell (1797–1875; *DNB*), FRS 1826, President of Geological Society 1835, married the daughter of Leonard Horner, also a geologist, 1832; his famous and widely influential *Principles of Geology*, 1830, progressively revised and enlarged to incorporate further discoveries, was then in its sixth edn (1840); the first American edn was published from this by Hilliard, Grey & Co, Boston, 1842, clearly with Lyell's authority. Travelled widely in America July 1841–Aug 1842, lecturing at the Lowell Institute and elsewhere; a report of his New York lectures of Apr 1842 was issued by the publishers of the *New York Tribune*; his year's researches

disposed to assist in giving it publicity, because of certain Thieves in books, called Wiley and Putnam,[1] having recently published a variety of similar statements, to which publicity was given by the Athenæum—and in which, they lie consumedly—after the true American fashion of smartness.

Always | Faithfully Your friend

Thomas Carlyle Esquire   CHARLES DICKENS

To JOHN DE GEX, 18 APRIL 1843

MS Mr W. A. Foyle.

Devonshire Terrace | Eighteenth April 1843

My Dear De Gex

In the last piece I saw at the Victoria, a murdering Brigand (of high moral sentiments) was urged by another murdering Brigand (of low moral sentiments) to slaughter a child, whom it was indispensable to the plot of the play—but not otherwise—to murder.[2] After a severe moral struggle, he said "I'll do it!"— whereat the audience were very much delighted, and applauded hugely; though I couldn't tell exactly why. I repeat the Brigand's sentiment; and I hope *my* audience[3] may be in the same humour.

Faithfully Yours always

John De Gex Esquire   CHARLES DICKENS

resulted in some 20 papers to the Geological Society. Though he says "I gave all my thoughts in the United States to my own science", his *Travels in North America* also included general observations, almost all favourable; he was especially struck by the expenditure on popular education and the size and literacy of the reading public. In *A Second Visit to the United States*, 1849, including the journal of his travels in 1845–6, he observed for the first time the growing strength of the cause of international copyright (II, 335–41), noted the "number of reprisals now made by English speculators", but still saw little amiss with the existing situation.

[1] They had published the *American Book Circular*, which contained a defence of American publishers against charges of piracy, and pointed out CD's use of Joseph Neal's *Charcoal Sketches* in *Pic-Nic Papers*, without acknowledgment; the *Athenæum*, 1 Apr 43, noticing this, suggested that CD was not responsible (rightly, as it was Colburn's doing: see Agreement, Vol. I, p. 665). Wiley & Putnam also published *Change for American*

Notes By a Lady, an attack on English society; unfavourably reviewed in the *Examiner*, 8 July 43, but the publishers extracted one approving phrase and quoted it in later advertisements as if it applied to the whole book, at which the *Examiner* protested.

[2] The Victoria, formerly the Coburg Theatre, was in the Waterloo Road; its gallery and "terrific combat, which is nightly encored" are mentioned in "The Streets—Night", *Sketches by Boz*, First Series, 1836; in 1840 described as "situated in one of the worst neighbourhoods, its audiences are of the lowest kind" (F. G. Tomlins, *A Brief View of the English Drama*, p. 60). Exotic melodrama about brigands and corsairs was typical of its productions before 1841 when Osbaldiston took it over and concentrated more on the domestic and nautical drama; but these particular brigands have not been found in any play performed from 1836 on.

[3] Not clear what CD refers to—not a public dinner; see *To* De Gex, 30 Mar, *fn.*

To THOMAS MITTON, 22 APRIL 1843

MS Huntington Library.

Devonshire Terrace | Twenty Second April 1843

My Dear Mitton

I have had a bad cold in my ears for some days, and woke up this morning with a most horrible affection of all the nerves on one side of my face (ear included) since which cheerful discovery, I have been roaming up and down stairs in perpetual, restless, uneasiness and pain.

This will throw me back in my work. Couldn't you manage to dine in the country with me, next *Saturday* instead of Tuesday? Consider, and let me know. Meanwhile I will reserve Henry's Invitation.[1]

Faithfully Always

Thomas Mitton Esquire   CD

To MISS BURDETT COUTTS, 24 APRIL 1843

MS Morgan Library.

Devonshire Terrace | Twenty Fourth April 1843.

My Dear Miss Coutts.

Mr. Marjoribanks was with me this morning; and I really cannot tell you how very much I feel your great kindness and interest in my behalf. I wrote to him, and not to you, in the first instance; because, feeling assured of your friendship, I was the more sensitive and delicate in troubling you, if I could help it.

I enclose such a note to you as Mr. Marjoribanks told me you wished to have.[2] Nor do I know that I can add anything to it, further than that I am prepared to catch thankfully at anything which promises a reasonable opening, no matter where.

We are much concerned to hear of Miss Meredith's illness. I am myself kept within doors by the doctor for a kind of rheumatism in the face, which penetrates into the depths of my ears, and makes me feel at times as if a beehive had been upset in the intricacies of my brain. But as divers small tortures are to be inflicted on me this morning, I look for a release into the open air tomorrow; and whenever I *do* get out, I shall walk straight to your door, and make my personal enquiries.

Pray let me recommend the Dragon in the Easter Piece[3] to your particular regards. I look upon him as the most comic animal of modern times. When he

---

[1] Mitton preferred Tues 2 May; see *To Austin*, 28 Apr.

[2] See next.

[3] J. R. Planché's *Fortunio and his Seven Gifted Servants* (published in *Extravaganzas*, 1879, II) at Drury Lane. There was "a most select dragon" performed by Mr Stilt: "gentlemanly . . . walks with a mincing gait" (*The Times*, 18 Apr), "carries his tail genteely under his arm" (*Examiner*, 22 Apr). During rehearsals Macready "knew everyone's part, and acted each in turn", according to Planché; his production of the piece was "very successful" (*Diaries*, II, 204). CD's children acted it in 1855 (N, II, 158).

gets drunk at the Fountain, he is Sublime—the Learned Pig[1] turns pale before
him, in his dullest moments.

Dear Miss Coutts | Always Faithfully Yours
CHARLES DICKENS

Miss Coutts.

To MISS BURDETT COUTTS, 24 APRIL 1843

MS Morgan Library. Enclosed with last.

Devonshire Terrace | Twenty Fourth April 1843

Dear Miss Coutts.

I have it very much at heart at this time to obtain some suitable and worthy
employment for a brother of mine[2]—just now of age—who has been bred a
Civil Engineer, and has for the last four years been constantly employed on one
of the great main lines of Railway, performing all the duties of assistant Engineer—drawing plans and executing them—levelling—constructing bridges—
and so forth; all of which, from the beginning of the work to its close, he has
done to the great satisfaction of those above him, as his testimonials fully shew,
and as I can most honestly avouch.[3]

The work on which he was engaged, being completed;[4] and the Profession
being, as I dare say you know, most horribly overstocked; he has applied to me
to exert any interest or influence I may possess in his behalf. And knowing the
kind interest you take in any application or design of mine, I have determined
to write to you to ask you if it be possible that you can assist me in this. I know
him to be possessed of great energy, industry, and ability; and I am more anxious
than I can tell you to procure him the means of exercising these qualities, either
at home or abroad.

I will not ask you to forgive my troubling you on such a subject; for if I were
not sure you had already done that, I could never have made up my mind to
trouble you at all.

I am always | Dear Miss Coutts
Yours faithfully and obliged
CHARLES DICKENS[5]

Miss Burdett Coutts.

---

[1] In 1784 Anna Seward and Dr Johnson
had discussed the learned pig exhibited at
Nottingham (*Boswell's Life of Johnson*, ed.
L. F. Powell, IV, 547–8). "Learned pigs"
were still common at fairs in the 1840s
and 1850s; they answered questions by
pointing to cards, letters, and persons in
the audience.

[2] Alfred, who was 21 on 11 Mar 43.

[3] See Vol. II, p. 223*n*.

[4] See *To* Beard, 11 July 42. He was still
unemployed in the autumn (*To* Mitton,
28 Sep 43) but by 1844 he had obtained
employment at York. He married Helen
Dobson (of Strensall, near York) in London on 16 May 46.

[5] Miss Coutts forwarded the letter to
Marjoribanks next day, asking if he "or any
of my friends in the Strand" could help
him: "I should be particularly glad to be
of any service to Mr. Dickens to whom of
course it must be a great object, as he has
his own family to provide for . . . I have
not [*thus*] doubt from what he says that
his Brother will be found as deserving &
competent as he says" (MS Morgan).

To THE STEWARDS OF THE ARTISTS' BENEVOLENT FUND,[1] 27 APRIL [1843]

Text from N, II, 23. *Date:* clearly 1843, from address; confirmed by reference to another Dinner (see *fn*). Wrongly given in N as 1847, a common misreading.

Devonshire Terrace, York Gate, Regent's Park
Twenty-Seventh April 184[3]

Mr. Charles Dickens presents his compliments to The Stewards of the Artists' Benevolent Fund, and begs to thank them for the honor they have done him in forwarding him an Invitation to the forthcoming Dinner.[2] It would have given him the very greatest pleasure to accept it, if he had not been already pledged to attend another Public Dinner in the City on the same day.[3]

To CHARLES BABBAGE, 27 APRIL 1843

MS British Museum.

Devonshire Terrace | Twenty Seventh April 1843

My Dear Sir

I write to you, *confidentially*, in answer to your note of last night; and the tenor of mine will tell you why.

You may suppose, from seeing my name in the Printed Letter[4] you have received, that I am favorable to the proposed Society. I am decidedly opposed to it. I went there on the day I was in the chair,[5] after much solicitation; and

---

[1] The Stewards included Lord Lansdowne, Lord Palmerston, Dilke, and W. J. Linton; the secretary was John Martin.

[2] The Anniversary Dinner at Freemasons' Hall announced for 6 May 43, with Lord John Russell in the chair, was in fact later postponed to 20 May when the Royal Academy Dinner was moved to 6 May. CD had been a Steward at the anniversary festival on 12 May 38, and took the chair in 1858 (*Speeches*, ed. K. J. Fielding, pp. 2, 265–9).

[3] The second annual Dinner of the Hospital for Consumption and Diseases of the Chest on 6 May at the London Tavern with the Earl of Arundel and Surrey in the chair; CD proposed the toast of the evening (*Speeches*, pp. 40–1).

[4] Robertson's letter accompanying the draft prospectus; does not survive, but probably similar to a later letter of 3 May, referring to the meeting of 8 Apr with CD in the chair.

[5] See *To* Beard, 7 Apr, *fn*. Carlyle had withdrawn from the committee in a letter of 7 Apr. 43, presumably to Robertson; he approved the prospectus as "unexceptionable in character" but thought it

offered little practical basis for any operation. On 1 May he wrote again declining to be a member of the Committee of the Society (Besant, *Essays and Historiettes*, pp. 282–3), and more forcibly in a letter to another correspondent: "I attended once for ten minutes, in a tavern at Charing Cross, a company of some thirty very ugly men, not above three of whom were known to me. I did admit, in a whisper, in answer to the 'Hon. Secretary's' whisper, that the thing Sir L. Bulwer said appeared to have reason in it; and thereupon, little edified by the physiognomy of the business, I took my hat and glided away without intention to return. About a month ago I formally declined to be a member" (Carlyle *to* Unknown Correspondent, 4 June 43; D. Wilson, *Carlyle on Cromwell and Others*, 1925, p. 222). Robertson, according to Mrs Carlyle (3 May 43), had been pestering Carlyle about it for some time: "time after time he has come here—*always out of season* (which is his peculiar faculty) to bore Carlyle into taking active part in something which he calls *Association of British Authors* . . . And so on Monday he came in at twelve and sat till three . . . when C. came down at three and was

being put into it, opened the Proceedings by telling the meeting that I approved of the Design in theory, but in practice considered it hopeless. I may tell you—I did not tell them—that the nature of the meeting, and the character and position of many of the men attending it, cried Failure trumpet-tongued[1] in my ears. To quote an expression from Tennyson, I may say that if it were the best society in the world, the grossness of some natures in it, would have weight to drag it down.[2]

In the wisdom of all you urge in the Notes you have sent me, taking them as statements of Theory, I entirely concur.[3] But in practice, I feel sure that the present Publishing system cannot be overset, until Authors are different men. The first step to be taken, is, to move as a body in the question of copyright— enforce the existing laws—and try to obtain better. For that purpose, I hold that the Authors and Publishers must unite, as the wealth, business-habits, and interests of that latter class are of great importance to such an end. The Longmans and Murray have been with me proposing such an association. That I shall support. But having seen the Cockspur Street Society, I am as well convinced of its invincible hopelessness as if I saw it written by a Celestial Penman in the book of Fate.

My Dear Sir | Always Faithfully Yours

Charles Babbage Esquire   CHARLES DICKENS

To SIR EDWARD LYTTON BULWER, 27 APRIL 1843

MS Lytton Papers.

Devonshire Terrace | Twenty Seventh April 1843

My Dear Sir Edward

I wish to speak with you in relation to that Brood of birds at the British Coffee House in Cockspur Street,[4] who have certainly taken my name in vain, and I

passing out *determined* not to see him, Robertson intercepted him in the Lobby and thrust a paper on him like a bailiff serving a writ. Had you seen C.'s look!! '*Oh Heavens*'! and then how he fell to brushing his hat saying the while—'Sir! I have told you already I will have nothing more to do with that business'—'Why?' says the other; 'Because nobody but a madman can expect any good out of it under the present circumstances!'" (*Letters to her Family*, pp. 122–3).

[1] *Macbeth*, I, vii, 19.

[2] "Locksley Hall", first published in *Poems*, 1842: "thou art mated with a clown, | And the grossness of his nature will have weight to drag thee down". Among the gross natures CD doubtless included Samuel Carter Hall and James Silk Buckingham.

[3] Babbage had evidently suggested various improvements in the Society, involving more cooperation between authors and publishers; he wrote to others on the sub-

ject, including Milnes and Charles Lyell; Lyell replied 10 May (MS BM).

[4] The Society of Authors. They met again on 29 Apr, H. F. Cary presiding, and elected a Provisional Committee to consider the constitution; this still included Bulwer. On 3 May Robertson circulated the proof of the Prospectus; and there was at least one further meeting, on 13 May. By then the Society was collapsing; letters quoted by Besant indicate widespread but vague support, mainly among minor authors, and few practical suggestions. James Silk Buckingham adopted some of Robertson's ideas for his proposed British and Foreign Institute, and held a private meeting on 31 May, perhaps referred to in Mrs S. C. Hall's letter to Robertson: "Mr. Hall and myself regret most truly that any opinion we should have expressed could give you pain. I knew that Mr. Dickens did not think your plan as certain as you did yourself, and persons may change their opinion without doing a wrong thing.

dare say have taken yours likewise. I also wish to impart to you the purport of some communications I have had from the Longmans and Murray.[1] At what time will you be at home this morning, if you can make it convenient to see me?

Faithfully Yours

Sir Edward Lytton Bulwer CHARLES DICKENS

To HENRY AUSTIN, 28 APRIL 1843*

MS Morgan Library.

Devonshire Terrace | Twenty Eighth April 1843

My Dear Henry

Mitton is going to dine with me in the country, next Tuesday.[2] Will you come and do likewise? And shall we meet in Southampton Buildings at 12? That is, unless you should be in this Neighbourhood in the morning, and will come here at halfpast Eleven.

Love to Letitia. | Always Faithfully

Henry Austin Esquire CHARLES DICKENS

To MESSRS BRADBURY & EVANS, 28 APRIL 1843*

MS Berg Collection.

Devonshire Terrace | Twenty Eighth April 1843

My Dear Sirs

Please send up to me on Monday Morning, for copy of next No.[3] and when you have it *all* in type, send proofs to Mr. Browne and Mr. Forster. In No. 4 page 108, there is a horrible mistake, which I think must be yours. "What do you go a lowerin the table for?" says Bailey in the type. "What do you go a lowerin' the table BEER[4] for", *my* Bailey says.[5]

Faithfully Yours always

Messrs. Bradbury & Evans. CHARLES DICKENS

Your confidence of success in the first instance prevented, perhaps, persons from saying all they thought and all they feared. Of *your* integrity of purpose there could be no doubt; and if Mr. Buckingham effects a good and provides for himself at the same time, he is—a careful man—and that is all. | Mr. Hall has been tempted to join them more than once, but he has not done so. I am sure he is ready now as ever to stand by you, though he fears, as he did at first, that your troops will not 'march'" (Besant, *Essays and Historiettes*, pp. 301–2).

[1] See *To* Longman, 17 May.
[2] See *To* Mitton, 22 Apr.
[3] This must refer to No. VI, the June No.; CD had been getting well ahead, probably because of his new project of sending Martin to America.
[4] Written very large.
[5] Ch. 9 in the Apr No. It was not corrected, but appears in the Errata of 1st edn, 1844, in the final No.; corrected in the Cheap edn (1852), but not in any reprint of 1844.

To FREDERICK DICKENS, 2 MAY 1843

MS John Rylands Library.

Devonshire Terrace. | Second May 1843

My Dear Frederick.

Your absence from here, has been your own act always.[1] I shall be perfectly glad to see you; and should have been, at any time.

Mitton and I are going to dine somewhere in the Country to day. If you like to join us, and can conveniently,—do. I will take the chance, and will send Topping up to you at half past 12 when I shall be in the carriage at the Treasury Door.

Affectionately Always
CD.

To THOMAS LONGMAN, 2 MAY 1843

Extract in Walter T. Spencer catalogue No. 104 (1901); *MS* 1 p.; dated Devonshire Terrace, 2 May 43.

Sir Edward Lytton was with me yesterday. I explained our views to him, and he is very much of our opinion in the matter. *Saturday Week* (he is going out of town in the meanwhile) he would be glad to attend a meeting.[2]

To JOHN FORSTER, [3 MAY 1843]

Extract in F, IV, i, 295. *Date:* 3 May 43 according to Forster.

I am deeply grieved about Black.[3] Sorry from my heart's core. If I could find him out, I would go and comfort him this moment.[4]

---

[1] No explanation of this; possibly connected with the bill sent to CD on 17 Feb 43 (see *To* Mitton, 17 Feb).

[2] Held at Longman's office on Wed 17 May.

[3] Dismissed from editorship of the *Morning Chronicle* by Sir John Easthope who wanted the post for Andrew Doyle, the foreign editor, his prospective son-in-law. W. C. Hazlitt in his story of Black's dismissal (*Four Generations of a Literary Family*, 1897, I, 282–3) attributed it to Black's indiscreet after-dinner speech at a banquet in Easthope's honour, when he told the company that "both of them had come up to London to seek their fortune and the only difference between them was that he had had shoes to his feet and Easthope had not". Black spent the rest of his life in retirement.

[4] Forster comments: "He did find him out; and he and a certain number of us did also comfort this excellent man after a fashion extremely English, by giving him a Greenwich dinner on the 20th of May; when Dickens had arranged and ordered all to perfection, and the dinner succeeded in its purpose, as in other ways, quite wonderfully. Among the entertainers were Sheil and Thackeray, Fonblanque and Charles Buller, Southwood Smith and William Johnson Fox, Macready and Maclise, as well as myself and Dickens" (F, IV, i, 295). The dinner did *not*, as stated by Forster, take place on 20 May (see *To* Macready, 16 May) but possibly on some later date, not known.

To DOUGLAS JERROLD, 3 MAY 1843

MS Comtesse de Suzannet.

Devonshire Terrace | Third May 1843

My Dear Jerrold.

Let me thank you, most cordially, for your books[1]—not only for their own sakes (and I have read them with perfect delight) but also for this hearty and most welcome mark of your recollection of the friendship we have established; in which light I know I may regard and prize them.

I am greatly pleased with your opening paper[2] in the Illuminated.[3] It is very wise, and capital; written with the finest end of that iron pen of yours; witty, much needed, and full of Truth. I vow to God that I think the Parrots of Society are more intolerable and mischievous than its Birds of Prey.[4] If ever I destroy myself, it will be in the bitterness of hearing those infernal and damnably good old times, extolled. Once in a fit of madness, after having been to a Public Dinner which took place just as this Ministry came in, I wrote the Parody[5] I send you enclosed, for Fonblanque. There is nothing in it but wrath; but that's wholesome—so I send it to you.

---

[1] According to Walter Jerrold (*Douglas Jerrold*, [1914], I, 346) these included *Cakes and Ale* (2 vols, 1842); it is in the inventory of CD's books made in 1844 (MS Major Philip Dickens).

[2] "Elizabeth and Victoria" in the first number of the *Illuminated Magazine*, May 43 (reprinted in *Chronicles of Clovernook*, 1846)—an ironical description of the "good old days".

[3] A monthly illustrated magazine of 64 pp. with a large page, and red, blue and gold title-page, price 1s; Herbert Ingram of the *Illustrated London News* was proprietor, and Jerrold editor, assisted by a sub-editor, George Hodder, who had "the practical responsibility of arranging the contents" (see his *Memories of my Time*, 1870, p. 29). It was designed to comment on "our social abuses and social follies", and "to speak to the MASSES of the people" (Preface to Vol. 1). The prospectus, which appeared widely in the press in Apr, emphasized the "strong and healthful" nature of the contents; there was to be no shrinking "from any subject with a social wrong at its core". Fiction and "ample reviews" were to be included; among the illustrators were Kenny Meadows, Leech, and Browne. The *Examiner* (5 Aug 43) noted a marked improvement after a bad first and a worse second number (see *To* Jerrold, 13 June); it was "well-written, carefully and ingeniously illustrated, and marvellously

cheap". In Apr 44 Horne described it as "not doing at all well ... They have a large but inadequate circulation" (Walter Jerrold, *Douglas Jerrold*, I, 362–3), although on 9 Sep 44 Jerrold told Hodder "The Mag. is rising ... last week it went up 1500" (Hodder, *op. cit.*, p. 32). Jerrold gave up the editorship in Oct 44 and it came to an end in 1845.

[4] CD repeated this figure in his speech at the Athenæum Soirée at Manchester on 5 Oct 43; attacking the view that learning is dangerous, he said "I do sometimes begin to doubt whether the parrots of society are not more pernicious to its interests than the birds of prey" (*Speeches*, p. 47).

[5] "The Fine Old English Gentleman", published anonymously in the *Examiner*, 7 Aug 41 (see Vol. II, p. 357*n*). Although there is considerable emphasis on the horrors and sufferings of past ages, there is no passage very close to Jerrold's paper. The parody was undoubtedly based not on any public dinner attended by CD in late July 41, but on the *Times* report (29 July 41) of a Conservative dinner at Stainton near Gloucester on 27 July, at which Sir A. Lechmere said "he trusted ... he should yet witness the return of the good old English times, when the nobleman afforded advice to his tenants, and identified himself with them", and the speech was followed by "Song, by Mr. Allan—'Fine Old English Gentleman'".

I am writing a little history of England[1] for my boy, which I will send you when it is printed for him, though your boys are too old to profit by it. It is curious that I have tried to impress upon him (writing, I dare say, at the same moment with you) the exact spirit of your paper. For I don't know what I should do, if he were to get hold of any conservative or High church notions; and the best way of guarding against any such horrible result, is, I take it, to wring the parrots' necks in his very cradle.

Oh Heaven, if you could have been with me at a Hospital Dinner[2] last Monday! There were men there—your City aristocracy—who made such speeches, and expressed such sentiments, as any moderately intelligent dustman would have blushed through his cindery bloom to have thought of. Sleek, slobbering, bow-paunched, overfed, apoplectic, snorting cattle—and the auditory leaping up in their delight![3] I never saw such an illustration of the Power of Purse, or felt so degraded and debased by its contemplation, since I have had eyes and ears. The absurdity of the thing was too horrible to laugh at. It was perfectly overwhelming. But if I could have partaken it with anybody who would have felt it as you would have done, it would have had quite another aspect—or would at least, like a "classical" mask (oh damn that word!)[4] have had one funny side to relieve its dismal features.

Supposing fifty families were to emigrate into the wilds of North America—yours, mine, and forty eight others: picked for their concurrence of opinion on all important subjects, and for their resolution to found a Colony of Common Sense. How soon would that Devil, Cant, present itself among them in one shape or other—the day they landed, do you say—or the day after?

That is a great mistake (almost the only one I know) in the Arabian Nights, where the Princess restores people to their original beauty by sprinkling them with the Golden Water.[5] It is quite clear that she must have made monsters of them by such a christening as that.

My wife is very sorry to hear of your daughter's illness,[6] and sends many kind

---

[1] The *Child's History of England* appeared in *Household Words* in 1851–3; its relation to the early draft is not known. The MS of Ch. 12 in CD's hand is in the Huntington Library, and of Chs 2 and 6 in the Forster Collection; handwriting shows that no part of these chapters was written in 1843.

[2] The seventh anniversary dinner of the Charterhouse Square Infirmary, held at the Albion Tavern on 1 May with Sir James Lushington in the chair (*The Times*, 2 May); various aldermen and sheriffs were present, but the speeches were not reported. CD had described a charity-dinner, satirically but with less disgust, in "Public Dinners" (*Evening Chronicle*, 7 Apr 35; *Sketches by Boz*).

[3] "Bankers and sheriffs and aldermen" heavily deleted by CD.

[4] CD mocks at the term "classical" in a way suggesting some private joke, in *Old Curiosity Shop*, Ch. 27, where, in reply to Nell's question whether waxwork is "funnier than Punch", Mrs Jarley says: "It isn't funny at all. . . . It's calm and—what's that word again—critical?—no—classical, that's it—it is calm and classical. No low beatings and knockings about, no jokings and squeakings like your precious Punches, but always the same, with a constantly unchanging air of coldness and gentility".

[5] CD has confused two parts of "The Story of Two Sisters who envied their Younger Sister": the Princess restores her brothers by sprinkling water on the stones, and "golden water" to make a fountain is one of the objects of the quest.

[6] Jerrold had two daughters, Jane Matilda, *b*. 29 Aug 1825, and Mary Anne, *b*. 21 Sep 1831.

messages to her and Mrs. Jerrold—whereof the best, is, that she hopes the latter will never stand upon ceremony, but always on something better.

My Dear Jerrold | Faithfully your friend

Douglas Jerrold Esquire   CHARLES DICKENS

To CLARKSON STANFIELD, 5 MAY 1843

MS University of Kentucky. *Address:* Clarkson Stanfield Esquire.

Devonshire Terrace | Fifth May 1843.

My Dear Stanfield

Mac told me (I mean Maclise: not Macready) of the party today;[1] and I should have been delighted to join it, had we not engaged to dine with Forster, previous to going to "Doory Lane".[2] There, however, I shall hope to see you in a double sense—firstly in your proper person; secondly, in your immortal screenery. To both of whom be all Love Honor and Glory, now and for evermore. Amen.

CHARLES DICKENS

To MRS GEORGE HOGARTH, 8 MAY 1843

Text from MDGH, III, 50-1.

Devonshire Terrace, 8th May, 1843.

My Dear Mrs. Hogarth,

I was dressing to go to church yesterday morning—thinking, very sadly, of that time six years[3]—when your kind note and its accompanying packet were brought to me. The best portrait that was ever painted would be of little value to you and me, in comparison with that unfading picture we have within us; and of the worst (which ——'s really is)[4] I can only say, that it has no interest in my eyes, beyond being something which she sat near in its progress, full of life and beauty. In that light, I set some store by the copy you have sent me; and as a mark of your affection, I need not say I value it very much. As any record of that dear face, it is utterly worthless.

I trace in many respects a strong resemblance between her mental features and Georgina's—so strange a one, at times, that when she and Kate and I are sitting together, I seem to think that what has happened is a melancholy dream from which I am just awakening. The perfect like of what she was, will never be again, but so much of her spirit shines out in this sister, that the old time comes back again at some seasons, and I can hardly separate it from the present.

After she died, I dreamed of her every night for many months—I think for the better part of a year—sometimes as a spirit, sometimes as a living creature,

---

[1] At the Athenæum, with Edwin Landseer, Eastlake and Macready, before going to the theatre (Macready, *Diaries*, II, 206).

[2] To see *Acis and Galatea, Comus* and *Fortunio* (see *To* Miss Coutts, 24 Apr); Stanfield was responsible for the scenery of *Acis* and *Comus*, and had "refreshed" it (*Diaries, ibid.*) for this special revival with Clara Novello as Galatea.

[3] The death of Mary Hogarth: see Vol. I, p. 65*n*.

[4] The only known painting was done after her death, perhaps from an earlier sketch, by Hablot K. Browne (see Vol. I, p. 65*n*).

never with any of the bitterness of my real sorrow, but always with a kind of quiet happiness, which became so pleasant to me that I never lay down at night without a hope of the vision coming back in one shape or other. And so it did. I went down into Yorkshire, and finding it still present to me, in a strange scene and a strange bed, I could not help mentioning the circumstance in a note I wrote home to Kate. From that moment I have never dreamed of her once,[1] though she is so much in my thoughts at all times (especially when I am successful, and have prospered in anything) that the recollection of her is an essential part of my being, and is as inseparable from my existence as the beating of my heart is.[2]

Always affectionately
[CHARLES DICKENS]

To WILLIAM BROWN,[3] 10 MAY 1843

Mention in *American Book Prices Current*, 1938–9; *MS* 1 p.; dated 10 May 43.

Thanking him warmly for the gift of a book.

To DAVID DICKSON,[4] 10 MAY 1843

Text from MDGH, 1, 89.

1, Devonshire Terrace, York Gate, Regent's Park,
May 10th, 1843

Sir,

Permit me to say, in reply to your letter, that you do not understand the intention (I daresay the fault is mine) of that passage[5] in the "Pickwick Papers" which has given you offence. The design of "the Shepherd" and of this and every other allusion to him is, to show how sacred things are degraded, vulgarised, and rendered absurd when persons who are utterly incompetent to teach the

---

[1] See Vol. 1, p. 366 and *n.*

[2] This sentence is quoted in F, XI, iii, 841, but with "greatly" added before "prospered".

[3] Perhaps the Dr William Brown who married Miss Meredith on 19 Dec 44.

[4] Possibly David Dickson, DD, writer, of St Cuthbert's, Edinburgh. The 1843 "Narrative" in MDGH, 1, 85, reads: "Mr. David Dickson kindly furnishes us with an explanation of the letter . . . 'It was . . . in answer to a letter from me, pointing out that the "Shepherd" [i.e. Stiggins] in "Pickwick" was apparently reflecting on the scriptural doctrine of the new birth'." That such criticisms were numerous is suggested by CD's forcible defence in the

Preface to the Cheap edn, 1847—a passage not in the 1837 Preface—in which he insists on the sharp distinction between "religion and the cant of religion", and protests against "that coarse familiarity with sacred things which is busy in the lips, and idle in the heart". The paragraph was retained unaltered in the shorter preface to the CD edn of 1867.

[5] *Pickwick Papers*, Ch. 22 (Mr Weller on his wife, under the Shepherd's influence): "She's got hold o' some invention for grown-up people being born again, Sammy —the new birth, I think they calls it . . . I should very much like to see your mother-in-law born again. Wouldn't I put her out to nurse!"

commonest things take upon themselves to expound such mysteries, and how, in making mere cant phrases of divine words, these persons miss the spirit in which they had their origin. I have seen a great deal of this sort of thing in many parts of England, and I never knew it lead to charity or good deeds.

Whether the great Creator of the world and the creature of his hands, moulded in his own image, be quite so opposite in character as you believe, is a question which it would profit us little to discuss. I like the frankness and candour of your letter, and thank you for it. That every man who seeks heaven must be born again, in good thoughts of his Maker, I sincerely believe. That it is expedient for every hound to say so in a certain snuffling form of words, to which he attaches no good meaning, I do not believe. I take it there is no difference between us.

Faithfully yours
[CHARLES DICKENS]

To J. H. FRISWELL,[1] 10 MAY 1843

Mention in Bangs & Co. catalogue, June 1902; *MS* 1 p. (3rd person); dated 10 May 43.

To EDWARD F. LEEKS,[2] 10 MAY 1843

MS Bowdoin College, Maine.

Devonshire Terrace | Tenth May 1843.
My Dear Sir
I am exceedingly sorry to say that circumstances over which I have no controul, and which oblige me to be otherwise engaged this evening, will prevent my having the pleasure I had expected, of attending your Anniversary Dinner.

Faithfully Yours
Edward. F. Leeks Esquire   CHARLES DICKENS

---

[1] James Hain Friswell (1825–78; *DNB*), author, son of William Friswell, attorney, of 93 Wimpole Street; at this time articled to John Rumley, an engraver on gold and silver plate; married Rumley's daughter in 1847. Friswell's own daughter, Laura, described him as an enthusiastic admirer of Thackeray and CD (*James Hain Friswell. A Memoir*, 1898, p. 13).

[2] Edward Frederick Leeks, solicitor, of 2 Charlotte Row, Mansion House. The dinner was the Anniversary Festival of the

St Ann's Society "for Educating, Clothing and Maintaining the Children of those once in prosperity, whether orphans or not", of which Leeks was secretary; it took place, with Lord Morpeth in the chair, on 10 May, the same day as the Literary Fund dinner which CD had also already accepted (*To* Blewitt, 6 Apr), but which he evidently did not attend; perhaps his mistake in accepting two dinners on the same date accounts for his attending neither.

To [?THOMAS LONGMAN], 10 MAY 1843*

MS New York University Library. *Address:* Substance of letter suggests Longman.

Devonshire Terrace. | Tenth May 1843.

My Dear Sir

I have glanced at the papers you send me; and they appear to be quite correct.

I did not forget yesterday, that I had promised to send to Murray;[1] but on my life I did not know, without entering into a regular history, what to write. Nor do I know now, unless it be the very short paragraph I send you on the other side,[2] which you might insert,[3] where that letter of yours comes out.

Faithfully Always
CD.

To THOMAS MITTON, 10 MAY 1843

MS University of Texas. *Address:* Thomas Mitton Esquire | 23 Southampton Buildings | Chancery Lane.

Devonshire Terrace | Tenth May 1843.

My Dear Mitton.

If tomorrow at 5, will suit you (as, in the event of my not hearing from you to the contrary, I shall take it for granted it will), I will sign, seal, and deliver, at that hour.[4] If you are engaged at that time, say when your leisure serves on Friday or Saturday.

Faithfully Yours always
Thomas Mitton Esquire   CHARLES DICKENS

To CHARLES SMITHSON, 10 MAY 1843

Text from N, I, 519.

1 Devonshire Terrace, York Gate, Regent's Park
Tenth May 1843

My Dear Smithson,

If you will act as my representative at the Font, I will gladly be supposed to make all manner of impossible promises for your blooming daughter,[5] in right of whom I cordially congratulate you and Mrs. Smithson. And as the captain

---

[1] Probably John Murray the publisher; the papers were perhaps connected with the meeting on 13 or on 17 May.

[2] Not now part of the letter.

[3] Probably in "Longman's Circular" mentioned in *To* Bulwer, 14 May.

[4] This is not the date of any known Agreement; possibly a new tenancy for CD's parents (cf. the troublesome family affairs mentioned in *To* Shoberl, 19 May). CD's accounts (MS Messrs Coutts) show a possibly related payment of £30 to

Mitton on 16 May; and on the previous day appears one of a mysterious series of payments (of which the first was 21 May 40), usually about £40, to "W. J. Roper", recurring at irregular intervals over the next four years, but not appearing when CD was abroad. (The only W. J. Roper in the London Directory is William John Roper, 14 Osnaburgh Street; he was Assistant Secretary of the Artists' General Benevolent Institution.)

[5] Mary, born 16 Mar 43.

of the ship in which Mr. William Taylor[1] served as an able seaman said of the lady who followed Mr. Taylor on board in man's attire, so I say of Mrs. Smithson that "I've wery[2] much applauded her for wot she's done." I hope *my* missis won't do so never no more: but that's nothing to the purpose.

We talk of invading you[3] for a day or two, some time before we go to Broadstairs, which fashionable movement takes place usually on the First of August. I have likewise made rash pledges to go to Scotland, but whether I shall carry out either design is at present hidden in the mists of time and monthly numbers.

Great changes have taken place here, during the many years that have elapsed since your retirement into Yorkshire. I am grey, and Kate is bald. Charles (you remember him a little boy?) was married some years ago to a fascinating girl (with no prospects)[4] and is just appointed the Government Inspector of Egyptian Balloons, which is a very good post. Mary's second husband is not quite equal to her first, poor fellow!—but in his capacity of chief clerk to the chief magistrate at Bow Street, which office I have filled, as you know, for nearly ten years, he is always near me, which is a great comfort, I find, in the decline of life.

Mr. Mitton after living on hard eggs for several years, under the delusion that he was fast approaching the workhouse, has married his only friend, the old charwoman whom he employed when you first left Southampton Buildings. I am told she beats him cruelly. These are a few of the alterations wrought by Time, you see!

Commend me heartily to all your house,—not forgetting Beauteous Billa,—and lay your hand for me, as apostolically as you can, on the head of my God-child.

Always my Dear Smithson— | Faithfully your friend
CHARLES DICKENS

To W. C. MACREADY, 11 MAY 1843*

MS Morgan Library.

Devonshire Terrace | Eleventh May 1843

My Dear Macready

I have proposed next Saturday Week, for poor Black's dinner[5] at Greenwich (the house we dined in the other day),[6] at 6 exactly. Will this suit you? I will take you down and bring you home, if you please.

Faithfully Ever
CD.

[1] A version of the ballad about Billy Taylor appeared in J. B. Buckstone's *Billy Taylor; or, the Gay Young Fellow*, a nautical burlesque burletta, acted 1829; Billy Taylor's fair lady follows him in disguise and shoots him when she discovers him to be false: "When the captain *com'd* for to hear on't | He werry much applauded her for what she'd done".

[2] N omits "wery"; supplied from extract in Sotheby's catalogue, June 1932.

[3] See *To* Maclise, 6 July 43.

[4] Catalogue extract reads "property".

[5] See *To* Forster, 3 May and *fn*.

[6] They had dined at Greenwich on 8 May with a party including Stanfield, Maclise, Forster ("who was *stentorian*"), Ainsworth and others (Macready, *Diaries*, II, 207).

To MISS BURDETT COUTTS, 12 MAY 1843*

MS Morgan Library.

Devonshire Terrace | Twelfth May 1843.
My Dear Miss Coutts

I am most earnestly obliged to you for your cordial kindness, which, in its spirit, I really cannot acknowledge sufficiently.

I will take care that my brother immediately acts upon the hint contained in the letter you sent me yesterday. It was a previous knowledge of the perfect truth of all that is stated there, in respect to Railway Making, that first suggested to me the expediency of finding him some other pursuit, if I possibly could. And I still think that if I could get him out to some better sphere of action—as to India—I should do him, as an active and intelligent young man, the best service. Whatever he may get, or fail to get, I cannot be more truly grateful to you than I am.

I called on you the other day, but, I fear, before the Wedding[1] was over. The wind having, at last, gone round to the South, I think and hope Miss Meredith will make a dashing recovery. Pray tell her, with my best wishes, that she is bound to do so.

Always Yours faithfully & obliged
Miss Coutts.   CHARLES DICKENS

To MACVEY NAPIER, 12 MAY 1843

MS British Museum.

1 Devonshire Terrace | York Gate Regents Park
Twelfth May 1843
My Dear Sir

Any day next week, I shall be truly delighted if you will breakfast or dine with me.[2] I will not bore you with a party. That I promise; and I do so, because I think no party will be a relief to you. Name your own hour.

But if you be already sufficiently engaged; do not, I beg, put yourself out of the way. It is a great misery to do so, I know; and in that case you must bind yourself to give me early notice of your next arrival in these parts.

Faithfully Yours
Professor Napier   CHARLES DICKENS

To JOHN WILSON,[3] 13 MAY 1843

Text from N, I, 521.

1 Devonshire Terrace, York Gate, Regent's Park
Private.   Thirteenth May 1843
My Dear Sir,

A few friends of Mr. Black (a countryman of yours) who has been Editor of the Morning Chronicle for nearly thirty years, are going to give him a *Strictly*

---

[1] Edward Marjoribanks, junior, married Marion Fenella Loch at St George's, Hanover Square, on 3 May.

[2] Napier was spending the first two or three weeks of May in London.

[3] Clearly not Professor Wilson (as stated

Private dinner at the Trafalgar Tavern at Greenwich next Saturday the Twentieth, at a quarter before 6 for 6 exactly. The party is composed of a few influential and private gentlemen who are his personal friends; and will not exceed fifteen in number.

I am one of the circle; and my object in writing to you is to ask you if you will allow me to carry you there, as my guest. You already know the majority of the Company—and would, I think, have pleasure in the Society of the remainder. On the other and more selfish hand, I must frankly tell you that I can think of nothing so appropriate and pleasant to all of us on such an occasion, as the presence of a National man like you who can carry an old Scotchman home again by one sound of your voice.

I will not offer any other apology to you for this request, than that very comprehensive one which lies in the assurance that I well know how valuable your time is, and how numerous your engagements are.

I should be happy to bring you home and to take you down. Oblige me with one line in answer at your early convenience.

Faithfully Yours
[CHARLES DICKENS]

To ROBERT WOOD,[1] [13 MAY 1843]

Mention in N, I, 521.

To SIR EDWARD LYTTON BULWER, 14 MAY 1843

MS Lytton Papers.

Devonshire Terrace | Fourteenth May 1843

My Dear Sir Edward.

By this time you will, I have no doubt, have received Longman's Circular.[2] Pray come,[3] and let us see if we can do anything reasonable.

Faithfully Yours always
CHARLES DICKENS

Sir Edward Lytton Bulwer
&c &c &c

---

in N, I, 521*n*), but John Wilson (1800–49; *DNB*), the Scottish vocalist: see Vol. I, p. 418 and *n*. "Wilson's Scottish Entertainments" were given regularly in the season at the Music-hall, Store Street, and at the Hanover-square rooms; in Apr 43 he was also at the Castle Hotel, Richmond; he had several programmes, such as "Jacobite Relics", "The Adventures of Prince Charles", "Highland Songs" and "Another Nicht wi' Burns". He was a steward at the Anniversary Festival of the Caledonian Asylum on 27 May 43 and contributed songs to the entertainment.

[1] Unidentified.

[2] Not traced.

[3] To the meeting of authors and publishers on 17 May.

To THOMAS MITTON, 14 MAY 1843

MS Huntington Library.

Devonshire Terrace | Sunday Evening | Fourteenth May 1843

My Dear Mitton

Here is as much as I can manage now.[1] I hope it will do.

When you see Moody,[2] will you tell him you can get him a cheque from me for £7, if he will take that in full. Should he say, yes, I will forthwith send you that separately. What I now enclose, is "between you and the Schoolmaster".[3]

Faithfully Always

Thomas Mitton Esquire CD.

To THE REV. HENRY COLMAN,[4] 16 MAY 1843

MS Harvard College Library.

1 Devonshire Terrace | York Gate Regents Park
Sixteenth May 1843.

Dear Sir.

The rain prevented me from being punctual yesterday; and you had left your lodgings before I reached them. I was very sorry to miss you, but glad you had not stood upon ceremony, and had taken me at my word.

Will you join our family dinner on Friday (which is, I am sorry to say, the first day we are disengaged) at half past five o'Clock? We shall be quite alone.

If there be, in the mean time, any Lion whose Den I can open for you, pray command me. I called on Sunday last, to say thus much and a great deal more, and to tell you I had been busy all the week, or I should have come to you sooner for Felton's sake. But unfortunately you were from home.

I shall be within doors tomorrow, from half past Eleven to Half past twelve. On other days, I usually leave off work at a quarter before Three in the afternoon, and go out at Three.

Believe me | Faithfully Yours

The Reverend | Henry Colman CHARLES DICKENS

---

[1] See *To* Mitton, 10 May 43, *fn.*

[2] Unidentified; payments to "Moody" appear in the accounts for 10 Feb 43 (£15.18.6) and 27 Jan 44 (£15.18.0).

[3] Not recorded, but meaning obvious: cf. "between you and me and the bedpost" (from 1830). CD's variant suggests that the payment may have concerned a real schoolmaster, perhaps at Exeter: see *To* Mitton, 3 Jan 42, *fn.*

[4] Henry Colman (1785–1849; *DAB*), Unitarian minister and writer on agriculture, from Boston; in Europe 1843–6 to investigate agricultural conditions. His letters (in *European Life and Manners*, 1850, I, 17) show that he dined with CD some time before 29 May. He visited Carlyle on 27 May (*Correspondence of Emerson and Carlyle*, p. 356n) and gave him valuable advice about his brother Alexander who was emigrating to farm in Canada (Carlyle *to* Colman, 17 June 43; *New Letters of Thomas Carlyle*, 1904, I, 293). CD wrote a satirical review of the American edition of Colman's book (also mocking at N. P. Willis) in the *Examiner*, 21 July 49 (*Miscellaneous Papers*, ed. B. W. Matz, pp. 153–161).

To THE REV. W. J. FOX,[1] 16 MAY 1843

Extract in Carnegie Book Shop catalogue No. 157; *MS* 1 p.; addressed to the Reverend W. J. Fox; dated [London], 16 May 43; marked Private.

Concerning the postponement of the friendly and private dinner *to Mr. Black.*

To W. C. MACREADY, 16 MAY 1843*

MS Morgan Library.

Devonshire Terrace | Sixteenth May 1843

My Dear Macready

Sheil,[2] Fonblanque, and I, have held a kind of Divan,[3] wherein we have determined that it will be better to *defer* the dinner to Black, for the present; in as much as some negociations[4] (having no reference, however, to his restoration) are pending between him and Easthope; and the dinner, however private and friendly, might give offence to the latter Potentate whose sickly soul was cradled in the Stock Exchange, and ran alone in Lombard Street.[5]

So the dinner, for the time, is off. And if it never comes on, until men are Men and Nature's Nobility are baronets, God help the Landlord who looks to profit from it.

Affectionately Your friend always

W. C. Macready Esquire   CHARLES DICKENS

To THOMAS LONGMAN, 17 MAY 1843*

MS Mr Arnold U. Ziegler.

Devonshire Terrace | Wednesday Seventeenth May | 1843.

My Dear Sir

If you and Murray should be together, before I come; pray consider the "two principles" which Dilke[6] informs me he intends to move in the opening and outset of the business.[7]

---

[1] William Johnson Fox (1786–1864; *DNB*), preacher, journalist and social reformer: see Vol. I, p. 387*n*. An obvious choice as a guest, since he was a long-standing friend of Forster and Macready and a colleague of Black's on the *Morning Chronicle*—which he also left about this time (Richard and Edward Garnett, *The Life of W. J. Fox*, 1910, p. 248).

[2] Richard Lalor Sheil (1791–1851; *DNB*), dramatist and MP, and co-author of "Sketches of the Irish Bar" in the *New Monthly* from 1823; friend of Macready's. A remarkable orator in spite of a "squeaking" voice "like a tin kettle" (S. C. Hall, *Retrospect of a Long Life*, 1883, I, 249–54).

[3] "An Oriental council of state" (*OED*, 1).

[4] Mackay (*Forty Years' Recollections*, I, 95) recalls that when Black had to leave the *Morning Chronicle*, his friends unsuccessfully tried to get him an appointment on the *London Gazette*; Easthope may have been concerned in this.

[5] Clearly a half-quotation, but untraced.

[6] Charles Wentworth Dilke (1789–1864; *DNB*), critic and antiquary: see Vol. I, p. 127*n*. As editor of the *Athenæum* he continued to give much space to the copyright question.

[7] The meeting at Longman's offices was briefly reported in the *Athenæum* of 20 May, doubtless by Dilke, as the "Association for the Protection of Literature"; CD was in the chair. A paper giving "proposed objects", list of subscribers, and resolutions

1. That a main object of the association is to advance the cause of International Copyright all over the World.

2. That as it protests against being robbed, it protests no less against robbing; and therefore*ᵃ* pledges itself by all its Members, not *ᵃ*to lay violent hands upon the property of any Foreign author whomsoever, without his permission in writing.

I cannot oppose either of these things, so far as I am concerned. Indeed I consider them unquestionably honorable and just, and calculated to give the association a high standing.

In haste | Faithfully Yours always

Thomas Longman Esquire   CHARLES DICKENS

To W. M. THACKERAY, [6–18 MAY 1843]

Mention in Thackeray *to* his mother, Mrs Carmichael Smyth, *Letters and Private Papers*, ed. G. N. Ray, II, 113. *Date:* On 20 May Thackeray wrote "Boz has written me a letter of compliments" (on his *Irish Sketch Book*,[1] published 5 May).

passed is in the Parrish Collection, Princeton University; the first resolution was "that it is expedient, with a due regard to the rights of literary property in all nations, to form an Association of Authors, Publishers, Printers, Stationers, and others connected with Literature, Art, and Science, or feeling an interest in their protection, to carry into effect, in the most complete manner, the provisions of the recent Acts in relation to infringement of Copyright, and the introduction into England and her Possessions abroad of pirated copies of English works". The *Athenæum* reported that a resolution declaring that "members would not knowingly either edit, print, or publish any work in which copyright exists, whether such copyright be vested *in a foreigner* or an Englishman, without the consent of the author or publisher, or sell a copy of any pirated work of such work" was shown to be impracticable by the publishers. The committee was to consist of Bulwer, G. P. R. James, CD, Marryat, Dilke and nine publishers; Bulwer, James and Marryat had been on the committee of the earlier society, while Dilke had been a member; G. P. R. James had also shown his support by the gesture of publishing, on 10 May, his 3-volume novel, *The False Heir*, at a guinea, in spite of Bentley's remonstrances, with a view to proving that prices would not be raised if foreign piratical editions were debarred, and dedicated it "to those Members of the Govern-

ment who gave the first real protection to our Literature". The names of Forster, Bradbury & Evans, Chapman & Hall, Hallam, Lockhart, Macaulay, and Moore are in the list of subscribers; J. S. Buckingham was present (*Examiner*, 29 July 43). John Blackwood wrote to his brother on 18 May 43 to say that he had heard from Dickinson that "the meeting . . . went off very languidly, the subscriptions still more so", and that Dilke had attacked Bentley for pirating an American book (Mrs Oliphant, *William Blackwood and his Sons*, 1897, II, 345). Hood had been present at the meeting, and probably was proposed for the Committee, but suspected that Colburn and Longman had objected because of what he had published on Copyright in June 42; he subsequently withdrew from the Association (MS Huntington; *Letters of Thomas Hood*, ed. P. Morgan, pp. 535–6; undated letters, but "Saturday" is clearly 20 May 43 and "Tuesday" either 30 May or 6 June 43).

*ᵃᵃ*These 7 words, on p. 3 of a folded sheet, are underlined in ink and "those printers & publishers who are present express their desire not to" is written opposite on p. 2 in an unknown hand.

[1] Thackeray, in some financial difficulty, was particularly anxious for the success of this volume, and asked various friends to review it (*Letters*, II, 103, 105, 106, 111); Laman Blanchard had already reviewed it "famously" in the May *Ainsworth's Magazine*, and Forster in the *Examiner* (four

To DR S. G. HOWE, 19 MAY 1843

Mention in Anderson Galleries catalogue, Dec 1917; *MS* 2 pp.; dated Devonshire Terrace, 19 May 43.

A cordial letter of greeting and invitation to dine.[1]

To D. M. MOIR, 19 MAY 1843

MS Brotherton Library, Leeds.

1 Devonshire Terrace | York Gate Regents Park
Nineteenth May 1843.

My Dear Sir

Very many thanks to you for your beautiful book,[2] and for your affectionate letter. I can very truly say that I have not received half as much pain from the sources you mentioned,[3] as I have received pleasure from any one piece in your volume, or any one sentence in your note. I have a strong spice of the Devil in me; and when I am assailed, as I think falsely or unjustly, my red hot anger carries me through it bravely, until I have forgotten all about it.

When I first began to write, too, I suffered intensely, from reading Reviews. And I made a solemn compact with myself, at last, that I would only know them, for the future, from such General report as might reach my ears. For five years[4] I have never broken this Rule, once. I am unquestionably the happier for it—and certainly lose no Wisdom.

columns, on 13 May; "his article is splendid"). Later favourable reviews included one in Jerrold's *Illuminated Magazine* for June, probably by Jerrold himself, calling it "the best book yet written upon Ireland" and "a great advance upon anything heretofore fallen from his pen". It was the first of Thackeray's books to go into a second edition.

[1] Howe had married Julia Ward on 26 Apr in New York; they sailed for Europe on the *Britannia* early in May, accompanied by her sister Annie Ward and their friend Horace Mann who had timed his own marriage to Mary Peabody so as to go with them. The Howes had just arrived at 31 Upper Baker Street, where Howe was confined to the house with an inflamed leg; in a letter to Sumner (25 May) Howe wrote, "As soon as we were installed here, we sent off our letters by a trusty messenger, and were soon favoured with the calls of the lettered", including Morpeth, "hearty, jovial, genial Kenyon" and the Montagus; CD "wrote an affectionate note as soon as he received my card, and sent his wife next day; . . . invited us to dine, but did not call for four days. I am fearful he has been damaged by flattery, and that he is, by the style of his living, endangering his *biler*, as the Kentucks say" (*Letters and Journals of Samuel Gridley Howe*, II, Boston, 1909, pp. 127–8). The Howes were generally feted; among the early visitors was Carlyle, and they met CD at dinners given by Rogers and by Edward Everett, the American ambassador.

[2] *Domestic Verses*: see *To* Moir, ?Jan–Feb 43 and *fn*. The volume, considerably enlarged by the addition of many other elegiac pieces, was published by Blackwood on 18 May. Copy (uninscribed) in CD's library at his death.

[3] Clearly Moir had expressed his sympathy with CD over adverse reviews of *American Notes*—perhaps especially over Warren's, in view of his own close association with *Blackwood's*. Moir would feel this the more keenly because of his own hesitation about publishing his elegies.

[4] Perhaps referring back to the *Quarterly's* article in Oct 37; but an obvious overstatement.

Upon the whole I have as little to complain of in this respect, as any man perhaps. I set your note against the worst thing[1] I have heard of within these six months—and find the balance in my favor.

It gives me great pleasure to read your account of Jeffrey.[2] I have ever found him a warm-hearted, zealous, kindly-natured friend, and I love him very much. I know no man who would be more truly and keenly alive to the tenderness and pathos of your verse.

God bless you and all your house! Mrs. Dickens unites with me in cordial regards to Mrs. Moir. And I am always

My Dear Moir
(For here I vow never to call you 'Sir' again)
Faithfully Your friend

D. M. Moir Esquire   CHARLES DICKENS

To J. C. PRINCE,[3] 19 MAY 1843

Extract in Sotheby's catalogue, July 1929; *MS*, 1 p.; dated Devonshire Terrace, 19 May 43.

I think *highly* of your tribute to Southey;[4] and was very much influenced by it, on reading it this morning.

To WILLIAM SHOBERL,[5] 19 MAY 1843*

MS Morgan Library.

1 Devonshire Terrace, | York Gate Regents Park
Nineteenth May 1843

Dear Sir

I am obliged to you for your note—and regret very much that I was not at home on either occasion of your calling here. But I have been constantly engaged in the adjustment of some family affairs;[6] and they have sadly interfered with my ordinary routine of business and recreation.

---

[1] *Blackwood's* and *Fraser's* were noted as the only bad reviews in *To* Felton, 31 Dec 42; the *Edinburgh* could now be added.

[2] CD met Jeffrey again on 25 May when he dined with Sydney Smith in the company of Lady Stepney, Fanny Kemble, and others (F. Kemble, *Records of Later Life*, 1882, III, 4).

[3] John Critchley Prince (1806–66; *DNB*), poet: see Vol. II, p. 246*n*. From 1845 to 1851 edited the *Ancient Shepherd's Quarterly Magazine* (Ashton-under-Lyne). On 15 May 44 was granted £40 from the Literary Fund, and another £20 on 20 May 46.

[4] Robert Southey had died on 21 Mar 43; Prince's tribute "On the Death of Robert Southey, Poet Laureate" appeared in *Dreams and Realities*, 1847, and evidently earlier in a periodical or newspaper, where CD read it—but not in *Bradshaw's Journal* or the *Oddfellows' Magazine* to which Prince was contributing at this date. According to R. W. Procter (*Literary Reminiscences and Gleanings*, 1860, p. 117) he wrote in Manchester magazines and newspapers under various pseudonyms—Britannicus, Harold Hastings, and Walter Wellbeck among them.

[5] William Shoberl (d. 1853), publisher: see Vol. II, p. 244*n*.

[6] See *To* Mitton, 10 May.

I have a great horror of "editing", and have much employment on my hands. I cannot therefore entertain the project[1] to which your note refers.

I shall not fail to remember, at your desire, that our correspondence on this head, is strictly private.

Believe me | Faithfully Yours

William Shoberl Esquire   CHARLES DICKENS

To T. N. TALFOURD, 20 MAY 1843†

MS Huntington Library.

Devonshire Terrace | Saturday Night Twentieth May | 1843.

My Dear Talfourd

*a*I am more vexed than I can tell you, that I overlooked a horrible engagement for Tuesday, the other night; and have only had it brought home to me today.*a*

I am a steward at the Dinner of the Deaf and Dumb Charity,[2] which comes off that very evening.[3] *That* I wouldn't mind; but, most unhappily one Dr. Howe[4] from America who invented the means of communicating with Laura Bridgman; the deaf, dumb, and blind girl at Boston; has come to London, just when I don't want him, for the express purpose of being carried to that dinner (in pursuance of a wild engagement made four thousand miles off) by *me*. But for this, he would have remained another week at Liverpool—as I devoutly wish he had.

*b*We were talking the other night, when we were last together, of the nuisance of these things. Previously to that, I had registered a Vow to have nothing more to do with them. But now,*b* I swear I will shun them like a Pestilence; and that I will make this, my Third Public Dinner[5] this year, my final appearance on the London Tavern Stage.

If I get away in decent time, will you let me in?

*c*AlwaysFaithfully | My Dear Talfourd
CHARLES DICKENS*c*

P.S. When *are* you going to let us into the secret of that unconfessed Tragedy?[6]

---

[1] Unidentified.

aa; bb; cc Not previously published.

[2] The Charitable and Provident Society for the Aged and Infirm Deaf and Dumb, on 23 May; CD proposed the health of the chairman, Lord Dudley Coutts Stuart (*Speeches*, ed. K. J. Fielding, pp. 41–2).

[3] Macready and Forster dined at Talfourd's chambers on 23 May (Macready, *Diaries*, II, 208)—perhaps a birthday dinner for Talfourd who usually had a joint celebration on 22 May with his son Frank (see Talfourd *to* Hunt, 18 May 44, *Correspondence of Leigh Hunt*, 1862, II, 11). Talfourd entertained very little at home in Spring 43 on account of his wife's ill-

health (Talfourd *to* Hunt, 11 Apr 44, MS BM).

[4] Howe was to have spoken at the dinner; but at the last minute was unable to attend even on crutches owing to "fever and ague" (*Letters and Journals*, II, 128).

[5] For the second, see *To* the Stewards of the Artists' Benevolent Fund, 27 Apr, *fn*.

[6] Talfourd had been working on *The Castilian* at least since 1840 and continued as late as 1850 (MS Diary, Reading Public Library). It was published in 1853, the year before his death, with a preface noting his use of Prescott's *Ferdinand and Isabella*, but was never performed.

To W. C. MACREADY, [25 MAY 1843]

Mention in Macready, *Diaries*, II, 208. *Date:* On 25 May Macready recorded: "Note from Dickens".[1]

To JOHN OVERS, 25 MAY 1843*

Text from typescript, Huntington Library.

Devonshire Terrace, | Twenty fifth May, 1843.

My Dear Mr Overs,

I have learned the value of a good and honest intention so well, that when I am assured of its deserving that character, I look upon it as a deed done. Do not therefore suppose that in my mind, you have left anything unaccomplished in the matter you wrote me of, a few days since. The measure of my gratification is as well filled up, as if I had the mark of recollection on my table.

I hope your wife is better. She has a fine season before her: and I hope is laying up a store of health, as peasants store up fuel, for the winter.

Faithfully yours,

Mr Overs.   CHARLES DICKENS

To CLARKSON STANFIELD, 25 MAY 1843[2]

MS Dartmouth College, New Hampshire.

Devonshire Terrace | Twenty Fifth May 1843.

My Dear Stanfield

No—no—no—Murder, murder! Madness and misconception—Any *one* of those subjects—not the whole. Oh blessed Star of Early Morning,[3] what do you think I am made of, that I should, on the part of any man, prefer such a pig-headed, calf-eyed, donkey-eared, imp-hoofed request!

Says my friend,[4] to me, "Will you ask *your* friend, Mr. Stanfield, what the damage of a little picture of that size, would be—that I may treat myself with the same—if I can afford it?"—Says I, "I will". Says he, "Will you suggest that I should like it to be *one* of those subjects?" Says I, "I will".

I am beating my head against the door, with grief and frenzy—and shall continue to do so, until I receive your answer.

Mrs. Stanfield has heard from Kate?[5]

Ever Heartily Yours
The Misconceived One.

[1] CD dined with Macready next day— with Stanfield, Maclise, Quin, Forster, and Helen Faucit.

[2] MDGH, I, 205 and N, II, 115 wrongly give as 1849.

[3] Also in *To* Felton, 31 Dec 42.

[4] Possibly T. J. Thompson, the only friend of CD's known to have com- missioned a picture from Stanfield (*To* Thompson, 15 Feb 44); on the other hand, no reason to think he could not have afforded even Stanfield's prices.

[5] Macready found "the Dickenses" at Stanfield's when he called on 28 May. The same evening CD, Stanfield, Maclise, and Forster dined with him (*Diaries*, II, 209).

To T. J. WATSON,[1] 25 MAY 1843

Extract in Sotheby's catalogue, Dec 1924; *MS* 1 p.; dated 1 Devonshire Terrace, York Gate, 25 May 43.

Pray do not forget your kind promise to dine here on Saturday next. We shall be quite a family party;[2] and our hour is half-past six.

To JOSEPH SOUL,[3] 26 MAY 1843

Text from N, 1, 523.

1 Devonshire Terrace, York Gate, Regents Park
Twenty-Sixth May 1843

Dear Sir,

I am greatly obliged to Mr. Abdy[4] for his kind and flattering recollection of me; and to you for conveying his welcome mark of it. I have not forgotten the Working School,[5] but have been so constantly engaged in a Private Working School of my own, wherein I am teacher and scholar too, that I have not been able to get there.

Faithfully yours
[CHARLES DICKENS]

---

[1] Named as a steward at the Anniversary dinner of the Society for the Aged and Infirm Deaf and Dumb on 23 May in the *Times* advertisement of 1 May.

[2] This was the dinner given for the Howes; Forster is the only other known guest. Julia Howe wrote on 30 May to her sister Louisa: "We had a pleasant dinner at Dickens's, on Saturday—a very handsome entertainment, consisting of all manner of good things. Dickens led me in to dinner—waxed quite genial over his wine, and was more natural than I ever saw him—after dinner we had coffee, conversation and music, to which I lent my little wee voice! We did not get home until half past eleven" (Laura Richards and Maud Howe Elliott, *Julia Ward Howe, 1819–1910*, New York, 1916, I, 84). In her own *Reminiscences 1819–99*, New York, 1900, p. 110, Julia Howe recalled the refrain of one of the comic songs sung after dinner, "Tiddy hi, tiddy ho, tiddy hi hum, | Thus was it when Barbara Popkins was young". Forster invited them to dine at his chambers with the Dickenses and Maclise—on which occasion Julia Howe addressed her husband as "darling", whereupon "Dickens slid down to the floor, and, lying on his back, held up one of his small feet, quivering with pretended emotion. 'Did she call him darling?' he cried" (*ibid.*).

[3] Joseph Soul (1805–81); Secretary of the Orphan Working School 1840–76; acted also as Secretary of the Alexandra Orphanage, established 1864, the two institutions being run as one.

[4] Possibly the Rev. John Channing Abdy, Rector of St John's, Southwark; or Edward Strutt Abdy (1791–1846; *DNB*), writer on America.

[5] Founded by the Rev. Edward Pickard in 1758 at Hoxton with accommodation for 20 boys; 20 girls were added later. "Working School" as the founder wished that the "orphans and other necessitous children" should learn some useful trade; its large building in the City Road to which it removed in 1773 contained workrooms and facilities for baking, brewing and washing. Boys were apprenticed at 14, girls trained for domestic service until they were 15 or 16. The school moved to Haverstock Hill 1847; created a Corporation by Act of Parliament 1848. Easthope was a Governor 1843; CD became a Life Governor 1844 by subscribing five guineas which entitled him to nominate children for admission and to a vote at each election.

To THE DUCHESS OF SUTHERLAND,[1] 26 MAY 1843*

MS William H. Robinson Ltd.

1 Devonshire Terrace | Twenty Sixth May 1843

Mr. Charles Dickens presents his compliments to the Duchess of Sutherland, and very much regrets that having an engagement for this evening which he cannot set aside, and which he has reason to fear will detain him late; he cannot have the honor and pleasure of availing himself of The Duchess of Sutherland's kindness. It is unnecessary for him to add that if it had been possible to forego his previous engagement, he would most gladly have relinquished it.

To T. J. THOMPSON, 26 MAY 1843

MS Huntington Library.

Devonshire Terrace | Twenty Sixth May 1843.[2]

My Dear Thompson

Read the enclosed,[3] and say Will it do?

Faithfully Always.

Anti Pusey[4]

To MISS BURDETT COUTTS, 28 MAY 1843*

MS Morgan Library.

Devonshire Terrace. | Twenty Eighth May 1843.

Dear Miss Coutts

Very many thanks to you for your kind note of yesterday. I will not fail to call on Captain Fitzroy,[5] and to carry my brother with me, at the appointed

---

[1] Harriet Elizabeth Georgiana Leveson-Gower (1806–68; *DNB*), third daughter of George Howard, sixth Earl of Carlisle; friend of Mrs Norton (see *To* Sumner, 31 July 42, *fn*). "The society which the Duchess gathered round her included a large and miscellaneous contingent from the ranks of literature, of science, and especially the rising section of philanthropists in politics, of which Lord Ashley . . . was the most remarkable" (George Douglas, Duke of Argyll, *Autobiography*, 1906, I, 223, under date 1843).

[2] N, II, 25 has 1847, incorrectly.

[3] Clearly either the MS or proof of CD's "anti-Pusey" article, "Report of the Commissioners appointed to inquire into the condition of the Persons variously engaged in the University of Oxford", published as an unsigned leader in the *Examiner*, 3 June 43 (*Miscellaneous Papers*, ed. B. W. Matz). The MS (Forster Collection, V & A) shows little revision, but comparison with the printed text shows

that a few changes and omissions were made in proof, softening the reference to the Thirty-nine articles by omitting "almost every one of which shall contradict the other", and substituting "Learned degrees" for "clerical degrees". Crabb Robinson saw it on 4 June, and read it aloud to the Austins as "a capital jeu d'esprit . . . The students are made out to be worse than the children in the Mines" (MS Diary, Dr Williams's Library).

[4] Pusey's sermon on the Eucharist, preached before the university at Christ Church, Oxford, on 14 May, had been delated to the Vice-Chancellor; the *Morning Chronicle* of 24 May reported this as a "sensation", under the heading "Dr Pusey's Public Profession of Roman Catholic Doctrine".

[5] Probably Captain Robert FitzRoy (1805–65; *DNB*), hydrographer and meteorologist, later vice-admiral; had sailed with Darwin on the *Beagle*; MP for Durham 1841; conservator of the Mersey

time. But I rather fear from what I read in the note you send me from Mr. Parkinson,[1] that I shall trouble him in vain.

I am delighted to hear that Miss Meredith is getting on so well, and beg to send her my best regards and congratulations. If she goes back any more, though by but the twentieth part of an inch, my faith in her is at an end, and my affections shall be transferred—as a mark of the wildest desperation—to Lady Sale.[2]

If you will permit me—which I shall take it for granted you will, unless I hear from you to the contrary—I will call on you at about Two on Wednesday: after I have seen Captain Fitzroy.

Dear Miss Coutts
Always Yours faithfully and obliged
CHARLES DICKENS

Miss Coutts.

To MISS BURDETT COUTTS, 2 JUNE 1843

MS Morgan Library.

Devonshire Terrace | Second June 1843

Dear Miss Coutts.

I will not weary you, at present, by saying anything more in the way of Thanks. I enclose a note, written according to Mr. Marjoribank's[3] suggestion. It is quite needless, I am sure, for me to add that I am fully sensible of its value, and of his kindness.

Lady Sale, I renounce for ever. And I here register a vow to look upon her henceforth with an eye, colder and duller than a Fish's. Nor will I ever envy her Husband—her dog—her maid—nor anything that is her's,[4] except the Memory of her departed Son in Law.[5] He must have had a blessed release; and I have no doubt is in an uncommon state of Peace. If his wife took after her mother, I believe more implicitly than I ever did, that every bullet has its billet, and that there is a Special Providence in the Fall of a Sparrow.[6]

If Miss Meredith will receive me in that Poet's apartment[7] you write of, on Sunday next; there will I be. I have pondered and reflected about the best time. Something seems to point in my mind to 3.[8] But if that something be wrong by

---

1842–3; appointed Governor of New Zealand 31 Mar 43, and left in July, arriving in Auckland at end of Dec. May have been consulted about prospects for Alfred in New Zealand.

[1] Possibly "Jas. Parkinson" of Lloyd's.

[2] Florentia (*b.* ?1790), daughter of George Wynde and wife of Sir Robert Henry Sale (1782–1845; *DNB*) who commanded the British forces in Afghanistan; her *Journal of the Disasters in Affghanistan, 1841–2*, published by Murray 15 Apr 43, describes the retreat. Lord Auckland was attacked, which CD may have disliked. Also, she was being lionized; Sydney Smith said "She'll be Sale by auction!"

(F. Kemble, *Records of Later Life*, I, 106), and "J. H. Siddons" [Stocqueler] described her as "a burly lady of middle age; a strong-minded woman, whose manners smacked of a barrack education" ("Random Recollections of a Life", *Harper's New Monthly*, Dec 62, XXVI, 76).

[3] Thus in MS.

[4] Cf. the 10th Commandment.

[5] Captain J. D. L. Sturt of the Engineers; married 1841, and died at Kabul in 1842.

[6] *Hamlet*, V, ii, 232.

[7] Perhaps the library: cf. refs to "library dinners" in Vol. II.

[8] Written very large.

the Horse Guards, all times are alike to me in such a pleasant case, and an anonymous figure received per post in the course of tomorrow, will be perfectly understood and gratefully attended to.

There is a terrible paper on Theodore Hook,[1] in the last Quarterly—admirably written—as I think, from its internal evidence, by Lockhart. I have not seen anything for a long time so very moving. It fills me with grief and sorrow. Men have been chained to hideous prison walls and other strange anchors 'ere now, but few have known such suffering and bitterness at one time or other, as those who have been bound to Pens. A pleasant thought for one who has been using this very quill all day!

Always Faithfully Yours | And earnestly obliged

Miss Coutts.   CHARLES DICKENS

To GEORGE FLETCHER,[2] 2 JUNE 1843

Extract in Carnegie Book Shop catalogue No. 119 (1944); *MS* 1 p.; dated Devonshire Terrace, 2 June 43.

I thank you very much for the book ... I have already one reason to read it with interest; and I have very little doubt that its own merit[3] will give me another.

To W. C. MACREADY, 2 JUNE 1843*

MS Morgan Library.

Devonshire Terrace | Second June 1843.

My Dear Macready.

It has been a matter of Life or Death with the Sanatorium[4]—which has done a World of Good, and if it can weather the storm, will do worlds more. We are going to have a dinner (Lord Lansdowne, I believe, in the chair)—and they are very anxious to have you for a steward, as being the distinguished head of a large class who come immediately within its objects.[5] For a similar reason, though it is

---

[1] *Quarterly Review*, May 1843, LXXII, 53–108; Lockhart was the author. Hook had died heavily in debt in 1841. The article, though sympathetic, dwells on his money troubles and the excesses of his life, and concludes that "the example of such talents, exerted so much to the delight of others, so little to their possessor's profit—of a career so chequered by indiscretion, and so darkly closed at a period so untimely—ought not, at all events, to be destitute of instructiveness". See Vol. II, p. 396*n*.

[2] George Fletcher, of Birmingham: see Vol. II, p. 416*n*. He had contributed to periodicals, but his collected writings were not published until 1857.

[3] A shorter extract in Carnegie catalogue No. 103 reads "merits".

[4] At the Annual Meeting of 29 May, CD had moved a resolution that other benevolent institutions should be invited to co-operate with the Sanatorium (*The Times*, 30 May).

[5] The dinner was held at the London Tavern on Thurs 29 June with Lord Ashley in the chair. CD proposed the health of the chairman: see *Speeches*, ed. K. J. Fielding, pp. 42–3. Macready went with CD, Forster, and Procter, and noted that "Dickens spoke the best, Forster very fairly, Dillon very well" (*Diaries*, II, 215). The other stewards included Browning, John Dillon, Forster, Lord Robert Grosvenor, Matthew Davenport Hill, Lord Lansdowne, Maclise, Lord Sandon, Lord Dudley Coutts Stuart and Dr Southwood Smith.

not so powerful in his case, I have secured Maclise. So, in the name of Wise Charity, and Church Mice—the Sanatorium represents the first; and I—being very poor—the second—let me put you down. I wouldn't ask you in behalf of any other Establishment.

The dinner is proposed for the last Wednesday *or* Thursday in June—this present Month.

Faithfully Ever
CD.

To THOMAS MITTON, 7 JUNE 1843

MS Huntington Library.

Devonshire Terrace | Wednesday Evening | Seventh June 1843.
My Dear Mitton

I duly received your first note; but I have been (as you never seem to think I am) busied and worried in a hundred ways; with scores of perplexing engagements[1] on my hands, and the American episode[2] in Chuzzlewit to wo[rk][3] at; which takes me at least [twic]e as long, every line of it, [as t]he ordinary current of [it w]ill.

I will try [to] come down to you tomorrow ev[cni]ng at 8. It is the first evening I have had for nights and nights; though every evening, I have meant to come down to you upon the next.

Faithfully Always
Thomas Mitton Esquire   CD.

To AMÉDÉE PICHOT,[4] 7 JUNE 1843

Text from *Le Neveu de ma Tante*, 3rd edn, Paris, 1851, I, viii–ix; presumably Pichot's translation: of CD's letters to him, only those in *Le Neveu de ma Tante* are in French.

Devonshire Terrace, York Gate, Regent's Park
7 juin 1843.
Mon cher monsieur,

Je serai vraiment heureux de recevoir votre visite et celle d'un gentleman aussi universellement connu que le *personnage noir*[5] dont vous me parlez dans votre

---

[1] With the Howes; and negotiations about the presentation of the Macready testimonial.

[2] Chs 16–17 in the July No.

[3] Narrow tears down centre of MS have removed several letters here supplied conjecturally.

[4] Amédée Pichot (1795–1877); editor of *Revue Britannique* since 1839, translator of many English writers, and author of books on England, including *Galerie des Personnages de Shakespeare*, 1843; friendly

with Thackeray (*Letters and Private Papers*, ed. Gordon N. Ray, II, 121–2).

[5] Paul Emile Daurand Forgues (1813–1883); literary and dramatic critic on *Le Commerce* in 1838 under the pseudonym "Old Nick"; then on *Le National* and *Charivari*, and a regular contributor to the *Revue Britannique* where he had an article on CD in Apr 43 (W. J. Carlton, "'Old Nick' at Devonshire Terrace", *D*, LIX [1963], 138–44).

billet. S'il vous convenait de venir lundi prochain à midi (je fais une petite absence à la campagne[1] dans l'intervalle), ce sera un grand plaisir pour moi de faire personnellement votre connaissance.[2]

Je vous remercie beaucoup de la *Cloche du Tocsin*,[3] ainsi que de tout ce que vous me dites d'obligeant et d'aimable.

Croyez-moi fidèlement à vous,

A M. Amédée Pichot.   CHARLES DICKENS

To THE BARONESS DE ROTHSCHILD,[4] [7 JUNE 1843]

Mention in *To* Miss Coutts, 9 June 43.

[1] This absence, presumably at Finchley, is not mentioned in other letters. CD and Forster were probably there together, CD coming up for the day on Fri 9 June.

[2] Three accounts of the visit were published, one in the London letter in the June *Revue Britannique* (written by a third member of the party who did not accompany Pichot and Forgues on this occasion), one by Forgues in *L'Illustration*, 1844, and one in the long prefatory notice added to the 3rd edition of Pichot's translation of *David Copperfield*, *Le Neveu de ma Tante*. All are drawn upon, and Forgues' is quoted in its entirety, in W. J. Carlton's article (above). Forgues thought the street dreary, "with frontages resembling a badly whitewashed sepulchre"; CD's house was "the most respectable". They were cordially greeted by CD at the door of his study, "an oval room, simply furnished". Pichot noticed the "splendid bookcases, filled with fine books, beautifully bound", and both observed a portrait which they supposed to be of Mrs Dickens (probably Laurence's drawing of her, but just possibly Browne's painting of Mary Hogarth). Like many observers, they were struck by CD's quick intelligence and vivaciousness, and the "bright, restless eyes" and generous smile; Pichot found it unexpected that an Englishman should make so much use of gesture (though "without going beyond the limits of British dignity") and was not surprised at learning later of his talent in private theatricals. Forgues felt that if he had met him by chance he might have thought him a head clerk, a smart reporter, a secret agent, a wily barrister or the manager of a troupe of strolling players; but these impressions were contradicted by his modest and frank conversation. CD was more ready to speak of his children (Charley entered the room at one point) than of his works, but discussed the translations of his books, mainly with polite approval, though excluding "a certain German version of *Nickleby* and *Oliver*" (by H. Roberts of Leipzig); he also spoke of mesmerism, and of prisons, giving them a letter of introduction to the Middlesex House of Correction (Coldbath Fields). They were pleased to learn of his intention of visiting France; this is the sole confirmation of the early forming of the project referred to in *To* Forster, 1 and 2 Nov, which may well have been encouraged by this flattering visit by French admirers.

[3] Title of the instalments of *Barnaby Rudge* translated by Pichot and published in *Revue Britannique*, Oct–Dec 42, collected in *Les Contes de Charles Dickens*, *deuxième série*, Paris, 1847. Pichot later translated CD's *Christmas Books*.

[4] Charlotte (*d.* 1884), wife (and cousin) of Lionel Nathan de Rothschild, banker and philanthropist (1808–71; *DNB*). Actively interested in various charities and left £120,000 to charity on her death.

To [AUGUSTUS TRACEY], 7 JUNE 1843*

MS University of Texas. *Address:* clearly to Lieutenant Tracey, Governor of Tothill Fields Bridewell.

1 Devonshire Terrace | York Gate Regents Park | Seventh June 1843. Governor.

Now, we don't want none of your sarse—and if you bung any of them tokes[1] of yours in this direction, you'll find your shuttlecock sent back as heavy as it came. Who wants your Bridewell umberellers? Do you suppose people can't perwide theirselves with crooked handles, without axing *you*? Who ever see your umbereller? *I* didn't. Go and look for it in the Gruel; and if it an't there, search the Soup. It an't so thick, but wot you'll find three and sixpence worth of ginghum[2] among the ox heads as you pave your garden with. Ah. Oh. Yes. No. Yor'ne too cheekish[3] by half Governor. That's where it is. You'd better take it out of yourself by a month and labour, on the Mill. If that don't answer, let off one of them blunderbusses in the office agin your weskut. *That's* what your complaint wants.

his

Villium   Gibbuns[4]

Mark.

Memorandum added by the Chaplain[5]

P.S.[6] The unfortunate man forgot to state that the umbrella was Found in his possession while he penned the above—that his wretched wife was as well as could be expected; also her sister—that he had determined not to ask the Governor in Dr Howe's behalf, for a ticket to the St. Giles's Lions[7] (thinking the said Doctor troublesome in that respect) but had conferred with Mr. Crea[8] according

---

[1] Pieces of dry bread (J. C. Hotten, *Slang Dictionary*, 1859); recorded as prison slang before 1830 by G. L. Chesterton (*Revelations of Prison Life*, 2nd edn, 1856, I, 240).

[2] An umbrella; not recorded in this sense in *OED* before 1861.

[3] Not recorded in *OED* before 1850 (Mayhew).

[4] If "William Gibbons" were the name of an actual prisoner, it would add to the joke.

[5] The chaplain of the Tothill Fields Bridewell was the Rev. George Henry Hine.

[6] "I forgot" cancelled here.

[7] Howe may have proposed this expedition to the "thieves' quarter" (see *Letters and Journals of Samuel Gridley Howe*, II, 132) during the visit he is known to have paid to Bridewell with the Dickenses and the Manns, almost certainly on 5 June (E. F. Williams, *Horace Mann*, New York, 1937, p. 250). Julia Howe recalled that CD, looking at the treadmill, said to Howe "My God! If a woman thinks her son may come to this, I don't blame her if she strangles him in infancy" (*Reminiscences*, p. 109).

[8] The head turnkey; see also *To* Tracey, 9 June. Mentioned as "Cree" in *To* Tracey, 10 June 47.

to the Governor's kind suggestion; and would write the Governor when the Night was fixed.

To MISS BURDETT COUTTS, 9 JUNE 1843*

MS Morgan Library.

Devonshire Terrace | Friday Ninth June 1843

Dear Miss Coutts.

I hasten to say, in answer to your kind note, that I wrote to the Baroness De Rothschild on *Wednesday Night*, proposing to call to day at Half Past Three. I did not name an earlier day, because on Tuesday and Wednesday the Baroness was engaged; and yesterday I was obliged to shut myself up, from 9 until 5.

I am truly sorry to hear that Miss Meredith is so slow—the more so, as I think it is quite a new complaint with her. But it must be a comforting reflection, both to her and you, that there are *outward* causes enough, in all conscience, to account for her tardy recovery. I suppose it is morally impossible to get rid of rheumatism while this terrible wetness prevails.[1]

I enclose you the little pamphlet[2] I spoke of—and will report progress when I have seen the Baroness.

                              Always Faithfully Yours
Miss Coutts.   CHARLES DICKENS

To AUGUSTUS TRACEY, 9 JUNE 1843*

MS University of Texas.

Devonshire Terrace | Ninth June 1843

My Dear Sir

Will you tell the watchful Crea (who always sits, by instinct, close to the door when he comes here, and looks as if he would like to lock it and keep the key) that at Halfpast Eleven tonight, a carriage—most probably a Brougham—will be waiting by St. Giles's Church; and that in that mysterious vehicle, he will find Dr. Howe and his friend expecting him, eagerly.

He is a cold-blooded fellow, that Howe—a regular American—and I wouldn't have taken the trouble to put even your friendly willingness to this test, but for your letter.[3]

---

[1] The "long-continued unfavourable weather" (seven rainy weeks) was commented on by the *Examiner*, 17 June.

[2] Possibly about the Sanatorium.

[3] Lower part of second leaf of folded sheet cut away, probably removing only ending and signature.

To DR S. G. HOWE, 9 JUNE 1843

Text from Laura E. Richards and Maud H. Elliott, *Julia Ward Howe, 1819–1910*, New York, 1916, I, 183.

Ninth June, 1843.

My Dear Howe,

Drive to-night to St. Giles's Church. Be there at half-past 11—and wait. One of Tracey's people will put his head into the coach after a Venetian and mysterious fashion, and breathe your name. Trust him to the death.

So no more at present from

The Mask[1]

To W. C. MACREADY, [?9 JUNE 1843]*

MS Morgan Library. *Date:* June 43 on handwriting; likely to be before Macready's last performance on 14 June; Macready mentions a call on 9 June (see *fn*).

My Dear Macready

Will *you* call *here*, if you are coming out?—The sooner after 12, the better.[2] I wod. come to you; but forgot last night, having appointed a man to call. Talfourd was sublimely ridiculous—a very comet of absurdity—last night.

Faithfully Always

CD.

To [? SIR FRANCIS AND LADY BURDETT], 10 JUNE 1843*

MS Bodleian Library.

Devonshire Terrace | Tenth June 1843.

Mr. Charles Dickens very greatly regrets that he cannot have the pleasure of accepting [Sir Francis & Lady Burdett's][3] kind Invitation for Wednesday;[4]

---

[1] No account of the expedition appears to survive, except that according to Laura Richards (*Letters and Journals*, II, 132) "The police said to the people, 'This gentleman has been eased!' and a thief would cry out, 'I wish I was the one who had eased him!'"

[2] "Called on Dickens, who told me of the Duke of Cambridge's proposal of presenting the testimonial at twelve for one on Monday 19th." (*Diaries*, II, 212). Entries of 6 and 7 June show calls from CD and Forster about the arrangements.

[3] The name has been cut out; "Sir Francis & Lady Burdett's" would fill the space, and would account for the presence of the letter among the Burdett papers. See also *To* [Lady Burdett], 13 Jan 43.

[4] On Wed 14 June CD went to the final performance (*Macbeth*) at Drury Lane, followed by Macready's farewell address

from the stage. This had been postponed on account of the Queen's command performance (of *As You Like It* and J. M. Morton's *Thumping Legacy*) on Monday— her first visit during Macready's management. Wednesday's audience, "scarcely less numerous and enthusiastic", were "anxious to hear from his own mouth an explanation of the cause of his retirement" (*Athenæum*, 17 June 43), and on his appearance as Macbeth gave him such a tremendous reception, that he was "never so affected by the expression of sympathy by an audience. When wearied with shouting, they changed the applause to a stamping of feet, which sounded like thunder; it was grand and awful! ... I think I never played Macbeth so well ... I spoke my speech, and retired with the same mad acclaim" (Macready, *Diaries*, II, 213). The speech (not described by

but on that evening his friend Mr. Macready retires from the direction of Drury Lane Theatre, and, for some considerable time,[1] from the English Stage—and it is an occasion in which he has so much interest and regret, that he cannot avoid being present.[2]

To GEORGE LAVAL CHESTERTON, [12 JUNE 1843]

Mention in *Revue Britannique*, Paris, June 1843, p. 702. *Date:* written during Pichot's and Forgues' call on CD (see *To* Pichot, 7 June 43, *fn*).

Introducing Amédée Pichot and Emile Forgues to the Governor of the Middlesex House of Correction.[3]

To W. C. MACREADY, 12 JUNE 1843*

MS Morgan Library. *Address:* W. C. Macready Esquire.

Twelfth June 1843

My Dear Macready.   Moore[4] will be very glad to receive your Invitation to the

Macready) made it clear that he was not complaining of lack of support for his Shakespearian productions; nightly receipts had been as good as in his last Covent Garden season and promised future and permanent success; but the rent was too high for the decayed state of the theatre when he took over, and the law gave to persons unacquainted with the drama "an irresponsible power over it". The *Athenæum* commented: "That such a manager as Mr. Macready should be compelled to retire by the treatment of the proprietors, whose property and patent rights he has done his utmost to uphold, cannot but excite surprise and regret, if not indignation. The case against the 'patent' monopoly of the two great houses has never been so strongly urged before; and Mr. Macready has given it 'a heavy blow and great discouragement'—let us hope that it will be fatal".

[1] Macready's proposed departure to America in the autumn, of which there had been earlier rumours, was officially announced in *The Times* on 5 July 43; meanwhile he was to "recruit his health by a total abstinence from professional labour".

[2] *Athenæum*'s diary entry concludes with "Dickens, H. Smith, Forster and Stanfield, Serle came into my room. They did not seem struck with the speech".

[3] The writer of the London letter dated 19 June in the *Revue Britannique* says they were to visit the prison on that day.

Forgues in *L'Illustration* (1844) also mentions the note to the Governor, and says: "thanks to his precious recommendation, we were received with as much attention and courtesy as though Prince Albert himself had taken the trouble to go with us" (W. J. Carlton, *D*, LIX, 143).

[4] Thomas Moore (1779–1852; *DNB*), poet, best known for his *Irish Melodies*, published in parts 1807–34, and well known to CD who often quotes from them and from *National Airs* (1825); CD possessed his works in the 12-vol. Paris edition of 1823–7 (*Library of CD*, ed. J. H. Stonehouse, p. 82). Awarded a pension in 1835; collected his poems in ten vols, 1840–1, and was engaged on *The History of Ireland* for *Lardner's Cabinet Cyclopaedia*, completed 1846. His home since 1817 had been Sloperton Cottage, Wilts, on Lord Lansdowne's estate, but he made extended visits to London each spring and was often at Rogers's. CD had probably first met him through Bentley in 1838 (see Vol. I, p. 460*n*) and both were members of the Siddons Committee in 1840–1. Moore was in London in Mar and again in June–July 43, constantly dining out in aristocratic and literary company and charming them with his conversation and songs. Jeffrey, who had once attacked his work, called him "the sweetest-blooded, warmest hearted, happiest, hopefullest creature that ever set fortune at defiance" (quoted without source by Charles Kent in the Cen-

Theatre,[1] though the chances seem against his being able to use it. His address is 31 Sackville Street.[2]

> Affectionately always
> CD.

To [MAJOR] H. S. STEPHENS,[3] 12 JUNE 1843

MS Huntington Library.

1 Devonshire Terrace | Twelfth June 1843.

Sir.

I have appointed the time kindly proposed by His Royal Highness,[4] for the presentation of the Testimonial[5] to Mr. Macready.[6] And I avail myself of the permission of His Royal Highness, to forward such facts connected with the Testimonial, as I conceive His Royal Highness may desire to know. To the best of my recollection, they include those points upon which his late Royal Highness The Duke of Sussex,[7] laid the greatest stress, and set the most value.

Mr. Smith, 12 Duke Street Lincolns Inn Fields, is the Working Silversmith, at whose house the Testimonial will be, after the day I mentioned in my former letter. In the mean time it is undergoing some process necessary to its completion.[8]

---

tenary edition of Moore's *Works*, 1879, p. xxvi). His domestic life was darkened by the death of his second son in Nov 42, after a long illness contracted in India, and the wildness of his eldest son who was heavily in debt and had joined the Foreign Legion.

[1] For an entertainment given by Macready after the command performance, to which many of his friends were invited, including Stanfield, Edwin and Charles Landseer, Stone, Maclise and CD (*Cerberus*, 17 June 43).

[2] The house of Lady Elizabeth Feilding, which she often lent him.

[3] Major Henry Sykes Stephens, one of the 13 equerries of the Duke of Cambridge. Listed as "Captain", in error, in the earlier of the two Royal Kalendars for 1843.

[4] Adolphus Frederick, Duke of Cambridge (1774–1850; *DNB*); well known as a supporter of public charities and for his interest in the arts.

[5] See *To* Miss Coutts, 28 Feb.

[6] The following notice in CD's hand (MS Suzannet) was presumably circulated to the company, or posted in the theatre: "TESTIMONIAL TO MR. MACREADY | The Committee for the management of this Testimonial, beg to inform the Ladies and Gentlemen engaged in The Theatre Royal Drury Lane, that it will be publicly presented to Mr. Macready, by His Royal Highness The Duke of Cambridge, in

Willis's Rooms King Street Saint James's, on Monday the 19th. Instant, at 12 o' clock at noon, for 1 precisely. | They will be happy to accommodate those Gentlemen of the Company who may wish to attend, upon the Platform; to which they will be admitted on presenting their cards to the Person in charge of it. | They will also be happy to make the best provision in their power, for the reception of those Ladies of the Company who may desire to be present. With this view, they request the favor of their registering their names with Mr. Serle, on or before Wednesday Evening the 14th. Instant. That Gentleman's list will be handed to the Committee on the conclusion of the night's Performances: and they will make their arrangements accordingly. | Saturday. Tenth June 1843".

[7] The Duke of Sussex, who was to have presented the testimonial, had died on 21 Apr 43.

[8] The inscription (given in press reports) read as follows: "To William Charles Macready, in commemoration of his management of the Theatre Royal, Covent Garden, in the seasons 1837–8 and 1838–9, when his personation of the characters, his restorations of the text, and his illustrations—by the best intellectual aids—of the historical facts and poetical creations of the plays of Shakespeare formed an epoch in theatrical annals, alike honorable to his own genius and elevating in its influence

Should His Royal Highness give me leave, it would afford me pleasure to attend there at any time His Royal Highness might appoint, to explain the views the Committee have had, in the selection of the Design.

> I have the honor to be | Sir,
> Your faithful Servant

Captain H. S. Stephens.   CHARLES DICKENS

To JAMES SILK BUCKINGHAM, 13 JUNE 1843

Facsimile in Henri Saffroy catalogue No. 52 (1967).

Devonshire Terrace | Thirteenth June 1843.

Dear Sir

I am much obliged to you for your kindness in forwarding me a prospectus of the British and Foreign Institute[1]—not the less so, because I cannot, at present, become a member of any New association.

> Faithfully Yours

James S. Buckingham Esquire   CHARLES DICKENS

To SIR EDWARD LYTTON BULWER, 13 JUNE 1843

MS Lytton Papers.

Devonshire Terrace | Thirteenth June 1843.[2]

My Dear Sir Edward

The Duke appoints *12 for 1*, instead of 1 for 2.

"There's no such thing"[3]—as an Honorary Secretary. Some phantom with

upon public taste, this testimonial is presented by the lovers of the national drama"; on the other side of the base *Troilus and Cressida*, III, iii, 115-23 was quoted.

[1] According to the *Transactions of the British and Foreign Institute*, 1845, the idea first occurred to Buckingham in 1825, when he was "in the habit of enjoying, at [his] residence ... frequent *Soirées Littéraires*"; he projected building plans and issued a prospectus in 1830, but gained no support (p. 2). He revived his plans in Apr 43, no doubt because of the scheme for a Society of Authors, whose members he evidently hoped, but failed, to attract. After a preliminary meeting 31 May at the residence of the Earl of Devon, a circular letter was issued to "those most distinguished ... and generally known ... as the friends and promoters of all literary, scientific, and useful undertakings"; this is what CD refers to. When 100 members were obtained a further meeting was held, and a formal Prospectus issued. The two objects were first to establish "a centre of Personal Intercourse" for gentlemen from

all countries, and second, frankly stated, "to secure for the Originator and Founder ... a permanent home and resting-place, after his varied and active life". Few literary men joined, though Milnes and Shelton Mackenzie were among those on the Committee (see *To* Milnes, 6 Aug); the first thousand members included Miss Mitford, Harriet Martineau, Behnes the sculptor, and Charles Martin the artist. A public meeting was held on 20 July (*op. cit.*, pp. 9-19); the *Athenæum's* comment on 12 Aug was that funds appeared inadequate and "the project appears to be crude, undigested, and even aimless". The Institute was formally opened in Hanover Square on 2 Feb 44 by the Prince Consort and published its rather grandiose *Transactions* in 1845, including 13 lectures by Buckingham and his account of the soirées. The Institute collapsed in 1846 for financial reasons; Buckingham blamed the constant attacks by *Punch*.

[2] Dated 1849, incorrectly, in N, II, 156.

[3] *Macbeth*, I, ii, 47.

that name, once flitted through the books at Coutts's, but has long since passed away;[1] and unlike old Aubrey's spectres left no "melodious twang" behind.[2]

I found two or three restless men, wandering in the depths of the Drury Lane Scenery last night, and plundered them of as many Guineas. They had heard of the Testimonial in their infancy, and thought it a pleasant fiction. One hoary sage had been a Member of the Committee of Taste,[3] he mournfully said.

Always | Faithfully Yours

Sir Edward Lytton Bulwer.   CHARLES DICKENS

To DOUGLAS JERROLD, 13 JUNE 1843

MS Brotherton Library, Leeds.

Devonshire Terrace | Thirteenth June 1843.

My Dear Jerrold.

Yes. You have anticipated my occupation. Chuzzlewit be damned,—High Comedy and five hundred pounds are the only matters I can think of.[4] I call it The One Thing Needful, or A Part is Better than the Whole. Here are the characters.

Old Febrile	—	Mr. Farren.[5]
Young Febrile (his son)	—	Mr. Hone.
Jack Hessians (his friend)	—	Mr. W. Lacy.

[1] William Brydone, the business manager dismissed by Macready in 1842, had been the honorary secretary of the Macready testimonial in 1840 (T. Marshall, *Lives of the Most Celebrated Actors and Actresses*, p. 24).

[2] John Aubrey, *Miscellanies*, 1696, p. 67, on the apparition which "being demanded, whether a good Spirit, or a bad? returned no answer, but disappeared with a curious perfume and most melodious Twang".

[3] For choosing the plate; on the model of the various Committees of Taste concerned with public memorials, e.g. for the Waterloo monument in 1826.

[4] Jerrold had written on 8 June from New Herne Bay, "Of course, you have flung *Chuzzlewit* to the winds, and are hard at work on a comedy. Somebody—I forget his name—told me that you were seen at the Haymarket door, with a wet newspaper in your hand, knocking frantically for Webster. Five hundred pounds for the *best* English comedy! As I think of the sum, I look loftily around this apartment of full 12 by 13—glance with poetic frenzy on a lark's turf that docs duty for a lawn—take a vigorous inspiration of the 'double Bromptons' that are nodding saucily, defyingly at me through the diamond panes,—and think the cottage, land, pig-stye, all are mine,—evoked from an ink-bottle, and labelled 'freehold', by the call of Webster! The only thing I am puzzled for, is a name for the property—a name that shall embalm the cause of its purchase. On due reflection, I don't think 'Humbug Hall' a bad one" (MS Mr Douglas Jerrold; part quoted in Walter Jerrold, *Douglas Jerrold*, I, 350-1, 353-4). Webster's competition had been announced early in June, with 1 Jan 44 as the closing date; the committee of judges included Kemble, Charles Young, and T. J. Serle. Jerrold contributed to *Punch*, 29 July 43, "Punch's Prize Comedy, The Academy of Scandal" (an attack on Lord William Lennox as a plagiarist) and A'Beckett published in 1844 "Scenes from the Rejected Comedies". By some of the Competitors", with parodies of Knowles, Jerrold, Talfourd, Planché, Fitzball, Boucicault, Hunt, Lemon, Bulwer and himself (reprinted as *A Quizziology of the British Drama*, 1846).

[5] "Farren, who began playing the old men at nineteen, and played them without a rival for nearly half a century" (G. H. Lewes, *On Actors and the Art of Acting*, 1875). Jerrold had written in the same letter, "Farren . . . boldly declares that to him the 'best' comedy would be that which enshrined the best old man".

Chalks (a landlord)	— Mr. Gough.
Hon. Harry Staggers	— Mr. Mellon
Sir Thomas Tip	— Mr. Buckstone
Swig	— Mr. Webster
The Duke of Leeds	—⎱ Mr. Coutts
Sir Smivin Growler	—⎰ Mr. Macready

Servants, gamblers, visitors &c

Mrs. Febrile	— Mrs. Gallot
Lady Tip	— Mrs. Humby
Mrs. Sour	— Mrs. W. Clifford
Fanny	— Miss A. Smith[1]

One scene, where Old Febrile tickles Lady Tip in the ribs, and afterwards dances out with his hat behind him, his stick before, and his eye on the pit, I expect will bring the house down. There is also another point—where Old Febrile, at the conclusion of his disclosure to Swig, rises and says "And now Swig, tell me, have I acted well?"—and Swig says "Well Mr. Febrile! Have you ever acted ill!"—which will carry off the piece.

Herne Bay.[2] Hum. I suppose it's no worse than any other place in this weather—but it *is* watery, rather—isn't it? In my mind's eye, I have the sea in a perpetual state of smallpox; and the chalk running downhill like town milk. But I know the comfort of getting to work "in a fresh place", and proposing pious projects to one's self, and having the more substantial advantage of going to bed early and getting up ditto, and walking about, alone. If there were a fine day, I should like to deprive you of the last-named happiness, and to take a good long stroll, terminating in a public house, and, whatever they chanced to have in it. But fine days are over, *I* think. The horrible misery of London in this weather, with not even a fire to make it cheerful, is hideous.

But I have my Comedy to fly to. My only comfort! I walk up and down the street at the back of the Theatre every night, and peep in at the Green Room Window—thinking of the time when "Dick—Ins"[3] will be called for, by excited hundreds, and won't come, 'till Mr. Webster[4] (half Swig and half himself) shall enter from his dressing room, and quelling the tempest with a smile, beseech

---

[1] With the exception of "Mr. Coutts" and "Mr. Hone" (unidentified), these are well-known actors and actresses, many of whom were or had been in Macready's company.

[2] Jerrold's letter began, "I write from a little cabin, built up of ivy and woodbine, and almost within sound of the sea. Here I have brought my wife and daughter, and have already the assurance that country air and sounds and sights will soon recover them". "Punch's Guide to the Watering Places" (30 July 42) described Herne Bay as a "juvenile town . . . many of the houses are not out of their scaffold poles", with "a wooden pier nearly twice the extent of the town".

[3] "Ins" written large.

[4] Benjamin Webster (1797–1882; *DNB*), actor, dramatist, and lessee of the Haymarket; see Vol. II, p. 71*n*. He had had the theatre completely remodelled, introducing gas lighting at great expense, and expected a brilliant season; but good plays were scarce, and he was anxious to attract new dramatists. The *Theatrical Journal*, although critical of the comedy prize, commented that "this truly English house has successfully stemmed the foreign tide, and bravely maintained its legitimate course of support to the English drama and English artists" (5 Aug 43).

that Wizard if he be in the house (here he looks up at my box) to accept the congratulations of the audience, and indulge them with a sight of the man who has got five hundred pound in money and it's impossible to say how much in laurel. Then I shall come forward and bow—once—twice—thrice—Roars of approbation—Brayvo—Brarvo—Hooray—Hoorar—Hooroar—one cheer more— and asking Webster home to supper shall declare eternal friendship for that public-spirited Individual—which Talfourd (the Vice) will echo with all his heart and soul and with tears in his eyes: adding in a perfectly audible voice, and in the same breath, that "he's a vewy wetched cweature, but better than Macweady any way, for *he* wouldn't play Ion[1] when it was given to him"— after which he will propose said Macweady's health in terms of red hot eloquence.

They have *not* sent me the Illustrated Magazine.[2] What do they mean by that? —You don't say your daughter is better, so I hope *you* mean that she is quite well. My wife desires her best regards. I am always My Dear Jerrold
Faithfully Your friend
The Congreve of the 19th. Century
(which I mean to be called in the Sunday Papers).

P.S. I shall dedicate it to Webster, beginning—"My dear Sir. When you first proposed to stimulate the slumbering dramatic talent of England, I assure you I had not the least idea"—&c—&c—&c.
P.S. I did your errand to Maclise,[3] who sends Regards and Thanks.

To WILLIAM LUCY,[4] 13 JUNE 1843

MS Mr Leslie Staples. *Address:* Mr. William Lucy | 25 College Green | Bristol.

Devonshire Terrace | Thirteenth June 1843

Mr. Charles Dickens sends his compliments to Mr. William Lucy, and begs to inform him, in reply to his letter, that Bailey Junior was liberally rewarded

---

[1] Macready did produce *Ion* in May 36, after some delays; CD's recollection perhaps confused it with *The Athenian Captive*, declined by Macready and produced by Webster (see Vol. I, p. 355).

[2] CD's slip for *Illuminated Magazine*; Jerrold asked whether the June number had been forwarded to him, and commented: "As for 'illuminations',—you have, of course, seen the dying lamps on a royal birthday-night; with the R burnt down to a P, and the W's very dingy W's indeed, even for the time of the morning. The 'illuminations' in my *Mag*: were very like these. No enthusiastic lamplighter was ever more deceived by cotton-wicks and train-oil, than I by the printer. However, I hope, in another month we shall be able to burn gas. Two of the proprietors were prize apes—but apes, laden and shod with gold. Fortunately, they are now out".

[3] Jerrold had written, "I have little more than a nodding acquaintance with Maclise, and therefore send the enclosed to him through you. I cut it out of the *Times* last summer in France, with the intention of forwarding it ... It appears to me to contain an admirable subject for a painter".

a a Written at top of p. 1, above address and date.

[4] The only William Lucy in the 1844 Directory is the Rev. William Lucy, of 10 Montague Parade, Bristol. A letter from Catherine to "W.L.", dated "Wednesday", shows that an earlier letter had been signed with initials only; she tells him that CD never answers an anonymous letter and that if W.L. "should wish to address Mr. Dickens in her own name, he will have pleasure in replying to her" (MS Mr Leslie C. Staples).

by the Miss Pecksniffs, and broke the bandboxes and damaged the luggage, in the greatness of his energy.[1]

To WILLIAM SANDYS,[2] 13 JUNE [1843]

Text from MDGH, I, 178–9. *Date:* 1843 on Devonshire Terrace and reference to Cornwall; wrongly given as 1847 in MDGH—a common misreading.

1, Devonshire Terrace, June 13th, 184[3].

Dear Sir,

Many thanks for your kind note. I shall hope to see you when we return to town, from which we shall now be absent (with a short interval in next month) until October.[3] Your account of the Cornishmen gave me great pleasure; and if I were not sunk in engagements so far, that the crown of my head is invisible to my nearest friends, I should have asked you to make me known to them. The new dialogue[4] I will ask you by-and-by to let me see. I have, for the present, abandoned the idea of sinking a shaft in Cornwall.[5]

I have sent your Shakesperian extracts to Collier.[6] It is a great comfort, to my thinking, that so little is known concerning the poet. It is a fine mystery; and I tremble every day lest something should come out. If he had had a Boswell, society wouldn't have respected his grave, but would calmly have had his skull in the phrenological shop-windows.

Believe me | Faithfully Yours
[CHARLES DICKENS]

[1] In Ch. 11, in the May No., the Miss Pecksniffs on leaving Todgers's present Bailey, on his solicitation, with a "liberal" gratuity: the reader had evidently inquired whether he damaged the luggage because he thought it inadequate.

[2] William Sandys (1792–1874; *DNB*), FSA, solicitor, practising in London in partnership with Charles Pearson at Serjeant's Inn. Miscellaneous publications included *A Selection of Christmas Carols, Ancient and Modern*, 1833, with an interesting introduction on local Christmas customs; it has been suggested that two of the carols gave CD hints for the *Carol*, because of their incidental references to misers and the words "He said, God bless us every one".

[3] CD slightly exaggerates the length of his absence from town, but was probably at Finchley again before leaving for Yorkshire.

[4] See *To* Cooke, 15 Dec 42, *fn*. Dialogues in dialect are included in Sandys's *Specimens of Cornish Provincial Dialect by Uncle Jan Treenoodle*, 1846; Sandys also made collections which were not published, used in Joseph Wright's *English Dialect Dictionary*.

[5] See *To* Forster, 12 Nov 42. But CD returned to Cornwall in Stave III of the *Carol*, and recalled the whole landscape near Land's End, at St Just: "a bleak and desert moor, where monstrous masses of rude stone were cast about, as though it were the burial-place of giants", with "a streak of fiery red" in the west "which glared upon the desolation for an instant, like a sullen eye"; in a miner's hut the family is round the fire singing an old Christmas song; beyond "the last of the land, a frightful range of rocks", stands "a solitary lighthouse" (the Longships) "upon a dismal reef of sunken rocks, some league or so from the shore, on which the waters chafed and dashed, the wild year through".

[6] John Payne Collier (1789–1883; *DNB*), Shakespeare critic and editor: see Vol. I, p. 31*n*. A fellow-member of the Shakespeare Society (see *To* Felton, 2 Mar 43) and mainly responsible for its publications. The "extracts" appeared in the *Shakespeare Society's Papers*, Vol. III, 1847, as Art. V, pp. 22–32, "Shakespeare illustrated by the Dialect of Cornwall", signed "William Sandys, Devonshire Street, 19th December, 1846".

To RICHARD MONCKTON MILNES, 17 JUNE 1843

MS Trinity College, Cambridge.

Parthenon Club | Seventeenth June 1843.

My Dear Milnes

The Duke of Cambridge gives Macready his "Testimonial" on Monday in Willis's rooms at 12 for one. Pray, as a Member of the Committee, come up to the Scratch.

Faithfully Yours

Richard Monckton Milnes Esquire   CHARLES DICKENS

To W. C. MACREADY, [19 JUNE 1843]

MS Morgan Library. *Date:* clearly the day of the presentation.

From the Chapel of the Jail | Monday Morning

Unhappy man.

Yes. I am of opinion that in your miserable condition, you might extend your remarks—so far, for instance, as to say what you had done in the Theatres, and tried to do. But whatever is easiest and most comfortable to yourself, will be the best course to take.[1]

You will be expected on the Scaffold at halfpast twelve. Enquire for the Committee Room—or the Sheriffs.

If you have anything on your mind, yet unrevealed, now is the time to throw the weight from off your conscience and make a clean breast.

Sympathetically Yours

The Ordinary[2]

---

[1] Macready had begun to compose his speech on 25 May; he spent the morning of 19 June working on and rehearsing it, "disheartened, dismayed, and despairing". He had a pleasant talk with the Duke of Cambridge in the committee-room; they entered the "great room" at one o'clock, as arranged; according to reports, the hall was full, the company including many of "the fair sex". "The Duke spoke better than I ever heard him" (*Diaries*, II, 214). He expressed the general gratitude for all that Macready had done to raise the theatre from its previous degradation, and regretted that he should have been obliged to give up the management of a national theatre. Macready, after "a short hesitation during which he seemed much overcome by his feelings", disclaimed "sordid motives" and expressed his wish to revive the taste for the legitimate drama; because of "absurd restrictions" he resigned the contest for the present, but was encouraged by public sympathy to contemplate its future renewal (*Times*, 20 June; *Athenæum*, 24 June). Macready thought his speech a failure and "drove home, weary and disgusted" (*Diaries, ibid.*). William Collins, the painter, who was on the platform, thought Macready looked "almost miserable" (Wilkie Collins, *Memoirs of the Life of William Collins, R.A.*, 1848, II, 235).

[2] i.e. the prison chaplain.

To GEORGE HOGARTH, 20 JUNE 1843*

MS Mr J. M. Dawkins. *Address:* George Hogarth Esquire | 8 Willows Place | Brixton.

1 Devonshire Terrace | York Gate Regents Park
Twentieth June 1843.

My Dear Hogarth.

I was obliged to go out very early yesterday morning to arrange for the presentation of Macready's Testimonial. In that way I missed you when you called.

Pray let Mr. Doyle[1] know that I have heard nothing said to his disadvantage, but on the contrary have learned on all hands, that he acted, in the business of the Chronicle Editorship, with the utmost consideration and manliness. When I first heard of Black's removal, I asked a deservedly distinguished man, in a conversation we had together, at the Athenæum one morning, "whether Mr. Doyle was friendly to him?"—meaning Black. I did so casually, and for information, really not knowing at that time in what relation they stood, with reference to each other. If this should have reached Mr. Doyle (which is very possible), and he supposes on that account that I am "under any wrong impression", undeceive him by all means, and assure him from me, that he is quite mistaken.

So very anxious have I been not to be supposed to cast the slightest blame on Mr. Doyle, that when I wrote certain notes postponing a Private Dinner a few friends had intended to give to Black;[2] I went out of my way to say, in so many words, that it was merely a mark of our personal regard, and had no reference whatever to any other Transaction or Individual. You know my old regard and esteem for Black, and can perfectly understand this to be the case. I should be greatly shocked and disgusted if I could suppose that my favorable feeling towards him, were considered by any man to include a disfavorable feeling towards his successor, or anybody else. Any such representation is very monstrous, wholly absurd, and from the crown of its head to the sole of its foot, unwarranted.

Affectionately Yours
George Hogarth Esquire   CHARLES DICKENS

To GEORGE CRUIKSHANK, 22 JUNE 1843

MS Colonel Richard Gimbel. *Address: Wait.* | George Cruikshank Esquire | 23 Amwell Street.

Devonshire Terrace | Twenty Second June 1843.

My Dear George

Can you, and will you, dine with me on Sunday, at 6 exactly? I shall have an American of the better sort[3]—and Maclise—and maybe two more. That's all.

---

[1] Andrew Doyle (1809–88), son of Andrew Doyle of Dublin; barrister; on the staff of the *Morning Chronicle* from Autumn 1842, editor 1843–8; married Louisa, the youngest of Easthope's three daughters, on 22 Aug 43.

[2] See *To* Forster, 3 May, and *To* Macready, 16 May.

[3] Thomas Gold Appleton (1812–84; *DAB*), essayist, poet and artist, of Boston; one of Channing's congregation and a friend of Emerson. He travelled much in Europe, collected books and works of art, and was known as a brilliant conversationalist. Had recently come to London bringing letters of introduction from Long-

I am obliged to make it Sunday, for we are going out of town soon; and the preparatory work leaves me no other day to dine upon.

United best regards to Mrs. C.

Faithfully Ever

CHARLES DICKENS

To T. B. BRINDLEY,[1] 26 JUNE 1843*

MS Brotherton Library, Leeds.

1 Devonshire Terrace | York Gate Regents Park
Twenty Sixth June 1843

My Dear Sir

In consequence of your book and kind letter having been sent to my Publishers (where parcels addressed to me, accumulate until there is a great heap to be opened) I have only just now received them. I need not assure you that this is the sole cause of the present tardy acknowledgment of your glowing Dedication.[2]

Although it puts my modesty to the blush, and makes it very rosy indeed, I am truly obliged to you for your earnest and fervent tribute. I am sure you mean and feel what you say; and this consoles me for not deserving it.

I shall not forget your request, with which I am delighted to comply. My booksellers shall find means of forwarding to you a couple of Volumes,[3] which pray put upon your shelves in remembrance of me.

Believe me Yours | Faithfully and obliged

Mr. T. B. Brindley   CHARLES DICKENS

---

fellow, who had just become engaged to his sister Fanny; to Forster Longfellow wrote: "You have many points of character that will make each other's society agreeable . . . he must see the rooms in Lincoln's Inn Fields . . . If possible make Appleton acquainted with Tennison. This he would like above all things; saving to know Cruikshank, which he would like still more" (*Letters of H. W. Longfellow*, ed. A. Hilen, II, 530). His letter to Forster of 24 May (announcing his engagement) asked him and CD to treat Appleton "with a double degree of kindness", and described him as "a most agreeable fellow, full of talent and wit"; a letter to Appleton, then in Germany, on 29 July shows that he had seen Cruikshank (*op. cit.*, II, 539, 548). Writing to Prescott on 1 July, Appleton mentioned "an agreeable breakfast" that day with Forster and a visit to "a young artist, Mr. Stone" (*Corre-*

spondence of W. H. Prescott, ed. R. Wolcott, pp. 373–4).

[1] Thomas Bardel Brindley, author and mesmerist, of Stourbridge; communicated particulars of his cures to the *Zoist* from Jan 44, having been encouraged to do so by Elliotson and Townshend.

[2] Of *The Omnipotence of the Deity and other Poems*, 3rd edn, 1843. The dedication speaks of "a mind of so gigantic an order . . . and profound knowledge of human life, in all its varied phases", and mentions CD's "kind permission to inscribe this volume" to him.

[3] One was a copy of *Barnaby Rudge*, inscribed "From Charles Dickens, Fourteenth December 1843" (J. C. Eckel, *The First Editions of the Writings of Charles Dickens*, 1913, p. 266). The gift was probably delayed at the binder's (Zaehnsdorf).

To FREDERICK DICKENS, [27 JUNE 1843]

Extract in American Art Association catalogue, Nov 1923;[1] *MS* 1 p; dated Devonshire Terrace, Tuesday Morning. *Date:* presumably the Tuesday before 1 July 43 (see *fn*).

Your friend's lines[2] on seeing poor Scott embark for his last voyage, are in a very worthy spirit, and do him honor. If it is likely to give any pleasure to know that I think so, pray tell him as much;

To JOHN FORSTER, [28 JUNE 1843]

Extract in F, IV, ii, 303. *Date:* 28 June according to Forster.[3]

I am so irritated, so rubbed in the tenderest part of my eyelids with bay-salt, by what I told you yesterday,[4] that a wrong kind of fire is burning in my head, and

---

[1] Accompanied, according to catalogue, by a letter from Frederick to "Chris Dowson" (4 pp., dated Sat 1 July 43, stating that "he encloses his brother's note returning the lines and that he was sorry Dowson could not accompany him to Drury Lane on the last night—mentions Macready and Sir James Graham"). Christopher Dowson, Jr (1807–48), always called Chris, of Chris. Dowson & Son, shipbuilders and proprietors, Bridge Dock, Limehouse; grandfather of Ernest Dowson, *b.* 1867. An intimate of Browning's, and like him one of "the Colloquials" (with Captain Pritchard, Alfred Domett, Joseph Arnould and Joseph Dowson, his younger brother), who met at the house of George Frederick Young at Limehouse; married Mary, Alfred Domett's sister, in 1836, and lived at Albion Terrace, Limehouse; had a country cottage at Woodford, Essex, where he was spending the summer. "He was of a nervous and mercurial temperament, devoted to the theatre and fond of entertaining his friends" (W. Hall Griffin and H. C. Minchin, *Life of Robert Browning*, 1910, pp. 80–1).

[2] Probably the verses composed by Joseph Dowson "On Seeing Sir W. Scott embark for Scotland, in a melancholy state of debility, July, 1832", and published in two newspapers, according to a letter of Chris Dowson to his sister, 13 July 1832 (Hall Griffin Papers, MS BM).

[3] Date confirmed by later references to financial difficulties, such as *To* Mitton, 22 July; also close to the completion of the half-year at which Chapman & Hall would be making up their accounts. Forster's references to the monthly Nos of *Chuzzlewit* (pp. 302–3) are confused and inaccurate; but in saying that the letter was written "on the eve of the seventh [number]" he would be correct, though not in adding "in which Mrs. Gamp was to make her first appearance". The seventh (July) number was the first all-American one; the June number had concluded with the voyage, and notice of Martin's intention had been given in the May number.

[4] The Agreement of 7 Sep 41 (see Vol. II, pp. 478–81) had contained a proviso that if the profits on the first five numbers of the next novel showed that Chapman & Hall's share was "not likely to liquidate the advance . . . within one month after completion of the work", the publishers could deduct £50 a month from the normal £200. Shortly before the seventh number was published, William Hall tactlessly referred to the possibility of putting this clause into effect. According to Forster, the sales of the first few numbers were a little over 20,000 in contrast to the 50,000 of *Nickleby*; Martin's visit to America raised them, but they never exceeded 23,000 (F, IV, ii, 302–3, and Arthur Waugh, *A Hundred Years of Publishing*, 1930, pp. 60–1). The reasons for the fall in the sale of *Chuzzlewit* in numbers have been the subject of some speculation. The two explanations canvassed by Ada Nisbet ("The Mystery of *Martin Chuzzlewit*" in *Essays . . . Dedicated to Lily B. Campbell*, Berkeley and Los Angeles, 1950), that readers' disappointment over one novel (in this case, *Barnaby*) affects the *next* novel, in a pattern of alternation, and

I don't think I *can* write.[1] Nevertheless, I am trying. In case I should succeed, and should not come down to you this morning, shall you be at the club or elsewhere after dinner? I am bent on paying the money. And before going into the matter with anybody I should like you to propound from me the one preliminary question to Bradbury and Evans.[2] It is more than a year and a half since Clowes[3] wrote to urge me to give him a hearing, in case I should ever think of altering my plans. A printer is better than a bookseller, and it is quite as much the interest of one (if not more) to join me. But whoever it is, or whatever, I am bent upon paying Chapman and Hall *down*.[4] And when I have done that, Mr. Hall shall have a piece of my mind.

To J. SPANTIN,[5] 30 JUNE 1843

Mention in N, I, 527

that CD had lost prestige and reputation with *American Notes*, cannot be sustained. *American Notes*, though it had some adverse reviews, sold four editions in two months; moreover it is unlikely that there was any considerable overlap between the purchasers of a travel-book and of shilling numbers. Forster's view that "the change to weekly issues", in 1840–1, was "the primary cause" (F, IV, ii, 302) and that CD's absence in America had not helped, is sound, if perhaps insufficient; also contributory were the continuance of the trade depression of 1842 (affecting publishers as different as John Murray, who had had to return accepted MSS to authors, and Bentley, who resorted to large remainder sales to Tegg), and the increased competition since 1839 from other serial novels both in numbers and in magazines. There remain, in Forster's phrase, "lulls too capricious for explanation". Reviews of *Chuzzlewit* month by month were favourable and attractive extracts were widely quoted in the press. Chapman & Hall were perhaps discouraged too soon, and certainly advertised the numbers much less than CD's earlier novels. They were themselves receiving lower revenue from advertisements: June, July, and August had only 8 pages each, Sep and Oct had 6 pages and an inset—a rather larger seasonal drop than is seen in *Nickleby* and *Dombey*.

[1] He was trying to get ahead with the August No. because of the coming Yorkshire holiday; the middle chapter, intro-

ducing Mrs Gamp, was in proof by 5 July (*To* Forster, 6–7 July).

[2] See Vol. I, p. 397*n*. Printers and (from 1842) proprietors of *Punch*, but not its official publishers until the issue of 18 Jan 45; they did not publish any books, even by *Punch* authors, until 1844, Jerrold's *Story of a Feather* being one of the first. *The Chimes* initiated CD's connection with them, which he later referred to as a special arrangement (*To* G. H. Lewes, 17 Feb 48). Their reception of CD's proposal was not very encouraging (F, IV, ii, 303); but some negotiations continued (see *To* Forster, 1 and 2 Nov 43).

[3] William Clowes (1779–1847; *DNB*) of Duke Street, Stamford Street, Blackfriars, founder of a large printing business, the first to use steam presses, of which he had 29 by 1839, each capable of turning out a thousand sheets an hour; printer to the Society for the Diffusion of Useful Knowledge since 1832. The firm became William Clowes & Sons in 1846 and the eldest son, also William (1807–83), may have been known to CD through the Printers' Pension Society of which he became a trustee in 1844. Nothing is known of the firm's approach to CD in 1841; their only later connection with him was as one of the two firms who printed the Charles Dickens edition.

[4] CD's accounts (MS Messrs Coutts) show that he received £100 on 1 July and £70 on 24 July.

[5] Unidentified.

To FREDERICK WILKINSON,[1] 30 JUNE 1843†

MS Dickens House.

London, 1 Devonshire Terrace, | York Gate, Regents Park
Thirtieth June 1843

Sir.

I am exceedingly sorry to have read your note incorrectly. I have no doubt
the mistake was mine.

Pray believe that I am quite *a*as much obliged by your polite communication,
as if you had offered me a Hundred Translations.*a*

Faithfully Yours

Frederick Wilkinson Esqre   CHARLES DICKENS

To JOHN MILES,[2] [30 JUNE or 1 JULY 1843]

Extract in N, I, 527, from catalogue source; dated Devonshire Terrace, June 1843.
Date: CD was still in London 30 June (see last); in *To* Beard, 18 July, he was back
from Yorkshire having been there "all the month".

It would have given me great pleasure to come to you today, if I had been
disengaged. But I am going into Yorkshire this evening[3] to pay a long-promised
visit

To THE COUNTESS OF BLESSINGTON, 5 JULY 1843*

MS The Carl H. Pforzheimer Library.

Easthorpe Park | Fifth July 1843

Dear Lady Blessington.

The sins of my youth (I was quite a boy when I made that ancient promise)[4]
rise up against me, fearfully.

If I can think of anything, though it be but a scrap of rhyme, I will send it
you by the end of the week. Keep me in your charitable and forgiving remembrance.

Many thanks to you for so kindly recollecting me in the matter of your new
book, Meredith.[5] I torture myself by wondering what its[6] about, and am all
impatience to read it.

---

[1] Possibly Frederick Wilkinson, barrister, 1 Stone Buildings, Lincoln's Inn.

aa Substantially as summarized in N, II,
31; wrongly dated 13 June 47.

[2] Of various persons of this name, the
most likely is John Miles (1813–86),
senior partner in Simpkin & Marshall, and
vice-president of the Booksellers' Provident
Association.

[3] CD presumably left in the morning, as
he advised Maclise to do: see *To* Maclise,
6 July.

[4] In 1840: see *To* Lady Blessington, 23
Nov 41 (Vol. II, p. 425 and *n*).

[5] *Meredith*, published by Longmans in
3 vols in early July 43: a novel of intrigue,
unlikely to interest CD unless for the
Italian setting of some chapters (where the
heroine and her governess are rescued
from brigands). On 21 Oct Longman told
Lady Blessington it was not a success
(A. Morrison, *The Blessington Papers*,
1895, p. 161). Lea & Blanchard had paid
her £50 for early sheets, and according to
Mrs Sigourney it was much admired in
America.

[6] Thus in MS.

Pray make my best regards to Count D'Orsay—and to your nieces—And believe me, with sincerity,

Faithfully Yours always

The | Countess of Blessington CHARLES DICKENS

To DANIEL MACLISE, 6 JULY 1843*

MS University of Texas.

Easthorpe Park, near Malton | Yorkshire | Sixth July 1843

My Dear Mac.

It is plain to me, that Smithson (who don't know you as I do) is living in the delusive idea that you are coming down here to see him. Now, if it *be* delusive, I wish you'd write and tell him so. But if it be not, I wish much more that you would write and say that much. For I am quite serious in saying that this is the most remarkable place of its size in England[1] and immeasurably the most beautiful; and that if you lose the opportunity of seeing it (they move next Autumn)[2] you will miss something which would certainly have been most suggestive and enjoyable to you. As to the rides—and they would mount you capitally—it is impossible to do them justice by description.

In the event of your coming, all you have to do, is to start from the Birmingham Railway, *for York*, at a quarter before Nine in the morning—and to write here, and say on what day. My present intention is to return home on Saturday Week,[3] but I should be delighted to stay longer, if you were coming.[4]

Tell me how you get on at the Palace, and whether you are knighted yet.[5] Kate and Georgy send their best regards.

Always My Dear Mac | Faithfully

Daniel Maclise Esquire CD

---

[1] "An uncommonly fine late C18 house of moderate size, attributed convincingly to *Carr* of York", i.e. John Carr (1723–1807; *DNB*), who also designed Harewood House "of three by three bays. The S front has a canted bay window in the middle. Its three ground-floor windows are arched. The ground-floor windows to the l. and r. of the bay are Venetian. All windows have Gibbs surrounds ... To the W the former main entrance ... Tuscan columns, a fluted frieze, and a pediment" (N. Pevsner, *The North Riding*, 1966). Severely damaged by fire 1967, its west wing alone survives.

[2] To Old Malton Abbey, from which CD wrote on 6 Apr 44 (*Mr and Mrs CD*, ed. W. Dexter, 1935, pp. 98–101).

[3] CD did not return until the Mon or Tues 17–18 July: see *To* Overs, 15 July and *To* Beard, 18 July.

[4] Maclise refers to this in a letter to Forster (MS Forster Collection, V & A): "A note from Dick to ask me to York—but it was no go alas".

[5] To encourage experiments in fresco, the Prince Consort in Apr 43 had invited several artists to decorate a small pavilion or summer-house in the grounds of Buckingham Palace, afterwards sometimes called Milton Villa. The central octagonal room (15.8 by 15.9 with a high vaulted ceiling) was to be decorated with illustrations of *Comus* by eight painters, Stanfield, Maclise, Landseer, Eastlake, Uwins, Sir William Ross (knighted 1842), Leslie, and Etty. According to Maclise in Alexander Gilchrist's *Life of William Etty, R.A.*,

To JOHN FORSTER, [6 or 7 JULY 1843]

Extracts in F, IV, i, 294. *Date:* "July 1843", and "from Yorkshire", according to
Forster; dated by reference in *To* Lady Blessington, 5 July.

Tell me what you think of Mrs. Gamp?[1] You'll not find it easy to get through
the hundreds of misprints in her conversation, but I want your opinion at once.
I think you know already something of mine. I mean to make a mark with her.

I have heard, as you have, from Lady Blessington, for whose behoof I have
this morning penned the lines I send you herewith. But I have only done so to
excuse myself, for I have not the least idea of their suiting her;[2] and I hope she
will send them back to you for the *Ex.*

1853 (II, 152), Etty disliked fresco-painting and found difficulty in mastering the technique; in July 44 his work was finally rejected by the Prince, and Dyce commissioned in his place. Thackeray was sarcastic about the low fees paid to the artists: "frescoes . . . which royalty . . . condescended to purchase at a price that no poor amateur would have the face to offer . . . forty pounds for pictures worth four hundred . . . condescending to buy works from humble men who could not refuse, and paying for them below their value!" ("Picture Gossip", *Fraser's*, June 45; *Works*, II, 649–50). Painting had begun in May 43 and in a letter of 15 July 43 Mary Ann Skerrett described the scene to Frances Trollope: "In front of one panel sits Leslie, at another Landseer, another Etty, another Maclise, and Stanfield, and Sir William Ross—always four at a time, doing frescos after designs of their own!" (Frances E. Trollope, *Frances Trollope*, 1895, II, 24). There was some duplication, both Leslie and Maclise choosing to depict the Lady under the spell (Maclise's design he reproduced in a painting, *Scene from Comus*, exhibited RA 1844). The designs are reproduced in *The Decorations of the Garden Pavilion* . . . engraved under the superintendence of L. Gruner. With an Introduction by Mrs. Jameson, 1846. The frescoes suffered from damp, and the pavilion was pulled down in 1928. In the letter to Forster quoted above Maclise wrote: "You know I am down *there* every day . . . I assure you I get on there in great favor—I told Dick that the King of the Belges bought my original—and complimented me on its composition!" According to Uwins (letter to Severn, 26 July 43; Sarah Uwins, *Memoir of Thomas Uwins*, 1858, II, 283) Maclise "who never touched fresco till he began his lunette, is painting it more perfectly than ever I have yet seen it, ancient or modern".

[1] First introduced in Ch. 19 in the Aug No., now evidently in proof. According to F, IV, i, 294, she was based on a nurse (not named) "hired by a most distinguished friend of his own, a lady, to take charge of an invalid very dear to her"—clearly Miss Coutts and Miss Meredith during the latter's illness of 1842–3. Forster says this nurse's "common habit" was "to rub her nose along the top of the tall fender" (see also *To* Miss Coutts, 5 Oct 46). Charles C. Osborne ("The Genesis of Mrs. Gamp", *D*, XXIII [1927], 27–30) mentions various other details, including the sniffs, the cucumber, and some of her sayings.

[2] Lady Blessington did accept the verses, which appeared under the title "A Word in Season" in *The Keepsake*; reproduced in F, IV, i, 294n, and in National edn, XXXVI, 476. The third verse, with its reference to a land of "brutal ignorance, and toil, and dearth" where those who should have "oped the door of charity and light" instead "Squabbled for words upon the altar-floor, | And rent The Book, in struggles for the binding", reflects CD's views on the arguments following the Second Report of the Children's Employment Commission (see *To* Napier, 16 Sep 43 and *fn*). The whole poem was quoted in several reviews, including the *Athenæum's*, 18 Nov 43, and the *Examiner's*, 25 Nov 43.

To W. C. MACREADY, 8 JULY 1843*

MS Morgan Library.

Easthorpe Park | Saturday Eighth July 1843
In haste.

My Dear Macready.

You will not suppose, I am certain, that I forgot your request,[1] the day before I left town.[2] But I had so much to do, that I was occupied until midnight, and went to bed quite weary and worn out. Since I have been here, I have done nothing but ride over all manner of country;[3] stroll among ancient Ruins; eat, drink, and sleep.

Your note finds me just setting out for Scarboro'. But having an hour to spare, I sketch hurriedly what I think you had best say. I have followed your own ideas closely, and have, indeed, seldom departed from them except when it occurred to me that they could be showily combined with mine.

Kate unites with me in best regards to Mrs. Macready, and all your house We shall be home, I think, this day Week.

Always My Dear Macready
Affectionately Your friend
W. C. Macready Esquire. CHARLES DICKENS

To JOHN BOWRING,[4] 15 JULY 1843*

MS The Carl H. Pforzheimer Library.

Easthorpe Park | Near Malton | Yorkshire. | Fifteenth July 1843.

My Dear Sir

I have been in this county for some weeks, and your kind note has only just

---

[1] Almost certainly in connection with the drafting of Macready's petition to Parliament against the clause in the new bill for regulating theatres, by which a justices' licence was declared no warrant for acting Shakespeare's plays within five miles of any patent theatre. The petition (of which many passages certainly read like CD's composition) traced his own experience over the last six years, showing the defects of the patent system under present conditions: "these persons have . . . used their trust as a mere piece of property, letting it out to any adventurer who would hire it . . . That by these means all kinds of degrading exhibitions, tending not to humanise and refine, but to brutalise and corrupt, the public mind, have been introduced upon the patent stage; with which practices of licentiousness and habits of debauchery, unknown at places of theatrical entertainment in any other civilised country, have also, by the same system, been connected as matters of

profit and gain"; his own management had shown that there was a public for the legitimate drama, and "whereas these patent holders are not able by themselves or their tenants to maintain the national drama in their theatres, yet they are armed by law with power to prevent your petitioner from exercising that his art or calling in any other theatre, and to declare that unless he live on such terms as they may prescribe to him, he shall not by his industry and the use of such abilities as he may possess, live at all". Macready had a conference at the Home Office with Manners Sutton on 24 July (*Diaries*, II, 216); the petition was presented on 8 Aug by Lord Beaumont, and the clause struck out on 14 Aug—a victory for Macready.

[2] See *To Miles*, ?30 June or 1 July, *hn*.

[3] *To Smithson*, 20 Sep, shows that he also visited Castle Howard.

[4] John Bowring (1792–1872; *DNB*), Benthamite Radical, first editor of the *Westminster Review*, MP for Bolton since

now reached me. If I had been in town, it would have given me much pleasure to accept your friendly Invitation.

Faithfully Yours

Dr. Bowring   CHARLES DICKENS

To THE EARL OF MULGRAVE, 15 JULY 1843*

MS The Marquis of Normanby.

Easthorpe Park, Near Malton
Fifteenth July 1843.

My Dear Lord Mulgrave.

We were at Mulgrave last Sunday afternoon. There we found the most hospitable and generous arrangements made for our reception—everybody on the look out for us—and the whole establishment with a lively Faith in our having come to stay a couple of days at least—all owing to your kind instructions in our behalf.

But I never dreamed of such a thing, when I wrote to you. All I intended, was, to stroll about the grounds and walk through the house. And being in that part as a mere bird of passage, and having (besides Mrs. Dickens and her sister) two friends with me, I went to Mulgrave solely with this view. So the bed was unslept in, and the dinner was untasted, and the wine was undrunk, and the buck was unattended in his Death next morning, and I, most probably, at the time of his violent decease, was returning to this place by the Whitby railroad.[1]

Pray receive my hearty thanks for your great kindness. We were perfectly charmed with Mulgrave, which is one of the most desirable and beautiful places[2]

1841, a founder of the anti-Corn Law League; knighted 1854. Described by Caroline Fox on their first meeting in 1838 as "a very striking-looking personage with a most poetical, ardent, imaginative forehead, and a temperament all in keeping". He told her that he knew CD well, and that he was "a brilliant creature with a piercing eye" (*Memories of Old Friends*, 1882, I, 64).

[1] This ran from Pickering, 14 miles from Easthorpe. Completed by local enterprise in 1836 as a single line for fixed engines and horse-drawn coaches resembling stage-coaches; the horses were used on the level and in moderate ascents; on steeper gradients the coach was hauled by a steam winding-engine, the counterweight being supplied by descending wagons or, as CD recalls in *To* Wilkie Collins, 28 Aug 61, by tanks of water mounted on wheels. It became part of the York and N. Midland railway and was supplied with locomotive engines in 1845. George A. Hobson in his life of the engin-

eer in charge of its construction describes its beautiful route, running for 24 miles "through the deep and sinuous gorges of the Eskdale, Goathland-dale, and New-towndale, the last a valley of ever-varying width with cliff-like sides, bordered for the most part with gloomy purple moors and in places with larch woods. The scenery . . . gives an impression of travelling in Scotland" (*Life of James Falshaw, Bt*, 1905, p. 57; see also *Illustrations of the Scenery on the Whitby and Pickering . . . from Drawings by G. Dodgson with a Short Description of the District and Undertaking*, 1836).

[2] The original early Georgian house, built for the Duchess of Buckingham in 1735, with two wings added in 1786–7 by Soane; in the 1790s the grounds had been landscaped with the help of Repton (with a castellated ha-ha) and the "mediaevalising" of the building begun with the addition of battlements and continued by William Atkinson's towers, turrets, and projecting entrance hall. CD would also have

I ever saw. I could ride about those woods, and look out upon the sea from that terrace, and write in that Library, for ever and a day. More I will report to you when we come home next week; but I could not avoid shaking hands with you by post, first, and telling you how much indebted we are to you.

Always Believe me | Faithfully Yours

The | Earl of Mulgrave.   CHARLES DICKENS

To JOHN OVERS, 15 JULY 1843*

Text from typescript, Huntington Library.

Easthorpe Park, | Near Malton, Yorkshire.
Fifteenth July, 1843.

Dear Mr Overs,

Your letter has only just now been forwarded to me here. I have been in this county for some weeks.

It gives me much sorrow to receive so bad an account of your doings—the more so, because my influence in respect of newspapers is most insignificant: my position suggesting to me the propriety of keeping aloof from them. But it has occurred to me that with the Doctor's[1] assistance, I may *possibly* be able to advance your object. And immediately on my return to town I will see him on the subject.

This will be very early next week. By Wednesday, or Thursday at latest, you shall hear from me again.

Faithfully Yours,

Mr J. A. Overs.   CHARLES DICKENS

To THOMAS BEARD, 18 JULY 1843

MS Dickens House. *Address:* Thomas Beard Esquire | 42 Portman Place | Edgeware Road.

Devonshire Terrace | Eighteenth July 1843

My Dear Beard

I have been in Yorkshire all the month, and am only just now in the receipt of your note. I address my answer to the old house: hoping that by this time you have come home, round and sound. You know who has always treated you successfully, and you know where that great physician is to be found, during the months of August and September. Kate agrees with me that to make your cure complete, there would be nothing like eight undisturbed weeks at Broadstairs with that distinguished man. Now, do think of this. There are a hundred things you could do for the paper on the Margin of the Sea—abstracting Parliamentary reports, and so forth—matters of great use in the Recess. The bedroom you had last year, is ready for you. The bathing machine beckons its wooden finger— and cocks its preposterous eye—on the sands. The tide rushes in, demanding

seen the ruins of the early 14th century castle in the grounds and the famous views of the moors and sea.

[1] Probably Elliotson.

to be breasted. Dick is all joviality, and very brown in the face from Northern toasting. Mac swears "he'll swim to the Goodwin Sands if HE will—there!" Forster asserts with dignified emphasis that "it is the very sort of thing my dear boy that Beard requires to set him on his legs". Timber makes himself as unlike a dog as possible, in confirmation of these sentiments. Topping forgets even "Mount Consumious"[1] at the Surrey Zoological Gardens (his crack subject just now) and overhearing these discussions, redly[2] remarks to me that "a little pickling 'ud make Mister Beard wot he used to be, wen we wos down at whats his name"—meaning Petersham[3]—in short, everything and everybody are decisive on the subject; so take the Sussex card[4] off your Portmanteau, and label it afresh Pashangermarjit.

Have you come back? If so, will you ride out on Sunday, and dine here afterwards? Say yes: and I will call for you at half past two.

I am so full of Broadstairs and your going there, that I have scarcely left room to say, with my regards to Mr. Blackburn, that we have sent out Powers of attorney to divers parts of India,[5] for the enforcement of the new law as far as my books are concerned; and that I don't think I can entertain any proposal for an arrangement, after handing the matter over to others by these means. But if he would like to make a distinct proposal, I will take counsel with the Publishers upon it.

Regards from all to all. Ever Faithfully My Dear Beard.

Thomas Beard Esquire   CD.

To MISS MARGARET GILLIES,[6] 21 JULY 1843*

MS Dickens House.

Devonshire Terrace | Twenty First July 1843.

Mr. Charles Dickens presents his compliments to Miss Gillies, and begs to say that he will have the pleasure of sitting to her, next Tuesday, at *12*.

---

[1] The firework display of Mount Vesuvius.

[2] Unmistakable in MS; presumably Topping was blushing.

[3] In June 39, at Elm Cottage; see Vol. I, pp. 552, 557.

[4] Beard was staying at Lewes where CD's letter had been forwarded.

[5] See *To* Mitton, 17 Jan 43. "J. Blackburn" (see Vol. II, p. 46*n*) in a letter to Beard from the Colonial Club, St. James's Square, 24 June 43, had said that the home agents of the *Englishman* had asked him, in view of the "recent enactments", whether CD would permit republication of his writings for a fee; he hesitated to approach him direct and asked Beard to do so. He also offered Beard some of the Himalayan plant *cheratah*, a tonic and febrifuge (MS Dickens House). The

Englishman was a Calcutta weekly periodical, formerly named *John Bull* and in 1838 owned and edited by J. H. Stocqueler.

[6] Margaret Gillies (1803–87; *DNB*), miniaturist and water-colour painter; had painted Wordsworth and stayed at Rydal Mount 1839, also Dr and Mrs Arnold; was a friend of the Howitts. Lived at Highgate with her sister Mary (*d.* 1870), a writer, who collaborated with Horne in stories for children by "Harriet Myrtle" 1844–8. Southwood Smith was a close friend and on his death left to them the charge of his grand-daughters, the Hills, of whom one, Gertrude, married the son of G. H. Lewes. According to F. N. L. Poynter, "Thomas Southwood Smith—the Man" (*Proceedings of the Royal Society of Medicine*, LV [1962], 381–92), he arranged for her to illustrate some of the scenes in the

To THOMAS MITTON, 22 JULY 1843

MS Huntington Library.

Devonshire Terrace | Saturday Twenty Second July | 1843.

My Dear Mitton

I want you to help me in money matters, until the 1st. of September; for several things have come crowding on me at once,[1] and although at any other time I wouldn't mind overdrawing my account at Coutts's, I cannot prevail upon myself to do so now, when she is exerting herself in behalf of Alfred. I needn't say why I will not exceed by sixpence the reduced monthly of C and H.[2]

Therefore what I want you to do, is, to draw £70 on account of that bill you have deposited at your banker's,—for me,—and to pay [it][3] into Coutts's. This will not [pu]t[4] you about, as you have already effected the necessary understanding with them. On the 1st. of September, as I have said, you shall have it back[5]—of course with whatever interest the bankers charge for the five or six weeks.

Faithfully Always
CD.

I am working like a Dragon.[6]

To MESSRS BRADBURY & EVANS, 24 JULY 1843

MS Dickens House.

Devonshire Terrace | Monday 24th. July 1843

Dear Sirs

Please to send a proof of the enclosed[7] to the Parthenon Club in Regent Street; this evening at 7 exactly. Mr. Forster and myself will be there together, and the boy can wait while it is corrected.

Faithfully Always
C.D.

Messrs. Bradbury & Evans.

Report of the 1842 Commission, and obtained for her the commission for CD's portrait. CD gave her six or seven sittings: Miss Gillies later recalled that he was "full of most agreeable and pleasant talk" and "completely won over" a little girl who was in the room (perhaps Gertrude, *b.* 1837) with his "amusing stories". She said that "Daniel Maclise came also on several occasions"; this was not after 23 Oct (see *To* Miss Gillies, that day). The miniature was exhibited at the RA May 44 and an engraving made from it by J. C. Armytage for Horne's *New Spirit of the Age,* published Apr 44 (F. G. Kitton, *CD by Pen & Pencil,* I, 50). Horne's book was already planned (see *To* Powell, 9 Oct 43) and CD may have known of it. Three more of the eight portraits in the two volumes were by Miss Gillies: Southwood Smith, Wordsworth, and Harriet Martineau.

[1] CD's accounts (MS Messrs Coutts) show that he had drawn cash for £20 on 5 July; his disbursements for the rest of the month came to about £60 and included £12 for Henry Burnett on 31 July.

[2] See *To* Forster, 28 June. This sentence clearly an afterthought; squeezing in words at foot of page, CD presumably omitted "payments" after "monthly" (N misreads as "mouths").

[3] Letter is torn and stained; a hole at centre fold has removed two letters here.

[4] Two letters missing; the "t" is clear.

[5] Mitton received the £70 on 5 Sep.

[6] At Ch. 20, the last of the August No.; see next.

[7] Either of Ch. 20, or a further proof of Ch. 19; there had been "hundreds of misprints" in Mrs Gamp's conversation (see *To* Forster, 6 or 7 July).

To JOHN DE GEX, 24 JULY 1843

Text from N, I, 529, checked from MS Sotheby's, May 1966.

Devonshire Terrace | Twenty Fourth July 1843.

My Dear De Gex.

I am truly sorry to be obliged to return the enclosed papers to you, without having written a Statement for the Charity.[1] But I have so much to do, and have been so beset by other Institutions to use my pen in their behalf also, that I really have no alternative. Trust me that if I could have done it by any reasonable means, I would.

Faithfully Yours

John De Gex Esquire   CHARLES DICKENS

To THOMAS MITTON, 24 JULY 1843

Extract in Sotheby's catalogue, May 1949; *MS* 2 pp; dated Devonshire Terrace, 24 July 43.

I finished my work on Saturday; having gone at it every morning at eight o'clock. I have great confidence in the story, and have just received some tremendous and elaborately written panegyrics on the same from Sydney Smith,[2] which from such an authority are worth having.

To JOHN OVERS, 24 JULY 1843*

Text from typescript, Huntington Library.

Devonshire Terrace, | Twenty fourth July, 1843.

Dear Mr Overs,

As soon as I returned to town, I fulfilled my promise, and saw the doctor on the subject of your last note. He agreed with me that there was a bare possibility of being able to do something with the newspaper proprietor[3] I mentioned to him, whom he knows better than I do. He said he would see him straightway. I have nothing further to report yet; but am waiting, still, to hear the result.

Faithfully yours,

CHARLES DICKENS

[1] Unidentified; De Gex is not known to have been interested in any particular charity.

[2] These have not survived; but see *To* Forster, 28 July, *fn*. Smith had written to CD on 1 July: "Excellent! nothing can be better! You must settle it with the Ameri-cans as you can, but I have nothing to do with that. I have only to certify that the number is full of wit, humour, and power of description" (*The Letters of Sydney Smith*, ed. Nowell C. Smith, II, 785).

[3] See *To* Overs, 3 Aug and *fn*.

To MISS BURDETT COUTTS, 26 JULY 1843

MS Morgan Library.

Devonshire Terrace | Twenty Sixth July 1843.

Dear Miss Coutts

I don't know whether you have seen an advertisement in the papers of this morning, signed by me and having reference to the family of Mr. Elton[1] the actor, who was drowned in the Pegasus. I consented last night to act as Chairman of a Committee[2] for the assistance of his children; and I assure you that their condition is melancholy and desolate beyond all painting.

He was a struggling man through his whole existence—always very poor, and never extravagant. His wife died mad, Three Years ago, and he was left a Widower with seven children—who were expecting his knock at the door, when a friend arrived with the terrible news of his Death.[3]

If in the great extent of your Charities, you have a niche left to fill up, I

---

[1] Edward William Elt, known as Elton (1794–1843; *DNB*), son of a schoolmaster, trained as a solicitor but became an actor in 1823. Engaged at Covent Garden 1837 and played Beauséant in Bulwer's *Lady of Lyons*; at Drury Lane from 1841. When the theatre closed on 14 June 43 took an engagement with W. H. Murray at the Edinburgh Theatre Royal, and while returning by sea to Hull was drowned on 19 July when the *Pegasus* struck a rock near Holy Island (*Times*, 24 and 25 July). CD had known him as Chairman and Treasurer of the Theatrical Fund (see *To* Elton, 30 Mar 43), and as a close friend of Laman Blanchard and Douglas Jerrold. Belonged to the Mulberry Club in the 1820s; Jerrold, a founder member, recalled their early friendship when both were "gaily struggling . . . Poor Elton! He was one of those men whose life was nearly always in the shade", and his "graceful intelligence . . . refined taste, and true love of literature . . . warm affections and high principle"; he quoted poems Elton had written for the Club (*Illuminated Magazine*, Sep 43, I, 253–5).

[2] According to George Hodder (*Memories of my Time*, 1870, pp. 142–7) CD was elected "by general acclamation" at the meeting at the Freemasons' Tavern, and "under his practical and business-like direction" a series of resolutions was drafted. There was to be a public benefit; Prince Albert's Treasurer and the Proprietors of Drury Lane were to be applied to; R. B. Perry was appointed Treasurer

and R. R. M'Ian Secretary. It was then discovered that M'Ian "was not quite so ready with his pen as he was with his pencil", and Mark Lemon summoned Hodder, who was dining in the neighbourhood, to take his place. "[CD] treated me with such friendly consideration," wrote Hodder, "and gave me all my instructions so clearly and succinctly, that I soon felt perfectly at ease by his side; and it was not unusual for me to write upwards of twenty letters in the course of an evening, showing how vigorously and determinedly the committee pursued their philanthropic mission". Their first advertisement appeared in the papers of 26 July and ran: "THE ORPHAN FAMILY of the late Mr. W. ELTON.—A Committee is formed for the purpose of arranging a BENEFIT for the seven fatherless and motherless CHILDREN of Mr. W. ELTON, late of the Theatre Royal, Drury Lane, a sufferer in the fatal wreck of the Pegasus. The performances will be announced as soon as possible; in the mean time offers of professional service on the occasion will be gratefully received, as well as subscriptions in money, by CHARLES DICKENS, Chairman".

[3] Elton had been twice married, and left six daughters, including Esther, Rosa and Rosalind, and one son (the youngest, aged 8). "On Saturday [22 July] his young daughters, in anticipation of his return, had decked his room with flowers" (*Britannia*, 29 July 43). The news reached them on Sunday.

believe in my heart this is as sad a case as could possibly be put into it. If you have not, I know you will not mind saying so to me.

Do not trouble yourself to answer this, as I will call upon you today between one and two. I called on Sunday last, to enquire after Miss Meredith; but seeing your carriage at the door, I left my card.—By the way—lingering at the street corner, was a very strange looking fellow, watching your house intently. I hope it was not Mr. Dunn.[1]

                    Dear Miss Coutts | Always Yours Faithfully & obliged
Miss Coutts.   CHARLES DICKENS

To SIR EDWARD LYTTON BULWER, 26 JULY 1843

MS Lytton Papers.

                              1 Devonshire Terrace | Twenty Sixth July 1843[2]
My Dear Sir Edward.

I am Chairman of a Committee whose object is, to open a Subscription and arrange a benefit for the relief of the seven destitute children of poor Elton (your Beauseant)[3] who was drowned in the Pegasus. They are exceedingly anxious to have the great assistance of your name; and if you will allow yourself to be announced as one of the Body,[4] I do assure you, you will help a very melancholy and distressful cause.

                              Faithfully Yours always
Sir Edward Lytton Bulwer   CHARLES DICKENS

To GEORGE CRUIKSHANK, 26 JULY 1843

MS Colonel Richard Gimbel.

                         Devonshire Terrace | Twenty Sixth July 1843
My Dear Cruikshank.

I am Chairman of a Committee whose object is to open a Subscription and arrange a benefit, for the relief of the seven destitute children of poor Elton the actor, who was drowned in the Pegasus. They are exceedingly anxious to have

---

[1] Richard Dunn (*d.* 1890); on his harassing of Miss Coutts, see Vol. II, p. 207*n*.

[2] Wrongly given as 1847 in N, II, 44.

[3] He had also played Louis XIII in Bulwer's *Richelieu* in 1839; was first considered for François, but Bulwer thought him not young enough, "Wig him as you will" (Bulwer *to* Macready, 10 Jan 39; *Bulwer and Macready*, ed. C. H. Shattuck, p. 118).

[4] An advertisement of 28 July listed the following as members of the Committee: W. H. Ainsworth, H. Allen, Robert Bell, W. B. Bernard, Laman Blanchard, J. B. Buckstone, John Cooper, George Cruik- shank, John Dillon, W. Farren, John Forster, T. Greenwood, J. P. Harley, R. Honner, Thomas Hood, Douglas Jerrold, R. Keeley, Mark Lemon, Charles and Thomas Landseer, Daniel Maclise, Charles Mathews, Kenny Meadows, B. W. Procter, Samuel Rogers, T. J. Serle, Frank Stone, Clarkson Stanfield, T. N. Talfourd, B. Webster, and Charles Young. Of those to whom CD's letters survive, Bulwer's name alone is lacking. The newspapers inserted the advertisements at a nominal price, and Cutts offered a free room at the Freemasons' Tavern (*Examiner*, 23 Dec 43).

the great assistance of your name; and if you will allow yourself to be announced as one of the body, I do assure you, you will help a very melancholy and distressful cause.

Faithfully Yours always

CHARLES DICKENS

*a*The committee meet tonight, at 8, at the Freemasons' Tavern.*a*

To J. P. HARLEY, 26 JULY 1843*

MS Huntington Library.

1 Devonshire Terrace. | Twenty Sixth July 1843.

My Dear Harley.

I am Chairman of a Committee whose object is, to open a Subscription and arrange a benefit for the relief of poor Elton's seven children. They are exceedingly anxious to have the great assistance of your name. Let them have it my good fellow for God's sake.

We meet at the Freemason's tonight at 8.

Faithfully Yours always

J. P. Harley Esquire   CHARLES DICKENS

To THOMAS HOOD, 26 JULY 1843*

MS Birthplace Museum, Portsmouth.

1 Devonshire Terrace | Twenty Sixth July 1843

My Dear Hood.

I am Chairman of a Committee whose object is, to open a Subscription and arrange a benefit for the relief of the seven destitute children (they have no mother) of poor Elton the actor, who was drowned in the Pegasus. They are exceedingly anxious to have the great assistance of your name; and if you will kindly allow yourself to be announced as one of the Body, I do assure you, you will help a very melancholy and distressful cause.

Faithfully Ever

CHARLES DICKENS

We meet at the Freemasons tonight at 8 oClock.[1]

---

aa Omitted in N, I, 530.

[1] Hood replied at once, offering his name: "I would add my purse, but unluckily just now there is nothing in it, thanks to B—" (his lawsuit with Baily), and regretting that as his article for the month was unfinished he could not attend at the Freemasons' Tavern. He recalled noticing Elton's "superior intelligence" when he was dramatic critic on the *Atlas* in 1826: "The name brought him vividly to my memory, along with the scene of the tragedy, which is familiar to me" (*Letters of Thomas Hood*, ed. P. Morgan, p. 546). A day or so later Jane Hood wrote: "Hood desires me to write—he being driven up into the last corner of the Magazine—and ask you as there is to be a benefit for the poor children of Mr. Elton whether you think a poetical address for the occasion written by him would be of any service—the idea has only just struck him" (MS Private).

To DANIEL MACLISE, 26 JULY 1843*

MS Benoliel Collection.

1 Devonshire Terrace | Twenty Sixth July 1843
My Dear Mac.

I am Chairman of a Committee whose object is, to open a Subscription and arrange a Benefit for the relief of poor Elton's children. They are exceedingly anxious to have your name as one of the body. Pray give me permission to announce it.

Faithfully Ever
Daniel Maclise Esquire   CD.

To W. C. MACREADY, 26 JULY 1843*

MS Morgan Library.

Devonshire Terrace | Twenty Sixth July 1843.
My Dear Macready.

I consented last night to be Chairman of a Committee for doing the best that *can* be done for the unfortunate family of that poor man, Elton. A couple of hours put the business into good shape; and I have written this morning to everybody I can think of.

Lumley[1] replies that he cannot allow the Singers to assist—but sends five guineas as his Subscription. Now, what do you think? I ask you for the guidance of my own opinion. Without the singers, wod. you run the hazard of opening Drury Lane if it is to be got for nothing—or would you accept an offer which has been made by Webster, of the Haymarket and the Lighting?[2]

Faithfully Always
W. C. Macready Esquire   CD

To SAMUEL ROGERS, 26 JULY 1843*

MS Free Library of Philadelphia.

1 Devonshire Terrace | Twenty Sixth July 1843
My Dear Mr. Rogers.

I am Chairman of a Committee whose object is, to open a Subscription and arrange a benefit for the relief of the seven destitute children (for they have no mother) of poor Mr. Elton the actor, who was drowned in the Pegasus. They are exceedingly anxious to have the great assistance of your name; and if you will kindly allow yourself to be announced as one of the Body, I do assure you you will help a very melancholy and distressful cause.

Faithfully Yours always
Samuel Rogers Esquire   CHARLES DICKENS

---

[1] Benjamin Lumley (1811–75; *DNB*), director of the Italian Opera at Her Majesty's Theatre since 1842.

[2] The offer of the theatre had been made at the meeting, and a resolution of thanks to Webster was passed. See *To* Cruikshank, 31 July, *fn.*

To CLARKSON STANFIELD, 26 JULY 1843

MS Rosenbach Foundation.

1 Devonshire Terrace | Twenty Sixth July 1843

My Dear Stanfield

I am Chairman of a Committee, whose object is, to open a Subscription and arrange a benefit for the relief of the seven destitute children of poor Elton the actor, who was drowned in the Pegasus. They are exceedingly anxious to have the great assistance of your name; and if you will allow yourself to be announced as one of the body, I do assure you you will help a very melancholy and distressful cause.

Faithfully Always
CHARLES DICKENS

The Committee meet tonight at the Freemasons', at 8 oClock.

To UNKNOWN CORRESPONDENT,[1] 26 JULY [1843]

Text from N, II, 44, from catalogue source, dated Devonshire Terrace, 26 July 47. *Date:* clearly 1843, with other Elton letters.

I am Chairman of a Committee, whose object is, to open a Subscription and arrange a benefit for the relief of the seven destitute children of poor Elton the actor who was drowned in the Pegasus. They are exceedingly[2] anxious to have the great assistance of your [name];[3] and if you will allow yourself to be announced as one of the body, I do assure you, you will help a very melancholy and distressful cause.

To W. C. MACREADY, 26 JULY 1843*

MS Morgan Library.

Devonshire Terrace | Wednesday Evening | Twenty Sixth July 43

My Dear Macready

I called at Forster's today, and found him in the act of writing to you, before going to Greenwich with Procter.[4] As soon as he told me what he was writing,

---

[1] Could be the letter to Cruikshank, or to Stanfield (see last) with postscript omitted; but CD clearly wrote many more letters of appeal than have survived.

[2] N reads "all exceedingly", almost certainly in error; cf. other letters.

[3] N reads "hands".

[4] Bryan Waller Procter (1787–1874; *DNB*), writer and lawyer: see Vol. I, p. 314*n*. Had moved to 13 Upper Harley Street from St John's Wood by Feb 43; "removed into a genteel house And gives large parties" according to Crabb Robinson on ?30 Mar 43 (*Correspondence with the Wordsworth Circle*, Oxford, 1927, I,

537). CD was probably at one such party on 21 Feb (see *To* Mitton, 20 Feb, *fn*) and certainly on 29 Mar: "We had an Omnium Gatherum including H:B: [*Brougham*?] We insignificants were not afraid of his 'Evil Eye' Dickens and other young poets & romancers were to be seen" (*ibid.*). Procter's prefatory Memoir and Essay appeared in *Works of Shakespeare* (ed. J. Ogden with introductions and notes on some plays by Horne, Elton, and Whitehead), published in parts by Robert Tyas, 1839–43, and complete in 3 vols, Sep 43.

I undertook to save him the trouble of going on, by communicating its substance to you in the strongest terms I cod. employ.

He had been thinking all day of your declining to act for Elton's family—*and had been considering it: not with any reference to them, but solely with reference to You.* And he says that if you do not act at that benefit, you will, in your position, do yourself irretrievable injury, and give your enemies a lever to use against you, which will be worked beyond all foreseeing.

I had a delicacy in telling you my opinion on this subject, for I thought it might be only mine. But when I find Forster so bent and set upon this opinion—and call to mind that the instant I heard of your refusal last night, I considered it the most rash and injudicious step that such a man as you could take—I should be wanting in the duty which my love for you prescribes, if I did not tell you plainly—along with him—that I think you have made a mistake, which I urge you to reconsider.

My Dear Macready everything that you urge as a reason for *not* playing, is a reason why you *should* play, and a reason why the grace of playing wod. be immeasurably the greater. I am confident you are in error.

Do think of this once more, and let me hear from you between this and a quarter to Eight, when I leave home to preside at the Meeting.[1]

                                            Faithfully Ever

W. C. Macready Esquire   CD

To JOHN [POVEY],[2] [27 or 28] JULY 1843

Extract in S. J. Davey's catalogue No. 42, (Dickens House, in Kitton's "Dickens Ana", III, 20); *MS* 1 p.; *Date:* 13 July 1843 according to catalogue, but certainly later; probably the day after one of the early meetings of the Elton committee. *Address:* "Pavey" in catalogue, clearly a misreading of "Povey".[2]

Your kind offer of assistance in behalf of poor Elton was joyfully and gratefully accepted by us all. I have sent—I mean, I will send immediately—your note to Serle, who is our acting manager.

---

[1] The letter is endorsed by Macready: "1843. | 26 July | Dickens | Elton's fam. Benefit | Refused", and Macready did not act at the Haymarket benefit on 2 Aug; Edgar Johnson's statement that he did so (*CD, his Tragedy and Triumph*, p. 457) is based on the mistaken recollection of Thomas Hood, Jr, and F. Broderip in *Memorials of Thomas Hood*, II, 158. There is no reference to the matter in Macready's *Diaries*; his refusal may be attributed to a fear of anti-climax after his recent farewell performance. Little comment appeared; the *Era*, 30 July 43, says he "felt himself compelled, by his recent announcement that he would not re-appear on the stage for some time, to decline".

[2] John Povey the actor (1799–1867), also a manager and agent (E. L. Blanchard, *Life and Reminiscences*, 1891, I, 338); known as "Honest John Povey". Probably the same as the Povey referred to by Macready in his *Diaries* while in America this year.

To MISS BURDETT COUTTS, 28 JULY 1843

MS Morgan Library.

1 Devonshire Terrace | Twenty Eighth July 1843.

My Dear Miss Coutts.

I will not attempt to tell you what I felt, when I received your noble letter last night.[1]

Trust me that I will be a faithful steward of your bounty; and that there is no charge in the Wide World I would accept with so much pride and happiness as any such from you.

I should be uneasy if I did not let you know that your letter being put in my hands at the Freemasons' last night where the committee were sitting,[2] I told them what it contained, *before* I arrived at your injunction of secrecy. But the gentlemen who were there, were far too much impressed by what I had conveyed to them, ever to betray your confidence, I am sure. I can answer for that.

Charley will be ready at the appointed time, and is counting the clock already.

Ever Dear Miss Coutts | Faithfully Yours

Miss Coutts.   CHARLES DICKENS

To JOHN FORSTER, [28 JULY 1843]

Extract in F, IV, ii, 308. *Date:* 28 July 43 according to Forster.

I write in haste, for I have been at work all day; and, it being against the grain with me to go back to America when my interest is strong in the other parts of the tale, have got on but slowly.[3] I have a great notion to work out with Sydney's favourite,[4] and long to be at him again.

---

[1] On 1 Aug *The Times* reported that Miss Coutts had forwarded a considerable sum, and the offer of her great patronage for any public school which the ages of the Elton children might fit them to enter. On 19 Aug the *Theatrical Journal* reported that a lady who wished to be anonymous had offered to keep the family for six months.

[2] Their second meeting. The *Examiner* of 29 July described the appeal, and added that "Mr. Murray . . . of the Edinburgh theatre . . . has appealed to the public there with a promptitude that does him great honour; and . . . Mr. Dickens no sooner heard of the proposed benefit in that city, than intent on aiding it, he wrote and forwarded an address to be spoken on the occasion". The Edinburgh benefit, originally advertised in the Edinburgh press from 22 July, for 5 Aug, was altered to 29 July, so that CD's offer would have been too late. Murray therefore offered the address to Alexander of the Theatre Royal, Glasgow, for their benefit, but he refused it (letter from Murray dated 5 Aug to the editor of the *Glasgow Chronicle*; *Caledonian Mercury*, 10 Aug) and declined to take part or to allow the theatre to be used. At the Glasgow benefit at the Free Trade Hall, 9 Aug, there was no address, and as a result no further record of it survives.

[3] He had only just begun work on the Sep No. (Chs 21–3), of which the whole is in America. The shift is abrupt: Ch. 20, the last in the Aug No., which has no American matter, ends with a loud knocking at Mr Pecksniff's door, while Ch. 21 opens with the "frank admission" that this knocking "bore no resemblance whatever to the noise of an American railway train at full speed".

[4] Sydney Smith had written to CD about Chuffey, who first appears in the May No.: "Chuffey is admirable. I never read a finer piece of writing; it is deeply pathetic and affecting" (possibly part of the

To MRS HOOD,[1] [?28 JULY 1843]*

MS (fragment) Mr Graham Storey. *Date:* June-July 1843 on handwriting; probably in reply to hers of ?27 July (see *To* Hood, 26 July, *fn*).

I shall be glad to hear from you, or to see you, next week.

Always Dear Mrs. Hood | Faithfully Yours
CHARLES DICKENS

To GEORGE CRUIKSHANK, 31 JULY 1843*

MS Mr Theodore Hewitson.

Devonshire Terrace | Thirty First July 1843

My Dear George.

I received your hearty letter in due course; and have begged the Secretary to send you, in the course of to day, some Circular Letters and Subscription Lists. Any money you can collect,[2] we shall be truly glad to receive.

I hope we are getting on as well as we could expect. Much depends on the benefits.[3] After one or two of them have come off, we shall know better where we are.

In haste | Always Faithfully Your friend
George Cruikshank Esquire   CHARLES DICKENS

To T. P. COOKE,[4] 3 AUGUST 1843

Mention in Anderson Galleries catalogue No. 1272 (1917); *MS* 1 p.; dated London, 3 Aug 43.

Acknowledging a contribution for Elton's children.[5]

letter referred to in *To* Mitton, 24 July; given by Forster in footnote, and attributed to April; wrongly placed as P.S. to letter of 6 Jan 43 in *The Letters of Sydney Smith*, ed. Nowell C. Smith, II, 776). Chuffey reappeared briefly in Ch. 26 at the end of the Oct No., with a hint of sympathy between him and Mercy Pecksniff, now married to Jonas. This is an interesting instance of planning ahead, for the "great notion", which makes Chuffey an agent of Jonas's exposure, is not worked out until the closing number.

[1] Jane Hood (1792–1846), sister of John Hamilton Reynolds, friend of Keats and Lamb; married 1825.

[2] Others were also active in collection; Blanchard wrote to P. G. Patmore on 6 Aug 43, "I have been writing night and day about the subscription for the children of my poor old friend Elton; it is most successful" (P. G. Patmore, *My Friends and Acquaintance*, 1854, III, 211).

[3] At the Haymarket, 2 Aug; the City of London, and the Surrey, 3 Aug; the Princess's, 4 Aug; Sadler's Wells, 5 Aug;

Astley's, 12 Aug. A night's receipts were also offered to the Fund by the New Strand, the Garrick and by Anderson, the "Wizard of the North", at the Adelphi.

[4] Thomas Potter ("Tippy") Cooke (1786–1864; *DNB*), actor; in the Navy 1796–1802; on the stage from 1804, mainly in melodramas; his most famous part was William in Jerrold's *Black-eyed Susan* 1829, first at the Surrey and then at Covent Garden, constantly revived; CD reviewed a revival at the Marylebone Theatre in the *Examiner*, 12 May 49 (*Miscellaneous Papers*, ed. B. W. Matz, p. 152); in 1857, at 71, Cooke played the part at a performance in remembrance of Jerrold (N, II, 865). Other favourite parts were Long Tom Coffin in *The Pilot*, Aubrey in the *Dog of Montargis*, and Harry Halyard in *My Poll and My Partner Joe*; "Christopher North" called him "the best sailor . . . that ever trod the stage". In Sep–Nov 43 was appearing in nautical melodramas at the Surrey Theatre with great success.

[5] Cooke gave three guineas to the Fund.

To VISCOUNT MORPETH, 3 AUGUST 1843

MS Mr George Howard.

1 Devonshire Terrace | York Gate Regents Park
Third August 1843.

Dear Lord Morpeth.

In acknowledging the safe receipt of your kind donation in behalf of poor Mr. Elton's orphan children,[1] I hope you will suffer me to address you with little ceremony, as the best proof I can give you of my cordial reciprocation of all you say in your most welcome note. I have long esteemed you, and been your distant but very truthful admirer; and trust me that it is a real pleasure and happiness to me to anticipate the time when we shall have a nearer intercourse.

Believe me | With sincere regard
Faithfully Your Servant

The | Viscount Morpeth CHARLES DICKENS

To JOHN OVERS, 3 AUGUST 1843*

MS Yale University Library.

Devonshire Terrace | Thursday Third August | 1843.

Dear Mr. Overs.

The Dr. has taken immense pains in the matter I wrote you of. The result is, that Mr. Young[2] of the Sun Newspaper requests you to call on him, next Saturday evening at 6. The office is in the Strand, and you must send up to him the enclosed card.

Be as plain; and as cheerful in your anticipations of him and yourself; as you can. Tell him what things of yours have been published, and fill him with the impression, so far as in you lies, that you desire to be useful. If you do anything for him, lay this to heart—never use a hard word, where an easy one will serve your turn.

Write to me at Broadstairs, and tell me what passed. If, at any time, you have anything to do for him that admits of so much leisure, let me see your Manuscript.

In great haste | Faithfully Yours always

Mr. J. A. Overs CD

To WILLIAM PULFORD,[3] 6 AUGUST 1843†

MS Colonel Richard Gimbel.

Broadstairs, Kent. | Sixth August 1843.

Dear Sir

In reply to your enquiry, I beg to say that what we are doing for the orphan Family of poor Mr. Elton, is simply this—endeavouring to get as much money as possible. We shall be truly glad to have some from you; and I have written to the Secretary, begging him to send you a Blank subscription List by Post.

---

[1] He gave £2 to the Fund.

[2] Murdo Young (?1791–1870), editor and proprietor: see Vol. II, p. 444*n*.

[3] The list of subscriptions published on 25 Aug includes "W. Pulford and Friends, £2.10".

I do not see that it is possible to *suggest* anything to Mr. Welch.[1] Whatever he could get for us, we would gratefully accept; but we have no means of sending professional people down to Brighton,[2] nor should we feel justified in incurring any risk in getting up a concert or other entertainment there. But I will not fail to make Mr. Welch's kind offer of service known to the Committee when they meet again on Monday week; and I can answer for their thanking him for his kindness.

Faithfully Yours

William Pulford Esquire   CHARLES DICKENS

To RICHARD MONCKTON MILNES, 6 AUGUST 1843*

MS Trinity College, Cambridge.

Broadstairs,[3] Kent. | Sixth August 1843.

My Dear Milnes

Behold the date of this. And say,—being here, and receiving your kind note only this morning—how *could* I breakfast with you yesterday?

I wish you would endorse this Card for me. Mr. Jerrold (who is a friend of mine, and a man of very great ability) wishes to join the British and Foreign Institute; and by the endorsement of an original member, can do so without ballot.[4] Therefore if you will affix your sign manual to this little bit of pasteboard, and send it me back again by return of post, you will truly oblige me.

My Dear Milnes | Faithfully Yours

R. M. Milnes Esquire   CHARLES DICKENS

To R. W. HONNER,[5] 6 AUGUST 1843

Extract in Sotheby's catalogue, July 1912; *MS* 1 p; dated Broadstairs, 6 Aug 43.

I am truly gratified by your account of the splendid result of the Benefit[6] at the Surrey Theatre in behalf of the orphan children of poor Mr. Elton—and so will the committee be, I am sure, when we meet again on Monday week.

---

[1] Presumably connected with a Brighton theatre, but not in Brighton Directory. "T. Welch, £3" appears in the same subscription list as Pulford.

[2] A benefit at the Brighton Theatre (proprietor J. F. Saville), 11 Aug, raised £45 (*Theatrical Journal*, 26 Aug 43).

[3] CD must have gone there on 1 or 2 Aug, returning for the night of 3 Aug: see *To* Miss Coutts, 7 Aug.

[4] After a meeting of the Institute on 2 Aug, an announcement in *The Times* (3 Aug) invited applications for membership at reduced terms for the first 250, and stated that the 100 original members, of whom Milnes was one, "have the privilege of introducing a limited number of friends without ballot . . . early application is desirable"; there was a card for applica-

tion. According to James Silk Buckingham, *An Appeal against Punch*, 1845, Jerrold, although elected at his own request, refused to take up his membership, because "he understood that the Institute was conducted very differently from what had been promised" (W. Jerrold, *Douglas Jerrold*, [1914], II, 420).

[5] Robert William Honner (1809–52; *DNB*), actor and manager: see Vol. I, p. 388*n*. Formerly lessee of Sadler's Wells (to 1842) and in 1845 at the City of London. A member of the Fund Committee, and spoke the prologue by Leman Rede before the benefit at the Surrey Theatre, where he was stage-manager, on 3 Aug. Subscribed 10s on 10 Oct.

[6] It raised £140.18.0.

To AMBROSE WILLIAMS,[1] 6 AUGUST 1843*

MS Free Library of Philadelphia.

Broadstairs, Kent. | Sixth August 1843

Dear Sir

Pray accept the best thanks of the Committee for your Address in behalf of poor Mr. Elton's children. It impressed me very favorably in the reading, as being appropriate, modest, and pathetic.

You will have seen that having had another and an earlier offer[2] we could not avail ourselves of your kindness. But we are not the less indebted to you, believe me.

Dear Sir | Faithfully Yours

Ambrose Williams Esquire   CHARLES DICKENS

To MISS BURDETT COUTTS, 7 AUGUST 1843

MS Morgan Library.

Broadstairs, Kent. | Monday Seventh August 1843

Dear Miss Coutts.

I went up to town last Thursday to preside at a Meeting of the Committee for poor Mr. Elton's children; but as I came back here next morning, I had no opportunity of calling on you.

Owing to the offensive conduct of Mr. Charles Mathews[3] and his estimable lady we were unable to use either Harley, the Keeleys, Mrs. Nisbett, or Mrs. Stirling at the Haymarket, although they had all been previously announced with Mr. Webster's full consent. The consequence was, that we were obliged at the last moment to alter an excellent bill; and the entertainments were very trash.[4] You will be glad to hear, however, that the receipts were £280; a very large sum in that Theatre, which when crammed to the very utmost will not hold more than £300. Including this sum, we had in hand on Thursday night, hard upon a thousand pounds; since which time the benefit at the Surrey[5] (the only return I have yet had) has produced a hundred and forty pounds more, and some additional private subscriptions have also come in.

Finding it exceedingly difficult in the midst of their trouble to arrive with

---

[1] Unidentified.

[2] Presumably of Hood's address at the Haymarket: see *To* Hood, 26 July, *fn*.

[3] Charles James Mathews (1803–78; *DNB*), actor and dramatist: see Vol. II, p. 385*n*. A member of the Fund Committee; but objected to the use of actors from other theatres.

[4] The "excellent bill" for 2 Aug, advertised in the *Morning Herald* on 1 Aug, contained *The Rivals*, with a combined cast of the best actors from Drury Lane and the Haymarket, including Farren,

Mathews, Anderson, Phelps, Harley, Buckstone, Webster, Mrs Glover, Vestris, and Mrs Nisbett, and an "interlude" by the Keeleys; the "trash" that took its place was W. B. Bernard's *Louison*, Webster's *Little Devil*, J. M. Morton's *The Double Bedded Room*, and Buckstone's *A Kiss in the Dark*, all in the current Haymarket repertory. Hood's address (*Poetical Works*, ed. W. Jerrold, 1906, pp. 622–3) was spoken by Mrs Warner.

[5] See *To* Honner, 6 Aug, *fn*.

anything like tolerable certainty at the weekly expenses of the family; last Thursday, I placed £10—the ten you sent me—in the hands of a lady[1] who knows them, and can be trusted to make a careful report: and begged her to account to me for it, and to get me an estimate by the time we meet again (next Monday) of their average bills. Before I see you on that head, I will visit the children myself. For I wish particularly to speak to the eldest girl[2] about it, and to be very careful that your assistance, is free from the controul of any relation or friend,[3] but such as she knows can be thoroughly trusted, and is kindly disposed towards them. I fancy I have observed some slight signs and tokens, which render this precaution indispensable.

This little place is very bright and beautiful—and I wish you and your Patient could see it this morning. I have been here six years, and have never had a Piano next door; but this fortune was too good to last, and now there is one close to the little bay window of the room I write in, which has six years' agony in every note it utters. I have been already obliged to take refuge on the other side of the house, but that looks into a street where the "Flies" stand, and where there are donkeys and drivers out of number. Their Music is almost as bad as the other, and between the two, I was driven into such a state of desperation on Saturday, that I thought I must have run away and deserted my family. The matter was not mended when the paper came down, with Mr. Thomas Duncombe's[4] tribute to the character and acquirements of Mr. Bunn;[5] which so exasperated me (though the two gentlemen are well worthy of each other's friendship) that I walked ten miles over burning chalk, before I could resume the least composure.

Charley and two hundred and fifty other children, are making fortifications in the sand with wooden spades, and picking up shells and sea weed. He is still full of his last visit to you, and brightened up like burnished copper at breakfast

---

[1] Possibly Mrs M'Ian, as wife of the Secretary; or Mrs S. C. Hall, whose "unceasing kindness to the orphan children" is mentioned by T. Marshall, *Lives of the Most Celebrated Actors and Actresses*, p. 158.

[2] The eldest girl was said by the *Morning Herald* to be 20, and was probably Esther.

[3] Elton's wife's mother had been dependent on him, as well as his own parents. The *Theatrical Journal* mentions a brother of Elton's, a bookseller in High St, Islington (Charles Henry Elt); another Elt (Thomas R.) kept the White Swan at 138 Salisbury Court, Fleet Street.

[4] Thomas Slingsby Duncombe (1796–1861; *DNB*), MP for Finsbury; presented the Chartists' petition in May 42; an active politician, popular speaker and writer of many pamphlets and letters to the press. The contrast between his aristocratic connections and radical views was often noted. He appeared unmistakably in "A Parliamentary Sketch" (*Sketches by Boz*, Second series, 1836): "That smart-looking fellow in the black coat with velvet facings and cuffs, who wears his *D'Orsay* hat so rakishly, is 'Honest Tom', a metropolitan representative".

[5] Alfred Bunn (1796–1860; *DNB*), theatrical manager: see Vol. I, p. 317n. Had just become lessee of Drury Lane; Macready had heard the news on 3 Aug: "This is, on the part of the committee, shameful—to the art, actors, and the public" (*Diaries*, II, 216). The *Morning Chronicle* (5 Aug), in reporting the debate on the Theatres Regulation Bill, gave Duncombe's tribute to Bunn: "Drury Lane Theatre had been taken in consequence of the introduction of this bill, by a gentleman of great experience in connection with the drama, and extremely well versed in dramatic literature; he meant Mr. Bunn".

when I asked him if he had any message to send. If I thought his love would *do* (he said) he should like to forward it. So I promised to convey it to you, in due form. I have some idea of writing him a Child's History of England,[1] to the end that he may have tender-hearted notions of War and Murder, and may not fix his affections on wrong heros, or see the bright side of Glory's sword and know nothing of the rusty one. If I should carry it out, I shall live in the hope that you will read it one wet day.

I fear the weather has been sorely against Miss Meredith; as indeed it has been against all invalids, Mrs. Dickens[2] included, who begs me to send her best remembrances. It would give us great pleasure to hear that Miss Meredith had left her room, though individually I must say that if I once knew of her eating two thirds of a roast chicken, and drinking three glasses of Wine, I would be content to leave all the rest to Herself and Good Fortune. I beg to be heartily remembered to her, and am ever dear Miss Coutts with high regard

Faithfully Yours

Miss Coutts. CHARLES DICKENS

To THOMAS MITTON, 10 AUGUST 1843

MS Huntington Library.

Broadstairs, Kent | Tenth August 1843.

My Dear Mitton

I have but a moment before the Post goes: having been at work the livelong day.

If the Insurance[3] be *not* for Chapman and Hall, let it drop. But if it be theirs, I think we had better let it be renewed; the account not having been wiped off to the extent we had looked for. If it be mine—decidedly No.

I shall come to town for a meeting of the Elton Committee, on Monday: returning next Morning. I will appoint a time for calling on you when I know my movements better—most likely by Sunday Night's Post from here. We have about £1500 in hand.

The next No.[4] is not so much to *my* taste as the last—being in America again. But I am making the best of it.

Faithfully Yours ever
CD.

---

[1] See *To* Jerrold, 3 May 43.
[2] Francis Jeffrey was born 15 Jan 44.
[3] Chapman & Hall had held one of CD's life assurance policies with the Britannia since 31 July 41, and two others since Jan 42 (see *To* Chapman & Hall, 1 Jan 42 and *fn*).
[4] Chs 21–3.

To MESSRS BRADBURY & EVANS, 13 AUGUST 1843

Extract in Sotheby's catalogue, July 1932; *MS* 1 p.; dated Broadstairs, 13 Aug 43.

I come up to town tomorrow for one night, and dine with Mr. Forster at 5. If you can send a proof of the accompanying MS[1] by that time, I should like to have it. . . . Punch is better than ever[2]

To JOHN FORSTER, [13 AUGUST 1843]*

MS Mr Alfred Essex. *Date:* clearly same day as last.

Broadstairs | Sunday.

My Dear Forster.

I shall come up by the Fame; we may dine at halfpast 5 to the moment—and I have little doubt that I shall be with you before then.

I have "Yeses" from Barham and Stanny. Thompson will be out of England. Stone uncertain, till tomorrow night. Edwin Landseer, very.

Have you asked Fox?[3]

Ever affecy.

John Forster Esquire   CD.

To THOMAS MITTON, [13 AUGUST 1843]*

MS University of Texas. *Date:* clearly same day.

Broadstairs | Sunday

My Dear Mitton

I shall come up by the Fame tomorrow, and will immediately call—it will be only a call I am sorry to say—on you. But I shall be in town again, soon.

I have nearly killed myself with laughing at what I have done of the American No.[4]—though how much comicality may be in my knowledge of its Truth,[5] I can't say. I seem to hear the people talking again.

Faithfully Ever

Thomas Mitton Esquire.   CD

---

[1] Probably Chs 21 and 22, as Ch. 23 was ready by 18 Aug (see *To* Bradbury & Evans, that day).

[2] The number of 12 Aug had an excellent cartoon showing O'Connell as Ondine in the Shadow Dance, and two humorous theatrical items which would appeal to CD, one of them a skit on the Theatres Regulation Bill.

[3] CD and Forster were arranging a farewell dinner to Macready for 26 Aug; all the possible guests named attended except Thompson. See *To* Crew, 24 Aug and *fn*.

[4] Ch. 21 introduces Mr La Fayette Kettle, General Choke, and the Watertoast Association, and Ch. 22 the Hominys; the arrival in Eden (Ch. 23) is not amusing.

[5] Ch. 21 was particularly topical this summer. In the Preface to the Cheap edn (1852) CD claims that the Watertoast Association was "a literal paraphrase of some reports of public proceedings in the United States (especially of the proceedings of a certain Brandywine Association), which were printed in the Times Newspaper in June and July 1843". Reports of various Repeal Associations meetings in New York and Philadelphia had been appearing in *The Times* from 30 June; on 7 July appeared a letter to O'Connell from the Brandywine Emett Repeal Association of Delaware, read at one of his meetings on 5 July. It referred to "a people whose very bosoms heave to overflowing with the chrystal stream of pure republicanism" and bid Ireland "with a voice of thunder

To MISS BURDETT COUTTS, 15 AUGUST 1843*

MS Morgan Library.

Broadstairs | Fifteenth August 1843.

Dear Miss Coutts.

I have satisfactorily ascertained that the weekly expenses of the Elton Family, will be, as nearly as possible, Three Pounds—not more. I have also taken the utmost care that not a farthing of the money shall be appropriated to any but the main and single purpose of their support; and that no man, woman, or child, shall interfere with its expenditure in any way. I will keep such a watch upon them as Argus could not have surpassed, though all his eyes had been melted down into one; and will take care that every shilling you entrust me with in their behalf, shall be satisfactorily accounted for.

You will be glad, I am sure, to hear that the Subscriptions and benefits together, will amount to a couple of Thousand Pounds.[1]

I shall come to town to see the children on Friday week; and if you are not otherwise engaged, will call on you next morning about one o'Clock. I sincerely hope Miss Meredith is better. She *ought* to be much better now, I think.

Always Dear Miss Coutts
Yours faithfully and obliged

Miss Coutts.

CHARLES DICKENS

To JOHN FORSTER, [15 AUGUST 1843]

Extract in F, IV, ii, 309. *Date:* 15 Aug according to Forster; but he is probably wrong in saying that it was accompanied by the "second chapter of his eighth [*error for ninth*] number".

I gather from a letter I have had this morning that Martin has made them all stark staring raving mad across the water.[2] I wish you would consider this.

---

sever the chains that bind her to the oppressor . . . Let England beware before it is too late". A letter was also read from the Wilmington Repeal Association calling England a "haughty Power" whose "Hydra folds . . . boa-like" oppressed and bound them. But when the Associations heard of O'Connell's anti-slavery speech of 10 May, there was a reaction and many such Associations were dissolved; this news was reported in *The Times* on 25 and 29 July.

[1] The amount collected by 25 Nov 43 was "£2380, exclusive of expenses" (*The Times*; CD's final advertisement). About half of this came from the benefits—the Haymarket's having been the most productive, with £281.17.0.

[2] The *Roscius* arrived at Liverpool on 11 Aug bringing American papers up to 25 July, and the *Caledonia* on 13 Aug,

having taken only 12 days. No. VII (Chs 16–17) was published by Harpers in New York soon after 19 July. Reviews appeared before the end of the month; Park Benjamin's *Brother Jonathan*, 29 July, referred to CD's "malignity and thorough hatred", "determination to distort and misrepresent", and "infuriated malice"; considered that the No. was "dull, vapid and feeble", but that there was "no occasion to work ourselves into a passion", as many editors of the daily press had done; judgment should be reserved till the next No. (for the whole review, see *D*, X [1914], 97–9). Philip Hone recorded in his diary, 29 July, that the chapter describing Martin's arrival—"what he saw, and heard, and did, and suffered, in this land of pagans, brutes, and infidels"—was just published; and he commented, "I was sorry to see it". He had taken CD's part on most occasions,

Don't you think the time has come when I ought to state that such public entertainments as I received in the States were either accepted before I went out, or in the first week after my arrival there; and that as soon as I began to have any acquaintance with the country, I set my face against any public recognition whatever but that which was forced upon me to the destruction of my peace and comfort—and made no secret of my real sentiments.

To H. K. BROWNE, [?15–18 AUGUST 1843]

MS Huntington Library. *Date:* probably between 15 Aug (his return to Broadstairs) and the completion of the No. on 18 Aug.[1]

2nd Subject[2]

The First Subject having shewn the settlement of Eden on paper, the second shews it in reality. Martin and Mark are displayed as the tenants of a wretched log hut (*for a pattern whereof, see a Vignette brought by Chapman and Hall*) in a perfectly flat swampy, wretched forest of stunted timber in every stage of decay, with a filthy river running before the door, and some other miserable loghouses indicated among the trees, whereof the most ruinous and tumbledown of all, is

"but he has now written an exceedingly foolish libel upon us, from which he will not obtain credit as an author, nor as a man of wit, any more than as a man of good taste, good nature, or good manners". He thought it "unmitigated trash" (*The Diary of Philip Hone*, ed. A. Nevins, p. 666; for his opinion of *American Notes*, see *To* Hone, 16 Sep 42, *fn*). Longfellow, writing to Appleton on 29 July, said that both CD and Forster were "living in a strange hallucination about this country, as you must have seen" (MS Houghton Library). English views were more varied: Macready had read the No. on the day of publication and did not like it: "It will not do Dickens good, and I grieve over it"; he also noted a letter from Miss Martineau, "angry with Dickens—and not unreasonably so". The Sep No. he thought powerful, but bitter and unfair to the majority of Americans—"How many answer to his description?" (*Diaries*, II, 215, 217, 218–219). But Carlyle wrote to Forster on 3 July, "The last *Chuzzlewit* on Yankeedoodledodom is capital. We read it with loud assent, loud cachinnatory approval! You may tell Dickens if you like" (MS V & A); and both the July and Sep Nos were widely praised and quoted in the English press. But Sydney Smith, in spite of what he had written to CD on the July No. (see *To* Mitton, 24 July), told Lady Carlisle in a letter of 17 Sep that he was

"very sorry for the turn Dickens' novel has taken. It seems as if he had gone over to America on purpose to raise a sum of money by exposing their ridicules" (transcript, MS Lord Halifax). The charge of ingratitude to his hosts (also made by Hone) was evidently common in American reviews, and Elizabeth Barrett, though defending his conduct in America, wrote on 7 Sep 13, ' It is his conduct *since*, which has used all this honor to dishonor himself—he is an ungrateful, an ungrateful man!' (*Elizabeth Barrett to Miss Mitford*, ed. Betty Miller, 1954, p. 198). CD had doubtless heard of American attacks on his ingratitude. These are satirized in "The American's Apostrophe to Boz", one of the Bon Gaultier ballads by Aytoun and Martin, first published in *A Book of Ballads*, 1845: "Did we spare our brandy-cocktails, stint thee of our whisky-grogs? . . . | Did the hams of old Virginny find no favour in thine eyes? | Came no soft compunction o'er thee at the thought of pumpkin pies?"

[1] The scene is at the close of Ch. 23, but could obviously be thought out in advance; and for such a scene Browne would need as long as possible.

[2] Heading "2nd Subject" is in CD's writing. Another hand, not Browne's, has written "Martin Chuzzlewit" [*thus*] over it, and Browne has written "Martin Chuzzlewit" to the right.

labelled BANK. And National Credit Office. Outside their door, as the custom is, is a rough sort of form or dresser, on which are set forth their pot and kettle and so forth: all of the commonest kind. On the outside of the house at one side of the door, is a written placard CHUZZLEWIT AND CO. ARCHITECTS AND SURVEYORS; and upon a stump of tree, like a butcher's block, before the cabin, are Martin's instruments—a pair of rusty compasses &c On a three legged stool beside this block, sits Martin in his shirt sleeves, with long dishevelled hair, resting his head upon his hands: the picture of hopeless misery—watching the river, as sadly remembering that it flows towards home. But Mr. Tapley, up to his knees in filth and brushwood, and in the act of endeavouring to perform some impossibilities with a hatchet, looks towards him with a face of unimpaired good humour, and declares himself perfectly jolly. Mark the only redeeming feature. Everything else dull, miserable, squalid, unhealthy, and utterly devoid of hope: diseased, starved, and abject.

The weather is intensely hot, and they are but partially clothed.[1]

To MESSRS BRADBURY & EVANS, 18 AUGUST 1843*

MS Victoria & Albert Museum (FC). *Address:* clearly to Bradbury & Evans (see 13 Aug).

Broadstairs | Friday 18 August 1843

Dr. Sirs.
    Proof with all speed

Faithfully
CD.[2]

To MISS BURDETT COUTTS, 20 AUGUST 1843*

MS Morgan Library.

Broadstairs. | Twentieth August 1843

Dear Miss Coutts
    I avail myself of the last moment before the post leaves, to say that I have just received your kind note, and that either you misread, or I miswrote mine. I said *Saturday Week*[3]—meaning next Saturday. I only mention it, lest you should think I had neglected my appointment.

---

[1] At the foot of the page another hand has written: "With 2 Sketches" and Browne has written in pencil "I can't get all this perspective in—unless you will allow of a long subject —— something less than a mile." Browne's sketch resembles the illustration except that the stump is larger and not growing in the ground, the Chuzzlewit placard is differently placed, and the other reads only "BANK". Beneath it is written (with two vertical lines indicating the width of the block) "too wide—cannot it be compressed by putting Martins label on the other side of the door and bringing Mark with his tree forwarder qy is that a hat on his head", and "the stump of the tree should be *in* the ground in fact a tree cut off two feet up [*rough sketch*]". The hand is neither CD's nor Browne's, but the substance of the comments suggests that they are CD's, perhaps dictated at the printing office to a member of the staff when CD was in London again 24–26 Aug. The required changes were made, but the hat looks exactly the same on the plate.

[2] Note written in pencil on the last page of MS of *Chuzzlewit* No. IX.

[3] CD was right; see *To* Miss Coutts, 15 Aug.

I am truly rejoiced to hear that Miss Meredith has made a rally; and am quite sure of her, *now*. Charley sends his best love.

The piano goes away on Friday. My mind misgives me that some other Instrument will take the house afterwards. I have seen a man looking at the bill, who has been heard playing the flute in the Evening under solitary cliffs.

Dear Miss Coutts | Ever Yours faithfully

Miss Coutts.   CHARLES DICKENS

To MR COOPER,[1] 21 AUGUST 1843

Mention in N, I, 533.

To FRANCIS CREW,[2] [24 AUGUST 1843]

Text (with corrected punctuation) from version by F. Crew, described by him as "something like this" (MS John Rylands Library; see *fn* below). Mention in S. F. Henkels catalogue No. 1492; *MS* 2 pp.; dated Devonshire Terrace, Thursday night—clearly the Thursday before the Macready dinner on 26 Aug.

Dear Sir

A few friends[3] will dine together at the Star and Garter, Richmond, on Saturday at four for the purpose of giving a farewell dinner to Mr Macready on

---

[1] Unidentified.

[2] Francis Crew, bookseller and stationer of 27 Lambs Conduit Street; an amateur tenor singer of some repute. CD wrote to him as a friend, but spelt his name "Crewe", on ?27 Nov 36: see Vol. I, p. 199. Recalled as singing Moore's songs at Offley's Tavern, Covent Garden, in about 1820 by John Timbs (*Walks and Talks about London*, 1865, pp. 180–2); at Offley's he learned from its author, one Churchill, "The Brave Old English Gentleman" "which he thoroughly made his own"; it was the subject of an action in the King's Bench, 13 June 1834 (C. H. Purday, "Some account of the Origin and Trial of the Old English Gentleman", MS note on BM copy of the song, and H. Phillips, *Musical and Personal Recollections*, I, 198–9)—the song parodied by CD in *Examiner* Aug 41: see Vol. II, p. 357*n*. Crew was a family friend, or perhaps a relation, of Fanny Brown, later Mrs Talbot, the well-known correspondent of Ruskin, but then a girl of 19, to whom he wrote a very full account of the occasion: see MS Rylands, mostly reproduced in "A Dickens Dinner Party, 1843", *Bulletin of John Rylands Library*, XXXVI, 1953–4, 9–14. Crew first gives CD's letter, then his own letter in reply, expressing pleasure at an "invitation so agreeable" and "unmixed

gratification to join a party where you are the presiding deity and Mr. Maccready [*thus*] the object of your protection", but asking to be one of the hosts rather than "a visitor". He then draws a sketch of the circular table indicating the position of the guests: CD, Macready, Dillon, H. P. Smith, Dr Quin, F. Crew, G. Raymond, Rev. W. J. Fox, Forster, Maclise, Landseer, Frank Stone, Rev. R. H. Barham, and C. Stanfield—briefly identifying each for the sake of his correspondent and his own pleasure in being one of so "brilliant" a company. (For Dillon, described by Crew as "a very clever as well as rich man", see next vol.) Crew next describes the dinner —"much Turtle and Venison and Lamb, and Ham and Goose and at least fifty other dishes ... Hock, Sherry, Moselle, Madeira, Champagne, Port &c ... Ices and Creams and Pine apples Melons and sundry other fruits"—and how, after "many witticisms and great laughter", CD proposed Macready's health: "and oh that I could convey to you even a distant idea of its brilliancy, of its lovely lights and shades of its enthusiasm and pathos, at once exciting our smiles and tears". In the course of his speech CD "playfully & wittily" conveyed his own opinion of America, begging Macready not to mention his name (see *To* Macready, 1 Sep),

his departure for America. It struck me on my journey to town from Broadstairs that your company would be a great acquisition to our party. I do not pretend to hide from you that I am in some measure selfish in this invitation, but yet I think you will derive some pleasure from such a meeting. You [cannot][1] but be aware how charmed I always am with your delightful voice, nor less admirable taste, and I would willingly afford my friends who will be present upon this occasion an example of them. Do not, however, look upon the reason of my asking the pleasure of your company, but come. You will by doing it very much oblige Yours most faithfully

CHARLES DICKENS

To THE GENTLEMEN OF THE STOCK EXCHANGE, 28 AUGUST 1843

MS Boston Public Library.

1 Devonshire Terrace, York Gate, Regents Park.
Twenty Eighth August 1843.

Gentlemen.

You are aware, I have no doubt, that a Public Subscription has been entered into, for the benefit of the Seven Orphan Children—all girls but one—of the late Mr. Elton, who was drowned in the Sad Shipwreck of the Pegasus. Their mother died insane some years since; and but for the friends they have found since their father's death, they would be quite destitute and unprotected.

The fund will be vested in three trustees—Edward Marjoribanks Esquire, Mr. Serjeant Talfourd, and myself. A committee of five gentlemen; all known to Mr. Elton and to the public; will be associated with them for promoting, by all means in their power, the welfare of these orphans, and the benevolent intentions of the Subscribers.

and "vividly painted" the affection of Macready's wife, children and friends. Mrs Barham reported to her daughter (MS copy Mr T. E. Barham Howe) that this "beautiful speech . . . set all the men *crying*". Crew, who rode home in Barham's carriage, related his comment: "'It was too glowing, too bright, too magnificent to be described, its wit astonished me, its pathos overpowered me, it contained all that was most excellent in his writings without a particle of its verbiage. Theodore Hook only could have surpassed it Hook spoke better than he wrote Dickens ('till now) has written better than he spoke I was ashamed of my tears, but shd have been more ashamed not to have cried.' Macready returned thanks more feelingly than eloquently". (His own version in *Diaries*, II, 218 is, "I had not had time before to ponder the circumstances of my departure, and I quite broke down under it. I could not speak for tears, or very inefficiently"). "After this speech all was silence for many seconds. Dickens cried out Pray, Crew, stifle this gloom you only can restore us to ourselves I sang 'Poor Jack' very badly, then again began the Reparte the wit the fun and it continued till 12 o'clock." Crew sang several other songs, and was most successful in "Molly Brallaghan"; among the "many songs by other parties" (e.g. Stanfield) were Landseer's rendering of "Lord Lovel and Lady Nancy Bell" and Barham's of "a portion of 'Robin Hood and the Bp of Hereford'" —he "left off before the Bp's punishment [*being tied up and made to sing a mass*] to Mr Fox's great regret". Macready called it "a most joyous evening . . . the warmest emotions of regard and regret pervaded the party".

[3] See above; Procter's inclusion might have been expected, but he was in the north on Commission of Lunacy business.

[1] MS reads "can".

I have refrained from addressing you until now, for I deemed it right to bring our plans thus far towards a practical conclusion, before I troubled you upon the subject. But I feel that I should be very imperfectly discharging my duty as Chairman of the Committee of this Fund, if I allowed the Subscription to come to a close, without soliciting the aid of a body of Gentlemen, always conspicuous for their Charity and Generosity, and always so nobly representing, in its best aspect, the Wealth of this great city.

Trust me, Gentlemen, that if you should feel disposed to assist the object I have thus briefly explained and have very much at heart, you will extend a helping hand to persons not unworthy of your notice; and may securely rely on as careful, and at the same time as tender and becoming an appropriation, of every farthing of the money, as even you yourselves could desire.[1]

I have the honor to be
Gentlemen | Your faithful Servant
CHARLES DICKENS

The Gentlemen | of | The Stock Exchange.

To W. H. MURRAY,[2] 29 AUGUST 1843†

MS Walter T. Spencer.

Broadstairs, Kent | Twenty Ninth August 1843

Dear Sir

As I do not know the address of Bishop Gillies;[3] and as the kind offer of that reverend Gentleman in reference to the disposal of one of poor Elton's children, was made through you; I shall feel much obliged to you if you will convey to him the purport of this communication.

The smaller committee to whom the immediate consideration of the family's necessities has been entrusted, have given their best and most grateful attention to the offer of Bishop Gillies. But they have come to the conclusion that as it would involve the necessity of one child being educated in the Roman Catholic persuasion, it is best for them to decline it.

In arriving at this opinion, they have not allowed themselves to be influenced by any religious opinions or scruples of their own: but have confined themselves to three points of consideration—firstly, how their father would have viewed such a proposal had he been happily alive—secondly, how the elder children regard it among themselves—and thirdly how far they would be justified in

---

[1] Published subscription lists do not specify the Stock Exchange as such, but name individual stockbrokers, including three Capels. See *To* Marjoribanks, 8 Sep.

[2] William Henry Murray (1790–1852; *DNB*), actor and manager: see Vol. II, p. 311*n*. Founder and director of Edinburgh Theatrical Fund; organized benefit performances for the Elton children in Edinburgh and Glasgow (see *To* Miss Coutts, 28 July) and had collected £100 in subscriptions; the Edinburgh benefit was a great success, "one of the most overflowing bumpers we ever witnessed" (*Edinburgh Advertiser*). Benefits and subscriptions totalled £322.18.1.

[3] Mis-spelt by CD. Bishop James Gillis (1802–64), coadjutor to the Vicar Apostolic of the Eastern district 1837, consecrated bishop, July 38.

introducing differences of faith and separations of opinion among persons too young to judge on such difficult matters, *for* themselves. The result is, what I have already stated.

They beg, at the same time, to return the Bishop their warm and cordial acknowledgements; and to assure him of their high esteem.

My Dear Sir | Faithfully Yours

W. H. Murray Esquire CHARLES DICKENS

To JOHN FORSTER, [?29 AUGUST 1843]

Extract in F, IV, i, 296. *Date:* according to Forster, "at the close of August", from Broadstairs,[1] and "a few days" before *To* Felton, 1 Sep; but clearly not earlier than 29 Aug, to allow time for a whole day since CD's return from London.

I performed an insane match against time of eighteen miles by the milestones in four hours and a half, under a burning sun the whole way. I could get no sleep at night, and really began to be afraid I was going to have a fever. You may judge in what kind of authorship-training I am to-day. I could as soon eat the cliff as write about anything.

To C. C. FELTON, 1 SEPTEMBER 1843

MS Berg Collection. *Address:* By the Caledonia Mail Packet | Professor Felton | Cambridge | Massachusetts | United States.

Broadstairs, Kent. First September 1843.

My Dear Felton. If I thought it in the nature of things that you and I could ever agree on paper touching a certain Chuzzlewitian question whereupon Forster tells me you have remarks to make, I should immediately walk into the same tooth and nail. But as I don't—I won't. Contenting myself with this prediction—that one of these years and days, you will write or say to me "My dear Dickens you were right, though rough, and did a world of good, though you got most thoroughly hated for it." To which I shall reply, "My dear Felton, I looked a long way off and not immediately under my nose, *a*and I value their hatred, being haters, just as much as I prized their love, being lovers—a little more indeed, for Nature formed them to be very constant in their prejudices, and not at all constant in their affections."*a* At which sentiment you will laugh, and I shall laugh; and then (for I foresee this will all happen in England) we shall call for another pot of porter, and two or three dozen of oysters.

Now don't you in your own heart and soul*b*—in that secretest of Feltonian chambers—*b*quarrel with me for this long silence? Not half so much as I quarrel with myself, I know; but if you could read half the letters I write to you

---

[1] Forster had probably been at Broadstairs recently: "Yesterday I promised Dickens to join him at Broadstairs this coming week" (Forster *to* Leigh Hunt, 19 Aug, MS BM).

aa; bb Not previously published.

in imagination, you would swear by me for the best of correspondents. The truth is, that when I have done my morning's work, down goes my Pen, and from that minute I feel it a positive impossibility to take it up again, until imaginary butchers and bakers wave me to my desk. I walk about brimful of letters, facetious descriptions, touching morsels, and pathetic friendships, but can't for the soul of me uncork myself. The Post-Office is my rock ahead. My average number of letters that *must* be written every day, is, at the least, a dozen. And you could no more know what I was writing to you spiritually, from the perusal of the bodily thirteenth, than you could tell from my hat what was going on in my head, or could read my heart on the surface of my flannel waistcoat.

This is a little fishing-place; intensely quiet; built on a cliff whereon—in the centre of a tiny semicircular bay—our house stands: the sea rolling and dashing under the windows. Seven miles out, are the Goodwin Sands (you've heard of the Goodwin Sands?) whence floating lights perpetually wink after dark, as if they were carrying on intrigues with the servants. Also there is a big lighthouse called the North Foreland on a hill behind the village—a severe parsonic light—which reproves the young and giddy floaters, and stares grimly out upon the sea. Under the cliff are rare good sands, where all the children assemble every morning and throw up impossible fortifications which the sea throws down again at high water. Old gentlemen and ancient ladies, flirt, after their own manner, in two reading rooms and on a great many scattered seats in the open air. Other old gentlemen look all day through telescopes and never see anything. In a bay-window in a one pair, sits from nine o'Clock to one, a gentleman with rather long hair and no neck-cloth who writes and grins as if he thought he were very funny indeed. His name is Boz. At one, he disappears, and presently emerges from a bathing machine, and may be seen—a kind of salmon-coloured porpoise—splashing about in the ocean. After that, he may be seen in another bay window on the ground floor, eating a strong lunch—after that, walking a dozen miles or so—or lying on his back in the sand, reading a book. Nobody bothers him unless they know he is disposed to be talked to; and I am told he is very comfortable indeed. He's as brown as a berry, and they *do* say, is a small fortune to the inn-keeper who sells beer and cold punch. But this is mere rumour. Sometimes he goes up to London (eighty miles or so, away) and then I'm told there is a sound in Lincolns Inn Fields at night, as of men laughing: together with a clinking of knives and forks and wine-glasses.

I never shall have been so near you since we parted aboard the George Washington, as next Tuesday. Forster, Maclise, and I—and perhaps Stanfield—are then going aboard the Cunard Steamer at Liverpool, to bid Macready good bye, and bring his wife away.[1] It will be a very hard parting. You will see and know him of course. We gave him a splendid dinner last Saturday at Richmond, whereat I presided with my accustomed grace. He is one of the noblest fellows in the world; and I would give a great deal that you and I should sit beside each other to see him play Virginius, Lear, or Werner—which I take to be, every one,

[1] Clearly written before CD received Marryat's letter (see next, and *To* Marryat, 6 Sep); but the close of the paragraph indicates his grounds for already thinking it inadvisable to go aboard.

the greatest piece of exquisite perfection that his lofty art is capable of attaining. His Macbeth, especially the last act, is a tremendous reality; but so indeed is almost everything he does.[1] You recollect perhaps that he was the guardian of our children while we were away. I love him dearly. *He has no letters from me: not even to you.*[2] Do not laugh, when I say that I have given him none, lest they should injure him; for I know how many head of vermin would eat into his heart if they could, that they might void their hatred even second-hand, upon a man I prized.[3] But pray tell Sumner, Ticknor, and such friends as you know I esteem, with what commendation and affectionate regard, I mention him through you.[4] If I could un-dedicate Nickleby, I would, until his return from America.*

You asked me, long ago, about Maclise. He is such a wayward fellow in his subjects,[5] that it would be next to impossible to write such an article as you were thinking of, about him. I wish you could form an idea of his Genius. One of these days, a book will come out—Moore's Irish Melodies[6]—entirely illustrated by him, on every page. *When* it comes, I'll send it to you. You will have some notion of him then. He is in great favor with the Queen, and paints secret pictures for her to put upon her husband's table on the morning of his birthday[7]

[1] All these parts except King Lear were acted by Macready in Boston.

* Not previously published.

[2] Mrs Macready called on Jane Carlyle on 19 Aug, asking if Carlyle could write him any letters; "she cannot bear the idea of his 'going merely as a player, without private recommendations'" (*Letters and Memorials*, I, 245). Carlyle wrote one to Emerson, referring to Macready's "dignified, generous, and every-way honorable deportment in private life" and concluding: "I have often said, looking at him as a manager of great London theatres, 'This Man, presiding over the unstablest, most chaotic province of English things, is the one public man among us who has dared to take his stand on what he understood to be *the truth*, and expect victory from that: he puts to shame our Bishops and Archbishops.' It is literally so" (*Correspondence of Emerson and Carlyle*, ed. J. Slater, p. 345). Macready presented the letter, with one from Harriet Martineau, on 16 Nov (*Letters of R. W. Emerson*, ed. R. L. Rusk, 1939, III, 223).

[3] There was some basis for this. A writer recently returned from America reported in the *Theatrical Journal* (11 Nov 43) that when Macready was expected, a number of New York critics "worked might and main to prejudice the playgoing public against him . . . indeed, one paper recommended, that as Macready was a friend of Dickens, they should give

him a reception accordingly". N. P. Willis contributed an attack on him to a Philadelphia paper (see Macready, *Diaries*, II, 233; 7 Nov 43). Nothing came of this opposition, owing to Macready's great success.

[4] Macready's *Diaries* mention frequent meetings with Felton and Sumner in Boston, and one with Ticknor.

[5] Maclise's paintings and drawings at this date include genre scenes, scenes from plays, numerous portraits, book illustrations (with a preference for fantasy and fairy tale) and some historical paintings; his work in fresco had only just begun (see *To* Maclise, 6 July) and his later concentration on epic and allegorical subjects could hardly have been foreseen.

[6] This edition was published in 1845 by Longman, who commissioned Maclise to do the designs. Moore's Preface speaks of his particular pleasure that "an Irish pencil has lent its aid to an Irish pen in rendering due homage to our country's ancient harp". For many of the preliminary sketches, according to Kate Perugini's recollections ("CD as a Lover of Art and Artists", *Magazine of Art*, N.S., Jan 1903, I, 128), CD, Catherine, and Georgina sat to him as models (perhaps in 1843)—but the illustrations are conventional figures, and do not look like portraits.

[7] Maclise in his letter to Forster about the pavilion in July (see *To* Maclise, 6 July, *fn*) says, "I have got a picture or two

—and the like. But if he has a care, he will leave his mark on more enduring things than Palace Walls.

And so Longfellow is married.[1] I remember her well; and could draw her portrait—in words—to the life. A very beautiful and gentle creature—and a proper love for a poet. My cordial remembrances and congratulations. Do they live in the house where we breakfasted?[2] *d*And does Longfellow find cold water as essential to matrimony as to a single life. I greatly desire to be enlightened on this head. *Do* ask him—in confidence. As to oysters—but I may be open to misconstruction, if I pursue that subject.*d*

I very often dream I am in America again; but strange to say, I never dream of you. I am always endeavouring to get home in disguise, and have a dreary sense of the distance. Apropos of dreams, is it not a strange thing if writers of fiction never dream of their own creations: recollecting I suppose, even in their dreams, that they have no real existence? *I* never dreamed of any of my own characters and I feel it so impossible, that I would wager Scott never did of his, real as they are. I had a good piece of absurdity in my head a night or two ago. I dreamed that somebody was dead. I don't know whom, but it's not to the purpose. It was a private gentleman and a particular friend; and I was greatly overcome when the news was broken to me (very delicately) by a gentleman in a cocked hat, top boots, and a sheet. Nothing else. "Good God", I said. "Is he dead!". "He is as dead Sir", rejoined the gentleman, "as a door-nail. But we must all die Mr. Dickens—sooner or later my dear Sir"—"Ah!" I said. "Yes. To be sure. Very true. But what did he die of?" The gentleman burst into a flood of tears, and said, in a voice broken by emotion, "He christened his youngest child, Sir, with a toasting-fork." I never in my life was so affected as at his having fallen a victim to this complaint. It carried a conviction to my mind that he never could have recovered. I knew that it was the most interesting and fatal malady in the world; and I wrung the gentleman's hand in a convulsion of respectful admiration—for I felt that this explanation did equal honor to his head and his heart!

What do you think of Mrs. Gamp? And how do you like the undertaker? I have a fancy that they are in your way. Oh Heaven such green woods as I was rambling among, down in Yorkshire, when I was getting that done, last July![3] For days and weeks, we never saw the sky but through green boughs; and all day long, I cantered over such soft moss and turf that the horse's feet scarcely made a sound upon it. We have some friends in that part of the country (close to Castle Howard, where Lord Morpeth's father dwells in state—*in* his Park indeed) who are the jolliest of the jolly: keeping a big old country house, with an ale cellar

---

to paint in addition". One of the pictures then commissioned was *Undine*, which the Queen gave to Prince Albert as a birthday present on 26 Aug 43 (Osborne Catalogue, 1876).

[1] On 13 July; he had sent CD the news on 15 June: "I am afraid you will think I have *repudiated*. It is not so. But of late my heart has turned my brains out of doors. I am to be married in a few weeks; and

take the liberty, in consequence, of neglecting my friends. This I trust you will forgive" (*Letters of H. W. Longfellow*, ed. A. Hilen, II, 542; although only a rough draft survives, no reason to suppose letter not sent).

[2] See *To* Forster, 30 Jan 42, *fn.*

dd Not previously published.

[3] Probably the proofs; see *To* Forster, 6 or 7 July.

something larger than a reasonable church, and everything like Goldsmith's bear dances, "in a concatenation accordingly". Just the place for you, Felton! We performed some madnesses there, in the way of forfeits, pic-nics, rustic games, inspections of ancient monasteries at midnight[1] when the moon was shining; that would have gone to your heart, and as Mr. Weller says, "come out on the other side."[2]

*e*I was going to say a great deal about Mrs. Felton, and the good it would do her to bring her to England, but Kate is going to write to her by this Mail:[3] which is much better. Our domestic news is slight but portentous. Coming events cast their shadows before. I have visions of a fifth child, sometimes.*e*

Write soon My Dear Felton, and if I write to you less often than I would, believe that my affectionate heart is with you always. Loves and regards to all friends, from Yours ever and ever CHARLES DICKENS

*f*P.S. I heard from Hamlet[4] by the last packet.[5] He seems to be a prey to Gentle Melancholy. But he was a Good fellow, and I believe as honestly and disinterestedly attached to me, as a Man could be. I wish you could have seen his lady love. Quite a practical joke, she was.*f*

To W. C. MACREADY, 1 SEPTEMBER 1843

MS Morgan Library.

Broadstairs | First September 1843.

My Dear Macready.

I have lately had great doubts of the propriety of my seeing you on board the Steamer. It will be crowded with Americans at this season of the year; and believe me, they are not the people you suppose them to be. So strongly have I felt that my accompanying you on board, would be, after the last Chuzzlewit, *fatal*[6] to your success, and certain to bring down upon you every species of insult and outrage, that I have all along determined within myself to remain in the Hotel, and charge the Landlord to keep my being there, a secret.

But this morning I have heard from Marryatt[7] to whom Stanfield had chanced

---

[1] According to T. P. Cooper, *With Dickens in Yorkshire* (York, [1913]), they visited Kirkham Abbey as well as Old Malton Abbey.

[2] "'Sights, Sir,' resumed Mr. Weller, 'as 'ud penetrate your benevolent heart, and come out on the other side'" (*Pickwick*, Ch. 16).

ee: ff Not previously published.

[3] A letter from Catherine to unknown correspondent, 2 Sep 43, "Charles has written to your husband and speaks for himself. My children are all well and enjoying themselves . . . We were so glad to hear of Mr. Longfellow's marriage"

(extract in C. F. Libbie catalogue, 17 Mar 1919), is almost certainly to Mrs Felton.

[4] George Putnam; see *To* Felton, 29 Apr 42, *fn*.

[5] Probably the *Independence*, which had arrived on 25 Aug, having left Boston on 9 Aug.

[6] Underlined twice.

[7] Mis-spelt thus in MS. Marryat may have been already in London; his letter to Forster, 24 Aug, shows that he expected to see him there after 28 Aug, and on 3 Sep he called on Macready (*Letters of Marryat*, I, 139; *Diaries*, II, 219).

to mention our Liverpool design.[1] And he so emphatically and urgently implores me, for your sake, not even to go to Liverpool, that I instantly renounce the delight of being among the last to say God bless you. For when a man who knows the country confirms me in my fears, I am as morally certain of their foundation in Truth and freedom from exaggeration, as I am that I live.

If you but knew one hundredth part of the malignity, the monstrous falsehood, the beastly attacks even upon Catherine;[2] which were published all over America, even while I was there, on my mere confession that the country had disappointed me—confessions wrung from me in private society, before I had written a word upon the people—you would question all this, as little as I do. Soon after you receive this, I hope to come to Clarence Terrace to shake you by the hand.[3]

And now my dear Macready, I have one request to make to you; the indisputable expediency of which is as clearly presented before my eyes, as if it were written in fire upon the wall: Whatever you see or hear stated of me—whatever is addressed to you or to anybody else in your presence—never contradict it, never take offence at it, never claim me for your friend, or champion me in any way.[4] I not only absolve you from any such office, but I distinctly entreat you to consider silence upon all such topics, your duty to those who are nearest and dearest to you. It is enough for me that while you are away, you hold me in your heart. I have no desire to be upon your lips. Nor have I the faintest glimmering of a wish that you should say any monstrous assertions to my disparagement are false, because you know them—knowing me—to be so. Every anxiety of my breast, points in an exactly opposite direction.

Further—do not write to me through the post, but enclose any letter to me, in some other one, and let it come that way. And do not be shaken out of this by your own prepossessions or by anything else. For I *know* that such precaution is necessary—though I do not know that I should have had the courage to tell you so, but for the indescribable earnestness of Marryatt, who gives expression, in a perfect agony of language, to every misgiving that has haunted me for months past.

Ever My Dear Macready | Your affectionate friend
CHARLES DICKENS

I wish to Heaven I could un-dedicate Nickleby until you come home again.

[1] Macready's diary entry for 1 Sep runs: "Forster told me at dinner that he had written a very strong letter to Dickens, endeavouring to dissuade him from accompanying me on board the steamship. I thought for Dickens's sake he was quite right, but did not feel the full . . . mischief to myself". On receiving the present letter on 2 Sep Macready noted that it was "generous, affectionate, and most friendly. But why did he say *Marryat* had written when it was *Forster*?" (*Diaries*, II, 218). Macready was needlessly suspicious, and failed to distinguish Forster's advice (not to go on board) from Marryat's ("not even to go to Liverpool"). Presumably CD did not mention Forster because the "strong letter" merely confirmed his own doubts.

[2] No such attacks have yet been traced.

[3] CD did so the next day (Macready, *Diaries*, II, 219): "Took leave of H. Smith and Dickens, who were most affectionate".

[4] Macready would not have defended *Chuzzlewit*; he had just read the Sep No., and thought it "as bitter as it is powerful . . . I am grieved to read the book" (*ibid.*). In his American diary entries there are scarcely any references to CD, though he met many of his friends; but shortly after landing he "defended and explained as I best could his morbid feeling about the States" to a Mr Penn, who said CD "must

To JOHN FORSTER, [?3 SEPTEMBER 1843]

Extract in F, IV, i, 296. *Date:* "from Broadstairs" according to Forster; presumably the day after their meeting in London 2 Sep (Macready, *Diaries*, II, 219).

Your main and foremost reason for doubting Marryat's judgment,[1] I can at once destroy. It had occurred to me many times; I have mentioned the thing to Kate more than once; and I had intended *not* to go on board, charging Radley to let nothing be said of my being in his house. I have been prevented from giving any expression to my fears by a misgiving that I should seem to attach, if I did so, too much importance to my own doings. But now that I have Marryat at my back, I have not the least hesitation in saying that I am certain he is right. I have very great apprehensions that the *Nickleby* dedication will damage Macready. Marryat is wrong in supposing it is not printed in the American editions, for I have myself seen it in the shop windows of several cities. If I were to go on board with him, I have not the least doubt that the fact would be placarded all over New York, before he had shaved himself in Boston. And that there are thousands of men in America who would pick a quarrel with him on the mere statement of his being my friend,[2] I have no more doubt than I have of my existence. You have only doubted Marryat because it is impossible for *any man* to know what they are in their own country, who has not seen them there.

To MISS BURDETT COUTTS, 5 SEPTEMBER 1843

MS Morgan Library. *Address:* Miss Burdett Coutts | (Lord De Grey's)[3] | Putney.

Broadstairs. | Fifth September 1843.

Dear Miss Coutts.

All of a sudden it occurred to me the other day that if I went to Liverpool with Macready they would bowstring his throat in New York; so tightly that not a word should come out of it upon the stage—and drive him out of the country, straightway. While I was deliberating whether this was probable in the abstract, or I was like Dennis (who after writing a satire on the French Nation, fled from

have been ungrateful, and therefore a bad man"; and a little later, suffering from the "unredeemed scoundrels" of the press, he noted, "I disagree with Dickens whilst I quite sympathize with his disgust at these wretches" (*Diaries*, II, 224, 231).

[1] Evidently Forster was reluctant to let CD give up the whole expedition, and thought Marryat exaggerated the danger. In introducing the letter he says nothing of his own earlier advice, which he had possibly forgotten: "a word from our excellent friend Captain Marryat, startling to all of us except Dickens himself, struck him out of our party". Stanfield and Maclise did not go either; Forster met Macready at Liverpool on 4 Sep, dined with him and his wife and sister, and alone

went on board the *Caledonia* on 5 Sep (*Diaries*, II, 220).

[2] American threats against CD were referred to in the introduction to "The American's Apostrophe to Boz" in *A Book of Ballads*, edited by Bon Gaultier, 1845 ("some of [the] more fiery spirits threw out playful hints as to the propriety of gouging the 'strannger', and furnishing him with a permanent suit of tar and feathers"), and such threats are burlesqued in the ballad itself. American violence was also the subject of several comic ballads in Bon Gaultier's "A Night at Peleg Longfellow's", *Fraser's*, Aug 43.

[3] Lord Lieutenant of Ireland; he had a house in Putney which was evidently let to Miss Coutts while he was out of London.

the English Coast on catching sight of a French ship in the distance: thinking it must be despatched to seize and bear him off)[1] the Postman brought me a note from Marryatt, adjuring me not to go, or Macready was "done for". As he knows the virtuous Americans pretty well and as I think I do too, I immediately abandoned my intention. And so it came to pass that I sat down to Chuzzlewit quietly, and am now in the heart of it. Under other circumstances I should have been reporting to you this week, touching the Ragged Schools.[2]

I find that they are only open on Sundays and Thursdays. Next Thursday *week*,[3] in the evening, I will take my seat among the fluttering rags of Saffron Hill. If I have finished my Number, and can remain in town next day, I will come out to Putney. If I should be obliged to return here on Friday morning, I will punctually write you a full account of the school, the pupils, and the masters; and all concerning them.[4]

Charley and his sisters desire their loves to be faithfully conveyed to you. The piano is gone, and the flute is out of hearing—at Dover. But a barrel organ, a monkey, a punch, a Jim Crow, and a man who plays twenty instruments at once and doesn't get the right sound out of any one of them, are hovering in the neighbourhood. Also a blind man who was in a Sea Fight in his youth; and after playing the hundredth psalm on a flageolet, recites a description of the Engagement.

Charley is so popular with the boatmen, that I begin to think of Robinson

---

[1] The satire was the play *Liberty Asserted*, 1704; the story is told in Cibber's *Lives* and in Swift's "Thoughts on Various Subjects" (*Polite Conversation*, ed. Herbert Davis and Louis Landa, 1957, p. 250).

[2] The first reference to them in CD's letters to Miss Coutts. *To* Southwood Smith, 6 Mar 43, shows CD's interest in the general problem, and he may have discussed writing an article on the subject for Macvey Napier when they met in May (*To* Napier, 12 Sep 43). The movement had begun many years before, but the name "Ragged School" was first used by S. R. Starey, a lawyer's clerk (*d.* 1904), Treasurer of Field-lane Ragged School (opened 1841), who appealed for help in an advertisement in *The Times* of 18 Feb 43: "RAGGED SCHOOLS.—FIELD-LANE SABBATH SCHOOL, 65, West-street, Saffron-hill.—A room has been opened and supported in this wretched neighbourhood for upwards of 12 months, and religious instruction imparted to the poor by a few laymen of the churches of England and Scotland and Protestant Dissenters. Their benevolent endeavours have been greatly blessed: about 50 (adults and children) assemble on the Sundays, likewise on Monday and Thursday evenings.

The application for admission far exceeds the room engaged, and the teachers are desirous of taking another adjoining, but are necessitated to APPEAL to the Christian public for pecuniary assistance to carry out their designs. Donations will be thankfully received by the Rev. P. Lorimer, 12, Colebrook-row, Islington; W. D. Owen, Esq., Secretary, 30, Great Sutton-street, Clerkenwell; or by the Treasurer, Mr. S. R. Starey, 17, Ampton-street, Gray's-inn-road. Left off garments sent to the schools will be carefully distributed". Starey subsequently wrote to Miss Coutts (*To* Starey, 12 Sep 43). In the Report of the Education Committee of the Statistical Society on the Borough of Finsbury (read 16 Jan 43) the special needs of the Saffron Hill area were noted ("proverbially the dirtiest in London; very possibly the dirtiest in the world"), but searches by three agents found "no dame or common day school", and made no reference to Starey's school. The best account of the movement is P. A. W. Collins, "Dickens and the Ragged Schools", *D*, LV (1959), 94–109.

[3] Underlined twice.

[4] See *To* Miss Coutts, 16 Sep 43.

Crusoe, and the propriety of living in-land. I saw him yesterday through a telescope, miles out at sea, steering an enormous fishing-smack, to the unspeakable delight of seven gigantic companions, clad in oilskin. Katey is supposed to be secretly betrothed, in as much as a very young gentleman (so young, that being unable to reach the knocker, he called attention to the door by kicking it) called the other evening, and being gratified in a mysterious, I may say quite a melodramatic, request, to speak with the Nurse, produced a live crab, which he said he had "promised her".

I hope Miss Meredith is past the fowl stage, and getting on towards beef. I beg to be cordially remembered to her.

Dear Miss Coutts | Always Yours faithfully and obliged

CHARLES DICKENS

To JOHN OVERS, 5 SEPTEMBER 1843

MS Huntington Library.

Broadstairs, Kent. | Fifth September 1843.

Dear Mr. Overs

I received your five pound note, quite safely, this morning. I take it for granted that if you could not comfortably afford to return it, you would never dream of sending it to me.

I shall be glad to hear whether you do anything satisfactory with Mr. Young. Don't you think you could suggest to him the feasibility of your writing some original articles in the paper? It is much read by working men in London. Couldn't you hit upon some subject of interest to them (and consequently to other people of liberal opinions) and suggest it to Mr. Young? I *fear*—this is strictly between ourselves—that your Guildhall attendance[1] may turn out unprofitable in more ways than one. But be as patient as you can, because the difficulty of holding any moderate recompense in that way (I mean the newspaper way) would be nothing to the difficulty of seizing it.

Faithfully Yours always

CHARLES DICKENS

I hadn't time to tell you the other day, how immeasurably better I thought you looking.

To FREDERICK MARRYAT, 6 SEPTEMBER 1843

MS University of Texas.

Broadstairs, Kent | Sixth September 1843.

My Dear Marryat,

A hundred thanks for your kind note, and the renewal of your hospitable invitation—and for your truly friendly suggestion in the joint matter of Macready and Liverpool. The same thought had occurred to me, but I felt it would

---

[1] Probably an attempt to obtain some police court reporting; there was a regular police court there, also occasional meetings of the Common Council.

seem so preposterous to people who didn't "know our country",[1] that I really lacked the courage to give it utterance. As soon as I heard what you had said, I resolved, of course, to keep away—and did so.

It gives me great pleasure to find that you like the tickling. I shall go in again before I have done, and give the Eagle a final poke under his fifth rib.[2]

I fear I cannot say with any degree of certainty, sooner than the *third* week in October for the pleasures of Langham;[3] but please God I shall be ready about the 19th. or 20th. I will make this known to Maclise and Forster; and we will send you a threatening letter when the time approaches.

Kate (that's Mrs. Dickens) is very thankful for your kind recollection of her, and begs me to say that she hopes to have the pleasure of knowing your daughter[4] well. I fear however that she will not be fit for travelling. A coming event casts its shadow before. Still she can't make up her mind to a capital *No*[5] yet.

My Dear Marryat | Cordially Yours
CHARLES DICKENS

To FREDERICK DICKENS, 7 SEPTEMBER 1843

MS Benoliel Collection.

Broadstairs | Seventh September 1843

My Dear Fred

I have only time to say that we are all well, and here is the Money. Best regards and loves to all at pleasant Easthorpe.

Acknowledge safe receipt.

Affy. always

Frederick Dickens Esquire   CD.

---

[1] General Choke in *Chuzzlewit*, Ch. 21 (in the No. just published) says, "You come from England, and you do not know my country".

[2] Chs 33–4 in the Jan No.; introducing Hannibal Chollop ("Our backs is easy ris. We must be cracked-up, or they rises, and we snarls"), Elijah Pogram and the literary ladies. The "final poke" at the American Eagle may be Mark's description of how he would paint it: "I should want to draw it like a Bat, for its short-sightedness; like a Bantam, for its bragging; like a Magpie, for its honesty; like a Peacock, for its vanity; like an Ostrich, for putting its head in the mud, and thinking nobody sees it" (Ch. 34).

[3] Marryat had a small farm at Langham near Blakeney in Norfolk, and settled there in 1843. It was a cottage in the Eliza-bethan style, thatched and gabled; the dining-room walls were covered with Stanfield's illustrations for *Poor Jack*. Marryat had also invited Forster, Landseer, Maclise and Stanfield, but it is unlikely that any of them went. The plan was broached in his letter to Stanfield in Aug (before the 24th). On 9 Oct he wrote to Forster: "Dickens said he would come in the third week in October, others the second—so how is it to be? . . . I shall be most happy to see them all; but . . . if it has become really inconvenient, from their engagements, I should be sorry that they should come down and consider it a bore" (Florence Marryat, *Life and Letters of Captain Marryat*, 1872, II, 141–3 and 147).

[4] Blanche, the eldest, mentioned in Marryat's letter to Stanfield.

[5] Written very large.

To MR CAPEL,[1] [8 SEPTEMBER 1843]

Mention in next.

Thanking him for Stock Exchange subscriptions to the Elton Fund.

To [EDWARD MARJORIBANKS], 8 SEPTEMBER 1843*

MS Morgan Library. *Address:* clearly written to Marjoribanks, a banker and a fellow trustee of the Elton Fund.

Broadstairs, Kent | Eighth September 1843.

My Dear Sir

I think the Stock Exchange Subscription, all things considered, an excellent one. I assure you I should have thought Twenty Pounds a *most* satisfactory result. The suggestion was truly valuable.

I have written by this post to Mr. Capel. I think we had better enter all their names in the book. Perhaps it would be well to bracket them, "Stock Exchange"? I return you the list.

A Misgiving came over me that the quondam Dr. Kaye,[2] while tinkering his name into something else, might have permanently taken off the handle. But in the days when I met him he wore that appendage; and I didn't like to apply my shears to it without authority.

I begin to be afraid from the tone of your letters that you are going to set up an opposition Chuzzlewit.[3] If your mind be made up, you won't believe anything I may say to dissuade you. But I assure you it's a poor trade—nothing like banking.

My Dear Sir | Always Faithfully Yours
CHARLES DICKENS

N.B. | The *Original* Boz. | All others are Counterfeits.

To UNKNOWN CORRESPONDENT,[4] 8 SEPTEMBER 1843*

MS Colonel Richard Gimbel.

Broadstairs, Kent. | Eighth September 1843

Sir.

I thank you for your welcome and obliging note; and I beg to inform you, in

---

[1] A member of one of the several firms of stockbrokers of this name, probably James Capel & Co, brokers to Coutts, in which David Marjoribanks, Edward's nephew, was a partner.

[2] James Phillips Kay-Shuttleworth, MD (1804–77; *DNB*); on his marriage to Janet, daughter of Robert Shuttleworth, on 24 Feb 42, he assumed her name and arms by royal licence. His work as an educational reformer began in 1841; CD wrote to him on 28 Mar 46 about Ragged Schools (see Vol. IV).

[3] Marjoribanks did not publish anything.

[4] Correspondent's name, written bottom left, has been removed by a strip being cut off the paper right across it. Tops of a few letters show at the cut edge.

reply, that Chuzzlewit, like Pickwick and Nickleby, will be completed in Twenty Numbers.[1]

Faithfully Yours
CHARLES DICKENS

To MADAME SALA,[2] [?AUGUST-SEPTEMBER 1843]

Mention in G. A. Sala, *Things I Have Seen and People I Have Known*, 1894, I, 59, as "from Broadstairs, or Brighton, or some other watering-place". *Date*: 1843, as Sala says he was "about fifteen" and that *Punch* had started "some two years previously"; in the period when CD was at Broadstairs and making occasional visits to London.

An amicable letter, making an appointment for Sala and his mother to meet him at ten o'clock on a given morning at the Euston Hotel.

To MACVEY NAPIER, 12 SEPTEMBER 1843

MS British Museum. *Address:* By favor of Thomas Hood Esquire | Professor Napier | Castle Street | Edinburgh.

Broadstairs, Kent. | Twelfth September 1843

My Dear Sir

I will not offer any apology for introducing to you, Mr. Hood—a personal friend of mine whom I greatly value; and a public friend of yours, I have not the least doubt, already. If his writings have not found for him greater favor in your eyes than any *I* could bespeak, then am I the most mistaken of Edinburgh citizens.

I am going to write to you in a week or two, upon the subject we spoke of when you were last in London,[3] in reference to which, an idea has now and then occurred to me: though I am yet sadly in want of your suggestive help.—In the meantime Mrs. Dickens begs to unite with me in cordial regards to yourself and daughter.[4] And I am always

My Dear Sir | Faithfully Yours
CHARLES DICKENS

Professor Napier.

[1] *Chuzzlewit* was so advertised before publication, but the few advertisements during 1843 did not mention it, and it is not stated on the covers. On 20 Jan 44 the *Athenæum* advt had "to be completed in Twenty Monthly Numbers", perhaps as a result of such inquiries.

[2] Henrietta Catherine Florentina Simon Sala (1788–1860), singer and actress: see Vol. I, p. 302*n*. Was singing at Brighton Town Hall (for the first time for some years) on 11 Sep 43; was also billed to sing at a Matinée Musicale, but "found she was obliged to leave for London" (*La Belle Assemblée*, Oct 43). According to Sala, she had written to CD reminding him of "the old St. James's Theatre days" and asking him to see her son, who wanted employ-ment as an artist. George Augustus (1828–96; *DNB*) was her youngest son; had been at school in Paris and then at the studio of Carl Schiller in Charlotte Street; was precocious and gifted, and his mother hoped to get him an introduction to Mark Lemon. In *Things I Have Seen* Sala describes the interview, recalling CD as "not quite the dandy and extremely youthful-looking 'Boz' whom I had seen in Braham's green-room on the first night of *The Village Coquettes*"; he says that CD gave him a letter of introduction to Lemon, but he was not taken on as a *Punch* illustrator.

[3] See *To* Napier, 12 May 43.

[4] Presumably the eldest of Napier's three daughters: see Vol. II, p. 354.

To THOMAS HOOD, 12 SEPTEMBER 1843

MS Berg Collection.

Broadstairs, Kent. | Twelfth September 1843

My Dear Hood

Since I received your first letter, I have been pegging away, tooth *and nail*, *at Chuzzlewit*. Your supplementary note[1] gave me a pang such as one feels when a friend has to knock twice at the street door, before anybody opens it.

There can be no doubt in the mind of any honorable man, that the circumstances under which you signed your agreement, are of the most disgraceful kind in so far as Mr. Colburn is concerned. There can be no doubt that he took a money-lending, bill-broking, Jew clothes-bagging, Saturday Night pawnbroking advantage of your temporary situation. There is as little doubt (so I learn from Forster who had previously given me exactly your version of the whole circumstances) that like most pieces of knavery, this precious document is a mere piece of folly, and just a scrap of wastepaper wherein Mr. Shoberl might wrap his dirty snuff.[2] But I am sorry—speaking with a backward view to the feasibility of placing you in a better situation with Colburn—that you flung up the Editorship of the Magazine. I think you did so at a bad time, and wasted your strength in consequence.

When a thing is done, it is of no use giving advice—not even when it can be as frankly rejected as mine can be by you. But have you *quite* determined to reject his offer of the Thirty Guineas per sheet? Have you placed it, or resolved to place it, out of your power to enter into such an arrangement if you should feel disposed to do so, bye and bye? On my word I would pause before I did so—and if I did, then, most decidedly, I would open a communication with Bentley, and try to get that Magazine.[3] For to any man, I don't care who he is, the

---

[1] Hood's second note, probably of 11 Sep, had mentioned his idea of reviewing *Chuzzlewit*, not in the *New Monthly*, because of his objections to the management, nor in the *Athenæum*, "for certain reasons", but possibly in the *Edinburgh*; no review appeared (MS Huntington; *Letters of Thomas Hood*, ed. P. Morgan, p. 554).

[2] CD is clearly answering the earlier of Hood's two letters, 5 Sep 43 (extracts from catalogue source, *op. cit.*, p. 553) complaining of the unfair terms of what Colburn, "the little Shylock", "dares to call an agreement" (of Sep 41) for the editing of the *New Monthly Magazine*. Hood had resigned the editorship in Aug because he disapproved of the way the magazine was conducted, resenting especially the interference of Colburn and Shoberl; Colburn was insisting that under their agreement Hood was bound to continue to contribute articles to the *New Monthly* after his resignation. Forster, who was acting as go-between in the negotiations, had had an "unsatisfactory" interview with Colburn on 14 Aug at which Colburn offered Hood 30 guineas a sheet for articles if he would consent to contribute without legal obligation—Colburn "to have the whole Copyright, and not to interfere with contributions elsewhere (excepting Bentley's and Ainsworth's Magazines)" (Forster *to* Hood, 14 Aug 43; MS Bristol Reference Library). Hood had made, and told CD as a secret, "an arrangement with Bradbury to contribute to 'Punch'. . . . light occasional work for odd times", but needed a regular source of income. Writing to Mrs Hood, 20 Sep 43, Hood says, "I hardly think Dickens understands why I resigned" (*op. cit.*, p. 561).

[3] Hood applied to Cunningham & Mortimer, publishers of *Ainsworth's Magazine*, of whose generosity to contributors he had heard from CD and Barham; he was surprised to receive a reply offering

Editorship of a Monthly Magazine, on tolerable terms, is a matter of too much moment, in its pecuniary importance and certainty, to be flung away as of little worth. It would be to me, I assure you.

I send you letters for Jeffrey and Napier.[1] If the former should not be in Edinburgh, you will find him at his country place, Craigcrooch,[2] within three or four miles of the City. Should you see Wilson, give him a hundred hearty greetings from me. And should you see the Blackwoods[3] don't believe a word they say to you. Moir (their Delta) is a very fine fellow, and you will like him much. In all probability he will come to see you, should he know of your being in Edinburgh.

A pleasant journey and a pleasant return! Mrs. Dickens unites with me in best regards to Mrs. Hood. And I am always

My Dear Hood | Faithfully Yours

Thomas Hood Esquire   CHARLES DICKENS

P.S. The light of Mr. Colburn's countenance has not shone upon *me* in these parts.[4] May I remain in outer darkness!

To T. J. SERLE, 12 SEPTEMBER 1843

MS Mr Peter Brandt.

Broadstairs. | Twelfth September 1843

My Dear Serle

I shall see you tomorrow evening, of course. Will you send Miss Elton the enclosed? She ought to have had it *last Friday*, but I had no memorandum of her address.

Faithfully Yours always

T. J. Serle Esquire   CHARLES DICKENS

him 16 guineas a sheet, "the highest terms the Magazine can afford", from Ainsworth, since CD had told him that Ainsworth was "out of the Editorship" and this had been confirmed by Barham and by Hurst of Colburn's. He wrote to CD to ask whether he knew "anything of the Ainsworth affair", and to have his view of it, telling him: "My *notion* is to see *Mortimer* tomorrow & know the rights of it—to decline the thing—& reopen an old arrangement with Bentley" (Hood *to* CD, [19 Oct 43]; *op. cit.*, pp. 569–70). On 21 Oct Hood applied for the editorship of *Bentley's* and was told that "Mr. Wilde" was editor (J. C. Reid, *Thomas Hood*, 1963, p. 203).

[1] Hood had asked particularly for these in his letter of 11 Sep.

[2] Thus in MS; Hood dined at Craigcrook with Jeffrey, "who sent his love"— and also "spent a very happy evening with Moir"; Wilson and Napier were away (Hood *to* CD, 19 Oct 43).

[3] Alexander (1805–43) and Robert (1807–52): see Vol. II, p. 317*n*. CD owed them a grudge for Warren's review of *American Notes*.

[4] Hood had written, "Hurst [*the publisher*] told me the other day Colburn had left Broadstairs, for he did not like it. Perhaps he met *you* in his walks".

To S. R. STAREY, 12 SEPTEMBER 1843

MS Boston Public Library.

Broadstairs, Kent. | Twelfth September 1843.

Sir.

I take a great interest in the advertizement of the Ragged School;[1] and am deeply impressed by a sense of the great benevolence and importance of the scheme. I have also promised a wealthy and influential person to whom you made application for support, that I would see your pupils, and take an opportunity of being present in the school. I do not suppose that you would consider a visit from me, likely to be prompted by idle curiosity; and I merely mention this latter circumstance as one that is likely to interest you.

I shall be in town on Thursday; and if you will kindly write me word (addressed to my house in town) at what hour that evening, I could visit the school and *see it in its usual aspect* without giving you any inconvenience, I will be punctual in coming—bringing two, or at most three friends, along with me, if I have your permission.[2]

I am Sir | Your faithful Servant

Mr. Samuel R. Starey   CHARLES DICKENS

To JOHN FORSTER, [?14 SEPTEMBER 1843]

Extract in F, IV, iii, 323. *Date:* according to Forster, 18 Feb 44; but neighbouring extracts contain other dating errors, and the only Nos in which Betsey Prig appears are Oct and Nov 43 and June 44. In this period the only recorded visit to the Ragged School (perhaps with "two, or at most three friends", and certainly with Stanfield) was on 14 Sep 43.

Stanfield and Mac have come in, and we are going to Hampstead to dinner. I leave Betsey Prig as you know, so don't you make a scruple about leaving Mrs. Harris.[3] We shall stroll leisurely up, to give you time to join us, and dinner will be on the table at Jack Straw's at four... In the very improbable (surely impossible?) case of your not coming, we will call on you at a quarter before eight, to go to the ragged school.

---

[1] See *To* Miss Coutts, 5 Sep; no advertisement later than that of 18 Feb has been found in *The Times* or *Morning Chronicle*; but E. Hodder (*Life and Work of the Seventh Earl of Shaftesbury*, 1886, I, 481–2) quotes under the date "February, 1843" a different advertisement, clearly somewhat later since, although the signatories are the same, the secretaryship had passed from Owen to Macdonald as in the advertisement of 30 Dec 43 (see *To* Starey, 29 Dec, *fn*). The later advertisement showed the average attendance to have gone up from 50 to 70; there was no Monday evening opening; and as well as appealing for donations it stated that those willing to assist as teachers would be cordially welcomed.

[2] For the visit, on which CD was accompanied by Stanfield, see *To* Miss Coutts, 16 Sep.

[3] CD either meant that any excuse of Forster's would be fictitious, or just possibly intended a reference to the projected life of Goldsmith (1848), already so long worked on as to warrant the joke.

To MISS BURDETT COUTTS, 16 SEPTEMBER 1843

MS Mr Roger W. Barrett.

Broadstairs | Sixteenth September 1843

Dear Miss Coutts.

I wished very much to have had the pleasure of coming to Putney on Friday, and to have remained there that night, in compliance with your kind Invitation. But when I got to town on Thursday, I had still an unfinished number on my hands and mind. So I came back here again yesterday—too late for the post, or I would have saved it, and written to you. Pray tell Miss Meredith, with my best regards, that I have written the second chapter in the next number, with an eye to her experiences.[1] It is especially addressed to them, indeed.

On Thursday night, I went to the Ragged School; and an awful sight it is.[2] I blush to quote Oliver Twist[3] for an authority, but it stands on that ground, and is precisely such a place as the Jew lived in. The school is held in three most wretched rooms on the first floor of a rotten house; every plank, and timber, and brick, and lath, and piece of plaster in which, shakes as you walk. One room is devoted to the girls: two to the boys. The former are much the better-looking—I cannot say better dressed, for there is no such thing as dress among the seventy pupils; certainly not the elements of a whole suit of clothes, among them all. I have very seldom seen, in all the strange and dreadful things I have seen in London and elsewhere, anything so shocking as the dire neglect of soul and body exhibited in these children. And although I know; and am as sure as it is possible for one to be of anything which has not happened; that in the pro-digious misery and ignorance of the swarming masses of mankind in England, the seeds of its certain ruin are sown, I never saw that Truth so staring out in hopeless characters, as it does from the walls of this place. The children in the Jails are almost as common sights to me as my own;[4] but these are worse, for they have not arrived there yet, but are as plainly and certainly travelling there, as they are to their Graves.

The Masters are extremely quiet, honest, good men. You may suppose they are, to be there at all. It is enough to break one's heart to get at the place: to say nothing of getting at the children's minds afterwards. They are well-grounded in the Scotch—the Glasgow—system[5] of elementary instruction, which is an

---

[1] Ch. 25 "Is in part Professional; and furnishes the Reader with some Valuable Hints in relation to the Management of a Sick Chamber". See *To* Forster, 6 or 7 July, *fn.*

[2] The visit is later described in *To* the Editor of the *Daily News*, 4 Feb 46, and "A Sleep to Startle Us", *Household Words*, 13 Mar 52 (*Miscellaneous Papers*, ed. B. W. Matz, 1914).

[3] Ch. 8. Fagin's house was in Saffron Hill, near Field Lane; the Field Lane Ragged School was at 65 West Street, Saffron Hill.

[4] See *To* Napier, below. A leading

article in the *Examiner* of 16 Sep 43, "Juvenile Imprisonment in the Metro-polis" (possibly by CD), deplored the neglect of juvenile prisoners, describing the case of three boys, the eldest nine years old, convicted of felony (stealing some toys from a shop), who had been in every prison in the metropolis in the last two years, but could not read or write.

[5] i.e. the methods introduced by David Stow (1793–1864; *DNB*) in the infant school and teachers' seminary which he opened in Glasgow in 1826 and 1827, and described in his book *The Training System, Moral Training School, and Normal*

excellent one; and they try to reach the boys by kindness. To gain their attention in any way, is a difficulty, quite gigantic. To impress them, even with the idea of a God, when their own condition is so desolate, becomes a monstrous task. To find anything within them—who know nothing of affection, care, love, or kindness of any sort—to which it is possible to appeal, is, at first, like a search for the philosopher's stone. And here it is that the viciousness of insisting on creeds and forms in educating such miserable beings, is most apparent. To talk of Catechisms, outward and visible signs, and inward and spiritual graces, to these children, is a thing no Bedlamite would do, who saw them. To get them, whose whole lives from the moment of their birth, are one continued punishment, to believe even in the judgment of the Dead and a future state of punishment for their sins, requires a System in itself.

The Masters examined them, however, on these points, and they answered very well—sometimes in a shout all at once, sometimes only one boy, sometimes half a dozen. I put a great many questions to them upon their answers, which they also answered very well. There was one boy, who had been selling Lucifer Matches all day in the streets—not much older than Charley—clad in a bit of a sack—really a clever child, and handsome too, who gave some excellent replies, though, of course, in language that would be very strange in your ears. Hardly any of them can read yet. For the masters think it most important to impress them at first with some distinction (communicated in dialogue) between right and wrong. And I quite agree with them. They sell trifles in the streets, or beg (or some, I dare say, steal) all day; and coming tired to this place at night, are very slow to pick up any knowledge. That they *do* come at all, is, *I* think, a Victory.

They knew about the Saviour, & the Day of Judgment. The little match boy told me that God was no respecter of persons, and that if he (the match boy) prayed "as if he meant it", and didn't keep company with bad boys, and didn't swear, and didn't drink, he would be as readily forgiven in Heaven, as the Queen would. They understood that the Deity was everywhere, and had knowledge of everything; and that there was something in them which they couldn't see or lay their hands on, which would have to account to him after they were dead. They were very quiet and orderly, while the Master said a little prayer; and sang a short hymn before they broke up. The singing was evidently a great treat, and the match boy came out very strong, with a Shake, and a Second.

I am happy to say I afforded great amusement at first—in particular by having a pair of white trousers on, and very bright boots. The latter articles of dress, gave immense satisfaction, and were loudly laughed at. Mr. Stanfield, who was with me,—in consequence of looking rather burly and fat in the small room—was received with a perfect cheer; and his sudden retirement, in consequence of being overcome by the closeness of the atmosphere, and the dread of Typhus Fever, was much regretted. When they saw that I was quite serious, and had an

Training Seminary (1836; 10th edn, 1854); these methods included group teaching, oral instruction beginning with concrete objects, and "learning by doing" (John Manning, *Dickens on Education*, 1959, pp. 128–9). Dr Kay (later Kay-Shuttleworth) visited it and recommended in 1841 a further Government grant.

interest in their answers, they became quiet, and took pains. They were still better-behaved on seeing that I stood with my hat off, before the master (though I heard one boy express his opinion that I certainly wasn't a barber, or I should have cut my hair); and so far as their behaviour is concerned, I should not have the least doubt of my ability—or that of anybody else who went the right way to work—to reduce them to order in five minutes, at any time.

The school is miserably poor, you may believe, and is almost entirely supported by the teachers themselves. If they could get a better room (the house they are in, is like an ugly dream); above all, if they could provide some convenience for washing; it would be an immense advantage. The moral courage of the teachers is beyond all praise. They are surrounded by every possible adversity, and every disheartening circumstance that can be imagined. Their office is worthy of the apostles.

My heart so sinks within me when I go into these scenes, that I almost lose the hope of ever seeing them changed. Whether this effort will succeed, it is quite impossible to say. But that it is a great one, beginning at the right end, among thousands of immortal creatures, who cannot, in their present state, be held accountable for what they do, it is *as* impossible to doubt. That it is much too squalid and terrible to meet with any wide encouragement, I greatly fear. There is a kind of delicacy which is not at all shocked by the existence of such things, but is excessively shocked to know of them; and I am afraid it will shut its eye on Ragged Schools until the Ragged Scholars are perfect in their learning out of doors, when Woe to whole garments.

I need not say, I am sure, that I deem it an experiment most worthy of your charitable hand. The reasons I have, for doubting its being generally assisted, all assure me that it will have an interest for you. For I know you to be very, very far-removed, from all the Givers in all the Court Guides between this, and China.

If you will let me know whether there is anything you would like me to do in the matter, I shall be truly rejoiced to do it—I shall certainly visit the school again; for some important topics have occurred to me, in reference to which, I want to offer strong suggestions to the Masters.

We return to town on the second of next month. I am going down to Manchester for a couple of days, on the fifth, to preside at the re-opening of their Athenæum, whereat some couple of thousand people are to be assembled.[1] If you are at Putney on the Third or Fourth, perhaps you will let me come to see you.

With best regards to Miss Meredith—and Mr. Young[2] if the bird of passage known by that name be still with you—I am always Dear Miss Coutts

Yours faithfully and obliged

Miss Coutts.   CHARLES DICKENS

---

[1] See *To* Miss Coutts, 13 Oct.

[2] Charles Mayne Young (1777–1856; *DNB*), actor: see Vol. I, p. 592*n*. CD met his son Julian at Miss Coutts's on 29 May 46 (Julian Charles Young, *A Memoir of Charles Mayne Young*, 1871, II, 108).

To MACVEY NAPIER, 16 SEPTEMBER 1843

MS British Museum.

Confidential

Broadstairs, Kent. | Sixteenth September 1843

My Dear Sir

I hinted in a letter of introduction I gave Mr. Hood the other day to you, that I had been thinking of a subject for The Edinburgh.[1]

Now, would it meet the purposes of the Review, to come out strongly against any system of Education, based exclusively upon the principles of the Established Church? If it would, I should like to shew why such a thing as the Church Catechism is wholly inapplicable to the state of ignorance that now prevails; and why no system but one, so general in great religious principles as to include all creeds, can meet the wants and understandings of the Dangerous Classes of Society.

This is the only broad ground I could hold, consistently with what I feel and think, on such a subject. But I could give, in taking it, a description of certain voluntary places of instruction, called "The Ragged Schools", now existing in London—and of the schools in Jails[2]—and of the ignorance presented in such places, which would make a very striking paper—especially if they were put in strong comparison with the effort making, by subscription, to maintain exclusive Church Instruction.[3] I could shew these people in a state so miserable and so neglected, that their very nature rebels against the simplest religion—and that to convey to them the faintest outlines of any system of distinction between Right and Wrong, is in itself a Giant's task, before which Mysteries and Squabbles for Forms, *must* give way. Would this be too much for the Review? I shall be glad to know what you think.

My Dear Sir | Faithfully Yours

Professor Napier

CHARLES DICKENS

P.S. We should have to find a peg[4] to hang the paper on.—Perhaps you know of one.

[1] The proposed article was several times postponed, and never written.

[2] CD refers to a class in Newgate in "A Visit to Newgate" (written Nov 35), in *Sketches by Boz*, 1st series (1836). Schools for boys and girls at Tothill Fields in charge of the chaplain were established on the National System in Nov 35; the children learnt and worked on alternate days. Chesterton had a probably similar school at Coldbath Fields. But the case described in the *Examiner* article, 16 Sep, shows that they were ineffective. In Jan 43 Graham sent a circular letter to Chairmen of Quarter Sessions directing that, in accordance with the Report of the Inspectors of Prisons, schools with qualified instructors should be established in all prisons. CD described what he had seen in *To* the Editor of the *Daily News*, 4 Feb 46.

[3] Lord Ashley's Factories Regulation Bill, following the second Report of the Commissioners, had been thrown out because of the impossibility of getting the agreement of the nonconformist interests to the education clauses, which left the control of schools in the hands of the Church. The first large advertisement of the National Society for Promoting the Education of the Poor in the Principles of the Established Church had appeared in *The Times*, 15 Aug 43, covering over four columns, including the address at the Special Committee of 5 July and an extensive list of subscribers.

[4] See *To* Napier, 24 Oct 43.

To A. VAN LEE,[1] 16 SEPTEMBER 1843

MS[2] Free Library of Philadelphia. *Address:* M. Avan Lee | Amsterdam.

1 Devonshire Terrace | York Gate—Regents Park
September 16th. 1843

Sir.

I beg to acknowledge the receipt of your obliging letter, and to thank you for the terms in which it is expressed.

I am compelled to add, however, that it is not in my power to enter into any arrangement for the transmission of early proofs of my wrtings, with a view to their translation abroad, unless some distinct proposal is made to my publishers, upon which in the ordinary course of business they can form an opinion and report the same to me in consulting my views upon the subject.[3]

I believe there are difficulties and objections in the way of such an arrangement, unless it were attended with a certain profit to them.

I am Sir | Your faithful Servant

M. Avan Lee[4] | Amsterdam   CHARLES DICKENS

To THOMAS MITTON, 17 SEPTEMBER 1843*

MS Morgan Library. *Address:* Thomas Mitton Esquire.

Broadstairs, Kent. | Seventeenth September 1843

My Dear Mitton

As soon as I receive Smithson's communication, I will answer it in the needful way.[5] It gives me great delight to find him yielding so readily to your proposition; and I must say that I think he has always behaved like a Man in this matter.[6]

I am not surprised at your having enjoyed yourself at Easthorpe, for it is a most enjoyable place. I never saw such varieties of scenery crowded within so small a space, as on the Whitby Railroad.[7] From Devonshire to the Scottish Highlands, all the grades and diversities are there.

They write to me from Manchester 'Thursday, October the Sixth'. But Thursday is the *Fifth*. I suppose, however, that they are more likely to be wrong in the day of the month than the day of the week. Supposing it is Thursday, we will go down on Wednesday (staying with Fanny) and return on Friday.[8]

---

[1] Author of books on art and printing published in 1845 and 1848, and translator of Vinet's anthology of French writers in 1852, all published at Amsterdam (Brinkman, *Alphabetische Naamlijst van Bocken* . . . Amsterdam, 1858).

[2] In another hand, presumably Alfred Dickens's, except for signature: see *To* Mitton, 28 Sep, *fn.*

[3] CD's novels were early translated into Dutch; an anonymous translation of *Martin Chuzzlewit* appeared in 1843–4.

[4] Thus in MS.

[5] See *To* Smithson, 20 Sep 43, and *To* Mitton, 28 Sep 43.

[6] In a letter of 31 May 44 CD reminded Mitton that "I was to hold a policy on your life for the amount of my liability under Smithson's bond". This bond was evidently entered into some time before Oct 41 when Mitton was purchasing the practice; the "Argus Policy", necessary for CD's "protection", is mentioned in *To* Mitton, 29 Oct 41 (see Vol. II, p. 414). Presumably the bond fell due in Sep 43 and Smithson had agreed to its renewal.

[7] See *To* Lord Mulgrave, 15 July.

[8] The Athenæum Soirée was on Thurs 5 Oct, and CD and Mitton stayed with the Burnetts 4–6 Oct.

The weather here is gorgeous, but the heat terrific. All well except Mrs. D who has ailed very much this time, and suffers a good deal.

The next Number,[1] bangs all the others!

Faithfully Ever

Thomas Mitton Esquire   CD.

To THE REV. JOHN SINCLAIR,[2] [?17 SEPTEMBER 1843]

Mention in next.

To T. J. SERLE, [?17 SEPTEMBER 1843]

MS Mr Peter Brandt. *Date:* 1843, as obviously referring to the Eltons;[3] CD returned 2 Oct, therefore Sep; 17 Sep the likeliest Sunday (see *To* Serle, 12 Sep and 24 Sep).

Broadstairs | Sunday

My Dear Serle

The writer of the enclosed is the Reverend John Sinclair. I have written to him, and told him that if we proceed in the matter before I return next month, one of the Committee will communicate with him. Will you, like a good Christian—either through yourself or that better Christian, Mrs. Serle—possess the two girls with the contents of the Printed Scrap? And if either of them should be ready to go, I suppose she had better, like Macbeth's visitors, go at once[4]— had she not?

Faithfully Yours always

T. J. Serle Esquire   CHARLES DICKENS

To CHARLES SMITHSON, 20 SEPTEMBER 1843*

MS Huntington Library.

Broadstairs | Twentieth September 1843.

My Dear Smithson.

He[5] is the most tremendous fellow in the world. I don't know what is to be done with him. Just before he left town, he came out in a waistcoat that turned

---

[1] Chs 24–6; it includes the marriage of Jonas and Mercy, a good deal of Mrs Gamp, and the Anglo-Bengalee Disinterested Loan and Life Insurance Company.

[2] John Sinclair (?1797–1875), chaplain to the Bishop of London and Vicar of Kensington; became Archdeacon of Middlesex in Nov 43. As Treasurer of the National Society was responsible for its schools, and also for the training college at Whitelands, Chelsea. Esther Elton was completing her training there in 1845.

[3] N, II, 237 misdates as 1850.

[4] *Macbeth*, III, iv, 118–19.

[5] The references to Brougham below and in *To* Mrs Burnett, 24 Sep, show that this is Thomas Mitton. The description resembles that of Montague Tigg, just introduced in *Chuzzlewit*, Ch. 26, with his flowered waistcoat and fingers clogged with brilliant rings. Perhaps Mitton's waistcoat was bought for the wedding of his sister Mary Ann (see *To* Mitton, 26 July 42), who married John Cooper, market gardener, at St James's, Piccadilly, on 4 Sep.

my whole mass of blood—a flowery waistcoat, with buttons like black eyes; I don't mean natural black eyes, but artificial ones. He has also a sea-weed coloured coat, against which human nature revolts and reason rebels. His trousers (especially at the knees) are a spectacle I wouldn't meet in a lonely place for the wealth of a Rothschild. His cravats would be rejected with scorn in Holywell Street. Any magistrate of intelligence (if there were such a thing) would commit him to the treadmill, on the evidence of his jewellery. There is a ring, like a lady bird in the dropsy, on one of his fingers (one of those that are always crooked: I think the third) which tempts me to stab him. I don't see the end of it. But it *must* be something awful.

I am going to Manchester on the fifth, to take the chair at a great set-out at their Athenæum, where a vast number of people are to be assembled. He wants to go with me. I have said "Yes". My mind is disturbed in consequence, so excuse the incoherence of this letter. Sometimes I wonder whether I could get him in, in a box; sometimes, a bag. Sometimes I think of making interest with the Railroad to put him in a wrong train and run him into Scotland. I fancy the Manchester people putting him on the platform, as a distinguished friend of mine from London. I see him standing there. I behold that boot (oh what a boot it is!) crossed over the other boot; one hand playing with that cruel watch-chain, and the crooked fingers of the other pushing up that bird's nest of hair, which meets a little rill of whisker. I see his countenance twisted up into an expression of auctioneering acuteness, while he mentally appraises the furniture, and ticks off the benches at "four and half each—I mean to say they shan't be more." I then give a great shriek, and fall upon the floor, where I am found by a disconsolate wife and four small children, in a state of mind bordering on distraction.

My best love, and all our best loves, to all at Easthorpe. We often talk of you. I think when I am a bachelor pro tem. I shall look in at one of the ground floor windows of the abbey with a carpet bag in my hand, and terrify Miss Thompson with what HE[1] would call high-strikes—oh!—but I think a great many things that never come to pass. Good God how green You must be! I don't mean you, but the country about you,—those exquisite leaves—and Castle Howard Park.[2] You see how incoherent I am. But I have told you why; so pity me.

I have been expecting, and am still expecting, Thompson here. I have his little dog; for I wished that an alliance shd. take place between her and Timber; but there seems to be an incompatibility—I don't know whether of temper, or taste. Its an uncommon nice dog, and regularly runs away twice a day—once after breakfast, and once after tea—always being brought back by the Police. We *have* a police here now. A.1. He wears an uniform. But it has been discovered that he hasn't any power (not being legally appointed)[3] so

---

[1] Written very large in ornamental capitals.

[2] See *To* Felton, 1 Sep.

[3] The Kent County Constabulary was not formed until 1857, 18 years after the passing of the "Permissive Act" which provided for the creation of county forces, although some cities and boroughs had their own police (*The Kent Police Centenary*, ed. R. L. Thomas, 1957, pp. 21, 114ff.). The appointment of the "police" at Broadstairs presumably failed in some way to comply with the provisions of the 1842 Act for the Appointment and Payment of Parish Constables, by which justices might require from parish over-

strong vagrants come over, and dare him to take 'em up. As they come on purpose, we find him rather an inconvenience than otherwise.

Among other similar invites, I have had a note from Ld. Brougham this morning, asking me to go on there, when I am at Manchester, *and take anyone I may have with me.* Shall I make them known to each other ? If Mrs. Smithson says Yes,—I will. Damme.—There!

Document enclosed.[1] Always My Dear Smithson

Cordially Yours
CHARLES DICKENS

To J. C. PRINCE, 22 SEPTEMBER 1843

Mention in N, I, 541; dated Broadstairs, 22 Sep 43.

CD hopes to be able to meet Prince when he comes to Manchester.[2]

To JAMES QUILTER[3], 22 SEPTEMBER 1843*

MS[4] Dickens House.

Broadstairs—Kent | September 22nd. 1843

Mr. Charles Dickens presents his Compts to Mr. Quilter and begs to thank him for his obliging note.[5] He can scarcely admit, however, that the unfortunate Postboy of Lincoln at all contravenes the great authorities in question,[6] as he came to his end by violent means, and not in the ordinary course of nature.

---

seers a list of men eligible to serve, while vestries decided whether one or more should be paid from the Poor Relief Funds (C. Reith, *A New Study of Police History*, 1956, pp. 253–4).

[1] See *To* Mitton, 17 Sep.

[2] Prince, now working at Blackburn, was at the Athenæum Soirée, and was introduced to CD during the interval at CD's request (*Manchester Guardian*, 7 Oct 43). He had contributed a poem to the *Athenæum Souvenir*, which was sold at the bazaar.

[3] James Quilter, clerk to the city magistrates of Lincoln.

[4] Letter in the same hand as *To* A. van Lee, 16 Sep, presumably Alfred Dickens's.

[5] Quilter had written on 20 Sep "to correct the false notion of your Friends Messrs. Weller and Sawyer respecting the immortality of Post Boys", enclosing the copy of an inscription in the churchyard at Nettleham—a village three miles from Lincoln, with a large Early English church (Quilter's draft; MS Dickens House). The inscription reads: "THO. GARDINER | POST BOY OF LINCOLN | BARBAROUSLY | MURDERED BY | ISAAC & THO. HALLAM | JAN. 3D 1732. | AGED 19." (text from headstone still to be seen in S.W. corner of the churchyard; Quilter's copy is not completely accurate).

[6] In *Pickwick Papers*, Ch. 51, Sam Weller, in conversation with Bob Sawyer, asks, "Never know'd a churchyard where there wos a postboy's tombstone, or see a dead postboy, did you?" and explains his theory about why no one ever sees a dead postboy or a dead donkey, "without goin' so far as to as-sert, as some wery sensible people do, that postboys and donkeys is both immortal".

To LORD BROUGHAM, 24 SEPTEMBER 1843*

MS Brotherton Library, Leeds.

Broadstairs, Kent. | Twenty Fourth September 1843

Dear Lord Brougham.

I have had much pleasure in the receipt of your kind note. I wish it were in my power to come on into Cumberland,[1] when I am as far upon the way as Manchester—there are few things I should like better—but I grieve to say that I am obliged to return to town on the day after the Meeting:[2] having been here for two months; and before then, in Yorkshire.

Since I had the pleasure of seeing you, I have gone very much about the Jails and byeplaces of London, and although they are old sights to me, am more than ever amazed at the Ignorance and Misery that prevail. I saw the other day the announcement of a New Treatise in your name upon the subject of Education,[3] which brings the theme to my mind.

I would that I were a Police Magistrate,[4] and could take and hold this question from such a 'vantage ground at its lowest and most wretched end. I think I should be a pretty good one, with my knowledge of the kind of people that come most commonly within their Jurisdiction; and I would never rest from practically shewing all classes how important it has become to educate, on bold and comprehensive principles, the Dangerous Members of Society. I have often had this desire in my mind, but never so strongly as now.

With many thanks for your kind remembrance, and begging to send my compliments to Lady Brougham[5]

I am always | Dear Lord Brougham
Faithfully Yours
CHARLES DICKENS

The | Lord Brougham.

---

[1] Brougham Hall, near Penrith.

[2] See *To* Ainsworth, 13 Oct 43, *fn*.

[3] No such announcement has been found; CD is perhaps thinking of *Political Philosophy*, Part II, by Henry, Lord Brougham, published in July by the Society for the Diffusion of Useful Knowledge, or of the third series of *Historical Sketches of Statesmen* . . . , published by Chapman & Hall (introduction dated 1 Oct).

[4] A serious intention, which persisted for some years: see *To* Lord Morpeth, 20 June 46 (MS Mr George Howard). An Act of 1840 had given power to extend districts and to appoint extra magistrates, who had, however, to be barristers of seven years' standing; the *Journal of the Statistical Society*, Dec 46, quotes, as an "admirable description" of the qualities required, part of the evidence of a former magistrate before the Commons Police Committee of 1834: "The value of his office does not consist more in the strict legal performance of his judicial and administrative duties than in the exercise of a sound discretion, and in the considerate application of the principles and feelings of humanity, as an adviser, an arbitrator, and a mediator. The hearing at a police-office may in some instances, especially to the young and misguided, be the opening of new views of life and new rules of conduct."

[5] Lady Brougham and Vaux (1786–1865); Mary Anne, widow of John Spalding and daughter of Thomas Eden (uncle of Lord Auckland); married 1819.

To MRS HENRY BURNETT, 24 SEPTEMBER 1843*

MS Mrs A. M. Stern.

Broadstairs | Sunday Twenty Fourth September | 1843.

My Dear Fanny.

I am declining all Invitations to peoples'[1] houses, about Liverpool and Manchester (it's one man's work to answer them); and hold myself bound to you, of course. They invited Lord Brougham who can't attend, but has written to ask me to go on to his place in Cumberland, and stay there—and to bring any friend I may have with me. I have been chuckling, ever since, over the notion of taking Mitton, and making Them known to each other.

I mean to leave town on the Wednesday Morning, and come direct to you. Will it not be best for us to dine upon the road? And should we stop at Ardwick[2] (if we can) or go on? And shall I bring John? I wish you would write me a line, addressed to Devonshire Terrace, by next Saturday's or Sunday's post, and enlighten me. I shall be home next Monday night.

Don't think of making Mitton a bed on the sofa, but get him one at the nearest public house, or any decent place. He would be wretched at the idea of putting you out of the way, I am sure.

Kate[3] sends her best love to yourself, and Burnett, and the children—to whom commend me kindly also. I hope Harry is getting on well.[4] I shall be delighted to renew our old facetiousness.[5]

To MISS BURDETT COUTTS, 24 SEPTEMBER 1843

MS Morgan Library.

Broadstairs | Twenty Fourth September 1843

My Dear Miss Coutts.

I shall be most glad to confer with you, about Little Nell;[6] and I will come out to Putney on Tuesday Afternoon, the Third, which will be the day after I return to town. But I solemnly protest against the number being read out of its proper course—especially as the first chapter is not mortally long. If Miss Meredith resorts to any such improper and unjustifiable courses, Pinch is a dead man from that moment.[7]

I will endeavour between this time, and when I have the pleasure of seeing you, to ascertain what you so kindly desire to know, in reference to the Ragged Schools. There are fewer girls than boys; but the girls are more numerous than

[1] Thus in MS.

[2] The suburb of Manchester in which the Burnetts lived. CD was evidently travelling by coach.

[3] MS reads "Kates".

[4] Henry Burnett recalled him as: "one of the happiest and brightest of children. . . . Nothing seemed ever to escape his observation. If he was taken into a room with people, he, like his always-busy uncle, noted every face and the dress each

person wore" (F. G. Kitton, *CD by Pen and Pencil*, I, 136).

[5] Signature and ending have been cut away.

[6] Unidentified; cannot be Esther Elton as stated by Edgar Johnson, *Letters from CD to Angela Burdett-Coutts*, 1955, p. 54n.

[7] The first chapter in the October No. (Ch. 24) concerns Tom Pinch and is 13 pages long.

you would suppose, and much better behaved—although they are the wretchedest of the wretched. But there is much more Good in Women than in Men, however Ragged they are. People are apt to think otherwise, because the outward degradation of a woman strikes them more forcibly than any amount of hideousness in a man. They have no better reason.

Mr. Rogers is[1] down here, with an old Schoolfellow, Mr. Maltby.[2] We have had some mutual tea-drinkings of a rather forlorn description: the same stories being related over and over again, at each festivity. But really Rogers walks about, in a most surprising manner. I find him, with a little cane under his arm, airing himself on the top of inaccessible cliffs, and trotting, with his head on one side and his chin on his waistcoat, down gulfs and chasms where few middle-aged Visitors penetrate. Sometimes I see him on the sand, hustled by beggars, and defending himself manfully against a host of Vagrants. And his occupation within doors is to make perpetual alterations in the Pleasures of Memory,[3] and blot them out again. "Everybody writes too fast,"[4] he says. It's the great pleasure of his life to think so.

Charley sends his best love, and so do his sisters. The unknown (who like a Greater Unknown[5] is called Walter) does the like, on the faith of their representations. Mrs. Dickens begs to add her best regards.

I don't wonder that Miss Meredith, in her weak state, has suffered from the heat. Everybody here, has been ill from the same cause.

Always Dear Miss Coutts | Yours most faithfully

Miss Coutts.   CHARLES DICKENS

To JOHN FORSTER, [24 SEPTEMBER 1843]

Extract in F, IV, i, 298 (*aa*), dated 24 Sep according to Forster; and extract in F, IV, i, 298 (*bb*), wrongly dated "at the close of the year". (Both the "sledge-hammer account" for Miss Coutts and the suggestion to Napier for an article were written on 16 Sep; CD would doubtless have reported on them both in the same letter to Forster.)

*a*I sent Miss Coutts a sledge-hammer account of the Ragged schools;[6] and as I saw her name for two hundred pounds in the clergy education subscription-list,[7] took pains to show her that religious mysteries and difficult creeds wouldn't do for such pupils. I told her, too, that it was of immense importance they should be washed. She writes back to know what the rent of some large airy premises would be, and what the expense of erecting a regular bathing or purifying place; touching which points I am in correspondence with the authorities. I have no doubt she will do whatever I ask her in the matter. She is a most excellent

[1] MS reads "in".

[2] William Maltby (1763-1854; *DNB*): see Vol. I, p. 643*n*.

[3] First published 1792; a revised edition was published with *Italy* in Dec 43.

[4] This was a common complaint of Rogers's; calling on CD later in the year he found him writing the *Carol*, and said "nothing was now written with care"

(P. W. Clayden, *Rogers and his Contemporaries*, 1889, II, 225).

[5] Sir Walter Scott. Miss Coutts had evidently not yet seen Walter Landor Dickens, b. 1841.

[6] See *To* Miss Coutts, 16 Sep.

[7] See *To* Napier, 16 Sep; Miss Coutts's subscription was in the second list.

creature, I protest to God, and I have a most perfect affection and respect for her.[a]

[b]I have told Napier I will give a description of them in a paper on education, if the *Review* is not afraid to take ground against the church catechism and other mere formularies and subtleties, in reference to the education of the young and ignorant. I fear it is extremely improbable it will consent to commit itself so far.[1b]

To G. CARR GLYN,[2] 24 SEPTEMBER 1843

Mention in Sotheby's catalogue, Mar 1904; *MS* 1 p.; dated 24 Sep 43.

In reference to CD's brother.[3]

To T. J. SERLE, 24 SEPTEMBER 1843

MS Mr Peter Brandt.

Broadstairs, Kent. | Twenty Fourth September 1843
My Dear Serle.

I wrote to this Mr. Griffiths,[4] as we agreed, politely declining. Whereupon, with the perseverance of a Fiend with a newly-ground pitchfork, he addresses the enclosed note, and accompanying pieces of Gold-beaters skin to me. If you think there is no reason for us to alter our opinion, I wish *you* would try him with a communication (as Secretary) again declining. Its quite clear to me, that he wants to make an advertizement[5] for himself of the little Eltons.

Always Faithfully Yours
CHARLES DICKENS

To S. R. STAREY, 24 SEPTEMBER 1843

MS Shaftesbury Society.

Broadstairs, Kent. | Twenty Fourth September 1843.
Dear Sir.

Allow me to ask you a few questions in reference to that most noble undertaking in which you are engaged—with a view, I need scarcely say, to its advancement and extended usefulness. For the present, I could wish them, if you please to be considered as put in confidence, but not to the exclusion of the

---

[1] Forster's comment after the extract, "His fears were well-founded", shows that he had forgotten why the article was not after all written.

[2] George Carr Glyn (1797–1873), later first Baron Wolverton, banker and railway director; chairman from 1837 of the London & Birmingham railway, amalgamated with other companies as the London & North Western 1844.

[3] Clearly in relation to Alfred's search for new employment.

[4] There were three firms of carvers and gilders of this name, one at 27 Drury Lane.

[5] CD would have seen in *Punch* of 9 Sep "Death and the Tailor", quoting and criticizing verses "On the Death of Mr. Elton" which culminated in a tasteless puff of L. Hyam, a tailor of Gracechurch Street.

gentlemen associated with you in the management of the Ragged School on Saffron Hill.[1]

It occurred to me when I was there as being of the most immense importance that if practicable the boys should have an opportunity of Washing themselves, before beginning their tasks.

Do you agree with me? If so, will you ascertain at about what cost, a washing-place—a large trough or sink, for instance, with a good supply of running water, soap, and towels,—could be put up? In case you consider it necessary that some person should be engaged to mind it, and to see that the boys availed themselves of it in an orderly manner, please to add the payment of such a person to the expence.

Have you seen any place, or do you know of any place, in that neighbourhood —any one or two good spacious lofts or rooms—which you would like to engage (if you could afford it) as being well suited for the school? If so, at what charge could it be hired, and how soon?

In the event of my being able to procure you the funds for making these great improvements, would you see any objection to expressly limiting Visitors (I mean visiting teachers—volunteers, whoever they may be—) to confining their questions and instructions, as a point of honor, to the broad truths taught in the School by yourself and the gentlemen associated with you? I set great store by this question, because it seems to me of vital importance that no persons, however well intentioned, should perplex the minds of these unfortunate creatures with religious Mysteries that young people with the best advantages, can but imperfectly understand. I heard a lady visitor, the night I was among you, propounding questions in reference to "the Lamb of God" which I most unquestionably would not suffer any one to put to my children: recollecting the immense absurdities that were suggested to my own childhood by the like injudicious catechizing.[2]

I return to town on Monday the second of next Month. If you write to me before then, please to address your letter here. If after that date, to my house in town.

With a cordial sympathy in your Great and Christian Labour, I am Dear Sir

Faithfully Yours

Mr. R. Starey

CHARLES DICKENS

To MESSRS CHAPMAN & HALL, 27 SEPTEMBER 1843*

MS Huntington Library.

Broadstairs | Twenty Seventh September 1843

Dear Sirs

I shall be much obliged to you, if you will get for me, and send to Devonshire

---

[1] Their names, as given in the advertisement, were the Rev. P. Lorimer, W. D. Owen, and P. Macdonald.

[2] Perhaps in the church or "platform assemblage" to which he was dragged to hear the powerful preacher "Boanerges" ("City of London Churches" in *The Uncommercial Traveller*, 1861); or possibly at the dame school in Rome Lane, Chatham (F, I, i, 4).

Terrace on Monday, those Volumes of The Library of Entertaining Knowledge, which contain "The Pursuit of Knowledge under difficulties".[1]

Faithfully Yours

Messrs. Chapman & Hall   CHARLES DICKENS

To THOMAS MITTON, 28 SEPTEMBER 1843*

MS Comtesse de Suzannet.

Broadstairs | Twenty Eighth September 1843

My Dear Mitton

He is certain to do it again.[2] There was no help but to pay it, as you so kindly did. But he is sure to do it again.

Even now, with the knowledge of him which I have so dearly purchased, I am amazed and confounded by the audacity of his ingratitude. He, and all of them, look upon me as a something to be plucked and torn to pieces for their advantage. They have no idea of, and no care for, my existence in any other light. My soul sickens at the thought of them.

There seems to be no hope of anything—or next to no hope—for Alfred,[3] yet. I had been debating in my own mind what to do for the present, and had resolved to give him a pound a week[4] and his boathire[5] to and fro, and to make use of him as a Secretary. I have tried him in that capacity here, and he does exceedingly well: being very quick, and very neat.[6] I think I should have proposed it to

[1] G. L. Craik's volumes, first published anonymously in 1830–1, are in the 1844 inventory of CD's library (MS Major Philip Dickens). He had long known the work (which is alluded to in *Pickwick*, Ch. 33, by the elder Weller when Sam is writing his valentine), but needed it for reference in his Manchester speech, where he lists examples of self-taught men (*Speeches*, ed. K. J. Fielding, p. 48).

[2] John Dickens was evidently again in debt; CD's account-book (MS Messrs Coutts) shows a payment to Mitton of £15.9.6 on 16 Oct (see also *To* Forster, ?17 Nov 43 and *fn*). He had written a begging letter, marked "Confidential", to Chapman & Hall from "The Manor House, Lewisham" on 9 July 43: "My dear Sirs. | It would add greatly to my comfort if I could procure a free transit Ticket by the Watermans Company for the year, the sum is Five Guineas, but the drains upon me from other sources & my limited means for supplying them, are so great and numerous, I cannot myself accomplish it. I will not enter into family matters, further than to say, that in a more satisfactory arrangement of them in a pecuniary point of view, this point has been overlooked. | As I am to be an in-

dependent Gentleman how am I to get rid of my time? Two or three hours a day, two or three days a week at the Museum, would be a great relief, but to walk to London & back to accomplish that object, is rather more than I can do with ease & Rheumatism at sixty. If you would be my surety to the Watermen well & good, and I should be grateful, if not why then I must doze away the future,—'who talks of future whose existence is already of the past,'—in my arm chair, in re-reading the works of 'Boz'. | Always Yours & obliged | JOHN DICKENS."

[3] See *To* Miss Coutts, 24 Apr.

[4] Payments of £5 to "Mr Alfred" on 20 and 30 Oct and of £7 on 11 Dec are recorded in CD's account-book.

[5] The natural route would be by the Greenwich steamer. "The Manor House" was an old wooden house facing the foot of Lewisham Hill, and said to have been the residence of a Mr Bennett, "a friend of Charles Dickens" (L. L. Duncan, *History of the Borough of Lewisham*, 1908, p. 76); it had been demolished by 1854.

[6] *To* A. van Lee, 16 Sep, and *To* Quilter, 22 Sep, are in what is presumably Alfred's hand.

him this very day. But his father's letter—a threatening letter, before God!—to me!—chokes the words in my throat.

What do you think of this? If you think it the best thing I can do, and should see my disinterested and most affectionate parent, will you undertake to tell him that his letter has disgusted me beyond expression; and that I have no more reference to anything he wants or wishes or threatens or would do or wouldn't do, in taking on myself this new Burden, than I have reference to the Bell of Saint Paul's Cathedral or the Statue at Charing Cross?

Nothing makes me so wretched, or so unfit for what I have to do, as these things. They are so entirely beyond my own controul, so far out of my reach, such a drag-chain on my life, that for the time they utterly dispirit me, and weigh me down.

I shall be punctual on Tuesday. In the meantime, perhaps I shall receive a line from you.

Faithfully Ever
CHARLES DICKENS

I received Smithson's communication, and answered it by Return.

To EDWARD WATKIN[1] AND PETER BERLYN, [?2 OCTOBER 1843]

Mention in Edward William Watkin, *Alderman Cobden of Manchester*, 1891, p. 123.
Date: CD would wait to write until he heard from Ardwick on Mon 2 Oct (see *To Mrs Burnett*, 24 Sep).

Desiring an interview for Wednesday night, October 4, at about 9 o'clock, to arrange for the meeting.[2]

[1] Edward William Watkin (1819–1901); became Director of the Athenæum 1843 and arranged soirées of the next three years. Published *A Plea for Public Parks*, 1843. Later, Secretary of the Trent Valley Railway and director of several railway companies; was one of the founders of the *Manchester Examiner*, 1843. MP 1864; knighted 1868 (*Men of the Time*, 10th edn, 1879). He and Peter Berlyn were joint honorary secretaries of the Bazaar Committee. In *Alderman Cobden of Manchester*, pp. 123–30, Watkin describes in detail their meeting with CD on 4 Oct; they went to the Burnetts' house with Samuel Giles (brother of William). "We were at once introduced by Mrs. Burnett to her brother, standing with one hand on the chimney-piece. He cordially welcomed us, and asked us to take some wine, and in passing the decanter, upset his own glass, and deluged a very pretty book lying on the table". CD inquired about the speakers, and "we talked of their several qualities in a free and laughing manner—Dickens elevating his eyebrows and nodding his head forward as the remarks struck him. An interjection as to the doubt he had in 'Pickwick' cast upon 'swarries' provoked a quick, funny glance". In the history of the Athenæum and its objects CD "appeared to take great interest" and said: "Well, we must do all we can to obtain the assistance of all classes; but if a *certain* party choose to oppose the education of the masses, we cannot help it. We must go on in spite of them. ... Such institutions are most necessary and most useful, and there is a too general desire to get the utmost possible amount of work out of men instead of a generous wish to give the utmost possible opportunity of improvement ... I must put it into them strong" or "give it them strong". CD mentioned his note from Brougham regretting his inability to attend the soirée, "but how would Cobden and Brougham consort or agree together? ... you should have Mr.

To GEORGE LOVEJOY,[1] 4 OCTOBER 1843

Summary in Sotheby's catalogue, Dec 1930; *MS* 1½ pp.; dated 1 Devonshire Terrace, 4 Oct 43.

Regretting that he cannot attend the opening of the new buildings of a Literary and Scientific Institution.[2]

To WILLIAM JERDAN,[3] 9 OCTOBER 1843

Extract in Anderson Galleries catalogue No. 2298; *MS* 1 p.; dated London, 9 Oct 43.

A thousand thanks for your kind and genial letter. I have been out of town, and only received it yesterday. It is not a weak cheer, but good cheer, strong cheer, heart cheer, and cheer I love to have.[4] It satisfies me more than I can tell you. My Dear Jerdan, Faithfully your friend,

[CHARLES DICKENS]

To THOMAS POWELL,[5] 9 OCTOBER 1843*

MS Mrs Caroline Trollope.

Devonshire Terrace | Ninth October 1843.

My Dear Sir

Mrs. Dickens is much beholden to you for your kind recollection of her, and

Bright there to make the set complete". On the evening of 5 Oct Watkin and Berlyn went to Burnett's in James Heywood's carriage and had some further talk with CD: "I told him that we should have invited a General Duff Green, an American now in Manchester, to attend the soirée but for the exasperation felt by Yankees ever since his 'exposure' of them. 'Ah, General Green, I know. Never mind —the Americans will thank me for it themselves in ten years hence.' ... On the way to the hall we talked of Hood and Jerrold. Dickens lamented Hood's ill-health and poverty, and much praised his writings; admired Jerrold and lauded *Punch*, which, he said, he generally 'saw before it was in print'. I tried to turn the talk upon America. Heywood asked about the society of the American Universities. Dickens praised it highly ... he had formed friendships amongst them which would last his life. He praised the society of Boston, and I think of New York and Philadelphia, and said the feeling against slavery was ... growing".

[2] For an account of the Athenæum soirée, see *To* Miss Coutts, 13 Oct and *fn.*

[1] Liberal agent at Reading; see Vol. II, p. 288*n*.

[2] Clearly Lovejoy had invited CD to the inaugural dinner at the opening of the great Public Hall on 24 Oct; the *Examiner*, 28 Oct, reported Talfourd's speech in which "he regretted, in common with his fellow townsmen, the absence of one whose genius was as universal as the nature he illustrated ... Charles Dickens".

[3] William Jerdan (1782–1869; *DNB*), editor of the *Literary Gazette*: see Vol. II, p. 207*n*.

[4] Probably Jerdan had written a letter praising the October *Chuzzlewit*. No review appeared in the *Literary Gazette*.

[5] Thomas Powell (1809–87), miscellaneous writer, embezzler and forger; ingratiated himself in literary circles until his defalcations at Thomas Chapman's were discovered in 1846 (see next vol.). In his reminiscences, "Leaves from my Life" (*Frank Leslie's Sunday Magazine*, New York, 1886), many details of which are inaccurate, he claimed a relationship to the Chapman family, and to have been employed by him since 1823 (unconfirmed, but he knew them by 1834). Married

for your elegant present.[1] She begs me to thank you most cordially. I should have done so, before now; but we have been out of town, and I returned only yesterday.

I shall not fail to keep a sharp eye on Horne.[2] Let him beware! If he gives

Frances Maria Machell 27 Feb 36. Published *Attempts at Verse*, anonymously, with Effingham Wilson, "an old friend of my father's", June 37, after consulting Wordsworth, whom he knew by 1836. By 1837 he was sending him presents of cheese; Powell's eldest son, Arthur Wordsworth (born 19 Jan 37, dead by 1842), may have been Wordsworth's godson. By 1839 Southwood Smith called him his "very dear friend" and had introduced him to Leigh Hunt; the pretext of helping Hunt in his financial difficulties increased Powell's literary connections. In Winter 1839–40 was engaged on *The Poems of Geoffrey Chaucer, Modernized* (1841), edited by Horne, and in collaboration with Hunt, Wordsworth, Leonhard Schmitz (Powell's brother-in-law), Elizabeth Barrett, and possibly others, Powell contributing three pieces. Contributed poems to the *Monthly Chronicle*, of which Bulwer was one of the proprietors and nominal editors, from 1840 until its demise in 1841. In 1842 published, probably at his own expense, two verse plays, *The Count de Foix* (dedicated to Lough, the sculptor) and *The Wife's Revenge* (dedicated to Talfourd) and a volume of *Poems*, mainly work previously published—also poems which he had acquired (possibly by purchase) from Horne and Hunt (*Letters of Robert Browning and Elizabeth Barrett*, I, 393) and verses published later as the work of Sophia Iselin. By this time Browning had met Powell through Talfourd and soon became "a constant visitor" at his house at Peckham; at some time "took pity on him and helped his verses into a little grammar and sense" (*Letters, ibid.*; J. C. Eckel, *The First Editions of CD*, p. 245, mentions some Powell proof sheets of a volume of verses corrected by Browning—now at Yale), and gave him his MS of Act I of *Colombe's Birthday* (which he sold with many other autographs, 6 Mar 48); Powell's next play, *The Blind Wife*, 1843, was dedicated to him. Browning later claimed to have "found him out earlier than most of his dupes" (*Letters of Robert Browning*, ed.

T. L. Hood, 1933, p. 225); but in June 43 Vincent Hunt was already somewhat suspicious and thought "a year's imprisonment for debt would do him good" (A. N. L. Munby, *Letters to Leigh Hunt from his Son Vincent*, 1934, pp. 25–6). That summer, became part-proprietor of the new *Foreign and Colonial Review*, later the *New Quarterly*, but was unreliable in his payment to contributors; later in the year published two more plays, *The Shepherd's Well* (Sep), with a verse prologue by Horne, and *Marguerite* (Dec), dedicated to Thomas Chapman. Most of his plays are named and praised as "reality tragedies" in the essay on Browning and Marston in *A New Spirit of the Age*. According to Shelton Mackenzie, Chapman arranged a party on 27 July 42, including CD and Powell, to see the restored Crosby Hall (W. J. Carlton, "A Note on Captain Cuttle", *D*, LXIV [1968], 152); but they may have met earlier through Southwood Smith or Talfourd. For Augustus Dickens's employment at Chapman's, see next vol.

[1] The epithet suggests that this was not one of Powell's usual presents of food.

[2] Richard Henry ("Hengist") Horne (1803–84; *DNB*), poet and journalist: see Vol. I, p. 500*n*. In 1842, having completed his collection of evidence for the Second Report of the Children's Employment Commission, was at work on a Shelleyan religious epic, *Ancient Idols, or the Fall of the Gods*, never published but surviving in MS; in Nov began to write his famous social epic *Orion*, published at the beginning of June 43, price one farthing (rising to a shilling with the fourth edn in July). Some months earlier Horne had begun to plan the collection of essays on leading contemporary figures which became *A New Spirit of the Age*, and by Oct contributions were being discussed between him and Elizabeth Barrett (*Letters of E. B. Barrett to R. H. Horne*, ed. S. R. Townshend Mayer, 1877, I, 147ff.). According to Powell, Mary Gillies, Robert Bell and Powell himself also contributed (Ann Blainey, *The Farthing Poet, R. H. Horne,*

me the least offence, I will unsay all I have said, everywhere, in praise of his report on youthful labour.¹ It will take a long time to do, but vengeance is strong, and Dickens persevering.

Believe me | Very Faithfully Yours

Thomas Powell Esquire

CHARLES DICKENS

To BERNHARD TAUCHNITZ,² 9 OCTOBER 1843

Extract in Kurt Otto, *Der Verlag Bernhard Tauchnitz, 1837–1912*, Leipzig, 1912.

London, 1, Devonshire Terrace | York Gate, Regents Park,
October 9th, 1843.

In reply to your letter I beg to say that if you will favour me with any distinct proposition . . . I shall be happy to give it *immediate* consideration.³

1968, p. 142). In June Leigh Hunt had been invited (L. A. Brewer, *My Leigh Hunt Library*, Iowa, 1938, pp. 285–9), but he declined. Miss Barrett's letters show that strict secrecy was supposed to be observed about authorship (*op. cit.*, I, 168) and up to Jan 44 she did not know that CD was included among the subjects; but Powell had evidently told CD. Horne (who does not mention Powell in connection either with *A New Spirit* or *Chaucer Modernized*) states, "The article upon CD was written entirely by myself" (*Letters, op. cit.*, I, 241); but *To* Horne, 13 Nov 43 may suggest that Powell had been collecting material for him. Horne had been suffering from ill-health and had been out of London for several weeks in Aug and Sep, first at Miss Mitford's (who found him a great nuisance) and then in Sussex; this was one cause of the delay in completing the *New Spirit*, but by Dec much of it was in proof.

¹ See *To* Southwood Smith, 6 Mar 43.

² The firm of Bernhard Tauchnitz of Leipzig, founded in 1837, began its Collection of British Authors Sep 41 with Bulwer's *Pelham*; *Pickwick, Oliver* and *American Notes* had appeared before the end of 1842, and *Nickleby* in June 43. Tauchnitz visited London in Summer 1843 and in July concluded agreements for authorized continental editions with several authors, including Bulwer, James, and Lady Blessington. Longmans' letters to Lady Blessington (A. Morrison, *The Blessington Papers*, 1895, pp. 160–1) show that they encouraged the plan, once satisfied that importation of these editions into England or the colonies could be prevented, and CD may have had their advice. Not all publishers agreed; John Blackwood opposed it, regarding it as "perfect folly" for publishers as a body to give up all chance of selling their editions abroad (letter of 26 July 43; M. Oliphant, *Annals of a Publishing House. William Blackwood and his Sons*, 1897, II, 353). Agreements evidently included the transmission of early proofs; the Tauchnitz *Christmas Carol* was advertised in Germany on 8 Dec 43 as an "edition sanctioned by the author", to appear "later this month, simultaneously with the London edition", and was published between 23 and 27 Dec; and *Martin Chuzzlewit* appeared in 2 vols (vols 57 and 58 of the "Collection") in 1844 (Vol. I by 21 June). For a full account of the firm see S. Nowell-Smith, "Firma Tauchnitz 1837–1900", *Book Collector*, xv (1966), 423–36.

³ CD is answering Tauchnitz's first approach to him (F, XI, ii, 807*n*); according to Forster, Tauchnitz always paid liberally.

To EDWARD WATKIN AND PETER BERLYN,
10 OCTOBER 1843

Text from facsimile in Edward William Watkin, *Alderman Cobden of Manchester*, 1891, p. 139.

London Devonshire Terrace | York Gate Regent's Park
Tenth October 1843

Dear Sirs

I am exceedingly glad to receive so good a report of our Athenæum prospects.[1] And I hope when I next hear from you, to learn that everything continues to realize your expectations.

Pray assure the Ladies' Committee and the Bazaar Committee, of the great gratification I have in their kind and flattering recollection of me.

Many thanks to you for the Manchester Newspapers—in which the proceedings of the other night, are remarkably well reported.[2] If you should see, or know, any of the gentlemen who attended for the Press, I wish you would say as much from me, in common justice.

Dear Sirs | Faithfully Yours
CHARLES DICKENS

Edward Watkins Esquire
Peter Berlyn Esquire

To W. HARRISON AINSWORTH, 13 OCTOBER 1843

MS Johns Hopkins University.

Devonshire Terrace | Thirteenth October 1843.

My Dear Ainsworth

I want very much to see you: not having had that old pleasure for a long time. I am at this moment deaf in the ears, hoarse in the throat, red in the nose, green in the gills, damp in the eyes, twitchy in the joints, and fractious in the temper, from a most intolerable and oppressive cold—caught the other day, I suspect, at Liverpool,[3] where I got exceedingly wet. But I will make prodigious efforts to get the better of it tonight, by resorting to all conceivable remedies. And if I succeed so far as to be only negatively disgusting tomorrow, I will joyfully present myself at 6, and bring my womankind along with me.

Cordially Yours
CHARLES DICKENS

William Harrison Ainsworth Esquire

[1] The *Manchester Guardian* of 11 Oct announced the total proceeds of the Bazaar, Soirée, and donations as £1820. The Bazaar in the Town Hall was open for the whole week.

[2] One was the *Guardian* of 7 Oct (see *To* Miss Coutts, 17 Oct), on which the report in *Speeches*, ed. K. J. Fielding, is mainly based. The full account in the *Examiner*

(14 Oct 43) is drawn from the *Manchester Times*.

[3] CD left Manchester on Fri 6 Oct and was back in London 8 Oct; why he visited Liverpool is not known—possibly to meet T. J. Thompson, or to see William Giles, who now had a school at Seacombe House, Cheshire.

To MISS BURDETT COUTTS, 13 OCTOBER 1843

MS Morgan Library.

Devonshire Terrace | Thirteenth October 1843

My Dear Miss Coutts.

The "Ragged" Masters are really very honest men. I infer from the enclosed,[1] that they fear they may not succeed in the long run, and are delicate of availing themselves of individual kindness, beyond the temporary help of a Subscription. But I may be wrong in this; and when I have done my month's work (with which I am now in spasms) I will see the writer, and talk to him more fully. This will be, very early, I hope, in the week after next.[2]

I have been thinking very much about Nell. Will you tell me whether you wish her to *learn* anything? I am not quite clear about that.—I mean, to learn a trade, or learn what is popularly called "her book".

A hideous cold has taken possession of me to an almost unprecedented extent. I am not exactly, like Miss Squeers, screaming out loud all the time I write;[3] but I am executing another kind of performance beginning with an s, and ending with a g; perpetually.

The Manchester Meeting, composed of men of all parties, was very brilliant I assure you. A thousand tickets were sold, and most of them admitted two,— many three,—persons.[4] I am strongly tempted to send you a local paper, containing all the Speeches. But modesty (a besetting sin with authors) prevents me.

---

[1] A letter from Starey informing CD of the result of his search for new premises which might be hired for the Ragged School (see *To* Starey, 24 Sep); he feared that "without taking some which would require money being laid out upon to adapt them to our wants we are not likely to succeed", and asked CD's advice on the best way of approaching the Committee of Council of Education for a grant towards such adaptation should it be thought desirable (Starey *to* CD, 10 Oct 43; MS Morgan).

[2] *To* Starey, 17 Oct, and Starey's reply probably took the place of this meeting.

[3] From Fanny Squeers's letter to Ralph Nickleby, *Nicholas Nickleby*, Ch. 15.

[4] The Soirée was to raise funds for the Athenæum, founded in 1835 and at first successful but recently in debt owing to the trade depression; CD's chairmanship was announced on 6 Sep, and tickets sold rapidly, so that it was held in the great Free Trade Hall and not in the institute's own rooms. CD referred in his speech to "the brilliant and beautiful spectacle" before him and emphasized the lack of party differences; he recalled the history of the Athenæum, and complimented Manchester on its foundation—"it is grand to know that while her factories re-echo with the clanking of stupendous engines and the whirl and rattle of machinery, the immortal mechanism of God's own hand, the mind, is not forgotten in the din and uproar, but is lodged and tended in a palace of its own". As Forster says (F, IV, i, 297), he "spoke mainly on a matter always nearest his heart, the education of the very poor" (having already in mind the two spectres of Ignorance and Want in the *Carol*), and recalled what he had seen in "certain jails and nightly refuges"; he attacked the axiom that a little learning was dangerous, and dwelt on its consolations to "men of low estate" such as Ferguson, Crabbe, Bloomfield, and Burns. The "men of all parties" were represented by speakers as diverse as Milner Gibson, Cobden, Disraeli, and James Crossley. Watkin relates how he and Berlyn on the previous day planned "a mixture of parties . . . we could place Mr. Cobden and Mr. James Crossley side by side, and thus make violent political opponents for once put aside their differences for the good of the Athenæum". Disraeli had not originally been invited to speak; Watkin's account shows that Cobden

It will be a comfort to Miss Meredith to know that my other rheumatic friend[1] who got well long before her—that is to say too soon—is turning all wrong again, just as she is turning all right. May I trouble you to tell her that my hair is growing,[2] and I'll never do so any more?

Charley and his sisters, entrust me with messages full of partially unintelligible enthusiasm. Mrs. Dickens begs me to say that if you can oblige her with your Drury Lane Box[3] for any performing night next week, she will take it as a great favor.

Always Dear Miss Coutts
Yours faithfully and obliged
CHARLES DICKENS

I was greatly pleased with Mr. Morier.[4]

---

discovered only on 5 Oct that he was staying at the Mosley Arms and asked Watkin to invite him to the soirée (E. W. Watkin, *Alderman Cobden of Manchester*, pp. 124, 130). Mrs Disraeli (letter of 24 Nov) says he declined, "and they sent a deputation of ladies, which, you know, he could not refuse; so he went, and made a fine speech for them—all said by far the finest—literary not political". He commented on the "miracle of machinery" by which his name was printed in the programme; held up the Medici and the great merchants of Venice as examples to Manchester in the patronage of art; and made a humorous reference to the ladies as the "Lancashire witches" which CD described as "very brilliant and eloquent" (*Manchester Guardian*, 7 Oct; W. F. Monypenny & G. E. Buckle, *Life of Benjamin Disraeli, Earl of Beaconsfield*, revised edn, 1929, I, 581–2). During the interval CD was "besieged by bevies of fair applicants for his autograph" (*Speeches*, p. 50). John Eustace Giles, his old schoolfellow and brother of his first schoolmaster, then spoke, and recalled the time when they "rambled through the same Kentish fields".

[1] Probably Forster; on 19 Oct Hood called on him and was "shocked to hear he was very ill—but could not make out exactly how—for they said he had undergone an operation—& his complaint was rheumatic" (Hood *to* CD, [19 Oct 43],

MS Huntington; *Letters of Thomas Hood*, ed. P. Morgan, p. 570). He was still ill on 21 Oct (Procter *to* Landor, MS V & A) and was not fully recovered for another two months (see *To* Forster, 10 Nov, *fn*). Jerrold was also suffering from rheumatism (see *To* Mrs Hurnall, 2 Nov).

[2] It was long in mid-Sep (*To* Miss Coutts, 16 Sep); perhaps he had it cut for the Manchester visit.

[3] Donizetti's *La Favorita*, with Grisi, followed by J. M. Morton's farce, *My Wife's Come*, with Harley, opened on 18 Oct. The report in the *Examiner*, 21 Oct, is almost certainly by CD, who perhaps offered it because of Forster's illness. He described the first three acts as "very heavy, very cold, and very noisy", the fourth as "natural, simple, and affecting" although "Miss Romer walked upon her knees to an extent which we never saw equalled, saving by the clown at Astley's". For complete text and commentary, see *D*, LXV (1969), 80–3.

[4] CD may not previously have met James Justinian Morier (?1780–1849; *DNB*), traveller and novelist, author of *Hajji Baba*, 1824 (a book well known to him), and contributor to *Bentley's*; he lived in Brighton. Or this may have been one of his brothers, two of whom were living in London—John Philip (1776–1853), retired from the diplomatic service, and William (1790–1864), captain RN.

To MISS BURDETT COUTTS, 17 OCTOBER 1843*

MS Morgan Library.

Devonshire Terrace. | Seventeenth October 1843.

Dear Miss Coutts.

In a scarlet fever of modesty, I send you two papers. The report in the Guardian, is, upon the whole, the better of the twain.

Certainly I would teach Nell, a *trade*. It is a matter of stupendous difficulty, however, to say what trade. I will keep the point in my mind, and after making some enquiries, report to you next week.

Undoubtedly if the Ragged School could obtain any assistance from the Government, it would be an immense thing. I am not sanguine in my hopes of any Government in such cases; but Lord Sandon[1] would be an excellent person to interest in Saffron Hill's[2] behalf, and I believe would be easily interested in any question involving so much misery. *Your* intervention would be most powerful.

I send you the advertisement,[3] and will duly forward your valuable donation.

Always Believe me | Most Faithfully Yours

Miss Coutts.   CHARLES DICKENS

P.S. I beg to inform Miss Meredith, (with my best regards) that my other rheumatic friend is of the sterner sex. But I have shrewd misgivings that *his* disorder is not rheumatism after all, though it has been treated as such. May I trouble you to keep the Manchester papers until you see me?

To MACVEY NAPIER, 17 OCTOBER 1843

MS British Museum. *Address:* Professor Napier | Castle Street | Edinburgh.

Devonshire Terrace. | Seventeenth October 1843.

My Dear Sir

My view of the case is precisely yours.[4] I know it would be very bad policy to hit the church unnecessarily in any tender place; and I have no inclination to do so.

I think you had best make up your *January* No. without reference to me, as I am not *certain* for that time. But in the course of that month you shall have the paper; and then you will suffer no uneasiness or chance of disappointment in reference to it.

---

[1] Dudley Ryder, 2nd Earl of Harrowby (1798-1882; *DNB*), married Miss Coutts's cousin, Lady Frances Stuart; philanthropist and interested in Lord Ashley's schemes for the betterment of factory conditions; patron of the National Society, and though not on the Committee of Council of Education, well known to its members as an influential member of the Tory party.

[2] MS reads "Saffron's Hill".

[3] See *To* Miss Coutts, 5 Sep.

[4] In an article on "The Ministry and the late Session" in the October *Edinburgh Review*, by Lord Monteagle (Thomas Spring-Rice), the "spirit of exclusiveness and of fanaticism" shown by the Church, the Government and the Dissenters was criticized, but without the kind of strictures on religious education and attacks on the National Society that CD had proposed in *To* Napier, 16 Sep.

I should say a dozen pages or thereabouts, will be the utmost extent of the article. That is not too long, I hope?

Mrs. Dickens sends you her best regards. We have been in Yorkshire, and in Kent; but are fixtures in London now, until next Summer.

My Dear Sir | Always Faithfully Yours

Professor Napier   CHARLES DICKENS

To S. R. STAREY, 17 OCTOBER 1843*

Text from typescript, Huntington Library.

Devonshire Terrace, | York Gate, Regents Park,
Seventeenth October 1843.

Dear Sir,

I very much regret that it is not more immediately within your power, and in that of the gentlemen who are associated with you, to carry out the object I hinted in my last. I have made the best interest in my power to bring your case before the council of education;[1] and although I am not very sanguine as to the result, I have no doubt that it will be considered there.

I have ten pounds for you, which is a subscription from Miss Burdett Coutts. As I do not like to send it by the post, I shall be glad if you will have the goodness to let it be called for here. I will leave it out in an envelope addressed to you,

Faithfully yours,

R. S. Starey Esquire.   CHARLES DICKENS

P.S. When you send for the money will you be good enough to forward a receipt.

To MISS MARGARET GILLIES, 23 OCTOBER 1843

MS Private.

Devonshire Terrace | Monday October Twenty Third | 1843.

Dear Miss Gillies

Tomorrow, Tuesday, at 3 o'Clock, I will dutifully present myself: having now got rid (almost) of a cold, which has ridden rough-shod—to use the favorite newspaper expression—over my features.

Would you like me to ask Mr. Maclise to look in, during the sitting? He has a mighty knowledge of my face, and expressed himself much struck with the

---

[1] The Minutes of the Committee of Council of Education (a committee of the Privy Council, set up in 1839) show no reference to Ragged Schools in 1843. In *To* the Editor of the *Daily News*, 4 Feb 46 (*Miscellaneous Papers*, ed. B. W. Matz, p. 20), CD refers to his attempt "to bring these Institutions under the notice of the Government", but says he "heard no more of the subject from that hour".

"spirit"[1] of your portrait as photographed.[2] "A very little bit"—he said, waving his hand in the air, something [?like an auc]tioneer,[3] and giving it a twist [at] the same time, "would make it ca-pi-tal".

Miss Gillies

Faithfully Yours always
CHARLES DICKENS

To T. BOYS,[4] 24 OCTOBER 1843

Mention in Parke-Bernet Galleries catalogue No. 1535 (1954); *MS* 1 p.; dated 24 Oct 43.

To MACVEY NAPIER, 24 OCTOBER 1843

MS British Museum. *Address:* Professor Napier | Muirestone House | Mid-Calder | by Edinburgh.

Devonshire Terrace | Twenty Fourth October 1843

My Dear Sir

I am extremely sorry to find that my proposal puts you to any inconvenience; but the fault is really not mine. You wrote me in answer to my letter,[5] that you were much oppressed by matter of all kinds and from a variety of distinguished sources (as I can readily understand)—but would "*endeavour*" to find room for me in the January Number. I immediately resolved not to give you that trouble, but to write the paper at my leisure, and send it to you for the Number following —really meaning to be considerate, and to meet your views, as I understood them. And I thought the postponement, rather advantageous than otherwise, as the mention of the subject in the Queen's Speech,[6] or the omission of it, would be alike a good reason for taking it up afresh. Accordingly I plunged headlong into a little scheme[7] I had held in abeyance during the interval which had elapsed between my first letter and your answer; set an artist[8] at work upon it; and put it wholly out of my own power to touch the Edinburgh subject until after Christmas is turned. For carrying out the notion I speak of, and being

---

[1] CD must already have known that the portrait was intended for Horne's *New Spirit of the Age*.

[2] Daguerre had pointed out in his *History and Practice of Photogenic Drawing*, 1839, that the new invention could be useful to the painter, who "will obtain, by this process, a quick method of making collections of studies", and by 1843 some portrait-painters and miniaturists had begun to use photographs to reduce the number of necessary sittings. CD had evidently been photographed in the chosen pose.

[3] Words obscured by large smear of ink.

[4] Either Thomas Shotter Boys (1803–1874; *DNB*), painter, who lithographed works of Stanfield, published *London as It Is*, 1842 (in CD's library at his death), and lived in Great Portland Street; or Thomas Boys, print-seller, 11 Golden Square, who published works of T. S. Boys, and whose Fine Art Distribution to subscribers was advertised to take place at Exeter Hall on 25 Oct.

[5] See *To* Napier, 16 Sep.

[6] i.e. in Feb 44. The subject was omitted.

[7] The first certain reference to the *Christmas Carol*, which Forster says was started "a week after his return from Manchester, where the fancy first occurred to him" (F, IV, i, 299). But see *To* Southwood Smith, 10 Mar 43 and *fn*.

[8] John Leech, the only illustrator.

punctual with Chuzzlewit, will occupy every moment of my working time, up to the Christmas Holidays.[1]

I hope you will see how this has come to pass; and that I acted *on your letter, distinctly.*

I did not fail to give your message to Hood, who thanks you very much, and greatly regrets having missed you.[2]

My Dear Sir | Faithfully Yours always

Professor Napier.   CHARLES DICKENS

To MRS CROWE,[3] 26 OCTOBER 1843†

MS Colonel Richard Gimbel.

London. 1 Devonshire Terrace | York Gate Regents Park
Twenty Sixth October 1843

My Dear Mrs. Crowe.

It can't be done. When there is unanimity among authors, perhaps it may be.[4] As that state of things may be expected to come to pass on the afternoon of the Last Day But One, I hope neither you nor I may live to see it.

You are not alone in your sufferings, nor does great success carry with it any exemption from such penalties. If you knew what my books have brought to others, and what they have brought to me, you would, as the Song says,

open your eyes
and die with surprise[5]

[a]—so I won't tell you; the more especially as I want you to get off your back with all speed, and be as well and merry as you can wish to be.

Believe me always | Faithfully Yours

Mrs. Crowe.   CHARLES DICKENS[a]

---

[1] The *Carol* was not finished till 2 Dec.

[2] Napier was away on Hood's Edinburgh visit.

[3] Catherine Crowe, *née* Stevens (1800–1876; *DNB*), novelist; lived in Edinburgh; best known for *Susan Hopley*, 1841, her first novel (see Vol. II, p. 256*n*), and *The Night Side of Nature*, 1848; contributed to *Household Words*, 20 Apr 50.

[4] Mrs Crowe had probably consulted CD about her troubles over *Susan Hopley* and may have inquired if the proposed Society for the Protection of Literature could help. *Susan Hopley* was first published by Saunders & Otley in 3 vols in 1841, and then in weekly numbers, monthly parts, and a three-shilling volume in 1842 by William Tait of Edinburgh, advertised as "Cheap Genuine Edition";

Sadleir (*XIX Century Fiction*, p. 101) suggests that Saunders & Otley had bought the copyright and sold or leased it to Tait, so that Mrs Crowe would gain little from its popularity. (She had also suffered from the use of her title in a penny serial by T. P. Prest, published by E. Lloyd, 1842, and a very popular dramatic version by G. D. Pitt, 1841, often played at the Victoria Theatre.) She returned to Saunders & Otley with *Men and Women, or Manorial Rights*, published 11 Dec 43 (favourably reviewed in the *Examiner*, 16 Dec).

[5] From Samuel Lover's song "Molly Carew", in *Songs and Ballads*, 1839, pp. 99–102.

[aa] Not previously published.

To JOHN FORSTER, [1 NOVEMBER 1843]

Text from F, IV, ii, 304–5. *Date:* 1 Nov according to Forster.

Don't be startled by the novelty and extent of my project. Both startled *me* at first; but I am well assured of its wisdom and necessity. I am afraid of a magazine—just now. I don't think the time a good one, or the chances favourable. I am afraid of putting myself before the town as writing tooth and nail for bread, headlong, after the close of a book taking so much out of one as *Chuzzlewit*. I am afraid I could not do it, with justice to myself. I know that whatever we may say at first, a new magazine, or a new anything, would require so much propping, that I should be *forced* (as in the *Clock*) to put myself into it, in my old shape. I am afraid of Bradbury and Evans's desire to force on the cheap issue of my books, or any of them, prematurely. I am sure if it took place yet awhile, it would damage me and damage the property, *enormously*. It is very natural in them to want it; but, since they do want it, I have no faith in their regarding me in any other respect than they would regard any other man in a speculation. I see that this is really your opinion as well; and I don't see what I gain, in such a case, by leaving Chapman and Hall.[1] If I had made money, I should unquestionably fade away from the public eye for a year, and enlarge my stock of description and observation by seeing countries new to me; which it is most necessary to me that I should see, and which with an increasing family I can scarcely hope to see at all, unless I see them now. Already for some time I have had this hope and intention before me; and though not having made money yet, I find or fancy that I can put myself in the position to accomplish it. And this is the course I have before me. At the close of *Chuzzlewit* (by which time the debt will have been materially reduced) I purpose drawing from Chapman and Hall my share of the subscription[2]—bills, or money, will do equally well. I design to tell them that it is not likely I shall do anything for a year; that, in the meantime, I make no arrangement whatever with anyone; and our business matters rest *in statu quo*. The same to Bradbury and Evans. I shall let the house if I can; if not, leave it to be let. I shall take all the family, and two servants— three at most—to some place which I know beforehand to be CHEAP and in a delightful climate, in Normandy or Brittany, to which I shall go over, first, and

---

[1] See *To* Forster, 28 June 43. Forster (IV, ii, 303–4) says that he had persuaded CD to "suspend proceedings" over his change of publishers till Oct; Bradbury & Evans had been taken by surprise when he communicated CD's proposal, and "replied by suggestions which were in effect a confession of . . . want of confidence in themselves", proposing a cheap re-issue of CD's works, and offering "to invest to any desired amount in the establishment of a magazine or other periodical to be edited by him". CD was probably right in thinking the time not favourable to a new magazine; the trade depression of 1842 still continued, and the sale of *Bentley's*

Miscellany, for example, had dropped by one-third. Cheap re-issues of the whole of an author's works to date were still uncommon; the only precedents were Marryat, whose six novels were published in Bentley's Standard Novels in 1838, and Bulwer, with ten novels collected in 1840–1 (Saunders & Otley, with Colburn), in imitation of the Standard Novels, appearing monthly at 6s a volume. Forster had assisted Bulwer in the early stages of the negotiations.

[2] The booksellers' subscription for the volume edition of *Chuzzlewit*, due to be published in July 44.

where I shall rent some house for six or eight months. During that time, I shall walk through Switzerland, cross the Alps, travel through France and Italy; take Kate perhaps to Rome and Venice, but not elsewhere; and in short see everything that is to be seen. I shall write my descriptions[1] to you from time to time, exactly as I did in America; and you will be able to judge whether or not a new and attractive book may not be made on such ground. At the same time I shall be able to turn over the story I have in my mind,[2] and which I have a strong notion might be published with great advantage, *first in Paris*[3]—but that's another matter to be talked over. And of course I have not yet settled, either, whether any book about the travel, or this, should be the first. "All very well," you say, "if you had money enough." Well, but if I can see my way to what would be necessary without binding myself in any form to anything; without paying interest, or giving any security but one of my Eagle[4] five thousand pounds; you would give up that objection. And I stand committed to no bookseller, printer, moneylender, banker, or patron whatever; and decidedly strengthen my position with my readers, instead of weakening it, drop by drop, as I otherwise must. Is it not so? and is not the way before me, plainly this? I infer that in reality you do yourself think, that what I first thought of is *not* the way? I have told you my scheme very baldly, as I said I would. I see its great points, against many prepossessions the other way—as, leaving England, home, friends, everything I am fond of—but it seems to me, at a critical time, *the* step to set me right. A blessing on Mr. Mariotti my Italian master, and his pupil!— If you have any breath left, tell Topping how you are.

To T. J. SERLE, 1 NOVEMBER 1843*

MS Mr C. D. B. Hawksley. *Address:* T. J. Serle Esquire | 9 Southampton Row | Russell Square.

1 Devonshire Terrace | First November 1843.

My Dear Serle.

Let us meet here on Saturday at half past Seven exactly, as an Elton Committee.

Faithfully Yours
                                                                     CHARLES DICKENS

T. J. Serle Esquire

---

[1] The first suggestion of the letters which became *Pictures from Italy*, 1846.

[2] If, as seems likely, this project was for a novel with a continental setting, it never matured, though it persisted for some years; alternatively, the first notion of *Dombey and Son* may already have been in his mind.

[3] In order to make some profit from a continental edition.

[4] The policy taken out on 18 Nov 41; cf. CD's use of his Britannia policy as security for Chapman & Hall.

To MISS BURDETT COUTTS, 2 NOVEMBER 1843

MS Morgan Library. *Address:* To be forwarded | Miss Burdett Coutts | Stratton Street | Piccadilly.[1]

Devonshire Terrace. | Second November 1843.

Dear Miss Coutts.

On going out to Putney yesterday, I was perfectly amazed to find that Miss Meredith had gone direct to Brighton[2] in the Garden chair. I trust she is better; and that your Ague has gone over to Holland, to settle there.

I enclose you a note[3] I have had from the Ragged Schoolmaster. I don't know what you may have said to Lord Sandon, or whether you would desire to shew it him. But I send it to you, on the chance.

Nell distracts me. It unfortunately happens that there is no Institution (that I know of, or can find out, at least) where such a girl could learn a trade. This throws one on a choice of trades. Then I think of tambour-working—then of stay-making—then of shoe-binding—then of ready made Linening—then of Millinery—then of Straw Bonnet Making[4]—then of Mrs Brownrigge[5]—then of surplus labor—and then I give it up, with a headache.

Would it not be a good plan—first, to find out what the child thinks herself, and then to cast about among your servants for instance, whether they have not some friend or relation who is, or who knows some other friend or relation who is, in a respectable little way of business that would do for her? I could very easily find out, by personal inspection, whether it promised well. None of our former handmaidens are settled in any trade, except a most respectable cook,[6] who married from us (in a cab—No. 74) and keeps a thriving shop, I am told, "in the general line". But there seems to be nothing to learn, in the general

---

[1] Re-addressed, in unknown hand, to 2 Eastern Terrace | Brighton.

[2] Dr Brown evidently accompanied her; Henry Crabb Robinson called on her on 17 Nov ("her love Mr. Browne was there") and dined with them on 18 Nov, Charles Young and Miss Coutts being present, and Miss Meredith "in spirits . . . though under the care of her medical friend Mr. Browne" (MS Diary, Dr Williams's Library).

[3] Starey had written on 18 Oct thanking CD for his letter of 17 Oct and for Miss Coutts's donation, and for "laying the subject before the Council of Education". At present he was unable to move the school to better premises, as proposed in *To* Starey, 24 Sep 43, but was negotiating with the landlord of "a large shed in West Street", which could be converted into a schoolroom for 300 or 400 pupils for about £90 (MS Morgan).

[4] These are typical instances of trades to which girls could be apprenticed, all appearing either in the *Report of the Children's Employment Commission* (Appx F) or the *Journal of the Statistical Society*'s report of an investigation of the earnings of single women and widows in 1845 (XI, 206). CD may have recalled the case of Mrs Hibner, a tambour-worker who murdered two little female apprentices from the parish of St Pancras in about 1827 (referred to in the *Memoir* of Captain E. P. Brenton, pp. 47–8, and in a report of one of his meetings in *The Times*, 6 Dec 38).

[5] Elizabeth Brownrigg, a midwife, hanged at Tyburn in 1767 for causing the death of one of her female apprentices. "Elizabeth Brownrigge", a skit on Newgate novels, appeared in *Fraser's*, Aug–Sep 32; sometimes wrongly attributed to Thackeray, but probably by Leigh Hunt.

[6] Unidentified.

line,[1] except making up infinitessimal[2] parcels of pepper, and chopping soap
into little blocks—and she can do that now, I dare say.

There's half a bonnet-shop in Tottenham Court Road, with an Inscription in
the window in these words—"Wonted a feamail Prentis with a premum". *That*
wouldn't do, perhaps?

This day week, I shall have paid the Eltons, the full amount you gave me.
One of the poor girls[3] is very ill, I am sorry to say, and seems consumptive.
Did you see the cruel hoax of the bottle?[4] We have the slip of paper which was
shut up in it; and it is not (they tell me) in his handwriting, or at all like it.
What strange minds those must be, which can find delight in such intolerable
cruelties—for which, and which only, if I had my will, I would flog at the
church-doors. After the President went down, Mrs. Power[5] had some new
letter, almost every day, saying that he had landed in Ireland, and was staying
at the Writer's house!

Dear Miss Coutts | Always Faithfully Yours

Miss Burdett Coutts.   CHARLES DICKENS

To JOHN FORSTER, [2 NOVEMBER 1843]

Text from F, IV, ii, 305–6. *Date:* 2 Nov according to Forster.

I expected you to be startled.[6] If I was startled myself, when I first got this
project of foreign travel into my head, MONTHS AGO,[7] how much more must
you be, on whom it comes fresh: numbering only hours! Still, I am very
resolute upon it—very. I am convinced that my expenses abroad would not be
more than half of my expenses here; the influence of change and nature upon
me, enormous. You know, as well as I, that I think *Chuzzlewit* in a hundred
points immeasurably the best of my stories. That I feel my power now, more
than I ever did. That I have a greater confidence in myself than I ever had.
That I *know*, if I have health, I could sustain my place in the minds of thinking
men, though fifty writers started up to-morrow. But how many readers do *not*
think! How many take it upon trust from knaves and idiots, that one writes too
fast, or runs a thing to death! How coldly did this very book go on for months,
until it forced itself up in people's opinion, without forcing itself up in sale![8] If

---

[1] Like Mrs Chickenstalker, in *The Chimes*, 1844, Fourth Quarter.

[2] Thus in MS.

[3] Not known which of the six Elton daughters this was; probably not Esther or Rosa. Perhaps an older half-sister, said to have been sent by CD to Nice, who married a doctor; Esther (as Mrs Nash) joined her there in or before 1854 (undated cutting in Fitzgerald collection, Eastgate House, No. 341).

[4] "A few days ago a bottle was picked up at Waborne on the Norfolk coast, which contained a piece of paper on which the following had been written, in all probability, by the gentleman whose name it

bears, almost at the last moment:—'Pegasus—God help us! She's sinking! The bottle's empty; 'twill swim, and we also into eternity! Farewell!—ELTON'" (*Observer*, 22 Oct 43).

[5] Widow of Tyrone Power (1797–1841; *DNB*), Irish comedian and dramatist: see Vol. II, p. 104*n*.

[6] Forster opposed the project with "such insufficient breath as was left" to him, and urged "far more consideration" (F, IV, ii, 305), evidently also suggesting that CD should wait until the proposed cheap edition had brought in more money.

[7] Perhaps in June: see *To* Pichot, 7 June.

[8] See *To* Forster, 28 June 43, *fn*.

I wrote for forty thousand Forsters, or for forty thousand people who know I write because I can't help it, I should have no need to leave the scene. But this very book warns me that if I *can* leave it for a time, I had better do so, and must do so. Apart from that again, I feel that longer rest after this story would do me good. You say two or three months, because you have been used to see me for eight years[1] never leaving off. But it is not rest enough. It is impossible to go on working the brain to that extent for ever. The very spirit of the thing, in doing it, leaves a horrible despondency behind, when it is done; which must be prejudicial to the mind, so soon renewed, and so seldom let alone. What would poor Scott have given to have gone abroad, of his own free will, a young man, instead of creeping there, a driveller, in his miserable decay![2] I said myself in my note to you—anticipating what you put to me—that it was a question *what* I should come out with, first. The travel-book, if to be done at all, would cost me very little trouble; and surely would go very far to pay charges, whenever published. We have spoken of the baby,[3] and of leaving it here with Catherine's mother. Moving the children into France could not, in any ordinary course of things, do them anything but good. And the question is, what it would do to that by which they live: not what it would do to them.—I had forgotten that point in the B. and E. negociation[4]; but they certainly suggested instant publication of the reprints, or at all events of some of them; by which of course I know, and as you point out, I could provide of myself what is wanted. I take that as putting the thing distinctly as a matter of trade, and feeling it so. And, as a matter of trade with them or anybody else, as a matter of trade between me and the public, should I not be better off a year hence, with the reputation of having seen so much in the meantime? The reason which induces you to look upon this scheme with dislike—separation for so long a time—surely has equal weight with me. I see very little pleasure in it, beyond the natural desire to have been in those great scenes; I anticipate no enjoyment at the time. I have come to look upon it as a matter of policy and duty. I have a thousand other reasons, but shall very soon myself be with you.

To MRS HURNALL,[5] 2 NOVEMBER 1843

Extract in Edwin A. Denham catalogue No. XII (1902).

The Story of a Feather[6] (which you so justly commend) is written by Mr. Jerrold, an author of great power, who has been laid up with rheumatic gout, but is getting better rapidly.

---

[1] This would be since the writing of *Sketches* in 1835; but Forster did not meet CD until the winter of 1836–7.

[2] Scott went abroad in his last illness in Oct 1831, after his second stroke, returning the following July to die in Sep 1832.

[3] The child expected in Jan.

[4] Possibly delayed payment for the cheap edition, as opposed to "instant publication".

[5] Unidentified: but see Vol. II, p. 263*n*.

[6] Jerrold's story was appearing as a serial in *Punch*, 5 Jan–16 Dec 43, with some breaks owing to his illness.

To J. C. PRINCE, 2 NOVEMBER 1843

Text from transcript by Mr Walter Dexter.

1 Devonshire Terrace | York Gate Regents Park
Second November 1843

Dear Sir,

I regret too, I assure you, that we had not the pleasure of a longer conversation when we became known to each other at Manchester.[1]

I should say that the chances of your being able to connect yourself with a London Magazine as a paid contributor, were very good. I would recommend you to send one or two pieces, with a short note, to the Editor of Blackwood's Magazine; and one or two to Mr. Ainsworth for insertion in *his* Magazine. That gentleman is a native of Manchester, and very likely, I think, to be interested in you. If Blackwoods say No, try if Tait will say Yes.[2]

My Dear Sir | Faithfully Yours
Mr. J. C. Prince.   CHARLES DICKENS

P.S. I have no connexion with any magazine myself, or I would gladly assist you.

To OCTAVIAN BLEWITT, 6 NOVEMBER 1843

MS Royal Literary Fund.

1 Devonshire Terrace | York Gate Regents Park
Sixth November 1843

My Dear Sir.

I have heard, with much distress, from Mr. Charles Whitehead,[3] that he finds it necessary to seek assistance from the Literary Fund.[4] And he has requested me to speak to my knowledge of him.

I know him to be a gentleman of very great accomplishments, and of very

---

[1] See *To* Prince, 22 Sep.

[2] No evidence of any contributions to these magazines has been found, but there were verses by Prince in the *Pictorial Times*, 25 Nov 43 (poem dated Ashton-under-Lyne, 16 Nov 43) and 24 Feb 44; Prince's next volume, *Dreams and Realities*, 1847, also included some poems contributed to *Bradshaw's Magazine, The Leisure Hour*, and the *Oddfellows' Magazine*.

[3] Charles Whitehead (1804–62; *DNB*), novelist, dramatist and poet: see Vol. I, p. 207*n*.

[4] Whitehead's letter of application for the third of his five grants described in detail the "circumstances of great distress" which compelled him to make this application. For the past six months he and his wife had been subsisting on the amount raised by the sale of his furniture and the help of his two sisters; he was now in debt and threatened with arrest by a creditor. His last grant (£15 in 1837) had been of essential service, "contributing to raise me to a certain position in the literary world from which, I believe, nothing but the extreme depression of the publishing trade could have displaced me". He was granted £20. A letter of 1852 shows that since 1844 he had been in Bentley's employment, "revising and correcting MSS. and giving my opinion upon works submitted to him", but was paid only "by the piece"; Bentley's *List* under 20 Sep 42 says "he read for the firm", without dates (K. J. Fielding, "Charles Whitehead and CD", *Review of English Studies*, N.S. III [1952], 141–54).

high original power as a writer of Fiction.[1] I have always considered him to be an author of remarkable ability; have read his productions with strong interest; and have borne my testimony to their merit on many occasions, when I little thought he would ever need such a service as this at my hands.

I have reason to know that he has been proud in his troubles, and has never obtruded them on the notice of his admirers. I am sure he is a man of too honorable and high a spirit to appeal to the Literary Fund, but on the pressure of strong necessity. And I can conscientiously and earnestly recommend his case.

If you think I can say more, or that it is desirable for me to address the Committee in any other form, I will gladly do it.

My Dear Sir | Faithfully Yours

O. Blewitt Esquire
CHARLES DICKENS

To R. W. OSBALDISTON,[2] 8 NOVEMBER 1843

Mention in *To* Perry, 10 Nov.

To P. B. TEMPLETON,[3] 8 NOVEMBER 1843*

MS University of Texas. *Address:* P. B. Templeton Esquire | Manchester Advertizer Office | Manchester.

London—1 Devonshire Terrace | York Gate Regents Park
Eighth November 1843.

Dear Sir

"Laid down by brutal ignorance, and held together like the Solid Rock, by years of this most wicked axiom"—certainly.[4] This wicked axiom, meaning, the axiom that a little Learning is a dangerous thing.

I have glanced at your book on Short Hand; and it seems to me a very good one—as indeed you practically shew it to be, in your excellent Reporting. But I am sorry that I feel obliged to lay my earnest entreaties on you, *not* to publish

---

[1] His best work, *Richard Savage*, serialized in *Bentley's* 1841–2, was published in Sep 42, dedicated to Elton, dramatized by the author and successfully put on at the Surrey Theatre Jan 43; *The Earl of Essex*, a historical romance, was published Apr 43, also by Bentley.

[2] R. W. Osbaldiston, manager of the Victoria Theatre, had perhaps not yet sent the proceeds of his benefit for the Eltons; the final statement about the Fund was in *The Times*, 25 Nov.

[3] Reporter on the *Manchester Times* (as well as the *Advertiser*) and writer on shorthand; see *To* Watkin and Berlyn, 10 Oct. Formerly a schoolmaster at Preston; two editions of his *Six Lessons on Short-Hand*,

a manual of Taylor's stenography, published in 1840; in the Preface he claimed to have had "many years' experience in Short-Hand writing, both for his own private purposes, and for the benefit of the public, in connection with the newspaper press in some of the largest towns in this country"; attacked Isaac Pitman's new shorthand system in 1840 and carried on a long controversy with him (A. Baker, *Life of Sir Isaac Pitman*, 1908, pp. 55–63); later became a reporter in USA.

[4] See *Speeches*, ed. K. J. Fielding, p. 47; at the end of the paragraph in which the "axiom" is quoted. The report in the *Advertiser* reads "actions".

this opinion. I have a great objection to seeing such things in Print as if I were asserting my infallibility. And I assure you that if I were to comply with one Twentieth part of such requests, my warmest admirers would be disgusted by the sight of my name: as I certainly should be myself.

Faithfully Yours

P. B. Templeton Esquire   CHARLES DICKENS

To EDWARD WATKIN AND PETER BERLYN, 8 NOVEMBER 1843*

Text from transcript by Mr Walter Dexter. *Address:* Edward Watkin Esquire | Peter Berlyn Esquire | The Athenæum | Manchester.

Devonshire Terrace | Eighth November 1843

Dear Sirs

I am extremely happy to hear that the Athenæum is going on so favourably. The half holiday and the gift of the membership by the Merchants as a reward for good behaviour, are vital points.[1] The latter does great honor, I think, to the gentlemen of Manchester.

I enclose an acknowledgment[2] of the elegant gift[3] I received in due course; and I shall be much obliged if you will entrust yourselves with its delivery.

Dear Sirs | Always Faithfully Yours

Edward Watkin Esquire   CHARLES DICKENS
Peter Berlyn Esquire

To P. E. PEMBERGUE,[4] 8 NOVEMBER 1843

Text from *Manchester Guardian*, 11 Nov 1843.

Devonshire Terrace, | Eighth November 1843

Dear Sir,

Allow me to most gratefully acknowledge the gift of a life membership of the Manchester Athenæum; and the flattering, and earnest terms in which it is bestowed on me, in the elegant testimonial to which your signature is attached. I cannot have a warmer interest in the prosperity of such an Institution than I had before, nor can anything enhance the pleasure I feel in the recollection of

---

[1] At Watkin's instigation, a weekly half-holiday had just been conceded to employees in warehouses; on 4 Nov the committee concerned held a meeting to adopt a vote of thanks. One firm had decided to present many of their young men with annual membership of the Athenæum and others followed suit (*Manchester Guardian*, 8 and 11 Nov 43).

[2] See next.

[3] The certificate of life membership "beautifully embossed on vellum ... mounted and inclosed in a chaste carved gilt frame, of a most elegant design", with the Manchester arms and the words "Literature and Science" and "For the Diffusion of Knowledge" (*Manchester Guardian*, 11 Nov 43). The *Guardian* of 11 Oct had reported that "owing to an oversight" CD had left on 6 Oct without having become a member, so the documents were to be despatched to him.

[4] Chairman of the Board of Directors of the Athenæum; not named in reports as present at the Soirée.

having presided at one of its festivals. But I am truly gratified by this mark of the regard and approbation of the directors, and shall ever prize it highly—trust me.

> I have the honor to be, dear sir,
> Your most obliged and faithful servant,
> CHARLES DICKENS

To JOHN FORSTER, [10 NOVEMBER 1843]

Extract in F, IV, ii, 306–7. *Date:* 10 Nov according to Forster.

I have been all day in *Chuzzlewit* agonies[1]—conceiving only. I hope to bring forth to-morrow. Will you come here at six? I want to say a word or two about the cover of the *Carol* and the advertising,[2] and to consult you on a nice point in the tale. It will come wonderfully I think. Mac will call here soon after, and we can then all three go to Bulwer's[3] together. And do, my dear fellow, do for God's sake turn over about Chapman and Hall, and look upon my project as *a settled thing*.[4] If you object to see them, I must write to them.

To R. B. [PERRY],[5] 10 NOVEMBER 1843

Extract in Anderson Galleries catalogue No. 2273 (1928); dated Devonshire Terrace, 10 November 1843.

I enclose you my account of subscriptions; the balance is paid into Coutts's.[6] I wrote to Mr. Osbaldistone the day before yesterday, but have not yet received an answer.

---

[1] Over Chs 30–2, including the exposure of Pecksniff to Tom Pinch.

[2] Chapman & Hall published it for CD on commission; the account for the binding was £180. The first edition was "bound in fine-ribbed cloth, blocked in blind and gold on front, in gold on spine . . . All edges gilt" (Sadleir, *XIX Century Fiction*, 1951, p. 104). For the advertising see *To* Mitton, 4 Dec, *fn*.

[3] If this sentence really belongs in this letter, the plan cannot have been carried out. Forster wrote to Bulwer on 20 Dec (the day after Bulwer's mother's death) regretting that they had not met for so long, "but I have just recovered from a long and severe illness—which kept me a three months' prisoner to the house and bed" (MS Lytton Papers); cf. Forster *to*

Leigh Hunt, 11 Nov, saying, "I have not been many days promoted from bed to sofa" (MS BM). *To* Bulwer, 25 Jan 44 (N, I, 562) also seems to rule out the possibility of any such intention.

[4] See *To* Forster, 1 Nov. Forster was reluctant because of the *Carol*: "at such a moment to tell them, short of absolute necessity, his intention to quit them altogether, I thought a needless putting in peril of the little book's chances" (F, IV, ii, 307).

[5] "Terry" in catalogue extract; but R. B. Perry was Treasurer of the Elton Fund.

[6] CD's accounts show 8 guineas paid to the Elton Fund on 11 Nov; he had paid £5 to "Mr Perry" on 28 July, presumably as his own donation.

To W. H. PRESCOTT, 10 NOVEMBER 1843*

MS Mr Linzee Prescott. *Address:* By Mail Steam Packet | W. H. Prescott Esquire | Boston | United States.

London. 1 Devonshire Terrace | York Gate Regents Park
Tenth November 1843.

Mr Dear Prescott.

I avail myself of a minute's leisure this morning, to acknowledge the receipt of your last kind note. I am afraid of putting it off until I have time to write a long reply; for how many boats would cross and recross the Atlantic before that came about, Heaven only knows.

I have received your noble book, through Mr. Rich.[1] It came here a few days ago. I am half way through it already, and *am full of delight and pleasure—* dreaming of it, talking of it, and thinking of it. It will exceed the warmest expectations of your warmest admirers, I am convinced.[2]

Your bargain with Bentley, amazes me! He has no copyright, you know, one moment after the publication of the work in America. You could not have got more, in the existing state of the law; and could have got much less with stupendous ease.[3] Moreover, the Brigand has really brought the book out in a handsome form, and done it justice.[4] For which I take off one of the seven hundred thousand imprecations I laid upon his head during the ancient intercourse between myself and him;[5] and leave him only six hundred and ninety nine thousand to wipe off by decent conduct.

The heartiest of Greek Professors has become strangely mute. I wrote him a

---

[1] The *History of the Conquest of Mexico*, published by Bentley in 3 vols on 28 Oct 43. In a letter of 15 Oct Prescott had asked for one of his 12 copies to go to CD (*Correspondence*, ed. R. Wolcott, p. 401); James Rich of Red Lion Square was his bookseller. CD's copy was in the Gad's Hill library at his death.

[2] CD's opinion of the work was widely shared, and it quickly won its permanent reputation, as a picturesque narrative delighting the general reader, as well as a major historical work. The favourable English reception gave Prescott great pleasure, especially a letter of praise from Hallam, "one of the head of the craft", and Lyell's comment, in a letter to Ticknor, that "every body in London is reading the Conquest of Mexico" (*The Literary Memoranda of W. H. Prescott*, ed. C. Harvey Gardiner, 1961, II, 115–16).

[3] See *To* Prescott, 2 Mar 43, *fn.* Bentley's payment of £650 was conditional on his being allowed to publish at least a fortnight before the American publication which in fact was on 6 Dec. It was somewhat higher than CD's own estimate of

what Prescott might expect, but well below his eventual receipts from Bentley for *Ferdinand and Isabella* (C. Harvey Gardiner, *Prescott and his Publishers*, Southern Illinois, 1959, p. 233). CD's views had been affected by his prejudice against Bentley as well as his wish to favour Chapman & Hall; a writer in the *Knickerbocker* (XXXV [1850], 277) says of Bentley: "No English publisher has brought out one half the number of American works; indeed the liberality of Mr. Bentley towards American authors is well known, and he is now identified with the literature of this country". Bentley and Prescott remained on good terms until Aug 56 when misunderstandings led to Prescott's leaving Bentley for Routledge.

[4] Prescott had stipulated that the *Conquest* should be as well produced as *Ferdinand and Isabella*, and was especially concerned about the portraits, maps and documents. The volumes were "handsomely bound in dark-blue cloth" with a design on the cover.

[5] In 1837–40.

beaming epistle of four sides of paper; and he introduces a friend[1] (after its receipt) with four lines! I am not quite certain whether he won't find himself in Chuzzlewit before long. At the best, I shall cut him off with an oyster.

What an unnatural villain you must be, to disparage Mrs. Prescott's eyes.[2] I shuddered when I read the passage. Her critical taste assures me that her mental eyes are brighter than Diamonds. To her physical organs of vision I have indited a Sonnet, which will be forwarded by the next mail. Being rather heavy, it will come as Goods.

Mrs. Dickens sends her love and best regards. We think of keeping the New Year, by having another child. I am constantly reversing the Kings in the Fairy Tales, and importuning the Gods not to trouble themselves: being quite satisfied with what I have. But they are *so* generous when they *do* take a fancy to one!

Longfellow has done quite right, and I commend him for it. My best remembrances to him, and all old friends in Boston.

Always My Dear Prescott | Faithfully Yours

W. H. Prescott Esquire CHARLES DICKENS

To SIR WILLIAM ALLAN,[3] 13 NOVEMBER 1843[4]

Text from Sir Theodore Martin, *Helena Faucit (Lady Martin)*, 1900, p. 117.

Devonshire Terrace, | York Gate, Regent's Park,
13th November 1843.

My Dear Allan,

I am very anxious to bespeak your kind offices in behalf of Miss Helen Faucit:[5] a young lady who is a much esteemed friend of ours, and whose great

---

[1] Probably Theodore Parker, who sailed for England in Sep 43; CD speaks of meeting him in *To* Felton, 2 Jan 44.

[2] Unexplained.

[3] Sir William Allan (1782–1850; *DNB*), historical painter: see Vol. II, p. 65*n*.

[4] F. G. Kitton, *CD by Pen and Pencil*, II, 159, and N, II, 128, read "1848".

[5] Helen (later Helena) Saville Faucit (1817–98; *DNB*), actress, and later (as Lady Martin) author of *On Some of Shakespeare's Female Characters*, 1885, was now rapidly advancing in her distinguished career. She was an unusually sensitive and intelligent actress as well as beautiful and accomplished. Youngest daughter of Saville Faucit and Harriet (*née* Diddear), both on the stage, but separated in her early childhood; as a girl, met Edmund Kean, and was encouraged by him to play Juliet at the Richmond Theatre. For many years was taught and advised by Percival Farren, brother of William, the actor (with whom her mother was living), and made her London début

with Kemble as Julia in Knowles's *Hunchback*, 1836. Macready first met her at Kean's funeral in 1833; she was his leading lady at Covent Garden 1836–8, and at the Haymarket 1839, 1841, her greatest successes being in Shakespeare and as the heroines of five of Bulwer's plays. Her part in *Strafford* (1837) led to a lifelong friendship with Browning. Illness interrupted her career in the winter of 1839–40 and "gross insinuations" in the press hinted at pregnancy and intimacy with Macready (*Diaries*, II, 40, 48, 49); the situation was complicated by her deep personal devotion to him, with which he dealt wisely. Macready's mature judgment of her in 1845 was "a very pleasing, clever, and good actress, but ... not a great one" (*Diaries*, II, 307–8). In his Drury Lane season of 1842–3 CD saw her as Lady Mabel in *The Patrician's Daughter* and in *King John*, *Comus*, and probably *Cymbeline*. On CD's death she recalled "how kind he was to me when we met in my very early days at Mr. Macready's,

abilities I hold in high regard. She is coming to Edinburgh to fulfil an engagement with Murray. If you and Miss Allan[1] can come to know her in private, I will answer for your having real pleasure in her society, and for your not taxing me with overrating her excellent qualities. I am "say[2] fond" of her, which I think—and as an Edinburgh citizen I *ought* to *know*[3]—is good Lowlan' Scotch.

Kate unites in this, and in kind loves to Miss Allan and yourself.

Always, my dear Allan, faithfully your friend,

CHARLES DICKENS

To R. H. HORNE, 13 NOVEMBER 1843

Text from MDGH, I, 93.

Devonshire Terrace, November 13th 1843.

Pray tell that besotted —— to let the opera sink into its native obscurity.[4] I did it in a fit of d——ble good nature long ago, for Hullah, who wrote some very pretty music to it. I just put down for everybody what everybody at the St. James's Theatre wanted to say and do, and that they could say and do best, and I have been most sincerely repentant ever since. The farce[5] I also did as a sort of practical joke, for Harley, whom I have known a long time. It was funny— adapted from one of the published sketches called the "Great Winglebury Duel," and was published by Chapman and Hall. But I have no copy of it now, nor should I think they have. But both these things were done without the least consideration or regard to reputation.[6]

I wouldn't repeat them for a thousand pounds apiece, and devoutly wish them to be forgotten. If you will impress this on the waxy mind of —— I shall be truly and unaffectedly obliged to you.

Always faithfully yours

[CHARLES DICKENS]

Mr. S. C. Hall's, and at his own house" (Theodore Martin, *Helena Faucit* (*Lady Martin*), p. 306). From 1840 she was on social terms with the Macreadys, and had dined there with the Dickenses on 28 May 43 (*Diaries*, II, 209). M'Ian, another early friend, also wrote to Edinburgh on her behalf, and his letter and CD's (of which she was unaware) were the means of Theodore Martin's first introduction to her (Martin, p. 117); they were married in 1851. The Edinburgh season, after a slow start on 14 Nov with *The Lady of Lyons*, was a triumphant success.

[1] Allan's niece: see Vol. II, p. 321.

[2] Martin reads "very": Kitton and N read "say" (for "sae"), obviously correctly.

[3] Thus in Kitton and N; Martin reads "know".

[4] In *A New Spirit of the Age*, 1844 (I,

46) Horne nevertheless wrote: "Few are perhaps aware that Mr. Dickens once wrote an Opera ... set to music very prettily by Hullah ... but, somehow, it vanished into space; albeit, at dusty old book-stalls [it may occasionally be found] labelled price three-pence". *The Village Coquettes* was published by Bentley in Dec 36: see Vol. I, p. 172*n*. The "besotted ——" referred to may have been Thomas Powell, who claimed to have written the essay on CD jointly with Horne.

[5] *The Strange Gentleman*. Horne said "it 'went off' in a smoke, with Harley wringing his hands at the top of the cloud" (*ibid.*).

[6] "Leaving these failures behind him with so light a pace that no one heard him moving off, and never once turning back his head" (*op. cit.*, p. 47).

To CHARLES SMITHSON, 14 NOVEMBER 1843

Text from transcript by Mr R. E. G. Woodman (*Times Literary Supplement*, 25 Jan 1947).

Devonshire Terrace, | Tuesday, Fourteenth November, 1843.

My Dear Smithson,

I wish you to know one or two facts and one or two opinions of mine, upon which (so far as I understand what Mitton tells me of your correspondence together) I have a natural desire to set you right.

Don't believe all you hear; and least of all believe the flying rumours that rise about Lewisham and Blackheath Hill.[1]

More than £2,000—in fact all the debt that is likely to exist at the expiration of Chuzzlewit—was advanced by Chapman and Hall to wrest the copyright of Oliver Twist from Bentley, and release me from the Magazine. It was advanced, more for their benefit than mine; for they had a fortune, and I had only an income from the work then in progress, which would have been greatly damaged by his flooding the town with Oliver in numbers.[2] The Clock, with a circulation more than equal to that of The Times multiplied by five, was certainly not a very profitable undertaking. But not from any onesidedness in the agreement, but because every calculation made by Chapman and Hall (who are preposterously ignorant of all the essentials of their business) was wrong, and the thing could not pay largely at the price. The Oliver agreement was of my own making, and so was the Pickwick. It was a consequence of the astonishing rapidity of my success and the steady rise of my fame that the enormous profits of these books should flow into other hands than mine. It has always been so (I speak from a knowledge of the lives of eminent and successful writers); and I cannot reasonably hope to be exempt from the curse which has fallen on all the Professors of Literature.

The Nickleby agreement turned out to be a terrible mistake, though at that time the stability of my success was not certain. But it was a mistake to which I was the chief party, and the blame of which mainly rests with me.[3]

I wish you to know that Bradbury and Evans would bring to my house £3,000[4] to-morrow morning. But I do not take it, and will not; simply because I wish to free myself by my own exertions, and not by the assistance of "The Trade."

I cordially approved of the project of confiding with you, because I had no reason to be delicate of your knowing these things; and had reason, I thought,

---

[1] i.e. from his parents: see *To* Mitton, 7 Dec 42, and 28 Sep 43. CD's accounts between Dec 43 and July 44 contain numerous payments to "Mrs. Jno Dickens" and "Lewisham". In order to moderate their demands he had perhaps exaggerated the difficulties of his financial position, and rumours had spread to Smithson through Fred.

[2] It is very doubtful that Bentley intended this; see Vol. I, pp. 647–8.

[3] The "mistake" was presumably in letting Chapman & Hall have the copyright for five years for £3000 (£150 a number). For the Agreements referred to, see Vol. I, pp. 655–62, 681, Vol. II, pp. 464–81.

[4] i.e. if he left Chapman & Hall for them, and agreed to early publication of a cheap edition.

to believe that if you had the money to put out at all, you would as soon advance
it for a short period to one in whose energy and honor you could confide, as you
would employ it in any other way. If you haven't got it to spare—you can't
send it.

But as I would not have been assisted on mistaken grounds, and would not
have had the money on any terms while you were wrong in your understanding
of anything connected with my position, so I do not like to close the matter in
any misconception and therefore I have written you this note.

My dear Smithson, | Faithfully yours,

Charles Smithson, Esquire.   CHARLES DICKENS

To JOHN FORSTER, [?17 NOVEMBER 1843]

Mention in F, IV, ii, 307. *Date:* according to Forster "a few days" after CD's
letter of 10 Nov; his letter of 19 Nov answered, "on the following day", Forster's
reply.

Describing with great bitterness one of his family's financial demands.[1]

To JOHN FORSTER, [19 NOVEMBER 1843]

Extract in F, IV, ii, 307–8. *Date:* 19 Nov according to Forster.

I was most horribly put out for a little while; for I had got up early to go at it,
and was full of interest in what I had to do. But having eased my mind by that
note to you, and taken a turn or two up and down the room, I went at it again,
and soon got so interested that I blazed away till 9 last night; only stopping ten
minutes for dinner! I suppose I wrote eight printed pages of *Chuzzlewit* yesterday. The consequence is that I *could* finish to-day, but am taking it easy, and
making myself laugh very much.[2]

To JOHN FORSTER, [20 NOVEMBER 1843]

Extract in F, IV, ii, 308. *Date:* the day after last according to Forster.[3]

I am quite serious and sober when I say, that I have very grave thoughts of
keeping my whole menagerie in Italy, three years.

---

[1] One of "many, never-satisfied, con-
stantly-recurring claims from family
quarters, not the more easily avoidable
because unreasonable and unjust" (F, IV,
ii, 307).

[2] He had evidently written the latter part
of Ch. 31 on 18 Nov, leaving Ch. 32, a
short Todgers chapter (five printed pages),
to write; Augustus Moddle would make
him "laugh very much".

[3] "The very next day, unhappily, there
came to himself a repetition of precisely
similar trouble in exaggerated form, and
to me a fresh reminder of what was gradually settling into a fixed resolve", says
Forster.

To GEORGE CRUIKSHANK, 21 NOVEMBER 1843*

MS Carl H. Pforzheimer Library. *Address:* George Cruikshank Esquire | 4 Clifton Terrace | near The Baths | Gravesend.

Devonshire Terrace | Twenty First November 1843.

My Dear George

Many Thanks for the Almanack,[1] in which you are prodigious.

I am afraid I may not be in the way tomorrow; and therefore write to you. For I am finishing a little Book for Christmas, and contemplate a Bolt, to do so in peace. As soon as I have done, I will let you know, and then I hope we shall take a glass of Grog together: for I have not seen you since I was grey.

Always Heartily Yours

George Cruikshank Esquire CHARLES DICKENS

To JOHN WILSON,[2] 24 NOVEMBER 1843*

MS Morgan Library.

Devonshire Terrace. | Friday Evening | Twenty Fourth November 1843.

Sir.

Allow me to ask whether you addressed a letter to me this morning, recommending a Petitioner from Scotland? If so, I grieve to assure you that my means are utterly inadequate to answer the enormous number of similar appeals that are made to me every day; and would be if my income were multiplied by four, and my blood-petitioners divided by six.[3] Do you know anything of this unhappy person's case, beyond what you have told me? And how do you know that?

Your obedient Servant

Mr. John Wilson. CHARLES DICKENS

To THOMAS MITTON, 25 NOVEMBER 1843*

MS University of Texas. *Address:* Thomas Mitton Esquire | 23 Southampton Buildings.

Twenty Fifth November 1843

My Dear Mitton

Let every bill be returned, with "No orders" noted on it; and let the answer be, that no such person is known at your office.

---

[1] Cruikshank's *Comic Almanac* for 1844, published by 18 Nov; CD may have been particularly struck by his satiric "Report on the Treatment of Pauper Children" (March) and "The Unexhibited Cartoon of Guy Fawkes".

[2] Not Professor Wilson or John Wilson the vocalist (see *To* Wilson, 13 May), but evidently a stranger; possibly one of the John Wilsons living in CD's neighbourhood at 16 Devonshire St and 41 Chester Terrace.

[3] That is, his parents, brothers, and one sister—presumably Fanny.

After that, he[1] must have the money to take them up, and must be seen to take them up, or he'll not do it. What after that, it is impossible to say. I am full of Grief.

On Monday Evening I will come to you. Your note found me in the full passion of a roaring Christmas scene![2]

Faithfully Ever

CD

To MISS MARION ELY, [29 NOVEMBER 1843]*

MS Berg Collection. *Date:* Since from Devonshire Terrace, the only possible Christmas book is the *Carol* or the *Cricket*; but by 1845 Miss Ely had seen CD act. Wednesday must be 29 Nov, as he is finishing the *Carol*, and refers to the dinner on 2 Dec (see below).

Devonshire Terrace | Wednesday Morning

My Dear Miss Ely.

Forgive my not having answered your kind note; but I have been working from morning until night upon my little Christmas Book; and have really had no time to think of anything but that.

I am much pleased by your sister's[3] recollection of me, and if I can possibly get to the "Theatre"[4] tonight (I have strong hopes of it, for I am finishing now) —trust me, I will. For I have such a passion for anything in the shape of Private Theatricals—Ah! You never saw me act!—as nobody but Mrs. Harris[5] ever had.

We dine on Saturday[6]—Kate begs me say, with her love to Mrs. Talfourd— at a Quarter before Seven.

Dear Miss Ely | Always Faithfully Yours

Miss Ely.   CHARLES DICKENS

---

[1] Presumably John Dickens.

[2] The date seems too late for the most "roaring" of the Christmas scenes, the Fezziwigs' ball in Stave II; the reference must be either to the Cratchits' Christmas dinner or the party at the nephew's in Stave III. Staves IV and V occupy 16 MS pages.

[3] Marion had at least three younger sisters, Rachael, Helen and Jane, and three brothers, one of whom was in India by 1846; the youngest was Talfourd Ely, whose uncle paid for his education at University College School (1851–4) and University College, London; according to Crabb Robinson Mrs Ely's "second daughter" married a solicitor named Stuck (*Memorials of John Towill Rutt*, 1845; Crabb Robinson MS Diary, Dr Williams's Library).

[4] Probably a performance in Talfourd's own house; on 13 Jan 46 Browning went to "Frank Talfourd's theatricals, and met Dickens and his set" (*Letters of Robert Browning and Elizabeth Barrett*, 1899, I, 394), and on 24 Jan 48 Crabb Robinson saw a performance of *Ion* in "a neat little theatre . . . in the large drawing room" (MS Diary).

[5] The mythical Mrs Harris had first appeared in Ch. 25 of *Chuzzlewit* (Oct No.).

[6] Recorded in Barham's Diary for 2 Dec (*Life and Letters of Richard Barham by his Son*, 1870, II, 167). Among the other guests were Sydney Smith, Fonblanque, Tagart, Maclise, Forster, and Rogers; Barham noted an amusing story about Sydney Smith and Colburn, but no other details.

To JOHN W. BOWDEN,[1] 2 DECEMBER 1843*

MS New York University Library.

1 Devonshire Terrace | York Gate Regents Park
Second December 1843.

Sir.

Being the person referred to, in your letter, I have much pleasure in complying with your request, for an Autograph[2]—as I should have had in any case.

Faithfully Yours

CHARLES DICKENS

John Bowden Esquire

To CHARLES MARTIN,[3] 2 DECEMBER 1843*

MS Huntington Library.

Devonshire Terrace | Second December 1843.

Dear Sir

I regret that I was not at home yesterday, when you called.

It will give me pleasure to see you Tomorrow (Sunday) at Two, or on Monday at half past Twelve.[4]

Faithfully Yours

CHARLES DICKENS

Charles Martin Esquire

[1] A schoolfellow of CD's at Wellington House in 1826–7; sent recollections of him to the *Daily News*, 21 Dec 71, recalling how they "used to write short tales" and "lend them to other boys to read", and "occasionally issued a small morning newspaper containing comic advertisements and scraps of news"; also mentioning Lane, the head tutor, who played the flute, and afterwards opened a school on his own account in Lambeth. Further recollections were communicated to Robert Langton: see *The Childhood and Youth of CD*, revised edn, 1912, pp. 88–90.

[2] Bowden mentions his letter in the *Daily News* (misdating it 1847) and refers to CD's reply.

[3] Charles Martin (1820–1906; *DNB*), portrait-painter; fifth surviving child of the painter John Martin; first exhibited at the RA 1834; assisted his father in his historical picture of the Coronation 1838, and was living with him in 1841. In America 1849–53, where he made numerous crayon portraits and became a friend of Longfellow and Irving; married his cousin Mary Anne Wilson, but deserted her; last exhibited at the RA 1896.

[4] Possibly their first meeting; but CD had met John Martin and an older son Leopold at Cruikshank's in 1836, according to Leopold's "Reminiscences of John Martin" (*Newcastle Weekly Chronicle*, 1889, quoted in M. L. Pendered, *John Martin, Painter*, 1923, p. 124). In 1843, according to Henry Vizetelly, Charles Martin was "a young fellow about town who at all times got himself up in the very pink of fashion . . . pushing his way into upper-class society" (*Glances back through Seventy Years*, 1893, i, 255). He commissioned Martin to make a series of portraits, "Living Litterateurs", for publication in his new periodical the *Pictorial Times*; the first, Samuel Lover's, appeared on 30 Mar 44, and CD's, the second, on 20 Apr. Other subjects included Talfourd, Lady Blessington, Rogers, Disraeli, Procter, Ainsworth, Lady Morgan and Hood; the descriptions, some of which were signed "Asper", were all written by Peter Cunningham, Martin's brother-in-law, who claimed to have seen CD first in "the heyday of his rising reputation" and would have known him as Treasurer of the Shakespeare Society. Some of the original drawings were reproduced in *Twelve Victorian Celebrities. A Series of Original Portraits by Charles Martin*, 1899, with an introductory note by Curzon Eyre describing his meeting with Martin, whose recollections he noted; Martin recalled that CD

To CHAPMAN & HALL, [2-4 DECEMBER 1843]

Mention in next. *Date:* written after seeing Bradbury on 2 Dec.

To THOMAS MITTON, 4 DECEMBER [1843]*

MS Morgan Library. *Date:* 1843 on reference to *Carol*; 4 Dec was a Monday.

Devonshire Terrace | Monday Fourth December

My Dear Mitton

Just now, as I was coming down to you, a man brought a note from Lady Holland: begging me to dine there today,[1] and to go and give her some advice this morning—Heaven knows what about. So I am obliged to turn my face Westward, and not Eastward. But I write to you for three reasons. First, to know whether anything has occurred. Secondly, what time tomorrow will suit you best for my calling on you. Thirdly, to ask you to turn over in your mind, between this and tomorrow, how I can best put £200 into Coutts's. For on looking into the matter this morning, for the first time these 6 weeks, I find (to my horror) that I have already overdrawn[2] my account. This month's money I have paid into the Eagle.[3] Next month's is bespoke. And therefore I must anticipate the Christmas Book, by the sum I mention, which will enable me to keep comfortable.

If it would[4] damage you, or bother you very much, to break the bill at Dixons[5] by that sum, suppose you give me your acceptance at 3 months for it, and I will tell them I want it discounted at Coutts's?[6] What do you think of this? The reason that I am pressed to do it, *at once* is, that I want it done, before I have any notice of my account being overdrawn—which is very important.

Of course, I could have double the sum from C and H, instantly. But I have been obliged to write them a most tremendous letter, and have told them not to answer it, or to come near me, but simply to do what I have ordered them. Can you believe that with the exception of Blackwood's, *the Carol is not advertized*

---

asked him if he knew what "a *convivial* glass of port wine" was, because "Samuel Carter Hall has just written asking if I will go and take one with him". Cunningham's article described CD as "small, but well-made; his look intelligent, and his eyes peculiarly expressive. He seemed scanning you, not obtrusively but unobservedly, from head to foot", and noted that "the pencils of Wilkie and Maclise have been employed to adorn his walls; his library is extensive". The portrait drawing of CD, now in the Huntington Library, is full-length, and shows him lounging in an arm-chair; the engraving in the *Pictorial Times* is reproduced in *D*, IV (1908), 58, and in B. W. Matz's edn of Forster's *Life*, I, 334.

[1] The Holland House Dinner Book (MS BM) shows that CD dined at 9 Great Stanhope Street, in a party of 12, including the St Aulaires, Sydney Smith, and Charles Greville.

[2] Not by more than a few pounds.

[3] The accounts show a payment of £124.11.8 on 4 Dec to the Eagle Company; on 1 Dec CD had received £100 from Chapman & Hall.

[4] Word confused; almost certainly "will" changed to "would".

[5] Probably the bankers, Dixon, Brooks, and Dixon, 25 Chancery Lane.

[6] "Bill on T. Mitton discod. £200", is in the accounts for 5 Dec (MS Messrs Coutts).

in One of the Magazines![1] Bradbury would not believe it when I told him on Saturday last. And he says that nothing but a tremendous push can possibly atone for such fatal neglence. Consequently, I have written to the Strand, and said—Do this—Do that—Do the other—keep away from me—and be damned.

I have shewn the book to two or three Judges[2] of very different views and constitutions. I have never seen men, personally and mentally opposed to each other, so unanimous in their predictions, or so hot in their approval.

I *can* come down to you before dinner to day—at 4 or 5. A word by Bearer. I wouldn't trouble you about the money, if it were not a case of necessity. But being so busy, I have let it pass until the very last moment. In March or so, please God, I shall be as rich as (a very moderate) Jew.

Faithfully Ever
CD.

To THOMAS MITTON, [6 DECEMBER 1843]

MS Huntington Library. *Date:* Coutts's had discounted the bill on 5 Dec (*To* Mitton, 4 Dec, *fn*). *Address:* Thomas Mitton Esquire.

Devonshire Terrace. | Wednesday

My Dear Mitton

I am extremely glad you *feel* the Carol.[3] For I knew I meant a good thing. And when I see the effect of such a little *whole* as that, on those for whom I care, I have a strong sense of the immense effect I could produce with an entire book. I am quite certain of that.

Bradbury predicts Heaven knows what. I am sure it will do me a great deal of good; and I hope it will sell, well.

The title page I have had materially altered.[4] They always look bad at first.

I had a letter from Coutts's yesterday afternoon to say that they had much

---

[1] The *Carol* had been first advertised in the *Examiner* on 18 Nov and in other weeklies on 25 Nov, but the omission of the magazines was serious, as there could be no later opportunity before publication. The monthlies should have carried announcements like the one between the plates and the text in the Dec No. of *Chuzzlewit*—a whole page, with the same wording as in the weeklies: "New Christmas Book by Mr Dickens. In December will be published . . . with Four Coloured Etchings and Woodcuts by Leech A CHRISTMAS CAROL In Prose. Being a Ghost Story of Christmas. . . . Price Five Shillings".

[2] Probably some of his guests on 2 Dec: see *To* Miss Ely, ?29 Nov, *fn*.

[3] The proofs were evidently lent to Mitton to read on 4 or 5 Dec. The MS

(with the words "My own, and only MS of the Book") was at some time presented to Mitton, bound in red morocco with "Thomas Mitton" on the cover; if, as Kitton says, it was presented "on publication", it was perhaps a token of gratitude for the loan, or possibly it was presented in the course of 1844, as a return for Mitton's help over the Chancery suits against the pirates. Mitton sold the MS in 1875; it is now in the Morgan Library.

[4] Probably from red and green to red and blue: see P. Calhoun and H. J. Heaney, "Dickens' Christmas Carol after a Hundred Years" (*Papers of the Bibliographical Society of America*, XXXIX [1945], 271–317). All known copies presented before publication have red and blue title pages and yellow end-papers. See *To* Leech, 14 Dec, *fn*.

pleasure in discounting the bill: though they were not in the habit of doing so, without the acceptance of a banker or large mercantile house.

Faithfully Ever
CD.

To W. HARRISON AINSWORTH, 7 DECEMBER 1843*

MS Morgan Library.

Devonshire Terrace. | Seventh December 1843.

My Dear Ainsworth.

Half past five. Sharp as Jack Sheppard, and bright as Jolly Nose.[1]
Loves to all.

Faithfully Always

William Harrison Ainsworth Esquire CHARLES DICKENS

To GEORGE CRUIKSHANK, 7 DECEMBER 1843

MS Colonel Richard Gimbel.

Devonshire Terrace | Seventh December 1843.

My Dear George.

Ainsworth, Thackeray, Maclise, and Forster—and maybe another or two—dine here, at a short notice, on Saturday next at *Half Past Five*, punctually. Come to my arms!

Faithfully Ever

George Cruikshank Esquire CHARLES DICKENS

To THOMAS HOOD, 7 DECEMBER 1843*

MS Folio Society.

Devonshire Terrace | Seventh December 1843

My Dear Hood.

It has not at all surprised me, that I have not heard from you. I know how busy you must be just now; and did not expect it.

I am glad I did not make your proposal to C and H. There can be no kind of doubt that your ballads should appear, in the first instance at all events, in your own Magazine.[2]

---

[1] The drinking song in Part II, Ch. 5, of *Jack Sheppard* begins "Jolly Nose! the bright rubies that garnish thy tip".

[2] Hood had written (on "Monday", presumably 4 Dec): "You will have wondered at not hearing from me; but the truth is after receivg your note, about Chapman & Hall, it struck me, that in case the arrangement for my Magazine was completed I ought to throw my new ballads into the periodical" (MS New York;

Letters of Thomas Hood, ed. P. Morgan, p. 577). Hood's letter of 11 Sep mentions his intention of bringing out "the Elm Tree Poem" by itself (first published *New Monthly Magazine*, Sep 42), and his plan of writing two others, "to be illustrated, like the German ones . . ." (*op. cit.*, p. 554). One of these may have been "The Haunted House", which appeared in *Hood's Magazine*, Jan 44.

Your prospectus[1] is *admirable*, and I hear but one opinion of it on all sides. Whatever you do, be early with your number.[2] Up to the scratch in good season!

Faithfully Ever
CHARLES DICKENS

Thomas Hood Esquire

To MR FOUNTAIN,[3] 12 DECEMBER 1843*

MS Mr H. E. Quick.

1 Devonshire Terrace | York Gate Regents Park
Twelfth December 1843

Sir.

I truly regret to say, that I have no present means of giving you any employment in your present occupation. But if I should have an opportunity, I will bear your letter in mind. Do not suppose I shall be the less mindful of it, because, in the pressure of laborious engagements, I acknowledge its receipt thus briefly.

Truly Yours
CHARLES DICKENS

Mr. Fountain

To W. M. THACKERAY, [?12–13 DECEMBER 1843]

Mention in Thackeray *to* Ainsworth, [Dec 43], *Letters and Private Papers*, ed. G. N. Ray, II, 132. *Date: see fn.*

Begs for a remission of the dinner.[4]

---

[1] Hood's letter of ?4 Dec continued: "As you will see by the enclosure, the Magazine is to be". The prospectus (reprinted in T. Hood Jr and F. Broderip, *Memorials of Thomas Hood*, II, 186–9) emphasized the purpose of light entertainment and disclaimed party spirit and comments on political and religious questions; "a critical eye will be kept on our current Literature,—a regretful one on the Drama, and a kind one on the Fine Arts". There was also a facetious advertisement of the opening number of 1 Jan 44, set out in the form of an auctioneers' catalogue, including, for example, the "CURIOUS TABLE | of Contents ... ARTICLES OF VIRTUE, | A Temperance Romance, especially addressed to the associations of the UNIQUE TEA SERVICE".

[2] "I have had quite as much—& a bittock—to do as fits my powers, you will suppose, and am still hard at work. | I am besides in all the anxieties of my Trial with Bailey which comes on this week. | Make Tom Pinch turn Author, and Pecksniff become a Publisher" (?4 Dec).

[3] Unidentified.

[4] Ray suggests that Thackeray's dinner was planned for 18 Dec to repay CD for the dinner on 9 Dec 43. Thackeray also wrote to Maclise on "Wednesday" (?13 Dec) from Jermyn Street, to which he had moved in that month, saying that "Ainsworth & Boz won't come & press for delay" (*op. cit.*, II, 133).

To JOHN LEECH, 14 DECEMBER 1843[1]

MS Benoliel Collection.

Devonshire Terrace | Fourteenth December 1843.

My Dear Sir

I do not doubt, in my own mind, that you unconsciously exaggerate the evil done by the colourers.[2] You can't think how much better they will look in a neat book, than you suppose. But I have sent a Strong Despatch[3] to C and H, and will report to you when I hear from them. I quite agree with you, that it is a point of great importance.

                                              Faithfully Yours
John Leech Esquire   CD

To DANIEL MACLISE, 17 DECEMBER 1843*

MS University of Texas.

Devonshire Terrace | Seventeenth December 1843

My Dear Mac.

I think of walking out to Ainsworth's this morning at a quarter before 2, and giving him his copy of the enclosed.[4] Will you come? I was writing this Morning until Three o'Clock.[5]

                                              Faithfully Ever
                                                     CD

To SAMUEL ROGERS, 17 DECEMBER 1843

MS Professor E. S. Pearson.

Devonshire Terrace | Seventeenth December 1843.

My Dear Mr. Rogers

If you should ever have inclination and patience to read the accompanying little book,[6] I hope you will like the slight fancy it embodies. But whether you do or no,[7] I am ever

                                        Your friend and admirer
Samuel Rogers Esquire   CHARLES DICKENS

---

[1] Wrongly dated 1847 in N, II, 63.

[2] Four of Leech's eight illustrations were etched on steel and the impressions afterwards coloured by hand (F. G. Kitton, *Dickens and his Illustrators*, p. 140). Maclise, in a letter to Forster of Oct–Nov 44 (MS Forster Collection, V & A), called the *Carol* "the very climax of vulgarity in its mise en planches", perhaps in reference to the colouring of the plates (not used for any later Christmas book) or more particularly the title-page with its red and blue type.

[3] Perhaps the same as the "tremendous letter" of 2–4 Dec: see *To* Mitton, 4 Dec.

[4] The *Carol*; see next.

[5] At *Chuzzlewit*, Chs 33–5, the last American number.

[6] CD presented at least 10 other copies before publication on 19 Dec: to Ainsworth, Carlyle, Miss Coutts, Fonblanque, Forster, Landor, Tagart, Talfourd, Thackeray, and Mrs Touchet. Many of these survive, and the inscriptions are given in P. Calhoun and H. J. Heaney, "Dickens' *Christmas Carol*", *Papers of the Bibliographical Society of America*, XXXIX (1945), 271–317. The Thackeray copy is inscribed "To W. M. Thackeray from Charles Dickens (Whom he made very happy once, a long way from home)"; Kitton (Introduction to facsimile edn of

To ANDREW BELL, 19 DECEMBER 1843*

Text from typescript, Huntington Library.

Devonshire Terrace,
Nineteenth December, 1843. | Tuesday Afternoon.

Dear Sir,

I have only this moment risen from the current number of Chuzzlewit; or I would have answered your note sooner.

I have no doubt that I shall be at home at eleven on Thursday morning, or at Eleven on Friday morning. I shall be glad to see you on either day. If both are inconvenient, let me know, and I will appoint another.

I have conceived a real regard for Bradbury and Evans, and am pained by your allusions to them. It is very possible that six months hence you will think more tenderly of them yourself.[1] But in any case, it is a subject I would rather avoid.

Faithfully yours,

Andrew Bell, Esquire.   CHARLES DICKENS

P.S. I am very glad you think so highly of the Carol.[2] It interested *me* exceedingly.

To CHARLES MACKAY, 19 DECEMBER 1843*

MS Morgan Library.

1 Devonshire Terrace | York Gate Regents Park
Nineteenth December 1843.

My Dear Mackay.

Believe me that your pleasure in the Carol,[3] so earnestly and spontaneously

Carol, 1890) says, without evidence, that it is "a pleasing reference to some verses by his friend which had affected him very much while abroad"; but the reference is more probably to Thackeray's "Dickens in France" in *Fraser's*, Mar 42 (see *To* Lady Holland, 23 Dec 42, *fn*). The mistaken statement that the Queen bought the inscribed copy was taken by Forster from Hotten in the 1st edn of the *Life* and corrected in later edns; the copy is now in Cornell University Library. Carlyle passed his copy on to Jane Carlyle's uncle John Welsh, to whom she wrote on 23 Dec 43: "My husband sends you the last literary nove : . . really a kind-hearted, almost poetical little thing, well worth any Lady or gentleman's perusal—somewhat too much imbued with the Cockney-admiration of *The Eatable*, but as Dickens writes for 'the greatest happiness of the greatest number' (of Cockneys) he could not be expected to gainsay their taste in that particular" (*Letters to her Family*, ed. L. Huxley, p. 167).

[7] Clayden says (*Rogers and his Contemporaries*, II, 239): "He did read it, and his nephew Henry Sharpe records what he said of it in a conversation at Broadstairs soon afterwards—'Dickens's "Christmas Carol" being mentioned, he said he had been looking at it the night before; the first half hour was so dull it sent him to sleep, and the next hour was so painful that he should be obliged to finish it to get rid of the impression. He blamed Dickens's style very much, and said there was no wit in putting bad grammar into the mouths of all his characters, and showing their vulgar pronunciation by spelling "are" "air", a horse without an h: none of our best writers do that'".

[1] Possibly Bell was thinking of a change in employment after another six months and wished to consult CD, who at this juncture would certainly not wish to be the confidant of any complaints against Bradbury & Evans.

[2] Bell would have seen proofs or an early copy.

expressed, gives me real gratification of heart. It has delighted me very much. I am sure you feel it; that your praise is manly and generous; and well worth having. Thank you heartily.

I was very much affected by the little Book myself; in various ways, as I wrote it; and had an interest in the idea, which made me reluctant to lay it aside for a moment. Your allusion to that inexorable Pot, tempts me into saying that the Subscription was large, and the demand great.[1]

I shall not forget your note, easily.

Always Faithfully Yours

Charles Mackay Esquire   CHARLES DICKENS

To T. N. TALFOURD, [?20 DECEMBER 1843]*

MS Cornell University Library. *Date:* Handwriting suggests 1843–4; perhaps refers to the party at Mrs Macready's on Tues 26 Dec.

At your chambers | Wednesday afternoon

My Dear Talfourd.

I thought it better, on consideration, not to urge Mrs. Talfourd again, to go to Mrs. Macready's,—as I threatened to do—when I left your house on Saturday. Not because I had the least doubt of her receiving it kindly, or being disposed to accede to a request of mine; but because I really was unwilling to associate myself with any subject disagreeable or irksome to her—I am here to tell you so, and to ask you whether you don't think I am right. And not finding you, I leave this note.

Ever Yours CD.

To FREDERICK DICKENS, [?20 or 27 DECEMBER 1843]

MS Benoliel Collection. *Date:* 1843–4 on handwriting; "quadrille" suggests Christmas season, and 23 and 30 Dec are possible Saturdays for the gathering.

Athenæum | Wednesday

My Dear Fred

Moses[2] is the most impudent dog in the world; and Moses's Son is another.

I am going to give Ainsworth's little daughters, a quadrille on Saturday. No party. Will you dine with that family and ours, at half after five?

Affectionately Always

Frederick Dickens Esquire   CD

---

[3] Mackay was a "sub-editor" on the *Morning Chronicle*, and it is possible that he wrote the review which appeared on 19 Dec; it is enthusiastic about the "message" of the *Carol*, and quotes extensively.

[1] For the sales, see *To* Mitton, 27 Dec.

[2] E. Moses and Son, tailors and outfitters, of 154–7 Minories and 83–6 Aldgate; well known for their versified advertisements. CD did not deal with them, but perhaps Frederick did and was being pressed for payment. A recent case had exposed the low pay given to their women shirtmakers, getting "good profits out of the vitals of the poor" (*Examiner*, 28 Oct 43), and is said to have inspired Hood's "Song of the Shirt", published in the Christmas No. of *Punch*.

To THE REV. WILLIAM HARNESS, 22 DECEMBER 1843

MS Comtesse de Suzannet.

Devonshire Terrace | Friday Decr. 22nd. 1843

My Dear Harness.

I have run short of copies of the Carol,[1] owing to the demand, or I would have sent you this before.

I forget your pretty niece's[2] christian name. When you have read the little book, send it me back with that information; and I will write the same on the title page.

Faithfully Yours

The Reverend William Harness. CHARLES DICKENS

To JOHN NOBLE,[3] 22 DECEMBER 1843

Mention in *Autograph Prices Current*, v, 1919–21; *MS* 1 p.; dated 22 Dec 43.

Refusing an invitation.

To T. J. PETTIGREW, 22 DECEMBER 1843*

MS Walter T. Spencer.

1 Devonshire Terrace | York Gate Regents Park
Twenty Second December 1843

My Dear Sir.

Many thanks for the ingenious and interesting book[4] you were kind enough to leave for me the other day (though I should have been better pleased if you had put your name in it); and which I have read with very great pleasure. I take some blame to myself for not having acknowledged it sooner, but I have been too closely engaged to do many things I ought to have done.

I mentioned the enclosed little book to Mrs. Pettigrew. It's such a small one,[5] that I was afraid I never should find it again.

Always Faithfully Yours

T. J. Pettigrew Esquire CHARLES DICKENS

---

[1] Other copies presented soon after publication were to Jeffrey and Elliotson on 21 Dec, to his sister Letitia on 22 Dec, and to Felton, Jerrold, Macready and Sydney Smith in the New Year.

[2] Mary, the daughter of Harness's brother, a captain in the Navy. Described by Mrs Hofland *c.* 1840 as "a lovely niece, as like her uncle thirty years ago as possible" (C. Duncan-Jones, *Miss Mitford and Mr. Harness*, 1955, p. 41). She had married, on 25 June 42, George Hogg of Biggleswade, who later took the family name of Archdale and lived at Scottowe

Hall, Norfolk. Forster refers to Harness's niece, Mrs Archdale, among the frequent visitors in the last years at Devonshire Terrace.

[3] John Noble (*d.* 1849), FSA: see Vol. I, p. 493*n*.

[4] Probably *On Superstitions connected with . . . Medicine and Surgery*, 1844, published Nov 43 and widely noticed.

[5] Perhaps a miniature book, like Schloss's *Bijou Almanac* (see Vol. II, p. 356*n*). Mrs Pettigrew (1786–1854) was formerly Elizabeth Reid; their youngest child was Emily, *b.* 1830.

To DANIEL MACLISE, 25 DECEMBER 1843*

MS University of Texas.

Devonshire Terrace | Christmas Day 1843.

Recreant of the Castle.

The banquet hour on this eventful day, is when the turret chimes denote Half Past Five. If, in accordance with a Sacred Custom, you dine with the Bozonian Knight be punctual. If with Royalty,[1] be hungry and be jovial— strange qualities, Sir Painter, at your Queenly boards!

Carol.

To WILLIAM BEHNES,[2] 26 DECEMBER 1843

MS Free Library of Philadelphia. *Date:* CD was mistaken in the day of the week; 26 Dec was a Tuesday in 1843.

Devonshire Terrace | Monday Twenty Sixth December | 1843.

My Dear Sir

I am obliged to remain at home this morning. Mrs. Dickens extremely unwell; and I am waiting to see the Doctor. Will you let our Engagement stand for the same hour tomorrow?[3]

Faithfully Yours

W. Behnes Esquire   CHARLES DICKENS

[1] Cf. *To* Maclise, 6 July 43. The Queen was at Windsor Castle, which adds to the joke.

[2] William Behnes (?1795–1864; *DNB*), sculptor: see Vol. I, p. 537n. Was teaching D'Orsay to model portrait busts; D'Orsay's first exercise was to copy Behnes's death-mask of the Duke of Sussex as a profile sketch in Apr 43, and he was at Behnes's studio in July when Macready sat to the sculptor (Willard Connely, *Count D'Orsay*, 1952, pp. 386–7; Macready, *Diaries*, II, 215). Behnes assisted him with the only large bust he exhibited, of Lady Canterbury ("The Story of a Spoilt Life", *Cornhill Magazine*, June 1864, IX, 689–701).

[3] Presumably CD was sitting for his bust, as also probably in 1839; but no more is heard of it; it was not exhibited at the RA (where Behnes had six busts in 1844) and no record of it has survived. His Osnaburgh Street studio was crowded and dusty, and deterred fashionable sitters: "ladies ... having seen the place once,

returned no more" (*Cornhill*, June 64). Behnes died in great poverty; his works were then "scattered to the winds; to be found only one by one, here and there, in the by-alleys of Art" (Henry Weekes, *Lectures on Art*, 1880, p. 311). G. A. Storey (*Sketches from Memory*, 1899, Ch. 2) recalled visits to Behnes's studio at the age of nine (i.e. about 1843), and seeing CD, "a bright, lively young man, good-looking and with dark flowing locks ... He ... seemed amused at the scene—and very much so when he caught sight of a small boy sitting in front of a foot [*of the Farnese Hercules*] almost as big as himself, with a bun on one side, and a large lump of clay on the other, which he was trying to thumb into shape ... He came and looked over me, patted me on the head and said some kind things, but I did not know who he was till afterwards". All he remembered of CD's conversation was "that he had been in an accident and the wheel was within two inches of his head as he lay on the ground, but he escaped uninjured".

To DANIEL MACLISE, 26 DECEMBER 1843*

MS Yale University Library.

Devonshire Terrace | Twenty Sixth December 1843.

My Dear Mac

How are you today? Better? If so, will you dine here at half past *Four*, preparatory to going to Macready's?[1]

Faithfully Ever

CD

To MISS BURDETT COUTTS, 27 DECEMBER 1843

MS Morgan Library.

Devonshire Terrace | Twenty Seventh December 1843.

Dear Miss Coutts.

If every Christmas that comes to you, only makes you, or finds you, one half as happy and merry as I wish you to be, you will be the happiest and merriest person in all the world. I should have sent you my seasonable wishes; but I feared (from not having heard from you) that Lady Burdett[2] was still very ill; and am exceedingly sorry to have the apprehension confirmed by your note.

Mrs. Dickens begs me to thank you for your kind remembrance of her, and to say that she will use the box *tonight*.[3] She is not very well, and I am glad of a pantomime or anything else that is likely to amuse her.

Charley is in great force, and, with his sisters, desires his hearty love. They all went, with us, last night to a juvenile party at Mrs. Macreadys,[4] and came out

---

[1] Mrs Macready's: see *To* Miss Coutts, 27 Dec.

[2] She died 12 Jan 44.

[3] To see Balfe's *The Bohemian Girl* and the pantomime *Harlequin and King Pepin*.

[4] Thus in MS. This was Nina Macready's birthday party, of which Jane Carlyle gave an account in letters to Jeannie Welsh: "It was the *very* most agreeable party that ever I was at in London—everybody there seemed animated with one purpose to make up to Mrs. Macready and her children for the absence of 'the Tragic Actor' and so amiable a purpose produced the most joyous results. Dickens and Forster above all exerted themselves till the perspiration was pouring down and they seemed *drunk* with their efforts! Only think of that excellent Dickens playing the *conjuror* for one whole hour—the *best* conjuror I ever saw—(and I have paid money to see several)—and Forster acting as his servant. This part of the entertainment concluded with a plum pudding made out of raw flour, raw eggs— all the raw usual ingredients—boiled in a gentleman's hat—and tumbled out reeking —all in one minute before the eyes of the astonished children and astonished grown people! that trick—and his other of changing ladies' pocket handkerchiefs into comfits—and a box full of bran into a box full of—a live guinea-pig!—would enable him to make a handsome subsistence let the bookseller trade go as it please—! Then the dancing—old Major Burns with his one eye—old Jerdan of the Literary Gazette, (escaped out of the Rules of the Queen's Bench for the great occasion!) the gigantic Thackeray &c. &c. all capering like *Maenades*!! Dickens did all but go down on his knees to make *me*—waltz with him! But I thought I did my part well enough in talking the maddest nonsense with *him*, Forster, Thackeray and Maclise —without attempting the Impossible— however *after supper* when we were all madder than ever with the pulling of crackers, the drinking of champagne, and the making of speeches; a universal

very strong—especially Charley who called divers small boys by their Christian names (after the manner of a Young Nobleman on the Stage) and indulged in numerous phases of genteel dissipation. I have made a tremendous hit with a conjuring apparatus, which includes some of Doëbler's best tricks, and was more popular last evening after cooking a plum pudding in a hat, and producing a pocket handkerchief from a Wine Bottle, than ever I have been in my life. I shall hope to raise myself in your esteem by these means.

Macready still continues as successful as it is possible to be. He is very well, and likes the people—which must be a great comfort to him.[1]

We are getting on steadily with the Elton's.[2] The sick one is quite restored to health.

I am very glad to hear that Miss Meredith has left that corner she was so long in turning, quite out of sight. Will you remember me, kindly and cordially to her?

I shall have a request—a petition I ought to say—to make to you before I

country dance was proposed—and Forster *seizing me round the waist*, whirled me into the thick of it, and *made* me dance!! like a person in the tread-mill who must move forward or be crushed to death! Once I cried out 'oh for the love of Heaven let me go! you are going to dash my brains out against the folding doors!' to which he answered—(you can fancy his tone)—'your *brains*!! who cares about their brains *here*? *let them go*!' | In fact the thing was rising into something not unlike the *rape of the Sabines*! (Mrs. Reid was happily gone some time) when somebody looked [at] her watch and exclaimed 'twelve o'clock!' Whereupon we all rushed to the cloak-room—and *there* and in the lobby and up to the last moment the mirth raged on—Dickens took home Thackeray and Forster with him and his wife '*to finish the night there*' and a *royal* night they would have of it I fancy!—ending perhaps with a visit to the watch-house. After all—the pleasantest company, as Burns thought, *are* the *blackguards*!—that is; those who have just a sufficient dash of blackguardism in them to make them snap their fingers at *ceremony* and 'all that sort of thing.' I question if there was as much witty speech uttered in all the aristocratic, conventional drawing rooms thro'out London that night as among us little knot of blackguardist literary people who felt ourselves above all rules, and independent of the universe!" (*Letters to her Family*, ed. L. Huxley, pp. 170–1). She also recalled seeing Mrs Reid "trying to indoctrinate one of Dickens's small children with *Socinian benevolence*—the child about the size of a quartern loaf was sitting on a low chair gazing in awestruck delight at the reeking plum-pudding which its Father had just produced out of 'a gentleman's hat.' Mrs. Reid leaning tenderly over her (as benevolent gentle-women understand how to lean over youth) said in a soft voice *professedly* for *its* ear, but loud enough for mine and everybody else's within three yards' distance—'Would not you like that there was such a nice pudding as that in every house in London to-night? I am sure *I* would!' The shrinking uncomprehending look which the little blouzy face cast up to her was inimitable—a whole page of protest against *twaddle*! if she could but have read it!" (*op. cit.*, p. 179).

[1] Macready's diary entries for Nov confirm his success; on 3 Nov he began to think of remaining till the summer (*Diaries*, II, 232) and in fact stayed till Sep 44. On the Americans, a typical entry is 21 Nov, "I liked almost all the people I saw" (II, 238). Reports of his success had been appearing in the English press; e.g. the *Examiner*, 18 Nov 43, quoted the *Morning Chronicle* and *Times* on the "very great sensation" in Philadelphia; 16 Dec, quoted from a Boston paper an enthusiastic account of his continued successes; and 30 Dec, an extract from a New York paper on *The Bridal*.

[2] Thus in MS.

finish the Chuzzlewit, which is very selfish, for it will give the book a new interest in my eyes.[1] But I will defer it, and all questions concerning the charities into which I have made enquiry for you, until you have more leisure for such subjects. I am sure this ancient Year must have been a very arduous one to you; and but for such occupations being their own reward, would have wearied you to a serious extent.

With every good wish

Believe me Dear Miss Coutts
Always Faithfully Yours

Miss Coutts.   CHARLES DICKENS

You will be glad to hear, I know, that my Carol is a prodigious success.[2]

To M. A. DE GOY,[3] 27 DECEMBER 1843*

MS Mr Robert L. Henderson. *Address:* M. A. De Goy | London Coffee House | Ludgate Hill.

Devonshire Terrace
Twenty Seventh December 1843.

Mr. Charles Dickens presents his compliments to M. A. De Goy, and begs to say that being engaged with friends in town and country just now, he cannot have the pleasure of making an appointment, without a previous delay which M. De Goy may find inconvenient and troublesome. But his Publishers, Messrs. Chapman and Hall 186 Strand will be happy to receive M. De Goy at any time, and have full power in the business. He begs to thank M. De Goy for his obliging note.

To THOMAS MITTON, 27 DECEMBER 1843

Text from N, I, 550.

Devonshire Terrace, | Twenty-Seventh December, 1843

My dear Mitton,

You will be glad to hear that I had a note from C and H on the twenty-fourth to say that the Carol was then in its Sixth Thousand;[4] and that as the orders

[1] *Chuzzlewit* was dedicated to Miss Coutts.

[2] See next *To* Mitton.

[3] André de Goy, minor writer and translator; his translations of three of CD's Christmas books were published in Paris, 1850—*Le Grillon du Foyer, Le Possédé et le pacte du fantôme* in one volume and *La Bataille de la Vie* in another, the latter also in a different series, 1854; contributed *La Bataille* and *Le Possédé* to *Contes de Noel* in Hachette's authorized collected edition 1857, and so presumably met CD in Apr 56 with other translators: see N, II, 759, 762. Also dramatized the *Battle* (with M. Mélesville) for perfor-mance at the Vaudeville, 1853, and translated *Jack Sheppard* as *Le Bandit de Londres*, 1851. Clearly he intended to translate the *Carol* in 1843-4; no such publication can be traced, and the earliest known is *Les Apparitions de Noel*, in *Revue Britannique*, May–June 1844, pp. 567–75, 670–92.

[4] According to F, IV, ii, 314–15, giving the accounts, the 1st edn was 6000; Forster was wrong in saying that it sold out on the day of publication, but might be correct in saying that "two thousand more . . . were sold before the close of the year".

were coming in fast from town and country, it would soon be necessary to re-print. I am very glad you saw the children the other day, and made them so happy. I have much to say in reference to your note of last Friday, but cannot say it better perhaps than when France draws nearer to us.[1] I shall see you within a day or two.

Ever faithfully
[CHARLES DICKENS]

To S. R. STAREY, 29 DECEMBER 1843*

MS Maggs Bros Ltd.

1 Devonshire Terrace | York Gate Regents Park.
Twenty Ninth December 1843

Dear Sir

I am exceedingly sorry that my engagements render it impossible for me to preside at the Meeting in behalf of the Field Lane School.[2] I regret that I did not know of it sooner; and that when the Superintendent[3] did me the favor to call here, he did not leave some card or note in explanation of his business. In which case I would have made an appointment with him immediately.

I can have no objection to your stating (as you desire it) that I have visited the School, and am deeply impressed with a sense of the vital importance of such Institutions. I have already taken measures for directing public attention to them, and urging their claims to the best of my ability.[4]

There can be no objection either, to the announcement of Miss Coutts's Subscription.

As I have not yet seen Lord Sandon (who I believe is still absent from town) I would recommend you to say no more in reference to your wish to obtain a Government Grant, and your hopes of success, than that application has been made through a private channel.

Faithfully Yours
CHARLES DICKENS

Mr. Samuel Robert Starey.

To FREDERICK DICKENS, 30 DECEMBER 1843*

MS Chicago University Library.

Devonshire Terrace. | Thirtieth December 1843.

My Dear Frederick.

You will find a *bed* in my dressing room on the Ground floor. The door will be on the latch; the gate open; and a light in the hall. I enclose you the latch key.

---

[1] See *To* Forster, 1 Nov.

[2] The second anniversary meeting took place on 3 Jan 44 "at the British School-rooms, Harp-alley, Farringdon-street", (*The Times*, 30 Dec 43); a note at the end of the advertisement added: "N.B. a large loft or shed wanted in this immediate neighbourhood". No report of the meeting has been found.

[3] Andrew Proven.

[4] Probably referring to his promised article for the *Edinburgh*.

In consequence of your putting off your request about money to so late a moment, and my not returning home until after the time you mentioned, I have not known what to do about it. And I fear to send it you with this: feeling that so strange a letter is not unlikely to be opened at any rate. For a post office order there is no time. Therefore, as you say nothing on the subject, I think it best not to send it. Of course you can have it, when you arrive.

Kate and Georgy send their loves to all. Kate is but poorly, and keeps at home. There was some talk of a Maltonian[1] hamper. If it has been sent, some fiend in human shape has got it, for we haven't.

The Carol is a prodigious success.

In haste, always affecy.
CD.

To H. G. ATKINSON,[2] 1843

Mention in Sotheby's catalogue, Dec 1935; *MS* 1 p.; dated Devonshire Terrace, 1843.

Thanking him for kind remembrances.

To JOHN BRADFORD,[3] 1843

Extract in Anderson Galleries catalogue No. 617 (1908); *MS* 1 p.; dated Devonshire Terrace, 1843.

I am glad to learn that I have ever given you pleasure

To UNKNOWN CORRESPONDENT, 1843

Extract in George D. Smith catalogue, 1901; *MS* 1 p.; dated London, 1843.

In case you should call to-morrow. I write a hasty line to tell you that contrary to my usual Sunday custom I shall not be at home.

To DANIEL MACLISE, [1843]*

MS Colonel Richard Gimbel. *Date:* Handwriting suggests 1843.

My Dear Mac

How in respect of dining at the Athenæum today? Can you call here, about 4?

Faithfully Ever

Wednesday Morning CD.

---

[1] From the Smithsons at Malton, Yorks.
[2] Unidentified.
[3] John Bradford, minor writer: see Vol. II, p. 426*n*.

APPENDIXES

A. DOCUMENTS CONCERNING INTERNATIONAL COPYRIGHT

MSS Berg Collection.[1]

MEMORIAL SENT TO DICKENS BY TWELVE BRITISH AUTHORS, 28 MARCH 1842

TO THE AMERICAN PEOPLE

We the undersigned, in transmitting to one of our most eminent English Authors the following Memorial for an International Copyright between the United States and Great Britain, are willing that our claims should be considered, apart from our interests in urging them.

Addressing a Great Nation—chiefly united to us by a common Ancestry; speaking the same language; and indebted to the same hereditary sources for models in literature, and authorities in science—we venture to hope that a Prayer which asks, for labours not less useful to America than Great Britain, those rewards which can only be proportionate to the estimation in which, by Americans, the labours may be held; will need little argument to advance it with the Legislature and People of the United States: provided that no counter-balancing disadvantage can be proved to arise from its concession.

Independently of grace or generosity to ourselves, we conclude that the question of International Copyright can only be viewed by enlightened Americans—first; as affecting the interests of American Authors—secondly; as influencing those of the American Reading Public.

With regard to the first. We respectfully submit that a greater curse cannot be inflicted on American Authors, nor a more serious injury on American Literature, than a state of Law which admits, gratuitously, the works of Foreign Authors in the same language. It is impossible that an American Writer can hope for adequate remuneration in any branch of Literature, so long as he can be met by the Publishers with a declaration that they can publish the best English Works without paying a farthing for the Copyrights. The necessary consequence must be, that the energy of American industry and genius, so remarkable in every other department of Human Intellect, will be greatly chilled and oppressed in the general departments of Literature. Against all possible exertion of Native Authors is arrayed a wholesale system of competition, existing only by means of Piracy and Smuggling. And we are convinced that the ultimate consequence of inundating the American Market with English Works for which no remuneration is paid to the Author, must be, the extinction of American Literature, as an adequate, independent, and honorable profession.

With regard to the second.—The only interest the American Public can have, is in the supply of English Works in as cheap a form as at present. And there can be no doubt that this would continue to be the case, were a Copyright

---

[1] Copies in CD's hand, immediately following his own letter of 27 Apr to the Editors of Four American Newspapers. Of the four copies made from CD's by Putnam, one owned by Comtesse de Suzannet was sold at Sotheby's, Nov 1971.

established. Works are sold at a low or a high price, not in proportion as there
is a copyright or not, but in proportion as they can obtain a larger or smaller
community of readers. The noble cultivation of the American People, which
forms a Reading Public almost commensurate with the entire population, renders
it the obvious interest of every author (and every publisher) to adapt his price to
the means of all his readers. And we venture to predict that were an International
Copyright established, not one popular English Work would be sold in the
United States, at a higher price than at present. So far, if this be true, the
American Public will be no losers. But will they be no gainers, if they have
removed from their own Writers and Men of Genius, the great impediment to a
purely National Literature?

We do not pause to enquire if there be any separate or oligarchical interests
against us in this Great Question; because we venture to trust that in a country
the Institutions of which, are based on foundations so broad, the minor and
selfish interests which cannot be supported by simple justice, are not suffered to
prevail. And also because we cannot conceive that concession to our Prayer
could disturb or invade one solitary Vested Right.

On the other hand, in our sanguine anticipations from a Legislature willing
to be just to others, and honorably jealous of the Fame of the people it represents
—in Arts and Letters no less than in Arms and Commerce—we look forward
with pleasure to the new and firm bond that the Law we pray for, must establish,
between our American Brotherhood and ourselves. Such a Law must, naturally
and obviously, bind the large body of our Writers to peace and amity with a
Public they may then justly consider as their own. And whatever tends to
connect the intelligence of one Country with that of another, must exert a
deeper and more permanent influence than they who superficially regard this
question as one of mere pecuniary profit to English Authors, can foresee; upon
the tranquillity and civilization of the World.

    (Signed)

EDWARD LYTTON BULWER.	HENRY HALLAM.
THOMAS CAMPBELL.	SYDNEY SMITH.
ALFRED TENNYSON.	H. H. MILMAN.
T. N. TALFOURD.	SAMUEL ROGERS.
THOMAS HOOD.	JOHN FORSTER.
LEIGH HUNT.	BARRY CORNWALL.

LETTER TO DICKENS FROM BRITISH AUTHORS

London 28th. March 1842.

Dear Dickens.

The deep interest we take in the efforts you have been making for the cause of
International Copyright, impels us to express to you, *our* earnest sympathy with
your course, and our cordial wishes for its success. Our feeling, like your own,
is not prompted merely by a desire that Authors on this side of the Atlantic
should obtain some palpable reward of their industry from the Mighty Public
who enjoy its fruits, but is exalted by the conviction that, on the issue, depends

the question whether the intellect of America shall speedily be embodied in a Literature worthy of its new-born powers, or shall be permitted to languish under disadvantages which may long deprive the World of the full developement of its greatness. Assured that in promoting this object, you will make the best return for that generous appreciation which your Genius has received from our Transatlantic brethren, and which we have learned with grateful and unmingled delight,

We are, | Your obliged and faithful Servants.

(To this, the same signatures are appended)

To Charles Dickens Esquire
   United States

LETTER TO DICKENS FROM CARLYLE[1]

Templand (for London) 26th. March 1842.

My Dear Sir.

We learn by the Newspapers that you everywhere in America stir up the question of International Copyright, and thereby awaken huge dissonance where all else were triumphant unison for you. I am asked my opinion of the matter, and requested to write it down in words.

Several years ago, if memory err not, I was one of many English Writers who, under the auspices of Miss Martineau, did sign a petition to Congress, praying for an International Copyright between the Two Nations—which, properly, are not Two Nations, but one—*indivisible* by Parliament, Congress, or any kind of Human Law or Diplomacy; being already united by Heaven's Act of Parliament, and the Everlasting Law of Nature and Fact. To that opinion I still adhere, and am like to continue adhering.

In discussion of the matter before any Congress or Parliament, manifold considerations and argumentations will necessarily arise; which to me are not interesting, nor essential for helping me to a decision. They respect the time and manner in which the thing should be; not at all whether the thing should be, or not. In an ancient Book, reverenced I should hope on both sides of the ocean, it was Thousands of Years ago, written down in the most decisive and explicit manner, "*Thou Shalt not Steal*". That thou belongest to a different "Nation" and canst steal without being certainly hanged for it, gives thee no permission to steal. Thou shalt not in any wise steal at all! So it is written down for Nations and for Men, in the Law Book of the Maker of this Universe. Nay, poor Jeremy Bentham and others step in here, and will demonstrate that it is actually our true convenience and expediency not to steal; which I for my share, on the great scale and on the small, and in all conceivable scales and shapes, do also firmly believe it to be. For example, if Nations abstained from stealing, what need were there of fighting—with its butcherings and burnings: decidedly the most expensive

---

[1] Forster "had it transcribed" before sending it out to CD, and published it in F, III, iii, 226–7. There are a number of small differences between the F text and CD's.

thing in this World? How much more two Nations which, as I said, are but one Nation, knit in a thousand ways by Nature and Practical Intercourse; indivisible brother elements of the same great SAXONDOM,[1] to which, in all honorable ways, be long life!

When Mr Robert Roy M'Gregor lived in the district of Menteith on the Highland Border, Two Centuries ago, he, for his part, found it more convenient to supply himself with beef by stealing it alive from the adjacent glens, than by buying it killed in the Stirling butchers' Market. It was Mr Roy's plan of supplying himself with beef in those days, this of stealing it. In many a little "Congress" in the district of Menteith there was debating, doubt it not, and much specious argumentation this way and that, before they could ascertain that, really and truly, buying was the best way to get your beef; which, however, in the long run, they did with one assent find it indisputably to be: and accordingly they hold by it to this day.

Wishing you a pleasant voyage, and a swift and safe return,

> I remain always, My Dear Sir
> Yours very sincerely
> THOMAS CARLYLE

To | Charles Dickens Esquire | In | The United States

---

[1] CD's copy reads "SAXENDOM", surely in error.

B. THE FORGED LETTER

NEW YORK EVENING TATTLER, 11 AUGUST 1842[1]

[Front page article]

BOZ'S OPINIONS OF US.

It was frequently remarked, while Boz was among us, gaining golden favors from all sorts of people, and absolutely surfeited with kindness—that very likely, when he returned home, he would show up the whole affair. His friends here, however, stoutly denied the possibility of such a thing; his amiability, modesty, frankness, good nature, and good breeding were all brought forth by the Boz faction as evidences that the result feared would never come to pass. How sadly have we been disappointed!

We don't know that we regret the consummation. It is undeniable, that the Americans are too much guided by impulse—too apt to pet and caress a foreign lion—too liable, in short, to make fools of themselves. Lessons of the kind Dickens is teaching them will soon remove these follies.

Let Boz—ungrateful as he has proved himself—let him be treated fairly. He no doubt came over here with the main purpose of effecting an international copyright: we are among those who believe that a law to that effect would be wise and righteous. He did not succeed in this scheme: he sees the American government, having the *power* to take advantage of the labor of foreign authors without remuneration, meanly, (as he thinks) shuffle off from giving those authors their due. Boz, too, cannot look upon the United States with any but English eyes; his likings, habits, uses, and tastes are not as ours. Therefore it is, that we say, let justice be done the man, and let all this go in palliation of his still unpardonable insolence.

One part of his letters, we especially like. It is that wherein he speaks of his having been sought after merely as a subject of curiosity, and for giving notoriety to "his keepers."

[1] Walt Whitman had been editor of the *Tattler* since his resignation 16 May 42 from the editorship of the *New York Aurora*, and must have sanctioned the three forged paragraphs which had appeared in the *Tattler* on 2 or 3 Aug (though possibly not knowing that they were forgeries), also this article of 11 Aug and the ten weak paragraphs which were now added in the pretence of at last giving the forged letter complete (see *To* Forster, ?30 or 31 Aug 42, *fn*, and below). Earlier, Whitman had shown himself to be one of CD's warm admirers. According to *Walt Whitman of the New York Aurora*, ed. J. J. Rubin and C. H. Brown (State College, Pa., 1950), he had replied, in "Dickens and Democracy" (*Aurora*, 2 Apr), to an attack in the Apr *Democratic Review* on the "atrocious exaggeration of [CD's] bad characters", arguing that there were indeed people just as bad (J. G. Bennett one of them). "Boz and Democracy", in *Brother Jonathan* (for which he is known to have wirtten), 26 Feb, signed "W.W.", must also have been his. It defended CD's low-life scenes, and spoke of Whitman's "love and esteem" for his writings: "Never having seen Boz in the body . . . I have long considered [him] as a personal friend". But probably Whitman, like other American editors, had disliked CD's circular letter to British Authors of 7 July and found its paragraph about the editors of the "mammoths" (early confused with the initial forged paragraphs) particularly offensive.

Another thing we cotton to in the letter. It is where he cuts into the flimsiness of our American aristocracy. Reader, look over that part of the epistle twice.

We shall now give the letter. Lest there may be some misunderstanding, we will add that there are *two* letters in the Chronicle from Mr. Dickens. The first one (which we do not publish because it has already appeared extensively in the papers) was written some time before the one that follows:

To the Editor of the Morning Chronicle.

Devonshire Terrace, Parkgate,[1] | July 15th, 1842.

Sir,

In my note, accompanying the circular you were kind enough to publish for me, I expressed an intention to address you again on the subject there treated on, and which I have so nearly at heart.

I feel no disposition to pick delicate terms, and use sweet phrases upon the matter; and I advise all of my craft to speak out openly in the same manner.

Why, then, should I conceal that I believe the Americans, in withholding from us our rights, act with a degree of meanness which is only equalled by its glaring iniquity? In truth, it is nothing more than *theft*. I regret to say this; and indeed I would not were it not my duty.

The great fault of the American people is their worship of pelf. Through my travels, I found that *in the larger cities the grand aim of the people seems to be *money making*. Every good desire, every refined wish, every aspiration for the lofty, and the pure, and the holy, is swallowed up in the great whirlpool of avarice. Before crossing the Atlantic, I had heard much of the *thriftiness* of our American offspring; but I must confess I was not prepared to see so much *meanness.**

Chivalry, and a high toned generosity never have taken root in the new world; at least there are no fruits borne. Admiring, as I often have, the deeds done by her brave men during her rebellion against the mother country, which ended in her independence, I expected to see some remains of that nobility of spirit in her present race. I found *none*.

It may be said that I, of all persons, ought to be blind to the dark spots of American character, treated as I have been by the American people. I do not agree with this view of the case; I did not seek their attentions, their dinners, and their balls. On the contrary, these things were forced upon me, many times to the serious inconvenience of myself and my party. The kindness of a friend, if it is troublesome and officious, often annoys as much as the injuries of an enemy. The Americans have most of the faults, both of the English and French, with very few of their virtues. I never thought that *I* was petted, merely for *myself*, but as a kind of *monster*, to look at, and be gazed about, and imbue my keepers with somewhat of the notoriety that enveloped myself. I can freely and confidently say that this was the case, almost without exception.

My books were never written for fops and the luxurious rich. I have always thought that much good might be done by selecting out characters from the lower walks of life, and embodying in their stories, how often it is that the beauty of innocence and integrity may be seen among the poor, and how many excuses there are for their vices, if they are vicious.

While in America, I of course could not rudely tell the aristocracy (for they have aristocracy there) among whom I was forced to move, what I really thought of them. Yet how nauseous was it to me, to see in a country which pretends to so much equality, (and whose laws really are imbued with it) an exemplification of the very silliest kind of mock *exclusiveness*.

Perhaps in the course of time the Americans will get over this. I hope so, I am sure. They should know that a classic simplicity of manners—a cutting loose from the stale and absurd ceremonies of European high life—a bold, and noble, and manly independence of foreign conventional usage, would become their people much better, and excite our admiration much more strongly than their present slavish truckling, and base spirit of imitation.

Though in my travels from city to city, I of course found much to be pleased with and astonished at, yet the total difference between our good old English customs, and the awkwardness, the uncouth manners, and the unmitigated selfishness which meet you everywhere in America, made my journey one of a good deal of annoyance. I do not think the Americans, as a people, have much good taste. To a person brought up among them, and in their own way, of course the glaring faults that strike a stranger do not appear; but to any well-bred man from abroad, the effect of the prevalent features of the American character is by no means agreeable.

But, sir, I find that I have wandered away from my text. I have indeed so much upon my mind upon the subject of my recent journey, as to itself alone, that I could hardly avoid saying what I have said.

And the best return I could make the people of the United States, even if all their attention to me had been shown out of pure kindness, would be to show them the utter folly of such conduct. A *man* is a *man*, and because he happens to have done a little good in the world, that is no reason why his fellow-creatures should fall down and worship him. The Americans profess to be good democrats; I say from my heart, I don't believe there is a country on the face of the earth where *man worship* prevails so much, and in so gross and disgusting a method!

There is really much misapprehension here with regard to what America really is. I do not believe that the books of travellers from this country there, have caused that misapprehension. On the contrary, I am of opinion that very few faults have been laid at their door, which do not honestly belong to them.

I shall address you again in a few days.

With respect, etc.

CHARLES DICKENS

C. MISCELLANEOUS

MINUTES OF THE MEETING HELD ON SS *BRITANNIA*
21 JANUARY 1842

Facsimile, *D*, xxv (1929), 288–9.

At a Meeting of the Passengers on board the Britannia Steam Ship, travelling from Liverpool to Boston: held in the Saloon of that Vessel on Friday the Twenty First of January 1842:

It was moved and seconded, That the Earl of Mulgrave do take the chair. The motion having been carried unanimously, The Earl of Mulgrave took the chair accordingly.

It was also moved, and seconded, and carried unanimously, That Charles Dickens Esquire be appointed Secretary and Treasurer to the Meeting.

The three following Resolutions were then proposed and seconded, and carried nem: con:

1. That gratefully recognizing the blessing of Divine Providence, by which we are brought nearly to the termination of our Voyage, we have great pleasure in expressing our high appreciation of Captain Hewett's nautical skill, and of his indefatigable attention to the management and safe conduct of the Ship, during a more than ordinarily tempestuous passage.

2. That a Subscription be opened for the purchase of a piece of Silver plate; and that Captain Hewett be respectfully requested to accept it, as a sincere expression of the sentiments embodied in the foregoing Resolution.

3. That a Committee be appointed to carry these Resolutions into effect; and that the committee be composed of the following gentlemen—Charles Dickens Esquire, E. Dunbar Esquire, and Solomon Hopkins Esquire.

The Committee having withdrawn and conferred with Captain Hewett, returned; and informed the Meeting that Captain Hewett desired to attend and express his thanks: which he did.

The amount of the subscriptions was reported at Fifty Pounds, and the List was closed. It was then agreed that the following Inscription should be placed upon the Testimonial to Captain Hewett.

This Piece of Plate | Was presented | to | Captain John Hewett | of | The Britannia Steam Ship, | By the Passengers | On board that Vessel, | In a Voyage | From Liverpool to Boston | In the month of January | 1842 | As a slight acknowledgment | of | His great ability | And skill | Under Circumstances | of much difficulty | And danger; | And as a feeble token | of | Their lasting gratitude.

Thanks were then voted to the chairman and to the Secretary; and the meeting separated.

CHARLES DICKENS

LETTER FROM MRS CHARLES DICKENS TO MRS HENRY BURNETT, 30 JANUARY 1842

Text from F. G. Kitton, *CD by Pen and Pencil*, 1890–2, 1, 39. *Address:* 3, Elm Terrace, Higher Ardwick,[1] Manchester, England. By *Britannia* Steamer.

Boston, January 30, 1842.

My dearest Fanny,

According to my promise, I lose no time in writing to you by the first steamer, to give you an account of our voyage and arrival in America. You cannot imagine what a dreadful voyage we had. We were eighteen days on our passage, and experienced all the horrors of a storm at sea, which raged frightfully for a whole night, and broke our paddle-boxes and the life-boat to pieces. I was nearly distracted with terror, and don't know what I should have done had it not been for the great kindness and composure of my dear Charles. It was very awful. I thought we should never see another day, but, thank God, we were spared, and you may imagine our relief and happiness when, towards morning, it gradually lulled, and although the ship was heaving terribly all day, owing to the heavy swell which follows a gale, all further danger from the wind was over.

You cannot think how our thoughts flew to our precious children and home during that terrible night. We met with another danger. Two or three nights after that, owing to an unskilful pilot, we ran aground, which caused great consternation, as we were surrounded by rocks, and very near the shore; we got free in a few minutes, and remained there at anchor all night. We were told, after the danger was past, that the sailors had taken off their jackets and shoes ready for a swim ashore. We were all very sick, and to crown all my miseries, I had a most awfully swoln face, and looked quite an object.

To turn to the brighter side of the picture, the reception Charles has met with is something not to be described. He is perfectly worshipped, and crowds follow him in the streets even. It will be the same, they tell us, all through America. The people are most hospitable, and we shall both be killed with kindness. We are constantly out two or three times in the evening. At New York they are going to give a public ball as well as a dinner, and we hear it is to be a very splendid affair. Sometimes we are quite knocked up, and long most ardently for dear Devonshire Terrace. I am already *very* homesick, but it is of no use yet I will not pretend to give you any account, dear Fan, of the manners and customs, and so on, as my powers of description are not great, and you will have it some day or other so much the better from Charles.

We long most ardently for letters, which we will receive about the middle of February. God grant that the darlings are well,—how my heart yearns for them!

I trust, dearest Fan, that you and yours are well. Charles joins me in most affectionate love to yourself and Burnett, and kiss your dear little ones for Aunt Kate. Do write me a long letter, and with a thousand good wishes,

Believe me, dearest Fanny, | Your truly attached Sister,

CATHERINE DICKENS

---

[1] Kitton reads "Hardwick".

INDEXES

INDEX OF CORRESPONDENTS

INDEX OF NAMES AND PLACES

Buildings, streets, districts etc are indexed under the town or city to which they belong, e.g. Blackheath under LONDON. If a separate entry is desirable, a cross-reference is given from the town to the separate entry, e.g. from LONDON: Finchley to FINCHLEY.

References to characters in Dickens's novels are listed as a sub-section under the title of the novel within the entry DICKENS, Charles: *Works.*

Abbreviations and symbols
The letter D stands for the name Dickens, CD for Charles Dickens. Initial letters are used to abbreviate the titles of Dickens's books, e.g. *AN* for *American Notes*, *MC* for *Martin Chuzzlewit.*

Those footnotes which contain the main particulars about a person or place are distinguished by an asterisk, e.g. 106n*, 314 & n*.

The sign ∼ is used to show that the reference which follows it is linked with the reference which precedes.

The names of Dickens's correspondents are printed in capitals.

P. W.

Bracher, Peter (cont.)
346n; 'The New York *Herald* and *American Notes*' 346n, 348n
Bradbury, John 165n
Bradbury, William 559n, 605(2)
BRADBURY & EVANS 517n*; printers of *AN* 319, 338n, 347n; ~ of *MC* 377 & n (handbills), 479 & nn, 525, 540, 543; proprietors of *Punch* 469n, 517n, 540; CD's proposal that they become his publishers 517 & n, 587 & n, 591 & n, 599 & n; ~ pained by Bell's allusions to 609 & n; also 492n
BRADFORD, John 617 & n
Bradshaw's Journal 494n
Bradshaw's Little Magazine 592n
Braham, John 65n, 558n
Brandon, Edgar E.: ed. *A Pilgrim of Liberty: . . . the Triumphal Tour of General Lafayette . . . in 1825* 120n
Brandywine Emett Repeal Association 540n
'Brave Old English Gentleman' *see* 'Fine Old. . . .'
Breese, Judge 196? ('a certain judge in St. Louis') & n
Bremer, Frederica: *The Homes of the New World* 403n
Bremner, John, baker 231? ('Mr Bremner') & n
Bremner & Till, tobacco brokers 231n
Brenton, Capt. Edward Pelham 436 & n*, 589n
Brenton, Sir Jahleel: *Memoir of Captain E. P. Brenton* 589n
BRESLAW ('BRESLEY'), John 74 & n
Brevoort, Henry 79n
Brewer, L. A.: *My Leigh Hunt Library* 579n
Brewster, William 194n
Bridal, The (Knowles) 614n
Bridgman, Laura 51n, 317 & nn, 413n, 495
Bright, John 577n
Brighton, Sussex: Miss Coutts and Miss Meredith at 589 & n; Theatre, Elton benefit at 536 & nn; Town Hall, Madame Sala at 558n; also 275n, 582n
BRINDLEY, Thomas Bardel 515n*; *The Omnipotence of the Deity and Other Poems* dedicated to CD 515 & n; *BR* presented to *ib.*
Brinkman, C.L.: *Alphabetische Naamlijst van Boeken . . .* 566n
Bristol: CD sees Longfellow off from 355n, 407 & n; also 212n, 362n, 511n
Britannia 527n
Britannia, S.S.: accommodation on 6–7 & n, 8–9 & n, 10, 11, 12, 88n, 178, 188, 226, 227; in Atlantic storm 11–13 & nn, 36–7 & n, 40–1 & n, 43, 88–9 & n, 93, 226–7; ~ runs aground 13–14, 43, 629; captain *see* Hewitt; chief steward 165 & n; CD plays accordion 165–6; doctor *see* Wiley;

Britannia, S.S. (cont.)
passengers 11, 12, 13n, 16n, 33n, 106n, 472 & n; ~ meeting of 14n, 628; stewardess *see* Bean, Mrs; also 33hn, 50hn, 92n, 325, 493n
Britannia Life Assurance Co. 2 & n, 88n, 162 & n, 437n, 539n, 588n
British Almanac for 1844, Companion to 472n
British and Foreign Institute 478n, 508 & n, 536 & n; *Transactions* 508n
Brittany 587
BRITTON, John 352n, 443n, 450 & n*
Broadstairs, Kent, also referred to as 'the Seaside', 'here', 'this place' 260n*
    CD's visits: (Aug–Sep 42) 255, 267, 273, 290, 292, 294, 298n, 300 & n, 301, 303hn & n, 304 & n, 309 & n (Minster), 319n, 320n, 324, 325 (races), 327, 328n, 329 (regatta) & n, 332, 336–7; ~ (Aug–Sep 43) 487, 535, 536 & n, 538, 545, 547 & n, 548 (CD's regime), 558hn, 570
    Albion Hotel 304n; Albion Street 255n; 273n; Barnes's Library 273n; Beard invited 264, 273, 304, 321, 523; Mrs Christian at 328 & nn; Colburn at 560 & n; Miss Collins, the Bather 163 & n, 308n; Cruikshank at 309; CD's praise of 260; Fletcher to be invited 305 & n; Forster at 310 & n, 547n; Maclise invited 277, 308, 310 & n; Police 568 & n; Rogers at 332n, 335, 572, 609n; the Terrace 255; also 5n, 584 ('Kent')
Broadway Journal 422n
Brock, Major-Gen. Sir Isaac 413 & nn
Brockway, John H. 135n
Broderip, Mrs (Frances Freeling Hood) and Thomas Hood, the younger: ed. *Memorials of Thomas Hood* 341n, 386n 532n, 607n
Brodie, Sir Benjamin 399n
Brooks, Sidney 3n
Brother Jonathan: Park Benjamin and 312n; on the lionising of CD 66n, 67n, 72n; *MC* reviewed (quot.) 541n; C. Mathews and 406 & n; piracy: of *AN* 286n, 346n; ~ of other works 230n, 232n, 258 & n, 274n, 292 ('piratical newspapers') & n; ~ declared contraband 292n; Whitman's defence of CD in 625n; also xii, 318n
BROTHERS IN UNITY Society, New Haven 36 & nn, 37, 44 ('public dinner'), 53n, 55, 68 ('engagement at Newhaven') & n
BROUGHAM and Vaux, Henry Peter Brougham, 1st Baron: as Chairman of the Society for the Diffusion of Useful Knowledge 6 & nn; interested in CD's American progress 42n, 144; his letter and pamphlet for Judge Story 51, 52n, 109, 144–5; speech on *Creole* case 145 & n; letter received from 248; social 270, 297 & n; ~ invites CD to Brougham

Glencoe, Argyllshire 171, 211, 239
Globe, The 262 & n
Gloucestershire: prisons 104n, 436 & nn
Glover, Mrs Julia 537n
GLYN, George Carr, later 1st Baron Wolverton 573 & n
Godey's Lady's Book 114n, 125n, 232n
Godley, J. R.: *Letters from America* xiiin, 139n, 363n
Godwin, Parke: *A Biography of William Cullen Bryant* 46n, 58n, 59n, 86n
Godwin, William: *Fleetwood* 107n; *Things as They Are: or, the Adventures of Caleb Williams* 107 & nn
Goldsmith, Oliver: *Citizen of the World, The* 174 ('Beau Tibbs') & n, 308n; *Essays:* 'The Genius of Love' 308 & n; *She Stoops to Conquer:* 'in a concatenation accordingly' 246 & n, 441, 551
Good Night's Rest, A see Gore, Mrs
Goodrich, Samuel Griswold, pseud. Peter Parley 341n*; and international copyright 238n, 243n, 341–2 & nn; *Recollections of a Lifetime* 243n, 341n, 342n
Goodwin Sands 524, 548
GORDON, Cuthbert C. 56 & n
Gore, Charles 399n
Gore, Mrs Charles Arthur (Catherine Moody): *A Good Night's Rest: or, Two in the Morning*, staged by Montreal Garrison company with title *Past Two o'Clock in the Morning* 216, 218, 231, 235, 236, 237n*, 244, 245n, 246 ('the interlude') & nn, 247 ('the piece') & n, 250n, 354 ('our theatricals') & n; also 232n
Gough, Mr, actor 510
GOY, André de 615 & n*
Gracie, Mr and Mrs Archibald 252n
Graham, Sir James 280n, 516n, 565n
Graham's Magazine: on *AN* xi; payment of contributors 232n; Poe editor and contr. 106n, 107nn, 108n, 194n; also 34n, 82n, 125n, 204n
Grant, Daniel 216 ('his brother') & nn
Grant, William 216 ('one of the . . . Cheeryble brothers') & nn*
GRANVILLE, Frederick 250n*; in Montreal theatricals 247n, 250n; at N.Y. farewell dinner 252n; passenger on *George Washington* 250–1, 354 & n; marriage 354n
Granville, Mrs Frederick (Isabella Sheldon) 354n
GRATTAN, Thomas Colley 15n*; invites CD to dine 15; escorts him in Boston 15n, 21n, 40n; speech at Boston dinner 15n, 67n; speech at Ashburton dinner 342 & nn; *Civilized America* 16n, 100n, 168n, 231n
Grattan, Mrs 16
Graves, William 175n

Gray, Francis C: dinner party for CD 19n, 24n, 27hn, 39n, 40n; also 33n
Great Fish River expedition 390n
Great Lakes, the: passage of, projected 130, 148, 153, 159, 161, 164; said to be stormy and sea-sicky 182, 184; also 151n
Great Mammoth Cave, Kentucky 153 & n
Great Prairie: crossing of, projected 148, 153, 159, 161; ∼ not recommended 182, 184, 188
Great Western, S.S. 212 & n, 271 & n, 317; Longfellow returns on 346 & n, 348, 351, 355n, 360n, 362n, 407 & n
Greeley, Horace 82n, 85n, 230n
Green, Gen. Duff 577n
GREEN, Edmund Brewster 23 & nn*, 61
Green, Edmund Fiske, later John Fiske 23n
Green, Joseph, picture framer 306 ('Maclise's framer') & n
Greenhill, W. G. 372n
Greenhow, Robert 160n*; CD's dinner engagment with xi, 113n, 131n, 160
Greenhow, Mrs Robert (Rose O'Neale) 160 & n*
Greenleaf, Mrs James (Mary Longfellow) 40n
Greenleaf, Simon 240n
GREENOUGH, William Whitwell 21 & nn*, 45
Greenwich, London: Crown and Sceptre 172; dinners: to Black 480n, 487, 489; ∼ to CD (9 July 42) 264 ('the business . . . last Saturday') & n, 272n, 292, 359n; ∼ other dinners or visits 385, 386n, 387, 487n, 531; fair 170, 172; 'Greenwich pensioner' 401 & n; steamer 575n; Thames at 181, 188; Trafalgar Tavern 489
Greenwood, Thomas Longdon 528n
Gregory, Barnard 441n*; editor *Satirist* 84n, 364n, 441n; hissed from the stage at Covent Garden 441 & nn, 444 ('scoundrel editor')
Greville, Charles 604n
Grey, 2nd Earl 15n, 266n
Grey, Lieut. Col. Charles 15 & n
GRIFFIN, George 54 & nn
Griffin, Dr George, 85th Foot 245 ('Tristram Sappy') & n
Griffin, Gerald: *Gisippus* 159 ('the tragedy') & n
Griffin, Rev. James 379n
Griffin, W. H., and H. C. Minchin: *Life of Robert Browning* 516n
GRIFFITH, Mrs Mary 77 & nn*
Griffiths, carver and gilder 573 & n
Griggs, E. L.: ed. *Collected Letters of Samuel Taylor Coleridge* 82n
Grimaldi, Joseph 244 & n
Grinnell, Minturn & Co., shipowners 251 & n
Grip, the raven 94n, 296 & nn

688